REGULATION OF BANK FINANCIAL SERVICE ACTIVITIES

CASES AND MATERIALS

Fourth Edition

. . .

By
Lissa L. Broome
Wachovia Professor of Banking Law
Director, Center for Banking and Finance
University of North Carolina

Jerry W. Markham
Professor of Law
Florida International University College of Law

AMERICAN CASEBOOK SERIES®

WEST®
A Thomson Reuters business

Mat #41046234

American Casebook Series is a trademark registered in the U.S. Patent and Trademark Office.

© West, a Thomson business, 2001, 2004, 2008
© 2011 Thomson Reuters
    610 Opperman Drive
    St. Paul, MN 55123
    1–800–313–9378
Printed in the United States of America

ISBN: 978–0–314–26608–8

For Adam Houston Broome and Anna Lamkin Broome
—L.L.B.

For Mollie and Sean Markham
—J.W.M.

PREFACE TO THE FOURTH EDITION

The current regulatory structure for bank financial services in the United States is not the result of any grand design or reasoned blueprint. Rather, bank regulation represents a long history of responses to financial crises, scandals, happenstance, personalities, and compromises among a broad and competing array of industry and governmental units. The result is multiple levels of state and federal regulation. This complicated regulatory picture is compounded by the fact that many banks now offer a broad range of financial products and services beyond those traditionally considered to be banking services. The Gramm–Leach–Bliley Act of 1999 expanded the financial services offered by banks to include securities, insurance, and merchant banking. These products and services are subject to a multitude of additional regulatory requirements administered by the appropriate "functional" regulators, including the Securities and Exchange Commission, the Commodity Futures Trading Commission, state securities and insurance regulators, as well as the various traditional bank regulators. This book seeks to pierce this regulatory thicket and identify some of the more significant regulatory requirements confronting banks offering both traditional services and this expanded array of products.

This fourth edition incorporates developments in bank legislation and regulation that have occurred through September 2010, including the Dodd–Frank Wall Street Reform and Consumer Protection Act enacted in July 2010. This legislation, the most significant banking legislation since the Great Depression, is discussed extensively in this edition. The financial crisis that began in 2007 and preceded Dodd–Frank is also reviewed in detail. The new edition is accompanied by a revised and expanded statutory supplement, which includes the major federal banking statutes, excerpts from the Dodd–Frank Act, and some of the relevant federal regulations.

Many people provided support for this project. We list some of them here at the risk of excluding others who made equally valuable contributions. Former UNC School of Law deans Gene Nichol and Judith Wegner established the *North Carolina Banking Institute* journal and the Center for Banking and Finance. Dean Jack Boger continues to provide crucial support to these endeavors. Those institutions have brought us into contact with a number of bank lawyers, each of whom has made his or her own special contribution to our learning, and hence to this book. Special thanks, however, are owed to Tony Gaeta, of Gaeta & Eveson, PA, and to Gene Katz of the Wells Fargo Corporation for providing much of the raw material for Chapter 8. We have also benefitted from our association with Joseph Smith, the Commissioner of Banks of North Carolina. Any errors are, of course, our own.

A number of research assistants worked on the first edition of this book, including Julie Kimbrough, Cam Lavin, Bettina Mumme, Jonathan Perry, Scott Schaaf, and Adam Whitten. For their extraordinary efforts, we especially thank Cindy Mabel and Adam Wheeler. Steve Lee provided assistance with the production of the second edition, and Chase Tweel with the production of the third edition. For this fourth edition, we thank Patrick Craig and Cheryl Chew of the UNC School of Law and Ryan Peiffer, Rigers Gjyshi (Senior Research Fellow), and George Sullivan (Presidential Management Fellow) at FIU College of Law.

ACKNOWLEDGMENTS

We are indebted to the following authors and publishers for their generosity in giving us permission to reprint excerpts from copyrighted materials:

Basel Committee on Banking Supervision, Recommendation for Trading and Derivatives Activities of Banks and Securities Firms <www.bis.org/publ/bcbs60.htm>. Bank for International Settlements, Basle, Switzerland. Reprinted with permission.

Lissa L. Broome, Government Investment in Banks: Creeping Nationalization or Prudent, Temporary Aid?, 4 FIU L. Rev. 409 (2009).

Lissa L. Broome & Jerry W. Markham, Banking and Insurance: Before and After the Gramm–Leach–Bliley Act, 25 J. Corp. L. 723 (2000). Reprinted with permission of the Journal of Corporation Law © (2000).

Lissa L. Broome, The Influence of the Enhanced Thrift Institution Powers on Commercial Bank Market Expansion, 67 N.C. L. Rev. 795 (1989). Reprinted with permission.

Lissa L. Broome, Redistributing Bank Insolvency Risks: Challenges to Limited Liability in the Bank Holding Company Structure, 26 U.C. Davis L. Rev. 935 (1993). Reprinted with permission.

John J. Byrne, Douglas W. Densmore & Jeffrey M. Sharp, Examining the Increase in Federal Regulatory Requirements and Penalties: Is Banking Facing Another Troubled Decade? 24 Cap. U. L. Rev. 1 (1995). Reprinted with permission.

E. Gerald Corrigan, Are Banks Special?, Federal Reserve Bank of Minneapolis, 1982 Annual Report Essay. Reprinted with permission.

Fannie Mae, The Industry <www.fanniemae.com>. Reprinted with permission.

Jose Gabilondo, Leveraged Liquidity: Bear Raids and Junk Loans in the New Credit Market, 34 J. Corp. L. 447 (2009). Reprinted with permission.

Peter G. Gosselin, Greenspan Legacy Rides on a Wobbly Economy, L.A. Times, July 8, 2001, at A1. Reprinted with permission.

Group of Thirty, Global Derivatives Study Group, Derivatives: Practices and Principles, July 1993. Reprinted with permission.

Cassandra Jones Havard, Back to the Parent: Holding Company Liability for Subsidiary Banks—a Discussion of the Net Worth Maintenance Agreement, the Source of Strength Doctrine, and the Prompt Corrective Action Provisions, 16 Cardozo L. Rev. 2353 (1995). Reprinted with permission.

James O. Johnston & Daniel Schott Schecter, In the Matter of Kaye, Scholer, Fierman, Hays & Handler: A Symposium on Government Regulation,

Lawyers' Ethics, and the Rule of Law, 66 S. Cal. L. Rev. 977 (1993). Reprinted with permission of the Southern California Law Review.

Jerry W. Markham, Merging the SEC and the CFTC—A Class of Cultures, 78 U. Cin. L. Rev. 537 (2009). Reprinted with permission.

Jerry W. Markham, Regulating Credit Default Swaps in the Wake of the Subprime Crisis, Working Paper Prepared for the International Monetary Fund Seminar on Current Developments in Monetary and Financial Law, Dec. 2, 2009. Reprinted with permission.

Jerry W. Markham, SEC v. Goldman Sachs & Co.—Serious Fraud or Just More Banker Bashing, 30 Fut. & Deriv. L. Rep. 8 (2010). Reprinted with permission.

Jerry W. Markham, The Subprime Crisis—Some Thoughts on a "Sustainable" and "Organic" Regulatory System, 4 FIU L. Rev. 381 (2009). Reprinted with permission.

Jerry W. Markham, Super–Regulator: A Comparative Analysis of Securities and Derivatives Regulation in the United States, the United Kingdom, and Japan, 28 Brook. J. Int'l L. 319 (2003). Reprinted with permission of the author.

Jerry W. Markham & David J. Gilberg, Federal Regulation of Bank Activities in the Commodities Market, 39 Bus. Law. 1719 (1984). Reprinted by Permission from the American Bar Association and the authors.

Patricia A. McCoy, A Political Economy of the Business Judgment Rule in Banking: Implications for Corporate Law, 47 Case W. Res. L. Rev. 1 (1996). Reprinted with permission.

Frederic S. Mishkin, Survey: Mastering Risk–7: Securing a safety net against economic free fall, Fin. Times (London), (Survey), June 7, 2000, at 2. Reprinted with permission.

NASDAQ, NASD Regulation Fines Citicorp Securities $25,000; Orders $300,000 in Disgorgement, press release, 1986. Reprinted with permission.

The North Carolina Banking Institute journal, published by the University of North Carolina School of Law, has granted permission for the following articles to be reprinted:

Chad F. Brown, Note, Bank Mergers in Concentrated Markets: The Role of Mitigating Factors, 2 N.C. Banking Inst. 345 (1998).

John L. Douglas, Cyberbanking: Legal and Regulatory Considerations for Banking Organizations, 4 N.C. Banking Inst. 57 (2000).

Michael Durrer, Asset–Backed Commercial Paper Conduits, 1 N.C. Banking Inst. 119 (1997).

Evan M. Gilreath, Note, The Entrance of Banks into Subprime Lending: First Union and The Money Store, 3 N.C. Banking Inst. 149 (1999).

Mark O. Henry, Note, The Impact of Statement of Financial Accounting Standards 133 on the Banking Industry, 3 N.C. Banking Inst. 291 (1999).

Richard R. Holley, III, Note, One–Card 101: Wachovia Hits the Pit and Becomes the Partner Bank of the UNC One Card, 4 N.C. Banking Inst. 371 (2000).

Paul J. Polking & Scott A. Cammarn, Overview of the Gramm–Leach–Bliley Act, 4 N.C. Banking Inst. 1 (2000).

David W. Roderer, Tentative Steps Toward Financial Privacy, 4 N.C. Banking Inst. 209 (2000).

Jaclyn Rodriguez, Note, The Credit Card Act of 2009: An Effective but Incomplete Solution Evidencing the Need for a Federal Regulator, 14 N.C. Banking Inst. 309 (2010).

Scott A. Sinder, The Gramm–Leach–Bliley Act and State Regulation of the Business of Insurance—Past, Present and ... Future? 5 N.C. Banking Inst. 49 (2001).

Michael D. White, What Will it Take for Bank Insurance to Succeed in the United States? 2 N.C. Banking Inst. 123 (1998).

Timothy L. O'Brien, Former Official in Bankers Trust Fraud Case Claims a Set–Up, N.Y. Times, Mar. 15, 1999, at B4. Copyright © 1999 by the New York Times Co. Reprinted by permission.

Bryan J. Orticelli, Note, Crisis Compounded by Constraint: How Regulatory Inadequacies Impaired the Fed's Bailout of Bear Stearns, 42 Conn. L. Rev. 647 (2009). Reprinted with permission.

Katherine Samolyk, Role of Commercial Banks in U.S. Credit Markets, FDIC, Future of Banking Study (2004). Reprinted with permission.

Herbert Stein, The Model of a Modern Central Banker, Wall St. J., Aug. 7, 1998, at A10. Republished with permission of the Wall Street Journal; permission conveyed through Copyright Permission Center, Inc.

Peter P. Swire, Bank Insolvency Law Now That it Matters Again, 42 Duke L.J. 469 (1992). Reprinted with permission.

Julie L. Williams & Mark P. Jacobsen, The Business of Banking: Looking to the Future, 50 Bus. Law. 783 (1995). Reprinted with permission.

Julie L. Williams & James F.E. Gillespie, Jr., The Business of Banking: Looking to the Future—Part II, 52 Bus. Law. 1279 (1997). Reprinted with permission.

Summary of Contents

                                                                            Page

Preface to the Fourth Edition --- v
Acknowledgments-- vii
Table of Cases--- xxxi

Chapter One.   The History of Banking Regulation in America ---- **1**
  1. The Role of Banks in Early America ------------------------------- 2
  2. The Creation of Banks in Early America --------------------------- 9
  3. The Civil War Era--- 15
  4. The Birth of the Federal Reserve System -------------------------- 30
  5. The New Deal Legislation --- 38
  6. Limitations on Geographic Expansion------------------------------- 44
  7. Regulation of Bank Holding Companies ----------------------------- 49
  8. Inflationary Pressures --- 52
  9. Geographic Barriers Fall-- 54
 10. The Changing Roles of Banks and Their Holding Companies ---------- 55
 11. Post September 11 -- 61
 12. The Financial Crisis and the Dodd–Frank Wall Street Reform and
       Consumer Protection Act of 2010 -------------------------------- 61
 13. Themes of Banking Regulation ------------------------------------- 67

Chapter Two.   Thrift and Credit Union Regulation ------------- **72**
  1. The History of Thrift and Credit Union Regulation --------------- 72
  2. Savings and Loan Crisis-- 95
  3. The Financial Crisis and the Dodd–Frank Act-------------------- 114
  4. Regulation of Thrifts and Credit Unions ----------------------- 114
  5. Review of Regulatory Themes ----------------------------------- 128

Chapter Three.   The Business of Banking----------------------- **132**
  1. Financial Intermediation ------------------------------------- 132
  2. Transaction Accounts --- 133
  3. Monetary Policy--- 134
  4. Characteristics of Banks ------------------------------------- 169
  5. Income Statement-- 172
  6. Balance Sheet--- 173
  7. Challenges to the Traditional Business of Banks -------------- 174

Chapter Four.   Bank Regulation Today ------------------------ **184**
  1. Regulatory Structure--- 184
  2. Holding Company Regulation ---------------------------------- 231
  3. Privacy-- 268
  4. Technology, the Internet, and E–Commerce-------------------- 282

Page

Chapter Five.   Bank Assets - **291**
1. Non–Loan Assets - 291
2. General Regulation of Loans - 300
3. Commercial Lending Concerns - 320

Chapter Six.   Consumer Lending - **369**
1. Usury - 371
2. Truth in Lending Act (TILA) - 387
3. Equal Credit Opportunity Act (ECOA) - 420
4. Redlining, the Home Mortgage Disclosure Act (HMDA), and the Community Reinvestment Act (CRA) - 429
5. Real Estate Settlement Procedures Act (RESPA) - 436
6. Subprime and Predatory Lending - 441
7. Payday Lending - 460

Chapter Seven.   Bank Liabilities and Capital - **465**
1. Deposits - 465
2. Non–Deposit Liabilities - 508
3. Payment Methods - 528
4. Bank Capital - 545

Chapter Eight.   Supervision, Enforcement and Failed Bank Resolution - **568**
1. Supervision - 568
2. Enforcement Powers - 577
3. Orderly Liquidation Authority for Systemically Significant Financial Companies - 589
4. Failed Bank Resolution - 593

Chapter Nine.   Geographic Expansion, Mergers, and Antitrust - **633**
1. Geographic Expansion - 633
2. The Riegle–Neal Act and Beyond - 658
3. Bank Mergers and Acquisitions - 662
4. Antitrust Review - 667
5. Director Interlocks - 695

Chapter Ten.   Trust and Other Activities - **700**
1. Banks as Trustees - 700
2. Fiduciary Standards - 708
3. Custodial Services - 723
4. Pension Fund Management - 726
5. Safe Deposit Boxes - 735
6. Fund Transfer Services - 740

Chapter Eleven.   Capital Market Activities - **746**
1. Historical Limitations - 746
2. The Gramm–Leach–Bliley Act (GLBA) - 767
3. Bank Securities Sales - 775
4. Margin Requirements - 796

		Page
5.	Clearing and Settlement	802
6.	Merger Activities	809
7.	Mutual Funds	811
8.	Hedge Funds and Private Equity	822
9.	Trust Indentures	837
10.	Commercial Paper	847

Chapter Twelve.   Derivatives — **851**

1.	Introduction to Derivatives	851
2.	Banks Enter the Derivatives Business	863
3.	Hedging	867
4.	The Treasury Amendment	873
5.	Over–The–Counter Derivatives	877
6.	Credit Default Swaps	885
7.	Accounting for Derivatives	892
8.	Fair Value Accounting	901

Chapter Thirteen.   Insurance — **905**

1.	Introduction to Insurance	905
2.	Bank Insurance Activities Prior to Gramm–Leach–Bliley	912
3.	The Gramm–Leach–Bliley Act	932
4.	The Dodd–Frank Act	948

Chapter Fourteen.   International Banking — **951**

1.	Foreign Bank Operations in the United States	951
2.	International Operations of United States Banks	967
3.	Comparative Regulation	978
4.	International Monetary System	1000
5.	Money Laundering	1011
6.	Financial Embargos	1029

Index — 1035

TABLE OF CONTENTS

	Page
PREFACE TO THE FOURTH EDITION	v
ACKNOWLEDGMENTS	vii
TABLE OF CASES	xxxi

Chapter One. The History of Banking Regulation in America ···· **1**

1. The Role of Banks in Early America ····· 2
    A. Medium of Payment ····· 2
        The Case of Mixed Money in Ireland ····· 3
        Craig v. Missouri ····· 6
    B. Lending Money ····· 8
2. The Creation of Banks in Early America ····· 9
    A. The Bank of the United States and Early State Chartered Banks ····· 9
    B. The Second Bank of the United States ····· 10
        M'Culloch v. Maryland ····· 11
    C. The Fight Over the Second Bus ····· 14
3. The Civil War Era ····· 15
    A. Bank Currency ····· 15
        Marine Bank v. Fulton Bank ····· 16
    B. Shinplasters and the Stamp Payments Act ····· 17
        United States v. Van Auken ····· 18
    C. Greenbacks as Legal Tender ····· 19
        Legal Tender Cases Knox v. Lee Parker v. Davis ····· 19
    D. The National Bank Act ····· 22
        First National Bank of Charlotte v. National Exchange Bank of Baltimore ····· 24
        Veazie Bank v. Fenno ····· 25
    E. Clearing Houses and Central Banks ····· 28
        Philler v. Patterson ····· 29
4. The Birth of the Federal Reserve System ····· 30
    A. Check Clearing ····· 32
        American Bank & Trust Co. v. Federal Reserve Bank of Atlanta ····· 32
    B. Federal Reserve Notes ····· 33
        Milam v. United States ····· 33
    C. Monetary Policy ····· 34
        Raichle v. Federal Reserve Bank of New York ····· 35
5. The New Deal Legislation ····· 38
    A. Creation of Federal Deposit Insurance ····· 38
        Hewitt v. United States ····· 38
    B. Strengthening the Federal Reserve System ····· 40
        Herbert Stein, The Model of a Modern Central Banker ····· 41
    C. Glass-Steagall Act Restrictions on Securities Activities ····· 42
    D. Interest Rate Restrictions ····· 44

Page

6. Limitations on Geographic Expansion 44
   First National Bank in St. Louis v. Missouri 44
   First National Bank of Logan v. Walker Bank & Trust Co. 46
7. Regulation of Bank Holding Companies 49
   A. Closely Related to Banking 49
      Cameron Financial Corp. v. Board of Governors of the Federal Reserve System 49
   B. The Douglas Amendment and Geographic Expansion by Bank Holding Companies 51
   C. Pressures on the Bank Holding Company Act 51
8. Inflationary Pressures 52
   Paine, Webber, Jackson & Curtis, Inc. v. Merrill Lynch, Pierce, Fenner & Smith, Inc. 52
9. Geographic Barriers Fall 54
10. The Changing Roles of Banks and Their Holding Companies 55
    A. Continuing Competitive Pressures 55
    B. The Gramm–Leach–Bliley Act and Financial Holding Companies ... 57
       Paul J. Polking & Scott A. Cammarn, Overview of the Gramm–Leach–Bliley Act 57
       Jerry W. Markham, Merging The SEC and CFTC—A Clash of Cultures ... 60
11. Post September 11 61
12. The Financial Crisis and the Dodd–Frank Wall Street Reform and Consumer Protection Act of 2010 61
    A. The Financial Crisis 61
    B. The Dodd–Frank Wall Street Reform and Consumer Protection Act of 2010 65
       (1) Financial Stability Oversight Council 65
       (2) Orderly Liquidation Authority 65
       (3) Expanded Powers of the Fed Over Nonbank Financial Companies 66
       (4) The Fed's Emergency Lending and the FDIC's Systemic Risk Determinations 66
       (5) Financial Market Utilities 66
       (6) Bureau of Consumer Financial Protection 66
       (7) Securities, Hedge Funds, Private Equity, Derivatives, Insurance 67
       (8) Corporate Governance and Executive Compensation 67
13. Themes of Banking Regulation 67
    A. Reasons for Major Banking Legislation 67
    B. Themes Inherent in Banking Legislation and Regulation 67
       (1) Concerns About Mixing Banking and Commerce 68
       (2) Limited Entry 68
       (3) Dual Chartering and Regulatory Arbitrage 68
       (4) Restrictions on Geographic Expansion 69
       (5) Concerns About Impermissible Concentrations of Economic Power 69
       (6) Safety and Soundness Regulation 70
       (7) Grandfather Provisions 70
          Questions and Notes 71

Page

Chapter Two.   Thrift and Credit Union Regulation **72**
1. The History of Thrift and Credit Union Regulation 72
   A.   Savings and Loans 72
        West Helena Savings & Loan Ass'n v. Federal Home Loan Bank Board   74
        North Arlington National Bank v. Kearny Federal Savings & Loan Ass'n 76
        Fidelity Federal Savings & Loan Ass'n v. de la Cuesta 77
   B.   Savings Banks 82
        Huntington v. National Savings Bank 83
   C.   Credit Unions 84
        La Caisse Populaire Ste. Marie (St. Mary's Bank) v. United States 85
        National Credit Union Administration v. First National Bank & Trust Co. 91
   D.   Other Institutions 95
2. Savings and Loan Crisis 95
   A.   Destructive Inflationary Pressures 95
        Biscayne Federal Savings & Loan Ass'n v. Federal Home Loan Bank Board 96
   B.   The First Round of Legislative Responses 98
        Lissa Lamkin Broome, the Influence of Enhanced Thrift Institution Powers on Commercial Bank Market Expansion 99
        In the Matter of Charles H. Keating, Jr. 102
   C.   The Second Round of Legislative Responses: Congress Gets Tough 105
        Spiegel v. Ryan 106
        United States v. Winstar Corp. 108
3. The Financial Crisis and the Dodd–Frank Act 114
4. Regulation of Thrifts and Credit Unions 114
   A.   Regulatory Structure 114
   B.   Characteristics of Thrifts and Credit Unions 115
   C.   Powers 115
        Questions and Notes 117
   D.   Conversion or Demutualization 119
        Dougherty v. Carver Federal Savings Bank 119
        Questions and Notes 123
   E.   Holding Companies 124
        Office of Thrift Supervision, Historical Framework for Regulation of Activities of Unitary Savings and Loan Holding Companies 124
5. Review of Regulatory Themes 128
   A.   Reasons for Major Legislation 128
   B.   Regulatory Themes 128
        (1)   Concerns About Mixing Banking and Commerce 129
        (2)   Limited Entry 129
        (3)   Dual Chartering and Regulatory Arbitrage 129
        (4)   Restrictions on Geographic Expansion 129
        (5)   Concerns About Impermissible Concentrations of Economic Power 130
        (6)   Safety and Soundness Regulation 130
        (7)   Grandfather Provisions 130
        Questions and Notes 130

Chapter Three.   The Business of Banking **132**
1. Financial Intermediation 132
   Questions and Notes 133

Page

2. Transaction Accounts --- 133
   Questions and Notes -- 134
3. Monetary Policy --- 134
   A. Structure of the Federal Reserve System ----------------------- 134
      Board of Governors of the Federal Reserve System The Federal Reserve
         System: Purposes and Functions ------------------------------- 135
      Federal Reserve Banks --- 137
   B. Reserve Requirements -- 137
      Board of Governors of the Federal Reserve System The Federal Reserve
         System: Purposes & Functions --------------------------------- 137
      First Bank and Trust Co. v. Board of Governors of Federal Reserve
         System -- 140
   C. Open Market Operations -- 142
      Board of Governors of the Federal Reserve System, The Federal Reserve
         System: Purposes & Functions --------------------------------- 142
      Riegle v. Federal Open Market Committee ------------------------- 144
   D. The Discount Rate and Federal Funds Rate ----------------------- 147
      Board of Governors of the Federal Reserve System, The Federal Reserve
         System: Purposes & Functions --------------------------------- 148
   E. The Goals of Monetary Policy and How It Affects the Economy   150
      Board of Governors of the Federal Reserve System, The Federal Reserve
         System: Purposes & Functions --------------------------------- 150
      Peter G. Gosselin, Greenspan Legacy Rides on A Wobbly Economy -------- 154
   F. Systemic Risk --- 156
      (1) Fed Intervention -- 156
          Frederic S. Mishkin, Survey: Mastering Risk: Securing a Safety Net
             Against Economic Free Fall -------------------------------- 156
          Lakonia Management Ltd. v. Meriwether --------------------- 157
          Board of Governors of the Federal Reserve System, 88th Annual
             Report to Congress 2001 ----------------------------------- 160
          Questions and Notes -- 162
      (2) Fed Intervention in the Wake of the Financial Crisis --------- 162
          Jerry W. Markham, The Subprime Crisis—Some Thoughts on a
             "Sustainable" and "Organic" Regulatory System ------------- 163
      (3) The Dodd–Frank Act and the Financial Stability Oversight
          Council -- 166
4. Characteristics of Banks -- 169
5. Income Statement --- 172
6. Balance Sheet -- 173
7. Challenges to the Traditional Business of Banks ------------------------- 174
   E. Gerald Corrigan, Are Banks Special? -------------------------------- 176
   Julie L. Williams & Mark P. Jacobsen, The Business of Banking: Looking to
      the Future --- 180
   Katherine Samolyk, The Evolving Role of Commercial Banks in U.S. Credit
      Markets -- 181
   Questions and Notes --- 183

Chapter Four.   Bank Regulation Today -------------------------------- **184**
1. Regulatory Structure --- 184
   A. Chartering a Bank --- 187
      (1) National Bank --- 187
      (2) State Bank -- 188
          Farmers Deposit Bank of Brandenburg v. Department of Banking
             and Securities --- 188
          Questions and Notes -- 192

Page

1. Regulatory Structure—Continued
 B. Bank Powers --- 192
  (1) The Business of Banking for National Banks ------------- 192
   Arnold Tours, Inc. v. Camp -------------------------------- 192
   NationsBank of North Carolina, N.A. v. Variable Annuity Life
    Insurance Co. --- 197
   Julie L. Williams & Mark P. Jacobsen, The Business of Banking:
    Looking to the Future -------------------------------- 201
   Julie L. Williams & James F.E. Gillespie, Jr., The Business of
    Banking: Looking to the Future–Part II ------------------ 203
   Questions and Notes ------------------------------------ 205
  (2) National Bank Act Preemption of State Law ------------- 206
   Barnett Bank of Marion County, N.A. v. Nelson ----------- 206
  (3) The OCC's Visitorial Powers --------------------------- 213
   Cuomo v. The Clearing House Association, LLC ------------ 214
  (4) Diversity Jurisdiction -------------------------------- 218
   Wachovia Bank, N.A. v. Schmidt ------------------------- 218
   Questions and Notes ------------------------------------ 220
  (5) Powers of State Banks -------------------------------- 222
   Questions and Notes ------------------------------------ 223
 C. Bank Subsidiaries -- 223
  (1) Bank Service Corporation ------------------------------ 223
  (2) Operating Subsidiary ---------------------------------- 224
   Watters v. Wachovia Bank, N.A. ------------------------- 224
  (3) Financial Subsidiary ---------------------------------- 229
   Questions and Notes ------------------------------------ 230
 D. Corporate Governance ------------------------------------- 230
2. Holding Company Regulation ------------------------------------- 231
 A. Bank Holding Companies ----------------------------------- 231
  Board of Governors of the Federal Reserve System v. Dimension Finan-
   cial Corp. -- 232
  National Courier Ass'n v. Board of Governors of the Federal Reserve
   System -- 237
 B. Financial Holding Companies ------------------------------ 239
  Board of Governors of the Federal Reserve System, Bank Holding
   Companies and Change in Bank Control ------------------- 242
  Federal Reserve System, The Goldman Sachs Group, Inc. Goldman
   Sachs Bank USA Holdings LLC, Order Approving Formation of Bank
   Holding Companies -------------------------------------- 244
 C. Additional Regulation for Systemically Significant Companies ---- 246
  Questions and Notes -------------------------------------- 247
 D. Functional Regulation ------------------------------------ 248
  Jerry W. Markham, The Subprime Crisis—Some Thoughts on a "Sus-
   tainable" and "Organic" Regulatory System --------------- 250
 E. Commercial Activities ------------------------------------ 251
  Questions and Notes -------------------------------------- 254
 F. Interaffiliate Relations --------------------------------- 255
  (1) Affiliate Transactions -------------------------------- 255
   Board of Governors of the Federal Reserve System, Interim Rules
    With Request for Public Comments ----------------------- 255
   Questions and Notes ------------------------------------ 256
  (2) Conflicts of Interest --------------------------------- 257
   Washington Steel Corp. v. TW Corp. --------------------- 257
   Questions and Notes ------------------------------------ 263

                                                                          Page

2. Holding Company Regulation—Continued
    (3) Anti–Tying 263
        Dibidale of Louisiana, Inc. v. American Bank & Trust Co. 265
        Questions and Notes 267
3. Privacy 268
    A. Disclosure to the Government 268
        Adams v. Board of Governors of the Federal Reserve Board 268
        Lopez v. First Union National Bank of Florida 270
    B. Disclosure to Private Parties 277
        David W. Roderer, Tentative Steps Toward Financial Privacy 277
        Questions and Notes 281
4. Technology, the Internet, and E–Commerce 282
    A. Technology 282
        Roger W. Ferguson, Jr., Information Technology In Banking and Super-
        vision 282
    B. Electronic Banking 286
        Federal Financial Institutions Examination Council, Information Tech-
        nology Examination Handbook E–banking 286
        Questions and Notes 289

Chapter Five.   Bank Assets **291**
1. Non–Loan Assets 291
    A. Real Estate 291
    B. Investments 291
        Marx v. Centran Corp. 292
        United States v. Iguchi 294
        Questions and Notes 298
2. General Regulation of Loans 300
    A. Lending Limits 300
        del Junco v. Conover 301
        Questions and Notes 306
    B. Insider Loans 306
        de la Fuente v. Federal Deposit Insurance Corp. 307
        Questions and Notes 312
    C. Lender Liability 312
    D. Environmental Lender Liability 313
        United States v. Fleet Factors Corp. 313
        Questions and Notes 317
    E. Accounting for Loan Loss Reserves 317
    F. Fair Value Accounting 319
3. Commercial Lending Concerns 320
    A. Loan Participations, Syndicated Loans, and Leveraged Loans 320
        Banco Espanol De Credito v. Security Pacific National Bank 321
        Jose Gabilondo, Leveraged Liquidity: Bear Raids and Junk Loans in the
        New Credit Market 324
        Questions and Notes 328
    B. Secondary Loan Market 329
        Freddie Mac, Our Business 333
        Questions and Notes 334
    C. Securitization 334
        Office of the Comptroller of the Currency, Comptroller's Handbook: Asset
        Securitization 335
        (1) Mortgage-Backed Securities 336

Page

3. Commercial Lending Concerns—Continued
    Ginnie Mae, What Are Mortgage–Backed Securities? 337
    Rockford Life Insurance Co. v. Illinois Department Of Revenue 337
    Securities Industry Ass'n v. Clarke 339
    *Federal Deposit Insurance Corporation, Breaking New Ground In
        U.S. Mortgage Lending* 342
    (2) Collateralized Mortgage Obligations 342
        Banca Cremi, S.A. v. Alex. Brown & Sons, Inc. 343
        *Jerry W. Markham, Regulating Credit Default Swaps in the Wake
            of the Subprime Crisis* 347
    (3) Other Asset–Backed Securities 351
        *Board of Governors of the Federal Reserve System, Term Asset–
            backed Securities Loan Facility* 352
        Michael Durrer, Asset-Backed Commercial Paper Conduits 354
    (4) Role of the Credit Rating Agencies 356
    (5) Special Concerns Related to Securitizations by Banks 359
        Questions and Notes 361
    D. Loan Protection and Surety Bonds 362
        JPMorgan Chase Bank v. Liberty Mutual Insurance Co. 363
        Questions and Notes 367

Chapter Six. Consumer Lending **369**
1. Usury 371
    A. National Banks 372
        Tiffany v. National Bank of Missouri 372
        *Marquette National Bank of Minneapolis v. First of Omaha Service
            Corp.* 374
        Smiley v. Citibank (South Dakota), N. A. 378
    B. State Banks 381
        Greenwood Trust v. Commonwealth of Massachusetts 381
        Questions and Notes 385
2. Truth in Lending Act (TILA) 387
    A. Open–End Versus Closed–End Credit 387
        Benion v. Bank One, Dayton, N.A. 387
    B. Fair Credit and Charge Card Disclosure Act 389
        *Statement by John P. Laware, Subcommittee on Consumer Affairs and
            Coinage of the Committee on Banking, Finance and Urban Affairs* 390
        *Jaclyn Rodriguez Note, Credit Card Act: The Credit Card Act of 2009:
            An Effective but Incomplete Solution Evidencing the Need for a
            Federal Regulator* 391
    C. Fair Credit Billing Act 395
        American Express Co. v. Koerner 395
        First National City Bank v. Mullarkey 398
    D. Home Equity Loan Consumer Protection Act (HELC) 400
        Consumers Union of the U.S., Inc. v. Federal Reserve Board 400
        Questions and Notes 402
    E. Rights and Remedies 403
        (1) Rescission 403
        (2) Damages 403
            Turner v. Beneficial Corp. 403
            Koons Buick Pontiac GMC, Inc. v. Nigh 406
        (3) Arbitration 411
            Green Tree Financial Corp.–Alabama v. Randolph 411
            Randolph v. Green Tree Financial Corp.–Alabama 416
            Questions and Notes 419

Page

3. Equal Credit Opportunity Act (ECOA) ---------------------------------- 420
   Markham v. Colonial Mortgage Service Co. ---------------------------- 420
   Latimore v. Citibank Federal Savings Bank -------------------------- 423
   Questions and Notes --- 428
4. Redlining, the Home Mortgage Disclosure Act (HMDA), and the
   Community Reinvestment Act (CRA) --------------------------------- 429
   Lee v. Board of Governors of the Federal Reserve System ------------ 430
   United States v. Chevy Chase Federal Savings Bank ----------------- 433
   Questions and Notes --- 434
5. Real Estate Settlement Procedures Act (RESPA) ---------------------- 436
   Heimmermann v. First Union Mortgage Corp. --------------------- 437
   Questions and Notes --- 440
6. Subprime and Predatory Lending ------------------------------------ 441
   Office of the Comptroller of the Currency, OCC Advisory Letter Al 2003–2 ---- 441
   United Companies Lending Corp. v. Sargeant ---------------------- 443
   Department of the Treasury, Office of the Comptroller of the Currency,
      Preemption Determination and Order --------------------------- 447
   Department of the Treasury, Office of the Comptroller of the Currency, Final
      Rule: Bank Activities and Operations; Real Estate Lending and Apprais-
      als -- 449
   Interagency Statement, Statement on Subprime Mortgage Lending ------------ 453
   Questions and Notes --- 459
7. Payday Lending -- 460
   Questions and Notes --- 463

Chapter Seven.   Bank Liabilities and Capital ---------------------- 465
1. Deposits --- 465
  A. Types of Deposit Accounts --- 465
     (1) Lifeline or Basic Accounts -------------------------------------- 466
     (2) Certificates of Deposit --- 467
        Marine Bank v. Weaver -- 467
     (3) Discriminatory Account Policies: The Truth in Savings Act -- 469
        Garcia-Harding v. Bank Midwest, N.A. ------------------------ 469
  B. Regulation of Deposit Accounts ----------------------------------- 471
     (1) Deposit Account Fees and ATM Fees --------------------------- 471
        Video Trax, Inc. v. Nationsbank, N.A. -------------------------- 472
        Bank of America v. City and County of San Francisco ----------- 478
        Questions and Notes --- 485
     (2) Check 21 --- 487
     (3) Deposit Interest Rate Regulation ------------------------------ 487
        CF Industries, Inc. v. Commissioner of Internal Revenue ---------- 488
        Questions and Notes --- 490
  C. Deposit Insurance --- 490
     (1) Amount of Coverage -- 491
     (2) FDIC Reserves --- 492
     (3) Deposit Insurance Assessments -------------------------------- 494
     (4) Who Is Covered --- 495
     (5) FDIC Guarantees --- 496
        Questions and Notes --- 496
  D. Brokered Deposits --- 496
     Gary Plastic Packaging Corp. v. Merrill Lynch, Pierce, Fenner & Smith,
       Inc. --- 497
     Faic Securities, Inc. v. United States ------------------------------- 500
     Questions and Notes --- 502

Page

1. Deposits—Continued
 E. Set–Off 503
  Farmers' National Bank v. Jones 503
 F. Escheat Laws 505
  Delaware v. New York 505
  Timothy L. O'Brien, Former Official in Bankers Trust Fraud Case
   Claims a Set–Up 507
  Questions and Notes 508
2. Non–Deposit Liabilities 508
 A. Federal Funds Bought 508
 B. Repos 508
  Securities and Exchange Commission v. Miller 508
  Manufacturers Hanover Trust Co. v. Drysdale Securities Corp. 514
  Bryan J. Orticelli, Note, Crisis Compounded by Constraint: How Regu-
   latory Inadequacies Impaired the Fed's Bailout of Bear Stearns 516
  Questions and Notes 517
 C. Bankers' Acceptances 518
  United States v. Dougherty 519
 D. Letters of Credit 521
  Federal Deposit Insurance Corp. v. Philadelphia Gear Corp. 521
  Centrifugal Casting Machine Co. v. American Bank & Trust Co. 524
  Questions and Notes 527
3. Payment Methods 528
 A. Credit and Debit Cards 528
  National Bancard Corp. v. VISA, U.S.A. 528
  In re Visa Check/Mastermoney Antitrust Litigation 532
  Questions and Notes 535
 B. Smart Cards or Stored Value Cards 536
  Richard R. Holley, III NOTE, One–Card 101: Wachovia Hits the Pit and
   Becomes the Partner Bank of the UNC One Card 536
  FDIC General Counsel's Opinion No. 8, Insurability of Funds Underly-
   ing Stored Value Cards and Other Nontraditional Access Mecha-
   nisms 538
 C. Electronic Transfers 539
  Bisbey v. D.C. National Bank 540
  Eisenberg v. Wachovia Bank, N.A. 541
  Questions and Notes 545
4. Bank Capital 545
 A. Evolution of Bank Capital Requirements 546
  (1) Inadequate Capital as an Unsafe and Unsound Practice 546
   First National Bank of Bellaire v. Comptroller of the Currency 546
   Federal Deposit Insurance Corp. v. Bank of Coushatta 549
  (2) Capital Ratios and the Basel Accord 551
   Board of Governors of the Federal Reserve System, Trading and
    Capital–Markets Activities Manual Capital Adequacy, Section
    2110.1 553
  (3) Basel II 554
  (4) The Government's Response to the Financial Crisis–the
    Troubled Asset Relief Program (TARP) 556
   Lissa L. Broome, Government Investment in Banks: Creeping Na-
    tionalization or Prudent, Temporary Aid? 556
  (5) The Financial Crisis and Basel III 561
  (6) The Dodd–Frank Act 562
   Questions and Notes 563

Page

4. Bank Capital—Continued
  B. Special Issues 565
    (1) Merchant Banking 565
    (2) Securitizations 565
    (3) Subordinated Debt 566
      Board of Governors of the Federal Reserve System, The Feasibility
        and Desirability of Mandatory Subordinated Debt 566
      Questions and Notes 567

Chapter Eight. Supervision, Enforcement and Failed Bank
  Resolution **568**
1. Supervision 568
  A. Camels Rating System 570
    Federal Deposit Insurance Corporation, Manual of Examination Policies 570
  B. Holding Company Regulation 575
    Federal Reserve Board of Governors, Bank Holding Company Rating
      System 575
  C. Systemically Significant Financial Institutions 576
2. Enforcement Powers 577
  A. History of Enforcement Activities 577
  B. Types of Enforcement Actions 579
    (1) Informal Supervisory and Enforcement Actions 579
    (2) Formal Enforcement Mechanisms 579
    (3) Conduct of the Administrative Process 582
      Matter of Seidman 583
      Questions and Notes 589
3. Orderly Liquidation Authority for Systemically Significant Financial
  Companies 589
  Statement of Sheila C. Bair, Chairman, Federal Deposit Insurance Corpora-
    tion, Financial Crisis Inquiry Commission 590
4. Failed Bank Resolution 593
  A. Open Bank Assistance 594
  B. Prompt Corrective Action 594
  C. Closure of Bank 595
  D. Resolution Methods 595
    Lissa Lamkin Broome, Redistributing Bank Insolvency Risks: Chal-
      lenges to Limited Liability in the Bank Holding Company Structure 595
    Scott C. Alvarez, General Counsel, Federal Reserve Board of Governors,
      Testimony Before the Financial Crisis Inquiry Commission 598
  E. Cross-Guarantees, the Controlling Company Guarantee Provi-
    sion, and Source of Strength 602
    Lissa Lamkin Broome, Redistributing Bank Insolvency Risks: Chal-
      lenges to Limited Liability In the Bank Holding Company Structure 602
    Cassandra Jones Havard, Back to the Parent: Holding Company Liabili-
      ty for Subsidiary Banks—A Discussion of the New Worth Maintenance
      Agreement, the Source of Strength Doctrine, and the Prompt Correc-
      tive action Provisions 605
    Questions and Notes 607
  F. Creditors and Priorities 607
    Peter P. Swire, Bank Insolvency Law Now That it Matters Again 608
  G. Liability of Institution–Affiliated Parties, Including Officers, Di-
    rectors, and Attorneys 611
    (1) Cease and Desist Order Against Institution–Affiliated Party 611
      James O. Johnston, Jr. & Daniel Schott Schecter, Introduction:
        Kaye, Scholer and the OTS— Did Anyone Go Too Far? 611

Page

4. Failed Bank Resolution—Continued
    (2) Actions by Conservator or Receiver to Recover Losses from
        Officers or Directors 615
        Resolution Trust Corp. v. Walde 615
    (3) Special Standards for Professional Negligence Actions
        Brought by Conservators or Receivers 619
        Patricia A. McCoy, A Political Economy of the Business Judgment
            Rule in Banking: Implications for Corporate Law 619
        Atherton v. Federal Deposit Insurance Corp. 621
    (4) Criminal Sanctions 624
        John J. Byrne, Douglas W. Densmore & Jeffrey M. Sharp, Examin-
            ing the Increase in Federal Regulatory Requirements and Penal-
            ties: Is Banking Facing Another Troubled Decade? 624
        Questions and Notes 628
  H. Claims by Debtors 628
      Peter P. Swire, Bank Insolvency Law Now That it Matters Again 629
      Motorcity of Jacksonville, Ltd. v. Southeast Bank N.A. 629
      Questions and Notes 632

Chapter Nine. Geographic Expansion, Mergers, and Antitrust ... 633
1. Geographic Expansion 633
  A. The History of In–State Branching Prior to Riegle–Neal 633
      First National Bank in Plant City v. Dickinson 634
      Clarke v. Securities Industry Ass'n 637
  B. Interstate Branching Prior to Riegle–Neal 642
      Conference of State Bank Supervisors v. Office of Thrift Supervision 642
      Bank One, Utah, N.A. v. Guttau 645
      Questions and Notes 650
  C. The History of Interstate Banking Prior to Riegle–Neal 650
      Northeast Bancorp, Inc. v. Board of Governors of the Federal Reserve
        System 650
      Questions and Notes 658
2. The Riegle–Neal Act and Beyond 658
  A. Repeal of the Douglas Amendment 659
  B. Interstate Branching 659
  C. The Ban on Interstate Branching for Deposit Production 661
      Questions and Notes 661
3. Bank Mergers and Acquisitions 662
  A. Form of Combination 663
  B. Business Issues 664
  C. Regulatory Approvals 666
      Questions and Notes 667
4. Antitrust Review 667
  A. Definition of the Relevant Market 669
      United States v. Philadelphia National Bank 669
      United States v. Connecticut National Bank 672
      Lissa Lamkin Broome, The Influence of Enhanced Thrift Institution
        Powers on Commercial Bank Market Expansion 675
  B. Convenience and Needs of the Community 676
      County National Bancorporation v. Board of Governors of the Federal
        Reserve System 676
      Jerry W. Markham, Regulating Credit Default Swaps in the Wake of the
        Subprime Crisis 681

Page

4. Antitrust Review—Continued
   C. Market Concentration -- 684
      Lissa Lamkin Broome, The Influence Of Enhanced Thrift institution Powers on Commercial Bank Market Expansion -- 684
      Board of Governors of the Federal Reserve System, Division of Research and Statistics -- 685
      Federal Reserve Board of Governors, Order Approving the Merger of Bank Holding Companies -- 687
   D. Mitigating Factors -- 690
      Chad F. Brown, Note, Bank Mergers in Concentrated Markets: The Role of Mitigating Factors -- 690
   E. Deposit Caps and Liability Concentration Limits ------------------ 693
      Questions and Notes -- 694
5. Director Interlocks -- 695
   BankAmerica Corp. v. United States -- 695
   Questions and Notes -- 699

Chapter Ten. Trust and Other Activities -- **700**
1. Banks as Trustees -- 700
   First National Bank of Bay City v. Fellows -- 700
   American Trust Co. v. South Carolina State Board of Bank Control -- 702
   Mullane v. Central Hanover Bank & Trust Co. -- 706
   Questions and Notes -- 707
2. Fiduciary Standards -- 708
   In re Bank of New York -- 709
   Matter of OnBank & Trust Co. -- 711
   First Alabama Bank of Montgomery, N.A. v. Martin -- 714
   Central National Bank of Mattoon v. United States Department of Treasury -- 719
   Questions and Notes -- 722
3. Custodial Services -- 723
   Comptroller of the Currency, Custody Services: Comptroller's Handbook -- 723
   Grede v. Bank of New York Mellon -- 725
4. Pension Fund Management -- 726
   Laborers National Pension Fund v. Northern Trust Quantitative Advisors, Inc. -- 727
   Questions and Notes -- 734
5. Safe Deposit Boxes -- 735
   National Safe Deposit Co. v. Stead -- 735
   Morgan v. Citizens' Bank of Spring Hope -- 738
   Questions and Notes -- 740
6. Fund Transfer Services -- 740
   Banca Commerciale Italiana, New York Branch v. Northern Trust International Banking Corp. -- 741
   Questions and Notes -- 744

Chapter Eleven. Capital Market Activities -- **746**
1. Historical Limitations -- 746
   A. Early Restrictions -- 746
      Block v. Pennsylvania Exchange Bank -- 746
   B. The Glass–Steagall Act -- 748
      Securities Industry Ass'n v. Board of Governors of the Federal Reserve System -- 749
      Investment Company Institute v. Camp -- 751

Page

1. Historical Limitations—Continued
    - (1) Brokering Securities ----- 753
        - *American Bankers Ass'n v. Securities and Exchange Commission* --- 753
        - *Securities Industry Ass'n v. Board of Governors of the Federal Reserve System* ----- 757
    - (2) Underwriting Securities ----- 759
        - *Securities Industry Ass'n v. Board Of Governors of the Federal Reserve System* ----- 759
    - C. Thrift Securities Activities ----- 764
        - *Securities Industry Ass'n v. Federal Home Loan Bank Board* ----- 765
        - Questions and Notes ----- 766
2. The Gramm–Leach–Bliley Act (GLBA) ----- 767
    - A. Background ----- 767
        - *CIT Group, Inc. v. Citicorp* ----- 767
    - B. Broker–Dealer Registration ----- 769
        - Questions and Notes ----- 770
    - C. Underwriting ----- 771
        - Questions and Notes ----- 772
    - D. Merchant Banking ----- 773
        - Questions and Notes ----- 774
3. Bank Securities Sales ----- 775
    - *In the Matter of Nations Securities and NationsBank, N.A.* ----- 776
    - *NASD Regulation Fines Citicorp Securities $25,000; Orders $300,000 in Disgorgement* ----- 779
    - *Press v. Chemical Investment Services Corp.* ----- 780
    - *Charter House, Inc. v. First Tennessee Bank, N.A.* ----- 782
    - *In re First Union Securities, Inc.* ----- 785
    - Questions and Notes ----- 788
    - *In the Matter of Deutsche Asset Management, Inc.* ----- 791
4. Margin Requirements ----- 796
    - *Securities and Exchange Commission, Response to an Inquiry from Senator John C. Danforth* ----- 797
    - *Schy v. Federal Deposit Insurance Corp.* ----- 799
5. Clearing and Settlement ----- 802
    - *Alex. Brown & Sons, Inc. v. Marine Midland Banks, Inc.* ----- 802
    - *In the Matter of the Chase Manhattan Bank, N.A.* ----- 805
    - *Fidelity Partners, Inc. v. First Trust Co. of New York* ----- 806
6. Merger Activities ----- 809
    - *Norwest Bank Minnesota v. Sween Corp.* ----- 809
7. Mutual Funds ----- 811
    - *In the Matter of the Bank of California, N.A.* ----- 813
    - *Olesh v. Dreyfus Corp.* ----- 814
    - Questions and Notes ----- 821
8. Hedge Funds and Private Equity ----- 822
    - A. Hedge Funds ----- 822
        - *Pension Committee of the University of Montreal Pension Plan v. Banc of America Securities LLC* ----- 824
        - *Jerry W. Markham, SEC v. Goldman Sachs & Co.—Serious Fraud or Just More Banker Bashing* ----- 828
        - Questions and Notes ----- 831
    - B. Private Equity ----- 833
    - C. Dodd–Frank Act Limits on Hedge Funds and Private Equity ----- 836
9. Trust Indentures ----- 837
    - *Zeffiro v. First Pennsylvania Banking and Trust Co.* ----- 838
    - *Elliott Associates v. J. Henry Schroder Bank & Trust Co.* ----- 840
    - *Racepoint Partners, LLC v. JPMorgan Chase Bank, N.A.* ----- 843
    - Questions and Notes ----- 846

Page

10. Commercial Paper... 847
    Ryder International Corp. v. First American National Bank........... 847
    Questions and Notes... 848

Chapter Twelve. Derivatives.. **851**
1. Introduction to Derivatives.. 851
    Merrill Lynch, Pierce, Fenner & Smith, Inc. v. Curran.............. 851
    Group of Thirty, Global Derivatives Study Group, Derivatives: Practices and
        Principles... 858
    Questions and Notes... 863
2. Banks Enter the Derivatives Business.................................. 863
    Jerry W. Markham & David J. Gilberg, Federal Regulation of Bank Activi-
        ties in the Commodities Markets................................. 863
    Questions and Notes... 866
3. Hedging.. 867
    OCC Bulletin 96–43, Credit Derivatives: Guidelines for National Banks..... 867
    Greene County Bank v. Federal Deposit Insurance Corp.............. 870
    Questions and Notes... 872
4. The Treasury Amendment... 873
    Dunn v. Commodity Futures Trading Commission...................... 873
    Questions and Notes... 877
5. Over–The–Counter Derivatives... 877
    Procter & Gamble Co. v. Bankers Trust Co.......................... 878
    Questions and Notes... 885
6. Credit Default Swaps.. 885
    Jerry W. Markham, Regulating Credit Default Swaps in the Wake of the
        Subprime Crisis... 885
    Questions and Notes... 892
7. Accounting for Derivatives.. 892
    Basel Committee on Banking Supervision, Recommendations for Public
        Disclosure of Trading and Derivatives Activities of Banks and Securities
        Firms.. 892
    Mark O. Henry, Note, The Impact of Statement of Financial Accounting
        Standards 133 on the Banking Industry........................... 893
    Questions and Notes... 896
8. Fair Value Accounting... 901

Chapter Thirteen. Insurance... **905**
1. Introduction to Insurance... 905
    A. The Business of Insurance...................................... 905
        New York Life Insurance Co. v. Statham........................ 905
    B. Regulation of Insurance—Background and History................. 908
        Scott A. Sinder, The Gramm–Leach–Bliley Act And State Regulation of
            the Business of Insurance................................... 909
    C. Insurance Expands Its Borders................................. 911
        Questions and Notes... 912
2. Bank Insurance Activities Prior to Gramm–Leach–Bliley............... 912
    Michael D. White, What Will It Take for Bank Insurance to Succeed in the
        United States?... 912
    A. National Banks... 916
        Saxon v. Georgia Ass'n of Independent Insurance Agents, Inc... 916
        Independent Insurance Agents of America v. Ludwig............. 918
        Office of the Comptroller of the Currency, OCC Interpretive Letter........ 920
        Questions and Notes... 923

Page

2. Bank Insurance Activities Prior to Gramm–Leach–Bliley—Continued
    B. State Banks 923
        Citicorp v. Board of Governors of the Federal Reserve System 924
    C. Nonbanking Subsidiary of a Bank Holding Company 931
        Questions and Notes 931
3. The Gramm–Leach–Bliley Act 932
    A. Nonbanking Subsidiary of a Holding Company 932
    B. National Banks and National Bank Subsidiaries 933
    C. State Banks and State Bank Subsidiaries 934
    D. State Regulation of Insurance 935
        Scott A. Sinder, The Gramm–Leach–Bliley Act and State Regulation of
          the Business of Insurance 935
        In re Lutheran Brotherhood Variable Insurance Products Co. Sales
          Practices Litigation 943
        Questions and Notes 946
4. The Dodd–Frank Act 948
    Financial Crisis Inquiry Commission, Preliminary Staff Report: Governmental Rescues of "Too–Big–to–Fail" Financial Institutions 948
    Questions and Notes 950

Chapter Fourteen. International Banking **951**
1. Foreign Bank Operations in the United States 951
    A. International Banking Act 951
        United States v. Lewis 951
        McHugh v. Westpac Banking Corp. 954
        Questions and Notes 956
    B. International Coordination of Regulation 956
        United States General Accounting Office, International Banking: Strengthening the Framework for Supervising International Banks 957
        United States v. BCCI Holdings (Luxembourg), S.A. 959
        United States v. Drogoul 962
        (1) Foreign Bank Supervision Enhancement Act 963
          United States General Accounting Office International Banking: Strengthening the Framework for Supervising International Banks 963
        (2) The Gramm–Leach–Bliley Act (GLBA) 965
        (3) Regulatory Framework 965
        (4) The Dodd–Frank Act 966
          Questions and Notes 966
2. International Operations of United States Banks 967
    Apfel v. Mellon 967
    Allied Bank International v. Banco Credito Agricola De Cartago 970
    Citibank, N.A. v. Wells Fargo Asia Ltd. 973
    Federal Deposit Insurance Corporation, The Globalization of the U.S. Banking Industry 976
    Questions and Notes 978
3. Comparative Regulation 978
    A. Japan 979
        Jerry W. Markham, Super Regulator: A Comparative Analysis of Securities and Derivatives Regulation in the United States, the United Kingdom, and Japan 980
    B. United Kingdom 984
        Financial Services Authority 984
        Financial Services Authority 985
        Financial Services Authority 985
        Questions and Notes 987

Page

3. Comparative Regulation—Continued
    C. Germany -- 988
        The New Federal [German] Financial Supervisory Authority (BAFIN) ---- 988
    D. European Union -- 995
        Questions and Notes --- 998
4. International Monetary System -- 1000
    Norman v. Baltimore & Ohio Railroad Co. ----------------------------- 1001
    Trans World Airlines, Inc. v. Franklin Mint Corp. ------------------------- 1005
    Elliott Associates, L.P. v. Banco De La Nacion ------------------------- 1007
    Questions and Notes -- 1010
5. Money Laundering --- 1011
    California Bankers Ass'n v. Shultz --------------------------------------- 1012
    Lee v. Bankers Trust Co. -- 1018
    United States v. Giraldi -- 1020
    United States v. One 1997 E35 Ford Van --------------------------------- 1023
    Questions and Notes -- 1029
6. Financial Embargos --- 1029
    Dames & Moore v. Regan -- 1029
    Banque San Paolo v. Iraqi State Co. for Food Stuff Trading ------------- 1030
    Questions and Notes -- 1032

INDEX --- 1035

TABLE OF CASES

The principal cases are in bold type. Cases cited or discussed in the text are in roman type. References are to pages. Cases cited in principal cases and within other quoted materials are not included.

Acorn v. Household Intern., Inc., 211 F.Supp.2d 1160 (N.D.Cal.2002), 420

Adams v. Board of Governors of Federal Reserve Bd., 855 F.2d 1336 (8th Cir.1988), **268**

Alex. Brown & Sons Inc. v. Marine Midland Banks, Inc., 1997 WL 97837 (S.D.N.Y.1997), **802**

Allied Bank Intern. v. Banco Credito Agricola de Cartago, 757 F.2d 516 (2nd Cir.1985), **970**

American Bankers Ass'n v. Lockyer, 412 F.3d 1081 (9th Cir.2005), 280

American Bankers Ass'n v. Lockyer, 2005 WL 2452798 (E.D.Cal.2005), 281

American Bankers Ass'n v. National Credit Union Admin., 271 F.3d 262, 350 U.S.App.D.C. 1 (D.C.Cir.2001), 94

American Bankers Ass'n v. S.E.C., 804 F.2d 739, 256 U.S.App.D.C. 194 (D.C.Cir.1986), **753**

American Bank & Trust Co. v. Federal Reserve Bank of Atlanta, 262 U.S. 643, 43 S.Ct. 649, 67 L.Ed. 1153 (1923), **32**

American Bar Ass'n v. F.T.C., 430 F.3d 457, 368 U.S.App.D.C. 368 (D.C.Cir.2005), 281

American Bell Intern., Inc. v. Islamic Republic of Iran, 474 F.Supp. 420 (S.D.N.Y.1979), 527

American Deposit Corp. v. Schacht, 84 F.3d 834 (7th Cir.1996), 923

American Exp. Co. v. Koerner, 452 U.S. 233, 101 S.Ct. 2281, 68 L.Ed.2d 803 (1981), **395**

American Trust Co., Inc. v. South Carolina State Bd. of Bank Control, 381 F.Supp. 313 (D.S.C.1974), **702**

Anderson Nat. Bank v. Luckett, 321 U.S. 233, 64 S.Ct. 599, 88 L.Ed. 692 (1944), 508

Apfel v. Mellon, 33 F.2d 805 (D.C.Cir.1929), **967**

Arnold Tours, Inc. v. Camp, 472 F.2d 427 (1st Cir.1972), **192**

Association of Banks in Ins., Inc. v. Duryee, 270 F.3d 397 (6th Cir.2001), 941

Association of Data Processing Service Organizations, Inc. v. Board of Governors of Federal Reserve System, 745 F.2d 677, 240 U.S.App.D.C. 301 (D.C.Cir.1984), 432

Atherton v. F.D.I.C., 519 U.S. 213, 117 S.Ct. 666, 136 L.Ed.2d 656 (1997), **621**

Banca Commerciale Italiana, New York Branch v. Northern Trust Intern. Banking Corp., 160 F.3d 90 (2nd Cir.1998), **741**

Banca Cremi, S.A. v. Alex. Brown & Sons, Inc., 132 F.3d 1017 (4th Cir.1997), **343**

Banco Espanol de Credito v. Security Pacific Nat. Bank, 973 F.2d 51 (2nd Cir.1992), **321**

Bankamerica Corp. v. United States, 462 U.S. 122, 103 S.Ct. 2266, 76 L.Ed.2d 456 (1983), **695**

Bank of America v. City and County of San Francisco, 309 F.3d 551 (9th Cir.2002), **478**

Bank of America, N.A. v. City of Daly City, Cal., 279 F.Supp.2d 1118 (N.D.Cal.2003), 280

Bank of California, N.A., In the Matter of The, 1993 WL 243770 (S.E.C. Release No.1993), **813**

Bank of New York, In re, 35 N.Y.2d 512, 364 N.Y.S.2d 164, 323 N.E.2d 700 (N.Y.1974), **709**

Bank One, Utah v. Guttau, 190 F.3d 844 (8th Cir.1999), **645**

BankWest, Inc. v. Baker, 446 F.3d 1358 (11th Cir.2006), 461

BankWest, Inc. v. Baker, 411 F.3d 1289 (11th Cir.2005), 461

BankWest, Inc. v. Baker, 324 F.Supp.2d 1333 (N.D.Ga.2004), 461

Banque San Paolo v. Iraqi State Co. for Food Stuff Trading, 1996 WL 735505 (S.D.N.Y.1996), **1030**

Barnett Bank of Marion County, N.A. v. Nelson, 517 U.S. 25, 116 S.Ct. 1103, 134 L.Ed.2d 237 (1996), **206, 919**

BCCI Holdings, Luxembourg, S.A., United States v., 69 F.Supp.2d 36 (D.D.C.1999), **959**

Beneficial Nat. Bank v. Anderson, 539 U.S. 1, 123 S.Ct. 2058, 156 L.Ed.2d 1 (2003), 386

Benion v. Bank One, Dayton, N.A., 144 F.3d 1056 (7th Cir.1998), **387**

Bilski v. Kappos, ___ U.S. ___, 130 S.Ct. 3218, 177 L.Ed.2d 792 (2010), 285

Bisbey v. D.C. Nat. Bank, 793 F.2d 315, 253 U.S.App.D.C. 244 (D.C.Cir.1986), **540**

Biscayne Federal Sav. & Loan Ass'n v. Federal Home Loan Bank Bd., 720 F.2d 1499 (11th Cir.1983), **96**

Blackfeet Nat. Bank v. Nelson, 171 F.3d 1237 (11th Cir.1999), 923

Block v. Pennsylvania Exchange Bank, 253 N.Y. 227, 170 N.E. 900 (N.Y.1930), **746**

Board of Governors of Federal Reserve System v. Dimension Financial Corp., 474 U.S. 361, 106 S.Ct. 681, 88 L.Ed.2d 691 (1986), 52, **232**

Bowler v. Hawke, 320 F.3d 59 (1st Cir.2003), 942

Braka v. Bancomer, S.N.C., 762 F.2d 222 (2nd Cir.1985), 973

Brown v. AVEMCO Inv. Corp., 603 F.2d 1367 (9th Cir.1979), 313

Brown v. Payday Check Advance, Inc., 202 F.3d 987 (7th Cir.2000), 464

Buckeye Check Cashing, Inc. v. Cardegna, 546 U.S. 440, 126 S.Ct. 1204, 163 L.Ed.2d 1038 (2006), 420

California Bankers Ass'n v. Shultz, 416 U.S. 21, 94 S.Ct. 1494, 39 L.Ed.2d 812 (1974), **1012**

Cameron Financial Corp. v. Board of Governors of Federal Reserve System, 497 F.2d 841 (4th Cir.1974), **49**

Canadyne–Georgia Corp. v. NationsBank, N.A. (South), 183 F.3d 1269 (11th Cir.1999), 317

Central Bank of Denver, N.A. v. First Interstate Bank of Denver, N.A., 511 U.S. 164, 114 S.Ct. 1439, 128 L.Ed.2d 119 (1994), 368

Central Nat. Bank of Mattoon v. United States Dept. of Treasury, 912 F.2d 897 (7th Cir.1990), **719**

Centrifugal Casting Mach. Co., Inc. v. American Bank & Trust Co., 966 F.2d 1348 (10th Cir.1992), **524**

CF Industries, Inc. and Subsidiaries v. Commissioner, T.C. Memo. 1991-568 (U.S.Tax Ct.1991), **488**

Chamber of Commerce of United States v. S.E.C., 443 F.3d 890, 370 U.S.App.D.C. 249 (D.C.Cir.2006), 812

Chamber of Commerce of United States v. S.E.C., 412 F.3d 133, 366 U.S.App.D.C. 351 (D.C.Cir.2005), 812

Charles H. Keating, Jr., Matter of, 1993 WL 724714 (O.T.S.), **102**

Charter House, Inc. v. First Tennessee Bank, N.A., 693 F.Supp. 593 (M.D.Tenn. 1988), **782**

Chase Manhattan Bank, N.A., In the Matter of, 1994 WL 559152 (S.E.C. Release No.1994), **805**

Checking Account Overdraft Litigation, In re, 694 F.Supp.2d 1302 (S.D.Fla.2010), 485

Chevron, U.S.A., Inc. v. Natural Resources Defense Council, Inc., 467 U.S. 837, 104 S.Ct. 2778, 81 L.Ed.2d 694 (1984), 205

Chevy Chase Federal Savings Bank, United States v., No. 94–1824–JG, Consent Decree (D.C. 1994), **433**

CIT Group, Inc. v. Citicorp, 20 F.Supp.2d 775 (D.N.J.1998), **767**

Citibank, N.A. v. Wells Fargo Asia Ltd., 495 U.S. 660, 110 S.Ct. 2034, 109 L.Ed.2d 677 (1990), **973**

Citicorp v. Board of Governors of Federal Reserve System, 936 F.2d 66 (2nd Cir. 1991), **924**

Clarke v. Securities Industry Ass'n, 479 U.S. 388, 107 S.Ct. 750, 93 L.Ed.2d 757 (1987), **637**

Cline v. Hawke, 2002 WL 31557392 (4th Cir. 2002), 942

Commodity Futures Trading Com'n v. Zelener, 373 F.3d 861 (7th Cir.2004), 876

Conference of State Bank Sup'rs v. Office of Thrift Supervision, 792 F.Supp. 837 (D.D.C.1992), **642**

Connecticut Nat. Bank, United States v., 418 U.S. 656, 94 S.Ct. 2788, 41 L.Ed.2d 1016 (1974), **672**

Consumers Union of United States, Inc. v. Federal Reserve Bd., 938 F.2d 266, 291 U.S.App.D.C. 1 (D.C.Cir.1991), **400**

Coronado v. Bank Atlantic Bancorp, Inc., 222 F.3d 1315 (11th Cir.2000), 276, 1020

County Nat. Bancorporation v. Board of Governors of Federal Reserve System, 654 F.2d 1253 (8th Cir.1981), **677**

Craig v. State of Missouri, 29 U.S. 410, 4 Pet. 410, 7 L.Ed. 903 (1830), **6**

Cuomo v. Clearing House Ass'n, L.L.C., ___ U.S. ___, 129 S.Ct. 2710, 174 L.Ed.2d 464 (2009), **214**

Currency Conversion Fee Antitrust Litigation, In re, 265 F.Supp.2d 385 (S.D.N.Y.2003), 877

Daccarett, United States v., 6 F.3d 37 (2nd Cir.1993), 1012

Dames & Moore v. Regan, 453 U.S. 654, 101 S.Ct. 2972, 69 L.Ed.2d 918 (1981), **1029**

de la Fuente v. F.D.I.C., 332 F.3d 1208 (9th Cir.2003), **307**

Delaware v. New York, 507 U.S. 490, 113 S.Ct. 1550, 123 L.Ed.2d 211 (1993), **505**

Delbrueck & Co. v. Manufacturers Hanover Trust Co., 609 F.2d 1047 (2nd Cir.1979), 745

del Junco v. Conover, 682 F.2d 1338 (9th Cir.1982), **301**

Department of Banking and Consumer Finance of State of Miss. v. Clarke, 809 F.2d 266 (5th Cir.1987), 641

Deutsche Asset Management, Inc., In the Matter of, Securities and Exchange Commission, Aug. 19, 2003, Investment Advisors Act of 1940, Release No. 2160, **791**

Dibidale of Louisiana, Inc. v. American Bank & Trust Co., New Orleans, 916 F.2d 300 (5th Cir.1990), **265**

Dougherty v. Carver Federal Sav. Bank, 112 F.3d 613 (2nd Cir.1997), **119**

Dougherty, United States v., 763 F.2d 970 (8th Cir.1985), **519**

Drogoul, United States v., 1 F.3d 1546 (11th Cir.1993), **962**

Dunn v. Commodity Futures Trading Com'n, 519 U.S. 465, 117 S.Ct. 913, 137 L.Ed.2d 93 (1997), **873**

E.E.O.C. v. Waffle House, Inc., 534 U.S. 279, 122 S.Ct. 754, 151 L.Ed.2d 755 (2002), 419

Eisenberg v. Wachovia Bank, N.A., 301 F.3d 220 (4th Cir.2002), **541**

Elliott Associates v. J. Henry Schroder Bank & Trust Co., 838 F.2d 66 (2nd Cir. 1988), **840**

Elliott Associates, L.P. v. Banco de la Nacion, 194 F.3d 363 (2nd Cir.1999), **1007**

Ellis v. Citizens' Nat. Bank of Portales, 25 N.M. 319, 183 P. 34 (N.M.1918), 528

Eternity Global Master Fund Ltd. v. Morgan Guar. Trust Co. of N.Y., 375 F.3d 168 (2nd Cir.2004), 869

FAIC Securities, Inc. v. United States, 768 F.2d 352, 247 U.S.App.D.C. 235 (D.C.Cir. 1985), **500**

Farmers Deposit Bank of Brandenburg v. Department of Banking and Securities, 669 S.W.2d 22 (Ky.App.1984), **188**

Farmers' Nat. Bank v. Jones, 234 Ky. 591, 28 S.W.2d 787 (Ky.1930), **503**

F.D.I.C. v. Bank of Coushatta, 930 F.2d 1122 (5th Cir.1991), **549**

F.D.I.C. v. Hurwitz, 384 F.Supp.2d 1039 (S.D.Tex.2005), 589

F.D.I.C. v. Philadelphia Gear Corp., 476 U.S. 426, 106 S.Ct. 1931, 90 L.Ed.2d 428 (1986), **521**

Fidelity Federal Sav. and Loan Ass'n v. de la Cuesta, 458 U.S. 141, 102 S.Ct. 3014, 73 L.Ed.2d 664 (1982), **77**

Fidelity Partners, Inc. v. First Trust Co. of New York, 142 F.3d 560 (2nd Cir.1998), **806**

First Alabama Bank of Montgomery, N.A. v. Martin, 425 So.2d 415 (Ala.1982), **714**

First Bank & Trust Co. v. Board of Governors of Federal Reserve System, 605 F.Supp. 555 (E.D.Ky.1984), **140**

First City Nat. Bank of Houston, United States v., 386 U.S. 361, 87 S.Ct. 1088, 18 L.Ed.2d 151 (1967), 668

First Eagle SoGen Funds, Inc. v. Bank for Intern. Settlements, 252 F.3d 604 (2nd Cir. 2001), 957

First Nat. Bank v. National Exch. Bank, 92 U.S. 122, 2 Otto 122, 23 L.Ed. 679 (1875), **24**

First Nat. Bank in Plant City, Fla. v. Dickinson, 396 U.S. 122, 90 S.Ct. 337, 24 L.Ed.2d 312 (1969), **634**

First Nat. Bank in St. Louis v. State of Missouri at inf. Barrett, 263 U.S. 640, 44 S.Ct. 213, 68 L.Ed. 486 (1924), **44**

First Nat. Bank of Bay City v. Fellows ex rel. Union Trust Co., 244 U.S. 416, 37 S.Ct. 734, 61 L.Ed. 1233 (1917), **700**

First Nat. Bank of Bellaire v. Comptroller of Currency, 697 F.2d 674 (5th Cir.1983), **546**

First Nat. Bank of Logan, Utah v. Walker Bank & Trust Co., 385 U.S. 252, 87 S.Ct. 492, 17 L.Ed.2d 343 (1966), **46**

First Nat. City Bank v. Mullarkey, 87 Misc.2d 1, 385 N.Y.S.2d 473 (N.Y.City Civ. Ct.1976), **398**

First Union Corp. v. SunTrust Banks, Inc., 2001 WL 1885686 (N.C.Super.2001), 664

First Union Securities, Inc., In re, Securities and Exchange Commission, Oct. 24, 2000, Securities Exchange Act of 1934 Release No. 43478, **785**

Fleet Factors Corp., United States v., 901 F.2d 1550 (11th Cir.1990), **313**

Fuente v. Federal Deposit Ins. Corp., 2005 WL 3159735 (9th Cir.2005), 311

Garcia–Harding v. Bank Midwest, N.A., 964 F.Supp. 1492 (D.Kan.1997), **469**

Gary Plastic Packaging Corp. v. Merrill Lynch, Pierce, Fenner & Smith, Inc., 756 F.2d 230 (2nd Cir.1985), **497**

Giraldi, United States v., 86 F.3d 1368 (5th Cir.1996), **1020**

Goldstein v. S.E.C., 451 F.3d 873, 371 U.S.App. D.C. 358 (D.C.Cir.2006), 823

Grede v. Bank of New York Mellon, 2009 WL 188460 (N.D.Ill.2009), 725

Greene County Bank v. F.D.I.C., 92 F.3d 633 (8th Cir.1996), **870**

Green Tree Financial Corp. v. Bazzle, 539 U.S. 444, 123 S.Ct. 2402, 156 L.Ed.2d 414 (2003), 420

Green Tree Financial Corp.–Alabama v. Randolph, 531 U.S. 79, 121 S.Ct. 513, 148 L.Ed.2d 373 (2000), **411**

Greenwood Trust Co. v. Commonwealth of Mass., 971 F.2d 818 (1st Cir.1992), **381**

Gutierrez v. Wells Fargo Bank, N.A., 2010 WL 3155934 (N.D.Cal.2010), 485

Harris Corp. v. National Iranian Radio and Television, 691 F.2d 1344 (11th Cir.1982), 527

Harvard College v. Amory, 26 Mass. 446 (Mass. 1830), 709

Heimmermann v. First Union Mortg. Corp., 305 F.3d 1257 (11th Cir.2002), **437**

Hepburn v. Griswold, 75 U.S. 603, 19 L.Ed. 513 (1869), 19

Hewitt v. United States, 110 F.2d 1 (8th Cir.1940), **38**

Household Credit Services, Inc. v. Pfennig, 541 U.S. 232, 124 S.Ct. 1741, 158 L.Ed.2d 450 (2004), 402

Hunt v. United States Securities & Exchange Commission, 520 F.Supp. 580 (N.D.Tex. 1981), 268

Hunter, In re, 4 N.Y.3d 260, 794 N.Y.S.2d 286, 827 N.E.2d 269 (N.Y.2005), 722

Huntington v. National Sav. Bank, 96 U.S. 388, 6 Otto 388, 24 L.Ed. 777 (1877), **83**

Iguchi, United States v., 125 F.3d 845 (2nd Cir.1997), 294
Independent Ins. Agents of America, Inc. v. Ludwig, 997 F.2d 958, 302 U.S.App.D.C. 268 (D.C.Cir.1993), **918**
In re (see name of party)
Investment Co. Institute v. Camp, 401 U.S. 617, 91 S.Ct. 1091, 28 L.Ed.2d 367 (1971), 708, **751,** 814
Investment Co. Institute v. Conover, 790 F.2d 925, 252 U.S.App.D.C. 364 (D.C.Cir.1986), 708, 726
Irving Bank Corp. v. Board of Governors of Federal Reserve System, 845 F.2d 1035, 269 U.S.App.D.C. 290 (D.C.Cir.1988), 667

Johnson v. Bank of Bentonville, 269 F.3d 894 (8th Cir.2001), 386
JPMorgan Chase Bank v. Liberty Mut. Ins. Co., 189 F.Supp.2d 24 (S.D.N.Y.2002), 363

K.M.C. Co., Inc. v. Irving Trust Co., 757 F.2d 752 (6th Cir.1985), 313
Koons Buick Pontiac GMC, Inc. v. Nigh, 543 U.S. 50, 125 S.Ct. 460, 160 L.Ed.2d 389 (2004), **406**

Laborers Nat. Pension Fund v. Northern Trust Quantitative Advisors, Inc., 173 F.3d 313 (5th Cir.1999), **727**
La Caisse Populaire Ste–Marie (St. Mary's Bank) v. United States, 425 F.Supp. 512 (D.N.H.1976), **85**
Lakonia Management Ltd. v. Meriwether, 106 F.Supp.2d 540 (S.D.N.Y.2000), **157**
Latimore v. Citibank Federal Sav. Bank, 151 F.3d 712 (7th Cir.1998), **423**
Lee v. Bankers Trust Co., 166 F.3d 540 (2nd Cir.1999), 276, **1018**
Lee v. Board of Governors of the Federal Reserve System, 118 F.3d 905 (2nd Cir. 1997), **430**
Legal Tender Cases (Knox v. Lee; Parker v. Davis), 79 U.S. 457, 20 L.Ed. 287 (1870), **19**
Lewis, United States v., 67 F.3d 225 (9th Cir.1995), **951**
Lopez v. First Union Nat. Bank of Florida, 129 F.3d 1186 (11th Cir.1997), **270**
Lopez v. Washington Mut. Bank, FA, 302 F.3d 900 (9th Cir.2002), 486
Lutheran Broth. Variable Ins. Products Co. Sales Practices Litigation, In re, 105 F.Supp.2d 1037 (D.Minn.2000), **943**

Manufacturers Hanover Trust Co. v. Drysdale Securities Corp., 801 F.2d 13 (2nd Cir.1986), **514**
Marine Bank v. Fulton Bank, 69 U.S. 252, 17 L.Ed. 785 (1864), **16**
Marine Bank v. Weaver, 455 U.S. 551, 102 S.Ct. 1220, 71 L.Ed.2d 409 (1982), **467**

Markham v. Colonial Mortg. Service Co., Associates, Inc., 605 F.2d 566, 196 U.S.App.D.C. 50 (D.C.Cir.1979), **420**
Marquette Nat. Bank of Minneapolis v. First of Omaha Service Corp., 439 U.S. 299, 99 S.Ct. 540, 58 L.Ed.2d 534 (1978), **374**
Marx v. Centran Corp., 747 F.2d 1536 (6th Cir.1984), **292**
Massachusetts Bankers Ass', Inc. v. Bowler, 392 F.Supp.2d 24 (D.Mass.2005), 943
Matter of (see name of party)
McHugh v. Westpac Banking Corp., 1995 WL 243339 (N.D.Ill.1995), **954**
M'Culloch v. Maryland, 17 U.S. 316, 4 L.Ed. 579 (1819), **11**
Merrill Lynch, Pierce, Fenner & Smith, Inc. v. Curran, 456 U.S. 353, 102 S.Ct. 1825, 72 L.Ed.2d 182 (1982), **851**
Milam v. United States, 524 F.2d 629 (9th Cir.1974), **33**
Miller v. Bank of America, 94 Cal.Rptr.3d 31, 207 P.3d 531 (Cal.2009), 486
Monarch Tile, Inc. v. City of Florence, 212 F.3d 1219 (11th Cir.2000), 317
Morgan v. Citizens' Bank of Spring Hope, 190 N.C. 209, 129 S.E. 585 (N.C.1925), **738**
Motorcity of Jacksonville, Ltd. v. Southeast Bank N.A., 120 F.3d 1140 (11th Cir. 1997), **629**
Mullane v. Central Hanover Bank & Trust Co., 339 U.S. 306, 70 S.Ct. 652, 94 L.Ed. 865 (1950), **706**

National Bancard Corp. (NaBanco) v. VISA, U.S.A., Inc., 596 F.Supp. 1231 (S.D.Fla.1984), **528**
National Courier Ass'n v. Board of Governors of Federal Reserve System, 516 F.2d 1229, 170 U.S.App.D.C. 301 (D.C.Cir. 1975), **237**
National Credit Union Admin. v. First Nat. Bank & Trust Co., 522 U.S. 479, 118 S.Ct. 927, 140 L.Ed.2d 1 (1998), **91**
National Safe Deposit Co. v. Stead, 232 U.S. 58, 34 S.Ct. 209, 58 L.Ed. 504 (1914), **735**
NationsBank of North Carolina, N.A. v. Variable Annuity Life Ins. Co., 513 U.S. 251, 115 S.Ct. 810, 130 L.Ed.2d 740 (1995), **197,** 923
NationsSecurities and NationsBank, N.A., In the Matter of, Securities Act of 1933, Release No. 7532 (May 4, 1998), **776**
New York Life Ins. Co. v. Statham, 93 U.S. 24, 3 Otto 24, 23 L.Ed. 789 (1876), **905**
New York Trust Co. v. Eisner, 256 U.S. 345, 41 S.Ct. 506, 65 L.Ed. 963 (1921), 1
Norman v. Baltimore & O.R. Co., 294 U.S. 240, 55 S.Ct. 407, 79 L.Ed. 885 (1935), **1001**
North Arlington Nat. Bank v. Kearny Federal Sav. & Loan Ass'n, 187 F.2d 564 (3rd Cir.1951), **76**
Northeast Bancorp, Inc. v. Board of Governors of Federal Reserve System, 472

U.S. 159, 105 S.Ct. 2545, 86 L.Ed.2d 112 (1985), **650**

Norwest Bank Minnesota, Nat. Ass'n v. Sween Corp., 118 F.3d 1255 (8th Cir. 1997), **809**

Olesh v. Dreyfus Corp., 1995 WL 500491 (E.D.N.Y.1995), **814**

OnBank & Trust Co., Matter of, 90 N.Y.2d 725, 665 N.Y.S.2d 389, 688 N.E.2d 245 (N.Y.1997), 714

OnBank & Trust Co., Matter of, 227 A.D.2d 20, 649 N.Y.S.2d 592 (N.Y.A.D. 4 Dept. 1996), **711**

One 1997 E35 Ford Van, VIN 1FBJS31L3VHB70844, United States v., 50 F.Supp.2d 789 (N.D.Ill.1999), **1023**

Paine, Webber, Jackson & Curtis, Inc. v. Merrill Lynch, Pierce, Fenner & Smith, Inc., 564 F.Supp. 1358 (D.Del.1983), **52**

Pension Committee of University of Montreal Pension Plan v. Banc of America Securities LLC, 568 F.3d 374 (2nd Cir.2009), 824

Perdue v. Crocker National Bank, 216 Cal. Rptr. 345, 702 P.2d 503 (Cal.1985), 471

Philadelphia Nat. Bank, United States v., 374 U.S. 321, 83 S.Ct. 1715, 10 L.Ed.2d 915 (1963), **669**

Philler v. Patterson, 168 Pa. 468, 32 A. 26 (Pa.1895), **29**

Press v. Chemical Investment Services Corp., 166 F.3d 529 (2nd Cir.1999), **780**

Procter & Gamble Co. v. Bankers Trust Co., 925 F.Supp. 1270 (S.D.Ohio 1996), **878**

Racepoint Partners, LLC v. JPMorgan Chase Bank, N.A., 14 N.Y.3d 419, 902 N.Y.S.2d 14, 928 N.E.2d 396 (N.Y.2010), 843

Raichle v. Federal Reserve Bank of New York, 34 F.2d 910 (2nd Cir.1929), **35**

Randolph v. Green Tree Financial Corp.-- Alabama, 244 F.3d 814 (11th Cir.2001), **416**

Ratzlaf v. United States, 510 U.S. 135, 114 S.Ct. 655, 126 L.Ed.2d 615 (1994), 1015

Regents of University of California v. Credit Suisse First Boston (U.S.A.), Inc., 482 F.3d 372 (5th Cir.2007), 772

Resolution Trust Corp. v. Walde, 18 F.3d 943, 305 U.S.App.D.C. 183 (D.C.Cir.1994), **615**

Riegle v. Federal Open Market Committee, 656 F.2d 873, 211 U.S.App.D.C. 284 (D.C.Cir.1981), **144**

Rockford Life Ins. Co. v. Illinois Dept. of Revenue, 482 U.S. 182, 107 S.Ct. 2312, 96 L.Ed.2d 152 (1987), **337**

Ryder Intern. Corp. v. First American Nat. Bank, 943 F.2d 1521 (11th Cir.1991), **847**

Safeco Ins. Co. of America v. Burr, 551 U.S. 47, 127 S.Ct. 2201, 167 L.Ed.2d 1045 (2007), 398

Saxon v. Georgia Ass'n of Independent Ins. Agents, Inc., 399 F.2d 1010 (5th Cir. 1968), **916**

Schwartz v. Visa Intern. Corp., 2003 WL 1870370 (Cal.Super. 2003), 877

Schwartz v. Visa Intern. Service Ass'n, 34 Cal. Rptr.3d 449 (Cal.App. 1 Dist.2005), 877

Schy v. Federal Deposit Ins. Corp., 465 F.Supp. 766 (E.D.N.Y.1977), **799**

S.E.C. v. CIBC Mellon Trust Co., SEC Litigation Release No. 19081 (Feb. 16, 2005), 808

S.E.C. v. J.P. Morgan Chase & Co., 2003 WL 21738802 (S.E.C. Release No.2003), 845

S.E.C. v. J.P. Morgan Securities, Inc., 2003 WL 22250420 (S.E.C. Release No.2003), 791

S.E.C. v. Miller, 495 F.Supp. 465 (S.D.N.Y. 1980), **508**

S.E.C. v. Pollet, SEC Litigation Release No. 19,199 (E.D.N.Y. Apr. 21, 2005), 774

S.E.C. v. United Ben. Life Ins. Co., 387 U.S. 202, 87 S.Ct. 1557, 18 L.Ed.2d 673 (1967), 911

S.E.C. v. Variable Annuity Life Ins. Co. of America, 359 U.S. 65, 79 S.Ct. 618, 3 L.Ed.2d 640 (1959), 911

Securities and Exchange Commission Release Notice, 2000 WL 1577345 (S.E.C. Release No.2000), **785**

Securities Industry Ass'n v. Board of Governors of Federal Reserve System, 839 F.2d 47 (2nd Cir.1988), **749, 759**

Securities Industry Ass'n v. Board of Governors of Federal Reserve System, 807 F.2d 1052, 257 U.S.App.D.C. 137 (D.C.Cir.1986), 849

Securities Industry Ass'n v. Board of Governors of Federal Reserve System, 468 U.S. 137, 104 S.Ct. 2979, 82 L.Ed.2d 107 (1984), 432, 848

Securities Industry Ass'n v. Board of Governors of Federal Reserve System, 468 U.S. 207, 104 S.Ct. 3003, 82 L.Ed.2d 158 (1984), **757**

Securities Industry Ass'n v. Clarke, 885 F.2d 1034 (2nd Cir.1989), **339**

Securities Industry Ass'n v. Federal Home Loan Bank Bd., 588 F.Supp. 749 (D.D.C.1984), **765**

Seidman, Matter of, 37 F.3d 911 (3rd Cir. 1994), **583**

Simms v. First Gibraltar Bank, 83 F.3d 1546 (5th Cir.1996), 428

Smiley v. Citibank (South Dakota), N.A., 517 U.S. 735, 116 S.Ct. 1730, 135 L.Ed.2d 25 (1996), **378**

Smith v. First Union Nat. Bank of Tennessee, 958 S.W.2d 113 (Tenn.Ct.App.1997), 485

Spiegel v. Ryan, 946 F.2d 1435 (9th Cir. 1991), **106**

State Farm Bank, F.S.B. v. Burke, 445 F.Supp.2d 207 (D.Conn.2006), 117

State Street Bank & Trust Co. v. Signature Financial Group, Inc, 149 F.3d 1368 (Fed. Cir.1998), 285

Stoneridge Inv. Partners, LLC v. Scientific–Atlanta, 552 U.S. 148, 128 S.Ct. 761, 169 L.Ed.2d 627 (2008), 368

Stoutt v. Banco Popular de Puerto Rico, 320 F.3d 26 (1st Cir.2003), 276, 1020

Strong Capital Management, Inc., In the Matter of, 2004 WL 1124933 (S.E.C. Release No.2004), 820

Synovus Financial Corp. v. Board of Governors of Federal Reserve System, 952 F.2d 426, 293 U.S.App.D.C. 70 (D.C.Cir.1991), 642

Szetela v. Discover Bank, 118 Cal.Rptr.2d 862 (Cal.App. 4 Dist.2002), 419

Tiffany v. National Bank of Missouri, 85 U.S. 409, 21 L.Ed. 862 (1873), **372**

Trans World Airlines, Inc. v. Franklin Mint Corp., 466 U.S. 243, 104 S.Ct. 1776, 80 L.Ed.2d 273 (1984), **1005**

Turner v. Beneficial Corp., 242 F.3d 1023 (11th Cir.2001), **403**

Union Bank For Savings & Investment (Jordan), United States v., 487 F.3d 8 (1st Cir. 2007), 1026

United Companies Lending Corp. v. Sargeant, 20 F.Supp.2d 192 (D.Mass.1998), **443**

United States v. _____ (see opposing party)

Van Auken, United States v., 96 U.S. 366, 6 Otto 366, 24 L.Ed. 852 (1877), **18**

Veazie Bank v. Fenno, 75 U.S. 533, 19 L.Ed. 482 (1869), **25**

Video Trax, Inc. v. NationsBank, N.A., 33 F.Supp.2d 1041 (S.D.Fla.1998), **471**

Visa Check/MasterMoney Antitrust Litigation, In re, 280 F.3d 124 (2nd Cir.2001), **532**

Visa U.S.A., Inc., United States v., 344 F.3d 229 (2nd Cir.2003), 535

Wachovia Bank v. Schmidt, 546 U.S. 303, 126 S.Ct. 941, 163 L.Ed.2d 797 (2006), **218**

Wachovia Bank, Nat. Ass'n v. Schmidt, 445 F.3d 762 (4th Cir.2006), 220

Wachovia Bank, Nat. Ass'n v. Schmidt, 545 U.S. 1113, 125 S.Ct. 2904, 162 L.Ed.2d 293 (2005), 661

Washington Nat. Building, Loan & Investment Ass'n v. Stanley, 38 Or. 319, 63 P. 489 (Or.1901), 72

Washington Steel Corp. v. TW Corp., 602 F.2d 594 (3rd Cir.1979), **257**

Watters v. Wachovia Bank, N.A., 550 U.S. 1, 127 S.Ct. 1559, 167 L.Ed.2d 389 (2007), 212, **224**

Wells Fargo Bank of Texas NA v. James, 321 F.3d 488 (5th Cir.2003), 486

West Helena Sav. and Loan Ass'n v. Federal Home Loan Bank Bd., 553 F.2d 1175 (8th Cir.1977), **74**

Winstar Corp., United States v., 518 U.S. 839, 116 S.Ct. 2432, 135 L.Ed.2d 964 (1996), **108**

Zeffiro v. First Pennsylvania Banking and Trust Co., 623 F.2d 290 (3rd Cir.1980), **838**

REGULATION OF BANK FINANCIAL SERVICE ACTIVITIES

CASES AND MATERIALS

Fourth Edition

CHAPTER ONE

THE HISTORY OF BANKING REGULATION IN AMERICA

■ ■ ■

The structure of banking regulation is quite complicated. There are a number of different types of depository institutions—banks, savings associations, savings banks, and credit unions. For each type of depository institution, a federal or state charter may be obtained. Each type of depository institution is regulated by a different regulatory body, and multiple regulatory bodies may regulate even a single type of depository institution, such as a bank. Many banks are owned by holding companies that are subject to their own regulatory oversight. Moreover, their non-banking subsidiaries may be subject to regulation by one or more non-banking regulators, such as a state insurance commissioner or the Securities and Exchange Commission. Notwithstanding these different and complicated regulatory structures, the financial results of these holding companies are reported to the public and to the companies' shareholders on a consolidated basis. The bank subsidiaries of the holding companies continue to report their own separate financial performance to the bank regulators and this information is publicly available on the website of the Federal Deposit Insurance Corporation.[1]

How did we get to such a place? As Justice Holmes once said, "a page of history is worth a volume of logic."[2] This chapter will, therefore, explore some of the history of the regulation of banking in America for the purpose of explaining how we arrived at our current regulatory structure. You may wish to read this chapter now—not for the facts and holdings of each case, but rather to see how banks and their regulation evolved over the course of our country's history—or later as background for the more specific subject matter chapters that follow. We will indicate in the later chapters, the relevant material from this chapter that you may wish to read or review for historical background.

Our major bank regulatory agencies were created over time, as were the different financial entities. The chart below indicates how and when

---

1. See http://www.fdic.govhttp://www.fdic.gov (click on tab for Industry Analysis).
2. New York Trust Co. v. Eisner, 256 U.S. 345, 349 (1921).

1

the regulators and entities came into existence. This chapter provides additional background on each action that resulted in a new regulator and new type of entity.

Action	Regulator	Entity
State laws	State	State banks
National Bank Act of 1862	Office of the Comptroller of the Currency (OCC)	National banks
Federal Reserve Act of 1913	Federal Reserve Board (FRB)	State member banks
Banking Act of 1933	Federal Deposit Insurance Corporation (FDIC)	State nonmember banks
Bank Holding Company Act of 1956	FRB	Bank holding companies
Gramm–Leach–Bliley Act of 1999 (GLBA)	FRB	Financial holding companies
Dodd–Frank Wall Street Reform and Consumer Protection Act of 2010	Financial Stability Oversight Council (FSOC or Council)	Nonbank financial companies and large, inter-connected bank holding companies
	Bureau of Consumer Financial Protection (BCFP)	Any entity (including nonbanks) that provides a consumer financial product or service

SECTION 1. THE ROLE OF BANKS IN EARLY AMERICA

The traditional role of banks is to facilitate the transfer of money, lend money, and help implement monetary policy. In the early days of the United States banks began to develop these three roles, in varying degrees.

A. MEDIUM OF PAYMENT

Money is at the center of banking. Banking thus involves, at least in the traditional sense, the transfer and storage of money, as well as the lending of that medium of exchange. Money itself is of ancient origin. Mesopotamians used silver as a currency as early as 2500 B.C., and the coin was developed as a unit of value in 650 B.C. in the Mediterranean country of Lydia. Spanish money in the form of coins (dinars) has been traced back to 722 A.D. Some seventy currencies circulated in Europe before the discovery of America. They included ecus and florins in many forms, ducats, pfennigs, Hellers, stuivers, weisspfennigs, blankes, pfunds, orrts, gulden, crona, anglots, and rose nobles. The gold florin of Florence was the most popular currency in the Mediterranean at the time of

Columbus' voyage, but the Spanish piece of eight would become the model for the American dollar.

Paper money was used in China at the time of Marco Polo's journeys in the thirteenth century. Bills of exchange were employed as a method of payment even before the discovery of America. A bill of exchange is simply an order drawn by one person that directs a second person to pay money to a third person. It is a method of payment very similar to a present-day check in that the drawer of a check gives an order to the bank to pay money to a third party, such as a merchant. In the case of a bill of exchange, the order to pay is given to someone, other than a bank, who owes the drawer money or who is willing to extend him credit.

The "legal tender" concept that developed from European societies also had broad-ranging effects on banking. Legal tender is a particular form of money or currency that a government has decreed must be accepted in payment of government or private debts. This assures governments a central role in controlling the money supply.

THE CASE OF MIXED MONEY IN IRELAND

Trin. 2 James I. A.D. 1605 [Davies's Reports].

Queen Elizabeth in order to pay the royal army which was maintained in this kingdom for several years, to suppress the rebellion of Tyrone, caused a great quantity of mixed money, with the usual stamp of the arms of the crown, and inscription of her royal stile, to be coined in the tower of London, and transmitted this money into this kingdom, with a Proclamation, bearing date 24 May, in the 43d year of her reign, by which her majesty declared and established this mixed money, immediately after the said proclamation, to be the lawful and current money of this kingdom of Ireland, and expressly commanded that this money should be so used, accepted and reputed by all her subjects and others, using any traffic or commerce within this kingdom; and that if any person or persons should refuse to receive this mixed money according to the denomination or valuation thereof, viz. shillings for shillings, six penny pieces for sixpenny pieces, & c. being tendered for payment of any wages, fees, stipends, debts, & c. they should be punished as contemners of her royal prerogative and commandment. And to the intent that this mixed money should have the better course and circulation, it was further declared by the same proclamation, that after the 10th day of June immediately following, all other money which had been current within this kingdom, before the said proclamation, should be cried down and annulled and esteemed as bullion, and not as lawful and current money of this kingdom.

In April, before this Proclamation was published, when the pure coin of England was current within this kingdom, one Brett of Drogheda, merchant, having bought certain wares of one Gilbert in London, became bound to the said Gilbert in an obligation of 200£. on condition that he should pay to the said Gilbert, his executors or assigns, 100£. sterling, current and lawful money of England, at the tomb of Earl Strongbow in

Christ–Church, Dublin, at a certain day to come; at which day and place, Brett made a tender of the 100£. in the Mixed Money of the new standard, in performance of the condition of the obligation; and whether this tender was sufficient to save the forfeiture of the obligation, or whether the said Brett should now, upon the change or alteration of money within this kingdom, be compelled to pay the said 100£. in other or better coin than in the mixed money, according to the rate and valuation of it, at the time of the tender, was the question at the council table, where the said Gilbert, who was a merchant of London, exhibited his Petition against the said Brett, for the speedy recovery of his debt aforesaid.

And, inasmuch as this case related to the kingdom in general, and was also of great importance in consideration and reason of state, Sir George Carew, then Lord Deputy and also Treasurer, required the Chief Judges (being of the privy council) to confer on and consider this Case, and to return to him their Resolution touching it; who upon conference and consideration on all the points of the said Proclamation, resolved, That the tender of the 100£. in the mixed money, at the day and place aforesaid, was good and sufficient in the law, to save the forfeiture of the said obligation, and that Brett should not be obliged at any time after, to pay other money in discharge of the debt, than this mixed money, according to the rate and valuation that it had, at the time of the tender; and this Resolution was certified by them to the lord-deputy, and the certificate entered in the Council–Book. And in this case divers Points were considered and resolved.

First, it was considered, that in every commonwealth, it is necessary to have a certain standard of money. [Cotton 4.] For no commonwealth can subsist without contracts, and no contracts without equality, and no equality in contracts without money. For although in the first societies of the world, permutation of one thing for another was used, yet that was soon found cumbersome, and the transportation and division of things was found difficult and impossible; and therefore money was invented, as well for the facility of commerce, as to reduce contracts to an equality. * * *

Secondly, it was resolved, That it appertaineth only to the King of England, to make or coin money within his dominions; [2 Ro. ab. 166. 1 Co. 146, 5 Co. 114. 1 H.H.P.C. 188.] so that no other person can do it without special license or commandment of the king; and if any person presume to do it of his own head, it is treason against the person of the king by the common law; and this appears by the stat. of 25 Edw. 3, c. 2, (which is only a declaration of the common law,) and by Glanvil, Britton and Bracton, before that statute, Stamford fol. 2 and 3. And in the case of Mines, Plowd, 316 a. this point is expressed more clearly, where as is said, That the king shall have mines of gold and silver; for if a subject had them, he by law could not coin such metals, nor stamp a print or value upon them, for it appertaineth to the king only to put a value upon coin, and make the price of the quantity, and to put a print to it; which being done the coin is current; and if a subject doth this it is high treason at common law, as appears, 23 Ass. p. 2 and it is high treason to the king, because he hath the sole power of making Money, & c.

And in this book three things are expressed which are requisite to the making of lawful money, viz. The authority of the Prince, the Stamp, and the value. But upon the consideration of the case in question, it was observed, that six things or circumstances ought to concur, to make lawful and current money, viz. 1. Weight 2. Fineness. 3. Impression. 4. Denomination. 5. Authority of the Prince. 6. Proclamation. [See 1 H. H. P. C. 196, that Proclamation is not always necessary.] For every piece of money ought to have a certain proportion of weight or poise, and a certain proportion of purity or fineness, which is called alloy; also every piece ought to have a certain form of impression, which may be knowable and distinguishable; for as wax is not a seal without a stamp, so metal is not money without an impression. * * *

And so it is manifest, that the kings of England have always had and exercised this prerogative of coining and changing the form, and when they found it expedient of enhancing and abasing the value of money within their dominions: and this prerogative is allowed and approved not only the common law, but also by the rules of the imperial law. * * *

And according to this resolution, several other cases on the same point were afterwards ruled and adjudged in the several Courts of Record in Dublin.

———

Money and banking in America have a long and tangled history. There was no money as we know it in America before the arrival of Columbus, and money was only slowly introduced to the "New World." The English colonies in particular were largely dependent on barter, foreign coins, and "bills of credit" (i.e., notes or promises to pay issued by the colonies). Commodities were sometimes used as legal tender at a value set by the colonial governments. An often cited description of this confusing monetary system noted that:

> They give the title of "merchant" to every trader, who rates his goods according to the time and species they pay in; viz., "pay"; "money"; "pay-as-money"; and "trusting." Pay is grain, pork and beef, etc., at the prices set by the General Court. Money is pieces-of-eight, ryals, Boston or Bay shillings, or "good hard money," as sometimes silver coin is called; also wampum, viz., Indian beads, which serve as change. Pay-as-money is provision aforesaid, one-third cheaper that the Assembly set it; and Trust, as they agree for at the time. When the buyer comes to ask for a commodity, sometimes before the merchant answers that he has it, he says, "is your pay ready?" Perhaps the chap replies, "yes." "What do you pay in?" says the merchant. The buyer having answered, then the price is set; as suppose he wants a 6d. knife, in "pay" it is 12d.; in "pay-as-money"

8d., and "hard-money," its own value, 6d. It seems a very intricate way of trade, and what the Lex Mercatoria had not thought of.[3]

Bills of credit issued by colonial governments to finance their operations were often authorized without adequate backing in revenues to fulfill their promises to pay. Those bills sharply depreciated in value and caused price inflation. During the Revolution, the Continental Congress and the warring colonies issued even more bills, notes, and other promises to pay in order to fund the war. That currency quickly depreciated in value because, like colonial bills of credit, there were few taxes or other revenues to back them. The result was massive inflation in prices, and the currency became almost worthless, giving rise to the expression: "not worth a continental dollar."

The colonies, of course, were able to persevere and obtain their independence. The newly independent states, were faced, however, with the challenge of creating a new system for governmental and private finance. One issue raised during the Constitutional debates was control by the federal government over monetary matters. The new federal government did not want a repetition of the issuance of inflationary bills of credit by the colonies. That concern was addressed by Article I, Section 10 of the Constitution. It stated that no State shall "coin money; emit bills of credit; [or] make anything but gold or silver coin a tender in payment of debts."

CRAIG v. MISSOURI

Supreme Court of the United States, 1830.
29 U.S. (4 Pet.) 410.

MR. CHIEF JUSTICE MARSHALL delivered the opinion of the Court.

* * * This brings us to the great question in the cause: Is the act of the legislature of Missouri repugnant to the constitution of the United States? * * *

The act under the authority of which the certificates loaned to the plaintiffs in error were issued, was passed on the 26th of June 1821, and is entitled "an act for the establishment of loan offices." [The act directed the state treasury to issue certificates that would be receivable in the discharge of taxes as debts due to the state. The certificates were issued by various loan offices which were authorized to loan the certificates to citizens of the state secured by mortgage or personal security. The loans bore interest at a rate not exceeding 6% per annum. The act provided for the gradual withdrawal of the certificates from circulation, and all the certificates have now been redeemed.] * * *

The clause in the constitution which this act is supposed to violate is in these words: "No state shall" "emit bills of credit."

---

3. Journal of Mrs. Knight, New Haven, 1704 A.D., quoted in Alexander Del Mar, The History of Money in America 78 (Cambridge Ency. Co. 1899).

What is a bill of credit? What did the constitution mean to forbid? * * *

At a very early period of our colonial history, the attempt to supply the want of the precious metals by a paper medium was made to a considerable extent; and the bills emitted for this purpose have been frequently denominated bills of credit. During the war of our revolution, we were driven to this expedient; and necessity compelled us to use it to a most fearful extent. The term has acquired an appropriate meaning; and "bills of credit" signify a paper medium, intended to circulate between individuals, and between government and individuals, for the ordinary purposes of society. Such a medium has been always liable to considerable fluctuation. Its value is continually changing; and these changes, often great and sudden, expose individuals to immense loss, are the sources of ruinous speculations, and destroy all confidence between man and man. To cut up this mischief by the roots, a mischief which was felt through the United States, and which deeply affected the interest and prosperity of all; the people declared in their constitution, that no state should emit bills of credit. If the prohibition means any thing, if the words are not empty sounds, it must comprehend the emission of any paper medium, by a state government, for the purpose of common circulation. * * *

We learn from Hutchinson's History of Massachusetts, vol. 1, p. 402, that bills of credit were emitted for the first time in that colony in 1690. An army returning unexpectedly from an expedition against Canada, which had proved as disastrous as the plan was magnificent, found the government totally unprepared to meet their claims. Bills of credit were resorted to, for relief from this embarrassment. They do not appear to have been made a tender; but they were not on that account the less bills of credit, nor were they absolutely harmless. The emission, however, not being considerable, and the bills being soon redeemed, the experiment would have been productive of not much mischief, had it not been followed by repeated emissions to a much larger amount. The subsequent history of Massachusetts abounds with proofs of the evils with which paper money is fraught, whether it be or be not a legal tender.

Paper money was also issued in other colonies, both in the north and south; and whether made a tender or not, was productive of evils in proportion to the quantity emitted. In the war which commenced in America in 1755, Virginia issued paper money at several successive sessions, under the appellation of treasury notes. This was made a tender. Emissions were afterwards made in 1769, in 1771, and in 1773. These were not made a tender; but they circulated together; were equally bills of credit; and were productive of the same effects. In 1775 a considerable emission was made for the purposes of the war. The bills were declared to be current, but were not made a tender. In 1776, an additional emission was made, and the bills were declared to be a tender. The bills of 1775 and 1776 circulated together; were equally bills of credit; and were productive of the same consequences.

Congress emitted bills of credit to a large amount; and did not, perhaps could not, make them a legal tender. This power resided in the states. In May 1777, the legislature of Virginia passed an act for the first time making the bills of credit issued under the authority of congress a tender so far as to extinguish interest. It was not until March 1781 that Virginia passed an act making all the bills of credit which had been emitted by congress, and all which had been emitted by the state, a legal tender in payment of debts. Yet they were in every sense of the word bills of credit, previous to that time; and were productive of all the consequences of paper money. * * *

A majority of the court feels constrained to say that the consideration on which the note in this case was given, is against the highest law of the land, and that the note itself is utterly void. In rendering judgment for the plaintiff, the court for the state of Missouri decided in favour of the validity of a law which is repugnant to the constitution of the United States. * * *

The judgment of the supreme court of the state of Missouri for the first judicial district is reversed; and the cause remanded, with directions to enter judgment for the defendants. * * *

JUSTICES JOHNSON, THOMPSON AND M'LEAN dissent. * * *

B. LENDING MONEY

Money lenders were an early type of banker. These individuals were not always popular because of the high rates of interest they charged. The Code of Hammurabi set limits on interest rates that varied from 20 to 33.33 percent. Both the Bible and the Qur'an contain prohibitions on usury. By 1100, the Catholic church declared that loaning money at interest was a sin. Later, this church declared that a person committing such a sin might have his soul saved through purgatory. It was said that the birth of purgatory was the "dawn of banking."[4]

The Great Forum in Rome had private bankers who kept sophisticated accounts, and checks may have been in use in Rome as early as 352 B.C. One of the first international banks was the Knights of the Templars, a religious order founded by the Crusaders in Jerusalem around 1118 A.D. The Templars built over 800 castles that stretched across Europe, the Mediterranean, England, and Jerusalem.

These fortresses provided a safe storage place for gold and silver. Deposits could be made at one castle and withdrawn from another. Loan agents also operated from these castles. Other banks appeared elsewhere in Europe. The Bank of Venice was established in 1171. The Bank of Genoa was founded a few centuries later. Seventy-two international banks had offices located in Florence by 1422 A.D. By 1397, the Medici Bank in Florence loaned money, established rates of exchange for various curren-

---

4. William Greider, Secrets of the Temple: How the Federal Reserve Board Runs the Country 172 (1987).

cies, and created a system that allowed merchants to transfer funds to other cities.

Prior to the creation of the Bank of England in 1694, goldsmiths were England's principal bankers. An English statute adopted in 1679 addressed itself to goldsmiths and others who borrowed money and loaned out the same for hire or profit. The legislation noted that these individuals were referred to as "bankers." Goldsmiths gave their customers receipts or "goldsmith's notes" that were payable on demand. Customers holding such receipts could give orders to the goldsmiths to assign their holdings to third parties, another early form of check. Goldsmiths also discovered that they could issue more receipts than they held gold for because the notes would not all be redeemed at the same time. This laid the foundation for modern bank lending practices.

SECTION 2.   THE CREATION OF BANKS IN EARLY AMERICA

The Constitution precluded the use of the State bills of credit that had served as money during the colonial period, but there was no federal currency to serve as a substitute, other than a limited number of coins. This initially meant that banks had to create a supply of money for commerce in America. There was one small problem—no real banks existed in America before the Revolution.[5] In the midst of that conflict, Robert Morris, the Superintendent of Finance for the Continental Congress, and Alexander Hamilton, who later became America's first Secretary of the Treasury, laid the groundwork for our existing bank structure. After reading Adam Smith's *The Wealth of Nations*, which was published in 1776, Hamilton became an advocate of a central bank that would help build America into a world power. Hamilton proposed such an institution in a letter to Robert Morris written while the Continental Army was in winter quarters. Morris set that plan in motion through the "Bank of North America," which began operations in 1782 and aided the Continental army during some of its darker hours.

A.   THE BANK OF THE UNITED STATES AND EARLY STATE CHARTERED BANKS

In 1790, after he became Secretary of the Treasury, Hamilton reported to Congress on measures needed to establish public credit for the new federal government. He recommended the creation of a "National Bank" that would become the "Bank of the United States." Hamilton used the

---

5. The Land and Manufacture Bank was created in 1740 in New England, but was shut down by colonial authorities, causing the financial ruin of Samuel Adams' father. Robert Harvey, A Few Bloody Noses: The American War of Independence 24, 92 (2001). Henry McCulloh unsuccessfully petitioned the North Carolina legislature in 1767 for the creation of a Bank for America that would be established as a branch of the Bank of England. T. Harry Garton, Banking in North Carolina: A Narrative History 24 (1987).

Bank of England as a model.[6] Hamilton wanted the Bank of the United States (BUS) to be a private bank. Congress approved Hamilton's recommendations and authorized the creation of a national bank in 1791. The cabinet of George Washington was divided over the issue of whether Congress had the power to create such a corporation. Alexander Hamilton, however, convinced the President to sign the bill and the BUS began operations.

The BUS was not the only bank in America. A number of banks were created with charters from the states in the years following the Revolution. North Carolina was the last state of the original thirteen to allow the chartering of banks, granting its first bank charter in 1804. Between 1782 and 1837, over 700 banks sprang up in the United States. Despite state bank competition, the BUS continued as the premier bank. It had branches in Boston, New York, Washington, Newport, Charleston, Savannah, and New Orleans. Ironically, the success of the BUS spelled its doom. It was a threat to the state banks that appeared in ever increasing numbers, and Congress refused to renew its charter in 1811. The expiration of the Bank's charter created a vacuum that was filled by even more state banks. Over 120 new banks were chartered between 1811 and 1815. Since there was no national currency, the notes issued by the state banks began circulating as a medium of exchange. State bank notes, however, were an unstable currency. As John Adams noted in 1799, "the fluctuations of our circulating medium have committed greater depredations upon the property of honest men than all the French piracies."[7] The state bank notes presented other problems, as illustrated in a letter written in 1818 describing the purchase of a pair of gloves in Washington, D.C.:

> The price was half a dollar per pair. I presented a Philadelphia one dollar note. It could not be taken without a discount of 2 1/2 per cent. I then tendered a Baltimore check, of the same amount.
>
> This being one hundred miles nearer was accepted. The storekeeper had no silver change; to remedy which he took a pair of scissors and divided the note between us! I enquired if the half would pass, and being answered in the affirmative, took it without hesitation, knowing the want of specie throughout the country, and being previously familiarized with Spanish dollars cut into every variety of size. I now find that demi-notes are common circulating medium.[8]

B. THE SECOND BANK OF THE UNITED STATES

Difficulties encountered during the War of 1812, when runs on banks for specie forced many banks to suspend payments in specie and when the

---

6. The Bank of England operated as a central bank for both the English government and private merchants. National banks existed in other countries, including Italy, Germany, France, and Holland.

7. Bray Hammond, Banks and Politics in America From the Revolution to the Civil War 36 (1957).

8. Alexander Mackie, Facile Princeps: The Story of the Beginning of Life Insurance in America 224 (1956).

Treasury had no one place to turn to for loans, resulted in the creation of a new Bank of the United States (the Second BUS) which existed from 1816 to 1836. The states did not react favorably toward this institution. Fourteen states passed laws that tried to prevent the Second BUS from collecting its debts. Six states tried to tax branches of the Second BUS located within their borders.

M'CULLOCH v. MARYLAND

Supreme Court of the United States, 1819.
17 U.S. (4 Wheat.) 316.

MR. CHIEF JUSTICE MARSHALL delivered the opinion of the Court.

In the case now to be determined, the defendant, a sovereign State, denies the obligation of a law enacted by the legislature of the Union, and the plaintiff, on his part, contests the validity of an act which has been passed by the legislature of that State. The constitution of our country, in its most interesting and vital parts, is to be considered; the conflicting powers of the government of the Union and of its members, as marked in that constitution, are to be discussed; and an opinion given, which may essentially influence the great operations of the government. No tribunal can approach such a question without a deep sense of its importance, and of the awful responsibility involved in its decision. But it must be decided peacefully, or remain a source of hostile legislation, perhaps of hostility of a still more serious nature; and if it is to be so decided, by this tribunal alone can the decision be made. On the Supreme Court of the United States has the constitution of our country devolved this important duty.

The first question made in the cause is, has Congress power to incorporate a bank? * * * yes

The power now contested was exercised by the first Congress elected under the present constitution. The bill for incorporating the bank of the United States did not steal upon an unsuspecting legislature, and pass unobserved. Its principle was completely understood, and was opposed with equal zeal and ability. After being resisted, first in the fair and open field of debate, and afterwards in the executive cabinet, with as much persevering talent as any measure has ever experienced, and being supported by arguments which convinced minds as pure and as intelligent as this country can boast, it became a law. The original act was permitted to expire; but a short experience of the embarrassments to which the refusal to revive it exposed the government, convinced those who were most prejudiced against the measure of its necessity, and induced the passage of the present law. It would require no ordinary share of intrepidity to assert that a measure adopted under these circumstances was a bold and plain usurpation, to which the constitution gave no countenance. * * *

The government of the United States, then, though limited in its powers, is supreme; and its laws, when made in pursuance of the constitution, form the supreme law of the land, "any thing in the constitution or laws of any State to the contrary notwithstanding."

Among the enumerated powers, we do not find that of establishing a bank or creating a corporation. But there is no phrase in the instrument which, like the articles of confederation, excludes incidental or implied powers; and which requires that every thing granted shall be expressly and minutely described. Even the 10th amendment, which was framed for the purpose of quieting the excessive jealousies which had been excited, omits the word "expressly," and declares only that the powers "not delegated to the United States, nor prohibited to the States, are reserved to the States or to the people;" thus leaving the question, whether the particular power which may become the subject of contest has been delegated to the one government, or prohibited to the other, to depend on a fair construction of the whole instrument. * * * A constitution, to contain an accurate detail of all the subdivisions of which its great powers will admit, and of all the means by which they may be carried into execution, would partake of the prolixity of a legal code, and could scarcely be embraced by the human mind. It would probably never be understood by the public. Its nature, therefore, requires, that only its great outlines should be marked, its important objects designated, and the minor ingredients which compose those objects be deduced from the nature of the objects themselves. * * * In considering this question, then, we must never forget, that it is *a constitution* we are expounding.

* * * To its enumeration of powers is added that of making "all laws which shall be necessary and proper, for carrying into execution the foregoing powers, and all other powers vested by this constitution, in the government of the United States, or in any department thereof."

* * * This clause, as construed by the State of Maryland, would abridge, and almost annihilate this useful and necessary right of the legislature to select its means. That this could not be intended, is, we should think, had it not been already controverted, too apparent for controversy. We think so for the following reasons:

1st. The clause is placed among the powers of Congress, not among the limitations on those powers.

2nd. Its terms purport to enlarge, not to diminish the powers vested in the government. It purports to be an additional power, not a restriction on those already granted. * * *

If a corporation may be employed indiscriminately with other means to carry into execution the powers of the government, no particular reason can be assigned for excluding the use of a bank, if required for its fiscal operations. * * *

After this declaration, it can scarcely be necessary to say, that the existence of State banks can have no possible influence on the question. No trace is to be found in the constitution of an intention to create a dependence of the government of the Union on those of the States, for the execution of the great powers assigned to it. * * *

After the most deliberate consideration, it is the unanimous and decided opinion of this Court, that the act to incorporate the Bank of the United States is a law made in pursuance of the constitution, and is a part of the supreme law of the land.

The branches, proceeding from the same stock, and being conducive to the complete accomplishment of the object, are equally constitutional. It would have been unwise to locate them in the charter, and it would be unnecessarily inconvenient to employ the legislative power in making those subordinate arrangements. The great duties of the bank are pre-scribed; those duties require branches; and the bank itself may, we think, be safely trusted with the selection of places where those branches shall be fixed; reserving always to the government the right to require that a branch shall be located where it may be deemed necessary.

It being the opinion of the Court, that the act incorporating the bank is constitutional; and that the power of establishing a branch in the State of Maryland might be properly exercised by the bank itself, we proceed to inquire * * * [w]hether the State of Maryland may, without violating the constitution, tax that branch? * * *

This great principle is, that the constitution and the laws made in pursuance thereof are supreme; that they control the constitution and the law of the respective States, and cannot be controlled by them. From this, which may be almost termed an axiom, other propositions are deduced as corollaries, on the truth or error of which, and on their application to this case, the cause has been supposed to depend. These are, 1st. That a power to create implies a power to preserve. 2nd. That a power to destroy, if wielded by a different hand, is hostile to, and incompatible with these powers to create and to preserve. 3d. That where this repugnancy exists, that authority which is supreme must control, not yield to that over which it is supreme. * * *

The power of Congress to create, and of course to continue, the bank, was the subject of the preceding part of this opinion; and is no longer to be considered as questionable.

That the power of taxing it by the States may be exercised so as to destroy it, is too obvious to be denied. But taxation is said to be an absolute power, which acknowledges no other limits than those expressly prescribed in the constitution, and like sovereign power of every other description, is trusted to the discretion of those who use it. But the very terms of this argument admit that the sovereignty of the State, in the article of taxation itself, is subordinate to, and may be controlled by the constitution of the United States. * * *

The sovereignty of a State extends to every thing which exists by its own authority, or is introduced by its permission; but does it extend to those means which are employed by Congress to carry into execution powers conferred on that body by the people of the United States? We think it demonstrable that it does not. * * *

We find, then, on just theory, a total failure of this original right to tax the means employed by the government of the Union, for the execution of its powers. The right never existed, and the question whether it has been surrendered, cannot arise. * * *

It has also been insisted, that, as the power of taxation in the general and State governments is acknowledged to be concurrent, every argument which would sustain the right of the general government to tax banks chartered by the States, will equally sustain the right of the States to tax banks chartered by the general government.

But the two cases are not on the same reason. The people of all the States have created the general government, and have conferred upon it the general power of taxation. The people of all the States, and the States themselves, are represented in Congress, and, by their representatives, exercise this power. When they tax the chartered institutions of the States, they tax their constituents; and these taxes must be uniform. But, when a State taxes the operations of the government of the United States, it acts upon institutions created, not by their own constituents, but by people over whom them claim no control. It acts upon the measures of a government created by others as well as themselves, for the benefit of others in common with themselves. * * *

The Court has bestowed on this subject its most deliberate consideration. The result is a conviction that the States have no power, by taxation or otherwise, to retard, impede, burden, or in any manner control, the operations of the constitutional laws enacted by Congress to carry into execution the powers vested in the general government. This is, we think, the unavoidable consequence of that supremacy which the constitution has declared.

We are unanimously of opinion, that the law passed by the legislature of Maryland, imposing a tax on the Bank of the United States, is unconstitutional and void. * * *

C. THE FIGHT OVER THE SECOND BUS

A financial panic in 1819 was blamed by some on the Second BUS's conservative lending practices. The Second BUS engendered further hostility when it foreclosed on large amounts of real estate after the panic. The appointment of Nicholas Biddle as president of the Second BUS in 1823 restored its stature. Biddle, a lawyer, wunderkind college student at age ten and editor of the Lewis & Clark journals, pursued an aggressive program of expansion. Under his leadership, the Second BUS had twenty-five branches by 1830 and conducted some twenty percent of all banking business in the United States. Despite that success, or perhaps because of it, the Second BUS became the center of a political battle that has reverberated through the centuries. President Andrew Jackson viewed the BUS as a "monster." Henry Clay, his political rival, wanted to make the BUS's charter a political issue to further his own presidential ambitions.

Clay and his supporters, including Daniel Webster, appeared to have control of both the House and the Senate. They rechartered the Second BUS in 1832, but Jackson vetoed the legislation. His veto was upheld, and he ordered the government's deposits to be removed from the Second BUS to state banks that were politically aligned with Jackson. These banks were derisively referred to by Jackson's opponents as the "pet" banks. At Clay's urging, Jackson was censured by the Senate for his deposit removal order, but Clay suffered a severe defeat when the Senate voted to expunge that censure from Senate records in 1837.

The struggle over the Second BUS set back the effort to create a central banking authority until the next century, and its demise led to another "bank mania." The number of state banks more than doubled between 1829 and 1837. Gradually, banking regulation was adopted at the state level to deal with the ever increasing number of state banks.

Massachusetts and New Hampshire prohibited unincorporated banks in 1799. New York imposed a similar measure in 1804. Those prohibitions were based on the English Bubble Act of 1720, which sought to curb speculative enterprises by requiring businesses to obtain a government approved charter before stock could be sold to the public or notes issued. New York later allowed banks to be incorporated without requiring a special charter from the state legislature. Several other states followed this "free banking" approach to chartering.[9]

More affirmative regulation was adopted.[10] States began requiring banks to report on their financial positions in the early 1800s. Massachusetts passed such a statute in 1803. New York set up a bank supervisory authority in 1829. Reserve requirements were imposed to assure that banks had specie on hand to meet depositor demands for withdrawals. The first insurance for bank depositors appears to have been the New York safety fund law that was passed in 1829. This effort proved inadequate, however, to deal with bank failures in the aftermath of the Panic of 1837.

SECTION 3. THE CIVIL WAR ERA

A. BANK CURRENCY

By the time of the Civil War, America's principal currency was the bank notes issued by some 1,600 state banks, which fluctuated in value according to their quality. James Haxby issued a Standard Catalog of Obsolete United States Bank Notes, 1782–1866. This catalog identified some 72,000 bank notes. The following account that appeared in a Buffalo newspaper in 1837 described the problems engendered by this currency:

---

9. Banking was not universally accepted. After its settlement, the Texas Constitution prohibited banks until 1904. Iowa, Arkansas, Oregon, and California prohibited banks before the Civil War.

10. After the Panic of 1837, several states adopted legislation that made bank stockholders liable for twice the amount of the par value of their shares in the event of a bank's failure. This was called "double liability." Double liability was also included in the National Banking Act when it was enacted during the Civil War.

An acquaintance who has recently been to the West, invested his funds in Buffalo bills * * * at 10 per cent discount. At Buffalo he exchanged his bills for specie at 5 per cent premium, which he sent back to New York and sold it at 12 per cent premium, making a net profit of 17 per cent.

He bought also a parcel of the Canada Joint Stock Bank notes at 25 per cent discount, which he turned to still better account.[11]

"In March, 1842, a $1 note from Planters Bank in Nashville, Tenn., would get you just 80 cents in Philadelphia, and a $1 note from State Bank of Illinois fetched just 50 cents."[12]

MARINE BANK v. FULTON BANK

Supreme Court of the United States, 1864.
69 U.S. (2 Wall.) 252.

In the spring of 1861, the Fulton Bank, of New York, sent for collection to the Marine Bank, Chicago, two notes, one of Cooley & Co., for $2000, and one of Hunt & Co., for $1037; both due May 1–4, in that year. The currency at Chicago had become at that time somewhat deranged, and consisted exclusively of bills of the Illinois banks. The Marine Bank, just afterwards, addressed a circular to its correspondents, informing them that, in the disturbed state of the currency, it would be impossible to continue remittances with the usual regularity, and that until further notice it would be compelled to place all funds received in payment of collections to the credit of its correspondents in such currency as was received in Chicago,—bills of the Illinois Stock Banks,—to be drawn for only in like bills. * * *

On the 21st April, 1862, that is to say, about a year after the collection made, the New York bank made a demand of payment from the Chicago bank, which was refused, unless the former bank would accept Illinois currency, now sunk fifty per cent. below par. * * *

MR. JUSTICE MILLER delivered the opinion of the Court.

* * * All deposits made with bankers may be divided into two classes, namely, those in which the bank becomes bailee of the depositor, the title to the thing deposited remaining with the latter; and that other kind of deposit of money peculiar to banking business, in which the depositor, for his own convenience, parts with the title to his money, and loans it to the banker; and the latter, in consideration of the loan of the money and the right to use it for his own profit, agrees to refund the same amount, or any part thereof, on demand. The case before us is not of the former class. It must be of the latter. The parties seem to have taken this view of it, as is shown by the reply made by the Chicago bank, May 1st and 6th, to the New York bank, when inquiring how the account stood.

---

11. Daily Commercial Advertiser (Buffalo, New York), July 10, 1837, at 2.
12. Lawrence Ingrassia, Exchequered Past, Wall St. J., Jan. 13, 1998, at 1.

The counsel have argued as to the effect of mixing the money of plaintiff with that of defendant. In the view we take of the matter, there was no such admixture. It being understood between the parties that, when the money was received, it was to be held as an ordinary bank deposit, it became by virtue of that understanding the money of the defendant the moment it was received.

But let us look for a moment at the equity of defendant's position. It receives this money when it is worth ninety cents on the dollar. It places it with its other money; and, perhaps, in the course of a week, all the specific bank bills it then had on hand are paid out by it. It uses it in paying the checks of its depositors, in other words, its debts at par.

It buys with it bills on New York, which it converts into exchange worth a premium. But it continues to receive of other parties this class of paper, though constantly depreciating. There is no legal necessity that it should do this. It only does so with a view to its own advantage.

When, however, it proves to be a loss instead of a profit, the bank says to the man whose money it had used profitably months before, "I claim to impose this loss on you. I insist on the right to pay the debt I owe you, not in the specific bank bills I received from you, nor in those of the same value which I received from you; but in bills of that general class, although, while I have been using the money, they have depreciated forty per cent." * * * [The Court found that the bank owed the depositor the sum collected, rather than the lower value of the now-depreciated bank notes that were originally deposited.]

A further problem was that many bank notes were counterfeited. Publications were available that identified counterfeit or altered bank notes. John Thompson's Bank Note Detector was one of the more popular services.

B. SHINPLASTERS AND THE STAMP PAYMENTS ACT

A continuing problem with bank note currency was the "shinplaster," a small denomination note issued by "wildcat" banks that did not have reserves adequate to back their issues. Because the notes were in such small denominations, they were often accepted without questioning the condition of the issuing bank, which frequently was doubtful. In 1835, the Secretary of the Treasury decreed that no bank notes of less than $5 in value would be accepted by the Treasury. Some states also sought to drive "shinplasters" and other worthless small notes out of existence by prohibiting their issuance. Alabama and the District of Columbia, for example, prohibited the circulation of bank bills in amounts less than $5. Alabama, however, allowed its own banks to issue such bills. Arkansas passed an anti-shinplaster statute in 1855. This bill created difficulties in the marketplace because shinplasters were about the only circulating currency that could be used to pay debts. In 1862, Congress prohibited shinplasters through enactment of the Stamp Payments Act, described in the following case.

UNITED STATES v. VAN AUKEN

Supreme Court of the United States, 1877.
96 U.S. (6 Otto.) 366.

MR. JUSTICE SWAYNE delivered the opinion of the Court.

The act of Congress of July 17, 1862, sect. 2 (12 Stat. 592; Rev. Stat. 711, sect. 3583), declares that "no private corporation, banking association, firm, or individual shall make, issue, circulate, or pay out any note, check, memorandum, token, or other obligation, for a less sum than one dollar, intended to circulate as money, or to be received or used in lieu of lawful money of the United States," and denounces as a penalty for the offence fine or imprisonment, or both.

Van Auken was indicted under this act for circulating the "obligations" of the Bangor Furnace Company, a corporation created by and under the laws of the State of Michigan, which obligations are alleged to be *in hoec verba*:—

"BANGOR, MICH., Aug. 15, 1874.

"The Bangor Furnace Company will pay the bearer, on demand, fifty cents, in goods, at their store, in Bangor, Mich.

(Signed)

"A. B. Hough, Pres.

"Chas. D. Rhoder, Treas." * * *

The grammatical construction and the obvious meaning are the same. The statute makes the offence to consist of two ingredients: 1. The token or obligation must be for a less sum than a dollar. 2. It must be intended to circulate as money, or in lieu of the money of the United States. Here the note is for "goods," to be paid at the store of the Furnace Company. It is not payable in money, but in goods, and in goods only. No money could be demanded upon it. It is not solvable in that medium. The sum of "fifty cents" is named, but merely as the limit of the value in goods demandable and to be paid upon the presentment of the note. Its mention was for no other purpose, and has no other effect. In the view of the law, the note is as if it called for so many pounds, yards, or quarts of a specific article. The limit of value, there being none other, gave the holder a range of choice as to the articles to be received in payment, limited only by the contents of the store. * * *

[The Court held that the indictment was defective since it alleged an obligation payable in money, while this obligation was one payable in goods.]

JUSTICE MILLER dissents. * * *

––––––––––

The Supreme Court's decision in *Van Auken* is not of just historical interest. An issue was raised in the 1990s as to whether the Stamp Payments Act of 1862 would interfere with electronic money. There was also the fear that electronic money could become the basis for the creation of another set of wildcat banks such as those existing before the Civil War.

C. GREENBACKS AS LEGAL TENDER

In 1862, Congress created the "greenback"—notes issued by the government that derived their name from the color of the back of the note. Over $400 million in greeenbacks were printed. Greenbacks were made legal tender and were one mechanism for funding the expenses of the Civil War. Although considered "legal tender," greenbacks were not redeemable in specie and their value fluctuated. The Supreme Court considered the legality of greenbacks in the so-called "legal tender" cases. In Hepburn v. Griswold, 75 U.S. (8 Wall.) 603 (1869) the Court initially held that the legal tender requirement was unconstitutional. The Chief Justice who wrote the majority opinion for the Court in the *Hepburn* case was none other than Salmon P. Chase, the former Secretary of the Treasury who had administered the introduction of the greenbacks and the legal tender requirement during the Civil War. That decision was soon under attack.

LEGAL TENDER CASES
KNOX v. LEE
PARKER v. DAVIS

Supreme Court of the United States, 1870.
79 U.S. (12 Wall.) 457.

MR. JUSTICE STRONG delivered the opinion of the Court.

The controlling questions in these cases are the following: Are the acts of Congress, known as the legal tender acts, constitutional when applied to contracts made before their passage; and, secondly, are they valid as applicable to debts contracted since their enactment? These questions have been elaborately argued, and they have received from the court that consideration which their great importance demands. It would be difficult to overestimate the consequences which must follow our decision. They will affect the entire business of the country, and take hold of the possible continued existence of the government. If it be held by this court that Congress has no constitutional power, under any circumstances, or in any emergency, to make treasury notes a legal tender for the payment of all debts (a power confessedly possessed by every independent sovereignty other than the United States), the government is without those means of self-preservation which, all must admit, may, in certain contingencies, become indispensable, even if they were not when the acts of Congress now called in question were enacted. It is also clear that if we hold the acts invalid as applicable to debts incurred, or transactions which have taken place since their enactment, our decision must cause, throughout the country, great business derangement, widespread distress, and the rankest injustice. The debts which have been contracted since February 25th, 1862, constitute, doubtless, by far the greatest portion of the existing indebtedness of the country. They have been contracted in view of the acts of Congress declaring treasury notes a legal tender, and in reliance upon that declaration. Men have bought and sold, borrowed and lent, and assumed every variety of obligations contemplating that payment might be made with such notes. Indeed, legal tender treasury notes have become the universal measure of values. If now, by our decision, it be established that these debts and obligations can be discharged only by gold coin; if, contrary to the expectation of all parties to these contracts, legal tender notes are rendered unavailable, the government has become an instrument of the grossest injustice; all debtors are loaded with an obligation it was never contemplated they should assume; a large percentage is added to every debt, and such must become the demand for gold to satisfy contracts, that ruinous sacrifices, general distress, and bankruptcy may be expected. These consequences are too obvious to admit of question. * * *

We do not propose to dilate at length upon the circumstances in which the country was placed, when Congress attempted to make treasury notes a legal tender. They are of too recent occurrence to justify enlarged description. Suffice it to say that a civil war was then raging which seriously threatened the overthrow of the government and the destruction of the Constitution itself. It demanded the equipment and support of large armies and navies, and the employment of money to an extent beyond the capacity of all ordinary sources of supply. Meanwhile the public treasury was nearly empty, and the credit of the government, if not stretched to its utmost tension, had become nearly exhausted. Moneyed institutions had advanced largely of their means, and more could not be expected of them. They had been compelled to suspend specie payments. Taxation was inadequate to pay even the interest on the debt already incurred, and it was impossible to await the income of additional taxes. The necessity was immediate and pressing. The army was unpaid. There was then due to the soldiers in the field nearly a score of millions of dollars. The requisitions from the War and Navy Departments for supplies exceeded fifty millions, and the current expenditure was over one million per day. The entire amount of coin in the country, including that in private hands, as well as that in banking institutions, was insufficient to supply the need of the government three months, had it all been poured into the treasury. Foreign credit we had none. We say nothing of the overhanging paralysis of trade, and of business generally, which threatened loss of confidence in the ability of the government to maintain its continued existence, and therewith the complete destruction of all remaining national credit. * * *

Here those who assert the unconstitutionality of the acts mainly rest their argument. They claim that the clause which conferred upon Congress power "to coin money, regulate the value thereof, and of foreign coin," contains an implication that nothing but that which is the subject of coinage, nothing but the precious metals can ever be declared by law to be money, or to have the uses of money. If by this is meant that because certain powers over the currency are expressly given to Congress, all other powers relating to the same subject are impliedly forbidden, we need only remark that such is not the manner in which the Constitution has always been construed. On the contrary it has been ruled that power over a particular subject may be exercised as auxiliary to an express power, though there is another express power relating to the same subject, less comprehensive. * * * To assert, then, that the clause enabling Congress to coin money and regulate its value tacitly implies a denial of all other power over the currency of the nation, is an attempt to introduce a new rule of construction against the solemn decisions of this court. So far from its containing a lurking prohibition, many have thought it was intended to confer upon Congress that general power over the currency which has always been an acknowledged attribute of sovereignty in every other civilized nation than our own, especially when considered in connection with the other clause which denies to the States the power to coin money, emit bills of credit, or make anything but gold and silver coin a tender in payment of debts. * * *

We come next to the argument much used, and, indeed, the main reliance of those who assert the unconstitutionality of the legal tender acts. It is that they are prohibited by the spirit of the Constitution because they indirectly impair the obligation of contracts. The argument, of course, relates only to those contracts which were made before February, 1862, when the first act was passed, and it has no bearing upon the question whether the acts are valid when applied to contracts made after their passage. The argument assumes two things,—first, that the acts do, in effect, impair the obligation of contracts, and second, that Congress is prohibited from taking any action which may indirectly have that effect. Neither of these assumptions can be accepted. It is true that under the acts, a debtor, who became such before they were passed, may discharge his debt with the notes authorized by them, and the creditor is compellable to receive such notes in discharge of his claim. But whether the obligation of the contract is thereby weakened can be determined only after considering what was the contract obligation. It was not a duty to pay gold or silver, or the kind of money recognized by law at the time when the contract was made, nor was it a duty to pay money of equal intrinsic value in the market. (We speak now of contracts to pay money generally, not contracts to pay some specifically defined species of money.) The expectation of the creditor and the anticipation of the debtor may have been that the contract would be discharged by the payment of coined metals, but neither the expectation of one party to the contract respecting its fruits, nor the anticipation of the other constitutes its obligation. There is a well-recognized distinction between the expectation of the parties to a contract and the duty imposed by it. Were it not so the expectation of results would be always equivalent to a binding engagement that they should follow. But the obligation of a contract to pay money is to pay that which the law shall recognize as money when the payment is to be made. If there is anything settled by decision it is this, and we do not understand it to be controverted. * * * Every contract for the payment of money, simply, is necessarily subject to the constitutional power of the government over the currency, whatever that power may be, and the obligation of the parties is, therefore, assumed with reference to that power. * * *

Closely allied to the objection we have just been considering is the argument pressed upon us that the legal tender acts were prohibited by the spirit of the fifth amendment, which forbids taking private property for public use without just compensation or due process of law. That provision has always been understood as referring only to a direct appropriation, and not to consequential injuries resulting from the exercise of lawful power. It has never been supposed to have any bearing upon, or to inhibit laws that indirectly work harm and loss to individuals. A new tariff, an embargo, a draft, or a war may inevitably bring upon individuals great losses; may, indeed, render valuable property almost valueless. They may destroy the worth of contracts. But whoever supposed that, because of this, a tariff could not be changed, or a non-intercourse act, or an embargo be enacted, or a war be declared? * * *

But, without extending our remarks further, it will be seen that we hold the acts of Congress constitutional as applied to contracts made either before or after their passage. In so holding, we overrule so much of what was decided in Hepburn v. Griswold, as ruled the acts unwarranted by the Constitution so far as they apply to contracts made before their enactment. * * *

JUSTICE BRADLEY, concurs. * * * CHIEF JUSTICE CHASE, dissents. * * * JUSTICE CLIFFORD, dissents. * * * JUSTICE FIELD, dissents. * * *

D. THE NATIONAL BANK ACT

Congress continued to address the national currency issue. It adopted the National Currency Act on February 25, 1863, to create a system of national banks. Congress concluded that a system of banks with federal charters was needed to provide a uniform circulating currency and financial stability. Upon deposit of bonds with the Secretary of the Treasury, a national bank was authorized to issue circulating notes that were valued at ninety percent of the amount of the current market value of bonds on deposit. These circulating notes could be used to pay most government obligations and were in effect legal tender. Large amounts of the "National Currency" notes were issued by the national banks in denominations that were often as small as $5 and $20 and looked very much like modern currency.

Those notes provided much of the Nation's paper currency until the creation of the Federal Reserve System.

The National Currency Act was replaced by the National Bank Act of 1864 (NBA) which set forth much of the modern regulation of national banks.

The NBA defined banking as including the activities of discounting and negotiating evidences of debt; receiving deposits; buying and selling exchange, coin and bullion; and loaning money on personal security. A bank engaging in such activities that desired to become a "national bank" was required to incorporate under a federal charter. National banks were required to have minimum capital ranging from $200,000 in cities of 50,000 or more to $50,000 in cities with a population of 6,000 or less. The NBA contained a number of restrictions on bank activities, including a prohibition on lending more than ten percent of the bank's capital to any one borrower for the purpose of investing in stocks.

The NBA required national banks to keep fifteen to twenty five percent of their deposits as a reserve.

Those reserves were required to be kept in lawful money of the United States. National banks could count as reserves funds deposited with other national banks (such as correspondent banks), but not funds deposited at state banks. The Office of the Comptroller of the Currency was directed to administer the NBA.

At the end of 1863, there were only sixty-six national banks and approximately fifteen hundred state banks. An early requirement that national banks bear numbers in their names and that "existing banks give up their original names and be designated by numbers, as if bankers long and successfully in business were without sentiment and would as soon bear a number as an old and honored name,"[13] clearly discouraged many banks from the national charter. When the rule was eliminated, the popularity of the national charter increased so that there were 469 national banks at the end of 1864. However, this historical artifact helps to account for the names of many banks, including the First National Bank of Charlotte (in the case below) and current institutions such as Fifth Third Bank, which has its antecedents in the Third National Bank, organized in 1863 and the Fifth National Bank, which received its name in 1888. These two institutions merged in 1908 to become the Fifth Third National Bank of Cincinnati. The bank is now a state chartered bank.

The creation of national banks raised issues as to the scope of their authority to engage in various banking activities.

---

13. Bray Hammond, Sovereignty and an Empty Purse: Banks and Politics in the Civil War 345 (1970).

FIRST NATIONAL BANK OF CHARLOTTE v. NATIONAL EXCHANGE BANK OF BALTIMORE

Supreme Court of the United States, 1875.
92 U.S. (2 Otto.) 122.

MR. CHIEF JUSTICE WAITE delivered the opinion of the Court.

The question presented for our consideration in this case is, whether a national bank, organized under the National Banking Act, may, in a fair and *bona fide* compromise of a contested claim against it growing out of a legitimate banking transaction, pay a larger sum than would have been exacted in satisfaction of the demand, so as to obtain by the arrangement a transfer of certain stocks in railroad and other corporations; it being honestly believed at the time, that, by turning the stocks into money under more favorable circumstances than then existed, a loss, which would otherwise accrue from the transaction, might be averted or diminished. * * *

A national bank can "exercise by its board of directors, or duly authorized officers or agents, subject to law, all such incidental powers as shall be necessary to carry on the business of banking, by discounting and negotiating promissory notes, drafts, bills of exchange, and other evidences of debt; by receiving deposits; by buying and selling exchange, coin, and bullion; by loaning money on personal security; and by obtaining, issuing, and circulating notes." Rev. Stat., sect. 5136, par. 7; 15 Stat. 101, sect. 8.

Authority is thus given to transact such a banking business as is specified, and all incidental powers necessary to carry it on are granted.

These powers are such as are required to meet all the legitimate demands of the authorized business, and to enable a bank to conduct its affairs, within the general scope of its charter, safely and prudently. This necessarily implies the right of a bank to incur liabilities in the regular course of its business, as well as to become the creditor of others. Its own obligations must be met, and debts due to it collected or secured. The power to adopt reasonable and appropriate measures for these purposes is an incident to the power to incur the liability or become the creditor. Obligations may be assumed that result unfortunately. Loans or discounts may be made that cannot be met at maturity. Compromises to avoid or reduce losses are oftentimes the necessary results of this condition of things. These compromises come within the general scope of the powers committed to the board of directors and the officers and agents of the bank, and are submitted to their judgment and discretion, except to the extent that they are restrained by the charter or by-laws. Banks may do, in this behalf, whatever natural persons could do under like circumstances.

To some extent, it has been thought expedient in the National Banking Act to limit this power. Thus, as to real estate, it is provided that it may be accepted in good faith as security for, or in payment of, debts previously contracted; but, if accepted in payment, it must not be retained more than five years. So, while a bank is expressly prohibited from loaning money upon or purchasing its own stock, special authority is given for the acceptance of its shares as security for, and in payment of, debts previously contracted in good faith; but all shares purchased under this power must be again sold or disposed of at private or public sale within six months from the time they are acquired.

Dealing in stocks is not expressly prohibited; but such a prohibition is implied from the failure to grant the power. In the honest exercise of the power to compromise a doubtful debt owing to a bank, it can hardly be doubted that stocks may be accepted in payment and satisfaction, with a view to their subsequent sale or conversion into money so as to make good or reduce an anticipated loss. Such a transaction would not amount to a dealing in stocks. It was, in effect, so decided in Fleckner v. Bank U.S., 8 Wheat. 351, where it was held that a prohibition against trading and dealing was nothing more than a prohibition against engaging in the ordinary business of buying and selling for profit, and did not include purchases resulting from ordinary banking transactions. For this reason, among others, the acceptance of an indorsed note in payment of a debt due was decided not to be a "dealing" in notes. Of course, all such transactions must be compromises in good faith, and not mere cloaks or devices to cover unauthorized practices. * * *

The intention of the NBA was to create a uniform system of banks and currency. One of the act's ardent supporters stated that the " 'national banks * * * were intended to supersede the state banks. Both can not exist together.' "[14] To ensure a system of national banks, the legislation imposed a tax of two percent on the notes issued by state banks. This tax had no effect on state bank note issuance and the tax was raised in 1865 to ten percent. At the ten percent rate, state banks ceased issuing state bank notes. The next case discusses a challenge to the tax on state bank notes.

VEAZIE BANK v. FENNO

Supreme Court of the United States, 1869.
75 U.S. (8 Wall.) 533.

MR. CHIEF JUSTICE CHASE delivered the opinion of the Court.

The necessity of adequate provision for the financial exigencies created by the late rebellion, suggested to the administrative and legislative departments of the government important changes in the systems of currency and taxation which had hitherto prevailed. These changes, more or less distinctly shown in administrative recommendations, took form and substance in legislative acts. We have now to consider, within a limited range, those which relate to circulating notes and the taxation of circulation. * * *

---

14. Bray Hammond, Sovereignty and an Empty Purse: Banks and Politics in the Civil War 347 (1970) (quoting Senator John Sherman of Ohio).

It will be seen that when the policy of taxing bank circulation was first adopted in 1863, Congress was inclined to discriminate for, rather than against, the circulation of the State banks; but that when the country had been sufficiently furnished with a National currency by the issues of United States notes and of National bank notes, the discrimination was turned, and very decidedly turned, in the opposite direction.

The general question now before us is, whether or not the tax of ten per cent., imposed on State banks or National banks paying out the notes of individuals or State banks used for circulation, is repugnant to the Constitution of the United States.

In support of the position that the act of Congress, so far as it provides for the levy and collection of this tax, is repugnant to the Constitution, two propositions have been argued with much force and earnestness.

The first is that the tax in question is a direct tax, and has not been apportioned among the States agreeably to the Constitution.

The second is that the act imposing the tax impairs a franchise granted by the State, and that Congress has no power to pass any law with that intent or effect. * * *

The tax under consideration is a tax on bank circulation, and may very well be classed under the head of duties. Certainly it is not, in the sense of the Constitution, a direct tax. It may be said to come within the same category of taxation as the tax on incomes of insurance companies, which this court, at the last term, in the case of Pacific Insurance Company v. Soule held not to be a direct tax.

Is it, then, a tax on a franchise granted by a State, which Congress, upon any principle exempting the reserved powers of the States from impairment by taxation, must be held to have no authority to lay and collect?

We do not say that there may not be such a tax. It may be admitted that the reserved rights of the States, such as the right to pass laws, to give effect to laws through executive action, to administer justice through the courts, and to employ all necessary agencies for legitimate purposes of State government, are not proper subjects of the taxing power of Congress. But it cannot be admitted that franchises granted by a State are necessarily exempt from taxation; for franchises are property, often very valuable and productive property; and when not conferred for the purpose of giving effect to some reserved power of a State, seem to be as properly objects of taxation as any other property.

But in the case before us the object of taxation is not the franchise of the bank, but property created, or contracts made and issued under the franchise, or power to issue bank bills. A railroad company, in the exercise of its corporate franchises, issues freight receipts, bills of lading, and passenger tickets; and it cannot be doubted that the organization of railroads is quite as important to the State as the organization of banks.

But it will hardly be questioned that these contracts of the company are objects of taxation within the powers of Congress, and not exempted by any relation to the State which granted the charter of the railroad. And it seems difficult to distinguish the taxation of notes issued for circulation from the taxation of these railroad contracts. Both descriptions of contracts are means of profit to the corporations which issue them; and both, as we think, may properly be made contributory to the public revenue.

It is insisted, however, that the tax in the case before us is excessive, and so excessive as to indicate a purpose on the part of Congress to destroy the franchise of the bank, and is, therefore, beyond the constitutional power of Congress.

The first answer to this is that the judicial cannot prescribe to the legislative departments of the government limitations upon the exercise of its acknowledged powers. The power to tax may be exercised oppressively upon persons, but the responsibility of the legislature is not to the courts, but to the people by whom its members are elected. So if a particular tax bears heavily upon a corporation, or a class of corporations, it cannot, for that reason only, be pronounced contrary to the Constitution.

But there is another answer which vindicates equally the wisdom and the power of Congress.

It cannot be doubted that under the Constitution the power to provide a circulation of coin is given to Congress. And it is settled by the uniform practice of the government and by repeated decisions, that Congress may constitutionally authorize the emission of bills of credit. It is not important here, to decide whether the quality of legal tender, in payment of debts, can be constitutionally imparted to these bills; it is enough to say, that there can be no question of the power of the government to emit them; to make them receivable in payment of debts to itself; to fit them for use by those who see fit to use them in all the transactions of commerce; to provide for their redemption; to make them a currency, uniform in value and description, and convenient and useful for circulation. These powers, until recently, were only partially and occasionally exercised. Lately, however, they have been called into full activity, and Congress has undertaken to supply a currency for the entire country.
* * *

Having thus, in the exercise of undisputed constitutional powers, undertaken to provide a currency for the whole country, it cannot be questioned that Congress may, constitutionally, secure the benefit of it to the people by appropriate legislation. To this end, Congress has denied the quality of legal tender to foreign coins, and has provided by law against the imposition of counterfeit and base coin on the community. To the same end, Congress may restrain, by suitable enactments, the circulation as money of any notes not issued under its own authority. Without this power, indeed, its attempts to secure a sound and uniform currency for the country must be futile.

Viewed in this light, as well as in the other light of a duty on contracts of property, we cannot doubt the constitutionality of the tax under consideration. * * *

JUSTICES NELSON and DAVIS dissent. * * *

_____

Although state bank notes were taxed out of existence by Congress, state banks continued to thrive. Congress seemed ignorant of the fact that state banks could profitably continue business even without issuing state bank notes since the more important monetary function could be supplied by "deposit credit transferable by check."[15] Transfers of money by check "was a monetary function of far greater volume and importance" than the issuance of state bank notes.[16] The increased use of checking accounts in the United States is one of the early examples of innovative products and services being developed to avoid existing regulatory regimes. Thus, state banks continued and one of the results of the NBA was a dual bank chartering system, rather than a unified federal banking system. As one historian noted, [the NBA fostered what is probably the greatest mass of redundant, otiose, and conflicting monetary legislation and the most complex structure of self-neutralizing regulatory powers enjoyed by any prominent country anywhere. It has put the federal government and the states in competition for the number and size of banks under their respective jurisdictions....][17]

E. CLEARING HOUSES AND CENTRAL BANKS

An important part of modern banking is the clearing and settlement of checks and electronic transfers for customers from one bank to another. An elaborate system now accomplishes these transactions swiftly and efficiently, but that has not always been the case. The clearing system is said to have begun long ago when two clerks accidentally met in a coffee house while taking a break from their rounds to collect funds for their banks. The clerks arranged an informal transfer of the obligations of their respective banks at this chance meeting, saving themselves a trip to the other's bank. They decided to continue this practice and were joined by other clerks. The Suffolk Bank of Boston created a more sophisticated clearing system in 1819 that sought to prevent state banks from over-issuing their bills.

The Suffolk Bank agreed to redeem the bills of New England country banks at par (full value), if those banks kept funds on deposit with the Suffolk Bank. Another innovation, the New York Clearing House, was created in 1853 by sixty-two banks. It, and similar organizations in other

---

15. Bray Hammond, Sovereignty and an Empty Purse: Banks and Politics in the Civil War 335 (1970).

16. Id.

17. Id. at 349–50.

cities, became a key part of the banking system. The bank clearing houses provided check clearing and other inter-bank services.

PHILLER v. PATTERSON

Supreme Court of Pennsylvania, 1895.
32 A. 26.

WILLIAMS, JUSTICE.

* * * An examination of the constitution or articles of association adopted by the banks forming the Clearing House Association of the Banks of Philadelphia shows the character and objects of the organization very clearly. In substance these articles amount to an agreement with each other by 38 national banks in the city of Philadelphia to facilitate and simplify the settlement of daily balances between them, for their mutual advantage. This agreement substitutes a settlement made at a fixed place and time each day by representatives of all the members of the association, in the place of a separate settlement by each bank with every other made over the counter. No other object is contemplated or provided for. * * * To carry this agreement into operation, it became necessary to determine the place and hour at which the settlement should be made. A suitable room was secured, fitted up with desks and other necessary appliances, at the expense of the associated banks, and a manager chosen to preside over it and direct the action of the clerks and runners when in session. This room is the clearing place or, in the language of the constitution of the association, the clearing house. It is the place where the representatives of the several banks meet, and where all balances are struck and settled daily between the banks composing the association.

At the close of each meeting the amount due to and from each bank is definitely ascertained. The debtor banks then pay over to the manager the gross balance due from them to settle their accounts with all the members of the association, and he makes distribution of the sum so received among the creditor banks entitled to receive them. * * * Among the economies in time and labor contemplated by the banks was a settlement of daily balances without the necessity for handling and counting the cash in every case. To provide for this, the banks agreed that they would deposit in the hands of certain persons, to be selected by them and to be called the "clearing-house committee," a sum of money, or its equivalent in good securities, at a fixed ratio upon their capital stock, to be used for payment of balances against them. For these sums the committee was to issue receipts or certificates in convenient sums, and these receipts or certificates were to be used in lieu of the cash they represented, which remained in the hands of the committee, pledged for the payment, when payment became necessary, of the certificates. The committee held the funds and securities deposited with them in trust for the special purpose of securing the payment, as far as they would reach, of the balances due from the bank making the deposit.

On the 24th day of September, 1873, the associated banks entered into another agreement with each other, by which, "for the purpose of enabling the banks, members of the Philadelphia Clearing House Association, to afford proper assistance to the mercantile and manufacturing community, and also to facilitate the inter-bank settlements resulting from the daily exchanges," they authorized the committee to receive from any member of the association additional deposits of bills receivable and other securities, and issue certificates therefor "in such amount and to such percentage thereof as may in their judgment be advisable." The additional certificates, if issued, they agreed to accept in payment of daily balances at the clearing house on the condition that the securities deposited therefor should be held by the committee "in trust as a special deposit, pledged for the redemption of the certificates issued thereupon." * * * This same method, or one identical in general outline, has been adopted by the banks in every great city in the United States and by many in other lands; and, as far as I am aware, it has nowhere been held that the method is illegal. On the contrary it has recommended itself by its economy of time and labor to the several banks and, by its incidental results in promoting mutual helpfulness and confidence, has come to be regarded with favor by the general public. * * * [The court concluded that] it was not a violation of law for the banks to arrange for their own daily settlements in the manner provided by the clearing-house agreement. * * *

Clearing house certificates, a form of promissory note backed by bank assets, were used as a means of relieving temporary tightening of the money supply. The value of the clearing house certificates was proven during the financial panics of 1873, 1884, 1890, and 1893, when the clearing houses performed some of the functions of a central bank during a time of monetary stringency.

SECTION 4. THE BIRTH OF THE FEDERAL RESERVE SYSTEM

Trust companies became popular at the turn of the century as a mechanism for avoiding the regulations and restrictions imposed on commercial bank activities. The Knickerbocker Trust Company, the third largest trust company in New York, with deposits in excess of $60 million, failed on October 22, 1907. Lillian Russell lost $75,000 in the failure.[18] Its insolvency touched off one of the worst financial panics in the history of the United States. The federal government appeared to be helpless in dealing with the crisis. Although the Secretary of the Treasury sought to act as a central banker, he had neither the resources nor the knowledge

---

18. H. Paul Jeffers, Diamond Jim Brady: Prince of the Gilded Age 294 (2001).

necessary to implement such policies successfully. Instead, the private sector had to rescue itself. That effort was led by J.P. Morgan, and he was later characterized as a "one-man Federal Reserve Bank" in stopping the panic.[19] Even so, the country was left shaken and stunned by the suddenness and force of that economic catastrophe. Senator Nelson Aldrich noted that the "country escaped by the narrowest possible margin from a total collapse of all credit and a wholesale destruction of all values." He stated that:

> To the great majority of the people of the country the blow came without a warning. Most of our banking institutions were in excellent condition, business of every kind was prosperous, labor was fully employed at satisfactory wages, industries of every kind were flourishing. Our people were full of hope and confidence for the future. Suddenly the banks of the country suspended payment, and acknowledged their inability to meet their current obligations on demand. The results of this suspension were felt at once; it became impossible in many cases to secure funds or credit to move crops or to carry on ordinary business operations; a complete disruption of domestic exchanges took place; disorganization and financial embarrassment affected seriously every industry; thousands of men were thrown out of employment, and the wages of the employed were reduced.[20]

Congress created a Monetary Commission to examine the causes of the Panic of 1907 and to propose measures to prevent such an occurrence in the future.[21] The Commission was chaired by Senator Aldrich. He conducted an extensive investigation that lasted almost four years. Senator Aldrich introduced legislation in 1912 that proposed the creation of a central banking authority in the United States. Ostensibly the result of the Monetary Commission's study, the bill had actually been written at a secret meeting of mostly commercial bankers held at a millionaires' club on Jekyll Island, Georgia.[22] They concluded that a federal banking system was needed to provide liquidity to the private banks in times of stress. The group eschewed a central bank that would be controlled by the government. Instead, they proposed a more decentralized system that would be owned by private bankers.

Following much debate and various compromises, the Federal Reserve Act of 1913 was enacted; it created a further division in bank regulation. In addition to state regulation, federal bank regulatory authority was split between the Treasury Department and the Federal Reserve System. The

---

19. Paul B. Trescott, Financing American Enterprise: The Story of Commercial Banking 127 (1963).

20. Senator Nelson W. Aldrich, The Work of the National Monetary Commission, 61st Cong., 2d Sess., S. Doc. No. 406, at 3–4 (1910).

21. Congress initially enacted the Aldrich–Vreeland Act of 1908, which established "National Currency Associations" to provide relief in times of stringency. The National Currency Associations were to provide emergency liquidity by allowing banks to issue credit notes against deposits of commercial paper, as well as government bonds.

22. The participants, disguised as duck hunters, arrived by private rail car.

Comptroller of the Currency at the Treasury retained responsibility for examining and regulating national banks.

A. CHECK CLEARING

The Federal Reserve System was given several responsibilities by its authorizing legislation, including the development of a more efficient national system of clearing checks and other bank instruments.

AMERICAN BANK & TRUST CO. v. FEDERAL RESERVE BANK OF ATLANTA

Supreme Court of the United States, 1923.
262 U.S. 643.

MR. JUSTICE BRANDEIS delivered the opinion of the Court.

* * * A large part of the checks drawn on country banks are sent to payees who reside in places other than that in which the drawee bank is located. Payment of such a check is ordinarily secured through the payee's depositing it in his local bank for collection. This bank ordinarily used, as the means for presenting the check to the drawee, a clearing house and/or correspondent banks. Formerly when the check was so presented, the drawee ordinarily paid, not in cash, but by a remittance drawn on his balance in some reserve city or by a credit with some correspondent. This process of collection yielded to the country bank a two-fold profit. It earned some profit by the small service charge called exchange, which it made for the remittance or the credit. And it earned some profit by using the depositor's money during the period (sometimes weeks) in which the check was traveling the often circuitous route, with many stops, from the payee's bank to its own, and also while the exchange draft was being collected. These avenues to profit are, in large measure, closed by the federal reserve banks' course of action. These banks do not pay any exchange charges to the drawee. And their superior facilities so shorten the time required to collect checks that the drawee bank's balances available for loans are much reduced. Largely because of the fact that the reserve banks thus make the collection without any deduction for exchange, most checks on country banks are now routed through the reserve banks. Although there is, as the District Court found, no intentional accumulation or holding of checks in order to embarrass, the advantages offered by the federal reserve banks have created a steady flow in increased volume of checks on country banks so routed.

That the action contemplated by the Federal Reserve Bank will subject the country banks to certain losses is clear. In order to protect them from the resulting loss it would be necessary to prevent the federal reserve banks from accepting the checks for collection. For these banks cannot be compelled to pay exchange charges or to abandon superior facilities.

The contention is that the injunction should issue, because it is *ultra vires* the federal reserve banks to collect checks on banks which are not members of the system or affiliated with it, through establishing an exchange balance, and which have definitely refused to assent to clearance at par. It is true that Congress has created in the reserve banks institutions special in character, with limited functions and with duties and powers carefully prescribed. Those in respect to the collection of checks are clearly defined. * * *

Federal reserve banks are, thus, authorized by Congress to collect for other reserve banks, for members, and for affiliated non-members, checks on any bank within their respective districts, if the check is payable on presentation and can in fact be collected consistently with the legal rights of the drawee without paying an exchange charge. Within these limits federal reserve banks have ordinarily the same right to present a check to the drawee bank for payment over the counter, as any other bank, state or national, would have. * * *

The findings of fact negative the charges of wrongful intent and of coercion. The Federal Reserve Bank has formally declared that it is willing, when presenting checks, to accept in payment a draft of the drawee bank upon its Atlanta correspondent or a draft upon any other solvent bank—if collectible at par. Country banks are not entitled to protection against legitimate competition. Their loss here shown is of the kind to which business concerns are commonly subjected when improved facilities are introduced by others, or a more efficient competitor enters the field. It is *damnum absque injuria.* As the course of action contemplated by the Federal Reserve Bank is not *ultra vires,* we need not consider whether lack of power, if it had existed, would have entitled plaintiffs to relief. * * *

B. FEDERAL RESERVE NOTES

The Federal Reserve Act sought to have its regional banks establish a more "elastic" currency by the issuance of Federal Reserve bank notes. Those notes became a part of the general circulation of currency, and today form the basis for our paper currency. The Federal Reserve Act also rescinded the power of national banks to issue their own notes which had previously served as currency.

MILAM v. UNITED STATES

United States Court of Appeals, Ninth Circuit, 1974.
524 F.2d 629.

Appellant has filed a substantial brief and an adequate reply brief and has argued his full share of allotted time in support for a demand that his $50.00 Federal Reserve Bank Note be redeemed in "lawful money" of the United States, which he says, in effect, must be gold or silver. Appellant refused appellees' tender of an equivalent value in Federal Reserve Notes.

Appellant's contentions, in our view, were put at rest close to a century ago in *Juilliard v. Greenman*, 110 U.S. 421, 448 (1884), in which it was said:

"... Under the power to borrow money on the credit of the United States, and to issue circulating notes for the money borrowed, its power to define the quality and force of those notes as currency is as broad as the like power over a metallic currency under the power to coin money and to regulate the value thereof. Under the two powers, taken together, *Congress is authorized to establish a national currency, either in coin or in paper, and to make that currency lawful money for all purposes, as regards the national government or private individuals....*" [Emphasis supplied.]

The power so precisely described in *Juilliard* has been delegated to the Federal Reserve System under the provisions of 12 U.S.C. § 411. Appellant's challenge to the validity of this legislation is meritless. Cf. 31 U.S.C. § 392.

While we agree that golden eagles, double eagles and silver dollars were lovely to look at and delightful to hold, we must at the same time recognize that time marches on, and that even the time honored silver dollar is no longer available in its last bastion of defense, the brilliant casinos of the houses of chance in the state of Nevada. Appellant is entitled to redeem his note, but not in precious metal. Simply stated, we find his contentions frivolous.

C. MONETARY POLICY

From its inception, the Federal Reserve System struggled with the issue of what constituted the correct monetary policy: to provide liquidity or to dampen speculation that might result in a bubble that would burst and precipitate a panic.[23] The country experienced an expansion after World War I that the Federal Reserve System tried to slow. At the same time, farm commodity prices fell, and a "commodity or inventory panic" resulted in a recession in the farm belt. The economy recovered by 1923, and it was thought that the Federal Reserve System had stabilized the situation and prevented a panic in the financial markets. This led to claims that financial panics were a thing of the past and that the Federal Reserve System could safely guide the economy during troubled times. Lending credence to this view, the Federal Reserve System sought to curb speculation in the stock market during the "speculative orgy of 1928 and 1929"[24] by limiting the availability of call market loans for margin trading.

---

23. The modern role of the Federal Reserve System in effectuating monetary policy is described further in Chapter 3.

24. S. Rep. No. 1455, 73d Cong., S. Rep. No. 73–1455, at 81 (1934).

RAICHLE v. FEDERAL RESERVE BANK OF NEW YORK

United States Court of Appeals, Second Circuit, 1929.
34 F.2d 910.

AUGUSTUS N. HAND, CIRCUIT JUDGE.

* * * The wrongs charged against the [the Federal Reserve Bank of New York] are (a) spreading propaganda concerning an alleged money shortage and increasing volume of collateral loans; (b) setting about to restrict the supply of credit available for investment purposes by engaging in open market transactions through the sale of its securities; (c) raising the rediscount rate for its member banks in order to reduce the volume of security loans; (d) coercing member banks to call collateral loans by declining to rediscount eligible commercial paper for such member banks.

Three principal questions must be considered:

(1) Are the foregoing acts, irrespective of the alleged purpose to reduce the volume of brokers' loans, within the power of the Federal Reserve Bank?

(2) If the acts are, generally speaking, lawful, are they rendered unlawful because the purpose was to reduce the volume of brokers' loans?

(3) Is the Federal Reserve Board a necessary party to the action?

The Federal Reserve Act marked the end of a long struggle and was thought to afford the solution of many difficulties. When the Independent Treasury Bill was passed in 1846, the effect was completely to divorce the government from all connection with the money market, by making it its own banker and by keeping government funds in the vaults of independent treasury office banks. The public then had to depend on state banks for currency and credit, with a result that in times of financial stress is well known.

To meet the necessities of Civil War, national banks were established. They became the official depositaries of the government and furnished an enlarged currency, because of their ability to issue circulating notes against government bonds deposited with the Treasurer of the United States. They were required to maintain reserves in certain cities, based upon a percentage of their deposits. As the government debts of the Civil War became liquidated, the means for issuing currency lessened, though the business requirements of the country were expanding. In such a situation business prosperity inevitably promoted monetary stringency. Moreover, as the reserves were deposited in relatively few banks in the metropolitan centers, when financial stringencies arose, pressure always came on the banks, their deposits would be withdrawn, the rates for call loans would advance, and a liquidation of collateral and depreciation of values would ensue.

While the national banking system was a great improvement over what went before, it provided no central regulating force, and furnished no adequate means for controlling interest rates, or preventing or lessening financial stringencies and panics. The usual method of furnishing funds needed for business was for the Treasury to deposit moneys from its vaults in the national banks and to withdraw these deposits, if they were used too much in speculation. This was a rather ineffectual way of dealing with complicated and difficult situations. It was dependent too much upon the determination of a single official and lacked the information and guidance that a scientific federal banking system would afford.

To remedy the difficulties we have mentioned, the Federal Reserve Act was passed. The Federal Reserve Banks have national charters and their stockholders are member banks. Each Federal Reserve Bank has nine directors, three chosen from the member banks, three selected as representatives from industry, and three designated by the Federal Reserve Board. * * *

The foregoing outline shows the broad purposes of the Act and the wide powers of supervision and control given to the Federal Reserve Board over the whole Reserve System. * * *

To carry out the purposes of the act, Federal Reserve Banks, subject to the supervision of the Federal Reserve Board, are authorized to act as government depositories and fiscal agents; to receive and maintain the legal reserves of member banks; upon endorsement of member banks to discount notes, drafts, and bills of exchange arising out of actual commercial transactions, but not "notes, drafts, or bills covering merely investments, or issued for the purposes of carrying or trading in stocks, bonds, or other investment securities, except bonds and notes of the government of the United States"; to make advances to member banks on their promissory notes for not more than 15 days at rates to be established by the Federal Reserve Banks, subject to the review and determination of the Federal Reserve Board, provided such promissory notes are secured by eligible paper, or by bonds, or notes of the United States, to receive Federal Reserve notes upon deposit of eligible paper, or gold, or gold certificates, provided a gold reserve of not less than 40 per cent. of such notes is maintained. USCA tit. 12, c.3, §§ 341–361.

Federal Reserve Banks may also, under rules and regulations prescribed by the Federal Reserve Board, engage in "open market operations"; that is to say, purchase and sell in the open market at home or abroad cable transfers and bankers' acceptances and bills of exchange of the kinds and maturities eligible for rediscount. They may deal in gold coin and bullion at home and abroad; buy and sell, at home and abroad, bonds and notes of the United States, and bills, notes, revenue bonds, and warrants with a maturity from date of purchase of not exceeding six months, issued by any state, county, district, political subdivision, or municipality in the United States, such purchases to be made in accordance with regulations prescribed by the Federal Reserve Board. They may purchase from member banks, and sell, bills of exchange arising out of commercial transactions, and may "establish from time to time, subject to review and determination by the Federal Reserve Board, rates of discount to be charged by the Federal Reserve Bank for each class of paper, which shall be fixed with a view of accommodating commerce and business.'} They may establish accounts with other Federal Reserve Banks, with the consent and upon the order and direction of the Federal Reserve Board, and, under regulations to be prescribed by said board, may open accounts and establish agencies in foreign countries for the purpose of purchasing, selling, and collecting bills of exchange. They may purchase and sell in the open market, either from or to domestic banks, firms, corporations, or individuals, acceptances of Federal Intermediate Credit Banks and of national agricultural credit corporations whenever the Federal Reserve Board shall declare that the public interest so requires. USCA, tit. 12, c. 3, §§ 353–357.

The foregoing provisions enable the Federal Reserve Banks, without waiting for applications from their member banks for loans or rediscounts, to adjust the general credit situation by purchasing and selling in the open market the class of securities that they are permitted to deal in. The power "to establish from time to time, subject to review and determination of the Federal Reserve Board, rates of discount to be charged by the Federal Reserve Bank," appears in the act (12 USCA § 357) with the open market powers. The two powers are correlative and enable the Federal Reserve Banks to make their rediscount rates effective. The sale of securities does not lessen the total amount of credit available, but, by necessitating payment to the Federal Reserve Banks, increases available credit in their hands, "with a view of accommodating commerce and business," as provided by the act. * * *

We can see no basis for the contention that it is a tort for a Federal Reserve Bank to sell its securities in the open market, to fix discount rates which are unreasonably high, or to refuse to discount eligible paper, even though its policy may be mistaken and its judgment bad. The remedy sought would make the courts, rather than the Federal Reserve Board, the supervisors of the Federal Reserve System, and would involve a cure worse than the malady. The bank, under the supervision of the board, must determine whether there is danger of financial stringency and whether the credit available for "commerce and business" is sufficient or insufficient. If it proceeds in good faith through open market operations and control of discount rates to bring about a reduction of brokers' loans, it commits no legal wrong. A reduction of brokers' loans may best accommodate "commerce and business." USCA tit. 12, c. 3, §§ 357. * * *

[Decree dismissed for failure to join the Federal Reserve Board as an indispensable party since the Federal Reserve Bank of New York is a governmental agency under the direction of the Federal Reserve Board.]

In its efforts to develop appropriate monetary policy, the Fed became involved in a power struggle among the regional Federal Reserve Banks that were initially given some autonomy from the Washington-based Federal Reserve Board. This internecine fight was compounded by the fact that the New York Federal Reserve Bank sought prominence over the Federal Reserve Board and other Reserve Banks in the system. Those banks resisted the New York Bank's dominance over monetary policy and sometimes pursued their own open market policies. This conflict proved a severe obstacle to effective monetary policy during and after the Stock Market Crash of 1929.

SECTION 5.   THE NEW DEAL LEGISLATION

Bank failures reached epidemic proportions after the Stock Market Crash of 1929. In December of 1930, the Bank of United States failed. It was the largest bank failure in history at that time. By 1932, one of every four banks in the United States had failed. Depositors lined up at the bank doors to remove their deposits. Banks often did not have enough cash on hand to meet those demands because their deposits were out on loan.[25]

Franklin Roosevelt was sworn in as President during the bank panic that struck America. President Roosevelt declared a national bank holiday on March 6, 1933 to bring a stop to the destructive run on bank deposits.

A.   CREATION OF FEDERAL DEPOSIT INSURANCE

The Banking Act of 1933 was enacted to strengthen the banking system and to allow the resumption of banking in the United States. Congress thought that depositor runs could be discouraged if customers had a federal guarantee that their deposits would be protected even if their bank failed. To that end, the Banking Act of 1933 created federal deposit insurance and established the Federal Deposit Insurance Corporation (FDIC) as a temporary agency of the federal government. The Banking Act of 1935 made the FDIC a permanent government agency. President Roosevelt, interestingly, initially opposed federal deposit insurance.

HEWITT v. UNITED STATES

United States Court of Appeals, Eighth Circuit, 1940.
110 F.2d 1, *cert. denied*, 310 U.S. 641.

SANBORN, CIRCUIT JUDGE.

The University Bank of Kansas City, Missouri, on the morning of June 30, 1937, was robbed by armed men who stole $3,955.71 of its funds. It was a State bank and its deposits were insured by the Federal Deposit Insurance Corporation of the United States. For that reason, the United States was interested. * * *

---

25. Frank Capra's movie, *It's a Wonderful Life,* starring Jimmy Stewart, was about such an event that threatened a small town thrift.

The sufficiency of the evidence to sustain the conviction is not challenged. Two of Hewitt's co-defendants, Karatasos and Newell, were witnesses against him. Their testimony was to the effect that, while Hewitt was not personally present when the robbery was committed, he had suggested, planned and financed it, had supplied the automobiles and one of the guns used in connection with its commission, had shared in the loot, and had endeavored to assist his co-defendants to escape the consequences of their crime. They testified that Hewitt had given assurances to the actual participants that the robbery could be committed without fear of burglar alarms or of the local police. Assuming that the facts were as the government's evidence indicated them to be, the guilt of the defendant Hewitt was proved beyond the possibility of any doubt. * * *

The government in the indictment undertook to charge the defendants in count one with having forcibly robbed the University Bank, a State bank the deposits of which were insured by the Federal Deposit Insurance Corporation of the United States, and in count two with having, while committing the robbery, put the lives of persons in jeopardy by the use of dangerous weapons. The indictment was defective in that in the first count the bank was alleged to be "a member of the Federal Deposit Insurance Corporation of the United States", and in the second count was alleged to be "a member of the F.D.I.C. of the United States." The indictment should have alleged in each count that the bank was a State bank the deposits of which were insured by the Federal Deposit Insurance Corporation of the United States. It is the defendant's contention that these defects in the indictment were fatal and that the demurrer to the indictment should have been sustained. The government argues that the defects were to be regarded as formal and technical and nonprejudicial. § 556, Tit. 18, U.S.C., 18 U.S.C.A. § 556.

Speaking with precision, the Federal Deposit Insurance Corporation has no members. It has stockholders (United States and Federal Reserve Banks), and it has insureds. In practical effect it is a mutual insurance company set up by the government, to be supported by assessments levied upon insured banks. The insured banks may be regarded as members of this insurance corporation in much the same way and to much the same extent as persons insured in a fraternal benefit society or in a mutual insurance company are considered and commonly referred to as members of those organizations. The banks are members of the Federal Deposit Insurance Corporation in the sense that their deposits are insured therein and that they are liable for assessments, and that through the medium of the corporation they furnish each other's depositors protection against losses. As a practical matter, no one was, and no one could have been, in any doubt as to what the government meant by the allegation in the indictment that the bank was a member of the Federal Deposit Insurance Corporation. The defendant was in no doubt as to the nature of the charge that was made against him. * * *

The contention that the designation of the Federal Deposit Insurance Corporation in the second count by its initials "F.D.I.C." rendered that count fatally defective, is, we think, without merit. * * *

B. STRENGTHENING THE FEDERAL RESERVE SYSTEM

Congress was also concerned about the effects of the dispute between the Federal Reserve Board in Washington and the New York Federal Reserve Bank on the nation's monetary policy. The death of Benjamin Strong, leader of the New York Federal Reserve Bank, in 1929 left a vacuum in policy. Charles Mitchell, the President of the National City Bank, was appointed as a director of the New York Federal Reserve Bank in 1929. After the Fed sought to restrict credit in 1929, Mitchell announced that National City Bank would loan $25 million into the call money market to provide liquidity. Its affiliate, National City Company, was the nation's largest distributor of securities at that time. This policy conflict along with other disputes between the Federal Reserve Board and the New York Federal Reserve Bank paralyzed monetary policy during a critical period before the Stock Market Crash of 1929 and rendered the Federal Reserve Board powerless to alleviate the effects of the crash.

To remedy this problem, Congress strengthened the independence of the Federal Reserve Board in the Banking Act of 1935. The Board of Governors of the Federal Reserve System (the Fed) was given responsibility for administration of the Federal Reserve System, settling the conflict between the Board and the Federal Reserve Banks. The Board received greater power to alter reserve requirements, the ability to broaden the lending powers of Federal Reserve Banks, and the power to regulate credit granted by banks and brokers to customers for the purpose of purchasing securities.

The Fed's grasp on the reigns of control over monetary policy was weak even after its powers were strengthened in 1935. The Fed was accused of pushing the country back into recession in 1937 with its restrictive policies. The Fed was also forced to bow to the Treasury Department on issues of monetary policy during World War II. In order to reduce government costs, the Treasury Department decreed that interest rates would be kept at artificially low levels. The Fed agreed to that policy until post-war inflation became more of a threat than high government borrowing costs. Friction between the Fed and the Treasury on this issue increased and had to be resolved through an inter-governmental agreement.

HERBERT STEIN, THE MODEL OF A
MODERN CENTRAL BANKER

Wall St. J.
Aug. 7, 1998, at A10.

William McChesney Martin, the former Federal Reserve Chairman who died on July 28, [1998,] was a key actor in one of the most dramatic events in the history of American economic policy. The time was 1951. After the most open struggle ever between the Federal Reserve and the executive branch, the two sides reached an agreement that gave the Fed the independence it needed to stabilize the American economy. * * *

The dispute was over the commitment of the Federal Reserve to support the price of government bonds. In 1941, after the U.S. entered World War II, the Federal Reserve and the Treasury agreed that the Fed would support the price of long-term Treasury bonds at a level that would keep their yield from rising above 2.5%, then the rate prevailing in the market, so that the government could finance the war.

Moreover, the Treasury Department was engaged in a great effort to sell savings bonds to the public on a patriotic basis. These bonds, designed for the small saver, bore a fixed interest of 2.9%, and it did not seem fair to allow large investors to earn more.

This policy had obvious implications. The need to provide for the war and avoid inflation demanded that private consumption and investment be curtailed, yet the Fed was not allowed to raise interest rates to achieve these goals. But to keep interest rates from rising, the Fed had to buy bonds and expand the money supply.

During the war the consequences of this policy were disguised, because prices, investments, and many items of consumption were under direct government control. But once controls were lifted the dangers in the policy, mainly the threat of inflation, became apparent, and calls for abandoning the support policy mounted.

The Truman administration resisted these calls. The Treasury liked having a guaranteed market for its issues at a low and certain interest rate. Leon Keyerling, then the chairman of the Council of Economic Advisers, believed that the antidote for inflation was growth brought about by an expansion of demand, so he opposed any restrictive policy from the Federal Reserve. But the main defender of the bond-support policy was President Truman himself: he recalled with pain how the bonds he had bought as an Army officer in World War I had fallen in value after the war's end. He did not want to see that happen to the veterans of World War II, or to anyone else.

The Board of Governors of the Federal Reserve did not publicly object to the policy in the first years after the war, although the president of the New York Fed was one of the leading critics. But when the Korean War heightened the danger of inflation, the board began to insist publicly on the need to be relieved of its commitment to support the price of bonds. The president called all members of the Board of Governors to the White House (I believe that has not happened at any other time) to explain to them why the bond-support should be continued. The board was not persuaded.

It is at this point that William McChesney Martin enters the story. A committee of Treasury and Fed officials was created to find a way out of the impasse, and Martin was on the Treasury team. He was ideally suited for the task. Although a Treasury official, he had not been in charge of debt management and had no personal commitment to the old policy. Financial markets trusted him because he had once been head of the New York Stock Exchange—the youngest ever. The Fed trusted him because he came from a Fed family, his father having been president of the St. Louis Federal Reserve Bank. Truman trusted him because he was from Missouri. And he was intelligent and honest.

Within a few weeks the committee reached what became known as the Treasury Federal Reserve Accord of 1951. It provided for a brief period of transition in which the Treasury could adapt to the new regime, after which the Fed would be relieved of its commitment to support the bond market and would be free to pursue its primary goals.

A little later the chairman of the Fed, Thomas McCabe, resigned, and Martin was named to replace him. There were at the time some skeptics, including several senators, who did not believe that Martin, "the Treasury's man," could be counted on to defend the independence of the Fed. Nineteen years of his chairmanship proved them wrong. * * *

C. GLASS-STEAGALL ACT RESTRICTIONS ON SECURITIES ACTIVITIES

In 1902, the Comptroller of the Currency ruled that a national bank could not act as an investment bank in underwriting securities. To avoid that restriction, some larger national banks formed affiliates to act as securities dealers—such as the National City Company formed by the National City Bank for this purpose. On November 6, 1911, Frederick W. Lehman, the Solicitor General of the United States, rendered an opinion to the Attorney General that the creation of National City Company violated banking laws. The National City Bank ignored that ruling. The Attorney General then adopted the Solicitor's opinion and was prepared to mount a formal challenge to the affiliate as being in violation of the national banking laws.

The Secretary of the Treasury, however, took the opposite position. President William H. Taft decided to let the issue die.

Thereafter, bank affiliates became heavily involved in the securities markets, especially during the speculative era of the 1920s. They maintained substantial sales staffs and were responsible for unloading vast amounts of securities on the public, resulting in large losses when the market crashed in 1929. This caused much concern in Congress, particularly when it appeared that numerous conflicts of interest existed between the banks and their securities affiliates.

The Glass–Steagall Act was enacted in 1933 as part of the Banking Act of 1933 which created federal deposit insurance and the FDIC. Glass–Steagall was comprised of four statutory sections that sought to separate commercial and investment banking. It is still not clear why Congress adopted this approach.

The Supreme Court has suggested that Congress was motivated by the failure of the Bank of United States and its securities affiliate—the City Financial Corporation. That affiliate, however, was not shown to have caused the bank's failure.[26] A second motivation for this legislation may have been Congressional annoyance with Charles Mitchell and the National City Company, the securities affiliate of the National City Bank, and Mitchell's defiance of the Federal Reserve Board's efforts to curb call money before the crash.

In any event, Section 16 of the Glass–Steagall Act limited the power of a commercial bank to engage in the "business of dealing in stock and securities," and it prohibited a national bank from buying securities, other than "investment securities," for its own account. Investment securities included obligations of the United States and general obligations of the states. In addition, Section 16 stated that a national bank "shall not underwrite any issue of securities or stock." Another provision of Glass–Steagall made Section 16 applicable to state banks that were members of the Federal Reserve System. Section 21 of the Glass–Steagall Act prohibited a securities firm from engaging in the banking business, and Section 20 prohibited commercial bank affiliates from being "principally engaged" in the "issue, floatation, underwriting, public sale or distribution" of securities.

Adoption of the Glass–Steagall Act resulted in dismemberment of several banks. For example, J.P. Morgan & Co. chose to become a commercial bank, while certain partners of the old firm split off and formed Morgan Stanley, an investment bank. Thereafter, "commercial" banking (broadly defined as taking deposits and making commercial loans) and "investment" banking (underwriting and dealing in securities) were separated. Some have suggested that this forced separation was a dramatic overreaction as later studies indicated that, in the aftermath of the Stock Market Crash of 1929, banks with securities affiliates failed at the same rate as banks without securities affiliates. Only 7.2% of the national banks that "actively dealt in securities failed, a far smaller percentage than that experienced by the national banks that did not conduct both commercial and investment banking."[27] Under this view, the Fed was to

---

26. A Federal Reserve Board official testified during the Glass–Steagall hearings that, while there had been abuses with bank affiliates, the Board did not advocate prohibiting banks from having securities affiliates.

27. George W. Benston, The Separation of Commercial and Investment Banking 32 (1990).

blame for the Great Depression because of its ineffectual response to financial crisis. In any event, the barrier between securities and banking eroded in later years, and Glass–Steagall's prohibitions were ultimately repealed.

D.   INTEREST RATE RESTRICTIONS

The Banking Act of 1933 prohibited the payment of interest on checking accounts and limited the rate of interest that banks and savings and loans could pay on savings accounts. The purpose of these limitations was to restrict the call money market, and to prevent banks from engaging in ruinous competition by bidding up deposit interest rates to attract deposits and then having to make risky loans to earn a high enough rate of return to pay the inflated deposit rate. The Fed implemented these statutory proscriptions in Regulation Q.

The Fed's Regulation Q restricted interest rates paid by banks on time deposits. Because of Regulation Q, banking was not viewed as a very complicated business in the 1950s. Industry observers claimed that bankers operated on a "3–6–3–3" rule. This meant that bankers borrowed money from their depositors at the Regulation Q interest rate of three percent and loaned it out at six percent, collecting the 3% spread. The bankers were then free to play golf by three o'clock since there was nothing else to do.

Advertising "premiums," such as toasters and other giveaways, were offered in the 1950s to attract new depositors, and to avoid some of the effect of Regulation Q interest rate ceilings. The Fed then began to regulate the maximum value of the premiums that could be offered and came close to banning them altogether as a result of "reports of large numbers of violations where shipping and handling costs were inflated to permit institutions to pay more than legal limits for gifts or where the prices of many gifts in a campaign were averaged to avoid legal limits."[28]

SECTION 6.   LIMITATIONS ON GEOGRAPHIC EXPANSION

FIRST NATIONAL BANK IN ST. LOUIS v. MISSOURI

Supreme Court of the United States, 1924.
263 U.S. 640.

MR. JUSTICE SUTHERLAND delivered the opinion of the Court.

The state of Missouri brought this proceeding in the nature of *quo warranto* in the state Supreme Court against the plaintiff in error to determine its authority to establish and conduct a branch bank in the City of St. Louis. The information avers that the bank was organized under the

---

28. Phil Battey & Laura Gross, Fed Fines Citibank $350,000; 1980 Premium Campaign Said to Violate Reg Q, Am. Banker, July 23, 1981, at 1.

laws of the United States and was and is engaged in a general banking business in that city at a banking house, the location of which is given; that, in contravention of its charter and of the act of Congress under which it was incorporated, it has illegally opened and is operating a branch bank for doing a general banking business in a separate building several blocks from its banking house, and proposes to open additional branch banks at various other locations, and that this is in violation of a statute of the State expressly prohibiting the establishment of branch banks. * * *

The Missouri statute provides "that no bank shall maintain in this state a branch bank or receive deposits or pay checks except in its own banking house." That the facts alleged in the information bring the case within that part of the statute which prohibits the maintenance of branch banks and that the statute applies to national banks is conclusively established by the decision of the state court, and we confine ourselves to the inquiry whether, as thus applied, the statute is valid.

National banks are brought into existence under federal legislation, are instrumentalities of the federal government and are necessarily subject to the paramount authority of the United States. Nevertheless, national banks are subject to the laws of a state in respect of their affairs unless such laws interfere with the purposes of their creation, tend to impair or destroy their efficiency as federal agencies or conflict with the paramount law of the United States. * * *

Clearly, the state statute, by prohibiting branches, does not frustrate the purpose for which the bank was created or interfere with the discharge of its duties to the government or impair its efficiency as a federal agency. This conclusion would seem to be self-evident but, if warrant for it be needed, it sufficiently lies in the fact that national banking associations have gone on for more than half a century without branches and upon the theory of an absence of authority to establish them. If the non-existence of such branches or the absence of power to create them has operated or is calculated to operate to the detriment of the government, or in such manner as to interfere with the efficiency of such associations as federal agencies, or to frustrate their purposes, it is inconceivable that the fact would not long since have been discovered and steps taken by Congress to remedy the omission. * * *

[The Court held that the state may enforce its statute prohibiting branching against the national bank.]

JUSTICE VAN DEVANTER, dissents. * * *

Stat. prohibiting branching

Many states continued to resist branching in favor of so-called "unit" banking—single bank units. These restrictions were sometimes evaded by the creation of "chain banks"—banks owned by common owners. The individual banks operating without branches usually established correspondent banking arrangements with other banks in order to conduct interstate and inter-city banking transactions. The correspondents borrowed from each other and referred business outside their geographical area. Most "country" banks were strongly dependent on their correspondent banking relationships in New York, which had become the nation's money center by the Civil War. Nevertheless, correspondent banking frustrated efforts by city banks and their clearing houses to stabilize liquidity during times of financial panic because country banks withdrew their deposits in times of trouble.

Other states permitted limited branching for state banks (such as within the same city or within a certain number of miles from the bank's main office). Some states permitted state banks to establish branches anywhere within the state. By 1920, the number of branch banks for state banks increased substantially. The Comptroller of the Currency pushed state legislation to limit branch banking by state banks because of his concern that unlimited state bank branch banking would mean the destruction of the national banking system. The American Bankers Association was a firm opponent of branch banking. In 1916, and again in 1922, it adopted resolutions against branches.

The next case discusses the McFadden Act of 1927, and its amendment as part of the Banking Act of 1933, directly addressing the issue of branching by national banks.

FIRST NATIONAL BANK OF LOGAN
v. WALKER BANK & TRUST CO.

Supreme Court of the United States, 1966.
385 U.S. 252.

MR. JUSTICE CLARK delivered the opinion of the Court.

These cases involve the construction of those portions of the National Banking Act, 12 U.S.C. § 36(c), which authorize a national banking association, with the approval of the Comptroller of the Currency, to establish and operate new branches within the limits of the municipality in which the bank is located, if such operation is "at the time authorized to State banks by the law of the State in question." Two national banks with their main banking houses in Logan and Ogden, Utah, respectively, seek to open branches in those municipalities. The Utah statute prohibits Utah banks, with certain exceptions not here relevant, from establishing branches except by taking over an existing bank which has been in operation for not less than five years. * * *

There has long been opposition to the exercise of federal power in the banking field. Indeed, President Jefferson was opposed to the creation of the first Bank of the United States and President Jackson vetoed the Act of Congress extending the charter of the second Bank of the United States. However, the authority of Congress to act in the field was resolved in the landmark case of McCulloch v. State of Maryland. There Chief Justice Marshall, while admitting that it does not appear that a bank was in the contemplation of the Framers of the Constitution, held that a national bank could be chartered under the implied powers of the Congress as an instrumentality of the Federal Government to implement its fiscal powers. The paramount power of the Congress over national banks has, therefore, been settled for almost a century and a half.

Nevertheless, no national banking act was adopted until 1863, and it was not until 1927 that Congress dealt with the problem before us in these cases. This inaction was possibly due to the fact that at the turn of the century, there were very few branch banks in the country. At that time only five national and 82 state banks were operating branches with a total of 119 branches. By the end of 1923, however, there were 91 national and 580 state banks with a total of 2,054 branches. The Comptroller of the Currency, in his Annual Report of 1923, recommended congressional action on branch banking. The report stated that if state banks continue to engage "in unlimited branch banking it will mean the eventual destruction of the national banking system. . . ." Soon thereafter legislation was introduced to equalize national and state branch banking. * * *

This bill failed to pass in the Senate and, although Congress continued to study the problem, it was not until 1927 that the McFadden Act was adopted. The bill originated in the House and, in substance, proposed that both national and state banks be permitted to establish "inside" branches within the municipality of their main banking facilities in those States that permitted branch banking at the time of the enactment of the bill. The intent of the Congress to leave the question of the desirability of branch banking up to the States is indicated by the fact that the Senate struck from the House bill the time limitation, thus permitting a subsequent change in state law to have a corresponding effect on the authority of national banks to engage in branching. The Senate Report concluded that the Act would permit "national banks to have branches in those cities where State banks are allowed to have them under State laws." In the subsequent Conference Committee, the Senate position was adopted. State banks which were members of the Federal Reserve System were also limited to "inside" branches. A grandfather clause permitted retention of branches operated at the date of enactment. The Act was finally passed on February 25, 1927, and became known as the McFadden Act of 1927, taking its name from its sponsor, Representative McFadden. * * *

During the economic depression there was much agitation that bank failures were due to small undercapitalized rural banks and that these banks should be supplanted by branches of larger and stronger banks. The Comptroller of the Currency advocated that national banks be permitted to branch regardless of state law. Senator Carter Glass held a similar belief and introduced a bill that would authorize national banks to organize branches irrespective of state law beyond and "outside" the municipality of its principal banking house. His proposal was strenuously opposed and was eventually defeated. It was not until the Seventy-third Congress that the Banking Act of 1933 was adopted. Senator Glass, the ranking member of the Senate Committee on Banking and Currency and the dominant banking figure in the Congress, was sponsor of the Act. In reporting it to the Senate for passage, he said, the Act "required that the establishment of branch banks by national banks in States which by law permit branch banking should be under the regulations required by State law of State banks." In a colloquy on the floor of the Senate with Senator Copeland as to the purpose of the Act (with reference to branch banking by national banks), Senator Glass said that it would be permissible "in only those States the laws of which permit branch banking, and only to the extent that the State laws permit branch banking." Moreover, to make it crystal clear, when Senator Copeland replied that "it permits branch banking only in those States where the State laws permit branch banking by State banks," Senator Glass was careful to repeat: *"Only in those States and to the extent that the State laws permit branch banking."*

As finally passed, the Act permitted national banks to establish outside branches if such branches could be established by state banks under state law. It is well to note that the same Act also removed the restriction on outside branch banking by state member banks previously imposed by the McFadden Act.

It appears clear from this resume of the legislative history of § 36(c)(1) and (2) that Congress intended to place national and state banks on a basis of "competitive equality" insofar as branch banking was concerned. Both sponsors of the applicable banking Acts, Representative McFadden and Senator Glass, so characterized the legislation. It is not for us to so construe the Acts as to frustrate this clear-cut purpose so forcefully expressed by both friend and foe of the legislation at the time of its adoption. To us it appears beyond question that the Congress was continuing its policy of equalization first adopted in the National Bank Act of 1864.

The Comptroller argues that Utah's statute "expressly authorizes" state banks to have branches in their home municipalities. He maintains that the restriction, in the subsequent paragraph of the statute limiting branching solely to the taking over of an existing bank, is not applicable to national banks. It is a strange argument that permits one to pick and choose what portion of the law binds him. Indeed, it would fly in the face of the legislative history not to hold that national branch banking is limited to those States the laws of which permit it, and even there "only to the extent that the State laws permit branch banking." Utah clearly permits it "only to the extent" that the proposed branch takes over an existing bank.

The Comptroller also contends that the Act supersedes state law only as to "whether" and "where" branches may be located and not the "method" by which this is effected. We believe that where a State allows branching only by taking over an existing bank, it expresses as much "whether" and "where" a branch may be located as does a prohibition or a limitation to the home office municipality. As to the restriction being a "method," we have concluded that since it is part and parcel of Utah's policy, it was absorbed by the provisions of §§ 36 (c)(1) and (2), regardless of the tag placed upon it. * * *

The McFadden Act only authorized national banks to branch "within a state" to the same extent as a state bank. National banks could not branch outside their home state. The authority of states to authorize branching by state banks was presumably limited in effect to the boundaries of that state. This assured that small communities would only be served by their local banks or banks located elsewhere in the state. Country banks were thus shielded from competition with the larger and better capitalized banks from money centers or from other states. More significantly, restrictions on branch banking resulted in a large number of very weak banks that were unable to cope with a serious economic downturn. Branch banking restrictions continued to confine interstate banking until late in the twentieth century.

SECTION 7. REGULATION OF BANK HOLDING COMPANIES

The Bank Holding Company Act (BHCA) was enacted in 1956 to limit the ability of banks to affiliate through common ownership with commercial enterprises not related to banking. A second purpose of the BHCA was to preclude banks from expanding geographically in contravention of the existing restrictions on bank branching. As enacted, the statute only applied to a company that owned more than one bank. So-called "one-bank holding companies" were brought within the statute by the 1970 amendments to the Bank Holding Company Act.

A. CLOSELY RELATED TO BANKING

The BHCA authorized the Fed to allow bank holding companies to acquire or retain ownership only of companies whose activities are "so closely related to banking or managing or controlling banks as to be a proper incident thereto." The Fed adopted Regulation Y to define such areas.

closely related to banking

CAMERON FINANCIAL CORP. v. BOARD OF GOVERNORS OF THE FEDERAL RESERVE SYSTEM

United States Court of Appeals, Fourth Circuit, 1974.
497 F.2d 841.

ADAMS, CIRCUIT JUDGE.

* * * [W]e must decide whether section 4(a)(2) of the Bank Holding Company Act extends so-called "grandfather" privileges to a bank holding

company which controlled, prior to June 30, 1968, a bank subsidiary that also engaged in limited courier activities, but which "spun-off" the courier activities to a nonbanking subsidiary subsequent to June 30, 1968. * * *

Prior to 1956, a bank holding company, then completely unregulated, was utilized to achieve geographical expansion and service diversification unattainable by its banking subsidiary alone because the banking subsidiary was subject to national or state regulation. Misgivings were developing among Congressmen that proliferation of the bank holding device was having anticompetitive effects in the economy. Banking resources were becoming increasingly concentrated and the combination in one enterprise of a major creditor in a locality, a bank, and another service business created a condition ripe for exploitation through tying relationships. In response to these concerns, Congress enacted the Bank Holding Company Act of 1956.

In essence, the Act brought multibank holding companies under the regulatory authority of the Federal Reserve Board. It limited the acquisition of banking subsidiaries and restricted the scope of allowable diversification. But the 1956 Act did not extend to *one*-bank holding companies. Since concentration of banking resources was facilitated by the acquisition of several banking subsidiaries, the bank holding company that controlled only one bank did not represent as significant a threat to competition as the multi-bank holding company. Further, the general small size, at the time, of one-bank holding companies and the absence of evidence of competitive abuse of the one-bank holding company device provided support in terms of the Act's objectives for exempting from the reach of the Act the holding companies that controlled only one bank.

But several large banks responded to the promise of stricter regulation as the result of court rulings limiting the authority of the Comptroller of the Currency to permit national banks wide-ranging entrepreneurial discretion by turning to the one-bank holding company device. "The nations largest banks," including the six largest, "rushed to form one-bank holding companies, many of which engaged in commercial and industrial enterprises not even arguably within banking powers, such as TV broadcasting, furniture manufacturing, and pizza parlors."[29] "In view of the large growth of the assets held by the one-bank holding company industry, and in view of the theoretical freedom of a one-bank holding company to engage in any business, or acquire anything it desires . . . ,"[30] Congress amended the Act [in 1970] to include within its regulatory scheme one-bank holding companies as well as the multi-bank holding companies already covered.

The 1970 Amendments were directed primarily at the portent of serious anticompetitive consequences presented by the trend of unregulated one-bank holding company proliferation and expansion. Congress was

---

29.   [n.16] [Note, Implementation of the Bank Holding Company Act Amendments of 1970: The Scope of Banking Activities, 71 Mich. L. Rev. 1170] at 1176.

30.   [n.17] [Quoting from S. Rep. No. 1084, 3 U.S.C.C.A.N. 5522 (1970).]

not, therefore, eager to effect a dramatic alteration of the existing organizational structure of the banking industry. Furthermore, Congress "felt that the one-bank holding companies existing at the time set in the clause, most of which were quite small, had not caused great problems and was thus reluctant to require them to undergo the hardships of divestiture, which would be particularly hard for small banks."[31]

Turning to an examination of how these considerations are reflected in the statutory scheme, we note that one-bank holding companies that seek to engage in nonbanking activities or to continue to engage in such activities initiated subsequent to the grandfather date of June 30, 1968, must seek Board approval pursuant to section 4(c)(8). * * *

In sum, since we agree with the Board that "subsidiary" in section 4(a)(2) does not refer to a banking subsidiary, Cameron's courier activities are not entitled to grandfather privileges under that section. Accordingly, Cameron's petition for review will be denied.

B. THE DOUGLAS AMENDMENT AND GEOGRAPHIC EXPANSION BY BANK HOLDING COMPANIES

The Douglas Amendment, part of the BHCA of 1956, effectively precluded a bank holding company from owning banks in more than one state. The practical ban it imposed on interstate banking was first eroded by state statutes on a state-by-state basis, and then later repealed by the Riegle–Neal Act of 1994.

Geographic expansion is discussed further in Chapter 9.

C. PRESSURES ON THE BANK HOLDING COMPANY ACT

The BHCA applied to a company that controlled a bank and limited the activities of that company to those that were "closely related to banking." This precluded common ownership of banks and other commercial enterprises, including securities firms.

The BHCA and its limitations could be avoided, however, if the "bank" failed to meet the BHCA definition of bank because it either accepted deposits or made loans, but not both. This permitted commercial firms and stock brokers to own so-called "nonbank banks," entitites with bank charters but not within the BHCA's definition of a "bank." Nonbank banks also evaded the Douglas Amendment's limitations on interstate banking. Gulf & Western acquired a California bank and sold its commercial loan portfolio so that it could become a nonbank bank and not be subject to the Bank Holding Company Act.

In 1983, J.C. Penney did essentially the same thing when it bought a national bank and sold its commercial loans. The brokerage firms Merrill

---

31. [n.19] Note, [supra note 25], at 1181.

Lynch, E.F. Hutton, Paine Webber, Drexel Burnham, Lambert and Shearson Lehman/American Express also operated nonbank banks.

In Board of Governors of the Federal Reserve System v. Dimension Financial Corp., 474 U.S. 361 (1986) (excerpted in Chapter 4), the Supreme Court struck down Fed regulations which defined "bank" in such a way as to include many of the so-called nonbank banks as contrary to the statutory definition of bank in the BHCA. Congress intervened shortly after the Supreme Court's decision by adopting the Competitive Equality Banking Act of 1987 (CEBA).

That Act curbed the use of nonbank banks by redefining the term "bank" in the BHCA to its present definition in 12 U.S.C.A. § 1841(c). Nonbank banks acquired before March 5, 1987 were grandfathered. These banks are sometimes referred to as "CEBA banks."[32]

SECTION 8.   INFLATIONARY PRESSURES

The Vietnam War and world economic events led to increased inflation in the 1960's. The interest rate ceilings imposed by the Banking Act of 1933 interfered with the ability of banks to attract deposits. Credit "crunches" occurred in which loan demand outstripped the amount of funds banks had available to lend. Banks could not attract sufficient deposits to meet loan demand at Regulation Q rates. This gave rise to a growing concern with "disintermediation" in which funds were drawn from deposit institutions such as banks and savings and loan associations ("S&Ls") and invested in other investments not subject to the Regulation Q caps, such as securities.

One source of competition for funds was money market funds. These are mutual funds that invest in short term money market instruments, such as Treasury bills, that pay interest to the investor. Money market funds allow their owners to receive interest at current market rates on idle funds, rather than earning nothing in a checking account or an artificially low rate when held in a savings deposit at a bank. The funds are also viewed as relatively safe, even though they do not benefit from the federal deposit insurance guarantee, because they are primarily invested in government securities with little or no risk of default.

In June 1976, money market funds held less than $3 billion. By December 1982, broker-dealers held over $230 billion in money market funds. Brokerage firms also used money market funds and related accounts to become effective substitutes for banks.

PAINE, WEBBER, JACKSON & CURTIS,
INC. v. MERRILL LYNCH, PIERCE,
FENNER & SMITH, INC.

United States District Court, District of Delaware, 1983.
564 F.Supp. 1358.

LATCHUM, CHIEF JUDGE.Plaintiff, Paine, Webber, Jackson and Curtis, Inc. ("Paine Webber"), brings this action pursuant to 28 U.S.C. §§ 2201–

---

32. See 2 Jane W. D'Arista, The Evolution of U.S. Finance, Restructuring Institutions and Markets 88, 308, 369 (1994).

2202 and Rule 57, Fed.R.Civ.P., seeking a declaratory judgment of noninfringement, invalidity and unenforceability of United States Patent No. 4,346,442 ("the '442 patent"), and ancillary injunctive relief against defendant Merrill Lynch, Pierce, Fenner & Smith, Inc. ("Merrill Lynch"), from initiating infringement litigation against and/or charging Paine Webber or any of its customers, officers, directors or employees with the infringement of the '442 patent. * * *

In 1977 Merrill Lynch offered to the public the Cash Management Account program ("CMA") which combined three financial services commonly offered by financial institutions and brokerage houses and included a brokerage security account (the "Securities Account"), several money market funds (the "Money Market Fund"), and a charge/checking account (the "Visa Account"). The Securities Account, the primary component of the CMA program, is a conventional Merrill Lynch margin account which may be used to purchase and sell securities and options on margin or on a fully-paid basis. * * *

The Money Market Fund is a conventional money market fund which provides the customer of the CMA with a choice of three CMA money market funds: * * * Each of these funds is a no-load, diversified, open-end management investment company registered under the Investment Company Act. The objectives of the funds are similar to the objectives of other money market funds (such as the Merrill Lynch Ready Assets Trusts). Each seek the safety of principal, liquidity and current income available from investing in a portfolio of money market securities. Dividends are declared daily and automatically reinvested in the Money Market Fund similar to the method by which the dividends are distributed, and reinvested in other money market funds.

The Visa Account is the third component of the CMA and is managed by Bank One of Columbus, N.A. ("Bank One"). Bank One issues a Visa card and checks to each person who is a CMA customer.

The card may be used to make purchases of merchandise or services at Visa-participating establishments or to obtain cash advances from any Visa-participating bank or branch. The CMA customer may draw checks upon his Visa Account for any purpose and the Visa card is similar to the conventional card in that the card is honored at more than the 100,000 worldwide bank branches in the Visa system, as well as the 3,000,000 business establishments accepting the Visa card.

No question exists that the three major components of the CMA were offered to the public prior to the marketing of the CMA by financial institutions and/or brokerage houses: one could have placed securities into a brokerage account, purchased shares in a money market fund, or obtained a Visa charge account. Merrill Lynch, however, argues that by combining the three components of the CMA, the customer receives synergistic benefits. According to Merrill Lynch, one of the advantages of the CMA is that all money generated in the Securities Account is automatically invested within a week into the Money Market Fund. This differs from a conventional brokerage account, which might not invest money generated from activity in the brokerage account and thus some money might remain in an account without yielding any financial return.

Another advantage of having an integrated financial service, as provided by the CMA, is that the cash balances in the Securities Account, shares in the Money Market Fund, and available margin loan value of the securities in the Securities Account are calculated when determining the amount of credit available in the Visa Account. * * *

Another advantage of the CMA, according to Merrill Lynch, is that those customers who subscribe to the CMA receive a monthly transaction statement from Merrill Lynch which details all CMA transactions during the preceding month. The statement describes securities and options bought and sold in the Securities Account, whether on margin or on a fully-paid basis, any other type of transaction effected in the Securities Account, margin interest charges, if any, Money Market Fund shares that were purchased or redeemed, dividends on Money Market Fund shares, purchases of merchandise or services that were made with the Visa card, checks drawn against the Visa Account and cash advances. * * *

[The court held that the data processing methodology for the CMA was patentable subject matter.]

Congress responded in various ways to the challenges posed by inflationary pressures on the traditional business of banking. These responses are described in more detail in Chapter 2. The statutory and regulatory responses to inflation were neither swift enough nor dramatic enough to save many depository institutions from insolvency. Bank and savings and loan failures were the highest since the Depression.

SECTION 9.   GEOGRAPHIC BARRIERS FALL

Regional, reciprocal interstate banking statutes were adopted by groups of states to encourage interstate banking within a defined region, consistent with the Douglas Amendment. These interstate compacts were found constitutional by the U.S. Supreme Court. See Chapter 9. Although this led to interstate banking on a regional basis, there were still no banks that had nationwide operations. Moreover, interstate *branches* were still restricted, although a handful of states adopted legislation that permitted reciprocal interstate branching.

The Riegle–Neal Interstate Banking and Branching Efficiency Act of 1994 finally opened the door to nationwide interstate banking. That legislation repealed the Douglas Amendment and allowed bank holding companies to acquire banks in any state. After July 1, 1997, interstate branching was also permitted, and this enabled bank holding companies with separate banks located in various states to consolidate the banks into one charter with interstate branches.

SECTION 10. THE CHANGING ROLES OF BANKS AND THEIR HOLDING COMPANIES

A. CONTINUING COMPETITIVE PRESSURES

The effect of competition on banking services was aptly summarized in a 1995 Treasury Department document, which noted that:

> The share of total private financial assets held by insured depository institutions has declined sharply, from about 60 percent in 1970 to less than 35 percent today.

> Only 15 percent of all financial assets held by households and the non-profit sector in 1994 was accounted for by insured deposits.

> Recent data show that, of the 20 largest financial firms in the United States, only 5 are commercial banks. Moreover, a number of diversified financial services firms own non-bank, thrift institutions, or industrial loan companies.

> The differences between the products of banks and non-bank financial firms have become increasingly blurred. The emergence of similar products by different firms operating under different regulatory regimes results in complicated competitive and regulatory issues.

> A number of commercial banks engage in little or no traditional banking—funding commercial loans with deposits. Rather, they specialize in trading activities, consumer finance, or fee-based services.

> Capital markets have become increasingly globalized, and financial markets in different countries have become more interdependent.

> Technological innovations such as remote banking and digital cash daily redefine the nature and delivery of financial services and the respective roles played by bank and non-bank firms. For example, the data processing firm EDS is the second largest owner/operator of ATMs in the U.S.[33]

The number of banks declined from almost 14,500 in 1984 to 8,600 1999. This statistic reflected the fact that a massive restructuring of the banking industry had occurred through mergers and acquisitions. A new form of bank—the "super regional"—emerged in the early 1990s. Super regional banks included Banc One Corporation, First Chicago/NBD Corpo-

---

33. Dept. of the Treasury, Memorandum for Members of the Secretary's Advisory Commission on Financial Services from Joan Affleck–Smith, Director, Office of Financial Institutions Policy (October 23, 1995).

ration, Fleet Financial, Norwest Corporation in Indianapolis, CoreStates, First Union, Wachovia Corporation, Wells Fargo and NationsBank. These enterprises became even more aggressive in seeking to expand their business base.

As the Twentieth Century came to a close, banks continued to rely less on their traditional lending business and more on developing other financial services. As will be seen in Chapter 11, the investment banking barriers in the Glass–Steagall Act were gradually eroded. Banks became involved in selling United States Treasury securities, leases and asset backed securities, municipal securities, corporate bonds, corporate equities and financial and precious metal futures, as well as bullion. They acted as private placement agents, sponsored closed end investment funds, and offered deposit accounts with returns that were tied to stock market performance. Other bank activities included eurodollar dealings, mergers and acquisitions, trust investments, automatic investment services, dividend investment services, financial advising, discount brokerage activities, swaps and research services. Chemical Bank reported revenues of $1 billion dollars based on proprietary trading activities in 1993. Bank of America made more profits from trading than from its lending activities.

The new role being played by banks was illustrated by a two page advertisement in the Wall Street Journal in February of 1998 that announced NationsBank's results for the prior year. In that year, the bank handled initial public offerings worth $4.5 billion; "follow-ons" worth $11.8 billion; high-grade securities underwritings of $30.6 billion; private placements worth $940 million; asset-backed securities underwritings at $22.5 billion; project finance of $5.7 billion; convertible securities underwritten in the amount of $3.7 billion; syndicated floating rate debt of $442 billion; real estate finance valued at $30.2 billion; high-yield ("junk bond") transactions worth $16.7 billion; and mergers and acquisitions worth $14.5 billion.[34]

In April 1998, Citicorp announced a planned merger with Travelers Group, Inc. which owned Salomon Brothers and Smith Barney, an investment banking firm formed by the merger of Salomon Brothers and Smith Barney. The value of this merger was set at $83 billion. Before its merger with Travelers Group, Citicorp had relationships with one in five households in the United States. The combined entity had more than 100 million customers worldwide, and it offered a wide range of products that varied from corporate finance to consumer banking and securities.[35] The merger of BankAmerica and NationsBank matched the Citigroup amalgamation in bank size. The Deutsche Bank also announced on November 23, 1998 that it was acquiring Bankers Trust for almost $10 billion. This merger created the world's largest financial services company.

---

34. 1997 Results—$559 Billion in Transactions, Wall St. J., Feb. 11, 1998, at A12.

35. Citigroup's initial existence was authorized under 12 U.S.C. § 1842(a) for a two-year period to permit divestiture of the Citigroup subsidiaries which were engaged in activities not "closely related to banking."

B. THE GRAMM–LEACH–BLILEY ACT AND FINANCIAL HOLDING COMPANIES

PAUL J. POLKING & SCOTT A. CAMMARN[36] OVERVIEW OF THE GRAMM–LEACH– BLILEY ACT

4 N.C. Banking Inst. 1 (2000).

The Gramm–Leach–Bliley Act (the "Act"), signed into law by President Clinton on November 12, 1999, represents the culmination of Congressional financial reform efforts spanning more than 30 years. The Act makes sweeping changes to federal statutes governing the scope of permissible activities and the supervision of banks, bank holding companies, and their affiliates. In particular, the Act lowers (although does not altogether eliminate) barriers between the banking and securities industries erected by the Banking Act of 1933 (popularly known as the "Glass–Steagall Act") and between the banking and the insurance industries erected by the 1982 amendments to the Bank Holding Company Act of 1956 (the "Bank Holding Company Act"). Some have described the Gramm–Leach–Bliley Act as the most important piece of federal banking legislation since the Depression. * * *

In any case, the Gramm–Leach–Bliley Act is undoubtedly significant: the Act expands the statutory powers of banks, bank subsidiaries, and bank holding companies, alters which (and how) federal agencies regulate banks and bank holding company activities through the concept of "functional regulation," curtails the power of the thrift charter, and imposes privacy restrictions on entire industries. * * *

Under the Gramm–Leach–Bliley Act, a bank holding company may *Permits banks to.* elect to become a "financial holding company" and thereby engage, directly or through a nonbank subsidiary, in any activity that is "financial in nature" or other activity that is complimentary or incidental thereto. * * *

As a result of these expanded activities granted to financial holding companies, the Gramm–Leach–Bliley Act effectively permits affiliation between bank holding companies, insurance companies, and securities firms, under the umbrella of a "financial holding company." However (except in the case of merchant banking investments), the Act continues to bar banking and commerce affiliations, i.e., affiliations between depository institutions and companies engaged in activities that are not "financial in nature." * * *

Bank holding companies are not compelled to elect "financial holding company" status. Bank holding companies that do not make such an election will continue to be regulated by the Federal Reserve Board as

---

36. At the time of publication, the authors were the General Counsel and Associate General Counsel of Bank of America Corporation.

such, and their permissible activities will continue be limited to those that are "closely related to banking" as prescribed by the Bank Holding Company Act and Federal Reserve Board orders and regulations in effect on November 11, 1999. Thus, the permissible scope of non-electing bank holding company activities is frozen as of the date of enactment of the Act. * * *

The Gramm–Leach–Bliley Act also expands the permissible activities of a subsidiary of a national bank. Currently, national banks may own an "operating subsidiary," which, for the most part, may engage only in those activities that are permissible for the national bank itself, i.e., activities that are "part of or incidental to the business of banking ... or other activities that are permissible for national banks or their subsidiaries under other statutory authority." By interpretation and regulation, the OCC has permitted a national bank to own a subsidiary engaged in activities that meet the above standard, even though separate statutory authority precludes a national bank from engaging in the same activity directly (referred to as a "Part 5 subsidiary").

The Gramm–Leach–Bliley Act preserves the existing authority of a national bank to own an operating subsidiary, and in addition permits the bank to own a "financial subsidiary"—a subsidiary that may engage in a broader range of activities that are "financial in nature." * * *

A financial subsidiary of a national bank may engage in any activity that either (i) is permissible for the bank itself, (ii) is listed as "financial in nature" under the Act, (iii) has been determined by the Treasury to be "financial in nature" (and the Federal Reserve Board has not disagreed), or (iv) is "incident" to a financial activity. However, a financial subsidiary may *not* engage in:

- Underwriting insurance (other than credit insurance) or issuing annuities;

- Real estate development or investment; or

- Merchant banking (although five years after enactment, a financial subsidiary may engage in merchant banking if the Federal Reserve Board and the Treasury concur).

A financial subsidiary therefore may engage in a wide range or activities previously barred to a national bank or its operating subsidiaries, such as:

- Underwriting or dealing in securities (including market-making);

- Organizing, sponsoring, or distributing a mutual fund;

- Selling insurance (including title insurance) outside a "place of 5,000";

- Engaging in real estate lease financing;

- Engaging in real estate brokerage;

- Operating a travel agency; and

● Providing management consulting services.

* * * The Act also permits FDIC-insured state-chartered banks to own a financial subsidiary, subject to generally the same requirements, conditions, and firewalls applicable to national banks. Of course, a state bank could not own a financial subsidiary unless permitted to do so by the law of the state in which the bank is chartered, although many states have adopted "wild card" statutes that would permit state bank ownership of a subsidiary if a similarly situated national bank could do so. * * *

The Act confers on the Federal Reserve Board the primary authority to examine and supervise a bank holding company, financial holding company, and their respective affiliates, other than its depository institution and "functionally regulated" affiliates. The "functionally regulated affiliates" (and their respective functional regulators) are:

● For a registered broker-dealer, investment adviser, or an investment company, the Securities and Exchange Commission (the "SEC");

● For a state-regulated insurance company, the state insurance authority; and

● For a CFTC regulated firm, the Commodity Futures Trading Commission.

The Federal Reserve Board's authority to require reports from, examine, or impose capital requirements on a functionally regulated affiliate of a bank holding company or financial holding company is significantly restricted. Similarly, the authority of the SEC or a state insurance authority to require reports from or examine a holding company or a nonbank subsidiary is restricted as well (unless such nonbank subsidiary is functionally regulated by the SEC or the state insurance authority). * * *

———————

Banks and their holding companies faced a multitude of regulators, from the traditional bank regulatory agencies—the Treasury (Comptroller of the Currency), the Fed, FDIC, and various state banking commissions—to the Securities Exchange Commission (SEC), state securities administrators, Securities Investor Protection Corporation (SIPC), the Commodity Futures Trading Commission (CFTC), state insurance regulators, state attorney generals, self-regulatory bodies (i.e., stock and commodity exchanges, the National Association of Securities Dealers (NASD) and the National Futures Association), as well as the Pension Benefit Guaranty Corporation, the Department of Justice (DOJ), and the Federal Trade Commission (FTC).

JERRY W. MARKHAM
Merging The SEC and CFTC—A Clash of Cultures
78 U. Cin. L. Rev. 537 (2009).

* * * Responding to widespread concerns over overlapping and unnecessary regulation in the existing regulatory structure, then-Secretary of the Treasury Henry M. Paulson, Jr. launched an initiative in October 2007 to consider how those concerns might be alleviated. The backdrop for that study was a widely expressed concern that excessive regulation in the United States was undermining the nation's competitive position in the world. * * *

The Treasury Department published its report in March 2008 (the "Treasury Blueprint").[37] * * * The Blueprint contrasted the functional regulatory approach in America with regulatory mechanisms abroad. England, Germany, Japan, and dozens of other countries use a single consolidated regulator, along with a central bank, to regulate; those countries eschew the "rules-based" approach used by most regulators in the United States. Rather, foreign regulators use a "principles-based" approach that sets broad regulatory goals and permits the industry to decide how to meet those goals. A principles-based approach reduces the need for volumes of regulations that seek to control every aspect of financial services operations * * *.

Instead of a single regulator, the Blueprint recommended that the United States adopt the "twin peaks" approach used in Australia and the Netherlands. This concept is attributed to Michael Taylor, a former official at the Bank of England who wrote a 1995 article entitled *'Twin Peaks': A Regulatory Structure for the New Century.*[38] The Twin Peaks approach is objectives-based and focuses on specific regulatory goals.

Twin Peaks envisions a central bank that focuses on prudential supervision, and a single business practices regulator that focuses on business conduct and consumer protection. From this the Treasury Blueprint created a "Three Peaks" approach that would have three separate bodies implementing three specific regulatory goals: (1) market stability regulation, (2) prudential financial regulation, and (3) business conduct regulation. This objectives-based approach would require consolidating and reshuffling the existing functional regulators in the United States into essentially three principal regulators. The market stability regulator would be the Federal Reserve Board. A new agency would be created for prudential financial regulation that would regulate financial institutions with a government guarantee, such as banks insured by the FDIC and broker-dealers insured by the Securities Investor Protection Corporation (SIPC). A new agency would also have to be created for the business

---

37. [n.2] Dep't of the Treasury, Blueprint for a Modernized Financial Regulatory Structure (2008), available at http://www.treas.gov/press/releases/reports/Blueprint.pdf.

38. [n. 53] Jill Treanor, Regulators back Taylor's twin-peaks theory, Independent (London), Oct. 29, 1996.

conduct regulator, which would create and apply principles-based regulation. * * *

The financial crisis that began in 2007 with the subprime mortgage crisis sidelined this effort.

SECTION 11. POST SEPTEMBER 11

The terrorist attacks of September 11, 2001, prompted Congress to enact the USA PATRIOT Act. That Act, signed by President Bush on October 26, 2001, included anti-money laundering and anti-terrorist financing provisions which are discussed in greater detail in Chapter 14.

The Patriot Act involved banks to a greater extent than ever before in law enforcement efforts. The Act's provisions requiring collection and disclosure of customer information stand in contrast to the Gramm–Leach–Bliley Act which placed restrictions on the ability of financial institutions to disseminate customer financial information to nonaffiliates.

SECTION 12. THE FINANCIAL CRISIS AND THE DODD–FRANK WALL STREET REFORM AND CONSUMER PROTECTION ACT OF 2010

A. THE FINANCIAL CRISIS

The twenty-first century began with the bursting of a stock market bubble in Internet and telecommunication stocks after a period of sharp interest rate increases by the Federal Reserve Board that threw the economy into a near recession. That crash was followed by a series of financial accounting scandals at the Enron, WorldCom, and other companies. Congress responded to those scandals with the Sarbanes–Oxley Act of 2002 that imposed costly corporate governance and accounting reforms on publicly traded companies.

In order to right the economy, the Fed drastically cut interest rates starting in 2001. The federal funds rate was 6.50% in 2000 but had been reduced to 1% by June 2003. This dramatic reduction in interest rates helped create a residential real estate bubble. The real estate bubble was fueled by liberal credit extensions at quite low initial "teaser" interest rates often to "subprime" borrowers with credit problems that disqualified them from obtaining a conventional mortgage.

Mortgage lenders and brokers, many of whom were not affiliated with banks, were able to make an increasing number of mortgage loans without concern for credit quality because they were able to immediately pool and sell the loans to securitization vehicles funded by investors who purchased mortgage-backed securities. The mortgage-backed securities were primarily debt securities. A single securitization produced a number of "tranches" of securities varying in interest rates and payment priority. The investors were repaid from payments made by mortgage holders on their mortgages, which were then paid out in the payment priority and amount prescribed by a particular security's tranche. Those tranches with the first priority to payment seemed very safe. The securities issued by the securitization were also frequently insured against default by "monoline" insurance companies with little capital, or hedged by a financial instrument called a credit default swap. Those protections allowed the "super senior" tranches in subprime securitizations to obtain AAA credit ratings from the leading credit rating agencies, making them highly marketable in the U.S. and Europe. Investors seeking a safe return, and discouraged by the low interest rates paid on Treasury securities in the low interest rate environment created by the Fed, flocked to these investments. As demand grew from institutional and foreign investors, mortgage brokers sought to generate even more mortgage loans and promoted "no-doc" or "low doc" loans that did not require the normal documentation of the borrower's creditworthiness—known as "liar loans."

There was, however, a major hidden flaw in the ratings process. The rating agencies used risk models for awarding the AAA rating that did not take into account the possibility of a major downturn in the real estate market. Moreover, the historical mortgage repayment information used in the models may have been based on prime rate borrowers repaying conventional mortgages, rather than subprime borrowers and the more exotic mortgage products that developed in that market.

Subprime mortgages were sometimes pooled to fund off-balance sheet commercial paper borrowings called "structured investment vehicles" (SIVs) or "asset-backed commercial paper" (ABCP). Banks, such as Citigroup, used short-term commercial paper borrowings to purchase mortgages held in their SIVs. Those commercial paper borrowings funded the mortgages and provided a profit through the spread between the higher rates paid by mortgages and the lower rates then existing in the commercial paper market. There was a flaw in these "carry trade" programs. In the event that commercial paper lenders refused to roll over their loans, the SIV would have to liquidate its mortgages. That roll over might not be possible in a credit crunch or major market downturn. Another danger was that short-term rates could rise faster than long-term rates, erasing the spread, or even inverting the payment stream.

In order to crush the real estate bubble that was feeding on low interest rates, Fed Chairman Alan Greenspan began a series of consecutive interest rate increases on June 30, 2004. Ben Bernanke, who replaced Alan Greenspan as the Chairman of the Federal Reserve Board on February 1, 2006, presided over still more interest rate increases. The effects of those actions were already manifesting themselves as Bernanke assumed office. The housing market experienced the largest decline in new home sales in nine years in the month after Bernanke became the Fed

Chairman. This did not deter the Fed. The Fed announced its seventeenth consecutive increase on June 29, 2006, increasing short-term rates to 5.25%. The effect of this onslaught on the real estate market turned into a financial crisis in 2007. Home sales and new residential construction slowed dramatically, and the market became glutted with unsold homes.

Construction firms, such as Toll Brothers, cut back their building programs, and the housing construction industry experienced its worst slump in forty years. Speculators who had been receiving unprecedented profits by buying and quickly reselling properties, often after only a cosmetic touch up, found that they could no longer flip their properties for a quick profit, and they were left holding highly depreciated properties. "Short" sales, in which foreclosed homes were sold for less than their outstanding mortgage balance, became common as speculators defaulted, and as homeowners could no longer meet their payments due to the rising interest rates. Subprime homeowners, in many instances, simply walked away from their homes and mortgages when the value of their home dropped below the amount of the mortgage, a condition known as being "underwater."

The growing crisis in the real estate market caused banks to tighten credit requirements and to cut back on credit extensions creating a credit crunch in the summer of 2007. Foreclosures continued to mount and subprime defaults skyrocketed. A crisis resulted in the financial markets when the SIVs were unable to roll over their commercial paper. As the crisis deepened, some SIVs tried to sell their mortgage collateral, but they could only do so at steep discounts. Concerned with losses from SIVs and mortgage-backed securities, banks reduced lending more, worsening the credit crunch that was causing funding problems throughout the economy.

Subprime problems spread abroad. European investors had purchased significant amounts of U.S. mortgage-backed securities, seeking a higher return than paid on U.S. Treasuries with the supposed safety of a AAA rating. As a result, however, some financial institutions there faced massive losses. Customers began a run on Northern Rock PLC in England in September 2007, after they became concerned with its mortgage exposure. That was the first bank run in England in over 100 years. Depositors withdrew $2 billion before the run was stopped by a $28 billion cash infusion from the Bank of England. The English government later nationalized Northern Rock, as well as the Royal Bank of Scotland. The Bank of England and the European Central Bank also worked in tandem with the Federal Reserve Board to make unlimited funds available to their banks for borrowing in order to ease the credit crunch.

Citigroup and Merrill Lynch announced billions of dollars in losses from subprime loans as 2007 ended, causing the removal of their CEOs and the injection of billions of dollars obtained from sovereign wealth funds to shore up their capital. Other financial institutions also announced billions of dollars of losses from subprime loans, including Morgan Stanley. Congress enacted a $160 billion economic stimulus package, which had little effect. The Fed was forced to arrange a dramatic takeover of Bear Stearns, one of the nation's largest brokerage firms, by JPMorgan Chase in March 2008. Bear Stearns was brought down by a liquidity crisis that arose after traders refused to roll over Bear Stearns' positions in the money market. Assets of clients were pulled from the firm in large amounts, and counterparties refused to trade with Bear Stearns because of concerns that it would fail. In order to close the deal, the Fed agreed to guarantee to JPMorgan some $30 billion of Bear Stearns assets. The Fed also threw open its discount lending window to investment banks, as well as to commercial banks, and accepted mortgage backed securities—the very instruments that led to the crisis—as good collateral.

The month of September 2008 was particularly devastating. Fannie Mae and Freddie Mac, purchasers and securitizers of home mortgage loans, were placed in government conservatorship. Merrill Lynch was taken over by Bank of America. The situation became a full-scale panic, after another giant brokerage firm, Lehman Brothers, failed. The Fed did not provide assistance as it did for the JPMorgan purchase of Bear Stearns, because it deemed Lehman Brothers incapable of providing adequate collateral in exchange for Fed credit. The American International Group Inc. (AIG), a giant global insurance firm, had to be rescued by the federal government at a cost of over $180 billion. The Reserve Primary Fund, a money market mutual fund, "broke-the-buck" when its net asset value fell below $1 per share and touched off an investor run on money market funds in which over $500 billion was withdrawn before the government stepped in to guarantee the funds. Wachovia Bank's failure was imminent and the government negotiated first with Citigroup, but the bank was ultimately purchased by Wells Fargo without government assistance.

That fateful month of September ended with an initial defeat in the House of Representatives of a proposed "bailout" bill. Just a few days later, however, on October 3, 2008, Congress enacted the Emergency Economic Stabilization Act (EESA). A key part of EESA was an unprecedented $700 billion bailout package called the Troubled Assets Relief Program ("TARP"). At the time the bill was passed, it was assumed that the money would be used to clean up the balance sheets of troubled financial institutions by buying their troubled loans and other assets. As the practicality of valuing these troubled loans became apparent, the Department of Treasury quickly changed course and used its discretion under TARP to inject capital by buying preferred stock of the largest financial institutions, including a $25 billion investment in Citigroup.

The initial stock investments failed to halt a stock market panic. Citicorp's stock dropped sixty percent in a single week, and its existence was threatened until the government stepped in to guarantee some $250 billion of its mortgage holdings and to inject another $20 billion in capital into the bank. General Motors and Chrysler also received substantial TARP funding, making the U.S. government the major shareholder in both companies.

The Federal Reserve Board introduced various new lending programs in order to restart the credit markets. The newly elected president, Barack Obama, also stepped into the crisis with an $838 billion stimulus package, but the subprime crisis bottomed out in March 2009 before that stimulus could have any effect.[39] Congress and the still new administration began considering a near complete revamping of the existing financial regulatory structure. President Obama issued a white paper describing a sweeping Regulatory Reform Plan in the summer of 2009. The discussion of financial reform legislation was dwarfed for most of 2009 by debate regarding health care reform legislation.

B. THE DODD–FRANK WALL STREET REFORM AND CONSUMER PROTECTION ACT OF 2010

Congress began work on regulatory reforms even before the financial crisis ended, but financial reform legislation was not enacted until July 2010.[40] The Dodd–Frank Wall Street Reform and Consumer Protection Act of 2010 (the Dodd–Frank Act) was massive in scope and touched nearly every aspect of finance. Most observers have called it the most significant and extensive regulation of financial institutions and Wall Street since the 1930s. The Dodd Frank Act will be discussed in detail in the chapters that follow, but some of its more significant aspects are highlighted here.

(1) Financial Stability Oversight Council

Dodd–Frank created a Financial Stability Oversight Council (FSOC or Council) that is chaired by the Secretary of the Treasury. The Council is discussed in greater detail in Chapter 3. Its purpose is to identify risks to the financial stability of the United States that could arise from the distress, failure, or ongoing activities of nonbank financial companies as well as large, interconnected bank holding companies. It is charged with eliminating the belief on the part of shareholders, creditors, and counterparties that the federal government will bail out a firm that is about to fail.

(2) Orderly Liquidation Authority

As will be discussed in greater detail in Chapter 8, the FSOC may also order the Fed to require too big to fail companies to divest some of their holdings if the company poses a "grave threat" to the financial stability of the United States. In the event a systemically significant company may not be saved, the Act provides for the orderly liquidation of the company without the possibility of a reorganization, in contrast to the perception

---

39. In May 2008, before the brunt of the financial crisis hit, the Dow Jones Industrial Average was over 13,000. On March 9, 2009, it hit its low point of 6440.

40. The House passed the legislation on June 30, 2010, followed by Senate approval on July 15, and president Obama's signature on July 21.

during the financial crisis that some institutions were deemed too big to fail and were bailed out by the federal government. The FDIC would serve as the receiver of such an institution preempting the U.S. Bankruptcy Code, which otherwise applies to nonbank failures when the failing company does not pose a systemic risk. An Orderly Liquidation Fund will be funded by assessments on fund claimants, and, if needed, other financial companies with consolidated assets of $50 billion or more, to cover the costs of resolving these failed institutions.

(3) Expanded Powers of the Fed Over Nonbank Financial Companies

The Dodd–Frank Act expands the power of the Fed over systemically significant non-bank financial companies, as discussed further in Chapters 3 and 4, recognizing the risks to the financial system from the failure or near failure of firms like Bear Stearns, Merrill Lynch, Lehman Brothers, and AIG, among others.

(4) The Fed's Emergency Lending and the FDIC's Systemic Risk Determinations

The Fed is limited in its emergency lending programs to providing liquidity only in a broad-based program as discussed in Chapter 3, and not to aid a particular failing financial company such as Bear Stearns or AIG.

Upon the written determination of the FDIC and the Fed, the FDIC is authorized to create a widely available program to guarantee obligations of solvent insured depository institutions or solvent depository institution holding companies, including any affiliates. This authority may be exercised during times of severe economic distress and is discussed in greater detail in Chapter 7.

(5) Financial Market Utilities

Dodd–Frank adds further regulatory supervision over systemically important payment, clearing, and settlement systems—so-called "financial market utilities"—to the Fed, SEC, or CFTC, as designated by the Council.

(6) Bureau of Consumer Financial Protection

The Dodd–Frank Act created a Bureau of Consumer Financial Protection (BCFP or Bureau) housed within the Fed, but to be headed by an independent director appointed by the President and confirmed by the Senate. The BCFP is tasked with implementing and enforcing federal consumer financial laws consistently for the purpose of ensuring that all consumers have access to markets for consumer financial products and services, and that markets for such products and services are "fair, transparent, and competitive." Non-bank entities will be regulated by the same rules as their bank competitors marketing similar products and services. The Bureau and the minimum mortgage lending standards set forth by the Act will be discussed further in Chapter 6. The application of state consumer protection rules to federally chartered financial institutions under Dodd–Frank will be explored in Chapter 4.

(7) Securities, Hedge Funds, Private Equity, Derivatives, Insurance

The Dodd–Frank Act also touches upon securities (see Chapter 11), hedge funds and private equity (see Chapter 11), derivatives (see Chapter 12), and Insurance (see Chapter 13) in significant ways.

(8) Corporate Governance and Executive Compensation

Dodd–Frank delves into corporate governance issues and executive compensation issues as well, expanding the presence of the federal government in these areas. Some of this expansion will be explored in Chapter 4.

SECTION 13.   THEMES OF BANKING REGULATION

A.   REASONS FOR MAJOR BANKING LEGISLATION

New banking laws seem to arise in two situations. First, the laws can result from a major financial calamity. For instance, the National Bank Act might be said to be the result of the dire financial need to find a source of funds to finance the Civil War.

The Federal Reserve Act resulted in part from the financial panic of 1907. The Banking Act of 1933, which included the Glass–Steagall provisions separating banking and securities and the creation of a system of federal deposit insurance, was a result of the 1929 stock market crash and the ensuing bank panic and Great Depression. The 1980s legislation discussed in Chapter 2 responded to the effects of inflation on the solvency of savings and loans and banks. The Dodd–Frank Act was passed in the wake of a severe financial crisis that began in 2007 and peaked in 2008 and 2009.

The second explanation for changes in banking laws relates to legislative and judicial responses to regulatory avoidance efforts. In some cases, loopholes that have been exploited by creative lawyering have been decisively closed. In other cases, Congress or the states have reacted to permit a particular activity to go forward unfettered, as when the Gramm–Leach–Bliley Act repealed the Glass–Steagall Act because the Fed's regulatory interpretation of it permitted (although in a limited manner) affiliations between banks and securities firms.

B.   THEMES INHERENT IN BANKING LEGISLATION AND REGULATION

No matter what the reason for the adoption of the major banking statutes, they each explicate one or more themes of banking regulation

These themes have been relatively constant over the course of history in the United States.

(1) Concerns About Mixing Banking and Commerce

Banks are creatures of limited powers, and these limited powers do not extend to general commercial activities. The limitations on bank powers set forth in the National Bank Act have remained relatively constant over time. Concern about the intermingling of banking and other commercial enterprise was expressed directly in the Glass–Steagall provisions of the Banking Act of 1933 (regarding the combination of securities and banking), and again in 1956 with the adoption of the Bank Holding Company Act which limited the activities of companies affiliated with banks by common ownership to those activities closely related to banking. Even the 1999 Gramm–Leach–Bliley Act, hailed as path-breaking modernization of financial regulation, reiterated this fundamental separation by limiting the affiliates of financial holding companies to those activities that are "financial in nature." The Dodd–Frank Act contained the so-called Volcker Rule limiting the ability of banks to engage in proprietary trading and investing in or owning private equity or hedge funds.

(2) Limited Entry

With the exception of a few states who formerly embraced a "free banking" approach to bank chartering, entry into the business of banking is limited. Not all charter applications are granted. One consequence of this regulatory theme is concern for the potential abuse of this limited monopoly power.

(3) Dual Chartering and Regulatory Arbitrage

Since the creation of the national charter during the Civil War, banks have been able to freely switch charters between the state and national system. Since the advent of the Federal Reserve System, state banks have been able to join or resign from Federal Reserve System membership as they see fit.

The result is a system of regulatory arbitrage where the most favored regulator and most favored rules of regulation may be easily selected by the regulated entity. On the one hand, this may result in healthy competition by the regulatory entities to provide effective regulatory oversight. On the other hand, some have compared this system to a "race to the bottom." In either case, competition does exist and in recent years the pressure has been to ensure "competitive equality" between the charter forms, which over time has diminished the distinctions between charter types.

A related issue is whether and to what extent a national bank is subject to the laws of the state in which it operates. Interestingly, the OCC did not issue a comprehensive rule on this subject until 2004. Chapter 4 discusses this issue of federal preemption of state laws, including the Dodd–Frank Act's attempt to balance state consumer protection efforts with the supremacy of federal law with respect to federally chartered institutions. As you continue your study of banking law, you should be alert to the tension between federal and state law. The discussion of usury limits on interest rates to be charged by banks in Chapter 6 explores a federal statute governing national banks that appears deferential to state law, but which was interpreted to provide a substantial advantage to national banks over state banks, at least until federal legislative relief "leveled the playing field" for state banks.

(4) Restrictions on Geographic Expansion

Perhaps in recognition of the limited monopoly afforded by restrictions on entry, banks have until recently been severely restricted in their efforts to expand geographically. The McFadden Act, as amended in 1933, permitted national banks to branch within a state to the same extent as state banks.

The McFadden Act, however, did not contemplate interstate branching. The Bank Holding Company Act of 1956 enacted the Douglas Amendment, which also deferred to state law, in this case to determine whether a bank holding company would be permitted to own separate banks in more than one state. At the time of its passage, and for many years thereafter, there were no state laws which enabled the creation of interstate bank holding companies. The Riegle–Neal Act of 1994 did away with most restrictions on interstate banking and interstate branching. The remaining restrictions on interstate branching for banks were removed by the Dodd–Frank Act of 2010. This is one of the only regulatory themes that has been rejected by modern banking legislation.

(5) Concerns About Impermissible Concentrations of Economic Power

Politically, there seems to have always been a concern that banks might become too large and thereby wield too much economic power or wield that power in an impermissible manner. This fear is evidenced in the debates about the first Bank of the United States and its successor. The restrictions on geographic expansion may also have been justified by the notion that banks should not expand too far and should not amass too much economic power. Moreover, this concern may also reflect the potential for the limited monopoly for banks created by restrictions on entry to be misused.

The Bank Holding Company Act of 1956 expressed concern about concentrations of economic power both in its enactment of the Douglas Amendment (effectively preventing interstate banking at the time) and the limitation of the activities of bank holding companies to those closely related to banking. As will be discussed in further detail in Chapter 9, the antitrust laws that apply to banks are in some ways more stringent than those that apply to regular commercial enterprises. It is also interesting that, although the Riegle–Neal Act of 1994 opened the door for interstate banking and interstate branching, it also imposed nationwide and state-wide deposit percentage caps on bank size.

Dodd–Frank addresses financial institution size in several different ways. Systemically important institutions, which may include large financial institutions and nonbank financial companies, are subject to oversight and review by the new Financial Stability Oversight Council and may be forced to liquidate, rather than receive government assistance to survive. Financial institutions with consolidated assets in excess of $50 billion may be assessed for costs incurred during the resolution of one of these institutions by the FDIC. Dodd–Frank also expands the insured deposit cap to include all insured depository institutions and not just banks, and by fashioning a ten percent consolidated liabilities cap.

(6) Safety and Soundness Regulation

Much of the regulation that you will read about in upcoming chapters is designed to help minimize the losses caused to the federal deposit system in the event of a bank failure. As an example, federal and state laws limit the percentage of a bank's capital that may be loaned to any one borrower. This limitation is a risk-spreading technique designed to ensure that banks have not put all their eggs in one basket so that the default of one borrower will not be ruinous to a particular bank's financial health. Much of the regulation animated by a desire to reduce or police bank risk for the purpose of minimizing the loss to the federal deposit insurance fund in the event of a bank failure was put into place after the creation of federal deposit insurance in 1933. Even prior to federal deposit insurance, however, the consequences of a particular bank's insolvency could have far-reaching effects on consumer confidence and lead to bank panics and runs. Therefore, bank regulators have long been concerned with minimizing bank risk and reducing the potential ill effects of bank failures on the economy. The Financial Stability Oversight Council created by the Dodd–Frank Act may order the break up of large systemically significant financial institutions or nonbank financial companies if the company poses a grave threat to the financial stability of the United States. Regulators may also establish leverage requirements and increase risk-based capital requirements for banks.

(7) Grandfather Provisions

Many of the major statutory enactments discussed in this chapter contain so-called "grandfather" provisions designed to preserve the ability of an entity previously operating within the law to continue its operations, even though a statute might forbid anyone not already conducting that activity from starting it anew. For instance, bank holding companies that were not subject to the Bank Holding Company Act until its 1970 amendment (covering one-bank holding companies) were able to grandfather their prior permissible, now impermissible, activities. Balanced against fairness to the entity conducting a formerly permissible activity is the resulting uneven playing field, where some entities may perform an activity, yet others may not. Two sets of rules also complicates regulatory oversight.

The Gramm–Leach–Bliley Act continued this practice most recently by grandfathering unitary thrift holding companies (discussed in Chapter 2). Once an entity has received the benefit of a grandfather provision, a related question is whether that grandfathered activity may be continued if ownership of the entity later changes. Recently adopted grandfather provisions usually directly address this question.

QUESTIONS AND NOTES

1.   Are there other themes that you believe underlie banking regulation in the United States?

2.   Evaluate each of these themes and decide whether each theme should continue to play a role in bank regulation or whether it should be replaced by an alternative regulatory approach? If you believe an alternative regulatory approach would be desirable, describe that approach.

3.   Are there other examples of these themes present in the material you have read so far? Consider these themes as you study additional banking regulation in the remaining chapters.

CHAPTER TWO

THRIFT AND CREDIT UNION REGULATION

∎ ∎ ∎

SECTION 1. THE HISTORY OF THRIFT
AND CREDIT UNION REGULATION

Savings and loans, savings banks, and credit unions are depository institutions that encourage savings, or "thrift," by their customers. Their customers are consumers, rather than businesses, and often have relatively small sums of money to deposit. The use of funds by thrift institutions was, until recently, limited to home loans or other loans for consumer purposes.

A. SAVINGS AND LOANS

Building and loan associations began as state chartered institutions before the Civil War. These institutions would later be joined by savings and loan associations (S&Ls). The first building and loan association in America was Oxford Provident Building Association, created in 1831 in Frankford, Pennsylvania. Members made monthly payments until they had paid in $500. That amount was then available for a loan, and members submitted bids for the use of those funds to purchase a home.

The First Permanent Building and Loan Association was chartered in 1843 in Charleston, South Carolina. Such "permanent" plans permitted members of the associations to maintain individual accounts. This allowed members to increase their savings as they desired. Thus, members were no longer restricted to making limited and specified contributions. A further variation was added under the "Dayton" plans, which allowed dividends to be paid from the earnings of the S&L. Some S&Ls later used a "permanent capital" structure in which stock was purchased by participants. In such organizations, the savings and loan member was treated like a shareholder in a corporation.

The purpose of a building and loan or savings and loan association was described in Washington National Building, Loan & Investment Ass'n v. Stanley, 63 P. 489 (Ore. 1901):

There is no distinction between a building and loan and savings and loan association, and the two appellations were used to designate but one class of societies, viz. those doing a savings and loan or investment business on the building society plan. Associations of this kind enable persons belonging to a deserving class, whose earnings are small, and with whom the slowness of accumulation discourages the effort, by the process of gradual and enforced savings to become, either at the end of a certain period, or by anticipation of it, the owners of homesteads. It is by reason of the peculiar character of this particular class of associations, and because of their capability, when conducted upon the plan which essentially distinguishes them from other organizations and business enterprises, that they have acquired, under the law, distinct and peculiar rights and privileges. * * *

A building association, as now existing, is defined by Thompson as "a private corporation designed for the accumulation, by the members, of their money, by periodical payments into its treasury, to be invested from time to time in loans to the members upon real estate for home purposes, the borrowing members paying interest, and a preference in securing loans over other members, and continuing their fixed periodical installments in addition; all of which payments, together with the nonborrower's payments, including fines for failure to pay such fixed installments, forfeitures for such continued failure of such payments, fees for transferring stock, membership fees required upon the entrance of the member into the society, and such other revenues, go into the common fund until such time as that the installment payments and profits aggregate the face value of all the shares in the association, when the assets, after the payment of the expenses and losses, are prorated among all the members, which, in legal effect, cancels the borrower's debt, and gives the nonborrower the amount of his stock" Thompson, Bldg. Assoc. (2 ed.) § 3. * * * The societies in this country were first organized under the plan evolved in England. * * *

By the end of 1928, over 12,000 thrift institutions in the United States held assets in excess of $8 billion. Over 1,700 of those institutions, however, failed during the 1930s. The Federal Home Loan Bank Board (FHLBB) was created by the Federal Home Loan Bank Act of 1932 to create a system of regional Federal Home Loan banks (similar to the Federal Reserve System) to meet the liquidity needs of its members. Congress also created a federal chartering system for S & Ls, bringing a dual chartering system to thrifts some 70 years after it was available for banks. Congress also created the Home Owners Loan Corporation (HOLC) in 1933 to deal with the failure of thrifts and their credit crisis. HOLC provided assistance to individuals who could not meet their mortgage payments. That agency refinanced home mortgages on more than one million homes between 1933 and 1936.

Other New Deal legislation arrived, including the National Housing Act of 1934, which created the Federal Housing Administration (FHA) and the Federal Savings and Loan Insurance Corporation (FSLIC). The FHA was chartered to protect mortgage lenders by guaranteeing full repayment of defaulted loans covered by the legislation. FSLIC insurance was designed to protect small depositors at thrifts by insuring their deposits up to $2,500. Membership in FSLIC was required for federally chartered S & Ls; state chartered associations could join if they chose to do so.

WEST HELENA SAVINGS & LOAN ASS'N v. FEDERAL HOME LOAN BANK BOARD

United States Court of Appeals, Eighth Circuit, 1977.
553 F.2d 1175.

HENLEY, CIRCUIT JUDGE.

These are appeals by the Federal Home Loan Bank Board (Board) and the Federal Savings and Loan Insurance Corporation (Corporation) from a joint judgment of the United States District Court for the Eastern District of Arkansas which ordered appellants to grant deposit insurance to the plaintiffs, West Helena Savings & Loan Association (West Helena) and Woodruff County Savings & Loan Association (Woodruff) as authorized by 12 U.S.C. § 1726 (a). * * *

Both the Board and the Corporation are agencies of the United States. The Board was created by the Federal Home Loan Bank Act of 1932, 12 U.S.C. §§ 1421 et seq. Its functions include the chartering of federal savings and loan associations, and the supervision and regulations of such associations. Another of its functions is to manage and direct the Corporation which was established by Title IV of the National Housing Act of 1934, 12 U.S.C. §§ 1724 et seq.

The purpose of the Corporation is to provide insurance for savings deposits in institutions that are eligible for the insurance that the Corporation provides. 12 U.S.C. § 1725(a).

Section 1726(a) provides that the Corporation shall insure the deposits in federal savings and loan associations, and that it "may" insure the deposits in certain other types of institutions including state chartered savings and loan associations.

Section 1726(c) sets up certain criteria for the rejection of applications for insurance. An application must be rejected if the Corporation, that is to say the Board, finds that the capital of the applicant is impaired or that its financial policies or management is unsafe. An application "may" be rejected if it is found that the character or management of the applicant or its home financing policy is inconsistent with economical home financing or with the purpose of the statute. The subsection states: "In considering applications for such insurance the Corporation shall give full consideration to all factors in connection with the financial condition of applicants and insured institutions, and shall have power to make such adjustments in their financial statements as the Corporation finds to be necessary."

The applications of the plaintiffs were not rejected on the basis of the criteria specifically set out in § 1726(c) but rather on the basis of agency findings that there was no public or community need for the proposed services and that to grant the insurance would create unacceptable insurance risks for the Corporation.

The position of the Board was, and is, that [it] has a broad discretion in passing on an application for insurance filed by a state chartered institution, and that it is not limited in the exercise of its discretion to a consideration of the specific criteria mentioned in § 1726(c) and may take into consideration "all factors" that are relevant including any lack of economic need for the services that the applicant would offer to the saving and borrowing public.

The Board evidently takes the view that if there is no need for the services to be provided by a state chartered institution, that institution is not likely to succeed, and that its failure, if it occurs, will or may imperil its deposits which would be covered by the Corporation's insurance if the application for the insurance should be granted. Going a step further, the Board is also evidently of the opinion that if existing services in a given area are needlessly duplicated, the duplication may result in the failure of both institutions with a loss to the deposits of both which would have to be covered by the Corporation if the deposits in both institutions were covered by insurance granted by the Corporation. * * *

Federally chartered savings and loan associations first came into existence with the passage of the Home Owners' Loan Act of 1933, 12 U.S.C. §§ 1461 et seq., and federal insurance with respect to deposits in savings and loan and similar associations was provided by Title IV of the National Housing Act of 1934, 12 U.S.C. § 1724 et seq.

Taken together, those two statutes created and contemplate the continued existence of a dual system of savings and loan associations with some associations being chartered by the Board and with others being chartered by state regulatory agencies. And although it was not required to do so, Congress provided that state chartered institutions should be eligible for federal deposit insurance, subject to the rejection criteria appearing in 12 U.S.C. § 1726(c).

Given such a system, at least as it operates in a state like Arkansas which requires a state chartered association to obtain federal deposit insurance before commencing business and which requires that business be commenced within a limited period of time, it seems unlikely that Congress intended for the Board in evaluating an initial application tendered by such an association after obtaining its charter to re-examine the underlying question of economic need for the proposed service and related questions which bear directly upon the propriety of the chartering of the association in the first instance. * * *

The judgment of the district court [ordering defendants to grant plaintiffs deposit insurance is affirmed.]

NORTH ARLINGTON NATIONAL BANK v. KEARNY FEDERAL SAVINGS & LOAN ASS'N

United States Court of Appeals, Third Circuit, 1951.
187 F.2d 564, *cert. denied*, 342 U.S. 816.

GOODRICH, CIRCUIT JUDGE.

This case involves the question whether a Federal savings and loan association may have a branch office. * * *

The basic statute is the Home Owners' Loan Act of 1933, 12 U.S.C.A. §§ 1461–1468. Provision for Federal savings and loan associations begins with Section 1464. The statute is one of the type which states a policy, provides for the project under consideration, lays down some general rules and prohibitions and leaves details to the Board which is authorized by Section 1463. The statutory delegation of authority to the Board has been held constitutional.

The statute does not give explicit authority to the Board to permit branch offices for associations set up under its guidance. There are words and phrases in the statute on which each side, respectively, relies to show that such authority was intended or, contra, not intended to be given. As evidencing the existence of authority for branch offices is Section 1464(c). This Section limits the selection of the security on which loans can be made to property within fifty miles of an association's home office. It is argued, with plausibility, that it would be meaningless to speak of a "home" office if that was the only kind of office the association could have. * * *

What is the practice with regard to branch offices? According to a committee report on a bill to amend the present act, only six states have statutes which prohibit the establishment of branch offices by building and loan associations. Thirteen states specifically authorize them and twenty-nine have not legislated upon the subject. Congress put the duty upon the Board to decide what was the best practice and to give consideration to it. The Board did so by authorizing branches under conditions set out in its Regulations. This, it seems to us, is a very strong argument for concluding that the authority to establish branch offices is vested in the Board, and by the very terms of the Congressional enactment. * * *

Finally, there is a consideration of a point on principle which may not be amiss in this highly technical business of statutory interpretation. We were pressed with the decisions under the National Banking Act to the effect that national banks could not under the original law have branches and that the privilege given to them to establish branches has been very strictly limited. All that is tied up with the historical reasons back of the establishment of national banks and the altogether different type of administrative control exerted over them. We do not think that the analogy drawn to the limitations of the powers of the national banks is very helpful in our questions here.

These savings and loan associations do some of the same things which banks do, obviously. But they do not do a general banking business. They are set up under the declared Congressional purpose to provide thrift institutions in which people may invest their funds and to provide for the financing of homes. There is no danger of any single association becoming a giant monopoly. Its investment area is limited. * * * It may well be that it is good practice, instead of chartering a large number of associations too small to carry on successfully, to let an established concern do business through branches for the convenience of its customers. If, under all the restrictions placed upon the Board by the statute, it seems to those charged with the decision that a branch office of an established association should be permitted, we think it would be unfortunate to construe the statute to prevent that exercise of business judgment. Such a construction would tend to defeat the policy declared in the legislation. [The dismissal of the motion seeking a declaratory judgment that a branch is not permitted for a federal savings and loan association is affirmed.]

The regulatory policy for federal savings and loans was expanded to permit federal S&Ls to branch freely throughout their state, and later was broadened to permit interstate branching as well. 12 U.S.C.A. § 1464(r); 12 C.F.R. § 556.5. Unlike commercial banking, where the McFadden Act deferred to the state branching scheme to determine the scope of a national bank's ability to branch within that state, federal savings and loans were not constrained by state law limits on branching. The result was that many states felt compelled to permit state chartered S & Ls statewide branching authority. As a practical matter, as the *North Arlington* case suggests, few S&Ls—federal or state—engaged in extensive branching.

The ability of a federal S&L to preempt state law on other fronts was a significant advantage for federal S&Ls as it was for national banks vis-a-vis their state chartered counterparts.

FIDELITY FEDERAL SAVINGS & LOAN ASS'N v. DE LA CUESTA

Supreme Court of the United States, 1982.
458 U.S. 141.

MR. JUSTICE BLACKMUN delivered the opinion of the Court.

At issue in this case is the pre-emptive effect of a regulation, issued by the Federal Home Loan Bank Board (Board), permitting federal savings and loan associations to use "due-on-sale" clauses in their mortgage contracts. * * *

The Board, an independent federal regulatory agency, was formed in 1932 and thereafter was vested with plenary authority to administer the Home Owners' Loan Act of 1933 (HOLA), 48 Stat. 128, as amended, 12

U.S.C. § 1461 et seq. Section 5(a) of the HOLA, 12 U.S.C. § 1464(a) (1976 ed., Supp. IV), empowers the Board, "under such rules and regulations as it may prescribe, to provide for the organization, incorporation, examination, operation, and regulation of associations to be known as 'Federal Savings and Loan Associations.'" Pursuant to this authorization, the Board has promulgated regulations governing "the powers and operations of every Federal savings and loan association from its cradle to its corporate grave." People v. Coast Federal Sav. & Loan Assn., 98 F.Supp. 311, 316 (SD Cal. 1951).

In 1976, the Board became concerned about the increasing controversy as to the authority of a federal savings and loan association to exercise a "due-on-sale" clause—a contractual provision that permits the lender to declare the entire balance of a loan immediately due and payable if the property securing the loan is sold or otherwise transferred. Specifically, the Board felt that restrictions on a savings and loan's ability to accelerate a loan upon transfer of the security would have a number of adverse effects: (1) that "the financial security and stability of Federal associations would be endangered if . . . the security property is transferred to a person whose ability to repay the loan and properly maintain the property is inadequate"; (2) that "elimination of the due on sale clause will cause a substantial reduction of the cash flow and net income of Federal associations, and that to offset such losses it is likely that the associations will be forced to charge higher interest rates and loan charges on home loans generally"; and (3) that "elimination of the due on sale clause will restrict and impair the ability of Federal associations to sell their home loans in the secondary mortgage market, by making such loans unsalable or causing them to be sold at reduced prices, thereby reducing the flow of new funds for residential loans, which otherwise would be available." 41 Fed. Reg. 6283, 6285 (1976). The Board concluded that "elimination of the due on sale clause will benefit only a limited number of home sellers, but generally will cause economic hardship to the majority of home buyers and potential home buyers." Ibid.

Accordingly, the Board issued a regulation in 1976 governing due-on-sale clauses. The regulation, now 12 CFR § 545.8–3(f) (1982), provides in relevant part:

> "[A federal savings and loan] association continues to have the power to include, as a matter of contract between it and the borrower, a provision in its loan instrument whereby the association may, at its option, declare immediately due and payable sums secured by the association's security instrument if all or any part of the real property securing the loan is sold or transferred by the borrower without the association's prior written consent. Except as [otherwise] provided in . . . this section . . . , exercise by the association of such option (hereafter called a due-on-sale clause) shall be exclusively governed by the terms of the loan contract, and all rights and remedies of the association and borrower shall be fixed and governed by that contract." * * *

Fidelity was not notified prior to each appellee's purchase of property; when it did learn of the transfer, it gave notice of its intent to enforce the due-on-sale clause. Fidelity expressed a willingness to consent to the transfer, however, if the appellee agreed to increase the interest rate on the loan secured by the property to the then-prevailing market rate. Each appellee refused to accept this condition; Fidelity then exercised its option to accelerate the loan. When the loan was not paid, Fidelity instituted a nonjudicial foreclosure proceeding.

In response, each appellee filed suit in the Superior Court of California for Orange County. Each asserted that, under the principles announced by the California Supreme Court in Wellenkamp v. Bank of America, 582 P. 2d 970 (1978), Fidelity's exercise of the due-on-sale clause violated California's prohibition of unreasonable restraints on alienation, Cal. Civ. Code Ann. § 711 (West 1982), "unless the lender can demonstrate that enforcement is reasonably necessary to protect against impairment to its security or the risk of default." 582 P. 2d, at 977. * * *

The pre-emption doctrine, which has its roots in the Supremacy Clause, U.S. Const., Art. VI, cl. 2, requires us to examine congressional intent. Pre-emption may be either express or implied, and "is compelled whether Congress' command is explicitly stated in the statute's language or implicitly contained in its structure and purpose." Jones v. Rath Packing Co., 430 U.S. 519, 525 (1977). Absent explicit pre-emptive language, Congress' intent to supersede state law altogether may be inferred because "[the] scheme of federal regulation may be so pervasive as to make reasonable the inference that Congress left no room for the States to supplement it," because "the Act of Congress may touch a field in which the federal interest is so dominant that the federal system will be assumed to preclude enforcement of state laws on the same subject," or because "the object sought to be obtained by the federal law and the character of obligations imposed by it may reveal the same purpose." Rice v. Santa Fe Elevator Corp., 331 U.S. 218, 230 (1947).

Even where Congress has not completely displaced state regulation in a specific area, state law is nullified to the extent that it actually conflicts with federal law. Such a conflict arises when "compliance with both federal and state regulations is a physical impossibility," Florida Lime & Avocado Growers, Inc. v. Paul, 373 U.S. 132, 142–143 (1963), or when state law "stands as an obstacle to the accomplishment and execution of the full purposes and objectives of Congress," Hines v. Davidowitz, 312 U.S. 52, 67 (1941). * * *

Federal regulations have no less pre-emptive effect than federal statutes. * * *

As even the Court of Appeal recognized, the Board's intent to preempt the *Wellenkamp* doctrine is unambiguous. The due-on-sale regulation plainly provides that a federal savings and loan "continues to have the power" to include a due-on-sale clause in a loan instrument and to enforce that clause "at its option." 12 CFR § 545.8–3(f) (1982). The

California courts, in contrast, have limited a federal association's right to exercise a due-on-sale provision to those cases where the lender can demonstrate that the transfer has impaired its security. * * *

In addition, the Board recently has "[confirmed]" that the due-on-sale practices of federal savings and loans "shall be governed exclusively by the Board's regulations in pre-emption of and without regard to any limitations imposed by state law on either their inclusion or exercise." 12 CFR § 556.9(f)(2) (1982). Thus, we conclude that the Board's due-on-sale regulation was meant to pre-empt conflicting state limitations on the due-on-sale practices of federal savings and loans, and that the California Supreme Court's decision in *Wellenkamp* creates such a conflict.[1]

The question remains whether the Board acted within its statutory authority in issuing the pre-emptive due-on-sale regulation. The language and history of the HOLA convince us that Congress delegated to the Board ample authority to regulate the lending practices of federal savings and loans so as to further the Act's purposes, and that § 545.8–3(f) is consistent with those purposes. * * *

Thus, in § 5(a) of the Act, Congress gave the Board plenary authority to issue regulations governing federal savings and loans:

> "In order to provide local mutual thrift institutions in which people may invest their funds and in order to provide for the financing of homes, the Board is authorized, under such rules and regulations as it may prescribe, to provide for the organization, incorporation, examination, *operation*, and *regulation* of associations to be known as 'Federal Savings and Loan Associations', or 'Federal mutual savings banks' ..., and to issue charters therefor, giving primary consideration to the best practices of local mutual thrift and home-financing institutions in the United States." 12 U. S. C. § 1464(a)(1) (1976 ed., Supp. IV) (emphasis added).

The broad language of § 5(a) expresses no limits on the Board's authority to regulate the lending practices of federal savings and loans. * * *

As we noted above, a savings and loan's mortgage lending practices are a critical aspect of its "operation," over which the Board unquestionably has jurisdiction. Although the Board's power to promulgate regulations exempting federal savings and loans from the requirements of state law may not be boundless, in this case we need not explore the outer limits of the Board's discretion. We have no difficulty concluding that the due-on-sale regulation is within the scope of the Board's authority under the HOLA and consistent with the Act's principal purposes. * * *

MR. JUSTICE POWELL took no part in the consideration or decision of this case.

---

1. [n. 14] Because we find an actual conflict between federal and state law, we need not decide whether the HOLA or the Board's regulations occupy the field of due-on-sale law or the entire field of federal savings and loan regulation.

MADAM JUSTICE O'CONNOR, concurring.

I join in the Court's opinion but write separately to emphasize that the authority of the Federal Home Loan Bank Board to pre-empt state laws is not limitless.[2] Although Congress delegated broad power to the Board to ensure that federally chartered savings and loan institutions "would remain financially sound," ante, at 168, it is clear that HOLA does not permit the Board to pre-empt the application of all state and local laws to such institutions. Nothing in the language of § 5(a) of HOLA, which empowers the Board to "provide for the organization, incorporation, examination, operation, and regulation" of federally chartered savings and loans, remotely suggests that Congress intended to permit the Board to displace local laws, such as tax statutes and zoning ordinances, not directly related to savings and loan practices. Accordingly, in my view, nothing in the Court's opinion should be read to the contrary.

MR. JUSTICE REHNQUIST, with whom MR. JUSTICE STEVENS joins, dissenting.   ↳ state's rights

* * * In declaring the due-on-sale clause enforceable as a matter of federal law, however, the Board has departed from the approach contemplated by Congress. Although Congress has authorized the Board to regulate the lending activities of federal savings and loan associations, there is no indication in the HOLA itself, or in its legislative history, that Congress has empowered the Board to determine whether and when federal law shall govern the enforceability of particular provisions contained in mortgages concluded by federal savings and loan associations. If anything, § 8 of the FHLBA indicates that it was Congress' understanding in 1932 that the enforceability of provisions in mortgages is a matter of state law. Contract and real property law are traditionally the domain of state law. Congress did not intend to create a federal common law of mortgages.

The Board's attempt to enforce due-on-sale clauses as a matter of federal law cannot be upheld as a regulation of mortgage lending practices of federal savings and loan associations. * * * California's rule regarding due-on-sale clauses is not invalid pursuant to the Supremacy Clause simply because it makes it difficult for lenders to eliminate unprofitable mortgage loans from their portfolios.

Although the Board has concluded that the California courts' limitations upon the enforceability of due-on-sale clauses is economically unsound, I cannot agree that Congress has enabled the Board to insulate federal savings and loans from California mortgage law merely by promulgating a regulation that declares these clauses to be enforceable. Discharge of its mission to ensure the soundness of federal savings and loans does not authorize the Federal Home Loan Bank Board to intrude into the

---

2. [*] At one point in today's opinion, the Court states that "we need not decide whether the HOLA or the Board's regulations occupy ... the entire field of federal savings and loan regulation." Ante, at 159, n. 14.

domain of state property and contract law that Congress has left to the States.

―――――――

Following the opinion in the *Fidelity Federal* case, the FHLBB adopted 12 C.F.R. § 545.2, which provided that the FHLBB had "plenary and exclusive authority" to "regulate all aspects of the operations of Federal associations as set forth in section 5(a) of the Home Owners' Loan Act of 1933, 12 U.S.C. 1464," and that the "authority is preemptive of any state law purporting to address the subject of the operations of a Federal association."

[handwritten margin note: Weakened by Dodd Frank]

In 1989, the FHLBB's regulatory authority over federal savings associations was transferred to the newly created Office of Thrift Supervision (OTS). The OTS replaced § 545.2 with an even more extensive regulation, 12 C.F.R. § 560.2(a). This regulation specifically provided that "[p]ursuant to sections 4(a) and 5(a) of the HOLA" the "OTS hereby occupies the entire field of lending regulation for federal savings associations," and that "federal savings associations may extend credit as authorized under federal law, including this part, without regard to state laws purporting to regulate or otherwise affect their credit activities." This notion of field preemption provided federal savings associations with a substantial advantage over their state-chartered counterparts. See Chapter 4 for a discussion of preemption of state laws for national banks.

The Dodd–Frank Act cut back on the preemption advantage for federally chartered institutions, specifically rejecting the authorities under sections 4 and 5 of HOLA (presumably including the regulation cited above), and providing that HOLA "does not occupy the field in any area of State law." Dodd–Frank, § 1046. Dodd–Frank provides that preemption determinations under HOLA shall now be made pursuant to the same laws and standards applicable to national banks regarding State law. As discussed further, in Chapter 4, these have been affected by Dodd–Frank, and appear to reduce the ability of nationally chartered banks and savings associations to preempt state law.

B. SAVINGS BANKS

In 1797, Jeremy Bentham concluded that small savings banks were needed to allow working families to accumulate savings. He thought these institutions should be owned by their depositors in a mutual form of ownership. The first state savings banks were formed in 1816 in Pennsylvania and Massachusetts. A variation of the savings bank arrived in the 1850s in the form of "penny" or "five cent" savings banks. These institutions allowed depositors to make deposits of less than a dollar. Such savings banks were especially popular with immigrants. Until recent years, state savings banks were only chartered in seventeen northeastern states. A federal charter was not available until 1978.[3]

―――――――

3. A federal charter was available in the District of Columbia prior to 1978.

HUNTINGTON v. NATIONAL SAVINGS BANK

Supreme Court of the United States, 1877.
96 U.S. 388.

MR. JUSTICE STRONG delivered the opinion of the Court.

The bill of the complainants assumes that, as personal representatives of William S. Huntington, deceased, they have an equitable ownership of one-sixteenth part of the franchises, property, and privileges of the defendant corporation, and that, as such representatives, they are entitled to call for an account of the profits made, and to demand payment to them of one-sixteenth part of the value of the franchises and property as well as profits. Whether this assumption is well founded or not,—whether the estate of their intestate has any pecuniary interest in the corporate franchise and property, can be determined only after a careful examination of the defendant's charter. The corporation was created by an act of Congress, approved May 24, 1870, entitled "An Act to incorporate the National Union Savings Bank of the District of Columbia." By that act, George H. Plant, William S. Huntington, and twenty-one other persons named, and their successors, were declared to be a body politic and corporate, under the corporate name mentioned, having succession, capable of suing and being sued, of having a common seal, and generally of doing and performing all things relative to the object of the institution lawful for any individual or body politic or corporate to do. * * *

It is to be noticed that the charter does not authorize the creation of any corporate stock or capital, nor does it contemplate the existence of any other than the deposits which may be made. The corporators are not required to contribute any thing. There are, of consequence, no shareholders. Not a word is said in the instrument respecting any dividends of capital, or even of profits, to others than the depositors. * * * The institution having no capital stock, whatever liability, if any, there may be to the corporators must be satisfied out of the profits made from the deposits. But the charter, when conferring the power to receive money on deposit, limits it to receiving for "the use and benefit of the depositors," and directs how it may be invested. It further declares that "the income or interest of all deposits shall be divided among the depositors or their legal representatives," not among the depositors and the corporators. It is true, the income or interest is to be divided among the depositors, "according to the terms of interest stipulated;" implying, perhaps, that the dividend may be less than the interest received by the corporation; but there is nothing in the charter that indicates the excess is for the benefit of the corporators. It is to provide for the necessary expenses of the institution authorized to be paid, and perhaps to raise a contingent fund to meet possible losses. * * *

We think the complainants have mistaken the nature of the corporation. It is not a commercial partnership, nor is it an artificial being the members of which have property interests in it, nor is it strictly eleemosynary. Its purpose is rather to furnish a safe depositary for the money of those members of the community disposed to intrust their property to its keeping. It is somewhat of the nature of such corporations as church-wardens for the conservation of the goods of a parish, the college of surgeons for the promotion of medical science, or the society of antiquaries for the advancement of the study of antiquities. Its purpose is a public advantage, without any interest in its members. The title of the act incorporating it indicates its purpose; namely, an act to incorporate a national savings bank: and the only powers given to it were those we have mentioned,—powers necessary to carry out the only avowed purpose, which was to enable it to receive deposits for the use and benefit of depositors, dividing the income or interest of all deposits among its depositors or their legal representatives. It is, like many other savings institutions incorporated in England and in this country during the last sixty years, intended only for provident investment, in which the management and supervision are entirely out of the hands of the parties whose money is at stake, and which are quasi benevolent and most useful, because they hold out no encouragement to speculative dealing or commercial trading. This was the original idea of savings banks. Scratchley's Treatise on Savings Banks, passim; Grant's Law of Bankers, 571, where, in defining savings banks, it is said the bank derives no benefit whatever from any deposit, or the produce thereof. Such are savings banks in England, under the statutes of 9 Geo. IV., c. 92, sect. 2, and 26 & 27 Vict., c. 87. Very many such exist in this country. Among the earliest are some in Massachusetts, organized under a general law passed in 1834, which contained a provision like the one in the act of Congress, that the income or profit of all deposits shall be divided among the depositors, with just deduction of reasonable expenses. They exist also in New York, Pennsylvania, Maine, Connecticut, and other States. Indeed, until recently, the primary idea of a savings bank has been, that it is an institution in the hands of disinterested persons, the profits of which, after deducting the necessary expenses of conducting the business, inure wholly to the benefit of the depositors, in dividends, or in a reserved surplus for their greater security. Such, very plainly, is the defendant corporation in this case. The complainants have, therefore, no pecuniary interest in it, and no right to the relief they ask. * * *

C.   CREDIT UNIONS

"Credit unions are cooperative institutions owned by their member-customers, both borrowers and savers. They differ from the commercial banks, which are owned by the stockholders and from the mutual thrift intermediaries, which are owned by the savers alone."[4] The principal

---

4. Financial Institutions and the Nation's Economy (FINE), Discussion of Principles, Committee on Banking, Currency and Housing, H. Rep. 94th Cong., 2d Sess. (committee print) 119 (June 1976).

business of credit unions is to provide small loans to their members. The first credit union in the United States was created in 1909 by St. Marie's Parish in New Hampshire. It was founded in response to a letter written to the governors of each state by President William Howard Taft in 1908. He asked the governors to allow the creation of credit unions in their states. The Massachusetts Credit Union Law was adopted in 1909 in response to that plea. It was designed to provide an alternative to the usurious money lenders for factory workers. Three other states adopted similar legislation by 1921.

The Federal Credit Union Act was enacted in 1934 to provide for national charters for credit unions. By then, forty-one states authorized state-chartered credit unions. The National Credit Union Administration (NCUA) charters and regulates federal credit unions. The National Credit Union Share Insurance Fund (NCUSIF) was established to insure deposits in federal credit unions, and state credit unions which wished to obtain federal deposit insurance. The legislation prohibited credit unions from offering banking services to anyone other than their members. Federal credit union membership was limited to groups having a "common bond" of occupation or association or to groups within a well-defined neighborhood or rural district. The amount of unsecured loans that could be made by credit unions was limited to $400.

Credit unions were exempted from federal income taxation in 1937 because at that time other mutual thrift institutions were exempt from tax.[5] This has afforded credit unions an advantage over other depository institutions and has been the subject of extensive litigation.

LA CAISSE POPULAIRE STE. MARIE (ST. MARY'S BANK) v. UNITED STATES

United States District Court, District of New Hampshire, 1976.
425 F.Supp. 512, *aff'd*, 563 F.2d 505 (1st Cir. 1997).

BOWNES, DISTRICT JUDGE.

This is an action to recover income taxes alleged to be erroneously and illegally assessed and collected by the Internal Revenue Service. The taxpayer claims that it is an exempt organization under Section 501(c)(14)(A) of the Internal Revenue Code. Jurisdiction is conferred on this court by 28 U.S.C. § 1346(a)(1). The issue is whether the plaintiff is a "credit union" within the meaning of Section 501(c)(14)(A) of the Internal Revenue Code.

The taxpayer, La Caisse Populaire Ste. Marie (St. Mary's Bank), was the first credit union organized in the country. Its charter from the State of New Hampshire on April 9, 1909, came just six days prior to the

---

5. Mutual savings and loans and savings banks were exempted from taxation by the Revenue Act of 1913. Congress eliminated the exemption from taxation for mutual savings associations in the Revenue Act of 1951, but retained the tax exemption for credit unions without any accompanying rationale.

enactment of a general credit union statute in Massachusetts. New Hampshire did not pass a general credit union statute until 1921. * * *

In 1962, the Internal Revenue Service recommended to the Secretary that the taxpayer's exempt status be revoked because it was not being operated as a credit union. The exemption granted in 1935 was revoked in a letter dated January 14, 1966. The taxpayer paid taxes in the years 1969 through 1974 in the following amounts: $0, $4,616.70, $3,824.25, $4,724.16, $32,826.00, and $2,974.00, respectively. The taxpayer filed claims for refunds for the years in question which were disallowed. This action was commenced on December 23, 1975.

The Internal Revenue Service claims that St. Mary's was not operated as a credit union during the years in question and that it was not entitled to the exemption.

Since it is the Government's position that the plaintiff functions as a bank and not as a credit union, it is necessary to examine the history and structure of both the banking system and the credit union movement in this country and the pertinent Federal and State statutes.

The dual bank regulatory system with which we find ourselves today is a result of the holding in McCulloch v. Maryland, 17 U.S. 316 (1819), that Congress was able to charter banks under the authority of the "necessary and proper" clause of Article I and the historical regulation of banks by states, reserved to them as a police power under the Constitution. * * *

As a result, both Congress and the states may charter a variety of financial institutions. Today there are three types of federally chartered financial institutions: national associations, federal savings and loan associations, and federal credit unions.

National associations, or national banks, are primarily commercial banks. * * * All national banks are subject to the rules of the Comptroller of the Currency, an official of the Treasury Department, and all must have their deposits insured by the Federal Deposit Insurance Corporation.

Varying amounts, depending upon the size of the locality in which the bank proposes to operate, are required to be contributed to the association in return for capital stock. 12 U.S.C. § 51. National banks are permitted to form branches pursuant to state law. 12 U.S.C. § 36. Apart from the reserve requirements of the respective bank regulatory agency, national banks are permitted to make loans or investments for all of the purposes permitted to any financial institution. Traditionally, national banks, like all commercial banks, have favored short-term business loans, although they are permitted and do maintain a smaller percentage of their assets in consumer loans, real estate loans, and others.

The other noteworthy feature about national banks, and other commercial banks, is that they are permitted to accept both demand deposits and time deposits. Demand deposits are deposits of funds which are payable on demand. Time deposits cannot legally be required to be paid until a certain time or day or a certain number of days after the deposit is made. In addition to these two kinds of deposits, a third, certificates of deposit, are time deposits for longer periods of time, usually yielding higher rates of interest. Most checking accounts are demand deposits. Savings accounts are always time deposits. * * *

The Federal Home Loan Bank Board was established in 1932 by the Federal Home Loan Bank Act. 12 U.S.C. § 1421 et seq. In 1933, it was given the authority to charter and supervise federal savings and loan associations. 12 U.S.C. § 1464 et seq. Savings and loan associations, in contrast with national banks and other commercial banks, were formed by Congress:

> In order to provide local mutual thrift institutions in which people may invest their funds and in order to provide for the financing of homes.... 12 U.S.C. § 1464(a).

Savings and loan associations still keep the great bulk of their assets in home mortgages. 12 U.S.C. § 1464(c). As mutual associations, they do not raise money through the sale of capital stock, but only through the solicitation of deposits. 12 U.S.C. § 1464(b)(1) and 12 C.F.R. § 543.3. The earned surplus technically belongs to the depositors, but, because dividend rates are restricted, they only receive them in regulated amounts unless the association is liquidated. The depositor-owners do not have any control over the management of the institution which is run by a self-perpetuating board of directors. 12 C.F.R. § 543.6. * * * The Federal Savings and Loan Insurance Corporation insures all federal savings and loan associations.

1934 was a fertile year for the creation of new financial institutions. Not only did Congress create federal savings and loan associations, but it also passed the Federal Credit Union Act. Federal credit unions are now regulated by the National Credit Union Administration which also insures many state chartered credit unions. One principal difference between credit unions and other federally chartered financial institutions lies in the democratic control and management of credit unions. Although savings and loan associations are also mutual associations, depositors do not have any say in the election of the directors who compose a self-perpetuating board. 12 U.S.C. §§ 1760 & 1761 mandate democratic control of all federal credit unions. * * *

Federal credit unions are not subject to taxation under the Internal Revenue Code. 26 U.S.C. § 501(c)(1) and 12 U.S.C. § 1768. 12 U.S.C. § 1759 requires that:

> Federal credit union membership shall be limited to groups having a common bond of occupation or association, or to groups within a well-defined neighborhood, community, or rural district.

The common bond requirement, together with the statutes which specify democratic control, are what most set federal credit unions apart from federal savings and loan associations.

The Federal Credit Union Act limits the loans which can be made and the assets which can be held by an institution chartered under its auspices. The most important limitation is that a credit union may only make loans to its members. Congress has also strictly limited the authority of credit unions to make long-term, real estate, and other loans. 12 U.S.C. § 1757. * * *

Perhaps the most important distinction to the members of a federal credit union is that they not only receive their regular interest payments, but they may also receive a share of surplus. 12 U.S.C. § 1763. This is, of course, subject to the credit union's maintenance of adequate reserves and other requirements imposed by the National Credit Union Administration.

Title XXXV of the New Hampshire Revised Statutes Annotated provides for the chartering of trust companies, guarantee savings banks, mutual savings banks, building and loan associations, and credit unions.

NH RSA 392 provides for the organization of "trust companies" which are New Hampshire's commercial banks. For the sake of brevity, I will not delineate each of the aspects of "trust companies." Suffice it to say that in corporate organization (capital stock), lending authority and policy, and general investment authority and policy, they are much the same as national banks. They also have similar authority with regard to the receipt of deposits and parallel authority with regard to branching and payment of interest on deposits. The most important distinctions between "trust companies" and national banks lie in the nature of their respective regulators, examiners, and reserve requirements. "Trust companies" are also eligible for insurance by the Federal Deposit Insurance Corporation and membership in the Federal Reserve.

New Hampshire statutes provide for two types of savings banks. Mutual savings banks are found in seventeen east coast states as well as New Hampshire. Guarantee savings banks are a hybrid institution indigenous to this state. Mutual savings banks are owned by their depositors and run by a self-perpetuating board of directors similarly to federal savings and loan associations. Guarantee savings banks are owned by stockholders who elect boards of directors which are responsible for the management of the day-to-day operations of the institutions.

Savings banks are designed primarily to make real estate loans, but they are also permitted to maintain a portfolio consisting of a large variety of other conservative investments.

The deposit authority of savings banks, which must be insured by the F.D.I.C., is similar to that of federal savings and loan associations. They have historically been denied checking account authority, but have recently been permitted to offer N.O.W. accounts.

Building and loan associations, which may also call themselves "co-operative banks" or "savings and loan associations," are organized very similarly to federal credit unions in that they are democratically controlled mutual institutions. In this, they are also similar to state chartered credit unions. Building and loan associations are similar to savings banks, both "mutual" and "guarantee," in that they are primarily restricted to real estate lending. Their nonreal estate loans are more greatly restricted than those of savings banks. Their real estate loans are also closely regulated. The deposit structure is similar to those of federal savings and loan associations.

There are two principal distinctions between credit unions and building and loan associations. The first lies in their loan authority. Credit unions are granted wider authority to make diverse loans. NH RSA 394:16 provides that credit unions:

> May make loans to its members on such terms and upon such security, real or personal, as the union may vote or its by-laws prescribe.

This service is performed principally by a "Credit Committee" which is unlike anything in the building and loan statute.

The second major difference is the State's parallel to the federal requirement of "common bond."

> The by-laws shall prescribe ... the conditions of residence or occupation which qualify persons for membership. . . .

There are no cases or available legislative history to help interpret this requirement, and there was little testimony about the requirement for a "common bond" in New Hampshire State chartered credit unions.

In 1850, Herman Schulze–Delitzsch, after being removed from his position as a Justice of the Peace in Delitzsch, Prussia, in 1849 as a result of radical political beliefs, formed a "co-operative purchasing society for master shoemakers to buy leather at wholesale prices." He also formed a separate "cooperative credit society" to meet "the great need for credit among craftsmen and small shopkeepers." The loans granted by Schulze–Delitzsch type credit unions were to be for "productive purposes." They were to be made to an artisan or merchant so that he could obtain the necessary materials to make a profit. These first credit unions were democratic in nature, run by the members on a one person, one vote basis. There was no requirement of common bond. Rather, the loans, which were always unsecured, were made on the basis of character "to all 'worthy seekers after credit, not limited to any one occupation, or social class. . . .' " Unlike financial institutions today, these credit unions operated on the "unlimited liability" of their members.

Friedrick Wilhelm Raiffeisen, former mayor of Heddesdorf, created the first agricultural credit union in 1864. The Heddesdorf credit union was organized with nominal capital subscriptions from its original membership and, like the Schulze–Delitzsch credit unions, borrowed on the "unlimited liability" of the members. These agrarian credit unions were not open to anyone; only owners of "tangible assets [real property]" were permitted to join. * * *

In 1866, Luigi Luzzatti, a professor at the University of Padua, opened a cooperative bank in Milan. Luzzatti rejected the principle of unlimited liability and the Schulze–Delitzsch dependence on high-priced shares. Officers served without pay, and Schulze–Delitzsch's principle of "character credit" was employed. By 1909, People's Bank of Milan was one of the largest banking institutions in Italy, with seventy unpaid officers and one hundred salaried clerks. It had almost 25,000 members, capital of nearly $2,000,000, and savings of over $32,000,000. Rural credit unions, similar to those organized by Raiffeisen, were also established in Italy.

The credit union movement finds its North American roots in La Caisse Populaire de Levis located across the St. Lawrence River from the City of Quebec. A stenographer-reporter from the Provencial House of Commons, Alphonse Desjardins, organized the credit union at Levis in 1900. He determined that the dichotomy between urban and rural credit unions prevalent in Europe at the time, should not prevail in Canada. In rejecting the principle of "unlimited liability," he said:

> "Our population is completely opposed to the idea of unlimited responsibility," and that he would never have been able to acquire supporters if ... [he] tried to have this principle accepted. * * *

St. Mary's Cooperative Credit Association was established on November 24, 1908, by Monsignor Pierre Hevey, Pastor of St. Mary's Church on the west bank of the Merrimack River in Manchester. The "West Side" then, as now, was occupied predominantly by French speaking Canadian immigrants and their descendants who had come to textile mills. With the assistance of Alphonse Desjardins, organizer of La Caisse Populaire de Levis, the Monsignor organized this country's first credit union which was incorporated less than one year later, on April 6, 1909, by an Act of the State Legislature. Chapter 303 of the Laws of 1909 define the authority of the corporation to accept deposits from and give loans to its members exclusively. Membership was initially restricted to residents of Manchester, but this provision was removed from St. Mary's charter in 1925. In 1917, the name of the institution was changed to La Caisse Populaire Ste. Marie to which the Legislature added the anglicized name "St. Mary's Bank," in 1925. * * *

At the same time as Monsignor Hevey was organizing his credit union, Edward Filene, a Boston merchant, was busy establishing a system of credit unions which was to become the nucleus of this country's credit union movement. By July, 1974, there were 23,028 state and federal credit unions with 28,700,000 members. * * *

St. Mary's is structurally the same as every other credit union which we have examined by statute or which has been discussed by any witness. There is no "capital stock." The shares owned by the members cannot appreciate in value. The cost of a share is $5.00 which is the same as it was when St. Mary's was established. Because St. Mary's will buy back any share for $5.00, there can be no gain or loss. This is the same structure which was initially approved as being "without capital stock" so that credit unions could be exempted under the general exemption for cooperative institutions.

St. Mary's is operated for "mutual purposes" within the meaning of the Code. Both borrowers and savers alike are required to be members of the institution and participate in the earnings of the institution by receiving dividends declared on capital shares. The members are the only owners.

St. Mary's is operated "without profit." The earnings are turned over to the members annually or invested on their behalf. The plaintiff is a nonprofit institution because all the earnings of the institution, after the deduction from net earnings of necessary and prudent reserves, are distributed to the members, borrowers and savers alike, or held for the benefit of all members in a surplus account for the purpose of dealing with future contingencies. * * *

Judgment is entered for the plaintiff in an amount equal to the amount of taxes paid for the years 1969 through 1974 * * * plus interest.

The credit union industry was the most rapidly growing segment of the financial system in the middle of the 1970s. At one point, there were more than 23,000 credit unions. The National Credit Union Administration permitted federal credit unions to expand their membership beginning in 1982 to include multiple unrelated employer groups. This reversed a longstanding interpretation that had restricted membership in national credit unions under the Federal Credit Union Act to persons having a common bond of occupation, association or residential area. The expanded operations of federal credit unions under the revised interpretation did not go unnoticed by banks jealous of the federal income tax exemption enjoyed by credit unions.

NATIONAL CREDIT UNION ADMINISTRATION v. FIRST NATIONAL BANK & TRUST CO.

Supreme Court of the United States, 1998.
522 U.S. 479.

MR. JUSTICE THOMAS delivered the opinion of the Court, except as to footnote 6.

Section 109 of the Federal Credit Union Act (FCUA), 48 Stat. 1219, 12 U.S.C. § 1759, provides that "[f]ederal credit union membership shall be limited to groups having a common bond of occupation or association, or to groups within a well-defined neighborhood, community, or rural district." Since 1982, the National Credit Union Administration (NCUA), the agency charged with administering the FCUA, has interpreted § 109 to permit federal credit unions to be composed of multiple unrelated employer groups, each having its own common bond of occupation. In this case, respondents, five banks and the American Bankers Association, have challenged this interpretation on the ground that § 109 unambiguously requires that the *same* common bond of occupation unite every member of an occupationally defined federal credit union. * * *

In 1934, during the Great Depression, Congress enacted the FCUA, which authorizes the chartering of credit unions at the national level and provides that federal credit unions may, as a general matter, offer banking services only to their members. Section 109 of the FCUA, which has remained virtually unaltered since the FCUA's enactment, expressly restricts membership in federal credit unions. In relevant part, it provides:

> "Federal credit union membership shall consist of the incorporators and such other persons and incorporated and unincorporated organizations, to the extent permitted by rules and regulations prescribed by the Board, as may be elected to membership and as such shall each, subscribe to at least one share of its stock and pay the initial installment thereon and a uniform entrance fee if required by the board of directors; *except that Federal credit union membership shall be limited to groups having a common bond of occupation or association, or to groups within a well-defined neighborhood, community, or rural district.*" 12 U.S.C. § 1759 (emphasis added).

Until 1982, the NCUA and its predecessors consistently interpreted § 109 to require that the *same* common bond of occupation unite every member of an occupationally defined federal credit union. In 1982, however, the NCUA reversed its longstanding policy in order to permit credit unions to be composed of multiple unrelated employer groups. See IRPS 82–1, 47 Fed. Reg. 16775 (1982). It thus interpreted § 109's common bond requirement to apply only to each employer group in a multiple-group credit union, rather than to every member of that credit union. See IRPS 82–3, 47 Fed. Reg. 26808 (1982). Under the NCUA's new interpretation, all of the employer groups in a multiple-group credit union had to be located "within a well-defined area," ibid., but the NCUA later revised this requirement to provide that each employer group could be located within "an area surrounding the [credit union's] home or a branch office that can be reasonably served by the [credit union] as determined by NCUA." IRPS 89–1, 54 Fed. Reg. 31170 (1989). Since 1982, therefore, the NCUA has permitted federal credit unions to be composed of wholly unrelated employer groups, each having its own distinct common bond.
* * *

By its express terms, § 109 limits membership in every federal credit union to members of definable "groups." Because federal credit unions may, as a general matter, offer banking services only to members, see, e.g., 12 U.S.C. §§ 1757(5)–(6), § 109 also restricts the markets that every federal credit union can serve. Although these markets need not be small, they unquestionably are limited. The link between § 109's regulation of federal credit union membership and its limitation on the markets that federal credit unions can serve is unmistakable. Thus, even if it cannot be said that Congress had the specific purpose of benefiting commercial banks, one of the interests "arguably . . . to be protected" by § 109 is an interest in limiting the markets that federal credit unions can serve. This interest is precisely the interest of respondents affected by the NCUA's interpretation of § 109. As competitors of federal credit unions, respondents certainly have an interest in limiting the markets that federal credit unions can serve, and the NCUA's interpretation has affected that interest by allowing federal credit unions to increase their customer base. [Therefore, respondents have standing to seek review of § 109.] * * *

Turning to the merits, we must judge the permissibility of the NCUA's current interpretation of § 109 by employing the analysis set forth in Chevron, U.S.A., Inc. v. Natural Resources Defense Council, Inc., 467 U.S. 837 (1984). Under that analysis, we first ask whether Congress has "directly spoken to the precise question at issue. If the intent of Congress is clear, that is the end of the matter; for the court, as well as the agency, must give effect to the unambiguously expressed intent of Congress." Id., at 842–843. If we determine that Congress has not directly spoken to the precise question at issue, we then inquire whether the agency's interpretation is reasonable. Because we conclude that Congress has made it clear that the *same* common bond of occupation must unite each member of an occupationally defined federal credit union, we hold that the NCUA's contrary interpretation is impermissible under the first step of *Chevron*.

As noted, § 109 requires that "federal credit union membership shall be limited to groups having a common bond of occupation or association, or to groups within a well-defined neighborhood, community, or rural district." Respondents contend that because § 109 uses the article "a"— "i.e., one"—in conjunction with the noun "common bond," the "natural reading" of § 109 is that all members in an occupationally defined federal credit union must be united by one common bond. Petitioners reply that because § 109 uses the plural noun "groups," it permits multiple groups, each with its own common bond, to constitute a federal credit union.

Like the Court of Appeals, we do not think that either of these contentions, standing alone, is conclusive. * * *

First, the NCUA's current interpretation makes the phrase "common bond" surplusage when applied to a federal credit union made up of multiple unrelated employer groups, because each "group" in such a credit union already has its own "common bond." * * * Put another way, in the multiple employer group context, the NCUA has read the statute as though it merely stated that "[f]ederal credit union membership shall be limited to occupational groups," but that is simply not what the statute provides. * * *

Finally, by its terms, § 109 requires that membership in federal credit unions "shall be limited." The NCUA's interpretation—under which a common bond of occupation must unite only the members of each unrelated employer group—has the potential to read these words out of the statute entirely. The NCUA has not contested that, under its current interpretation, it would be permissible to grant a charter to a conglomerate credit union whose members would include the employees of every company in the United States. Nor can it: Each company's employees would be a "group," and each such "group" would have its own "common bond of occupation." Section 109, however, cannot be considered a *limitation* on credit union membership if at the same time it permits such a *limitless* result.

For the foregoing reasons, we conclude that the NCUA's current interpretation of § 109 is contrary to the unambiguously expressed intent of Congress and is thus impermissible under the first step of *Chevron*. The judgment of the Court of Appeals is therefore affirmed.

Justice O'CONNOR, with whom Justices STEVENS, SOUTER, AND BREYER join, dissenting. * * *

———————

This opinion proved to be quite unpopular. Congress adopted the Credit Union Membership Access Act of 1998 and reversed the Supreme Court's decision by permitting multiple groups each with their own common bond to join together in a single credit union. The statute, however, restricted the size of each group (in a multi-group credit union) to no more than 3,000. 12 U.S.C.A. § 1759(d).

In American Bankers Ass'n v. National Credit Union Administration, 271 F.3d 262 (D.C. Cir. 2001), the D.C. Circuit upheld NCUA regulations implementing the Credit Union Membership Access Act of 1998. The ABA challenged the NCUA rule for failure to count family and household members within the 3000—member limit, but the D.C. Circuit determined that the statute did not unambiguously require that family and household members be counted towards the 3,000—member limit. The court also upheld a rule that the membership of grandfathered federal credit unions existing as of August 7, 1998, was not limited to those who had joined the group as of that date, but could include new members if they joined a *group* that was in existence on that date.

The NCUA recognizes single common-bond credit unions, composed of one group with a common bond of occupation or association; multiple common bond credit unions with more than one group if each group has within that group a common bond of occupation or association and the number of members of each group when it is first included does not exceed 3,000; and a community credit union that consists of people or organizations "within a well-defined local community, neighborhood, or rural district." 12 U.S.C.A. § 1759(b). By the end of 206, almost one-quarter of all credit unions were based on community charters. Also eligible for membership in a credit union are members of the immediate family or household of an eligible credit union member. Id. at § 1759(e)(1). Once a person becomes a member of a credit union, he or she remains a member until he or she withdraws or is expelled from membership. Id. § 1759(e)(2).

D. OTHER INSTITUTIONS

Other financial institutions that conducted banking operations appeared in America. The "Morris Plan" was created in 1910 by Arthur Morris at the Fidelity Loan & Trust Company in Norfolk, Virginia. Under the Morris plan, small one-year loans were made to workers. The loans were repaid in monthly or weekly installments. Before a loan would be granted, the borrower had to have two cosigners and prove he was creditworthy. Interest was deducted in advance from the loan proceeds. The interest rate was supposed to be six percent, but with the advance deduction and the use of weekly or monthly payments, actual rates were often in excess of eleven percent. Within ten years, Morris Plan banks were operating in thirty-seven states. So-called "labor banks" were also organized by trade unions for their members. There were thirty-three such banks in the United States by 1927 with assets of over $120 million.

Congress established a Postal Savings Bank system in 1910. These banks provided small depositors with a safe place for their savings. The Postal Savings Banks were allowed to keep five percent of their deposits as a reserve fund in the United States Treasury, and they could invest up to thirty percent of their deposits in government securities. In 1911, postal savers were offered the opportunity to exchange their savings account deposits for 2.5 percent, twenty-year government bonds. The bonds dropped almost immediately in price as interest rates rose. Even so, by 1916, there were some $80 million of deposits in the Postal Savings Banks. The Postal Savings System was discontinued in 1966.[6]

SECTION 2.   SAVINGS AND LOAN CRISIS

A. DESTRUCTIVE INFLATIONARY PRESSURES

In the late 1970s, inflation increased market interest rates and seriously impaired the earnings of banks and thrifts. Interest rates became increasingly volatile in 1979 when the Fed announced that it would attempt to control inflation by restricting the growth in the money supply, rather than by maintaining interest rates. One effect of inflation was that depositors withdrew their funds from depository institutions, where interest rates were capped by Regulation Q at 5 1/4% for banks and 5 1/2% for thrifts,[7] and invested the funds in money market mutual funds. In March of 1980, those funds were paying the Treasury bill rate of return, which

---

6. The remaining 580,000 accounts were transferred to the Department of the Treasury in 1967. In 1983, Congress enacted a one-year statute of limitations for the filing of claims for unpaid accounts formerly maintained in the Postal Savings System.

7. The slight differential for thrifts was intended to assist in attracting deposits to the thri industry for home mortgage lending.

was between fourteen and fifteen percent. "To meet withdrawal demands, some depository institutions borrowed money at high market interest rates or sold, at large discounts, assets earning below-market interest rates, such as low-interest-rate mortgage loans."[8] By 1981, most thrifts were losing money. Eighty-one thrifts failed that year, and over 250 failed in 1982.

BISCAYNE FEDERAL SAVINGS & LOAN ASS'N v. FEDERAL HOME LOAN BANK BOARD

United States Court of Appeals, Eleventh Circuit, 1983.
720 F.2d 1499, *cert. denied*, 467 U.S. 1215 (1984).

FAY, CIRCUIT JUDGE.

This case is a consolidated appeal from two orders entered in the United States District Court for the Southern District of Florida. It has its origin in a dispute over the Federal Home Loan Bank Board's (FHLBB or "the Board") appointment, pursuant to 12 U.S.C. § 1729(b) (1982), of the Federal Savings and Loan Insurance Corporation (FSLIC) as federal receiver for a federally chartered association, Biscayne Federal Savings and Loan Association ("Biscayne"). * * *

Biscayne began experiencing financial difficulties with the rise of interest rates in the late 1970's. These difficulties were endemic to the savings and loan ("S & L") industry, as the historical practice by S & Ls of accepting savers' deposits, paying interest at low fixed rates on those deposits and then reinvesting the deposits in long-term loans with slightly higher fixed rates left the S & Ls vulnerable to the effects of the recent inflationary spiral. Many of these institutions were unable to overcome the changes in the financial market which resulted from the rising interest rates and widespread deregulation of that market. Investors in the late 1970's began moving their funds out of S & Ls and into other liquid investments which produced higher rates of return. As funds were depleted from the S & Ls, most of those institutions were unable to make new loans and were forced to borrow money elsewhere at high market rates to support their existing loan commitments.

Caught up amid the industry upheaval, Biscayne in July 1981 reported the first annual loss in its history, and its positive net worth of $31,850,000 began to erode. In light of the continuing losses projected, Kaufman & Broad, Inc., a multinational corporation and Biscayne's majority shareholder, contacted the FHLBB to discuss possible strategies for recapitalizing Biscayne. From July of 1981 through March of 1983, Biscayne, through Kaufman & Broad, and the Board negotiated unsuccessfully in search of a mutually acceptable plan to save Biscayne from receivership. During that time, Biscayne's net worth dropped from a positive $24 million to a negative $30 million.

---

8. Lissa Lamkin Broome, The Influence of Enhanced Thrift Institution Powers on Commercial Bank Market Expansion, 67 N.C. L. Rev. 795, 800 (1989).

At 2:05 p.m. on April 6, 1983, after Biscayne's net worth had dropped below a record negative $30 million, the Board appointed the FSLIC as receiver for Biscayne pursuant to 12 U.S.C. § 1729(b) (1982) on the grounds that Biscayne was insolvent and in an unsafe and unsound condition. It is undisputed that Biscayne's negative net worth as of this date constituted statutory insolvency as defined in 12 U.S.C. § 1464(d)(6)(A)(i) (1982). Shortly thereafter, the FSLIC as receiver took possession of the property and assets of Biscayne and conveyed them to a new federal mutual association, New Biscayne Federal Savings and Loan Association of Miami ("New Biscayne"). Within hours after the FSLIC had taken possession, Biscayne and Kaufman & Broad as its principal shareholder filed an action pursuant to 12 U.S.C. § 1464(d)(6)(A) seeking an order requiring the Board to remove the receiver. Joined as defendants were the Board and the FSLIC in both its receivership and corporate capacities. The plaintiffs also filed a motion for a temporary restraining order (TRO) which would prevent the Board from acting upon Biscayne's assets. On April 12, 1983, after conducting several hearings on preliminary motions, the district court entered an order which denied Biscayne's motion for a TRO but which enjoined the Board and the FSLIC from selling or otherwise disposing of Biscayne's assets pending the outcome of a trial on the merits. The defendants FHLBB and the FSLIC immediately appealed from that order. * * *

We find that in actions brought under § 1464(d)(6)(A), the sole question properly before the district court and this Court is whether a statutory ground authorizing the appointment of the FSLIC exists. The statute, while authorizing a role for the courts in review of appointment decisions, does not expressly define the scope of judicial review. However, the limits of such a review seem clearly apparent: a determination as to whether one of the statutory grounds has been met. When one of the stated grounds relied upon by the Board is statutory insolvency, as is the case here, the issue for the courts should be a straightforward one: whether the association in question was statutorily insolvent at the time of the FSLIC's appointment.

In this case statutory insolvency was established at the first pre-trial hearing in the district court, since plaintiffs at that time stipulated to the fact of Biscayne's insolvency as of April 6, 1983. Any allegations by plaintiffs as to Biscayne's liquidity at that time or as to its potential to pull itself out of its dire circumstances are simply irrelevant. Section 1464, in our opinion, gives courts *very* limited jurisdiction, permitting a suit by an association subject to the Board's intervention for solely one purpose— that of ascertaining whether a statutory ground exists to support the Board's action. The statute does not require the Board to negotiate with or set guidelines for restructuring a failing association. The undisputed satisfaction of a statutory ground for the appointment of a receiver, coupled with the fact that there was no finding by the trial court that the Board's "outrageous conduct" in any way contributed to Biscayne's insolvent status as of April 6, thus renders the district court without authority to proceed further. * * *

In Count III the plaintiff contends that the Board, in view of the protracted negotiations between Biscayne and its staff and the absence of any exigent circumstances surrounding Biscayne's financial straits, should have undertaken a less drastic remedy than receivership for Biscayne. * * * As we emphasized above, there is nothing in the statute at issue here which authorizes a court to second-guess the Board's choice of action as to a failing savings and loan association once the requirements of § 1729(b) and, by incorporation, § 1464, have been met with regard to that association. The discretion available under this legislation has been delegated to the Board, not the courts.

[handwritten margin note: deference to the Board]

———

The woes suffered by depository institutions in times of inflation were not limited to thrifts. Bank failures increased as well. The National Bank of San Diego, with almost $1 billion in deposits, failed in December of 1973. The Bank of the Commonwealth in Detroit had to be rescued by the FDIC. First Pennsylvania Bank, the oldest bank in the United States, began to fail in April of 1980. The bank had used short-term borrowings and deposits to fund its purchase of long-term bonds. In order to rescue First Pennsylvania Bank, a group of banks agreed to loan it $500 million and to extend a credit line of another $1 billion.

B. THE FIRST ROUND OF LEGISLATIVE RESPONSES

Congress responded at first with legislation designed to increase the ability of thrifts to attract deposits and to generate additional and higher earnings. This legislative period was marked by a general loosening of the traditional asset and liability powers of thrifts. Banks also benefitted from much of this loosening of restrictions. This response proved inadequate to stem the increasing tide of thrift and bank failures. Congress later concluded that some institutions had misused the privileges the first round of legislation granted them. A second round of legislation followed that strengthened bank and thrift regulatory supervision and enforcement, placing a premium on strong capital.

The first round of legislation occurred in three pieces: The Financial Institutions Regulatory and Interest Rate Control Act of 1978 (FIRIRCA), the Depository Institutions Deregulation and Monetary Control Act of 1980 (DIDMCA), and the Garn–St Germain Depository Institutions Act of 1982 (Garn–St Germain). In FIRIRCA, banking regulators authorized the issuance of six-month money market certificates by depository institutions. These certificates required a minimum investment of $10,000, and their maximum interest rates varied with the rate on Treasury bills. This

[handwritten margin note: money mkt certs   not capped]

allowed large investors to receive a market interest rate on their idle funds.

DIDMCA created the Depository Institutions Deregulation Committee (DIDC) to facilitate the elimination of the Regulation Q federal limitations on maximum rates of interest payable on deposits. 12 U.S.C. §§ 3501, 3502. The DIDC removed existing ceilings on interest rates for certain deposits. Interest could still not be paid on commercial checking accounts, but banks could issue certificates of deposit in negotiable form to institu-tional borrowers; this resulted in the creation of a secondary market in those instruments. DIDMCA also authorized depository institutions, including thrifts and credit unions, to offer NOW accounts—negotiable orders of withdrawal (the functional equivalent of checks) drawn on an interest-bearing savings account. These accounts effectively permitted the payment of interest on checking accounts for consumers. The amount of deposit insurance coverage offered by the FDIC and FSLIC was increased from $40,000 to $100,000 per account in an effort to attract large deposits back into depository institutions.

The lifting of interest rate ceilings on deposits provided the opportunity for commercial banks and thrifts to compete for funds at market rates with other institutions. Deposit brokers assisted the S & Ls in that effort. Before 1980, the FHLBB had limited brokered deposits to five percent of an S & L's total deposits, but that limit was later eased.

Once deposit interest caps were lifted, depository institutions needed to be able to earn interest rates on their loans that would be high enough to offset the increasing cost of deposits in times of inflation. Thrifts were granted increased lending authority to augment other changes being made to expand their traditional mortgage lending base.[9]

LISSA LAMKIN BROOME
THE INFLUENCE OF ENHANCED THRIFT INSTITUTION POWERS ON COMMERCIAL BANK MARKET EXPANSION

67 N.C. L. Rev. 795 (1989).

* * * Thrift institutions were especially disadvantaged by inflation. Rising market interest rates made deposits more costly, yet the statutory requirement that thrifts devote the principal portion of their assets to long-term, fixed-rate mortgage loans constrained earnings from those deposits. Existing home mortgage loans could not be repriced to meet the increasing costs of attracting deposits. * * *

The Monetary Control Act also granted federally chartered thrifts opportunities to make short-term loans to help alleviate their mismatch in

---

9. Initially, thrifts were prohibited from making mortgages on property outside a 50 mile radius from their home office, but that limit was extended to 100 miles in 1960. In 1970, thrifts were allowed to lend statewide; nationwide lending was permitted in 1983.

deposit and loan maturities. The Act gave federally chartered thrifts the power to invest a limited percentage of their assets in secured or unsecured consumer loans and loans secured by improved nonresidential real estate. In addition, the Act granted federally chartered thrifts trust and fiduciary powers and the authority to provide credit card services. Finally the Act granted federal savings banks the authority to devote a small percentage of their assets to commercial loans and to offer demand deposits to those commercial loan customers.

Apparently finding the 1980 measures insufficient, Congress enacted the Garn–St Germain Act in 1982 to grant thrifts even greater powers. This Act expanded consumer loan authority for federal thrifts to thirty percent of assets and enlarged nonresidential real estate loan authority to forty percent of assets. Finally, the Act authorized federal thrifts to devote up to ten percent of assets to secured or unsecured loans for commercial purposes and to offer non-interest-bearing demand deposits to their commercial loan customers. * * *

Congress recognized in the Garn–St Germain Act that the financial condition of some depository institutions was so poor that only special measures might preserve these institutions. Accordingly, the Act authorized, in certain circumstances, the acquisition of a failed thrift or bank by either a bank holding company or a savings and loan holding company on an interstate basis overriding other federal statutory provisions that might limit such interstate and interindustry acquisitions.

The 1980 and 1982 legislation also affected the powers of state-chartered thrifts in the majority of states that had "wild card" provisions authorizing state thrifts to engage in those activities permitted their federally chartered counterparts. Many of the states without wild card provisions authorized similar extensive powers for their state-chartered thrifts through specific legislation.

The enhancement of thrift powers in the 1980 and 1982 legislation gave thrifts the ability to offer products and services that previously had been provided exclusively by commercial banks. These products and services included checking accounts, nonresidential real estate loans, nonmortgage consumer loans (including credit card loans), commercial loans, and the ability to exercise trust and fiduciary powers. * * *

As S&Ls' capital positions continued to weaken, the FHLBB reduced the capital requirement from 5% to 4% of assets in 1980, and to 3% in 1982. In addition, the Board encouraged the use of so-called "regulatory accounting practices" (RAP), a departure from generally accepted accounting practices (GAAP).

The Federal Home Loan Bank Board encouraged mergers of healthy institutions with financially troubled S&Ls. Over 700 mergers occurred between 1981 and 1982, but this did not stop the industry's decline. The financial difficulties of S&Ls continued to mount, raising concerns that the Federal Savings and Loan Insurance Corporation (FSLIC) would not have sufficient funds to pay insured deposits. In March 1982, Congress passed a joint resolution stating that the full faith and credit of the United States would stand behind FSLIC and the FDIC.

Thrifts were successful in attracting deposits once the Regulation Q interest rate limits were phased out. Thrift deposits increased by sixty percent between 1983 and 1986. This continued the pressure on S&Ls to broaden their search for investments with a higher rate of return. Thrift managers concluded that the best way to regain profitability was to increase the spread between interest rates paid on insured depositor funds and the amount received from the investment of those funds. That was accomplished by placing depositor funds into high risk investments that offered a chance for a higher rate of return. State regulators encouraged such activity by loosening restrictions on the investment powers of thrifts. Two of the most progressive states in that regard were California and Texas. California relaxed its restrictions to allow thrifts to invest in stock and debt instruments of corporations up to twenty-five percent of the thrift's gross capital. However, no more than ten percent of a thrift's investments could be made in any one corporation. This opened the door for investment in "junk" (now called high-yield) bonds by thrifts.

S&Ls became a favorite dumping ground for junk bonds. S&Ls owned about seven percent of outstanding junk bonds at one point. Those holdings were concentrated into a few large S&Ls. Columbia Savings of Beverly Hills, California, in particular, helped finance various corporate raiders through junk bond purchases with insured deposits of customers. It announced a loss of $591 million at the end of the 1980s. The so-called "go-go thrifts" of this era began investing in a broad range of speculative investments that included oil drilling operations. S&Ls bought worthless assets from their own executives and cronies in "trash-for-cash" deals. Brokered deposits funded much of this growth.

Cracks in the S&L industry's profitability continued to widen. In 1984, FSLIC paid out some $2.5 billion to depositors as a result of thrift insolvencies. By then, over thirty percent of all FSLIC insured institutions were operating at a loss. Over 700 S&Ls became insolvent in 1985. S&Ls lost some $7 billion in 1987. The crisis was exacerbated by changes in accounting standards that allowed the S&Ls to mask the magnitude of their problems. In the early stages of the crisis, the government's strategy was to change regulatory accounting principles to overstate capital and understate the extent of insolvency in the thrift industry. This reduction of capital reserves allowed thrifts to grow explosively without increasing their capital base. This soon led to problems and the regulators began to revise their course.

At the end of the 1980s, collapsing real estate values exposed the extent of the problems facing S&Ls, and hundreds of S&Ls failed. A majority of the distressed thrift associations were in California and the

Southwest, particularly Texas. Those failures were caused in many cases by irresponsible investment activities. Vernon Savings and Loan Association in Texas was one of the worst abusers of the loosened restrictions. Vernon invested in high risk real estate projects using funds obtained through deposit brokers. At first, Vernon was highly profitable, but losses then mounted. Members of its board of directors and management were later indicted for fraud. Their enormous questionable expenditures included a beach house and personal travel. One Vernon executive, Don Dixon, took a two-week culinary tour of France at the S&L's expense, and he bought jets and other luxuries. When Vernon was taken over by the government, ninety-six percent of its loans were in default. Taxpayers were stuck with a bill of $1.3 billion.

American Diversified Savings Bank in California held over $1.1 billion in federally insured assets. Of those assets, $800 million were used to make worthless loans. North American Savings and Loan Association failed in 1988. The individuals that organized this entity sold properties through it for $40 million that they bought for just $3.65 million. The American Savings & Loan Association in California, controlled by Charles Knapp, had $6.6 billion in mortgage backed securities in its portfolio in 1984. The S&L sustained large losses on those securities when interest rates rose. Centrust Savings Bank in Miami bought $1.4 billion in junk bonds from Drexel Burnham. The disaster following deregulation of the S&Ls was called the "greatest scandal in the history of American banking."[10]

IN THE MATTER OF CHARLES H. KEATING, JR.

Director's Order, Office of Thrift Supervision, 1993.
1993 WL 724714 (O.T.S.).

The failure of Lincoln Savings and Loan Association, Irvine, California ("Lincoln"), which will cost the taxpayers an estimated $2.6 billion, resulted in large measure from insider abuses, including those that are the subject of this enforcement proceeding. Lincoln was the wholly owned subsidiary of its holding company, American Continental Corporation ("ACC").

Charles H. Keating, Jr. ("Keating" or "Respondent") was the Chairman of the Board and controlling shareholder of ACC at all relevant times, and he was also President and Chief Executive Officer of ACC from September 1981 through May 1985. Keating's domination of the holding company enabled him to control Lincoln and use it—and its federal deposit insurance guarantee—as if it were his private coffer.

In the matter before the Acting Director, the Special Trial Division ("Enforcement Counsel") of the Office of Thrift Supervision ("OTS") seeks an order against Keating to cease and desist and directing restitution and an order of prohibition based on two transactions evidencing

---

10. Robert Emmet Long, Banking Scandals: The S&Ls and BCCI 9 (1993).

egregious insider abuse. The record conclusively demonstrates that Keating deliberately manipulated Lincoln for his personal financial benefit in defiance of his fiduciary responsibilities and with a disregard for the law and for the institution's safety and soundness.

First, Keating personally and, in combination with others, caused certain Lincoln subsidiaries to loan funds to the Hotel Pontchartrain Limited Partnership ("HPLP") on terms disastrous for the lenders. HPLP was a tax shelter in which Keating, his immediate family and other officers and directors of ACC, Lincoln, and its subsidiaries were limited partners. The subsequent failure of HPLP to repay the loan resulted in losses to Lincoln of approximately $24.2 million.

Second, motivated by his desire to sell his ACC stock, Keating directed officers and directors of ACC and Lincoln to cause an Employee Stock Ownership Plan established for the benefit of ACC and Lincoln employees (the "ESOP") to borrow $20 million. An essential element of the transaction was Lincoln's pledge of assets and guarantee of $15 million of the ESOP's debt. ACC, however, appointed the ESOP's Trustee, and ACC and Keating controlled the Administrative Committee that was responsible for making decisions on behalf of the ESOP. The ESOP used the proceeds of the loan to purchase ACC stock from insiders. When the ESOP defaulted on its obligations following ACC's bankruptcy, Lincoln lost approximately $12.2 million. * * *

Keating's conduct involved reckless disregard for banking laws and regulations, willful and continuing disregard for the safety and soundness of Lincoln, and conclusively demonstrates his unfitness to participate in the conduct of the affairs of Lincoln or any other depository institution. Based on the administrative record and the applicable statutory standards, the Acting Director concludes that a cease and desist order requiring restitution of $36,398,738.76 and a prohibition order should issue against Respondent. * * *

Bank failures also continued. In 1982, the failure of Penn Square Bank, a small shopping center bank in Oklahoma, threatened the entire banking system. The oil embargo had made energy lending popular, and Penn Square had grown rapidly through sales to other banks of "participations" in loans made to oil businesses. Continental Illinois, a large Chicago bank, purchased over $1 billion in loan participations from Penn Square. Chase Manhattan Bank purchased another $275 million; "SeaFirst", a Seattle bank, purchased several hundred million dollars; Michigan National Bank had about $200 million; and Northern Trust Company of Chicago had another $125 million of participations from Penn Square. Banking regulators closed Penn Square on July 5, 1982, when it became clear that its portfolio of loans was largely uncollectible. The FDIC announced that only deposits of up to $100,000 would be protected by the government. This was the first time the FDIC had not rescued a failing institution and protected all of the depositors and creditors, regardless of deposit size or insurance limits. Some 140 credit unions, 48 savings and loans, and 47 commercial banks had substantial unsecured deposits at the Penn Square Bank when it closed.

Among the hardest hit banks, Seafirst had to be merged with the Bank of America. A run began on deposits at Continental Illinois, and concerns were raised about Manufacturers Hanover Bank, where another run began. A group of banks extended a $5.5 billion line of credit to the Continental Illinois Bank to ease this dangerous situation. The Treasury added another $2 billion, but Continental Illinois had other problems. A run by depositors on that bank's assets began on May 9, 1984. On a single day, $1 billion in funds from Asia were withdrawn from the bank. A rescue of Continental Illinois was led by Morgan Guaranty. That institution, and several other banks, made $4.5 billion available to Continental in order to restore confidence in its viability. Continental was then the seventh largest bank in the country, and the government could not let it fail, lest confidence in the entire financial system be undermined. Such a failure, it was feared, would drag down at least sixty other banks. The Fed loaned Continental Illinois $8 billion and announced that all depositors would be paid, regardless of their deposit size. The total amount of support given to Continental Illinois exceeded $12 billion, but the run on Continental Illinois continued. An effort to merge Continental with other large banks failed. The FDIC then effectively nationalized Continental by taking control of its equity capital. The government removed management, and stability was restored.

Continental's problems exposed a new danger in the financial system. The bank had only about $4 billion of insured deposits when it ran into financial difficulties. An additional $36 billion in deposits at the bank were not insured because they were business checking or correspondent banking accounts with balances in excess of the insurance limit. Most of those funds were owned by large institutional investors. Withdrawals by those institutions could quickly impair the liquidity of even the largest bank. The institutions were aware of the danger to their uninsured deposits, and began a run on Continental. That bank run was different from those experienced early in the century. Instead of small depositor lines forming at teller windows, modern institutions could be drained of funds almost instantly as banks and other institutions withdrew funds by electronic wire transfers.

Problems continued in the banking industry. BankAmerica Corp. had been the largest, most profitable bank in the world in 1980. Six years later, it posted a loss of more than $1 billion. Between 1980 and 1985, the Bank of America had to write off over $4 billion in bad loans and an additional $7 billion in Latin American loans were in doubt. Other large money center banks had similar problems, and additional stress fractures appeared. Over forty banks failed each year during the middle of the 1980s. The number of "problem" depository institutions on the FDIC "watch" list rose substantially. In 1984, the FDIC had a list of over 500

"Problem" banks – no gold star for you

problem banks; that number soon increased to 800. By 1986, over 1,000 institutions were on the FDIC watch list.

C. THE SECOND ROUND OF LEGISLATIVE RESPONSES: CONGRESS GETS TOUGH

In 1987, Congress passed the Competitive Equality Banking Act (CEBA). This act recapitalized FSLIC, which had experienced massive losses from the rash of thrift insolvencies. The amount pledged by Congress was, however, too little, too late. In 1989, FSLIC was abolished by the Financial Institutions Reform, Recovery, and Enforcement Act (FIRREA) and its deposit insurance function was assumed by the FDIC. The legislation directed the FDIC to create and regulate two separate deposit insurance funds—the Bank Insurance Fund (BIF) to insure the deposits of banks and the Savings Association Insurance Fund (SAIF) to insure the deposits of savings associations. "Savings association" was the new term coined in FIRREA for savings and loans and savings banks. The federal regulatory structure for savings associations was revamped with a new agency, the Office of Thrift Supervision (OTS), replacing the FHLBB. The OTS was made part of the Department of Treasury in tandem with the Treasury-supervised OCC. The powers of state chartered savings and loans were limited to those powers Congress had authorized for federally chartered savings associations. Finally, FIRREA created the Resolution Trust Corporation (RTC). This temporary government agency was charged with the management and disposal of the assets of failed institutions. The RTC began its business with $125 billion in government funding, which grew over time to $160 billion.

FIRREA also permitted bank holding companies to purchase healthy thrift institutions. The hope was perhaps that banks would find thrift acquisition an attractive way to expand deposits.[11] Bank acquisitions of thrifts were not very significant. Banks could grow faster through mergers with other banks, which were usually larger than thrifts. Barriers to interstate banking were breaking down, affording banks expansion opportunities in new markets. Many savings and loans were still organized in mutual form, which also complicated the purchase process.

Congress enacted the Crime Control Act of 1990, which included Title XXV, known as the Comprehensive Thrift and Bank Fraud Prosecution and Taxpayer Recovery Act of 1990. This Act expanded the ability of federal regulators to combat financial fraud.

In 1991, the Federal Deposit Insurance Corporation Improvement Act (FDICIA) was passed. It recapitalized the FDIC, which had experienced massive losses from bank and thrift failures. FDICIA reasserted the importance of adequate capital for depository institutions and instituted an enforcement scheme based on prompt corrective action for institutions

---

11. See Lissa Lamkin Broome, Private Market Solutions to the Savings and Loan Crisis: Bank Holding Company Acquisitions of Savings Associations, 59 Fordham L. Rev. S111 (1991).

with declining capital. The statute also established a system of risk-based assessments for deposit insurance, rather than a flat rate for each depository institution. FDICIA placed restrictions on brokered deposits and limited the activities of state chartered banks as principal to those permitted for national banks.

Ultimately, inflationary pressures eased. The insolvent depository institutions were sold to healthy institutions, with some assets being retained and later sold by the RTC. In the five-year period following the enactment of FIRREA, 747 thrifts with $403 billion of assets were closed or sold. The RTC completed its mission and was closed in 1995, one year ahead of schedule. The statutory reforms put in place by FIRREA and FDICIA placed much tighter controls over depository institutions and attempted to deal with problem institutions before they were hopelessly insolvent. A great deal of litigation took place pursuant to the new statutes.

SPIEGEL v. RYAN

United States Court of Appeals, Ninth Circuit, 1991.
946 F.2d 1435, *cert. denied*, 503 U.S. 970 (1992).

NORRIS, CIRCUIT JUDGE.

In 1989 Congress enacted the Financial Institutions Reform, Recovery and Enforcement Act ("FIRREA"), Pub. L. No. 101–73, 103 Stat. 183 (1989). Among other things, FIRREA created the Office of Thrift Supervision ("OTS") to take over many of the savings and loan regulatory tasks previously handled by the Federal Home Loan Bank Board, which the statute abolished. Congress also armed the OTS with expanded powers to deal with the crisis that had gripped the nation's savings and loan industry. In this appeal we resolve a dispute over the OTS's statutory authority to issue a temporary cease and desist order requiring a former officer of a savings and loan association to make restitution in the sum of $21 million pending an administrative hearing to determine whether a permanent cease and desist order should issue. We also consider whether the Temporary Order constituted a pre-hearing deprivation of property that violated due process of law.

On November 28, 1989, the OTS launched a formal investigation of Columbia Savings and Loan Association ("Columbia") and Thomas Spiegel ("Spiegel"), its former chairman and chief executive officer. On July 5, 1990, the OTS issued a "Notice of Charges and Hearing and Notice of Intention to Remove and Prohibit, and to Direct Restitution, and Notice of Assessment of Money Penalty" ("Notice of Charges"). This notice, *inter alia*, alleged that Spiegel misappropriated corporate assets and committed other violations of banking laws, and set September 4, 1990 as the date for the commencement of an administrative hearing to determine whether the OTS should issue a permanent cease and desist order against Columbia and/or Spiegel. On the same day, the OTS issued a "Temporary Order to Cease and Desist" (the "Temporary Order"), which required Spiegel, *inter alia*, to make restitution to Columbia in the amount of approximately $21 million, by no later than 12 o'clock noon the next day, July 6. The Temporary Order provided that this restitution could be accomplished by a cash payment to Columbia, the establishment of an escrow account, or the posting of a letter of credit or bond.

On July 6, Spiegel filed a complaint in the United States District Court for the Central District of California seeking injunctive relief from the Temporary Order. * * *

The Temporary Order required that Spiegel make restitution in an amount exceeding $21 million, or else face daily-accruing money penalties. The order gave him the option of paying Columbia cash, establishing an escrow account, or posting a bond or letter of credit, pending the outcome of the administrative proceedings determining whether the OTS would issue a permanent order. The district court held that the Temporary Order violated the due process clause. We disagree. * * *

Spiegel argues that he was entitled to a predeprivation hearing. As a general rule, it is true that due process requires a hearing before a person may be deprived of her property. See Fuentes v. Shevin, 407 U.S. 67, 90 (1972). "In a few limited situations," however, the Supreme Court has "allowed outright seizure without opportunity for a prior hearing." Id. at 90–91. We must determine, then, whether this case presents an " 'extraordinary situation[]' that justif[ies] postponing notice and opportunity for a hearing." Id. at 90. * * *

We also agree with the district court that Congress, in authorizing temporary restitution orders pending an administrative hearing, acknowledged a need for prompt action against officers and directors formally charged by the OTS with misconduct harmful to a troubled savings institution. In this case, the temporary restitution order was based upon findings by the OTS's examiners that Spiegel caused Columbia to lend $28 million to a personal friend without adequate collateral, resulting in a loss to Columbia of $5 million, and that he caused Columbia to purchase four condominiums, a jet airplane and a collection of 100 guns, all for his personal enjoyment. In addition, he was charged with accepting inflated compensation, including a $2.4 million bonus in 1989. A year later, shortly after his departure as chairman and chief executive officer, Columbia's financial condition had deteriorated to the point that it was insolvent in the amount of $215 million. In light of the gravity of the charges against Spiegel, it was not unreasonable for the OTS to issue the Temporary Order simultaneously with the Notice of Charges in order to avoid the risk that he would dissipate his assets or attempt to put them beyond the government's reach. * * *

We disagree, however, with the district court's decision that the Temporary Order did not provide "substantial assurance that the deprivation is not baseless or unwarranted." *Mallen*, 486 U.S. at 240. Rather, we agree with the OTS that "substantial assurance" that the charges were not "baseless or unwarranted" was provided by a combination of factors:

the OTS was required to meet specific statutory requirements before issuing the order, the decision to issue the order was made by the head of the agency expert in these matters, and his decision was supported by detailed findings of Spiegel's misconduct following a long investigation by the OTS's examiners, the results of which were submitted to the district court under penalty of perjury. * * *

We, therefore, conclude that the State in this case "has kept strict control over its monopoly of legitimate force," *Fuentes*, 407 U.S. at 91, and hold that the OTS' prehearing deprivation of property does not violate due process under *Fuentes*. * * *

RYMER, CIRCUIT JUDGE, with whom HALL, CIRCUIT JUDGE, joins, concurring. * * *

———

The RTC sold the assets of the failed S&Ls through an army of lawyers, banks, insurance companies and real estate brokers. In just one year, the RTC had disposed of the assets of more than 340 insolvent S&Ls and received more than $110 billion from those sales.

FIRREA mandated a get-tough attitude on capital and accounting practices. Enforcement of the new rules forced many thrifts to recognize that prior regulatory practices had masked their insolvency.

UNITED STATES v. WINSTAR CORP.

Supreme Court of the United States, 1996.
518 U.S. 839.

MR. JUSTICE SOUTER delivered the Opinion of the Court.[12]

The issue in this case is the enforceability of contracts between the Government and participants in a regulated industry, to accord them particular regulatory treatment in exchange for their assumption of liabilities that threatened to produce claims against the Government as insurer. Although Congress subsequently changed the relevant law, and thereby barred the Government from specifically honoring its agreements, we hold that the terms assigning the risk of regulatory change to the Government are enforceable, and that the Government is therefore liable in damages for breach.

We said in Fahey v. Mallonee, 332 U.S. 245, 250 (1947), that "banking is one of the longest regulated and most closely supervised of public callings." That is particularly true of the savings and loan, or "thrift," industry, which has been described as "a federally-conceived and assisted system to provide citizens with affordable housing funds." H. R. Rep. No. 101–54, pt. 1, p. 292 (1989) (House Report). Because the contracts at issue in today's case arise out of the National Government's efforts over the last

---

12. [eds.] Justice O'Connor did not join Parts IV–A and IV–B.

decade and a half to preserve that system from collapse, we begin with an overview of the history of federal savings and loan regulation.

The modern savings and loan industry traces its origins to the Great Depression, which brought default on 40 percent of the Nation's $20 billion in home mortgages and the failure of some 1,700 of the Nation's approximately 12,000 savings institutions. In the course of the debacle, Congress passed three statutes meant to stabilize the thrift industry [and created the FHLBB, the federal charter for savings and loans, and the FSLIC]. * * *

The resulting regulatory regime worked reasonably well until the combination of high interest rates and inflation in the late 1970's and early 1980's brought about a second crisis in the thrift industry. Many thrifts found themselves holding long-term, fixed-rate mortgages created when interest rates were low; when market rates rose, those institutions had to raise the rates they paid to depositors in order to attract funds. When the costs of short-term deposits overtook the revenues from long-term mortgages, some 435 thrifts failed between 1981 and 1983.

The first federal response to the rising tide of thrift failures was "extensive deregulation," including "a rapid expansion in the scope of permissible thrift investment powers and a similar expansion in a thrift's ability to compete for funds with other financial services providers." Breeden, Thumbs on the Scale: The Role that Accounting Practices Played in the Savings and Loan Crisis, 59 Ford. L. Rev. S71, S72–S74 (1991) (describing legislation permitting nonresidential real estate lending by thrifts and deregulating interest rates paid to thrift depositors). Along with this deregulation came moves to weaken the requirement that thrifts maintain adequate capital reserves as a cushion against losses, see 12 CFR § 563.13 (1981), a requirement that one commentator described as "the most powerful source of discipline for financial institutions." Breeden, supra, at S75. The result was a drop in capital reserves required by the Bank Board from five to four percent of assets in November 1980, see 45 Fed. Reg. 76111, and to three percent in January 1982, see 47 Fed. Reg. 3543; at the same time, the Board developed new "regulatory accounting principles" (RAP) that in many instances replaced generally accepted accounting principles (GAAP) for purposes of determining compliance with its capital requirements. According to the House Banking Committee, "[t]he use of various accounting gimmicks and reduced capital standards masked the worsening financial condition of the industry, and the FSLIC, and enabled many weak institutions to continue operating with an increasingly inadequate cushion to absorb future losses." The reductions in required capital reserves, moreover, allowed thrifts to grow explosively without increasing their capital base, at the same time deregulation let them expand into new (and often riskier) fields of investment.

While the regulators tried to mitigate the squeeze on the thrift industry generally through deregulation, the multitude of already-failed savings and loans confronted FSLIC with deposit insurance liabilities that threatened to exhaust its insurance fund. According to the General Accounting Office, FSLIC's total reserves declined from $6.46 billion in 1980 to $4.55 billion in 1985, when the Bank Board estimated that it would take $15.8 billion to close all institutions deemed insolvent under GAAP. By 1988, the year of the last transaction involved in this case, FSLIC was itself insolvent by over $50 billion. And by early 1989, the GAO estimated that $85 billion would be needed to cover FSLIC's responsibilities and put it back on the road to fiscal health. In the end, we now know, the cost was much more even than that. See, e. g., Horowitz, The Continuing Thrift Bailout, Investor's Business Daily, Feb. 1, 1996, p. A1 (reporting an estimated $140 billion total public cost of the savings and loan crisis through 1995).

Realizing that FSLIC lacked the funds to liquidate all of the failing thrifts, the Bank Board chose to avoid the insurance liability by encouraging healthy thrifts and outside investors to take over ailing institutions in a series of "supervisory mergers." Such transactions, in which the acquiring parties assumed the obligations of thrifts with liabilities that far outstripped their assets, were not intrinsically attractive to healthy institutions; nor did FSLIC have sufficient cash to promote such acquisitions through direct subsidies alone, although cash contributions from FSLIC were often part of a transaction. Instead, the principal inducement for these supervisory mergers was an understanding that the acquisitions would be subject to a particular accounting treatment that would help the acquiring institutions meet their reserve capital requirements imposed by federal regulations.

Under GAAP there are circumstances in which a business combination may be dealt with by the "purchase method" of accounting. The critical aspect of that method for our purposes is that it permits the acquiring entity to designate the excess of the purchase price over the fair value of all identifiable assets acquired as an intangible asset called "goodwill." In the ordinary case, the recognition of goodwill as an asset makes sense: a rational purchaser in a free market, after all, would not pay a price for a business in excess of the value of that business's assets unless there actually were some intangible "going concern" value that made up the difference. * * * Goodwill recognized under the purchase method as the result of an FSLIC-sponsored supervisory merger was generally referred to as "supervisory goodwill."

Recognition of goodwill under the purchase method was essential to supervisory merger transactions of the type at issue in this case. Because FSLIC had insufficient funds to make up the difference between a failed thrift's liabilities and assets, the Bank Board had to offer a "cash substitute" to induce a healthy thrift to assume a failed thrift's obligations. * * *

Supervisory goodwill was attractive to healthy thrifts for at least two reasons. First, thrift regulators let the acquiring institutions count supervisory goodwill toward their reserve requirements under 12 CFR § 563.13

(1981). This treatment was, of course, critical to make the transaction possible in the first place, because in most cases the institution resulting from the transaction would immediately have been insolvent under federal standards if goodwill had not counted toward regulatory net worth. From the acquiring thrift's perspective, however, the treatment of supervisory goodwill as regulatory capital was attractive because it inflated the institution's reserves, thereby allowing the thrift to leverage more loans (and, it hoped, make more profits). * * *

[T]he rationale for recognizing goodwill stands on its head in a supervisory merger: ordinarily, goodwill is recognized as valuable because a rational purchaser would not pay more than assets are worth; here, however, the purchase is rational only because of the accounting treatment for the shortfall. * * * As some in Congress later recognized, "[g]oodwill is not cash. It is a concept, and a shadowy one at that. When the Federal Government liquidates a failed thrift, goodwill is simply no good. It is value-less. That means, quite simply, that the taxpayer picks up the tab for the shortfall." 135 Cong. Rec. 11795 (1989) (remarks of Rep. Barnard). To those with the basic foresight to appreciate all this, then, it was not obvious that regulators would accept purchase accounting in determining compliance with regulatory criteria, and it was clearly prudent to get agreement on the matter. * * *

Although the results of the forbearance policy, including the departures from GAAP, appear to have been mixed, it is relatively clear that the overall regulatory response of the early and mid–1980's was unsuccessful in resolving the crisis in the thrift industry. As a result, Congress enacted the Financial Institutions Reform, Recovery, and Enforcement Act of 1989 (FIRREA), Pub. L. 101–73, 103 Stat. 183, with the objects of preventing the collapse of the industry, attacking the root causes of the crisis, and restoring public confidence.

FIRREA made enormous changes in the structure of federal thrift regulation by (1) abolishing FSLIC and transferring its functions to other agencies; (2) creating a new thrift deposit insurance fund under the Federal Deposit Insurance Corporation (FDIC); (3) replacing the Bank Board with the Office of Thrift Supervision (OTS), a Treasury Department office with responsibility for the regulation of all federally insured savings associations; and (4) establishing the Resolution Trust Corporation (RTC) to liquidate or otherwise dispose of certain closed thrifts and their assets. More importantly for the present case, FIRREA also obligated OTS to "prescribe and maintain uniformly applicable capital standards for savings associations" in accord with strict statutory requirements. § 1464(t)(1)(A). In particular, the statute required thrifts to "maintain core capital in an amount not less than 3 percent of the savings association's total assets," § 1464(t)(2)(A), and defined "core capital" to exclude "unidentifiable intangible assets," § 1464(t)(9)(A), such as goodwill. Although the reform provided a "transition rule" permitting thrifts to count "qualifying supervisory goodwill" toward half the core capital requirement, this allowance was phased out by 1995. §§ 1464(t)(3)(A). According to the House Rep., these tougher capital requirements reflected a congressional judgment that "to a considerable extent, the size of the thrift crisis resulted from the utilization of capital gimmicks that masked the inadequate capitalization of thrifts." HR,310.

The impact of FIRREA's new capital requirements upon institutions that had acquired failed thrifts in exchange for supervisory goodwill was swift and severe. * * *

This case is about the impact of FIRREA's tightened capital requirements on three thrift institutions created by way of supervisory mergers. Respondents Glendale Federal Bank, FSB, Winstar Corporation, and The Statesman Group, Inc., acquired failed thrifts in 1981, 1984, and 1988, respectively. After the passage of FIRREA, federal regulators seized and liquidated the Winstar and Statesman thrifts for failure to meet the new capital requirements. Although the Glendale thrift also fell out of regulatory capital compliance as a result of the new rules, it managed to avoid seizure through a massive private recapitalization. Believing that the Bank Board and FSLIC had promised them that the supervisory goodwill created in their merger transactions could be counted toward regulatory capital requirements, respondents each filed suit against the United States in the Court of Federal Claims, seeking monetary damages on both contractual and constitutional theories. That court granted respondents' motions for partial summary judgment on contract liability, finding in each case that the Government had breached contractual obligations to permit respondents to count supervisory goodwill and capital credits toward their regulatory capital requirements. * * *

The Federal Circuit found that "[t]he three plaintiff thrifts negotiated contracts with the bank regulatory agencies that allowed them to include supervisory goodwill (and capital credits) as assets for regulatory capital purposes and to amortize that supervisory goodwill over extended periods of time." 64 F.3d, at 1545. * * *

We accept the Federal Circuit's conclusion that the Government breached these contracts when, pursuant to the new regulatory capital requirements imposed by FIRREA, 12 U.S.C. § 1464(t), the federal regulatory agencies limited the use of supervisory goodwill and capital credits in calculating respondents' net worth. 64 F.3d, at 1545. * * *

The Government argues for reversal, first, on the principle that "contracts that limit the government's future exercises of regulatory authority are strongly disfavored; such contracts will be recognized only rarely, and then only when the limitation on future regulatory authority is expressed in unmistakable terms." Brief for United States 16. Hence, the Government says, the agreements between the Bank Board, FSLIC, and respondents should not be construed to waive Congress's authority to enact a subsequent bar to using supervisory goodwill and capital credits to meet regulatory capital requirements.

The argument mistakes the scope of the unmistakability doctrine. The thrifts do not claim that the Bank Board and FSLIC purported to bind Congress to ossify the law in conformity to the contracts; they seek no injunction against application of FIRREA's new capital requirements to them and no exemption from FIRREA's terms. They simply claim that the Government assumed the risk that subsequent changes in the law might prevent it from performing, and agreed to pay damages in the event that such failure to perform caused financial injury. The question, then, is not whether Congress could be constrained but whether the doctrine of unmistakability is applicable to any contract claim against the Government for breach occasioned by a subsequent Act of Congress. The answer to this question is no. * * *

The Government's final line of defense is the sovereign acts doctrine, to the effect that " '[w]hatever acts the government may do, be they legislative or executive, so long as they be public and general, cannot be deemed specially to alter, modify, obstruct or violate the particular contracts into which it enters with private persons.' " Horowitz v. United States, 267 U.S. at 461 (quoting Jones v. United States, 1 Ct. Cl. 383, 384 (1865)). Because FIRREA's alteration of the regulatory capital requirements was a "public and general act," the Government says, that act could not amount to a breach of the Government's contract with respondents.

The Government's position cannot prevail, however, for two independent reasons. The facts of this case do not warrant application of the doctrine, and even if that were otherwise the doctrine would not suffice to excuse liability under this governmental contract allocating risks of regulatory change in a highly regulated industry. * * *

We affirm the Federal Circuit's ruling that the United States is liable to respondents for breach of contract. Because the Court of Federal Claims has not yet determined the appropriate measure or amount of damages in this case, we remand for further proceedings.

––––––––––

Although a majority of the *Winstar* cases have been resolved, relatively few have been resolved by settlement rather than litigation. As of the beginning of 2006, the government had paid out over $1.6 billion in cases in which the plaintiffs sought an aggregate of $50 billion in damages. The government believes the costs of defending these suits—estimated at between $430 million and $513 million—is money well-spent. Ethan Zindler, Decade later, Goodwill Suits Still Stuck in Court, Am. Banker, Jan. 24, 2006.

SECTION 3. THE FINANCIAL CRISIS AND THE DODD–FRANK ACT

The subprime mortgage crisis that began in 2007[13] was generated in part by adjustable rate mortgage loans (ARMs), many of which were originated by savings associations and savings banks that defaulted in large numbers as the Federal Reserve Board increased interest rates and as initial "teaser" rates were reset. Some large savings associations failed as a result of those exposures.

WaMu failed, gov't sold it to JPMorgan

The Office of Thrift Supervision (OTS) witnessed a number of failures on its watch during the subprime crisis. Washington Mutual, the largest savings and loan in the United States failed and was seized by the OTS on September 25, 2008. Its operations were sold to JPMorgan Chase. Countrywide Financial operated the nation's third largest savings and loan and was taken over by the Bank of America in 2008 when it appeared that Countrywide was about to fail. Another massive failure occurred at IndyMac, which cost taxpayers some $11 billion after it was taken over by the OTS. These institutions had engaged in reckless lending practices that led to their failure. Those failures thoroughly discredited OTS.

The Dodd–Frank Act abolished the Office of Thrift Supervision. The OTS authority over savings and loan holding companies was transferred to the Fed, and the OCC received OTS's powers over federal savings associations.

SECTION 4. REGULATION OF THRIFTS AND CREDIT UNIONS

A. REGULATORY STRUCTURE

In 1978, Congress made it possible for state savings banks to convert to a federal savings bank charter in the Financial Institutions Regulatory and Interest Rate Control Act of 1978. This was the first recognition of a federal charter for savings banks. In 1989, the creation of the OTS included the ability to charter a de novo (or new) federal savings bank. A federal savings bank is also regulated by the OTS. In the aftermath of the savings and loan crisis, many states created a state savings bank charter. These state savings banks are more bank-like than thrift-like and are regulated by the state bank regulatory authority and at the federal level by the FDIC. 12 U.S.C. § 1813(e).

fed.

st.

Savings associations are defined as including federal savings and loans, federal savings banks, and state chartered savings and loans. 12

---

13. For a further description of these events see Jerry W. Markham, VI A Financial History of the United States: The Subprime Crisis (2006–2009) (2011).

U.S.C. § 1813(b). In 1989, the regulatory authority over these institutions was transferred from the Federal Home Loan Bank Board to a new agency within the Department of the Treasury, the Office of Thrift Supervision (OTS). The Dodd–Frank Act abolished the OTS and provides for the transfer of its supervisory and rulemaking authority over federal savings associations to the Office of the Comptroller of the Currency (OCC), the regulator of nationally chartered banks. Dodd–Frank Act, § 312. The OCC is required to designate a Deputy Comptroller for the supervision and examination of federal savings associations. The OCC also receives the OTS rulemaking authority over state chartered savings associations, although their supervision at the federal level was transferred to the Federal Deposit Insurance Corporation (FDIC), which also is the federal supervisor of state chartered banks. The transfer from the OTS to the OCC and FDIC is to be completed by one year after Dodd–Frank's enactment, or on July 21, 2011. Id. § 311.[14]

B. CHARACTERISTICS OF THRIFTS AND CREDIT UNIONS

In 1980, there were 4,319 total thrifts and over half of those institutions were state chartered. In 2009, by contrast, the number of total thrifts was down to 1,173 and only forty percent were state chartered.

Savings associations and savings banks may be stock corporations or mutual institutions. In 1980, there were 3,211 mutual thrifts. In 2010, however, there remained only 506 mutual thrifts. The most recent OTS regulations on conversions may be found at 12 C.F.R. pts. 563b. The conversion process (sometimes called "demutualization") is described in Section E. infra.

In 1980, there were over 15,000 credit unions. In 2009, that number had declined to 7,554. All credit unions are mutual institutions. Some credit unions have converted to a mutual thrift charter because of difficulties in meeting the membership requirements, a desire for broader lending authority, or the wish to convert to a stock institution in the future. The NCUA amended its regulations on conversions of credit unions to mutual savings banks to require disclosure of changes in voting rights, potential benefits to insiders and the possibility of a subsequent conversion to a stockholder owned institution. Some have suggested that these changes are designed to discourage conversion.

---

14. The Secretary of the Treasury may, after consultation with other federal financial regulators, communicates to the Senate Committee on Banking and the House Financial Services Committee a later transfer date that is not more than 18 months after enactment. Dodd–Frank, § 311.

C. POWERS

The lending and investment powers of federal savings associations is set forth at 12 U.S.C.A. § 1464. There are still limitations on the lending and investment authority of federal thrifts that make the thrift charter more restrictive than the bank charter. For instance, commercial loans are limited to twenty percent of a federal thrift's assets, consumer loans (other than home mortgages, credit cards, and education loans) are limited to thirty-five percent of assets, and nonresidential real property loans may not exceed 400% of the thrift's capital. State thrift powers are set forth under state law, but since FIRREA in 1989, state thrift powers may not exceed the powers of federal thrifts. The Dodd–Frank Act does not eliminate the savings association charter. All existing OTS regulations, orders, and other issuances are transferred and shall be enforced by the relevant agency until they are "modified, terminated, set aside, or superseded" by the OCC, a court, or by operation of law. Id. § 316. It will be interesting to see whether thrifts remain as separate entities or whether over time most convert to a bank charter since savings associations will be regulated by a bank regulator (the OCC or the FDIC) rather than the OTS as a regulator focused exclusively on savings associations.

The adoption of field preemption by the OTS and nationwide branching without any state control of branching within the state enhanced the appeal of the federal savings association charter as a nationwide platform for delivering retail credit products. In, 2003, J.P. Morgan & Co. established a federal savings bank for just this purpose. This strategy was abandoned, however, after J.P. Morgan merged with Bank One and converted its JPMorgan Bank from a New York state bank charter to a national bank charter. The Dodd–Frank Act provides, however, that federal savings associations no longer benefit from field preemption and are subject to the same, new preemption standards applicable to national banks, Dodd–Frank, § 1045. Although a savings association that becomes a bank may retain its branches that it operated immediately before the conversion to a bank charter, id. § 341, a national or state bank is also permitted under Dodd–Frank to establish interstate branches with regard to state requirements for interstate branching, id. § 613.

Credit unions are even more restricted in their lending authority. 12 U.S.C.A. § 1757. Loans may only be made to credit union members, who must meet quite specific membership requirements. Loans to members for business purposes are limited in the aggregate to the lesser of 1.75 times the credit union's actual net worth or 12.25% of the credit union's total assets. 12 U.S.C.A. § 1757a; 12 C.F.R. § 723.16. State chartered credit unions are subject to similar limitations under state law.

Regulation of Depository Institutions[15] 2009

Type	Number	Primary Regulator	Federal Regulator
Commercial Banks	6,669		
National	1,426	OCC	OCC
State Member	834	State	FRB
State Nonmember	4,409	State	FDIC
Savings Associations and Savings Banks	1,173		
Federal	701	OTS/OCC*	OTS/OCC*
State Savings Associations	64	State	OTS/FDIC*
State Savings Banks	408	State	FDIC
Credit Unions	7,554		
Federal	4,714	NCUA	NCUA
State	2,840	State	NCUA

* Under the Dodd–Frank Act, the supervisory functions of the OTS will be transferred to the OCC and the FDIC.

QUESTIONS AND NOTES

1. State Farm Bank, FSB, a federal savings bank headquartered in Bloomington, Illinois and owned by State Farm Insurance Company, operates nationwide through its insurance company's agents, but without any traditional bank branches. The OTS general counsel issued a legal opinion on October 25, 2004, which State Farm Bank relied upon to argue that it need not register its independent securities agents selling jumbo certificates of deposit (in amounts of greater than $100,000) under the laws of eighteen separate states. OTS, P–2004–7, Authority of a Federal Savings Association to Perform Banking Activities Through Agents Without Regard to State Licensing Requirements, Oct. 25, 2004, available at <www.ots.treas.gov/docs/5/560404.pdf>. After intense opposition to this plan was expressed by state officials, State Farm initially agreed to register its independent agents under the applicable securities laws in the eighteen states. The company then litigated the preemption issue in Connecticut, Ohio, and the District of Columbia. The first court to rule, the United States District Court of Connecticut, sided with the OTS and ruled that state licensing laws are preempted as to State Farm's exclusive agents. State Farm Bank, F.S.B. v. Burke, 445 F.Supp.2d 207 (D. Conn. 2006). After reading the OCC's new preemption standard under Dodd-Frank in Chapter 4 which will be applicable to federal savings associations regulated by the OCC, consider whether the state securities agent registration requirement would be a "state consumer financial law" under § 1044 of Dodd–Frank and subject to the new OCC preemption standard.

15. Sources: FDIC Statistics on Banking, available at <www2.fdic.gov/idasp/index.asp> (More Key Statistics) (as of July 22, 2010); OTS: 2009 Fact Book, available at <http://www.ots.treas.gov/_files/481165.pdf> (as of Dec. 31, 2009); NCUAA 2009 Yearend Statistics for Federally Insured Credit Unions <http://www.ncua.gov/Resources/Reports/statistics/Yearend2009.pdf> (as of Dec. 31, 2009).

2. What do you think will happen to the thrift industry upon the transfer of the OTS rulemaking and supervisory functions to the OCC and FDIC? Will savings associations convert to bank charters for the benefit of greater lending authority? Will the separate regulations relating to savings associations be maintained by the OCC and FDIC or replaced with their bank regulatory standards?

3. The requirements relating to field of membership for a federal credit union charter, Chartering and Field of Membership Manual, are available at Appendix B to 12 C.F.R. § 701. In addition to common bonds of occupation, association, and community, the Manual describes Low–Income Credit Unions and Credit Unions Serving Underserved Areas.

4. The nonprofit and tax-exempt status of credit unions allows them to offer interest rates on loans that are lower than and deposit interest rates that are higher than their bank competitors. A July 23, 2007 report from the Treasury Department concluded that taxing credit unions would result in an additional $19 billion in government revenue over the next ten years. See also U.S. Government Accountability Office, Credit Unions: Greater Transparency Needed on Who Credit Unions Serve and on Senior Executive Compensation Arrangements GAO–07–29 (Nov. 30, 2006).

5. Credit unions accumulate capital by retaining earnings over time. As for other financial institutions, there is a required ratio they must maintain of capital to assets. If deposits and loans of a credit union grow more rapidly than retained earnings, the credit union risks falling below its minimum capital requirements. Currently, a credit union's net worth must be 7% of its assets for the credit union to be considered well-capitalized. 12 U.S.C. § 1790d. This is higher than the minimum capital required for a bank to be considered well-capitalized. The National Credit Union Administration has proposed reducing the capital levels so that a capital to asset ratio of 5% or above would constitute well-capitalized. Legislative change would be necessary to weight the assets against which capital must be held according to risk, as is done for banks and thrifts.

6. Some credit unions have converted to a mutual thrift charter. Part of the motivation for conversions may be to take advantage of the lower capital requirements for thrift institutions, or the possibility that if the mutual thrift later converts to a stock thrift, additional capital to fuel expansion could be raised through stock issuance. In 2005, the NCUA invalidated a vote to convert by seventy-one percent of a Texas' credit union's members voting because the disclosure statement mailed to members with the ballot was improperly folded. John Reosti, Showdown on Disputed Credit Union Conversion, Am. Banker, June 23, 2005. A subsequent lawsuit against the NCUA by the credit union was settled when the NCUA agreed to the conversion in exchange for the dismissal of the lawsuit. John Reosti, In Brief: NCUA, Tex. Credit Unions Settle Cases, Am. Banker, Sept. 1, 2005.

The NCUA responded with a final rule on conversion, including specifics on how to give notice to credit union members of the proposed conversion and how to provide notice of arguments opposing the proposed conversion. 12 C.F.R. pt. 708a. Legislation to restrict the NCUA's authority over conversions has been proposed, and the NCUA has testified against that legislation citing the substantial benefits retained by the former credit union officers and directors if the credit union converts to a mutual savings bank that subsequently goes public. According to the NCUA, in twenty-one of the most recent twenty-nine credit union to mutual savings bank conversions, the mutual savings bank has subsequently converted to a stockholder owned savings bank, and the officers and directors of the former credit union have retained twenty-five percent or more of the equity of the institution. Luke Mullins, Hearing Explores Executives' Gains in CU Conversions, Am. Banker, May 12, 2006. See Michael W. Briggs, Credit Union Conversions: Charter Choices and Controversy, 10 N.C. Banking Inst. 1 (2006).

D. CONVERSION OR DEMUTUALIZATION

The adoption of FIRREA caused many thrifts to convert from mutual ownership to stock companies in order to raise the funds needed to meet FIRREA's increased capital requirements. It was later claimed that many insiders had profited from these conversions to the detriment of the depositors, who were more clearly considered the owners of the mutual institution. The stock was said to be underpriced in many of these conversions and it was alleged that the managers bought more than their fair share of the underpriced stock. Because of such criticism, federal regulators toughened appraisal standards for conversions. Other problems arose with respect to mutual-to-stock conversions.

DOUGHERTY v. CARVER FEDERAL SAVINGS BANK

United States Court of Appeals, Second Circuit, 1997.
112 F.3d 613.

Cardamone, Circuit Judge.

This appeal arises out of the conversion by defendant Carver Federal Savings Bank (Carver or Bank) from the mutual to the stock form of ownership in the fall of 1994. In connection with that transaction, Carver issued 2,314,375 shares of common stock to investors at a price of $10 per share. Plaintiffs Robert L. Dougherty, Joseph Uminer and Norman Gomberg each subscribed for and purchased Carver stock at the $10 price, purchasing respectively $150,000, $86,800 and $350,300 worth of Carver stock, only to see the stock lose a substantial portion of its value in the first week of public trading.

Plaintiffs then brought separate securities fraud class actions in the United States District Court for the Southern District of New York (Motley, J.) alleging that the offering circular used by Carver to sell its stock contained material misstatements and omissions in violation of federal and state securities laws. Because the Office of Thrift Supervision (OTS) approved Carver's application to convert to stock form, the district court, relying on 12 U.S.C. § 1464(i)(2)(B), which designates the Court of Appeals as the exclusive forum for judicial review of final OTS conversion approvals, dismissed the plaintiffs' claims for lack of subject matter jurisdiction in an opinion reported at 909 F.Supp. 197 (1996). OTS approval of Carver's conversion from mutual form to stock form did not decide the issues raised by plaintiffs' securities fraud claims. Hence, we reverse.

To put this case in proper perspective, it is helpful to discuss briefly at the outset the conversion process in general and the manner in which the regulatory framework governing such conversions has evolved.

Federal savings associations come in two forms—mutual associations and stock associations. Mutual associations differ from ordinary stock corporations in that they have no stock or shareholders, but instead are operated for the mutual benefit of their depositors, who elect the board of directors. Stock savings associations, in contrast, are like ordinary stock corporations—they are owned and controlled by persons holding their stock. See Ordower v. Office of Thrift Supervision, 999 F.2d 1183, 1185 (7th Cir. 1993) (discussing mutual form of ownership); Charter Fed. Savings & Loan Ass'n v. Office of Thrift Supervision, 912 F.2d 1569, 1570 (11th Cir. 1990) (same). The present action arises from defendant Carver's decision to convert from mutual form to stock form. In a conversion of this sort, a mutual association exchanges its mutual charter for a stock charter and issues stock to investors, who then become the owners of the association.

The regulatory and legislative environment for such conversions has varied over the years. Initially, all federal savings associations were in mutual form. When Congress first enacted the Home Owners' Loan Act of 1933 (HOLA), 12 U.S.C. § 1461 et seq., permitting the formation of federal savings associations, it provided for only one form of charter—the mutual charter—and provided no mechanism for converting to stock form. This changed in 1948, when the legislature amended HOLA to permit federal mutual associations to convert to state stock associations. See Charter Fed. Savings & Loan Ass'n, 912 F.2d at 1571.

The initial experience with conversions raised troubling problems. In this initial period, the question of who owned the net worth that had been accumulated over years and how to dispose of it in a conversion to a stock corporation was not well regulated. There was great temptation to raid the billions of dollars in industry accumulation of net worth. In fact, an independent study commissioned by Congress revealed that in the majority of pre–1963 conversions, the group of insiders initiating the conversion appropriated "a large part" of the net worth. S. Rep. No. 93–902 (1974) (additional views of Sen. William Proxmire). As a result a moratorium was placed on conversions in 1963.

A decade later, Congress began to lift the ban, which was completely eliminated in 1976. See Charter Fed. Savings & Loan Ass'n, 912 F.2d at 1571. Conversions resumed under a new set of comprehensive regulations adopted by the Federal Home Loan Bank Board. Initially, concerned with insider abuse, federal regulators were wary of conversions. As time went on these officials became increasingly attracted to the procedure as a means for shoring up the capital position of undercapitalized savings associations. This trend became more pronounced with the advent of the savings and loan crisis of the late 1970s and early 1980s. Faced with the prospect of widespread savings association failures, federal regulators loosened the conversion regulations to make it easier and more attractive for banks to take advantage of the procedure to raise capital. See Conversions From Mutual to Stock Form, 59 Fed. Reg. 22,725, 22,725–26 (1994) (to be codified at 12 C.F.R. pts. 563b & 575) (interim final rule with request for comments, May 3, 1994) (discussing evolution of regulatory environment) [hereafter Proposed 1994 Regulations].

In this environment, conversions became very popular. Over 300 federal savings institutions converted between 1990 and 1994, raising nearly $5 billion in the process, see Mutual Depository Institution Conversion Protection Act of 1994: Hearings on S. 1801 Before the Senate Comm. on Banking, Housing and Urban Affairs, 103 Cong. (1994) (statement of Jonathan L. Fiechter, Acting Director, Office of Thrift Supervision), and in the decade between 1984 and 1994, the number of savings associations in mutual form nationwide dropped by roughly 56 percent. See Mutual-to-Stock Conversions of State Nonmember Savings Banks, 59 Fed. Reg. 30,357 (1994) (FDIC notice and request for comments) (noting decrease to 1,100 mutual associations in 1994 from more than 2,500 in 1984).

Eventually, Congress passed the Financial Institutions Reform, Recovery, and Enforcement Act of 1989 (FIRREA), Pub. L. No. 101–73, 103 Stat. 183 (1989), which restructured the regulation of the savings association industry by, inter alia, abolishing the Federal Home Loan Bank Board (Bank Board) and vesting many of its functions in the newly-created Office of Thrift Supervision, see FIRREA § 301 (establishing OTS), § 401 (abolishing Bank Board). With time, the thrift undercapitalization problem abated and the industry returned to solvency. With the crisis past, the OTS, concerned anew with insider abuses, tightened its conversion procedures through interim final rules issued in May 1994, see Proposed 1994 Regulations, supra, 59 Fed. Reg. at 22,725. Those rules were adopted in final form in November 1994. See Conversions from Mutual to Stock Form, 59 Fed. Reg. 61,247 (1994) (to be codified at 12 C.F.R. pts. 563b & 575) (final rule, Nov. 30, 1994). Carver's conversion to stock form took place in the midst of this regulatory rule-tightening, but was completed before the adoption of the final rule.

In early 1994, defendant Carver was one of the largest African–American owned financial institutions in the United States, but had not yet converted from mutual to stock form. Although the mutual form of ownership has certain advantages—among other things, it offers near-complete takeover protection—Carver, like many other mutual banks, decided to convert to stock form to raise capital by selling its stock to investors. Converting to stock form allows a savings bank to operate in a more traditional manner, provides the capital necessary to acquire branches more readily and strengthens the bank's ability to recruit and retain quality managers using stock-based incentives such as employee stock option plans. See C. Thomas Long et al., Conversions and Securities Offerings of Savings and Loan Associations, C418 ALI–ABA 411, 421–422 (1989) (discussing advantages and disadvantages of converting to stock form). * * *

The centerpiece of a mutual-to-stock conversion is the issue and sale of the converted institution's capital stock to investors and, as one might expect, a key feature of any conversion plan is the price at which that capital stock will be offered. OTS regulations require a converting institution to "issue and sell its capital stock at a total price equal to the estimated pro forma market value of such stock in the converted savings association." § 563b.3(c)(1) (1994). To determine what this estimated value should be, OTS regulations direct the issuer to obtain an appraisal performed by a party "independent of the applicant, experienced and expert in the area of corporate appraisal, and acceptable to the [OTS]." § 563b.7(f)(1)(i) (1994). Although OTS regulations have since been amended to restrict the use of underwriters who will be selling the stock and their affiliates to serve as conversion appraisers, the regulations in effect at the time of Carver's conversion had no such restrictions. Compare § 563b.7(f)(2) (1996) ("No affiliate of an appraiser may act as an underwriter or selling agent unless procedures are followed and representations made to ensure that an appraiser is separate from the underwriter or selling agent affiliate and the underwriter or selling agent affiliate does not make recommendations or in any way impact the appraisal.") with § 563b.7(f)(2) (1994) ("A [party] will not be considered as lacking independence for the reason that such [party] will participate in effecting a sale of capital stock under the plan of conversion. . . ."). Carver accordingly was free to hire Capital Resources Group, Inc.—a direct affiliate of Capital Resources, the sales agent for the transaction—as the "independent" appraiser.

Despite the potential conflict of interest in allowing the deal underwriter or its affiliate to act as the conversion appraiser, Carver's offering circular did not disclose to potential investors the relationship between Capital Resources Group and Capital Resources. Instead, the offering circular referred to Carver's appraiser, without qualification, as "independent" and advised potential investors that the aggregate offering price of Carver's stock would be based upon an "independent appraisal." * * *

Because of the regulatory controls imposed on savings institutions by banking legislation and the jurisdiction exercised over such institutions by bank regulatory agencies like the OTS, Congress has expressly exempted securities issued by savings and loan banks from registration with the SEC as a condition to their offer and sale under the Securities Act of 1933. See 15 U.S.C. § 77c(a)(5)(A). Carver was thus not required to register the stock issued in its conversion with the SEC. However, Carver's stock is not exempt from the securities law antifraud provisions, including § 12(2) of the Securities Act, 15 U.S.C. § 77l(a)(2), and § 10(b) of the Exchange Act, 15 U.S.C. § 78j(b), and Rule 10b–5, 17 C.F.R. § 240.10b–5. See Tcherepnin v. Knight, 389 U.S. 332, 340–41, 19 L. Ed. 2d 564, 88 S. Ct. 548 (1967); see also §§ 12(2) and 17(c) of the Securities Act, 15 U.S.C. 77l(a)(2), 77q(c) (expressly including these exempted securities within antifraud coverage). Savings association spokesmen appearing before Congress in the 1930s "emphatically endorsed the coverage of [savings] associations under the . . . antifraud provisions," Tcherepnin, 389 U.S. at 340, and when it enacted the Exchange Act, Congress intended the antifraud provisions to act as a "shield" to protect savings association investors against "unscrupulous or unqualified promoters," id. at 345–46.

Stock issued pursuant to a mutual bank's conversion to a stock corporation is no exception. Nothing in the statutory scheme governing mutual savings bank conversions divests a district court's jurisdiction under the securities laws for claims alleging fraud in a converting bank's sale of its stock. * * *

Simply put, OTS approval of a conversion does not lift from the shoulders of the bank, its managers and agents the obligation to conduct the sale of its stock in an honest and straightforward manner so that investors are not misled. See *Ordower*, 999 F.2d at 1188.

However, because every conversion involves the preparation of an offering circular and a proxy statement, there is a danger that some litigants seeking review of the OTS decision to approve or disapprove the plan of conversion will recast the allegations in their complaints to assert securities fraud claims in order to circumvent the exclusive review provisions contained in the conversion statute. To prevent this end-run around § 1464(i)(2)(B), other circuits have cautioned trial courts to review carefully the substance of securities fraud causes of action allegedly arising out of a conversion in order to ensure that by means of artful pleading litigants do not obtain prohibited district court review of an OTS conversion approval.

Thus, in deciding a motion to dismiss for lack of subject matter jurisdiction in reliance on 12 U.S.C. § 1464(i)(2)(B), attention must be focused on what issues the agency has actually decided. Subject matter jurisdiction to decide an issue raised in a securities fraud lawsuit arising out of a mutual-to-stock conversion is lacking in the district court only when (1) the OTS, acting within its authority, has actually considered and decided the same issue, and (2) the resolution of that issue is essential to the agency's decision to approve or disapprove the conversion. * * *

[The court held that shareholders' claims that the offering circular was false and misleading were within the jurisdiction of the district court.]

QUESTIONS AND NOTES

1. In a standard mutual-to-stock conversion, a mutual becomes 100% owned by its stockholders. In some cases, where the institution may not be able to effectively deploy so much additional capital, conversions have been structured in two steps. The two-step conversion is the most popular conversion format. First, a mutual holding company is formed, which sells 49% of its stock to the public. The second step is a subsequent offering of the remaining stock to the public. Mutuals seek to convert to raise additional capital and expand their business or to position themselves for sale. Eighty percent of converted mutuals have been acquired in the three-to-five year period following conversion. Laurie Kulikowski, An Unexpected Comeback for One–Step Conversions, Am. Banker, May 23, 2006.

2. A stockbroker was found guilty of conspiracy to commit mail fraud and of securities fraud by recruiting a mutual savings banks' depositors to accept money from an investor to buy stock in the converting institution and split the profits in the appreciated stock following the conversion. Mutual savings bank depositors are prohibited by law from transferring their ability to subscribe to purchase shares in the converted institution to non-depositors. Karen Krebsback, Prosecution: Fourth Conviction in NHSB Case Shakes Up Industry, US Banker 10 (Sept. 2006). See also Peter Lattman, Ex–Star Analyst Sentenced To Prison for IPO Caper, Wall St. J., Aug. 6, 2007 (describing the conviction of a former stock analyst for a similar crime).

E. HOLDING COMPANIES

OFFICE OF THRIFT SUPERVISION
HISTORICAL FRAMEWORK FOR REGULATION OF
ACTIVITIES OF UNITARY SAVINGS AND LOAN
HOLDING COMPANIES

<www.ots.treas.gov/docs/4/48035.html>.

The term "unitary savings and loan holding company" or "unitary thrift holding company" is a shorthand description of a corporate structure in which a company (or group of companies) controls a single savings association. The significance of this structure is that the holding company may engage in any legitimate business activity that it chooses; it is free from the activities restrictions that apply to bank holding companies.

Why Congress has chosen, as it considers regulation of the holding companies of insured depository institutions, to treat unitary thrift holding companies differently from bank holding companies is the subject of this memorandum. The evolution of the unitary thrift holding company as a structure warranting different regulatory treatment reflects a number of changing public policy considerations that have been before Congress in the last thirty to forty years.

Initially, Congress was concerned with the perceived dangers presented by multiple holding companies, as opposed to unitary holding companies, even where the subsidiary was a bank. When Congress first enacted legislation in 1967 to regulate savings and loan holding companies, unitary or one-bank holding companies were exempt from the Bank Holding Company Act ("BHCA") and its restrictions on unrelated business activities. To qualify as a bank holding company at that time, a company had to control two or more banks. Partially in recognition that the BHCA restrictions applied only to multi-bank holding companies, Congress imposed activities restrictions only on multiple savings and loan holding companies.

Congress also recognized, however, the difference between, on the one hand, the traditional thrift focus on home mortgage lending and ancillary consumer services and, on the other hand, the commercial lending and more wide-ranging business-oriented services provided by banks. In recent years, the major thrust of legislation has been aimed not at curbing the unrelated business activities of thrift holding companies, but rather at reinforcing the residential and consumer lending mission of their subsidiary associations. Congress first imposed a "qualified thrift lender test" ("QTL test") of "thriftness" on savings associations in 1987. Failure of a savings association to meet the QTL test can lead to substantial operational sanctions for a subsidiary thrift, and, more significantly, to required divestiture of non-banking business activities for the parent unitary holding company. Two years later, Congress barred thrifts from making loans or extension of credit to affiliates engaged in non-banking activities.

The contemporaneous legislative history of the BHCA reflects different concerns. These have been framed as potential systemic threats presented by large one-bank and multi-bank holding companies that may form powerful banking/industrial conglomerates and possibly monopolize commercial credit. Congress has not historically expressed the same concern with respect to the interrelationship of activities of unitary savings and loan holding companies. * * *

The statutory exemption for the unrelated activities of unitary thrift holding companies remained unaffected for fifteen years following its adoption in 1968. During this period, holding company formations accelerated as conversions of associations from the mutual to stock form gradually increased, aided by the ability of Federal associations for the first time to convert to the stock form without relinquishing their Federal charters. With the enactment of the Garn–St Germain Depository Institutions Act of 1982 ("DIA"), the FHLBB was granted the authority to issue de novo Federal stock charters. Thereafter, the stock charter became the preferred form of organization in the savings and loan business and the use of the unitary holding company format grew accordingly.

The DIA, however, also imposed the first statutory condition on unitary thrift holding companies' exemption from unrelated business activities. Where a subsidiary savings association failed to qualify as a domestic building and loan association under the Internal Revenue Code, after a period of three years for compliance, its parent holding company and any of the parent's nonthrift subsidiaries were limited to the activities permitted for multiple holding companies.

Five years later the enactment of the Competitive Equality Banking Act of 1987 ("CEBA") brought the QTL test, a measure of an association's "thriftness." The QTL test is keyed to a percentage of a subsidiary thrift's assets devoted to "qualified thrift investments" ("QTI"). This test performed the same function as the DIA's requirement of qualification as a domestic building and loan association. That is, the subsidiary thrift of a unitary holding company was required to meet the test; otherwise, the holding company would be treated essentially as a bank holding company. Under the CEBA QTL test, QTI are defined generally to include residential real estate loans and other housing related investments. Largely prompted by the rapid expansion in powers of both state and federally chartered savings institutions in the early 1980s, the QTL test was intended partially to complement companion CEBA provisions aimed at closing the so-called "nonbank bank" loophole in the BHCA.

The QTL test was further refined by the Financial Institutions Reform, Recovery and Enforcement Act of 1989, ("FIRREA"), which also moved the statutory location of the SLHCA from Title IV of the NHA, major portions of which were repealed, into a new Section 10 of the Home Owners' Loan Act ("HOLA"). Without discussing the intricacies of the QTL test, it is sufficient to observe that the penalty imposed on a unitary thrift holding company for the failure of the QTL test by its subsidiary association is mandatory registration and treatment of the parent company as a bank holding company, beginning one year after the failure. For many unitaries, the confinement of their unrelated business activities to those permissible for bank holding companies could have a disastrous impact by causing the forced sale of either the subsidiary thrift or other profitable entities.

Although the effect of a subsidiary thrift's failure of the QTL test on a parent unitary holding company can be quite severe, one significant conclusion can be inferred from requiring compliance with the QTL test. Implicit in the QTL test is a Congressional determination that ownership of a single savings association by a firm engaged in commercial activities does not raise the types of concerns regarding the mixture of banking and commerce and the monopolization, or discriminatory availability, of commercial credit that led to enactment of the BHCA of 1956 and its extension to one-bank holding companies by the BHCA Amendments of 1970.

Recent OTS reports to Congress suggest that the unitary thrift holding company structure has encouraged notable but not overwhelming investment by non-banking firms in home mortgage and consumer lending. Of a total of over 600 unitary holding companies as of June 30, 1977, only 102 unitary companies were actively engaged in nonbanking activities, and these companies together owned 64 thrifts. The range of nonbanking activities by these unitary holding companies varies. Several, but fewer than half, of the 102 companies engage in financial activities such as insurance sales and underwriting, investments, mutual fund management and investor services, and broker-dealer operations. A greater number of unitary holding companies have affiliates that do business in non-financial areas, predominantly real estate and related services. Other non-financial activities of these unitary companies include management services, hotel operations and development, and wood products. In surveying many of these holding companies, OTS discovered that the subsidiary thrift contributes either a minimal amount to holding company revenue (less than 10% in 41% of the cases) or significant amount (over 50% in 56% of the companies surveyed). As these figures show, the OTS experience with holding companies engaged in non-banking activities has been modest. Since the enactment of the savings and loan reform legislation in 1989 and the creation of OTS, unitary thrift holding companies have not as a class presented special supervisory problems.

The Gramm–Leach–Bliley Act (GLBA) closed the unitary thrift holding company loophole that permitted the common ownership of a thrift and a general commercial enterprise. 12 U.S.C.A. § 1467a(c)(9). Unitary thrift holding companies that existed or had applied for a thrift charter by May 4, 1999, may continue their unitary thrift holding company activities pursuant to a grandfather provision. The grandfathered unitary holding company status terminates, however, upon a change in control. Wal-Mart's application for a federal thrift charter did not meet the statutory deadline. Approximately eighty-five percent of all thrift holding companies are exempt from the statutory activity restrictions contained in the Home Owners' Loan Act for thrift holding companies because they are either grandfathered unitary thrift holding companies or thrift holding companies that acquired all or all but one of their thrift subsidiaries in acquisitions assisted by federal regulators. The Dodd–Frank Act requires that financial activities conducted by a grandfathered unitary thrift holding company be placed in a new intermediate holding company that is subject to Fed regulation as a savings and loan holding company. Dodd–Frank § 626. The parent of the new intermediate holding company is expected to act as a "source of strength" to the new intermediate holding company, and is subject to limited reporting obligations to the Fed and limited enforcement actions by the Fed. Further, any transactions between the parent holding company and the new intermediate holding company are subject to the Fed's affiliate transaction limitations.

The remainder of thrift holding companies—the so-called "non-exempt" holding companies—are subject to activity limitations. The non-exempt thrift holding companies may engage in the financial in nature activities permitted for financial holding companies in § 1843(k) and in any of the activities listed in 12 U.S.C.A. § 1467a(c)(2). The latter list of activities includes any activity approved by the Fed for bank holding companies under 12 U.S.C.A. § 1843(c) of the Bank Holding Company Act, unless prohibited or limited by the OTS director by regulation. The OTS director initially limited thrift holding company activities pursuant to this authority to only those activities permitted under § 1843(c)(8) as closely related to banking. In 2007, however, the OTS finalized a regulation that permitted thrift holding companies to engage in any activity permitted for a bank holding company by the Fed under other subjections of § 1843(c), including those that authorize bank holding companies with foreign operations to engage in certain activities. 12 C.F.R. § 584.2–2(a). Thus, non-exempt thrift holding companies may engage in activities permitted to a bank holding company and to the "financial in nature" activities listed in § 1843(k)(4).

The Dodd–Frank Act, as part of its dissolution of the OTS, transfers supervision of savings and loan holding companies to the Fed, which also supervises bank holding companies. Dodd–Frank Act, § 312.

SECTION 5.   REVIEW OF REGULATORY THEMES

The regulatory themes applicable to banks should also be examined in the context of the statutes relating to thrift institutions.

A. REASONS FOR MAJOR LEGISLATION

It was previously suggested that much banking legislation resulted either in response to a financial calamity or in response to law evasion (by either closing a loophole or making the evasive activity specifically permissible). This same pattern holds true in the legislation dealt with in this chapter. The birth of the federal charter for thrifts came during the New Deal legislation that responded to the Great Depression and attempted to help solidify the system for home loan lending in America. The savings and loan crisis of the 1980s resulted in a spate of legislative activity as well.

DIDMCA of 1980 authorized NOW accounts which had been created as a way around the prohibition of the payment of interest on checking accounts and the inability to then offer checking accounts at thrifts. Thus, it presents one example of law avoidance leading to explicit law change.

The NCUA relaxed the "common bond" requirements for federal credit union membership. The Supreme Court struck down the regulations as in excess of the NCUA's statutory authority. Congress promptly responded with the Credit Union Membership Access Act which reinstated by statute the NCUA's previous regulatory definition of the common bond requirement.

Financial calamity in the form of the savings and loan crisis lead to the demise of the FHLBB as the federal regulator of thrifts and its replacement by the OTS in 1989. Just over twenty years later, the financial crisis that began with the subprime lending crisis, resulted in a similar regulatory reshuffling, with the OTS's functions transferred to the OCC (rulemaking and supervision of federal savings associations and rulemaking for state savings association), the FDIC (supervision of state savings associations), and the Fed (rulemaking and supervision of savings and loan holding companies).

B. REGULATORY THEMES

The regulatory themes introduced in Chapter 1 are repeated in much of the legislation discussed in this chapter.

(1) Concerns About Mixing Banking and Commerce

Until just recently, a unitary savings and loan holding company could engage in banking through a QTL thrift and any other commercial enterprise. This mixture may still continue for a grandfathered unitary holding company. Congress reasserted its concern about such combinations when it closed the unitary thrift holding company loophole in GLBA.

(2) Limited Entry

Like banks, thrifts must apply for a charter. Not all charters are granted. An example of the potential for limitation on entry is the *West Helena Savings & Loan* case reprinted earlier in this chapter where the FHLBB initially decided to deny the deposit insurance applications of two state chartered thrifts because there was not a sufficient need in the relevant markets for their services. This decision was overturned since the stated reason for insurance denial was not one of the permissible factors for insurance denial listed in the statute. Still, it is an example of the hoops that depository institutions must jump through before they may begin business.

(3) Dual Chartering and Regulatory Arbitrage

It is interesting to note that the dual chartering option was not available for savings and loans and credit unions until the 1930s and that it was not until 1978 that a federal charter became available for a savings bank. Nevertheless, the dual chartering system for thrifts and credit unions is now well entrenched. There even exists a second level of regulatory arbitrage among the different types of depository institutions. Savings and loans may convert to the state savings bank charters; credit unions may convert to a mutual thrift charter; and there are sometimes conversions by thrifts to banks and vice-versa. The Dodd–Frank Act may reduce arbitrage as the OCC is the federal regulator of national banks and federal savings associations. It remains to be seen, however, whether the OCC will retain regulations that preserve the distinct character of federal savings associations, or whether those associations will voluntarily convert to a national bank charter. It also remains to be seen whether the OCC will issue or organizers will seek any new federal savings association charters. Some financial reform proposals debated prior to the adoption of Dodd–Frank Act would have abolished the thrift charter altogether.

(4) Restrictions on Geographic Expansion

As discussed in *North Arlington National Bank*, federal thrifts have long been afforded the right to branch throughout the state in which they are located, regardless of the branching privileges afforded by state law to state thrifts. This is in contrast to the McFadden Act which limits national banks to the same in-state branching as available for state banks within the state. Federal savings association are now also afforded the right to establish out-of-state branches. 12 U.S.C.A. § 1464(r). They received this right prior to the passage in 1994 of the Riegle–Neal Interstate Branching and Banking Efficiency Act. If a savings association converts to a bank, the Dodd–Frank Act preserves the ability of the bank to retain branches that were permissible to it as a federal savings association. Id. § 341.

(5) Concerns About Impermissible Concentrations of Economic Power

Thrift institutions were initially statutorily circumscribed so that they could not grow too large or gain too much economic power. For instance, home mortgage loans originally could be secured only by property located within 50 miles of the thrift's office. These limits were gradually eliminated. Restrictions on accepting demand deposits constrained the growth of thrift deposits until the development of the NOW account. Remaining investment and loan limitations may serve in part to prevent impermissible concentrations of economic power in thrift institutions. The growth of credit unions is constrained by the common bond and other specific membership requirements.

(6) Safety and Soundness Regulation

Much of the regulation relating to thrifts and credit unions attempts to protect the safety and soundness of the deposit insurance funds. Limits on the lending authority of thrifts are motivated in part by this concern. Whether these limits will be retained by the OCC post-Dodd–Frank, or whether savings associations convert to a bank charter where they are not subject to asset limits, remains to be seen.

(7) Grandfather Provisions

An example of grandfather provisions in the regulation of thrifts is the GLBA provision grandfathering in existing unitary thrift holding companies and preserving their ability to mingle banking and commerce. A heated debate took place prior to GLBA's passage regarding whether these grandfather rights should be transferable to a new entity upon a change in control. Congress determined that the grandfather rights would end upon a change in control. In any event, we continue to operate under a system where there is one set of rules for one type of unitary thrift holding companies and another set of rules for the grandfathered institutions.

QUESTIONS AND NOTES

1. What are the remaining distinctions between banks, savings associations and credit unions? Will these distinctions be maintained after Dodd–Frank?

2. Does it make sense to maintain multiple types of depository institutions with multiple regulatory structures? What would be a preferable regulatory structure? The dissolution of the OTS in Dodd–Frank was, in part, justified by the failures of OTS-regulated institutions during the financial crisis and in part by the dwindling number of institutions subject to OTS

oversight. Is the first reason alone a sufficient justification for the demise of the OTS given that banks subject to OCC supervision like Citibank and Bank of America survived the financial crisis only with extraordinary financial support from the government? In terms of simplifying the regulatory structure for financial institutions, was the OTS model one that should have been preserved instead of abolished? The OTS regulated state and federal savings associations as well as their holding companies. In contrast, banks are subject to regulation by the OCC (nationally chartered), Fed (state member), or FDIC (state nonmember), and their holding companies are overseen by the Fed. Is the bank regulatory model more efficient or effective?

3.   What other examples of the regulatory themes listed above did you find when you considered the material in this chapter?

4.   How does the legislation passed during the savings and loan crisis deal with the fundamental problem faced by banks and thrifts that fund fixed-term loans (assets) with short-term or on demand deposits (liabilities)?

5.   Banks have long argued that credit unions enjoy an unfair competitive advantage that includes tax-exempt status and an exemption from the Community Reinvestment Act. Does the nonprofit status of credit unions justify this favorable treatment?

CHAPTER THREE

THE BUSINESS OF BANKING

■ ■ ■

SECTION 1. FINANCIAL INTERMEDIATION

There are two characteristics that distinguish banks from other financial institutions: financial intermediation and checking accounts. Financial intermediaries pool financial resources from those with excess funds and make those funds available for use by others who need additional funds. The intermediary provides a matchmaking service for which it charges a fee or interest. Intermediaries have information and expertise that enable them to make realistic evaluations of market and credit risks as they select among competing investment opportunities.

Financial intermediaries fall into two broad categories: depository institutions and nondepository institutions. For depository institutions— banks, thrifts, and credit unions—the principal source of funds is deposits, and the principal use of funds is to make loans. A depository institution profits from the spread between its cost of funds (the interest paid on deposits) and the yield on the funds (the interest earned on loans). Nondepository financial intermediaries—including insurance companies, pension funds, and finance companies—receive their funds from sources other than customer deposits. Insurance companies, for instance, receive premiums from their customers. Pension funds operate with pension contributions made by current employees, and finance companies operate with funds supplied by lenders and shareholders.

The opposite of intermediation is direct investment. A person making a direct investment finds a way to profitably use his excess funds, either by making a direct loan to or direct investment in a person or entity in need of additional funds. Since an intermediary need not be compensated, the investor and borrower in a direct investment may share in this savings through a higher return on the investment and a lower cost source of funds. Direct investment, although increasingly popular as an alternative to intermediation, is not always a feasible alternative. For instance, if a law student receives a $500 check for her birthday, she may not have the time or expertise to find a suitable direct investment. Moreover, even if she did have the time and expertise to engage in a direct investment, $500 would not satisfy the investment needs of many people or entities. If, instead, she deposits the money in a bank account, she will earn a modest rate of interest on the $500, and the bank can pool her $500 with other deposited funds and make the larger sum available to a borrower at a rate in excess of the interest it pays the law student for the use of the deposited funds. Moreover, as we will see, this deposit is insured by the federal government against loss, unlike most direct investments. There are other advantages of intermediation, such as the intermediary's ability to diversify risk by investing the pooled funds in a variety of direct investments and greater liquidity.

QUESTIONS AND NOTES

1. Which investment, intermediated or direct, is more likely to have a higher return? Why?

2. For the consumer, what are some of the advantages of the bank deposit (an intermediated investment) over a direct investment?

SECTION 2.   TRANSACTION ACCOUNTS

A unique characteristic of depository institutions is that checking and savings accounts provide their primary source of funds. Checking accounts are sometimes referred to as transaction accounts because the customer may *transact* business by using a check to pay a third party. Checking accounts are also sometimes referred to as demand deposits because deposited funds must be repaid to the depositor upon demand. Checking accounts held by individuals, not-for-profit entities, or governmental entities may earn interest.[1] The payment of interest is not authorized for business checking accounts until July 21, 2011 when § 627 of the Dodd–Frank Act allowing such payments is effective. The Dodd–Frank Act, however, will provide unlimited deposit insurance on non-interest-bearing transaction accounts until December 31, 2012. Dodd–Frank Act, § 343. Commercial depositors will, therefore, need to choose between earning interest on deposit accounts that offer $250,000 deposit insurance coverage and non-interest bearing accounts that offer unlimited deposit insurance coverage. Savings accounts do not offer a transaction feature such as check-writing privileges. Although in practice the customer may withdraw funds from a savings account on demand, as a matter of law the institution may require seven days written notice of the customer's withdrawal prior to honoring it.[2] Checking accounts were originally a product unique to banks. This distinguished them from other depository institutions such as thrifts and credit unions, which were permitted only to offer savings accounts. However, all depository institutions now offer transaction ac-

---

1. 12 U.S.C. § 1832 (authorizing depository institutions to pay interest only on transaction accounts held by individuals and not-for-profit entities). See also 12 U.S.C.A. § 371a (member banks); 12 U.S.C.A. § 1828(g) (insured nonmember banks and insured branches of foreign banks); 12 U.S.C.A. § 1464(b)(1)(B) (federal savings associations).

2. Regulation D, 12 C.F.R. § 204.2(d)(1).

counts. Transaction accounts with unlimited check writing privileges are provided exclusively by depository financial institutions.[3]

Banks do not retain all the funds their customers deposit, but instead put much of that money to work by loaning it to borrowers. There is, however, a legal reserve requirement set by the Federal Reserve Board that banks must maintain in vault cash or on deposit at their regional Federal Reserve bank. That requirement is normally set at approximately 10% of deposits.[4] Thus, a bank is likely to have only this minimum amount of cash on hand. If depositors decided to withdraw most of a bank's deposits at one time, the bank would not have enough cash on hand to satisfy those requests. Before the creation of federal deposit insurance, there were sometimes "runs" on banks if depositors feared that their bank would run out of its cash reserves. Bank runs or panics have largely disappeared following the advent of federal deposit insurance.

QUESTIONS AND NOTES

1. Where do you maintain a checking account? Is this a depository or nondepository institution? Is it a bank, savings association, or credit union? What interest rate did your checking account earn as shown on your most recent statement?

2. Do you also have a savings account? Why or why not? Has a bank ever refused immediate access to your savings account funds when you have asked to make a transfer or withdrawal? What interest rate does your savings account earn? Is it a fixed rate or does it fluctuate with market rates?

3. What are other ways of paying for goods and services? What advantages does a checking account have over other payment mechanisms?

SECTION 3.   MONETARY POLICY

A.   STRUCTURE OF THE FEDERAL RESERVE SYSTEM

The Federal Reserve Board of Governors (FRB) is the entity empowered with the authority and tools to establish and implement our country's monetary policy. The FRB's monetary policy is in part implemented through banks. The Federal Reserve System was created by Congress in 1913. The Board of Governors of the Federal Reserve System is made up of seven members who are appointed by the President, confirmed by the

---

3. Some securities firms offer checking accounts through affiliated banks. Prior to the adoption of the Gramm–Leach–Bliley Act of 1999, which endorsed common ownership of banks and securities firms, securities firms offered a competing service, the cash management account. This operated much like a bank checking account, but contained certain limitations not applicable to a checking account.

4. By statute the Fed may set the reserve requirement (for the portion of the depository institution's transaction accounts in excess of $25 million) between eight and fourteen percent. 12 U.S.C.A. § 461(b)(2). By regulation, the current reserve requirement is three percent for transaction account balances less than $45.8 million and ten percent for transaction account balances over $45.8 million. Reg. D, 12 C.F.R. § 204.9.

Senate, and serve for fourteen-year terms. The Chairman and Vice Chairman are designated by the President and confirmed by the Senate for four-year terms. The Dodd–Frank Act created a Vice Chairman for Supervision, who will be a member of the Fed designated by the President to develop policy recommendations regarding "supervision and regulation of depository institution holding companies and other financial firms" supervised by the Fed, as well as oversee their supervision and regulation. Dodd–Frank, § 1108. The Federal Reserve system is governed by the Board of Governors and composed of twelve regional Federal Reserve Banks. After Dodd–Frank, regional Federal Reserve Bank directors elected by member banks will no longer be allowed to vote for the president of their regional Federal Reserve Bank. Dodd–Frank Act, § 1107. The presidents will be selected by the other board members, with the approval of the Fed.

In addition to monetary policy, the Fed performs multiple supervisory, regulatory, and enforcement functions. The FRB is the primary federal regulator of state chartered banks that are members of the Federal Reserve System. State chartered banks that are not members of the Federal Reserve System are regulated at the federal level by the FDIC. The state chartering authority is the primary regulator of any banks chartered in that state. The FRB also serves as the regulator of bank holding companies and financial holding companies under the Bank Holding Company Act of 1956, as discussed in greater detail in Chapter 4. Following the Dodd–Frank Act, a new Fed supervisory framework over systemically important nonbank financial companies was established. Moreover, under Dodd–Frank the Fed will supervise savings and loan holding companies (previously the province of the OTS). The FRB's issuance of consumer protection regulations pursuant to the Truth in Lending Act (TILA) and other consumer protection statutes, as discussed further in Chapter 6, was transferred by Dodd–Frank to a new Bureau of Consumer Financial Protection. The new BCFP will act as an independent bureau within the Fed with authority over any person offering or providing a financial product or service to a consumer. Finally, since its creation in 1913, the FRB has issued Federal Reserve Notes—our currency—through its regional banks, supplanting the issuance of national bank notes.

BOARD OF GOVERNORS OF THE FEDERAL RESERVE SYSTEM
THE FEDERAL RESERVE SYSTEM: PURPOSES AND FUNCTIONS

Ninth Edition, 2005.
<www.federalreserve.gov/pf/pf.htm>.

* * * A network of twelve Federal Reserve Banks and their Branches (twenty-five as of 2004) carries out a variety of System functions, including operating a nationwide payments system, distributing the nation's currency and coin, supervising and regulating member banks and bank holding companies, and serving as banker for the U.S. Treasury. * * * Besides carrying out functions for the System as a whole, such as administering nationwide banking and credit policies, each Reserve Bank acts as a depository for the banks in its own District and fulfills other District responsibilities.

* * * Congress chartered the Federal Reserve Banks for a public purpose. The Reserve Banks are the operating arms of the central banking system, and they combine both public and private elements in their makeup and organization. As part of the Federal Reserve System, the Banks are subject to oversight by Congress. * * *

The income of the Federal Reserve System is derived primarily from the interest on U.S. government securities that it has acquired through open market operations. Other major sources of income are the interest on foreign currency investments held by the System; interest on loans to depository institutions; and fees received for services provided to depository institutions, such as check clearing, funds transfers, and automated clearinghouse operations.

After it pays its expenses, the Federal Reserve turns the rest of its earnings over to the U.S. Treasury. About 95 percent of the Reserve Banks' net earnings have been paid into the Treasury since the Federal Reserve System began operations in 1914. * * * In 2003, the Federal Reserve paid approximately $22 billion to the Treasury. * * *

The FOMC [Federal Open Market Committee] is charged under law with overseeing open market operations, the principal tool of national monetary policy. * * *

The FOMC is composed of the seven members of the Board of Governors and five of the twelve Reserve Bank presidents. The president of the Federal Reserve Bank of New York is a permanent member; the other presidents serve one-year terms on a rotating basis. * * * The FOMC * * * by tradition elects the Chairman of the Board of Governors as its chairman and the president of the Federal Reserve Bank of New York as its vice chairman. * * *

FEDERAL RESERVE BANKS

Available at www.federalreserve.gov/otherfrb.htm.

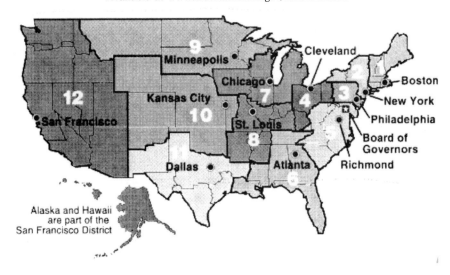

Alaska and Hawaii
are part of the
San Francisco District

Three tools are used by the FRB to implement monetary policy through banks: reserve requirements, open market operations, and the discount rate.

B.   RESERVE REQUIREMENTS

BOARD OF GOVERNORS OF THE FEDERAL RESERVE SYSTEM THE FEDERAL RESERVE SYSTEM: PURPOSES & FUNCTIONS

Ninth Edition, 2005.
<www.federalreserve.gov/pf/pf.htm>.

Requiring depository institutions to hold a certain fraction of their deposits in reserve, either as cash in their vaults or as non-interest-bearing balances at the Federal Reserve, does impose a cost on the private sector. The cost is equal to the amount of forgone interest on these funds—or at least on the portion of these funds that banks hold only because of legal requirements and not to meet their customers' needs. * * *

[Before 1980,] only banks that were members of the Federal Reserve System were subject to reserve requirements established by the Federal Reserve. The regulatory structure and competitive pressures during a period of high interest rates were putting an increasing burden on member banks. The situation fostered the growth of deposits, especially the newly introduced interest-bearing transaction deposits, at institutions other than member banks and led many banks to leave the Federal

Reserve System. Given this situation, policy makers felt that reserve requirements needed to be applied to a broad group of institutions for more effective monetary control—that is, to strengthen the relationship between the amount of reserves supplied by the Federal Reserve and the overall quantity of money in the economy.

The Monetary Control Act of 1980 (MCA) ended the problem of membership attrition and facilitated monetary control by reforming reserve requirements. Under the Act, all depository institutions are subject to reserve requirements set by the Federal Reserve, whether or not they are members of the Federal Reserve System. The board of Governors may impose reserve requirements solely for the purpose of implementing monetary policy. The required reserve ratio may range from 8 percent to 14 percent on transaction deposits and from 0 percent to 9 percent on nonpersonal time deposits. * * *

Following the passage of the MCA in 1980, reserve requirements were not adjusted for policy purposes for a decade. In December 1990, the required reserve ratio on nonpersonal time deposits was pared from 3 percent to 0 percent, and in April 1992 the 12 percent requirement on transaction deposits was trimmed to 10 percent. These actions were partly motivated by evidence suggesting that some lenders had adopted a more cautious approach to extending credit, which was increasing the cost and restricting the availability of credit to some types of borrowers. By reducing funding costs and thus providing depositories with easier access to capital markets, the cuts in reserve requirements put banks in a better position to extend credit.

Although reserve requirement ratios have not been changed since the early 1990s, the level of reserve requirements and required reserve balances has fallen considerably since then because of the widespread implementation of retail sweep programs by depository institutions. Under such a program, a depository institution sweeps amounts above a predetermined level from a depositor's checking account into a special-purpose money market deposit account created for the depositor. In this way, the depository institution shifts funds from an account that is subject to reserve requirements to one that is not and therefore reduces its reserve requirement. With no change in its vault cash holdings, the depository institution can lower its required reserve balance, on which it earns no interest, and invest the funds formerly held at the Federal Reserve in interest-earning assets.

The Financial Services Regulatory Relief Act of 2006 amended the Federal Reserve Act to provide that balances maintained at a Federal Reserve Bank by depository institutions may earn interest at a rate less than or equivalent to the general level of short-term interest rates. 12 U.S.C.A. § 461(b)(12). The effective date of this provision was initially October 1, 2011, but it was moved up to October 1, 2008 by the Emergency Economic Stabilization Act of 2008. Interest is paid on required reserves and excess reserves that banks may lend to each other at the so-called federal funds rate. From the end of 2008 through mid–2010, the interest rate on both required reserves and excess reserves has been 25 basis points. In June 2010, the discount rate was 75 basis points and the targeted federal funds rate was between 0 and 25 basis points.

[handwritten: what is a basis point? .01%]

During the financial crisis, the liquidity facilities created by the Fed, and described further later in this Chapter, resulted in a large increase in excess reserves. As a result, on some occasions open market operations were not successful in preventing the federal funds rate from falling to levels far below the target rate set by the Fed. By paying interest on excess balances, there is no incentive for institutions to arrange federal funds transactions at a rate lower than the interest rate paid by the Fed, allowing the Fed to keep the actual federal funds rate closer to the targeted rate. The Fed supported paying interest on reserves, even though this increases the Fed's costs, because of the inefficiencies the Fed perceived in the retail sweep account programs described above. As of July 21, 2011, banks may, in turn, pay interest on commercial demand deposits.

[handwritten: banks can pay int. on comm. checking accnts]

The requirement that only a fraction of the money on deposit be kept in reserves is referred to as fractional reserve banking. A simple example illustrates how fractional reserves help increase the money supply. Suppose the law student who received a $500 gift decided to forego her limited direct investment opportunities and instead took advantage of the financial intermediation function offered by her local bank. She deposited the $500 in a checking account at Bank 1. Bank 1 reserved $50 of that to meet the reserve requirement and kept that $50 accessible in vault cash or on deposit at Bank 1's regional Federal Reserve bank. The remaining $450 might be used by Bank 1 to loan money to Borrower A. Borrower A deposits the $450 loan proceeds in its account at Bank 2. Bank 2 reserves $45 dollars against that deposit and the remaining $405 is loaned out by Bank 2 to Borrower B. The cycle continues. The original $500 deposit, subject to a 10% reserve requirement, can create up to $5,000 in new money.[5]

[handwritten: Magic]

The money supply can be decreased or increased by raising or lowering the reserve requirement.[6] If the reserve requirement were increased to 20%, Bank 1 would need to reserve $100 against the $500 deposit, and would only have $400 to loan out. Borrower A would get a smaller loan and his bank, Bank 2, would reserve $80 against the $400 deposit and loan out only $320 to Borrower B. The potential creation of

---

5. Assume that the money is deposited and reloaned *ad infinitum* so that ultimately the entire $500 gift is now held as required reserves in the banking system. To determine how much money is created by this fractional reserve system of banking, solve for A in the following equation: 10% x A = $500. A = $5,000.

6. Reserve requirements are set by Federal Reserve Board Regulation D, 12 C.F.R. pt. 204.

money would be reduced from $5,000 (when the reserve requirement was just 10%) to $2,500.[7]

FIRST BANK AND TRUST CO. v. BOARD OF GOVERNORS OF FEDERAL RESERVE SYSTEM

United States District Court, Eastern District of Kentucky, 1984.
605 F.Supp. 555.

WILHOIT, JUDGE.

* * * This action concerns the validity of the MCA [Monetary Control Act] of 1980, and as amended in 1982. In its pertinent parts, the MCA extended reserve requirements to all banks in the United States whether the bank was a member of the Federal Reserve System or not. Prior to 1980, a dual system of reserve requirements for banks was in existence. Banks that were members of the Federal Reserve were required to post reserves in accordance with the regulations of the Board. Banks not a member of the Federal Reserve could keep reserves in accordance with state banking laws. All nationally chartered banks are required to be members of the Federal Reserve and comply with its reserve requirements. State-chartered banks could be members of the Federal Reserve, but if they were not, they did not have to comply with the Board's reserve requirements.

This dual system has been in existence for some time. In recent years it began to be unprofitable for many banks to maintain membership in the Federal Reserve System because of the relatively high cost of services provided by the Federal Reserve, and more importantly, because of the growing loss of profits occasioned by Federal Reserve's relatively high percentage of required reserves, many banks began to leave the System.

Prior to 1980, First Bank was a nationally chartered bank. Because of the greater amount of idle reserves it had to hold being a member of the Federal Reserve, First Bank's Board of Directors in 1979, decided to withdraw from the System and seek a state charter. The bank's shareholders approved the Board of Director's decision on February 26, 1980. A state charter was obtained March 3, 1980, and on the same day, the Bank withdrew its reserve balances from the Federal Reserve Bank of Cleveland, relinquishing its stock in the system.

The rising tide of "bank flight" from the Federal Reserve System did not escape Congress' attention. Indeed, in 1979, at least five bills appeared in Congress aimed at correcting the Federal Reserve's growing lack of control over the money supply. * * *

The Conference Committee Report of the MCA, which was rendered on March 21, 1980, and which includes the provisions under dispute in this lawsuit, re-imposed mandatory reserve requirements. The Conference

---

7. The formula now reflects the assumed increase in the reserve requirement. Solve for A to determine the maximum amount of money to be created: 20% of A = $500. A = $2,500

Report was approved by both houses of Congress and signed into law by President Carter on March 31, 1980.

The pertinent provisions of the MCA, as finally passed and signed by the President, provide that <u>non-member banks shall be allowed an</u> eight-<u>year phase-in of the mandatory reserve requirements</u>. Member banks, however, were not given any phase-in period and had to maintain reserves in accordance with federal regulations as always. * * *

[handwritten: 7 yr phase-in]
[handwritten: MCA reg. member]
[handwritten: parties to suit]

On June 13, 1980, First Bank petitioned the Board for a determination that it had withdrawn from membership prior to July 1, 1979 [so that pursuant to Board regulations it would be eligible for the eight-year phase-in of reserve requirements or a "hardship exemption" from immediate application of the reserve requirements. The Board <u>denied both</u> requests and this appeal followed.] * * *

[handwritten: bd: no phase-in for First Bank]

It is clear from the legislative history behind the MCA that one of the principle [sic] purposes of the Act was to equalize the inequities between the amount of reserves required to be kept by non-member banks vis-a-vis member banks. In attempting to equalize these inequities, by establishing mandatory reserve requirements for all banks, Congress intended to curb the rising tide of bank flight from the Reserve System. Bank flight created what many, including Congress, perceived to be an alarming decrease in the amount of the nation's money supply directly controllable by the Federal Reserve Board. The equalization brought about by the MCA, albeit accomplished through a phase-in for non-member banks, has the <u>effect of reducing the attractiveness</u> for member banks to withdraw from <u>the System</u>. There is no longer any significant competitive advantage to be gained by forfeiting Reserve membership in favor of a state charter. With fewer banks, therefore, "fleeing" from the Reserve System, the Board is assured of not losing anymore [sic] <u>control over the nation's money</u> supply via its member banks.

Pursuant to the intent behind the MCA, it is clear Congress had a rational purpose in picking a date prior in time to the Act's enactment for determining which banks would be deemed member or non-member banks for purposes of the Act's phase-in provision. First of all, Congress wanted to curb bank flight and therefore was not going to reward banks that had recently withdrawn from the System in anticipation of Congress' imposing mandatory reserve requirements. More importantly, Congress wanted to equalize the inequitable differences in the amount of reserves required of member and non-member banks. Congress no longer wanted member banks to be at a competitive disadvantage with their non-member counterparts. At the same time, Congress did not want to impose mandatory reserves on non-member banks effective immediately without some transitional, phase-in provisions to ease the financial hardship that might be occasioned on non-member banks having to increase their required reserves. The phase-in provisions of the Act allow non-member banks the opportunity to gradually post the increased reserves required of them by the federal government. * * *

[Because there is a rational basis for this legislative scheme,] [t]here is, therefore, no equal protection or retroactive (due process) problems with the MCA, either as originally enacted or amended. Although the Bank's complaint—that it has been inequitably treated vis-a-vis other *state* banks because it was not permitted a phase-in period for posting reserves while other state banks were permitted such a phase-in—is a compelling and logical argument, the Court does not believe the argument raises a substantial constitutional question. There being a rational basis for requiring the Bank to post its reserves without a phase-in, the Court believes the argument is a matter best settled in the political arena. * * *

Consequently, the Court * * * agrees with the Board with regard to the validity of the MCA and the regulatory scheme promulgated pursuant thereto. * * *

C. OPEN MARKET OPERATIONS

BOARD OF GOVERNORS OF THE FEDERAL RESERVE SYSTEM
THE FEDERAL RESERVE SYSTEM: PURPOSES & FUNCTIONS

Ninth Edition, 2005.
<www.federalreserve.gov/pf/pf.htm>.

* * * For open market operations to work effectively, the Federal Reserve must be able to buy and sell quickly, at its own convenience, in whatever volume may be needed to keep the federal funds rate at the target level. These conditions require that the instrument it buys or sells be traded in a broad, highly active market that can accommodate the transactions without distortions or disruptions to the market itself.

The market for U.S. Treasury securities satisfies these conditions. The U.S. treasury securities market is the broadest and most active of U.S. financial markets. Transactions are handled over the counter, not on an organized exchange. Although most of the trading occurs in New York City, telephone and computer connections link dealers, brokers, and customers—regardless of their location—to form a global market.

The overall size of the Federal Reserve's holdings of Treasury securities depends principally on the growth of Federal reserve notes; however, the amounts and maturities of the of the individual securities held depends on the FOMC's preferences for liquidity. * * * At the end of 2004, the Federal Reserve's holdings of Treasury securities were about evenly weighted between those with maturities of one year or less and those with maturities greater than one year. * * *

If staff projections indicate that the demand for balances is likely to exceed the supply of balances by a large amount for a number of weeks or months, the Federal Reserve may make outright purchases of securities or arrange longer-term repurchase agreements to increase supply. Conversely, if the projections suggest that demand is likely to fall short of supply, then the Federal Reserve may sell securities outright or redeem maturing securities to shrink the supply of balances.

* * * If the funds rate is likely to move away from the target rate, then the Desk will arrange short-term repurchase agreements, which add balances, or reverse repurchase agreements, which drain balances, to better align the supply of and demand for balances. If the funds rate is likely to remain close to the target, then the Desk will not arrange a short-term operation. Short-term temporary operations are much more common than outright transactions because daily fluctuations in autonomous factors or the demand for excess reserve balances can create a sizable imbalance between the supply of and demand for balances that might cause the federal funds rate to move significantly away from the FOMC's target.

The Federal Reserve tends to conduct far more outright purchases than outright sales or redemptions of securities primarily because it must offset the drain of balances resulting from the public's increasing demand for Federal Reserve notes. * * *

When the projections indicate a need to drain Federal Reserve balances, the Desk may choose to sell securities or to redeem maturing securities. Sales of securities are extremely rare. By redeeming some maturing securities, rather than exchanging all of them for new issues, the Federal Reserve can reduce the size of its holdings gradually without having to enter the market. Redemptions drain Federal Reserve balances when the Treasury takes funds out of its accounts at depository institutions, transfers those funds to its account at the Federal Reserve, and then pays the Federal Reserve for the maturing issues. * * *

[handwritten margin note: Sale of Securities is rare]

The Federal Reserve frequently arranges repurchase agreements to add Federal Reserve balances temporarily. In these transactions, it acquires a security from a primary dealer under an agreement to return the security on a specified date. Most repurchase agreements have an overnight term, although short-term repurchase agreements with maturities of two to thirteen days are also arranged to address shortages in Federal Reserve balances that are expected to extend over several days. Longer-term repurchase agreements are used to address more persistent needs. The Federal Reserve accepts Treasury, federal agency, and mortgage-backed securities guaranteed by federal agencies as collateral for its repurchase agreements.

[handwritten margin note: Repurchase Agreements]

When the Federal Reserve needs to absorb Federal Reserve balances temporarily, it enters into reverse repurchase agreements with primary dealers. These transactions involve selling a Treasury security to a primary dealer under an agreement to receive the security back on a specified date. As in repurchase agreement transactions, these operations are arranged on an auction basis. When the Federal Reserve transfers the collateral (usually a Treasury bill) to the dealer, the account of the dealer's clearing bank at the Federal Reserve is debited, and total Federal

Reserve balances decline. When the transaction unwinds, the account of the dealer's clearing bank is credited and total balances increase. * * *

Each weekday, beginning at around 7:30 a.m., two groups of Federal Reserve staff members, one at the Federal Reserve Bank of New York and one at the Board of Governors in Washington, prepare independent projections of the supply of and demand for Federal Reserve balances. The manager of the System Open Market Account and the group in New York are linked in a telephone conference call with members of the staff at the Board of Governors and with a Federal Reserve Bank president who is currently a member of the FOMC. Participants in the call discuss staff forecasts for Federal Reserve balances and recent developments in financial markets. They pay special attention to trading conditions in the federal funds market, particularly to the level of the federal funds rate in relation to the FOMC's target. In light of this information, they determine a plan for open market operations. The decision is announced to the markets at around 9:30 a.m., at the same time that the Desk solicits offers from dealers. * * *

The stock and bond markets react sharply to changes in interest rates. Those markets closely follow the Fed's actions on rates and respond to changes in the Fed's "bias" on raising or lowering rates. Due to the sensitivity of this information, it is closely guarded. The FOMC now issues a statement shortly after each meeting, however, that includes the FOMC's "assessment of the risks in the foreseeable future to the attainment of its long-term goals of price stability and sustainable economic growth."[8] Minutes of an FOMC meeting are released a few days following the next regularly scheduled meeting. The Fed also publishes its "Beige Book," which contains assessments of the condition of the economy in each of the Federal Reserve districts and is thought to provide insight on what may affect the bias of the Fed on interest rates. The Fed Chairman testifies before Congress in February and July of each year on monetary policy. These semiannual Monetary Policy Reports may be found on the Fed's website, <www.federalreserve.gov/boarddocs/hh/>.

RIEGLE v. FEDERAL OPEN MARKET COMMITTEE

United States Court of Appeals, District of Columbia Circuit, 1981.
656 F.2d 873, *cert. denied*, 454 U.S. 1082.

ROBB, CIRCUIT JUDGE.

This case presents the question whether a United States Senator has standing to challenge the constitutionality of the procedures established by the Federal Reserve Act, 12 U.S.C. § 221 et seq. (1976) for the appointment of the five Reserve Bank members of the Federal Open Market Committee. * * *

---

8.   <www.federalreserve.gov/fomc/>.

The Federal Reserve System, which was created by Congress in 1913 as this nation's central bank, is comprised of public and private entities organized on a regional basis with federal supervisory authority. The System includes a seven-member Board of Governors, the twelve regional Federal Reserve Banks, the FOMC, the Federal Advisory Council, and approximately 5,500 privately-owned member commercial banks. The primary role of the System in the conduct of monetary policy is to facilitate the achievement of national economic goals through influence on the availability and cost of bank reserves, bank credit, and money. Three basic mechanisms employed by the System to implement monetary policy are open market operations, regulation of member bank borrowing from the Federal Reserve Banks, and establishment of member bank reserve requirements. The most flexible and potentially significant of these tools is open market transactions.

[handwritten margin note: 3 mechs to control monetary policy]

Open market trading, which consists of the purchase and sale of government and other securities in the financial markets by the Reserve Banks, is exclusively directed and regulated by the FOMC. 12 U.S.C. § 263(b) (1976). The FOMC, like the System as a whole, is constituted to reflect both public and private interests. Since 1935 the FOMC has been composed of the seven members of the Board of Governors of the Federal Reserve System, 12 U.S.C. § 241 (1976), who are appointed by the President with the advice and consent of the Senate, and five representatives of the Federal Reserve Banks, who are elected annually by the boards of directors of the Banks. 12 U.S.C. § 263(a) (1976). Since 1942 Congress has required that the five Reserve Bank members of the FOMC be either presidents or first vice presidents of the Reserve Banks. 12 U.S.C. § 263(a). The Reserve Banks are private corporations whose stock is owned by the member commercial banks within their districts. 12 U.S.C. § 321 (1976). These member commercial banks elect six of the nine members of the board of directors of each Reserve Bank, and the Board of Governors of the Federal Reserve System selects the remaining three. 12 U.S.C. §§ 302, 304 (1976). The presidents and first vice presidents of the Reserve Banks, although selected by the respective boards of directors, are subject to the approval, suspension, and removal authority of the Board of Governors. 12 U.S.C. §§ 341, 248 (1976). In short, the FOMC consists of seven members who hold their offices by virtue of presidential appointments confirmed by the Senate, and five members who are elected by the boards of directors of the Banks and who hold their offices subject to the approval of the Board of Governors. 12 U.S.C. § 263(a).

The securities transactions directed by the FOMC have a significant effect on the financial markets. In 1974, for example, the FOMC alone was responsible for approximately $19.4 billion in outright transactions in U.S. Government Securities. These transactions potentially affect the value of the dollar, foreign exchange rates, interest rates, investment, and employment. Approximately every 45 days, the FOMC formulates its monetary policy objectives for the immediate future by setting targets for growth rates in the money supply and the range of variance in the Federal Funds rate (the member banks' rate for overnight loans of excess reserves to other banks). The FOMC then issues a domestic policy directive to the Federal Reserve Bank of New York for the management of the System Open Market Account, which is a central entity representing the open market transaction interests of the twelve Reserve Banks. The manager of the Account, who maintains daily contact with Federal Reserve staff members in Washington, engages in financial transactions designed to achieve the monetary conditions sought by the FOMC. Reserve Banks are prohibited under the Act from engaging in any open market transactions except those directed by the FOMC through the Account. 12 U.S.C. § 263(b).

Considering the substantial economic power wielded by the FOMC, it is not surprising that controversy over the balance between public and private control of the Committee has existed since its creation. As originally constituted, the FOMC was privately dominated, consisting solely of representatives of the twelve Reserve Banks. Banking Act of 1933, 48 Stat. 162. This arrangement was unsatisfactory to those who favored greater governmental control over disposition of Reserve Bank funds. During debates on the Senate floor preceding passage of the Banking Act of 1935, 49 Stat. 684, Chairman Carter Glass of the Senate Banking Committee (a supporter of Reserve Bank control of the FOMC) explained the legislative compromise between public (Board of Governors) and private (Reserve Bank) interests which produced the present procedure for constituting the FOMC:

> (We are) amazed to have it proposed that the Federal Reserve Board alone should constitute the open-market committee of the system. . . . The Government of the United States has never contributed a dollar to one of the Reserve Banks; yet it is proposed to have the Federal Reserve Board, having not a dollar of pecuniary interest in the Reserve funds or the deposits of the Federal Reserve banks or of the member banks . . . to make such disposition of the reserve funds of the country, and in large measure the deposits of the member banks of the country, as they may please. . . . In order to reconcile bitter differences there was yielding, and we have now proposed an open-market committee composed of all 7 members of the Federal Reserve Board and 5 representatives of the regional reserve banks.

79 Cong. Rec. 11778 (1935).

Despite the passage of the compromise represented by the Banking Act of 1935, the debate over public and private control of the FOMC has continued during the past 48 years. The late Congressman Wright Patman, Chairman of the House Banking Committee, asserted in 1938 that the Reserve Bank members of the FOMC did not represent the "people's interest." Mr. Patman's successor, Congressman Henry S. Reuss, has made several unsuccessful attempts, both in Congress by amendment of 12 U.S.C. § 263(a) and in the federal courts, to require that the five Reserve Bank members of the FOMC be appointed with the advice and consent of the Senate pursuant to the Appointments Clause. United States Constitution, Art. II, sec. 2, cl. 2. Based on his belief that the work of the FOMC "is essentially a governmental function, and should not be exercised by private people," Mr. Reuss in 1976 introduced the "Federal Reserve Reform Act," H.R. 12934, 94th Cong., 2d Sess. (1976), which in part would have required that the five Reserve Bank seats on the FOMC be limited to Bank presidents appointed by the President with the advice and consent of the Senate. The House Banking Committee defeated this provision on April 30, 1976. Mr. Reuss then brought an action in federal court seeking, in part, to have 12 U.S.C. § 263(a) declared unconstitutional. The District Court dismissed the action on the ground that the Congressman lacked standing to sue either in his capacity as a congressman or as a private bondholder. Reuss v. Balles, 73 F.R.D. 90 (D.D.C.1976) (Parker, J.), aff'd, 584 F.2d 461, cert. denied, 439 U.S. 997 (1978). On April 1, 1980 Congressman Reuss introduced another bill, H.R. 7001, which would amend 12 U.S.C. § 263(a) in the manner sought by Senator Riegle in this case: a prohibition on voting by the five Reserve Bank members of the FOMC. This legislation was not enacted.

Senator Riegle instituted the present suit on July 2, 1979 (prior to the introduction of H.R. 7001 by Congressman Reuss) in the United States District Court for the District of Columbia, seeking injunctive relief in the form of an absolute prohibition on voting by the Reserve Bank members of the FOMC. In an opinion by District Judge Gesell, the court dismissed the action for lack of standing. * * *

We hold that Senator Riegle has standing to bring this action but exercise our equitable discretion to dismiss the case on the ground that judicial action would improperly interfere with the legislative process. * * *

D. THE DISCOUNT RATE AND FEDERAL FUNDS RATE

In addition to purchasing government securities through open market operations to increase the supply of reserves ("nonborrowed reserves"), the FRB may also increase the supply of so-called "borrowed reserves" by lending to banks at a rate of interest called the discount rate.

Until 1980, the discount window was open only to banks that were members of the Federal Reserve System—national banks and state banks that had elected to become members and purchase stock in their regional Federal Reserve Bank. After the Depositary Institutions and Monetary Control Act of 1980, however, access to the discount window was opened to all institutions. As discussed further in this chapter, in times of "unusual and exigent circumstances," the FRB may extend credit under certain conditions to "any individual, partnership, or corporation." Section 13(3), Federal Reserve Act, 12 U.S.C.A. § 343. This authority was invoked during the financial crisis—not without controversy—and was limited by the Dodd–Frank Act.

BOARD OF GOVERNORS OF THE
FEDERAL RESERVE SYSTEM
THE FEDERAL RESERVE SYSTEM:
PURPOSES & FUNCTIONS

Ninth Edition, 2005.
<www.federalreserve.gov/pf/pf.htm>.

The Federal Reserve's lending at the discount window serves two primary functions. It complements open market operations in achieving the target federal funds rate by making Federal Reserve balances available to depository institutions when the supply of balances falls short of demand. It also serves as a backup source of liquidity for individual depository institutions.

Although the volume of discount window borrowing is relatively small, it plays an important role in containing upward pressures on the federal funds rate. If a depository institution faces an unexpectedly low balance in its account at the Federal Reserve, either because the total supply of balances has fallen short of demand or because it failed to receive an expected transfer of funds from a counterparty, it can borrow at the discount window. This extension of credit increases the supply of Federal Reserve balances and helps to limit any upward pressure on the federal funds rate. At times when the normal functioning of financial markets is disrupted—for example after operational problems, a natural disaster, or a terrorist attack—the discount window can become the principal channel for supplying balances to depository institutions.

The discount window can also, at times, serve as a useful tool for promoting financial stability by providing temporary funding to depository institutions that are having significant financial difficulties. If the institution's sudden collapse were likely to have severe adverse effects on the financial system, an extension of central bank credit could be desirable because it would address the liquidity strains and permit the institution to make a transition to sounder footing. Discount window credit can also be used to facilitate an orderly resolution of a failing institution. An institution obtaining credit in either situation must be monitored appropriately to ensure that it does not take excessive risks in an attempt to return to profitability and that the use of central bank credit would not increase costs to the deposit insurance fund and ultimately the taxpayer.

In ordinary circumstances, the Federal Reserve extends discount window credit to depository institutions under the primary, secondary, and seasonal credit programs. The rates charged on loans under each of these programs are established by each Reserve Bank's board of directors every two weeks, subject to review and determination by the Board of Governors. The rates for each of the three lending programs are the same at all Reserve Banks, except occasionally for very brief periods following the Board's action to adopt a requested rate change * * *

Primary credit is available to generally sound depository institutions on a very short-term basis, typically overnight. * * * Depository institutions are not required to seek alternative sources of funds before requesting occasional advances of primary credit, but primary credit is expected to be used as a backup, rather than a regular, source of funding.

The rate on primary credit has typically been set 1 percentage point above the FOMC's target federal funds rate, but the spread can vary depending on circumstances. Because primary credit is the Federal Reserve's main discount window program, the Federal Reserve at times used the term *discount rate* specifically to mean the primary credit rate.

Reserve Banks ordinarily do not require depository institutions to provide reasons for requesting very short-term primary credit. Borrowers are asked to provide only the minimum information necessary to process a loan, usually the required amount and term of the loan. * * *

Primary credit may be extended for longer periods of up to a few weeks if a depository institution is in generally sound financial condition and cannot obtain temporary funds in the market at reasonable terms. Large and medium-sized institutions are unlikely to meet this test.

Secondary credit is available to depository institutions that are not eligible for primary credit. It is extended on a very short-term basis, typically overnight. Reflecting the less-sound financial condition of borrowers of secondary credit, the rate on secondary credit has typically been 50 basis points above the primary credit rate, although the spread can vary as circumstances warrant. Secondary credit is available to help a depository institution meet backup liquidity needs when its use is consistent with the borrowing institution's timely return to a reliance on market sources of funding or with the orderly resolution of a troubled institution's difficulties. Secondary credit may not be used to fund an expansion of the borrower's assets. * * *

The Federal Reserve's seasonal credit program is designed to help small depository institutions manage significant seasonal swings in their loans and deposits. Seasonal credit is available to depository institutions that can demonstrate a clear pattern of recurring swings in funding needs throughout the year—usually institutions in agricultural or tourist areas. Borrowing longer-term funds from the discount window during period of seasonal need allows institutions to carry fewer liquid assets during the rest of the year and make more funds available for local lending.

The seasonal credit rate is based on market interest rates. * * *

By law, depository institutions that have reservable transaction accounts or nonpersonal time deposits may borrow from the discount window. * * *

By law, all discount window loans must be secured by collateral to the satisfaction of the lending Reserve Bank. Most loans that are not past due and most investment-grade securities held by depository institutions are acceptable as collateral.

A second source for credit is borrowing in the federal funds market. A bank with excess reserves deposited at its regional Federal Reserve Bank may lend the excess to institutions who need additional reserves. The FRB uses open market operations to achieve a targeted interest rate for this "federal funds" lending market. Ultimately, the discount rate and the federal funds rate affect market interest rates such as the prime rate and LIBOR. The prime rate is the interest rate banks charge to large corporations for short-term loans. LIBOR stands for the London Inter-bank Offered Rate and is the rate of interest banks charge each other for loans of Eurodollars (U.S. dollars held abroad).

E. THE GOALS OF MONETARY POLICY AND HOW IT AFFECTS THE ECONOMY

BOARD OF GOVERNORS OF THE FEDERAL RESERVE SYSTEM THE FEDERAL RESERVE SYSTEM: PURPOSES & FUNCTIONS

Ninth Edition, 2005.
<www.federalreserve.gov/pf/pf.htm>.

The goals of monetary policy are spelled out in the Federal Reserve Act, which specifies that the Board of Governors and the Federal Open Market Committee should seek "to promote effectively the goals of maximum employment, stable prices, and moderate long-term interest rates." Stable prices in the long run are a precondition for maximum sustainable output growth and employment as well as moderate long-term interest rates. When prices are stable and believed likely to remain so, the prices of goods, services, materials, and labor are undistorted by inflation and serve as clearer signals and guides to the efficient allocation of resources and thus contribute to higher standards of living. Moreover, stable prices foster saving and capital formation, because when the risk of erosion of asset values resulting from inflation—and the need to guard against such losses—are minimized, households are encouraged to save more, and businesses are encouraged to invest more.

Although price stability can help achieve maximum sustainable output growth and employment over the longer run, in the short run some tension can exist between the two goals. Often, a slowing of employment is accompanied by lessened pressures on prices, and moving to counter the weakening of the labor market by easing policy does not have adverse inflationary effects. Sometimes, however, upward pressures on prices are developing as output and employment are softening—especially when an adverse supply shock, such as a spike in energy prices, has occurred. Then, an attempt to restrain inflation pressures would compound the weakness in the economy, or an attempt to reverse employment losses would aggravate inflation. In such circumstances, those responsible for monetary policy face a dilemma and must decide whether to focus on defusing price pressures or on cushioning the loss of employment and output. Adding to the difficulty is the possibility that an expectation of increasing inflation might get built into decisions about prices and wages, thereby adding to inflation inertia and making it more difficult to achieve price stability. * * *

The initial link in the chain between monetary policy and the economy is the market for balances held at the Federal Reserve Banks. Depository institutions have accounts at their Reserve Banks, and they actively trade balances held in these accounts in the federal funds market at an interest rate known as the federal funds rate. The Federal Reserve exercises considerable control over the federal funds rate through its influence over the supply of and demand for balances at the Reserve Banks. * * *

Short-term interest rates, such as those on Treasury bills and commercial paper, are affected not only by the current level of the federal funds rate but also by expectations about the overnight federal funds rate over the duration of the short-term contract. As a result, short-term interest rates could decline if the Federal Reserve surprised market participants with a reduction in the federal funds rate, or if unfolding events convinced participants that the Federal Reserve was going to be holding the federal funds rate lower than had been anticipated. Similarly, short-term interest rates would increase if the Federal Reserve surprised market participants by announcing an increase in the federal funds rate, or if some event prompted market participants to believe that the Federal Reserve was going to be holding the federal funds rate at higher levels than had been anticipated. * * *

It is for these reasons that market participants closely follow data releases and statements by Federal Reserve officials, watching for clues that the economy and prices are on a different trajectory than had been thought, which would have implications for the stance of monetary policy.

Changes in short-term interest rates will influence long-term interest rates, such as those on Treasury notes, corporate bonds, fixed-rate mortgages, and auto and other consumer loans. Long-term rates are affected not only by changes in current short-term rates but also by expectations about short-term rates over the rest of the life of the long-term contract. Generally, economic news or statements by officials will have a greater impact on short-term interest rates than on longer rates because they typically have a bearing on the course of the economy and monetary policy over a shorter-period; however, the impact on long-term, rates can also be considerable because the news has clear implications for the expected course of short-term rates over a long period.

Changes in long-term interest rates also affect stock prices, which can have a pronounced effect on household wealth. Investors try to keep their investment returns on stocks in line with the return on bonds, after allowing for the greater riskiness of stocks. For example, if long-term interest rates decline, then, all else being equal, returns on stocks will exceed returns on bonds. Moreover, lower interest rates may convince investors that the economy will be stronger and profits higher in the near future, which should further lift equity prices.

Furthermore, changes in monetary policy affect the exchange value of the dollar on currency markets. For example, if interest rates rise in the United States, yields on dollar assets will look more favorable, which will lead to bidding up of the dollar on foreign exchange markets. The higher dollar will lower the cost of imports to U.S. residents and raise the price of U.S. exports to those living outside the United States. Conversely, lower interest rates in the United States will lead to a decline in the exchange value of the dollar, prompting an increase in the price of imports and a decline in the price of exports.

Changes in the value of financial assets, whether the result of an actual or expected change in monetary policy, will affect a wide range of spending decisions. For example, a drop in interest rates, a lower exchange value of the dollar, and higher stock prices will stimulate various types of spending. Investment projects that businesses believed would be only marginally profitable will become more attractive with lower financing costs. Lower consumer loan rates will elicit greater demand for consumer goods, especially bigger-ticket items such as motor vehicles. Lower mortgage rates will make housing more affordable and lead to more home purchases. They will also encourage mortgage refinancing, which will reduce ongoing housing costs and enable households to purchase other goods. When refinancing, some homeowners may withdraw a portion of their home equity to pay for other things, such as a motor vehicle, other consumer goods, or a long-desired vacation trip. Higher stock prices can also add to household wealth and to the ability to make purchases that had previously seemed beyond reach. The reduction in the value of the dollar associated with a drop in interest rates will tend to boost U.S. exports by lowering the cost of U.S. goods and services in foreign markets. It will also make imported goods more expensive, which will encourage businesses and households to purchase domestically produced goods instead. All of these responses will strengthen growth in aggregate demand. A tightening of monetary policy will have the opposite effect on spending and will moderate growth of aggregate demand.

If the economy slows and employment softens, policy makers will be inclined to ease monetary policy to stimulate aggregate demand. When growth in aggregate demand is boosted above growth in the economy's potential to produce, slack in the economy will be absorbed and employment will return to a more sustainable path. In contrast, if the economy is showing signs of overheating and inflation pressures are building, the Federal Reserve will be inclined to counter these pressures by tightening monetary policy—to bring growth in aggregate demand below that of the economy's potential to produce—for as long as necessary to defuse the inflationary pressures and put the economy on a path to sustainable expansion.

While these policy choices seem reasonably straightforward, monetary policy makers routinely face certain notable uncertainties. First, the actual position of the economy and growth in aggregate demand at any point in time are only partially known, as key information on spending, production, and prices becomes available only with a lag. * * * Second, exactly how a given adjustment in the federal funds rate will affect growth in aggregate demand—in terms of both the overall magnitude and the timing of its impact—is never certain. * * * Third, the growth in aggregate supply, often called the growth in potential output cannot be measured with certainty. Key here is the growth of the labor force and associated labor input, as well as underlying growth in labor productivity. Growth in labor input typically can be measured with more accuracy than underlying productivity; for some time, growth in labor input has tended to be around the growth in the overall population of 1 percentage point per year. However, underlying productivity growth has varied considerably over recent decades, from approximately 1 percent or so per year to somewhere in the neighborhood of 3 percent or even higher, getting a major boost during the mid-and late 1990s from applications of information technology and advanced management systems. * * *

After several unsuccessful governmental efforts to deal with the problem of inflation in the wake of the Vietnam War, Fed Chairman Paul Volcker, appointed by President Carter in 1979, decided to take decisive action.

In October, 1979, the Federal Reserve Board made an historic decision which threw the financial markets into chaos. Prior to that time, the Federal Reserve Board had attempted to use monetary policy to control interest rates. On October 6, 1979 a—Saturday—the Fed held a special meeting to change this policy and decided, in effect, to unregulate interest rates and allow them to move with as much volatility as the market permitted. A Shearson affiliate Vice President, William Melton, in his book, Inside the Fed: Making Monetary Policy (1985), describes the changes in the financial markets after this Fed decision as traumatic. He adds:

> Over the course of the week following the Saturday Night Special, markets remained thin and illiquid, while bond rates, which jumped an unprecedented 30 basis points over the weekend, continued to rise ... [The fed] funds rate, formerly the focal point of the Fed's cautious concern for interest-rate stability, was now changing 50 to 100 basis points—or more!—per day.[9]

Although the Fed's new policy curbed inflation, it also sent the country into a recession. Nevertheless, interest rates did drop eventually, and the economy later began a record period of growth.

---

9. Campbell v. Shearson/American Express, Inc., 1985 Fed. Sec. L. Rep. (CCH) ¶ 92,303 (E.D. Mich. 1985), aff'd in part and rev'd in part, 829 F.2d 38 (6th Cir. 1987).

PETER G. GOSSELIN
GREENSPAN LEGACY RIDES ON A
WOBBLY ECONOMY

L.A. Times, July 8, 2001, at A1.

* * * No sooner had the Federal Reserve chairman won that Oscar for Washington power brokers—a worshipful book published in November by Washington Post editor Bob Woodward[10]—than the U.S. economy, which Greenspan is as responsible as anybody for managing, began to unravel in earnest.

Now the 75–year-old economist is in a frantic scramble to keep the country from slipping into recession and to preserve his reputation, which until recently was among the most sterling of any public official's in the land.

His efforts are haunted by two dark possibilities. The first is that interest rate cuts, which the Fed has been wielding more fiercely than at any time in almost two decades, are blunt weapons against current conditions. The second is that the golden age of economic growth, which Greenspan desperately wants to be remembered as having ushered in, turns out not to have been so golden after all. * * *

Still, the consensus is that Greenspan will pull off another turn-around. The economy looks as if it will avoid an outright contraction, although it may grow only 1% to 1.5% [in 2001] compared with an annual average of better than 4% during the late 1990s. Many Americans—for example, home buyers—are behaving as if nothing is wrong. At the 4.5% rate announced [July 6, 2001], the nation's unemployment is still about a point and a half below its five-decade average. The Dow Jones industrial average is about 12% off its all-time high, but it still closed [on July 6] above 10,200. So what's the problem?

The problem, as Greenspan knows, is that corporate America has fallen into a deep funk from which it shows few signs of emerging quickly. Its worries threaten to do some serious economic harm.

Where only a few years ago companies were stocking up on technology and workers, now they're laying off employees and slashing everything from capital spending to corporate expense accounts. Where once they posted double-digit growth in profits and spectacular share price increases, now they waste no time to warn they won't make their own already-reduced earnings targets.

Greenspan and the Fed got pummeled this spring for having helped cause this corporate reversal of fortune. Critics charged that the central bank let stocks and the economy get out of hand by keeping interest rates too low in 1998 and early 1999. Then it caused both to stall by raising rates too high in the rest of 1999 and the first half of 2000. And finally, it

---

10. [eds.] Bob Woodward, Maestro: Alan Greenspan's Fed and the American Economic Boom (2000).

failed to keep the two from tumbling by not starting to slash rates until early this year.

Those attacks largely have abated now that the Fed has whacked a full 2 3/4 points from its key signal-sending interest rate. The latest quarter-point cut June 27[, 2001] in the fed funds rate came along with the promise of still more if necessary. The reductions have been the swiftest and steepest by the central bank since 1982.

But what has taken the place of the criticism seems more frightening: a sneaking suspicion that rate cuts can't make much difference when the problem is that companies think they already have spent too much and consumers feel poorer because a stock bubble has burst.

There always has been a possibility that the Fed's rate cut weapon could lose some of its edge, and not just because of the peculiar circumstances of the current downturn. The Fed system was designed for a world in which people needing money borrowed it from banks, which are extremely sensitive to Fed action; today two-thirds of the country's credit comes from the stock and bond markets.

In Greenspan's defense, he has regularly reminded congressional committees and others that the Fed's power to manage growth is limited. And, in public, he has deflected most of the praise that came his way with the boom of the late 1990s. * * *

[I]f, as many analysts expect, the economy revives late this year or early next, he probably will be credited with having gotten the country across another rough patch. Together with his expert handling of the 1987 stock market crash and the 1998 global financial contagion, the current period could add to his reputation for being one of the most effective central bankers the country has ever had. * * *

[I]if the economy's troubles turn out to be more deeply rooted, it could take a lot longer than the three years remaining in Greenspan's term as Fed chairman to work them out. The delay could cost him the legacy he wants. * * *

———————

Ben Bernanke was sworn in to replace Alan Greenspan as Chairman of the Federal Reserve's Board of Governors on February 1, 2006. The economy remained strong under Chairman Bernanke until a credit crunch occurred in the summer of[2007 precipitated by rising defaults on subprime mortgage loans and ratings downgrades of mortgage-backed securities. In August 2007, the Fed approved a temporary reduction of 50 basis points in the discount rate to narrow the spread between the targeted federal funds rate and the discount rate from 100 to 50 basis points. The Fed also announced that the term of discount window advances would be increased to up to 30 days, and subject to renewal. The purpose of this announcement was to restore confidence and orderly conditions in the financial markets. The country's four largest banking companies—Citigroup, Bank of America, JPMorgan Chase, and Wachovia—each borrowed $500 million shortly thereafter even though each had substantial liquidity and access to lower-cost funding sources. The borrowings were meant to show the utility of discount window borrowing to inject liquidity into the financial system.

F. SYSTEMIC RISK

(1) Fed Intervention

The Fed fills the role of a central bank by intervening to provide liquidity in times of crisis. It has assumed this role where events create a "systemic risk," i.e., a threat to the entire financial system. For example, in 1980, the Fed gave tacit approval to a syndicated loan by banks to the members of the Hunt family of Dallas, Texas after they suffered financial problems as a result of a failed attempt to manipulate the world price of silver. Silver prices had gone from under $10 per ounce to $50 and then plunged back under $11. The Hunts owed huge sums to their brokers and banks, and the viability of some of those institutions was threatened. A syndicated loan of $1.1 billion was arranged to provide liquidity to the Hunts so that the could meet their immediate obligations. This stabilized the situation.[11] Paul Volcker, the Fed chairman at the time, helped to arrange a $1.1 billion loan to the Hunt brothers from a consortium of banks which would pay their debts. The Fed was criticized in a Business Week editorial which argued that the Hunts should have been treated like other speculators and been forced to liquidate their other assets to cover their losses. Mary Fringis, Hunts Play Court Card as Hard Times Bite, Fin. Times, July 8, 1986, 1, at 29.

FREDERIC S. MISHKIN
SURVEY: MASTERING RISK:
SECURING A SAFETY NET AGAINST ECONOMIC FREE FALL

Fin. Times (London), (Survey), June 7, 2000, at 2.

For the financial system to remain healthy, managers of financial companies must actively manage the risks they face to keep their companies viable. * * * However, there are potentially highly dangerous shocks beyond the control of individual managers that can strike the financial system as a whole. The collective term for these threats is systemic risk.

Who should manage such risks? Obviously only government can do so. The question is: how should they manage them and what role does this imply for government involvement in the financial system? * * *

The systemic risk created by panics can be limited by government provision of a safety net for the banking system. One common way to do

---

11. See 23 Jerry W. Markham & Thomas Lee Hazen, Broker–Dealer Operations Under Securities and Commodity Law § 2.07[4] (1999).

this is through government-guaranteed deposit insurance. If depositors will not suffer losses when a bank fails, they have no incentive to start a run on the bank even when they are concerned about the bank's health: they still get 100 cents on the dollar no matter what happens. Deposit insurance can therefore short-circuit bank runs and prevent bank panics.

Another way of providing a government safety net is through what is called the "lender of last resort." Faced with a potential banking panic, the central bank can provide liquidity to financial institutions to keep them afloat. It should only do so when these institutions are solvent, but illiquid, or when the government needs time to marshal the funds to close institutions down or take them over in an orderly manner. In recent years, the US Federal Reserve has engaged in its role as lender of last resort several times. For example, in 1984 it lent Dollars 5 bn to the Continental Illinois National Bank to prop it up.

Central banks can also act as lender of last resort to prevent systemic risk, even when another part of the financial system—and not the banking system—is threatened. The most important recent example of this was the Federal Reserve's intervention immediately after the stock market crash of October 19 1987. Just before the market opened on October 20, Alan Greenspan, chairman of the Federal Reserve Board, announced the Federal Reserve System's "readiness to serve as a source of liquidity to support the economic and financial system." Liquidity was injected into the system and banks were encouraged to lend to stockbrokers who needed large amounts of funds (Dollars 1.5 bn for Kidder Peabody and Goldman Sachs alone) to clear their customers' margin accounts. The market immediately recovered and the business cycle continued.

Another example occurred in autumn 1998 immediately after the Russian financial crisis and the near-failure of the Long Term Capital Management hedge fund simultaneously roiled US capital markets. Then the Fed also took pre-emptive action to avoid systemic risk by lowering its federal funds rate by 75 basis points. * * *

Although a government safety net is able to keep systemic risk from spinning out of control, it is a mixed blessing. A safety net creates the well-known problem of moral hazard common to all insurance arrangements. When a financial institution knows government will come to its rescue, it has incentives to take on greater risk because the government will bail it out. Provision of a safety net can thus lead to precisely that outcome the safety net is intended to prevent. * * *

LAKONIA MANAGEMENT LTD. v. MERIWETHER

United States District Court, Southern District of New York, 2000.
106 F. Supp. 2d 540.

SCHEINDLIN, JUDGE.

This action arises out of the near-collapse in September 1998 of the initially heralded, and now infamous, Long Term Capital Hedge Funds (the "LTC Funds" or "Funds"). Plaintiff Lakonia Management Limited ("Lakonia") is a former investor in the Funds. Plaintiff alleges that defendants—individuals, partnerships and corporations associated with the Funds—violated sections 1962(b) and 1962(d) of the Racketeer Influenced and Corrupt Organizations Act ("RICO"), 18 U.S.C. § 1962(b), (d), by engaging in a fraudulent scheme to gain control of the Funds and to "squeeze out" plaintiff and other investors for insufficient consideration. In addition to its federal RICO claims, plaintiff asserts related state law claims for breach of fiduciary duty. * * *

Defendant Meriwether[12] is a recognized expert in sophisticated investment strategies. In 1993, Meriwether, joined by a group of nine similarly renowned financiers, started the LTC Funds.

The Funds were composed of various domestic and foreign corporate entities. These entities operated through a bi-level master fund/feeder fund structure as follows. Investors purchased shares in one of several feeder funds. The feeder funds in turn invested substantially all of their assets in a single master fund—defendant LTC Portfolio—which utilized the capital to make sophisticated and highly-leveraged investments. * * *

Pursuant to its investment strategy, LTC Management leveraged the assets of LTC Portfolio, taking on "huge" amounts of debt. For example, in 1996, LTC Portfolio's leverage ratio was approximately 30 to 1. That is, LTC Portfolio carried $30 of debt for every $1 of available capital.

From late winter 1994 through spring 1998, LTC Management's strategy worked well. Investors earned profits of 20% in 1994; 43% in 1995; 41% in 1996 and 17% in 1997. By fall 1997, the reported capital of LTC Portfolio was approximately $7 billion. Similarly, by November 30, 1997, the value of Lakonia's investment in LTC V had increased from $50,039,887 to $137,931,042—a profit of $87,891,155. * * *

On August 17, 1998, Russia devalued the ruble and declared a debt moratorium. Russia's actions precipitated an international financial crisis.

Among other things, the Russian debt moratorium sparked a "flight to quality" by investors; that is, investors sought safe, high-quality investments and avoided risk. The Complaint alleges that this flight to quality caused

---

12. [eds.] The defendant, John Meriwether, has a colorful past. As recounted by Michael Lewis, while a bond trader at Salomon, Meriwether loved to play a game with the other bond traders called "Liar's Poker" that involved guessing the serial number on a dollar bill. The game is based on bluffing the other players. Reportedly, John Gutfreund, the CEO of Salomon, challenged Meriwether one day to "One hand, one million dollars, no tears." Meriwether is said to have responded, "If we're going to play for those kind of numbers, I'd rather play for real money. Ten million dollars. No tears." Gutfreund declined to play for those stakes. Michael Lewis, Liar's Poker 13–17 (1989).

In 1991, Meriwether, then head of Fixed Income Trading, Gutfreund, and Salomon's president, Thomas Strauss, were forced to resign from Salomon as part of a settlement with the SEC involving false bids by Salomon during auctions for Treasury bonds. Gutfreund was barred from association with any broker/dealer, Strauss was barred for six months, and Meriwether for three months. In the Matter of John H. Gutfreund, Thomas W. Strauss and John W. Meriwether, [1992 Transfer Binder] Fed. Sec. L. Rep. (CCH) ¶ 85,067 (Dec. 3, 1992).

credit risk spreads and liquidity premiums [to rise] sharply in markets around the world. The size, persistence, and pervasiveness of the widening of risk spreads represented an extreme deviation from the risk management models employed by the [LTC Funds], which were based on assumptions that did not take into account such dramatic circumstances but rather were historical in nature. As a result, the [LTC Funds] (and other market participants) suffered losses in individual markets that greatly exceeded what conventional (so called value at risk) models, estimated during more stable periods, suggested were probable.

The flight to quality "also resulted in a substantial reduction in the liquidity of many markets, which made it difficult for the [LTC Funds] to reduce exposure quickly without incurring further ('fire sale') losses—particularly given the large positions it held in certain markets." At the same time, the Funds were finding it difficult to raise capital or to obtain additional financing.

By the end of August 1998, LTC Portfolio's available capital was $2.3 billion compared to $4.7 billion in December 1997—a loss of equity totaling more than fifty percent. * * *

By September 21, the Funds' liquidity situation had deteriorated further. That evening, defendants Goldman Sachs, J.P. Morgan and Merrill Lynch met with Peter Fisher of the Federal Reserve to discuss various options for salvaging the Funds. The meeting continued the following day with the added participation of [Federal Reserve Bank of New York] President McDonough and defendant UBS AG.

The group of commercial banks and government representatives focused primarily on a salvage option called the "consortium approach." Under the consortium approach, a group of the Funds' major creditors—namely, the thirteen Bank Defendants—would recapitalize LTC Portfolio by investing $3.6 billion in a newly created feeder fund and a newly created limited liability company (collectively, the "New Funds"). The New Funds would then invest their combined $3.6 billion in LTC Portfolio in exchange for (i) a 90% interest in the assets of LTC Portfolio; and (ii) operational control of LTC Management. The original investors in LTC Portfolio would retain an aggregate 10% interest in the master fund. * * *

One day later, on September 24, the Bank Defendants formalized their consortium offer and collectively invested $3.6 billion in the New Funds as described above. The New Funds in turn invested $3.6 billion in LTC Portfolio in exchange for a 90% equity stake in LTC Portfolio and operational control of LTC Management. The remaining 10% equity stake was held by the original investors in LTC Portfolio, including LTC V.

Following the Bank Defendants' recapitalization, the financial health of the Funds greatly improved. By February 26, 1999, LTC Portfolio had earned returns of more than 20%. By March 30, 1999, the Funds' risk dropped by more than 50%, and the value of LTC Portfolio's assets increased to $5 billion. The Bank Defendants announced that, as a result of the reduction in risk and an increase in the value of LTC Portfolio's net assets, they anticipated returning some capital to investors during the second half of 1999.

In a letter dated June 17, 1999, Meriwether notified plaintiff and "the original 1994 investors" that their shares would be mandatorily redeemed "in the near future." On July 6, 1999, the "Funds eliminated the interests of all of its outside investors, including the plaintiff, by redeeming their interests with a $300 million redemption payment." Pursuant to the redemption, Lakonia received $8,157,379. Thus, Lakonia ultimately recouped $63,728,925—a 27% return on its original investment of $50,039,887. Also on July 6, the Funds made a $1 billion payment to the Bank Defendants. The payment represented a return of 27.5% of the Bank Defendants' $3.6 billion investment in the Funds. * * *

[handwritten margin note: Lakonia got > 8.1 million (a 27% Rtn.)]

[The court concluded that the plaintiff-shareholder lacked individual standing to asset claims under RICO, and that the plaintiff-shareholder failed to allege the predicate acts for mail and wire fraud with sufficient particularity to state a claim under RICO.] For the foregoing reasons, defendants' motions to dismiss are granted in their entirety. The Clerk of the Court is directed to close this case.

BOARD OF GOVERNORS OF THE FEDERAL RESERVE SYSTEM 88TH ANNUAL REPORT TO CONGRESS 2001

April, 2002.

* * * [Immediately following the terrorist] attacks on the World Trade Center and Pentagon on Tuesday, September 11, * * * many financial markets effectively ceased operations. But with Fedwire and other wholesale payments networks remaining open, securities dealers and banks faced a continuing need to obtain funding for large pre-existing positions that they typically finance on an overnight basis. Communications disruptions prevented many borrowers from having normal access to their investor base for the first few days after September 11, even among those not directly affected by the attacks, and the impaired ability of a major clearing bank to process funds and securities transfers for itself and on behalf of its customers created additional uncertainties. Banks and dealers, uncertain about their general cash position or the availability of financing, tended to refrain from making cash outlays until later than normal in the day. In the federal funds market, several of the major brokers ceased operations for a time, and many large banks resorted to arranging trades directly with one another.

Although not fully back to normal levels of operating efficiency, the payments and communications infrastructure most critical to the function of the financing market had recovered considerably by Monday, September 17, and participation levels were much improved.

* * * The level of float in the banking system, normally around $1 billion, peaked at $47 billion on that Thursday [September 13] as a result of the temporary curtailment of air traffic nationwide. * * *

On the morning of September 11, the Federal Reserve issued a public release stating, "The Federal Reserve System is open and operating. The discount window is available to meet liquidity needs," to encourage banks to view the discount window as a source of liquidity. * * *

From Wednesday through the following Monday, the sizes of open market operations were aimed at satisfying all the financing that dealers wished to arrange with the Desk, in order to mitigate to the extent possible the disruptions to normal trading and settlement arrangements. * * * To more effectively serve as a source of financing of last resort and to help encourage dealers to continue to intermediate on behalf of some of their own customers, the Desk operated relatively late in the day, after dealers had a good opportunity to assess their full financing needs and to secure all available financing in the market.

* * * Fed balances before borrowing were extraordinarily elevated from Wednesday [September 16] though Monday [September 17]. But even with such high levels of Fed Balances, severe dislocations that interfered with their distribution in the first few days after the attacks caused many banks to borrow at the discount window to cover overdraft positions. As a result, levels of adjustment borrowing soared to record levels on Tuesday and Wednesday.

* * * This excess [in Fed balances] was highly concentrated at a small number of institutions that accumulated high balances as a result of an inability to make payments or to sell funds in the first days after the attacks, and it did not reflect any desire to hold huge excess balances. * * *

From Tuesday, September 11, through most of Thursday, September 13, market participants in both the government securities RP [repurchase] markets and in the federal funds market simply priced their trades at the target fund rate, a response to the attacks that likely helped maintain some order in these markets. The high levels of excess balances * * * first began to weigh heavily on the funds rate during late trading on Thursday and again on Friday, although through Monday, September 17, morning rate generally reverted back to the target. Thereafter, extremely low rates prevailed * * * for several days, falling even below 1 percent. These low rates in large measure reflected misperceptions that the Desk was continuing to provide high levels of balances. * * * Several episodes of rates being pushed higher in late-day trading, induced by the relatively low levels of Fed balances the Desk was leaving in place, were needed to nullify these perceptions and to bring the funds rate back up closer to the target. * * *

The decision on whether to intervene when there is a systemic risk may hinge on political concerns, as demonstrated by the failure of Enron Corp. in December 2001. At the time of that crisis, the economy was under stress, approaching recession, and the stock market was in freefall. The September 11 terrorist attacks had crippled large segments of the economy, including the airlines, which received government support following September 11. This suggested a precedent for Enron, particularly since the failure of a company as large as Enron and with such a high profile raised concerns that a market panic could occur. Several Enron officials were close to the Bush administration. Ken Lay, Enron's chief executive officer, was a personal friend of President George W. Bush and his father, former President George H.W. Bush. Lay had been offered a cabinet position in the senior Bush's administration and was co-chairman of his unsuccessful reelection campaign in 1992. Thomas E. White, a retired brigadier general in the United States Army and executive assistant to the chairman of the Joint Chiefs of Staff, was a senior Enron official before joining the Bush administration as Secretary of the Army. Despite those close ties, Enron's efforts to obtain a governmental rescue were rejected. Federal Reserve Chairman Alan Greenspan, Treasury Secretary Paul O'Neill, and Commerce Secretary Don Evans all turned down Enron's pleas for aid.

QUESTIONS AND NOTES

1. Who are the current Chairman and Vice–Chairman of the Fed? When do their terms expire?

2. In what Federal Reserve Bank district is your city located?

3. When did the Fed last announce an action intended to affect monetary policy? What was the action and what was it intended to do?

4. What are the current federal funds and discount rates? How do those rates compare to rates one year ago and five years ago? How do these rates compare to the prime rate and LIBOR?

5. Why are banks essential in implementing the monetary policy of the Fed?

6. Look at the paper currency in your wallet. Is there a difference in newer currency and older currency regarding the designation of the Federal Reserve Bank? The phrase, "In God We Trust" was added to paper currency in 1955 at the direction of Congress. There have been periodic attacks on constitutional grounds as constituting the establishment of a religion. "In God We Trust" was placed on U.S. coins in 1864 at the request of Salmon P. Chase, then Secretary of the Treasury.

7. The Fed returns a large portion of its income to the U.S. Treasury. Over 90% of its income is interest earned on government securities acquired in open market operations. Additional income includes services to depository institutions and foreign currency earnings.

(2) Fed Intervention in the Wake of the Financial Crisis

The financial crisis raised renewed concerns over systemic risk.

JERRY W. MARKHAMTHE SUBPRIME CRISIS—SOME THOUGHTS ON A "SUSTAINABLE" AND "ORGANIC" REGULATORY SYSTEM
4 FIU L. Rev. 381 (2009).

* * * In 2003, investment bankers purchased and issued over $230 billion in subprime securitizations, almost double that of the prior year. At first, the investment bankers were well rewarded for this effort. They were happily reporting large profits in 2004 and 2005 from subprime lending and proprietary trading activities. Their executives were given huge bonuses, but then the market turned.

There was danger here that was real and apparent. Subprime loans were often funded by the lender at short-term rates and then loaned to the subprime borrower at higher long-term rates. This allowed a profit from the spread between the two, *i.e.* long term interest rates are normally higher than short-term rates. As long as yield spreads are constant, that spread creates a steady stream of profits from the CDOs created to fund subprime mortgages. However, that advantage becomes a liability when short-term interest rates rise faster than long term rates, cutting that profit margin. That is exactly what happened when the Federal Reserve Board raised short-term interest rates, with seventeen straight increases between June 2004 and June 2006.

Those interest rate increases had a twofold effect. CDOs funded with short-term paper were no longer profitable and refunding became a problem with the arrival of the credit crunch in 2007. Those rate increases also placed pressure on subprime borrowers because many of those loans were offered at "teaser" rates that would be reset at much higher rates than subprime lenders would be unable to afford. In the rising market accompanying the real estate bubble, borrowers had been able to refinance their homes, pulling additional equity of the homes that allowed them to service their debt and buy other, often unneeded, items. They lost that ability as housing prices declined when the bubble broke.

Subprime borrowers then became delinquent on their loans in increasingly large numbers and many of those delinquent loans went into foreclosure. By December 2008, about 4.5 percent of all first lien mortgages were 90 days or more delinquent or in foreclosure. One in ten Alt–A mortgages were delinquent and more than 20 percent of subprime mortgages were delinquent or in foreclosure. The number of foreclosures in 2008 reached nearly 2.25 million, up from an annual rate of only about one million per year before the subprime crisis. In Lee County, Florida, judges were authorizing 1,000 foreclosures per day.

The effects of the Federal interest rate increases were devastating to the large investment banks. The thirty years following the first Bear Stearns offering of securitized subprime loans would destroy that venerable firm and push Wall Street into the subprime crisis. Merrill Lynch then had to be rescued by Bank of America, which then had to be rescued by the government as losses at Merrill Lynch continued to grow. The banking giant Wachovia was brought down by losses from a subprime lender Wachovia had bought to gain market share in such lending. Wachovia had to be rescued by Wells Fargo. Washington Mutual failed and was rescued by JPMorgan Chase. Fannie Mae and Freddie Mac were placed in conservatorship. European banks, including UBS AG suffered massive losses. The Royal Bank of Scotland had to be nationalized.

In a market test of systemic risk, the government allowed Lehman Brothers to fail, which touched off a frightful panic in the credit markets and on the stock exchanges. A horrifying run began on the money market funds, after the Reserve Primary Fund announced that it would "break-the-buck" because of losses from exposures to Lehman Brothers debt. That panic was quelled only after the government announced it would be guaranteeing money market funds.

In total, large investment banks wrote down over $150 billion in subprime mortgages by March 2008, and that amount was expected to double. The stock values of most large financial institutions were smashed. The last two large independent investment banking firms, Morgan Stanley and Goldman Sachs, converted to bank-holding companies in order to qualify for government bailouts. Citigroup also sustained massive loses from subprime structured investment vehicles ("Sivs" or more appropriately "SIEVs") and was saved only by a massive federal rescue package. That giant financial supermarket, which had become a market model, is being split up into more traditional lines. The contagion spread to the American International Group, which had to be bailed out by the federal government with a $170 billion rescue package.

Credit markets were frozen and liquidity became absent. The federal government mounted a momentous effort to deal with this crisis. Over a period of several months, interest rates were slashed down to near zero, unprecedented in U.S. history. Credit lending facilities were made available to financial service firms that were non-prime dealers, and later those facilities were extended to commercial firms when the commercial paper markets froze after the collapse of Lehman Brothers. A facility was also created to purchase asset-backed commercial paper from money market mutual funds. After an initial rejection, the [Troubled] Asset Relief Program ("TARP"), the $700 billion bailout program for financial service firms, was passed by Congress to inject capital into those struggling institutions. FDIC insurance was increased to $250,000, and an FDIC guarantee was extended to debt issuance by financial service firms. This, of course, created an increased, moral hazard.

In the meantime, the economy fell into recession. Unemployment rates were up [to almost ten percent], while sales and manufacturing were trending sharply downward. The housing market was in a near historic slump as new housing starts dwindled to a fifty-year low and existing home sales dropped. This had a ripple effect throughout the economy as construction workers were laid off, real estate agents idled, mortgage brokers closed, and other direct and indirect participants in the real estate market were sidelined. The automakers were also in extremis as automobile sales plunged. Chrysler and General Motors were saved from bankruptcy, [but only] temporarily, by a cash infusion from the federal government in the waning days of the Bush administration. * * *

The Fed stepped into the breach and authorized a number of new credit and liquidity programs. As a result of funding these programs, the Fed's balance sheet exploded, with its assets increasing from $907 billion on September 3, 2008, to $2.26 trillion a little over three months later on December 17, 2008. Near the end of July 2010, the Fed's assets were up to $2.33 trillion. This increase is accounted for, in part, by the Fed's dramatic increase in discount window lending. It also created the Term Auction Facility (TAF) in December 2007 as a longer-term source of funds for depository institutions to complement its short-term discount window lending. TAF credit originally carried a 28–day term, and later there was an option for 84–day credit. The Fed required collateral for TAF loans and the interest rate paid by the depository institution was determined by an auction of the available funds to eligible depository institutions. The final TAF auction was conducted on March 8, 2010.

The Fed also utilized its power to extend credit to "any individual partnership, or corporation," in time of "unusual and exigent circumstances" under section 13(3) of the Federal Reserve Act, 12 U.S.C.A. § 343. Pursuant to this authority, the Fed created several broad-based credit and liquidity facilities, some of which are described below. The most up-to-date information about these programs may be found at http://www.federalreserve.gov/monetarypolicy/bst.htm.

(1) Asset–Backed Commercial Paper Money Market Mutual Fund Liquidity Facility (ABCP MMMF). This facility made non-recourse loans on asset-backed commercial paper to curb panic in money market funds after the Reserve Primary Fund was unable to redeem shares at par value. This facility was closed on February 1, 2010.

(2) Commercial Paper Funding Facility (CPFF). This facility was created in October 2008 to buy unsecured commercial paper from corporate issuers through a special purpose vehicle. This facility is administered by the Federal Reserve Bank of New York. No new loans have been made under this facility after February 1, 2010.

(3) Term Asset–Backed Securities Loan Facility (TALF). This facility made non-recourse loans available to banks and commercial firms, including hedge funds, secured by collateral that included credit card debt, consumer loans, and student loans. No additional credit is being extended under this program.

(4) Term Securities Lending Facility (TSLF). This facility made credit available from overnight to up to 28–days and allowed primary dealers to

use illiquid collateral to secure their borrowings. Primary dealers are the securities broker-dealers that sell and buy securities to and from the Federal Reserve Bank of New York. The TSLF was closed on February 1, 2010.

(5) Mortgage-backed Purchase Program. Under this program the Fed bought direct obligations of Fannie Mae, Freddie Mac, and the Federal Home Loan Banks. As the result of the Fed's tremendous commitment to this program by the summer of 2010, it held mortgage-backed securities with a face value of over $1.1 trillion. Some observers are concerned that the magnitude of this investment has the potential to affect the Fed's interest rate policy since the value of the mortgage securities portfolio will decline by over $50 billion for each 1% increase in interest rates.[13] Selling these securities at face value before any interest rate increase reduces their face value, however, will drain money from a still weak economy.

In addition to these programs, the Fed used its Section 13(3) authority to provide targeted credit to Bear Stearns to facilitate its acquisition by JP Morgan Chase & Co., American International Group, Inc. (AIG) a large insurance firm and counter-party in a number of credit default swaps, Citigroup, and Bank of America. These credit extensions to particular institutions were criticized by many as government bailouts of institutions deemed too big to fail. The Fed refused to provide assistance to Lehman Brothers prior to its bankruptcy on September 15, 2008, on the basis that Lehman did not have adequate collateral for the amount of credit that it needed. Just two days later, however, section 13(3) was invoked by the Fed to provide assistance to AIG The uncertainty regarding when Fed assistance would be provided and when it would not sent the stock market into free fall.

(3) The Dodd–Frank Act and the Financial Stability Oversight Council

Congress responded to the systemic risk issues raised by the financial crisis in the Dodd–Frank Act. The Fed's emergency lending authority under section 13(3) of the Federal Reserve act was limited by section 1101 of the Dodd–Frank Act to permit assistance only to a "participant in any program or facility with broad-based eligibility." Presumably, aid to individual companies such as Bear Stearns and AIG will no longer be permitted. The Fed, in consultation with the Treasury Department, is required to adopt regulations for emergency lending programs or facilities consistent with this requirement and for the purpose of providing liquidity to the financial system, and not to aid a failing financial company. The collateral given as security for emergency loans must be sufficient to protect taxpayers from losses, and the new regulations must ensure that any such program is terminated in a "timely and orderly" fashion.

---

13. Binyamin Appelbaum, Mortgage Securities It Holds Pose Sticky Problem for Fed, N.Y. Times, July 22, 2010.

Insolvent borrowers are not eligible for this Fed credit. Treasury approval is also a prerequisite of any Fed liquidity or credit facility.[14]

In a similar fashion, the Dodd–Frank Act, in sections 1104–06, limits the FDIC's ability to offer general liquidity to an insured depository institution in times of financial distress, terminating the FDIC's ability to bypass the least cost resolution of a failing financial institution when its failure would have a "serious adverse effect on economic conditions or financial stability" and FDIC assistance pursuant to this systemic risk provision would "avoid or mitigate such adverse effects." The FDIC, under Dodd–Frank may, upon the written determination of the FDIC and the Fed, create a widely available program to guarantee obligations of solvent insured depository institutions or solvent depository institution holding companies. Dodd–Frank Act, § 1105 (known as a Section 1105 Program). This authority may be exercised during times of severe economic distress (a "liquidity event"), except that a guarantee of obligations may not include the provision of equity in any form. The maximum amount of such a guarantee program is to be set by the President and approved by Congress by joint resolution. A "liquidity event" is defined as an "exceptional and broad reduction" in the general ability of financial market participants to sell financial assets without an unusual and significant discount; or to borrow using financial assets as collateral without an "unusual and significant increase in margin," or an "unusual and significant reduction" in the ability of financial market participants to obtain unsecured credit.

The centerpiece of the Dodd–Frank Act's treatment of systemic risk was the creation of the Financial Stability Oversight Council (FSOC or the Council) that is chaired by the Secretary of the Treasury. The Council will be assisted by a newly-created Office of Financial Research (OFR) that will gather and analyze information for the Council. The voting members of the Council are the heads of the Fed, OCC, FDIC, SEC, CFTC, Federal Housing Finance Agency, the National Credit Union Administration, the new Bureau of Consumer Financial Protection, and an independent member appointed by the President and knowledgeable about insurance.[15] The Council is tasked with identifying risks to the financial stability of the United States. The Council is also charged with identifying systemically significant non-bank financial companies and making recommendations to the Fed on prudential standards. The Council is to act by majority vote except for some actions that require a supermajority. The supermajority is defined as two-thirds of the voting members, plus the vote of the Secretary

---

14. The Government Accountability Office (GAO) is required by the Dodd–Frank Act to conduct a one-time audit of all Federal Reserve emergency lending that took place during the financial crisis. The GAO was also given on-going authority to audit emergency lending, discount window lending, and open market transactions.

15. The five non-voting members of the Council are the Director of the OFR, the Director of a new Federal Insurance Office (FIO) within the Department of the Treasury, a state insurance commissioner, a state banking supervisor, and a state securities commissioner. Dodd–Frank Act § 111.

of the Treasury, effectively giving the Treasury Secretary a veto over any Council actions requiring supermajority approval.

The Dodd–Frank Act expands the power of the Fed over large nonbank financial companies, recognizing the risks to the financial system from the failure or near failure of such firms like Bear Stearns, Merrill Lynch, Lehman Brothers, and AIG, among others. If 85% of a company's consolidated revenues or assets are derived from "activities that are financial in nature," the Council may designate by the supermajority vote described above the company as a "nonbank financial company." Nonbank financial companies will be required to register with the Fed and are subjected to enhanced regulation and supervision regarding systemic risk issues. The factors to be considered by the Council in making the nonbank financial company designation include the company's relationship with bank holding companies and other nonbank financial companies, and the company's importance as a source of credit and liquidity for the financial system. The Fed is authorized to require reports and conduct examinations of the activities of nonbank financial companies and recommend enforcement actions by their functional regulator or take its own action if the functional regulator fails to respond. The Fed is further authorized to establish prudential risk standards for these nonbank financial companies.

The Council will also subject "large, interconnected" bank holding companies to additional supervision by the Fed. Bank holding companies, including foreign banking organizations, with consolidated assets of $50 billion or more may be designated by the Council as "large, interconnected bank holding companies" and subject to additional supervision by the Fed which will include additional capital, leverage, and liquidity requirements, along with resolution plans (referred to as "living wills"), asset concentration limits, and periodic stress testing.

The Council may also by supermajority vote permit the Fed to order these systemically significant companies to divest some of their holdings if the company poses a "grave threat" to the financial stability of the United States. This extraordinary power is to be used only as a last resort. In the event a company may not be saved, the Dodd–Frank Act provides for the orderly liquidation of the company without the possibility of a reorganization. Thus, these systemically significant institutions will be allowed to fail in contrast to the perception that during the financial crisis some institutions were deemed too big to fail. In an orderly liquidation, the FDIC is appointed as receiver of the covered financial institution, preempting the U.S. Bankruptcy Code, which will continue to apply to financial companies (other than banks) that do not pose a systemic risk.[16] An Orderly Liquidation Fund will be funded by assessments on fund claimants and, if needed, risk-based assessments on financial companies with consolidated assets of $50 billion or more. The FDIC will use the fund to reimburse any amounts it borrowed from the Treasury under its exercise of the orderly

---

16. The FDIC must appoint SIPC to act as trustee for the liquidation of a broker-dealer in any orderly liquidation of a broker-dealer pursuant to this authority.

liquidation authority. This orderly liquidation authority may also be applied by the Council to any financial company whose failure the Council deems to "pose a significant risk to the financial stability of the United States."

SECTION 4. CHARACTERISTICS OF BANKS

Banks may not operate without a government charter. That charter is provided by the Office of the Comptroller of the Currency (OCC) for a national bank or by the banking commissioner of one of the states for a state-chartered bank. State banks outnumber national banks, but national banks control 70% of all banking assets (up from 57% in 2004).

Depository Institutions Number and Asset Size[17]

Institution	Number	Assets (in millions)
National Banks	1,426	$8,498,282
State Member	834	1,671,281
State Nonmember	4,409	1,942,556
Total Banks	**6,669**	**$12,112,120**
U.S. Branches of Foreign Banks	**10**	**$28,018**
Federal Savings	745	$925,800
State Savings	402	318,514
Total Savings	**1,147**	**$1,244,314**
Federal Credit Unions	4,714	$482,684
State Credit Unions	2,840	402,069
Total Credit Unions	**7,554**	**$884,753**

The number of banks has declined in recent years, from 14,496 in 1984 to less than half that—6,669—in 2010. The number of U.S. commercial bank branches, however, increased from 41,799 in 1984 to 83,320 in 2010. This decrease in the number of banks is due in large part to the numerous bank mergers and acquisitions that followed the repeal of interstate banking and branching restrictions. The number of savings institutions and credit unions has also experienced a similar decline over time. For instance, in 1991, there were 2,560 savings institutions, while only 1,147 remained in 2010. The proliferation of regulations in recent years, and the costs associated with the new regulatory compliance, impacts smaller institutions more severely than larger institutions and may be an additional factor leading to further consolidation in the industry. Moreover, the financial crisis spawned a number of bank failures, reducing the total number of banks and leading to acquisitions of

---

17. Sources: FDIC Statistics on Banking, available at <www2.fdic.gov/idasp/index.asp> (More Key Statistics) (number of financial institutions as of July 22, 2010; financial data as of March 31, 2010); <http://www.ncua.gov/Resources/Reports/statistics/Yearend2009.pdf> (as of Dec. 31, 2009).

banks with depleted capital that were unable to maintain minimum capital standards on their own.

The chart demonstrates the relative numbers and asset sizes of the various types of depository institutions. There are more credit unions than any other type of depository institution, but credit unions are the smallest depository institutions in asset size. State nonmember banks outnumber state member and national banks, but are also generally smaller institutions in assets.

As the next chart demonstrates, banks with less than $1 billion in assets constitute ninety-two percent of all commercial banks, but control only 10% of all bank assets. The remaining banks (just over 8% in number) control 90% of all bank assets. The four largest banks control nearly half—45%—of all bank assets. There are a number of criteria for measuring bank size. Asset size is most commonly used. Rankings occur on various other factors, however, including deposits and market capitalization.[18]

Approximately 95% of all bank assets are under the control of holding companies. There remain a number of independent banks not owned by holding companies, but these tend to be small, community-oriented banks. For those banks owned by holding companies, the financial results for the holding company are reported on a consolidated basis and today include sources of revenue from a variety of financial activities, such as securities and insurance, in addition to traditional banking activities.

Size of FDIC Insured Commercial Banks[19]

	< $100 mill in assets	$100 mill to $1 bill	$1 bill to $1 trillion	> $1 trillion
Number	2,469	3,780	519	4
Percent	36%	56%	8%	<1%
Assets (in mills)	$138,700	$1,098,100	$5,441,871	$5,407,829
Percent	1%	9%	45%	45%

---

18. Market capitalization is the product of the number of shares of stock outstanding of the bank or its holding company multiplied by the current market price of those shares.

19. Assets and Liabilities of FDIC–Insured Commercial Banks at <www2.fdic.gov/qbp/2010mar/qbp.pdf> (as of Match 31, 2010); banks with assets over $1 trillion found at <www2.fdic.gov/idasp/main.asp?formname=inst> (as of March 31, 2010).

Bank and Thrift Holding Companies by Assets[20]   2010

Rank	Institution	Assets (Thousands)
1	Bank of America Corp.	$2,340,667,014
2	JPMorgan Chase & Co.	2,135,796,000
3	Citigroup Inc.	2,002,213,000
4	Wells Fargo & Company	1,223,630,000
5	The Goldman Sachs Group, Inc.	880,677,000
6	Morgan Stanley	819,719,000
7	Metlife, Inc.	565,566,452
8	Barclays Group US Inc.	427,837,000
9	Taunus Corporation	364,079,000
10	HSBC North America Holdings Inc.	345,382,871

Included on the list above is one insurance company that owns a bank, MetLife; three foreign holding companies, Barclays Group US, the U.S. holding company for the U.K.-based bank, Taunus Corporation, the North American subsidiary of Germany's Deutsche Bank AG, and HSBC North America Holdings, the holding company for the U.K.'s HSBC Bank; and two investment banks that became bank holding companies during the financial crisis—Goldman Sachs Group and Morgan Stanley.[21] Citigroup lost its position as the largest bank holding company during the financial crisis as JPMorgan Chase & Co. acquired two struggling firms in Bear Stearns and Washington Mutual (itself formerly in the top ten), and Bank of America merged with the ailing investment bank, Merrill Lynch. Wells Fargo bought the failing Wachovia and more than doubled its asset size moving further up the list.

The next chart, the list of the largest commercial banks ranked by assets, is slightly different. There are now four commercial banks with over $1 trillion in assets, with a significant fall-off in size to the commercial bank ranked fifth in asset size. These four institutions combined account for 45% of all assets controlled by commercial banks. In 2004, then-FDIC Chairman Powell commented on the consolidation trend:

> Since 1985 the number of community banks declined by half, from over 14,000 to just over 7,000 today. In 1985, the top ten banking organizations held 16 percent of industry deposits. Today their share is 40 percent. * * * We could well see a banking industry with a few institutions having assets in the trillions of dollars and perhaps only half as many community banks as we have today. * * * [W]e believe a disparity of this magnitude among banking organization requires us to rethink the way we administer the deposit insurance system.[22]

---

20. Top 50 Bank Holding Companies at <www.ffiec.gov/nicpubweb/nicweb/Top50Form.aspx> (as of June 30, 2010).

21. This conversion to bank holding company status is discussed further in Chapter 4, Section 2.

22. Donald E. Powell, Remarks Before the National Association for Business Economics, Mar. 26, 2004 (available at <www.fdic.gov/news/news/press/2004/pr3004.html>).

Commercial Banks by Assets[23]

Rank	Institution	Assets (Thousands)
1	JPMorgan Chase Bank, NA	$1,674,523,000
2	Bank of America, NA	1,496,322,329
3	Citibank, NA	1,171,094,000
4	Wells Fargo Bank, NA	1,065,890,000
5	U.S. Bank, NA	277,509,284
6	PNC Bank, NA	254,518,132
7	FIA Card Services, NA	212,895,604
8	HSBC Bank USA, NA	183,562,481
9	The Bank of New York Mellon	162,064,000
10	SunTrust Bank	160,993,399

SECTION 5. INCOME STATEMENT

On a quarterly and annual basis, banks or their holding companies prepare an income statement showing income and expenses for the relevant time period. Traditionally, banks have earned most of their income from the interest charged on loans. The income statement reports net interest income which is the gross interest received by the bank less the expenses incurred to produce that interest income such as interest paid on deposits. An increasingly important source of income for banks is fee income charged for other services. These include services related to the traditional bank account, such as account maintenance fees, bounced check charges and so on. The fees also include charges for a broader range of financial services offered by the bank or through its holding company affiliates, such as commissions on insurance sales, commissions on sales of securities, fees for trading foreign currency, and fees for underwriting bond and stock issuances.

The basic business of banking is profitable when a bank's cost of funds (interest paid on deposits) is less than what the bank earns on those funds (interest charged on loans). The savings and loan crisis of the 1980s demonstrated that there is a great deal of instability built into the basic business model of a depository institution. The source of funds—deposits—are short-term in nature. Most deposits may be withdrawn by the customer upon demand. The cost of these funds is variable. The interest rate the bank pays its customers on deposits fluctuates with market interest rates. On the other hand, the use of the funds is often for fixed-rate loans which are usually for a specific term, which, in the case of home mortgage loans, can be as long as thirty years. When market interest rates are increasing, such as during a time of inflation, the bank must pay ever-increasing rates of interest to retain the funds of its depositors, but cannot re-price the fixed interest rate portion of its loan portfolio. It is not

---

23. Top 100 Banks and Thrifts Nationally by Asset Size at <www2.fdic.gov/idasp/main.asp> (financial data as of March 31, 2010).

surprising, then, that depository financial institutions continually seek other—hopefully more stable—sources of income.

Bank efforts to increase non-interest income have been largely successful. In 1989, 31% of banks' net income came from non-interest income; in 1999, that percentage had increased to 43%, and it increased further to 46% in 2005.

As you examine the income statement of a bank, you may notice that personnel expenses are often the largest expense item other than interest expenses. The merger and acquisition frenzy among banks in recent decades is attributable in part to the ability to combine two banks and eliminate overlapping personnel and the associated expenses. An unfortunate aftermath of most bank merger transactions is that many bank employees lose their jobs, especially when there is significant geographic overlap between the merging banks.

Once expenses are subtracted from income, the bank or holding company determines whether it will pay a dividend to shareholders and the size of any dividend. The dividend payment is taken from the net income amount. The resulting figure is referred to as retained earnings. This amount is an addition to capital. If expenses exceed income, the resulting loss reduces the firm's capital.

Certain financial ratios are helpful in evaluating a bank's performance and in making comparisons among banks. The net interest margin is the difference between the average rate earned on loans and the average interest rate paid on deposits. The higher that margin, the better. It is typical for the margin to be close to 4%. The net interest margin for the banking industry fell from 4.69% in 1992, to 4.10% by year-end 2003, to 3.39% for the second quarter of 2007. The overhead efficiency ratio is calculated by dividing the noninterest expenses (such as employee salaries and other operating expenses) by the bank's total revenue. The lower that percentage, the better. The leanest banks have ratios in the 35–40% range. Many banks have ratios of 60–70%, however. Larger banks tend to have lower efficiency ratios than smaller banks because of economies of scale. On the other hand, if the banks earns a high percentage of its income from fee-based businesses rather than the interest-rate spread, its efficiency ratio may be higher because fee-based businesses may require substantial investments in technology or higher, commission-based compensation.

One item found on a bank's income statement may be a deduction from revenue for "loan loss reserves." This deduction is one that depends on management's discretionary forecast of loans that are likely to result in a loss. Loan loss reserves are discussed further in Chapter 5.

SECTION 6. BALANCE SHEET

Another important measure of a bank's performance and its financial condition is the balance sheet. The asset side of a bank's balance sheet shows the valuation of the bank's assets at the end of each quarter and annually. A bank's assets include cash, investments (including government securities owned by the bank), real estate (such as the bank premises), and loans. In most banks, loans are the largest asset of the bank.

The other half of a bank's balance sheet must balance with the asset total. The other half includes the bank's liabilities, such as its deposits (the money it owes back to its depositors upon their demand for repayment) and any other debt. Also on the other half of the balance sheet is the bank's equity capital. Equity capital includes the amounts paid to the bank by its shareholders when the stock was initially issued, debt incurred by the bank that is subordinated to its other debt (and thus bears many of the loss-bearing characteristics of the contributions of the shareholders), and retained earnings.

Banks are highly leveraged firms. This means they have a relatively large amount of liabilities compared to the capital that they hold. A bank must be in compliance with regulatory minimum capital levels, which are described in more detail in Chapter 7. Because of this high leverage, banks are particularly susceptible to increases in the interest they must pay on their liabilities. If that cost rises to more than the bank earns on its assets, the bank will experience the "dark side" of leverage. If the bank's cost of funds is less than what it earns, it has "leveraged" the capital provided by its shareholders, through borrowing, and thereby increased the return on the shareholders' equity.

In examining a bank's balance sheet, there are several financial ratios that may prove helpful. The debt to equity ratio measures the amount of leverage on the balance sheet. It was thought that many large financial services firms had over-leveraged themselves before the subprime crisis and were unable to respond to the liquidity crunch that dried up their funding sources. In response to those concerns the Dodd–Frank Act authorized the Fed to establish leverage ratios limiting debt to equity of no more than 15 to 1. The return on equity (ROE) is the amount of money that is earned by the bank divided by the dollar amount of equity capital. Analysts generally expect banks to have an ROE of 15% or above; in good years many banks have enjoyed ROE's in excess of 20%. The return on assets is earnings divided by total assets. The ROA is expected to be 1% or above. Most banks like to have an ROA of 1.25–1.30%.

SECTION 7. CHALLENGES TO THE TRADITIONAL BUSINESS OF BANKS

The traditional function of banks—to serve as a financial intermediary and to provide transaction services—is under attack on a number of fronts. Many former bank loan customers are now able to bypass the bank as an intermediary and obtain money directly from the capital markets at a lower rate. Large corporate borrowers may now borrow funds for working capital purposes in the commercial paper market rather than seeking a line of credit from a bank. Commercial paper is the name of a promissory note issued by a borrower to a lender for a short term loan, typically with a maturity of less than 270 days. Commercial paper lenders may include insurance companies and pension funds. Some large corporate borrowers access the capital markets directly by securitizing their assets, rather than borrowing from a bank using those assets as collateral.

The success of banks as financial intermediaries may be traced in part to their expertise in evaluating potential borrowers (an advantage that depositors who provide the funds the banks loan may not have), the information available to them about the borrower and about general market conditions, and their access to deposits with which to fund loans. Technological innovations in recent years have erased many of these advantages formerly held by banks. For instance, sophisticated credit scoring programs are available to bank and nonbank lenders. Technology permits information to be readily disseminated, digested, and analyzed. To the extent that information confers expertise, the expertise advantage of banks may also be reduced. Moreover, large quantities of funds are available from other institutions (insurance companies and mutual funds) that also have adequate information and expertise to evaluate credit and market risks.

Banks have also faced challenges to their former monopoly as the provider of transaction accounts. As previously noted, since the early 1980s other depository institutions, such as savings and loans, have been able to offer transaction accounts. Securities brokers developed cash management accounts which provided features similar (although not identical) to a checking account and caused many depositors to forego keeping large deposits at a bank for relatively little interest in exchange for increased earnings opportunities through a brokerage account, even though the number of transactions might be limited in number or require a minimum amount per transaction. Today, many securities brokers have affiliated with banks through common ownership to offer FDIC-insured deposit accounts to their customers, taking money out of traditional banks in favor of the captive bank owned by the securities firm. One result of this competition for deposit dollars is that banks are relying increasingly on other funding sources, such as brokered deposits and commercial paper. In 1992, 95% of banks had core deposits[24] in excess of 65% of assets. At the end of 2000, only 75% of all banks had an equivalent percentage of core deposits, indicating the increased reliance by banks on other funding sources The rates banks must pay on commercial paper and brokered deposits are generally more volatile than the interest paid on core deposits. This can result in reduced earnings when interest rates increase for a bank relying heavily on non-core deposit funding sources.

---

24. Core deposits are those that are considered stable and thus provide a long-term source of funds.

E. GERALD CORRIGAN[25]
ARE BANKS SPECIAL?

Federal Reserve Bank of Minneapolis, 1982 Annual Report Essay.
<www.minneapolisfed.org>.

The recent evolution of the financial structure in the United States has produced two competing points of view regarding the proper direction for further change. On the one hand, there is the view that the "financial services industry"—encompassing banks, thrifts, brokers, investment banks, and insurance companies—should be looked at as a single entity. * * *

The competing, if not opposing, view is that banks are indeed special. This view holds that specialization of financial institutions has worked well and, at least in some cases, specialization may still be more efficient and also better serve the public interest. This view is associated with the historical separation of banking from commerce and from investment banking. In general, this "separation doctrine" in banking grew out of concerns about concentration of financial power, possible conflicts of interest, and the appropriate scope of risks banks should incur in the face of the special trusteeship falling on institutions that engage in the lending of depositors' money. In a shorthand way, as pertains to banks and the banking system, these concerns are typically captured by the phrase, "safety and soundness." * * *

What Makes Banks Special? Reduced to essentials, it would appear that there are three characteristics that distinguish banks from all other classes of institutions—both financial and nonfinancial. They are:

Banks offer transaction accounts.

Banks are the backup source of liquidity for all other institutions.

Banks are the transmission belt for monetary policy. * * *

Only banks issue transaction accounts; that is, they incur liabilities payable on demand at par and are readily transferable by the owner to third parties. The owner of a transaction account can demand and receive currency in the face amount deposited in the account; write a check in the full amount of the account; or perhaps most importantly the owner of the account can transfer the full amount of the account to a third party almost instantaneously by wire transfer. The liquidity, mobility, and acceptability of bank issued transaction accounts permit our diverse economic and financial system to work with the relative ease and efficiency to which we are accustomed. Moreover, in periods of financial stress, the capacity to quickly move transaction account balances to third parties takes on special significance by providing elements of flexibility and certainty in making and receiving payments that help to insure that financial disruptions do not spread. Individual banks can also create these

---

25. [eds.] At the time this article was written, Mr. Corrigan was the President of the Federal Reserve Bank of Minneapolis.

highly liquid and mobile balances through their lending function. The capacity to "create" liabilities with these characteristics is vital to the ongoing needs of commerce, but it takes on special significance in periods of financial stress.

Because of the peculiarities of law and regulation, not all classes of transaction accounts have the same precise legal or regulatory characteristics. The "demand deposit" is the purest form of transaction account, since, for example, negotiable order of withdrawal (NOW) accounts and some share drafts at mutual organizations have restrictions on the extent to which they are payable on demand. * * * If a financial asset satisfies the functional test of being payable on demand at par and readily transferable to a third party, it should—for those purposes—be a "transaction" balance. * * *

[T]he critical difference between banks and other classes of financial institutions rests with the capacity of banks to incur (and to create) liabilities that are payable on demand at par and that are readily transferable to third parties. The resulting mismatch of the maturities of assets and liabilities makes banks particularly vulnerable to sudden drains on deposits that can jeopardize their solvency. In practice, depositors—reinforced by the public policy safety net—have demonstrated tendencies to drain deposits from particular banks only when confronted with the reality or the perception of losses growing out of asset management problems and/or poor management of banking organizations. Thus, while the deposit taking function of banks is what makes them unique, the integrity of that process depends upon the risks, real and perceived, associated with the lending and related activities of the banking system as a whole and its capacity to absorb shocks in the short run.

* * * [E]xperience also suggests that public confidence in the ability of banks to meet their deposit obligations is ultimately related to the quality of bank assets and to the overall financial condition of the bank. This relationship takes on additional importance when it is recalled that banks can also create, through their lending activities, transaction deposits. Indeed, in a very real way banks are the primary source of liquidity for all other classes and sizes of institutions, both financial and nonfinancial.

The extent to which banks play this role cannot be judged simply by looking at the number and value of loans on the books of banking organizations. For these purposes, contingent credit obligations of banks, such as loan commitments and standby letters of credit, must be considered in virtually the same light as direct loans. These standby credit facilities are, for example, the arrangements which permit most financial markets and institutions to function as they do. It is highly unlikely that the commercial paper market would function very well were it not for the presence of standby bank credit facilities obtained by those corporations that issue commercial paper. Similarly, it is very difficult to imagine that even the best managed and capitalized broker/dealers could handle their day-to-day business with the efficiency that is now so common without ready access to bank lines of credit. The same, of course, applies to nonfinancial corporations. Indeed, while all such institutions may over time, have access to a wide variety of funding sources, direct or standby bank credit facilities are the cornerstone upon which these alternative sources of credit rest. If there are problems in one segment of the credit network, institutions will simply shift their borrowing activities elsewhere in the network. However, if the problem is in the banking sector, banks must either turn to each other or to the central bank. * * *

[V]irtually all other financial markets and other classes of institutions are directly or indirectly dependent on the banking system as their standby or backup source of credit and liquidity. Banks can fulfill this function for a variety of reasons, including their relative ease of access to deposit and nondeposit sources of funding. However, experience suggests that the capacity to provide this function or more directly, to provide access to these markets and sources of funding—like the integrity of the deposit taking function—is ultimately related to the overall financial strength of banks and the quality of bank assets. This role of banks as a standby source of liquidity takes on special significance in periods of stress and in this light underscores the importance of rigorous and impartial credit judgments by banks. This, in turn, provides a particularly relevant context in which concerns about the commingling of banking and other interests should be evaluated.

As the preceding discussion suggests, there is a direct link between banks and the central bank arising in part from the central banks' lender of last resort function. More broadly the fact that banks are subject to reserve requirements places the banking system in the unique position of being the "transmission belt" through which the actions and policies of the central bank have their effect on financial market conditions, money and credit creation, and economic conditions generally. To put it somewhat differently, the required reserves of the banking system have often been described as the fulcrum upon which the monetary authority operates monetary policy. The reserves in the banking system also serve the complementary purpose of providing the working balances which permit our highly efficient financial markets to function and to effect the orderly end-of-day settlement of the hundreds of billions of dollars of transactions that occur over the course of each business day.

* * * [A]lthough recent developments may have introduced elements of slack into the transmission belt. For example, the proliferation of close substitutes for bank-issued transaction accounts narrows the effective scope of reserve coverage. The narrowed reserve coverage can introduce more slippage into the process of monetary control, and it also means that a relatively smaller reserve base is supporting a larger flow of payments. Similarly the deregulation of the liability side of banks' balance sheets seems to imply that, in order to achieve a given degree of monetary restraint, a higher level of market interest rates is required than might otherwise have been the case. Further, increased leverage of banking organizations may work in the direction of introducing slippage into the

monetary control process, in that a larger volume of credit flows may be associated with some given rate of growth of "money". Finally, higher leverage and greater risk exposure may weaken the capacity of the banking system to adjust to and to absorb the changes in credit market conditions that must accompany periodic monetary restraint. * * *

Over time, a variety of tests have been used for the purpose of defining a bank. These tests ranged from a charter test to the functional test of issuing demand deposits and making commercial loans. At one time, each of these tests was satisfactory. However, currently neither existing statutes nor regulations seem to contain a definition that is satisfactory.

A satisfactory definition of a bank must start with a clear recognition of the essential functions provided by such institutions. From the earlier discussion, it is clear that the single characteristic of banks that distinguishes them from other classes of institutions is that they issue transaction accounts; that is, accounts that in law, in regulation, or in practice are payable on demand at par and are readily transferable to third parties. A powerful case can be made that the definition of a bank should stop right there: a bank is any organization that is *eligible* to issue transaction accounts. If an institution meets this test, it would (1) be eligible for government deposit insurance; (2) have direct access to the discount window; (3) be subject to the Feds' reserve requirements; and (4) have direct access to the Federal Reserves' payments services, particularly the wire transfer system. For these purposes, an appropriate statute would have to redefine transaction accounts. At a minimum, such a definition would have to include conventional demand deposits, NOW accounts, and share drafts. It might also include the new money market deposit accounts (MMDAs) and, depending on the standards of definition, perhaps even MMMFs [money market mutual funds] or other nonbank institutional arrangements that provide "check" writing capabilities.

* * * Taken by itself, there is nothing unique or special about the asset side of a banks' balance sheet, except for the limits on the scope of asset acquisition powers discussed below. Concerns about the nature and risk characteristics of bank assets arise in the context of the unique nature of bank liabilities, the need to preserve the integrity of the deposit taking function, and the special trusteeship growing out of that function. Thus, while it may be appropriate from the standpoint of public policy to limit the asset powers of banks to certain less risky activities, the definition of a bank need only deal with the liability side of the balance sheet. * * *

By this definition, existing commercial banks, thrifts, and credit unions would be considered "banks." * * * Treating thrifts and certain other institutions as "banks" raises a host of difficult and politically charged issues relating to regulatory treatment, tax status, divestiture, and grandfathering arrangements. However, for purposes of this discussion, the fact that certain "nonbank" financial institutions are, for a variety of reasons, banks does not require immediate or perhaps even parallel regulation. Rather, the suggestion would be that there is an essential core of regulation that should apply more or less equally to this broader class of institutions which provides essential banking functions. * * *

JULIE L. WILLIAMS & MARK P. JACOBSEN[26]
THE BUSINESS OF BANKING: LOOKING TO THE FUTURE

50 Bus. Law. 783 (1995).

* * * The scope of the business of banking is not merely an interesting theoretical issue. As all are aware, the financial services industry is continuing to evolve rapidly. If banks do not keep up, they will become obsolete. While the present condition of the U.S. banking industry is generally strong, the banking industry has experienced a long-term secular decline in its traditional activities. In the last twenty-five years, the share of credit market assets held by banks has dropped in half. The decline of U.S. banks in the international markets has been equally dramatic.

Why? When many of the current restrictions on bank activities were put in place, they reflected a compromise of sorts. While banks were restricted in the activities they could conduct and were subject to significant regulation, they also were the preeminent providers of transaction services and lending products commonly associated with banking. The first half of this bargain remains largely intact, but not the latter. As a result of fundamental economic developments, legislative and regulatory changes, and advancements in technology, banks now face competition from nonbanking organizations in almost all of their activities. And because banks face greater restrictions, more intense examinations, higher regulatory costs, and broader obligations in connection with their lending and deposit-taking activities, nonbank organizations frequently have the competitive upper hand.

Banks have seen, and may continue to see, their market share of commercial and industrial loans erode. The banking industry's most stable and successful corporate customers now turn to the cheaper commercial paper market (which is dominated by investment banks, insurance companies, and other nonbank institutions), Euromarkets, and foreign banks when they need funds. These markets and organizations have no intrinsic advantages over commercial banks. They simply operate under less regulation and hence have more flexibility and generally lower costs. The loss of these high-quality customers to nonbanking organizations affects banks beyond their bottom lines. It shifts bank lending portfolios into areas of greater risk, ultimately affecting the relative safety and soundness of the industry.

---

26. Julie Williams is the First Senior Deputy Comptroller and the Chief Counsel of the Office of the Comptroller of the Currency, the regulator of nationally chartered banks.

The situation is little better with banks' traditional consumer business. In the past two decades, consumers have invested hundreds of billions of dollars in uninsured nonbank money market accounts and mutual funds, which can offer more attractive returns than deposits. Nonbank firms offer check-writing services through their cash management accounts. Many nonbanking entities (e.g., finance companies, retailers that sell on credit, and mortgage companies) have become major players in the consumer credit market. Once more, the nonbank competition has been inching banks into increasingly more risky business areas. Having lost a substantial share of the secured consumer credit market (e.g., motor vehicle loans and home mortgages), banks have turned increasingly toward the revolving-credit market, where the credit is unsecured. Even in this market, though, the competition with nonbanks is intense, narrowing the returns.

Banks' continuing ability to serve their customers and to play a meaningful role in the national economy hinges on their ability to respond to changing markets and customer needs. Without the ability to retain existing customers and to attract new business, banks will continue to shrink relative to other financial service providers, or take on higher risks within the scope of their permissible activities, or both. The former will diminish access to credit for many borrowers dependant on banks, such as small businesses. The latter could undermine the industry's safety and soundness. From the perspective of both industry viability and the customer benefits that flow from healthy competition, the issue of whether banks can offer a competitive range of products and services is a vital, practical concern. * * *

KATHERINE SAMOLYK
THE EVOLVING ROLE OF COMMERCIAL BANKS
IN U.S. CREDIT MARKETS

FDIC, Future of Banking Study, FOB–2004–01.1.
<www.fdic.gov/bank/analytical/future/index.html>.

* * * This paper assesses concerns that banks are becoming less important in U.S. credit markets, using available data to quantify the importance of commercial banks as credit providers—to quantify their "market share." Certainly as the debt capacity of the U.S. economy expanded in the 1980s, the share of nonfinancial-sector debt that was directly funded by banks declined. This decline was associated with a dramatic increase in the extent to which lending to households and businesses became securitized—that is, standardized, pooled, and funded by the issue of securities. The shift away from traditional intermediation towards asset securitization reflects not only changing credit technologies but also the activity of government-sponsored enterprises. The shift towards funding credit through securities markets also reflects fundamental changes in how individuals accumulate assets, due to changes in technology, pension regulations, and demographics.

Long-term instruments such as home mortgages are arguably better suited to securitization as a funding mode because of the maturity mismatch inherent in depository institution funding. However, it is harder to make the same case for the private securitization of some other types of loans—for example, credit card receivables. Nevertheless, banks play a prominent role in this type of securitization activity, so this may be a way for banks to fund loans effectively by issuing secured debt while they continue to be involved in all other aspects of the provision of credit (including the relationship with the customer and the responsibility for maintaining the quality of the pool of loans being funded). This alternative funding mode has allowed banks to make more loans than they would have been able to if they had relied on deposits alone as a funding source.

Thus, although commercial banking's on-balance-sheet activity has declined as a piece of the credit-market pie, the industry's off-balance-sheet activities are a growing source of income. Hence the ultimate finding of this study must be that banking is evolving but does not appear to be declining. Even according to some fairly traditional measures, the commercial banking industry remains remarkably important in funding credit flows in the United States—especially credit flows to nonfinancial businesses.

What, then, can we say about the future of banking? Although the extent to which commercial banks directly fund nonfinancial sectors in our economy has been stable since 1993, such stability does not preclude future declines. Future increases in the economy's debt capacity are not likely to take the traditional form of intermediation. Thus, it will continue to be important for researchers to study the evolving roles banks play in our financial sector, the risks these roles pose for the industry, and the implications of these evolving roles for broader financial stability. For example, policy makers very much need evidence about the risks inherent in the unbundling and repackaging of credit and about the implications of these risks.

The secular shift by banks toward funding business lending that is collateralized by real estate represents a shift to a type of lending that has been associated with localized banking-sector problems. This association is likely to be most problematic for community banks, which are more geographically focused in their activities, than for larger banking companies operating a wide range of profit centers over broader geographic areas. In general, off-balance-sheet activities imply an ever more critical role for large banking organizations.

The services that commercial banks provide in enhancing the liquidity and credit quality of claims funded elsewhere undoubtedly reflect the industry's unique status in our financial sector. The role of banks in making credit marketable indicates that commercial banking remains a critical force in the modern flow of funds that has contributed to the broader availability of credit in the U.S. economy.

QUESTIONS AND NOTES

1. Download from the SEC's Edgar database or your bank's own website your bank or holding company's most recent 10–Q (quarterly report) or 10–K (annual report). Calculate or note the following for that institution:

(a) Percent of total net income attributable to net interest income.

(b) Percent of total net income attributable to personnel expense.

(c) List the sources of noninterest income. What is the primary source of noninterest income?

(d) If the bank paid a dividend, what is the annual percentage return to shareholders of the dividend based on the bank's current market price?

(e) The net interest margin.

(f) The overhead efficiency ratio.

(g) The amount of loan loss reserves.

(h) Return on assets.

(i) Return on equity.

2. Based on the information you just collected, evaluate the biggest challenges facing the continuing success of this bank.

3. Mr. Corrigan updated his essay "Are Banks Special?," excerpted earlier in this chapter, in 2000, <www.minneapolisfed.org>. Does Mr. Corrigan believe that banks are still special after the passage of the Gramm–Leach–Bliley Act in 1999?

CHAPTER FOUR

BANK REGULATION TODAY

■ ■ ■

SECTION 1.   REGULATORY STRUCTURE

Banks are subject to a number of different regulators. The table below shows that there are two different *primary* regulators of banks. For banks that have elected a state charter, there is also a primary *federal* regulator. One of three different federal regulators will be the primary federal regulator of the bank, depending on how the bank is organized. It is no wonder that banking law is a lawyer's paradise.

Bank Regulatory Structure

Bank Type	Primary Regulator	Primary Federal Regulator
National	OCC	OCC
State Member	State	Fed
State Nonmember	State	FDIC

A bank's regulator (or one of its regulators if it is a state chartered bank) will have responsibility for chartering, examining, supervising, and enforcing applicable laws with respect to the bank. The OCC is the Office of the Comptroller of the Currency,[1] an agency within the U.S. Department of the Treasury. The Fed is the Federal Reserve Board of Governors (sometimes referred to as the FRB). The FDIC is the Federal Deposit Insurance Corporation. Each state has its own regulatory entity for state chartered banks. That same state entity may also regulate state savings

---

1.   The word "comptroller" is a variation of "controller." Over time, "comptroller" because associated with the holder of a government office. Originally, both words were pronounced "con-TROLL-er." Now, however, many pronounce the M and the P in comptroller. Either pronunciation is recognized, but do not be surprised if you still hear "comptroller" pronounced like "controller."

associations and credit unions, depending upon how the state has organized its depository regulatory structure.

The Federal Financial Institutions Examination Council (FFIEC) was created in 1979 pursuant to the Financial Institutions Regulatory and Interest Rate Control Act of 1978 (FIRA). The FFIEC's purpose is to set uniform principles for federal examination of financial institutions and to make recommendations to promote uniformity in supervision. The FFIEC is an interagency body composed of the Comptroller of the Currency, the Chairman of the FDIC, a Fed governor designated by the Fed Chairman, the Director of the Bureau of Consumer Financial Protection (BCFP, the division of the Fed created by the Dodd–Frank Act to regulate consumer financial products or services),[2] the Director of the National Credit Union Administration (NCUA, the federal regulator of credit unions), and, since the passage of the Financial Services Regulatory Relief Act of 2006, the chairperson of the State Liaison Committee. The State Liaison Committee is composed of five representatives of state financial institution regulatory agencies. 12 U.S.C.A. § 3303(a).

A national bank receives its charter from the OCC; a state bank receives its charter from the state in which its principal place of business is to be located. The availability of a charter choice is the hallmark of what is commonly referred to as the "dual banking system." Only state chartered banks existed until 1864 when the national charter option was created with the passage of the National Bank Act. Although many expected national banks to then predominate and for state banks to convert to the national charter, competition between the two chartering systems continued and remains intense even today. National banks control 70% of all bank assets, but only 21% of banks have a national charter. A bank may fairly easily convert from one charter to the other.

A state chartered bank is primarily regulated by the state bank regulator in the state where the bank's principal place of business is located. A state bank is not exempt from federal regulation, however. If the state bank has elected to become a member of the Federal Reserve System then its primary federal regulator is the Federal Reserve Board (the Fed) and the bank is referred to as a "state member" bank. If the state bank has elected not to join the Fed, then its primary federal regulator is the Federal Deposit Insurance Corporation (FDIC), and the bank is referred to as a "state nonmember" bank. Most state banks are state nonmember banks. The privileges of Federal Reserve membership (such as access to the discount window and assistance with check clearing) have, since the 1980s, been available to all banks, whether or not Fed members. Sometimes banks owned by a holding company elect Fed membership so that the bank's primary federal regulator and the holding company's regulator will be the same—the Fed.

---

2. Dodd-Frank Act, at § 1091 (substituting the Director of the BCFP for the Director of the OTS on the FFIEC). Before the creation of the BCFP in the Dodd–Frank Act, this spot was held by the Director of the Office of Thrift Supervision, whose functions were transferred to other federal financial regulatory agencies under Dodd–Frank.

[handwritten margin note: Most banks are corps - but can be S-corps]

Most banks are organized as corporations. Indeed, that is currently the only permissible organizational structure for a national bank and for banks in many states. Banks may elect S Corporation status, which permits a bank to pass-through its income and losses to its shareholders so that they may avoid the taxation of corporate earnings at the corporate level and again when the earnings are paid out to shareholders as dividends. S corporations are subject to numerous limitations, including a maximum of 100 shareholders.[3] A handful of states permit a bank to be organized as a limited liability company (LLC). The advantages of such a structure include pass-through treatment of earnings and losses without the restrictions of the S corporation. Since 1996, business entities not specifically classified as corporations may elect partnership tax treatment through an LLC, but IRS regulations classify as a corporation (ineligible for pass-through treatment) a state-chartered entity operating as a bank if any of its deposits have FDIC insurance. Treas. Reg. § 301.7701–2 & –3. The IRS regulation must be changed before bank LLCs are a realistic optional organizational structure.[4]

By statute, the FDIC may only supply deposit insurance to a depository institution engaged in the business of receiving deposits. 12 U.S.C. § 1815. A depository institution includes a state bank which "is *incorporated* under the laws of any State." 12 U.S.C. § 1813(a)(2) (emphasis added). The FDIC amended its regulations to facilitate the formation of bank LLCs by providing that a bank chartered as an LLC pursuant to state law is deemed to be "incorporated" in the state if under the state's law the LLC has attributes of perpetual succession, centralized management, limited liability, and freely transferable interests. 12 C.F.R. § 303.15.

[handwritten margin note: Limited powers - statute reg'd activities]

A bank is a creature of limited powers. A bank may only engage in activities specifically authorized for it by its chartering authority by statute, regulation, or application. To the extent that a bank wishes to engage in activities beyond its approved banking powers, it may consider conducting a broader range of activities (again subject to statutory authorization and regulatory approval) in a subsidiary of the bank, or the bank may form a holding company to own the stock of the bank and the stock of one or more sister corporations engaged in nonbanking activities. Some banks conduct nonbanking activities in subsidiaries of the bank as well as in sister corporations owned by a common holding company. Many banks are owned by holding companies, but a number of banks, especially recently chartered banks, are independently owned by individual shareholders (sometimes called "stand-alone" banks).

A bank may own service corporations, operating subsidiaries, and financial subsidiaries. It is possible that a financial subsidiary may engage in a broad range of financial activities under the Gramm–Leach–Bliley Act of 1999.

---

3. 26 U.S.C.A. § 1361(b).

4. See T. Scott Kummer, Note, Should the IRS Continue to Deny Banks the Benefits of the LLC Structure? 8 N.C. Banking Inst. 325 (2004).

A number of factors are relevant in choosing between the national or state charter, whether at the formation stage or later, when considering the possibility of a charter conversion. These factors include available powers and authorized activities, the amount of fees assessed by the primary regulator, ease of access to the regulator, sophistication of the regulator, and the number of regulators. It is obvious that these factors play out differently for different institutions, leading some to choose the national charter and the remainder a state charter.

[margin note: choosing Nat'l / St. charter]

As previously noted, state chartered banks have a state regulator as well as a federal regulator (either the Fed or the FDIC), while national banks have only a single regulator (the OCC). National banks may be able to preempt state laws that limit the ability of a national bank to exercise the powers granted to it under federal law. This advantage was limited somewhat by the Dodd–Frank Act of 2010, and is discussed more fully below. Some bankers view the OCC as a more "sophisticated" regulator that is more comfortable dealing with the issues raised by the larger banks, most of whom have a national charter.

On the other hand, a bank and its officers are likely to find that their access to a state regulator is much greater than to the OCC, even though the OCC has regional offices. Regulatory response time may also be shorter at the state level than with the OCC. It is certainly easier to meet with a regulator in your own state than one that may be headquartered in another state in the region. Others suggest a state may act as a "laboratory for experimentation" where an innovative practice may be approved by a state regulator and later adopted at the federal level for national banks upon successful completion of the state experiment. Banks are examined on an annual basis and the examination fees paid by many state banks are often less than those paid by national banks.[5] For a small bank, this cost difference weighs heavily in favor of the state charter.

[margin note: St. charter has shorter response time from regulator; Examination Fees]

A.   CHARTERING A BANK

(1) National Bank

The National Bank Act provisions relating to chartering are found at 12 U.S.C. §§ 21–23, 26–27 & 53. More specific information is set forth in 12 C.F.R. § 5.20. The bank must also apply to the FDIC for federal deposit insurance. The factors to be considered by the FDIC in connection with an application for deposit insurance are set forth at 12 U.S.C. § 1816. The OCC forms relating to chartering a new bank are collected at <www.occ.treas.gov/corpapps/forms.htm>. A new bank must raise capital. Bank offerings are exempted from the securities laws. The OCC's offering regulations are set forth at 12 C.F.R. pt. 16.

---

5. See Connie Edwards Josey, Note, State v. National Banks: The Battle Over Examination Fees, 6 N.C. Banking Inst. 463 (2002).

(2) State Bank

State banks are chartered pursuant to the procedures set forth in the relevant state's laws. The factors considered are often quite similar to those set forth for chartering a national bank. A deposit insurance application must also be made. Usually any issues in a bank charter application are resolved at the application stage. On rare occasion, there is litigation over an approval or denial of a charter application.

FARMERS DEPOSIT BANK OF BRANDENBURG v. DEPARTMENT OF BANKING AND SECURITIES

Court of Appeals of Kentucky, 1984.
669 S.W.2d 22.

CLAYTON, JUDGE.

The Farmers Deposit Bank of Brandenburg appeals from a judgment of the Franklin Circuit Court affirming the decision of the Department of Banking and Securities to approve the bank charter application of the proposed Meade County Bank (the "proposed bank"). An application for a Bank Charter and Federal Deposit Insurance (the "application") was filed with the Department of Banking and Securities (the "Department") on December 9, 1982. Named as incorporators in the application are the appellees: J.D. Tobin, Jr.; J.D. Tobin, Sr.; Kenneth Heavrin; Leroy Humphrey; James Michael Jones; and David Ridenour. A notice of opposition to the application was filed with the Department that same month by the appellant, Farmers Deposit Bank of Brandenburg (the "Farmers Deposit Bank" or "Farmers").

Pursuant to the instructions of the Commissioner of the Department, an office review and field investigation of the application were conducted by a banking investigator for the Department. The investigator's report, dated January 10, 1982, includes a review of the proposed bank's financial history and condition, proposed management, public convenience and advantage, reasonable probability for successful operation, and capital requirements. The report concludes that "[a]ll factors addressed by the application and investigation thereof appeared favorable."

On March 7, 1983, a public hearing was held before a hearing officer of the Department as required by KRS 287.061. * * * The hearing officer subsequently entered Findings of Fact and Conclusions of Law recommending issuance of a bank charter. To quote a portion of language of the hearing officer, "[t]he projections favorable, proposed management has experience, and there is community support." The Commissioner of the Department subsequently adopted the hearing officer's recommendations. Farmers Deposit Bank appealed the Commissioner's decision to Franklin Circuit Court, which affirmed the Commissioner's ruling.

Farmers Deposit Bank now seeks reversal of the lower court's decision arguing that (1) the proposed bank's application does not meet the criteria of KRS 287.050(1); (2) the ownership of the Tobins in the proposed bank contravenes KRS 287.030; and (3) the approval of the proposed bank's application is arbitrary and capricious given the lack of significant or substantial changes in Meade County since 1976, the year in which the Department disapproved an application for a new bank in Meade County. * * *

We begin with an examination of the three statutory elements found in KRS 287.050. Both parties have stipulated the satisfaction of the first of these criteria, the "financial standing, moral character and capacity of the incorporators,"KRS 287.050. It is the second and third element, the reasonable assurance of success and the public convenience and advantage which the appellant draws into contention. The appellant's arguments regarding the second element of KRS 287.050(1), the reasonable assurance of sufficient volume of business, fall neatly into two categories. The first of these categories contains expert financial testimony on deposit growth and projected profits. The second one includes general testimony on relevant economic and demographic factors.

Distilled to its essence, the testimony of the appellant's first financial expert, Hamilton [a CPA], is that the proposed bank cannot be successfully operated at the 8.4% historical deposit growth rate of Meade County nor even at the more favorable deposit growth rate of 10%, the total deposit growth rate in the tri-county area of Meade, Breckinridge, and Hardin Counties. Stewart [a CPA], the second of the appellant's financial experts, contends that the proposed bank incorporators are overly optimistic in their projections on deposits, spread between return of assets and cost of funds, and loan losses. Farmers Deposit Bank additionally criticizes the testimony of the appellees' financial expert, Professor McGee [University of Kentucky, Professor of Economics], questioning the soundness of his reliance on a 12.6% personal income growth rate and "penetration ratio" estimates to project deposit growth of the proposed bank.

We have reviewed the appellees' financial projections and the bank investigator's and hearing officer's comments concerning them. None of the appellant's expert financial testimony, nor arguments founded thereon, has convinced us that these projections are improperly based, overly optimistic, or unsound. Professor McGee's reliance on the Meade County personal income growth rate to determine deposit growth is not unwarranted given the unique nature of the current banking climate in Meade County. As the record repeatedly reveals, Meade County has an unusually low 24% penetration ratio (bank deposits as a percentage of personal income), less than half the Kentucky average of 52%. While some of the discrepancy between the two ratios can be explained by the banking necessities of Meade countians who maintain accounts in financial institutions in adjacent Hardin and Breckinridge counties, the remaining portion of the ratio discrepancy appears attributable to the inefficiency of Farmers Deposit Bank in attracting new deposits. Therefore, to rely on the historic growth rate of deposits in the Farmers Deposit Bank is unrealistically conservative. On this point, we join with the hearing officer who in his Finding of Fact states,

> The appellant's deposit projections are based on growth in personal income, rather than the more common measure of growth of deposits in the county. But, use of such a measure is not unreasonable in light of the county's extraordinarily low penetration rate.

As for the accuracy of the proposed bank's projections on the amount of deposits, spread between asset return and costs of funds, and loan losses, these figures fall well within acceptable limits. As the comparative analysis of the bank investigator's report reveals, First State Bank of Irvington and Farmers Deposit Bank have closely similar performance percentages. Where the proposed bank's projections were found to be overly optimistic, i.e., loan losses and cost for computer services, they were adjusted with the result that the proposed bank's revised projections still showed a profit. Thus, based upon a review of arguments grounded in expert financial testimony we hold there to be substantial evidence of a reasonable assurance of a sufficient volume of business for the proposed bank to be successful. KRS 287.050(1).

With regard to the general testimony on demographic and economic conditions in Meade County, Farmers Deposit Bank argues that the county's agriculturally based economy and population growth are stagnant. What little growth there has been, it argues, is located in the eastern portion of the county, where most workers are commuters who bank outside Meade County at their place of business. In contrast to McGee's testimony regarding substantial population and personal income growth during the 1975–1980 period, Farmers Deposit Bank points out that during the most recent years unemployment in Meade County has increased while per capita income has actually decreased.

In response, we note that while population growth in the county may be currently stagnant, it is still projected to increase at a rate in excess of the state average throughout the year 2000. Moreover, the population growth that has already occurred during the 1975–1980 period has resulted in a Meade County bank-to-customer ratio of 1–to–22,854. The state average is 1–to–3,300. Therefore, while population growth may have temporarily decreased, the size of the existing populace appears more than sufficient to support an additional bank. The concentration of that growth in eastern Meade County does not convince us otherwise. A review of the letters supporting the establishment of a new bank reveals that many Meade countians who are presently banking outside the county do so because of the lack of an alternative in Meade County. Their current banking habits are the result of necessity, not preference. Thus, the proposed bank's customers are not strictly limited to customers in the immediate Brandenburg area. The population growth in eastern Meade County is a fertile source of new customers for a bank willing to accommodate their needs. The recent increase in unemployment and concurrent decrease in per capita income in Meade County are simply not of sufficient magnitude nor duration to cause us to reject the assumptions and financial projections of the appellees. Both the expert financial testimony and general testimony on population and demographics support the conclusion of the lower court that a reasonable assurance of sufficient volume of business is supported by substantial evidence.

We turn now to the third element of the statutory criteria of KRS 287.050(1), public convenience and advantage. Lengthy discussion of this element of the statute is unnecessary as the record presents overwhelming evidence that public convenience and advantage will be promoted by opening the proposed bank. There is a definite need for increased banking hours in Meade County. The letters of many of the local merchants and citizens now banking outside the county indicate that their banking habits are the result of the inadequate service and hours of the Farmers Deposit Bank. Farmers failed experiment with Saturday banking hours, which ended in 1969, long before the influx of population in the mid–1970's, is more possibly a commentary upon the performance of Farmers than the desires of the banking populace of Meade County. The historic exodus of the citizens of Guston, Payneville, Ekron, Flaherty, and Muldraugh to banks outside Meade County indicates to us those individuals' dissatisfaction with the present banking services available. Several of the letters from citizens in outlying areas of Meade County reflect this view. In short, it is clear that a new bank with increased hours and Saturday banking would greatly service the public convenience and advantage.

Farmers Deposit Bank next argues that the ownership of the Tobins in the proposed bank contravenes KRS 287.030. This statute provides in pertinent part that no person who owns more than one half of the capital stock of one bank shall own or acquire directly or indirectly any capital stock in another bank. KRS 287.030.

At present the Tobins' individual stock ownership in the First State Bank of Irvington, in the aggregate, equals eighty percent (80%). They will together own sixty percent (60%) of the proposed bank, thirty percent (30%) each. Neither J.D. Tobin, Sr., nor J.D. Tobin, Jr., individually owns nor will own more than fifty percent (50%) in either bank. Farmers, however, argues that they should be considered as one person within the definition of that term in KRS 287.030. "Person" as defined by KRS 287.030 includes a natural person, partnership, corporation, association, business trust, voting trust, or similar organization. Nowhere on the face of the statute is there mentioned a father/son relationship, nor any familial relationship for that matter. From the wording of the statute it appears that the legislature had in mind only the formal, more traditional, legal relationships. * * * Thus, the opportunity for bank stock manipulation through family control appears to have been of little concern to the legislature. We are equally untroubled by such a possibility.

In its final argument, Farmers Deposit Bank maintains that, contrary to the requirements of Williams v. Cumberland Valley National Bank, Ky.App., 569 S.W.2d 711 (1978), the Commissioner failed to set forth adequate findings of significant or substantial changes since 1976, the year in which the Department denied an application for a new bank in Meade County. We disagree. Our review of the record and the hearing officer's findings reveals that in the seven years since 1976 the growth in population and personal income in Meade County has been exceptional, far above the state average. Furthermore, a completely different, highly qualified group of incorporators supports the present application. Nor does the appellant's stipulation of their qualifications remove them from consideration as a substantially changed circumstance. The hearing officer properly included them in the Findings of Fact. These changed conditions are more than sufficient to be termed substantial within the confines of *Williams,* supra.

The judgment of the Franklin Circuit Court is affirmed. All concur.

QUESTIONS AND NOTES

1. What do the National Bank Act OCC regulations on bank chartering say about the issue addressed in the *Farmers Deposit Bank* case—the reasonable assurance of the proposed bank's success and public convenience and advantage?

2. Compare N.Y. Banking Law §§ 24 & 28–b with the OCC and Kentucky requirements.

3. In the aftermath of the financial crisis, few investors are interested in supporting new banks. Find your state banking supervisor's website and determine how many state chartered banks are operating in your state and when the last new state bank charter was granted.

B. BANK POWERS

Historically, a major factor in choosing between a state and national charter was which charter contained the most flexible and expansive powers. The competition between the OCC and state chartering authorities for bank charters based on powers was significantly reduced, however, by the passage of the Federal Deposit Insurance Corporation Improvement Act of 1991 (FDICIA), which attempted to limit state banks to those activities authorized for their national bank counterparts. 12 U.S.C. § 1831a. Because state bank powers are capped by the powers authorized for national banks, the source for national bank powers and their expansion over time must be carefully examined.

(1) The Business of Banking for National Banks

ARNOLD TOURS, INC. v. CAMP
United States Court of Appeals, First Circuit, 1972.
472 F.2d 427.

HAMLEY, CIRCUIT JUDGE.

This class action involves the authority of national banks to engage in the travel agency business. The plaintiffs are Arnold Tours, Inc., and forty-one other independent travel agents of Massachusetts engaged in the travel agency business.

One of the defendants is William B. Camp, Comptroller of the Currency (Comptroller). * * * The other defendant is South Shore National Bank (South Shore), a national banking association chartered by the United States Government, with a principal place of business in Quincy, Massachusetts, and with twenty-seven branch offices throughout Massachusetts. South Shore has been engaged in the travel agency business, operating it as a department of the bank, since November, 1966, after having bought out the fourth largest travel bureau in New England. * * *

The parties are in agreement that if there is any statutory authority for national banks to engage in the travel agency business, it is to be found in the following language contained in 12 U.S.C. § 24, Seventh, a provision of the National Bank Act (Act):

"Seventh. To exercise ... all such incidental powers as shall be necessary to carry on the business of banking...."

The Comptroller relied upon the quoted statutory words in his 1963 ruling that national banks could engage in the travel agency business. Thus, paragraph 7475 of the Comptroller's Manual for National Banks (1963), which is now codified as 12 C.F.R. § 7.7475, reads:

"§ 7.7475 National banks acting as travel agents

"Incident to those powers vested in them under 12 U.S.C. 24, national banks may provide travel services for their customers and receive compensation therefor. Such services may include the sale of trip insurance and the rental of automobiles as agent for a local rental service. In connection therewith, national banks may advertise, develop, and extend such travel services for the purpose of attracting customers to the bank."

In holding that 12 U.S.C. § 24, Seventh, did not authorize national banks to engage in the travel agency business the district court, in its opinion, first focused attention on the nature of South Shore's travel agency operation. * * *

The district court then observed that

"To say that conduct of a [travel agency] ... is a *sine qua non* to the successful operation of a national bank is a self-refuting proposition, especially in view of the fact that on the defendants' own claim only 122 national banks out of the many hundreds if not thousands in existence were providing travel agency services in 1967."

The Comptroller argues that the district court applied an erroneous legal standard in reviewing the Comptroller's construction of the "inciden-

essential

tal powers" clause of the National Bank Act (12 U. S.C. § 24, Seventh), as indicated by the court's above-quoted use of the term *sine qua non.*

We are in agreement with the Comptroller that a *sine qua non* standard would be an inappropriate measure of a national bank's incidental powers under 12 U.S.C. § 24, Seventh. While the pertinent language of that section refers to all such incidental powers "as shall be necessary to carry on the business of banking," we do not believe "necessary" was there used to connote that which is indispensable. * * *

In our opinion, these decisions [of prior courts discussed in an omitted portion of the case] amply demonstrate that a national bank's activity is authorized as an incidental power, "necessary to carry on the business of banking," within the meaning of 12 U.S.C. § 24, Seventh, if it is convenient or useful in connection with the performance of one of the bank's established activities pursuant to its express powers under the National Bank Act. If this connection between an incidental activity and an express power does not exist, the activity is not authorized as an incidental power.

This brings us to a consideration of the question of whether the operation of a travel agency business, such as that conducted by South Shore, may reasonably be said to be convenient or useful in connection with the performance of one of the bank's established activities in the exercise of its express powers.

While the Comptroller and South Shore do not concede that such a relationship between an incidental and an express power must exist, they suggest ways in which they believe a travel agency business is directly related to a national bank's normal banking operations. In presenting this view, they pursue two lines of argument. One of these is an effort to equate the basic functions performed by travel agencies with functions which have historically been performed by banks. The other is based on the premise that a substantial number of banks have, for a long time, been providing travel agency services. * * *

[W]hile national banks provide certain agency and informational services they are normally of a kind which are germane to the financial operations of the bank in the exercise of its express powers. There are, of course, instances in which banks have, as a convenience to their regular customers, and without additional compensation, obtained railroad, steamship or airline tickets for such customers, or provided information helpful to such customers in connection with their travels. But incidental good will service of this kind cannot reasonably be equated with the operation of a modern travel agency for profit. In short, there is a difference between supplying customers with financial and informational services helpful to their travel plans and developing a clientele which looks to the bank not as a source of general financial advice and support but as a travel management center.

The Comptroller asserts that one of the central purposes of the National Bank Act, enacted during the Civil War, was to serve as a unifying force to the nation and that the draftsmen of the Act contemplated that the Act would fulfill its unifying purpose by, among other things, facilitating interstate commerce and "facilitating travel."[6]

As a reading of these documents demonstrates, the objective of establishing a "unifying force" and "facilitating travel" were viewed in those early years, not as being attainable through the operation of a banking travel service, but as being attainable through the establishment and circulation of a national currency. Prior to the National Currency Act of 1863, now also known as the National Bank Act, there was no national currency and financial transactions were largely conducted through the medium of bank notes issued by state banks. The establishment of a national currency provided a form of legal specie acceptable throughout the country, and it was this which provided the desired "unifying force" and assisted in "facilitating travel."

South Shore asserts that banks in the United States have been offering travel services to their customers since at least 1865, when the Security National Bank in Sheboygan, Wisconsin, formally established its bank travel department. According to South Shore, in the ensuing years of the nineteenth century and the period preceding World War I, numerous other banks began to offer travel services largely to accommodate the great number of imigrants [sic] arriving in this country. * * *

The limited and largely uncompensated services of this kind, rendered by banks during this period, bear very little resemblance to the functioning of a modern travel agency. Moreover, it was not until 1959 that the Comptroller of the Currency ruled that national banks could engage in a regular travel agency business. * * *

Despite the Comptroller's sanction, since 1959, of the operation of travel agency businesses by national banks, only one hundred twenty-two out of about four thousand seven hundred national banks were engaged in that business in 1967, when this action was brought. This is far from persuasive evidence that the operation of travel service departments is useful and convenient to the functioning of normal banking services under the express powers granted by the National Bank Act.

The Comptroller and South Shore urge us * * * to accord great weight to the Comptroller's construction, in 12 C.F.R. § 7.7475, of the "incidental powers" provision, 12 U.S.C. § 24, Seventh.

We fully recognize the principle to which defendants refer. But, as the Supreme Court said in Zuber v. Allen, 396 U.S. 168, at 192–193 (1969):

> "While this Court has announced that it will accord great weight to a departmental construction of its own enabling legislation, espe-

---

6. [n.10] * * * The words "facilitating travel" appear in the Secretary of the Treasury's Annual Report for 1863, where, in reviewing the purposes of the Act, the Secretary said: "Impelled, therefore, by a profound sense of the present necessity of a national currency to the successful prosecution of the war against rebellion, and of its utility at all times in protecting labor, cheapening exchanges, facilitating travel, and increasing the safety of all business transactions ... the Secretary recommended, in two successive reports, the authorization of national banking associations, to which the capital of the corporations now issuing notes for circulation might be transferred, with advantage to the parties in interest as well as to the general public."

cially a contemporaneous construction ... it is only one input in the interpretational equation....

"The Court may not, however, abdicate its ultimate responsibility to construe the language employed by Congress."

In view of the many considerations which lead to a contrary conclusion, as reviewed above, the lack of essential articulation supporting the Comptroller's 1963 ruling, issued without opinion or accompanying statement, and in the light of the lack of uniformity in the Comptroller's own interpretation of the statute, we conclude that the Comptroller's current interpretation, as embodied in 12 C.F.R. § 7.7475, is not entitled to dispositive deference.

Defendants urge that Congress has long been aware of the Comptroller's regulation authorizing national banks to provide travel agency services and has often considered, but failed to enact, proposed legislation which would have amended the Act expressly to prohibit national banks from providing such services.

As the Supreme Court said in Zuber v. Allen, 396 U.S. 168, 185 (1969), "[l]egislative silence is a poor beacon to follow in discerning the proper statutory route." From the materials which are before us we cannot determine whether any committee or subcommittee of Congress rejected, on the merits, the proposal to overturn the Comptroller's ruling that national banks could engage in the travel agency business. It may well have been that this ruling was simply viewed as an inconsequential aberration which would probably involve very few national banks and hence was not deserving of legislative attention. We think that, under the circumstances, a much more reliable guide to the correct statutory construction of 12 U.S.C. § 24, Seventh, is to be found in what the national banks, as a whole, were doing about the travel agency business. As indicated above, all but a tiny fraction of them have avoided this activity. * * *

We conclude that the district court did not err in entering a declaratory judgment to the effect that it is illegal for a national bank to operate a full-scale travel agency since such an operation is not an exercise of the incidental powers referred to in 12 U.S.C. § 24, Seventh. For the same reason the district court did not err in determining that 12 C.F.R. § 7.7475 is invalid to the extent that it is construed by the Comptroller as authorizing a national bank to operate a full-scale travel agency. These determinations in no way limit banks in rendering banking services for travelers, such as the sale of travelers' checks and foreign currency, the making of travel loans, issuance of letters of credit, and providing gratis travel information.

In view of these determinations the district court did not err in permanently enjoining South Shore from engaging in the travel agency business and in requiring South Shore to divest itself of its travel department. * * *

In our view the disposition should be reasonably expeditious, but a limit should not be set which would be oppressive or inequitable. * * *

NATIONSBANK OF NORTH CAROLINA, N.A. v. VARIABLE ANNUITY LIFE INSURANCE CO.

Supreme Court of the United States, 1995.
513 U.S. 251.

Handwritten margin note: Banks occ.l sell annuities (not = insurance as spec. in 12 USC §92)

MADAME JUSTICE GINSBURG delivered the opinion of the Court.

These consolidated cases present the question whether national banks may serve as agents in the sale of annuities. * * *

*Handwritten margin note: * Bus of banking " is not lim. to those in Nat'l Bank Act*

Petitioner NationsBank of North Carolina, N.A., a national bank based in Charlotte, and its brokerage subsidiary sought permission from the Comptroller of the Currency, pursuant to 12 CFR § 5.34 (1994), for the brokerage subsidiary to act as an agent in the sale of annuities. Annuities are contracts under which the purchaser makes one or more premium payments to the issuer in exchange for a series of payments, which continue either for a fixed period or for the life of the purchaser or a designated beneficiary. When a purchaser invests in a "variable" annuity, the purchaser's money is invested in a designated way and payments to the purchaser vary with investment performance. In a classic "fixed" annuity, in contrast, payments do not vary. Under the contracts Nations-Bank proposed to sell, purchasers could direct their payments to a variable, fixed, or hybrid account, and would be allowed periodically to modify their choice. The issuers would be various insurance companies.

The Comptroller granted NationsBank's application. He concluded that national banks have authority to broker annuities within "the business of banking" under 12 U.S.C. § 24 Seventh. He further concluded that § 92, addressing insurance sales by banks in towns with no more than 5,000 people, did not impede his approval; for purposes of that provision, the Comptroller explained, annuities do not rank as "insurance." * * *

As the administrator charged with supervision of the National Bank Act, see §§ 1, 26–27, 481, the Comptroller bears primary responsibility for surveillance of "the business of banking" authorized by [12 U.S.C.] § 24 Seventh. We have reiterated:

> " 'It is settled that courts should give great weight to any reasonable construction of a regulatory statute adopted by the agency charged with the enforcement of that statute. The Comptroller of the Currency is charged with the enforcement of banking laws to an extent that warrants the invocation of this principle with respect to his deliberative conclusions as to the meaning of these laws.' " Clarke v. Securities Industry Assn., 479 U.S. 388, 403–404 (1987) (quoting Investment Company Institute v. Camp, 401 U.S. 617, 626–627 (1971)).

Under the formulation now familiar, when we confront an expert administrator's statutory exposition, we inquire first whether "the intent of Congress is clear" as to "the precise question at issue." Chevron U.S.A. Inc. v. Natural Resources Defense Council, Inc., 467 U.S. 837, 842, (1984). If so, "that is the end of the matter." Ibid. But "if the statute is silent or ambiguous with respect to the specific issue, the question for the court is whether the agency's answer is based on a permissible construction of the statute." Id. at 843. If the administrator's reading fills a gap or defines a term in a way that is reasonable in light of the legislature's revealed design, we give the administrator's judgment "controlling weight." Id., at 844.

In authorizing NationsBank to broker annuities, the Comptroller invokes the power of banks to "broker a wide variety of financial investment instruments," which the Comptroller considers "part of [banks'] traditional role as financial intermediaries," and therefore an "incidental powe[r] . . . necessary to carry on the business of banking." 12 U.S.C. § 24 Seventh. The Comptroller construes the § 24 Seventh authorization of "incidental powers . . . necessary to carry on the business of banking" as an independent grant of authority; he reads the specific powers set forth thereafter as exemplary, not exclusive.

VALIC argues that the Comptroller's interpretation is contrary to the clear intent of Congress because the banking power on which the Comptroller relies–"broker[ing] financial investment instruments"–is not specified in § 24 Seventh. According to VALIC, the five specific activities listed in § 24 Seventh after the words "business of banking" are exclusive– banks are confined to these five activities and to endeavors incidental thereto. VALIC thus attributes no independent significance to the words "business of banking." We think the Comptroller better comprehends the Act's terms.

The second sentence of § 24 Seventh, in limiting banks' "dealing in securities," presupposes that banks have authority not circumscribed by the five specifically listed activities. Congress' insertion of the limitation decades after the Act's initial adoption makes sense only if banks already had authority to deal in securities, authority presumably encompassed within the "business of banking" language which dates from 1863. VALIC argues, however, that the limitation was imposed by the Glass–Steagall Act of 1933, and that the power Glass–Steagall presupposed was specifically granted in the McFadden Act of 1927. While the statute's current wording derives from the Glass–Steagall Act, see Act of June 16, 1933, ch. 89, § 16, 48 Stat. 184, the earlier McFadden Act does not bolster VALIC's case, for that Act, too, *limited* an activity already part of the business national banks did. See Act of Feb. 25, 1927, § 2(b), 44 Stat. 1226 ("*Provided*, That the business of buying and selling investment securities shall hereinafter be limited to buying and selling without recourse. . . ."). * * *7

---

7. [n.2] We expressly hold that the "business of banking" is not limited to the enumerated powers in § 24 Seventh and that the Comptroller therefore has discretion to authorize activities

As we have just explained, the Comptroller determined, in accord with the legislature's intent, that "the business of banking" described in § 24 Seventh covers brokerage of financial investment instruments, and is not confined to the examples specifically enumerated. He then reasonably concluded that the authority to sell annuities qualifies as part of, or incidental to, the business of banking. National banks, the Comptroller observed, are authorized to serve as agents for their customers in the purchase and sale of various financial investment instruments, and annuities are widely recognized as just such investment products.

By making an initial payment in exchange for a future income stream, the customer is deferring consumption, setting aside money for retirement, future expenses, or a rainy day. For her, an annuity is like putting money in a bank account, a debt instrument, or a mutual fund. Offering bank accounts and acting as agent in the sale of debt instruments and mutual funds are familiar parts of the business of banking. See, e.g., Securities Industry Assn. v. Board of Governors, FRS, 468 U.S. 207, 215 (1984) ("Banks long have arranged the purchase and sale of securities as an accommodation to their customers."); First Nat. Bank of Hartford v. Hartford, 273 U.S. 548, 559–560 (1927) (banks have authority to sell mortgages and other debt instruments they have originated or acquired by discount).

In sum, modern annuities, though more sophisticated than the standard savings bank deposits of old, answer essentially the same need. By providing customers with the opportunity to invest in one or more annuity options, banks are essentially offering financial investment instruments of the kind congressional authorization permits them to broker. Hence, the Comptroller reasonably typed the permission NationsBank sought as an "incidental powe[r] ... necessary to carry on the business of banking."[8]

In the alternative, VALIC argues that 12 U.S.C. § 92 (1988 ed., Supp. V) bars NationsBank from selling annuities as agent. That section provides:

> "In addition to the powers now vested by law in [national banks] any such [bank] located and doing business in any place the population of which does not exceed five thousand inhabitants ... may ... act as the agent for any fire, life, or other insurance company authorized by the authorities of the State in which said bank is located to do business in said State, by soliciting and selling insurance and collecting premiums on policies issued by such company...."

The parties disagree about whether § 92, by negative implication, precludes national banks located in places more populous than 5,000 from

---

beyond those specifically enumerated. The exercise of the Comptroller's discretion, however, must be kept within reasonable bounds. Ventures distant from dealing in financial investment instruments–for example, operating a general travel agency—may exceed those bounds.

8. [n.4] Assuring that the brokerage in question would not deviate from traditional bank practices, the Comptroller specified that NationsBank "will act only as agent, ... will not have a principal stake in annuity contracts and therefore will incur no interest rate or actuarial risks." Comptroller's Letter 48a.

selling insurance. We do not reach this question because we accept the Comptroller's view that, for the purpose at hand, annuities are properly classified as investments, not "insurance."

Again, VALIC contends that the Comptroller's determination is contrary to the plain intent of Congress, or else is unreasonable. In support of its position that annuities are insurance, VALIC notes first that annuities traditionally have been sold by insurance companies. But the sale of a product by an insurance company does not inevitably render the product insurance. For example, insurance companies have long offered loans on the security of life insurance, but a loan does not thereby become insurance.

VALIC further asserts that most States have regulated annuities as insurance and that Congress intended to define insurance under § 92 by reference to state law. Treatment of annuities under state law, however, is contextual. States generally classify annuities as insurance when defining the powers of insurance companies and state insurance regulators. But in diverse settings, States have resisted lump classification of annuities as insurance.

As our decisions underscore, a characterization fitting in certain contexts may be unsuitable in others. Moreover, the federal banking law does not plainly require automatic reference to state law here. The Comptroller has concluded that the federal regime is best served by classifying annuities according to their functional characteristics. Congress has not ruled out that course, see *Chevron*, 467 U.S., at 842, courts, therefore, have no cause to dictate to the Comptroller the state-law constraint VALIC espouses.

VALIC further argues that annuities functionally resemble life insurance because some annuities place mortality risk on the parties. Under a classic fixed annuity, the purchaser pays a sum certain and, in exchange, the issuer makes periodic payments throughout, but not beyond, the life of the purchaser. In pricing such annuities, issuers rely on actuarial assumptions about how long purchasers will live.

While cognizant of this similarity between annuities and insurance, the Comptroller points out that mortality risk is a less salient characteristic of contemporary products. Many annuities currently available, both fixed and variable, do not feature a life term. Instead they provide for payments over a term of years; if the purchaser dies before the term ends, the balance is paid to the purchaser's estate. Moreover, the presence of mortality risk does not necessarily qualify an investment as "insurance" under § 92. For example, VALIC recognizes that a life interest in real property is not insurance, although it imposes a mortality risk on the purchaser. Some conventional debt instruments similarly impose mortality risk. * * *

The Comptroller's classification of annuities, based on the tax deferral and investment features that distinguish them from insurance, in short, is at least reasonable. A key feature of insurance is that it indemnifies loss.

As the Comptroller observes, annuities serve an important investment purpose and are functionally similar to other investments that banks typically sell. And though fixed annuities more closely resemble insurance than do variable annuities, fixed annuities too have significant investment features and are functionally similar to debt instruments. Moreover, mindful that fixed annuities are often packaged with variable annuities, the Comptroller reasonably chose to classify the two together.

We respect as reasonable the Comptroller's conclusion that brokerage of annuities is an "incidental powe[r] ... necessary to carry on the business of banking." We further defer to the Comptroller's reasonable determination that 12 U.S.C. § 92 is not implicated because annuities are not insurance within the meaning of that section. * * *

JULIE L. WILLIAMS[9] & MARK P. JACOBSEN
THE BUSINESS OF BANKING:
LOOKING TO THE FUTURE

50 Bus. Law. 783 (1995).

The basic framework that governs the powers and permissible activities of national banks was, at last, resolved by the United States Supreme Court's recent decision in NationsBank v. Variable Annuity Life Insurance Co. (VALIC). Ending over 100 years of muddled precedent and conflicting commentary, the unanimous Court held that the "business of banking" is not limited to those activities and powers expressly enumerated in the National Bank Act (Act). Rather, the Court found that the business of banking is an expansive concept and that the powers enumerated in the Act are merely illustrative. The Court's decision also reaffirmed that courts should accord substantial deference to reasoned decisions by the Comptroller of the Currency (Comptroller) interpreting the powers of national banks under the National Bank Act. Together, these two components of the VALIC decision give the Comptroller the ability to allow the business of banking conducted by national banks to evolve and to service developing markets and emerging customer needs. The key issue now is how to identify the activities that fit within the VALIC framework. Specifically, a test is needed to determine whether a particular activity is part of or incidental to the business of banking and therefore within the Comptroller's discretion to permit. * * *

While VALIC confirmed that the business of banking is a broad, evolving concept, it did relatively little to flesh out how far that business might extend. The many cases preceding VALIC, on the other hand, while they often had difficulty interpreting the powers clause, articulated useful considerations relevant to the question of whether a new activity falls within the business of banking. The essential reasoning of these courts (as well as the bank regulators) over the past century can be synthesized to three key factors, namely (i) whether the activity in question is functionally equivalent to, or a logical outgrowth of, a recognized bank power; (ii)

---

9. Julie Williams is the First Senior Deputy Comptroller and Chief Counsel of the OCC.

whether the activity benefits bank customers and/or is convenient or useful to banks; and (iii) whether the activity presents risks of a type similar to those already assumed by banks. * * *

The traditional scope of bank powers has been defined by practice and by the courts. *VALIC* refers to "dealing in financial investment instruments." The *Arnold Tours* court affirmed that the business of banking "primarily involves the performance of financial transactions pertaining to money or substitutes thereof." Judge Cardozo had written that the business of banking involves the substitution of the "[bank's] own credit, which has general acceptance in the business community, for the individual's credit, which has only limited acceptability." The Supreme Court earlier stated that the function of banks was to, *inter alia*, finance commerce and act as private depositories. In addition, courts have permitted new activities that were "useful," "convenient," or "functionally equivalent" to activities already permissible. * * *

Caselaw has endorsed new activities that have grown out of customer needs and demands and that promote customer convenience. Similarly, courts have recognized that the business of banking also includes activities that would promote the convenience of the bank's business for itself. Therefore, if an activity: (i) increases service, convenience, or options for bank customers; (ii) responds to new customer needs or demands; (iii) lowers the cost to banks of providing a product or service; or (iv) enhances bank safety and soundness, it should be viewed favorably as being part of the business of banking. * * *

Moreover, it should be expected that even new activities that present risks of a nature similar to those banks traditionally have assumed will be evaluated carefully by bank regulators. While banks have taken on additional and different types of risks over time, this evolution has been gradual. Regulators typically monitor new activities with care, even when the activities represent new forms of traditional risks, until they are comfortable that the risks can be appropriately managed by the bank and adequately supervised by the regulator.

Thus, while the theoretical scope of banking powers is broad, the pace of evolution of banking powers will be influenced by the overarching concern of ensuring that new activities do not imperil the safety and soundness of the banking industry. The delicate task facing bank regulators is to allow innovation in a safe and sound manner, without smothering new activities with unnecessarily burdensome restrictions that undermine the benefits, to banks and their customers, of allowing banks to develop and offer new products and services.

To survive, and to fulfill their role as catalysts for the nation's economy, banks must evolve to meet the changing needs of their customers. Fortunately, the *VALIC* decision makes clear that national banks have this ability. The scope of the future business of banking is potentially quite broad and the post-*VALIC* regime for analyzing permissible bank activities should be sufficiently flexible to allow banks to develop and deliver financially related products and services on a competitive, profitable, and safe and sound basis.

JULIE L. WILLIAMS & JAMES F.E. GILLESPIE, JR. THE BUSINESS OF BANKING: LOOKING TO THE FUTURE–PART II

52 Bus. Law. 1279 (1997).

* * * Before *VALIC*, the standard used to determine whether an activity was "incidental" had been developed by the First Circuit Court of Appeals in Arnold Tours, Inc. v. Camp. The First Circuit made two significant holdings on the scope of the incidental powers. First, the court held that the term "necessary" in 12 U.S.C. § 24(Seventh) should be construed in a broad and flexible manner to include "incidental" activities that are "convenient or useful" in conducting authorized activities. Second, however, the court held that "incidental" activities must be convenient or useful to one of the activities *expressly* authorized and enumerated in 12 U.S.C. § 24(Seventh).

The second aspect of the *Arnold Tours* test (requiring that incidental powers be based *solely* upon enumerated powers) has long been criticized as overly restrictive. The OCC has concurred in this criticism. Clearly, however, the *VALIC* decision mandates that the second aspect of the *Arnold Tours* test be modified to accommodate *VALIC*'s recognition of the "business of banking" as a separate authority. *VALIC* requires that the test be realigned as follows: an activity is validly "incidental" if it is convenient or useful to the "business of banking" including, but not limited to, the powers specifically enumerated in the National Bank Act. Thus, it is necessary to distinguish analytically between activities that are part of the "business of banking" and those that are "incidental to the business of banking." * * *

Case law purporting to discuss "incidental" powers must be re-examined in light of this distinction and in light of the reformulated *Arnold Tours* test. The courts frequently have confused or combined concepts of the "business of banking" and "powers incidental to the business of banking." Following the second aspect of the *Arnold Tours* test, courts tended to characterize all *non-enumerated* powers as "incidental" powers even though some activities held to be "incidental" clearly fell within the business of banking, e.g., where the activity was a functional equivalent of an established power such as lending.

In light of *VALIC*, it is now clear that incidental activities are activities that are permissible for national banks not because they are part of the "business of banking," but rather because they are somehow "necessary" (i.e., "convenient or useful") to the business of banking. Thus, as will be developed below, "incidental" activities must necessarily include those activities that would not otherwise be permitted as part of the "business of banking."

A reexamination of case law on national bank incidental powers indicates three broad categories of incidental activities. Specifically, an activity has been found to be incidental to the performance of the "business of banking" where it:

Incidental Activities

    (i) facilitates the operations of a bank as a business enterprise;

    (ii) enhances the efficiency and quality of the content or delivery of banking services or products; or

    (iii) optimizes the use and value of a bank's facilities and competencies, or enables the bank to avoid economic waste in its banking franchise. * * *

Technology is one of the core forces transforming the banking industry. It is changing fundamentally the content and the execution of the business of banking and the competitive dynamics of that business. This transformation also demonstrates the modern-day scope and flexibility of national banks' incidental powers. * * *

Banks are adopting emerging technologies both to meet customer demands for improved and more convenient service and also to realize potential cost efficiencies provided by those technologies. As one example, remote delivery of products and services is increasingly important to enhance efficiencies and maintain profitability. Several different types of technologies, such as Internet banking, are emerging. * * * Banks are also beginning to experiment with new payments systems such as stored-value and smart card systems.

Technology is also changing fundamentally the marketplace in which banks compete and the nature of their competitors. Technology is driving a convergence of information-related industries, including banking, telecommunications, and software firms. For example, banks already are facing increasing competition from non-banks that offer payment services that build upon the bank supplied payments system, but add features that provide customers additional information, convenience, and timeliness. To meet this competition, banks face pressure to develop banking products that "wrap information and other value-added elements around" traditional payment services.

The role of technology in modern banking provides contemporary examples of the importance of banks' incidental powers and illustrates the different components of the incidental powers concept discussed above. The analysis of the scope of these components actually begins, however, with a review of the importance of technology to the "business of banking." * * * [A] developmental and organic relationship exists between the business of banking and activities incidental thereto: incidental activities evolve with the ever-evolving business of banking, enhancing and supporting that business, and in some respects signal its next phase. * * *

Over time, some incidental electronic activities can become part of the business of banking simply because of the nature of the close relationship that originally made them incidental. * * * Walter Wriston observed that, "information about money is getting to be as important [for the business of banking] as money itself." This trend will undoubtedly continue as innovation and changing market demands cause previously incidental electronic activities to become absorbed into the business of banking. * * *

QUESTIONS AND NOTES

1. It is very important to note the discussion of Chevron, U.S.A., Inc. v. Natural Resources Defense Council, Inc., 467 U.S. 837 (1984), in the *VALIC* case. Although prior to *Chevron* most courts afforded "substantial deference" to the interpretations of statutes by administrative agencies, in practice courts often did not defer to the agency's decision. The *Arnold Tours* case is an example of one of many cases where a court believed it was free to disagree with the agency's conclusion and to find it inconsistent with the statutory authority. After *Chevron* there have been relatively few instances of a court overturning an agency's interpretation of an ambiguous statute. When courts have reversed the agency it has usually been based on the first step of *Chevron*, finding that the statutory language is not ambiguous and affording no special weight to the agency's interpretation of the clear language.

2. The OCC's website <www.occ.treas.gov> provides access to the OCC's interpretations and actions. See "Activities Permissible for a National Bank," available at <www.occ.treas.gov/corpapps/BankAct.pdf> and "Significant Legal, Licensing, and Community Development Precedents for National Banks," available at <www.occ.treas.gov/sigpre.pdf>.

3. A national bank's power to own real estate is also limited by statute. See 12 U.S.C. §§ 29, 371d. This limitation is discussed further in Chapter 5.

4. An OCC regulation provides that it is "part of the business of banking under 12 U.S.C. 24(Seventh) for a national bank to act as a finder, bringing together interested parties to a transaction," 12 C.F.R. § 7.1002(a), but that the finder authority "does not enable a national bank to engage in brokerage activities that have not been found to be permissible for national banks," id. § 7.1002(c). How does this authority affect the ability of a bank to offer travel agency or real estate brokerage services?

5. The authors of the previous two articles from the Business Lawyer argue that the "business of banking" should be an evolving concept. Do you agree?

6. OCC Bulletin 2004–20, Risk Management of New, Expanded, or Modified Bank Products and Services: (May 10, 2004), available at <www.occ. treas.gov/ftp/bulletin/2004–20.txt> reminds banks of the processes that they should follow to manage the risks associated with new products and services.

(2) National Bank Act Preemption of State Law

BARNETT BANK OF MARION COUNTY, N.A. v. NELSON

Supreme Court of the United States, 1996.
517 U.S. 25.

MR. JUSTICE BREYER delivered the opinion of the Court.

The question in this case is whether a federal statute that permits national banks to sell insurance in small towns pre-empts a state statute that forbids them to do so. To answer this question, we must consider both ordinary pre-emption principles, and also a special federal anti-pre-emption rule, which provides that a federal statute will *not* pre-empt a state statute enacted "for the purpose of regulating the business of insurance"—*unless* the federal statute "*specifically relates to the business of insurance.*" McCarran–Ferguson Act, 15 U.S.C. § 1012(b) (emphasis added). We decide that the McCarran–Ferguson Act's special anti-pre-emption rule does not govern this case, because the federal statute in question "specifically relates to the business of insurance." We conclude that, under ordinary pre-emption principles, the federal statute pre-empts the state statute, thereby prohibiting application of the state statute to prevent a national bank from selling insurance in a small town.

In 1916 Congress enacted a federal statute that says that certain national banks "may" sell insurance in small towns. It provides in relevant part:

"In addition to the powers now vested by law in national [banks] organized under the laws of the United States *any such* [*bank*] located and doing business in any place [with a population] ... [of not more than] five thousand ... *may*, under such rules and regulations as may be prescribed by the Comptroller of the Currency, *act as the agent for any fire, life, or other insurance company* authorized by the authorities of the State ... to do business [there], ... by soliciting and selling insurance ... * * * Act of Sept. 7, 1916 (Federal Statute), 39 Stat. 753, as amended, 12 U.S.C. § 92 (emphases changed).

In 1974 Florida enacted a statute that prohibits certain banks from selling most kinds of insurance. It says:

"No [Florida licensed] insurance agent ... who is associated with, ... owned or controlled by ... a financial institution shall engage in insurance agency activities...." Fla. Stat. § 626.988(2) (Supp.1996) (State Statute).

The term "financial institution" includes

"any bank ... [except for a] bank which is not a subsidiary or affiliate of a bank holding company and is located in a city having a population of less than 5,000...." § 626.988(1)(a).

Thus, the State Statute says, in essence, that banks cannot sell insurance in Florida—except that an *unaffiliated* small town bank (i.e., a bank that is not affiliated with a bank holding company) may sell insurance in a small town.

In October 1993 petitioner Barnett Bank, an "affiliated" national bank which does business through a branch in a small Florida town, bought a Florida licensed insurance agency. The Florida State Insurance Commissioner, pointing to the State Statute (and noting that the unaffiliated small town bank exception did not apply), ordered Barnett's insurance agency to stop selling the prohibited forms of insurance. Barnett, claiming that the Federal Statute pre-empted the State Statute, then filed this action for declaratory and injunctive relief in federal court.

The District Court held that the Federal Statute did not pre-empt the State Statute, but only because of the special insurance-related federal anti-pre-emption rule. The McCarran–Ferguson Act, which creates that rule, says:

> "No act of Congress shall be construed to invalidate, impair, or supersede any law enacted by any State for the purpose of regulating the business of insurance, or which imposes a fee or tax upon such business, unless such Act specifically relates to the business of insurance...." McCarran–Ferguson Act; § 2(b), 59 Stat. 34, 15 U.S.C. § 1012(b).

The District Court decided both (1) that the Federal Statute did not fall within the McCarran–Ferguson Act's exception because it did not "specifically relat[e] to the business of insurance"; and (2) that the State Statute was a "law enacted ... for the purpose of regulating the business of insurance." Barnett Banks of Marion County, N.A. v. Gallagher, 839 F.Supp. 835, 840–841, 843 (M.D.Fla.1993) (internal quotation marks omitted). Consequently, the McCarran–Ferguson Act, in the District Court's view, instructs courts not to "constru[e]" the Federal Statute "to invalidate" the State Statute. 15 U.S.C. § 1012(b). The Eleventh Circuit Court of Appeals, for similar reasons, agreed that the Federal Statute did not pre-empt the State Statute. Barnett Bank of Marion County, N.A. v. Gallagher, 43 F.3d 631, 634–637 (1995).

We granted certiorari due to uncertainty among lower courts about the pre-emptive effect of this Federal Statute. We now reverse the Eleventh Circuit.

We shall put the McCarran–Ferguson Act's special anti-pre-emption rule to the side for the moment, and begin by asking whether, in the absence of that rule, we should construe the Federal Statute to pre-empt the State Statute. This question is basically one of congressional intent. Did Congress, in enacting the Federal Statute, intend to exercise its constitutionally delegated authority to set aside the laws of a State? If so, the Supremacy Clause requires courts to follow federal, not state, law. U.S. Const., Art. VI, cl. 2; see California Fed. Sav. & Loan Assn. v. Guerra, 479 U.S. 272, 280–281 (1987) (reviewing pre-emption doctrine).

Sometimes courts, when facing the pre-emption question, find language in the federal statute that reveals an explicit congressional intent to pre-empt state law. More often, explicit pre-emption language does not appear, or does not directly answer the question. In that event, courts must consider whether the federal statute's "structure and purpose," or nonspecific statutory language, nonetheless reveal a clear, but implicit, pre-emptive intent. A federal statute, for example, may create a scheme of federal regulation "so pervasive as to make reasonable the inference that Congress left no room for the States to supplement it." Rice v. Santa Fe Elevator Corp., 331 U.S. 218, 230 (1947). Alternatively, federal law may be in "irreconcilable conflict" with state law. Rice v. Norman Williams Co., 458 U.S. 654, 659 (1982). Compliance with both statutes, for example, may be a "physical impossibility," or, the state law may "stan[d] as an obstacle to the accomplishment and execution of the full purposes and objectives of Congress." Hines v. Davidowitz, 312 U.S. 52, 67 (1941).

In this case we must ask whether or not the Federal and State Statutes are in "irreconcilable conflict." The two statutes do not impose directly conflicting duties on national banks—as they would, for example, if the federal law said, "you must sell insurance," while the state law said, "you may not." Nonetheless, the Federal Statute authorizes national banks to engage in activities that the State Statute expressly forbids. Thus, the State's prohibition of those activities would seem to "stan[d] as an obstacle to the accomplishment" of one of the Federal Statute's purposes—unless, of course, that federal purpose is to grant the bank only a very *limited* permission, that is, permission to sell insurance *to the extent that state law also grants permission to do so.*

That is what the State of Florida and its supporting *amici* argue. They say that the Federal Statute grants national banks a permission that is limited to circumstances where state law is not to the contrary. In their view, the Federal Statute removes only federal legal obstacles, not state legal obstacles, to the sale of insurance by national banks. But we do not find this, or the State's related, ordinary pre-emption arguments, convincing.

For one thing, the Federal Statute's language suggests a broad, not a limited, permission. That language says, without relevant qualification, that national banks "may . . . act as the agent" for insurance sales. 12 U.S.C. § 92. It specifically refers to "rules and regulations" that will govern such sales, while citing as their source not state law, but the federal Comptroller of the Currency. It also specifically refers to state regulation, while limiting that reference to licensing–not of banks or insurance agents, but of the insurance companies whose policies the bank, as insurance agent, will sell.

For another thing, the Federal Statute says that its grant of authority to sell insurance is in "addition to the *powers* now vested by law in national [banks]." Ibid. (emphasis added). In using the word "powers," the statute chooses a legal concept that, in the context of national bank legislation, has a history. That history is one of interpreting grants of both enumerated and incidental "powers" to national banks as grants of authority not normally limited by, but rather ordinarily pre-empting, contrary state law.

Thus, this Court, in a case quite similar to this one, held that a federal statute permitting, but not requiring, national banks to receive savings deposits, pre-empts a state statute prohibiting certain state and national banks from using the word "savings" in their advertising. Franklin Nat. Bank of Franklin Square v. New York, 347 U.S. 373, 375–379, (1954) (Federal Reserve Act provision that national banks "may continue . . . to receive . . . savings deposits" read as "declaratory of the right of a national bank to enter into or remain in that type of business").

In defining the pre-emptive scope of statutes and regulations granting a power to national banks, these cases take the view that normally Congress would not want States to forbid, or to impair significantly, the exercise of a power that Congress explicitly granted. To say this is not to deprive States of the power to regulate national banks, where (unlike here) doing so does not prevent or significantly interfere with the national bank's exercise of its powers. See, e.g., Anderson Nat. Bank v. Luckett, 321 U.S. 233, 247–252 (1944) (state statute administering abandoned deposit accounts did not "unlawful[ly] encroac[h] on the rights and privileges of national banks"); McClellan v. Chipman, 164 U.S. 347, 358 (1896) (application to national banks of state statute forbidding certain real estate transfers by insolvent transferees would not "destro[y] or hampe[r]" national banks' functions); National Bank v. Commonwealth, 76 U.S. (9 Wall.) 353, 362, (1869) (national banks subject to state law that does not "interfere with, or impair [national banks'] efficiency in performing the functions by which they are designed to serve [the Federal] Government").

Nor do these cases control the interpretation of federal banking statutes that accompany a grant of an explicit power with an explicit statement that the exercise of that power is subject to state law. See, e.g., 12 U.S.C. § 36(c) (McFadden Act) (authorizing national banks to operate branches, but only where state law authorizes state banks to do so); § 92a(a) (Comptroller of Currency may grant fiduciary powers "by special permit to national banks applying therefor, when not in contravention of State or local law"). Not surprisingly, this Court has interpreted those explicit provisions to mean what they say. See, e.g., First Nat. Bank in Plant City v. Dickinson, 396 U.S. 122, 131 (1969) (under McFadden Act, state branching restrictions apply to national banks); First Nat. Bank of Logan v. Walker Bank & Trust Co., 385 U.S. 252, 260–261(1966) (same); see also Van Allen v. Assessors, 70 U.S.(3 Wall.) 573, 586 (1865) (enforcing 1864 amendments to National Bank Act expressly authorizing state taxation of national bank shares). * * *

Finally, Florida and its supporters challenge this interpretation by arguing that special circumstances surrounding the enactment of the

Federal Statute nonetheless demonstrate Congress' intent to grant only a limited permission (subject to state approval). They point to a letter to Congress written by the Comptroller of the Currency in 1916. * * *

Although the letter mentions that enlarging the powers of small national banks will help them "better compete with local State banks," it primarily focuses upon small town national banks' need for added revenue–an objective met by a broad insurance-selling authority that is not limited by state law. The letter refers to limitations that *federal* regulation might impose, but it says nothing about limitations imposed by *state* regulation or *state* law. The letter makes clear that authority to sell insurance in small towns is an added "incidental power" of a national bank–a term that, in light of this Court's then-existing cases, suggested freedom from conflicting state regulation. * * *

In light of these considerations, we conclude that the Federal Statute means to grant small town national banks authority to sell insurance, whether or not a State grants its own state banks or national banks similar approval. Were we to apply ordinary legal principles of pre-emption, the federal law would pre-empt that of the State.

We now must decide whether ordinary legal principles of pre-emption, or the special McCarran–Ferguson Act anti-pre-emption rule, governs this case. The lower courts held that the McCarran–Ferguson Act's special anti-pre-emption rule applies, and instructs courts not to "construe" the Federal Statute to "invalidate, impair, or supersede" that of the State. 15 U.S.C. § 1012(b). By its terms, however, the Act does not apply when the conflicting federal statute "*specifically relates to the business of insurance.*" Ibid. (emphasis added). In our view, the Federal Statute in this case "specifically relates to the business of insurance"—therefore the McCarran–Ferguson Act's special anti-pre-emption rule does not apply.

Our conclusion rests upon the McCarran–Ferguson Act's language and purpose, taken together. Consider the language—"specifically relates to the business of insurance." In ordinary English, a statute that says that banks may act as insurance agents, and that the Comptroller of the Currency may regulate their insurance-related activities, "relates" to the insurance business. The word "relates" is highly general, and this Court has interpreted it broadly in other pre-emption contexts.

More importantly, in ordinary English, this statute *"specifically"* relates to the insurance business. * * *

Finally, using ordinary English, one would say that this statute specifically relates to the *"business of insurance."* The statute explicitly grants national banks permission to "act as the agent for any fire, life, or other insurance company," to "solici[t] and sel[l] insurance," to "collec[t] premiums," and to "receive for services so rendered ... fees or commissions," subject to Comptroller regulation. 12 U.S.C. § 92. * * *

Consider, too, the McCarran–Ferguson Act's basic purposes. The Act sets forth two mutually reinforcing purposes in its first section, namely, that "continued regulation and taxation by the several States of the business of insurance is in the public interest," and that "*silence* on the part of the Congress shall not be construed to impose any barrier to the regulation or taxation of such business by the several States." 15 U.S.C. § 1011 (emphasis added). The latter phrase, particularly the word "silence," indicates that the Act does not seek to insulate state insurance regulation from the reach of all federal law. Rather, it seeks to protect state regulation primarily against *inadvertent* federal intrusion–say, through enactment of a federal statute that describes an affected activity in broad, general terms, of which the insurance business happens to constitute one part.

The circumstances surrounding enactment of the McCarran–Ferguson Act suggest the same. Just prior to the law's enactment, this Court, in United States v. South–Eastern Underwriters Assn., 322 U.S. 533 (1944), held that a federal antitrust law, the Sherman Act, applied to the business of insurance. The Sherman Act's highly general language said nothing specifically about insurance. See 15 U.S.C. § 1 (forbidding every "contract, combination ... or conspiracy, in restraint of trade or commerce among the several States"). The Sherman Act applied only to activities in or affecting interstate commerce. Many lawyers and insurance professionals had previously thought (relying, in part, on this Court's opinion in Paul v. Virginia, 75 U.S.(8 Wall.) 168, 183 (1868), and other cases) that the issuance of an insurance policy was not a "transaction of commerce," and therefore fell outside the Sherman Act's scope.

In reaction to *South-Eastern Underwriters*, Congress "moved quickly," enacting the McCarran–Ferguson Act "to restore the supremacy of the States in the realm of insurance regulation." [Department of Treasury v.] Fabe, [508 U.S.] at 500, 113 S.Ct., at 2207. But the circumstances we have just described mean that "*restor[ation]*" of "supremacy" basically required setting aside the unanticipated effects of *South-Eastern Underwriters*, and cautiously avoiding similar unanticipated interference with state regulation in the future. It did not require avoiding federal pre-emption by future federal statutes that indicate, through their "specific relat[ion]" to insurance, that Congress had focused upon the insurance industry, and therefore, in all likelihood, consciously intended to exert upon the insurance industry whatever pre-emptive force accompanied its law. * * *

The language of the Federal Statute before us is not general. It refers specifically to insurance. Its state regulatory implications are not surprising, nor do we believe them inadvertent. * * * Consequently, considerations of purpose, as well as of language, indicate that the Federal Statute falls within the scope of the McCarran-Ferguson Act's "specifically relates" exception to its anti-pre-emption rule. * * *

For these reasons, the judgment of the Court of Appeals is reversed.

The *Barnett Bank* case identified as a significant benefit of a national bank charter the ability to use the National Bank Act to preempt state laws that "prevent or significantly interfere with the national bank's exercise of its powers." The issue of preemption of state law by the OCC for national banks (and the OTS for federal savings associations using the field preemption standard) gained increased attention and the OCC received many inquiries regarding the applicability of state law to national banks. In 2004, the OCC issued a final rule on this subject that provided: "state laws that obstruct, impair, or condition a national bank's ability to fully exercise its powers to conduct activities authorized under Federal law do not apply to national banks." 12 C.F.R. § 7.0009(b) (2010).[10] Most observers interpreted this language as a significant expansion on the language quoted above from *Barnett* Bank and the OCC applied the standard to broadly preempt state laws. The Federal Register release explaining the new rule, however, described the language as a "distillation of the various preemption constructs articulated by the Supreme Court," including those cited in *Barnett*, and maintained that the regulation's language was not "in any way inconsistent" with the *Barnett* standard.[11]

The Dodd–Frank Act significantly reduced the ability of national banks and federal savings associations to rely upon federal preemption of state consumer financial laws[12] in what the Act termed a "clarification" of state law preemption standards. The field preemption standard for federal savings associations was specifically overruled. Dodd–Frank Act, § 1046. Consistent with the transfer of the regulatory authority over federal savings associations from the OTS to the OCC, federal savings associations are now subject to the same "laws and legal standards applicable to national banks regarding the preemption of State law." Id.

Dodd–Frank provides in section 1044 that state consumer financial laws are preempted in three separate situations. First, if a state consumer financial law's application would have a discriminatory effect on national banks in comparison with a bank chartered by that state it is preempted. Second, if applying the Supreme Court's standard in the *Barnett Bank* case, the state consumer financial law "prevents or significantly interferes with the exercise by the national bank of its powers," as determined by a court or by an OCC regulation or order on a case-by-case basis, it is preempted. And third, if the state consumer financial law is preempted by a provision of a Federal law other than this portion of the Dodd–Frank

[handwritten margin note: 3 ways to preempt st. (consumer Law)]

---

10. The OCC also indicated that operating subsidiaries of national banks were not subject to state laws that were preempted for the national bank. 12 C.F.R. § 7.4006 (2010). This rule was upheld by the Supreme Court in Watters v. Wachovia Bank, N.A., 550 U.S. 1 (2007), but was overruled by the Dodd–Frank Act, as discussed in greater detail later in this Chapter.

11. Department of the Treasury, Office of the Comptroller of the Currency, Final Rule: Bank Activities and Operations; Real Estate Lending and Appraisals, 69 Fed. Reg. 1904 (Jan. 13, 2004) (codified at 12 C.F.R. pts. 7 and 34).

12. A state consumer financial law is defined in Dodd–Frank as a state law that does not directly or indirectly discriminate against national banks and that "directly and specifically regulates the manner, content, or terms and conditions of any financial transaction (as may be authorized for national banks to engage in), or any account related thereto, with respect to a consumer." Dodd–Frank Act, § 1044.

Act. At least quarterly, the OCC must publish a list of its preemption determinations then in effect to increase transparency regarding preemption. Every five years, the OCC must review its preemption decisions and submit a report to the Senate Banking Committee and the House Financial Services Committee about whether it intends to continue, rescind, or amend its prior preemption determinations.

Dodd–Frank also set standards for the courts in reviewing OCC preemption decisions, stating that the court shall assess the validity of such determinations, depending upon the "thoroughness evident in the consideration of the agency, the validity of the reasoning of the agency, the consistency with other valid determinations made by the agency, and other factors which the court finds persuasive and relevant to its decision." Dodd–Frank Act, § 1044. The OCC's preemption decision must be supported by substantial evidence made on the record and in accordance with the *Barnett Bank* standard.

[handwritten margin note: Reviews OCC preemp]

(3) The OCC's Visitorial Powers

On the same day the OCC's final rule on preemption of state law was issued in 2004, the OCC also issued a new final rule with respect to its exclusive power to visit, regulate, and enforce national banks' compliance with federal and state laws. In that issuance, the OCC concluded that even if a state law is *not* preempted with respect to a national bank, "enforcement of a national bank's compliance with a [state] law that would govern the content or the conditions for conduct of a national bank's Federally-authorized banking business is within the OCC's exclusive purview." Department of the Treasury, Office of the Comptroller of the Currency, Final Rule: Bank Activities and Operations, 69 Fed. Reg. 1895 (Jan. 13, 2004) (codified at 12 C.F.R. § 7.4000).

The OCC also maintained that this result was consistent with the Riegle–Neal Act. Riegle–Neal, enacted in 1994, freed banks and their holding companies from operating within a single state and permitted them to engage in interstate banking and branching. That statute provides:

(A) In general

The laws of the host State regarding community reinvestment, consumer protection, fair lending, and establishment of intrastate branches shall apply to any branch in the host State of an out-of-State national bank to the same extent as such State laws apply to a branch of a bank chartered by that State, except—

(i) When Federal law preempts the application of such State laws to a national bank; * * *

(B) Enforcement of applicable State laws

The provisions of any State law to which a branch of a national bank is subject under this paragraph *shall be enforced, with respect to such branch, by the Comptroller of the Currency.*

12 U.S.C. § 36(f)(1) (emphasis added). The OCC maintained in its final rule release on visitorial powers that

> Thus, although Riegle–Neal section 36(f) clarifies that the laws of the host state regarding community reinvestment, consumer protection, and fair lending would be applicable to branches of an out-of-state national bank located in the host state, unless preempted, the Riegle–Neal Act further and unambiguously provides that it is the OCC that has the authority to enforce such laws to the extent they are not preempted.

Department of the Treasury, Office of the Comptroller of the Currency, Final Rule: Bank Activities and Operations, 69 Fed. Reg. 1895 (Jan. 13, 2004) (codified at 12 C.F.R. 7.4000).

The Supreme Court considered the challenge of a state attorney general to the OCC's visitorial powers rule in the case excerpted below.

CUOMO v. THE CLEARING HOUSE ASSOCIATION, LLC

Supreme Court of the United States, 2009.
129 S.Ct. 2710.

JUSTICE SCALIA delivered the opinion of the Court.

In 2005, Eliot Spitzer, Attorney General for the State of New York, sent letters to several national banks making a request "in lieu of subpoena" that they provide certain non-public information about their lending practices. He sought this information to determine whether the banks had violated the State's fair-lending laws. Spitzer's successor in office, Andrew Cuomo, is the petitioner here. Respondents, the federal Office of the Comptroller of the Currency ("Comptroller" or "OCC") and the Clearing House Association, a banking trade group, brought suit to enjoin the information request, claiming that the Comptroller's regulation promulgated under the National Bank Act prohibits that form of state law enforcement against national banks.

The United States District Court for the Southern District of New York entered an injunction in favor of respondents, prohibiting the attorney general from enforcing state fair-lending laws through demands for records or judicial proceedings. The United States Court of Appeals for the Second Circuit affirmed. 510 F.3d 105 (2007). We granted certiorari. The question presented is whether the Comptroller's regulation purporting to pre-empt state law enforcement can be upheld as a reasonable interpretation of the National Bank Act.

Section 484(a) of Title 12, U.S.C., a provision of the National Bank Act, reads as follows:

> "No national bank shall be subject to any visitorial powers except as authorized by Federal law, vested in the courts of justice or such as shall be, or have been exercised or directed by Congress or by either House thereof or by any committee of Congress or of either House duly authorized."

The Comptroller, charged with administering the National Bank Act, adopted, through notice-and-comment rulemaking, the regulation at issue here designed to implement the statutory provision. Its principal provisions read as follows:

> "§ 7.4000 Visitorial powers.
>
> "(a) *General rule.* (1) Only the OCC or an authorized representative of the OCC may exercise visitorial powers with respect to national banks, except as provided in paragraph (b) of this section. State officials may not exercise visitorial powers with respect to national banks, such as conducting examinations, inspecting or requiring the production of books or records of national banks, or prosecuting enforcement actions, except in limited circumstances authorized by federal law. However, production of a bank's records (other than non-public OCC information under 12 CFR part 4, subpart C) may be required under normal judicial procedures.
>
> "(2) For purposes of this section, visitorial powers include:
>
> "(i) Examination of a bank;
>
> "(ii) Inspection of a bank's books and records;
>
> "(iii) Regulation and supervision of activities authorized or permitted pursuant to federal banking law; and
>
> "(iv) Enforcing compliance with any applicable federal or state laws concerning those activities." 12 C.F.R. § 7.4000 (2009).

By its clear text, this regulation prohibits the States from "prosecuting enforcement actions" except in "limited circumstances authorized by federal law."

Under the familiar *Chevron* framework, we defer to an agency's reasonable interpretation of a statute it is charged with administering ... There is necessarily some ambiguity as to the meaning of the statutory term "visitorial powers," especially since we are working in an era when the prerogative writs—through which visitorial powers were traditionally enforced—are not in vogue. The Comptroller can give authoritative meaning to the statute within the bounds of that uncertainty. But the presence of some uncertainty does not expand *Chevron* deference to cover virtually any interpretation of the National Bank Act. We can discern the outer limits of the term "visitorial powers" even through the clouded lens of history. They do not include, as the Comptroller's expansive regulation would provide, ordinary enforcement of the law. * * *

In sum, the unmistakable and utterly consistent teaching of our jurisprudence, both before and after enactment of the National Bank Act, is that a sovereign's "visitorial powers" and its power to enforce the law are two different things. There is not a credible argument to the contrary.

And contrary to what the Comptroller's regulation says, the National Bank Act pre-empts only the former.

The consequences of the regulation also cast doubt upon its validity. No one denies that the National Bank Act leaves in place some state substantive laws affecting banks. But the Comptroller's rule says that the State may not *enforce* its valid, non-pre-empted laws against national banks. The bark remains, but the bite does not.

The dissent admits, with considerable understatement, that such a result is "unusual." "Bizarre" would be more apt. As the Court said in [First National Bank in] St. Louis [v. Missouri]:

> "To demonstrate the binding quality of a statute but deny the power of enforcement involves a fallacy made apparent by the mere statement of the proposition, for such power is essentially inherent in the very conception of law." 263 U.S., at 660.

In sharp contrast to the "unusual" reading propounded by the Comptroller's regulation, reading "visitorial powers" as limiting only sovereign oversight and supervision would produce an entirely commonplace result-the precise result contemplated by our opinion in *St. Louis* which said that if a state statute is valid as to national banks, "the corollary that it is obligatory *and enforceable* necessarily results." Id. at 659–660 (emphasis added). Channeling state attorneys general into judicial law-enforcement proceedings (rather than allowing them to exercise "visitorial" oversight) would preserve a regime of exclusive administrative oversight by the Comptroller while honoring in fact rather than merely in theory Congress's decision not to pre-empt substantive state law. This system echoes many other mixed state/federal regimes in which the Federal Government exercises general oversight while leaving state substantive law in place.

* * * "Visitorial powers" in the National Bank Act refers to a sovereign's supervisory powers over corporations. They include any form of administrative oversight that allows a sovereign to inspect books and records on demand, even if the process is mediated by a court through prerogative writs or similar means. The Comptroller reasonably interpreted this statutory term to include "conducting examinations [and] inspecting or requiring the production of books or records of national banks," § 7.4000, when the State conducts those activities in its capacity as supervisor of corporations.

When, however, a state attorney general brings suit to enforce state law against a national bank, he is not acting in the role of sovereign-as-supervisor, but rather in the role of sovereign-as-law-enforcer. Such a lawsuit is not an exercise of "visitorial powers" and thus the Comptroller erred by extending the definition of "visitorial powers" to include "prosecuting enforcement actions" in state courts, § 7.4000.

The request for information in the present case was stated to be "in lieu of" other action; implicit was the threat that if the request was not voluntarily honored, that other action would be taken. All parties have assumed, and we agree, that if the threatened action would have been unlawful the request-cum-threat could be enjoined. Here the threatened action was not the bringing of a civil suit, or the obtaining of a judicial search warrant based on probable cause, but rather the Attorney General's issuance of subpoena on his own authority under New York Executive Law, which permits such subpoenas in connection with his investigation of "repeated fraudulent or illegal acts . . . in the carrying on, conducting or transaction of business." See N.Y. Exec. Law Ann. § 63(12) (West 2002). That is not the exercise of the power of law enforcement "vested in the courts of justice" which 12 U.S.C. § 484(a) exempts from the ban on exercise of supervisory power.

Accordingly, the injunction below is affirmed as applied to the threatened issuance of executive subpoenas by the Attorney General for the State of New York, but vacated insofar as it prohibits the Attorney General from bringing judicial enforcement actions.

The judgment of the Court of Appeals is affirmed in part and reversed in part.

JUSTICE THOMAS, with whom THE CHIEF JUSTICE, JUSTICE KENNEDY, and JUSTICE ALITO join, concurring in part and dissenting in part.

* * * [T]he only disputed question is whether the statutory term "visitorial powers" is ambiguous and, if so, whether OCC's construction of it is reasonable.

The majority concedes that there is "some ambiguity as to the meaning of the statutory term 'visitorial powers.'" Yet it concludes that OCC's interpretation of § 484(a) is not entitled to deference because the Court "can discern the outer limits of the term 'visitorial powers' even through the clouded lens of history" and these outer definitional limits "do not include . . . ordinary enforcement of the law." I cannot agree. The statutory term "visitorial powers" is susceptible to more than one meaning, and the agency's construction is reasonable. * * *

———————

The Dodd–Frank Act adopts the Supreme Court's decision in *Cuomo v. Clearing House Association,* providing in section 1047 that OCC visitorial rights shall *not* be construed as "limiting or restricting the authority of any attorney general (or other chief law enforcement officer) of any state to bring an action against a national bank in a court of appropriate jurisdiction to enforce an applicable law and to seek relief as authorized by such law." The same standard is made applicable by the Act to federal savings associations.

(4) Diversity Jurisdiction

WACHOVIA BANK, N.A. v. SCHMIDT

Supreme Court of the United States, 2006.
546 U.S. 303.

MADAME JUSTICE GINSBURG delivered the opinion of the Court.

* * * Petitioner Wachovia Bank, National Association (Wachovia), is a national banking association with its designated main office in Charlotte, North Carolina. Wachovia operates branch offices in many States, including South Carolina.

The litigation before us commenced when plaintiff-respondent Daniel G. Schmidt III and others, citizens of South Carolina, sued Wachovia in a South Carolina state court for fraudulently inducing them to participate in an illegitimate tax shelter. Shortly thereafter, Wachovia filed a petition in the United States District Court for the District of South Carolina, seeking to compel arbitration of the dispute. As the sole basis for federal-court jurisdiction, Wachovia alleged the parties' diverse citizenship. See 28 U.S.C. § 1332. The District Court denied Wachovia's petition on the merits; neither the parties nor the court questioned the existence of federal subject-matter jurisdiction. On appeal, a divided Fourth Circuit panel determined that the District Court lacked diversity jurisdiction over the action; it therefore vacated the judgment and instructed the District Court to dismiss the case.

The Court of Appeals' majority observed that Wachovia's citizenship for diversity purposes is controlled by § 1348, which provides that "national banking associations" are "deemed citizens of the States in which they are respectively located." As the panel majority read § 1348, Wachovia is "located" in, and is therefore a "citizen" of, every State in which it maintains a branch office. Thus Wachovia's branch operations in South Carolina, in the majority's view, rendered the bank a citizen of South Carolina. Given the South Carolina citizenship of the opposing parties, the majority concluded that the matter could not be adjudicated in federal court.

Circuit Judge King dissented. He read § 1348 and its statutory precursors to provide national banks with "the same access to federal courts as that accorded other banks and corporations." [388 F.3d] at 434. On his reading, Wachovia is a citizen only of North Carolina, the State in which its main office is located, not of every State in which it maintains a branch office; accordingly, he concluded, Wachovia's petition qualified for federal-court adjudication.

We granted certiorari to resolve the disagreement among Courts of Appeals on the meaning of § 1348. * * *

[A]s part of the 1948 Judicial Code revision, Congress enacted § 1348 in its current form. Act of June 25, 1948, 62 Stat. 933. The provision now reads:

The district courts shall have original jurisdiction of any civil action commenced by the United States, or by direction of any officer thereof, against any national banking association, any civil action to wind up the affairs of any such association, and any action by a banking association established in the district for which the court is held, under chapter 2 of Title 12, to enjoin the Comptroller of the Currency, or any receiver acting under his direction, as provided by such chapter.

All national banking associations shall, for the purpose of all other actions by or against them, be deemed citizens of the States in which they are respectively located.

28 U.S.C. § 1348.

The Fourth Circuit panel majority advanced three principal reasons for deciding that Wachovia is "located" in, and therefore a "citizen" of, every State in which it maintains a branch office. First, consulting dictionaries, the Court of Appeals observed that "[i]n ordinary parlance" the term "located" refers to "physical presence in a place." 388 F.3d, at 416–417. Banks have a physical presence, the Fourth Circuit stated, wherever they operate branches. Next, the court noted, "Section 1348 uses two distinct terms to refer to the presence of a banking association: 'established' and 'located.'" Id., at 419. "To give independent meaning" to each word, the court said, "it is most reasonable to understand the place where a national bank is 'established' to refer to a bank's charter location, and to understand the place where it is 'located' to refer to the place or places where it has a physical presence." Ibid. Finally, the Court of Appeals stressed that in Citizens & Southern Nat. Bank v. Bougas, 434 U.S. 35 (1977), this Court interpreted the term "located" in the former venue statute for national banks, see 12 U.S.C. § 94 (1976 ed.), as encompassing any county in which a bank maintains a branch office. 388 F.3d, at 419–420. Reasoning that "the jurisdiction and venue statutes pertain to the same subject matter, namely the amenability of national banking associations to suit in federal court," the panel majority concluded that, "under the *in pari materia* canon[,] the two statutes should be interpreted" consistently. Id., at 422.

* * * To summarize [our disagreement with the Fourth Circuit panel majority], "located," as its appearances in the banking laws reveal, is a chameleon word; its meaning depends on the context in and purpose for which it is used.

In the context of venue, "located" may refer to multiple places, for a venue prescription, *e.g.*, the current and former 12 U.S.C. § 94, presupposes subject-matter jurisdiction and simply delineates *where* within a given judicial system a case may be maintained. See, e.g., 28 U.S.C. § 1391(c) (for venue purposes, "a corporation shall be deemed to reside in any judicial district in which it is subject to personal jurisdiction at the time the action is commenced").

In contrast, in § 1348, "located" appears in a prescription governing not venue but federal-court subject-matter jurisdiction. Concerning access to the federal court system, § 1348 deems national banks "citizens of the States in which they are respectively located." There is no reason to suppose Congress used those words to effect a radical departure from the norm. An individual who resides in more than one State is regarded, for purposes of federal subject-matter (diversity) jurisdiction, as a citizen of but one State. Similarly, a corporation's citizenship derives, for diversity jurisdiction purposes, from its State of incorporation and principal place of business. § 1332(c)(1). It is not deemed a citizen of every State in which it conducts business or is otherwise amenable to personal jurisdiction. Reading § 1348 in this context, one would sensibly "locate" a national bank for the very same purpose, *i.e.*, qualification for diversity jurisdiction, in the State designated in its articles of association as its main office.

Treating venue and subject-matter jurisdiction prescriptions as *in pari materia,* the Court of Appeals majority overlooked the discrete offices of those concepts. The resulting Fourth Circuit decision rendered national banks singularly disfavored corporate bodies with regard to their access to federal courts. The language of § 1348 does not mandate that incongruous outcome, nor does this Court's precedent.

For the reasons stated, the judgment of the United States Court of Appeals for the Fourth Circuit is reversed, and the case is remanded for further proceedings consistent with this opinion.

On remand from the Supreme Court, the Fourth Circuit ruled that Schmidt's state law claims against Wachovia were not barred by the arbitration provisions in two documents because the state law claims lacked a sufficient relationship with those documents. Therefore, the Fourth Circuit affirmed the district court's decision to deny Wachovia's petition for an order compelling arbitration of the claims in federal court invoking the court's diversity jurisdiction. Wachovia Bank, N.A. v. Schmidt, 445 F.3d 762 (4th Cir. 2006).

The Financial Services Regulatory Relief Act of 2006 gives federal chartered savings associations and savings banks the same access to federal courts as national banks. 12 U.S.C.A. § 1464(x) (for purposes of diversity jurisdiction, a "federal savings association shall be considered to be a citizen only of the State in which such savings association has its home office").

QUESTIONS AND NOTES

1. Prior to Dodd–Frank, federal savings associations were subject to 12 C.F.R. § 560.2(a), which set forth the occupation of the field or field preemption standard:

Occupation of the field. Pursuant to sections 4(a) and 5(a) of the HOLA, 12 U.S.C. 1463(a), OTS is authorized to promulgate regulations that preempt state laws affecting the operations of federal savings associations when deemed appropriate to facilitate the safe and sound operation of federal savings associations, to enable federal savings associations to conduct their operations in accordance with the best practices of thrift institutions in the United States, or to further other purposes of the HOLA. To enhance safety and soundness and to enable federal savings associations to conduct their operations in accordance with best practices (by efficiently delivering low-cost credit to the public free from undue regulatory duplication and burden), OTS hereby occupies the entire field of lending regulation for federal savings associations. OTS intends to give federal savings associations maximum flexibility to exercise their lending powers in accordance with a uniform federal scheme of regulation.

12 C.F.R. § 560.2(a). After Dodd–Frank, federal savings associations are subject to the new preemption standard for national banks.

2. Why did it take the OCC until 2004 to issue a preemption regulation? As you think about this question, consider the effect of advances in technology and the removal of limitations on interstate banking.

3. The Dodd–Frank Act provisions regarding preemption of state laws only cover "state consumer financial laws." What preemption standards apply to other state laws that may be applicable to national banks and federal savings associations—the *Barnett Bank* standard or the language of the OCC's pre-Dodd–Frank regulation, "obstruct, impair, or condition?"

4. Broad preemption of state laws enhanced the ability of national banks and federal savings associations to operate in multiple states. Consider the consequences of the new preemption provisions on the multi-state operations of federally chartered banks and savings associations. Will compliance with multiple state standards increase the cost of credit to consumers? Will a state with an onerous consumer financial law find that federal institutions withdraw from operations in that state to avoid compliance with the state's law? Will banks and savings associations operating in multiple states adopt the standards set forth in the strictest law of the states in which it operates so they will only have to comply with one standard? Will banks and savings associations conducting business in multiple states lobby for federal (hence uniform) consumer protection standards to avoid being subject to a number of different state laws? See V. Gerard Comizio & Helen Y. Lee, Understanding the Federal Preemption Debate and a Potential Uniformity Solution, Business Law Brief, Spring/Summer 2010 (advocating the creation and adoption of a Uniform Banking and Consumer Protection Code to create uniform state banking regulation and achieve conformity with federal banking law).

The Bureau of Consumer Financial Protection (BCFP) created by the Dodd–Frank Act has the power to issue rules regarding consumer protection. As discussed in greater detail in Chapter 6, these rules will not preempt state consumer protections laws; rather, they will provide a floor for acceptable conduct and banks and other providers of consumer financial services will be subject to more stringent state law requirements that may be applicable in the states where they do business.

5. Pursuant to the *Cuomo* case, a state attorney general may not issue a subpoena to request information from a national bank, but may bring an

action to enforce any state law that applies to the national bank and has not been preempted. Dodd–Frank endorses this standard in interpreting the OCC's exclusive visitorial powers and extends it also to federal savings associations. Will federally chartered banks and savings associations be subject to potentially frivolous lawsuits by state attorneys general if they lack the subpoena power to explore the viability of a particular lawsuit?

6. What happens to state banks in states with "wild card" or parity statutes (that give state banks parity with national banks) when the OCC preempts the application of a state law for a national bank? Does the state bank get the benefit of the preemption under the parity provision?

7. Assume a state law provides that a lender may not encourage a borrower to default on an existing loan while in the process of refinancing that loan (a practice sometimes used in so-called predatory lending). Would the state law be preempted as to a national bank under the Dodd–Frank standard ("prevent or significantly interfere with the national bank's exercise of its powers")? Would the state law be preempted as to a national bank under the OCC's prior rule ("obstruct, impair, or condition" a national bank's exercise of its powers)?

(5) Powers of State Banks

The powers of state chartered banks are those powers granted by state statute. You may wish to find the statute in your state that sets forth the powers of state chartered banks. States formerly viewed bank powers as a potential way to compete with the national bank charter. Banks might be attracted to the state bank charter if it authorized a broader range of activities than those available under the National Bank Act. The potential obviously existed for a "race to the bottom" with states attempting to outdo each other for the most expansive state charter. This powers "arms race" was largely curtailed with the passage of the Federal Deposit Insurance Corporation Improvement Act of 1991 (FDICIA). FDICIA amended section 24 of the Federal Deposit Insurance Act to provide that the activities of a state-chartered bank *as principal* are limited to the activities of a national bank. FDICIA § 303, 12 U.S.C. § 1831a. The statute still permits state chartered banks to engage in *agency* activities authorized by their state. Moreover, the statute specifically permits activities beyond those permitted to national banks upon application to the FDIC if the FDIC finds that the bank is well capitalized and concludes that the activity poses no risk to the safety and soundness of the federal deposit insurance fund. Id. § 1831a(a)(1). The FDIC has entertained and granted a number of these exemptions and permitted state banks additional powers beyond those authorized for national banks. A listing is contained on the FDIC's web site.[13] It is important to note that new activities must also be approved by the state regulator, who often has great discretion and may disapprove the new activity based on considerations of safety and soundness.

---

13. See <www.fdic.gov/regulations/laws/bankdecisions/InvestActivity/index.html>.

One result of FDICIA's limit of state bank activities to those of national banks was that many states adopted national bank parity (or "wild card") statutes providing that state banks may engage in the same activities as national banks. In fact, all but a few states now have such parity provisions in their state bank statutes.[14]

QUESTIONS AND NOTES

1. Find the bank "powers" provision for banks chartered in your state. Does it contain a national bank parity provision? Does the statute afford powers parity with any other type of institution such as a federal savings association or other state chartered bank? If not, are the powers granted more limited than or greater than those afforded to national banks?

2. About thirty states permit real estate brokerage for a state chartered bank. Would real estate brokerage for a state chartered bank be precluded by the operation of the FDICIA provision discussed above?

3. Do you bank with a state or national bank? You can tell from the name of a bank whether it has a national charter or a state charter. All national associations must have in their legal name "national," "national association," or "N.A."(short for national association).

4. Banks sometimes "flip" their charter from national to state or state to national. You should keep your eyes open for conversion activity. J.P. Morgan Chase & Co.'s lead bank subsidiary, formerly the largest state chartered bank in the country, converted to a national bank headquartered in Ohio following its merger with Bank One. Chase was a national bank prior to its merger with Chemical Bank when it assumed Chemical Bank's New York state bank charter.

C. BANK SUBSIDIARIES

Both national and state banks are permitted to own the stock of subsidiary corporations under certain conditions. Subsidiaries of banks are general business corporations and not chartered banks. Therefore, they may not accept deposits. Banks may establish three different types of subsidiaries—a bank service corporation, an operating subsidiary or a financial subsidiary.

(1) Bank Service Corporation

A bank service corporation is subject to the Bank Service Corporation Act, 12 U.S.C.A. §§ 1861–67. A bank service corporation provides services to its bank owner and/or to other depository institutions, including "check and deposit sorting and posting, computation and posting of interest and other credits and charges, preparation and mailing of checks, statements, notice and similar items, or any other clerical, bookkeeping, accounting, statistical, or similar functions performed for a depository institution." 12 U.S.C.A. § 1863.

---

14. See generally Christian A. Johnson, Wild Card Statutes, Parity and National Banks–The Renascence of State Banking Powers, 26 Loy. U. Chi. L.J. 351 (1995).

(2) Operating Subsidiary

The Supreme Court case excerpted below explains the history relating to national bank operating subsidiaries prior the Dodd–Frank Act. In 1966, the OCC permitted a national bank to establish an operating subsidiary as part of its incidental authority under 12 U.S.C. § 24(7) to engage in activities in that subsidiary that were permissible for the bank to engage in directly. In 1996, the OCC broadened that authority to permit some activities in the operating subsidiary that were not permissible for the national bank parent. In the GLBA of 1999, Congress created a new type of bank subsidiary, a financial subsidiary, and the expansion of powers for the national bank operating subsidiary authorized in 1996 was curtailed. In 2001, the OCC adopted 12 C.F.R. § 7.4006, subjecting operating subsidiaries to state laws only to the same extent "those laws apply to the parent national bank." In 2004, the OCC adopted the standard for preempting any state law if it would "obstruct, impair, or condition" a national bank's ability to exercise its powers to conduct its banking business under federal law. The OCC stated in the rule release that national bank operating subsidiaries are subject to the same terms and restrictions of state law as their parent banks. In the following case, the Supreme Court considered whether a Michigan law requiring nonbank mortgage providers to register with the state's financial services regulator and submit to state supervision applied to Wachovia Mortgage, an operating subsidiary of Wachovia Bank, N.A.

WATTERS v. WACHOVIA BANK, N.A.

Supreme Court of the United States, 2007.
550 U.S. 1.

MADAME JUSTICE GINSBURG delivered the opinion of the Court.

* * * Wachovia Bank is a national banking association chartered by OCC. Respondent Wachovia Mortgage is a North Carolina corporation that engages in the business of real estate lending in the State of Michigan and elsewhere. Michigan's statutory regime exempts banks, both national and state, from state mortgage lending regulation, but requires mortgage brokers, lenders, and servicers that are subsidiaries of national banks to register with the State's Office of Insurance and Financial Services (OIFS) and submit to state supervision. From 1997 until 2003, Wachovia Mortgage was registered with OIFS to engage in mortgage lending. As a registrant, Wachovia Mortgage was required, *inter alia,* to pay an annual operating fee, file an annual report, and open its books and records to inspection by OIFS examiners. * * *

On January 1, 2003, Wachovia Mortgage became a wholly owned operating subsidiary of Wachovia Bank. [Three months later, Wachovia Mortgage advised the State of Michigan that it was surrendering its mortgage lending registration. Because it had become an operating subsidiary of a national bank, Wachovia Mortgage maintained, Michigan's registration and inspection requirements were preempted.] Watters responded with a letter advising Wachovia Mortgage that it would no longer be authorized to conduct mortgage lending activities in Michigan.

Wachovia Mortgage and Wachovia Bank filed suit against Watters, in her official capacity as commissioner, in the United States District Court for the Western District of Michigan. They sought declaratory and injunctive relief prohibiting Watters from enforcing Michigan's registration prescriptions against Wachovia Mortgage, and from interfering with OCC's exclusive visitorial authority. * * *

While conceding that Michigan's licensing, registration, and inspection requirements cannot be applied to national banks, Watters argues that the State's regulatory regime survives preemption with respect to national banks' operating subsidiaries. Because such subsidiaries are separately chartered under some State's law, Watters characterizes them simply as "affiliates" of national banks, and contends that even though they are subject to OCC's superintendence, they are also subject to multistate control. We disagree.

Since 1966, OCC has recognized the "incidental" authority of national banks under § 24 Seventh to do business through operating subsidiaries. See 31 Fed.Reg. 11459–11460 (1966); 12 CFR § 5.34(e)(1) (2006) ("A national bank may conduct in an operating subsidiary activities that are permissible for a national bank to engage in directly either as part of, or incidental to, the business of banking. . . ."). That authority is uncontested by Michigan's commissioner. OCC licenses and oversees national bank operating subsidiaries just as it does national banks. § 5.34(e)(3) ("An operating subsidiary conducts activities authorized under this section pursuant to the same authorization, terms and conditions that apply to the conduct of such activities by its parent national bank.").

In 1999, Congress defined and regulated "financial" subsidiaries; simultaneously, Congress distinguished those national bank affiliates from subsidiaries-typed "operating subsidiaries" by OCC—which may engage only in activities national banks may engage in directly, "subject to the same terms and conditions that govern the conduct of such activities by national banks." Gramm–Leach–Bliley Act (GLBA), § 121(a)(2), 113 Stat. 1378 (codified at 12 U.S.C. § 24a(g)(3)(A)). For supervisory purposes, OCC treats national banks and their operating subsidiaries as a single economic enterprise. OCC oversees both entities by reference to "business line," applying the same controls whether banking "activities are conducted directly or through an operating subsidiary."

* * * Watters seeks to impose state regulation on operating subsidiaries over and above regulation undertaken by OCC. But just as duplicative state examination, supervision, and regulation would significantly burden mortgage lending when engaged in by national banks, so too would those state controls interfere with that same activity when engaged in by an operating subsidiary. * * *

The NBA is thus properly read by OCC to protect from state hindrance a national bank's engagement in the "business of banking" whether conducted by the bank itself or by an operating subsidiary, empowered to do only what the bank itself could do. The authority to engage in the business of mortgage lending comes from the NBA, § 371, as does the authority to conduct business through an operating subsidiary. See §§ 24 Seventh, 24a(g)(3)(A). That Act vests visitorial oversight in OCC, not state regulators. § 484(a). State law (in this case, North Carolina law), all agree, governs incorporation-related issues, such as the formation, dissolution, and internal governance of operating subsidiaries. And the laws of the States in which national banks or their affiliates are located govern matters the NBA does not address. But state regulators cannot interfere with the "business of banking" by subjecting national banks or their OCC-licensed operating subsidiaries to multiple audits and surveillance under rival oversight regimes.

Watters' alternative argument, that 12 CFR § 7.4006 violates the Tenth Amendment to the Constitution, is unavailing. As we have previously explained, "[i]f a power is delegated to Congress in the Constitution, the Tenth Amendment expressly disclaims any reservation of that power to the States." New York v. United States, 505 U.S. 144, 156 (1992). Regulation of national bank operations is a prerogative of Congress under the Commerce and Necessary and Proper Clauses. The Tenth Amendment, therefore, is not implicated here.

For the reasons stated, the judgment of the Sixth Circuit is Affirmed.

Justice Thomas took no part in the consideration or decision of this case.

Justice Stevens, with whom Chief Justice Roberts and Justice Scalia join, dissenting.

* * * In 1966, the Comptroller of the Currency took the position "that a national bank may acquire and hold the controlling stock interest in a subsidiary operations corporation" so long as that corporation's "functions or activities . . . are limited to one or several of the functions or activities that a national bank is authorized to carry on." 31 Fed.Reg. 11459 (1966). The Comptroller declined to read the categorical prohibition on national bank ownership of stock to foreclose bank ownership of operating subsidiaries, finding authority for this aggressive interpretation of national bank authority in the "incidental powers" provision of 12 U.S.C. § 24 Seventh. See 31 Fed.Reg. 11460.

While Congress eventually restricted some of the new corporate structures, it neither disavowed nor endorsed the Comptroller's position on national bank ownership of operating subsidiaries. Notwithstanding the congressional silence, in 1996 the OCC once again attempted to expand national banks' ownership powers. The agency issued a regulation permitting national bank operating subsidiaries to undertake activities that the bank was *not* allowed to engage in directly. 12 CFR §§ 5.34(d), (f) (1997).

Congress overruled this OCC regulation in 1999 in the Gramm–Leach–Bliley Act (GLBA), 113 Stat. 1338. The GLBA was a seminal piece of banking legislation inasmuch as it repealed the Glass–Steagall Act's ban on affiliations between commercial and investment banks. More relevant to this case, however, the GLBA addressed the powers of national banks to own subsidiary corporations. The Act provided that any national bank subsidiary engaging in activities forbidden to the parent bank would be considered a "financial subsidiary," and would be subjected to heightened regulatory obligations. The GLBA's definition of "financial subsidiaries" excluded those subsidiaries that "engag[e] solely in activities that national banks are permitted to engage in directly and are conducted subject to the same terms and conditions that govern the conduct of such activities by national banks." § 24a(g)(3).

By negative implication, then, only subsidiaries engaging in purely national bank activities-which the OCC had termed "operating subsidiaries," but which the GLBA never mentions by name-could avoid being subjected to the restrictions that applied to financial subsidiaries. Taken together, these provisions worked a rejection of the OCC's position that an *operating* subsidiary could engage in activities that national banks could not engage in directly. See § 24a(g)(3). Apart from this implicit rejection of the OCC's 1996 regulation, however, the GLBA does not even mention operating subsidiaries.

In sum, Congress itself has never authorized national banks to use subsidiaries incorporated under state law to perform traditional banking functions. Nor has it authorized OCC to "license" any state-chartered entity to do so. The fact that it may have acquiesced in the OCC's expansive interpretation of its authority is a plainly insufficient basis for finding preemption. * * *

In my view, the most pressing questions in this case are whether Congress has delegated to the Comptroller of the Currency the authority to preempt the laws of a sovereign State as they apply to operating subsidiaries, and if so, whether that authority was properly exercised here. See 12 CFR § 7.4006 (2006) ("State laws apply to national bank operating subsidiaries to the same extent that those laws apply to the parent national bank") * * * I must consider (as did the four Circuits to have addressed this issue) whether an administrative agency can assume the power to displace the duly enacted laws of a state legislature.

To begin with, Congress knows how to authorize executive agencies to preempt state laws. It has not done so here. Nor does the statutory provision authorizing banks to engage in certain lines of business that are "incidental" to their primary business of accepting and managing the funds of depositors expressly or implicitly grant the OCC the power to immunize banks or their subsidiaries from state regulation. See 12 U.S.C. § 24 Seventh. For there is a vast and obvious difference between rules authorizing or regulating conduct and rules granting immunity from regulation. The Comptroller may well have the authority to decide whether the activities of a mortgage broker, a real estate broker, or a travel agent should be characterized as "incidental" to banking, and to approve a bank's entry into those businesses, either directly or through its subsidiaries. But that lesser power does not imply the far greater power to immunize banks or their subsidiaries from state laws regulating the conduct of their competitors. * * *

In any event, neither of the two justifications the OCC advanced when it promulgated 12 CFR § 7.4006 withstand *Chevron* analysis.[15] First, the OCC observed that the GLBA "expressly acknowledged the authority of national banks to own subsidiaries" that conduct national bank activities " 'subject to the same terms and conditions that govern the conduct of such activities by national banks.' " 66 Fed.Reg. 34788 (quoting 12 U.S.C. § 24a(g)(3)). * * * According to the OCC, "[a] fundamental component of these descriptions of the characteristics of operating subsidiaries in GLBA and the OCC's rule is that state laws apply to operating subsidiaries to the same extent as they apply to the parent national bank." 66 Fed.Reg. 34788.

This is incorrect. As explained above, the GLBA's offhand use of the "same terms and conditions" language says nothing about preemption. Nor can the OCC's incorporation of that language into a regulation support the agency's position: "Simply put, the existence of a parroting regulation does not change the fact that the question here is not the meaning of the regulation but the meaning of the statute." Gonzales v. Oregon, 546 U.S. 243, 257 (2006). * * *

Second, the OCC describes operating subsidiaries "as the equivalent of departments or divisions of their parent banks," 66 Fed.Reg. 34788, which, through the operation of 12 U.S.C. § 484(a), would not be subject to state visitorial powers. The OCC claims that national banks might desire to conduct their business through operating subsidiaries for the purposes of "controlling operations costs, improving effectiveness of supervision, more accurate determination of profits, decentralizing management decisions [and] separating particular operations of the bank from other operations." It is obvious, however, that a national bank could realize *all* of those benefits through the straightforward expedient of dissolving the corporation and making it in fact a "department" or a "division" of the parent bank.

Rather, the primary advantage of maintaining an operating subsidiary as a separate corporation is that it shields the national bank from the operating subsidiaries' liabilities. For that reason, the OCC's regulation is about far more than mere "corporate structure," or "internal governance." It is about whether a *state* corporation can avoid complying with *state* regulations, yet nevertheless take advantage of *state* laws insulating its owners from liability. The federal interest in protecting depositors in national banks from their subsidiaries' liabilities surely does not justify a

---

15. [eds.] The dissent earlier concluded that the OCC's regulation does not merit *Chevron* deference.

grant of immunity from laws that apply to competitors. Indeed, the OCC's regulation may drive companies seeking refuge from state regulation into the arms of federal parents, harm those state competitors who are not lucky enough to find a federal benefactor, and hamstring States' ability to regulate the affairs of state corporations. As a result, the OCC's regulation threatens both the dual banking system and the principle of competitive equality that is its cornerstone. * * *

The Dodd–Frank Act overruled *Watters*. The Act specifically provides that "a State consumer financial law shall apply to a subsidiary or affiliate of a national bank ... to the same extent that the State consumer financial law applies to any person, corporation, or other entity subject to such State law." Dodd–Frank Act, § 1044. Under § 1046 of Dodd–Frank, the same rule will apply to a subsidiary or affiliate of a federal savings association.

(3) Financial Subsidiary

GLBA authorized a broad range of new activities for holding companies that qualified as financial holding companies (FHC). Holding companies are discussed later in this Chapter. These new activities were to be performed in subsidiaries of the FHC and subject to FRB oversight. In a compromise with the OCC, some, but not all, of the activities were permitted for newly minted "financial subsidiaries" of national banks, 12 U.S.C.A. § 24a, or state banks, 12 U.S.C.A. § 1831w.

A financial subsidiary may engage in activities that are "financial in nature," or "incidental" to a financial activity. 12 U.S.C.A. § 24a. Authorized activities include those activities permissible for the subsidiaries of bank holding companies, activities permissible for a bank holding company to conduct abroad (other than real estate development or real estate investment), securities activities, and insurance agency activities (without the limitations of 12 U.S.C.A. § 92), and any additional activities subsequently determined by the Treasury Department and the Fed to be financial in nature. Unlike the subsidiaries of FHC's, financial subsidiaries may not engage in insurance underwriting, annuity issuance, or merchant banking. GLBA invited Congress to review the merchant banking prohibition five years after GLBA's enactment, but Congress took no action to remove the prohibition.

To establish a financial subsidiary, a bank and each depository institution affiliate must be well-capitalized and well-managed. 12 U.S.C.A. § 24a(a)(2)(D). The equity investment of the bank in the financial subsidiary is not counted for purposes of computing the bank's capital requirements. The theory is that insured deposits of the bank (gathered at below-market interest rates because of FDIC insurance coverage) should not be used to fund financial subsidiary activities. There are additional limits on the size of the financial subsidiary in relation to the parent bank,

12 U.S.C.A. § 24a(a)(2)(D), and requirements that the 100 largest banks meet certain credit standards before being allowed to establish a financial subsidiary, 12 U.S.C.A. § 24a(a)(3).

QUESTIONS AND NOTES

1. What is likely to happen to activities conducted in national bank operating subsidiaries that prior to Dodd–Frank were not subject to state law restrictions?

2. For additional information, see Office of the Comptroller of the Currency, Related Organizations: Comptroller's Handbook (2004), available at <www.occ.treas.gov/handbook/RelatedOrg.pdf>.

D. CORPORATE GOVERNANCE

The Sarbanes–Oxley Act applies to all publicly traded corporations, including banks, savings associations and bank holding companies which have registered their securities with the OCC, FDIC, FRB, or OTS pursuant to the Securities Exchange Act of 1934, 15 U.S.C. § 78(i). Enacted in 2002 in the wake of the corporate scandals involving Enron, WorldCom, and others, the Sarbanes–Oxley Act substantially strengthened corporate governance procedures. It was followed by additional SEC rulemaking as well as revised listing standards relating to corporate governance by the New York Stock Exchange (NYSE) and the National Association of Securities Dealers (NASD) (now named the Financial Industry Regulatory Authority–FINRA).

A nonpublic bank with assets in excess of $500 million must comply with banking laws and regulations added in the wake of the savings and loan crisis that are similar to those found in Sarbanes–Oxley. See 12 U.S.C. § 1831m; 12 C.F.R. pt. 363. For nonpublic banks with assets less than $500 million, the situation is slightly more complicated.[16] These small, nonpublic banks are exempt from the special banking law provisions cited above and are not covered by the Sarbanes–Oxley Act. The FDIC, however, believes that these small, nonpublic banks for whom it is the primary federal regulator (state nonmember banks) should adhere to practices similar or identical to those identified in the Sarbanes–Oxley Act. Financial Institution Letter 17–2003 (Mar. 5, 2003), available at <www.fdic.gov/news/news/financial/2003/fil0317.html>. The other three banking regulators (Fed, OCC, and OTS) have issued a joint guidance in which they advise the small nonpublic banks for which they are the primary federal banking regulator to merely periodically review their corporate governance and auditing practices. Federal Reserve Board, SR Letter 03–8 (May 5, 2003), available at <www.federalreserve.gov/board docs/SRLETTERS/2003/sr0308.htm>.

---

16. See generally Jonathan A. Treadway, Note, Problems with Potential Application of Selected Provisions of the Sarbanes–Oxley Act of 2002 to Small, Non–Public Banking, 8 N.C. Banking Inst. 165 (2004).

Approximately 7% of all publicly traded banks and thrifts became private institutions between the beginning of 2003 and through the first few months of 2006, compared with 2% of all public companies. Those making the shift have often cited the additional compliance costs associated with Sarbanes–Oxley.[17]

Title IX of Dodd–Frank contains some additional corporate governance provisions that are applicable to all publicly held companies, including publicly held banks or bank holding companies. This marks an additional federal expansion into corporate governance, which was previously the exclusive province of state corporate law. The Securities and Exchange Commission (SEC) is required to adopt rules requiring public companies to disclose in their annual proxy statements why they have either different persons or the same person serving in the roles of the chief executive officer and chairman of the board. The SEC may (but is not required to) issue rules that would require public companies to include shareholder nominees for board seats in the company's proxy (a "proxy access" rule). In addition, Dodd–Frank touches upon executive compensation, requiring that public companies hold a nonbinding vote to approve the compensation of key executives ("say on pay"), including golden parachutes, and to be subject to "clawbacks" of incentive compensation paid based on financial statements that are later restated because of error. The attention to executive compensation continues scrutiny of compensation that began as part of the government's investment in the preferred stock of banking organizations through the Troubled Asset Relief Program (TARP) in the midst of the financial crisis in 2008–09. TARP investments will be discussed in Chapter 7.

SECTION 2. HOLDING COMPANY REGULATION

A. BANK HOLDING COMPANIES

A bank holding company (BHC) is defined in the Bank Holding Company Act of 1956 (BHCA) as "any company which has control over any bank." 12 U.S.C.A. § 1841(a)(1). "Control," "company," and "bank" are all defined terms in the BHCA. There are numerous exceptions from the definition of bank that exclude many institutions that have a national or state bank charter. 12 U.S.C.A. § 1841(c)(2). The Fed has regulatory authority over bank holding companies and their nonbanking subsidiaries.

Over 90% of the banking assets in the United States are owned by bank holding companies or financial holding companies. Most new banks

---

17. The SEC and the Public Company Accounting Board are considering ways to ease the burden of Section 404 (compliance with internal controls) for smaller public companies. See Ben Jackson, SEC Offers Small Banks Internal Controls Leeway, Am. Banker, Dec. 14, 2006. See al-Rob Garver, SEC 404 Decision Leads to Tough Choice, Am. Banker, May 24, 2006; F Implications of the Sarbanes–Oxley Act for Public Companies and the U.S. Banking ᵀ FDIC Outlook 11 (Fall 2005).

and many community-oriented banking institutions are not owned by holding companies. The decision to form a holding company is a complex one. The costs associated with formation, the additional regulatory oversight that is provided to the holding company by the SEC (since the holding company is a general business corporation usually with publicly traded stock) and by the Fed (which oversees bank holding companies), and the additional restrictions discussed later in this chapter relating to relationships among affiliates in the holding company structure can be substantial deterrents to bank holding company formation. On the other hand, the holding company structure helps to facilitate acquisitions of other banks, permits multi-bank structures, and allows for expansion into certain nonbanking activities (discussed more fully below). Moreover, the holding company may be able to access the commercial paper market, raise capital through the issuance of trust-preferred securities, and facilitate stock redemptions. Other advantages may be present depending on the particular state laws governing a state chartered bank.

The BHCA limits a bank holding company to the ownership of one or more banks and the "shares of any company the activities of which had been determined by the [Federal Reserve] Board by regulation or order . . . as of the day before November 12, 1999, to be so closely related to banking as to be a proper incident thereto." 12 U.S.C.A. § 1843(c)(8). The regulation listing the activities found by the Fed to be closely related to banking is Regulation Y, 12 C.F.R. Part 225. 12 C.F.R. § 225.22 lists certain exempt nonbanking activities, and 12 C.F.R. § 225.28 contains a listing of permissible nonbanking activities. (Both of these sections are reprinted in the statutory and regulatory supplement that accompanies this casebook.) Prior to the enactment of the Gramm–Leach–Bliley Act of 1999 (GLBA), BHCs could apply to the Fed for approval to perform additional activities (not already listed in Reg. Y) that the Fed determined to be "closely related to banking." GLBA discontinued this practice and froze the scope of permissible activities for a bank holding company to those permitted on November 11, 1999.

BOARD OF GOVERNORS OF THE FEDERAL RESERVE SYSTEM v. DIMENSION FINANCIAL CORP.

Supreme Court of the United States, 1986.
474 U.S. 361.

MR. CHIEF JUSTICE BURGER delivered the opinion of the Court.

* * * Section 2(c) of the Bank Holding Company Act defines "bank" as any institution "which (1) accepts deposits that the depositor has a legal right to withdraw on demand, and (2) engages in the business of making commercial loans." 70 Stat. 133, as amended, 12 U.S.C. § 1841(c).

This case is about so-called "nonbank banks"—institutions that offer services similar to those of banks but which until recently were not under Board regulation because they conducted their business so as to place themselves arguably outside the narrow definition of "bank" found in

§ 2(c) of the Act. Many nonbank banks, for example, offer customers NOW (negotiable order of withdrawal) accounts which function like conventional checking accounts but because of prior notice provisions do not technically give the depositor a "legal right to withdraw on demand." 12 U.S.C. § 1841(c)(1). Others offer conventional checking accounts, but avoid classification as "banks" by limiting their extension of commercial credit to the purchase of money market instruments such as certificates of deposit and commercial paper.

In 1984, the Board promulgated rules providing that nonbank banks offering the functional equivalent of traditional banking services would thereafter be regulated as banks. 49 Fed. Reg. 794. The Board accomplished this by amending its definition of a bank, found in "Regulation Y," in two significant respects. First, the Board defined "demand deposit" to include deposits, like NOW accounts, which are "as a matter of practice" payable on demand. 12 CFR § 225.2(a)(1)(A) (1985). Second, the Board defined the "making of a commercial loan" as "any loan other than a loan to an individual for personal, family, household, or charitable purposes," including "the purchase of retail installment loans or commercial paper, certificates of deposit, bankers' acceptances, and similar money market instruments." 12 CFR § 225.2(a)(1)(B) (1985). * * *

The Bank Holding Company Act of 1956, 12 U.S.C. § 1841 et seq., vests broad regulatory authority in the Board over bank holding companies "to restrain the undue concentration of commercial banking resources and to prevent possible abuses related to the control of commercial credit." S. Rep. No. 91–1084, p. 24 (1970). The Act authorizes the Board to regulate "any company which has control over any bank." 12 U.S.C. § 1841(a)(1).

The breadth of that regulatory power rests on the Act's definition of the word "bank." The 1956 Act gave a simple and broad definition of bank: "any national banking association or any State bank, savings bank, or trust company." 12 U.S.C. § 1841(c) (1964 ed.). Experience soon proved that literal application of the statute had the unintended consequence of including within regulation industrial banks offering limited checking account services to their customers. These institutions accepted " 'funds from the public that are, in actual practice, repaid on demand.' " Although including these institutions within the bank definition was the "correct legal interpretation" of the 1956 statute, the Board saw "no reason in policy to cover such institutions under this act." Congress agreed, and accordingly amended the statutory definition of a bank in 1966, limiting its application to institutions that accept "deposits that the depositor has a legal right to withdraw on demand."

The 1966 definition proved unsatisfactory because it too included within the definition of "bank" institutions that did not pose significant dangers to the banking system. Because one of the primary purposes of the Act was to "restrain undue concentration of . . . commercial credit," it made little sense to regulate institutions that did not, in fact, engage in the business of making commercial loans. S. Rep. No. 91–1084, p. 24 (1970). Congress accordingly amended the definition, excluding all institutions that did not "engag[e] in the business of making commercial loans." Since 1970 the statute has provided that a bank is any institution that

> "(1) accepts deposits that the depositor has a legal right to withdraw on demand, and (2) engages in the business of making commercial loans." 12 U. S. C. § 1841(c). * * *

In 1984, the Board initiated rulemaking to respond to the increase in the number of nonbank banks. After hearing views of interested parties, the Board found that nonbank banks pose three dangers to the national banking system. First, by remaining outside the reach of banking regulations, nonbank banks have a significant competitive advantage over regulated banks despite the functional equivalence of the services offered. Second, the proliferation of nonbank banks threatens the structure established by Congress for limiting the association of banking and commercial enterprises. See 12 U.S.C. § 1843(c)(8) (bank holding company can purchase nonbanking affiliate only if entity "closely related to banking"). Third, the interstate acquisition of nonbank banks undermines the statutory proscription on interstate banking without prior state approval. 49 Fed. Reg. 794, 835–836 (1984). Since the narrowed statutory definition required that both the demand deposit and the commercial loan elements be present to constitute the institution as a bank, the Board proceeded to amend Regulation Y redefining both elements of the test. * * *

The Board amended its definition of "demand deposit" primarily to include within its regulatory authority institutions offering NOW accounts. A NOW account functions like a traditional checking account—the depositor can write checks that are payable on demand at the depository institution. The depository institution, however, retains a seldom exercised but nevertheless absolute right to require prior notice of withdrawal. Under a literal reading of the statute, the institution—even if it engages in full-scale commercial lending—is not a "bank" for the purposes of the Holding Company Act because the prior notice provision withholds from the depositor any "legal right" to withdraw on demand. The Board in its amended definition closes this loophole by defining demand deposits as a deposit, not that the depositor has a "legal right to withdraw on demand," but a deposit that "as a matter of practice is payable on demand."

In determining whether the Board was empowered to make such a change, we begin, of course, with the language of the statute. If the statute is clear and unambiguous "that is the end of the matter, for the court, as well as the agency, must give effect to the unambiguously expressed intent of Congress." Chevron U.S.A., Inc. v. Natural Resources Defense Council, Inc., 467 U.S. 837, 842–843 (1984). The traditional deference courts pay to agency interpretation is not to be applied to alter the clearly expressed intent of Congress.

Application of this standard to the Board's interpretation of the "demand deposit" element of § 2(c) does not require extended analysis.

By the 1966 amendments to § 2(c), Congress expressly limited the Act to regulation of institutions that accept deposits that "the depositor has a legal right to withdraw on demand." 12 U. S. C. § 1841(c). The Board would now define "legal right" as meaning the same as "a matter of practice." But no amount of agency expertise—however sound may be the result—can make the words "legal right" mean a right to do something "as a matter of practice." A *legal* right to withdraw on demand means just that: a right to withdraw deposits without prior notice or limitation. Institutions offering NOW accounts do not give the depositor a legal right to withdraw on demand; rather, the institution itself retains the ultimate legal right to require advance notice of withdrawal. The Board's definition of "demand deposit," therefore, is not an accurate or reasonable interpretation of § 2(c).

Section 2(c) of the Act provides that, even if an institution accepts deposits that the depositor has a legal right to withdraw on demand, the institution is not a bank unless it "engages in the business of making commercial loans." Under Regulation Y, "commercial loan" means "any loan other than a loan to an individual for personal, family, household, or charitable purposes," including "the purchase of retail installment loans or commercial paper, certificates of deposit, bankers' acceptances, and similar money market instruments."

The purpose of the amended regulation is to regulate as banks institutions offering "commercial loan substitutes," that is, extensions of credit to commercial enterprises through transactions other than the conventional commercial loan. * * *

As the Board's characterization of these transactions as "commercial loan substitutes" suggests, however, money market transactions do not fall within the commonly accepted definition of "commercial loans." The term "commercial loan" is used in the financial community to describe the direct loan from a bank to a business customer for the purpose of providing funds needed by the customer in its business. The term does not apply to, indeed is used to distinguish, extensions of credit in the open market that do not involve close borrower-lender relationships. * * *

Nothing in the statutory language or the legislative history, therefore, indicates that the term "commercial loan" meant anything different from its accepted ordinary commercial usage. The Board's definition of "commercial loan," therefore, is not a reasonable interpretation of § 2(c).

Unable to support its new definitions on the plain language of § 2(c), the Board contends that its new definitions fall within the "plain purpose" of the Bank Holding Company Act. Nonbank banks must be subject to regulation, the Board insists, because "a statute must be read with a view to the 'policy of the legislation as a whole' and cannot be read to negate the plain purpose of the legislation." The plain purpose of the legislation, the Board contends, is to regulate institutions "functionally equivalent" to banks. * * *

The "plain purpose" of legislation, however, is determined in the first instance with reference to the plain language of the statute itself. Application of "broad purposes" of legislation at the expense of specific provisions ignores the complexity of the problems Congress is called upon to address and the dynamics of legislative action. * * *

Rather than defining "bank" as an institution that offers the functional equivalent of banking services, however, Congress defined with specificity certain transactions that constitute banking subject to regulation. The statute may be imperfect, but the Board has no power to correct flaws that it perceives in the statute it is empowered to administer. Its rulemaking power is limited to adopting regulations to carry into effect the will of Congress as expressed in the statute.

If the Bank Holding Company Act falls short of providing safeguards desirable or necessary to protect the public interest, that is a problem for Congress, and not the Board or the courts, to address. * * * Our present inquiry, however, must come to rest with the conclusion that the action of the board in this case is inconsistent with the language of the statute. * * *

Congress responded to this opinion in the Competitive Equality Banking Act of 1987 (CEBA). In CEBA, the term "bank" was defined for purposes of the BHCA to include an FDIC-insured bank, which eliminated the idea of a nonbank bank, but grandfathered in existing institutions (sometimes referred to as CEBA banks as well as nonbank banks). CEBA provided an alternative definition of bank as an institution that is "engaged in the business of making commercial loans" and "accepts demand deposits or deposits that the depositor may withdraw by check or similar means for payment to third parties or others." 12 U.S.C.A. § 1841(c)(1).

[handwritten margin note: legal right changed to include Now accounts]

In September 2008, the Fed issued a policy statement spelling out with more particularity how it would interpret "controlling influence," one of the tests to determine whether a company has "control" over a bank thereby becoming a bank holding company and subject to the BHCA's limitations on activities other than those that are closely related to banking. Federal Reserve Board of Governors, Policy Statement on Equity Investments in Banks and Bank Holding Companies, http://www.federalreserve.gov/newsevents/press/bcreg/bcreg20080922b1.pdf. This statement was issued during the midst of the financial crisis when the banking industry was in desperate need of capital. The statement was intended to provide greater guidance to private equity investors, engaged in multiple nonbanking activities, about how much they could invest in banks without being considered to be in "control" of the bank and subject to the BHCA.

NATIONAL COURIER ASS'N v. BOARD OF GOVERNORS OF THE FEDERAL RESERVE SYSTEM

United States Court of Appeals, District of Columbia Circuit, 1975.
516 F.2d 1229.

McGOWAN, CIRCUIT JUDGE.

The Bank Holding Company Act of 1956, which generally prohibits bank holding companies from owning shares in companies other than banks, allows such ownership where the activities of the non-bank affiliate have been found by the Federal Reserve Board to be "so closely related to banking or managing or controlling banks as to be a proper incident thereto." 12 U.S.C. § 1843(c)(8) (1970). In the regulation herein challenged on direct review, the Board has enlarged the activities heretofore found by it to be "closely related."[18] The addition consists of certain courier or high speed transportation services[19] for

(i) the internal operations of the holding company and its subsidiaries;

(ii) checks, commercial papers, documents, and written instruments (excluding currency or bearer-type negotiable instruments) as are exchanged among banks and banking institutions;

(iii) audit and accounting media of a banking or financial nature and other business records and documents used in processing such media.

12 C.F.R. § 225.4(a)(11) (1974).

A fourth category of service that may be provided by bank-affiliated couriers is contained in the following "interpretation," also added to Regulation Y by the contested order:

(T)he furnishing of courier services for non-financially-related material upon the specific, unsolicited request of a third party when courier services are not otherwise reasonably available may be regarded as an incidental activity of a bank-related courier.

Id. § 225.129.

For the reasons stated below, the regulation under attack is upheld in part, and in part held invalid. * * *

Courier services were described in the statement accompanying the Board's order as the "transportation of any item with a critical time schedule, provided such items are small in bulk, light in weight, and

---

18. [n.1] The order in issue amends "Regulation Y," in which there are already listed a number of "closely related" activities. See 12 C.F.R. § 225.4 (1974). These include, for example, certain kinds of property leasing, insurance brokerage and underwriting, and financially related data processing. Id. §§ 225.4(2)(6), (8)-(10).

19. [eds.] Express or courier companies have long been closely allied with banks because of their transportation of money, checks and bills. Wells Fargo is an example of a bank that evolved from an express company. Jerry W. Markham, A Financial History of the United States: From Christopher Columbus to the Robber Barons (1492–1900) 197–98 (2001).

require only ordinary security measures." The items which are carried by
courier service in far the greatest volume are financial documents and
records—particularly banking instruments—which require speedy transportation from one place of business to another. It thus appears that the
nation's banks are by far the largest consumers of courier services,
accounting for more than half of that industry's sales. The industry itself
is about thirty years old, and has thus far remained largely independent of
the banks, though it is dominated by a very few firms.

Of the three categories of courier services that the Board has found to
be "closely related" to banking, the first, that of courier services "for the
internal operations of the holding company and its subsidiaries," is not in
issue. The provision of services by one bank affiliate is expressly allowed
by Section 4(c)(1)(C) of the statute. 12 U.S.C. § 1843(c)(1)(C) (1970).

The second category is that of courier services "for checks, commercial papers, documents, and written instruments (excluding currency or
bearer-type instruments) as are exchanged among banks and banking
institutions." What is meant are the so-called "cash letters" in which one
bank transmits all the checks, drafts, and money orders that must be
cleared or otherwise processed at another bank. * * *

The third category of "closely related" courier services are those "for
audit and accounting media of a banking or financial nature and other
business records and documents used in processing such media." The
term "media" appears simply to refer to the physical form (paper documents, magnetic tapes, etc.) in which the financial data to be processed
are conveyed. * * *

The fourth category of authorized courier services, that contained in
the Board's separate "interpretation," is largely self-explanatory. Bank-
affiliated couriers may carry non-financially related material if requests
for such service are unsolicited and it is not otherwise reasonably available. Any doubt as to the lack of limitation on the kind of material that
may be carried under this heading was erased by the press release
accompanying the Board's order, which gave as examples "human blood,
exposed and processed film, repair parts and cut flowers."

* * * As to what kinds of connections may qualify [as closely related],
at least the following seem to us within the statutory intent:

    1. Banks generally have in fact provided the proposed services.

    2. Banks generally provide services that are operationally or
functionally so similar to the proposed services as to equip them
particularly well to provide the proposed service.

    3. Banks generally provide services that are so integrally related
to the proposed services as to require their provision in a specialized
form.

We turn, then, to the question of whether the Board has rationally
found such connections in this case.

* * * [With regard to financially related data processing materials]: There is no question that courier service for data processing material has been found "closely related to banking" not because of its connection to banking *per se* but because of its relation to financial data processing, an activity banks are permitted to engage in. We are not so much bothered by the illogic reasoning (which could be overcome by simply asserting that the data processing industry as a whole is "closely related to banking") as we are by the danger, pressed on us by petitioners, that if the Board is permitted to string together a chain of close relations, the limitation means nothing.

Certainly the Board will not be permitted to tack one close relation on to another indefinitely, but we cannot forbid it in this case. The relations are of distinctly different kinds. That of financial data processing to banking may be thought of as horizontal, in the sense that these are parallel and kindred financial services. That of banking to the transportation of cash letters, and of financial data processing to the transportation of audit and accounting media, may be thought of as vertical, in the sense that transportation is a non-financial service necessary to the provision of financial services. Rather than threaten infinite repetition, the Board's reasoning seems rather to complete the missing fourth side of a square. More persuasive than its symmetry, however, are the practical realities it reflects. The record suggests that in many cases check processing and financially related data processing are carried on at the same locations and by the use of the same equipment. It would seem anomalous to require that similar material, quite possibly generated by a single customer and destined for a single bank computer, be transported by two separate couriers. * * *

The petition for review is denied in all respects with the exception that the so-called "interpretation" added to Rule Y [relating to nonfinancial courier services] is set aside. * * *

B. FINANCIAL HOLDING COMPANIES

A financial holding company (FHC) is a new type of bank holding company created by the Gramm–Leach–Bliley Act of 1999 (GLBA) that meets certain additional requirements. 12 U.S.C. §§ 1841(p), 1843(l)(1). All of a financial holding company's depository subsidiaries must be well capitalized, well managed, and have Community Reinvestment Act (CRA)[20] ratings of satisfactory or above. Id. § 1843(l). The Dodd–Frank Act extends these requirements to the FHC itself. Dodd–Frank Act, § 606. A BHC must file an application to be certified as an FHC. As of June 2010 the Fed reported that 524 companies, including foreign institutions, had been certified as FHC's. The current list is available at <www.federal reserve.gov/generalinfo/fhc>.

---

20. The CRA mandates that a bank meet the credit needs of its entire community, including low-and moderate-income neighborhoods. 12 U.S.C.A. § 2903. The CRA is discussed further in Chapter 6.

An FHC may offer a broader range of services than a traditional BHC. An FHC may engage in, or own a company that engages in, any activity that is "financial in nature or incidental to such financial activity; or complementary to a financial activity and does not pose a substantial risk to the safety or soundness of depository institutions or the financial system generally." Id. at § 1843(k)(1).[21]

A specific list of financial activities is set forth in § 1843(k)(4) and includes all activities permitted for a BHC, activities permitted for a BHC in foreign countries, securities, insurance (underwriting and agency), issuing annuities, mutual fund activities, insurance company portfolio investments, and merchant banking.[22] By regulation, the Fed has identified the activities permitted for a BHC by regulation and by order as closely related to banking, and those activities permitted for a BHC in foreign countries. 12 C.F.R. § 225.86(a) & (b). The foreign activities list includes providing nonfinancial management consulting services, operating a travel agency in connection with financial services, and organizing, sponsoring and managing a mutual fund. Additional activities may be considered "financial in nature" upon the joint determination of the Treasury Department and the Fed.

A final source of authority for FHC activities is 12 U.S.C. § 1843(k)(5). The regulation implementing that rule is at 12 C.F.R. § 225.86(e). The Dodd–Frank Act requires that a FHC obtain Fed approval prior to the purchase of a company engaged in financial activities if the acquired company's assets exceed $10 billion. Dodd–Frank Act, § 604. Recall that financial subsidiaries of banks are empowered to engage in this same set of activities, other than underwriting insurance, issuing annuities, real estate development and real estate investment activities, and merchant banking. 12 U.S.C. §§ 24a & 1831w.

According to the Fed, as of 2003 more than 160 FHC's were engaged in insurance agency activities, 50 in securities underwriting and dealing, 26 in insurance underwriting, and 26 in merchant banking.[23]

Prior to the passage of GLBA, Citigroup was formed by the combination of Citicorp (the BHC that owned Citibank) and Travelers Group, an insurance company. At this time, however, a BHC was not permitted to own an insurance underwriter such as Travelers. Nevertheless, the BHCA permits a company that becomes a bank holding company pursuant to an acquisition of a bank to retain a business that was not closely related to banking for two years following the acquisition in order to divest itself of the impermissible business in an orderly manner. 12 U.S.C.A. § 1843(a)(2). It is also possible to apply to the Fed for up to three one-year extensions of this authority. This historic merger was consummated in 1998 prior to the passage of GLBA in 1999. GLBA, of course, permitted

---

21. One difference between the subsidiaries of an FHC and a financial subsidiary of a bank is that the latter may not conduct activities "complementary" to a financial activity.

22. See 12 C.F.R. §§ 225.170 et seq. (merchant banking).

23. Board of Governors of the Federal Reserve System, Report to the Congress on Financial Holding Companies under the Gramm–Leach–Bliley Act 3 (Nov. 2003).

this combination of insurance underwriting and banking in a BHC that qualified as a FHC. Citigroup made a risky bet that Congress would act before the BHCA would have required it to divest either its bank subsidiary or insurance underwriting subsidiary.

Following GLBA, most BHCs submitted applications to be designated FHCs. Even though FHCs could engage in financial in nature activities, relatively few expanded their operations further. Following its creation in 1998, Citigroup grew and prospered. The merger between Citibank and Travelers was motivated in part by the possibility of cross-selling insurance products to bank customers, and bank products to insurance customers. It was probably the cross-selling between Citibank corporate lenders and the investment bankers at Travelers' Salomon Smith Barney that contributed the most benefit to Citigroup's bottom line, however. Ultimately, Citigroup spun off much of its insurance business since the return on insurance assets was not as high as the return on banking and investment banking assets. During the financial crisis, Citigroup floundered and was rescued by an initial $25 billion infusion of TARP money, followed shortly thereafter by an additional $20 billion investment under a special TARP program for systemically significant institutions. A few months later in January 2009, Bank of America became the second and only other bank holding company to receive this extraordinary additional government investment.

If the FHC fails to maintain a well capitalized or well managed rating, then corrective action by the Fed will be imposed on the institution. 12 C.F.R. § 225.83. If the FHC is unable to correct its deficiencies, the Fed may order the FHC to divest itself of any subsidiary institutions that are out of compliance. If the FHC fails to meet the CRA-rating requirement, then the FHC is prohibited from commencing any activities that are "financial in nature." 12 C.F.R. § 225.84.

In 2000, PNC Financial Services was designated a financial holding company. In 2002, however, it restated its earnings at the request of the Fed to recognize losses on bad loans that had previously not been reported as losses because the loans had been transferred to three off-balance sheet special purpose vehicles. The Fed and the OCC announced that the holding company and bank were no longer in compliance with the financial holding company standards set forth in GLBA. The downfall for PNC was apparently the agencies' characterization that PNC was no longer "well managed," at least from an accounting and risk management basis.[24] As a consequence of this characterization, PNC had 180 days to return to compliance and in the interim was unable to engage in new activities or make new investments without the Fed's prior approval. Further, any new activities so approved would be subject to specific limitation as ordered by the Fed. If PNC had failed to come into compliance in a timely manner, then regulators could have required PNC to

---

24. See Joyita R. Basu, Note, Accounting for and Disclosure of Special Purpose Entities by Financial Holding Companies: Lessons from PNC Financial Services, 7 N.C. Banking Inst. 177 (2003).

divest itself of subsidiaries engaged in activities permitted only to financial holding companies or to discontinue those particular lines of business.

Fifth Third Bancorp was also the subject of regulatory scrutiny that potentially threatened its status as a financial holding company and the ability of its bank to maintain financial subsidiaries. Among other things, Fifth Third agreed to improved risk management, accounting controls and technology. Both Fifth Third and PNC are now considered in full compliance with GLBA.

The Fed has had few opportunities since the passage of GLBA to consider what additional activities might be "financial in nature." The Fed has determined, however, that acting as a "finder" is "incidental to a financial activity," and is thus a permitted activity for a FHC.

BOARD OF GOVERNORS OF THE FEDERAL RESERVE SYSTEM BANK HOLDING COMPANIES AND CHANGE IN BANK CONTROL

65 Fed. Reg. 80735 (Dec. 22, 2000) (codified at 12 C.F.R. § 225.86(d)).

The Gramm–Leach–Bliley Act (Pub. L. 106–102, 113 Stat. 1338 (1999)) ("GLB Act") amended the Bank Holding Company Act (12 U.S.C. § 1841 et seq.) ("BHC Act") to allow a bank holding company or foreign bank that qualifies as a financial holding company to engage in a broad range of activities that the GLB Act defined as financial in nature or incidental to a financial activity. The GLB Act also provides that the Board, in consultation with the Secretary of the Treasury ("Secretary"), may determine that additional activities are financial in nature or incidental to a financial activity and, thus, permissible for a financial holding company.[25] * * *

National banks and many state banks are permitted to act and have acted as a finder in nonfinancial transactions for many years. Opportunities to provide finder services and interest in acting as a finder have grown dramatically with advances in technology and the increased use of the Internet. Thus, banking organizations, which in the past largely have served as a finder by providing statement stuffers and other marketing materials of sellers of various products and services or by helping to identify service providers as an accommodation to customers, have begun to explore the opportunity to act as a finder electronically on a broader scale. Financial holding companies have argued that acting as a finder,

---

25. [n.1] See 12 U.S.C. 1843 (k)(2). In determining whether to authorize an additional activity, the GLB Act directs the Board to consider: (1) the purposes of the GLB and BHC Acts; (2) the changes or reasonably expected changes in the marketplace in which financial holding companies compete; (3) the changes or reasonably expected changes in technology for delivering financial services; and (4) whether the proposed activity is necessary or appropriate to allow a financial holding company to compete effectively with companies seeking to provide financial services in the United States, efficiently deliver financial information and services through technological means, and offer customers any available or emerging technological means for using financial services or for the document imaging of data. The Board also may consider other information that it considers relevant to its determination.

particularly electronically, offers increased opportunities for financial holding companies to cross sell financial products and services or to enhance the attractiveness to customers of the financial holding company's own electronic web site. Commenters asserted that authorizing FHC's to act as a finder as proposed would facilitate competition between FHC's and nonbanking companies to provide customers with a wide range of financial services. One commenter stated that the new authority particularly would benefit FHC's affiliated with community banks, which often are knowledgeable about the business interests of third parties with whom they deal. In this way, finder services have become incidental to financial activities.

After carefully reviewing the public comments on the finder proposal, the Board has adopted a final rule that provides that acting as a finder, as defined in the rule, is an activity that is incidental to a financial activity and therefore permissible for financial holding companies to conduct. Under the GLB Act, the Board may not determine that an activity is financial in nature or incidental to a financial activity if the Secretary notifies the Board in writing that the Secretary believes the activity is not financial in nature, incidental to a financial activity, or otherwise permissible under section 4 of the BHC Act. The Secretary must notify the Board of the Secretary's determination within 30 days of receiving notice from the Board, or within such longer period as the Board may allow under the circumstances. The Board has provided the Secretary with notice of the proposed activity as required by the GLB Act and the Secretary has informed the Board in writing that the Secretary does not object to the final rule as adopted. * * *

[See 12 C.F.R. § 225.86(d) in the Statutory and Regulatory Supplement that accompanies this casebook.].

A joint proposal by the Fed and the Treasury Department to permit FHC's and financial subsidiaries to engage in real estate brokerage and management services met with widespread opposition.[26] A record number of comment letters were received opposing the proposal. This regulatory proposal was not considered further because of annual appropriations legislation that barred Treasury from using its budget to finalize the proposed rule.

The Fed permitted Citigroup to retain all of its voting shares of Phibro, Inc., a company that engages in commodity-related activities, including trading in physical commodities, such as oil, natural gas, agricultural products, and other nonfinancial commodities, concluding that these activities are complementary to a financial activity (buying and selling, as principal, permissible commodity derivative contracts) within GLBA. Federal Reserve System, Citigroup Inc., Order Approving Notice to Engage in

----

26. 66 Fed. Reg. 307 (Jan. 3, 2001) (to be codified at 12 C.F.R. pts. 225 & 1501).

Activities Complementary to a Financial Activity, available at <www. federalreserve.gov/boarddocs/press/orders/2003/20031002/attachment. pdf>. Citigroup had owned Phibro pursuant to the temporary grandfather authority of 12 U.S.C. § 1843(a)(2). Citigroup sold Phibro to Occidental Petroleum in late 2009, after receiving criticism that its main trader, Andrew Hall, earned $100 million in compensation in 2009.

GLBA permits nonbanking firms to purchase banks, but the limitation of the firms' other activities to those that are financial in nature, the oversight by the Fed, and the Fed's seeming unwillingness to move aggressively in approving new activities as financial in nature may explain the initial reluctance of nonbanking entities to acquire banks and become financial holding companies. Charles Schwab & Co., MetLife, and Franklin Resources were the most notable nonbanking companies to acquire banks pursuant to GLBA's authority prior to the financial crisis.[27]

Investment banks suffered during the financial crisis. Bear Stearns was sold to JPMorgan Chase in March 2008 with Fed assistance, and Bank of America announced its purchase of the ailing Merrill Lynch on September 15, 2008, one day after Lehman Brothers filed for bankruptcy protection after the Fed refused to bail it out. The two remaining independent investment banking companies—Goldman Sachs and Morgan Stanley—elected to become bank holding companies since during this turbulent time oversight by the Fed under the BHCA reassured investors. Although the Fed ruled on these applications on September 21, 2008, prior to the passage of EESA in early October, it was no doubt important to Goldman and Morgan Stanley to be in a position to benefit from government support expected to be provided in that bill to the banking industry. Each institution received a $10 billion investment in preferred stock from government-provided TARP funds on October 28, 2008, and each repurchased the stock from the government less than a year later on June 17, 2009. Other firms—GMAC, CIT Group, American Express, and Discover Financial Services—also became bank holding companies.

FEDERAL RESERVE SYSTEM
THE GOLDMAN SACHS GROUP, INC.
GOLDMAN SACHS BANK USA HOLDINGS LLC
ORDER APPROVING FORMATION OF BANK
HOLDING COMPANIES

Sept. 21, 2008.

The Goldman Sachs Group, Inc. ("Goldman") and Goldman Sachs Bank USA Holdings LLC ("Goldman Holdings") each has requested the Board's approval under section 3 of the Bank Holding Company Act ("BHC Act") (12 U.S.C. § 1842) to become a bank holding company on conversion of Goldman Sachs Bank USA, Salt Lake City, Utah ("Goldman Bank"), to a state-chartered bank.[28] Goldman Bank currently operates as

---

27. Board of Governors of the Federal Reserve System, Report to the Congress on Financial Holding Companies under the Gramm–Leach–Bliley Act 3 (Nov. 2003).

28. [n.1] Goldman Holdings is a wholly owned subsidiary of Goldman through which Goldman owns all of the voting stock of Goldman Bank.

an industrial loan company that is exempt from the definition of "bank" under the BHC Act.[29]

Goldman, with total consolidated assets of approximately $1.1 trillion, engages in investment banking, securities underwriting and dealing, asset management, trading and other activities through a variety of subsidiaries both in the United States and overseas. Its principal subsidiaries include Goldman Sachs & Co., New York, New York, a broker-dealer registered with the Securities and Exchange Commission under the Securities Exchange Act of 1934.

Goldman Bank has total consolidated assets of approximately $25 billion and has deposits of approximately $23 billion. Goldman Bank engages primarily in extending credit, including corporate loans and loan commitments, and taking deposits of the type permissible under the exception in section 2(c)(2)(H) of the BHC Act for an industrial loan company. * * *

In light of the unusual and exigent circumstances affecting the financial markets, and all other facts and circumstances, the Board has determined that emergency conditions exist that justify expeditious action on this proposal. For the same reasons, and in light of the fact that this transaction represents the conversion of an existing subsidiary of the applicants from one form of depository institution to another, the Board has waived public notice of this proposal. * * *

The Board consistently has considered capital adequacy to be an especially important aspect in analyzing financial factors. Goldman is adequately capitalized, and all Goldman entities that are subject to regulatory capital requirements currently exceed the relevant requirements. In addition, Goldman Bank currently is well capitalized under applicable federal guidelines. Goldman Bank also would be well capitalized on a pro forma basis on consummation of the proposal. * * *

Goldman engaged in a wide range of nonbanking activities that have been determined to be financial in nature, incidental to a financial activity, or complementary to a financial activity pursuant to section 4(k) of the BHC Act.[30] These activities include, among other things, underwriting, dealing, and making a market in securities; providing financial, investment, or economic advisory services; acting as a placement agent in the private placement of securities; engaging in merchant banking activities; acting as a principal in foreign exchange and in derivative contracts based on financial and nonfinancial assets; and making, acquiring, or brokering loans or other extensions of credit.[31]

Goldman expects promptly to file an election to become a financial holding company pursuant to sections 4(k) and (l) of the BHC Act and section 225.82 of the Board's Regulation Y Section 4 of the BHC Act by its

---

29. [n. 2] See 12 U.S.C. § 1841(c)(2)(H).

30. [n. 11] See 12 U.S.C. § 1843(k).

31. [n.12] See 12 U.S.C. § 1843(k)(4)(C), (E), and (H); 12 C.F.R. 225.28(b)(1) and (b)(8)(ii) and 225.171 et seq.

terms provides any company that becomes a bank holding company two years to conform its nonbanking investments and activities to the requirements of section 4 of the BHC Act, with the possibility of three one-year extensions.[32] Goldman must conform to the BHC Act any impermissible nonfinancial activities it may conduct within the time requirements of the Act. * * *

Based on the foregoing, and in light of all the facts of record, the Board has determined that the applications under section 3 of the BHC Act should be, and hereby are, approved. * * *

C. ADDITIONAL REGULATION FOR SYSTEMICALLY SIGNIFICANT COMPANIES

The Dodd–Frank Act provides that "large, interconnected bank holding companies," should be subject to enhanced supervision and prudential standards. If a bank holding company's assets exceed $50 billion it will be considered to be in this category. As of the summer of 2010, that threshold encompasses almost forty institutions, including many of the new bank holding company converts such as Goldman Sachs, Morgan Stanley, and GMAC. In fact, the Dodd–Frank Act includes a provision that has been termed the "Hotel California" provision in section 117. If a bank holding company had consolidated assets above the $50 billion threshold on January 1, 2010, and if it had received financial assistance under TARP, then like a guest at the Hotel California, "you can check out anytime you like, but you can never leave."[33] In other words, if the institution sold its bank subsidiary or converted it to an entity not considered a bank under the BHCA, it would still be treated as a systemically significant nonbank financial company that would still be subject to Fed oversight and the heightened supervision and prudential standards. Dodd–Frank Act, § 117.

Most significantly, under Dodd–Frank the Fed gains oversight over systemically significant *nonbank* financial companies that formerly escaped Fed purview since they were not bank holding companies. These companies are now subject to Fed registration, reporting, examination, and enforcement. Dodd–Frank Act, § 115. The new Financial Stability Oversight Council (FSOC or Council) (described in Chapter 3) is charged with designating these nonbank financial companies. Dodd–Frank Act, § 113. The designation of such a company by the FSOC requires a supermajority vote that must include the affirmative vote of the Treasury Secretary. The criteria to be considered by the FSOC include "material financial distress" at the nonbank financial company, or a determination that the "nature, scope, size, scale, concentration, interconnectedness, or mix of the activities ... could posed a threat to the financial stability of the United States." Dodd–Frank Act, § 113. As a threshold matter,

32. [n. 13] 12 U.S.C. § 1843(a)(2).

33. These lyrics are from the 1977 Eagles song, Hotel California.

however, the company must be "predominantly engaged" in financial activities and will be found to meet this test if 85% or more of its consolidated revenues or assets are attributable to financial in nature activities as defined in the BHCA, 12 U.S.C.A. § 1843(k)(4). Other factors that the FSOC must consider in making the nonbank financial company designation are listed in § 113. Suffice it to say that a great deal of discretion is vested in the FSOC in making this determination. The obvious intent is to ensure that entities like Bear Stearns, Lehman Brothers, and AIG are subjected to heightened supervision so that the Fed could forestall a crisis.

Once designated by the FSOC as a nonbank financial company, the company has 180 days to register with the Fed. The Fed is required to implement "prudential standards" for these systemically significant bank holding companies and nonbank financial institutions. The FSOC may make recommendations about the heightened standards to the Fed and may recommend a higher asset threshold for certain prudential standards. In any event, the statute requires the Fed to establish heightened standards for these institutions regarding risk-based capital and leverage limits, liquidity, risk management, resolution plan, credit exposure reporting, and concentration limits. The Fed is given the discretion to impose additional heightened standards related to contingent capital, enhanced disclosures, and short-term debt limits.

Nonbank financial holding companies will not be subject to the general prohibition of the BHC prohibiting participation in nonfinancial activities. The Fed, may however require that the nonbank financial company form an intermediate holding company, that all financial activities of the company be placed under the intermediate holding company, and that the intermediate holding company be fully subject to the BHCA. Dodd–Frank Act, § 113.

QUESTIONS AND NOTES

1.   Compare the powers of a financial subsidiary of a bank and a subsidiary of an FHC. If a BHC qualified as an FHC and owned a bank that had or could establish a financial subsidiary, out of which entity or entities could the following activities be conducted: insurance underwriting, insurance agency, merchant banking, and securities underwriting?

2.   To the extent an activity could be conducted in more than one entity, what are the factors that might influence the choice between different permissible entities?

3.   Should a bank be able to conduct a financial activity in an operating subsidiary or must financial activities be conducted by banks in a financial subsidiary?

4.   How are new activities determined to be "financial in nature?" See 12 U.S.C.A. § 1843(k)(2) & (k)(3).

5.   What are the advantages to becoming a FHC over remaining a BHC?

6. What nonbank financial companies has the FSOC designated as systemically significant? Has the Fed completed regulations with heightened prudential standards for systemically significant bank holding companies and nonbank financial companies?

D. FUNCTIONAL REGULATION

As one source notes:

> The regulatory structure of the United States is said to be functional because regulators supervise by line of business such as banking, insurance, or securities trading. The structure is said to be competitive because there are usually multiple regulators responsible for a single function, for example, banking services. Regulatory responsibilities are widely dispersed among several regulators on the federal as well as the state level of government.

Walter W. Eubanks, Federal Financial Services Regulatory Consolidation: An Overview, Congressional Research Service, CRS–5 (Aug. 17, 2005).

GLBA endorses the concept of "functional" regulation, as opposed to "entity" regulation. Thus, if the function that is being performed involves the sale of securities, the SEC regulates that function even if it is being performed by an entity, such as a bank or an insurance company, that is not a securities firm. The obvious advantages to this approach are fairness and regulatory expertise. It is only fair that the same functions are regulated the same way, no matter what type of financial entity is performing the function. Functional regulation helps to reduce one form of regulatory arbitrage by artificially placing an activity in a particular entity to avoid a disfavored regulator. Moreover, regulation of the function will presumably be performed by the regulator with the greatest expertise in that function. A "functionally regulated subsidiary" under GLBA is a company that is not a bank or a bank holding company, but that is either a broker or dealer, investment advisor, investment company, insurance company, or an entity subject to regulation by the Commodity Futures Trading Commission (CFTC). 12 U.S.C.A. § 1844(c)(5).

Non-functionally related subsidiaries of a bank holding company or a thrift holding company under Dodd–Frank must be examined by the Fed in the same manner and with the same frequency as if the entity was an insured depository institution. Dodd–Frank Act, § 605.

Functional regulation of securities dealing is provided by the repeal of the bank exception from the definitions of "broker" and "dealer" in the Securities Exchange Act of 1934, 15 U.S.C.A. § 78c(a)(4)-(5). The SEC is also granted jurisdiction over any "new hybrid product," that the SEC determines to be a security but which the SEC has not previously treated as a security, which is not an "identified banking product" and is not an equity swap. 12 U.S.C.A. § 78o(i).

Insurance activities, including those being conducted by a national bank, are regulated by the state insurance regulator. 15 U.S.C.A. § 6711.

Discrimination by the state insurance regulator against FHC's or depository institutions is prohibited. 15 U.S.C.A. § 6701(c) & (d). In anticipation of the inevitable turf conflict between a federal bank regulator and the state insurance regulator, GLBA provides for an expedited review of such a conflict in a U.S. Court of Appeals, and provides that the standard for review shall be "without unequal deference." This review standard negates the usual "controlling weight" standard of review given to a federal agency's interpretation of an ambiguous statute under *Chevron*. 15 U.S.C.A. § 6714. Federal regulators are not totally excluded from the regulation of insurance, however, as GLBA mandates the adoption by the federal bank regulators of consumer protection regulations relating to the sale of insurance. 12 U.S.C.A. § 1831x(a).[34] See Chapter 13 for a discussion of the Federal Insurance Office created by the Dodd–Frank Act.

GLBA also recognizes that comprehensive regulation is still necessary. Even though an entity may be subject to regulation by many different functional regulators, and an FHC by even more functional regulators, it is important for one regulator to have the big picture. The Fed has retained this role as the "umbrella supervisor" over the entire FHC. 12 U.S.C.A. § 1844(c).[35] In this role, the Fed may request reports, conduct examinations, and intervene to take action to redress unsound practices under certain circumstances. 12 U.S.C.A. §§ 1844(c), 1831v(a), 1848a. During the financial crisis, many felt that the Fed's umbrella supervision was too severely limited. Accordingly, Dodd–Frank enhances the Fed's authority to examine functionally regulated subsidiaries. Dodd–Frank Act, § 604.

There are, however, potential problems with functional regulation. Innovative products do not always fit neatly into a single functional category.[36] Moreover, entity regulation has not disappeared as a result of GLBA. Thus, a bank is still chartered and examined by one or more bank regulators, and may have its securities and insurance activities subject to additional functional regulators. Add to this mix the role of the Fed with its expanded oversight granted under Dodd-Frank, as "umbrella supervisor," and the potential for regulatory conflict is great. A single entity may discover that being subject to multiple functional regulators is unduly burdensome, and this may result in a competitive disadvantage for FHC's vis-a-vis foreign firms who are supervised by a unified regulator. Fear of the Fed's intrusion may have led some financial firms to avoid purchasing a bank in favor of entering banking via acquisition or chartering of a bank-like institution that is excluded from the definition of a "bank" for

---

34. See Joint Rule on Consumer Protections for Depository Institutions Sales of Insurance, 65 Fed. Reg. 75,822 (Dec. 4, 2000) (codified at 12 C.F.R. pts. 14, 208, 343 & 536).

35. FRB Supervisory Letter, Framework for Financial Holding Company Supervision, SR 00–13 (Aug. 15, 2000).

36. See Lissa L. Broome & Jerry W. Markham, Banking and Insurance: Before and After the Gramm–Leach–Bliley Act, 25 J. Corp. L. 724, 777 (2000) (describing the changing characterization of variable annuity products as (1) securities, (2) mutual funds subject to the Investment Company Act, and (3) part of the business of banking; Heidi Mandanis Schooner, Regulating Risk Not Function, 66 U. Cin. L. Rev. 441 (1998).

purposes of the BHCA. After Dodd–Frank, however, the FSOC may designate systemically significant nonbank financial companies that will become subject to Fed regulation, supervision, and enforcement.

As described in Chapter 1, the Treasury Department published a report in March 2008 that sought to change the system of functional regulation in the United States to a "Twin Peaks" approach.[37]

Jerry W. MarkhamThe Subprime Crisis—Some Thoughts on a "Sustainable" and "Organic" Regulatory System
4 FIU L. Rev. 381 (2009).

* * * The subprime crisis has given rise to a cry for more regulation, whatever its form and whatever its efficacy. Fortunately, there is all ready on the table a proposal by the Treasury Department for a comprehensive reform of U.S. financial services regulation that reflects common sense, rather than hysteria. That proposal was a result of a study conducted by Treasury in response to concerns over the existing financial regulatory system. Ironically, those concerns were focusing on the effects of too much regulation, particularly the Sarbanes–Oxley Corporate Reform Act of 2002.

As a part of its study, the Department sought public comment on a number of issues concerning the existing financial regulatory structure. Of particular interest was the Department's request for comment on whether the "increasing convergence of products across the traditional 'functional' regulatory lines of banking, insurance, securities, and futures" justifies changes in the regulatory system to assure that regulatory boundary lines do not unnecessarily inhibit competition. The Department received over 350 comment letters on this topic. This was obviously a subject that the financial community thought was important.

The Treasury Department then published its "Blueprint" for financial services regulatory reform that recommended a broad restructuring of this chaotic financial services regulatory structure. Not surprisingly, the Blueprint expressed concern that functional regulation was ineffective and was undermining America's traditional competitive advantage in financial services. The Blueprint prophetically asserted that functional regulation "exhibited several inadequacies, the most significant being the fact that no single regulator possesses all of the information and authority necessary to monitor systemic risk, or the potential that events associated with financial institutions may trigger broad dislocation or a series of defaults that affect the financial system so significantly that the real economy is adversely affected."

The Blueprint contrasted the functional regulatory approach in America with regulatory mechanisms abroad. England, Germany, Japan and dozens of other countries use a consolidated regulator, along with a

---

37. Dep't of the Treasury, Blueprint for a Modernized Financial Regulatory Structure (2008), available at http://www.treas.gov/press/releases/reports/Blueprint.pdf.

central bank, to impose regulation through a single rulebook approach. Those countries also eschew the "rules-based" approach used by most of the multitude of regulators in the United States. Rather, those overseas regulators use a "principles" based approach that generally prescribes the goals of regulation and allows the industry to choose how to reach those goals.

Interestingly, the Treasury Blueprint declined to adopt a single regulator approach, probably because of objections by the existing regulators. Instead, the Blueprint recommended that the United States adopt a so-called "Twin Peaks" approach to regulation that is used in Australia and the Netherlands. The Twin Peaks approach is objectives-based and focuses on specific regulatory goals. The concept of twin peaks envisions some regulatory consolidation, particularly through the creation of bodies that would focus on prudential supervision, market stability and a single business practices regulator that would govern business conduct and consumer protection. * * *

The Treasury Blueprint faced other obstacles. It was issued just before the subprime crisis was in full bloom, so it did not fully address the problems in that market. The Blueprint did recommend that mortgage brokers be regulated and that Fannie Mae and Freddie Mac be restructured, a recommendation that came before their failure. There were other players that attracted regulatory interest outside the Blueprint as the subprime crisis exploded. These included the non-bank lenders that built the subprime market in the 1990s, many of which failed on their own, such as the Countrywide Financial Group that had to be rescued by Bank of America, and many others which were acquired by and caused the failure of the large investment banks. * * *

The Obama Administration followed up with a report of its own on regulatory reform, which shifted the focus of legislation onto increased regulatory requirements rather than less as sought by the Treasury Blueprint. Dep't of Treasury, A New Foundation: Rebuilding Financial Supervision and Regulation (July 17, 2009). The resulting Dodd–Frank Act expanded the power of the Fed over large non-bank financial companies. The Fed is authorized to require reports and conduct examinations of their activities and recommend enforcement actions by their functional regulator or take it own action if the functional regulator fails to respond. The Fed is further authorized to establish prudential risk standards for these nonbank financial companies and to direct divestiture of assets in order to accomplish an orderly resolution in the event of failure.

E. COMMERCIAL ACTIVITIES

GLBA expanded the scope of holding company activities from those that are "closely related to banking" to those that are "financial in nature." Nonfinancial activities (i.e., commercial activities), however, are generally not permitted for FHC's. Senator Gramm—one of the sponsors of the GLBA—predicts that GLBA's separation of financial and nonfinancial activities will prove as anachronistic as Glass–Steagall's separation of commercial banking and investment banking. Representative Leach, however, is quite firm in his conviction that it would be a serious mistake to permit the common ownership of financial firms and commercial enterprises. The financial crisis reinvigorated this debate, with come calling for the revival of the Glass–Steagall Act's separation of commercial banking and investment banking that ended in 1999 with the enactment of GLBA.

It is possible for a commercial firm that becomes a FHC to retain its commercial activities for a minimum of ten years, with a potential five-year extension for a total of fifteen years of commingling of banking and nonfinancial activities. 12 U.S.C.A. § 1843(n)(7). To qualify for this grandfather provision, however, the FHC must be "predominantly engaged" in financial activities. 12 U.S.C.A. § 1843(n)(1). An FHC meets this test if at least 85% of its annual gross revenues (excluding the revenues of its depository subsidiaries) are received from financial activities. 12 U.S.C.A. § 1843(n)(2). This revenue requirement must be met on a continuing basis.

A further opportunity for entry into nonfinancial activities is by an expansive interpretation of "financial in nature." Moreover, FHCs may engage in activities that are "complementary to a financial activity." As discussed above, the Fed has approved trading in certain commodities as complementary to the financial activity of buying and selling as principal permissible commodity derivative contracts. An additional, and potentially large, breach in the wall separating financial from nonfinancial activities is GLBA's authorization of merchant banking investments for FHCs. This authority is discussed further in Chapter 11.

Historically, commercial firms enjoyed banking privileges through the unitary thrift holding company loophole and through nonbank banks. Even though both "loopholes" have since been legislatively closed, 200 or so unitary thrift holding companies have been grandfathered by GLBA and nonbank banks were grandfathered by the Competitive Equality Banking Act of 1987 (CEBA). These entities continue to provide opportunities to examine whether the combination of financial and nonfinancial activities is dangerous or harmful. Grandfathered unitary thrift holding companies include Nordstrom's department store, which owns Nordstrom FSB of Scottsdale, Arizona, and State Farm Insurance Company, which owns State Farm Bank. Grandfathered unitary thrift holding companies were afforded all the FHC powers without oversight by the Fed prior to the Dodd–Frank Act. Dodd–Frank requires that a unitary holding company's financial activities be operated by an intermediate holding company that will be subject to Fed regulation as a thrift holding company. Dodd–Frank Act, § 626.

Numerous entities chartered as banks remain excepted from the definition of "bank" under the BHCA. 12 U.S.C.A. § 1841(c)(2). Therefore, it is still possible for a commercial firm to own one of these "nonbank banks," escape characterization as an FHC, and escape GLBA's limitation of FHCs to activities that are "financial in nature." Even after GLBA freed securities firms to buy banks, many firms eschewed the opportunity in favor of limited purpose trust banks or industrial loan companies that would permit bank-like operations without FHC designation and FRB supervision and oversight. Goldman Sachs owned an industrial loan company, for instance. Since an industrial loan company is not considered a bank under the BHCA, Goldman Sachs was not a BHC or an FHC, and was not subject to Fed supervision and regulation. During the financial crisis, however, as described earlier in this Chapter, Goldman Sachs converted its industrial loan company to a bank and its application to become a BHC was approved by the Fed.

The Fed and the FDIC have squared off against industrial loan companies. The Fed opposed legislation that would benefit industrial loan companies by granting them de novo interstate branching authority and the ability to offer interest-bearing NOW accounts to commercial customers. The Fed's opposition was based on its view that industrial loan companies are not adequately supervised since their holding companies are not subject to FRB oversight. The FDIC, which provides deposit insurance and is the federal regulator of industrial loan companies, rejected the Fed's claim.[38] The debate continued with a GAO report that concluded that ILCs were a risk to the deposit insurance fund. GAO, Industrial Loan Corporations: Recent Asset Growth and Commercial Interest Highlight Differences in Regulatory Authority, GAO–05–621, Sept. 15, 2005.

Wal–Mart's attempt to purchase an industrial loan company in California was thwarted when California enacted a statute preventing nonfinancial firms from owning California chartered industrial loan companies.[39] Four other states, however, authorize industrial loan companies–Colorado, Minnesota, Nevada, and Utah–and Wal–Mart soon announced that is was seeking to charter an ILC in Utah. Its application to the FDIC for deposit insurance generated numerous comments and much controversy, although Wal–Mart maintained that the ILC's purpose was simply to process credit, debit, and check payments at a cheaper rate than could be offered by third party providers. The FDIC announced a moratorium on the consideration of applications by ILCs for deposit insurance in the summer of 2006. 71 Fed. Reg. 43,482 (Aug. 1, 2006). The moratorium was extended by the FDIC through January 31, 2008. 72 Fed. Reg. 5290 (Feb.

---

38. See Federal Deposit Insurance Corporation, The FDIC's Supervision of Industrial Loan Companies: A Historical Perspective, Supervisory Insights (Summer 2004), available at <www.fdic.gov/regulations/examinations/supervisory/insights/index.html>; Rob Blackwell, Greenspan Digs In on Fight Over ILC Charters, Am. Banker, July 15, 2003; Rob Blackwell, Powell Remarks Heat Up Battle Over ILC Powers, Am. Banker, June 2, 2003.

39. Rob Blackwell, Industrial Charter Could be Wal–Mart's Way In, Am. Banker, Apr. 17, 2003.

5, 2007). Wal–Mart withdrew its ILC application in March 2007 after the FDIC announced that it was extending its moratorium on ILC applications from commercial firms.

Wal–Mart did not give up. In June 2007, the company announced that it was opening 1,000 MoneyCenters in its stores that would provide online bill paying, payday check cashing, stored value Visa cards, and other financial services. H. Michael Jalili, Wal–Mart Details Its MSB Plans, Am. Banker, June 21, 2007. A Wal–Mart subsidiary also obtained a banking license in Mexico. Anna Gelpern, Wal–Mart Bank in Mexico: Money to the Masses and the Home–Host Battle, 39 Conn. L. Rev. 1513 (2007).

The Dodd–Frank Act imposed a moratorium on FDIC applications for deposit insurance filed after November 23, 2009, for an industrial loan company, credit card bank, or trust bank by a commercial firm that derives less than 15% of its consolidated revenue from financing activities. Dodd–Frank Act, § 603. The moratorium lasts for three years after the enactment of Dodd–Frank on July 21, 2010. The agencies are also prohibited from approving any application for a change of control of such a nonbank bank by a commercial firm. The GAO is required to prepare a study regarding the regulatory structure governing nonbank banks.

QUESTIONS AND NOTES

1. Should holding companies be permitted to engage in financial and nonfinancial activities without restriction? What were the historical reasons justifying the separation of banking and commerce? How do advances in technology impact on this question? Compare the views of Professors Wilmarth and White. Compare Arthur E. Wilmarth, Jr., Wal–Mart and the Separation of Banking and Commerce, 39 Conn. L. Rev. 1539 (2007) (arguing that the ownership of ILCs by large commercial firms creates risks for the financial system and the economy by spreading the federal safety net to the commercial sector, encouraging conflicts of interest in loans and investments by the ILC to benefit their commercial affiliates, and subjecting the ILCs to contagious losses of confidence for any problems suffered by the commercial firm), with Lawrence J. White, Should Wal–Mart, Real Estate Brokers, and Banks Be in Bed Together? A Principles–Based Approach to the Issues of the Separation of Banking and Commerce (July 2007), available at <ssrn.com/author=15117> (arguing that an activity should be permitted for a holding company that owns a bank if the financial transactions between the bank and the holding company are closely monitored by bank regulators).

2. What are the advantages of permitting some companies to engage in a mixture of banking and commerce through the grandfathered provisions described above? Do these grandfathered entities have an unfair competitive advantage over FHC's that generally may engage only in financial activities?

3. Why have regulators tried to block Wal–Mart's entry into banking? It is a well-run company that has provided great value to its customers and is unlikely to be a rogue bank. Critics assert that this action is being taken solely to protect the banking industry from competition at the expense of the

consumer. Peter J. Wallison, Carveout Reveals ILC Bill's True Nature, Am. Banker, June 29, 2007. Where Wal–Mart has offered check cashing services, check cashing fees in the market have fallen by 50%.

F.　INTERAFFILIATE RELATIONS

(1) Affiliate Transactions

BOARD OF GOVERNORS OF THE FEDERAL RESERVE SYSTEM, INTERIM RULES WITH REQUEST FOR PUBLIC COMMENTS

66 Fed. Reg. 24,229 (May 11, 2001).

* * * Sections 23A and 23B of the Federal Reserve Act are intended to limit the risks to an insured depository institution ("institution") from transactions with its affiliates.[40] Sections 23A and 23B also limit the ability of an institution to transfer to its affiliates the subsidy arising from the institution's access to the Federal safety net.

Section 23A achieves these goals in three major ways. First, it limits the aggregate amount of an insured depository institution's "covered transactions" with any single affiliate (other than a financial subsidiary of the institution) to no more than 10 percent of the institution's capital and surplus, and the aggregate amount of covered transactions with all affiliates combined (including financial subsidiaries of the institution) to no more than 20 percent of the institution's capital and surplus. Covered transactions include purchases of assets from an affiliate, extensions of credit to an affiliate, guarantees issued on behalf of an affiliate, and certain other transactions that expose an institution to an affiliate's credit or investment risk.

Second, the statute requires all covered transactions between an insured depository institution and its affiliates to be on terms and conditions that are consistent with safe and sound banking practices, and prohibits an institution from purchasing low-quality assets from its affiliates. Finally, the statute requires that an insured depository institution's extensions of credit to affiliates and guarantees issued on behalf of affiliates be appropriately secured by a statutorily defined amount of collateral.

Section 23B protects an insured depository institution by requiring that transactions between the institution and its affiliates be on market terms; that is, on terms and under circumstances that are substantially the same, or at least as favorable to the institution, as those prevailing at

---

40.　[n.1] Section 23A originally was enacted as part of the Banking Act of 1933 and applied only to banks that were members of the Federal Reserve System. Congress amended the Federal Deposit Insurance Act in 1966 to extend section 23A to insured nonmember banks. 12 U.S.C. 1828(j). In 1989, Congress further extended the coverage of section 23A to insured savings associations. 12 U.S.C. 1468. Congress enacted section 23B of the Federal Reserve Act as part of the Competitive Equality Banking Act of 1987, and has subsequently expanded its scope to cover the same set of depository institutions as are covered by section 23A.

the time for comparable transactions with *unaffiliated* companies. The market terms requirement of section 23B applies to any covered transaction (as defined in section 23A) with an affiliate as well as a broad range of other transactions, such as a sale of securities or other assets to an affiliate and a contract for the payment of money or furnishing of services to an affiliate.

Until its issuance of Regulation W in 2002,[41] the Fed's regulatory guidance in this area came solely through legal rulings and advisory letters relating to specific cases. Regulation W provides the Fed with authority to exempt transactions from 23A and Regulation W "if it finds such exemptions to be in the public interest and consistent with the purposes of section 23A." 12 C.F.R. § 223.43(a). Pursuant to its exemption authority, the Fed granted exemptions from the rule precluding lending more than 10% of capital to any one affiliate, to permit major banking institutions to provide liquidity to their securities affiliates in the wake of the credit tightening following the subprime lending crisis that surfaced in the summer of 2007. See www.federalreserve.gov/BoardDocs/LegalInt/FederalReserveAct/2007/ for the exemption letters sent to many large financial holding companies. Bank of America, N.A., for instance, was permitted to temporarily exceed the 10% of capital limit so long as the bank's loans to its securities affiliate were overcollateralized, guaranteed by the holding company, and did not exceed 30% of the bank's regulatory capital. Section 23A applies to insured nonmember banks pursuant to 12 U.S.C.A. § 1828(j). The FDIC proposed a new regulation in 2004 that would permit the FDIC to administer, interpret, and grant exemptions from Regulation W for insured nonmember banks.

In the Dodd–Frank Act Congress amended Sections 23A and 23B to limit the Fed's unilateral authority to grant exemptions from the affiliate transaction restrictions. The Fed is required to act with the FDIC and the primary regulator of the bank in issuing exemptions. Dodd–Frank Act, § 608. Further, the amendments expanded the scope of the affiliate transaction restrictions. "Covered transactions" were expanded to include securities lending or borrowing transactions with affiliates, all derivatives transactions with affiliates an expansion from just credit derivatives transactions, and eliminates the exception from the quantitative limits of Section 23A previously given to transactions between a bank and a financial subsidiary of the bank. Dodd–Frank Act, §§ 608 & 609.

QUESTIONS AND NOTES

Why are Congress and the banking regulators concerned about transactions between affiliates? What is wrong with an extension of credit by a

---

41. 67 Fed. Reg. 76604 (Dec. 12, 2002) (codified at 12 C.F.R. pt. 223) (reprinted in this book's Statutory and Regulatory Supplement).

member bank at a lower rate of interest to a securities subsidiary owned by the same holding company? Does Regulation W prohibit such a loan? Under what terms could a securities subsidiary borrow money from an affiliated bank?

(2) Conflicts of Interest

The potential for conflicts of interest increases as banks and their holding companies expand in size and engage in an increasingly broad range of activities. An article on intrabank conflicts describes the "informational conflict" and notes that there may be concerns if a bank disseminates nonpublic information it has about one of its borrowers (a) within its loan department, (b) to third parties such as a potential acquiror of the borrower, or (c) to a different department such as a trust department that recommends investments to its customers.[42] The article discusses the use of "ethical walls" or "screening devices" to restrict the flow of nonpublic information about a bank's customer within a bank that is also doing business with the customer's competitor or potential acquirer.

WASHINGTON STEEL CORP. v. TW CORP.

United States Court of Appeals, Third Circuit, 1979.
602 F.2d 594.[43]

GIBBONS, CIRCUIT JUDGE.

In this appeal we consider the limits, if any, imposed by law on a commercial bank which wishes to advance funds to one client in order to facilitate that client's takeover of another of the bank's clients. The appeal is taken from a preliminary injunction prohibiting appellant Chemical Bank (Chemical) from participating in a loan to Talley Industries, Inc., and TW Corporation, its wholly owned subsidiary, (Talley), the proceeds of which were to be used for the purchase by Talley of the outstanding shares of stock of appellee Washington Steel Corporation (Washington). Because we take a narrower view than did the district court of the limits on Chemical's lending authority, and because, on the present record, no facts support the trial court's order, we reverse the grant of preliminary relief and remand for further proceedings.

On January 15, 1974, Washington executed a credit agreement with Pittsburgh National Bank, Chemical, and Morgan Guaranty Trust Company, pursuant to which the banks agreed to lend Washington up to $10,000,000. Pittsburgh National was the lead bank in that transaction, agreeing to advance 55% of the funds. The credit agreement identified Pittsburgh National as "agent" of the lenders for purposes of the loan. Chemical agreed to advance 22.5% of the funds, or an amount up to $2,250,000. * * *

---

42. Peter C. Buck & Krista R. Bowen, Intrabank Conflicts of Interest, 3 N.C. Banking Inst. 31 (1999).

43. Overruled on other grounds, Clark v. K–Mart Corp., 979 F.2d 965, 967 n.4 (3d Cir. 1992).

In connection with its participation in the loan to Washington, Chemical received certain information from Washington, some of which was nonpublic in nature. This information included a May, 1973 Study produced by Washington, providing cash flow and earnings projections for Washington through 1982. In addition, Washington supplied Chemical with quarterly statements of its financial affairs as well as a year-end statement dated December 28, 1978 for the fiscal year ending September 30, 1978.

Besides participating as one of three banks lending money to Washington, Chemical also served as one of two registrars for its common stock. Its function as registrar was to ensure that no more than the authorized number of Washington shares of stock were issued.

Over the years, Chemical has also been the lead bank in loans to Talley. In January, 1979, Talley decided to endeavor to acquire Washington. On or about January 13, 1979, Talley spoke to Paul Fitzgerald, a Vice President at Chemical. Fitzgerald was the principal Chemical liaison to Talley, having worked on four or five Talley loan agreements during the prior seven years. At that time Talley discussed a possible acquisition of an unnamed company. Two days later, on January 15, Fitzgerald met with Talley representatives at the offices of Chemical's legal counsel. A discussion was held as to whether Chemical might participate in financing Talley's proposed acquisition of Washington, which was for the first time identified as the proposed acquisition target. An attorney for Talley indicated a belief that Chemical had an ongoing business relationship with Washington. * * *

Later in the day of January 15, Fitzgerald and other members of the Chemical Corporate Banking Department discussed in greater detail the possibility of financing the proposed acquisition. One of the persons attending this meeting was John Roach, District Director for Western Pennsylvania, who supervised the Washington Steel account at Chemical. Roach indicated that there was a loan outstanding to Washington Steel in which Pittsburgh National was the lead bank and Chemical and Morgan Guaranty were participants. Roach also stated that he could not be sure what Washington Steel's reaction would be to the Talley offer. At the conclusion of the meeting, a senior officer of the Chemical Corporate Banking Division made a policy decision that the Bank was not precluded from participating in the proposed loan, assuming that the loan was justified from the standpoint of Talley's creditworthiness.

Thereafter, Fitzgerald and his staff performed a credit analysis of Talley. Concluding that the company was a favorable credit risk, senior credit officials approved the loan commitment. * * *

By letter delivered on January 19, 1979, Talley communicated to Washington management and directors its proposal for a merger of the two companies to be accomplished by Talley's paying $36.00 per share of common stock to the shareholders of Washington. This offer was rejected by Washington's management. * * *

On January 26, 1979, Talley renewed its offer to merge with Washington, this time proposing to pay $37.50 per share of common stock. * * *

On January 31, 1979, Washington's management sent a letter to its shareholders urging rejection of the Talley offer. It reiterated this position in a February 1 newspaper advertisement. On February 5, 1979, Washington brought the instant suit in the United States District Court for the Western District of Pennsylvania. In pertinent part, Washington contended * * * that Chemical had violated its fiduciary duty to Washington in that it had allegedly misused confidential information obtained from Washington in deciding to finance the tender offer. Washington sought an injunction to foreclose the tender offer. * * *

Characterizing Chemical's participation in the Talley loan as "egregious and unethical conduct," the trial court preliminarily enjoined Chemical from further involvement in the loan to Talley. The court indicated that it was granting the injunctive relief only on the basis of count 3, which alleged a breach of a supposed common law fiduciary duty arising from the receipt of confidential information.

On February 16, 1979, the district court required Washington to post a $2,000,000 bond as a prerequisite to the issuance of the preliminary injunction.[44] * * *

The trial court granted the preliminary injunction on the ground that Chemical had violated a common law fiduciary duty to Washington. While the court's opinion did not make clear its precise origins or nature, Washington urges two possible theories in support of such a duty. First, it maintains that Chemical, by receiving confidential information in connection with its loan to Washington, impliedly assumed a duty not to act on behalf of another company whose purpose was to "subver[t] . . . Washington Steel's . . . capital development program. . . ." Second, Washington urges that even if there is no such *per se* rule which forbids a bank in Chemical's position from advancing the efforts of one client to merge with another, nonetheless there is a duty, which Chemical violated, not to misuse confidential information supplied by the target company.

The trial court ruled that, as a matter of law, Chemical "had a duty not to act adversely to the interests of Plaintiff Washington Steel under the circumstances. . . ." As noted above, the court seemed to derive this duty from Chemical's role as a registrar of Washington stock as well as from its receipt of information supplied by Washington in connection with a commercial loan. On appeal Washington does not rely on Chemical's role as registrar in urging a *per se* fiduciary duty. Rather, it contends that, having entrusted Chemical with the May, 1973 Study projecting future earnings as well as periodic financial reports, Washington reasonably expected Chemical to take no actions adverse to the continued viability of the Company. Whatever expectations it may have entertained, however,

---

44. [eds.] Washington received an offer from another company and Talley withdrew its offer. The Court of Appeals found the appeal was not moot since appellants wished to recover damages on the injunction bond. This finding has since been overruled. Id.

we cannot fairly imply a duty whose sweep is as broad and whose restrictions are as severe as that urged by Washington. * * *

[T]he only case to have actually considered the legal issues raised by Washington has squarely rejected identical contentions. See American Medicorp, Inc. v. Continental Illinois Nat'l Bank, No. 77 C 3865 (N.D.Ill. Dec. 30, 1977). In that case, American Medicorp sought to forestall efforts by Humana, Inc. to acquire its outstanding common stock. Toward that end, American Medicorp moved to enjoin Continental Bank from financing the proposed Humana tender offer. American Medicorp pointed out that Continental had lent it money over the years, performed "other banking services," and, in the course of these dealings, "acquired a file of 'non-public' financial and other information furnished by the plaintiff." American Medicorp contended that "making a loan to a company which desires to take over the control of one of Continental's customers which has supplied confidential data to the bank is a *per se* breach of a fiduciary obligation which should be enjoined." The district court rejected this contention, noting that plaintiff had failed to come forward with a single case "supporting a complete prohibition against lending money to a company seeking to take over one of the bank's customers which has provided it with 'non-public' information." The court noted that "[d]espite the stringent governmental regulations to which Federal banks are subject today, this limitation has not been imposed."

We agree with the court in *American Medicorp*. Not only is the *per se* rule urged by Washington wholly unprecedented, but, in addition, its application is objectionable on important policy grounds. To imply a common law fiduciary duty of banks not to deal with competitors of their borrowers, or even just potential acquirers of those borrowers, could wreak havoc with the availability of funding for capital ventures. See Note, Bank Financing of Involuntary Takeovers of Corporate Customers: A Breach of a Fiduciary Duty?, 53 Notre Dame Lawyer 827, 835 (1978). Companies seeking to insulate themselves from takeovers, or even from ordinary competition, could simply arrange for a series of loans from most of the major banks, supplying those banks with the requisite non-public information. Under the *per se* rule urged by Washington, the banks would thereby be foreclosed from financing competitors and potential acquirers of the borrowing firms. As the *American Medicorp* court recognized, such a result "would tend to burden the free flow of bank financing and the ability which a bank now has to deal with customers who may have adverse interests to other customers."

Moreover, even if the rule Washington proposes were sound public policy, it would hardly be the province of this court to say so in the context of this present litigation. First, establishing a *per se* common law fiduciary duty of banks to their borrowers seems archetypically within the domain of legislative judgment. * * * In addition, even were we to presume to venture into this area, we would be reluctant to do so as a matter of state common law, as the trial court apparently did and as Washington urges on appeal. Given the need for uniform rules in an area so vital to our national economy as banking, any state common law rule that we might imply would likely give way to the preemptive force of federal law. Moreover, there is every reason to believe that Congress is aware of this issue and has begun the difficult process of effecting a legislative solution. In addition, the Comptroller of the Currency has recently proposed a regulation for national banks which suggests ways of restricting the use of confidential information obtained from one client on behalf of another. See Proposed Treas.Reg. § 9.7(d), 42 Fed.Reg. 56,338 (1977), reprinted in Herzel & Colling, The Chinese Wall and Conflict of Interest in Banks, 34 Bus.Law. 73, 100 (1978). The Board of Governors of the Federal Reserve System has adopted a similar statement for state member banks. See 43 Fed.Reg. 12,755 (1978), cited in Herzel & Colling, supra, at 100. These developments evince a concern at the national level with the issues raised by Washington. Any common law fiduciary duty which we might imply would, in all probability, have to yield to whatever national policies might emerge from these deliberations.

Accordingly, we reject the contention that Chemical, having received confidential information from Washington in connection with its participation in a loan to that company, was necessarily precluded from financing the efforts of Talley to merge with Washington.

Besides urging a *per se* rule of fiduciary duty, Washington supports the preliminary injunction on the theory that Chemical allegedly misused Washington's confidential information in arranging the loan to Talley. * * *

We turn, therefore, to the remaining questions, whether the Chemical officers in evaluating the loan to Talley used confidential information obtained from Washington, and, if so, whether such use was ground for a preliminary injunction. Washington contends that Chemical should be deemed to have used the information. * * *

We do not accept Washington's contentions. There was, first of all, no showing that those Chemical officers who were involved with the loan to Talley made any use of the information provided by Washington. We refuse to presume such use on the unsupported assumption that, in view of Talley's ostensibly weak financial condition, Chemical would not have decided to make the loan to Talley had it not known of Washington's assertedly bright future. All the evidence on this record suggests otherwise; it was Talley's, and not Washington's financial standing that encouraged Chemical to move ahead. Chemical was "eminently familiar with Talley," having "done business with them for years." Chemical performed a "worse-case" analysis of Talley's ability to repay the loan. That analysis convinced Chemical of Talley's ability to cover its debt service. In performing that analysis, Chemical considered only Washington's current dividend payout; it made no assumptions about a change in Washington's dividend rate.

Roach's silence at the January 15 meeting does not alter this conclusion. What more, after all, could Roach do at that meeting to safeguard the information? The evidence establishes that Roach said nothing at the meeting beyond the fact that there was a loan relationship with Washington and that he did not know what Washington's reaction to the Talley offer would be. Moreover, Mr. Fitzgerald testified that his staff was instructed not to talk to anyone who worked on the Washington account, nor was it to look at any files kept on the target company. Fitzgerald himself had no access to Washington files. Indeed, both Roach and his assistant John Watkins submitted affidavits stating that they had personally secured all of the Washington files and kept them out of the possible sight of those persons working on the Talley loan. Thus we do not share appellee's view that Chemical used the Washington information in deciding to make the loan to Talley.

But assuming, arguendo, that such use occurred, we reject for a more fundamental reason Washington's contention. We do not believe that a bank violates any duty it may owe to one of its borrowers when it uses information received from that borrower in deciding whether or not to make a loan to another prospective borrower. First, like the *per se* rule adopted by the trial court and discussed above, the promulgation of a rule restricting the dissemination of confidential information within the loan department of a bank is neither the proper province of a court nor an appropriate subject for state law adjudication. More critically, the adoption of such a rule would make unwise banking policy. To prohibit a bank from considering all available information in making its own loan decisions might engender one or both of two undesirable outcomes. First, it might force banks to go blindly into loan transactions, arguably violating its duties to its own depositors. Alternatively, such a rule might discourage banks from lending money to any company which expresses an interest in purchasing shares of stock of another of the bank's customers. The adverse implication of this result for the free flow of funds is precisely the reason why we rejected the *per se* rule urged by Washington. Bank credit is, after all, the largest part, by far, of the national money supply.

Of course, we intimate no view on whether a bank may be foreclosed from disseminating confidential information to a *separate* bank department, such as the trust department, whose function it is to recommend particular investments to its clients. Such dissemination of insider information arguably might violate Section 10(b) of the Securities and Exchange Act of 1934 and the S.E.C.'s rule 10b–5. 17 C.F.R. 240.10b–5. See Herzel & Colling, supra, at 86; Lipton & Mazur, The Chinese Wall Solution to the Conflict Problems of Securities Firms, 50 N.Y.U.L.Rev. 459, 475 (1975). So, too, might the dissemination of such information to the acquiring company itself. Neither of these issues, however, is presented in this appeal. * * * In making loans, unless it is to take imprudent risks with the funds on deposit with the bank, the commercial loan department must be free to make full use of the information available to it. * * * Thus, we hold only that the use within that loan department of information received from one borrower, in evaluating a loan to another

borrower, does not, without more, state a cause of action against the bank.
* * *

QUESTIONS AND NOTES

1. A conflict of interest may be a decision to lend money to an officer, director, or major shareholder of bank. This conflict is discussed further in Chapter 5 in the section on insider loans.

2. Conflicts of interest may arise between a bank that has a trust department (see Chapter 10) that must act as a fiduciary and other aspects of a bank's operations. See 12 C.F.R. § 9.12 on self-dealing and conflicts of interest.

(3) Anti–Tying

Section 106 of the Bank Holding Company Act as amended in 1970 prohibits so-called "tying" arrangements. 12 U.S.C.A. §§ 1972 & 1975. "Tying" arrangements are considered to be anti-competitive. In a tying arrangement, the purchase of one product (the "desired product") is conditioned upon (or "tied" to) the purchase of another product (the "tied product"). A prohibited tying arrangement also occurs when a product or service is offered at a discount that is conditioned on the purchase of another product or service. Congress was concerned that banks might use their ability to offer bank products, particularly credit, in a coercive manner that would provide them a competitive advantage in markets for nonbanking products.

Section 106 does allow banks to impose conditions on a customer that are a part of prudent banking practice. For example, a requirement that customers adopt financial controls is permissible. Restrictions on other borrowings are permissible if the restrictions are imposed for the bank's protection. The tying of certain "traditional bank products" is also allowed. This includes tying arrangements involving loans, discounts, deposits, or trust services, provided that the products are offered by the bank and that they are available for purchase as separate products. For example, a bank could offer a lower interest rate on a loan on the condition that the customer maintain a deposit account with the bank. A bank could discount the price of its brokerage services on the condition that the customer also use a traditional bank product. Nevertheless, brokerage services and the traditional bank product must be separately available to customers. Credit card subsidiaries of a bank may also discount interest rates and fees on credit cards to customers who purchase traditional banking services from the bank.

Representative Dingell, the ranking member of the House Committee on Energy and Commerce requested in August 2002 that Chairman Greenspan of the Fed and Comptroller Hawke of the OCC respond to the question of whether a bank may condition its extension of a line of credit to a borrower on being included in a bond or stock underwriting deal by the borrower without violating the anti-tying restrictions. The regulators responded that "if banks were to condition the price of credit on a customer obtaining investment banking or other products or services from an affiliate, with certain exceptions, this condition would violate section 106 [12 U.S.C. § 1972]." They also noted the possibility that underpricing credit extensions to obtain business for other holding company units could constitute an unsafe and unsound practice, and that there might be a violation of Section 23B, 12 U.S.C. § 371c–1, if the credit extension is underpriced and the proceeds of the credit are used for the benefit of a holding company affiliate. The regulators committed to undertake a review of this tying issue at some of the country's largest banks.

The Government Accounting Office (GAO) (now known as the Government Accountability Office) also agreed to update its 1997 report on tying, Bank Oversight: Few Cases of Tying Have Been Detected, GAO/GGD–97–58 (May 8, 1997). The new report, Bank Tying: Additional Steps Needed to Ensure Effective Enforcement of Tying Provisions, GAO–04–4 (October 2003), found that some customers' tying complaints involved "lawful ties between traditional banking products rather than unlawful ties." The GAO recommended that since direct evidence of a tying relationship would rarely be available, bank regulators consider procedures by which they could obtain indirect evidence of tying relationships, including publication of contact points within bank regulatory agencies to answer questions from banks and bank customers and to receive complaints from bank customers. In addition, the GAO suggested that examination of loan pricing behavior might be helpful since low-priced credit could indicate a violation of the tying statute.

The National Association of Securities Dealers (NASD) (now known as FINRA, the Financial Industry Regulatory Authority) announced that it would investigate allegations relating to tying of bank credit and investment banking activities to determine whether NASD member firms were adhering to the NASD requirement of operating under "just and equitable principles of trade."

The Federal Reserve Board issued a proposed interpretation and supervisory guidance with request for public comment on tying considerations. 68 Fed. Reg. 52024 (Aug. 29, 2003).[45] This marks the Fed's first comprehensive guidance on Section 106. The proposed interpretation provides that

> section 106 prohibits a bank from imposing a condition on a prospective borrower that requires the borrower to do any of the following in order to obtain a loan from the bank—
>
> - Purchase an insurance product from the bank or an affiliate of the bank (a prohibited tie);

---

45. See Richard K. Kim, The Federal Reserve's Proposed Interpretation Regarding the Anti–Tying Restrictions of Section 106 of the Bank Holding Company Act Amendments of 1970, 8 N.C. Banking Inst. 1 (2004); David R. Kinman, Note, Tying: Enhancing Competition Through the Bank Holding Company, 8 N.C. Banking Inst. 215 (2004).

- Obtain corporate debt or equity underwriting services from an affiliate of the bank (a prohibited tie);

- Sell the bank or an affiliate of the bank a piece of real estate unrelated to the requested loan (a prohibited reciprocity arrangement); or

- Refrain from obtaining insurance products or securities underwriting services from a competitor of the bank or from a competitor of an affiliate of the bank (a prohibited exclusive dealing arrangement).

The interpretation has not been finalized.

DIBIDALE OF LOUISIANA, INC. v. AMERICAN BANK & TRUST CO.

United States Court of Appeals, Fifth Circuit, 1990.
916 F.2d 300.

POLITZ, CIRCUIT JUDGE.

* * * Each of the general antitrust statutes contains a provision that prohibits certain conditional transactions, or tying arrangements, in which the seller of one product (the tying product) conditions the sale of that product on the consumer's purchase or provision of another (the tied product). 15 U.S.C. § (Sherman Act section 1); 15 U.S.C. § 14 (Clayton Act section 3); 15 U.S.C. § 45 (Federal Trade Commission Act section 5). Although the scope of these provisions encompasses the banking industry as well as commerce in general, their applicability in the banking context is problematic. See 9 E. Kintner and J. Bauer, Federal Antitrust Law, § 68.6 at 135–136. First, Clayton Act section 3 regulates only the sale or lease of goods, not services. Second, recent case law imposing stricter evidentiary burdens on Sherman and Clayton Act plaintiffs, see Jefferson Parish Hosp. Dist. No. 2 v. Hyde, 466 U.S. 2 (1984); United States Steel Corp. v. Fortner Enterprises, Inc. (*Fortner II*), 429 U.S. 610 (1977), renders successful tying claims under these statutes difficult to attain. Third, the unique nature of the banking industry renders it more important to prohibit conditional transactions in that context than in other less sensitive sectors of the economy. Kintner & Bauer, § 68.6 at 136.

Congress enacted the anti-tying provisions of the BHCA "to provide specific statutory assurance that the use of the economic power of a bank will not lead to a lessening of competition or unfair competitive practices." S. Rep. No. 1084, 91st Cong., 2d Sess. 16, reprinted in 1970 U.S.Code Cong. & Admin.News 5519, 5535. The economic power of the banking industry stems from the aggregate control of banks over credit. In light of this unique economic role that banks play, Congress perceived conditional transactions involving credit as inherently anti-competitive, operating to the detriment of banking and non-banking competitors alike; thus the anti-tying provisions were intended to regulate conditional transactions in the extension of credit by banks more stringently than had the Supreme

Court under the general antitrust statutes. S. Rep. No. 1084, 1970 U.S.Code Cong. & Admin.News at 5558 (Letter of Assistant Attorney General Richard McLaren). See Fortner Enterprises, Inc. v. United States Steel Corp. (*Fortner I*), 394 U.S. 495 (1969) (stopping short of declaring tie-ins involving credit to be illegal *per se*).

Central to this more stringent regulation of the banking industry was Congress's decision to exclude from the bank anti-tying provisions the market share and anti-competitiveness requirements which were the cornerstone of tying claims under the general antitrust statutes. To establish an illegal tying arrangement in violation of section 1 of the Sherman Act a plaintiff must establish: (1) that the defendant possesses market power over the tying product sufficient to force (i.e. coerce) the consumer into purchasing a tied product or engaging in a reciprocal deal with the seller; and (2) that the alleged arrangement forecloses "a substantial volume of commerce." Jefferson Parish Hosp., 466 U.S. at 13–16. In contrast, a plaintiff claiming an unlawful tie-in or reciprocal dealing requirement under section 1972 may recover without demonstrating the tying bank's market power or the anti-competitive effect of the alleged arrangement.

The fact that Congress, in enacting the anti-tying provisions of the BHCA, sought to regulate a specific industry out of a recognition of that industry's aggregate economic power and unique economic role, undergirds our interpretation of the "condition or requirement" language central to Dibidale's appeal. To restrict the scope of those words to tying arrangements in which a seller is literally forced to purchase or provide a tied product or service in order to obtain credit would vitiate that section's intended role for, as Congress recognized, a tying arrangement may squelch competition whether coercive or not:

> [T]ie-ins may result from actual coercion by a seller or from a customer's realization that he stands a better chance of securing a scarce and important commodity (such as credit) by "volunteering" to accept [or provide] other products or services rather than seeking them in the competitive market place. *In either case, competition is adversely affected, as customers no longer purchase a product or service on its own economic merit.*
>
> Reciprocity, which involves the induced provision of products and services by the customer rather than his acceptance of other products and services, may also come about in these involuntary or "voluntary" manners.

Conf.Rep. No. 1747, 91st Cong., 2d Sess., reprinted in 1970 U.S.Code Cong. & Admin.News 5561, 5569 (emphasis added).

Nonetheless, American Bank and First National contend that Congress deliberately excluded these "voluntary" tying arrangements from the scope of section 1972 when it adopted the so-called Bennett amendment. As originally drafted, section 1972 prohibited banks from extending credit on the "condition, agreement, or understanding" that the customer would accept or provide some other product or service. The Bennett amendment replaced these words with the phrase "condition or requirement." As the comments of Senator Bennett make clear, however, the purpose of the amendment was to exclude from the scope of section 1972 the extreme case in which a plaintiff alleges nothing more than the mere simultaneity of transactions between bank and borrower:

> The elimination of the words "condition or understanding," and the substitution of the word "requirement," are intended to eliminate possible inferences and implications of tie-ins and exclusive dealing arrangements based on a bank's performance of two or more services for a particular customer, or the bank's providing a service to the customer and receiving a deposit or other service from the customer at the same time. The bill as amended would require that a condition or requirement imposed by the bank must be demonstrated in order to prove that a violation of the section has occurred.

116 Cong. Rec. 32124, 32125.

From the foregoing we conclude that in order to defend against an adverse summary judgment on its claim under 12 U.S.C. § 1972(a)(D), Dibidale need only allege and offer adequate summary judgment proof upon which the trier-of-fact could find that the hiring of Theriot was in fact a condition or requirement of its securing the desired loan from American Bank.[46]

* * * Dibidale's evidence, both direct and circumstantial, including the fact that American Bank approved the loan one day after Dibidale hired Theriot, renders summary judgment inappropriate herein. We do not now resolve this genuine issue of material fact; that remains for the trier-of-fact.

JONES, CIRCUIT JUDGE, dissents. * * *

QUESTIONS AND NOTES

1. Banks that wish to participate in bond or stock underwriting for a customer are sometimes expected by the customer to also participate in loan commitments or line of credit facilities to the customer. Does this violate the anti-tying restrictions? In its spinoff of Agere Systems, Inc., Lucent Technologies, Inc. required its underwriters to supply $1.1 billion in loans. Many traditional investment banks did not want to undertake such a commitment, but financial holding companies are usually happy to participate on those terms.

2. Although bank regulators and the GAO have not uncovered evidence of improper tying, a survey by the Association of Financial Professionals released in June 2004 indicated that one-half of the companies responding to its credit access survey had either been denied credit or had credit terms changed to their detriment because they did not provide other business to the bank.

---

46. This paragraph was added on rehearing by 941 F.2d 308 (5th Cir. 1991).

3. If credit is extended by a nonbank lending subsidiary of a bank or financial holding company on the condition that the borrower utilize another product provided by the holding company, is 12 U.S.C.A. § 1972 violated? Does this suggest an easy way around the statute and explain the widely held perception that improper tying frequently occurs?

4. Industry efforts to obtain an exemption from the proposed anti-tying rules for large sophisticated borrowers broke down over difficulties in defining a large borrower. Patrick Rucker, Griping Over Unfinished Tying Rules, Am. Banker, May 23, 2006. Perhaps the only fine issued by the Fed for illegal tying was a $3 million fine assessed against WestLB AG, a U.S. branch of a German bank, in August 2003 for tying bank credit to using the bank as a co-manager of offerings of syndicated debt securities. Id.

SECTION 3. PRIVACY

A. DISCLOSURE TO THE GOVERNMENT

The Right to Financial Privacy Act of 1978 (RFPA), 12 U.S.C.A. § 3401 et seq., limited the power of federal government agencies to obtain access to individual financial records. Banks were required to notify their customers if the government sought information concerning their accounts. In Hunt v. U.S. SEC, 520 F.Supp. 580, 601 (N.D. Tex. 1981), the SEC was found to have violated this statute when it improperly obtained the bank records of wealthy members of the Hunt family of Dallas, Texas, who were under investigation for attempting to manipulate the silver market. The court stated that "[t]he basic thrust of the Act is that customers of financial institutions are entitled to notice of any government request for their financial records and an opportunity to challenge the request."

ADAMS v. BOARD OF GOVERNORS OF THE FEDERAL RESERVE BOARD

United States Court of Appeals, Eighth Circuit, 1988.
855 F.2d 1336.

Gibson, Circuit Judge.

The issue in this case is whether the Board of Governors of the Federal Reserve System was subject to the procedural requirements of the Right to Financial Privacy Act, 12 U.S.C. §§ 3401–3422 (1982), when it reviewed financial records of Stephen Adams, Alfred T. Burke and Merritt Gates maintained by American National Bank of St. Paul, Minnesota, on three occasions in 1982 and 1983. These records related to loans made by American National to these individuals for purchases of voting stock in Bank of Montana Systems, a bank holding company. Through these urchases, Adams ultimately obtained control over Montana Systems. The rict court granted summary judgment and ruled that the Board was ot from the Financial Privacy Act because it had reviewed the records in the exercise of its supervisory functions with respect to American National and Montana Systems, see 12 U.S.C. § 3413(b), and because American National was required to report the information under the Change in Bank Control Act, 12 U.S.C. § 1817(j) (1982). See 12 U.S.C. § 3413(d). On appeal Adams, Burke and Gates argue that the Board examined the records for the purpose of investigating Adams personally, and that this renders the supervisory agency exception of section 3413(b) inapplicable. They also argue that section 3413(d) applies only to withholding of records or information, and that American National fully complied with the reporting requirements of the Change in Control Act. We affirm the judgment entered by the district court. * * *

The Right to Financial Privacy Act provides that, subject to specified exceptions, "no Government authority may have access to or obtain copies of, or the information contained in the financial records of any customer from a financial institution" unless certain procedural requirements, set forth in sections 3404 through 3408, are satisfied. 12 U.S.C. § 3401. Among the exceptions is that provided in section 3413(b), which states: "Nothing in this chapter prohibits examination by or disclosure to any supervisory agency of financial records or information in the exercise of its supervisory, regulatory, or monetary functions with respect to a financial institution." In addition, section 3412(d) provides that "[n]othing in this chapter prohibits any supervisory agency from exchanging examination reports or other information with another supervisory agency." Supervisory agency is defined, in section 3401(6), to include the Board and the Comptroller to the extent that they have statutory authority to examine the financial condition or business operations of a particular financial institution. The questions before us, therefore, are whether the Board and the Comptroller had statutory authority to examine American National or Montana Systems when they exchanged the American National loan files of Adams, Burke and Gates, and whether the Board was exercising such authority when it later examined these files directly. * * *

Under the Bank Holding Company Act, 12 U.S.C. §§ 1841–1850 (1982), the Board has general authority to supervise and regulate the financial condition and business operations of bank holding companies such as Montana Systems, e.g., 12 U.S.C. § 1844(b), (e), and it may examine such companies and their subsidiaries under 12 U.S.C. § 1844(c). In addition, the Change in Control Act gives the Board specific authority to approve or disapprove acquisitions of control of bank holding companies proposed by any person, "acting directly or indirectly or through or in concert with one or more other persons * * *." 12 U.S.C. § 1817(j)(1). The Board may disapprove such acquisitions if "the financial condition of any acquiring person is such as might jeopardize the financial stability of the bank or prejudice the interests of the depositors of the bank." 12 U.S.C. § 1817(j)(7)(C). With these powers, there is no question that the Board is a supervisory agency with respect to Montana Systems under section 3401(6), and that it has particular authority to supervise Adams' acquisition of control and to review his financial condition insofar as it may affect the company's financial stability.

We are also satisfied that the Board was "exercising" this authority within the meaning of section 3413(b) when it reviewed the American National loan files of Adams, Burke and Gates relating to their purchases of Montana Systems stock. The record makes clear that the Board's ultimate concern with regard to Adams' acquisition was to ensure the safety and soundness of Montana Systems and its subsidiary banks, and that the Board was particularly concerned with the level of Adams' debt financing. The Board's notice of charges alleged that if Adams acquired control of a majority of Montana Systems' voting stock and the election of a majority of its directors, he would be capable of diverting funds from the company or its subsidiary banks by increasing dividend payments and management fees, authorizing unwarranted loans, or other means to meet his debt service requirements. The Board further alleged that such action could prejudice the company, its other shareholders, its subsidiary banks, and their depositors. The record also demonstrates that the purpose of the Board's examinations of the American National loan files was to monitor and verify Adams' compliance with his commitment to the Board, which was an express condition of the Board's decision to approve his acquisition and was explicitly designed to limit his debt service requirements. These concerns are well within the scope of the Board's supervisory authority with respect to Montana Systems under the Bank Holding Company Act, e.g., 12 U.S.C § 1844(e), and the Change in Control Act, e.g., 12 U.S.C. § 1817(j)(7)(C). * * *

Subsequent legislation directed at money laundering limited the privacy expectations of bank customers vis-a-vis the government when there was suspected criminal activity. The following case demonstrates the interplay between RFPA, the Electronic Communication Privacy Act of 1986 (ECPA), 18 U.S.C.A. § 2501 et seq., and the Annunzio–Wylie Anti–Money Laundering Act of 1992, 31 U.S.C.A. § 5318(g).

LOPEZ v. FIRST UNION NATIONAL BANK OF FLORIDA

United States Court of Appeals, Eleventh Circuit, 1997.
129 F.3d 1186.

CARNES, CIRCUIT JUDGE.

* * * The FedWire Fund Transfer System is an electronic funds transfer system which permits large dollar fund transfers by computer-to-computer communications between banks. First Union is a bank within the FedWire Fund Transfer System and uses "electronic storage" to maintain the contents of an electronic funds transfer. On September 2, 1993, and November 30, 1993, First Union received an electronic wire transfer of funds for credit to Lopez's account. On both occasions, First

Union provided United States law enforcement authorities with access to the contents of those electronic transfers. First Union made these disclosures based solely on the "verbal instructions" of federal law enforcement authorities.

On February 3, 1994, a United States Magistrate Judge issued a seizure warrant directing First Union to freeze Lopez's account and conduct an inventory of it. Pursuant to the seizure warrant, First Union again provided United States law enforcement authorities access to the contents of the electronic funds transfers sent to Lopez that were being held in electronic storage. On June 6, 1995, First Union surrendered the $270,887.20 balance of Lopez's First Union account to the United States. The United States subsequently filed a civil forfeiture case against Lopez, which was resolved by a stipulation that $108,359 of Lopez's account was forfeited to the United States while $162,532.20 was returned to her.* * *

In 1986, Congress clarified the existence of privacy rights in electronic communications by enacting the [Electronic Communication Privacy Act, 18 U.S.C. § 2501 et seq.] ECPA, which provides "protection against the unauthorized interception of electronic communications." Sen. Rep. No. 99–541 at 3555. Among other things, the ECPA defines the conditions in which an electronic communications service may divulge the contents of electronic communications, see, e.g., 18 U.S.C. § 2702; 18 U.S.C. 2511, defines the conditions in which the government is entitled to access an individual's electronic communications, see 18 U.S.C. § 2703, and provides a civil cause of action for anyone injured by a violation of the act's substantive provisions, see 18 U.S.C. 2707.

In counts I and II of her complaint, Lopez alleges that First Union violated her rights under the ECPA. In count I, she specifically alleges that First Union violated 18 U.S.C. § 2702(a)(1), which provides that "a person or entity providing an electronic communication service to the public shall not knowingly divulge to any person or entity the contents of a communication while in electronic storage by that service." The complaint alleges that First Union provided an electronic communication service and that First Union provided the United States access to "the contents of information in electronic storage, including the contents of electronic communications pertaining to ... Lopez."

First Union contends that count I fails to state a viable claim under 18 U.S.C. § 2702(a)(1), because it is not an electronic communication service. We reject that contention which amounts to nothing more than a denial of the allegations in Lopez's complaint. Accepting all allegations in the complaint as true as we are required to do at this stage, we conclude that Count I states a violation of 18 U.S.C. § 2702(a)(1).[47]

---

47. [n.2] Nor does the fact that Congress amended the ECPA in 1996 to specifically exclude electronic funds transfers from the definition of an "electronic communication," see 18 U.S.C. § 2510(15) (1996), prevent Count I from stating a claim under § 2702(a)(1). That amendment did not take effect until 1996, well after the events giving rise to this case.

In count II, Lopez alleges that First Union infringed her rights under the ECPA by violating 18 U.S.C. § 2703 and 18 U.S.C. § 2711(3)(a). Section 2703 defines the conditions in which an electronic communication service may disclose electronic communications to the government. If the electronic communication service has held the contents of an electronic communication in electronic storage for one hundred eighty days or less, it may disclose that electronic communication to the government only pursuant to a federal or state warrant. See 18 U.S.C. § 2703(a). In count II, Lopez alleges that, on the same day funds were electronically transferred to her account, First Union disclosed contents of those electronic funds transfers in electronic storage pursuant to "verbal instructions" instead of a warrant. She also alleges that the disclosures were made on the same day that funds were electronically transferred to her account, which means the communication disclosed had been held in electronic storage for less than one hundred eighty days. Those allegations are sufficient to state a prima facie claim under 18 U.S.C. § 2703.

However, the allegations of count II of the complaint are not sufficient to state a claim under 18 U.S.C. § 2511(3)(a). That section provides that "an electronic communication service . . . shall not intentionally divulge the contents of any communication . . . *while in transmission* on that service to any person or entity other than an addressee or intended recipient of such communication." 18 U.S.C. § 2511(3)(a) (emphasis added). That proscription is not violated unless the communication is divulged "while in transmission." Neither count II nor any other part of the complaint alleges that First Union disclosed Lopez's electronic communications "while in transmission." Instead, count II alleges that First Union disclosed the contents of electronic communications held in electronic storage.

Alleging that First Union disclosed a communication held in "electronic storage," which violates § 2702(a)(1), is not equivalent to alleging that First Union disclosed a communication in "transmission," which would violate § 2511(3)(a). Because the complaint does not allege that First Union disclosed communications while in transmission, it fails to state a claim under § 2511(3)(a).

In United States v. Miller, 425 U.S. 435, 443 (1976), the Supreme Court held that individuals have no Fourth Amendment expectation of privacy in their financial records while those records are in the hands of third parties. That decision prompted Congress to enact the Right to Financial Privacy Act, 12 U.S.C. §§ 3401 et seq., ("the RFPA"), which provides individuals with some privacy rights in financial records that are in the hands of third parties. Among other things, the RFPA defines the conditions in which financial institutions may disclose an individual's financial records, see 12 U.S.C. § 3403, defines the conditions in which government officials may access an individual's financial records, see 12 U.S.C. § 3402, and provides a civil cause of action for anyone injured by a violation of the act's substantive provisions, see 12 U.S.C. § 3417.

In count III of her complaint, Lopez alleges First Union violated her rights under the RFPA by disclosing her financial records under conditions not authorized by the RFPA. First Union does not argue that Lopez has failed to allege a prima facie violation of the RFPA. Instead, it contends that count III should be dismissed because the alleged disclosures are protected by 12 U.S.C. § 3403(c), another section of the RFPA. Under § 3403(c), a financial institution possessing information relevant to a possible violation of law involving one of its accounts is permitted to make a disclosure of that information to law enforcement. However, the disclosure permitted is limited to the name of the account holder and "the nature of any suspected illegal activity." 12 U.S.C. § 3403(c). Because the complaint alleges that First Union went beyond that and disclosed actual financial records pertaining to Lopez's account (i.e., the electronic funds transfers communications, the contents of which were held in electronic storage), First Union's alleged disclosures are not protected by 12 U.S.C. § 3403(c). Accordingly, count III of Lopez's complaint states a claim under the RFPA.

The Annunzio–Wylie Anti–Money Laundering Act of 1992, 31 U.S.C. § 5318(g), provides * * * "[t]he [Treasury] Secretary may require any financial institution * * * to report any suspicious transaction relevant to a possible violation of law or regulation." * * * The three safe harbors provided by § 5318(g)(3) supply an affirmative defense to claims against a financial institution for disclosing an individual's financial records or account-related activity. Financial institutions are granted immunity from liability for three different types of disclosures:

(i) A disclosure of any possible violation of law or regulation,

(ii) A disclosure pursuant to § 5318(g) itself, or

(iii) A disclosure pursuant to any other authority.

The district court dismissed Lopez's complaint after concluding that the safe harbor provisions of § 5318(g)(3) protected First Union's disclosures of her account activity. Lopez contends that the district court's holding is erroneous for two reasons. First, she contends that § 5318(g)(3)'s safe harbor provisions apply only to disclosures of currency transactions. If that is true, First Union's disclosure of electronic transfers and the contents of transfers held in electronic storage are not protected by any of the safe harbor provisions of § 5318(g)(3). Second, Lopez contends that even if the Act does cover more than currency transactions, First Union's disclosures do not fall within one of the three categories of disclosures for which § 5318(g)(3) grants immunity. * * *

Lopez's contention that § 5318(g)(3) protects disclosures of currency transactions only is at odds with the text and purpose of the Annunzio–Wylie Act. The text of § 5318(g)(3) neither explicitly nor implicitly suggests that Congress intended to limit the safe harbor to disclosures of currency or to any specific kind of transaction. To the contrary, the text of that subdivision indicates Congress deliberately did *not* limit the safe harbor to disclosure of any specific type of transaction. For example,

§ 5318(g)(3) provides that a financial institution is entitled to immunity for a disclosure of "*any* possible violation of law." 31 U.S.C. § 5318(g)(3) (emphasis added). As we have recently had occasion to explain, when used in a statute, "the adjective 'any' is not ambiguous; it has a well-established meaning." * * * Thus § 5318(g)(3) protects disclosure of a violation of law regardless of whether it involves a cash transaction, electronic transfers, or any other type of transaction. Section 5318(g)(3)'s scope is not limited merely to disclosures of currency transactions.

Moreover, we agree with the district court that the purpose underlying the Act is inconsistent with Lopez's proposed construction. The district court reasoned as follows:

> [A]ccording to the comments of Congressman Neal regarding the enactment of 31 U.S.C. § 5318(g), banks have long been encouraged to report suspicious transactions to the appropriate authorities. See Cong.Rec. E57–02 (1993). Therefore, to ensure compliance from the banks, the safe harbor provision was added in order to protect a bank when it reports a suspicious transaction. Id. "The goal of this new law is to have banks work with international efforts to stop the global movement of drug money. Money laundering is an international problem. Money knows no borders and flows freely from one country to another. The United States has long recognized that, and has worked hard to ensure cooperation from foreign governments and financial institutions to assure that money launderers have no place to hide." Id.

> The Court finds that if Congress intended to limit this statute solely to "currency transactions" as asserted by Plaintiff, it would severely restrict the ability of a bank to report suspicious transactions without the fear of liability. As Plaintiff notes in her response to Defendant's motion, "[i]n 1994, some 72 million fund transfers with a total value of $211 trillion were moved over Fedwire." Thus, the effectiveness of the anti-money laundering act would be substantially limited if it applied only to cash transactions, since electronic fund transfers, the contents of which are held in electronic storage, are the means by which large dollar funds are transferred between the Federal Reserve and the service providers (i.e., originating banks, intermediary banks, and beneficiary banks)

Lopez v. First Union National Bank, 931 F. Supp. 860, 864 (S.D. Fla. 1996). * * *

The Annunzio–Wylie Act does not provide a financial institution blanket immunity for any disclosure of an individual's financial records. Instead, a financial institution is entitled to immunity only if its disclosure falls within one of the three safe harbors set forth in § 5318(g)(3). Lopez's complaint alleges that First Union disclosed Lopez's financial records twice in response to nothing more than "verbal instructions" of government officials and once pursuant to a seizure warrant. Under the facts alleged in Lopez's complaint, First Union's two disclosures in response to "verbal instructions" of government officials do not fit within any of § 5318(g)(3)'s three safe harbors. However, its disclosure pursuant to the seizure warrant is protected by § 5318(g)(3)'s third safe harbor.

The first safe harbor provision protects a financial institution's "disclosure of a possible violation of law or regulation." 31 U.S.C. § 5318(g)(3). As the use of the adjective "possible" indicates, a financial institution's disclosure is protected even if it ultimately turns out there was no violation of law. In order to be immune from liability, it is sufficient that a financial institution have a good faith suspicion that a law or regulation may have been violated, even if it turns out in hindsight that none was. By extending immunity to a financial institution's disclosure of a suspected violation of law or regulation, the first safe harbor encourages financial institutions to voluntarily play a role in combating money laundering and other crimes.

The problem for First Union at this stage of the litigation is that it is stuck with the allegations of the complaint. Those allegations do not show that First Union had a good faith suspicion that a law or regulation may have been violated. * * * First Union contends, however, that the first safe harbor should protect disclosures made in response to "verbal instructions" of government officials. It argues that law enforcement's demand for financial records should, by itself, be sufficient to give a financial institution a good faith basis to suspect a possible violation of law or regulation. The hidden premise of that argument is that Congress intended the first safe harbor to protect disclosures made pursuant to government officials' unexplained request or unvarnished instructions for financial records. That premise is flawed.

As we will discuss below, the second and third safe harbors protect from liability in situations where the government has and exercises the legal authority to demand disclosure of financial records. If we accepted First Union's premise that Congress intended the first safe harbor to protect disclosures made pursuant to any and all government demands, it would render the other two safe harbor provisions superfluous. * * *

The second safe harbor provision protects a financial institution's "disclosure pursuant to this subsection." 31 U.S.C. § 5318(g)(3). Disclosures "pursuant to this subsection" are disclosures required by the Office of the Treasury Secretary under the rule-making authority vested in the Treasury Secretary by 31 U.S.C. § 5318(g)(1) * * *. In February 1996, the Treasury Secretary issued regulations under this sub-section. See 31 C.F.R. § 103.21 (1996). * * *

However, the complaint alleges that First Union's disclosures occurred in 1993 and 1994. Because the Treasury Secretary's regulations under § 5318(g)(1) were not in effect at the time those alleged disclosures were made, the second safe harbor provision cannot immunize First Union's disclosures.

The third safe harbor provision protects a financial institution's disclosure pursuant to "any other authority." 31 U.S.C. § 5318(g)(3).

Because the second safe harbor protects disclosures pursuant to the legal authority of the Treasury Secretary's regulations, "other authority" means authority other than the Treasury Secretary's regulations. The "other authority" must be *legal* authority, because authority means "[r]ight to exercise powers," Black's Law Dictionary 133 (6th Ed. 1991), and in our system based on rule of law, the right to exercise power is derived from law, e.g., statutes, regulations, court orders, etc. Hence, for a financial institution's disclosure to fall within the confines of the third safe harbor, the financial institution must be able to point to a statute, regulation, court order, or other source of law that specifically or impliedly authorized the disclosure. If it cannot do so, the disclosure is not entitled to the protection of the safe harbor.

* * * Clearly, a disclosure in response to a seizure warrant is protected by the third safe harbor. The seizure warrant represented a judicial determination that the government had a legal right to obtain Lopez's financial records. First Union was neither required nor permitted to sit in review of the court's legal determination. It is immune from any liability for any disclosures made pursuant to the seizure warrant, which was issued on February 3, 1994.

However, First Union's earlier disclosures are a different matter, because disclosures in response to nothing more than the "verbal instructions" of government officials are not protected by the third safe harbor. * * *

In sum, we hold that First Union's disclosures of Lopez's financial records in response to nothing more than the "verbal instructions" of government officials are not protected by § 5318(g)(3)'s safe harbors, except that its disclosure pursuant to the seizure warrant is protected by the third safe harbor. * * *

———————

See also Coronado v. BankAtlantic Bancorp., Inc., 222 F.3d 1315 (11th Cir. 2000) (holding that a grand jury subpoena of an individual's private financial records was proper authority for the financial institution to release the records under the Annunzio–Wylie safe harbor provisions). The Eleventh Circuit's conclusion in *Lopez* that the safe harbor only applied if the financial institution had "a good faith suspicion that a law or regulation had been violated," *Lopez*, 129 F.3d at 1192–93, was rejected in Lee v. Bankers Trust Co., 166 F.3d 540 (2d Cir. 1999) (excerpted in Chapter 14). The *Lee* court stated "the safe harbor provision of the Annunzio–Wylie Act does not limit protection to disclosures based on a good faith belief that a violation has occurred." 166 F.3d at 544–45. The *Lee* court's position was adopted by the First Circuit in Stoutt v. Banco Popular de Puerto Rico, 320 F.3d 26 (1st Cir. 2003). Chapter 14 discusses money laundering restrictions and the requirement that banks report the suspicious activities of their customers to bank regulators.

The USA Patriot Act was signed by President Bush on October 26, 2001, in the wake of the devastating acts of terrorism that struck the United States on September 11, 2001. This Act, discussed in greater detail in Chapter 14, amended the RFPA to exempt from RFPA production and disclosure requests from government authorities authorized to conduct investigations related to Federal criminal law.

B. DISCLOSURE TO PRIVATE PARTIES

Disclosure of financial information to credit reporting agencies is regulated by the Fair Credit Reporting Act of 1970 (FCRA), 15 U.S.C.A. § 1681–1681f. Disclosure of financial information to a financial institution's affiliates and non-affiliates is addressed in the Gramm–Leach–Bliley Act of 1999, 15 U.S.C.A. §§ 6801–6827.

DAVID W. RODERER
TENTATIVE STEPS TOWARD FINANCIAL PRIVACY

4 N.C. Banking Inst. 209 (2000).

Until [November 1999], no federal law purported to ensure the privacy of personal financial information routinely entrusted by individuals to their bankers and other financial services providers. In most part, the concept of privacy pertaining to personal financial information has remained legally undeveloped, and seemingly beyond public consciousness or concern. In the waning hours at the last Congressional session, however, that changed. Spurred by the alleged misuse of account information by one lender, Congress enacted a hydra-headed regulatory scheme with a mandate to establish minimum federal safeguards for the capture, use, and sharing of financial information about customers by a wide range of businesses. Belatedly engrafted onto the provisions of the financial services modernization law, now formally known as the Gramm–Leach–Bliley Act, the new federal policy regime builds upon recent legal developments and bank regulatory pronouncements that sought to encourage certain financial services providers to voluntarily adopt and abide by announced privacy standards. * * *

The new federal law, embodied in Title V of the Gramm–Leach–Bliley Act, is comprised of five elements:

- an "affirmative and continuing obligation" is purportedly established for each financial institution "to respect the privacy of its customers and to protect the security and confidentiality" of customers' non-public personal information;

- a written privacy policy is mandated to be adopted and disclosed by each financial institution that transfers non-public personal information to unaffiliated entities, except as authorized by the new law;

- an "opt out" mechanism is required to be provided to individual customers concerning information transfers to unaffiliated parties, subject to various exceptions;

- the transfer of account numbers and access codes to telemarketers and other unaffiliated third parties is prohibited, except to credit bureaus; and

- a prohibition on pretext calling, or customer "identity theft," to obtain personal financial information through false or fraudulent means. * * *

The federal privacy safeguards are honeycombed with exceptions, leaving the new regime, despite its reassuring public appearance, to be significantly less than comprehensive. Most conspicuously, the privacy provisions of the new law do not apply to all consumer information, but only to so-called "non-public personal information." The term appears broadly inclusive: encompassing all personally identifiable financial information that is provided to a financial institution by a customer, or results from any transaction with the customer, or is otherwise obtained by the financial institution. However, the term does not include information covered by one of several statutory exemptions.

Seemingly most enormous is the exemption of all "public information," which at least one legal commentator has already speculated may exclude any information available over the Internet. Moreover, all information "derived from" public information is exempted as well. Those exclusions, in particular, blithely ignore the substantial threat to privacy posed, not by access to specific bits of information, but rather by the compilation and sharing through modern technologies of otherwise available data affecting individuals—the development of which is arguably the greater threat to privacy, and is yet unaffected by the new law.

Moreover, the full range of federal privacy safeguards does not apply to information sharing by financial institutions with either affiliates or third-party providers and servicers of the institution. A disclosure of an institution's privacy policies is mandated in order for an institution to share information with third parties, including aligned marketers, but prior notice is not required. In addition, so long as a financial institution discloses that it will share customer information with its third-party service providers, its customers are given no way under the new law to opt out of or prohibit such sharing. The statutory requirement that an institution enter into confidentiality agreements with service providers with whom it shares customer information is likely of little or no benefit to bank customers not party to such agreements. * * *

The enactment of the new law was heralded by many as effecting sweeping protections for consumer privacy. In signing the new law, President Clinton cautioned, however, against assuming it to be the final word on the subject. The financial services industry and its very effective advocates are likely to be disappointed, however, in any hope that the federal law will establish enduring, uniform standards under which business can be conducted without further disruptive legal and regulatory encumbrances. * * *

One reason for forming an FHC is to enjoy the benefits of cross-marketing the products of the commonly owned affiliates. Concerns about customer privacy of financial information potentially endangered the cross-marketing advantages for FHCs. After long debate, Congress adopted Title V of GLBA, which sets forth various requirements designed to protect the privacy of customers of financial institutions. 15 U.S.C.A. § 6801. Financial institutions are defined as institutions, "the business of which is engaging in financial activities as described in section 1843(k) of Title 12," 15 U.S.C.A. § 6809(3)(A). GLBA preserves the ability of an FHC to share customer information among its affiliates. 15 U.S.C.A. § 6802(a). Customers may, however, opt out of having their financial information shared with non-affiliates. 15 U.S.C.A. § 6802(b)(1)(B). The opt out right must be given to a customer along with the institution's privacy policy when a new customer relationship is established and annually thereafter. States may adopt more stringent privacy regulations than those set forth in GLBA, and a more stringent state scheme will control. 15 U.S.C.A. § 6807.

A handful of states have statutes that require a consumer to "opt in" before the consumer's financial institution may share information about the consumer with others. The Federal Trade Commission (FTC)[48] considered the effect of a Connecticut statute, Section 36a–42, which, subject to certain exceptions, prohibits the disclosure of "financial records" to "any person" unless the customer has authorized the disclosure. GLBA preserves a state statute that is not "inconsistent" with the privacy provisions of GLBA. 15 U.S.C. § 6807(a). The FTC determined that the Connecticut statute is not inconsistent with GLBA since a financial institution may comply with both the state statute and the federal statute.

> Thus where Connecticut law prohibits disclosure and federal law permits disclosure, a Connecticut financial institution can comply with both laws by not disclosing the consumer's nonpublic personal information. Likewise, where federal law prohibits disclosure and state law permits disclosure, the financial institution can comply with both laws by not disclosing the information. Here, compliance by Connecticut financial institutions with both the federal and state requirements is not physically impossible.

FTC Preemption Determination, June 7, 2002. <www.ftc.gov/privacy/glbact/conn020607.htm>. Interestingly, the FTC did not apply 15 U.S.C. § 6807(b) to afford the "greater protection under State law," since it found that § 6807(b) need only be resorted to if the state statute is "inconsistent" with GLBA.

Congress enacted the Fair Credit Reporting Act (FCRA), 15 U.S.C. § 1681, to reduce abuses in the use of credit reports that are relied upon

---

48. The FTC enforces consumer protection laws at the federal level, including antitrust laws, to ensure that markets are free from restrictions that harm consumers and that consumers are not subject to fraud, or unfair or deceptive business practices. The FTC enforces the GLBA privacy provisions and the FCRA as to entities subject to those laws that are not otherwise regulated by one of the federal bank regulatory agencies.

widely by firms that extend consumer credit. The statute allows consumers to examine the contents of their files and correct any inaccuracies. The Consumer Credit Reporting Reform Act of 1996 revised almost every section of FCRA. It requires consumer lenders to provide notice of adverse action on a credit decision where the decision was based on information shared with other creditors, and preempts most state laws governing credit information sharing.

In Bank of America, N.A. v. Daly City, 279 F.Supp.2d 1118 (N.D. Cal. July 29, 2003) (judgment later vacated and appeal dismissed), Bank of America and Wells Fargo challenged several municipal ordinances requiring customers of financial institutions to "opt in" before their information could be shared with affiliates or with non-affiliates. The court found that FCRA "expressly preempt[ed] State laws that impose a requirement or prohibition on information-sharing among affiliates," and "prohibited States from providing any additional protection to consumers in that context." In the court's view, "state and local governments are free to enact law affording some protection to consumer privacy greater than that provided by federal law," under GLBA, "but not with regard to the disclosure of information to affiliates."

The FCRA preemption provision relied on in the Bank of America case was set to expire on January 1, 2004, but was extended by Congress in the Fair and Accurate Credit Transactions Act of 2003 (FACT Act). See 15 U.S.C.A. § 1681t.[49]

A California state statute (SB1), that went into effect July 1, 2004, provided consumers a right to opt-out of having their financial information shared with affiliates and opt-in to consent to the disclosure of financial information to non-affiliates. Since GLBA defers to stricter state privacy statutes, in American Bankers Association v. Lockyer, 412 F.3d 1081 (9th Cir. 2005), the opt-in requirement was challenged under the FCRA, as amended by the FACT Act. The federal law as amended provides that state law may not interfere with the "exchange of *information* among persons affiliated by common ownership or common corporate control." 15 U.S.C. § 1861t(b)(2) (emphasis added). The Ninth Circuit held that the California statute was preempted by FCRA insofar as the California statute attempts to regulate the communication of "information" between affiliates as it is used in FCRA. FCRA information includes information about "creditworthiness, credit standing, credit capacity, character, general reputation, personal characteristics or mode of living." 15 U.S.C. § 1681a(d)(1). The court remanded to the district court to determine whether, after applying this definition of "information," any portion of the California statute survives preemption.

On remand, the district court concluded that the state's "affiliate sharing provision does not survive preemption and, even if some limited applications could be saved, they cannot be severed from the remainder of

---

49. The FACT Act also presents the federal response to the growing problems associated with identity theft.

the statute." American Bankers Association v. Lockyer, 2005 WL 2452798 (E.D. Cal. 2005).

QUESTIONS AND NOTES

1. The federal financial institution regulators have issued regulations regarding their enforcement of the GLBA privacy policy. Under Dodd–Frank, however, the new Bureau of Consumer Financial Protection (BCFP) has the exclusive rulemaking authority for the GLBA privacy provisions.

2. Find the privacy policy your financial institution sent you. If you did not save the brochure or pamphlet describing the privacy policy you can probably obtain a copy from your financial institution's web site. What must you do to opt out of having your information shared with non-affiliates? Should you exercise this right? Some institutions have elected not to provide an opt-out notice because they do not share customer information with non-affiliates. Why might some institutions have adopted this policy? Is there anything, other than interest in protecting customer information, that might justify such a decision? Some institutions have announced they do not share information even within the FHC.

Many consumers have not taken advantage of available opt-out provisions. Perhaps the privacy notices disseminated by financial institutions are not user-friendly. See Eric Poggemiller, Note, The Consumer Response to Privacy Provisions in Gramm–Leach–Bliley: Much Ado About Nothing? 6 N.C. Banking Inst. 617 (2002).

The federal banking agencies, the SEC, the FTC, and the CFTC issued an Interagency Proposal for Model Privacy Form Under the Gramm–Leach–Bliley Act, 72 Fed. Reg. 14940 (proposed Mar. 29, 2007), as corrected by 72 Fed. Reg. 16875 (Apr. 5, 2007), to provide a safe harbor for institutions that use the model form. The model form and safe harbor were mandated by the Regulatory Relief Act of 2006. Has the BCFP endorsed the use of a model form?

3. The FTC's attempt to require law firms to send privacy notices to their clients if they engage in financial activities such as tax preparation and estate planning was rebuffed in American Bar Ass'n v. Federal Trade Comm'n, 430 F.3d 457 (D.C. Cir. 2005). Lawyers and law firms that are service providers to financial institutions are still required to safeguard and protect any personal financial information they obtain in the course of their representation. This is consistent with a lawyer's existing duty of confidentiality pursuant to state rules of professional conduct.

4. Has your state adopted, or have under consideration, any GLBA-type privacy provisions?

SECTION 4. TECHNOLOGY, THE INTERNET, AND E–COMMERCE

A. TECHNOLOGY

The remarks below are from the then-Vice Chairman of the Federal Reserve Board of Governors and provide an overview of the evolving role of technology in the banking industry.

ROGER W. FERGUSON, JR.
INFORMATION TECHNOLOGY IN
BANKING AND SUPERVISION

Financial Services Conference 2000, St. Louis University.
October 20, 2000.
<www.federalreserve.gov/boarddocs/
speeches/2000/20001020.htm>.

* * * More than most other industries, financial institutions rely on gathering, processing, analyzing, and providing information in order to meet the needs of customers. Given the importance of information in banking, it is not surprising that banks were among the earliest adopters of automated information processing technology. The technological revolution in banking actually began in the 1950s, well before it began in most other industries, when the first automated bookkeeping machines were installed at a few U.S. banks. Automation in banking became common over the following decade as bankers quickly realized that much of their labor-intensive, information-handling processes could be automated on the computer. A second revolution occurred in the 1970s with the advent of electronic payments technology. Recognizing the importance of information security, the financial services industry during the late 1970s and early 1980s was also the first to implement encryption technologies on a widespread basis. The euphoria surrounding the Internet today seems very similar to that era, when the first nationwide credit card and electronic funds transfer systems were built.

As we could in earlier decades, we can identify three main reasons financial institutions are investing in technology. First, as in the 1950s and 1960s, they anticipate reductions in operating costs through such efficiencies as the streamlining back-office processing and the elimination of error-prone manual input of data. Second, institutions see opportunities to serve their current customers and attract new customers by offering new products and services as well as enhancing the convenience and value of existing products and services. Third, with more powerful data storage and analysis technologies, institutions are able to develop and implement sophisticated risk—and information-management systems and techniques.

While in hindsight it is clear that many of the earlier investments met those objectives, it is unclear whether today's most highly touted investments have done so, or will do so in the future. For example, the rush to set up Internet banks of a few years ago seems to have slowed, tempered by the experience of the few pioneers in this area, who found that although technology risks and hurdles are surmountable, the basic imperative of making a profit is often not. Smart cards are another example of an innovation that, although widely heralded several years ago as the next new personal banking device, has yet to be proved a convenient substitute for currency and coin.

Overall, the impact of the current technology investment boom in the financial services sector is difficult to assess. We know that productivity in financial services, like productivity in the rest of the service sector, is very hard to measure. The problem is due partly to the difficulty of measuring output accurately when the quality of service is changing as a result of such factors as greater convenience and speed and lower risk. Measuring output in the financial services sector is particularly controversial because so many services, such as deposits, provide services directly to customers and at the same time fund loans. Moreover, measuring the inputs used to produce outputs is difficult. We have not, for example, traditionally required from financial institutions, as part of the supervisory process, any reporting of technology-related investments and expenditures. Lack of consistent data significantly limits systematic industrywide or peer group analysis by supervisors or economic researchers that would shed light on some of these questions.

As I consider the very recent, admittedly mixed, experience of the financial services sector with technologies—looking at the examples of Internet banking, on-line banking, smart cards, and ATMs—it seems that several lessons emerge. First, many of the investments have been made to automate existing processes, but the challenge of fundamentally rethinking the process from start to finish—the so-called core process redesign that is necessary to reap the full benefit of the current generation of technologies—has proved daunting. This is in part because many of the services that banks are attempting to automate currently are "joint goods," that is, the production and consumption of the product or service depend on the inputs or behaviors of many players outside of the bank and even outside of the financial industry. For example, the flow of services from checks depends on a complex of economic actors, including consumers willing to write checks, merchants willing to accept them, and an infrastructure in place to clear and settle them. Attempting to automate part of the check process by imaging or to replace checks with a single instrument, such as the debit card, requires cooperation among all the organizations that support a checking transaction. Internet banks are another example of these interdependencies. Many Internet banks have discovered that they are using any savings in "brick and mortar" operating costs to pay "bounties," or fees, to other Internet sites that refer new customers and to operate call centers to field the customer inquiries that invariably arise.

Another lesson from the history of technology in banking is that so many of the costs in banking are shared across products, and even across customers. Therefore, an investment that might have a positive impact on one customer base or product may not have the desired impact on the overall cost base. I believe that the early history of ATMs illustrates this lesson. The ATM was originally introduced as a way to reduce costs of the branch network. Although the ATM succeeded in moving small-value withdrawal transactions from branches, that accounted for only a portion of the customers served and the transactions performed by a branch network. Therefore, early ATM networks added cost without substituting for branch networks. For ATMs to become truly economically attractive, they had to evolve to offer a fuller range of products for a greater proportion of bank customers. Indeed, ATMs now offer more services and more locations, and they have started to make a positive return on investment.

The third possible lesson from the history of technology in banking is that banking services may be a class of services for which demand and supply interact so that new supply creates additional demand. Clearly, creating different channels for retail access to banking services, such as branches, PC banking, phone banking, ATMs, and the Internet, has neither significantly reduced the demand for any of those channels nor led to significant bank cost savings. This situation may in part reflect banks' reluctance to use pricing as an incentive for customers to change their behavior and move to newer technologies. However, it may also reflect the fact that the increased convenience of these different channels is simply translating into a permanent increase in consumer welfare and not necessarily into a permanent increase in revenue or a permanent reduction in costs. In this regard, banks that are not early adopters will admit privately that their investments in new technologies for customer access are largely defensive measures. New channels, such as on-line banking, are not generally leading to increases in the customer base at banks that offer them; instead, customers (particularly the most sophisticated who have ready access to technology) have begun to expect these services and may readily switch providers if their expectations are not met. Thus, banks have recognized that they need to offer the conveniences of newer technologies merely to retain their existing customers.

Federal Reserve research has found an interesting caveat to the above statement: Banks that either are early adopters of new technologies or are particularly effective at using such technologies do have temporarily higher revenues but do not have cost savings. Revenue enhancements are the foundation of higher profitability. The elevation of profitability is expected to be temporary, however. As others adopt similar technologies, rates of return on new investment fall, and profitability for all banks returns to normal. The net result is an increase in consumer welfare but, as I have just stated, not a long-term reduction in cost or a long-term increase in profitability.

The fourth lesson is that the mixed effect of technology in banking more recently may simply reflect the fact that technology can replace relatively simple, repetitive functions, such as the basic calculations and internally oriented back-office support functions that were automated initially. But so much of banking still involves higher-level judgements. These are judgments that can be informed by the types of computations performed by computers, but ultimately they cannot be made by computers. Risk management, reserving policy and underwriting larger C & I loans are, it appears, areas in which technology is an important adjunct to the judgment of experienced managers but ultimately is not a replacement for the experience a banker brings to the undertaking. This is reflected in the fact that risk modeling seems to be further advanced for market risk than for credit risk.

We know that investments in newer technologies must be made to modernize existing operations, to face competitive challenges, and to meet customer expectations. Indeed, some of these investments will also be made in the hope of achieving cost savings and other efficiencies. However, I would suggest that bank management needs to enter these investments recognizing that the full benefits may not be gained quickly; may, if gained, be competed away; and may, indeed, not be captured at all. History teaches that costs may emerge long before expected revenues, and that operational risk can either decrease or increase as a result of making major technology investments. * * * [B]ank managers would be wise to monitor carefully the progress of large technology projects, marking major milestones clearly and holding technology management accountable. Given the size, complexity, and business risk of many modern technology investments, these investments clearly should be a top management interest and are a top management responsibility. * * *

In 1998, the Federal Circuit Court of Appeals injected patent law into banking by holding that business methods are patentable. State Street Bank & Trust Co. v. Signature Financial Group, Inc., 149 F.3d 1368 (Fed. Cir. 1998), cert. denied, 525 U.S. 1093 (1999). In *State Street* the court held that software implementing a mutual fund management business practice was patentable because it creates a "useful, concrete and tangible result." Before *State Street*, patents were issued only for an invention, machine or device. After *State Street*, many banks had to pay licensing fees to holders of patents on previously widely used business practices methods, many of which were embedded in bank proprietary software.[50] In 2005, Data Treasury filed suits against a number of banks alleging infringement of their patents on digital check processing technology. In 2010 in Bilski v. Kappos, 130 S.Ct. 3218 (2010), five justices rejected the *State Street* test. Bilski tried to patent the concept of hedging risk and the application of that hedging concept to energy markets. The Court found that the claims were not patentable because they are "attempts to patent

---

50. See Deborah Bach, AT & T patent Settlement Worries Financial Firms, Am. Banker, Jan. 5, 2001 (discussing AT & T's settlement agreement with an inventor who held patents on numerous systems commonly used by banks).

abstract ideas." The Court provided little guidance, however, with respect to what was an abstract idea and what was not. Several justices wanted to reject altogether the notion that business methods could be patentable, but this view was not embraced by a majority of the Court. The Court also rejected the Federal Circuit's en banc holding in *Bilski* that would find a process patentable *only if* "(1) it is tied to a particular machine or apparatus, or (2) it transforms a particular article into a different state or thing." This test may describe a category of patentable processes, the Court said, but it should not be used as the only test for patentability.

B. ELECTRONIC BANKING

Many banks offer banking services delivered via the Internet. "Bricks and clicks" is the characterization given to banks which have elected to offer banking services through the traditional branch system—the "bricks"—and to offer an additional point of customer access via an Internet web site—the "clicks." The number of U.S. households banking online continues to grow.

A few banks have been chartered with the express purpose of offering Internet-only access. Whether Internet account access is the optional or exclusive method of accessing the customer's bank account, similar issues are raised by the Internet presence: insuring the security and privacy of account information, and preventing fraudulent access to the account. For financial institutions doing business exclusively in cyberspace, there are also issues of where the bank is deemed located and what is an appropriate way to measure compliance with the Community Reinvestment Act (requiring that the bank meet the credit needs of the low and moderate income members of its local community). Internet only banks have met with less success that initially predicted. One such bank, the BestBank, failed in 1998. NetBank failed in 2007 as the result of faulty lending practices. At the time, it was the largest bank failure in fourteen years. In theory, the absence of multiple branches means that the operating costs of internet banks in terms of facilities and personnel are far less than the costs incurred by their brick and mortar competitors. These cost savings are passed on to customers in the form of lower loan rates and higher deposit interest rates. Some of the pioneering internet-only banks found, however, that customers demanded additional physical facilities such as ATMs, branches, or call centers. The resulting increases in costs undermined the ability to compete based on price.

FEDERAL FINANCIAL INSTITUTIONS EXAMINATION COUNCIL INFORMATION TECHNOLOGY EXAMINATION HANDBOOK E–BANKING

August 2003.

* * * [E]-banking is defined as the automated delivery of new and traditional banking products and services directly to customers through

electronic, interactive communication channels. E-banking includes the systems that enable financial institution customers, individuals or businesses, to access accounts, transact business, or obtain information on financial products and services through a public or private network, including the Internet. Customers access e-banking services using an intelligent electronic device, such as a personal computer (PC), personal digital assistant (PDA), automated teller machine (ATM), kiosk, or Touch Tone telephone. While the risks and controls are similar for the various e-banking access channels, this booklet focuses specifically on Internet-based services due to the Internet's widely accessible public network. Accordingly, this booklet begins with a discussion of the two primary types of

Internet websites: informational and transactional.

Informational websites provide customers access to general information about the financial institution and its products or services. Risk issues examiners should consider when reviewing informational websites include

- Potential liability and consumer violations for inaccurate or incomplete information about products, services, and pricing presented on the website;

- Potential access to confidential financial institution or customer information if the website is not properly isolated from the financial institution's internal network;

- Potential liability for spreading viruses and other malicious code to computers communicating with the institution's website; and

- Negative public perception if the institution's on-line services are disrupted or if its website is defaced or otherwise presents inappropriate or offensive material.

Transactional websites provide customers with the ability to conduct transactions through the financial institution's website by initiating banking transactions or buying products and services. Banking transactions can range from something as basic as a retail account balance inquiry to a large business-to-business funds transfer. * * *

Since transactional websites typically enable the electronic exchange of confidential customer information and the transfer of funds, services provided through these websites expose a financial institution to higher risk than basic informational websites. Wholesale e-banking systems typically expose financial institutions to the highest risk per transaction, since commercial transactions usually involve larger dollar amounts. In addition to the risk issues associated with informational websites, examiners reviewing transactional e-banking services should consider the following issues:

- Security controls for safeguarding customer information;

- Authentication processes necessary to initially verify the identity of new customers and authenticate existing customers who access e-banking services;

- Liability for unauthorized transactions;

- Losses from fraud if the institution fails to verify the identity of individuals or businesses applying for new accounts or credit online;

- Possible violations of laws or regulations pertaining to consumer privacy, anti-money laundering, anti-terrorism, or the content, timing, or delivery of required consumer disclosures; and

- Negative public perception, customer dissatisfaction, and potential liability resulting from failure to process third-party payments as directed or within specified time frames, lack of availability of online services, or unauthorized access to confidential customer information during transmission or storage. * * *

In addition to traditional banking products and services, financial institutions can provide a variety of services that have been designed or adapted to support e-commerce. * * * [T]he most common support services [are]: weblinking, account aggregation, electronic authentication, website hosting, payments for e-commerce, and wireless banking activities. * * *

[E-banking risks include:]

Transaction/Operations Risk. Transaction/Operations risk arises from fraud, processing errors, system disruptions, or other unanticipated events resulting in the institution's inability to deliver products or services. This risk exists in each product and service offered. The level of transaction risk is affected by the structure of the institution's processing environment, including the types of services offered and the complexity of the processes and supporting technology. * * *

Credit Risk. Generally, a financial institution's credit risk is not increased by the mere fact that a loan is originated through an e-banking channel. However, management should consider additional precautions when originating and approving loans electronically, including assuring management information systems effectively track the performance of portfolios originated through e-banking channels. * * *

Liquidity, Interest Rate, Price/Market Risks. Funding and investment-related risks could increase with an institution's e-banking initiatives depending on the volatility and pricing of the acquired deposits. The Internet provides institutions with the ability to market their products and services globally. Internet-based advertising programs can effectively match yield-focused investors with potentially high-yielding deposits. But Internet-originated deposits have the potential to attract customers who focus exclusively on rates and may provide a funding source with risk characteristics similar to brokered deposits. An institution can control this potential volatility and expanded geographic reach through its deposit contract and account opening practices, which might involve face-to-face meetings or the exchange of paper correspondence. * * *

Compliance/Legal Risk. Compliance and legal issues arise out of the rapid growth in usage of e-banking and the differences between electronic and paper-based processes. E-banking is a new delivery channel where the laws and rules governing the electronic delivery of certain financial institution products may be ambiguous or still evolving. * * *

Strategic Risk. A financial institution's board and management should understand the risks associated with e-banking services and evaluate the resulting risk management costs against the potential return on investment prior to offering e-banking services. Poor e-banking planning and investment decisions can increase a financial institution's strategic risk. Early adopters of new e-banking services can establish themselves as innovators who anticipate the needs of their customers, but may do so by incurring higher costs and increased complexity in their operations. Conversely, late adopters may be able to avoid the higher expense and added complexity, but do so at the risk of not meeting customer demand for additional products and services. * * *

Reputation Risk. An institution's decision to offer e-banking services, especially the more complex transactional services, significantly increases its level of reputation risk. * * *

QUESTIONS AND NOTES

1. The OCC's rules regarding the conduct of electronic banking activities by national banks may be found at 12 C.F.R. §§ 7.5000–.5010.

2. The OCC has approved a broad range of activities for national banks that fall in the general realm of e-banking. These approvals are detailed on a special section of the OCC's website, <www.occ.treas.gov/netbank/net bank.htm>.

3. E-commerce has invoked experiments with alternative payment systems such as electronic "coins" that may be downloaded from the customer's bank account to his computer's hard drive and stored value (or "smart") cards. Interestingly, such new methods of transferring payment may implicate the Stamp Payments Act of 1862, 18 U.S.C.A. § 336, discussed in Chapter 1, which makes the private issuance of any "note, check, memorandum, token, or other obligation, for a less sum than $1, intended to circulate as money or to be received or used in lieu of lawful money of the United States" a criminal offense. The government could enforce this act to discourage the creation of electronic money or it could enact new legislation to override the Act.

4. The Federal Electronic Signatures in Global and National Commerce Act of 2000 (E–Sign), 15 U.S.C.A. §§ 7001–06, 7021, 7031, provides that electronic signatures and electronic records will in most cases satisfy legal requirements for writings and signatures.

Many states have also enacted versions of the Uniform Electronic Transactions Act (UETA) which was sponsored by the National Conference of

Commissioners on Uniform State Laws. E–Sign contemplates that states, through legislation such as UETA, may add additional consumer protections that are consistent with the federal law. See R. David Whitaker, An Overview of Some Rules and Principles for Delivering Consumer Disclosures Electronically, 7 N.C. Banking Inst. 11 (2003); Jean Braucher, Replacing Paper Writings With Electronic Records in Consumer Transactions: Purposes, Pitfalls and Principles, 7 N.C. Banking Inst. 29 (2003).

5. The OCC approved an application by Zions First National Bank to establish an operating subsidiary to provide an online service for secure, web-based document storage and retrieval for both consumer and business customers. These electronic safety deposit boxes or "e-boxes" were approved by the OCC because providing physical safe deposit boxes has long been considered part of or incidental to the business of banking, and because pursuant to prior rulings national banks may use electronic means to perform any services expressly or incidentally authorized for national banks. OCC Conditional Approval No. 479 (July 27, 2001) (citing OCC Conditional Approval No. 289 (Oct. 2, 1998)).

6. In response to several high profile breaches of customer data security, the federal banking agencies issued the Interagency Guidance on Response Programs for Unauthorized Access to Customer Information and Customer Notice, 70 Fed. Reg. 15736 (Mar. 29, 2005). See also Interagency Guidelines Establishing Information Security Standards, Small Entity Compliance guide, available at <www.federalreserve.gov/boarddocs/press/bcreg/2005/20051214/attachment.pdf>. Still to be decided is how this guidance interacts with state laws requiring the institution to notify its customers of a data security breach. Over thirty states currently have breach notification laws. National standards would be preferred by banks operating in multiple states, but it remains to be seen whether Congress will ever be able to agree on the appropriate approach. See Satish M. Kini & James T. Shreve, Notice Requirements: Common Themes and Differences in the Regulatory and Legislative Responses to Data Security Breaches, 10 N.C. Banking Inst. 87 (2006).

CHAPTER FIVE

BANK ASSETS

■ ■ ■

The majority of most banks' assets are loans. Traditionally, most of a bank's income came from the interest earned on its loans. Other assets held by a bank may also contribute to earnings directly (such as investments) or indirectly (such as bank premises and office equipment). This chapter briefly discusses some of the non-loan assets commonly found on a bank's balance sheet, explores some of the general regulations that apply to bank loans, and considers some specific issues related to commercial lending. Regulations that pertain to consumer loans are discussed in Chapter 6.

SECTION 1. NON–LOAN ASSETS

A. REAL ESTATE

The largest non-loan asset owned by most banks is real estate. A national bank, however, is limited by 12 U.S.C.A. § 29, in the type and amount of real estate it may own to the real estate needed for its premises, and to real estate that it may have foreclosed upon in its lending business. The amount that a bank may have invested in its premises may not exceed the amount of the bank's capital stock. 12 U.S.C. § 371d. Section 371d also applies to state member banks. The real estate that a bank owns pursuant to foreclosure on defaulted loans is sometimes referred to as "other real estate owned," or OREO.

B. INVESTMENTS

National banks are specifically permitted to own, without limitation in amount, "Type I" investment securities. 12 U.S.C.A. § 24(Seventh); 12 C.F.R. pt. 1. Investment securities are marketable debt instruments that are not predominantly speculative in nature. Type I investment securities are obligations of the United States or general obligations of any state or political subdivision of the state. Type II investment securities include certain revenue bonds issued by a state. Type III investment securities may be issued by private issuers, and include corporate bonds as well as municipal revenue bonds and mortgage-backed securities. Type III securities must be of investment grade, or its credit equivalent, to be eligible for bank purchase. The Type II and Type III securities of any one obligor owned by a bank may not exceed 10% of the bank's capital stock and unimpaired surplus. These investment security ownership limitations apply also to state member banks pursuant to 12 U.S.C.A. § 335. The relevant provisions of 12 C.F.R. pt. 1 are included in the Statutory and Regulatory Supplement that accompanies this casebook.

MARX v. CENTRAN CORP.

United States Court of Appeals, Sixth Circuit, 1984.
747 F.2d 1536, *cert. denied*, 471 U.S. 1125 (1985).

CONTIE, CIRCUIT JUDGE.

* * * The parties stipulated to the following facts. Defendant Central National Bank of Cleveland (C.N.B.) is a national banking association chartered by the United States. C.N.B. is also a member of the Federal Reserve System. Defendant Centran is a bank holding company as defined in 12 U.S.C. § 1841(a). Centran owns all of the shares of common stock of C.N.B. and, in addition, owns all or substantially all of the stock of several other Ohio banks. Centran is incorporated in the state of Delaware and is qualified to do business in Ohio. Centran stock has been publicly traded since 1972. Marx bought 200 shares of Centran stock in 1978 on the open market. Centran has approximately 9,000 shareholders and has issued over 4,000,000 shares of common stock. The individual defendants are officers and members of the board of directors of Centran and C.N.B.

This litigation has its origins in an investment scheme undertaken by C.N.B. in 1980. The plan was to obtain leverage by incurring debt during a time of decreasing interest rates and using the assets acquired from the incurred liabilities to buy long-term, fixed-rate governmental obligations. Operating on the assumption that interest rates would fall, C.N.B. believed that the debt required to maintain this portfolio would eventually decrease. That is, the liability would be "rolled over" to progressively lower interest rates. At the same time, the rate of return on the governmental obligations, because it was fixed, would not be affected by the declining interest rates. It was also hoped that the market value of the governmental obligations would rise as interest rates fell.

As events turned out, interest rates did not fall but instead rose and the liabilities were "rolled over" in the wrong direction, increasing C.N.B.'s short-term liabilities. The rate of interest on the short-term liabilities eventually exceeded the rate of return from the investments they were used to maintain, creating a negative carrying cost. At the same time, the market value of the long-term, fixed-rate governmental obligations fell. This resulted in further losses to C.N.B. when it attempted to liquidate some of its investments. The net result was a loss to C.N.B. of over $50,000,000. These losses sustained by C.N.B. decreased the value of its stock and impaired its ability to pay dividends to Centran. As a result, the value of Centran's stock was diminished and Centran's ability to pay dividends was also restricted. * * *

The short-term liabilities which C.N.B. incurred in order to finance the purchase of the governmental obligations arose as follows. Although the money used to buy the securities was nominally "borrowed," the precise method of obtaining the funds was more complicated than that characterization might suggest. First, C.N.B. obtained "Federal Funds Purchased." Banks which are a part of the Federal Reserve System are required to maintain a minimum deposit overnight in Federal Reserve Banks to clear drafts. Banks which are short of the minimum overnight deposit at the end of a day often "buy" funds from banks which have a surplus. This benefits both banks. The bank which is short in its deposit account obtains the necessary funds through a simple transaction. Because the overnight accounts pay no interest, the "selling" bank obtains a return on its capital which it would otherwise lose. At the opening of business the next day, the "borrowing" bank "sells" back the funds to the "lending" bank and pays a charge for the use of the funds which amounts to interest. The second method of obtaining funds was through the use of Sale and Repurchase Agreements, informally known as Repos. When a bank wants a short-term secured loan, it may sell a security to a lender and at the same time agree to repurchase the security at a later date for a higher price. The lender is secured by owning the security and the bank has the use of the capital generated by the sale. The price differential between the sale and the repurchase amounts to an interest payment.

Marx's claims flow from these events. He claims that the investment scheme * * * violated several banking statutes and regulations as well as the directors' common law fiduciary duties. * * * Marx claims damages by reason of the diminution in value of his shares of Centran caused by the losses suffered by C.N.B. due to its investment portfolio. * * *

The district court held that Marx does have a direct and derivative cause of action for alleged violations of 12 U.S.C. § 24. This result is obviously correct. 12 U.S.C. § 93 (a) expressly provides that directors of national banks who "knowingly violate" the "provisions of this chapter" of title 12 of the United States Code, "shall be held liable in [their] personal and individual capacity for all damages which *the association, its shareholders, or any other person*, shall have sustained in consequence of such violation." Thus, it is "beyond dispute that under proper circumstances Section 93 creates a direct cause of action by the shareholders against the directors of a national bank." Harmsen v. Smith, 542 F.2d 496, 500 (9th Cir. 1976) (citing Chesbrough v. Woodworth, 244 U.S. 72 (1917)). Since § 24 is within "this chapter," that is, since both § 24 and § 93 are contained in chapter 2 of title 12 of the United States Code, it is clear that Marx may maintain a cause of action both directly and derivatively for the benefit of Centran for violations of § 24.

The district court correctly determined, however, that the defendants did not violate § 24. That statute provides, in pertinent part:

> * * * That the association *may purchase for its own account invest-
> ment securities under such limitations and restrictions as the Comp-
> troller of the Currency may by regulation prescribe.*

12 U.S.C. § 24(seventh) (emphasis added). The statute also provides some
specific limitations on a national bank's power to invest in securities. A
national bank may not hold investment securities of any single obligor in
excess of "10 per centum of its capital stock actually paid in and unimpaired and 10 per centum of its unimpaired surplus fund." Id. Section 24
exempts certain governmental obligations from the ten-percent limitation.

> The limitations and restrictions herein contained as to dealing in,
> underwriting and purchasing for its own account, investment securi-
> ties *shall not apply to obligations of the United States, or general
> obligations of any State or any political subdivision thereof. . . .*

Id. (emphasis added). The Comptroller of the Currency has provided
regulations implementing these statutory commands. The regulations
designate "obligations of the United States, or general obligations of any
State or of any political subdivision thereof," referred to in § 24(seventh),
as "Type I securities." See 12 C.F.R. § 1.3(c). Obligations which may not
be characterized as "obligations of the United States, or general obligations of a State or of a political subdivision thereof" are defined as Type
II or Type III securities. See id., § 1.3(d), (e). The regulations restate the
statutory command that Type I securities are not subject to the ten-
percent limitation but that Type II and III securities are. See 12 C.F.R.
§§ 1.4, 1.7.

The parties stipulated that the bulk of the investment portfolio in
question, "about 75%," consisted of Type I securities. As to the Type II
and Type III securities, "no single purchase approached the 10% limit."
The stipulation further provided that "the Court may assume no violation
of 12 C.F.R. 1.1 et seq. with respect to Type II and Type III Municipal
Bonds, and treat the Securities Portfolio increase in Municipal Bond
holding as though all purchases with short-term borrowings were purchases of Type I securities."

It is clear from these stipulations that no violation of § 24(seventh)
occurred. Most of the obligations purchased were not subject to the ten-
percent limitation and the remaining purchases did not exceed the ten-
percent limitation. The district court correctly held that the defendants
did not violate 12 U.S.C. § 24(seventh). * * *

UNITED STATES v. IGUCHI

United States Court of Appeals, Second Circuit, 1997.
1997 WL 593018 (unpublished).

KAPLAN, CIRCUIT JUDGE.

Toshihide Iguchi appeals from the district court's judgment of conviction following his guilty plea to one count of misapplication of bank funds
in violation of 18 U.S.C. § 656, one count of making false entries in bank

books and records in violation of 18 U.S.C. § 1005, one count of money laundering in violation of 18 U.S.C. § 1956(a)(1)(B)(i), two counts of conspiracy to commit various banking law crimes, each in violation of 18 U.S.C. § 371, and one count of forfeiture in violation of 18 U.S.C. § 982. Iguchi was sentenced to 48 months imprisonment, five years supervised release, a $2 million fine, $300 in special assessments, and directed to make restitution in the amount of $570,000.

From 1979 to 1995, Iguchi was the head of the Securities Custody Department of the New York branch of The Daiwa Bank, Ltd. (Daiwa), a Japanese banking institution. During much of that time, he was authorized by Daiwa to trade securities subject to established position and loss limits. Iguchi engaged in trading far beyond his limitations and suffered losses in excess of $1 billion. He concealed the losses from Daiwa pursuant to a complex scheme of selling securities without authorization and falsifying Daiwa's books and records. When appellant confessed his scheme of unauthorized trading and concealment to Daiwa officials in July 1995, his employer did not tell him to inform U.S. regulatory and law enforcement agencies, but instead directed Iguchi to continue concealing the losses. Several months later Daiwa disclosed its losses to U.S. law enforcement authorities. Iguchi's cooperation with the authorities during the course of their subsequent investigation in part led to the 24–count indictment brought against Daiwa. Daiwa pled guilty to 16 counts and paid a $340 million fine—the largest criminal fine in history.

On appeal, Iguchi challenges the district court's imposition of the $2 million fine, arguing that the record made clear his financial inability to pay such a large amount of money. See U.S.S.G. § 5E1.2(a) (mandating the imposition of a fine in all cases "except where the defendant establishes that he is unable to pay and is not likely to become able to pay any fine"). We have recognized that a sentencing court may impose a fine upon an indigent defendant based on the realistic possibility that the individual will be able to pay in the future, such as where the defendant committed a "highly publicized crime [and] might be able to generate future income from books or movies about [the] crime." United States v. Wong, 40 F.3d 1347, 1383 (2d Cir. 1994) (internal quotations omitted). Although the district court acknowledged Iguchi's financial limitations, it also implicitly recognized that he should be able to obtain employment in the future. In addition, the sentencing court acknowledged Iguchi's opportunity to make money "in a world driven by notoriety," in apparent recognition of the reported millions Barings Bank trader Nicholas Leeson earned on book and movie deals after committing crimes similar to Iguchi's. Thus, the imposition of a $2 million fine, to be paid in installments contingent upon Iguchi's future earnings, was not illegally imposed. * * *

The judgment is affirmed.

Former Fed Chairman Paul Volcker was selected to serve as the head of President Obama's Economic Recovery Advisory Board in the wake of the financial crisis. Volcker wanted to separate commercial banking from investment banking and to preclude commercial banks from owning or trading risky securities. Senate Banking Committee Chairman, Chris Dodd, adopted the Volcker approach in the Senate's financial reform bill. When the House and Senate conference met to resolve the differences among their bills, after a marathon twenty-two hours of negotiations on June 25, 2010 they cut back on the Volcker proposal.

Volker Rule §619 of Dodd Frank

The basic thrust of the resulting Volcker Rule, as set forth in Section 619 of the Dodd–Frank Act, is to restrict banking entities from proprietary trading and to ban certain bank relationships with hedge funds and private equity funds. These limitations are, however, subject to a variety of exemptions. The Act defines "proprietary trading" as engaging as a principal for the trading account of the bank in buying or selling any security, derivative, commodity contract, or option on any of the above, or any other security or financial instrument that will be designated by rule by the federal banking agencies, the SEC, and the CFTC. A "trading account" is an account used for acquiring securities and instruments "principally for the purpose of selling in the near term," Dodd–Frank Act, § 619, so holding the covered instruments for investment is permitted. A "banking entity" includes an FDIC-insured institution, a bank holding company, and any affiliate or subsidiary of an insured bank of bank holding company.[1]

Proprietary trading that's permitted

There are numerous exemptions from the bank on proprietary trading that are termed "permitted activities." These exemptions include transactions in: (1) U.S. government or agency obligations, obligations of GSEs (like Fannie Mae), and obligations of states or political subdivisions; (2) securities in connection with underwriting or market-making activities so long as consistent with the near term demand of clients and customers; (3) risk-mitigating hedging activities in connection with holdings of the banking entity; and (4) securities held on behalf of customers. Since a BHC may own an insurance company under GLBA, and the insurance company would also be considered a "banking entity" subject to Dodd–Frank's proprietary trading limitations, the Act also exempts from the ban, proprietary trading by any regulated insurance company or its affiliate for the insurance company's general account.

Dodd–Frank also bans a banking entity from acquiring or retaining an equity, partnership, or other ownership interest in or sponsoring a hedge fund or private equity fund. The funds that are covered by this bank include those from an issuer that would be considered an investment company under the Investment Company Act (ICA) but for an exemption under the ICA in Section 3(c)(1) (exempting funds with fewer than 100 beneficial owners in the U.S.), Section 3(c)(7) (exempting funds with

---

1. An institution that functions only in a trust or fiduciary capacity is not subject to the rule. A non-U.S. bank or bank holding company that has a U.S. insured depository institution subsidiary, branch, agency, or commercial lending company is subject to the rule's limitations.

owners who are considered "qualified purchasers" such as institutions and individuals with large investment portfolios), or such other funds designated by rule by the federal banking agencies, the CFTC, and the SEC. The Dodd–Frank Act bans on investments in these covered funds by banking entities, also prohibits banking entities from sponsoring such funds. A banking entity is a fund sponsor if it is (1) a "general partner, managing member or trustee of a fund," (2) able "to select or to control . . . a majority of the fund's directors, trustees, or management," or (3) shares a name or variation of a the name with the fund for marketing or other purposes.

The Volcker Rule's ban on banking entities investing in or sponsoring private equity and hedge funds is subject to several exemptions. There is an exemption that permits banking entities to make *de minimis* investments so long as the entity's aggregate investment in all covered funds is less than three percent of the bank's Tier 1 capital. There is a fiduciary exemption that permits a banking entity to sponsor a private equity or hedge fund and serve as a general partner or managing member, subject to numerous conditions, including that the banking entity provides investment advisory or fiduciary services, does not have an equity interest in the fund greater than the three percent *de minimis* amount, and the fund is offered only to customers of the banking entity. Banking entities are also permitted to invest in Small Business Investment Companies "designed primarily to promote the public welfare."

The exemptions that are afforded to the bank on proprietary trading and investing in or sponsoring covered funds will not be available if the exempt activity involves a "material conflict of interest," exposes the banking entity to "high risk" assets or trading strategies, poses a threat to the safety and soundness of the banking entity, or poses a threat to the financial stability of the U.S. The definitions of the terms in quotes will be determined by agency rulemaking.

A nonbank financial company designated as systemically significant by the FSOC is not a banking entity subject to the restrictions outlined above, but it is subject to more stringent capital adequacy requirements and FRB quantitative limits on proprietary trading and private equity and hedge fund activities.

Rulemaking to implement the Volcker Rule is to be completed by the federal banking agencies, the SEC, and the CFTC within nine months of the completion of the FSOC's study regarding the Volcker Rule.[2] The prohibitions of the Volcker Rule will take effect on the earlier of twelve months after the final rules are issued or two years after enactment of Dodd–Frank. Following the rules' effective date, banking entities will have two years to bring their investments and activities into compliance with the rule. The Fed may extend this deadline for up to three additional one year increments.

---

2. The FSOC study is to be completed within six months of the enactment of the Dodd–Frank Act.

QUESTIONS AND NOTES

1. Why are banks' real estate investments limited by purpose and by amount? How does real estate differ from other bank assets?

2. In an interpretive letter, the OCC opined that if a national bank's use of space in an office complex dropped from 22% of the space to 11%, and the bank was acting in good faith and not trying to evade the restrictions on bank ownership in real estate, its investment in the office complex would be permissible. OCC, Interpretive Letter #1034 (July 2005).

3. Three additional OCC interpretive letters have generated controversy about the application of section 29. See Rick Jackson, Note, National Banks in Commercial Real Estate Market: Alarm over the OCC's Recent Expansion of National Banks' Powers May be Premature, 11 N.C. Banking Inst. 183 (2007). In one letter, Bank of America was granted permission to develop an office building that would house a hotel that would be used in part by employees and visitors to the bank's headquarters city of Charlotte, North Carolina. OCC Interpretive Letter #1045 (Dec. 2005). By its terms, the letter appears to authorize the bank to own the hotel itself and contract with another company (the Ritz–Carlton) to manage the hotel, rather than to merely authorize the bank to lease the excess space in its office building to the hotel chain. The OCC concluded that providing cost-efficient lodging for bank visitors is "a legitimate business concern for the Bank" and would fall within section 29's authorization for a national bank to hold such real estate "as shall be necessary for its accommodation in the transaction of its business."

A second letter issued to PNC Bank authorized the bank to develop a mixed-use office building with retail space, office space, hotel space, and condominiums to be sold by an unaffiliated real estate broker. OCC Interpretive Letter #1044 (Dec. 2005). The bank justified the mixed use project as the most economically viable project for its location (with the revenue from the condominium sales as crucial for the financing of the project) and as an important part of a downtown rejuvenation effort. The OCC concluded that if "including the condominiums is necessary to the economic viability of the development of the Proposed Premises, then their construction and sale should not be prohibited by 12 U.S.C. § 29."

In the third letter, Union Bank of California was permitted to acquire a 70% equity interest of a wind farm, including any leaseholds and easements acquired by the wind farm company. OCC Interpretive Letter #1048 (Jan. 2006). The equity investment was apparently necessary to maximize the use of available tax credits. Any interest in real estate acquired by the bank was, according to the OCC, an integral part of the authorized banking activity, which was providing financing to the project.

Critics of these interpretations, including several members of Congress, believe the OCC went too far in its authorizations, breaching the separation of banking and commerce, permitting impermissible real estate investments, and authorizing inappropriate merchant banking investments. Joe Adler, Legislators Question OCC Realty Rulings, Am. Banker, Sept. 28, 2006.

4. Do any states permit greater real estate ownership authority for their state chartered banks? How would this authority fare under FDICIA's limitation of state bank powers? You may wish to consult the FDIC website to see if the FDIC ever permitted a well-managed and well-capitalized state bank to engage in state-authorized real estate powers in excess of those available to a national bank.

5. Why are banks permitted to own investment securities? Does it surprise you to learn that the authorization for bank ownership of investment securities described above was endorsed in section 16 of the Glass–Steagall Act of 1933, codified at 12 U.S.C.A. § 24(Seventh)? This portion of the Act was not repealed by GLBA. The securities activities of banks and their holding companies are explored in greater detail in Chapter 11.

6. You may wish to look at the asset side of your bank's most recent balance sheet to see what percentage of its assets are loans, cash, investment securities, and real estate. Are there other assets listed as well? What are they? Do they contribute to bank earnings directly or only indirectly?

7. A 2002 OCC interpretive letter permits national banks to buy and hold equity securities that banks do not generally have the authority to hold for the purpose of hedging "customer-driven, bank-permissible equity derivative transactions." OCC Interpretive Letter No. 935 (May 14, 2002) (citing OCC Interpretive Letter No. 892 (Sept. 13, 2000)). Is this interpretation consistent with the Volcker Rule?

8. Analyze whether the OCC's authorization to purchase Type III securities is consistent with the Volcker Rule.

9. How might the Volcker Rule negatively impact banks and bank holding companies? Is the rule likely to have a bigger effect on bank holding companies like Bank of America and JPMorgan Chase or the financial crisis-era bank holding companies like Morgan Stanley and Goldman Sachs?

10. The federal banking agencies are required by Dodd–Frank § 620 to submit a study to the FSOC, the Senate Banking Committee, and the House Financial Services Committee reviewing the investments undertaken ban banking entities, their risks, and the risk mitigation activities used by the banking entities. The study must consider the effect of these investments on the safety and soundness of the banking entity and additional restrictions that may be necessary to address those safety and soundness concerns.

11. In 1919, prior to imposition of the Glass–Steagall Act, Trust Company of Georgia received $110,000 in stock of Coca–Cola as its fee for serving as the investment banker in Coke's initial public offering of stock. The SunTrust bank vault also houses the secret formula for Coca–Cola. Trust Company, now SunTrust, has been permitted to retain its investment in Coke, and at one point the investment was worth over $2 billion. SunTrust had been unwilling to sell the stock because of the large tax gain it would recognize on sale. Tax law changes, retroactive to January 1, 2003, reducing the tax rate on dividend income from 40% to 15% will substantially benefit SunTrust's bottom line. See David Boraks, After a Legal Taste Test, SunTrust Sticks to Coke, Am. Banker, June 16, 2003. Others have suggested that the Coke stock is like a poison pill since any potential acquirer of SunTrust would have to factor in

the Coke stock's market value in the purchase price for SunTrust. Valerie Baulerlein, SunTrust Without Coke?, Wall St. J., May 17, 2007. Nevertheless, in the spring of 2007, SunTrust sold 9% of its Coke stock and pledged to use the proceeds to fund buybacks of SunTrust stock. Id. Additional Coke stock sales have been made by SunTrust to help strengthen its balance sheet.

SECTION 2. GENERAL REGULATION OF LOANS

The items discussed in this section are applicable to commercial as well as consumer loans.

A. LENDING LIMITS

The amount of credit that one bank may extend to one borrower is limited by statute and regulation. For national banks, the limitations are set forth in 12 U.S.C.A. § 84, and 12 C.F.R. pt. 32 (included in the Statutory and Regulatory Supplement). Section 84 provides that the basic limit for loans[3] to one borrower is 15% of the bank's unimpaired capital and unimpaired surplus. An additional 10% of capital and surplus may be loaned to the same borrower if it is fully secured by "readily marketable collateral." The OCC regulations refer to this amount as the "combined general limit." 12 C.F.R. § 32.3(a). OCC regulations provide that collateral is readily marketable if it consists of financial instruments that may be sold with reasonable promptness at a fair market value determined by quotations based upon actual transactions on an auction or daily bid and ask price. 12 C.F.R § 32.2(a). Financial instruments include stocks, notes, bonds and debentures traded on a national securities exchange, commercial paper, negotiable certificates of deposit and shares in money market or mutual funds. 12 C.F.R. § 32.2(j). Finally, 12 U.S.C.A. § 84(c) excepts from the lending limit certain delineated loans which have been adjudged to be virtually risk-free. For instance, loans fully secured by United States Treasury obligations do not count in the calculation of loans to one borrower (LTOB).

Thirty-eight states provide state banks with lending limits in excess of the national bank limit under § 84. One reason for this may be to enhance the attractiveness of the state charter, especially for smaller banks for which the 15% of capital lending limit may preclude numerous loans. Within eighteen months after Oklahoma raised its basic lending limit from 20% to 30% of capital, ten national banks converted to the Oklahoma state charter.[4] The OCC countered with a pilot program permitting national banks with main offices in states that have a higher lending limit for residential real estate, small business, or unsecured loans than the § 84(c) rate, to make loans at the higher state rate. In 2007, the OCC published

---

3. Lending limits apply to contractual commitments to lend as well as to fully funded loans.

4. Nicole Duran, OCC to Pilot Higher Limit on Bank Loans, Am. Banker, June 11, 2001.

an interim rule making the temporary program permanent.[5]

Sometimes, loans made to different borrowers must be aggregated for determining compliance with the LTOB rules. For instance, if the proceeds of a loan to Jones are to be used for the direct benefit of Smith, the amount of the Jones loan and the amount of any loans to Smith must be added together to determine if the bank is lending too much for the benefit of Smith. In addition, if a common enterprise exists between different borrowers, the loans made to them for the benefit of that common enterprise must be added together. Thus, if Smith, Jones, and Brown all borrow money from the same bank to use to start a business together, the three loans must be added together to determine if the lending limit has been violated as to their common enterprise.

The board of directors of a bank, through its loan committee, monitors lending limits. If there is a violation of the lending limit, board members may be required to indemnify the bank for any losses it has suffered from the loans.

If a potential loan is so large it would exceed the bank's lending limit, the bank may decide to sell participations in the loan or syndicate the loan so that the bank's exposure to the borrower is limited to an amount less than its LTOB limit, and so that the bank may still have a lending relationship at some level with the borrower.

DEL JUNCO v. CONOVER

United States Court of Appeals, Ninth Circuit, 1982.
682 F.2d 1338, *cert. denied*, 459 U.S. 1146 (1983).

FLETCHER, CIRCUIT JUDGE.

In December 1979, a periodic examination by the Comptroller of the Currency ("Comptroller") of the Los Angeles National Bank ("Bank") disclosed a possible violation of the provisions of 12 U.S.C. § 84. Section 84 limits the amount that a bank can lend to a single borrower to 10% of the bank's capital stock. At issue was whether three of the Bank's loans were really to the same entity and whether, when added together, they exceeded the bank's legal lending limit.

The loans were to Rehbock Lewis ("Lewis"), President of Fame Furniture Co., Inc.; Fame Furniture Co., Inc. ("Fame"); and Ralph Ware ("Ware"), Treasurer of Fame. The chart below sets forth the date, borrower, and amount of each loan, as well as the legal lending limit of the bank at the time of each loan and the amount by which the loans, when aggregated, exceeded the legal lending limit.

The legality of the Lewis loan for $225,000 has never been at issue, as that loan did not exceed the legal lending limit of the bank when it was made. However, if the Lewis, Fame, and Ware loans could be aggregated, then the latter two loans would exceed the Bank's lending limit.

---

5. 72 Fed. Reg. 31441 (June 7, 2007) (to be codified at 12 C.F.R. § 32.7 and requesting comment on any other changes that should be considered for the final rule).

The Comptroller first requested the Directors of the Bank to indemnify the Bank for any losses sustained as a result of the two excess loans; the Directors refused. The Comptroller then began a formal cease and desist action against the Directors and the Bank by issuing a Notice of Charges. The Bank and Directors answered, and the Comptroller moved for summary judgment in an agency proceeding.

Date Granted	Borrower	Amount	Lending Limit	Excess Amount
1/19/79	Lewis	225,000		
5/9/79	Fame	225,000		
	Subtotal	450,000	272,866	177,134
6/1/79	Ware	125,000		
	Present Balance	575,000	277,108	297,892

In the agency proceeding, the Bank and Directors admitted that they knew that the proceeds of the Fame and Lewis loans were to be used for the benefit of Fame. On these facts, the Administrative Law Judge (ALJ) ruled that it was proper to aggregate the Lewis and Fame loans so as to constitute a violation of 12 U.S.C. § 84. * * * [After] an evidentiary hearing * * * the ALJ determined that the Ware loan was used for the benefit of Fame. Accordingly, the ALJ recommended that the Comptroller issue a cease and desist order, that the Directors indemnify the Bank for the Fame and Ware loans, that the Bank recover costs of collection fees, and that the Bank recover attorneys' fees that it had paid for the Directors' defense.

Although the Comptroller agreed with the ALJ's findings, he disagreed as to the proper construction of section 84 with regard to reducing the Directors' liability. Both the Comptroller and the ALJ agreed that the potential liability of the Directors equalled $350,000 the sum of the two excess loans. The ALJ would have permitted the Directors to reduce their liability of $350,000 by offsetting a checking account of Fame and by selling bonds assigned as security to the Ware loan. The Comptroller, however, concluded that the Directors' potential $350,000 liability could not be reduced by the Bank's recoveries until the legal but unsecured Lewis loan had been fully repaid with interest. * * *

The regulation that implements the lending statute provides that "obligations of a corporation must be combined with any other extension of credit *the proceeds of which are used for the benefit of the corporation.*" 12 C.F.R. § 7.1310(c) (3) (1981) (emphasis added). The issue presented by this regulation is whether there was substantial evidence to support a finding that the $125,000 loan to Ware, the Treasurer of Fame, was "used for the benefit of the corporation."

The Comptroller found:

The hearing record clearly discloses the purpose and use of proceeds of the Ware loan. Mr. Ware, Fame's treasurer, testified that Fame's checking account at another bank was overdrawn. Accordingly, he and Mr. Lewis, Fame's president, went to the Bank to procure another loan. The Bank's vice president and senior lending officer, Mr. Jewett, informed Lewis and Ware that the Bank could not make an additional loan to Fame or to Mr. Lewis without violating the Bank's legal lending limit. Therefore, Mr. Ware's "name was used for the loan papers to borrow the money." As agreed, the Bank put the Ware loan proceeds directly into Fame's corporate checking account. * * * Mr. Jewett testified that he knew the proceeds were "going to go through Mr. Ware to Fame." On these facts, the Comptroller agrees with the ALJ's finding and conclusion that the deposit of the Ware loan proceeds directly into Fame's corporate checking account shows that the proceeds were used for the benefit of Fame.

The evidence of the corporation's overdrawn account, the corporation's search for another loan, the action and knowledge of the Bank's lending officer, and the deposit of the loan proceeds directly into Fame's account is substantial enough to support the Comptroller's finding.

Thus, because sufficient evidence supported the finding that the Ware loan was for the benefit of Fame, that loan could be aggregated with other Fame loans to calculate whether an excess loan had been made.

* * * The Directors argue that (a) indemnification is an improper remedy because the Directors did not "knowingly violate" the banking laws; (b) if indemnification is a proper remedy, then the Directors must be allowed to reduce their liability on the illegal loans by offsetting a checking account and selling collateral, even though the legal unsecured loan remains unpaid; (c) the Comptroller lacks authority to order that collection and attorneys' fees be paid to the Bank.

In the past, violations of the excess lending rule in 12 U.S.C. § 84 (1976) have been enforced through district court proceedings made possible by 12 U.S.C. § 93 (1976 & Supp. IV 1980). Section 93, which is derived from the National Bank Act of 1864, imposes liability on directors for knowingly violating or knowingly permitting violations of the banking laws. Here, however, the Comptroller, in an enforcement proceeding, is seeking to indemnify the Bank through the application of 12 U.S.C. § 1818(b) (1) (Supp. IV 1980). Although in effect since 1950, section 1818(b) (1) was significantly amended in 1978 to extend the coverage of cease and desist orders, which had previously applied only to a bank, to include a bank's directors. On its face, § 1818(b) (1) requires no knowledge on the part of the wrongdoer. The provision simply allows the Comptroller "to take affirmative action to correct the conditions resulting from any such violation or practice."

Defendants argue, however, that 12 U.S.C. § 1818(b) imports the scienter requirement of § 93 when the Comptroller seeks to impose personal liability on bank directors for exceeding bank lending limits. We need not and do not resolve that question today. Even if the "knowingly" standard of 12 U.S.C. § 93 applies to an 1818(b) enforcement proceeding, we agree with the Comptroller that defendants are liable here.

The Supreme Court has enunciated the scienter requirement of § 93:

> Under the rule settled by familiar decisions of this court, in order for the Bank to prevail in this action it must appear not only that the liabilities of a person, company, firms, etc., to the Bank for money borrowed were permitted to exceed the prescribed limit, but that defendant, while a director, participated in or assented to the excessive loan or loans not through mere negligence but knowingly and in effect intentionally ... with this qualification, that if he deliberately refrained from investigating that which it was his duty to investigate, any resulting violation of the statute must be regarded as "in effect intentional," ....

Corsicana National Bank v. Johnson, 251 U.S. 68, 71–72 (1919) (citations omitted).

The Directors had knowledge of the identity of the borrowers, knowledge that all the loan proceeds were to be used by one company, and knowledge of the loan amounts and the bank's loan limits. The defendants have maintained that, because the loans were made on separate occasions, they failed to aggregate the loans. However, 12 U.S.C. § 84 requires the aggregation of loans to a single entity. Directors of a national bank operate in an area closely regulated by federal law, and cannot maintain ignorance of the law as a defense.

Since the scienter requirement of § 93 has been satisfied, whatever requirement § 1818(b) may have imported from § 93 has also been satisfied.

The Directors' potential liability is limited to $350,000—the difference between the total credit extension to Fame ($575,000) and the amount of the legal Lewis loan ($225,000). The Comptroller takes the position that the Directors' potential loss of $350,000 cannot be reduced by recoveries until the legal loan to Lewis has been repaid with interest.

In the instant case, the purpose underlying 12 U.S.C. § 84—protection of a bank's assets—will be furthered if the Directors are not allowed to extinguish their liability until the legal Lewis loan, which is unsecured, is fully repaid. The policy of protecting bank assets would be frustrated if the Directors were allowed to make, as they did, an unsecured but legal loan to the borrower, then to use, or agree to the use of, the borrower's assets to secure further credit extensions that are illegal. Such a procedure would permit the Directors to protect themselves fully against any exposure resulting from the illegal loans while substantially increasing the risk that the bank would be unable to recover the amount of its legal loan. The fiduciary responsibility of the Directors of the bank precludes them from protecting themselves against liability at the bank's expense. The security arrangement was in derogation of that responsibility. Thus, the Directors may not use the borrower's assets to extinguish their own liability to the bank.

Here, the Directors ignored the recommendation of the Comptroller and the bank president's advice that the first loan to be paid off should be that of Rehbock Lewis and not Fame Furniture, since the stockholders might claim that this loan was paid to limit the liabilities of the Directors. The Comptroller's remedy is appropriate, because any other remedy could create a conflict of interest between the Bank and its Directors. * * *

The Comptroller's decision and final order to cease and desist are affirmed. Substantial evidence supported the Comptroller's finding that the three loans could be aggregated as loans to a single business. Furthermore, the Comptroller, in fashioning a remedy, acted within the scope of his authority to correct conditions resulting from the Directors' violation of the banking laws.

The Dodd–Frank Act adds to the "loans and extensions of credit" subject to the national bank lending limits, credit exposure that arises from a derivative transaction, repurchase agreement, reverse repurchase agreement, securities lending transaction, or some securities borrowing transaction. Dodd–Frank Act, § 610. The Act further provides that state banks may only engage in derivatives transactions if the chartering state's lending limit law "takes into consideration" derivatives transaction credit exposures. Dodd–Frank Act, § 611. This provision will not go into effect for several years after Dodd–Frank's enactment to give states the opportunity to amend their definitions of credit exposure in their lending limit laws.

Title I of Dodd–Frank limits the credit exposure of systemically significant BHCs and nonbank financial companies to any unaffiliated company to 25% of the institution's capital stock and surplus, although the Fed is empowered to set a lower limit by regulation. Dodd–Frank Act, § 165(e). Credit exposure is defined broadly here, as in Section 610, and also includes all purchases or investments in securities issued by the company. There is also an attribution provision that requires that, if the proceeds of any transaction with a person are used for the benefit of or transferred to an unaffiliated company, the extensions of credit to that person are attributed to the extensions of credit to the company. The attribution rule imposes a significant tracking and monitoring burden on these systemically significant companies. The systemically significant companies must also submit to the Fed and FDIC a Credit Exposure Report that identifies significant credit exposures of the company to other companies. The fed may issue regulations exempting transactions from the definition of credit exposure if it deems the exemption to be in the public interest. In any event, these Title I provisions relating to credit exposure limits for systemically significant institutions will not become effective until three years after the July 21, 2010 enactment of Dodd–Frank, and the Fed is authorized to extend this effective date for up to two additional years.[6]

QUESTIONS AND NOTES

1.   Why are loans to one borrower limited? Are lending limits a finely crafted tool to reduce bank risk or a blunt-edged risk reduction tool? Why?

2.   Why does the statute allow additional loans above the basic limit if secured by readily marketable collateral? Why is the collateral that is accepted for this purpose limited to that which is considered "readily marketable?"

3.   Why are some loans (those identified in 12 U.S.C.A. § 84(c)), excluded from the lending limit calculation altogether?

4.   Assume a bank's unimpaired capital and surplus is $10 million. What is the bank's basic lending limit to one borrower? If the bank makes a $1 million loan to Brown secured by real estate, is this within the basic limit? If the loan is $2 million and is fully secured by real estate is this loan within the lending limit? Assume now that the bank has made a $1 million loan to Brown secured by real estate, a $500,000 unsecured loan to Jones, and a $250,000 unsecured loan to Smith, and that all the loans are going to be used for the common purpose of opening up a paintball course to be operated by Brown, Smith, and Jones. Is there a lending limit problem? What if the $1 million loan to Brown is secured by $1 million in IBM stock instead of by real estate?

5.   Should the OCC seek to amend 12 U.S.C.A. § 84, to provide that national bank lending limits are the same as the state lending limits in the state in which the national bank is headquartered, rather than try to accomplish this change by regulation?

6.   Check your state's law on lending limits for state chartered banks to see if the loans and extensions of credit subject to the limits include derivatives transaction. If your state does not amend its lending limit within the time period designated by Dodd–Frank, how will state banks be at a disadvantage?

7.   How do concentration limits imposed on systemically significant institutions by Dodd–Frank change the lending limits otherwise applicable to systemically significant BHCs and to nonbank financial companies?

B.   INSIDER LOANS

Loans to insiders of the bank are permitted, subject to certain regulations. The reason for the regulation may be that we do not want banks to make unsound credit decisions because of insider pressure and

---

6.   Until this effective date, institutions—systemic and otherwise—will be guided by the Board of Governors of the Federal Reserve System, Interagency Guidance on Correspondent Concentration Risk, 75 Fed. Reg. 23764 (May 4, 2010) (relating to interbank credit exposures).

we do not want banks to have their earnings reduced as a result of self-dealing on more favorable terms than would be available to other bank customers. 12 U.S.C.A. § 375a regulates loans to executive officers of the bank, and 12 U.S.C.A. § 375b regulates loans to a broader group which includes, in addition to executive officers, directors, and principal shareholders. By their terms, these statutes apply to member banks (i.e., national banks and state member banks). The limitations apply also to every nonmember insured bank in the same manner and to the same extent as if the bank were a member bank. 12 U.S.C.A. § 1828(j)(2). Regulation O implements these statutory provisions. 12 C.F.R. pt. 215.

Section 375b places limits on the loans that may be made to executive officers, directors, and principal shareholders. Executive officers are defined by regulation to include any person who participates or has the authority to participate in major policymaking functions, other than as a director. Unless excluded by board resolution or the bank's by-laws from major policy-making functions, the following will be considered executive officers: the chairman of the board, the president, every vice president, the cashier, the secretary, and the treasurer. Principal shareholders are defined as those who own more than 10% of any class of voting stock. Loans to this group of borrowers must be on substantially the same terms as those for other borrowers. The board must approve these insider loans in advance of the loan. Finally, loans to insiders in the aggregate may not exceed the amount of the bank's unimpaired capital and surplus. 12 U.S.C.A. § 375b(5).

Section 375a sets forth some additional limits on loans to executive officers. Such loans must not be on terms more favorable than loans to other borrowers. The executive officer must submit a detailed financial statement, and the loan must be reported to the board.[7]

The Sarbanes–Oxley Act, which was enacted in the wake of the bankruptcies of prominent corporations rocked by fraud and accounting irregularities such as Enron and WorldCom, prohibits loans to officers and directors, but specifically exempts loans made by institutions subject to Regulation O on insider lending. Sarbanes–Oxley Act, § 402 (codified at 15 U.S.C. § 78m(k)). The SEC has adopted Rule 13k–1 to provide an exemption from Sarbanes–Oxley for insider lending by foreign banks.

DE LA FUENTE v. FEDERAL DEPOSIT INSURANCE CORP.

United States Court of Appeals, Ninth Circuit, 2003.
332 F.3d 1208.

WARDLAW, CIRCUIT JUDGE.

Roque De La Fuente II petitions for review of an order of the Board of the Federal Deposit Insurance Corporation ("Board") removing him as a

---

7. Section 601 of the Financial Services Regulatory Relief Act of 2006 eased several statutory reporting requirements relating to loans to executive officers. See 72 Fed. Reg. 30470 (June 1, 2007) (codified at 12 C.F.R. pt. 215).

director of First International Bank ("FIB") and forbidding him from participating in, voting shares of, or serving on the board of any federally regulated bank for life. The Board found that De La Fuente had used his position at FIB to secure several loans in excess of applicable limits for entities in which he and his close associates were interested, as well as to engage in other self interested lending practices. * * *

De La Fuente became a board member of FIB, formerly known as People's Bank, on March 30, 1987, and served in that position until he was removed. This appeal centers around twelve FIB loans and two loan-related transactions, all of which occurred between 1990 and 1995, involving entities in which De La Fuente, his family, or his close associates were interested.

The loans that formed the basis for the removal action are (in chronological order):

(1) a May 17, 1990 loan in the amount of $1 million to the Roque de la Fuente Alexander Trust ("Fuente Alexander Trust"), a revocable trust set up by De La Fuente's father in which De La Fuente had a 25% contingent interest.

(2) an October 8, 1990 loan in the amount of $1 million to Rancho de la Fuente International Industrial Park ("Fuente/ IIP"), an entity owned by De La Fuente's mother through offshore corporations. De La Fuente's mother is a housewife who lives in Mexico City and does not participate in the operations of Fuente/IIP. Jose Luis Andreu, one of De La Fuente's close associates—who is also vice president of American International Enterprises ("AIE"), a company solely owned by De La Fuente—is the agent for Fuente/IIP.

(3) a December 26, 1990 loan in the amount of $400,000 to Rancho Vista del Mar, Inc. ("RVDM"), another entity owned by De La Fuente's mother through offshore corporations. As he is for Fuente/IIP, Andreu is the company's agent. RVDM has no employees.

(4) a January 24, 1992 loan in the amount of $800,000 to RVDM.

(5) a July 15, 1992 loan in the amount of $1.6 million to RVDM.

(6) September 9, 1992 personal loan to De La Fuente in the amount of $800,000.

(7) a July 20, 1995 loan in the amount of $763,000 to the Fine Particle Technology Corporation ("FPTC"), a company of which De La Fuente owned 5.6%. De La Fuente transferred his interest in FPTC into trusts for his children in 1995. Among FPTC's other shareholders are Andreu (24.42%), and Isaias Zapata (5.02%), another close De La Fuente associate. Andreu is also the president of FPTC, and has been a director and board chairman. This company also has no employees.

(8) an August 11, 1995 loan in the amount of $1.35 million to FPTC.

(9) an October 27, 1995 loan in the amount of $750,000 to National Enterprises, Inc. ("NEI"), an entity of which De La Fuente was the sole owner. De La Fuente transferred his interest in NEI into his children's trusts in 1995. The trustees at relevant times were Zapata and Sidney Schwartz, another close De La Fuente associate, who is currently the chairman of the FIB board. Schwartz is also a director of NEI.

(10) a November 8, 1995 loan in the amount of $600,000 to FPTC.

(11) a December 18, 1995 loan in the amount of $200,000 to C.T. Produce, Inc. ("C.T.Produce"), an entity of which Andreu is a director, and which is engaged in a joint venture with NEI.

(12) a December 28, 1995 loan in the amount of $800,000 to FPTC.

The Board's removal order was based on two additional transactions involving collateral for FIB loans:

(13) a 1994 FIB decision to accept the substitution of inferior substitute collateral to secure a loan the bank had made to RVDM (the "Collateral Substitution Transaction"); and

(14) a 1995 FIB decision to allow a non-creditworthy NEI employee to assume liability for a loan the bank had made to the Parking Company of America ("PCA Transaction"). * * *

The Board correctly found that De La Fuente "controlled" all of the loan recipients, and that the loans therefore violated the provisions of Regulation O, 12 C.F.R. § 215.1–.13. Regulation O restricts the ability of member banks in the Federal Reserve system (as well as nonmember, FDIC-insured banks such as FIB, see 12 U.S.C. § 1828(j)(2)) to extend credit to their "insider[s]." 12 C.F.R. § 215.4(a). The regulation defines "insider," in turn, as "an executive officer, director, or principal shareholder, and includes any related interest of such a person," id. § 215.2(h); a "[r]elated interest" is defined to include "[a] company that is controlled by that person," id. § 215.2(n)(1). Under the regulation, a person controls a company, when *inter alia* he or she owns 25% or more of the shares of a company, id. § 215.2(c)(1)(i), or "[h]as the power to exercise a controlling influence over the management or policies of the company," id. § 215.2(c)(1)(iii). The regulation also creates certain rebuttable presumptions of control for persons who own more than 10% of the stock in a company. Id. § 215.2(c)(2).

The Board found that De La Fuente controlled FPTC by owning, controlling, or having the power to vote 25% or more of its shares, under § 215.2(c)(1)(i). With respect to the other loans (except the loan to C.T. Produce), the ALJ found that the borrowing entities were "actual [ly] control[led]" by De La Fuente, which the Board determined constituted a finding of exercising a controlling influence under § 215.2(c)(1)(iii).

De La Fuente argues that because the regulation contains rebuttable presumptions of control in § 215.2(c)(2) for persons who own more than 10% of a company's shares, it creates a "safe harbor" insulating people who do not fall within the rebuttable presumption (i.e., De La Fuente) from a finding of control under § 215.2(c)(1)(iii). We disagree. Subsection 215.2(c)(1) establishes the test for control.[8] The following subsection, § 215.2(c)(2), sets forth a list of circumstances from which "control" is to be presumed.[9] "Control" may be established if a proper finding under the first subsection is made, or if one of the requirements of the second subsection is met and the presumption of control is not rebutted. De La Fuente would have us disregard the test in the first subsection because he was not *presumed* to have control under the second subsection. This is illogical. To read the regulation in this manner would render portions of the regulation surplusage, and would defeat the plain purpose of the regulatory scheme. * * *

[W]e conclude that the finding of control underlying the Board's conclusion that FIB's four loans to FPTC (totaling over $3 million in one year) violated Regulation O and Section 23A is supported by substantial evidence. Because De La Fuente owned, controlled, or had the power to vote 25% or more of FPTC's shares, FPTC was an affiliate or related interest of De La Fuente's under Regulation O, 12 C.F.R. § 215.2(c)(1)(i), and Section 23A, 12 U.S.C. § 371c(b)(3)(A)(i).

De La Fuente owned 5.6% of FPTC, which he transferred to trusts for his children in 1995. Among FPTC's other share holders are Andreu (24.42%) and Zapata (5.02%), both close associates and frequent business partners of De La Fuente's. Andreu is also the president of FPTC, and has been a director and board chairman. The company has no employees.

---

8. [n. 2] Subsection 215.2(c)(1) provides:

Control of a company or bank means that a person directly or indirectly, or acting through or in concert with one or more persons:

(i) Owns, controls, or has the power to vote 25 percent or more of any class of voting securities of the company or bank;

(ii) Controls in any manner the election of a majority of the directors of the company or bank; or

(iii) Has the power to exercise a controlling influence over the management or policies of the company or bank.

Id. § 215.2(c)(1).

9. [n.3] Subsection 215.2(c)(2) provides:

A person is presumed to have control, including the power to exercise a controlling influence over the management or policies, of a company or bank if:

(i) The person is:

(A) An executive officer or director of the company or bank; and

(B) Directly or indirectly owns, controls, or has the power to vote more than 10 percent of any class of voting securities of the company or bank; or

(ii)(A) The person directly or indirectly owns, controls, or has the power to vote more than 10 percent of any class of voting securities of the company or bank; and

(B) No other person owns, controls, or has the power to vote a greater percentage of that class of voting securities.

Id. § 215.2(c)(2).

Andreu purchased his share in FPTC with funds drawn on the account of Witec Patents (a company of which De La Fuente was a part owner, and of which Andreu eventually became president) supported by the votes of De La Fuente and Zapata.

Furthermore, one business day after FIB's directors were faced with $500 per day fines as a result of noncompliance with an FDIC cease-and-desist order, FPTC purchased two loans from FIB, saving it from the payment of the penalties. In addition, FPTC diverted $600,000 of a loan it received to De La Fuente (on undisclosed terms), who used the funds to pay down an unrelated loan, not connected with FPTC. Finally, both the ALJ and the Board found that "Andreu represented to [a third party] that FPTC was one of the 'De La Fuente' companies."

De La Fuente attempts to provide innocent explanations for this evidence, arguing that it could be consistent with a scenario in which he did not control FPTC. However, when the evidence is susceptible to more than one rational interpretation, we will not substitute our judgment for that of the agency. It is a reasonable inference from the evidence as a whole and the very structure of FPTC that De La Fuente controlled FPTC. As the trier of fact, the ALJ was in a superior position to evaluate any conflicting testimony and assess De La Fuente's arguments that FPTC's actions were not controlled by his interests. * * *

It is premature for us to consider De La Fuente's remaining claim, that the Board abused its discretion in banning him for life from the banking industry. We acknowledge that the Board concluded that "findings of violations of either Regulation O or section 23A, standing alone, would support" its decision, and further that "any one or combination of [the] loans that, in addition to the $800,000 [personal loan], would violate the lending limits of either Regulation O or section 23A ... would suffice to justify [De La Fuente's] removal and prohibition." We also cannot help but note that De La Fuente's use of FIB as his personal piggy bank was in shocking disregard of sound banking practices and the law to the detriment of depositors, shareholders, and the public. Nevertheless, we remand this matter to the Board for it to consider, in light of this disposition, whether this extraordinary sanction remains deserved.

Following remand, the FDIC permanently banned De La Fuente from banking. The Ninth Circuit denied his petition for review of this order in an unpublished decision, 156 Fed.Appx. 44 (9th Cir. 2005). The Ninth Circuit found that De La Fuente's actions justified a permanent ban and that the FDIC had adequately considered De La Fuente's argument in imposing the ban that the improper loans were profitable and did not result in losses to the bank.

The broadening of "extension of credit" to include derivatives, repurchase agreements, and other instruments described above for lending limit purposes under Dodd–Frank, also applies for purposes of the insider lending restrictions. Dodd–Frank Act, § 610. In addition, Dodd–Frank extends restrictions relating to lending transactions with insiders to asset purchases from or to insiders—any executive officer, director, or principal shareholder. Dodd–Frank Act, § 615. Any such purchase from an insider or sale to an insider must be on market terms and if the transaction is greater than ten percent of the institution's capital and surplus, must receive advance approval by a majority of the institution's disinterested directors.

QUESTIONS AND NOTES

1.　It is interesting to consider why Congress choose to regulate insider loans rather than to either prohibit such loans outright, or permit loans to insiders on more favorable conditions than to others. For instance, many department store employees receive an employee discount for merchandise purchased at the department store. Why don't bank insiders receive an equivalent benefit? Is there a practical reason why loans to insiders are not prohibited?

2.　Notice the different treatment of national banks, state member banks, and state nonmember banks relating to regulation of real estate ownership, investment security ownership, lending limits, and insider loans. In a dual banking system, will there always be pressure to equalize regulatory treatment? If so, are there any remaining advantages to maintaining both a state and national system of regulation?

C.　LENDER LIABILITY

Sometimes a disappointed borrower elects to pursue legal action against his bank. In some cases, lawsuits have been brought because the bank failed to make an advance to a borrower when requested. In other instances, the borrower has sued when the bank has declared a loan in default, or when the bank has repossessed the collateral for the loan, or otherwise acted to enforce the bank's rights against the borrower. In most instances, a bank takes action based on what it views as its rights under the loan contract with the borrower. When disputes have arisen, however, some borrowers have alleged that the bank breached its contractual duty to act in good faith or that the bank committed the tort of bad faith breach of contract. The good faith duty may be implied into a contract by the common law or by the Uniform Commercial Code. Section 1–203 of the UCC provides that "[e]very contract or duty [within the UCC] imposes an obligation of good faith in its performance or enforcement." Section 1–208 further provides:

A term providing that one party ... may accelerate payment or performance or require collateral or additional collateral "at will" or "when he deems himself insecure" or in words of similar import shall be construed to mean that he shall have power to do so only if he in good faith believes that the prospect of payment of performance is impaired.

Tort claimants may be entitled to punitive damages, in addition to compensatory damages.

Some plaintiffs found success pursuing these claims which were referred to under the general rubric of "lender liability."[10] The tension in the cases obviously comes from the bank's exercise of contractual rights under the loan contract and the borrower's contention that the bank's exercise of such rights was improper, not in good faith, or designed to take advantage of the borrower. Lender liability litigation has not been as successful in recent years. Banks may have improved their practices as a result of some of the early litigation. For instance, most banks no longer include in their loan agreements provisions which permit acceleration at will, or demands for additional collateral "at will" or when the lender "deems itself insecure." By removing this discretion and relying instead on defined events of default or explicit conditions to trigger a demand for additional collateral, banks have foreclosed potential liability for good faith violations under § UCC 1–208. In the case of a consumer borrower, it is also possible for a lender to run afoul of some of the federal consumer protection legislation discussed in more detail in Chapter 6. In the aftermath of the financial crisis, banks again find themselves the target of suits by unhappy borrowers and depositors. Much of the current litigation is related to subprime mortgages.

D. ENVIRONMENTAL LENDER LIABILITY

A special form of lender liability seeks to hold the lender liable under the federal environmental statutes for the costs of cleanup of environmental waste. In addition to the federal statutes, there may also be similar state statutes that impose liability. Environmental lender liability is a greater concern in the commercial lending context where commercial real property is taken as collateral than in the consumer context.

UNITED STATES v. FLEET FACTORS CORP.

United States Court of Appeals, Eleventh Circuit, 1990.
901 F.2d 1550, *cert. denied,* 498 U.S. 1046 (1991).

KRAVITCH, CIRCUIT JUDGE.

Fleet Factors Corporation ("Fleet") brought an interlocutory appeal from the district court's denial of its motion for summary judgment in this suit by the United States to recover the cost of removing hazardous waste from a bankrupt textile facility. The district court denied summary

---

10. See K.M.C. Co. v. Irving Trust Co., 757 F.2d 752 (6th Cir. 1985) (lender's failure to advance funds pursuant to the loan agreement without notice to the borrower is subject to the UCC's good faith requirement); Brown v. AVEMCO Investment Corp., 603 F.2d 1367 (9th Cir. 1979) (applying the good faith requirement of UCC 1–208 to an acceleration pursuant to a specific provision of the loan contract); Special Project: Lender Liability: A Survey of Common–Law Theories, 42 Vand. L. Rev. 855 (1989).

judgment because it concluded that Fleet's activities at the facility might rise to the level of participation in management sufficient to impose liability under the Comprehensive Environmental Response Compensation and Liability Act ("CERCLA"), 42 U.S.C. §§ 9601–57 (1982 & West Supp.1988), despite the statutory exemption from liability for holders of a security interest. We agree with the district court that material questions of fact remain as to the extent of Fleet's participation in the management of the facility; therefore, we affirm the denial of Fleet's summary judgment motion.

In 1976, Swainsboro Print Works ("SPW"), a cloth printing facility, entered into a "factoring" agreement with Fleet in which Fleet agreed to advance funds against the assignment of SPW's accounts receivable. As collateral for these advances, Fleet also obtained a security interest in SPW's textile facility and all of its equipment, inventory, and fixtures. In August, 1979, SPW filed for bankruptcy under Chapter 11. The factoring agreement between SPW and Fleet continued with court approval. In early 1981, Fleet ceased advancing funds to SPW because SPW's debt to Fleet exceeded Fleet's estimate of the value of SPW's accounts receivable. On February 27, 1981, SPW ceased operations and began to liquidate its inventory. Fleet continued to collect on the accounts receivable assigned to it under the Chapter 11 factoring agreement. In December 1981, SPW was adjudicated a bankrupt under Chapter 7 and a trustee assumed title and control of the facility.

In May 1982, Fleet foreclosed on its security interest in some of SPW's inventory and equipment, and contracted with Baldwin Industrial Liquidators ("Baldwin") to conduct an auction of the collateral. Baldwin sold the material "as is" and "in place" on June 22, 1982; the removal of the items was the responsibility of the purchasers. On August 31, 1982, Fleet allegedly contracted with Nix Riggers ("Nix") to remove the unsold equipment in consideration for leaving the premises "broom clean." Nix testified in deposition that he understood that he had been given a "free hand" by Fleet or Baldwin to do whatever was necessary at the facility to remove the machinery and equipment. Nix left the facility by the end of December, 1983.

On January 20, 1984, the Environmental Protection Agency ("EPA") inspected the facility and found 700 fifty-five gallon drums containing toxic chemicals and forty-four truckloads of material containing asbestos. The EPA incurred costs of nearly $400,000 in responding to the environmental threat at SPW. On July 7, 1987, the facility was conveyed to Emanuel County, Georgia, at a foreclosure sale resulting from SPW's failure to pay state and county taxes.

The government sued Horowitz and Newton, the two principal officers and stockholders of SPW, and Fleet to recover the cost of cleaning up the hazardous waste. The district court granted the government's summary judgment motion with respect to the liability of Horowitz and Newton for the cost of removing the hazardous waste in the drums. The government's motion with respect to Fleet's liability, and the liability of Horowitz and Newton for the asbestos removal costs was denied. Fleet's motion for summary judgment was also denied. The district court, *sua sponte*, certified the summary judgment issues for interlocutory appeal and stayed the remaining proceedings in the case. Fleet subsequently brought this appeal challenging the court's denial of its motion for summary judgment. * * *

The Comprehensive Environmental Response Compensation and Liability Act was enacted by Congress in response to the environmental and public health hazards caused by the improper disposal of hazardous wastes. United States v. Maryland Bank & Trust Co., 632 F.Supp. 573, 576 (D.Md.1986); S.Rep. No. 848, 96th Cong., 2d Sess. 2 (1980), U.S.Code Cong. & Admin.News 1980, p. 6119. The essential policy underlying CERCLA is to place the ultimate responsibility for cleaning up hazardous waste on "those responsible for problems caused by the disposal of chemical poison." Allis Chalmers, 893 F.2d at 1316. Accordingly, CERCLA authorizes the federal government to clean up hazardous waste dump sites and recover the cost of the effort from certain categories of responsible parties. Maryland Bank & Trust Co., 632 F.Supp. at 576. * * *

CERCLA also imposes liability on "any person who at the time of disposal of any hazardous substance owned or operated any ... facility at which such hazardous substances were disposed of...." 42 U.S.C. § 9607(a)(2). CERCLA excludes from the definition of "owner or operator" any "person, who, without participating in the management of a ... facility, holds indicia of ownership primarily to protect his security interest in the ... facility." 42 U.S.C. § 9601(20)(A). Fleet has the burden of establishing its entitlement to this exemption. Maryland Bank & Trust, 632 F.Supp. at 578; see United States v. First City National Bank of Houston, 386 U.S. 361, 366 (1967). There is no dispute that Fleet held an "indicia of ownership" in the facility through its deed of trust to SPW, and that this interest was held primarily to protect its security interest in the facility. The critical issue is whether Fleet participated in management sufficiently to incur liability under the statute. * * *

Under the standard we adopt today, a secured creditor may incur section 9607(a)(2) liability, without being an operator, by participating in the financial management of a facility to a degree indicating a capacity to influence the corporation's treatment of hazardous wastes. It is not necessary for the secured creditor actually to involve itself in the day-to-day operations of the facility in order to be liable—although such conduct will certainly lead to the loss of the protection of the statutory exemption. Nor is it necessary for the secured creditor to participate in management decisions relating to hazardous waste. Rather, a secured creditor will be liable if its involvement with the management of the facility is sufficiently broad to support the inference that it could affect hazardous waste disposal decisions if it so chose. * * *

Our ruling today should encourage potential creditors to investigate thoroughly the waste treatment systems and policies of potential debtors. If the treatment systems seem inadequate, the risk of CERCLA liability will be weighed into the terms of the loan agreement. Creditors, therefore, will incur no greater risk than they bargained for and debtors, aware that inadequate hazardous waste treatment will have a significant adverse impact on their loan terms, will have powerful incentives to improve their handling of hazardous wastes.

Similarly, creditors' awareness that they are potentially liable under CERCLA will encourage them to monitor the hazardous waste treatment systems and policies of their debtors and insist upon compliance with acceptable treatment standards as a prerequisite to continued and future financial support. Once a secured creditor's involvement with a facility becomes sufficiently broad that it can anticipate losing its exemption from CERCLA liability, it will have a strong incentive to address hazardous waste problems at the facility rather than studiously avoiding the investigation and amelioration of the hazard. * * *

We agree with the court below that the government has alleged sufficient facts to hold Fleet liable under section 9607(a)(2). From 1976 until SPW ceased printing operations on February 27, 1981, Fleet's involvement with the facility was within the parameters of the secured creditor exemption to liability. During this period, Fleet regularly advanced funds to SPW against the assignment of SPW's accounts receivable, paid and arranged for security deposits for SPW's Georgia utility services, and informed SPW that it would not advance any more money when it determined that its advanced sums exceeded the value of SPW's accounts receivable.

Fleet's involvement with SPW, according to the government, increased substantially after SPW ceased printing operations at the Georgia plant on February 27, 1981, and began to wind down its affairs. Fleet required SPW to seek its approval before shipping its goods to customers, established the price for excess inventory, dictated when and to whom the finished goods should be shipped, determined when employees should be laid off, supervised the activity of the office administrator at the site, received and processed SPW's employment and tax forms, controlled access to the facility, and contracted with Baldwin to dispose of the fixtures and equipment at SPW. These facts, if proved, are sufficient to remove Fleet from the protection of the secured creditor exemption. Fleet's involvement in the financial management of the facility was pervasive, if not complete. Furthermore, the government's allegations indicate that Fleet was also involved in the operational management of the facility. Either of these allegations is sufficient as a matter of law to impose CERCLA liability on a secured creditor. The district court's finding to the contrary is erroneous. * * *

Contrary to the positive results the *Fleet Factors* court expected to flow from its decision, there was a chilling effect on lending where land was necessary for collateral, especially where the land was used or had been used for commercial purposes. All such lending did not end, but its cost certainly increased as lenders demanded environmental inspections or audits prior to accepting commercial real property as collateral. The EPA issued a regulation in April 1992 that rejected the broad language of *Fleet Factors* about the capacity (even though unexercised) of influencing management decisions about the disposal of hazardous wastes. In 1994, however, a United States Appeals Court found the regulation to be invalid.[11] Undaunted, the EPA announced that its CERCLA enforcement policy would follow the substance of the invalid regulation. Congress amended CERCLA, effective September 30, 1996, to negate the management participation theory of liability.[12] Under the amended standard, "merely having the capacity to influence, or the unexercised right to control ... operations" is not participation in management.[13] 42 U.S.C. § 9601(20)(F)(i)(II).

[handwritten note: Not mgmt.]

In 2002, the Small Business Liability Relief and Brownfields Revitalization Act required the EPA to define acceptable due diligence to provide a defense for a buyer to federal liability for a contaminated site. The final EPA rule specified an "All Appropriate Inquiries-compliant Phase I Report" that detailed the required due diligence prior to acquiring property. The FDIC issued its updated "Guidelines for An Environmental Risk Program" to reflect these changes. FIL–98–2006 (Nov. 13, 2006), available at <www.fdic.gov/news/news/financial/2006/fil06098a.pdf>.

QUESTIONS AND NOTES

1. HSBC Bank USA, N.A. settled an environmental liability action brought by the New York Attorney General for $850,000 in civil penalties and $115,680 in costs. The bank seized the operating funds of its borrower. The Attorney General alleged that the bank was liable for waste at the borrower's abandoned manufacturing facility because the bank had participated in management of the facility. The bank did not admit to liability in the settlement. John Herzfeld, State Sends "Message" in Getting HSBC Bank to Pay $966,000 for Chemical Plant, Banking Daily (BNA), May 31, 2007.

E. ACCOUNTING FOR LOAN LOSS RESERVES

Each quarter, bank management determines the estimated dollar amount of expected losses on loans. This amount is reported on the

---

11. Kelley v. Environmental Protection Agency, 15 F.3d 1100 (D.C. Cir. 1994), cert. denied, 513 U.S. 1110 (1995).

12. Asset Conservation, Lender Liability, and Deposit Insurance Protection Act of 1996, Pub. L. No. 104–208, 110 Stat. 3009.

13. See Monarch Tile, Inc. v. City of Florence, 212 F.3d 1219, 1221–22 n.2 (11th Cir. 2000); Canadyne–Georgia Corp. v. NationsBank, N.A. (South), 183 F.3d 1269 (11th Cir. 1999) (regarding liability of banks acting as fiduciaries).

quarterly income statement as the provision for loan losses. It is a tax deductible expense item that reduces net income for the quarter. The amount allocated for loan losses is then added to the loan loss reserve fund reflected on the bank's balance sheet. This reserve acts as an offset to the value of the loans reported by the bank on the asset side of its balance sheet. As losses are actually experienced on loans, they are deducted from the reserve account. If a collection is made on a loan that was previously reserved for, the amount of the collection is added to the loan loss reserve account.

In 1998, the SEC required SunTrust Banks, Inc. to restate its earnings for three years and reduce its loan loss reserve account by $100 million before the SEC would grant approval to SunTrust's merger with Crestar Financial Corp. The SEC alleged that SunTrust's loan loss reserves were artificially high and had been inflated by SunTrust to permit it to "manage" its earnings to meet the quarterly earnings expectations set by stock analysts. In theory a bank could inflate its earnings by reducing the amount allocated in the current quarter to loan losses and relying on money placed into its loan loss reserve "cookie-jar" to cover any expected loan losses.[14]

The SEC was concerned about meaningful disclosure to investors. The federal banking regulators, on the other hand, viewed the reduction of SunTrust's loan loss reserves quite differently. In general, the banking regulators applaud loan loss reserve accounts as an appropriate and prudent risk management technique to guard against loan losses.

In July 1999, the SEC and the federal banking regulators issued a joint statement that loan loss reserves should be set in accordance with generally accepted accounting practices (GAAP), but recognized that setting the figure is a judgment exercised by bank management.[15] Thereafter, the American Institute of Certified Public Accountants (AICPA) began a project to clarify the accounting standards regarding loan loss reserves. Initial drafts were criticized as not giving enough deference to the experience of management in setting the reserve figure. The banking agencies issued a policy statement in 2001 providing guidance on the appropriate methodologies for calculating and reporting loan loss reserves.[16]

In June 2003, the Accounting Standards Executive Committee (AcSEC) of the AICPA issued for public comment proposed Statement of Position, "Accounting for Credit Losses" (SOP). AcSEC received almost 300 comment letters and decided to drop its overhaul of the accounting rule and proceed only on drafting guidance to improve disclosures. AcSEC

---

14. In late 1998, Arthur Levitt, then the chairman of the SEC, characterized loan loss reserves as "cookie-jar" reserves.

15. Joint Interagency Letter to Financial Institutions, July 12, 1999, available at <www.occ.treas.gov/ftp/release/99–65.pdf>. The banking agencies have also issued an Interagency Guidance on Certain Loans Held for Sale, Mar. 26, 2001, at <www.occ.treas.gov/ftp/bulletin/2001–15a.pdf>. The regulators are concerned that, as credit quality falls, banks may be tempted to move bad loans into their trading accounts rather than increase their loan loss reserves.

16. Notice of Final Interagency Policy Statement. 66 Fed. Reg. 35629 (July 6, 2001).

recommended that the Financial Accounting Standards Board (FASB) reconsider FAS 5, "Accounting for Contingencies." In September 2006, the AICPA dropped a project on loan loss reserve disclosure, "Proposed Statement of Position, Disclosures Concerning Credit Losses Related to Loans," concluding that the proposed disclosures would be too burdensome. Some of the proposed disclosures would have been of the geographical breakdown of loans and of the industry sectors of commercial loans.

In 2004, the federal banking agencies issued an interagency statement updating bankers on the status of these efforts to clarify loan loss accounting reiterating the banking agencies':

> longstanding supervisory guidance [that] financial institutions must maintain an [allowance for loan and lease losses] ALLL at a level that is appropriate to absorb estimated credit losses inherent in the loan and lease portfolio. Arriving at such an allowance involves a high degree of management judgment and results in a range of estimated losses. Accordingly, prudent, conservative, but not excessive, loan loss allowances that represent management's best estimate from within an acceptable range of estimated losses are appropriate.

Interagency Statement, Update on Accounting for Loan and Lease Losses (Mar. 1, 2004) (Federal Reserve SR 04–05). This was followed by an Interagency Policy Statement on the Allowance for Loan and Lease Losses (Dec. 13, 2006), available at <www.fdic.gov/news/news/press/2006/pr06115 b.pdf> and accompanying questions and answers document, available at <www.fdic.gov/news/news/press/2006/pr06115a.pdf>.

Many banks discovered during the financial crisis that they had inadequate reserves to cover the amount of loan defaults they experienced. Perhaps in response, the SEC sent a letter to Chief Financial Officers to companies in the summer of 2009 suggesting that in the light of the "current economic environment" they reassess their valuation of loan loss reserves. The Financial Accounting Standards Board (FASB) and the International Accounting Standards Board (IASB) circulated exposure drafts that propose changes to the current method of calculating loan loss reserves. The FASB proposal provides that loan loss allowances are to be based on expected losses rather than incurred losses.

F. FAIR VALUE ACCOUNTING

Fair value accounting is sometimes referred to as "mark-to-market" accounting. Under current accounting rules, loans a bank expects to hold to maturity are report at their amortized cost subject to the loan loss reserve amount described above. The fair value of these assets is discussed only in footnotes to the financial statements. Assets held for sale in the near term are reported at fair value, with unrealized gains or losses included in earnings. Assets that are neither in the trading account or expected to be held to maturity are classified as "available-for-sale" and are reported at fair value. Unrealized gains or losses for these assets do not flow through to bank earnings, but are reported as a component of shareholders equity called "Other Compensation Income" (OCI). During the financial crisis, some financial institutions struggled with the mark-to-market determination for assets held in their trading accounts for which there was effectively no market. The accounting standards required that "exit price" be used for these assets, which is difficult to determine in an illiquid market.

The FASB exposure draft, Accounting for Financial Instruments and Revisions to the Accounting for Derivative Instruments and Hedging Activities, proposes that for assets that will be held to maturity, a loan loss allowance account be maintained with changes to that account flowing through to earnings. Moreover, the fair value of assets would be reported under the proposal, with changes to fair value recorded in OCI. The American Bankers Association is concerned that marking all loans to their fair market value will have a significant impact on bank equity through the OCI component of shareholders' equity.

SECTION 3.   COMMERCIAL LENDING CONCERNS

A.   LOAN PARTICIPATIONS, SYNDICATED LOANS, AND LEVERAGED LOANS

Borrowers who need to borrow a lot of money often must arrange a multi-lender transaction. As banks have gotten bigger, so have their lending limits, but there may be times when a credit facility exceeds the lending limit of one bank. Banks also wish to diversify their loan portfolios and may not wish to extend credit to one borrower up to the maximum legal amount. In such cases, the lead lender may sell participating interests in the loan to other lenders or may arrange a syndicated credit facility.[17]

In a loan participation, the loan is negotiated between the borrower and the lead lender. The lead lender subsequently sells a percentage of the loan that has already been made to one or more participants. The borrower may not be aware that there are other participants in the loan, as the lead lender maintains the relationship with the borrower, and collects loan payments from the borrower to remit to the purchaser of the loan participation its pro rata share of the loan payments. Often, these loans are secured and the collateral underlying the loan helps to protect the purchaser of the loan participation. The loan participant is considered to have a double-risk exposure—to the borrower and to the lead lender. The Financial Accounting Standards Board (FASB) considered whether the portion of the loan purchased in the participation should nevertheless be accounted for as an asset of the lead lender.[18] Banks objected strongly

---

17.   See Megan Elizabeth Jones, Note, Bankers Beware: The Risks of Syndicated Credits, 3 N.C. Banking Inst. 169 (1999).

18.   If the full value of the loan remained an asset of the lead lender, then the lead lender would be required to hold capital against the full value of the loan, not just the portion of the loan

to this proposal and FASB will continue to treat loan participations as sales by the lead lender; however, the participation contracts must specify that the transaction is not a loan or other financing.

In a syndicated loan, each lender is a member of the syndicate and a party to the loan documents. The borrower has a direct contractual relationship with each member of the lending syndicate. Syndicated credit facilities often involve a revolving credit arrangement used by the borrower for working capital and a term loan that is used to refinance the borrower's existing debt. The "pieces" of a syndicated credit are generally $50 million or more in amount.

The lead lender in a loan participation or the administrative agent in a syndicated loan may charge a fee based on a percentage of the loan for the work performed. Thus, the bank is able to add fee income from facilitating the multi-lender credit transaction to its interest spread revenue from the loan.

BANCO ESPANOL DE CREDITO v. SECURITY PACIFIC NATIONAL BANK

United States Court of Appeals, Second Circuit, 1992.
973 F.2d 51, *cert. denied*, 509 U.S. 903 (1993).

ALTIMARI, CIRCUIT JUDGE.

* * * In 1988, Security Pacific extended a line of credit to Integrated permitting Integrated to obtain short-term unsecured loans from Security Pacific. Security Pacific subsequently made a series of short-term loans to Integrated. Security Pacific sold these loans, in whole or in part, to various institutional investors at differing interest rates. Resales of these loans were prohibited without Security Pacific's express written consent. The practice of selling loans to other institutions is known as "loan participation." Short-term loan participation permits a primary lender such as Security Pacific to spread its risk, while at the same time allowing a purchaser with excess cash to earn a higher return than that available on comparable money market instruments. Security Pacific, as manager of the loans, earned a fee equal to the difference between the interest paid by the debtor and the lower interest paid to the purchaser.

Security Pacific assumed no responsibility for the ability of Integrated to repay its loans. Indeed, each purchaser of loan participations was required to enter into a Master Participation Agreement ("MPA"), which contained a general disclaimer providing, in relevant part, that the purchaser "acknowledges that it has independently and without reliance upon Security [Pacific] and based upon such documents and information as the participant has deemed appropriate, made its own credit analysis."

In late 1988, Integrated began to encounter financial difficulties. In April 1989, Security Pacific refused a request by Integrated to extend

retained by the lead lender. See William H. Isaac, Questioning the Definition of "True Sales," Am. Banker, July 20, 2004.

further credit. Despite this refusal, Security Pacific continued to sell loan participations on Integrated's debt. Indeed, from mid-April through June 9, 1989, Security Pacific sold seventeen different loan participations to plaintiffs-appellants. Unable to obtain enough working capital, Integrated began defaulting on its loans on June 12, 1989. Integrated subsequently declared bankruptcy. * * *

As a result of Integrated's default, two sets of investors, who had purchased the seventeen loan participations, initiated separate actions against Security Pacific in the United States District Court for the Southern District of New York. Contending that the loan participations were "securities" within the meaning of the Securities Act of 1933 ("the 1933 Act"), plaintiffs sought to rescind their purchase agreements by alleging that Security Pacific had failed to disclose to them material facts about Integrated's financial condition in violation of § 12(2) of the 1933 Act. 15 U.S.C. § 77l(2). Plaintiffs also claimed that Security Pacific's failure to disclose constituted a breach of Security Pacific's implied and express contractual duties under its MPA's, and a breach of Security Pacific's duty to disclose material information based on superior knowledge. Based on these common law claims, plaintiffs sought to recover their investment plus unpaid interest. * * *

Section 2(1) of the 1933 Act provides in pertinent part:

> [u]nless the context otherwise requires—(1) the term "security" means any note ... evidence of indebtedness, ... investment contract, ... or any certificate of interest or participation in ... any of the foregoing.

15 U.S.C. § 77b(1). It is well-settled that certificates evidencing loans by commercial banks to their customers for use in the customers' current operations are not securities. See, e.g., Reves v. Ernst & Young, 494 U.S. 56, 65 (1990) citing Chemical Bank v. Arthur Andersen & Co., 726 F.2d 930, 939 (2d Cir.), cert. denied, 469 U.S. 884 (1984). However, as the district court noted, a participation in an instrument might in some circumstances be considered a security even where the instrument itself is not. See Banco Espanol de Credito, 763 F.Supp. at 41.

With respect to loan participations, the district court reasoned that "because the plaintiffs ... did not receive an undivided interest in a pool of loans, but rather purchased participation in a specific, identifiable short-term Integrated loan, the loan participation did not have an identity separate from the underlying loan." Id. at 42. Thus, Judge Pollack reasoned, because under Chemical Bank the loans to Integrated were not securities, the plaintiffs' purchase of discrete portions of these loans could not be considered securities.

On appeal, plaintiffs concede that traditional loan participations do not qualify as securities. Instead, plaintiffs contend that the peculiar nature of Security Pacific's loan participation program—which aimed at the sale of 100% of its loans through high speed telephonic sales and often pre-paid transactions—qualified these loan participations as securities.

Specifically, plaintiffs argue that the loan participations sold by Security Pacific are more properly characterized as securities—in the nature of "notes"—as enumerated in § 2(1) of the 1933 Act.

In examining whether the loan participations could be considered "notes" which are also securities, the district court applied the "family resemblance" test set forth by the Supreme Court in *Reves*, 494 U.S. 63 at 63–67. Under the family resemblance test, a note is presumed to be a security unless an examination of the note, based on four factors, reveals a strong resemblance between the note and one of a judicially-enumerated list of instruments that are not securities. Id. at 65. If the note in question is not sufficiently similar to one of these instruments, a court must then consider, using the same four factors, whether another category of non-security instruments should be added to the list. Id. at 67. The four *Reves* factors to be considered in this examination are: (1) the motivations that would prompt a reasonable buyer and seller to enter into the transaction; (2) the plan of distribution of the instrument; (3) the reasonable expectations of the investing public; and (4) whether some factor, such as the existence of another regulatory scheme, significantly reduces the risk of the instrument, thereby rendering application of the securities laws unnecessary. Id. at 66–67.

In addressing the first *Reves* factor, the district court found that Security Pacific was motivated by a desire to increase lines of credit to Integrated while diversifying Security Pacific's risk, that Integrated was motivated by a need for short-term credit at competitive rates to finance its current operations, and that the purchasers of the loan participations sought a short-term return on excess cash. Based on these findings, the district court concluded that "the overall motivation of the parties was the promotion of commercial purposes" rather than an investment in a business enterprise. Banco Espanol de Credito, 763 F.Supp. at 42–43.

Weighing the second *Reves* factor * * * [t]he plan of distribution specifically prohibited resales of the loan participations without the express written permission of Security Pacific. This limitation worked to prevent the loan participations from being sold to the general public, thus limiting eligible buyers to those with the capacity to acquire information about the debtor. This limitation also distinguishes Gary Plastic Packaging v. Merrill Lynch, Pierce, Fenner & Smith, Inc., 756 F.2d 230 (2d Cir. 1985), which involved a secondary market for the instruments traded in that case.

With regard to the third factor—the reasonable perception of the instrument by the investing public—the district court considered the expectations of the sophisticated purchasers who signed MPA's and determined that these institutions were given ample notice that the instruments were participations in loans and not investments in a business enterprise. Id.

Finally, the district court noted that the Office of the Comptroller of the Currency has issued specific policy guidelines addressing the sale of loan participations. Thus, the fourth factor—the existence of another regulatory scheme—indicated that application of the securities laws was unnecessary. Id.

Thus, under the *Reves* family resemblance analysis, as properly applied by the district court, we hold that the loan participations in the instant case are analogous to the enumerated category of loans issued by banks for commercial purposes and therefore do not satisfy the statutory definition of "notes" which are "securities." Since the loan participations do not meet the statutory definition of securities, plaintiffs may not maintain their action for relief under § 12(2) of the 1933 Act.

* * * Turning to plaintiffs' contractual and other common-law claims, we agree with the district court that the waiver provision in the MPA's signed by the loan participants specifically absolved Security Pacific of any responsibility to disclose information relating to Integrated's financial condition. Moreover, as an arms length transaction between sophisticated financial institutions, the law imposed no independent duty on Security Pacific to disclose information that plaintiffs could have discovered through their own efforts. See, e.g., Aaron Ferer & Sons v. Chase Manhattan Bank, 731 F.2d 112, 122 (2d Cir. 1984). * * *

OAKES, CHIEF JUDGE, dissenting: * * *

JOSE GABILONDOLEVERAGED LIQUIDITY: BEAR RAIDS AND JUNK LOANS IN THE NEW CREDIT MARKET

34 J. Corp. L. 447 (2009).

* * * Leveraged loans are secured, floating-rate loans (typically priced off LIBOR) that are syndicated between commercial banks and nonbank lenders such as hedge funds and investment banks. Corporate borrowers may seek these loans for many reasons. Start-up companies may be unable to secure investment-grade ratings. Or cyclical businesses may need capital during a low point in their operations. Firms exiting bankruptcy or "fallen angels"—formerly investment-grade issuers that have been notched down—may be relegated here until the issuer's financial prospects improve. Leveraged loan issuance is cyclical in the direction that Minsky predicted—increasing during economic expansion and risk-taking. Issuance also correlates with trends in mergers and acquisitions and recapitalizations, two common forms of "shareholder-friendly" upstreaming.

Like the junk bonds that financed the takeovers of the 1980s, leveraged loans rest on the assumption that lending at a subinvestment grade (albeit at a floating rate) is fine, so long as the rate reflects the default risk and is diversified in a portfolio. How borrowers, lenders, traders, and brokers came to think about leveraged loans reflects the semantic shifts that come with financial euphoria. The financial prefix "leverage" came to substitute for the harsher sounding "subinvestment grade" or, worse still, "junk" before the word "loan." Rather than thinking in terms of "credit supply" and borrower "demand for credit," the loans became "supply" for which (leveraged) investment demand competed, completing the semantic shift thanks to the growth of secondary markets. Indeed, even global financial regulators have adopted the custom of using "leveraged" as a substitute for "subinvestment grade" when it comes to these loans. These loans are another example of the kind of financial innovation that, according to Minsky, "regulates the pace of movement out of hedge and into speculative finance," and, presumably, Ponzi finance too.[19] Much as the petro-liquidity of the 1970s led to this type of investment demand, this last leverage wave led to increasingly complex products that were further removed from their underlying cash flows.

In 2006, the leveraged loan market represented about one-fifth of the overall corporate loan market and equaled about one-half of overall bond issuance. Had the trends in the first half of 2007 continued throughout the year, the volume of leveraged loans would have exceeded that of high-yield bonds. Leveraged loans have their own trade group—the Loan Syndications & Trading Association (LSTA). LSTA promotes standardization of loan and settlement documentation, credit ratings for loans, Committee on Uniform Securities Identification Procedures (CUSIP) numbers for loans, and benchmark indices. Credit rating agencies helped to promote these loans by rating them, beginning with S & P in 2000. Within a few years, specialized recovery ratings had developed to supplement the projected default rate with estimates of how much an investor would recover in the event of default. Anticipating such ratings by several decades, Hickman's bond research had also considered the effective recovery rate on defaulted bonds.[20]

The arranger of the leveraged loan gets a fee of 1.5%–2.5% for putting the loan together, more than the fees charged for investment-grade loans, which may have no arranger fees. Initially, leveraged loans included a revolving credit line and an amortizing term loan—so called "pro rata" tranches that bank investors preferred. While banks prefer to hold pro rata tranches, nonbank investors have tended to prefer junior tranches that did not amortize, had longer terms, and often lower security. So it has tended to be nonbank institutional investors who provided the riskier financing, a trend borne out by a finding in a 2006 federal review of syndicated lending that generally the credit quality of syndicated loans held by banks increased while that held by nonbanks decreased. Indeed, nonbank investors have become so dominant in these loans that "by early 2002, most [leveraged] loans were structured without an amortizing term loan component, and while the typical structure still included a revolver, it was usually a much smaller share of the overall package than would have been the norm in the past."[21]

19.　[n.301] [Hyman P.] Minsky, [Stabilizing an] Unstable Economy, at 212 [(1986)].

20.　[n.309] [W. Braddock] Hickman, [Trends and Cycles in Corporate Bond Financing] 2–4 [(Nat'l Bureau of Economic Research, Inc., Occasional Paper No. 37, 1952)].

21.　[n.314] [Stephen A.] Lumpkin, [The Integration of the Corporate Bond and Commercial Loan Markets, Fin. Mkt. Trends, Nov. 2003, at 69.]

The Loan Pricing Corporation classifies as leveraged those loans with BB, BB/B, and B or lower ratings. Others use the loan's spread over a reference rate at the time the loan is made, typically a spread of between 125 to 275 basis points over a reference rate. Not surprisingly, leveraged loans correlate most closely as an asset class to high-yield (junk) bonds, despite formal differences between the two. For example, most leveraged loans may be prepaid without penalty while high-yield bonds may not be callable by the issuer at all, or only occasionally, and then subject to a premium. These loans generally have a shorter term than high-yield bonds These loans may also have more financial covenants than do high-yield bonds.

The participation of commercial banks in originating leveraged loans has declined, in part because of investments in regulatory capital to dispose of subinvestment grade assets. At the same time, nonbank investors became interested in leveraged loans because of their high rates and secured status. For example, hedge funds became active in both the primary and secondary markets for leveraged loans, adding both liquidity and the risk that this liquidity will suddenly evaporate. It was nonbank demand for these loans that led to the concept of the "institutional loan" to refer to the funding provided by them. The S & P/LSTA Leveraged Loan Index tracks only the institutional sector of the leveraged loan market, not the bank sector, suggesting that nonbank lenders are, indeed, changing the structure of credit, much as the Fed's decision to fund the Bear deal implies.

Both junk bonds and leveraged loans rest on financial logic that Braddock Hickman demonstrated in his early studies of borrowing cycles. Hickman's cycle study looked at bond issuance over the prior 50–year period of his study and found that the realized yield on the most senior secured obligations exceeded that of the least secured obligation in all but 2 of the 12 four-year blocks during which the study period was divided. In other words, bond issuers had paid too much for the senior secured financing given that lenders should have been willing to accept a lower rate of return in exchange for collateralized risk. And the yield spread between the most secured bonds and the lowest ranked unsecured securities was not as large as one would have expected. Both results seemed counterintuitive in that they did not reflect the idea that return should be proportional to financial risk. In fact, though, they were an early demonstration of financial diversification of risk through Markowitz's portfolio theory. And Hickman's findings about returns from high-yield instruments would help Michael Milken to promote junk bonds 30 years later. Moody's Investor Services revisited and corroborated Hickman's findings in 2004 when explaining how it distinguishes between investment-grade and speculative bonds.

Between June and August 2007, leveraged loans faced their first major market liquidity crisis: origination dried up, loan products traded at a discount in the secondary market, and traders shorted loan indices. As activity slowed in the secondary market, these loans became stranded on the books of originating lenders, including banks. Surges in volume delayed trade settlement to an average of 17 days after the trade date. Banks with contractual duties to fund future leveraged loans found themselves choosing between paying "break-up fees" to walk away from the deal or to honor their commitments to originate the loans.

In the secondary market for leveraged loans, buyers and sellers deal in previously-issued loans, sometimes at a discount over the loan's par value based on changes in interest rates or the borrower's creditworthiness. The secondary market for these loans grew during the past decade. For example, the number of par value loans for which three or more market-makers made quotes increased ten-fold from 82 in 1998 to over 880 in 2007. Much of this trading happens right after the initial allocation of a loan (as investors adjust their holdings to reach their target), but, at the peak of the borrowing cycle, there had also been subsequent secondary trading, more so than with investment-grade loans. Reporting of secondary loan transactions—along the lines of what is common in the equity markets—still does not occur systematically, so more is known about price quotes than about actual trades.

As in the origination market, in the secondary market nonbank investors are more active than banks. As this market grew, investment banks that had traded these loans as brokers for the accounts of others began to take more proprietary positions in the loans. The same seems to be true for hedge funds that specialize in the credit market exposures.

Investment vehicles called "collateralized loan obligations" (CLO) played a key role in the secondary market by buying leveraged loans to collateralize the issuance of their own securities. Such CLOs may have accounted for over one-fifth of all secondary market demand for the loans. Compared with other forms of asset-backed securities like mortgage-backed securities and collateralized-debt obligations, CLOs tend to contain a more diverse set of receivables whose prepayment characteristics are harder to predict. Most frequently, CLOs buy leveraged loans based on one, two, or three month LIBOR. And CLOs seem to hold a disproportionate share of loans with fewer covenants used for "shareholder-friendly" activities. Although modest, a secondary market in which interests in CLOs trade has also developed. Just as there are balance sheet and synthetic collateralized-debt obligations, CLOs may also be structured around a real portfolio of loans (so-called "balance sheet" CLOs) or hold an unrelated pool of securities as collateral but issue securities priced off of loan obligations (so-called "synthetic" CLO). * * *

Private equity[22] investors often turned to leveraged loans for financing. The value of leveraged loans was triple the amount of money raised

---

22. Limitations placed by Dodd–Frank on bank investments in private equity funds are discussed further in Chapter 11.

through junk bond offerings in 2005. The leveraged loan market exploded in 2006, with new issues totaling nearly $500 billion in value, a fifty-eight percent increase over 2005. The amount of leveraged loans held in institutional portfolios jumped by nearly $150 billion in 2006. Further leverage was added to the market through "second lien" loans that paid higher spreads than the typical leveraged loan, but that were subordinated to other lenders. The leveraged loan market continued to boom in 2007 until the credit crunch shut it down. In the first quarter of 2007, $183 billion was raised through leveraged loans. By mid–2007, outstanding leveraged loans totaled almost $500 billion, of which about fifty percent were below investment grade.

Citigroup underwrote $114 billion in leveraged loans for private equity borrowers in 2007, earning fees of about $850 million. Banc of America Securities was the underwriter of $145 billion in leveraged loans in 2007, but was bested by JPMorgan Chase, which underwrote $217 billion in such offerings. By then private equity groups had become prime bank customers, accounting for about eighteen percent of bank revenue from investment banking activities. Leveraged loans were not made only to private equity groups. In January 2006, Georgia Pacific Corp. borrowed $11 billion through a leveraged loan syndication.

The leveraged loan market was badly damaged by the credit crunch in 2007 and then by the subprime crisis in 2008. The top ten leveraged loan underwriters had almost $200 billion in exposure from leveraged loans on their own books, and were forced to write off a portion of those loans. However, things could have been much worse for the banks. In 1995, commercial banks held over seventy percent of syndicated loans, but by 2007, they held only thirteen percent of their successor, leveraged loans. Hedge funds and other institutional investors had taken large positions in leveraged loans, but dumped those investments at steep discounts in order to raise cash in 2008.

QUESTIONS AND NOTES

1. What is the current market for syndicated loans? The Loan Syndications and Trading Association website is a good resource on the syndicated lending market, <www.lsta.org>.

2. Are large banks or small banks more likely to participate in loan participations? Are large banks or small banks more likely to participate in syndications?

3. JP Morgan, Bank of America, and Citigroup were the top three originators of syndicated loans in 2006, accounting for over one-half of the market.

4. More than half of the purchasers of syndicated loans are institutional investors. This group has helped develop a non-binding set of practices for amending syndicated loan agreements to respond to frustrations with agent banks asking for approval of amendments on short notice and with little

information. Amendments to syndicated loan agreements often require a 51% majority of the debtholders. These guidelines suggest a conference call to discuss amendments with forty-eight hours advance notice of the call, a standard five business days for syndicate members to approve the amendment, followed by written notice of the outcome of the vote on the amendment. The "Standard Amendment Procedures" was published by the Loan Syndications and Trading Association.

B.   SECONDARY LOAN MARKET

Banks and thrifts are vulnerable to interest rate risk when they fund long-term, fixed-rate loans with deposits for which they must pay interest based on prevailing market interest rates. This risk is especially pronounced for institutions that do a lot of mortgage lending. Most home mortgage loans are made at a fixed interest rate, often with a term of thirty years. The interest rate risk may be reduced by selling loans in the secondary market or by securitizing loans.

Two of the largest purchasers of home mortgage loans in the secondary market are Fannie Mae and Freddie Mac, as government-sponsored enterprises (GSEs).

The National Housing Act of 1934 established the Federal Housing Administration (FHA). Its principal function is to insure home mortgage loans made by private lenders. The Act also provided for the chartering of one or more national mortgage associations to buy and sell the mortgages insured by the FHA. Pursuant to this authority, the National Mortgage Association was formed in 1938. This entity became the Federal National Mortgage Association in 1948, and in 1954 its ownership structure was converted to mixed-ownership with the government owning the preferred stock and private shareholders owning the corporation's common stock. In 1968, this corporation was divided into two different entities—the Government National Mortgage Association (Ginnie Mae) to be owned by the government within the Department of Housing and Urban Development, and the Federal National Mortgage Association (which adopted its nickname—Fannie Mae—as its official name) to be privately owned.[23] The 1968 Charter Act provided Fannie Mae the authority to issue Mortgage–Backed Securities (MBS). Ginnie Mae does not purchase mortgage loans or issue mortgage-backed securities, rather it acts solely as a guarantor of mortgage-backed securities issued by approved institutions.

Fannie Mae's role expanded when it became a private corporation in 1968 and began to buy conventional mortgage loans not subject to any special governmental programs (such as government insurance or government guarantee). In 1970, Fannie Mae's stock began trading on the New York Stock Exchange and it was authorized to create a secondary market in conventional mortgages. In 1970, Congress chartered the Federal Home Loan Mortgage Corporation (now called Freddie Mac) to buy conventional

(handwritten margin notes: Fannie Mae: Fed'l Nat'l Mortgage Ass'n; Freddie Mac: Fed'l Home Loan mortgage Corp.)

---

23. Fannie Mae's government-owned stock was retired.

oversees Fannie & Freddie

mortgages from federally insured financial institutions. In 1972, Freddie Mac began its mortgage-backed securities program.

In 1992, Congress created the Office of Federal Housing Enterprise Oversight (OFHEO), an agency within the Department of Housing and Urban Development (HUD), to oversee Fannie Mae and Freddie Mac and ensure their adequate capitalization and safe operation. As government-sponsored enterprises, Fannie Mae and Freddie Mac were able to raise money to fund their secondary market activities at lower rates than competing financing institutions. Each GSE benefited from exemption from state and local taxes, exemption from SEC registration of securities, and access to a $2.5 billion line of credit provided by the U.S. Treasury. The amount and propriety of this implicit government subsidy were the subject of some criticism. Peter Wallison, a senior fellow at the American Enterprise Institute, was one prominent critic. He raised concerns over the financial viability of Fannie Mae and Freddie Mac, and the systemic threat they posed, for a number of years.[24]

The 1992 legislation that created OFHEO also required Fannie Mae and Freddie Mac to meet certain goals to provide for the housing needs of low-and moderate-income borrowers, and to ensure housing credit for certain underserved areas.

OFHEO set $730 bill. cap on mortgage holdings

In the wake of significant accounting irregularities, the CEO, CFO and president of Freddie Mac resigned in 2003. Fannie Mae also reported in 2003 a $1.3 billion error in calculating unrealized gains. In late 2004, an accounting scandal at Fannie resulted in the ouster of its CEO and CFO. As a result of these accounting irregularities, OFHEO imposed an approximately $730 billion cap on the mortgage assets that could be held by each company. Nonetheless, Fannie Mae was one of the country's largest corporations in terms of assets. In 2007, Fannie Mae and Freddie Mac had combined mortgage assets of close to $1.5 trillion.

The financial crisis placed tremendous pressure on Fannie Mae and Freddie Mac when many borrowers defaulted on the home mortgage loans they held.[25] By early 2008, it was estimated that about 40% of the mortgages held or guaranteed by the GSEs were subprime mortgages. Defaults on these mortgages also negatively impacted the banks holding the MBS issued by Fannie Mae and Freddie Mac. For the GSEs, losses began to mount. Fannie Mae reported a loss for the first quarter of 2008 of $2.2 billion. On March 19, 2008, OFHEO eased the stiffer capital requirements that had been imposed on Fannie Mae and Freddie Mac as a result of their earlier accounting problems. This change allowed them to invest in additional mortgages valued at $200 billion.

---

24. Serving Two Masters, Yet Out of Control (Peter J. Wallison, ed. 2001); Peter J. Wallison, Thomas H. Stanton & Bert Ely, Privatizing Fannie Mae, Freddie Mac, and the Federal Home Loan Banks (2004).

25. For a further description of these events see Jerry W. Markham, VI A Financial History of the United States: The Subprime Crisis (2006–2009) (2011).

OFHEO warned in April 2008 that, while Fannie Mae and Freddie Mac had made improvements in their systems and operations, they still were of "significant supervisory concern." Although it eased their capital requirements only a few months previously, OFHEO advised Congress in May 2008 that Fannie Mae and Freddie Mac's capital was insufficient for the risks they faced and that taxpayers could be left footing a big bill. More concern was raised in May 2008, after the *New York Times* published a front-page article questioning whether Fannie Mae and Freddie Mac might be endangered by the growing problems in the mortgage market.[26] The article pointed out that the two GSEs were handling more than eighty percent of all mortgages sold to investors in the first quarter of 2008. This was twice the percentage of such sales in 2006. To counter concerns over its financial stability, Fannie Mae announced that it was raising $6 billion in additional capital. This was in addition to the $7 billion it raised in December 2007 through the sale of preferred stock. That did not stabilize the situation.

On July 10, 2008, the government announced that Freddie Mac was technically insolvent and that Fannie Mae would be shortly. The Housing and Economic Recovery Act of 2008 (HERA), enacted at the end of July 2008, replaced OFHEO with the new Federal Housing Finance Agency (FHFA) to strengthen government oversight over the two FSEs and the twelve regional Federal Home Loan Banks (FHLBs). HERA legislation further authorized an unlimited credit line to Fannie Mae, Freddie Mac, and the FHLBs. The Treasury Department was also authorized to purchase stock in Freddie Mac and Fannie Mae in order to support their capital, and HERA established procedures for placing Fannie Mae and Freddie Mac into government conservatorship. These measures did not stop the hemorrhaging. Both GSEs continued to report losses and Fannie Mae announced that it would reduce its mortgage purchases, dealing another blow to the collapsing housing market.

Secretary Paulson stated on August 10, 2008 that he did not plan to inject capital into Fannie and Freddie, but less than a month later, on Sunday, September 8, 2008, the Treasury Department seized control of both Fannie Mae and Freddie Mac. They were placed in conservatorship and their executives were replaced. James Lockhart, the Director of the newly created FHFA, was given control over these failed institutions. At this point, Fannie Mae and Freddie Mac had suffered more than $14 billion in losses in 2008, and their stock values had dropped more than ninety percent.

The Treasury Department created a new secured lending credit facility for Fannie Mae and Freddie Mac. Loans from that facility were to be collateralized by mortgage-backed securities issued by Freddie Mac or Fannie Mae or advances made by the FHLBs. Fannie Mae was also easily able to sell $7 billion in two-year notes after it was placed into conserva-

---

26. Charles Duhigg, Doubts Raised on Big Backers of Mortgages, N.Y. Times, May 6, 2008, at A1.

torship but only because of its government backing. The Treasury Department further agreed to purchase up to $100 billion of senior preferred stock in both Fannie Mae and Freddie Mac and to provide up to $200 billion in capital to support their obligations through 2012.

Treasury's funding, in the neighborhood of $150 billion in the summer of 2010, is intended to ensure that the GSEs can continue to provide liquidity and stability to housing and mortgage markets. As a result of the Treasury funding, the government owns about 80% of Fannie Mae and Freddie Mac. Fannie and Freddie are obligated to pay a 10% annual dividend on their government shares, an amount that exceeded their net income even in their most profitable years. As of mid–2010, the Fed and Treasury had purchased over $1.4 trillion in MBS from Fannie and Freddie since their government conservatorship began in September 2008. The government later announced that it was suspending purchases of Fannie Mae and Freddie Mac obligations and was, instead, lifting the $400 billion ceiling on its commitment to those GSEs. The government agreed to supply capital to them on an as needed basis, thereby creating an unlimited guarantee of their operations.

The Treasury Department is preparing a legislative proposal for dealing with the failed GSEs. This subject, although one of the most significant in terms of government investments during the financial crisis, was not considered in the Dodd–Frank Act. The Dodd–Frank Act requires the Treasury to submit a report to the Senate Banking Committee and the House Financial Services Committee on options for ending the government conservatorship of Fannie Mae and Freddie Mac while minimizing the costs to taxpayers. The report must consider options, such as:

(A) the gradual wind-down and liquidation of such entities;

(B) the privatization of such entities;

(C) the incorporation of the functions of such entities into a Federal agency;

(D) the dissolution of Fannie Mae and Freddie Mac into smaller companies; or

(E) any other measures the Secretary [of the Treasury] determines appropriate.

Dodd–Frank Act, § 1074.

The GSEs, notwithstanding their problems, play a huge role in home mortgage finance. Fannie Mae helps to ensure that money is available to fund home mortgage loans first by buying mortgages from lenders and second by issuing Mortgage–Backed Securities (MBS) to lenders in return for pools of mortgage loans. In the first case, lenders receive cash to use to make additional mortgage loans, and in the second case, lenders who receive the MBS have a liquid asset that they may hold or sell. Fannie Mae funds these purchase by issuing debt securities to investors. Until the mortgage crisis, these MBS were attractive investments for banks as safe, liquid, and earning a higher return than Treasury securities. Banks were also permitted to hold lower capital for MBS issued by Fannie Mae or Freddie Mac than for the mortgages themselves.

Freddie Mac touts the public policy benefits of its business lines in the excerpt below.

FREDDIE MAC OUR BUSINESS

www.freddiemac.com/corporate/company_profile/our_business/.

* * * First, we have been a consistent market presence, providing mortgage liquidity in a wide range of economic environments. This has become significant during the credit crunch that began in mid–2007 and resulted in the exit of most other mortgage funders from the market. Indeed, in 2009 Freddie Mac and Fannie Mae funded 72 percent of all new home loans and an even higher percentage of multifamily loans.

Second, consumers have enjoyed uninterrupted access to long term, fixed rate mortgages. Banks and other depositories tend to hold shorter term, floating rate assets in their loan portfolios. These institutions finance long-term, fixed-rate mortgages (i.e., 15–, 20–and 30–year terms) largely by selling them into the secondary market, where Freddie Mac and Fannie Mae securitize and guarantee the loans. In 2009, long term, fixed-rate mortgages comprised 97 [percent] of new home loans.

Third, consumers have typically paid less on home loans funded by Freddie Mac or Fannie Mae. Because investors usually place a greater value on our mortgage securities, we have been able to pass this premium ultimately along to homebuyers in the form of lower mortgage rates. During normal or flush markets, where there are many sources of mortgage funds, homebuyer savings on our loans have averaged about 0.30 percent (or 30 basis points) compared to loans that exceed our loan limits. During the credit crunch that began in 2007, however, mortgage rate savings have been high as 1.84 percent (or 184 basis points). At year-end 2009, consumers were paying 0.91 percent (or 91 basis points) less on loans backed by Freddie Mac and Fannie Mae.

Fourth, consumers are able to refinance their loans when mortgage rates decline. Because of the nature of long-term, fixed-rate mortgages, homeowners are protected against rising interest rates but are able to take advantage of declining rates through refinancing. In 2009, Freddie Mac refinanced $379 billion in home loans for 1.7 million families who reduced their annual mortgage payments by $2,600 on average. In other words, mortgage refinanced enabled by Freddie Mac in 2009 created $4.5 billion in homeowner savings.

Fifth, all these benefits accrue the most to families of modest financial means. The majority of home loans that we fund support low-and moderate-income families, reflecting affordable housing goals set forth by the federal government. Further, more than four in five multifamily loans

support renters earn at or below the area median income where they live.
* * *

1. Prior to the government conservatorship of Fannie Mae and Freddie Mac, their "implicit" government subsidy was criticized. What did we learn about this government subsidy following their September 2008 conservatorship? Is it still implicit?

2. Go to the Fannie Mae website and see if you can determine the maximum amount single-family home mortgage that Fannie Mae will purchase. The amount of the mortgage may vary by whether it is located in a designed high-cost area or a high-cost state.

3. What are the current proposals to reform the GSEs? Are the Fed and Treasury still buying GSE MBS?

4. Fannie Mae and Freddie Mac do not purchase individual subprime mortgages, but they have purchased some of the investment grade securities issued in private securitizations of subprime mortgages. As of September 2007, the two companies together held about $170 billion in securities backed by pools of subprime mortgage pools.

C. SECURITIZATION

Banks may be interested in selling loans in the secondary market or securitizing the loans. In a securitzation, a bank or other lender sells a pool of loans. The purchaser of the pool places the loans into a securitization vehicle, often called a special purpose vehicle (SPV) or special purpose entity (SPE) that "securitizes" the loans by selling securities to investors (primarily debt securities). The proceeds from the sale of securities are used to pay for the pool of loans. The borrowers on the loans make payments on the loans to the SPV and a servicer of loans appointed by the SPV collects the payments and uses them to fund the principal and interest payments to the investors who own the debt securities.

Securitizing loans has a number of advantages for banks. They receive cash from the sale of the loan pool that may be used to make new loans and earn new loan origination fees. The bank no longer bears the risk of default on the loans sold or any risk from changing interest rates if the loans were made at a fixed rate (as opposed to an adjustable rate) of interest. Banks often serve as the servicer of the loans that they sold, earning fees for the servicing. This role as servicer has raised concerns of conflict of interest where a bank is servicing a loan on a property for another lender on which the servicing bank has a second mortgage. This conflict is claimed to have frustrated refinancing of delinquent first mortgages. Gretchen Morgenson, In This Play, One Role is Enough, N.Y. Times, August, 15, 2010, at B1.

Small banks may not generate a sufficient number of loans to form a large enough pool of loans for a securitization. These banks may, however, elect to sell loans into the secondary market to a GSE or private purchaser that may ultimately combine them with other loans that are then used to back a securitization. Larger banks sell loans into the secondary market and sometimes securitize loan pools that have been internally generated.

OFFICE OF THE COMPTROLLER OF THE CURRENCY COMPTROLLER'S HANDBOOK: ASSET SECURITIZATION

Nov. 1997.
<www.occ.treas.gov/handbook/assetsec.pdf>.

The market for mortgage-backed securities was boosted by the government agencies that stood behind these securities. To facilitate the securitization of nonmortgage assets, businesses substituted private credit enhancements. First, they overcollateralized pools of assets; shortly thereafter, they improved third-party and structural enhancements. In 1985, securitization techniques that had been developed in the mortgage market were applied for the first time to a class of nonmortgage assets—automobile loans. A pool of assets second only to mortgages, auto loans were a good match for structured finance; their maturities, considerably shorter than those of mortgages, made the timing of cash flows more predictable, and their long statistical histories of performance gave investors confidence.

The first significant bank credit card sale came to market in 1986 with a private placement of $50 million of bank card outstandings. This transaction demonstrated to investors that, if the yields were high enough, loan pools could support asset sales with higher expected losses and administrative costs than was true within the mortgage market. Sales of this type—with no contractual obligation by the seller to provide recourse—allowed banks to receive sales treatment for accounting and regulatory purposes (easing balance sheet and capital constraints), while at the same time allowing them to retain origination and servicing fees. After the success of this initial transaction, investors grew to accept credit card receivables as collateral, and banks developed structures to normalize the cash flows.

The next growth phase of securitization will likely involve nonconsumer assets. Most retail lending is "securitizable" because cash flows are predictable. Today, formula-driven credit scoring and credit monitoring techniques are widely used for such loans, and most retail programs produce fairly homogeneous loan portfolios. Commercial financing presents a greater challenge. Because a portfolio of commercial loans is typically less homogeneous than a retail portfolio, someone seeking to invest in them must often know much more about each individual credit, and the simpler tools for measuring and managing portfolio risk are less effective. Nonetheless, investment bankers and asset originators have proven extremely innovative at structuring cash flows and credit enhancements. Evidence of this can be seen in the market for securitized commercial real estate mortgages. Commercial real estate is one of the fastest-growing types of nonconsumer assets in the securitization markets, which fund approximately 10 percent of commercial mortgage debt.

The evolution of securitization is not surprising given the benefits that it offers to each of the major parties in the transaction.

For Originators. Securitization improves returns on capital by converting an on-balance sheet lending business into an off-balance-sheet income stream that is less capital intensive. Depending on the type of structure used, securitization may also lower borrowing costs, release additional capital for expansion or reinvestment purposes, and improve asset/liability and credit risk management.

For Investors. Securitized assets offer a combination of attractive yields (compared with other instruments of similar quality), increasing secondary market liquidity, and generally more protection by way of collateral overages and/or guarantees by entities with high and stable credit ratings. They also offer a measure of flexibility because their payment streams can be structured to meet investors' particular requirements. Most important, structural credit enhancements and diversified asset pools free investors of the need to obtain a detailed understanding of the underlying loans. This has been the single largest factor in the growth of the structured finance market.

For Borrowers. Borrowers benefit from the increasing availability of credit on terms that lenders may not have provided had they kept the loans on their balance sheets. For example, because a market exists for mortgage-backed securities, lenders can now extend fixed rate debt, which many consumers prefer over variable rate debt, without overexposing themselves to interest rate risk. Credit card lenders can originate very large loan pools for a diverse customer base at lower rates than if they had to fund the loans on their balance sheet. Nationwide competition among credit originators, coupled with strong investor appetite for the securities, has significantly expanded both the availability of credit and the pool of cardholders over the past decade.

―――――――

Several examples of securitization are described below.

(1) Mortgage-Backed Securities

Fannie Mae and Freddie Mac each issue mortgage-backed securities (MBS). MBS issued by these entities are sometimes referred to as "agency" securities. Ginnie Mae also participates in the MBS market by guaranteeing MBS.

GINNIE MAE
WHAT ARE MORTGAGE–BACKED SECURITIES?

<www.ginniemae.gov>.

Mortgage-backed securities (MBS) are pools of mortgages used as collateral for the issuance of securities in the secondary market. MBS are commonly referred to as "pass-through" certificates because the principal and interest of the underlying loans is "passed through" to investors. The interest rate of the security is lower than the interest rate of the underlying loan to allow for payment of servicing and guaranty fees. Ginnie Mae MBS are fully modified pass-through securities guaranteed by the full faith and credit of the United States government. Regardless of whether the mortgage payment is made, investors in Ginnie Mae MBS will receive full and timely payment of principal as well as interest.

Ginnie Mae MBS are created when eligible mortgage loans (those insured or guaranteed by FHA [Federal Housing Administration], the VA [Department of Veterans Affairs], RHS [Rural Housing Service] or PIH [Office of Public and Indian Housing]) are pooled by approved issuers and securitized. Ginnie Mae MBS investors receive a pro rata share of the resulting cash flows (again, net of servicing and guaranty fees). * * *

The creation of MBS was an important development for banks and thrifts. This securitization technique facilitated the raising of capital for the mortgage market. The Secondary Mortgage Market Enhancement Act of 1984 attempted to bolster MBS by exempting such securities from margin requirements and by allowing banks to invest in these secondary mortgage market obligations.

ROCKFORD LIFE INSURANCE CO. v. ILLINOIS
DEPARTMENT OF REVENUE

Supreme Court of the United States, 1987.
482 U.S. 182.

MR. JUSTICE STEVENS delivered the opinion of the Court.

This case involves financial instruments commonly known as "Ginnie Maes." These instruments are issued by private financial institutions, which are obliged to make timely payment of the principal and interest as set forth in the certificates. The Government National Mortgage Association (GNMA) guarantees that the payments will be made as scheduled. The question presented today is whether these instruments are exempt from state taxation under the constitutional provision of intergovernmental tax immunity, or under the relevant immunity statute.

The instruments involved here are standard securities bearing the title "Mortgage Backed Certificate Guaranteed by Government National Mortgage Association." True to that title, the instruments contain a provision in which GNMA pledges the "full faith and credit of the United States" to secure the timely payment of the interest and principal set forth in the instrument. The purpose of the guarantee, and the function of GNMA, which is a wholly owned government corporation within the Department of Housing and Urban Development, is to attract investors into the mortgage market by minimizing the risk of loss.[27] See 12 U.S.C. § 1716(a). There is uncontradicted evidence in the record supporting the conclusion that GNMA's guarantee is responsible for the ready marketability of these securities. That guarantee is not the primary obligation described in the instrument, however. The duty to make monthly payments of principal and interest to the investors falls squarely on the issuer of the certificate.[28]

The issuer of the certificate is a private party, generally a financial institution, that possesses a pool of federally guaranteed mortgages. Those individual mortgages are the product of transactions between individual borrowers and private lending institutions. It is this pool of private obligations that provides the source of funds, as well as the primary security, for the principal and interest that the issuer promises to pay to the order of the holder of the instrument. After a pool of qualified mortgages is assembled by a qualified issuer, the issuer enters into an agreement with GNMA authorizing the issuer to sell one or more certificates, each of which is proportionately based on and backed by all the mortgages in the designated pool, and each of which is also guaranteed by GNMA. The issuer thereafter may sell the "mortgage-backed certificates" to holders such as Rockford. The issuer administers the pool by collecting principal and interest from the individual mortgagors and remitting the amounts specified in the certificates to the holders. GNMA's costs for the regulatory duties is covered by a fee charged to the issuer. Unless the issuer defaults in its payments to the holder of a certificate, no federal funds are used in connection with the issuance and sale of these securities, the administration of the pool of mortgages, or the payments of principal and interest set forth in the certificates.

Under the type of Ginnie Maes involved in this case, the issuer is required to continue to make payments to the holders even if an individual mortgage in the pool becomes delinquent. In such event, the issuer may

---

27. [n. 4] "The Mortgage–Backed Securities Program provides a means for channeling funds from the Nation's securities markets into the housing market. The U.S. Government full faith and credit guaranty of securities makes them widely accepted in those sectors of the capital markets that otherwise would not be likely to supply funds to the mortgage market. The funds raised through the securities issued are used to make residential and other mortgage loans. Through this process, the program serves to increase the overall supply of credit available for housing and helps to assure that this credit is available at reasonable interest rates." Dept. of Housing and Urban Development, Handbook GNMA 5500.1 Rev. 6, GNMA I Mortgage Backed Securities Guide 1–1 (1984) (hereinafter GNMA Guide).

28. [n. 5] * * * The Ginnie Maes held by Rockford, are "modified pass-through securities" that provide for the payment of specific amounts whether or not timely collections are made from the individual mortgagors in the pool. GNMA also guarantees "straight pass-through securities" which provide that the issuer shall pay the holders of the securities the amounts collected from the pool, "as collected," less specified administrative costs. See 24 CFR § 390.5(a) (1986); GNMA Guide, at 1–1.

pursue its remedies against the individual mortgagor, or the guarantor of the mortgage, but the issuer does not have any rights against GNMA. GNMA's guarantee is implicated only if the issuer fails to meet its obligations to the holders under the certificates. In that event the holder proceeds directly against GNMA, and not against the issuer. But the risk of actual loss to GNMA is minimal because its guarantee is secured not only by the individual mortgages in the pool but also by the separate guarantee of each of those mortgages, and by a fidelity bond which the issuer is required to post. See 24 CFR § 390.1 (1986). * * *

[The Court concluded that Ginnie Maes are not exempt from state taxation in part because the government obligation as a guarantor is secondary and contingent.]

Larger banks may have originated a sufficient pool of mortgages to issue their own MBS. These securities are sometimes referred to as non-agency securities. MBS are sometimes referred to as SMBS, with "S" designating single-family home mortgage loans. Securities backed by commercial real estate are referred to as commercial mortgage-backed securities or CMBS.

SECURITIES INDUSTRY ASS'N v. CLARKE

United States Court of Appeals, Second Circuit, 1989.
885 F.2d 1034, *cert. denied*, 493 U.S. 1070 (1990).

MESKILL, CIRCUIT JUDGE.

* * * Mortgage pass-through certificates are used by banks as a mechanism for selling mortgage loans. A number of mortgage loans previously originated by a bank are placed in a pool. The bank then transfers the pool to a trust. In exchange for the pool, the trustee transfers to the bank pass-through certificates. These certificates represent fractional undivided interests in the pool of mortgage loans. The certificates may then be sold publicly or privately.

After sale of the certificates, the mortgage loans are often serviced by the originator-bank. In such a case, the bank collects the loan payments and "passes through" the principal and interest on a pro rata basis to the certificate holders. In doing so, the bank may deduct service or other fees.

Use of this mechanism has important benefits for banks, benefits that have resulted in its increasing popularity and use. Because residential mortgage loans typically are of long duration, banks traditionally have bought and sold the loans to facilitate management of their assets and liabilities. Use of the pass-through certificate mechanism makes the sale of these loans easier. Individual loans do not have to be sold separately, and buyers may find it more efficient and less risky to purchase interests in a pool of mortgages instead of single mortgages.

A Prospectus and Prospectus Supplement dated January 23, 1987 described the offering of approximately $194 million of Security Pacific Mortgage Pass–Through Certificates, Series 1987–B.

The Prospectus provided for the creation of a pool consisting of conventional, fixed-rate residential mortgage loans. "Each Mortgage Loan [would] be selected by [SPN Bank] for inclusion in the Mortgage Pool from among those originated by [SPN Bank] in the ordinary course of [SPN Bank's] lending activities as carried on in its offices in California." Certain characteristics of the mortgages to be selected were specified.

The Prospectus provided that, at the time of issuance of the series, "[SPN Bank] will assign the Mortgage Loans in the Mortgage Pool evidenced by that series to the Trustee. . . . The Trustee will, concurrently with such assignment, authenticate and deliver Certificates evidencing such series to [SPN Bank] in exchange for the Mortgage Loans." The freely transferable certificates would represent fractional undivided interests in the Trust Fund.

Limited credit support for the issue was to be provided either by (1) an irrevocable letter of credit issued by SPN Bank, (2) a limited guaranty issued by an entity other than SPN Bank, or (3) third-party mortgage insurance purchased by SPN Bank in its role as servicer of the mortgage loans. If SPN Bank provided its own letter of credit, the coverage was to be no more than ten percent of the initial aggregate principal balance of the mortgage pool. Any risk of delinquency or default not covered by these mechanisms of credit support would be borne by the certificate holders. * * *

SIA is a national trade association. * * * SIA stated [in a letter to the Comptroller] its belief that SPN Bank's participation in the transaction constituted a violation of the Glass–Steagall Act. The letter asked the Comptroller to review the transaction and "declare the bank's involvement in it to be contrary to the Glass–Steagall Act." * * *

The Comptroller correctly concluded that SPN Bank has the express power under the national banking laws to sell its mortgage loans. In 1982, Congress amended 12 U.S.C. § 371(a) to provide that "[a]ny national banking association may make, arrange, purchase or sell loans or extensions of credit secured by liens on interests in real estate, subject to such terms, conditions, and limitations as may be prescribed by the Comptroller of the Currency by order, rule, or regulation." Legislative history indicates that the amendment was intended to "simplif[y] the real estate lending authority of national banks by deleting rigid statutory requirements. Section 403 [which amended 12 U.S.C. § 371] is intended to provide national banks with the ability to engage in more creative and flexible financing, and to become stronger participants in the home financing market." S.Rep. No. 536, 97th Cong., 2nd Sess. 27 (1982), reprinted in 1982 U.S.Code Cong. & Admin.News 3054, 3081; see also id. at 60, 1982 U.S. Code Cong. & Admin. News at 3114. * * *

In determining that the use of mortgage pass-through certificates to sell mortgage loans fell within SPN Bank's "incidental powers" under 12 U.S.C. § 24 (Seventh), the Comptroller turned to the test adopted in *Arnold Tours*, 472 F.2d at 432. There, the First Circuit framed the inquiry as follows: in order to be authorized under section 16's "incidental powers" provision, a national bank's activity must be "convenient [and] useful in connection with the performance of one of the bank's established activities pursuant to its express powers under the National Bank Act." Id.

Although he applied the test of *Arnold Tours*, the Comptroller argued that that test is unnecessarily restrictive of the powers of national banks. * * * We have no need to address the Comptroller's position that the *Arnold Tours* test is overly restrictive, as we believe that the proper test is no more restrictive than *Arnold Tours* and we agree with the Comptroller that SPN Bank's activities here satisfied even the *Arnold Tours* test.

We have little difficulty concluding that SPN Bank's use of the pass-through certificate mechanism is "convenient [and] useful in connection with the performance of" its power to sell its mortgage loans. See *Arnold Tours*, 472 F.2d at 432. Indeed, SIA does not appear to argue otherwise. The pass-through certificate mechanism permits the bank to offer purchasers an interest in a pool of mortgage loans, rather than just single mortgage loans. The popularity of the mechanism confirms what seems apparent, that many investors who might be wary of the risk of investing in a single mortgage loan will be willing to invest in a pool of loans. With the increased marketability that pass-through certificates make possible comes increased liquidity, an important benefit as banks face the task of funding long term mortgage loans with short term deposits. We thus conclude that the Comptroller's view that SPN Bank's "incidental powers" authorized its activity in the transaction at issue here was reasonable.

The Comptroller properly recognized that once he determined that SPN Bank's activity was authorized under section 16 [12 U.S.C.A. § 24] (Seventh), he did not need to analyze the transaction under section 21 [12 U.S.C.A. § 378(a)(1)].[29] "[S]ection 21 cannot be read to prohibit what section 16 permits. . . . Therefore, if we find that the [Comptroller] acted reasonably in concluding that section 16 permits [SPN Bank's] activities, that is the end of our analysis." See Securities Industry Ass'n v. Board of Governors, 807 F.2d 1052, 1057 (D.C.Cir. 1986), cert. denied, 483 U.S. 1005 (1987) (*Bankers Trust II*). This is so because section 21 "was not intended to require banks to abandon an accepted banking practice that was subjected to regulation under § 16." *ICI*, 450 U.S. at 63; see also

---

29. [eds.] Sections 16 and 21 of the Glass–Steagall Act were its principal provisions separating commercial and investment banking. Section 21 provides that it is unlawful for an entity engaged in securities issuing or underwriting to engage at the same time in the business of receiving deposits. 12 U.S.C.A. § 378(a)(1).

Bankers Trust I, 468 U.S. at 149 ("§ 16 and § 21 seek to draw the same line"). * * *

The Gramm–Leach–Bliley Act of 1999 expressly declared that a "financial in nature" activity for a financial holding company or a financial subsidiary is "[i]ssuing or selling instruments representing interests in pools of assets permissible for a bank to hold directly." 12 U.S.C.A. § 1843(k)(4)(D).

FEDERAL DEPOSIT INSURANCE CORPORATION BREAKING NEW GROUND IN U.S. MORTGAGE LENDING

FDIC Outlook 21 (Summer 2006).

* * * Following the elimination of Regulation Q, control of the mortgage market shifted dramatically in the 1980s from savings institutions to banks and to federal government-sponsored enterprises (GSEs), which played a major role in the creation of mortgage-backed securities (MBS). These securitizations further opened the U.S. mortgage market to investors, introducing considerable new liquidity. By 2005, almost 68 percent of home mortgage originations were securitized. This reliance on securitization underscores its importance as a risk-management tool that allows lenders to shift mortgage credit risk and interest rate risk to investors who have greater risk tolerance.

A significant development in the mortgage securities market is the recent and dramatic expansion of "private-label" MBS, which are securitized by entities other than the GSEs and do not carry an explicit or implicit guarantee. Total outstanding private-label MBS represented 29 percent of total outstanding MBS in 2005, more than double the share in 2003. Of total private-label MBS issuance, two-thirds comprised nonprime loans in 2005, up from 46 percent in 2003. With the increased exposure to private-label MBS and a large share of higher-risk nontraditional mortgages being securitized in this sector, investors appear willing to assume greater risk in their search for yield.

The legislative changes and increased use of securitization during the 1980s significantly altered the mortgage market by facilitating product innovation and expanding mortgage credit availability. The increased liquidity provided by securitization allowed lenders to offer credit to more borrowers, because lenders were no longer limited to lending on their deposit base. Lenders not only could increase their underwriting of traditional mortgages, but also were able to develop new mortgage products to appeal to borrowers seeking nontraditional features. * * *

(2) Collateralized Mortgage Obligations

As explained in the following case, the securities sold to investors in a collateralized mortgage obligation (CMO) have been divided into separate maturity classes called tranches. The cash flows for each tranche are paid out in a predetermined order, making some tranches more risky than others. The classic form of the "pass through" MBS differs from CMOs in that the payments received on the mortgages in the MBS pool are passed-through to the investors on a pro rata basis. There are not different tranches of securities with different priorities for payment.

BANCA CREMI, S.A. v. ALEX. BROWN & SONS, INC.

United States Court of Appeals, Fourth Circuit, 1997.
132 F.3d 1017.

MAGILL, SENIOR CIRCUIT JUDGE.

Banca Cremi, S.A., Institucion de Banca Multiple, Grupo Financiero Cremi and Banca Cremi Grand Cayman (together, the Bank) purchased a number of collateralized mortgage obligations (CMOs) through John Isaac Epley, a broker with the brokerage firm of Alex. Brown & Sons, Incorporated (Alex. Brown). Although most of its CMO purchases were profitable, the Bank lost money on six CMO purchases after the market in CMOs collapsed in 1994. The Bank brought suit in the district court against Epley and Alex. Brown, alleging that Epley and Alex. Brown had committed securities fraud in violation of § 10(b) of the Securities and Exchange Act of 1934, 15 U.S.C. § 78j(b), and Rule 10b–5, 17 C.F.R. § 240.10b–5, by making material misrepresentations and omissions regarding the CMOs, by selling securities that were unsuitable, and by charging excessive markups. The Bank also alleged Texas state common-law tort claims for fraud, negligence, negligent misrepresentation, and breach of fiduciary duty, and a claim based on the Maryland Securities Act. The district court granted Epley and Alex. Brown's motion for summary judgment on all of the Bank's claims, and the Bank now appeals. We affirm.

CMOs, first introduced in 1983, are securities derived from pools of private home mortgages backed by U.S. government-sponsored enterprises. From 1987 to 1993, U.S. government-sponsored CMO issuances grew dramatically, from $900 million to $311 billion per year. The market in CMOs largely collapsed in 1994, and in 1995 new issuances fell to $25.4 billion.

Historically, investments in fixed-rate home mortgages have not been attractive to institutional investors. Investors in most fixed-rate securities benefit when interest rates fall. The fixed-rate security then earns interest at a rate higher than decreased prevailing rates. However, unlike other fixed-rate investments such as U.S. treasuries, fixed-rate home mortgages do not benefit from declines in interest rates. Because home mortgages may be freely prepaid, home owners frequently refinance their homes to take advantage of a drop in interest rates. When the mortgage is prepaid, the investor's funds are returned. If the investor seeks to reinvest those funds, as would be the case with most institutional investors, they must be reinvested at the low prevailing rate, rather than earning interest at the higher rate of the original mortgage. This is called the "prepayment risk."

If interest rates rise, home mortgages are generally not refinanced, and they lose value just like any other fixed-rate security. Thus, investments in home mortgages perform poorly both when interest rates rise and when they fall.

CMOs concentrate the prepayment risk in some securities in order to reduce that risk in other securities. In so doing, CMOs were designed to make home mortgage investments more attractive to institutional investors, increase the liquidity in the secondary home mortgage market, and reduce the interest costs to consumers buying homes.

A CMO issuer begins with a large pool of home mortgages, often worth billions of dollars. Each pool of home mortgages generates two streams of income. The first income stream is the aggregate of all interest payments made on the underlying mortgages. The second income stream is the aggregate of all principal payments made on the underlying mortgages. These income streams are divided into numerous CMO "tranches," which are the securities sold to investors. To determine what portion of the two income streams are received by an investor in a CMO tranche, each tranche has two unique formulae: one that determines the tranche's interest rate, and the other that determines the tranche's principal repayment priority.

The interest rate on a CMO tranche can be a fixed rate, a floating rate, or a rate that floats inversely to an index rate. Floating interest rates can also be leveraged, meaning that the interest rate shifts more dramatically than the index rate. For example, where a floating rate CMO is leveraged by a multiplier of two, the CMO's interest rate will increase by two percent when the index rate increases by one percent.

The tranche's principal repayment priority determines when the tranche will receive principal payments made on the underlying mortgages. Each principal payment is divided among all of the tranches in a CMO issuance. High priority tranches receive principal payments first. Support tranches receive principal payments last. Because of this, support tranches are the most sensitive to "extension risk." Extension risk is the opposite of prepayment risk: when interest rates rise, the expected maturity of the support tranche CMO increases, often dramatically.

CMO tranches are categorized into classes which have similar properties and risks. The least risky is the planned amortization class (PAC). PACs have little prepayment risk, and appeal to institutional investors for this reason. Two of the riskiest classes of CMOs, inverse floaters and inverse interest-only strips, are at issue in this litigation.

Inverse floaters have a set principal amount and earn interest at a rate that moves inversely to a specified floating index rate. Inverse floaters will often be leveraged, so a small increase in interest rates causes a dramatic decrease in the inverse floating rate. Usually, inverse floaters are also support tranches, so an increase in interest rates causes their maturity date to extend. Inverse floaters earn high returns if interest rates decline or remain constant, but lose substantial value if interest rates increase.

Inverse interest-only strips (inverse IOs) do not receive principal payments. The interest rate for an inverse IO floats inversely to a specified index rate, like an inverse floater. Interest is calculated by reference to the outstanding principal amount of another reference tranche. As the reference tranche is paid off, the principal on which the inverse IO earns interest decreases accordingly. Like an inverse floater, a rate increase reduces the inverse IO's floating rate. According to some investors, a rate increase also reduces prepayment of the reference tranche, extending the maturity of the inverse IO and, ultimately, increasing the total interest payments made on the inverse IO.

Inverse floaters were first introduced in 1986. Inverse IOs were introduced in 1987. Markets for both of these securities remained strong in the environment of decreasing or stable interest rates that predominated between 1986 and the beginning of 1994. On February 4, 1994, the Federal Reserve Board increased short-term interest rates for the first time in five years. Over the next nine months, short-term rates increased by a total of 2.5 percent, from 3 percent to 5.5 percent. In response to the rate increases, a wave of selling hit bond markets and investors in all types of bonds suffered significant losses.

CMOs were particularly hard hit, for a variety of reasons. The jump in rates halted mortgage prepayments. This in turn extended the average maturity of all CMOs, including, most dramatically, support tranche CMOs such as inverse floaters. Because of their degree of leverage, certain CMOs were extremely sensitive to the interest rate jumps, and their holders flooded the market after the first interest rate increase. CMO liquidity, which had never been a problem in the stable or declining interest rate environment that had existed since their introduction, dried up as all CMO holders tried to sell. The fear of liquidity problems built on itself, reducing the number of willing purchasers during the critical period after the Federal Reserve Board increased interest rates. In April 1994 an investment fund which primarily invested in CMOs filed for bankruptcy, reporting near total losses of its $600 million CMO investment. As a result of these incidents, the market in CMOs virtually collapsed in 1994. * * *

Despite its extensive investment experience and extraordinary resources, the Bank nevertheless contends that, while it may be sophisticated in certain types of investments, it was not sophisticated in CMO investments. * * *

We reject this argument. The Bank's [international investment transactions] unit, whose function was to invest Bank funds in dollar-denominated investments, employed three well-educated investment professionals to select a sound, but profitable, investment strategy. [These professionals] conducted a thorough, independent investigation of the benefits and risks of CMO investments by attending seminars, purchasing treatises on the subject, and developing a multi-step review process for each CMO investment. Rather than blindly relying on Epley and Alex. Brown, the record shows that the Bank rejected Epley's suggested investments far more often than it accepted them. Indeed, the Bank consulted with five other brokerage houses regarding CMO investments, and each of these brokerage houses gave the Bank detailed information describing the benefits and the risks of CMO investments. After a year of trading in CMOs, the Bank displayed a knowledge and an aggressiveness that belie its current claim that it did not understand CMO investments. * * *

In sum, in this case the Bank had access to an extraordinary wealth of information regarding CMOs. With few exceptions, the depth and breadth of this information illustrated one overriding point: investments in CMOs, while potentially very profitable, were undoubtedly highly risky. As a sophisticated business entity handling five billion dollars of other people's money, the Bank had the advice of its own employees and a horde of the defendants' competitors. Nevertheless, the Bank invested in CMOs through arm's length dealings with the defendants. While the vast majority of these investments were profitable for the Bank, a half-dozen proved disastrously timed, and the Bank now alleges that its misfortune resulted from its justifiable naivete in listening to the defendants' purported lies.

As in any "action[ ] for fraud, reliance on false statements must be accompanied by a right to rely." Foremost Guar. Corp. v. Meritor Sav. Bank, 910 F.2d 118, 125 (4th Cir. 1990). Here, the Bank lost its right to rely by its own recklessness. The Bank continued to purchase CMOs after it had sufficient information, given its sophistication, to be well apprised of the risks it would face were interest rates to rise. Given that the Bank was aware of the risks involved in investing in CMOs, the Bank was not justified in relying on Epley and Alex. Brown's alleged omissions and misstatements. Accordingly, we affirm the district court's grant of summary judgment against the Bank on this claim. * * *

For the foregoing reasons, the district court's grant of summary judgment is affirmed.

———

Another type of debt security backed indirectly by pools of home mortgage loans is a CDO, or collateralized debt obligation. The issuer acquires high-yield, high risk tranches of the debt securities issued in a CMO, then issues securities (debt and equity) backed by the pool of CMO securities.

JERRY W. MARKHAM
REGULATING CREDIT DEFAULT SWAPS IN THE WAKE OF THE SUBPRIME CRISIS

A Working Paper Prepared for the International Monetary Fund Seminar on Current Developments in Monetary and Financial Law, Washington, D.C., Dec. 2, 2009.

* * * Securitization provided the banks with a way to move subprime loans off their balance sheets, and it allowed lenders to shift mortgage risks to investors with greater risk tolerance. The amount of securitized subprime mortgages grew from about $11 billion in 1994 to over $100 billion in 2002. Bear Stearns made its first subprime securitization offering in 1997 for mortgages totaling $385 million, and it underwrote an additional $1.9 billion in securitizations over the next ten months. "By 2005, almost 68 percent of home mortgage originations were securitized."[30] The FDIC noted, in 2006, that:

> A significant development in the mortgage securities market is the recent and dramatic expansion of "private-label, [mortgage-backed securities] MBS" ... Total outstanding private-label MBS represented 29 percent of total outstanding MBS in 2005, more than double the share in 2003. Of total private-label MBS issuance, *two thirds comprised non-prime loans in 2005*, up from 46 percent in 2003.[31]

The securitization process was carried out through CDOs that were distributed through "warehouse" operations, in which mortgages were purchased from non-bank originators by investment banks and then resold through securitizations. These warehousing operations became a part of an unregulated "shadow banking" system.[32] A shareholder report by UBS AG described its CDO facility as follows:

> In the initial stage of a CDO securitization, the [CDO] desk would typically enter into an agreement with a collateral manager. UBS sourced residential mortgage backed securities ("RMBS") and other securities on behalf of the manager. These positions were held in a CDO Warehouse in anticipation of securitization into CDOs. Generally, while in the Warehouse, these positions would be on UBS's books with exposure to market risk. Upon completion of the Warehouse, the securities were transferred to a CDO special-purpose vehicle, and structured into tranches. The CDO desk received structuring fees on the notional value of the deal, and focused on Mezzanine ("Mezz") CDOs, which generated fees of approximately 125 to 150 bp (compared with high-grade CDOs, which generated fees of approximately 30 to 50 bp)....

---

30. [n. 31] FDIC, Breaking New Ground in U.S. Mortgage Lending, FDIC Outlook 21 (Summer 2006) (emphasis supplied).

31. [n. 32] Id.

32. [n. 33] These warehousing operations often involved the purchase on non-bank subprime mortgage originations by investment banks like Bear Stearns and Merrill Lynch. See Paul Muolo & Mathew Padilla, Chain of Blame (2008) (describing these warehousing operations).

Under normal market conditions, there would be a rise and fall in positions held in the CDO Warehouse line as assets were accumulated ("ramped up") and then sold as CDOs. There was typically a lag of between 1 and 4 months between initial agreement with a collateral manager to buy assets, and the full ramping of a CDO Warehouse.[33]

Subprime CDOs were broken up into separate tranches. The less secure tranches were required to absorb any larger than expected losses from mortgage defaults, providing a cushion from loss for the most secure tranche, called the "Super–Senior." As a result of this credit enhancement feature, the Super–Seniors were considered to be more credit-worthy than the underlying subprime mortgages themselves. The use of multiple payment stream tranches for a securitization was not a novel concept. "Collateralized mortgage obligations" (CMOs), also known as "real estate mortgage investment conduits" (REMICs), a product that divided principal and interest payments from the mortgages placed in the pool into different payment streams.

Mortgage principal and interest payments were not passed through to CMO investors pro rata, as was the case for the original GNMA pass through mortgage certificates. Instead, the CMO mortgage payments were divided into separate tranches with varying payment streams and with differing maturities, seniority, subordination, and other characteristics. The CMO market was crushed in 1994 after the Fed increased short-term interest rates for the first time in five years. Some of the tranches in the CMOs were so complex that Goldman Sachs had to use multiple super-computers to run simulations of cash flows under different interest-rate scenarios. That problem presaged the valuation issues that would emerge during the subprime crisis in 2007.

* * * With the credit enhancement of a CDS [credit default swap],[34] the credit rating agencies often gave the Super Seniors their highest triple-A rating. This was the same credit rating enjoyed by the federal government, which signaled to the world that a default on those Super Senior tranches was highly unlikely. Unfortunately, the rating agencies' risk models for awarding the triple-A rating on CDOs did not take into account the possibility of a major downturn in the real estate market. That flaw was not spotted until the subprime crisis arose.

A risk model developed by David Li did for CDOs what the Black–Scholes model did for options. Seemingly, it allowed a supposed precise mathematical computation of the risks posed by these instruments. That and other Gaussian Copula risk models failed, however, to predict the massive losses sustained by commercial banks in the United States, and Europe, from their exposures to subprime CDOs. Fail they did, but there was no cabal using a secret formula to deceive investors. Moody's actually published its CDO risk assessment model (CDOROM), which became the industry standard, on the Internet in 2004. The whole world was free to

---

33.   [n. 34] UBS AG, Shareholder Report on UBS's Write–Downs § 4.22 (2008).

34.   [eds.] A type of derivative discussed further in Chapter 12.

discover its flaws but, except for a few naysayers, the model went pretty much unchallenged.

The mathematical model used to rate CDOs proved to be badly flawed. Critics charged that these models were defective because they relied on historical prices generated by a rising market. That Pollyanna approach overlooked the possibility of a hundred-year, "perfect" storm, which arrived in the form of the subprime crisis. The possibility of such an unusual event was called a "fat tail" or "outlier." They were also called "black swans," as a metaphor for the widely held belief that there was no such thing as a black swan, until explorers reached Australia and found just such a bird.[35] The probability of an outlier was considered so small that they were ignored by the credit assessors. Lloyd Blankfein, the CEO at Goldman Sachs, also asserted that many financial institutions had erred in outsourcing their risk management to the rating agencies. He believed that the rating agencies had diluted their triple-A rating by giving that rating to over 64,000 structured finance instruments, while only twelve operating companies in the world had such a rating.

The high credit ratings given to the Super Senior tranches posed another problem. These securities were hard to market due to their lower interest rates, which was a function of their triple-A rating. That problem was solved after bank regulators in the United States allowed favorable capital treatment of Super Seniors on bank balance sheets, provided that the Super Senior had a triple-A credit rating. This regulatory blessing removed any residual concerns on the part of the banks of undue risk from Super–Seniors and created a demand for the Super Seniors by banks here and abroad. As a result, a large portion of the Super Senior tranches were held on the books of many major investment banks such as Citigroup, Merrill Lynch, UBS AG and Lehman Brothers.

* * * Fair value pricing [of CDOs on bank balance sheets] was resulting in a pro-cyclical progression of write-downs [during the subprime crisis] that bore no relation to actual value. As Peter Wallison, an American Enterprise Institute Fellow, noted in the midst of the subprime crisis:

> As losses mounted in subprime mortgage portfolios in mid–2007, lenders demanded more collateral. If the companies holding the assets did not have additional collateral to supply, they were compelled to sell the assets. These sales depressed the market for mortgage-backed securities (MBS) and also raised questions about the quality of the ratings these securities had previously received. Doubts about the quality of ratings for MBS raised questions about the quality of ratings for other asset-backed securities (ABS). Because of the complexity of many of the instruments out in the market, it also became difficult to determine where the real losses on MBS and ABS actually resided. As a result, trading in MBS and ABS came virtually to a halt

---

35. [n. 50] See Nassim Nicholas Taleb, The Black Swan: The Impact of the Highly Improbable (2007).

and has remained at a standstill for almost a year. Meanwhile, continued withdrawal of financing sources has compelled the holders of ABS to sell them at distressed or liquidation prices, even though the underlying cash flows of these portfolios have not necessarily been seriously diminished. As more and more distress or liquidation sales occurred, asset prices declined further, and these declines created more lender demands for additional collateral, resulting in more distress or liquidation sales and more declines in asset values as measured on a mark-to-market basis. A downward spiral developed and is still operating.[36]

"The difficulty in putting a value on loans, securities, and exotic financial instruments banks were carrying on their books became one of the most debilitating features of the Great Panic" in 2008.[37] Critics of fair value accounting charged that, because liquidity in subprime investments had dried up as the subprime crisis blossomed, the only prices available for "fair value" accounting were fire sale prices from desperate sellers. Those prices in no way reflected the actual value of the Super Seniors as measured by their cash flows or defaults. One accountant complained to the FASB that: "May the souls of those who developed FASB 157 burn in the seventh circle of Dante's Hell." Warren Buffett likened mark-to-market requirements for measuring bank regulatory capital to throwing "gasoline on the fire in terms of financial institutions." Paul Volcker, the former Fed Chairman was also an opponent of fair value accounting for banks.

The SEC gave some interpretative relief on September 23, 2008. The Emergency Economic Stabilization Act passed on October 3, 2008 required the SEC to conduct a study of mark-to-market accounting and authorized suspension of that requirement. However, a debate arose over whether a suspension was appropriate, and the SEC subsequently announced that it had decided not to suspend mark-to-market accounting. Its staff stated that: "Rather than a crisis precipitated by fair value accounting, the crisis was a 'run on the bank' at certain institutions, manifesting itself in counterparties reducing or eliminating the various credit and other risk exposures they had to each firm."[38] * * *

At the end of the first quarter in 2009, the delinquency rate for subprime mortgages, *i.e.*, those with payments more than sixty days overdue, was sixteen percent, but CDOs had been sold for as little as twenty-one cents on the dollar. This defies explanation. Fifty percent or more of the value of the sixteen percent of homes foreclosed should be recovered in foreclosure proceedings. Moreover, the Super Seniors were modeled to withstand a loss in foreclosure of four percent or more, plus

---

36. [n. 68] [Peter J. Wallison, Fair Value Accounting: A Critique, Fin. Services Outlook, July 2008.]

37. [n. 69] [David] Wessel, [In Fed We Trust] 128 (2009).

38. [n. 76] SEC Office of the Chief Accountant, Division of Corporate Finance, Report and Recommendations Pursuant to Section 133 of the Emergency Economic Stabilization Act of 2008: Study on Mark–To–Market Accounting 3 (2008).

many Super Seniors had four percent or more in CDS coverage. Even adding in a big risk discount for the new junk bond status of these once triple-A Super Seniors does not justify the steep discounts at which these instruments were dumped on the market.

This analysis is, admittedly, over-simplistic, but it does seem to suggest that the massive write-downs of the Super Seniors were driven by panic and had no ties to the actual value of many of these securities.

The Dodd–Frank Act defined three terms commonly used in securitizations—"asset-backed security," "securitizer," and "originator." As "asset-backed security" is a "fixed-income or other security collateralized by any type of self-liquidating financial asset" including a loan, mortgage, or secured or unsecured receivable "that allows the holder of the security to receive payments that depend primarily on cash from the asset." Dodd–Frank Act, § 941. The "securitizer" is the issuer of an asset-backed security, and the "originator" is the person who by an extension of credit "creates a financial asset that collateralizes an asset-backed security and sells an asset to the securitizer." Id.

Dodd–Frank introduced a risk retention requirement, reacting to the concern that securitizations had contributed to a decline in credit quality because the loan originators were "originating to distribute" rather than "originating to hold," and so had little concern with the risk of default on the loans in the securitized pool. The Act requires that originators retain at least 5% of the credit risk on the loan pool. Dodd–Frank Act, § 941. Some have referred to this as requiring originators to have "skin in the game."

"Qualified residential mortgages" are exempt from this risk retention requirement. That phrase will be defined in rulemaking, but the relevant agencies are guided by statutory factors that indicate a lower risk of default. Qualified residential mortgages may not allow balloon payments, negative amortization, prepayment penalties, interest-only payments, and other features that have been demonstrated to exhibit a higher risk of borrower defaults.

The Dodd–Frank Act prohibits underwriters or sponsors of asset-backed securities from engaging in any transaction that would be a material conflict of interest with respect to any investor for one year from the date of the first closing of the sale of the asset-backed security. Dodd–Frank Act, § 621. The conflicts of interest Congress was trying to prevent may include those at issue in matters like the SEC's action against Goldman Sachs that was settled in July 2010 for $550 million, discussed further in Chapter 11.

(3) Other Asset–Backed Securities

The concepts on which MBS and CDOs rely may be applied to almost every form of asset or revenue stream that could be included in a pool and sold in units as a security. Among assets being securitized are credit card balances, student loans, automobile loans, computer and airplane leases, mobile homes, vacation time shares, recreational vehicle loans, and royalties due artists from future record sales. An extensive illustration of a securitization of car loans may be found in Steven L. Schwarcz, Bruce A. Markell & Lissa Lamkin Broome, Securitization, Structured Finance and Capital Markets (2004).

The financial crisis resulted in a freezing of the liquidity of many of these asset-backed securities. In order to restore that sector of the credit market, the Federal Reserve Board created a new program called the Term Asset Backed Securities Loan Facility (TALF), in which the Federal Reserve Bank of New York (FRBNY) made non-recourse fully secured loans using a special purpose vehicle to purchase the loan collateral from the FRBNY. This program made secured, non-recourse loans available to banks and commercial firms, including hedge funds. The permissible securities that could be used for collateral for such loans included securities issued in securitizations of credit card debt, consumer loans, and student loans with a AAA-rating. The use of the rating agencies as the arbiter of collateral quality for these loans seemed a bit strange in light of the ongoing regulatory attacks on the rating agencies' failures in rating CDOs. Moreover, since the loans were non-recourse, the Fed bears any losses (above a small haircut on the collateral in setting their loan value) in the event of a decline in the value of the collateral. This program was closed on June 30, 2010, with $43 billion in outstanding loans. At that time, there had been no losses on TALF and all the outstanding loans were well collateralized.

BOARD OF GOVERNORS OF THE FEDERAL RESERVE SYSTEMTERM ASSET–BACKED SECURITIES LOAN FACILITY

<www.federalreserve.gov/monetarypolicy/bst_lendingother.htm>.

In November 2008, the Federal Reserve announced the creation of the Term Asset–Backed Securities Loan Facility (TALF) under section 13(3) of the Federal Reserve Act. The TALF is a funding facility that issues loans with a term of up to five years to holders of eligible asset-backed securities (ABS). The TALF is intended to assist the financial markets in accommodating the credit needs of consumers and businesses of all sizes by facilitating the issuance of ABS collateralized by a variety of consumer and business loans; it is also intended to improve the market conditions for ABS more generally. * * * The Federal Reserve Board has authorized extensions of credit through the TALF until June 30, 2010, for loans collateralized by newly issued commercial mortgage-backed securities (CMBS) and through March 31, 2010, for loans collateralized by all other TALF-eligible securities. * * *

Eligible collateral initially included U.S. dollar-denominated ABS that (1) are backed by student loans, auto loans, credit card loans, and loans guaranteed by the Small Business Administration (SBA) and (2) have a credit rating in the highest investment-grade rating category from two or more approved rating agencies and do not have a credit rating below the highest investment-grade rating category from a major rating agency. The loans provided through the TALF are non-recourse loans, meaning that the borrower's obligation to repay the loan can be fulfilled by surrendering the collateral. Borrowers commit their own risk capital in the form of "haircuts" against the collateral, which serve as the borrower's equity in the transaction and act as a buffer for absorbing any decline in the collateral's value in the event the loan is not repaid.

TALF LLC has committed, for a fee, to purchase all ABS surrendered to the FRBNY in conjunction with a TALF loan at a price equal to the TALF loan plus accrued but unpaid interest. Purchases of these securities are funded first through the commitment fees received by the LLC and any interest the LLC has earned on its investments. In the event that such funding proves insufficient, the U.S. Treasury's Troubled Asset Relief Program (TARP) will provide additional subordinated debt funding to the TALF LLC to finance up to $20 billion of asset purchases. Subsequently, the FRBNY will finance any additional purchases of securities by providing senior debt funding to TALF LLC. Thus, the TARP funds provide credit protection to FRBNY. Because the FRBNY is the primary beneficiary of the TALF LLC, the assets and liabilities of the LLC are consolidated onto the books of the FRBNY. * * *

On February 10, 2009, the Federal Reserve Board announced that it would consider expanding the size of the TALF to as much as $1 trillion and potentially broaden the eligible collateral to encompass other types of newly issued AAA-rated asset-backed securities, such as ABS backed by commercial mortgages or private-label (non-agency) ABS backed by residential mortgages. Any expansion of the TALF would be supported by the Treasury providing additional funds from the TARP.

On March 19 [2009], the Federal Reserve Board announced that starting in April, the set of eligible collateral for TALF loans was being expanded to include ABS backed loans or leases related to business equipment, leases of vehicle fleets, floorplan loans, and mortgage servicing advances. * * *

[Eligible collateral was expanded later in 2009 to include previously issued securities-so called "legacy securities" expected to include non-agency RMBS that were originally rated AAA and outstanding commercial mortgage-backed securities and ABS that are rated AAA; newly issued CMBS and securities backed by insurance premium finance loans; ABS backed by student loans; ABS backed by loans guaranteed by the Small Business Administration; and certain high-quality CMBS issued before January 1, 2009 (legacy CMBS).]

On August 17 [2009], the Federal Reserve and the Treasury announced that they were holding in abeyance any further expansion in the types of collateral eligible for the TALF.

On December 4, the Federal Reserve announced a formal process for determining the set of rating agencies whose ratings would be accepted for establishing the eligibility of ABS to be pledged as collateral to the TALF. Another change announced at that time requires the FRBNY to conduct a formal risk assessment of all proposed collateral in addition to continuing to require that collateral for TALF loans receive two AAA ratings from TALF-eligible NRSROs. These changes were intended to promote competition among credit rating agencies, ensure appropriate protection against credit risk for the U.S. taxpayer, and ensure that TALF collateral continues to comply with the existing high standards for credit quality, transparency, and simplicity of structure.

MICHAEL DURRER
ASSET-BACKED COMMERCIAL PAPER CONDUITS

1 N.C. Banking Inst. 119 (1997).

Asset securitization through commercial paper conduits began in the early 1980s in order to securitize credit card receivables. The concept expanded through the rest of the decade with conduit programs introduced by several money center banks, including 1st Chicago, Continental Bank and Security Pacific. This expansion has continued in the 1990s and includes many conduits sponsored by European and Japanese banks as well as several regional banks in the United States. As of the end of 1996, roughly 160 ABCP [Asset Backed Commercial Paper] programs had approximately $150 billion in asset-backed commercial paper outstanding. In addition to the growth in size, the market for ABCP has experienced diversification in the types of assets securitized. Conduit programs now issue commercial paper backed by a variety of asset classes, including trade receivables, automobile and consumer loans, corporate loans, and leases. The industry is also exploring additional asset types to securitize. Examples include 12b–1 fees (management fees for mutual funds), tax liens and utility fees. Although not in commercial paper conduit form, the singer and songwriter David Bowie recently raised $55 million from asset-backed notes secured by future royalties on his songs.

The purpose of asset securitization through issuance of commercial paper is to provide a flexible and economic source of funding for financial institutions and companies that create or acquire financial assets. ABCP, like term asset-backed securities, often offer a lower cost of funds to an issuer than conventional bank loans or from the sale of whole portfolios of assets. By converting credit cards receivables or trade receivables, for example, into broadly traded commercial paper, the owner of those assets gains access to a larger source of capital in the form of the institutional investors that participate in the commercial paper market. In addition, the credit enhancement and liquidity provided to ABCP * * * enable issuers to obtain funds from short-term capital markets at lower interest rates than from other sources. Commercial paper also offers flexibility to issuers with respect to the amount, timing and duration of borrowings. Within an existing conduit program, ABCP generally can be issued on short notice, in large or small amounts and with maturities of from 30 to 90 days. Some institutions and companies use ABCP to warehouse mortgage loans, auto loans or leases, using ABCP to fund the origination or acquisition of these assets until they have created a pool large enough to sell or securitize in a term structure (that is, a securitization in which [the] fixed-term securities [that] are issued have medium to long maturities). Finally, an important aspect of asset securitization is to remove assets from the owner's balance sheet. An ABCP conduit can be structured to permit the transfer of assets from the owner to the conduit entity to be treated as a sale for accounting purposes. * * *

The most important form of protection against credit related losses is the credit enhancement facility. Credit enhancement facilities most frequently take the form of a letter of credit provided by a bank or syndicate of banks which may include the Sponsor. Credit enhancement may also be provided by cash-collateralized guarantees from the Sponsor or by financial guarantee insurance policies issued by monoline insurance companies. Early ABCP conduits sometimes offered credit enhancement against 100% of the amount of commercial paper issued; however, it is more common recently to find partial credit enhancement in the range of 10% to 15% of the maximum amount of commercial paper issuable by a conduit program. The rating agencies establish the amount of credit enhancement required for a given conduit based on models of the expected timing and severity of losses on the receivables. Their analyses take into account the various credit risks of the receivables of each Seller and the strength of each Seller's origination and servicing operations. Credit enhancement facilities are contracted for by an ABCP Vehicle for the benefit of all commercial paper holders, and can therefore be used to cover losses on receivables of any Seller in the program. * * *

Subprime mortgages were sometimes pooled to fund off-balance sheet commercial paper borrowings. Banks, such as Citigroup, used short-term commercial paper borrowings to purchase mortgages held in their called "structured investment vehicles" (SIVs), or "asset-backed commercial paper" (ABCP), as they were sometimes called. Those mortgages then funded the commercial paper borrowings and provided a profit through the spread between the higher rates paid by mortgages and the lower rates then existing in the commercial paper market. ABCPs provided advantages to issuers, including access to funds at interest rates lower than that charged by commercial banks. ABCP programs became popular because the commercial paper market was usually quite liquid, and issuers had a great deal of flexibility in the timing and duration of their offerings in that market.

The commercial paper market grew from $1.5 trillion in 2005 to $2.25 trillion in August 2007. The ABCP market issued about $1.2 trillion of that amount when the credit crunch struck in 2007. That market shrank to a little over $800 million by December of 2007, and many programs were frozen and caused massive losses. As Citigroup discovered, there was a serious risk present under such an arrangement. Commercial paper is a short-term instrument, while the assets in a SIV pool that funded the commercial paper had a much longer maturity. This mismatch required the commercial paper issued by the pool to be continually rolled over until the pool self-liquidated as mortgages were paid off, or, in the case of SIVs, refunded with additional long-or medium-term assets. In the event of a crisis in the money markets, however, such a roll over might not be possible. In that case, the issuer would be faced with the problem of selling the assets, which might be illiquid or sold at fire sale prices. As a guard against such an event, some banks provided a loan facility to pay off the commercial paper holders. This left the bank holding the bag should the assets decline in value below the amount extended under that credit facility and in excess of any credit protection. As the crisis deepened some SIVs tried to sell their mortgage collateral, but they could only do so at steep discounts.

The largest of the Citigroup SIVs were based in the Cayman Islands. Citigroup moved some $50 billion in SIVs onto its balance sheet during the subprime crisis, but that action only served to place more unneeded pressure on Citigroup's capital. Citigroup had also sold "liquidity puts" on $25 billion of its SIVs that entitled investors in the SIVs to put the notes back to Citigroup at par. Several other large financial institutions, including Merrill Lynch, Bear Stearns, and UBS, had to write off billions of dollars in losses from SIVs and collateralized debt obligations (CDOs).

(4) Role of the Credit Rating Agencies

The credit rating agencies, which include Moody's, Standard & Poor's, and Fitch, had become the arbiters of the interest rate paid by companies when borrowing money. A company's credit status, as perceived by the ratings agencies, also measured their acceptance as a counterparty with other businesses. The higher the rating, the more exposure a counterparty would accept in trading or dealing with the rated company. Although the particular ratings names vary somewhat from one credit rating agency to another, the rating scale adopted by Standard & Poor's is a commonly used reference point. The S&P ratings range from AAA, AA, A, BBB, BBB-, BB+, BB, B, CCC, CC, C, to D, with AAA signifying "extremely strong capacity to meet financial commitments" and D denoting "payment default." Standard & Poor's, Credit Ratings Definitions and FAQS, <www.standardandpoors.com>. A BBB-rating is considered by market participants to be the lowest investment grade. A lower rating means more risk to investors, and they therefore demanded higher interest payments to compensate for that risk. It was, consequently, important to the issuer to receive the highest possible rating for its issues. As discussed earlier in this Chapter, national banks may purchase for investment debt issued by private issuers only if it is investment grade. Investment grade is also required for some other types of investors like pension funds. It was also important to maintain those ratings, because a downgrade would result in a sharp drop in the value of the bond or other debt instrument being rated. If a security is downgraded from investment grade to below investment grade, some investors are required by laws or investment guidelines to sell, putting further downward pressure on the market. Lower ratings could also impair the liquidity of instruments, as investors might be reluctant to buy them at anything other than fire sale prices because of the uncertainty of their performance.

The importance of the credit rating agencies grew when government regulators began using their ratings as regulatory tools. The SEC recognized this role of the rating agencies by designating them as Nationally Recognized Statistical Ratings Organizations (NRSROs). In addition to the NBA's investment requirement for national banks, the SEC limited money market investments to short-term debt instruments highly rated by the NRSROs. An internal SEC study found that there were forty-four references in its rules and forms to NRSROs.

Congress also adopted the NRSRO concept by defining an eligible "mortgage related security," in the Secondary Mortgage Market Enhancement Act of 1984, as being rated in one of the two highest rating categories by at least one NRSRO. In 1995, Fannie Mae allowed the use of a title insurer with a favorable credit rating from at least one independent credit rating agency. The Federal Deposit Insurance Act adopted the concept by defining "investment grade" corporate obligations as being rated in one of the four highest categories by at least one NRSRO. The U.S. Department of Education also uses NRSRO ratings to set eligibility standards for institutions seeking to participate in student financial aid programs.

The credit rating agencies' assessments of creditworthiness did not always prove to be reliable. For example, the rating agencies maintained their high rating for the Enron Corp. until just before its spectacular collapse. After the Enron affair, Congress passed the Credit Rating Agency Reform Act of 2006. That legislation required credit rating agencies to register with the SEC and to provide the SEC with their performance measurement statistics, rating methodologies, a code of ethics, and their financial statements. The credit rating agencies were also required to adopt procedures for the prevention of the misuse of inside information and to deal with conflicts of interest, such as their fee arrangements. The SEC was given rulemaking authority to deal with conflicts of interest. Tying practices, such as requiring payment for additional services in order to obtain or retain a rating, were prohibited.

Congress became dissatisfied with the rating agencies once again when they began a massive downgrading of the subprime mortgage securities. Those downgrades affected thousands of mortgage securitizations totaling some $1.5 trillion in value.

The massive number of subprime credit rating downgrades suggested that something was wrong at the rating agencies that gave the Super Senior tranches such high ratings and then switched and downgraded them to junk bond status. Some members of Congress demanded that the SEC investigate the rating agencies. A study released by the SEC in July 2008 found that the rating agencies had been careless in their approach to rating structured investment vehicles (SIVs). The SEC found that the rating agencies were understaffed and overwhelmed by the large number of subprime securitized offerings. The risks of the subprime securitizations were often not fully measured by the rating agencies.

Treasury Secretary Henry J. Paulson stated that he would be seek additional regulation of the rating agencies, including different ratings categories for mortgage-backed securities, the disclosure of conflicts of interest, and explanation of the basis for the ratings. He also wanted the rating agencies to assume a more aggressive regulatory role over loan originators. The President's Working Group on Financial Markets endorsed this plan. The SEC adopted some changes that required the rating agencies to take additional steps to mitigate conflicts of interest, to require more disclosures on their rating processes, and to disclose the performance of their ratings.

The Dodd–Frank Act further justified its additional regulation of rating agencies because the ratings agencies are financial "gatekeepers" and should be subject to the same standards of liability and oversight as auditors, securities analysts, and investment bankers. The legislative justification statement also noted that the misrating of structured products had contributed substantially to the subprime crisis. Dodd–Frank Act, § 931.

Among other things, rating agencies must strengthen their internal controls and attest to their effectiveness in an annual report filed with the SEC. The SEC was directed to establish an Office of Credit Ratings, and the SEC must conduct examinations of credit rating agencies at least once a year. The SEC is required to adopt rules governing the procedures and methodologies, including qualitative and quantitative data and models, used by the rating agencies. Disclosure of rating methodologies is also required.

A last minute change in the legislation made the ratings agencies liable for their quality of their ratings under the Securities Act of 1933 in the same manner as accountants are liable for accounting statements included in registration statements. This caused all three of the rating agencies to suspend the use of their ratings for asset-backed bonds, which froze that $1.4 trillion dollar asset-backed securities market for several days. The SEC intervened waiving for six months the requirement that credit ratings be included in bond offering documents.

Pursuant to what is called the Franken Amendment, the SEC will study whether some independent entity should assign credit rating agencies to rate CDOs. Some members of Congress had hoped the Dodd–Frank Act would require such an assignment to help eliminate the rating agencies' incentive to rate highly to attract business. The Comptroller General is assigned to report on alternatives to the credit rating agencies, including the creation of an independent professional analyst organization. Dodd–Frank also requires that all statutory or regulatory references to credit ratings by Nationally Recognized Statistical Rating Organizations (NRSROs, the way credit rating agencies are referenced in statutes) to be replaced by a reference to "meets the standards for creditworthiness as established by [the relevant federal regulator.]"

(5) Special Concerns Related to Securitizations by Banks

Valuation of Retained Interests. The benefits to banks of securitization were previously discussed. There are also significant risks associated with this structured financing technique. Of special concern to the OCC and other bank regulatory agencies is the valuation of retained interests from securitizations on a bank's balance sheet.[39] FASB announced that retained interests should be initially measured at fair value.[40]

Reclaiming Sold Loans on a Bank's Insolvency. If an insured depository institution becomes insolvent, the FDIC is appointed as its receiver. The federal bankruptcy code does not apply, but resolution of the insolvency is dealt with under the statutory and regulatory authority of the FDIC in its capacity as receiver. A regulation issued in 2000 clarified that under certain circumstances the FDIC could not reclaim loans previously sold into a securitization by the now-insolvent depository institution. 12 C.F.R. § 360.6. The FDIC has issued a Notice of Proposed Rulemaking to revise 12 C.F.R. § 360.6 to take into account a modification of accounting standards and a 2004 amendment to the Federal Deposit Insurance Act. See FDIC, Notice of Proposed Rulemaking With Request for Comments, 75 Fed. Reg. 27471 (May 17, 2010).

Guidance Regarding Reputational Risks. Interagency guidance from the federal bank regulatory agencies and the SEC on complex structured finance products cautions banks to analyze the reputation risks of aiding customers in devising structures to evade legal requirements or act unethically. Further, the guidance provides that a bank's board should set the bank's threshold for risk and that a senior risk-control committee be formed to approve complex structured deals. The final version of this interagency statement states that:

> Financial markets have grown rapidly over the past decade, and innovations in financial instruments have facilitated the structuring

---

39. Interagency Guidance on Asset Securitization, Dec. 13, 1999, FIL–109–99, available at <www.fdic.gov/news/news/financial/1999/fil99109.html>.

40. FASB Statement No. 133, and reconsideration of its "Application of Statement 133 to Beneficial Interests in Securitized Financial Assets." See the discussion of fair value accounting earlier in this Chapter.

of cash flows and allocation of risk among creditors, borrowers, and investors in more efficient ways. Financial derivatives for market and credit risk, asset-backed securities with customized cash flow features, specialized financial conduits that manage pools of assets, and other types of structured finance transactions serve important purposes, such as diversifying risk, allocating cash flows and reducing cost of capital. As a result, structured finance transactions, including the more complex variations of these transactions, now are an essential part of U.S. and international capital markets.

When a financial institution participates in a CSFT [Complex Structured Finance Transaction], it bears the usual market, credit, and operational risks associated with the transaction. In some circumstances, a financial institution also may face heightened legal or reputational risk if the customer's regulatory, tax or accounting treatment for the CSFT, or disclosures concerning the CSFT in its public filings or financial statements, do not comply with applicable laws, regulations or accounting principles.

Interagency Statement on Sound Practices Concerning Elevated Risk Complex Structured Finance Activities, 72 Fed. Reg. 1372 (Jan. 11, 2007).

Avoiding Consolidation of Loans Sold on Books of Selling Bank. Another accounting issue in a securitization is whether the liabilities of the special purpose entity (SPE) issuing debt securities in the capital market have to be consolidated with the financial statements presented by the bank or other originator of the assets. For qualified SPEs under FAS 140 (so-called QSPEs), consolidation is not required. For other SPEs, the view had been that consolidation was required if the originator controlled the SPE through voting interests. The SEC, however, expressed the view that nonconsolidation was inappropriate if the majority owner of the SPE (a third party other than the originator) had made only a nominal investment in the SPE. FASB later clarified that in most cases an investment of 3% of the entity's assets exceeded the nominal requirement.

In January 2003, FASB issued Interpretation No. 46, Consolidation of Variable Interest Entities (FIN 46), followed by FIN 46–R in December 2003. In July 2004, an interagency final rule excluded "ABCP program assets consolidated under FIN 46–R and any associated minority interests from risk-weighted assets and tier 1 capital, respectively, when sponsoring banking organizations calculate their tier 1 and total risk-based capital ratios." 69 Fed. Reg. 44908 (July 28, 2004).

The capital exclusion of ABCP programs by the bank regulators encouraged the use of these programs to engage in "carry" trades with securitized subprime mortgages. The originating bank would borrow funds in the short-term commercial paper market to purchase long-term mortgages. The bank could then obtain a profit between the difference in the usually lower interest rate paid on the commercial paper and the usually higher rate received from the subprime mortgages. This created a money machine and some $1.2 trillion of commercial paper was used to support ABCP programs when the subprime crisis arose.

The income stream to the banks from ABCPs depended on the assumptions that: long as short-term rates would remain below long-term rates; that defaults on the securitized subprime mortgages would occur at predicted rates; and that the short-term commercial paper could be continually rolled over to support the longer term mortgages. Several banks, including Citigroup, developed large ABCP programs. Those programs were decimated during the financial crisis when the assumptions upon which they were based collapsed. The value of the subprime mortgages in the programs had to be marked down drastically, short-term rates advanced against long-term rates, and the commercial paper market froze.

The result was that the bank ABCP programs caused massive losses. The lack of liquidity also caused concern for money market funds holding ABCP. To alleviate these concerns, the Fed created the Commercial Paper Funding Facility that purchased three-month asset backed commercial paper from eligible issuers. An Asset–Backed Commercial Paper Money Market Fund Liquidity Facility (AMLF) was also created that that made non-recourse loans to banks on ABCP commercial paper so that the banks could repurchase that paper from the money market funds.

As a result of these problems, and to recognize new accounting standards FAS 166 and FAS 167, bank regulators removed the exclusion from risk-weighted assets and Tier 1 capital explaining:

> recent events have raised serious questions about the original rationale for allowing the exclusion of consolidated ABCP programs from risk-weighted assets. As the agencies noted in the NPR [Notice of Proposed Rulemaking], the 2004 implementation of the ABCP exclusion was based on the agencies' belief that sponsoring banking organizations' risk exposure to these entities was limited to their contractual exposure. However, as a result of some banking organizations having provided implicit support to a number of ABCP programs they sponsored during the recent financial turmoil, the agencies have observed that the premise of a contractual limit on risk was incorrect for some ABCP programs.

75 Fed. Reg. 4636, 4643 (Jan. 28, 2010).

Additional issues relating to regulatory capital requirements and securitizations are discussed in Chapter 7.

QUESTIONS AND NOTES

1.   Are large banks or small banks more likely to securitize loans?

2. May banks buy securities (such as Type III investment securities) issued in a securitization? What are the limitations on the amount and kinds of securities a bank may purchase for its own account?

3. What are the risks to banks of securitizing assets?

4. The massive losses experienced by large financial institutions during the financial crisis were attributed in substantial part to their retained interests in subprime securitizations that were AAA-rated, the so-called "Super Seniors." For example, fifty percent of UBS AG's $18.7 billion in write-offs from U.S. mortgage exposure was due to Super Seniors. UBS AG, Shareholder Report on UBS's Write–Downs § 4.2.3 (2008). Merrill Lynch's U.S. CDO subprime net exposure consisted primarily of its Super Senior CDO portfolio. Merrill Lynch, 2008 Annual Report (Form 10–K) 27 (2008). As of September 30, 2007, Citigroup held "approximately $55 billion in U.S. sub-prime direct exposure, $43 billion of which was due to exposures in the most Super Senior tranches of CDOs." Kenneth C. Johnston, et al., The Subprime Morass: Past Present and Future, 12 N.C. Banking Inst. 125, 135 (2008). Of Citigroup's $14.3 billion pre-tax loss (net of hedges) in 2008 from subprime-related direct exposure, $12 billion was attributable to "net exposures to the super senior tranches of CDOs ... derivatives on asset-backed securities or both." Citigroup, Inc., 2008 Annual Report (Form 10–K) 18 (2008).

5. A variation of the mortgage-backed security is the "covered bond." However, covered bonds are distinguished from other mortgage-backed securities by the fact that the mortgages underlying the covered bond remain on the balance sheet of the issuing financial institution. Such bonds were first issued in Germany in 1770. http://europe.pimco.com/LeftNav/Bond + Basics/2006/ Covered + Bond + Basics.htm. It has been argued that requiring mortgages to stay on the issuing bank's books would have precluded the massive issuance of the subprime mortgage-backed securities that wreaked havoc during the financial crisis. Why would that have been the case?

D. LOAN PROTECTION AND SURETY BONDS

Lenders employ a variety of mechanisms to protect themselves from the risk that the borrower will not repay the loan when due. Usual devices include taking real or personal property as collateral for the loan that may then be repossessed and sold by the lender to satisfy the debt or requiring that the debtor's loan be guaranteed by a third party who promises to pay the lender in the event the debtor does not. Letters of credit (discussed in Chapter 7) are another credit enhancement mechanism. Surety bonds may also be used to protect a lender's interest. These bonds, usually issued by an insurance company, act as a guarantee to deliver the obligation of the debtor, or something in the place of that obligation, in the event the debtor defaults on the loan. The specifics of the insurance arrangement are set forth in the contract between the parties.

Surety bonds made the headlines in connection with the bankruptcy of Enron. Several offshore companies were used by JPMorgan Chase Bank, Mahonia Ltd. and Mahonia Natural Gas Ltd., to enter into a series of "forward sales contracts" with subsidiaries of Enron. In return for an immediate payment of cash to the Enron subs, the Enron subs promised to deliver to the offshore companies oil and gas at a future date. Enron's obligations to make these deliveries were covered by eleven different surety bonds. A few days after Enron filed for bankruptcy, the JPMorgan Chase subs sought payment on the surety bonds. The sureties refused. JPMorgan brought suit against the insurance companies on over $1 billion in surety bond obligations.

JPMORGAN CHASE BANK v. LIBERTY MUTUAL INSURANCE CO.

United States District Court, Southern District of New York, 2002.
189 F.Supp.2d 24.

RAKOFF, DISTRICT JUDGE.

By this lawsuit, plaintiff JPMorgan Chase Bank, for and on behalf of Mahonia Limited and Mahonia Natural Gas Limited (collectively "Mahonia"), seeks to compel the eleven defendant insurance companies (collectively the "Sureties") to pay Mahonia over $1 billion, pursuant to six surety bonds (the "Bonds") that guaranteed the obligations of Enron Natural Gas Marketing Corporation and Enron North America Corporation (collectively "Enron") on six corresponding natural gas and crude oil forward sales contracts (the "Contracts") entered into between June, 1998 and December, 2000.

According to plaintiff, the facts are simple and straightforward. Under each of the Contracts, Mahonia paid Enron a set sum in return for subsequent deliveries of natural gas or crude oil extending over many months. To insure against the risk that Enron might default in part or whole on its promise to deliver the gas and oil, Mahonia not only obtained contractual guarantees from Enron to make monetary payments in the event of such failures but also simultaneously obtained from the Sureties the Bonds here in issue, which guaranteed payment to Mahonia upon any default by Enron.

In due course, Enron did indeed default, following which, on December 7, 2001, plaintiff, on behalf of Mahonia, sent written notices to the Sureties demanding payment in accordance with the terms of the Bonds. When the sureties demurred, plaintiff brought this lawsuit and promptly moved for summary judgment in Mahonia's favor, contending that, by the express terms of the Bonds, the Sureties' obligation to pay was immediate and unconditional.

In response to the motion, defendants allege quite different facts. They allege that, unbeknownst to the Sureties at the time they issued the Bonds, the Contracts between Mahonia and Enron were part of a fraudulent arrangement by which simple loans to Enron by plaintiff's predecessor, the Chase Manhattan Bank ("Chase"), were disguised as sales of assets. Specifically, they allege that Chase lent Mahonia the money used to pay Enron on the Contracts, and that, at the very time Enron was contracting to sell to Mahonia future deliveries of gas and oil, Enron was secretly contracting to repurchase the very same gas and oil from one or more entities commonly controlled with Mahonia, at a price equal to what was owed by Mahonia to Chase on the loan. The net effect was simply a series of loans from Chase to Enron; but by disguising them as sales of assets, Enron could book them as revenue while Chase and Mahonia could, among other things, induce the Sureties to issue Bonds that would effectively guarantee repayment of the loans—something the Sureties were otherwise forbidden to do under applicable New York law (which here governs). See § § N.Y. Ins. Law 1102, 1113(16)(E); 6901(a)(1)(A) (McKinney 2000). In short, defendants allege that the Bonds were the product of fraudulent inducement and fraudulent concealment by the plaintiff.

Fraudulent inducement and fraudulent concealment are familiar defenses to contractual performance. Yet, New York law does not permit a contracting party to lightly evade its contractual obligations by simply crying "fraud." Thus, for example, under New York law, a claim for breach of contract cannot be converted into a fraud claim by simply alleging that the promisor intended not to perform its promise. Also, of particular relevance here, New York law will not permit a sophisticated party that, in negotiating a contract, has expressly disclaimed reliance on specific oral representations extrinsic to the contract to thereafter claim that the fraudulence of these representations is a defense to contractual performance.

Here, defendants, in seeking to defeat plaintiff's motion for summary judgment on the grounds of fraudulent inducement and/or fraudulent concealment, face three principal hurdles.

First, paragraph 7 of each of the Bonds states, in pertinent part:

The obligations of each Surety hereunder are absolute and unconditional, irrespective of the value, validity or enforceability of the obligations of [Mahonia] under the [corresponding Contract] or Enron under [its separate guarantees] or any other agreement or instrument referred to therein and, to the fullest extent permitted by applicable law, irrespective of any other circumstance whatsoever that might otherwise constitute a legal or equitable discharge or defense of a surety in its capacity as such.

Disclaimer language similar to this was given effect in the decision of the New York Court of Appeals in Citibank, N.A. v. Plapinger, 485 N.E.2d 974 (1985), in which * * * the Court held that corporate officers who had signed guarantees of corporate debt containing such language could not escape payment by arguing that they had been fraudulently induced to sign the guarantees in reliance on the lenders' unfulfilled oral promises to extend a further line of credit to the corporation.

But neither *Plapinger* nor its progeny, avails plaintiff here, for several reasons. To begin with, a full and fair reading of *Plapinger* makes plain that it does *not* stand for the extraordinary proposition—the logical extension of plaintiff's interpretation—that a general sweeping disclaimer can serve to disclaim any and all extrinsic fraud between sophisticated parties. * * *

Here, * * * even if one assumes *arguendo* that the disclaimers in paragraph 7 of the Bonds preclude reliance on the representations in the underlying Contracts of which the Sureties knew or were on notice, there is no suggestion that the Sureties knew or were on notice of the allegedly circular arrangements between Mahonia, Enron, and other entities that transformed what purported to be insurable sales contracts into disguised loans that the Sureties were prohibited by law from insuring.

Furthermore, nothing in the doctrine of *Plapinger* precludes a defense of fraudulent inducement or concealment premised on fraudulent misrepresentations in the Bonds themselves. Here, each of the Bonds is expressly premised on Mahonia's having entered with Enron into a gas or oil "Inventory Forward Sale Contract" and expressly recites that once all the contracted-for gas or oil "is fully delivered" the Sureties' obligations will cease. Plainly implicit in these representations is the assertion that the Sureties are being asked to insure the sale and future delivery of a commodity, rather than being asked to insure, unlawfully, a disguised loan transaction.

In short, nothing in the broad disclaimer language of the Bonds excludes the defense—whether characterized as a defense of fraudulent inducement or fraudulent concealment—that the insured arrangements were a total sham whose reality was totally concealed from the Sureties.

Second, plaintiff points out that under New York Insurance Law, a surety that illegally guarantees repayment of a loan is still obligated to make good on that surety. See N.Y. Ins. Law § 1303. But as the few cases applying this provision indicate, this is a statutory embodiment of the familiar equitable principle that a wrongdoer, whether willful or negligent, should not benefit from his own wrongdoing. By contrast, there is no reason to believe that the statute applies to an innocent, unknowing insurer who is fraudulently induced to illegally insure loans that the insurer has no reason to believe were loans at all. To put it another way, there is nothing to suggest that the statute was intended to change prior law and preclude an insurer from raising a fraud-in-the-inducement defense—a radical change that, absent legislative history, the legislature can not be supposed to have intended.

Third, plaintiff argues that defendants' allegations of fraud are too speculative and unsupported by admissible evidence to rebut the solid showing plaintiff has made in support of plaintiff's motion for summary judgment. Even if this were true, however, it would not preclude the Court from refusing to enter summary judgment on plaintiff's behalf at this time for defendants have provided a reasonable justification for further discovery. In particular, defendants have offered substantial evidence that, even while plaintiff was moving with alacrity to obtain summary judgment, defendants were repeatedly rebuffed in their informal attempts to obtain the information regarding the underlying transactions needed to confirm (or refute) defendants' theory.

In any event, despite such obstacles, defendants have managed to obtain some important evidence that, taken most favorably to them (as it must be for purposes of this motion), inferentially but materially supports their theory. For example, with respect to the last of the six underlying Contracts here in question, which was entered into between Enron and Mahonia on December 28, 2000, defendants have obtained evidence that, on that very same day, Enron entered into an agreement with an entity called Stoneville Aegean Limited ("Stoneville") to purchase from Stoneville the identical quantities of gas that Enron was that same day agreeing to sell to Mahonia, to be delivered to Enron on the very same future dates as Enron was supposed to deliver the same quantities of gas to Mahonia.

The fact that Enron would be simultaneously buying from Stoneville the very gas it was selling to Mahonia becomes even more suspicious when considered in light of the further evidence adduced by defendants to the effect that both Mahonia and Stoneville—offshore corporations set up by the same company, Mourant & Company—have the same director, Ian James, and the same shareholders.

What, finally, turns suspicion to reasonable inference is defendants' further evidence that, whereas Mahonia agreed in its Contract with Enron to pay Enron $330 million for the gas at the moment of contracting (December 28, 2000), Enron, in its agreement with Stoneville, agreed to pay Stoneville $394 million to buy back the same quantities of gas on the same delivery schedule—but with the $394 million to be paid at specified future dates.

Taken together, then, these arrangements now appear to be nothing but a disguised loan—or at least have sufficient indicia thereof that the Court could not possibly grant judgment to plaintiff.

* * * Accordingly, plaintiff's motion for summary judgment is hereby denied. * * *

———————

The case was settled after it was submitted to the jury, but before the jury reached a decision. JPMorgan reduced its claim by some $400 million in settling the case and accepted the sureties' claims against Enron as a part of the settlement, thereby reducing the sureties' obligations even further. The company also took a $1.3 billion charge against earnings to cover the settlement and other Enron-related exposure.[41] JPMorgan agreed to pay Enron's bankruptcy trustee $350 million in settlement of claims that JPMorgan had assisted Enron in disguising its financial situation. This followed an earlier $2.2 billion settlement with plaintiffs who had filed a class action alleging that JPMorgan had helped Enron

———————

41. Christopher Oster & Randall Smith, Enron Deals Cost J.P. Morgan; Bank Takes $1.3 Billion Charge, Wall St. J., Jan. 3, 2003, at A1.

finance special purpose entities and fail to disclose billions of dollars in debt. Citigroup entered into a $2 billion settlement in the same suit. Matthias Rieker, JPM Chase, TD Settle an Enron Lawsuit, Am. Banker, Aug. 17, 2005.

Enron obtained $8.6 billion in cash from its prepay transactions between 1992 and 2000. The prepay transactions were designed to increase Enron's cash flows in order to match its mark-to-market earnings. "[P]repays were the quarter-to-quarter cash flow lifeblood of Enron,"; providing over half of Enron's year 2000 flow of funds from operations.[42] These transactions provided almost all of Enron's net operating cash flow in 1999 and almost a third in the year 2000. The prepays—which totaled over $4 billion in 2000—were reported by Enron as liabilities from price risk management on Enron's balance sheet, rather than as debt. As a result, "Enron's key credit ratios were enhanced significantly."[43] "The prepay technique was a powerful tool employed by Enron to maintain investment grade rating."[44]

Before engaging the surety companies, JPMorgan Chase used standby letters of credit from banks for the same purpose under other prepay contracts with Enron. Under those letters of credit, the banks were required to pay if Enron defaulted on its delivery obligations. One of the syndicates refused to pay $165 million after Enron defaulted and JPMorgan sued the syndicate in England. The English judge ruled that the prepay transactions had been properly accounted for by Enron and that U.S. securities laws were not violated by that accounting treatment.

QUESTIONS AND NOTES

1. Another credit enhancement is a financial guaranty insurance policy issued by a "monoline" insurance company. Such insurance companies initially insured state and municipal bond offerings against default. The insurance allowed municipalities to issue AAA-rated bonds, which lowered their funding costs because they could not otherwise obtain such a rating. This business was successful for the insurer because the default rate on municipal securities, at least before the financial crisis, was less than one percent of the outstanding issues each year. The monoline insurers branched into guaranteeing subprime mortgage securitizations. Like the rating agencies, monolines used models to predict the expected rate of defaults on the subprime securitizations as the actuarial basis for setting premium payments. Those loss rates were quite low in the rising housing market before the financial crisis because of low teaser interest rates that had not reset, and frequent refinancings to take advantage of valuation increases that could be used to defer defaults. As a result, the monoline models proved to be inadequate in predicting the losses that would be experienced during the financial crisis and the monoline insurers were unable to cover all of the obligations they had insured.

---

42. Second Interim Report of Neal Batson, Court–Appointed Examiner, In re Enron Corp. 45, No. 01–16034 (AJG) (Bankr. S.D.N.Y. Jan. 21, 2003).

43. Id.

44. Id. at 62.

2. As described in Chapter 12, another form of credit protection appeared in the form of credit default swaps that were at the center of the financial crisis.

3. The United States Supreme Court held in Stoneridge Investment Partners, LLC v. Scientific–Atlanta, Inc., 552 U.S. 148 (2008), that shareholders may not recover from secondary parties like banks on a theory of "scheme liability." The Court found no implied rights of action under Section 10(b) of the Securities Exchange Act unless the shareholders relied on the secondary parties' deceptive acts, such as by relying on public representations by the secondary parties or when the secondary parties had some duty to disclose to the shareholders. The Dodd–Frank Act requires the Government Accountability Office (GAO) to prepare a report exploring whether the Supreme Court's decision in *Stoneridge* should be legislatively overturned. In addition, Section 929 Z of Dodd–Frank requires the GAO to conduct a study on whether Congress should permit a private right of action against a person who aids or abets another in a violation of the federal securities laws. Such legislation would overturn another Supreme Court decision denying such a right. Central Bank v. First Interstate Bank, 511 U.S. 164 (1994). Dodd–Frank also added aiding and abetting liability, which is already contained in the Securities Exchange Act of 1934, to the Securities Act of 1933 and the Investment Advisers Act of 1940. See Dodd–Frank Act, §§ 929 M & N. The standard of proof for intent for aiding and abetting was changed from "knowingly" to "recklessly." Id. § 929 O.

CHAPTER SIX

CONSUMER LENDING

■ ■ ■

Consumer lending can be a regulatory minefield for banks. Because of the imbalanced bargaining position between a consumer borrower and a bank, Congress has adopted a number of laws to protect consumers from overreaching. State statutes may apply as well. Many law schools have an entire course devoted to consumer credit laws. The discussion set forth in this chapter is meant to be illustrative of some of the issues associated with consumer lending rather than an exhaustive treatment of this complex subject.

The FDIC has commented on the positive and negative effects of the "consumer lending revolution." The primary positive outcome is the greater availability of credit to a broader cross-section of the population. The negative consequences include higher debt loads and an increase in the average riskiness of consumer loan portfolios. As of 2003, FDIC-insured banks held approximately $2.6 trillion in consumer and mortgage loans. FDIC, FYI–An Update on Emerging Issues in Banking, Evaluating the Consumer Lending Revolution (Sept. 17, 2003), available at <www.fdic.gov/bank/analytical/fyi/2003/index.html>.

The FDIC pointed to five significant trends that led to the "revolution" in consumer lending: deregulation, general purpose credit cards, credit scoring, pricing according to risk, and securitization.

Deregulation includes the *Marquette* ruling, discussed in the next section, that permitted interest rates to be charged according to the laws of the lender's state, rather than the laws in the borrower's state. This result led some states to relax interest rate restrictions to remain attractive homes to lenders.

General purpose credit cards that can be used at any time for any purpose, although common today, mushroomed in availability after the *Marquette* decision. There were 5 billion credit card solicitations mailed in 2001, more than five times the number mailed in 1990. Increase in credit card access across income levels has also resulted in increased credit card debt.

Credit scoring and improved technology permitted fully automated consumer loan underwriting beginning in the 1990s. A credit score predicts the likelihood that the borrower will repay a loan and is based on historical performance from borrowers with similar characteristics.

Risk-based pricing uses credit scores to better estimate borrower risk and price consumer loans to compensate for the additional risk. With a more finely segmented market, lower-risk individuals do not subsidize loans to higher-risk individuals through overpriced credit.

Securitization allows consumer credit, including mortgages, credit card receivables, and auto loans to be pooled into trusts and financed through debt instruments sold to investors worldwide. Credit scoring has assisted in the structuring and pricing of these debt instruments. Securitization reduces funding costs for consumer loans by diversifying risks and increasing liquidity.

The supervisor and enforcement of federal consumer financial protection laws is in the midst of a radical restructuring. The Dodd–Frank Act created a Bureau of Consumer Financial Protection (BCFP or Bureau) in the Fed, headed by an independent Director appointed by the President and confirmed by the Senate. The Director will be a member of FSOC and the board of directors of the FDIC. The Bureau will be funded by annual transfers from the earnings of the Fed, rather than assessments from the regulated entities, and insulated from the political appropriations process. The BCFP is tasked with implementing and enforcing "Federal consumer financial laws consistently for the purpose of ensuring that all consumers have access to markets for consumer financial products and services and that markets for consumer financial products and services are fair, transparent, and competitive." Dodd–Frank Act, § 1021. The Bureau is to protect consumers from "unfair, deceptive, or abusive acts and practices." Id.

The BCFP will regulate the offering and provision of consumer financial products or services under the federal consumer financial laws. The BFFP will also oversee enforcement of laws requiring nondiscriminatory access to credit for individuals and communities. The rulemaking authority for most of the federal laws discussed in this Chapter is transferred to the BCFP, including TILA, ECOA, HMDA, and RESPA. The BCFP has independent authority to write rules governing consumer protection for customers of all persons who offer consumer financial services or products. Thus, nonbank entities will be regulated by the same rules as their bank competitors marketing similar products. The BCFP must consult with other regulators before a proposal is issued. Only the FSOC, however, may set aside a BCFP regulation and then only by a supermajority vote.

The BCFP was given authority to supervise, examine, and enforce regulations for banks and credit unions with assets of over $10 billion, and nonbank entities such as all mortgage-related businesses (including lenders, servicers, and mortgage brokers), payday lenders, student lenders (who will be overseen by a Private Education Loan Ombudsman), debt collectors, and consumer reporting agencies. The relevant federal financial agency will continue to supervise, examine, and enforce federal consumer protection laws for smaller banks with assets of less than $10 billion to ensure that these smaller institutions will be subject to a single supervisor. The BCFP, however, may appoint its own examiners to participate in examinations conducted by the relevant federal financial regulatory agency on a sampled basis. The Dodd–Frank Act exempts a number of entities from the BCFP's authority. These include entities regulated by the SEC, the CFTC, the Farm Credit Administration, a state insurance regulator, or a state securities commissioner. Automobile dealers and some other sellers of nonfinancial services who offer consumer financial services in connection with those sales and do not routinely assign the credit to an unaffiliated third party financing source are also exempt. Dodd–Frank Act, § 1029.

State laws offering greater protection to consumers than BCFP rules are not preempted. The BCFP rules will be considered the floor and the more stringent state laws will also apply to banks and other consumer financial service providers. As discussed in detail in Chapter 4, federally chartered banks and savings and loans will be able to preempt state consumer protection laws if the new Dodd–Frank standards on preemption are satisfied. State attorneys general are also authorized to bring civil actions against federally chartered financial institutions to enforce BCFP regulations.

SECTION 1.   USURY

Usury regulation relates to the amount of interest a lender may charge a borrower. The original meaning of "usury" forbade charging any interest at all. Modern usage, however, equates usury with the charging of excessive interest as that has been defined by state regulation. The states approach usury regulation in different ways. Some states, such as Delaware and South Dakota, place no limit on the rate of interest that may be charged on a loan. The justification for this approach is that regulation is not needed in a market-based economy; natural market competition will ensure competitive and reasonable interest rates. Moreover, in times of inflation, fixed upper limits on interest rates may make borrowed funds totally unavailable if market rates exceed the fixed interest rate limit.

Other states, however, believe that borrowers need protection from lenders, in addition to disclosure of interest rates. These states do not believe market competition alone is enough to protect borrowers, who are often at a competitive disadvantage with lenders. Some believe that charging excessively high interest is morally wrong, perhaps based upon the biblical passage that lending money at interest between brothers was forbidden.[1] Even in those states that regulate interest rates on loans,

---

1. See Deuterotomy 23:20 ("Unto a stranger thou mayest lend upon usury; but unto thy brother thou shalt not lend upon usury...."). Under Islamic law, (Sharia) interest is prohibited on loans.

there are often exemptions from such regulation for corporate borrowers or for large loans, under the theory that corporate borrowers or those who borrow large sums of money are likely to be sophisticated enough to bargain for a reasonable rate of interest.

A. NATIONAL BANKS

A national bank may charge the rate of interest allowed in the state where it is located. 12 U.S.C. § 85. This provision of the National Bank Act has been subject to much interpretation, as the cases that follow demonstrate. The penalty for taking usurious interest is set forth in 12 U.S.C. § 86.

TIFFANY v. NATIONAL BANK OF MISSOURI

Supreme Court of the United States, 1874.
85 U.S. (18 Wall.) 409.

MR. JUSTICE STRONG delivered the opinion of the Court.

* * * The question, therefore, is whether the thirtieth section of the act of Congress of June 3d, 1864, relative to National banking associations, clearly prohibits such associations in the State of Missouri from reserving and taking a greater rate of interest than 8 per cent., the rate limited by the laws of that State to be charged by the banks of issue organized under its laws. It is only in case a greater rate of interest has been paid than the National banking associations are allowed to receive that they are made liable to pay twice the interest. The act of Congress enacts that every such association "may take, receive, reserve, and charge on any loan or discount made, or upon any note, bill of exchange, or other evidences of debt, interest at the rate allowed by the laws of the State or Territory where the bank is located, and no more; except that where, by the laws of any State, a different rate is limited for banks of issue, organized under State laws, the rate so limited shall be allowed for associations organized in any such State under the act." What, then, were the rates of interest allowed in Missouri when the loans were made by the defendants that are alleged to have been usurious? It is admitted to have been 10 per cent. per annum, allowed to all persons, except banks of issue organized under the laws of the State, and they were allowed to charge and receive only 8 per cent.

The position of the plaintiff is, that the general provision of the act of Congress that National banking associations may charge and receive interest at the rate allowed by the laws of the State where they are located, has no application to the case of these defendants, and that they are restricted to the rate allowed to banks of issue of the State, that is, to 8 per cent. This, we think, cannot be maintained. The act of Congress is an enabling statute, not a restraining one, except so far as it fixes a maximum rate in all cases where State banks of issue are not allowed a greater. There are three provisions in section thirty, each of them enabling. If no rate of interest is defined by State laws, 7 per cent. is allowed to be charged. If there is a rate of interest fixed by State laws for lenders *enabling stat.* generally, the banks are allowed to charge that rate, but no more, except that if State banks of issue are allowed to reserve more, the same privilege is allowed to National banking associations. Such, we think, is the fair construction of the act of Congress, entirely consistent with its words and with its spirit. It speaks of allowances to National banks and limitations upon State banks, but it does not declare that the rate limited to State banks shall be the maximum rate allowed to National banks. There can be no question that if the banks of issue of Missouri were allowed to demand interest at a higher rate than 10 per cent. National banks might do likewise. And this would be for the reason that they would then come within the exception made by the statute, that is, the exception from the operation of the restrictive words "no more" than the general rate of interest allowed by law. But if it was intended they should in no case charge a higher rate of interest than State banks of issue, even though the general rule was greater, if the intention was to restrict rather than to enable, the obvious mode of expressing such an intention was to add the words "and no more," as they were added to the preceding clause of the section. The absence of those words, or words equivalent, is significant. Coupled with the general spirit of the act, and of all the legislation respecting National banks, it is controlling. It cannot be doubted, in view of the purpose of Congress in providing for the organization of National banking associations, that it was intended to give them a firm footing in the different States where they might be located. It was expected they would come into competition with State banks, and it was intended to give them at least equal advantages in such competition. In order to accomplish this they were empowered to reserve interest at the same rates, whatever those rates might be, which were allowed to similar State institutions. This was considered indispensable to protect them against possible unfriendly State legislation. Obviously, if State statutes should allow to their banks of issue a rate of interest greater than the ordinary rate allowed to natural persons, National banking associations could not compete with them, unless allowed the same. On the other hand, if such associations were restricted to the rates allowed by the statutes of the State to banks which might be authorized by the State laws, unfriendly legislation might make their existence in the State impossible. A rate of interest might be prescribed so low that banking could not be carried on, except at a certain loss. The only mode of guarding against such contingencies was that which, we think, Congress adopted. It was to allow to National associations the rate allowed by the State to natural persons generally, and a higher rate, if State banks of issue were authorized to charge a higher rate. This construction accords with the purpose of Congress, and carries it out. It accords with the spirit of all the legislation of Congress. National banks have been National favorites. They were established for the purpose, in part, of providing a currency for the whole country, and in part to create a market for the loans of the General government. It could not have been intended, therefore, to expose them to the hazard of unfriendly legislation by the States, or to ruinous competition with State banks. On the contrary, much has been done to insure their taking the place of State banks. The latter have been substantially taxed out of existence. A duty has been imposed upon their issues so large as to manifest a purpose to compel a withdrawal of all such issues from circulation. In harmony with this policy is the construction we think should be given to the thirtieth section of the act of Congress we have been considering. It gives advantages to National banks over their State competitors. It allows such banks to charge such interest as State banks may charge, and more, if by the laws of the State more may be charged by natural persons.

The result of this is that the defendants, in receiving 9 per cent. interest upon the loans made by them, have not transgressed the act of Congress, consequently they are under no liability to the plaintiff.

MARQUETTE NATIONAL BANK OF MINNEAPOLIS v. FIRST OF OMAHA SERVICE CORP.

Supreme Court of the United States, 1978.
439 U.S. 299.

MR. JUSTICE BRENNAN delivered the opinion of the Court.

The question for decision is whether the National Bank Act, Rev. Stat. § 5197, as amended, 12 U.S.C. § 85, authorizes a national bank based in one State to charge its out-of-state credit-card customers an interest rate on unpaid balances allowed by its home State, when that rate is greater than that permitted by the State of the bank's nonresident customers. The Minnesota Supreme Court held that the bank is allowed by § 85 to charge the higher rate. We affirm.

The First National Bank of Omaha (Omaha Bank) is a national banking association with its charter address in Omaha, Neb. Omaha Bank is a card-issuing member in the BankAmericard plan. This plan enables cardholders to purchase goods and services from participating merchants and to obtain cash advances from participating banks throughout the United States and the world. Omaha Bank has systematically sought to enroll in its BankAmericard program the residents, merchants, and banks of the nearby State of Minnesota. The solicitation of Minnesota merchants and banks is carried on by respondent First of Omaha Service Corp. (Omaha Service Corp.), a wholly owned subsidiary of Omaha Bank.

Minnesota residents are obligated to pay Omaha Bank interest on the outstanding balances of their BankAmericards. Nebraska law permits Omaha Bank to charge interest on the unpaid balances of cardholder accounts at a rate of 18% per year on the first $999.99, and 12% per year on amounts of $1,000 and over. Minnesota law, however, fixes the permissible annual interest on such accounts at 12%. To compensate for the reduced interest, Minnesota law permits banks to charge annual fees of up to $15 for the privilege of using a bank credit card.

The instant case began when petitioner Marquette National Bank of Minneapolis (Marquette), itself a national banking association enrolled in the BankAmericard plan, brought suit in the District Court of Hennepin County, Minn., to enjoin Omaha Bank and Omaha Service Corp. from soliciting in Minnesota for Omaha Bank's BankAmericard program until such time as that program complied with Minnesota law. Marquette claimed to be losing customers to Omaha Bank because, unlike the Nebraska bank, Marquette was forced by the low rate of interest permissible under Minnesota law to charge a $10 annual fee for the use of its credit cards. * * *

Omaha Bank is a national bank. * * * The interest rate that Omaha Bank may charge in its BankAmericard program is thus governed by federal law. The provision of § 85 called into question states

> "Any association may take, receive, reserve, and charge on any loan or discount made, or upon any notes, bills of exchange, or other evidences of debt, interest at the rate allowed by the laws of the State, Territory, or District *where the bank is located....*" * * * (Emphasis supplied.)

Section 85 thus plainly provides that a national bank may charge interest "on any loan" at the rate allowed by the laws of the State in which the bank is "located." The question before us is therefore narrowed to whether Omaha Bank and its BankAmericard program are "located" in Nebraska and for that reason entitled to charge its Minnesota customers the rate of interest authorized by Nebraska law.

There is no question but that Omaha Bank itself, apart from its BankAmericard program, is located in Nebraska. Petitioners concede as much. The National Bank Act requires a national bank to state in its organization certificate "[t]he place where its operations of discount and deposit are to be carried on, designating the State, Territory, or district, and the particular county and city, town, or village." Rev.Stat. § 5134, 12 U.S.C. § 22. The charter address of Omaha Bank is in Omaha, Douglas County, Neb. The bank operates no branch banks in Minnesota.[2] * * *

The State of Minnesota, however, contends that this conclusion must be altered if Omaha Bank's BankAmericard program is considered: "In the context of a national bank which systematically solicits Minnesota residents for credit cards to be used in transactions with Minnesota merchants the bank must be deemed to be 'located' in Minnesota for purposes of this credit card program."

We disagree. Section 85 was originally enacted as § 30 of the National Bank Act of 1864, 13 Stat. 108. The congressional debates surrounding the enactment of § 30 were conducted on the assumption that a national bank was "located" for purposes of the section in the State named in its organization certificate. Omaha Bank cannot be deprived of this location merely because it is extending credit to residents of a foreign State.

---

2. [eds.] At the time of this case, interstate branching was not permitted.

Minnesota residents were always free to visit Nebraska and receive loans in that State. It has not been suggested that Minnesota usury laws would apply to such transactions. Although the convenience of modern mail permits Minnesota residents holding Omaha Bank's BankAmericards to receive loans without visiting Nebraska, credit on the use of their cards is nevertheless similarly extended by Omaha Bank in Nebraska by the bank's honoring of the sales drafts of participating Minnesota merchants and banks. Finance charges on the unpaid balances of cardholders are assessed by the bank in Omaha, Neb., and all payments on unpaid balances are remitted to the bank in Omaha, Neb. Furthermore, the bank issues its BankAmericards in Omaha, Neb., after credit assessments made by the bank in that city.

Nor can the fact that Omaha Bank's BankAmericards are used "in transactions with Minnesota merchants" be determinative of the bank's location for purposes of § 85. The bank's BankAmericard enables its holder "to purchase goods and services from participating merchants and obtain cash advances from participating banks throughout the United States and the world." Minnesota residents can thus use their Omaha Bank BankAmericards to purchase services in the State of New York or mail-order goods from the State of Michigan. If the location of the bank were to depend on the whereabouts of each credit-card transaction, the meaning of the term "located" would be so stretched as to throw into confusion the complex system of modern interstate banking. * * * The mere fact that Omaha Bank has enrolled Minnesota residents, merchants, and banks in its BankAmericard program thus does not suffice to "locate" that bank in Minnesota for purposes of 12 U.S.C. § 85.

Since Omaha Bank and its BankAmericard program are "located" in Nebraska, the plain language of § 85 provides that the bank may charge "on any loan" the rate "allowed" by the State of Nebraska. Petitioners contend, however, that this reading of the statute violates the basic legislative intent of the National Bank Act. At the time Congress enacted § 30 of the National Bank Act of 1864, 13 Stat. 108, so petitioners' argument runs, it intended "to insure competitive equality between state and national banks in the charging of interest." This policy could best be effectuated by limiting national banks to the rate of interest allowed by the States in which the banks were located. Since Congress in 1864 was addressing a financial system in which incorporated banks were "local institutions," it did not "contemplate a national bank soliciting customers and entering loan agreements outside of the state in which it was established." Therefore to interpret § 85 to apply to interstate loans such as those involved in this case would not only enlarge impermissibly the original intent of Congress, but would also undercut the basic policy foundations of the statute by upsetting the competitive equality now existing between state and national banks.

We cannot accept petitioners' argument. Whatever policy of "competitive equality" has been discerned in other sections of the National Bank Act, see, e. g., First Nat. Bank v. Dickinson, 396 U.S. 122, 131 (1969);

First Nat. Bank of Logan v. Walker Bank & Trust Co., 385 U.S. 252, 261–262 (1966), § 30 and its descendants have been interpreted for over a century to give "advantages to National banks over their State competitors." Tiffany v. National Bank of Missouri, 18 Wall. 409, 413 (1874). "National banks," it was said in *Tiffany*, "have been National favorites."[3] The policy of competitive equality between state and national banks, however, is not truly at the core of this case. Instead, we are confronted by the inequalities that occur when a national bank applies the interest rates of its home State in its dealing with residents of a foreign State. These inequalities affect both national and state banks in the foreign State. Indeed, in the instant case Marquette is a national bank claiming to be injured by the unequal interest rates charged by another national bank. Whether the inequalities which thus occur when the interest rates of one State are "exported" into another violate the intent of Congress in enacting § 30 in part depends on whether Congress in 1864 was aware of the existence of a system of interstate banking in which such inequalities would seem a necessary part.

Close examination of the National Bank Act of 1864, its legislative history, and its historical context makes clear that, contrary to the suggestion of petitioners, Congress intended to facilitate what Representative Hooper termed a "national banking system." Cong.Globe, 38th Cong., 1st Sess., 1451 (1864). * * *

Although in the debates surrounding the enactment of § 30 there is no specific discussion of the impact of interstate loans, these debates occurred in the context of a developed interstate loan market. As early as 1839 this Court had occasion to note: "Money is frequently borrowed in one state, by a corporation created in another. The numerous banks established by different states are in the constant habit of contracting and dealing with one another.... These usages of commerce and trade have been so general and public, and have been practiced for so long a period of time, and so generally acquiesced in by the states, that the Court cannot overlook them...." Bank of Augusta v. Earle, 13 Pet. 519, 590–591 (1839). * * *

We cannot assume that Congress was oblivious to the existence of such common commercial transactions. We find it implausible to conclude, therefore, that Congress meant through its silence to exempt interstate loans from the reach of § 30. We would certainly be exceedingly reluctant to read such a hiatus into the regulatory scheme of § 30 in the absence of evidence of specific congressional intent. Petitioners have adduced no such evidence.

Petitioners' final argument is that the "exportation" of interest rates, such as occurred in this case, will significantly impair the ability of States to enact effective usury laws. This impairment, however, has always been

P: impairs St. ability to legis.

---

3. [n.26] The "most favored lender" status for national banks under *Tiffany* has since been incorporated into the regulations of the Comptroller of the Currency. See 12 CFR § 7.7310(a) (1978).

implicit in the structure of the National Bank Act, since citizens of one State were free to visit a neighboring State to receive credit at foreign interest rates. This impairment may in fact be accentuated by the ease with which interstate credit is available by mail through the use of modern credit cards. But the protection of state usury laws is an issue of legislative policy, and any plea to alter § 85 to further that end is better addressed to the wisdom of Congress than to the judgment of this Court.

SMILEY v. CITIBANK (SOUTH DAKOTA), N. A.

Supreme Court of the United States, 1996.
517 U.S. 735.

Mr. Justice Scalia delivered the opinion of the Court.

Section 30 of the National Bank Act of 1864, Rev. Stat. § 5197, as amended, 12 U.S.C. § 85, provides that a national bank may charge its loan customers "interest at the rate allowed by the laws of the State ... where the bank is located." In Marquette Nat. Bank of Minneapolis v. First of Omaha Service Corp., 439 U.S. 299 (1978), we held that this provision authorizes a national bank to charge out-of-state credit-card customers an interest rate allowed by the bank's home State, even when that rate is higher than what is permitted by the States in which the cardholders reside. The question in this case is whether § 85 also authorizes a national bank to charge late-payment fees that are lawful in the bank's home State but prohibited in the States where the cardholders reside—in other words, whether the statutory term "interest" encompasses late-payment fees.

Petitioner, a resident of California, held two credit cards—a "Classic Card" and a "Preferred Card"—issued by respondent, a national bank located in Sioux Falls, South Dakota. The Classic Card agreement provided that respondent would charge petitioner a late fee of $15 for each monthly period in which she failed to make her minimum monthly payment within 25 days of the due date. Under the Preferred Card agreement, respondent would impose a late fee of $6 if the minimum monthly payment was not received within 15 days of its due date; and an additional charge of $15 or 0.65% of the outstanding balance on the Preferred Card, whichever was greater, if the minimum payment was not received by the *next* minimum monthly payment due date. Petitioner was charged late fees on both cards.

These late fees are permitted by South Dakota law, see S.D. Codified Laws §§ 54–3–1, 54–3–1.1 (1990 and Supp.1995). Petitioner, however, is of the view that exacting such "unconscionable" late charges from California residents violates California law, and in 1992 brought a class action against respondent on behalf of herself and other California holders of respondent's credit cards, asserting various statutory and common-law claims.[4] * * *

---

4. [n.1] By way of common-law claims, petitioner's complaint alleged breach of duty of good faith and fair dealing; unjust enrichment; fraud and deceit; negligent misrepresentation; and

On March 3, 1995, which was after the California Superior Court's dismissal of petitioner's complaint, the Comptroller of the Currency noticed for public comment a proposed regulation dealing with the subject before us, see 60 Fed.Reg. 11924, 11940, and on February 9, 1996, which was after the California Supreme Court's decision, he adopted the following provision:

"The term 'interest' as used in 12 U.S.C. § 85 includes any payment compensating a creditor or prospective creditor for an extension of credit, making available of a line of credit, or any default or breach by a borrower of a condition upon which credit was extended. It includes, among other things, the following fees connected with credit extension or availability: numerical periodic rates, late fees, not sufficient funds (NSF) fees, overlimit fees, annual fees, cash advance fees, and membership fees. It does not ordinarily include appraisal fees, premiums and commissions attributable to insurance guaranteeing repayment of any extension of credit, finders' fees, fees for document preparation or notarization, or fees incurred to obtain credit reports." 61 Fed.Reg. 4869 (to be codified in 12 CFR § 7.4001(a)).

Petitioner proposes several reasons why the ordinary rule of deference should not apply to this regulation. First, petitioner points to the fact that this regulation was issued more than 100 years after the enactment of § 85, and seemingly as a result of this and similar litigation in which the Comptroller has participated as *amicus curiae* on the side of the banks. The 100–year delay makes no difference. To be sure, agency interpretations that are of long standing come before us with a certain credential of reasonableness, since it is rare that error would long persist. But neither antiquity nor contemporaneity with the statute is a condition of validity. We accord deference to agencies under *Chevron*, not because of a presumption that they drafted the provisions in question, or were present at the hearings, or spoke to the principal sponsors; but rather because of a presumption that Congress, when it left ambiguity in a statute meant for implementation by an agency, understood that the ambiguity would be resolved, first and foremost, by the agency, and desired the agency (rather than the courts) to possess whatever degree of discretion the ambiguity allows. See *Chevron*, supra, at 843–844. Nor does it matter that the regulation was prompted by litigation, including this very suit. Of course we deny deference "to agency litigating positions that are wholly unsupported by regulations, rulings, or administrative practice," Bowen v. Georgetown Univ. Hospital, 488 U.S. 204, 212 (1988). The deliberateness of such positions, if not indeed their authoritativeness, is suspect. But we have before us here a full-dress regulation, issued by the Comptroller himself and adopted pursuant to the notice-and-comment procedures of the Administrative Procedure Act designed to assure due deliberation, see

breach of contract. It also alleged violation of Cal. Bus. & Prof.Code Ann. § 17200 (West Supp.1996) (prohibiting unlawful business practices) and Cal. Civ.Code Ann. § 1671 (West 1985) (invalidating unreasonable liquidated damages).

5 U.S.C. § 553. That it was litigation which disclosed the need for the regulation is irrelevant.

Second, petitioner contends that the Comptroller's regulation is not deserving of our deference because "there is no rational basis for distinguishing the various charges [it] has denominated interest ... from those charges it has denominated 'non-interest.'" As an analytical matter, it seems to us perfectly possible to draw a line, as the regulation does, between (1) "payment compensating a creditor or prospective creditor for an extension of credit, making available of a line of credit, or any default or breach by a borrower of a condition upon which credit was extended," and (2) all other payments. To be sure, in the broadest sense all payments connected in any way with the loan—including reimbursement of the lender's costs in processing the application, insuring the loan, and appraising the collateral—can be regarded as "compensating [the] creditor for [the] extension of credit." But it seems to us quite possible and rational to distinguish, as the regulation does, between those charges that are *specifically assigned* to such expenses and those that are assessed for simply making the loan, or for the borrower's default. In its logic, at least, the line is not "arbitrary [or] capricious," and thereby disentitled to deference under *Chevron*, see 467 U.S., at 844. * * *

Petitioner argues that the late fees charged by respondent do not constitute "interest" because they "do not vary based on the payment owed or the time period of delay." We do not think that such a limitation must be read into the statutory term. Most legal dictionaries of the era of the National Bank Act did not place such a limitation upon "interest." See, e.g., 1 J. Bouvier, A Law Dictionary 652 (6th ed. 1856) ("The compensation which is paid by the borrower to the lender or by the debtor to the creditor for ... use [of money]"). The definition of "interest" that we ourselves set out in Brown v. Hiatts, 15 Wall. 177, 185, 21 L.Ed. 128 (1873), decided shortly after the enactment of the National Bank Act, likewise contained no indication that it was limited to charges expressed as a function of time or of amount owing: "Interest is the compensation allowed by law, or fixed by the parties, for the use or forbearance of money or as damages for its detention." See also Hollowell v. Southern Building & Loan Assn., 120 N.C. 286 (1897) ("[A]ny charges made against [the borrower] in excess of the lawful rate of interest, whether called 'fines,' 'charges,' 'dues,' or 'interest,' are in fact interest, and usurious").

Petitioner suggests another source for the asserted requirement that the charges be time-and-rate-based: What is authorized by § 85, she notes, is the charging of interest "at the rate allowed" by the laws of the bank's home State. This requires, in her view, that the interest charges be expressed as functions of time and amount owing. It would be surprising to find such a requirement in the Act, if only because it would be so pointless. Any flat charge may, of course, readily be converted to a percentage charge—which was indeed the basis for 19th-century decisions holding that flat charges violated state usury laws establishing maximum "rates." See, e.g., Craig v. Pleiss, 26 Pa. 271, 272–273 (1856). And there is no apparent reason why home-state-approved percentage charges should be permissible but home-state-approved flat charges unlawful. In any event, common usage at the time of the National Bank Act prevents the conclusion that the Comptroller's refusal to give the word "rate" the narrow meaning petitioner demands is unreasonable. * * *

[The Court concluded that the Comptroller's regulation defining late fees as interest was entitled to deference and that the Comptroller's interpretation of § 85 was not unreasonable.]

The BCFP is prohibited by the Dodd–Frank Act from establishing usury limits on loans, preserving the exportation of interest rates under 12 U.S.C. § 85 (national banks—discussed above) and § 1831d (state banks—discussed below).

B. STATE BANKS

Greenwood Trust was decided before *Smiley* and under the authority of 12 U.S.C.A. § 1831d, a provision comparable to section 85 but applicable to state banks.

GREENWOOD TRUST v. COMMONWEALTH OF MASSACHUSETTS

United States Court of Appeals, First Circuit, 1992.
971 F.2d 818, *cert. denied*, 506 U.S. 1052 (1993).

SELYA, CIRCUIT JUDGE.

* * * The pertinent facts are largely undisputed. Plaintiff-appellant Greenwood Trust Company (Greenwood) is a Delaware banking corporation. Its deposits are insured by the Federal Deposit Insurance Corporation. Through a wholly owned subsidiary, Greenwood offers an open end credit card—the Discover Card—to customers nationwide. More than one hundred thousand of its cardholders live in Massachusetts.

The terms and conditions applicable to use of the Discover Card are spelled out in a Cardmember Agreement. The Agreement stipulates, *inter alia*, that the holder must make a minimum monthly payment, calculated by reference to the credit-card balance outstanding from time to time, on or before a designated due date. Failure to make this payment in a timeous fashion constitutes a default. If the default is not cured within twenty days, a ten-dollar late charge is automatically assessed. * * *

The Massachusetts statute is straightforward. It provides that: "No creditor shall impose a delinquency charge, late charge, or similar charge on loans made pursuant to ... an open end credit plan." Mass.Gen.L. ch. 140, § 114B.

On the other hand, section 521 [of the Depository Institutions Deregulation and Monetary Control Act of 1980 (DIDA)] is equally uncompromising:

In order to prevent discrimination against State-chartered insured depository institutions, including insured savings banks, ... with respect to interest rates, ... such State bank[s] ... may, notwithstanding any State constitution or statute which is hereby preempted for the purposes of this section, take, receive, reserve, and charge on any loan or discount made, or upon any note, bill of exchange, or other evidence of debt, interest at a rate of not more than 1 per centum in excess of the discount rate on ninety-day commercial paper in effect at the Federal Reserve bank in the Federal Reserve district where such State bank ... is located or at the rate allowed by the laws of the State, territory, or district where the bank is located, whichever may be greater.

12 U.S.C. § 1831d(a) (1988 & Supp.1990).

In Gibbons v. Ogden, 22 U.S. (9 Wheat.) 1 (1824), Chief Justice Marshall declared that, under the rubric of the Supremacy Clause, state laws which "interfere with, or are contrary to the laws of Congress, made in pursuance of the constitution," are preempted and, therefore, invalid. Id. 22 U.S. (9 Wheat.) at 211. * * *

Our conclusion that the proper analysis in this case reduces to an inquiry into express preemption is unaffected by the fact that the inquiry requires us to interpret the terms "interest" and "interest rates" as they are employed in section 521. While uncertainty about the meaning of interstitial terms in the text of a federal statute may affect the scope of express preemption, it does not bear directly on the character of Congress's preemptory intent. In other words, so long as Congress's intent to effect preemption remains clear and manifest, uncertainty which pertains only to the contours of the ensuing preemption does not necessitate an alteration of a reviewing court's basic analytic approach.

We must still resolve the crucial question of *what* state laws are preempted. Put specifically, is a state law banning the imposition of late charges a law regulating "interest" within the purview of section 521? If so, chapter 140, § 114B is preempted.

This inquiry necessarily reduces to ascertaining what Congress meant by the word "interest" in drafting section 521. In divining this legislative intent, it is incumbent upon us to "begin with the language employed by Congress and the assumption that the ordinary meaning of that language accurately expresses the legislative purpose." Morales v. Trans World Airlines, Inc., 112 S.Ct. 2031, 2036 (1992). In the process, however, we should not wear blinders: if there is "good reason to believe" that Congress intended to deviate from the ordinary meaning of the language selected, then a reviewing court must follow the congressional lead. * * *

The preamble to section 521 states that the law was created "to prevent discrimination against State-chartered insured depository institutions, including insured savings banks." To understand the reference, we examine the historical context.

As the 1970s wound down, the Nation was caught in the throes of a devastating credit crunch. Interest rates soared. Nevertheless, state lending institutions were constrained in the interest they could charge by state usury laws which often made loans economically unfeasible from a lender's coign of vantage. National banks did not share this inhibition because they could charge whatever interest rates were allowed under the National Bank Act of 1864, and specifically, those rates which were permitted under Bank Act § 85, 12 U.S.C.§ 85 (1988). Since section 85 authorized national banks to use interest rates set by reference to federal discount rates, state institutions were at an almost insuperable competitive disadvantage.

Congress tried to level the playing field between federally chartered and state-chartered banks when it enacted DIDA. See 126 Cong.Rec. 6,907 (1980) (section 521 will "allow[ ] competitive equity among financial institutions, and reaffirm[ ] the principle that institutions offering similar products should be subject to similar rules") (statement of Sen. Bumpers); 126 Cong.Rec. 6,900 (1980) (section 521 should "provide[ ] parity, or competitive equality, between national banks and State[-]chartered depository institutions on lending limits") (statement of Sen. Proxmire). To achieve this objective, Congress engrafted onto DIDA's bare bones, at several points, language taken from the Bank Act. Section 521, modeled on section 85 of the Bank Act, was the site of one such transplantation. The parallelism was not mere happenstance. To the exact contrary, Congress made a conscious choice to incorporate the Bank Act standard into DIDA.

The historical record clearly requires a court to read the parallel provisions of DIDA and the Bank Act *in pari materia*. It is, after all, a general rule that when Congress borrows language from one statute and incorporates it into a second statute, the language of the two acts should be interpreted the same way. So here. What is more, when borrowing of this sort occurs, the borrowed phrases do not shed their skins like so many reinvigorated reptiles. Rather, "if a word is obviously transplanted from another legal source, whether the common law or other legislation, it brings the old soil with it." Frankfurter, Some Reflections on the Reading of Statutes, 47 Colum.L.Rev. 527, 537 (1947). Because we think it is perfectly plain that this portable soil includes prior judicial interpretations of the transplanted language, Bank Act precedents must inform our interpretation of words and phrases that were lifted from the Bank Act and inserted into DIDA's text.

While we believe that several principles inherent in section 85 were transfused into section 521, the critical item for present purposes is the principle of exportation. This principle, solidly embedded in the language and purpose of both acts, provides the mechanism whereby a bank may continue to use the favorable interest laws of its home state in certain transactions with out-of-state borrowers. * * *

Section 521 allows a state bank to charge interest "at the rate allowed by the laws of the State . . . where the bank is located." We think this is a fairly clear indication that, if a state-law definition of interest is applicable, it must emanate from Delaware law. We so hold, much bolstered by the recognition that section 85 "adopts the entire case law of [a state bank's home] state interpreting the state's limitations on usury; it does not merely incorporate the numerical rate adopted by the state." First Nat'l Bank v. Nowlin, 509 F.2d 872, 876 (8th Cir.1975). * * *

Delaware law explicitly incorporates late charges into the definition of interest and allows lenders to assess such fees against credit-card customers. See Del.Code Ann. tit. 5, § 950 (1985 & Supp.1990). Thus, were we to look to Delaware law for help in fathoming the meaning of "interest" and "interest rates," late charges would be included. In that event, section 114B's prohibition on late fees would be nullified by section 521's express preemption of state laws limiting exported interest rates.

Federal common law brings us to precisely the same result. Several courts, in analyzing the language of section 85 of the Bank Act, have had little trouble in construing the term "interest" to encompass a variety of lender-imposed fees and financial requirements which are independent of a numerical percentage rate. * * *

We need not grease the rails. Given our conclusion that DIDA § 521 should be interpreted *in pari materia* with its direct lineal ancestor, section 85 of the Bank Act, and given, also, the litany of cases extending section 85 to a wide variety of fees and charges associated with the extension and maintenance of credit, we see no reason to define either the term "interest" or the term "interest rates," for purposes of section 521, in a manner that excludes late fees. * * *

With respect to the specific scope of section 521's preemption, section 85 of the Bank Act long ago laid the track upon which the parties must now travel. Section 85's preemption acts as a cowcatcher by brushing aside states' attempts to regulate "interest rates" charged by national banks. Included within those displaced state laws are regulations regarding flat fees analogous to late charges. In passing DIDA, Congress expressly placed section 521 on the same footing. Hence, "interest" in section 521 encompasses late fees charged to credit-card customers. Section 114B, which prohibits the assessment of late charges, thereby regulates the interest a bank may charge in a more restrictive manner than federal law permits.

We need go no further. For the reasons set forth above, it is patent that the state statute is on a collision course vis-a-vis section 521. Given the imperatives of the Supremacy Clause, the whistle sounds loud and clear. Section 114B must yield. It is preempted.

QUESTIONS AND NOTES

1. What is the maximum rate of interest that may be charged in your state for a consumer credit transaction? If your state law does not regulate interest rates, you may wish to look at Chapter 24 of the North Carolina General Statutes for an example of a detailed usury scheme.

2. In states that maintain restrictive usury laws, which lenders are subject to those rates? Do such state laws have any practical utility? Are consumer borrowers who reside in such states actually being protected from excessive interest?

3. If you have a credit card, look on the bank to see the name and location of the issuing bank. A Citi MasterCard, for instance, may be issued by a Citi-owned bank located in Nevada, rather than the flagship New York-based bank. Why would Citigroup maintain a bank in Nevada for the purpose of issuing credit cards? What is the maximum rate of interest that may be charged on a consumer credit transaction under Nevada law?

4. Some retailers issue credit cards through bank subsidiaries. How does a retailer own a bank and other nonbanking and nonfinancial businesses? See 12 U.S.C.A. § 1841(c)(2)(F). As discussed in Chapter 4, Dodd–Frank imposed a three-year moratorium on FDIC applications for deposit insurance for a credit card bank by a commercial firm. Dodd–Frank Act, § 603.

5. OCC regulation 12 C.F.R. § 7.4006 provides that state laws apply to a national bank's operating subsidiary to the same extent they apply to the national bank parent. Section 1044 of Dodd–Frank however, provides that a state consumer financial law shall apply to a national bank subsidiary to the same extent the law applies to any corporation subject to the state law. Given this, will national bank operating subsidiaries be able to export interest rates under 12 U.S.C. § 85 after Dodd–Frank?

6. Patricia Heaton, a Louisiana resident, brought suit against Monogram Credit Card Bank of Georgia, a Georgia state chartered bank owned by General Electric, claiming that Monogram is not entitled to export Georgia's interest rates and late fees under § 1831d because monogram is not a "state bank" entitled to the benefits of that statute. According to the plaintiff, federal law defines a state bank as an "institution engaged in the business of receiving deposits." The Georgia law under which Monogram was chartered states that the credit-card bank may take deposits only from affiliates. The plaintiff asserts that since the only deposits Monogram had were $670 million from other G.E. units, it did not meet the "state bank" definition. The FDIC argues, based on an opinion letter issued by its general counsel, that a bank is a "state bank" if it holds one or more nontrust deposits in an aggregate amount of at least $500,000. Following the issuance of this opinion letter, the FDIC completed a formal rulemaking process to promulgate a regulation to this effect. 66 Fed. Reg. 54,645 (Oct. 31, 2001) (codified at 12 C.F.R. § 303.14).

What is the banking statute that provides the federal definition of a "state bank"? How is General Electric operating a bank along with its other nonbanking and nonfinancial operations?

7. Section 731 of the Gramm–Leach–Bliley Act (GLBA), codified at 12 U.S.C.A. § 1831u(f) permits state chartered banks to charge the same rate of interest as any out-of-state bank that has a branch within the state, but only in the limited circumstance that the state has a "constitutional provision that sets a maximum lawful annual percentage rate of interest ... at not more than 5 percent above the discount rate for 90–day commercial paper in effect at the Federal reserve bank for the Federal reserve district in which such State is located." Arkansas is a state (perhaps the only one) with such a constitutional provision. In Johnson v. Bank of Bentonville, 269 F.3d 894 (8th Cir. 2001), the Eighth Circuit upheld the GLBA provision from attack under the Commerce Clause and held that it was permissible for Congress to preempt a provision of a state constitution. See Amanda K.S. Hill, Note, State Usury Laws: Are They Effective in a Post–GLBA World? 6 N.C. Banking Inst. 411 (2002).

8. A borrower brought suit against a national bank in state court for violation of the state's usury law. The United States Supreme Court held that removal of the case to federal court was proper because 12 U.S.C. §§ 85 and 86 preempted the claim under state law and provided the exclusive cause of action for usury against a national bank. Beneficial National Bank v. Anderson, 539 U.S. 1 (2003). Therefore, the usury claim against a national bank "arises under" federal law.

9. In October 2006, President Bush signed into law the John Warner National Defense Authorization Act for Fiscal Year 2007, Pub. L. No. 109–364, 120 Stat. 2083. Section 670 of that Act (codified at 10 U.S.C. § 987) and referred to as the Talent Amendment, caps the annual percentage rate that may be charged to a covered member of the armed forces (a member of the armed forces on active duty or active Guard or Reserve duty) or a dependent of such member for certain consumer credit at 36%.

The Department of Defense, in consultation with the banking agencies, prepared implementing regulations. Limitations on Terms of Consumer Credit Extended to Service Members and Dependents, 72 Fed. Reg. 50580 (Aug. 31, 2007) (codified at 32 C.F.R. pt. 232). The regulations limit the covered consumer credit transactions to certain closed-end credit, including payday loans, vehicle title loans, and tax refund anticipation loans. The cost of the loan must be disclosed as the Military Annual Percentage Rate (MAPR) and may not exceed 36%. A creditor who relies on a "covered borrower identification statement" in determining that the borrower is subject to the MAPR limitation falls within a safe harbor, unless the creditor receives documentation as part of the transaction that indicates that the borrower is not a "covered borrower."

Although banks had hoped to be expressly excluded in the regulations from compliance with the Talent Amendment, most banks are effectively excluded because they do not usually offer the covered consumer credit products. Home mortgage loans, purchase money loans (including auto loans), and open-end credit such as credit cards are excluded from coverage by the regulations.

Why did Congress feel that the cost of credit to service members and their dependents should be limited? Does this open the door for other national usury legislation?

SECTION 2. TRUTH IN LENDING ACT (TILA)

A number of federal and state laws exist to protect consumers in their credit relationships with banks and other lenders. One of the most important is the Truth In Lending Act (TILA), 15 U.S.C.A. § 1601 et seq., enacted in 1968. TILA has been amended numerous times, including a major rewrite in 1980 (effective October 1, 1982) as part of the Depository Institutions Deregulation and Monetary Control Act of 1980 (DIDMCA). The purpose of TILA is to require creditors to disclose to consumers the true cost of credit. TILA mandates the inclusion of all credit-related charges in calculating the annual percentage rate (APR) and the total finance charge for an extension of credit. These disclosures were intended to allow an informed comparison of credit choices. Prior to the Dodd–Frank Act, the Fed issued regulations under TILA, referred to collectively as Regulation Z, 12 C.F.R. pt. 226. Dodd–Frank transfers TILA rulemaking authority to the BCFP.

A. OPEN–END VERSUS CLOSED–END CREDIT

BENION v. BANK ONE, DAYTON, N.A.

United States Court of Appeals, Seventh Circuit, 1998.
144 F.3d 1056, *cert. denied*, 525 U.S. 963.

POSNER, CHIEF JUDGE.

This appeal presents an important interpretive question under the Truth in Lending Act and one on which we are unable to find any appellate decisions. Mr. and Mrs. Benion bought a satellite dish from Superior Satellite, an authorized dealer in products distributed by EchoStar Communications. The price of the dish was around $3,000 and in addition the Benions paid $1,000 for a year's worth of programming transmitted by satellite. The Benions didn't want to pay cash for these purchases, and so applied for an "EchoStar" credit card. This card is offered by Bank One in conjunction with Echo Acceptance (EchoStar's consumer financing arm). The Benions' application was accepted on the spot and they were given the card with a credit limit of $4,500, a few hundred dollars above the price of their purchases. The EchoStar card may be used at any of the hundreds of authorized retail dealers in EchoStar products. But EchoStar requires that the first use of the card include the purchase of a satellite dish, which usually costs at least $2,000, and limits subsequent purchases to goods and services that can be used in conjunction with the dish, such as a television set, video recorder, or television programming (a pay channel, for example). In the papers accompanying the sale to the Benions, the interest rate that Bank One charges on the unpaid balance of credit card debt—a variable rate that at the time of the sale and the issuance of the card to the Benions was about 19 percent—was disclosed, but not the total finance charge (roughly, the dollar amount of the interest) that the credit card holder would incur if the debt were paid off at the minimum rate permitted.

The Benions weren't happy with their purchase and refused to pay anything toward the satisfaction of their credit card debt, precipitating a legal squabble between them and Superior, Echo Acceptance, and Bank One. The squabble has mushroomed into a class action by the Benions on their own behalf and that of some 50,000 other users of the EchoStar card, claiming that the disclosures made to users concerning the cost of credit violate the Truth in Lending Act, 15 U.S.C. § 1601 et seq., and the Illinois Consumer Fraud Act, 815 ILCS 505/1 et seq. The district judge granted summary judgment for the defendants on both claims. 967 F.Supp. 1031 (N.D. Ill. 1997). He held that the state fraud claim was derivative from the Truth in Lending Act and fell with it. Id. at 1037. The plaintiffs do not challenge the derivative status of the fraud claim in their opening brief, and so we shall not have to consider that claim further.

The Truth in Lending Act has separate disclosure requirements for "open-end" and "closed-end" credit transactions. The requirements for the latter are more onerous (compare 15 U.S.C. § 1637 with id. § 1638), and include stating the total finance charge. Id., § 1638(a)(3); 12 C.F.R. § 226.18(d). If the credit arrangements with the Benions are classified as closed end, the Act was violated; otherwise not.

An open-end credit plan, the category that includes legitimate credit-card credit and revolving credit more broadly, is a financing plan under which the creditor "reasonably contemplates repeated transactions." 15 U.S.C. § 1602(i). * * *

It is beyond contestation that the bank (the only Truth in Lending defendant) hoped and expected, and *reasonably* expected, to have at least some repeat transactions with the holders of the EchoStar card. The card was usable at any dealer in a nationwide chain of dealers. Bank One had an aggressive marketing strategy designed to promote repeat purchases, which was very much in its financial self-interest. The bank had studied the performance of EchoStar's financing plan in an earlier incarnation and had obtained statistics which showed that repeat purchases had been an increasing fraction of total purchases under the plan. And, although we must not confuse hindsight with foresight, what actually happens is some evidence of what was reasonably expected to happen, and so it is relevant though not determinative to note that 20 percent of all holders of the EchoStar card issued by Bank One who used the card at least once (some never used it) made one or more additional purchases with the card after the initial purchase. The Benions bought only one year's worth of programming; it was likely that they would use the card to buy programming for the next year.

As neither the statute nor the regulation specifies a minimum level of "repeated transactions," it is apparent from the uncontradicted evidence just recited that the defendants have complied with the letter of the law. It is also apparent that a law which fixed a minimum level of repeat purchases for credit to qualify as open end would place the "private label" (as distinct from bank) credit card business in jeopardy unless it threw in the towel and made the disclosures required for closed-end credit. For the issuer could never be sure that consumer dissatisfaction, or a switch by consumers to an alternative method of financing, wouldn't cause repeat purchases to fall below the threshold fixed by the law. The jeopardy would be particularly great for new cards. Not only couldn't consumer acceptance be assured; the level of repeat purchases would necessarily be slight at the outset, since a repeat purchase cannot be made before the first purchase. In fact the percentage of purchases with the EchoStar card that are repeat purchases has grown since the card was introduced. * * *

The Benions [argue] that the defendants were trying to evade the Truth in Lending Act by conditioning the first use of the card on the purchase of a big-ticket item and then limiting subsequent purchases to products related to the initial purchase. They invite us to consider the enormous loophole that would be created if auto dealers could finance the purchase of an automobile by issuing a credit card conditioned on the holder's using it to buy an automobile from the dealer (or, as here, other dealers in the same product), and could justify this as open-end credit by pointing out that purchasers of automobiles buy parts and service from either the same dealer or other dealers in the same make of automobile. But if such a method of financing big-ticket purchases would be an abuse of the open-end credit provision of the Truth in Lending Act, as we may assume it would be, it could be curbed only by changing the regulatory scheme, for example by specifying a minimum ratio of subsequent purchases to original purchase. * * *

There may be cases in which the issuer of the card does not reasonably contemplate any repeat purchases; an example would be a sale of aluminum siding by a company that sells nothing else. The statute and regulation take care of that case, which in fact is specifically mentioned in the staff commentary. 12 C.F.R. pt. 226.2(a)(20)3, supp. I. They do not address the case in which the issuer reasonably contemplates repeat purchases though fewer than it would if it were financing sales by a department store or other general retail dealer.

Affirmed.

B. FAIR CREDIT AND CHARGE CARD DISCLOSURE ACT

The Fair Credit and Charge Card Disclosure Act of 1988, 15 U.S.C. § 1637, offers additional protection to consumers.

STATEMENT BY JOHN P. LAWARE[5]
SUBCOMMITTEE ON CONSUMER AFFAIRS AND COINAGE
OF THE COMMITTEE ON BANKING, FINANCE AND URBAN AFFAIRS

U.S. House of Representatives.
77 Fed. Res. Bull. 983 (1991).

In March 1989, the Fair Credit and Charge Card Disclosure Law amendments to the Truth in Lending law went into effect. Before these amendments were enacted, consumers sometimes did not receive full disclosure of the credit terms on their card accounts until after they had received a credit card accessing the account.

The Fair Credit and Charge Card Disclosure Act requires that card issuers provide early disclosure of rate and other cost information to potential cardholders. The disclosures generally must be provided in direct mail or telephone applications and preapproved solicitations and in applications made available to the general public. Most of the required disclosures must be provided in the form of a table that the Board prescribes to allow easy comparison of the terms offered by different card issuers. * * *

Under the current Truth in Lending Act, creditors that mention specific costs in advertisements for any type of open-end credit product must also disclose other relevant cost information. Under this "trigger term" approach, a card issuer that advertises its annual percentage rate, for example, must also disclose any minimum finance charge, transaction fee, or similar charge. The Board by regulation also requires that any fee for membership or participation be disclosed.

In general credit card advertisements, when no specific costs are stated, the law does not mandate that any other cost information be provided. In addition, if creditors advertise that certain fees are *not* charged on an account, no additional disclosures are required. For example, a card issuer may advertise that no annual fee is imposed on a card account, without disclosing the rate. Or a card issuer may represent in an advertisement that the annual percentage rate on its accounts is "low," without providing additional disclosure. Consequently, although the Truth in Lending Act and the Board's implementing regulation generally require uniform disclosure of cost information in credit advertisements, they do not require full cost information about credit and charge cards in all advertisements—only in those in which the advertiser triggers the need for further detail. * * *

The Board believes that the current disclosure scheme under the Truth in Lending Act gives consumers ample opportunity to ascertain and review account terms before being obligated on a card account. The

---

5. [eds.] Member, Board of Governors of the Federal Reserve System.

advertising rules provide for the uniform disclosure of credit terms when specific costs are mentioned. The Fair Credit and Charge Card Disclosure Act requires disclosure of key terms in those situations in which card issuers are aggressively marketing their card accounts—for example, in direct mail or telephone campaigns. In addition, the Truth in Lending Act has always required that consumers receive full disclosure before they become obligated on open-end plans. Moreover, the Board by regulation has provided that, if full disclosure is not given beforehand, a consumer may reject the plan once disclosures are received and the creditor must refund any membership fee that has already been paid. * * *

Currently, creditors are required to provide consumers with advance notice of changes in rates and other key cost terms initially required to be disclosed under the Truth in Lending Act. The notice must be provided at least fifteen days before a change takes effect. The act itself does not require this notification. The change in terms requirement, which the Board established by regulation, has been in effect since 1969. * * *

Congress sought to provide additional protection to credit card holders from hidden and excessive fees.

JACLYN RODRIGUEZ NOTE, CREDIT CARD ACT: THE CREDIT CARD ACT OF 2009: AN EFFECTIVE BUT INCOMPLETE SOLUTION EVIDENCING THE NEED FOR A FEDERAL REGULATOR

14 N.C. Banking Inst. 309 (2010).

* * * In response to controversial practices such as providing disclosures that are hard to comprehend and poorly organized, President Obama signed into law the Credit Card Accountability, Responsibility, and Disclosure Act of 2009 (CARD Act). The CARD Act amends the Truth in Lending Act (TILA) to "establish fair and transparent practices relating to the extension of credit under an open end consumer credit plan, and for other purposes."[6] Key elements of the CARD Act require plain language disclosures for rate increases and fees, and implementation of protective measures for consumers, such as advanced notice requirements prior to a rate increase. * * *

In response to demands for stronger consumer protection, Congress, the FRB and other key federal bank regulators responded with reforms designed to curb many of the card industry's controversial practices. First, on December 18, 2008, the FRB and Office of Thrift Supervision approved an interagency final rule (Final Rule) that banned five "unfair" practices used by credit card issuers. * * *

In a companion move, the FRB amended Reg. Z to require better consumer disclosures for credit cards. These amendments to TILA, which

---

6. [n. 8] Credit Card Accountability Responsibility and Disclosure Act of 2009, Pub. L. No. 111–24, 123 Stat. 1734, 1734 (2009).

will also become effective July 1, 2010, cover "applications and solicitation; account-opening; period statements, change-in-terms notices; and advertising."[7] * * *

Prior to the CARD Act, card issuers were allowed to charge different interest rates for purchases, cash advances, and balance transfers. This often left the average cardholder with multiple interest rates on one card. Credit card issuers typically allocated payments to the lowest rate of interest, making cardholders fully pay off their lower interest balances before applying payment to the higher rates of interest. This increased the total amount of interest paid to the credit card issuer, extending the time it took consumers to pay down their debt. A recent study conducted by the Center for Responsible Lending found that only three percent of borrowers understood credit card issuers' payment allocation policies.

The CARD Act addresses this controversial practice: credit card issuers are required to apply the amounts in excess of the minimum payment to the highest interest rate balances. * * *

Since the early 2000s, credit card issuers have used "universal default clauses" that allow credit card companies to increase interest rates based on factors other than the customer's payment history with the credit card issuer. Such clauses are often included in the fine print and hard to decipher. For example, if a cardholder failed to make a timely payment to another creditor or the borrower's credit score declined, the credit card company could increase the interest rate it charged the cardholder. While the six largest credit card issuers stopped using this practice prior to the enactment of the CARD Act, four of the six stated that they would instead raise interest rates through a change-in-terms, which unlike universal default may require prior notification to the customer. * * *

The CARD Act prohibits universal default clauses. If instead, an issuer increases the annual percentage rate (APR) based on the credit risk of the cardholder, the issuer must have methodologies to monitor those factors to determine whether a subsequent decrease is appropriate. The issuer must also monitor accounts whose APR has increased since January 1, 2009 every six months to determine whether factors contributing to the increase have changed. * * *

Another common practice employed by the card industry was to apply penalty rates retroactively to prior purchases in response to cardholder behavior that allegedly presented a "greater risk of loss." For example, one issuer told the GAO [Government Accountability Office] that if a cardholder made a late payment or went over his credit limit, the issuer automatically increased the cardholder's interest rate, and the increased rate applied to purchases that had not yet been fully paid off. Similarly, in April 2004, Discover told its customers that it "reserved the right to look back eleven months for a late payment that could justify the increase." Retroactive interest rate increases were especially harsh on consumers

---

7. [n. 27] [Barkley Clark & Barbara Clark, New Credit Card Rule Outlaws Five] "Unfair" Practices, [Clarks' Bank Deposit and Payments Monthly, Dec. 2008,] at 4–5.

who had a large balance. One expert stated that this practice was particularly problematic during the recession, as many consumers have less available cash.

Default interest rates, which are set in the cardholder agreement and represent the maximum interest rate a card issuer can charge in response to a violation of the cardholder agreement, have grown tremendously. Of all the credit cards reviewed by GAO as of 2005, only one did not include default interest rates. The levels of default interest rates, which have risen in recent years, averaged around 27.3 percent in 2005 and were much higher than typical non-default interest rates.

Under the CARD Act retroactive interest rate increases are prohibited except in certain conditions. A new rate may be applied retroactively if the cardholder fails to make a minimum payment within sixty days after the due date. * * *

Under the CARD Act, credit issuers are also prohibited from increasing the APR in the first year of the account, except for promotional rates (which must last at least six months) unless payment is sixty days late. If the account has been open for more than a year, only four situations permit an issuer to increase the APR for new transactions: "(1) an expiration of a specified period of time, (2) a variable rate, (3) completion or failure of a workout, or (4) a [sixty]-day delinquency on the account provided that the cardholder can cure to the previous APR after six months of timely payment."[8]

If an issuer is going to increase the card's APR for future balances, it must provide at least a forty-five day notice prior to the effective date of the increase. However, no advance notice is required if the increase is for a variable rate card, the completion or failure of a temporary hardship arrangement, or the expiration of an introductory rate.

Forty-five day advance notice is also required of any "significant change" in terms, which includes a fee increase. Since the term "significant change" is not defined in the CARD Act, the FRB will have to amend Reg. Z to provide for the definition. The CARD Act requires the notice to be clear and it must inform the cardholder of her right to decline the increase in interest rate by closing her account. The cardholder must then be allowed to pay off the balance within five years, under the previous interest rate, although the issuer may double the minimum payment.

Another problematic practice used by credit cards is to provide disclosures that are hard to comprehend, poorly organized and formatted, and unnecessarily detailed and long. While credit card companies are required to provide information that helps cardholders understand the terms and costs of their contracts, the GAO found that the structure of the disclosures prevented cardholders from understanding the costs associated with their cards. Although the average American adult reads at an

---

8. [n. 72] [Barkley Clark & Barbara Clark, Credit] Card Act [of 2009] Will Prohibit [Many] Widespread Practices, [Clarks' Bank Deposit and Payments Monthly, Apr. 2009,] at 6; Sec. 101(b); § 171(b)(4) (effective February 22, 2010).

eighth-grade level, most credit card disclosures were written at a tenth-grade level or higher. The credit card disclosure documents were excessively complicated, included more detail than necessary, and used complex terms when only simple ones were necessary. For example, one card member agreement used the phrase "rolling consecutive twelve billing cycle period" rather than using "over the course of the next twelve billing statements" or "next twelve months." Excessive detail both lengthened and complicated the disclosure document. Experts determined that this excess information made consumers less likely to read or understand the information presented. * * *

The CARD Act requires contract terms be disclosed in language that credit cardholders can easily understand to assist them in avoiding unnecessary costs. For example, the CARD Act requires that credit card issuers highlight fees cardholders may be charged as well as the reason they might be charged those fees. Issuers must include a written statement such as: "Minimum Payment Warning: Making only the minimum payment will increase the amount of interest you pay and the time it takes to repay your balance." Credit card issuers are also required to show the implications associated with paying only the minimum required payment: how many months it would take and the total cost including interest and principal payments. They must also disclose how much a cardholder would have to pay each month in order to pay off the entire balance in thirty-six months. Finally, issuers must provide a toll-free telephone number where the cardholder can receive "credit counseling and debt management services."[9] This information must appear in a prominent location on the billing statement.

The CARD Act also requires that late payment deadlines be shown in a clear manner. A statement must include the date on which payment is due or, if different, the date on which a late payment fee will be charged, together with the fee to be charged if the payment is made after that date. Also, if a credit card company has changed any of the terms of the account since the card was last renewed, it must provide disclosures within a specified period either as part of the customer's billing statement or via a separate document.

Double-cycle billing is the practice, previously used by some card issuers, of charging interest on debt already paid by a consumer, resulting in higher interest payments. This does not affect consumers who either pay in full or carry balances from month-to-month since there is either no balance to charge interest or interest is always accruing. Instead, this practice does affect those consumers who pay off their balance one month but not the next. The CARD Act * * * prohibit[s] double-cycle billing.

Before the passage of the CARD Act, credit card issuers had two options when a cardholder exceeded his credit limit. Card issuers could either decline the transaction or allow it and charge a fee. The issuers that charged over-the-limit fees provided for them in the credit card agree-

---

9. [n. 95] Sec. 201(a), § 127(b)(11)(B)(iv).

ment. Yet many cardholders would not learn about the penalty until they went over their credit limit. Disproportionately high over-the-limit fees were common and could be up to twenty-five dollars for a $300 credit limit.

The CARD Act states that card issuers may not charge an over-the-limit fee for a particular credit card transaction unless the consumer "opts-in" and allows the cardholder to complete the relevant transaction. Therefore, unless a cardholder gives the bank authorization to allow a purchase that puts her over her credit limit, the issuer cannot charge an over-the-limit fee. If the cardholder chooses to "opt-in," notice must be given regarding the right to revoke the "opt-in" every time the cardholder is charged an over-the-limit fee. The Act's prohibition applies even if interest charges or fees put the cardholder over the credit limit.

Due to these provisions in the CARD Act, American Express and Discover both have announced that they will no longer charge a fee when consumers exceed their spending limit. This is most likely because the cost of building a mechanism where consumers can opt-in, as required by the CARD Act, exceeds the over-the-limit fees they might subsequently recover. Experts believe that credit card issuers may start implementing membership programs that charge an annual fee in exchange for a waiver of over-the-limit fees.

C. FAIR CREDIT BILLING ACT

AMERICAN EXPRESS CO. v. KOERNER

Supreme Court of the United States, 1981.
452 U.S. 233.

MR. JUSTICE BLACKMUN delivered the opinion of the Court.

The question presented is whether a creditor must follow the requirements specified in 1974 by the Fair Credit Billing Act, Pub. L. 93–495, Tit. III, 88 Stat. 1511, for the correction of billing errors, when both a corporation and an individual officer are liable for a debt.

The Fair Credit Billing Act added a number of provisions to the Truth in Lending Act (TILA), Pub. L. 90–321, Tit. I, 82 Stat. 146. A primary provision, and the one at issue in this case, is § 161(a), as so added. 88 Stat. 1512, 15 U. S. C. § 1666(a). This section applies whenever a creditor transmits to an obligor "a statement of the obligor's account in connection with an extension of consumer credit." If the obligor believes that the statement contains a billing error, he then may send the creditor a written notice setting forth that belief, indicating the amount of the error and the reasons supporting his belief that it is an error. If the creditor receives this notice within 60 days of transmitting the statement of account, § 161(a) imposes two separate obligations upon the creditor. Within 30 days, it must send a written acknowledgment that it has received the notice. And, within 90 days or two complete billing cycles, whichever is shorter, the creditor must investigate the matter and either make appropriate corrections in the obligor's account or send a written explanation of its belief that the original statement sent to the obligor was correct. The creditor must send its explanation before making any attempt to collect the disputed amount.

A creditor that fails to comply with § 161(a) forfeits its right to collect the first $50 of the disputed amount including finance charges. § 161(e), 15 U. S. C. § 1666(e). In addition, § 161(d) provides that, pursuant to regulations of the Federal Reserve Board, a creditor operating an "open end consumer credit plan" may not restrict or close an account due to an obligor's failure to pay a disputed amount until the creditor has sent the written explanation required by § 161(a).

Every creditor under an "open end consumer credit plan" must disclose the protections available under § 161 to the obligor. This disclosure must occur at the time the account is opened and at semiannual intervals thereafter. See § 127(a)(8), 15 U. S. C. § 1637(a)(8).

This case presents a dispute over the applicability of § 161. The relevant facts, as the District Court noted, are largely undisputed. On November 16, 1965, prior to the enactment of the TILA, John E. Koerner & Co., Inc., applied for a credit card account with petitioner American Express Company. The application was for a "company account" designed for business customers. The Koerner Company asked American Express to issue cards bearing the company's name to respondent Louis R. Koerner, Sr., and four other officers of the corporation. Respondent was required to sign a "company account" form, agreeing that he would be jointly and severally liable with the company for all charges incurred through the use of the company card that was issued to him. American Express, before issuing the cards, investigated the company's credit rating, but not that of respondent or the other officers.

American Express billed the Koerner Company for all charges arising from the use of the five cards issued for the company account. It sent a monthly statement showing the total due and listing individual subtotals for each of the five users. Although respondent employed his card mostly for business-related expenses, he used it occasionally for personal expenses. When he did so, he paid for these items by sending his personal check to American Express. Charges for his business-related expenses were paid by the company.

In 1975, a dispute arose between the Koerner Company and American Express concerning charges that appeared on the company account. American Express had billed the company for flight insurance for three business trips made by company employees, and for renewal fees for two of the cards that the company claimed were no longer desired. The total amount in dispute, which the company refused to pay, was $55. Company officials wrote to American Express several times about this. The record does not indicate that American Express responded in any way prior to November 1976.

On September 28, 1976, respondent attempted to use his card to purchase a plane ticket for a business trip. After getting in touch with American Express, the ticket agent requested that respondent speak by telephone with an American Express employee. This employee informed respondent that the account was canceled because of delinquency in payment. She instructed the ticket agent to cut respondent's card in two and return it to him.

Shortly thereafter, respondent filed this action in the United States District Court for the Eastern District of Louisiana. He alleged that American Express had canceled the account because of the Koerner Company's refusal to pay the disputed charges and in retaliation for the many complaints that had been made by the company in its attempt to resolve the dispute. Jurisdiction was based upon § 130 of the TILA, 15 U.S.C. § 1640, which provides for the recovery of actual damages sustained by any person as the result of a creditor's failure to comply with various provisions of the TILA, including § 161, and grants jurisdiction of such actions to the federal district courts. The complaint sought damages of $25,000 for "inconvenience, mental anguish, grief, aggravation, and humiliation." Respondent, invoking diversity jurisdiction, also sought damages under Louisiana law. * * *

The threshold inquiry under § 161(a) is whether the creditor has transmitted to an obligor "a statement of the obligor's account in connection with an extension of consumer credit." If there has been no extension of "consumer credit," the section imposes no obligation upon a creditor, and the creditor is free to adopt its own procedures for responding to a customer's complaint about a billing error. We conclude that, on the undisputed facts of this case, respondent has failed to show that American Express has extended him "consumer credit" in any relevant transaction. Section 161(a), therefore, is not applicable to the dispute between these parties.

In order for there to be an extension of consumer credit, there first must be an extension of "credit." The TILA's definition of "credit" is contained in § 103(e), 15 U.S.C. § 1602(e): "The term 'credit' means the right granted by a creditor to a debtor to defer payment of debt or to incur debt and defer its payment." Thus, a credit card company such as American Express extends credit to an individual or an organization when it opens or renews an account, as well as when the cardholder actually uses the credit card to make purchases. When the account is opened or renewed, the creditor has granted a right "to incur debt and defer its payment"; when the card is used, the creditor has allowed the cardholder "to defer payment of debt."

An extension of credit is an extension of "consumer credit" if the conditions specified in the statute's definition of "consumer" are also satisfied. Section 103(h) of the TILA, 15 U. S. C. § 1602(h), defines "consumer" as follows:

"The adjective 'consumer,' used with reference to a credit transaction, characterizes the transaction as one in which the party to whom credit is offered or extended is a natural person, and the money, property, or services which are the subject of the transaction are primarily for personal, family, household, or agricultural purposes."

Two elements thus must be present in every "consumer credit" transaction: the party to whom the credit is extended must be a natural person, *and* the money, property, or services received by that person must be "primarily for personal, family, household, or agricultural purposes." We therefore conclude that the Court of Appeals erred in holding respondent to be a "consumer" without deciding whether American Express had extended him credit primarily for any of the purposes specified in § 103(h). If it had considered this issue, the only permissible conclusion for it to reach would have been that the undisputed facts of this case establish that the threshold requirement of § 161(a)—an "extension of consumer credit"—has not been satisfied because none of the credit transactions relevant to the billing dispute was entered into "primarily" for consumer purposes. * * *

———————

The Fair Credit Reporting Act requires notice to any consumer subjected to "adverse action ... based in whole or in part on any information contained in a consumer [credit] report." 15 U.S.C. § 1681m(a). Anyone who "willfully" fails to provide such notice is civilly liable to the consumer. 15 U.S.C. § 1861n(a). The Supreme Court has held that "reckless" conduct will constitute a willful violation of this provision. Safeco Ins. Co. of America v. Burr, 127 S.Ct. 2201 (2007).

FIRST NATIONAL CITY BANK v. MULLARKEY

New York City Civil Court, 1976.
385 N.Y.S.2d 473.

BARDY, JUDGE.

Plaintiff sues the defendant for $581.26, principal balance due on a credit card, and for an additional 20% or $116.25 counsel fees.

Defendant in his answer denies owing 90% of the credit card claim made by plaintiff.

On the trial the plaintiff called the defendant solely to ask if he requested a credit card to which defendant responded affirmatively. The plaintiff then called as witness its auditor who testified that, according to the account records of the plaintiff, the defendant owed a credit card balance of $581.26 and thereupon rested.

The defendant testified that six charges dated December 16, 1973 totaling $498.63 were charges not made by him, and that said charges were due to an "unauthorized use of his credit card." He testified that on

January 23, 1974 he reported his credit card was lost and received from a Miss Berlin a number 55575 in connection with such report.

The General Business Law of the State of New York (§ 512) incorporates and makes an integral part of the State's law with respect to credit cards the Truth in Lending Act and the regulations thereunder, enacted by the Congress (Consumer Credit Protection Act, US Code, tit. 15, § 1601 et seq.).

Pursuant to statute 15 U.S.C.A.—Section 1643, subdivisions "b", "c", and "d" of section 1643 of title 15 of the United States Code, the burden of proof is on the card issuer to show that the use was authorized or, if the use was unauthorized, then the burden of proof is on the card issuer to show that the conditions of liability for the unauthorized use of a credit card as set forth in subdivision (a) of this section, have been met.

In subdivision "a" referred to above, the conditions of liability for the unauthorized use of a credit card which plaintiff has the burden to meet are:

(a) That the defendant accepted the credit card;

(b) That the liability is not in excess of $50;

(c) That the card issuer gives adequate notice to the cardholder of the potential liability;

(d) That the card issuer has provided the cardholder with a self-addressed, prestamped notification to be mailed by the cardholder in the event of loss or theft of the credit card;

(e) That the unauthorized use occurs before the cardholder has notified the card issuer that an unauthorized use of the credit card has occurred or may occur as the result of loss, theft, or otherwise;

(f) The card issuer has provided a method whereby the user of such card can be identified as the person authorized to use it.

The said section 1643 goes on further to say that "[f]or purposes of this section, a cardholder notifies a card issuer by taking such steps as may be reasonably required in the ordinary course of business to provide the card issuer with the pertinent information whether or not any particular officer, employee, or agent of the card issuer does in fact receive such information."

The express intent of the Congress in enacting the "Truth in Lending Act" was to protect the consumer or cardholder against charges for unauthorized use of his or her credit card, and to limit his or her liability for such unauthorized use to a maximum of $50 providing, however, that the credit card issuer has complied with certain conditions precedent as set forth in the statute.

Certainly there is room for fraud if a cardholder is unscrupulous or dishonest, and in a multimillion dollar enterprise—such as credit extension—credit card issuers are or should be aware of the existence of individuals who are credit risks, and should make the necessary investigation prior to the issuance of credit cards.

However, the "Truth in Lending Act" was intended to protect the vast majority of credit cardholders who, in the main, are honest and should not be penalized for the dishonesty of a few.

Accordingly, it is the court's opinion based upon the evidence herein and the pertinent Federal and State statutes and case law, that the limit of the defendant's liability with respect to the unauthorized charges of December 16, 1973 totaling $498.63—is $50. On the evidence herein, the plaintiff is entitled to the sum of $82.63 credit card charges which the defendant has not disputed, plus the additional sum of $50 (the statutory limit of liability on the unauthorized charges) as hereinbefore indicated, for a total sum of $132.63.

Judgment for the plaintiff in the sum of $132.63.

D. HOME EQUITY LOAN CONSUMER PROTECTION ACT (HELC)

CONSUMERS UNION OF THE U.S., INC. v. FEDERAL RESERVE BOARD

United States Court of Appeals, District of Columbia Circuit, 1991.
938 F.2d 266.

SILBERMAN, CIRCUIT JUDGE.

This appeal from the district court challenges regulations issued by the Board of Governors of the Federal Reserve System implementing the amendments to the Truth in Lending Act ("TILA") concerning open-end home equity loans. Appellant asserts that the regulations are inconsistent with the statute. * * *

Open-end home equity loans ("HELs") are financial instruments whose popularity among ordinary consumers skyrocketed in the last few years, in large part because of the Tax Reform Act of 1986. That legislation made interest deductions on personal loans generally unavailable except with respect to residential housing indebtedness. Consequently, many consumers discovered tax advantages in converting an unsecured line of credit with their bank into a line of credit secured by the residence. The vast majority of these loans are not taken out to secure the actual purchase of the home, and therefore many of the borrowers do not need the principal of the loan distributed to them at once. They often prefer to have the ability to draw on their line of credit as needed; these loans are described as open-ended. The HEL differs from the traditional mortgage loan—also known as a closed-end loan—in which the borrower takes out the entire sum at the outset and then makes interest and principal payments on that fixed amount over the life of the loan.

The interest on the amounts advanced under an HEL is known as the annual percentage rate ("APR") and is the sum of two elements. The first element is the index, which can be one of the several publicly available proxies for the bank's cost of funds, that is, for the current interest rate. The second element is the margin, which is a fixed percentage generally designed to cover the bank's expenses and allow for a profit on the loan. The index fluctuates with the changes in the interest rate but the margin stays constant at the level set in the HEL contract. To guarantee the consumer against unlimited rises in the APR, the agreements must provide for a ceiling which the APR cannot exceed regardless of the rise in the index, see 12 U.S.C. § 3806, and often also provide for a limitation on annual increases in the APR. These limitations are known, respectively, as lifetime and annual caps. As the HEL market is highly competitive, banks often attempt to attract customers by offering to charge discount APRs for an initial period of the loan ("teasers") or by reducing the margin charged to "preferred customers."

Of course, an open-end home equity loan is simply the consumer equivalent of a secured commercial line of credit. The large scale transplantation of a sophisticated commercial instrument into the consumer finance area, although generally beneficial to consumers by providing them with additional options for the management of their financial affairs, also exposes them to large additional risks: possible misinformation by the lender, possible misunderstanding of the precise terms of the loan, or just plain improvidence in assuming too great a burden of repayment (a burden which often appears more manageable than it actually is). As the consequence to a consumer may be the loss of his home, Congress decided that additional regulation of the banks' credit practices in the specific area of HELs was necessary and enacted certain amendments to the Truth in Lending Act. See Home Equity Loan Consumer Protection Act of 1988 [HELC], Pub. L. No. 100–709, 102 Stat. 4725. The Federal Reserve Board was delegated authority to implement the amendments through promulgation of its regulations. * * *

The dispute between the Consumers Union and the banks offering HELs (whose position was partially adopted by the Board) might be thought to center on the flexibility that banks would have in tailoring loans to particular customers whose high credit rating, ownership of other accounts with the bank, or other attributes, enable them to receive more favorable terms than the terms offered to the other customers. The banks did not wish to disclose in pre-application literature their actual margins, or their actual caps because they wished to be free to give favorable treatment to more creditworthy customers. The banks also were concerned that a regulatory regime which eliminates their power to change the terms of the loan (even when the power to make changes upon certain triggering events was granted by the terms of the HEL contract) might expose the banks to the risk of being obliged to advance credit where it was understood at the outset of the contract that banks would not lend if the triggering events occurred. The most important power given to the banks was to withhold credit at a rate below the bank's cost of funds, as in the case of the APR going above the level of a cap. * * * And, finally, lenders were concerned that a requirement of publishing their discount or teaser rates and all repayment options would be terribly burdensome, indeed, infeasible, because discount (or promotional) rates change rapidly to stay abreast of the competition, and repayment options proliferate in response to market pressures.

Consumers Union argues that any terms in an HEL which are not disclosed in printed materials handed out by banks (called pre-application disclosures) will be less than adequate for two reasons. The customer will not be able to take home that material and pore over it at the "kitchen table." And oral disclosures such as those prompted by the "ask about" questions may be impossible to police: the statute permits a consumer to abandon a loan application without incurring liability for the application fees within three business days if the bank changes the terms of the actual loan from those disclosed to the customer at the start of the application process, see 15 U.S.C. § 1637a(a)(6)(B), but if the key terms at the initial stage are presented orally, it will be difficult for the consumer to demonstrate the bank's duplicity. * * *

The court in the *Consumers Union* case generally found in favor of the Fed but remanded for further consideration two issues dealing with how creditors disclose an initial discounted "teaser" rate, and the payment examples that must be furnished in the preapplication disclosures. After this litigation concluded, the Fed decided after a rulemaking effort to leave unchanged the regulatory provisions requiring that a discount or "teaser" rate be disclosed without requiring disclosure of the amount of the discount, and continued to limit the payment examples that must be provided to the consumer. 57 Fed. Reg. 34676 (Aug. 6, 1992) (codified at 12 C.F.R. pt. 226).

QUESTIONS AND NOTES

1. Does TILA regulate the fairness of consumer credit transactions?

2. Why must the finance charge be disclosed for closed-end credit transactions but not for open-end transactions?

3. Find your credit card agreement and see if it complies with the CARD Act. Do you think its disclosures are transparent? Can you determine the default rate of interest, the late payment fee, the over-limit fee (if any), and how your payments are allocated to outstanding balances?

4. In Household Credit Services, Inc. v. Pfennig, 541 U.S. 232 (2004), the plaintiff alleged that a $29 per month fee she was charged for exceeding her $2,000 credit card credit limit should have been considered part of the finance charge, rather than being posted to her account as a new purchase on which additional finance charges were assessed. The Supreme Court upheld a provision of the Fed's Regulation Z in which the Fed stated that over-line fees are not included in the definition of the term "finance charge." The Sixth

Circuit Court of Appeals had found that the over-line fee differed from the other fees excluded from the definition of "finance charge" in the Fed's regulation since the lender acquiesced in the extension of credit above the credit limit and assessed a fee as a result. 295 F.3d 522 (6th Cir. 2002). Such a fee, the Sixth Circuit reasoned, was imposed as an extension of credit, and thus within the definition of a finance charge. The Supreme Court held, however, that the statutory definition of "finance charge" was ambiguous and that the Fed' regulation interpreting that language should be upheld since it was not arbitrary or capricious. The Supreme Court ignored much case law to the effect that in TILA cases, ambiguity should be decided in favor of the consumer.

5. The Fed issued its final rules mandated by the CARD Act, effective August 22, 2010. 75 Fed. Reg. 37526 (June 29, 2010).

E. RIGHTS AND REMEDIES

(1) Rescission

TILA affords a homeowner an absolute right to rescind any transaction—such as a home equity loan or a home improvement credit sale—where the home is taken as collateral, within three days of the extension of credit. 15 U.S.C.A. § 1635(a). If the TILA disclosures were not properly made, however, this right to rescission may extend for up to three years. 15 U.S.C.A. § 1635(d). The right to rescind the consumer credit contract does not extend to a credit transaction financing the purchase of a home.

[handwritten margin note: 3 days to rescind]

The lender loses its lien on the property if the consumer gives a valid notice of rescission. This deprives the lender of its right to foreclose on the property for nonpayment of the debt. In addition, the lender is required to return to the borrower, or credit to the borrower's account, all finance, interest and other charges (including brokers' fees) associated with the loan. This often results in a dramatic reduction of the loan balance. As the lender is required to return for the benefit of the consumer what it received as a result of the credit transaction, so to is the consumer required to return to the lender the loan proceeds or the fair market value of the property received. In the case of a home improvement loan, the fair market value of the property received at the time of rescission may be less than the original amount of the credit.

[handwritten margin note: Lender to rtn. collateral — consumer must rtn. loan $]

(2) Damages

TURNER v. BENEFICIAL CORP.

United States Court of Appeals, Eleventh Circuit (en banc), 2001.
242 F.3d 1023, *cert. denied*, 534 U.S. 820.

BARKETT, CIRCUIT JUDGE.

This case arises out of Turner's purchase of a satellite dish system from Star Vision, Inc., prompted by a newspaper advertisement which indicated that monthly charges for this service would be $39.95. The

[handwritten margin note: Must p detrimentally rely on agreement to prevail under TILA claim? → yes - statute lang "as a result" shows intent.]

financing of the dish and the monthly service were to be provided through an agreement between Beneficial National Bank ("Beneficial") and Star Vision by way of an "Excel" credit card issued by Beneficial which could be used only to purchase goods and services from Star Vision. When the satellite system was delivered, the invoice reflected a monthly bill of $48.36, as did the Excel bill from Beneficial. With the Excel card, Turner had received TILA disclosure statements, but Turner alleges that these disclosures failed to reveal the true cost of financing the purchase of the satellite dish.[10]

Although Turner concedes that she did not read Beneficial's disclosure statements at the time of receipt and therefore did not rely on them, she claims that she is entitled to damages for Beneficial's failure to provide disclosure statements that complied with the requirements of the law under TILA. Beneficial does not dispute Turner's claim that the disclosures were improper. Instead it points out that, because Turner did not read the disclosure statements, she did not rely upon them to her detriment and thus could not have suffered actual injury as a result of Beneficial's TILA violation. The district court found that detrimental reliance is a necessary element of Turner's claim for actual damages under TILA and denied class certification on that claim. * * *

A court can certify a class only when the requirements of Rule 23(a) and at least one of the alternative requirements of Rule 23(b) are satisfied. Jackson v. Motel 6 Mutipurpose, Inc., 130 F.3d 999, 1005 (11th Cir. 1997). Turner maintains that all of the requirements of Rule 23(a) are satisfied and that the class also satisfies Rule 23(b)(3), which requires that questions of law or fact common to all members of the class predominate over questions pertaining to individual members. Finding that Turner's inability to prove detrimental reliance precluded her from satisfying the typicality and adequacy requirements of Rule 23(a)(3) and (4), the district court refused to certify a class on Turner's claim for actual damages under TILA.

The TILA provision governing actual damages reads:

> Except as otherwise provided in this section, any creditor who fails to comply with any requirement imposed under this part ... with respect to any person is liable to such person in an amount equal to
> ...
> (1) any actual damage sustained by such person as a result of the failure; ....

15 U.S.C. § 1640(a)(1) (1998).

In addition to allowing for actual damages, TILA provides three other remedies for violations of its provisions. First, TILA empowers the Federal Trade Commission as its overall enforcement agency, 15 U.S.C. § 1607(c),

---

10. [n. 2] Specifically, Turner contends that, pursuant to 15 U.S.C. § 1638, Beneficial should have disclosed: (1) the number of payments; (2) the amount of each monthly payment; (3) the amount financed; (4) the total finance charge; (5) the total of payments; and (6) the total sales price.

and provides other federal agencies with enforcement authority over specific categories of lenders. 15 U.S.C. § 1607(a). The enforcing agencies are authorized to require the creditor to "make an adjustment to the account of the person to whom credit was extended, to assure that such person will not be required to pay a finance charge in excess of the finance charge actually disclosed or the dollar equivalent of the annual percentage rate actually disclosed, whichever is lower." 15 U.S.C. § 1607(e)(1). Second, TILA imposes criminal liability on persons who willfully and knowingly violate the statute. 15 U.S.C. § 1611. Finally, TILA creates a private cause of action for statutory damages, which may be assessed in addition to any actual damages awarded. 15 U.S.C. § 1640(a)(2)(A).

Crim. Liability for Willful TILA violation

As necessary, Congress has amended TILA to ensure that it provides for a fair balance of remedies. Specifically, in 1974, Congress amended TILA to permit private litigants, both as individuals and in class actions, to sue for any actual damages sustained "as a result" of a TILA violation. 15 U.S.C. § 1640(a)(1). In 1980, Congress further amended TILA, this time capping defendants' liability for statutory damages. TILA now provides that the ceiling on statutory damages in a class action applies to all class actions arising out of the same TILA violation. Truth in Lending Simplification and Reform Act of 1980, Pub. L. No. 96–221 §§ 615(a)(1), 94 Stat. 132 (March 31, 1980).[11] Congress placed this ceiling on a defendant's statutory liability in a class action so that courts would no longer have to "choose between denying class actions altogether or permitting multi-million dollar recoveries against defendants for minor or technical violations." McCoy v. Salem Mortgage Co., 74 F.R.D. 8, 10 (E.D. Mich. 1976). Under this regime, statutory damages provide at least a partial remedy for all material TILA violations; however, actual damages ensure that consumers who have suffered actual harm due to a lender's faulty disclosures can be fully compensated, even if the total amount of their harm exceeds the statutory ceiling on TILA damages. In this case we assume that the statutory ceiling has already been reached, and the sole issue presented is whether a plaintiff must show detrimental reliance on a faulty TILA disclosure in order to be eligible for an award of actual damages.

Most courts that have addressed the issue have held that detrimental reliance is an element in a TILA claim for actual damages. See, e.g., Perrone v. General Motors Acceptance Corp., 232 F.3d 433, 436–40 (5th Cir. 2000); Stout v. J.D. Byrider, 228 F.3d 709, 718 (6th Cir. 2000); Peters v. Jim Lupient Oldsmobile Co., 220 F.3d 915, 917 (8th Cir. 2000); Bizier v.

---

11. [n.5] Under TILA Section 1640(a)(2)(A)(i), Turner would be entitled to individual statutory damages equal to "twice the amount of any finance charge in connection with the transaction." However, as lead plaintiff in a class action, the entire range of statutory damages for the class are limited to:

> such amount as the court may allow, except that as to each member of the class no minimum recovery shall be applicable, and the total recovery under this subparagraph in any class action or series of class actions arising out of the same failure to comply by the same creditor shall not be more than the lesser of $500,000 or 1 per centum of the net worth of the creditor;....

15 U.S.C. § 1640 (a)(2)(B).

Globe Financial Services, Inc., 654 F.2d 1, 4 (1st Cir. 1981) (dicta). This Circuit, however, has not joined the courts that have so held. Ransom v. S & S Food Center, Inc. of Florida, 700 F.2d 670, 677 (11th Cir. 1983). * * *

We now reconsider whether detrimental reliance is required for a TILA claim for actual damages. We note that the statute provides that a plaintiff is entitled only to "any actual damages sustained . . . as a result" of a TILA violation. 15 U.S.C. § 1640(a)(1). We find that this language indicates that the statute's authors intended that plaintiffs must demonstrate detrimental reliance in order to be entitled to actual damages under TILA. The legislative history behind the 1995 amendments to TILA supports our reading of the actual damages provision. It states:

> Section 130(a) of TILA allows a consumer to recover both actual and statutory damages in connection with TILA violations. Congress provided for statutory damages because actual damages in most cases would be nonexistent or extremely difficult to prove. To recover actual damages, consumers must show that they suffered a loss because they relied on an inaccurate or incomplete disclosure.

H.R. Rep. No. 193,104, 104th Cong., 1st Sess. (1995). The legislative history emphasizes that TILA provides for statutory remedies on proof of a simple TILA violation, and requires the more difficult showing of detrimental reliance to prevail on a claim for actual damages. * * * We hold that detrimental reliance is an element of a TILA claim for actual damages, that is a plaintiff must present evidence to establish a causal link between the financing institution's noncompliance and his damages.

For the foregoing reasons, the district court's denial of class certification on Turner's TILA claim for actual damages is affirmed.

KOONS BUICK PONTIAC GMC, INC. v. NIGH

Supreme Court of the United States, 2004.
543 U.S. 50.

MADAME JUSTICE GINSBURG delivered the opinion of the Court.

* * * Congress enacted TILA in 1968, as part of the Consumer Credit Protection Act, Pub.L. 90–321, 82 Stat. 146, as amended,15 U.S.C. § 1601 et seq., to "assure a meaningful disclosure of credit terms so that the consumer will be able to compare more readily the various credit terms available to him and avoid the uninformed use of credit," § 102, codified in 15 U.S.C. § 1601(a). The Act requires a creditor to disclose information relating to such things as finance charges, annual percentage rates of interest, and borrowers' rights, see §§ 1631–1632, 1635, 1637–1639, and it prescribes civil liability for any creditor who fails to do so, see § 1640. As originally enacted in 1968, the Act provided for statutory damages of twice the finance charge in connection with the transaction, except that recovery could not be less than $100 or greater than $1,000. The original civil liability provision stated:

> "(a) [A]ny creditor who fails in connection with any consumer credit transaction to disclose to any person any information required

under this chapter to be disclosed to that person is liable to that person in an amount . . . of

> "(1) twice the amount of the finance charge in connection with the transaction, except that liability under this paragraph shall not be less than $100 nor greater than $1,000. . . ." Pub.L. 90–321, § 130, 82 Stat. 157.

In 1974, Congress amended TILA's civil-liability provision, 15 U.S.C. § 1640(a), to allow for the recovery of actual damages in addition to statutory damages and to provide separate statutory damages for class actions. Pub.L. 93–495, § 408(a), 88 Stat. 1518. Congress reworded the original statutory damages provision to limit it to individual actions, moved the provision from § 1640(a)(1) to § 1640(a)(2)(A), and retained the $100/$1,000 brackets on recovery. In order to account for the restructuring of the statute, Congress changed the phrase "under this paragraph" to "under this subparagraph." The amended statute provided for damages in individual actions as follows:

> "(a) [A]ny creditor who fails to comply with any requirement imposed under this chapter . . . is liable to such person in an amount equal to the sum of—

>> "(1) any actual damage sustained by such person as a result of the failure;

>> "(2)(A) in the case of an individual action twice the amount of any finance charge in connection with the transaction, except that the liability under this subparagraph shall not be less than $100 nor greater than $1,000. . . ." § 408(a), 88 Stat. 1518.

A further TILA amendment in 1976 applied truth-in-lending protections to consumer leases. Congress inserted a clause into § 1640(a)(2)(A) setting statutory damages for individual actions relating to consumer leases at 25% of the total amount of monthly payments under the lease. Again, Congress retained the $100/$1,000 brackets on statutory damages. * * *

Following the insertion of the consumer lease provision, courts consistently held that the $100/$1,000 limitation remained applicable to all consumer financing transactions, whether lease or loan.

In 1995, Congress amended TILA's statutory damages provision once more. The 1995 amendment, which gave rise to the dispute in this case, added a new clause (iii) at the end of § 1640(a)(2)(A), setting a $200 floor and $2,000 ceiling for statutory damages in an individual action relating to a closed-end credit transaction "secured by real property or a dwelling." Truth in Lending Act Amendments of 1995, Pub.L. 104–29, § 6, 109 Stat. 274. These closed-end real estate loans, formerly encompassed by clause (i), had earlier been held subject to the $100/$1,000 limitation. Section 1640(a), as amended in 1995, thus provides for statutory damages equal to

> "(2)(A)(i) in the case of an individual action twice the amount of any finance charge in connection with the transaction, (ii) in the case of

an individual action relating to a consumer lease . . . 25 per centum of the total amount of monthly payments under the lease, except that the liability under this subparagraph shall not be less than $100 nor greater than $1,000, or (iii) in the case of an individual action relating to a credit transaction not under an open end credit plan that is secured by real property or a dwelling, not less than $200 or greater than $2,000. . . ." * * *

open end
secured

In 1997, the Seventh Circuit, in Strange v. Monogram Credit Card Bank of Ga., 129 F.3d 943, held that the meaning of clauses (i) and (ii) remained untouched by the addition of clause (iii). The Seventh Circuit observed that prior to the addition of clause (iii) in 1995, "[c]ourts uniformly interpreted the final clause, which established the $100 minimum and the $1,000 maximum, as applying to both (A)(i) and (A)(ii)." Id., at 947. The 1995 amendment, the Seventh Circuit reasoned, "was designed simply to establish a more generous minimum and maximum for certain secured transactions, without changing the general rule on minimum and maximum damage awards for the other two parts of § 1640(a)(2)(A)." Ibid. As *Strange* illustrates, TILA violations may involve finance charges that, when doubled, are less than $100. There, double-the-finance-charge liability was $54.27, entitling the plaintiff to the $100 minimum.

On February 4, 2000, respondent Bradley Nigh attempted to purchase a used 1997 Chevrolet Blazer truck from petitioner Koons Buick Pontiac GMC. Nigh traded in his old vehicle and signed a buyer's order and a retail installment sales contract reflecting financing to be provided by Koons Buick. * * * [The]contract contained an improperly documented charge of $965 for a Silencer car alarm Nigh never requested, agreed to accept, or received. Nigh made no payments on the Blazer and returned the truck to Koons Buick.

K included improper charge of $965 for silencer alarm; did not make payments

On October 3, 2000, Nigh filed suit against Koons Buick alleging, among other things, a violation of TILA. Nigh sought uncapped recovery of twice the finance charge, an amount equal to $24,192.80. Koons Buick urged a $1,000 limitation on statutory damages under § 1640(a)(2)(A)(i). The District Court held that damages were not capped at $1,000, and the jury awarded Nigh $24,192.80 (twice the amount of the finance charge).

A divided panel of the Fourth Circuit affirmed. The Court of Appeals acknowledged that it had previously interpreted the $1,000 cap to apply to clauses (i) and (ii). * * * According to the majority: "The inclusion of the new maximum and minimum in (iii) shows that the clause previously interpreted to apply to all of (A), can no longer apply to (A), but must now apply solely to (ii), so as not to render meaningless the maximum and minimum articulated in (iii)." [319 F.3d] at 127. The Court of Appeals therefore allowed Nigh to recover the full uncapped amount of $24,192.80 under clause (I). * * *

We granted certiorari to resolve the division between the Fourth Circuit and the Seventh Circuit on the question whether the $100 floor and $1,000 ceiling apply to recoveries under § 1640(a)(2)(A)(i). We now reverse the judgment of the Court of Appeals for the Fourth Circuit.

Statutory construction is a "holistic endeavor." United Sav. Assn. of Tex. v. Timbers of Inwood Forest Associates, Ltd., 484 U.S. 365, 371 (1988). "A provision that may seem ambiguous in isolation is often clarified by the remainder of the statutory scheme—because the same terminology is used elsewhere in a context that makes its meaning clear, or because only one of the permissible meanings produces a substantive effect that is compatible with the rest of the law." United Sav. Assn. of Tex., 484 U.S., at 371. In this case, both the conventional meaning of "subparagraph" and standard interpretive guides point to the same conclusion: The $1,000 cap applies to recoveries under clause (i).

Congress ordinarily adheres to a hierarchical scheme in subdividing statutory sections. This hierarchy is set forth in drafting manuals prepared by the legislative counsel's offices in the House and the Senate. The House manual provides:

> "To the maximum extent practicable, a section should be broken into—
>
> > "(A) subsections (starting with (a));
> >
> > "(B) paragraphs (starting with (1));
> >
> > "(C) subparagraphs (starting with (A)); _" total recovery under this subff "_
> >
> > "(D) clauses (starting with (i))...." House Legislative Counsel's Manual on Drafting Style, HLC No. 104–1, p. 24 (1995).
>
> * * *

Congress followed this hierarchical scheme in drafting TILA. The word "subparagraph" is generally used to refer to a subdivision preceded by a capital letter, and the word "clause" is generally used to refer to a subdivision preceded by a lower case Roman numeral. Congress applied this hierarchy in § 1640(a)(2)(B), which covers statutory damages in TILA class actions and states: "[T]he total recovery _under this subparagraph_ ... shall not be more than the lesser of $500,000 or 1 per centum of the net worth of the creditor...." (Emphasis added.) In 1995, Congress plainly meant "to establish a more generous minimum and maximum" for closed-end mortgages. _Strange,_ 129 F.3d, at 947. On that point, there is no disagreement. Had Congress simultaneously meant to repeal the longstanding $100/$1,000 limitation on § 1640(a)(2)(A)(i), thereby confining the $100/ $1,000 limitation solely to clause (ii), Congress likely would have flagged that substantial change. At the very least, a Congress so minded might have stated in clause (ii): "liability under this clause."

The statutory history resolves any ambiguity whether the $100/$1,000 brackets apply to recoveries under clause (i). Before 1995, clauses (i) and (ii) set statutory damages for the entire realm of TILA-regulated consumer credit transactions. Closed-end mortgages were encompassed by clause (I). * * *

There is scant indication that Congress meant to alter the meaning of clause (i) when it added clause (iii). By adding clause (iii), Congress sought to provide *increased recovery* when a TILA violation occurs in the context of a loan secured by real property. See, *e.g.,* H.R.Rep. No. 104–193, p. 99 (1995) ("[T]his amendment increases the statutory damages available in closed end credit transactions secured by real property or a dwelling. . . ."). "[T]here is no canon against using common sense in construing laws as saying what they obviously mean." Roschen v. Ward, 279 U.S. 337, 339 (1929) (Holmes, J.). It would be passing strange to read the statute to cap recovery in connection with a closed-end, real-property-secured loan at an amount *substantially lower* than the recovery available when a violation occurs in the context of a personal-property-secured loan or an open-end, real-property-secured loan. The text does not dictate this result; the statutory history suggests otherwise; and there is scant indication Congress meant to change the well-established meaning of clause (i).

For the reasons stated, the judgment of the Court of Appeals for the Fourth Circuit is reversed, and the case is remanded for further proceedings consistent with this opinion.

Concurring opinions of Mr. Justice Stevens, with whom Mr. Justice Breyer joins, concurring; Mr. Justice Kennedy, with whom Mr. Chief Justice Rehnquist joins, concurring; and Mr. Justice Thomas are omitted.

Mr. Justice Scalia dissenting.

* * * The ultimate question here is not the meaning of "subparagraph," but the scope of the exception which contains that term. When is "liability under this subparagraph" limited by the $100/$1,000 brackets? In answering that question, I would give dispositive weight to the structure of § 1640(a)(2)(A), which indicates that the exception is part of clause (ii) and thus does not apply to clause (I). * * *

The structure of subparagraph (A) provides the best indication of whether the exception is part of clause (ii). In simplified form, the subparagraph reads: "(i) . . . , (ii) . . . , or (iii). . . ." Clauses (i), (ii), and (iii) are separated by commas, and an "or" appears before clause (iii). It is reasonable to conclude that the exception—which appears between "(ii)" and the comma that precedes "or (iii)"—is part of clause (ii). In fact, the Court admits in passing that the exception appears "*in* clause (ii)." (Emphasis added). Yet the Court's holding necessarily assumes that the exception somehow stands outside of clause (ii)—someplace where its reference to "subparagraph" can have a different effect than "clause" would. The Court effectively requires the exception to be either part of clauses (i) and (ii) simultaneously, or a part of subparagraph (A) that is not within any of the individual clauses. * * *

As the Court noted earlier this year: "If Congress enacted into law something different from what it intended, then it should amend the statute to conform it to its intent. It is beyond our province to rescue Congress from its drafting errors, and to provide for what we might think is the preferred result." Lamie v. United States Trustee, 540 U.S. 526, 542

(2004) (internal quotation marks and alteration omitted). I would apply the exception only to the clause with which it is associated and affirm the judgment of the Court of Appeals.

(3) Arbitration

GREEN TREE FINANCIAL CORP.- ALABAMA v. RANDOLPH

P. argues △ violated TILA by failing to disclose a finance charge & E COA by requiring Arb.

Supreme Court of the United States, 2000.
531 U.S. 79.

MR. CHIEF JUSTICE REHNQUIST delivered the opinion of the Court.

* * * Respondent Larketta Randolph purchased a mobile home from Better Cents Home Builders, Inc., in Opelika, Alabama. She financed this purchase through petitioners Green Tree Financial Corporation and its wholly owned subsidiary, Green Tree Financial Corp.-Alabama. Petitioners' Manufactured Home Retail Installment Contract and Security Agreement required that Randolph buy Vendor's Single Interest insurance, which protects the vendor or lienholder against the costs of repossession in the event of default. The agreement also provided that all disputes arising from, or relating to, the contract, whether arising under case law or statutory law, would be resolved by binding arbitration.[12]

mandatory arb. clause

Randolph later sued petitioners, alleging that they violated the Truth in Lending Act (TILA), 15 U.S.C. § 1601 et seq., by failing to disclose as a finance charge the Vendor's Single Interest insurance requirement. She later amended her complaint to add a claim that petitioners violated the Equal Credit Opportunity Act, 15 U.S.C. §§ 1691–1691f, by requiring her to arbitrate her statutory causes of action. She brought this action on behalf of a similarly situated class. In lieu of an answer, petitioners filed a motion to compel arbitration, to stay the action, or, in the alternative, to dismiss. The District Court granted petitioners' motion to compel arbitration, denied the motion to stay, and dismissed Randolph's claims with prejudice. The District Court also denied her request to certify a class. 991 F.Supp. 1410 (M.D. Ala. 1997). * * *

---

12. [n.1] The arbitration provision states in pertinent part: "All disputes, claims, or controversies arising from or relating to this Contract or the relationships which result from this Contract, or the validity of this arbitration clause or the entire contract, shall be resolved by binding arbitration by one arbitrator selected by Assignee with consent of Buyer(s). This arbitration Contract is made pursuant to a transaction in interstate commerce, and shall be governed by the Federal Arbitration Act at 9 U.S.C. Section 1. Judgment upon the award rendered may be entered in any court having jurisdiction. The parties agree and understand that they choose arbitration instead of litigation to resolve disputes. The parties understand that they have a right or opportunity to litigate disputes through a court, but that they prefer to resolve their disputes through arbitration, except as provided herein. THE PARTIES VOLUNTARILY AND KNOWINGLY WAIVE ANY RIGHT THEY HAVE TO A JURY TRIAL EITHER PURSUANT TO ARBITRATION UNDER THIS CLAUSE OR PURSUANT TO A COURT ACTION BY ASSIGNEE (AS PROVIDED HEREIN). The parties agree and understand that all disputes arising under case law, statutory law, and all other laws, including, but not limited to, all contract, tort, and property disputes will be subject to binding arbitration in accord with this Contract. The parties agree and understand that the arbitrator shall have all powers provided by the law and the Contract."

The [Eleventh Circuit Court of Appeals] then determined that the arbitration agreement failed to provide the minimum guarantees that respondent could vindicate her statutory rights under the TILA. Critical to this determination was the court's observation that the arbitration agreement was silent with respect to payment of filing fees, arbitrators' costs, and other arbitration expenses. On that basis, the court held that the agreement to arbitrate posed a risk that respondent's ability to vindicate her statutory rights would be undone by "steep" arbitration costs, and therefore was unenforceable. * * *

We now turn to the question whether Randolph's agreement to arbitrate is unenforceable because it says nothing about the costs of arbitration, and thus fails to provide her protection from potentially substantial costs of pursuing her federal statutory claims in the arbitral forum. Section 2 of the [Federal Arbitration Act] FAA provides that "[a] written provision in any maritime transaction or a contract evidencing a transaction involving commerce to settle by arbitration a controversy thereafter arising out of such contract . . . shall be valid, irrevocable, and enforceable, save upon such grounds as exist at law or in equity for the revocation of any contract." 9 U.S.C. § 2. In considering whether respondent's agreement to arbitrate is unenforceable, we are mindful of the FAA's purpose "to reverse the longstanding judicial hostility to arbitration agreements . . . and to place arbitration agreements upon the same footing as other contracts." Gilmer v. Interstate/Johnson Lane Corp., 500 U.S. 20, 24 (1991).

In light of that purpose, we have recognized that federal statutory claims can be appropriately resolved through arbitration, and we have enforced agreements to arbitrate that involve such claims. See, e.g., Rodriguez de Quijas v. Shearson/American Express, Inc., 490 U.S. 477 (1989) (Securities Act of 1933); Shearson/American Express, Inc. v. McMahon, 482 U.S. 220 (1987) (Securities Exchange Act of 1934 and Racketeer Influenced and Corrupt Organizations Act); Mitsubishi Motors Corp. v. Soler Chrysler–Plymouth, Inc., 473 U.S. 614 (1985) (Sherman Act). We have likewise rejected generalized attacks on arbitration that rest on "suspicion of arbitration as a method of weakening the protections afforded in the substantive law to would-be complainants." Rodriguez de Quijas, supra, at 481. These cases demonstrate that even claims arising under a statute designed to further important social policies may be arbitrated because " 'so long as the prospective litigant effectively may vindicate [his or her] statutory cause of action in the arbitral forum,' " the statute serves its functions. See Gilmer, supra, at 28 (quoting Mitsubishi, supra, at 637).

In determining whether statutory claims may be arbitrated, we first ask whether the parties agreed to submit their claims to arbitration, and then ask whether Congress has evinced an intention to preclude a waiver of judicial remedies for the statutory rights at issue. See Gilmer, supra, at 26; Mitsubishi, supra, at 628. In this case, it is undisputed that the parties agreed to arbitrate all claims relating to their contract, including claims involving statutory rights. Nor does Randolph contend that the TILA evinces an intention to preclude a waiver of judicial remedies. She contends instead that the arbitration agreement's silence with respect to costs and fees creates a "risk" that she will be required to bear prohibitive arbitration costs if she pursues her claims in an arbitral forum, and thereby forces her to forgo any claims she may have against petitioners. Therefore, she argues, she is unable to vindicate her statutory rights in arbitration.

It may well be that the existence of large arbitration costs could preclude a litigant such as Randolph from effectively vindicating her federal statutory rights in the arbitral forum. But the record does not show that Randolph will bear such costs if she goes to arbitration. Indeed, it contains hardly any information on the matter.[13] As the Court of Appeals recognized, "we lack ... information about how claimants fare under Green Tree's arbitration clause." 178 F.3d at 1158. The record reveals only the arbitration agreement's silence on the subject, and that fact alone is plainly insufficient to render it unenforceable. The "risk" that Randolph will be saddled with prohibitive costs is too speculative to justify the invalidation of an arbitration agreement.

* * * The Court of Appeals therefore erred in deciding that the arbitration agreement's silence with respect to costs and fees rendered it unenforceable.[14] * * *

MADAME JUSTICE GINSBURG, with whom JUSTICES STEVENS and SOUTER join, and with whom JUSTICE BREYER joins as to parts, concurring in part and dissenting in part.

* * * The Court today deals with a "who pays" question, specifically, who pays for the arbitral forum. The Court holds that Larketta Randolph bears the burden of demonstrating that the arbitral forum is financially inaccessible to her. Essentially, the Court requires a party, situated as Randolph is, either to submit to arbitration without knowing who will pay for the forum or to demonstrate up front that the costs, if imposed on her, will be prohibitive. As I see it, the case in its current posture is not ripe for such a disposition.

The Court recognizes that "the existence of large arbitration costs could preclude a litigant such as Randolph from effectively vindicating her federal statutory rights in the arbitral forum." But, the Court next

---

13. [n. 6] In Randolph's Motion for Reconsideration in the District Court, she asserted that "[a]rbitration costs are high" and that she did not have the resources to arbitrate. * * * Randolph plainly failed to make any factual showing that the American Arbitration Association would conduct the arbitration, or that, if it did, she would be charged the filing fee [$500 for claims under $10,000] or arbitrator's fee [$700 per day] that she identified. These unsupported statements provide no basis on which to ascertain the actual costs and fees to which she would be subject in arbitration. * * *

14. [n.7] We decline to reach respondent's argument that we may affirm the Court of Appeals' conclusion that the arbitration agreement is unenforceable on the alternative ground that the agreement precludes respondent from bringing her claims under the TILA as a class action. The Court of Appeals did not pass on this question, and we need not decide here issues not decided below. Roberts v. Galen of Va., Inc., 525 U.S. 249 (1999) (per curiam).

determines, "the party resisting arbitration bears the burden of proving that the claims at issue are unsuitable for arbitration" and "Randolph did not meet that burden." In so ruling, the Court blends two discrete inquiries: First, is the arbitral forum *adequate* to adjudicate the claims at issue; second, is that forum *accessible* to the party resisting arbitration.

Our past decisions deal with the first question, the *adequacy* of the arbitral forum to adjudicate various statutory claims. See, e.g., Gilmer v. Interstate/Johnson Lane Corp., 500 U.S. 20 (1991) (Age Discrimination in Employment Act claims are amenable to arbitration); Shearson/American Express Inc. v. McMahon, 482 U.S. 220 (1987) (Claims under Racketeer Influenced and Corrupt Organizations Act and Securities Exchange Act are amenable to arbitration). These decisions hold that the party resisting arbitration bears the burden of establishing the inadequacy of the arbitral forum for adjudication of claims of a particular genre. See *Gilmer*, 500 U.S. at 26; *McMahon*, 482 U.S. at 227. It does not follow like the night the day, however, that the party resisting arbitration should also bear the burden of showing that the arbitral forum would be financially inaccessible to her.

The arbitration agreement at issue is contained in a form contract drawn by a commercial party and presented to an individual consumer on a take-it-or-leave-it basis. The case on which the Court dominantly relies, *Gilmer*, also involved a nonnegotiated arbitration clause. But the "who pays" question presented in this case did not arise in *Gilmer*. Under the rules that governed in *Gilmer*—those of the New York Stock Exchange—it was the standard practice for securities industry parties, arbitrating employment disputes, to pay all of the arbitrators' fees. See Cole v. Burns Int'l Security Servs., 105 F.3d 1465, 1483 (CADC 1997). Regarding that practice, the Court of Appeals for the District of Columbia Circuit recently commented:

> "[I]n *Gilmer*, the Supreme Court endorsed a system of arbitration in which employees are not required to pay for the arbitrator assigned to hear their statutory claims. There is no reason to think that the Court would have approved arbitration in the absence of this arrangement. Indeed, we are unaware of any situation in American jurisprudence in which a beneficiary of a federal statute has been required to pay for the services of the judge assigned to hear her or his case." Id. at 1484.

The form contract in this case provides no indication of the rules under which arbitration will proceed or the costs a consumer is likely to incur in arbitration. Green Tree, drafter of the contract, could have filled the void by specifying, for instance, that arbitration would be governed by the rules of the American Arbitration Association (AAA). Under the AAA's Consumer Arbitration Rules, consumers in small-claims arbitration incur no filing fee and pay only $125 of the total fees charged by the arbitrator. All other fees and costs are to be paid by the business party. Other national arbitration organizations have developed similar models for fair cost and fee allocation. It may be that in this case, as in *Gilmer*, there is a standard practice on arbitrators' fees and expenses, one that fills the blank space in the arbitration agreement. Counsel for Green Tree offered a hint in that direction. ("Green Tree does pay [arbitration] costs in a lot of instances...."). But there is no reliable indication in this record that Randolph's claim will be arbitrated under any consumer-protective fee arrangement.

As a repeat player in the arbitration required by its form contract, Green Tree has superior information about the cost to consumers of pursuing arbitration. * * * In these circumstances, it is hardly clear that Randolph should bear the burden of demonstrating up front the arbitral forum's inaccessibility, or that she should be required to submit to arbitration without knowing how much it will cost her.

As I see it, the Court has reached out prematurely to resolve the matter in the lender's favor. If Green Tree's practice under the form contract with retail installment sales purchasers resembles that of the employer in *Gilmer*, Randolph would be insulated from prohibitive costs. And if the arbitral forum were in this case financially accessible to Randolph, there would be no occasion to reach the decision today rendered by the Court. Before writing a term into the form contract * * * or leaving cost allocation initially to each arbitrator, as the Court does, I would remand for clarification of Green Tree's practice.

The Court's opinion, if I comprehend it correctly, does not prevent Randolph from returning to court, postarbitration, if she then has a complaint about cost allocation. If that is so, the issue reduces to when, not whether, she can be spared from payment of excessive costs. Neither certainty nor judicial economy is served by leaving that issue unsettled until the end of the line.

For the reasons stated, I dissent from the Court's reversal of the Eleventh Circuit's decision on the cost question. I would instead vacate and remand for further consideration of the accessibility of the arbitral forum to Randolph.

———

The BCFP, created by the Dodd–Frank Act, was directed to conduct a study on the use of mandatory pre-dispute arbitration in the connection with offering or providing a consumer financial service. Dodd–Frank Act, § 1028. After conducting that study, the BCFP may prohibit or restrict pre-dispute arbitration agreements that are connected with the providing of consumer financial products or services. The BCFP is, however, prohibited from restricting a consumer from entering into a voluntary arbitration agreements after a dispute has arisen. Id.

RANDOLPH v. GREEN TREE FINANCIAL CORP.–ALABAMA

United States Court of Appeals, Eleventh Circuit, 2001.
244 F.3d 814.

IS arb. clause unenforceable if it precludes class actions?

CARNES, CIRCUIT JUDGE.

[On remand from the United States Supreme Court, the Eleventh Circuit declined to consider Randolph's argument that she should be permitted to seek classwide relief in any arbitration because this issue was not argued on the initial appeal.] * * * The issue is whether an arbitration agreement that bars pursuit of classwide relief for TILA violations is unenforceable for that reason. The two principal decisions bearing upon this issue are Gilmer v. Interstate/Johnson Lane Corp., 500 U.S. 20 (1991), and Bowen v. First Family Financial Services., Inc., 233 F.3d 1331 (11th Cir. 2000).

In *Gilmer,* the Supreme Court set out the standards for determining whether a federal statutory claim is subject to arbitration. The Court stated that "[i]t is now clear that statutory claims may be the subject of an arbitration agreement, enforceable pursuant to the FAA," and went on to instruct us that:

① *Bop on*

> Although all statutory claims may not be appropriate for arbitration, "[h]aving made the bargain to arbitrate, the party should be held to it unless Congress itself has evinced an intention to preclude a waiver of judicial remedies for the statutory rights at issue." ... If such an intention exists, it will be discoverable in the text [of the statute], its legislative history, or an "inherent conflict" between arbitration and the [statute's] underlying purposes.

Gilmer, 500 U.S. at 26 (citations omitted). The *Gilmer* Court also held that the burden is on the party opposing arbitration to show that Congress intended to prevent waiver of a judicial forum in favor of an arbitral forum for the statutory claims. Id. The Court explained that an "inherent conflict" between the policies underlying a federal statute and the enforcement of an agreement to arbitrate claims under that statute does not exist simply because the statute "is designed not only to address individual grievances, but also to further important social policies ... [because] so long as the prospective litigant effectively may vindicate [his or her] statutory cause of action in the arbitral forum, the statute will continue to serve both its remedial and deterrent function." Id. at 27–28.

In light of those *Gilmer* standards, we addressed in *Bowen* the issue of whether the text of TILA and its legislative history, or an inherent conflict between TILA and the FAA, would render an arbitration clause unenforceable, and we concluded that they did not. 233 F.3d at 1334, 1338. *Bowen* involved claims made under ECOA, 15 U.S.C. § 1691, et seq., a necessary premise of which was the proposition "that the TILA grants consumers a non-waivable right to litigate, individually and through a class action, any claims arising under the statute." Id. at 1335. In deciding whether TILA created such a "right," we considered the plaintiffs' arguments about the role of class actions in the TILA enforcement scheme. We acknowledged that the text of TILA specifically contemplates class actions as evidenced by the fact that the statute caps the amount of statutory damages available in a TILA class action. The cap on those damages was enacted in order to overcome courts' reluctance to certify TILA class actions in light of the potentially crippling statutory damage awards which might otherwise result. We also considered in *Bowen* TILA's legislative history "which stresses the importance of class action procedures in the TILA scheme," and which the plaintiffs argued was an indication that "Congress intended to guarantee consumers access to individual lawsuits and class actions to allow them to serve as private attorneys general in enforcing the provisions of the TILA, thereby furthering the policy goals of the statute."

But after discussing TILA's text and legislative history relating to class action remedies in *Bowen,* we reasoned as follows:

> [W]e recognize, of course, that a class action is an available, important means of remedying violations of the TILA. See 15 U.S.C. § 1640. However, there exists a difference between the availability of the class action tool, and possessing a blanket right to that tool under any circumstance.... An intent to create such a "blanket right," a non-waivable right, to litigate by class action cannot be gleaned from the text and the legislative history of the TILA.

Id. at 1337–38 (citations and quotations omitted). We said that "[w]hile the legislative history of § 1640 shows that Congress thought class actions were a significant means of achieving compliance with the TILA, ... it does not indicate that Congress intended to confer upon individuals a non-waivable right to pursue a class action nor does it even address the issue of arbitration." Id. at 1338. We also concluded that the "private attorneys general" aspect of TILA's enforcement scheme did not require a different conclusion. Id.

In light of the *Bowen* decision and for the reasons set out in our opinion in that case, Randolph cannot carry her burden of showing either that Congress intended to create a non-waivable right to bring TILA claims in the form of a class action, or that arbitration is "inherently inconsistent" with the TILA enforcement scheme. We did say in *Bowen* that our holding went "no further than the [ECOA] § 1691(a)(3) issue" and "[did] not reach the issue of whether an agreement to arbitrate is unenforceable with respect to TILA claims on the ground that there is an inherent conflict between arbitration and the ... underlying purposes of the TILA."[15] Id. at 1338–39. But there is no good reason why our analysis

---

15. [n.1] In *Bowen,* we had no occasion to address whether an arbitration clause precluding class actions was enforceable in the TILA context because we found that the plaintiffs in that case had no standing to pursue their TILA claims. Id. at 1341. The basis for this holding was that "there [was] no allegation that [the defendant] ha[d] invoked, or threatened to invoke, the arbitration agreement to compel the plaintiffs to submit any claim to arbitration." Id. at 1339.

in *Bowen* of the interplay between arbitration, class actions and TILA in the context of ECOA claims premised on TILA violations does not apply with equal force to pure TILA claims. Randolph simply repeats the arguments that we considered in *Bowen* concerning the same statutory text, the same legislative history, and the same policy concerns. We have already rejected those arguments because they do not establish that Congress intended to preclude the arbitration of TILA claims, even where arbitration would prevent the claims from being brought in the form of a class action.

3rd Circuit agrees

Our thinking in this respect is consistent with the Third Circuit's decision that "[arbitration] clauses are effective even though they may render class actions to pursue statutory claims under the TILA ... unavailable." Johnson v. West Suburban Bank, 225 F.3d 366, 369 (3d Cir. 2000), cert. denied, U.S. , 121 S. Ct. 1081 (2001). On the way to that conclusion, the Third Circuit held that nothing in the text of TILA created a non-waivable right to bring a class action, and although the plaintiff argued that the legislative history "demonstrates the centrality of class actions to the TILA's effective enforcement," the court concluded that history "falls short of demonstrating irreconcilable conflict between arbitration and the TILA." Id. at 371–73. There is no irreconcilable conflict, because the public policy goals of TILA can be vindicated through arbitration, and the statute contains other incentives—statutory damages and attorneys fees—for bringing TILA claims. Id. at 373–74. Not only that, but TILA also provides for enforcement by administrative agencies. Id. at 375. For these reasons, the Third Circuit concluded in *Johnson,* as we have here, that Congress did not intend to preclude parties from contracting away their ability to seek class action relief under the TILA. Id. at 378.

Giving consideration to FAA, as rec'd by SCOTUS

What the Supreme Court said in the present case reinforces our decision. In reversing our earlier decision, the Court emphasized the "liberal federal policy favoring arbitration agreements," which is embodied in the FAA, and noted that it had previously "rejected generalized attacks on arbitration that rest on 'suspicion of arbitration as a method of weakening the protections afforded in the substantive law to would-be complainants.'" *Green Tree*, 121 S.Ct. at 521–22. See also *Johnson*, 225 F.3d at 376 ("Insofar as Congress's intent, broadly contemplated, is concerned, we must give equal consideration to Congress's policy goals in enacting the FAA."). According to the Supreme Court, the last time this case was before us we made the mistake of giving too little weight to the FAA's pro-arbitration policy. We decline to make the same mistake again. Giving full weight to the congressional policy embodied in the FAA, we hold that a contractual provision to arbitrate TILA claims is enforceable even if it precludes a plaintiff from utilizing class action procedures in vindicating statutory rights under TILA. * * *

They did have standing to pursue the claim that the defendant's requirement that they sign an arbitration agreement constituted discrimination with respect to a credit transaction in violation of ECOA, and it was that claim that we addressed in *Bowen*. Id. at 1334–38.

QUESTIONS AND NOTES

1. Arbitration agreements, such as the one at issue in *Green Tree Financial*, have numerous benefits for a lender. Traditional discovery is not available. In some states, punitive damages are not permitted in an arbitration. In addition, arbitration is often cheaper (for the lender) and resolved more quickly than litigation. Should arbitration be enforced when it effectively precludes a class action? One lender's attorney has argued that class actions are not needed to police the behavior of banks who are overseen by federal bank regulators. Do you agree?

2. The Supreme Court held in EEOC v. Waffle House, Inc., 534 U.S. 279 (2002), that an arbitration agreement between an employer and employee for employment-related disputes did not bar the EEOC from seeking victim-specific judicial relief, including backpay, reinstatement, and damages in an enforcement action. The court stated:

> It is an open question whether a settlement or arbitration judgment would affect the validity of the EEOC's claim or the character of relief the EEOC may seek. The only issue before this Court is whether the fact that [the employee] has signed a mandatory arbitration agreement limits the remedies available to the EEOC. The text of the relevant statutes provides a clear answer to that question. They do not authorize the courts to balance the competing policies of the ADA [Americans with Disabilities Act] and the FAA [Federal Arbitration Act] or to second-guess the agency's judgment concerning which of the remedies authorized by law that it shall seek in any given case.

Id. at 297. What does this holding suggest about the ability of the BCFP to pursue relief against lenders who have violated TILA?

3. A California Court of Appeals held in a far-reaching decision that an arbitration provision added to a consumer's credit card agreement was unconscionable since it precluded the consumer from pursuing a class action. Szetela v. Discover Bank, 118 Cal.Rptr.2d 862 (Ct. App. 2002), *cert. denied*, 537 U.S. 1226 (2003) (applying California law in an action seeking class-wide relief for breach of contract, breach of the implied covenant of good faith and fair dealing, fraudulent or negligent misrepresentation, and deceptive business practices). The court found procedural unconscionability since the consumer was presented the clause on a "take it or leave it basis," and found substantive unconscionability because the provision "violates fundamental notions of fairness." Id.

> By imposing this clause on its customers, Discover has essentially granted itself a license to push the boundaries of good business practices to their furthest limits, fully aware that relatively few, if any, customers will seek legal remedies, and that any remedies obtained will only pertain to that single customer without collateral estoppel effect. The potential for millions of customers to be overcharged small amounts without an effective method of redress cannot be ignored.

Id. A federal district court in California, held a short time later that an arbitration provision in borrower's loan contract was unconscionable and unenforceable under California law. Acorn v. Household International, Inc., 211 F.Supp.2d 1160 (N.D. Cal. 2002) (seeking class wide relief for alleged "predatory lending" practices in violation of California statutes and constituting common law fraud, deceit, negligent misrepresentation, and unjust enrichment). The court found that the clause contained various one-sided provisions, including a prohibition on class actions, and the continuing availability to the lender of judicial remedies for foreclosure. Are these cases consistent with the Eleventh Circuit's decision in *Green Tree Financial?*

4. In Green Tree Financial Corp. v. Bazzle, 539 U.S. 444 (2003), a plurality of the Supreme Court remanded two cases for the arbitrator to determine whether the arbitration clause of the consumer credit contract forbids class-based arbitration. Two separate class-based arbitrations had resulted in class awards of almost $11 million and over $9 million. Some have noted the potential unfairness of a class arbitration where members of the class do not participate in the arbitration and unlike a class action in court, there is no right to appeal. Eric Moglinicki, Arbitration Issue Up in Air After Green Tree Ruling, Am. Banker, June 27, 2003. Many lenders have arbitration provisions, unlike the one at issue here, that specifically forbid class-wide arbitration.

Some lenders routinely include class arbitration waivers in credit card agreements or other loan documents. Some courts have enforced the waivers and some have not. JAMS, one of three major arbitration companies, announced in November 2004 that it would not enforce clauses prohibiting class arbitrations. In March 2005, after receiving intense pressure from the defense bar, JAMS withdrew that policy and announced that its arbitrators would apply the law regarding the issue on a case-by-case basis in each jurisdiction.

5. The United States Supreme Court held in Buckeye Check Cashing, Inc. v. Cardegna, 546 U.S. 440 (2006), that an arbitrator, not a state court, must decide whether a contract containing an arbitration provision is voidable under state law for another reason such as usury.

SECTION 3.   EQUAL CREDIT OPPORTUNITY ACT (ECOA)

Adopted in 1974, the Equal Credit Opportunity Act, 15 U.S.C.A. §§ 1691–1691f (ECOA), prohibits discrimination in extending credit on the basis of sex or marital status. It was later broadened to prohibit discrimination on the basis of race, color, religion, national origin, age, public assistance income, or exercise of rights under the Consumer Credit Protection Act, 15 U.S.C.A. § 1691(a).

MARKHAM v. COLONIAL MORTGAGE SERVICE CO.

United States Court of Appeals, District of Columbia Circuit, 1979.
605 F.2d 566.

SWYGERT, CIRCUIT JUDGE.

The Equal Credit Opportunity Act, 15 U.S.C. §§ 1691, et seq., prohibits creditors from discriminating against applicants on the basis of sex or marital status. We are asked to decide whether this prohibition prevents creditors from refusing to aggregate the incomes of two unmarried joint mortgage applicants when determining their creditworthiness in a situation where the incomes of two similarly situated married joint applicants would have been aggregated. The plaintiffs in this action, Jerry and Marcia Markham, appeal the judgment of the district court granting defendant Illinois Federal Service Savings and Loan Association's motion for summary judgment. We reverse. * * *

In November 1976, plaintiffs Marcia J. Harris and Jerry Markham announced their engagement and began looking for a residence in the Capitol Hill section of Washington, D.C. One of the real estate firms which they contacted, defendant B.W. Real Estate, Inc., found suitable property for them, and in December 1976, Markham and Harris signed a contract of sale for the property.

Upon the recommendation of B.W. Real Estate, plaintiffs agreed to have defendant Colonial Mortgage Service Co. Associates, Inc. (Colonial Mortgage) conduct a credit check. Plaintiffs subsequently submitted a joint mortgage application to Colonial Mortgage, who in turn submitted it to Colonial Mortgage Service Company (Colonial–Philadelphia), a business entity located in Philadelphia and not a party to this action.

In March 1976, Colonial–Philadelphia had entered into an agreement with defendant Illinois Federal Service Savings and Loan Association (Illinois Federal), whereby Illinois Federal agreed to purchase certain mortgages and trust deeds offered it by Colonial–Philadelphia. Pursuant to this agreement, Colonial–Philadelphia offered plaintiffs' mortgage application to Illinois Federal.

Plaintiffs and B.W. Real Estate had decided that February 4, 1977 would be an appropriate closing date for the purchase of the Capitol Hill residence. Accordingly, plaintiffs arranged to terminate their current leases, change mailing addresses, and begin utility service at the new property. On February 1, the loan committee of Illinois Federal rejected the plaintiffs' application. On February 3, the eve of the settlement date, plaintiffs were informed through a B.W. Real Estate agent that their loan application had been denied because they were not married. They were advised that their application would be resubmitted to the "investor"— who was not identified—on February 8, but that approval would be contingent upon the submission of a marriage certificate.

On February 8, the Illinois Federal loan committee reconsidered the plaintiffs' application, but again denied it. A letter was sent that date from Illinois Federal to Colonial–Philadelphia, which letter stated that the application had been rejected with the statement: "Separate income not sufficient for loan and job tenure."

On February 9, 1977 plaintiffs filed this suit, alleging violation of the Equal Credit Opportunity Act. After the district court separately granted the motions of Illinois Federal and the other defendants for summary judgment on May 25, 1978, plaintiffs brought this appeal.

We address first the appeal from the district court's summary judgment entered in favor of Illinois Federal. The district court concluded as a matter of law that plaintiffs could not state a claim under the Equal Credit Opportunity Act even if they showed that Illinois Federal's refusal to aggregate their incomes resulted, in whole or in part, in the denial of their loan application. This conclusion was based on the premise that creditors need not ignore the "special legal ties created between two people by the marital bond." It was the court's conclusion that under Illinois law the mere fact of marriage provides creditors with greater rights and remedies against married applicants than are available against unmarried applicants. Presumably the district court believed that this excused Illinois Federal under 15 U.S.C. § 1691d(b), which allows a creditor to take "[s]tate property laws directly or indirectly affecting creditworthiness" into consideration in making credit decisions.

We fail to see the relevance of any special legal ties created by marriage with respect to the legal obligations of joint debtors. This was not an instance where a single person is applying for credit individually and claiming income from a third party for purposes of determining creditworthiness. In such an instance, the absence of a legal obligation requiring continuance of the income claimed by the applicant from the third party would reflect on the credit applicant's creditworthiness. Inasmuch as the Markhams applied for their mortgage jointly, they would have been jointly and severally liable on the debt. Each joint debtor would be bound to pay the full amount of the debt; he would then have a right to contribution from his joint debtor. See 4 A. Corbin, Contracts §§ 924, 928 (1951). While it may be true that judicially-enforceable rights such as support and maintenance are legal consequences of married status, they are irrelevancies as far as the creditworthiness of joint applicants is concerned. Illinois Federal would have had no greater rights against the Markhams had they been married, nor would the Markhams have had greater rights against each other on this particular obligation. Thus, inasmuch as the state laws attaching in the event of marriage would not affect the creditworthiness of these joint applicants, section 1691d(b) may not be used to justify the refusal to aggregate the plaintiffs' incomes on the basis of marital status.

We turn to a consideration of whether the Equal Credit Opportunity Act's prohibition of discrimination on the basis of sex or marital status makes illegal Illinois Federal's refusal to aggregate plaintiffs' income when determining their creditworthiness. Illinois Federal contends that neither the purpose nor the language of the Act requires it to combine the incomes of unmarried joint applicants when making that determination.

We start, as we must, with the language of the statute itself. 15 U.S.C. § 1691(a) provides:

> It shall be unlawful for any creditor to discriminate against any applicant, with respect to any aspect of a credit transaction
>
> > (1) on the basis of ... sex or marital status

This language is simple, and its meaning is not difficult to comprehend. Illinois Federal itself has correctly phrased the standard in its brief: The Act forbids discrimination "on the basis of a person's marital status, that is, to treat persons differently, all other facts being the same, because of their marital status...." Illinois Federal does not contend that they would not have aggregated plaintiffs' income had they been married at the time. Indeed, Illinois Federal concedes that the law would have required it to do so. Thus, it is plain that Illinois Federal treated plaintiffs differently—that is, refused to aggregate their incomes—solely because of their marital status, which is precisely the sort of discrimination prohibited by section 1691(a)(1) on its face.

Despite the section's clarity of language, Illinois Federal seeks to avoid a finding of prohibited discrimination by arguing that it was not the Congressional purpose to require such an aggregation of the incomes of non-married applicants. It can be assumed, *arguendo*, that one, perhaps even the main, purpose of the act was to eradicate credit discrimination waged against women, especially married women whom creditors traditionally refused to consider apart from their husbands as individually worthy of credit. But granting such an assumption does not negate the clear language of the Act itself that discrimination against *any* applicant, with respect to *any* aspect of a credit transaction, which is based on marital status is outlawed. When the plain meaning of a statute appears on its face, we need not concern ourselves with legislative history, especially when evidence of the legislation's history as has been presented to us does not argue persuasively for a narrower meaning than that which is apparent from the statutory language. We believe that the meaning of the words chosen by Congress is readily apparent.

Illinois Federal expresses the fear that a holding such as we reach today will require it to aggregate the incomes of all persons who apply for credit as a group. Lest it be misinterpreted, we note that our holding is not itself that far-reaching. It does no more than require Illinois Federal to treat plaintiffs—a couple jointly applying for credit—the same as they would be treated if married. We have not been asked to decide what the effect of the Act would have been had plaintiffs not applied for credit jointly. Nor do we have before us a question of whether the Act's marital status provision in any way applies to a situation where more than two people jointly request credit. We hold only that, under the Act Illinois Federal should have treated plaintiffs—an unmarried couple applying for credit jointly—the same as it would have treated them had they been married at the time. * * *

LATIMORE v. CITIBANK FEDERAL SAVINGS BANK

United States Court of Appeals, Seventh Circuit, 1998.
151 F.3d 712.

POSNER, CHIEF JUDGE.

Helen Latimore, a black woman, brought a suit charging racial discrimination in real estate lending by Citibank and two of its employees, in violation of an assortment of federal civil rights laws including the Equal Credit Opportunity Act, 15 U.S.C. § 1691(a)(1), and the Fair Housing Act, 42 U.S.C. § 3605(a), (b). The district court granted summary judgment for the defendants. Latimore's appeal requires us to consider what the prima facie case of credit discrimination is, that is, how much evidence a plaintiff must submit in order to withstand a motion for summary judgment. There is no reason to think that the answer will be different depending on the particular civil rights statute sued under.

Owner of a home in a largely black neighborhood on the south side of Chicago, Latimore applied to Citibank for a $51,000 loan secured by the home. She satisfied Citibank's standards for creditworthiness, but the bank's rules also required that the ratio of the appraised value of the security (Latimore's home) to the amount of the loan not exceed 75 percent. The bank's appraiser, defendant Kernbauer, appraised the property at only $45,000, yielding a loan-to-value ratio of 113 percent. When defendant Lundberg, the account executive handling Latimore's application, informed her that the appraised value of the home was too low to support a loan in the amount sought, Latimore told Lundberg that the house had been appraised less than a year earlier for $82,000. Lundberg asked Latimore for the appraisal report, and when Lundberg received it she sent it together with Kernbauer's report to the bank's appraisal review department. The department declined to overrule Kernbauer's appraisal, on the ground that the comparable sales on which the $82,000 appraisal had been based weren't really comparable, because they involved property more than six blocks from Latimore's home. And so Latimore did not receive the loan. Some months later she applied for a loan from another bank, which appraised her home at $79,000 and made her the loan, though for a smaller amount than she had sought from Citibank ($46,000 instead of $51,000) and at a one percent higher interest rate. The damages sought are the additional interest plus certain consequential damages.

In most discrimination cases, the plaintiff can establish a prima facie case either by presenting evidence of having been actually discriminated against on some forbidden ground such as race or by satisfying the *McDonnell Douglas* standard. See, e.g., McDonnell Douglas Corp. v. Green, 411 U.S. 792 (1973). Under that standard, in a typical case of employment discrimination, involving say the denial of a promotion to a black employee, the plaintiff would have to show only that he was qualified for the promotion and that a white got it instead, and the burden would then be on the employer to come forth with a noninvidious reason for why the white rather than the black got the promotion. Although the *McDonnell Douglas* standard originated and evolved in cases involving racial discrimination in employment, it has been extended to all sorts of other discrimination not even limited to the employment setting. * * *

[W]holesale transposition of the *McDonnell Douglas* standard to the credit discrimination context would display insensitivity to the thinking behind the standard. Normally the burden of producing evidence of each element of the plaintiff's claim is on the plaintiff. There has to be a reason for shifting the burden to the defendant. It is not reason enough that essential evidence is in the defendant's possession and would be difficult for the plaintiff, even with the aid of modern pretrial discovery, to dig out of the defendant. Before the defendant may be put to the burden of producing evidence, the plaintiff has to show that there is some ground for suspecting that the defendant has indeed violated the plaintiff's rights. Otherwise we would have a regime of precomplaint discovery. Anyone could put anyone else to the burden of producing evidence without having anything better than a hope and a prayer that the evidence would establish a violation.

The fact that a qualified black is passed over for promotion in favor of a white has been thought sufficiently suspicious to place on the defendant the minimum burden of presenting a noninvidious reason why the black lost out. But it is the competitive situation—the black facing off as it were against the white—that creates the (minimal) suspicion, and there is no comparable competitive situation in the usual allegation of credit discrimination. Latimore was not competing with a white person for a $51,000 loan. A bank does not announce, "We are making a $51,000 real estate loan today; please submit your applications, and we'll choose the application that we like best and give that applicant the loan." If a bank did that, and a black and a white each submitted an application, and the black's application satisfied the bank's criteria of creditworthiness and value-to-loan ratio yet the white received the loan, we would have a situation roughly parallel to that of a *McDonnell Douglas* case. And when we have an approximation to such a situation, a variant of the *McDonnell Douglas* standard may apply, as we shall see. But such cases are rare, and this is not one of them. The Supreme Court has reminded us that *McDonnell Douglas* was not intended to be a straitjacket into which every discrimination case must be forced kicking and screaming. See, e.g., McDonnell Douglas Corp. v. Green, supra, 411 U.S. at 802 n.13. In Diaz v. Fort Wayne Foundry Corp., 131 F.3d 711, 712–13 (7th Cir. 1997), we pointed out the unsuitability of the *McDonnell Douglas* framework when there is no basis for comparing the defendant's treatment of the plaintiff with the defendant's treatment of other, similarly situated persons.

The reason the bank—the (principal) defendant—urges adoption of the standard is that it construes it to require that Latimore show not only that she was creditworthy by the bank's standards, which she was, but also that she satisfied the bank's appraiser, which she did not, about the value of her house. There is no question that to be a qualified borrower—the counterpart to a worker who is performing to his employer's satisfaction in the employment discrimination context—the plaintiff has to meet the lender's requirements for collateral as well as to establish personal creditworthiness. But Citibank does not require that the borrower satisfy *its* appraiser; it requires only that the appraised value bear a specified relation to the amount of the loan sought, and the opinion of its own appraiser is not conclusive evidence of that value. The bank is willing to consider evidence from other sources and to overrule its own appraiser. The bank's appraisal review department could have overruled Kernbauer; that's why the bank has an appraisal *review* department.

Latimore argues, in her own variant of *McDonnell Douglas* (so strong is the magnetic field of that opinion), that all she had to show in order to withstand summary judgment was that her house was in a minority neighborhood, an appraisal (but not necessarily the defendant's) estimated the value of the house to be at least as great as the loan, the plaintiff was creditworthy, yet the loan was rejected. This cannot be right either, and not only because creditors rarely lend up to the value of the collateral and because there is nothing remotely suspicious about the bank's 75 percent rule. Appraisals are fallible, and if banks reposed automatic, unthinking trust in all third-party appraisals they would not employ their own appraisers, as Citibank does. No reasonable suspicion of racial discrimination can arise from the mere fact of a discrepancy between an appraisal conducted by another bank and the appraisal made by Citibank's employee.

Latimore's proposed prima facie case, like the bank's, lacks any comparison between the treatment of blacks and the treatment of whites. At the heart of *McDonnell Douglas* is the idea that if the black is treated worse than the white in a situation in which there is no *obvious* reason for the difference in treatment (such as that the black lacks an essential qualification for the promotion), there is *something* for the employer to explain; and although the competitive situation which invites and facilitates comparison is usually missing from credit discrimination cases, sometimes there will be another basis for comparison. Suppose, for example, that Latimore and Eromital (who is white), apply at roughly the same time for roughly the same-sized loan from the same Citibank office. The two prospective borrowers are equally creditworthy and the collateral they offer to put up is appraised at the same amount. Both applications are forwarded to Ms. Lundberg and she turns down Latimore's application and approves Eromital's. The similarity in the situations of the white and the black would be sufficient to impose on Citibank a duty of explaining why the white was treated better. No effort at such a comparison was attempted here.

So neither *McDonnell Douglas* nor the kind of *McDonnell Douglas* knock off which we have just sketched * * * is available here. But that does not end the case. It is always open to a plaintiff in a discrimination case to try to show in a conventional way, without relying on any special doctrines of burden-shifting, that there is enough evidence, direct or circumstantial, of discrimination to create a triable issue. And Latimore has tried to do that. She hired an expert to conduct a retrospective appraisal, that is, an appraisal of the value of her home at the time that Citibank appraised it. The expert came in with an appraisal of $62,000. But this gets her nowhere. Under the bank's 75 percent rule, which Latimore doesn't claim to be racially discriminatory, a $62,000 appraisal would not support a $51,000 loan; 75 percent of $62,000 is $46,500 (almost exactly what she got from the other bank, but at a higher interest rate). Real estate appraisal is not an exact science, moreover, and so the fact that Citibank's appraisal was lower than someone else's does not create an inference of discrimination. For all that appears, Citibank uses conservative appraisal methods—perhaps in order to keep interest rates low, for remember that while Latimore did succeed eventually in obtaining a loan on her house, she had to pay a higher interest rate and on a smaller loan than she wanted.

Latimore argues that Citibank exhibited favoritism toward white would-be borrowers. The specific contention is that these white borrowers were similarly situated to Latimore in the sense of wanting loans of the same amount secured by property having the same appraised value, but that Lundberg went out of her way to help them raise the appraised value of their property and she didn't go out of her way to help Latimore. Specifically, when she reported to a white borrower that the appraised value of his property was too low to support the loan he was seeking, she would encourage him to find additional "comparables" (comparable sales) of which the bank's appraiser might not have known, in order to justify an increase in the appraised value. But remember that when Lundberg informed Latimore of the results of Kernbauer's appraisal, Latimore told her about the other appraisal, and Lundberg urged her to send that in. The fact that Latimore had gotten a higher appraisal implied additional comparables, since appraisals of residential real estate are based on comparable sales. By asking for the higher appraisal, Lundberg was in effect encouraging Latimore to submit additional comparables. It was not Lundberg's fault that they turned out not to satisfy the bank's definition of comparability. She did for Latimore what she did for white people in Latimore's position.

One last bit of "evidence" must be considered. It concerns the notes on which Kernbauer based his appraisal. Kernbauer stored them in a filing cabinet in his office. Later the branch in which he worked was closed, and according to Citibank the notes were lost in the turmoil of the closing. The bank retained the report containing the appraisal and produced the report to the plaintiff in the course of discovery proceedings. The notes, along with the report itself, were required to be retained for 25 months after the denial of Latimore's application, 12 C.F.R. § 202.12(b)(1)(i), and the loss of the notes occurred within that period. The violation of a record retention regulation creates a presumption that the missing record contained evidence adverse to the violator. But Citibank's explanation, which was not controverted, showed that the disappearance of Kernbauer's notes was inadvertent, and an inadvertent failure to comply with the regulation is not a violation of it. 12 C.F.R. § 202.14(c). So the presumption did not attach.

Taking all the evidence as favorably to the plaintiff as the record permits, no reasonable jury could find that she was turned down because of her race; and so the grant of summary judgment to the defendants must be affirmed. * * *

* * *

The Supreme Court has yet to consider this issue. Counsel for Latimore did not seek certiorari in the Supreme Court even though there is a split in the circuits on the application of the *McDonnell-Douglas* standard to credit discrimination cases.[16]

QUESTIONS AND NOTES

1. Since the co-author of this book and his wife were the plaintiffs in the *Markham* case, we can report that after the D.C. Circuit rendered the opinion excerpted above, the case was dismissed by the district court because there were other non-discriminatory grounds for denying the loan (plaintiffs had been in their jobs for less than one year and had little credit history). The Markhams received their home loan, however, and at an interest rate slightly lower than that stated in the original commitment. Why did the lender persist in refusing to aggregate the income of Markham and his fiancé? Should the ECOA apply to a decision not to aggregate the income of a same sex couple in a state that does not sanction same sex unions as marriage? Would a failure to aggregate be an ECOA violation for discrimination based on sex under the *Markham* case?

2. How should the plaintiff in the *Latimore* case have attempted to prove her claim of race discrimination? Judge Posner commented on the absence of a "competitive" situation in the application for an extension of credit? Do you agree that the lack of a competitive situation is significant?

3. Should the lender in *Latimore* have been required to make a credit counter-offer at a lower principal amount and higher interest rate? Who determines the loan amount and the interest rate—the borrower or the lender?

4. Regulation B implementing the ECOA prohibits banks from collecting race and gender data from small-business loan applicants, presumably so race and gender would not influence the credit decision. Consumer advocate groups, however, have repeatedly asked the Fed to revise Regulation B to collect this information so that it may be analyzed to uncover illegal discrimination, but it had always declined.

Some ECOA enforcement efforts relating to business lending, however, have been successful. The Justice Department and Fifth Third Bancorp settled a suit brought by the Justice Department alleging that Old Kent Financial Corp. (now owned by Fifth Third) had refused to make small business loans in predominantly African–American areas of Detroit. The case was the first filed under the ECOA and the Fair Housing Act to focus on commercial lending. John Reosti, Fifth Third Settles Loan Bias Suit, Am.

---

16. See Simms v. First Gibraltar Bank, 83 F.3d 1546 (5th Cir.), cert. denied, 519 U.S. 1041 (1996); see generally Erin Elisabeth Dancy, Note, Latimore v. Citibank Federal Savings Bank: A Journey Through the Labyrinth of Lending Discrimination, 3 N.C. Banking Inst. 233 (1999).

Banker, May 20, 2004. As part of the settlement, Fifth Third agreed to spend over $3 million during a three-year period on marketing and subsidizing small business and home mortgage loan programs in Detroit. It also agreed to open three branches in Detroit.

Congress amended the ECOA in the Dodd–Frank Act to require that creditors determine in an application for credit from a small business, whether it is women- or minority-owned. This information is submitted to the BCFP and may, in the aggregate, be publicly disclosed. Dodd–Frank Act, § 1071.

5.   It may be a violation of the ECOA and its implementing regulation, Regulation B, 12 C.F.R. pt. 202, to require the signature of a credit applicant's spouse on any credit instrument if the applicant qualifies for the credit on his or her own. Non-applicant spouses may be required to sign if collateral is necessary for the extension of credit, and under state property laws the spouse needs to sign to transfer the collateral interest to the creditor. See FDIC, Financial Institution Letter, Guidance on Regulation B Spousal Signature Requirements, available at <www.fdic.gov/news/news/financial/2004/fil 0604a.html>.

The FDIC downgraded a state bank's Community Reinvestment Act (CRA—discussed in the next section) rating because of a bank-wide practice of discrimination on the basis of marital status. Joe Adler, Marital Discrimination Charge, Am. Banker, July 9, 2007.

SECTION 4.   REDLINING, THE HOME MORT-GAGE DISCLOSURE ACT (HMDA), AND THE COMMUNITY REINVESTMENT ACT (CRA)

"Redlining" is the name given to the practice of drawing a red line around a certain location on a map and refusing to make loans against property located within the red-lined area, regardless of the creditworthiness of the loan applicant. The Home Mortgage Disclosure Act of 1975 (HMDA), 12 U.S.C.A. §§ 2801–06, requires depository institutions in metropolitan areas to disclose the race, gender, and income level of all mortgage applicants. This legislation was meant to prohibit "redlining." HMDA data is publicly available and may be used to identify potentially discriminatory lending patterns and practices. Banks were required to report data on loan pricing; specifically, the spread between the annual percentage rate (APR) on the loan and the rate on a Treasury security of comparable maturity, beginning on 2004 HMDA reports. This pricing data is only required, however, for "higher-priced" loans, defined as first lien loans where the spread is more than three percentage points and for second lien loans where the spread is more than five percentage points.[17] The BCFP assumes HMDA rulemaking responsibility pursuant to the Dodd–Frank Act.

---

17.   See generally Henry M. Jay, Note, Full Disclosure: How Should Lenders Respond to the Heightened Reporting Requirements of the Home Mortgage Disclosure Act?, 10 N.C. Banking Inst. 247 (2006).

Adopted in 1977, the Community Reinvestment Act (CRA), 12 U.S.C.A. §§ 2901–06, requires the appropriate Federal banking agency to assess the bank's record of "meeting the credit needs of its entire community, including low-and moderate-income neighborhoods, consistent with the safe and sound operation of the institution." 12 U.S.C.A. § 2903(a)(1). This legislation was passed after charges were made that banks did not make credit available to minority neighborhoods.[18]

The regulators determine a bank's CRA rating based on an evaluation of its lending, investments, and services. CRA ratings range from Outstanding, Satisfactory (High and Low), Needs to Improve, to Substantial Noncompliance.[19] Since 1989, the ratings have been a matter of public record. Pursuant to regulations effective September 1, 2005,[20] "intermediate small banks" with assets from $250 million to $1billion in assets are evaluated under a more flexible lending test and a newly-created community development test.[21] Banks under $250 million in assets are evaluated only on a lending test.

The CRA is effectively enforced only when the regulatory agencies evaluate the applications of banks or thrifts to expand their facilities by establishing a new branch, or purchasing or merging with another depository institution.[22] The relevant federal banking agencies remain responsible for the CRA examination and rating after the Dodd–Frank Act. Since the CRA applies only to banks and savings associations, this function was not transferred to the BCFP.

LEE v. BOARD OF GOVERNORS OF THE FEDERAL RESERVE SYSTEM

United States Court of Appeals, Second Circuit, 1997.
118 F.3d 905.

VAN GRAAFEILAND, CIRCUIT JUDGE.

At issue herein are two petitions brought pursuant to section 9 of the Bank Holding Company Act ("BHCA"), 12 U.S.C. § 1848, and section

18. Laura T. Beyer, Note, The Community Reinvestment Act: A Boost to Low-and Moderate–Income Communities, A Setback for Minority–Owned Banks, 1 N. C. Banking Inst. 387 (1997).

19. Regulators have sometimes been criticized for awarding too many Outstanding CRA ratings. In 1998, almost 25% of the FDIC-supervised banks received an Outstanding. Jennifer Coogan, FDIC Gets Stingy with 'Outstanding' CRA Grade, Am. Banker, Mar. 9, 2004. In 2007, this percentage for all banks and thrifts was 12%, but only .5% were graded in the bottom two categories. Testimony of Sandra Braunstein, Director, Division of Consumer and Community Affairs (May 21, 2007), available at <http://www.federalreserve.gov/BoardDocs/Testimony/2007/20070521/default.htm>

20. 70 Fed. Reg. 44256 (Aug. 2, 2005) (codified at 12 C.F.R. pt. 24 (OCC), pt. 228 (FRB), pt. 345 (FDIC)).

21. The dollar figures will be adjusted for inflation. In 2007, the cut-offs were $258 million and $1.033 million. Some banks are critical of this new approach, arguing that the intermediate small bank category is complex and that the banking regulators have no statutory authority to impose the new community development test. Hannah Bergman, CRA Plan Criticized as Adding Complexity, Am. Banker, June 8, 2005.

22. See Joseph Moore, Note, Community Reinvestment Act and Its Impact on Bank Mergers, 1 N.C. Banking Inst. 412 (1997).

10(j) of the Home Owners' Loan Act ("HOLA"), 12 U.S.C. § 1467a(j), seeking to overturn three orders of the Board of Governors of the Federal Reserve System ("the Board") and one order of the Director of the Office of Thrift Supervision ("OTS") * * * [relating to] the Board's orders approving Chase Manhattan Corporation's application to acquire certain businesses controlled by United States Trust Corporation ("UST") * * * [and] the Board's order approving the merger of Chase into Chemical Banking Corporation. On May 16, 1996, this Court consolidated the two petitions for argument and decision. * * *

Because the transaction involved a merger of two bank holding companies and Chase's acquisition of a banking subsidiary, U.S. Trust Company of New York ("USTNY"), Chase was required to obtain the Board's approval pursuant to section 3 of the BHCA, 12 U.S.C. § 1842. Under this section, the Board, after receiving the recommendation of the Office of the Comptroller of the Currency ("OCC") or the applicable state supervisory agency, must evaluate an application pursuant to a number of factors: the anti-competitive effects of the proposal, the financial and managerial resources of the company and the banks involved and the "needs of the community to be served." 12 U.S.C. § 1842(c)(2). * * *

Under the Board's regulations implementing the BHCA, the public must be given notice of an application and may submit comments to the Board. See 12 C.F.R. § 262. Petitioner Inner City Press/Community on the Move ("ICP"), an association of low-income residents of New York City, presented the Board and OTS with a number of objections to both the Chase–UST applications and the Chase–Chemical applications. ICP's concerns were based principally on the Community Reinvestment Act ("CRA"), 12 U.S.C. § 2901 et seq. The CRA provides that "regulated financial institutions have [a] continuing and affirmative obligation to help meet the credit needs of the local communities in which they are chartered." 12 U.S.C. § 2901(a)(3). To police this obligation, the CRA provides that a federal regulatory agency must "assess the institution's record of meeting the credit needs of its entire community, including low- and moderate-income neighborhoods ... and ... take such record into account in its evaluation of an application for a deposit facility by such institution." 12 U.S.C. § 2903(a)(1) & (2). Nearly identical regulatory schemes implementing the CRA have been adopted by the Board and OTS. See 12 C.F.R. § 228 et seq.; id. § 563e et seq. * * *

For the reasons hereinafter discussed, we believe that petitioners have failed to demonstrate standing to pursue this litigation. However, because we are satisfied that petitioners' claims are without merit and it is important that the issues arising out of the several mergers finally be disposed of, we will address the lack-of-merit issue as an alternate ground for dismissing the petitions. * * *

The CRA is an amorphous statute. Its pronouncement that "regulated financial institutions have [a] continuing and affirmative obligation to help meet the credit needs of the local communities in which they are chartered," 12 U.S.C. § 2901(a)(3), is not a directive to undertake any particular program or to provide credit to any particular individual. The statute, rather, is precatory:

> It is the purpose of this chapter to require each appropriate Federal financial supervisory agency to use its authority when examining financial institutions, to encourage such institutions to help meet the credit needs of the local communities in which they are chartered consistent with the safe and sound operation of such institutions.

12 U.S.C. § 2901(b). As petitioners concede, the CRA does not create a private right of action to enforce any of its terms. Moreover, any attempt to glean substance from the CRA is met with the reality that the statute sets no standards for the evaluation of a bank's contribution to the needs of its community. H.R. Conf. Rep. No. 95–634, at 76, reprinted in 1977 U.S.C.C.A.N. 2965, 2995 ("This title ... [is] designed to encourage more coordinated efforts between private investment and federal grants and insurance in order to increase the viability of our urban communities.").
* * *

Examining alternately the merits of the petitions, we are satisfied that the orders at issue warrant affirmance, especially in light of our deferential standard of review. Under the BHCA, the Board's findings are conclusive so long as they are supported by substantial evidence. 12 U.S.C. § 1848. This standard has been described as a "specific application" of the "arbitrary and capricious" standard of review familiar in the administrative law context. See Association of Data Processing Serv. Orgs. v. Board of Governors, 745 F.2d 677, 683 (D.C. Cir. 1984). Although we, of course, have the ultimate say on the legal issues involved in this proceeding, the Board is the agency responsible for federal regulation of the national banking system, and its interpretation of pertinent federal statutes is entitled to substantial deference. Securities Industry Ass'n v. Board of Governors, 468 U.S. 137, 142 (1984). Pursuant to 12 U.S.C. § 1467a(j), an OTS order under HOLA is reviewed under the standards set out in the Administrative Procedure Act ("APA"), 5 U.S.C. § 701 et seq. Under the APA, administrative action is reviewable to the extent it is "arbitrary, capricious, an abuse of discretion, or otherwise not in accordance with law." 5 U.S.C. § 706(2)(A).

As stated above, the CRA imposes an obligation on a federal regulatory agency to "assess the institution's record of meeting the credit needs of its entire community, including low and moderate-income neighborhoods" and to "take such record into account in its evaluation of an application for a deposit facility by such institution." 12 U.S.C. § 2903(a)(1) & (2). After reviewing the orders at issue, we have no doubt that this mandate was carried out in these cases.

Each of the Board orders at issue clearly addresses the relevant institutions' CRA records in its analysis of the convenience and needs of the communities to be served, as required by section 3 of the BHCA. For example, the Board's order approving the Chase–Chemical merger is seventy-two pages long, forty-five pages of which are devoted to an exhaustive analysis of Chase and Chemical's performance in meeting the goal of the CRA.

We find no error in the Board's reference to prior CRA evaluations conducted by the OCC, a major focus of both petitions' attack on the Board's assessment of Chase. For one thing, Congress has directed the Board to use OCC examinations in its evaluation of BHCA applications. 12 U.S.C. § 1844(c). Insofar as the Board's regulations reflect interest in potentially stale information, the record reveals that the Board considered its comprehensive analysis of Chase's CRA performance in an earlier proceeding, 81 Fed. Res. Bull. 467 (1995), in connection with the instant applications. Petitioners cite no authority to contravene this practice, and, as a court with an ever-expanding docket, we believe that an agency should be permitted to develop efficient means of resolving recurring issues so long as the essential fairness of the proceeding is not affected thereby. In any event, it is clear that the Board did not "abdicate" its duties under the CRA by taking into account either the OCC evaluations or its prior order. The orders at issue reflect an independent, detailed assessment of Chase's CRA record. * * *

For the reasons expressed above, we hold that petitioners have not demonstrated standing to challenge he orders at issue. * * *

UNITED STATES v. CHEVY CHASE
FEDERAL SAVINGS BANK

United States District Court, District of Columbia District, 1994.
No. 94–1824–JG, Consent Decree.
<www.usdoj.gov/crt/housing/documents/chevychasesettle.htm>.

This decree is entered, upon consent of the parties, to resolve claims of the United States that Chevy Chase Federal Savings Bank and the B.F. Saul Mortgage Company [herein after referred to as the Bank and Mortgage Company] violated the Fair Housing Act, 42 U.S.C. 3601–3619, and the Equal Credit Opportunity Act, 15 U.S.C. 1691–1691f, by discriminating on the basis of race in home mortgage financing and other types of credit transactions in the Washington, D.C. metropolitan area. The United States contends that the Bank and Mortgage Company have considered the racial composition of residential areas in determining where to market their products, and have avoided doing business in areas where African American persons reside. The United States further alleges that the challenged practices and policies are intended to deny, and have the effect of denying, an equal opportunity to residents of African American neighborhoods, on account of the racial identity of the neighborhood, to obtain mortgage financing and other types of credit transactions. The totality of the policies or practices challenged are commonly referred to as redlining.

In June 1993, the United States began the investigation that resulted in this lawsuit. Before and after that date the Bank and Mortgage Company initiated an aggressive effort to market their products to African

American residential areas. Most notably, the Bank and Mortgage Company have opened three Chevy Chase Bank branches and four B.F. Saul Mortgage Company offices in African American residential neighborhoods of the Washington, D.C. metropolitan area, and have engaged in an aggressive campaign to solicit business in African American neighborhoods. Those efforts will be continued and expanded by the terms of this Consent Decree.

By this decree, the Bank and Mortgage Company have committed to a remedial plan by which they will take all reasonable actions to obtain a market share of mortgage loans in African American neighborhoods, that is comparable to the Bank and Mortgage Company's market share in white residential areas. * * *

The Bank and Mortgage Company will invest $11,000,000.00 in the African American community of the Washington, D.C. metropolitan area during the five year consent decree period to settle the claims of the United States for the damage caused by the alleged redlining, and in furtherance of their commitment to better serve this community. This investment will be undertaken through a combination of subsidized lending programs directed to Washington, D.C. metropolitan area African American neighborhoods and the opening of new bank branches and mortgage offices in these neighborhoods. * * *

Chevy Chase and the Mortgage Company adamantly deny that any act or omission on their part as alleged in the government's complaint or this consent decree as violative of federal law was motivated in any way by discriminatory intent or racial bias. The Bank and Mortgage Company have agreed to the undertakings set forth in the Consent Decree to settle the government's claims against them and because they believe the affirmative lending actions and practices described will enable them to better serve the African American community. * * *

QUESTIONS AND NOTES

1. The Fed analyzed the 2004 HMDA data which included loan pricing information for the first time. The Fed determined that blacks and Hispanics disproportionately received high interest rates on home mortgage loans. The Fed acknowledged that the HMDA data does not include information on credit scores, loan-to-value ratios, or borrower debt-to-income ratios that could account for the rate disparity. Two hundred lenders, including one hundred banks, will be subject to additional scrutiny by their federal regulators based on these disparities. "The 2005 HMDA data, like the 2004 data, indicate that black and Hispanic borrowers are more likely, and Asian borrowers less likely, to obtain loans with prices above the pricing thresholds than are non-Hispanic white borrowers." Robert B. Avery, et al., Higher–Priced Home Lending and the 2005 HMDA Data, 2006 Fed. Res. Bull. A123, A159 (Sept. 8, 2006). The Justice Department reportedly has several active HMDA pricing investigations underway. Cheyenne Hopkins, Justice Department Moves Over HMDA Data Said Near, Am. Banker, Feb. 21, 2007. The HMDA data is available at <www.ffiec.gov/hmda/default.htm>.

2. Each bank regulatory agency has comparable regulations relating to CRA. 12 C.F.R. pt. 25 (OCC); 12 C.F.R. pt. 228 (Fed); 12 C.F.R. pt. 345 (FDIC); 12 C.F.R. pt. 563e (OTS).

3. A significant aspect of GLBA, is that it requires that a bank holding company's depository subsidiaries have received CRA ratings of Satisfactory or better as a precondition of a BHC becoming an FHC. 12 U.S.C.A. § 1843(*l*)(2). Section 1843(*l*)(2) also must be satisfied to form a financial subsidiary of a national or state bank, 12 U.S.C.A. §§ 24a(a)(7), 1831w(a).

4. As a policy matter, is CRA sound legislation? Are fair lending laws sufficient or is something more needed? For many years an academic debate has existed as to whether CRA requires improper credit rationing by mandating loans that are not justified in a competitive market, or whether it is a necessary requirement to correct imperfections in the market. See Jonathan R. Macey & Geoffrey P. Miller, The Community Reinvestment Act: An Economic Analysis, 79 Va. L. Rev. 291 (1993) (the CRA is not needed because credit-worthy borrowers will find credit from willing lenders); N. Keith Hylton & Vincent D. Rougeau, Lending Discrimination: Economic Theory, Econometric Evidence, and the Community Reinvestment Act, 85 Geo. L.J. 237, 253–62 (1996) (reviewing the viewpoint that CRA is necessary to correct imperfections in credit markets).

5. Should credit unions be subject to the CRA? See C. Blythe Clifford, Note, The Community Reinvestment Act & Credit Unions, 4 N.C. Banking Inst. 545 (2000).

6. Should the CRA apply to nondepository financial services institutions? What distinguishes banks and savings associations from other financial services institutions that might justify application of CRA to just these institutions?

7. Even banks with satisfactory or outstanding CRA records are not immune from objections filed by CRA-watchdog groups. Since in the business world "time is money" and protests delay merger approval, many banks announce significant CRA commitments along with the merger announcement or in the face of CRA protests. Should CRA have specific enforcement provisions or only play a role in the review of applications for bank expansion?

At the time of the creation of Citigroup, Citibank and Travelers Group announced a ten-year, $115 billion commitment to lending and investment in low-and moderate-income communities and to small businesses. Travelers Group pledged that its nonbank businesses (not subject to the CRA) would actively support a broad range of community development activities. Travelers pledged to expand the availability of commercial and homeowners insurance coverage and to provide special pricing to low-and moderate-income customers.

Bank of America's 2004 merger with FleetBoston Financial Corp. was accompanied by a $750 billion, ten-year CRA pledge. That figure was eclipsed by a later announcement by J.P. Morgan Chase & Co. that it would pledge $800 billion over ten years in connection with its merger with Bank One Corp.

As described in Chapter 9, debate has arisen over whether the CRA forced commercial banks into the subprime market, resulting in massive losses and nearly destroying the entire financial system.

8. Perhaps in response to what some observers saw as "CRA extortion" in the bank merger context, Congress, at the behest of Senator Gramm, passed a CRA "sunshine" provision. 12 U.S.C.A. § 1831y. This portion of GLBA requires that banks file annual reports on all grants greater than $10,000 and loans greater than $50,000 to community groups where there has been a communication by that group to the bank or its regulator questioning the adequacy of the bank's CRA record.

9. Limited purpose or wholesale banks that do not engage in consumer lending, will obviously have difficulty complying with CRA. How do the regulations require such institutions to satisfy the CRA?

10. The assessment area in which the bank's CRA performance is judged is defined by the bank. What is the justification for this? On what basis would a challenge to the assessment area be justified? Traditionally, the assessment area has been geographically based. This has posed a problem for Internet-only banks. Is a geographic-based assessment area meaningful for an Internet bank? What alternative ways could an Internet bank's assessment area be defined? Although this issue was on the radar screen at the time of GLBA, Congress did not address it there. See Will Keyser, Note, The 21st Century CRA: How Internet Banks are Causing Regulators to Rethink the Community Reinvestment Act, 4 N.C. Banking Inst. 545 (2000).

11. Does the *Chevy Chase* enforcement action allege any specific acts of discriminatory lending? Is the activity at issue a violation of the ECOA, the FHA, or the CRA?

12. The Riegle–Neal Community Development and Regulatory Improvement Act of 1994 sought to improve community development by creating a fund that would support community development financial institutions serving low income areas. These institutions included community credit unions and "micro-finance funds" that supplied capital to low income communities.[23] The Treasury Department was authorized to allocate $382 million to such lenders over a four year period, starting in 1994.

SECTION 5. REAL ESTATE SETTLEMENT PROCEDURES ACT (RESPA)

The Real Estate Settlement Procedures Act (RESPA), 12 U.S.C.A. § 2601–17, was enacted in 1974. Its purpose was to require disclosure to consumers of the costs associated with real estate closings so that they might avoid "unnecessarily high settlement charges caused by certain abusive practices." 12 U.S.C.A. § 2601(a). Disclosures must be made in every settlement involving a federally related mortgage loan. The settlement costs must be disclosed on a HUD–1 Form. Regulation X, 24 C.F.R.

---

23. Banking on the Poor, The Economist, June 27, 1998, at 28; see generally Calvin Cunningham, Note, How Banks Can Benefit from Partnership with Community Development Financial Institutions: The Bank Enterprise Awards Program, 3 N.C. Banking Inst. 261 (1999).

§ 3500.8(a). The BCFP assumes rulemaking authority for RESPA following the Dodd–Frank Act.

HEIMMERMANN v. FIRST UNION MORTGAGE CORP.

United States Court of Appeals, Eleventh Circuit, 2002.
305 F.3d 1257, *cert. denied,* 539 U.S. 970 (2003).

EDMONDSON, CHIEF JUDGE.

First Union Mortgage Corporation appeals the district court's grant of class certification to a class of plaintiffs seeking damages for First Union's alleged violation of Section 8 of the Real Estate Settlement Procedures Act (RESPA). See 12 U.S.C. § 2601, et. seq. We accepted jurisdiction over this appeal. We review a district court's certification of a class for abuse of discretion. For a district court to apply the wrong legal standard is an abuse of discretion. We vacate the grant of class certification.

This case is one of several dealing with RESPA's effect on the legality of the payment of Yield Spread Premiums (YSP) by mortgage lenders to mortgage brokers. For a detailed discussion of YSP's and their role in the real estate mortgage market, see Culpepper v. Inland Mortgage Co., 132 F.3d 692, 694 (11th Cir. 1998) (*Culpepper I*) and Culpepper v. Irwin Mortgage Corp., 253 F.3d 1324, 1326 (11th Cir. 2001) (*Culpepper III*). A YSP is a payment made by a lender to a broker in exchange for that broker's delivering a mortgage that is above the "par rate" being offered by the lender. Briefly stated, the payment is typically a certain percentage of the total amount of the loan; the exact percentage is determined by the extent to which the actual interest rate exceeds the par rate. These YSP's potentially violate Section 8(a) of RESPA, which prohibits the payment of kickback fees and referrals in association with mortgage lending.

In *Culpepper III*—argued the same day as this case—we concluded that class certification in a case alleging a violation of RESPA was appropriate where the payment of a YSP was based solely upon the amount by which the loan rate exceeded the par rate and where the payment of the YSP was not tied to specific services provided by the broker. Because whether this standard was satisfied could be determined on a class-wide basis, we concluded that the district court in *Culpepper III* did not err by granting class certification. See *Culpepper III*, 253 F.3d at 1332.

Shortly after our *Culpepper III* ruling, the Department of Housing and Urban Development issued a Statement of Policy (the 2001 SOP),[24] purportedly clarifying a Statement of Policy issued in 1999 (the 1999 SOP).[25] Our ruling in *Culpepper III* had relied heavily on the 1999 SOP.

---

24. [n.2] Real Estate Settlement Procedures Act Statement of Policy 2001–1: Clarification of Statement of Policy 1999–1 Regarding Lender Payments to Mortgage Brokers, and Guidance Concerning Unearned Fees Under Section 8(b), 66 Fed. Reg. 53,052 (Oct. 18, 2001).

25. [n.3] Real Estate Settlement Procedures Act Statement of Policy 1999–1 Regarding Lender Payments to Mortgage Brokers, 64 Fed. Reg. 10,080, 10,080 (March 1, 1999).

According to First Union, the 2001 SOP is at odds with the outcome of *Culpepper III* and compels a different result in this case.

Before we address the substance of the 2001 SOP, we must determine its applicability to this case. Although the 2001 SOP raises some concerns about the retroactive application of agency interpretations, about the deference given to policy statements, and about the ability of an agency interpretation to overrule prior circuit precedent, we ultimately conclude that nothing prevents the application of the 2001 SOP to this case.

The 2001 SOP was promulgated after the transactions that gave rise to this litigation and after the district court's ruling on the issue of class certification. But because we accept that both the 2001 SOP and the statement it interprets, the 1999 SOP, are clarifications of existing law and not new rules or regulations, no problem with the retroactive application of the statements exists. * * *

An additional preliminary question is what deference, if any, should be given to the 2001 SOP.

No deference is to be given to an agency interpretation that is at odds with the plain meaning of the statute being interpreted. See Chevron, U.S.A., Inc. v. Natural Resources Defense Council, Inc., 467 U.S. 837 (1984). But RESPA does not, by its plain language, speak to the standard for determining whether the payment of a YSP violates the Act. Section 8(a) of RESPA simply prohibits kickbacks and referral fees, see 12 U.S.C. § 2607; Section 8(c) allows payment "for services actually performed in the making of a loan." The question of how to determine when a YSP is an illegal kickback and when it is a legally permissible payment for services actually performed is not specifically addressed in RESPA. Our ruling in Culpepper III did not purport to rely squarely upon the plain language of Section 8 of RESPA, but rather upon an *interpretation* of RESPA's language and of the "ambiguous" 1999 SOP. See Culpepper III, 253 F.3d at 1329–1330. The plain language of RESPA does not prevent us from giving deference to the 2001 SOP.

A question also exists about whether the 2001 SOP is the kind of agency statement to which the courts should give broad deference. In United States v. Mead Corp., 533 U.S. 218 (2001), the Supreme Court wrote that "administrative implementation of a particular statutory provision qualifies for Chevron deference when it appears that Congress delegated authority to the agency generally to make rules carrying the force of law, and that the agency interpretation claiming deference was promulgated in the exercise of that authority." *Mead*, 121 S. Ct. at 2171. RESPA contains an express delegation of congressional authority: the statute authorizes the Secretary of HUD "to prescribe such rules and regulations, *to make such interpretations*, and to grant such reasonable exemptions for classes of transactions, as may be necessary to achieve the purposes of this chapter." 12 U.S.C. § 2617(a) (emphasis added). HUD regulations identify a "statement of policy" as a document that embodies such a "rule, regulation, or interpretation" under RESPA's delegation of authority. See 24 C.F.R. § 3500.4(a)(1)(ii).

Because the power to issue interpretations is expressly delegated in RESPA, the 2001 SOP carries the full force of law. As a result, we give deference to the 2001 SOP. * * *

We also reject the argument that the 2001 SOP is due no deference because it is inconsistent with earlier expressions of HUD's position. We cannot say that the 2001 SOP is "inconsistent" with the 1999 SOP. The 1999 SOP was "ambiguous." The 2001 SOP clarifies that ambiguity. * * *

We also reject the argument that the 2001 SOP is inconsistent with clear congressional intent and, therefore, is due no *Chevron* deference. We cannot say that HUD's interpretation violates Congress's clear intent in enacting RESPA. One of RESPA's stated goals is "the elimination of kickbacks or referral fees that tend to increase unnecessarily the costs of certain settlement services." 12 U.S.C. § 2601(b)(2). The test laid out in the 2001 SOP, which does ban fees in excess of what would be reasonable compensation for the broker's service, seems to fulfill that ultimate goal. In addition, nothing in the language of RESPA itself compels the conclusion that HUD's test for the legality of YSP's—admittedly more lenient than that adopted in *Culpepper III*—violates congressional intent.

That we may have determined in *Culpepper III* that a different interpretation of RESPA (in our view) is better or more consistent with the statutory language does not require—or even allow—us to reject HUD's interpretation. "The resolution of ambiguity in a statutory text is often more a question of policy than of law." Florida Manuf. Housing Ass'n, Inc. v. Cisneros, 53 F.3d 1565, 1572 (11th Cir. 1995) . That we may prefer a different interpretation is not enough to deny deference to the agency interpretation. We conclude, therefore, that the 2001 SOP is entitled to Chevron deference.

We also conclude that the rule announced in the 2001 SOP can, in effect, overrule the holding of *Culpepper III*. "Courts generally must defer to an agency statutory interpretation that is at odds with circuit precedent, so long as the agency's answer is based on a permissible construction of the statute." Satellite Broadcasting and Communications Ass'n of America v. Oman, 17 F.3d 344, 347 (11th Cir. 1994).

We conclude that the substance of the 2001 SOP compels a different result in this case than the result in *Culpepper III*. The 2001 SOP explicitly rejects the foundation of *Culpepper III*: "neither Section 8(a) of RESPA nor the 1999 [SOP] supports the conclusion that a yield spread premium can be presumed to be a referral fee based solely upon the fact that the lender pays the broker a yield spread premium that is based upon a rate sheet, or because the lender does not have specific knowledge of what services the broker has performed." 2001 SOP, 66 Fed. Reg. at 53,055.

According to the 2001 SOP, the first step in assessing whether RESPA has been violated is to determine whether the broker has provided goods or services of the kind typically associated with a mortgage transaction. Contrary to the conclusion in *Culpepper III*, the lender and the broker need not be able to tie the YSP payment to specific services provided. If this first step is satisfied, the fact-finder must proceed to the second step: determining whether the total compensation paid to the broker is reasonably related to the total value of the goods or services actually provided. See 2001 SOP, 66 Fed. Reg. at 53,055.

Based on the 2001 SOP, we conclude that the district court did abuse its discretion in granting class certification in this case. Federal Rule of Civil Procedure 23(a) identifies four requirements which must be satisfied before a class can be certified. These elements are the requirements: "(1) the class is so numerous that joinder of all members is impracticable, (2) there are questions of law or fact common to the class, (3) the claims or defenses of the representative parties are typical of the claims or defenses of the class, and (4) the representative parties will fairly and adequately protect the interests of the class." Fed. R. Civ. P. 23(a).

In this case, the district court concluded that the requirements were met. The district court determined that common questions of fact were dominant because the class representative alleged these things: 1) for each class member's loan, the amount of the YSP was based solely upon the amount by which the loan rate exceeded the par rate; and 2) for each class member's loan, the YSP was not tied directly to specific additional services provided by the broker.

The 2001 SOP, however, makes clear that facts such as those alleged are not sufficient to establish a violation of RESPA. Instead, it is necessary to determine whether compensable services were provided by the broker and whether the total amount of broker compensation was reasonable in the light of the circumstances of each loan. In granting class certification, the district court therefore applied what we now see as an improper legal standard. The district court therefore abused its discretion when it granted class certification. * * *

* * * Therefore, the district court's grant of class certification is hereby vacated, and we remand for further proceedings consistent with this opinion.

QUESTIONS AND NOTES

1. In 2002, it was estimated that roughly 60% of all mortgages were arranged through mortgage brokers, and that of these mortgages, 80–90% carried yield spread premiums, Erick Berquist, Lenders Relieved by Yield–Spread Ruling, Am. Banker, Sept. 24, 2002. Senator Schumer alleged in 2007 that Countrywide Financial, then the nation's largest home mortgage lender, provided inappropriate incentives to mortgage brokers to steer consumers into high cost products, such as a commission of 1% of the loan's value when the

borrower agreed to a three-year prepayment penalty. Richard Cowden, Schumer Says Countrywide Must Take Steps to End Abusive Subprime Lending Practices, Banking Daily (BNA), Aug. 30, 2007.

The Dodd–Frank Act now prohibits compensation to a mortgage originator that varies based on the loan's terms (other than the principal amount of the loan). Dodd–Frank Act, § 1403. The Act does not expressly mention yield spread premiums. The Fed also adopted rules in August 2010 that prohibit yield spread premiums.

2. The Dodd–Frank Act defines a mortgage originator to include any person who takes a mortgage loan application, assists a consumer in applying or obtaining a mortgage loan, or offers or negotiates the terms of the mortgage loan. Dodd–Frank Act, § 1401. A real estate broker and a creditor are not originators. The originator must be licensed under any applicable state and federal licensing laws, including the Secure and Fair Enforcement for Mortgage Licensing Act of 2008 (SAFE Act).

3. Why might a lender use a mortgage broker?

SECTION 6.   SUBPRIME AND PREDATORY LENDING

Subprime lending is the name used to describe the credit extended to borrowers who do not meet traditional lending criteria. Because of the increased risk of default from such borrowers, subprime loans generally are priced higher than prime loans. Lenders, including some banks, who serve the subprime market provide credit to those who might otherwise not be able to obtain credit from a traditional bank lender. Some subprime lenders may overreach and lend only on terms and rates that are inconsistent with the risks they are undertaking. This practice is referred to as predatory lending.

The subprime segment of the home mortgage market grew from less than 5% of all mortgages in 1994 to almost 20% in 2007. As subprime lending increased, so did unsavory lending practices characterized as predatory lending. The OCC provided guidance about practices that might indicate predatory lending in OCC Advisory Letter AL 2000–7 (July 25, 2000), and elaborated on a definition of predatory lending in the 2003 Advisory Letter excerpted below.

OFFICE OF THE COMPTROLLER OF THE CURRENCY
OCC ADVISORY LETTER AL 2003–2

February 21, 2003.
<www.occ.treas.gov/ftp/advisory/2003–2.pdf>.

* * * The terms "abusive lending" or "predatory lending" are most frequently defined by reference to a variety of lending practices. Although it is generally necessary to consider the totality of circumstances to assess whether a loan is predatory, a fundamental characteristic of predatory lending is the aggressive marketing of credit to prospective borrowers who

simply cannot afford the credit on the terms being offered. Typically, such credit is underwritten predominantly on the basis of the liquidation value of the collateral, without regard to the borrower's ability to service and repay the loan according to its terms absent resorting to that collateral. This abusive practice leads to "equity stripping." * * *

While such disregard of basic principles of loan underwriting lies at the heart of predatory lending, a variety of other practices may also accompany the marketing of such credit.

- Loan "flipping"—frequent refinancings that result in little or no economic benefit to the borrower and are undertaken with the primary or sole objective of generating additional loan fees, prepayment penalties, and fees from the financing of credit-related products;

- Refinancings of special subsidized mortgages that result in the loss of beneficial loan terms;

- "Packing" of excessive and sometimes "hidden" fees in the amount financed;

- Using loans terms or structures—such as negative amortization—to make it more difficult or impossible for borrowers to reduce or repay their indebtedness;

- Using balloon payments to conceal the true burden of the financing and to force borrowers into costly refinancing transactions or foreclosures;

- Targeting inappropriate or excessively expensive credit products to older borrowers, to persons who are not financially sophisticated or who may be otherwise vulnerable to abusive practices, and to persons who could qualify for mainstream credit products and terms.

- Inadequate disclosure of the true costs, risks and, where necessary, appropriateness to the borrower of loan transactions;

- The offering of single premium credit life insurance; and

- The use of mandatory arbitration clauses. * * *

The regulation of predatory lending may come from state or federal sources. At the state level there may be an "unfair and deceptive acts and practices" statute (modeled after the Federal FTC Act) which can serve as the general authority for regulation of predatory lending concerns. Some states regulate mortgage brokers, which may provide an avenue for regulating predatory lending practices. In recent years states have enacted their own predatory lending statutes. As of 2004, 32 states and the District of Columbia had statutes regulating predatory lending practices.[26]

---

26. All the state statutes apply by their terms to banks, except for Indiana's, which exempts banks and credit unions.

UNITED COMPANIES LENDING CORP. v. SARGEANT

United States District Court, District of Massachusetts, 1998.
20 F.Supp.2d 192.

YOUNG, DISTRICT JUDGE.

* * * United Companies Lending Corporation ("United") makes, sells, and services refinancing, first lien residential mortgage loans which are used primarily for debt consolidation, home improvement, or major household purchases. United is licensed to do business in Massachusetts as a mortgage lender. United operates in the subprime market making loans to consumers who have a higher credit risk than borrowers in the prime market.

Subprime loans are more costly to the lender to originate, sell, and service than traditional "A credit" loans. In the subprime market, the lenders evaluate the credit-worthiness of a borrower "by establishing various risk classifications with associated pricing parameters." There is no standard set of credit risk assessment criteria as exists in the prime market. The subprime market typically takes into consideration a potential borrower's 1) credit history; 2) the household debt-to-income ratio if the loan is approved; and 3) the combined loan-to-value ratio for home equity loan and other mortgage debt on the property. "Standards vary, however, within the subprime market, and different lenders may assign different weights for each of these factors, for a given credit grade. (One firm's 'B' loans may look like another firm's 'C' loans.)"

Subprime loans have higher securitization costs associated with the sale of these loans on the private secondary market compared to loans in the prime market because they are "nonconforming" loans. United loans are also sold "with recourse" in the event of a default by the borrower. As a result of these terms, the risk to the lender on a subprime loan is substantially higher than on a prime loan. "Due to the higher risks and costs associated with subprime loans, the total cost of such loans to the borrower—as reflected in the Annual Percentage Rate ("APR")—is generally higher than the cost of loans by traditional lenders such as banks. Such costs typically include interest, origination fees or 'points' and other fees associated with the closing of the loan."

Daisy Sargeant ("Sargeant") is the owner of a New England triple-decker in Dorchester, Massachusetts. She resides on the second floor and rents out the first floor and third floor apartments for $600.00 per month each. Desiring to make improvements to the interior and the exterior of the house, she responded to an advertisement in the Boston Herald regarding the availability of loans. She contacted the toll-free number in the advertisement and received a mortgage application. The advertisement was placed by a California-based mortgage broker, John P. McIntyre ("McIntyre"). McIntyre referred Sargeant's name to David Richard ("Richard"), a United mortgage loan originator located at the Warwick,

Rhode Island office. Richard contacted Sargeant. Richard is the United agent with whom Sargeant dealt in obtaining the mortgage loan at issue.

On August 9, 1995, Sargeant completed the loan application and executed disclosure documents related to the loan. Sargeant was classified as a "C" borrower by United. On August 23, 1995, United approved Sargeant's loan. A title search disclosed an undischarged mortgage on the property, however, as well as unpaid real estate taxes. United states that McIntyre negotiated with the lien holder who agreed to accept $5000 as payment in full. United reapproved the loan, and the closing was held in Warwick, Rhode Island, on September 29, 1995.

Sargeant thus obtained a loan from United for $134,700. The mortgage had an adjustable interest rate with an initial rate of interest of 10.99%. The loan provided that the rate could be adjusted upward one percent every six months with a maximum interest rate of 16.99%. The initial annual percentage rate charged on the mortgage was 13.556%. The loan proceeds were disbursed as follows: $15,681 was applied to the home improvements upon their completion; $4,910 was applied to pay off credit card debt; and $93,000 was applied to two prior mortgages on her residence. According to the settlement statement, Sargeant was assessed a brokerage fee payable to United in the sum of $13,461.40. United claims that this entry is incorrect and that the $13,461.40 was paid to United as an origination fee or "points." Sargeant was also charged a broker's fee in the amount of $4,150 made payable to McIntyre. Her total closing costs and fees equaled $23,029.87. Her initial mortgage payments were $1,281. Her previous mortgage payments were $956 per month.

Sargeant fell behind in the repayment of her loan and United initiated foreclosure proceedings against her. Sargeant then filed a consumer complaint with the Consumer Protection and Antitrust Division of the Massachusetts Attorney General's Office.

After the filing of this Complaint, the Attorney General, on behalf of the Commonwealth of Massachusetts, commenced an action against United in the Massachusetts Superior Court sitting in and for the county of Suffolk seeking, *inter alia*, to enjoin United 1) from making any mortgage loans in violation of Mass. Gen. Laws ch. 184, § 17D and the Mortgage Brokers and Mortgage Lenders Regulations of the Attorney General, 904 C.M.R. § 8.00 et seq., and 2) from making any mortgage loans in violation of Mass. Gen. Laws ch. 183, § 63. A preliminary injunction issued in that case on January 24, 1997, prohibiting United from taking any further action in foreclosing on Sargeant's property and requiring it to notify the Commonwealth thirty days prior to a foreclosure sale on any other residential property.

At this point, United went forum shopping. It commenced this defendant class action suit against Daisy Sargeant and all persons similarly situated, seeking a declaratory judgment that 940 C.M.R. § 8.06(6) is void and unenforceable, that the mortgage loan origination fee or points charged to Sargeant were lawful and proper, and that a judgment of default against Sargeant on the mortgage note was therefore appropriate. Sargeant counterclaimed, asking for a declaration that the mortgage transaction was an unfair or deceptive act because it was unconscionable pursuant to 940 CMR § 8.06(6), and that rescission of the mortgage loan is therefore permissible. * * *

Here, the Attorney General has promulgated regulations governing the activities of mortgage brokers and mortgage lenders which apply to "any mortgage lender or broker advertising or doing business within Massachusetts, regardless of whether or not the lender or broker maintains an office in Massachusetts." 940 C.M.R. 8.02. Regulation 8.06(6) ("the Regulation"), which became effective August 1, 1992, states that:

> It is an unfair or deceptive practice for a mortgage broker or lender to procure or negotiate for a borrower a mortgage loan with rates or terms which *significantly deviate from industry-wide standards* or which are *otherwise unconscionable*. (emphasis added).

This is the regulation that United challenges in this case. * * *

The fact that the charging of points is permissible where there is disclosure, without requiring the direct correlation between the amount charged and the services rendered, does not imply that such points may be charged without limit or that the charging of certain points does not constitute an unfair act. The Attorney General's regulations may proscribe even good faith business practices that could be unfair or deceptive. The Regulation does not prevent the charging of points but, instead, furthers the underlying policy of Chapter 93A "to ensure an equitable relationship between consumers and persons engaged in business." The authorization of a particular act or practice by statute—here, the charging of points on a residential mortgage—does not mean that certain extreme applications of such practice may not be found unfair or deceptive. * * * [C]ompetitive market forces were not ensuring fair origination fees but instead, due to market failure, widespread mortgage lending abuses were present in Massachusetts. * * *

The Attorney General's Regulation attempts to prevent the charging of excessive origination fees or points in residential mortgage loan transactions which increase the debt obligation of the consumer and the potential for default. United argues that a limitation on the permissible origination fee or points charged would cause United either to charge a higher interest rate, thus increasing the cost of the loan to the consumer, or to withdraw from the Massachusetts mortgage market altogether, with the consequence that consumers like Sargeant could not obtain the loans and necessary credit to "get back on their feet." United argues that this cost outweighs the benefits of the Regulation and that the Regulation is thus inconsistent with the applicable Federal law [the FTC's unfair and deceptive trade practice statute, 15 U.S.C. § 45(a)(1)]. This Court disagrees.

Evidence in the record indicates that in 1995, the period when the loan transaction took place, the majority of subprime lenders did not charge ten points on loans but rather charged five points or less. The payment of points can result in a lower contract rate, but the payment of points does increase the annual percentage rate or the effective rate of interest. This is so because the debt service is based on the face amount of the loan rather than on the net amount of the loan or the amount actually received by the buyer. Thus, contrary to United's assertion, points do not reduce the annual percentage rate but increase it. Points have the effect of reducing the amount of money advanced by the lender while raising the effective interest rate. Although points may be necessary to raise the loan yield in order to obtain a return that is competitive with other types of loans, a two-fold increase above the average points charged by subprime market lenders is not necessary to achieve this objective, especially when the mortgage loan is an adjustable rate mortgage as opposed to a fixed mortgage. * * *

The origination fee charged by United constituted an unfair and deceptive trade practice as the points charged substantially deviated from industry-wide practice in Massachusetts. Therefore, Sargeant is entitled to actual damages of $13,461.40 plus interest. McIntyre was not entitled to a brokerage fee as he failed to provide Sargeant with the requisite disclosure. Such failure to disclose constitutes an unfair and deceptive trade practice in violation of Mass. Gen. Laws ch. 93A, § 2(a) and a violation of the disclosure requirements of Mass. Gen. Laws ch. 183, § 63. Therefore, Sargeant is entitled to actual damages of $4,150.00 plus interest. Sargeant is also entitled to reasonable attorney's fees in prosecuting to her Chapter 93A claims.

Upon reflection, as the question of unconscionability is a close one, the matter is a fact-specific expression of Massachusetts common law, and an equally just ground of decision between these particular parties is available, this Court refrains from expressing an opinion on the issue of unconscionability. * * *

A court sitting in equity, however, is necessarily empowered to do complete justice as between the parties. Here, Daisy Sargeant initiated neither the state nor the federal action. She only filed a consumer complaint with the Massachusetts Attorney General who, appreciating the seriousness of the matter, filed suit on behalf of all the citizens of the Commonwealth in the Massachusetts Superior Court. It was United who went forum shopping, and named Sargeant as the representative of the defendant class in the federal court. The Attorney General chose not to litigate here and Sargeant was thus left to fend for herself, ultimately vindicating the Attorney General's regulation generally as well as successfully rebuking the application of United's attempted unfair and deceptive acts to her. While she is entitled to her attorney's fees in prosecuting her counter-claim under Chapter 93A, this cannot adequately compensate her for alone bearing the full burden of this complex litigation. * * * The Court therefore awards Sargeant an opportunity similar to, albeit not as complete as, recission. Should Sargeant, within six months of the date of this order, tender to United the outstanding principal (not interest) due on the loan as of the date of this order as well as interest thereon at the contract rate from this date, the mortgage shall be discharged and the mortgage note satisfied. * * *

An anti-predatory lending law effective in Georgia October 1, 2002—which was then described as the "country's strictest law against predatory lending"—resulted in many lenders deciding not to make "high-cost" loans in Georgia because of the severe penalties provided in the law, including criminal penalties.[27]

The OTS preempted the Georgia Fair Lending Act (GFLA) as it applied to federal thrifts making covered loans in Georgia pursuant to its "occupation of the field" regulation.[28] The OCC followed suit in August, 2003, and simultaneously proposed for comment rules regarding predatory lending practices.[29]

DEPARTMENT OF THE TREASURY OFFICE OF THE COMPTROLLER OF THE CURRENCY, PREEMPTION DETERMINATION AND ORDER

68 Fed. Reg. 46264 (Aug. 5, 2003).

* * * GFLA does not apply to National City [the bank requesting preemption] or to any other bank or national bank operating subsidiary that engages in real estate lending activities in Georgia. * * *

In brief, the reasons supporting our Determination and Order are as follows:

- National banks' authority to engage in real estate lending activities derives exclusively from Federal law. Under applicable Federal preemption principles, based on the Supremacy Clause of the U.S. Constitution and articulated by the U.S. Supreme Court, a state law may not modify a Congressional grant of power to national banks by limiting, conditioning, or otherwise impermissibly affecting a national bank's exercise of that power.

- The Federal statute that authorizes national banks' real estate lending activities, 12 U.S.C. 371, precludes application of many provisions of the GFLA to national banks. First, by its terms, the statute grants real estate lending power unconditioned by the application of any state's law. * * * [T]he text of the statute specifically gives the OCC authority to determine the "restrictions and requirements" that apply to national banks' real estate lending activities. The exclusion of state authority in this regard is consistent with the history of the statute, which has, since its inception,

---

27. Erick Bergquist, Ga. Predator Law Drives Out Some Lenders, Am. Banker, Oct. 1, 2002.

28. OTS, Preemption of Georgia Fair Lending Act, P–2003–1, Jan. 21, 2003, available at <www.ots.treas.gov/docs/56301.pdf> (citing 12 C.F.R. § 560.2(a)).

29. 68 Fed. Reg. 46119 (proposed Aug. 5, 2003) (to be codified at 12 C.F.R. pts. 7 & 34).

imposed only Federal limits and conditions on national banks' real estate lending activities.

- National banks' real estate lending standards are subject to a comprehensive Federal regulatory framework that addresses the types of abusive and predatory practices that the GFLA seeks to prohibit. In addition, the OCC has recently issued detailed guidance applicable to national banks' mortgage originations, use of mortgage brokers, and purchases of loans from others. This guidance targets abusive and predatory practices and will be administered by the OCC as part of its comprehensive supervision of national banks, in addition to the already-applicable Federal restrictions on high-cost real estate lending, Federal consumer protections and disclosure requirements that apply to all home mortgage lending, and Federal standards that require national banks to base lending decisions on the borrower's ability to repay and not the foreclosure value of the collateral.

- The OCC regulations implementing 12 U.S.C. 371 currently provide that certain types of state laws do not apply to national banks. For instance, part 34 of our rules says expressly that state laws concerning the schedule for the repayment of principal and interest and state laws concerning the term to maturity of a loan do not apply to national banks. Thus, Federal law, comprised of the statute and OCC regulations, already preempts the GFLA provisions that modify a national bank's real estate lending authority by imposing limits or restrictions that concern the schedule for repayment of principal and interest or the term to maturity of a loan. * * *

- Some provisions of the GFLA purport to limit the interest a national bank may charge for certain types of loans. As the Supreme Court has recently reaffirmed, the rate of interest that is permissible for national banks is determined exclusively by Federal law, at 12 U.S.C. 85. Section 85 permits national banks to charge the most favorable rate permitted by the laws of the state in which the bank is located, regardless of where the borrower is located. Under this standard, National City uses the most favored lender rates of Indiana, not Georgia, and thus is not subject to limits on the rates of interest imposed by the GFLA. * * *

- Other provisions of the GFLA purport to limit the non-interest fees a national bank may charge in connection with certain types of loans. These provisions are preempted because they are inconsistent with national banks' well recognized authority to establish non-interest fees pursuant to the national bank powers provisions of 12 U.S.C. 24(Seventh) and the OCC's rules that govern national bank fees.

- The GFLA is also preempted with respect to national bank operating subsidiaries. Federal law authorizes national banks to conduct through operating subsidiaries activities that are permissible for the bank itself. Activities conducted through operating subsidiaries are subject to the same terms and conditions as apply to the parent bank and, pursuant to OCC regulations, are subject to state law only to the extent that the parent bank is subject to state law. * * *

The GFLA became effective October 1, 2002. As originally enacted, the GFLA restricted the ability of creditors or servicers to charge certain fees and engage in certain practices for three categories that it defined: "home loans," "covered home loans," and "high-cost home loans." Whether a loan was covered by one of these categories depended on the annual percentage rate and the amount of points and fees charged.[30] All "home loans" were subject to certain restrictions on the terms of credit and loan-related fees, including prohibitions on the financing of credit insurance, debt cancellation or suspension coverage, and limitations on late fees and payoff statement fees. * * *

"High-cost home loans" were subject to the restrictions on "home loans" and "covered home loans," as well as numerous disclosure requirements and restrictions on the terms of credit and loan-related fees. Creditors were required to disclose to borrowers that the loan is high-cost, and borrowers were required to be provided with certain loan counseling before the creditor could make the loan. In addition, the GFLA prohibited certain pre-payment penalties; balloon payments; negative amortization; increases in interest rates after default; advance payments from loan proceeds; fees to modify, renew, extend, amend, or defer a payment; and accelerating payments at the creditor's or servicer's sole discretion. * * *

DEPARTMENT OF THE TREASURY OFFICE OF THE COMPTROLLER OF THE CURRENCY, FINAL RULE: BANK ACTIVITIES AND OPERATIONS; REAL ESTATE LENDING AND APPRAISALS

69 Fed. Reg. 1904 (Jan. 13, 2004).
(codified at 12 C.F.R. pts. 7 and 34).

The OCC shares the view of the commenters that predatory and abusive lending practices are inconsistent with national objectives of encouraging home ownership and community revitalization, and can be devastating to individuals, families, and communities. We will not tolerate such practices by national banks and their operating subsidiaries. Our Advisory Letters on predatory lending,[31] our pioneering enforcement positions resulting in substantial restitution to affected consumers, and the anti-predatory lending standards adopted in this final rule reflect our

---

30.   [n.3] See GFLA Sec. 7–6A–2.

31.   [n.68] See [OCC Advisory Letter 2003–2, Guidelines for National Banks to Guard Against Predatory and Abusive Lending Practices, Feb. 21, 2003, and OCC Avisory Letter 2003–3, Avoiding Predatory and Abusive Lending Practices in Brokered and Purchased Loans, Feb. 21, 2003, both available at <www.occ.treas.gov/advlst03.htm>.]

commitment that national banks operate pursuant to high standards of integrity in all respects. The provisions of this final rule, clarifying that certain state laws are not applicable to national banks' operations, do not undermine the application of these standards to all national banks, for the protection of all national bank customers—wherever they are located.

Advisory Letters 2003–2, which addresses loan originations, and 2003–3, which addresses loan purchases and the use of third party loan brokers, contain the most comprehensive supervisory standards ever published by any Federal financial regulatory agency to address predatory and abusive lending practices and detail steps for national banks to take to ensure that they do not engage in such practices. As explained in the Advisory Letters, if the OCC has evidence that a national bank has engaged in abusive lending practices, we will review those practices not only to determine whether they violate specific provisions of law such as the Homeowners Equity Protection Act of 1994 (HOEPA), the Fair Housing Act, or the Equal Credit Opportunity Act, but also to determine whether they involve unfair or deceptive practices that violate the FTC Act. Indeed, several practices that we identify as abusive in our Advisory Letters—such as equity stripping, loan flipping, and the refinancing of special subsidized mortgage loans that originally contained terms favorable to the borrower—generally can be found to be unfair or deceptive practices that violate the FTC Act. * * *

* * * [E]vidence that national banks are engaged in predatory lending practices is scant. Based on the absence of such information—from third parties, our consumer complaint database, and our supervisory process—we have no reason to believe that such practices are occurring in the national banking system to any significant degree. Although several of the commenters suggested this conclusion is implausible given the significant share of the lending market occupied by national banks, this observation is consistent with an extensive study of predatory lending conducted by the Department of Housing and Urban Development (HUD) and the Treasury Department,[32] and even with comments submitted in connection with an OTS rulemaking concerning preemption of state lending standards by 46 State Attorneys General. * * *

✳ The OCC is firmly committed to assuring that abusive practices—whether in connection with mortgage lending or other national bank activities—continue to have no place in the national banking system. * * *

---

32. [n.73] A Treasury–HUD joint report issued in 2000 found that predatory lending practices in the subprime market are less likely to occur in lending by—

banks, thrifts, and credit unions that are subject to extensive oversight and regulation * * *. The subprime mortgage and finance companies that dominate mortgage lending in many low-income and minority communities, while subject to the same consumer protection laws, are not subject to as much federal oversight as their prime market counterparts—who are largely federally-supervised banks, thrifts, and credit unions. The absence of such accountability may create an environment where predatory practices flourish because they are unlikely to be detected. Departments of Housing and Urban Development and the Treasury, "Curbing Predatory Home Mortgage Lending: A Joint Report" 17–18 (June 2000). * * *

Sec. 7.4008   Lending.

* * *

(c) Unfair and deceptive practices. A national bank shall not engage in unfair or deceptive practices within the meaning of section 5 of the Federal Trade Commission Act, 15 U.S.C. 45(a)(1), and regulations promulgated thereunder in connection with loans made under this Sec. 7.4008. * * *

Sec. 34.3   General rule.

* * *

(b) A national bank shall not make a consumer loan subject to this subpart based predominantly on the bank's realization of the foreclosure or liquidation value of the borrower's collateral, without regard to the borrower's ability to repay the loan according to its terms. A bank may use any reasonable method to determine a borrower's ability to repay, including, for example, the borrower's current and expected income, current and expected cash flows, net worth, other relevant financial resources, current financial obligations, employment status, credit history, or other relevant factors.

(c) A national bank shall not engage in unfair or deceptive practices within the meaning of section 5 of the Federal Trade Commission Act, 15 U.S.C. 45(a)(1), and regulations promulgated thereunder in connection with loans made under this part. * * *

Preemption of state efforts to regulate predatory lending by the OCC and OTS for national banks and federal thrifts increased the attention on a solution at the federal level that would apply uniformly to all lenders. While Congress considered a federal legislative response, the banking agencies and other federal regulators continued to craft their own guidance.

One federal tool is the FTC Act which prohibits "unfair and deceptive acts and practices." Although the authority of the federal banking agencies to enforce the FTC's Act was in question just several years ago,[33] the federal banking agencies now seem confident in their enforcement authority.[34]

TILA, RESPA, the ECOA, and the CRA also provide extensive regulation of residential mortgage lending transactions. In 1994, TILA was amended to add the Home Ownership Equity Protection Act (HOEPA), which includes special limits and additional disclosures for nonpurchase

---

33. See McNeill Y. Wester, Note, OCC v. Providian National Bank: Enforcement of the FTC's Unfair and Deceptive Trade Practices Statute by the OCC, 5 N.C. Banking Inst. 373 (2001).

34. 12 C.F.R. §§ 7.4008(c) & 34.3(c) (OCC); FRB and FDIC, Unfair or Deceptive Acts or Practices by State–Chartered Banks (Mar. 11, 2004) (finding authority to enforce the FTC Act pursuant to 12 U.S.C.A. §§ 1818(b)(1), (e)(1) & (i)(2)).

money home mortgage loans, such as refinancings, second mortgages, and home equity lines of credit. The Fed amended Regulation Z, effective October 1, 2002, to provide that HOEPA was applicable to first mortgage nonpurchase money loans with an APR of 10% or more above that on treasury securities of comparable maturity, and that HOEPA was applicable to loans secured by second or subordinate mortgages on the borrower's home when the APR was 8% or more above that on comparable treasury securities. In addition, HOEPA is applicable if the loan's points or fees are 8% or more of the loan amount. The amended regulation adds to the fee calculation the cost of optional credit life insurance. Finally, the revised regulations ban refinancing (or "flipping") of a HOEPA loan within the first year after it is closed, unless the refinancing is in the borrower's interest. See 66 Fed. Reg. 65,604 (Dec. 20, 2001) (codified at 12 C.F.R. pt. 226). Furthermore, a purchaser of a loan that violates HOEPA may be liable for the HOEPA violation.

The OCC issued guidelines under 12 U.S.C. § 1831p–1, which sets forth standards for safety and soundness, Establishing Standards for Residential Mortgage Lending Practices, 70 Fed. Reg. 6329 (Feb. 7, 2005) (12 C.F.R. pt. 30, App. C) (effective April 8, 2005).

> The Guidelines describe particular practices inconsistent with sound residential mortgage lending practices. They also describe other terms and practices that may be conducive to predatory, abusive, unfair, or deceptive lending practices, depending on the circumstances, and which, accordingly, warrant a heightened degree of care by lenders.

Id. If a national bank or its operating subsidiary fails to meet a standard set forth in the guidelines, the OCC may issue a Notice of Deficiency and require the institution to submit a compliance plan to the OCC for its approval. Noncompliance with an approved plan may trigger other OCC enforcement actions, including civil money penalties.

An Interagency Guidance on Nontraditional Mortgage Product Risks, 71 Fed. Reg. 58609 (Oct. 4, 2006), addressed nontraditional mortgage products that have increased from 2% of the mortgage loan market in 2000 to approximately 30% of the market in 2006. In high-priced real estate markets, it is estimated that nontraditional mortgages account for half of the mortgage loan volume.[35] The guidance applies to "interest-only mortgage loans" and "payment option ARMs" which are defined in an Appendix to the guidance as:

> Interest-only Mortgage Loan—A nontraditional mortgage on which, for a specified number of years (e.g., three or five years), the borrower is required to pay only the interest due on the loan during which time the rate may fluctuate or may be fixed. After the interest-only period, the rate may be fixed or fluctuate based on the prescribed index and payments include both principal and interest.

---

35. See Mara Der Horvanesian's article, Nightmare Mortgages, Bus. Wk., Sept. 11, 2006, at 70.

Payment Option ARM—A nontraditional mortgage that allows the borrower to choose from a number of different payment options. For example, each month, the borrower may choose a minimum payment option based on a "start" or introductory interest rate, an interest-only payment option based on the fully indexed interest rate, or a fully amortizing principal and interest payment option based on a 15–year or 30–year loan term, plus any required escrow payments. The minimum payment option can be less than the interest accruing on the loan, resulting in negative amortization. The interest-only option avoids negative amortization but does not provide for principal amortization. After a specified number of years, or if the loan reaches a certain negative amortization cap, the required monthly payment amount is recast to require payments that will fully amortize the outstanding balance over the remaining loan term.

Id. at 58618.

The guidance cautions institutions to evaluate the borrower's ability to repay at the "fully indexed rate, assuming a fully amortizing repayment schedule," and that for products the may permit negative amortization, "the repayment analysis should be based upon the initial loan amount plus any balance increase that may accrue from the negative amortization provision." Id. at 58614.

Some of the principles of this statement were applied in the summer of 2007 to an interagency statement that applied to a broader set of mortgage products.

INTERAGENCY STATEMENT
STATEMENT ON SUBPRIME MORTGAGE LENDING

72 Fed. Reg. 37569 (July 10, 2007).

* * * The Agencies are concerned borrowers may not fully understand the risks and consequences of obtaining products that can cause payment shock.[36] In particular, the Agencies are concerned with certain adjustable-rate mortgage (ARM) products typically offered to subprime borrowers that have one or more of the following characteristics:

- Low initial payments based on a fixed introductory rate that expires after a short period and then adjusts to a variable index rate plus a margin for the remaining term of the loan;[37]

- Very high or no limits on how much the payment amount or the interest rate may increase ("payment or rate caps") on reset dates;

---

36. [n.10] Payment shock refers to a significant increase in the amount of the monthly payment that generally occurs as the interest rate adjusts to a fully indexed basis. Products with a wide spread between the initial interest rate and the fully indexed rate that do not have payment caps or periodic interest rate caps, or that contain very high caps, can produce significant payment shock.

37. [n.11] For example, ARMs known as "2/28" loans feature a fixed rate for two years and then adjust to a variable rate for the remaining 28 years. The spread between the initial fixed interest rate and the fully indexed interest rate in effect at loan origination typically ranges from 300 to 600 basis points.

Limited or no documentation of borrowers' income; Product features likely to result in frequent refinancing to maintain an affordable monthly payment; and/or

- Substantial prepayment penalties and/or prepayment penalties that extend beyond the initial fixed interest rate period.

Products with one or more of these features present substantial risks to both consumers and lenders. These risks are increased if borrowers are not adequately informed of the product features and risks, including their responsibility for paying real estate taxes and insurance, which may be separate from their monthly mortgage payments. The consequences to borrowers could include: being unable to afford the monthly payments after the initial rate adjustment because of payment shock; experiencing difficulty in paying real estate taxes and insurance that were not escrowed; incurring expensive refinancing fees, frequently due to closing costs and prepayment penalties, especially if the prepayment penalty period extends beyond the rate adjustment date; and losing their homes. Consequences to lenders may include unwarranted levels of credit, legal, compliance, reputation, and liquidity risks due to the elevated risks inherent in these products. * * *

Subprime lending is not synonymous with predatory lending, and loans with the features described above are not necessarily predatory in nature. However, institutions should ensure that they do not engage in the types of predatory lending practices discussed in the Expanded Subprime Guidance. Typically, predatory lending involves at least one of the following elements:

- Making loans based predominantly on the foreclosure or liquidation value of a borrower's collateral rather than on the borrower's ability to repay the mortgage according to its terms;

- Inducing a borrower to repeatedly refinance a loan in order to charge high points and fees each time the loan is refinanced ("loan flipping"); or

- Engaging in fraud or deception to conceal the true nature of the mortgage loan obligation, or ancillary products, from an unsuspecting or unsophisticated borrower.

Institutions offering mortgage loans such as these face an elevated risk that their conduct will violate Section 5 of the Federal Trade Commission Act (FTC Act), which prohibits unfair or deceptive acts or practices. * * *

Prudent qualifying standards recognize the potential effect of payment shock in evaluating a borrower's ability to service debt. An institution's analysis of a borrower's repayment capacity should include an evaluation of the borrower's ability to repay the debt by its final maturity at the fully indexed rate,[38] assuming a fully amortizing repayment sched-

---

38. The fully indexed rate equals the index rate prevailing at origination plus the margin to be added to it after the expiration of an introductory interest rate. For example, assume that a

ule.[39]

One widely accepted approach in the mortgage industry is to quantify a borrower's repayment capacity by a debt-to-income (DTI) ratio. An institution's DTI analysis should include, among other things, an assessment of a borrower's total monthly housing-related payments (e.g., principal, interest, taxes, and insurance, or what is commonly known as PITI) as a percentage of gross monthly income. * * *

Recognizing that loans to subprime borrowers present elevated credit risk, institutions should verify and document the borrower's income (both source and amount), assets and liabilities. Stated income and reduced documentation loans to subprime borrowers should be accepted only if there are mitigating factors that clearly minimize the need for direct verification of repayment capacity. Reliance on such factors also should be documented. Typically, mitigating factors arise when a borrower with favorable payment performance seeks to refinance an existing mortgage with a new loan of a similar size and with similar terms, and the borrower's financial condition has not deteriorated. Other mitigating factors might include situations where a borrower has substantial liquid reserves or assets that demonstrate repayment capacity and can be verified and documented by the lender. * * *

Communications with consumers, including advertisements, oral statements, and promotional materials, should provide clear and balanced information about the relative benefits and risks of the products. This information should be provided in a timely manner to assist consumers in the product selection process, not just upon submission of an application or at consummation of the loan. * * *

* * * Consumers should be informed of:

- Payment Shock. Potential payment increases, including how the new payment will be calculated when the introductory fixed rate expires.[40]

- Prepayment Penalties. The existence of any prepayment penalty, how it will be calculated, and when it may be imposed.

---

loan with an initial fixed rate of 7% will reset to the six-month London Interbank Offered Rate (LIBOR) plus a margin of 6%. If the six-month LIBOR rate equals 5.5%, lenders should qualify the borrower at 11.5% (5.5% + 6%), regardless of any interest rate caps that limit how quickly the fully indexed rate may be reached.

39. The fully amortizing payment schedule should be based on the term of the loan. For example, the amortizing payment for a "2/ 28" loan would be calculated based on a 30–year amortization schedule. For balloon mortgages that contain a borrower option for an extended amortization period, the fully amortizing payment schedule can be based on the full term the borrower may choose.

40. [n.23] To illustrate: a borrower earning $42,000 per year obtains a $200,000 "2/28" mortgage loan. The loan's two-year introductory fixed interest rate of 7% requires a principal and interest payment of $1,331. Escrowing $200 per month for taxes and insurance results in a total monthly payment of $1,531 ($1,331 + $200), representing a 44% DTI ratio. A fully indexed interest rate of 11.5% (based on a six-month LIBOR index rate of 5.5% plus a 6% margin) would cause the borrower's principal and interest payment to increase to $1,956. The adjusted total monthly payment of $2,156 ($1,956 + $200 for taxes and insurance) represents a 41% increase in the payment amount and results in a 62% DTI ratio.

- Balloon Payments. The existence of any balloon payment.

- Cost of Reduced Documentation Loans. Whether there is a pricing premium attached to a reduced documentation or stated income loan program.

- Responsibility for Taxes and Insurance. The requirement to make payments for real estate taxes and insurance in addition to their loan payments, if not escrowed, and the fact that taxes and insurance costs can be substantial. * * *

The interagency statements and guidances were directed only to banks and were not mandatory. Nonbank lenders could operate in this arena in states that did not have anti-predatory lending legislation. Thus, predatory lending continued, largely unabated by these regulatory efforts.

In the first six months of 2007, mortgage foreclosures were up 58% over the same period in 2006. By the summer of 2007, it was estimated that 13% of subprime mortgage loans were in or near foreclosure. A number of factors contributed to this increase, including poorly underwritten loans to borrowers who stated their income, but did not supply any documentation of their income (so-called "no doc" or "low doc" loans). Market conditions also played a role, as the increase in housing prices slowed, and in some areas, prices decreased. Finally, the low "teaser" rates on some adjustable rate loans reset to higher rates, increasing the payments beyond what the borrowers could afford. Regulators responded to this increase by encouraging financial institutions to enter into constructive workout arrangements with borrowers who may not be able to meet their mortgage payment obligations and forestall the devastation of foreclosure. Interagency Statement, Working with Mortgage Borrowers, Apr. 18, 2007, available at <www.occ.treas.gov/ftp/bulletin/2007–14. html>.

The mortgage market itself was shocked by the increase in foreclosures. Some mortgage lenders who retained residuals from mortgage loan securitizations suffered the first losses on their investments when mortgages in the securitized loan pool defaulted. Credit rating agencies downgraded some of the debt instruments issued by loan pools that contained subprime loans or securities issued in subprime mortgage securitizations. Some subprime mortgage originators failed. As a result, investors were reluctant to buy new securities and the availability of mortgage credit decreased.

The mortgage foreclosure problem was soon termed a "crisis."[41] Voluntary modifications and renegotiations of mortgage terms were encouraged, but in some cases mortgage loans that were held in a securitization vehicle could not be modified. The servicers (often the banks or

---

41. See Kathryn E. Johnson & Carolyn E. Waldrep, Note, The North Carolina Banking Institute Symposium on the Foreclosure Crisis: Overview, 14 N.C. Banking Inst. 191 (2010).

others who originated the loans) who received the mortgage payments and distributed them to the investors, were sometimes prohibited by the pooling and servicing agreements governing the securitization from modifying the mortgages in the loan pool. Many servicers did not have adequate personnel to work on modifications even when they were permitted. If there was a second lien—a junior mortgage or line of credit—on the property, sometimes the second lienholder stood in the way of a modification, since its lien was usually extinguished in a modification by the decline in the value of the property. The Federal government's response to the crisis included the Hope for Homeowners Act, which was part of the Housing and Economic Recovery Act of 2008. The idea behind this act was to encourage refinancing of troubled mortgages for borrowers who could afford a new FHA-insured loan. The program was remarkably unsuccessful, in part because of steep fees imposed upon the refinancing borrower and complexities in the program's requirements. In February 2009, the Obama Administration announced its Making Home Affordable plan, as a part of its overall financial stability plan responding to the financial crisis. One aspect of the plan was call the Home Affordable Modification Program (HAMP). The goal of HAMP is to reduce a borrower's mortgage payments so that his total debt payments do not exceed 31% of his pre-tax income. A trial modification period must be successfully completed, before a permanent mortgage modification is made. Not as many permanent mortgage modifications as hoped have resulted from HAMP. Congress enacted the Helping Families Save their Homes Act on May 20, 2009. This Act instituted adjustments to the prior programs to increase incentives for servicers and lenders to participate, and granted immunity to servicers from lawsuits claiming they wrongfully modified loans in the securitized mortgage pool. The immunity is available so long as the servicer can show that investors in the securitization would be better off as a result of the modification.[42]

Many states responded to the foreclosure crisis with their own efforts to provide relief to underwater borrowers. Some efforts have been more successful than others. Unfortunately, many of the mortgages that were modified became delinquent again in a few months. So long as negative equity in homes and high unemployment—a lethal combination—continue, the foreclosure crisis will likely persist.

In Title XIV of the Dodd–Frank Act, the Mortgage Reform and Anti–Predatory Lending Act, Congress directly addressed many of the problems with mortgage lending practices and predatory loans highlighted above. Of great significance, the BCFP has regulation, examination, and enforcement authority over any person that offers a financial product or service to a consumer. Thus, mortgage lenders, mortgage servicers, and mortgage brokers, even though not affiliated with a bank, are regulated by the BCFP. Title XIV of Dodd–Frank applies to all mortgage related products

---

42. See Leila A. Hicks, Note, The North Carolina Banking Institute Symposium on the Foreclosure Crisis: The Unintended and Unconstitutional Consequences of the Helping Families Save Their Homes Mortgage Servicers Litigation Safe Harbor, 14 N.C. Banking Inst. 237 (2010).

and services and not just to subprime or predatory loans, although "non-qualified" and "high-cost" mortgage loans are subject to additional restrictions.

Dodd–Frank provides as a general matter that a mortgage loan may not be made without the lender making a reasonable and good faith determination that the consumer borrower has the ability to repay the loan. Dodd–Frank Act, § 1411. This determination should include an examination of the consumer's credit history, income and expected income, debt-to-income ratio, employment status, and other available financial resources. Moreover, the lender must verify the borrower's income that it relies upon in making the ability to repay determination using tax returns or third-party income documentation. This requirement may affect community banks that use a model of "character" lending that is based on their personal knowledge and experience with local borrowers instead of mathematical formulas.

A "qualified" mortgage loan is defined in Dodd–Frank generally as a fixed-rate, conventional mortgage with points and fees that are 3% or less of the loan balance where the borrower is within a debt-to-income ratio set forth by the BCFP. Dodd–Frank Act, § 1412. An adjustable rate mortgage could also be a qualified mortgage if the borrower qualified for the loan based on the maximum interest rate permitted under the loan during its first five years and if the loan's payment schedule had it fully paid off (amortized) by the due date. There are several advantages for the lender who makes a "qualified mortgage." First, if the mortgage is a qualified mortgage, the lender may assume that the ability to repay standard has been satisfied. Secondly, there is an exemption for qualified mortgages from the originator's requirement to retain 5% of the risk when mortgages are sold by the lender. Dodd–Frank Act, § 941.

For a "high-cost" mortgage loan, the lender is subject to additional restrictions regarding prepayment penalties and balloon payments and is subject to additional prohibitions including charging fees to modify or defer a payment, making the loan without required pre-loan counseling, and financing of points and fees. A "high-cost" loan finding is triggered by excessive interest (an annual percentage rate 6.5% above the average prime offer as published by the BCFP), excessive points and fees (more than 5% of the transaction amount for loans greater than $20,000), or an onerous prepayment penalty (where the lender may charge a prepayment penalty more than three years after the closing date or the prepayment penalty exceeds more than 2% of the prepaid amount). Dodd–Frank Act, § 1431.

On first lien mortgage loans where the loan amount is within the conforming limit[43] and the annual percentage rate (APR) is more than 1.5% above the average prime offer, there must be an escrow established for the borrower to prepay on a monthly basis a pro rata portion of the

---

43. The conforming loan amount is the maximum principal amount of a loan that Fannie Mae or Freddie Mac will purchase pursuant to their guidelines.

annual property taxes and property and casualty insurance on the home. Dodd–Frank Act, § 1461. If the loan is greater than the conforming loan amount and the APR is more than 2.5% above the average prime offer, the tax and insurance escrow must be maintained.

The Dodd–Frank Act also places additional restrictions on the actions of servicers, including, for instance, requiring them to send an accurate pay-off statement to the borrower within a reasonable time after it is requested, not to exceed seven days after the borrower's written request.

As discussed in the prior section on RESPA, the Dodd–Frank Act now prohibits compensation, sometimes referred to as a yield spread premium, to a mortgage originator that varies based on the loan's terms (other than the principal amount of the loan). Dodd–Frank Act, § 1403. The BCFP will also adopt rules to prohibit a mortgage originator from steering a consumer who would be eligible for a "qualified mortgage" to a non-qualified mortgage loan, and from steering a consumer to a loan that has predatory characteristics, such as excessive fees or abusive terms.

QUESTIONS AND NOTES

1.   Sargeant was awarded attorneys fees of almost $80,000, 32 F.Supp.2d 21 (D. Mass. 1999), in the case reprinted earlier in this section. The court rejected United's argument that attorneys fees should not be awarded because Sargeant's attorneys' representation was undertaken on a *pro bono* basis.

2.   In their article, A Tale of Three Markets: The Law and Economics of Predatory Lending, 80 Tex. L. Rev. 1255 (2002), Professors Kathleen C. Engel and Patricia A. McCoy propose as a remedy for predatory lending:

> a duty of suitability in subprime mortgage lending. In fashioning a suitability remedy, we draw on the suitability requirement in securities and insurance to impose a similar obligation on subprime lenders and brokers, albeit one that is tailored to the subprime mortgage market. This new duty of suitability puts the onus of preventing predatory lending on those who can afford it most cheaply (i.e., predatory lenders and brokers) by authorizing the federal government and aggrieved victims to sue for loan reformation, disgorgement, and damages. In addition, we propose formation of an industry self-regulatory organization under federal supervision to promote the development of best-practices rules. Our position is that suitability successfully balances the need to curb predatory lending and the need to encourage beneficial market activity.

Is the Dodd–Frank Act's requirement that the lender determine that the borrower has the ability to repay the mortgage loan a form of suitability requirement? A "qualified mortgage" is not subject to the ability to repay standard, but are there other safeguards in place that help to ensure that the loan is suitable for the borrower?

3.   Compare the provisions of the Dodd–Frank Act related to a "high-cost" mortgage loan in the Dodd–Frank Act, § 1431, to a state anti-predatory lending law, and then advise a mortgage lender in that state whether it is subject to both statutes and how it would comply with both.

4. Among the non-traditional mortgages are "reverse mortgages" that allow homeowners to make monthly borrowings using the equity in their home as security. These loans are directed to retirees who do not want to sell their homes but need more income and would like to draw down on the appreciation in the value of their property. How, if at all, do the recent Interagency statements affect these products?

The Dodd–Frank Act requires the BCFP to conduct a study of reverse mortgages and their suitability for borrowers. See generally Annie E. Nelson, Note, Reverse Mortgages: Changes Brought About by the Housing and Economic Recovery Act, 13 N.C. Banking Inst. 337 (2009). The BCFP is directed to identify and prohibit abusive practices associated with such loans and to provide for integrated disclosure standards. Dodd–Frank Act, § 1076. The legislation also provides for grants to develop means to protect seniors from misleading marketing material.

5. The Dodd–Frank Act also addressed the role of appraisers. During the subprime mortgage crisis, many appraisals were fraudulently or incompetently inflated. In addition to banning false appraisals, the legislation requires an appraisal before high-risk mortgage loans may be made, and a second appraisal is required in some instances. Dodd–Frank Act, §§ 1471–73. Appraisers must be certified or licensed by a state and are subject to independence principles designed to remove conflicts of interest with loan originators.

6. The Dodd–Frank Act requires the HUD Secretary to prepare a study on shared appreciation mortgages in which the lender shares in equity appreciation of the home at the time of its sale in exchange for reduced or no interest payments. Dodd–Frank Act, § 1406.

SECTION 7. PAYDAY LENDING

Payday loans are often made by nonbanks. By definition, the borrower must have a checking account at a bank. The payday lender loans the borrower an amount, say $100, in return for the borrower's check in the amount of $115, dated the date of the borrower's next payday. The borrower gets an immediate loan for a short term without putting up any security. Usually no credit check or loan application is involved. The lender receives a very high return on an annualized basis. In the example just given, the annual percentage rate (APR) is 390% if the loan is outstanding for two weeks. One reason for the popularity of payday loans is that borrowers who maintain low balances in their checking accounts are fearful of writing bad checks and incurring the high bad check fees charged by their bank and the recipient of the bad check.

The payday lending industry was virtually non-existent fifteen years ago. In 2007, however, payday lenders earned about $6 billion per year in revenue. State regulation of payday lenders is uneven. Some states prohibit outright the practices of payday lenders by capping interest rates on small loans or specifically prohibiting payday lending. Some states regulate payday lending by specific statutes. Finally, a third group of states does not regulate payday lending at all.[44]

Where state laws limit payday lending, some payday lenders have partnered with banks in states that do not prohibit the high interest rate loans. In the typical partnership, the bank makes the loan to the out-of-state customer and sells it to the payday lender who solicited the customer. The exportation of the bank's interest rate from its home state to the customer's state follows under 12 U.S.C.A. §§ 85 & 1831d, discussed earlier in this chapter.

Payday lenders sought to enjoin the application of a Georgia statute regulating payday lending, arguing that it was preempted for out-of-state banks pursuant to the federal interest rate exportation statutes. BankWest, Inc. v. Baker, 324 F.Supp.2d 1333 (N.D.Ga. 2004) (holding that payday lenders and their bank partners were not entitled to a preliminary injunction to prevent the application of the law because 12 U.S.C.A. § 1831d did not preempt the Georgia payday lending legislation). The Eleventh Circuit affirmed the district court's decision and upheld the Georgia law. The Georgia law makes any loan to a consumer pursuant to an agency relationship between an in-state payday store and an out-of-state bank subject to the Georgia usury limits if the in-state agent holds a "predominate economic interest" in the revenue (defined as over 50% of the revenue) generated by the loan. BankWest v. Baker, 411 F.3d 1289 (11th Cir. 2005). The court found that since the in-state payday store retained 81% of the loan revenue, the in-state payday store is subject to the Georgia usury laws which would forbid the loan at the payday loan rates. The court refused to give deference to the FDIC's position, stating that it does "not defer to agency positions, whether formal or informal, on preemption issues." Id. at 1300. The dissent disagreed with the court's preemption analysis and argued that under the facts

> BankWest is the true lender. It is not only identified as such in the loan documents, but it also performed all of the critical loan decision-making functions, supplies all of the funds for the loan, is the only one exposed to any loss of principal, and has borne most of the loan losses that have actually occurred.

Id. at 1314.

BankWest had been accepted to be reheard *en banc* by the Eleventh Circuit when the State of Georgia suggested that the appeal was moot. The *en banc* court vacated its order granting rehearing and remanded to the panel to consider mootness. On remand, the panel dismissed the appeal as moot and vacated the district court decision. BankWest, Inc. v. Baker, 446 F.3d 1358 (11th Cir. 2006). Pursuant to the 2005 FDIC Guidelines (discussed below) that limited the number and duration of payday loans, the out-of-state banks had ended their relationship with their in-state payday store partners, thus ending the case and controversy.

---

44. See generally Scott A. Schaaf, Note, From Checks to Cash: The Regulation of the Payday Lending Industry, 5 N.C. Banking Inst. 339 (2001).

The North Carolina Commissioner of Banks ruled that Advance America, Cash Advance Centers of North Carolina, Inc., although operating in North Carolina through an out-of-state bank, is not a bank entitled to take make loans at a rate of interest forbidden in North Carolina, but authorized for an out-of-state bank in its home state under 12 U.S.C. § 1831d.[45]

The OCC, the OTS, and the Fed expressed concern about banks making their charters available for the purpose of exporting favorable usury laws to payday loan outlets located in usury-restrictive states. See Office of the Comptroller of the Currency, Advisory Letter 2000–10 Payday Lending (Nov. 27, 2000) (detailing some of the risks of payday lending, including credit risk, transaction risk, concentration risk, reputation risk, and compliance and legal risks). The OCC entered into consent orders with Eagle National Bank located in Darby, Pennsylvania, and Goleta National Bank in California, in which the banks agreed to cease their payday lending activities. In the case of Eagle National Bank, the OCC found that by concentrating in payday lending, the bank had risked its financial viability, that it had relinquished supervision of this program to a third party provider (Dollar Financial Group), and that its payday lending program violated a number of standards of safe and sound banking. Fact Sheet: Eagle National Bank Consent Order (Jan. 3, 2002), <www.occ.treas.gov/ftp/release/2002–01a.doc>.

On the other hand, although the OCC issued an order requiring Peoples National Bank in Paris, Texas, to cease and desist from making payday loans and issued it an "unsatisfactory" examination rating, Peoples was the most profitable small bank in Texas due to the dramatic increase in its interest income since it entered into payday lending. The bank's payday loans are marketed and serviced by Advance America Cash Advance Centers.[46] Pursuant to the OCC's cease and desist order, Peoples ended its association with Advance America and paid $175,000 in civil money penalties. In 2004, Peoples converted to a state charter.

The FDIC has not interfered with state nonmember banks wishing to engage in payday lending partnerships, although it issued guidelines for those partnerships in 2003.[47] At that time, approximately eleven state nonmember banks were engaged in payday lending partnerships. The FDIC issued revised payday lending guidance effective July 1, 2005. The guidelines stated that "providing high-cost, short-term credit on a recurring basis to customers with long-term credit needs is not responsible lending and increases banks' credit, legal, reputational and compliance risks." FDIC, Guidelines for Payday Lending, FIL–14–2005 (Mar. 1, 2005),

---

45. In re: Advance America, Cash Advance Centers of North Carolina, Inc. Docket No: 05–008:CF (Dec. 22, 2005), available at <www.nccob.org/NCCOB/ConsumerIndustries/CheckCashers/AdvanceAmerica.htm>. See also Scott A. Hefner, Payday Lending in North Carolina: Now You See It, Now You Don't, 11 N.C. Banking Inst. 263 (2007).

46. John Reosti, Fighting for Payday Loans, Am. Banker, Oct. 22, 2002.

47. Federal Deposit Insurance Corporation, Guidelines for Payday Lending, available at <www.fdic.gov/news/news/financial/2005/fill405a.html>.

available at <www.fdic.gov/news/news/financial/2005/fil1405a.html>. The guidelines specifically provide that FDIC-supervised institutions that engage in payday lending must submit a plan that details how they will address the new guidance, including its requirement that banks ensure that payday loans not be made to customers who have had payday loans outstanding from any lender for a total of three months out of the previous twelve months. This limits a customer to no more than six two-week loans in a year.

In 2007, the FDIC issued Affordable Small–Dollar Loan Guidelines, available at <www.fdic.gov/news/news/press/2007/pr07052a.html> to encourage banks to develop loan products of under $1,000, with interest rates below 35%, and with pay periods lasting beyond a single pay cycle. The FDIC noted that there is high demand for reasonably priced small-dollar loans and that providing such products to existing bank customers, "can help institutions retain these customers and avoid the reputation risk associated with high-cost products." Those institutions that participate in a two-year pilot program offering these products are eligible for favorable CRA consideration.

In 2006, Congress enacted legislation, described in Section 1 of this Chapter, limiting the interest rate that may be charged on payday loans to service members and their dependents to 36%.

A "covered person" subject to the BCFP under the Dodd–Frank Act includes any nondepository institutions that offer or provide payday loans to consumers. See Dodd–Frank Act, § 1024. The BCFP may require reports from payday lenders and examine them to ensure compliance with consumer financial protection laws. Moreover, they are subject to the rulemaking authority of the BCFP.

The Treasury Secretary is authorized in Dodd–Frank to establish demonstration programs for low-cost, small dollar value loans to consumers to provide alternatives to more costly loans like payday loans. Dodd–Frank Act, §§ 1204–05. These loans must be made on terms that are "reasonable" and in accordance with "reasonable" lending practices. Grants will be made available to assist in establishing these demonstration programs. Grantees must provide financial literacy and education opportunities to consumers who receive loans from them.

QUESTIONS AND NOTES

1.   Should banks be serving this market need as suggested by the FDIC? Could banks provide a competing product or should banks instead reduce the fee charged for a bad check? Should banks encourage all customers to have overdraft lines of credit? Are the bounce protection programs offered by banks (described further in Chapter 7) merely payday lending programs in disguise?

2.   Bank regulators and consumer advocates criticize payday loans for having an excessively high interest rate. Bank regulators also worry that payday loans expose banks to excessive credit losses and may therefore be

"unsafe and unsound." Are these two concerns inconsistent with each other? Could it be argued that the high costs are necessary to compensate for the risk and ensure the banks will not suffer undue credit losses? See Creola Johnson, Payday Loans: Shrewd Business or Predatory Lending? 87 Minn. L. Rev. 1 (2002).

3. The greatest concern for payday loans seems to be for borrowers who do not have enough funds in their checking account to honor the post-dated check when it is due, and thus "rollover" the loan for an additional two-week period upon the payment of an additional fee. This dramatically adds to the already high APR for the initial loan. The typical payday loan borrower takes out seven loans per year. Christopher Conkey, Payday Lenders Strike a Defensive Pose, Wall St. J., Feb. 21, 2007.

4. Does TILA apply to payday loans, requiring disclosure of the typically high APR? See Brown v. Payday Check Advance, Inc., 202 F.3d 987 (7th Cir. 2000) (applying TILA to a payday lending transaction); Thomas A. Wilson, Note, The Availability of Statutory Damages Under TILA to Remedy the Sharp Practice of Payday Lenders, 7 N.C. Banking Inst. 339 (2003) (discussing the application of TILA to payday loans and the availability of statutory damages under TILA).

5. According to the Center for Responsible Lending, payday loans cost borrowers $4.2 billion per year in excessive fees. Center for Responsible Lending, Financial Quicksand: Payday lending sinks borrowers in debt with $4.2 billion in predatory fees every year (Nov. 30, 2006), available at <www.responsiblelending.org/payday-lending/research-analysis/rr012–Financial_Quicksand–1106.pdf>.

6. The financial crisis resulted in much new regulation and imposed restrictions on payday and other high interest consumer loans. As one report noted:

> On July 1, [2010,] Arizona will force changes on the state's 595 payday-loan stores—outfits that make high-interest loans against future paychecks—that could effectively put them out of business. Wisconsin banned small loans backed by car titles that led many people to lose their vehicles. Arkansas, Maine and New York joined other states in putting curbs on tax preparers who offer costly loans against expected tax refunds. * * *

> "It's a pace of regulatory output we've never seen before in the consumer area," says Richard Hackett, who teaches consumer-finance law at Boston University's Morin Center for Banking and Financial Law.

Sudeep Reddy, Upheaval Sweeps Consumer Finance, Wall St. J., June 25, 2010.

CHAPTER SEVEN

BANK LIABILITIES AND CAPITAL

■ ■ ■

The funds for a bank's operations come from its liabilities and capital. Bank liabilities consist of deposit and non-deposit liabilities. Bank customers with checking and savings accounts at a bank lend the amounts on deposit to the bank. In return, the bank may pay interest on those accounts and promises to repay the customer upon the customer's demand to withdraw the funds. In addition to deposits, banks receive funds from the federal funds market, repurchase agreements, and subordinated notes and debentures. A bank's capital is its permanent source of funds that need not be paid back to any person. When a bank is formed and sells stock, the proceeds received from that initial stock offering constitute the bank's paid in capital. If the bank has net income in a particular year, its board of directors will determine how much of that income, if any, to pay out to shareholders in the form of a dividend. Whatever net income is left after any dividend payments is called retained earnings and is added to a bank's capital. Conversely, if a bank suffers a loss, the amount of the loss is deducted from the capital account. Sufficient capital is necessary to support a bank's operations and provide an adequate cushion to absorb any losses in income experienced by the bank.

SECTION 1. DEPOSITS

A. TYPES OF DEPOSIT ACCOUNTS

Banks offer various kinds of deposit products. Demand deposits are called transaction accounts and offer check-writing privileges. From the time of the Banking Act of 1933 until July 21, 2011, interest was not permitted on demand deposits. The Dodd–Frank Act, however, permits the payment of interest beginning one year from the date of its enactment. Dodd–Frank Act, § 627. Since that Act also provides unlimited deposit insurance on non-interest bearing transaction accounts through December 31, 2012, business customers will need to select between earning interest on deposit accounts that offer $250,000 deposit insurance coverage, and forgoing interest for unlimited deposit insurance. Dodd–Frank Act, § 343. Interest bearing transaction accounts available to individual customers

465

earn int
or
unlimited coverage

include NOW (negotiable order of withdrawal) accounts. Accounts that do not offer check-writing privileges include passbook savings, retail time deposits, and retail certificates of deposit (CDs), as well as wholesale negotiable CDs that are sold usually in minimum $100,000 denominations and for which there is a recognized secondary market. Sometimes a distinction is made between "core" deposits and non-core deposits. Core deposits are stable deposits that are unlikely to leave the bank for a higher interest rate elsewhere. These deposits include all the deposit types listed above other than "brokered" deposits (discussed in more detail later in this Chapter) and wholesale negotiable CDs.

Core deposits are declining for most banks. One reason for this decline is that many customers have shifted their excess funds from bank products to higher-yielding investments offered by others. Banks have therefore increased their reliance on wholesale funding sources, which often carry higher interest costs than core deposits. The interest rate paid on FDIC-insured deposits is lower than the rate paid on other liabilities because the FDIC insurance eliminates the risk of nonpayment to the depositor. Moreover, there is an increased risk of losing wholesale funding to other institutions that pay higher rates or are perceived as better credit risks.

(1) Lifeline or Basic Accounts

A 2009 FDIC Survey estimated that 7.7% of U.S. households are unbanked, with another 17.9% underbanked.[1] The percentages are substantially higher for minority households: 54% of black households and 43.3% of Hispanic households are unbanked or underbanked. Low-income households account (with annual incomes below $30,000) account for 71% of the unbanked households. The most common reason given in the survey for not being banked was the feeling that the respondents did not have enough money to need a bank account. The respondents who used alternative financial service providers like check cashers cited the convenience, speed, and cost as the reasons they used these services. The various account fees that some banks charge their customers, including account maintenance fees for low balance accounts and overdraft fees for bounced checks, also discourage some populations from having bank accounts. See generally Michael S. Barr, Banking the Poor, 21 Yale J. on Reg. 121 (2004).

Notwithstanding the substantial population to be served, many banks have been reluctant to embrace programs to serve this customer segment. To the extent banks have not fulfilled the market need, alternative businesses, such as check cashers, have rushed to fill the void. It is estimated that the unbanked and underbanked segment of the population

---

1. FDIC, FDIC National Survey of Unbanked and Underbanked Households (Dec. 2009). "Unbanked" households were identified as those where no one in the household has a checking or savings account. "Underbanked" households were defined as households in which someone has a bank account, but in which alternative financial services such as check cashers or payday lenders are used at least once a year.

spend $11 billion annually on fees charged for "alternative" financial transactions at check cashing outlets and other such businesses.[2]

Title XII of the Dodd–Frank Act is titled, Improving Access to Mainstream Financial Institutions and authorized a program of grants to promote initiatives designed to increase access by low-and moderate-income individuals to accounts at federally insured banks that are appropriate to meet the financial needs of such persons. Dodd–Frank Act, § 1204.

(2) Certificates of Deposit

Certificates of deposit (CDs) evidence the deposit of funds in a bank for a stated period of time at a specified rate of interest. CDs have maturity dates that vary from a few days to several years. Common maturities are three months, six months, one year, three years and five years. A certificate of deposit is redeemable only at maturity. Upon redemption, the holder receives the principal amount invested plus accrued interest. Banks may impose penalties for early withdrawal of funds.

CDs

MARINE BANK v. WEAVER

Supreme Court of the United States, 1982.
455 U.S. 551.

Mr. CHIEF JUSTICE BURGER delivered the opinion of the Court.

We granted certiorari to decide whether two instruments, a conventional certificate of deposit and a business agreement between two families, could be considered securities under the antifraud provisions of the federal securities laws.

Respondents, Sam and Alice Weaver, purchased a $50,000 certificate of deposit from petitioner Marine Bank on February 28, 1978. The certificate of deposit has a 6–year maturity, and it is insured by the Federal Deposit Insurance Corporation.[3] The Weavers subsequently pledged the certificate of deposit to Marine Bank on March 17, 1978, to guarantee a $65,000 loan made by the bank to Columbus Packing Co. Columbus was a wholesale slaughterhouse and retail meat market which owed the bank $33,000 at that time for prior loans and was also substantially overdrawn on its checking account with the bank. * * *

$50K CD
6yr

The definition of "security" in the Securities Exchange Act of 1934 is quite broad. The Act was adopted to restore investors' confidence in the financial markets, and the term "security" was meant to include "the many types of instruments that in our commercial world fall within the

---

2. Ann Carrns, Branching Out: Banks Court a New Client: The Low–Income Earner, Wall St. J., Mar. 16, 2007.

3. [n.1] The certificate of deposit pays 7 1/2% interest and provides that, if the bank permits early withdrawal, the depositor will earn interest at the bank's current savings passbook rate on the amount withdrawn, except that no interest will be paid for the three months prior to withdrawal. When the Weavers purchased the certificate of deposit, it could only be insured up to $40,000 by the FDIC. The ceiling on insured deposits is now $100,000. Act of Mar. 31, 1980, Pub. L. 96–221, 94 Stat. 147, § 308(b)(1), 12 U.S.C. § 1724(b) (1976 ed., Supp. IV).

ordinary concept of a security." H. R. Rep. No. 85, 73d Cong., 1st Sess., 11 (1933); quoted in United Housing Foundation, Inc. v. Forman, 421 U.S. 837, 847–848 (1975). The statutory definition excludes only currency and notes with a maturity of less than nine months. It includes ordinary stocks and bonds, along with the "countless and variable schemes devised by those who seek the use of the money of others on the promise of profits. . . ." SEC v. W.J. Howey Co., 328 U.S. 293, 299 (1946). Thus, the coverage of the antifraud provisions of the securities laws is not limited to instruments traded at securities exchanges and over-the-counter markets, but extends to uncommon and irregular instruments. Superintendent of Insurance of New York v. Bankers Life & Casualty Co., 404 U.S. 6, 10 (1971); SEC v. C.M. Joiner Leasing Corp., 320 U.S. 344, 351 (1943). We have repeatedly held that the test " 'is what character the instrument is given in commerce by the terms of the offer, the plan of distribution, and the economic inducements held out to the prospect.' " SEC v. United Benefit Life Ins. Co., 387 U.S. 202, 211 (1967), quoting SEC v. C.M. Joiner Leasing Corp., supra, at 352–353.

The broad statutory definition is preceded, however, by the statement that the terms mentioned are not to be considered securities if "the context otherwise requires. . . ." Moreover, we are satisfied that Congress, in enacting the securities laws, did not intend to provide a broad federal remedy for all fraud. Great Western Bank & Trust v. Kotz, 532 F.2d 1252, 1253 (CA9 1976).

The Court of Appeals concluded that the certificate of deposit purchased by the Weavers might be a security. * * * The Court of Appeals also concluded that a certificate of deposit is similar to any other long-term debt obligation commonly found to be a security. In our view, however, there is an important difference between a bank certificate of deposit and other long-term debt obligations. This certificate of deposit was issued by a federally regulated bank which is subject to the comprehensive set of regulations governing the banking industry. Deposits in federally regulated banks are protected by the reserve, reporting, and inspection requirements of the federal banking laws; advertising relating to the interest paid on deposits is also regulated. In addition, deposits are insured by the Federal Deposit Insurance Corporation. Since its formation in 1933, nearly all depositors in failing banks insured by the FDIC have received payment in full, even payment for the portions of their deposits above the amount insured.

We see, therefore, important differences between a certificate of deposit purchased from a federally regulated bank and other long-term debt obligations. The Court of Appeals failed to give appropriate weight to the important fact that the purchaser of a certificate of deposit is virtually guaranteed payment in full, whereas the holder of an ordinary long-term debt obligation assumes the risk of the borrower's insolvency. The definition of "security" in the 1934 Act provides that an instrument which seems to fall within the broad sweep of the Act is not to be considered a security if the context otherwise requires. It is unnecessary to subject issuers of bank certificates of deposit to liability under the antifraud provisions of the federal securities laws since the holders of bank certificates of deposit are abundantly protected under the federal banking laws. We therefore hold that the certificate of deposit purchased by the Weavers is not a security. * * *

(3) Discriminatory Account Policies: The Truth in Savings Act

GARCIA-HARDING v. BANK MIDWEST, N.A.

United States District Court, District of Kansas, 1997.
964 F.Supp. 1492.

VRATIL, DISTRICT JUDGE.

Plaintiff Therisa Garcia–Harding initiated this action under Title VII of the Civil Rights Act of 1964, 42 U.S.C. § 2000e et seq. ("Title VII"), claiming that her former employer, defendant Bank Midwest, N.A. ("Bank Midwest"), harassed and discriminated against her on the basis of her national origin, Mexican–American. * * *

Bank Midwest requires customer service representatives to be cautious when opening accounts, especially accounts with small cash deposits or no cash deposits, because such accounts are frequently opened for fraudulent purposes. A customer service representative can refuse to open an account if he or she believes that the person attempting to open the account intends to defraud the bank or the merchant community. Bank Midwest represents to the public that it has no minimum balance requirement, however, and customer service representatives are not supposed to require a minimum deposit to open an account.[4] In addition, Bank Midwest does not require a waiting period before a customer can receive an ATM card; ATM cards are to be "instant" cards.

Contrary to these policies, Cooley [an assistant bank manager] instructed customer service representatives at 5th and Minnesota to require a $100 deposit from customers and wait 30 days before issuing ATM cards. Cooley claims that this instruction resulted from her mistaken belief regarding bank policy and that she reversed her instruction as soon as she discovered her mistake. Plaintiff alleges that in issuing the instruction Cooley intended to discriminate against certain bank customers. The walk-in population at 5th and Minnesota was mostly African–American, and plaintiff claims that customer service representatives applied Cooley's instruction inconsistently and based on appearances so as to have a disparate, deleterious effect on minority customers.

---

4. [n. 4] Pursuant to the Truth in Savings Act of 1991, contained in the Federal Deposit Insurance Corporation Improvement Act of 1991, 12 U.S.C. § 4301 et seq., and Regulation DD [12 C.F.R. pt. 230] promulgated thereunder, depository institutions must provide certain disclosures to consumers so that they may make meaningful comparisons among depository institutions and informed decisions about accounts at those depository institutions. Among other things, depository institutions are required to disclose minimum balance requirements to open an account. Although the record is unclear on this point, the Court assumes for purposes of this Memorandum and Order that Bank Midwest's disclosures under Regulation DD provide that Bank Midwest does not require a minimum deposit to open an account.

Compliance meeting) [handwritten]

On November 21, 1995, the bank's Internal Compliance Committee held a meeting. At the meeting, plaintiff learned that bank policy was to require no minimum deposit to open an account. Fisher [an assistant vice president in Deposit Operations responsible for ensuring that tellers were complying with bank procedures] stated at the meeting that the branch at 78th and State was requiring a $100 deposit and that such requirement violated the bank's disclosures. Plaintiff stated that 5th and Minnesota was doing the same thing. Fisher and Mike Majors, who was in charge of compliance, instructed those in attendance at the meeting that such practices violated the bank's disclosures and must stop. Plaintiff claims that management did not follow up on this issue and that management's attitude at the meeting was unconcerned.

P claims [handwritten]

Plaintiff claims that when she complained to Cooley about the minimum deposit and the ATM waiting period, Cooley told her that it was her branch and she could do what she wanted. Cooley denies this, and claims that as soon as plaintiff informed her that the bank's disclosures prohibited an initial minimum deposit, she stopped requiring one and instructed other customer service representatives to do likewise. * * *

[Plaintiff was terminated for insubordination] Kansas public policy prohibits terminating an employee in retaliation for the good faith reporting to company management or law enforcement authorities of a serious infraction of rules, regulations or laws pertaining to public health, safety or general welfare, i.e., whistleblowing. Palmer v. Brown, 752 P.2d 685 (1988). To maintain an action under this doctrine, plaintiff must prove that a reasonably prudent person would have concluded that her co-worker or employer was engaged in activities in violation of rules, regulations, or laws pertaining to public health, safety, and the general welfare; that the employer had knowledge of the employee's reporting of such violation prior to the employee's discharge; and that the employee was discharged in retaliation for making the report. Id. Defendant does not deny that plaintiff reported to bank management that some of its employees discriminated against customers on the basis of race. Defendant does not deny that such acts, if true, would constitute a serious infraction of laws pertaining to the general welfare.[5] Defendant only denies that it terminated plaintiff in retaliation for making such a report. As discussed above, plaintiff has raised an issue of fact as to defendant's motive for terminating her. Consequently, plaintiff's whistleblower claim cannot be summarily dismissed. * * *

Must prove [handwritten]

---

5. [n.11] Neither party has addressed whether an employee who reported to bank management a violation of Regulation DD disclosures alone would fall under the protection of the Palmer whistleblower doctrine. The Court need not decide that issue for purposes of this Memorandum and Order, but expects that the parties will brief the issue in their trial briefs so that the Court can rule upon it, the parties can present evidence accordingly, and the Court can instruct the jury appropriately.

B. REGULATION OF DEPOSIT ACCOUNTS

(1) Deposit Account Fees and ATM Fees

Banks increasingly rely on deposit-related fees as additional sources of income. Some banks impose account maintenance fees on certain types of accounts. Most banks assess fees for various extraordinary events such as stop payment orders, checks written against insufficient funds, or deposited checks that are dishonored. These fees average around $30, but are sometimes more. According to a Fed survey, surcharges for using the ATM of another bank are imposed by three-quarters of all banks.

Some states and municipalities have attempted to regulate bank fees under consumer protection statutes or regulations. National banks and the OCC have joined forces to challenge some of these laws, arguing that the National Bank Act preempts this sort of state legislation. The OCC's regulation at 12 C.F.R. § 7.4002 requires a bank to consider the cost (including its profit margin) in providing the service, the deterrent effect on customer behavior, the enhancement of the bank's competitive position in accordance with its marketing strategy, and the maintenance of the safety and soundness of the institution in setting reasonable non-interest charges and fees.

In the OCC's 2004 preemption regulations, it explicitly set forth the broad preemption standard that "state laws that obstruct, impair, or condition a national bank's ability to fully exercise its Federally authorized deposit-taking powers are not applicable to national banks." 12 C.F.R. § 7.4007(b)(1) (2010). The Dodd–Frank Act in Section 1044, as discussed in Chapter 4, cut back somewhat on this preemption standard for national banks.

Bank customers have challenged bank fees on various grounds. In Perdue v. Crocker National Bank, 702 P.2d 503 (Cal. 1985), appeal dismissed, 475 U.S. 1001 (1986), the California Supreme Court ignored the OCC's then brand new interpretive ruling, 12 C.F.R. § 7.4002, and found that Crocker's imposition of a $6 fee for an insufficient funds check could constitute price unconscionability since the plaintiff alleged that the charge amounted to a 2000% percent profit for the bank (substantive unconscionability) and there might have been an absence of meaningful choice based on ineffective disclosure of the charge (procedural unconscionability). The court remanded the case for a hearing to develop the underlying facts. The case was settled at considerable cost to Wells Fargo (which had acquired Crocker in 1986). Wells Fargo agreed to refund millions of dollars to customers who could prove they paid fees for writing bad checks. Attorneys estimated the settlement would cost Wells Fargo $10 million.[6] Another line of attack on allegedly excessive NSF fees is based on usury.

---

6. Michael A. Robinson, Wells Fargo Agrees to Refund Millions in Bad Check Fees, Am. Banker, Apr. 20, 1987.

VIDEO TRAX, INC. v. NATIONSBANK, N.A.

United States District Court, Southern District of Florida, 1998.
33 F.Supp.2d 1041, *aff'd*, 205 F.3d 1358 (11th Cir.),
cert. denied, 531 U.S. 822 (2000).

GOLD, DISTRICT JUDGE.

THIS CAUSE is before the Court upon cross motions for summary judgment by Plaintiff, Video Trax, Inc. ("Plaintiff"), and Defendant NationsBank, N.A. ("Defendant"). Plaintiff brought this class action pursuant to the National Bank Act, 12 U.S.C. §§ 85 and 86 (the "Bank Act"). Plaintiff alleges that the Overdraft Item Fee (the "OD fee") on checking accounts charged by Defendant, a national banking association, was actually a subterfuge to exact a usurious rate of interest in violation of the Bank Act. Defendant avers that the OD fee was an administrative cost to cover the processing of checks drawn in excess of the collected balance in a depositor's account, and was not interest as contemplated by the Bank Act and Florida's usury statute, §§ 687.01, et seq., Fla. Stat. Therefore, according to Defendant, since the OD fee is not "interest," it is not usurious. * * *

As a threshold matter, except as the term "interest" relates to credit transactions, such as loans or credit card services, no provision of federal law discusses bank charges for NFS [sic] checks, or, for that matter, bank charges for any service performed for depositors of checking accounts.

"Interest" as used in the Bank Act includes:

any payment compensating a creditor or prospective creditor for an extension of credit, making available of a line of credit, or any default or breach by a borrower of a condition upon which credit was extended. It includes, among other things, the following fees connected with credit extension or availability: numerical periodic rates, late fees, not sufficient funds (NSF) fees, overlimit fees, annual fees, cash advance fees, and membership fees. . . .

12 C.F.R. § 7.4001(a) (1997).[7] Because the OD fees were not imposed in connection with a credit transaction, the fees are not interest as defined by the Bank Act. Rather, the fee arises from the terms of the deposit agreements, which incorporate the schedule of fees. These types of charges are addressed by 12 C.F.R. § 7.4002, which provides:

(a) Customer charges and fees. A national bank may charge its customers non-interest charges and fees, including deposit account service charges. . . .

(b) Considerations. The establishment of non-interest charges and fees, and the amounts thereof, *is a business decision to be made by each bank, in its discretion, according to sound banking judgment and safe and sound banking principles.* A bank reasonably establishes non-interest charges and fees if the bank considers the following factors, among others:

(1) The cost incurred by the bank, plus a profit margin, in providing the service;

---

7. [eds.] The regulation was revised slightly in 2001. See 66 Fed. Reg. 34791 (July 2, 2001) (codified at 12 C.F.R.§ 7.4001(a)).

(2) The deterrence of misuse by customers of banking services;

(3) The enhancement of the competitive position of the bank in accordance with the bank's marketing strategy; and

(4) The maintenance of the safety and soundness of the institution.

(c) Interest. Charges and fees that are "interest" within the meaning of 12 U.S.C. 85 are governed by § 7.4001 and not by this section.

The OD fees charged by Defendant are precisely those described in § 7.4002.

Moreover, the fees at issue substantially satisfy the reasonableness factors set forth in 12 C.F.R. § 7.4002(b). Defendant's "Noninterest Income Project" report states that the bank's primary concern "is the extensive daily aggregate work effort by the branches and officers expended in the processing of NSF/OD transactions . . . [which] requires substantial review and intervention by the branches and officers." Defendant determined that the decision to pay or return a check "sends a distinct message to the customer as to whether their behavior is to be encouraged or discouraged."

Analyzing the pattern of customer behavior and recognizing the additional financial risk to the bank, Defendant concluded that, since the majority of the potential overdraft checks are eventually honored, and the fact that the bank receives no additional fees when the item is presented a second time, honoring the check the first time provides little additional risk. Nevertheless, Plaintiff challenges Defendant's application of the considerations prescribed in § 7.4002(b), claiming that the fees are excessive for the services rendered. Plaintiff alleges that the cost analysis, based on the amount of the OD fee and the actual expense incurred by Defendant for processing an overdrawn check, does not justify the amount of the fee imposed. However, <u>Plaintiff has presented no evidence to substantiate its accusation that the OD fees were unconscionable and were imposed in contravention of the considerations required for analyzing and assessing the propriety of the fees.</u>[8]

Even if Plaintiff proffered competent evidence of profit percentages, such evidence does not automatically prove that the fees were unreasonable. In fact, the Code of Federal Regulations permit nationally chartered

[handwritten margin notes: P: ① Excessive fee for service ② No evidence by P to support AND banks allowed to add profit margin to OD admin. cost]

---

8. [n.5] Plaintiff complains that Defendant has not produced documentation of cost versus profit analysis. However, 12 U.S.C. § 484 provides that "no national bank shall be subject to any visitorial powers except as authorized by Federal Law." Cases construing this section do not clarify when an unauthorized person or agency may, without violating this section, examine bank records for a limited purpose. Thus, it is possible that § 484 may serve to limit Plaintiff's ability to examine records by way of discovery. Nevertheless, Defendant has represented that the cost analysis records requested by Plaintiff do not exist. Therefore, Plaintiff was required to support its argument of the unreasonableness of the amount of the OD fee using other methods.

banks to recover the "cost incurred" for processing bad checks, "plus a profit margin." 12 C.F.R. § 7.4002(b)(1).

Additionally, national banks are required to set non-interest charges and fees based on the "maintenance of the safety and soundness of the institution." 12 C.F.R. § 7.4002(b)(4). Defendant's OD fees are a fair and efficient method of allocating the administrative costs consequent to processing checks presented against insufficient funds. Depositors who maintain insufficient balances create operational costs directly attributable to their failure to comply with the terms of their agreement. Banks must adopt systems to track such behavior and respond to it appropriately. Since banks must refrain from engaging in unsafe and unsound practices, see 12 U.S.C. § 1818(e), it is more than conceivable that a charge for overdrawn checks which is low enough to avoid attack as unreasonable would fail to discourage the writing of such checks. * * *

Plaintiff argues that, by honoring checks for which insufficient funds exist in a checking account, Defendant was actually extending credit to Plaintiff. This extension of credit, according to Plaintiff, is synonymous with a loan. Therefore, the OD fee assessed on these "loans" constitutes interest. Accordingly, since the OD fee charged by Defendant exceeded the lawful rate of interest permitted in Florida, it was usurious.

Plaintiff relies heavily on Smiley v. Citibank (S.D.), N.A., 517 U.S. 735, (1996), to support its contention that a loan was extended in connection with its checking account. The Court finds Plaintiff's reliance on Smiley is misplaced. * * *

Here, the Court faces a different issue. The late fees at issue in Smiley arose from that plaintiff's relationship with the bank as a credit *card holder*, an arrangement which unambiguously is based on "an extension of credit, making available of a line of credit, or any default or breach by a borrower of a condition upon which credit was extended." 12 C.F.R. § 7.4001(a). A credit card holder fits neatly into the debtor role in a creditor/debtor relationship, which is essential to invoke § 85 of the Bank Act. In the instant case, Defendant's OD fees stem from a deposit agreement between a bank and one or more of its depositors. Although a creditor/debtor relationship exists, the roles are reversed: the bank is the debtor and the depositor is the creditor. Thus, the threshold question is whether the OD fees in this case are "connected with credit extension or availability," 12 U.S.C. § 7. 4001(a), and accordingly, whether the usury laws apply at all.

Significantly, the Smiley Court approved the definition of "interest" found in 12 C.F.R. § 7.4001, which includes a reference to NSF charges. However, § 7.4001 clearly provides that NSF fees are interest if, and only if, the fee is a "payment compensating a creditor . . . for an extension of credit." 12 C.F.R. § 7.4001(a). In the present case, the NSF and OD fees charged to Plaintiff were not compensating Defendant for an extension of credit. The fees were charged for the processing of bad checks. Thus, the

holding and reasoning of the Supreme Court in *Smiley* is inapplicable.
* * *

Plaintiff would argue that the word "loan" is intentionally broad, and covers all circumstances in which there has been a *de facto* loan. Plaintiff urges that even Defendant considers the honoring of checks drawn against overdrawn accounts an "unsecured extension of credit." Such a broad interpretation of this term places form over substance, in contravention of the intent and purpose behind the usury laws.

Although a loan may exist regardless of the form of the transaction, "whether or not [a] transaction constitutes a loan, is to be determined from the surrounding facts in the particular case." Calcasieu–Marine Nat'l Bank of Lake Charles v. American Employers' Ins. Co., 533 F.2d 290, 297 (5th Cir. 1976) (quoting source omitted). Courts should not interpret the transaction in a manner which would defeat the probable intentions of the parties. See id. at 296.

The classic definition of a loan is "a contract by which one delivers a sum of money to another and the latter agrees to return at a future time a sum equivalent to that which he borrows." In re Grand Union Co., 219 F. 353, 356 (2d Cir. 1914). Moreover, "to constitute a loan, there must be a contract whereby, in substance one party transfers to the other a sum of money which that other agrees to pay absolutely, *together with such additional sums as may be agreed upon for its use.*" Id. (emphasis added). Essentially, it is a contractual arrangement between two parties.

Must be a k if it's a loan [handwritten annotation]

In contrast, a check "is a contract in writing by which the drawer contracts with the payee that the bank will pay to the payee therein the amount designated on presentation." Sawgrass Builders, Inc. v. Realty Coop., Inc., 323 S.E.2d 243, 244 (Ga. Ct. App. 1984) (quoting source omitted). Unlike a loan note, which is a promise by the maker to pay a specified sum and described as a two-party instrument—the parties being the maker and a payee—a check constitutes an order on a third party, a bank, to pay a specified sum and is a three-party instrument—the parties being a drawer, a drawee or payor bank, and a payee. The differences between these types of instruments and underlying transactions are apparent in the respective definitions promulgated in the Uniform Commercial Code. Compare UCC § 3–104(f) (1990) (definition of check) with UCC § 3–104(e) (1990) (definition of note).

The Supreme Court has noted the dichotomy between loan documentation and checks. See Don E. Williams Co. v. Commissioner of Internal Revenue, 429 U.S. 569 (1977). In that case, the Court declared that:

> The promissory note, even when payable on demand and fully secured, is still, as its name implies, only a promise to pay, and does not represent the paying out or reduction of assets. A check, on the other hand, is a direction to the bank for immediate payment, is a medium of exchange, and has come to be treated for federal tax purposes as a conditional payment of cash.

Id. at 582–83.

When a bank honors a check, it reasonably expects the check to be paid in the normal course of business. See Pioneer Valley Savings Bank v. Indemnity Ins. Co., 225 F. Supp. 404, 411 (N.D. Iowa 1964), affd, 343 F.2d 634 (8th Cir. 1965). Checks, as the most common items handled by banks, are handled in bulk as cash items on the assumption that they will be honored in most cases; provisional credits are entered immediately at all stages of the collection process, and become final without further action upon payment by the drawee bank. See Calcasieu–Marine Nat'l Bank, 533 F.2d at 300 (citation omitted).

The Court cannot agree with Plaintiff's argument that the deposit agreement relative to Plaintiff's checking account treats an overdraft as an application for advance credit. The implementation of OD and NSF fees was based on the banking industry's awareness that a depositor often writes checks under the mistaken belief that he has, or will have, sufficient funds to cover the check, without any intent to apply for credit. The imposition of the fee is solely contingent upon the depositor's failure to comply with the terms of the deposit agreement, which require the maintenance of sufficient funds to cover all checks presented. * * *

In sum, as a matter of law, the Court finds that the payment of OD fees as consideration for honoring checks presented against overdrawn accounts is not the payment of interest under the deposit agreement. * * * [The court granted summary judgment in favor of NationsBank. The Eleventh Circuit affirmed based on the district court's opinion].

———

Consumers concerned about incurring overdraft fees may apply for an overdraft line of credit. In the event a check is presented for payment that would overdraw the customer's account, the bank pays the check and loans the consumer on the line of credit the amount necessary to cover the overdraft. This is the most cost effective way for a consumer to protect herself from bouncing checks and the fees that will be assessed for NSF checks by the bank and the check's payee. The line of credit is subject to TILA and the interest rate charge is often around 18%. A consumer must apply and qualify for this service based on their credit experience. Another overdraft protection option is setting up a linked account whereby overdrafts in the checking account will be covered by a transfer from another account maintained at the same bank, such as a savings account. Banks sometimes charge a transfer fee (usually around $5) whenever a transfer is necessary. Most banks, however, according to a 2008 FDIC study[9] automatically enroll their customers (although customers may opt-out) in a "bounce protection program" in which the bank has discretion on whether to cover a customer's bounced check, point-of-sale debit transac-

9. FDIC, FDIC Study of Bank Overdraft Programs (Nov. 2008).

tion, or ATM withdrawal when there are not sufficient funds in the customer's account and can charge the customer a bounce protection fee (usually equivalent in amount to the NSF fee) to cover the item. In the case of a check, this may save the customer the embarrassment of bouncing a check and possibly incurring another fee assessed by the check's payee.

Under TILA regulations, the fees assessed for the overdraft program are not considered finance charges subject to TILA disclosure or state usury limitations. Reg. Z, 12 C.F.R. pt. 205. The FRB issued final amendments to Regulation DD, which implements the Truth in Savings Act. 70 Fed. Reg. 29582 (May 24, 2005) (codified at 12 C.F.R. pt. 230). The FRB stated that it might consider application of TILA and Regulation Z to overdraft programs in the future. The FRB also distinguished between programs that were "promoted" by banks, through advertising and pamphlets, and programs that were not so promoted. For the former, the bank would need to provide certain disclosures and report the aggregate current and year-to-date overdraft fees in periodic statements to customers. For overdraft protection programs that were not promoted by the bank, the bank need only disclose when and how fees would be charged in account information materials.

The Fed revised Regulation E, effective July 1, 2010, to require customers of overdraft protection programs to opt-in to overdraft protection for payment of overdrafts created by ATM transactions or one-time debit card purchases. 12 C.F.R. pt. 205. If a consumer is enrolled in an overdraft protection program but does not opt-in, she will not incur overdraft and related charges by inadvertently overdrawing an account with an ATM withdrawal or a discretionary debit card purchase. Rather, the transaction will just not be consummated because of lack of sufficient funds and no NSF charges or bounce protection fees will be incurred. The Fed reasoned that consumers would want to avoid incurring the charges associated with the overdraft protection program for ATM and debit card purchases and would prefer to have the transaction refused instead because of insufficient funds. The FDIC followed this Fed action with proposed guidelines that would apply to state chartered, nonmember banks supervised by the FDIC. FDIC, Financial Institution Letter, FIL–47–2010, Overdraft Payment Programs and Consumer Protection (Aug. 11, 2010). This proposed guidance provide that customers be able to opt out of overdraft programs and that banks monitor a customer's usage of any overdraft program. The bank would need to discuss other, less costly options with any customer who used the overdraft program at least six times within a one-year period and then give the customer a reasonable period to decide whether to continue with the overdraft protection program.

cities regulation of ATMs was preempted by fed'l law

BANK OF AMERICA v. CITY AND COUNTY OF SAN FRANCISCO

United States Court of Appeals, Ninth Circuit, 2002.
309 F.3d 551 (9th Cir. 2002), *cert. denied*, 538 U.S. 1069 (2003).

SNEED, CIRCUIT JUDGE.

This appeal arises from the passage of municipal ordinances (the "Ordinances") by the cities of San Francisco and Santa Monica (the "Cities") prohibiting banks from charging ATM fees to non-depositors. Bank of America, Wells Fargo Bank, and the California Bankers Association (the "Banks") filed an action against the Cities seeking to invalidate the Ordinances. * * *

In October and November of 1999, the cities of Santa Monica and San Francisco enacted virtually identical ordinances prohibiting "financial institutions" from charging ATM fees to non-depositors. The Ordinances define financial institutions as "any bank, savings association, savings bank, credit union, or industrial loan company," and target California's two largest banks, Bank of America and Wells Fargo Bank.

These Ordinances are enforced through private rights of action. Under the Ordinances, any consumer who pays an unlawful ATM fee may sue for "actual damages" of not less than $250 plus attorney fees and costs. In addition, punitive damages of up to $5,000 are allowed where the financial institution has engaged in a "pattern of willful violations." The Ordinances also permit consumers and municipal officials to seek injunctive relief. * * *

The Cities allege that ATM fees charged to non-depositors harm consumers. They point out that non-depositors are charged twice for using an ATM.[10] They insist that ATM fees unduly burden the elderly, the disabled, and the poor because of their "lower mobility and [their] relative lack of choice over which ATMs to use."

The Cities also allege that ATM fees undermine competition in the local banking industry. The Cities argue that smaller banks and credit unions lose market share to larger banks because depositors seeking to avoid ATM fees transfer their accounts to banks that operate more ATMs in the Cities.

The Banks reject the Cities' characterization of the ATM market. They claim that ATMs are net "cost centers" for banks who on average lose between $8,000 and $11,000 annually per ATM. The Banks also dispute the Cities' contention that ATM fees have led to greater concentration in the local banking industry.

---

10. [n.1] When a non-depositor uses an ATM owned by Wells Fargo Bank or Bank of America, he is charged a total of $3.50 for the transaction. Three categories of fees are involved in this transaction: (1) a $1.50 "surcharge" is charged by the bank operating the ATM, (2) a $2.00 "foreign fee" is charged by the customer's home bank for using an ATM operated by another bank, and (3) a $0.50 "interchange fee" is paid by the home bank to the bank operating the ATM. The Ordinances prohibit only the $1.50 surcharge ("ATM fee").

Additionally, the Banks argue that their ability to compete is impaired by the Ordinances. The Ordinances' definition of financial institution does not include all ATM operators. For instance, credit card companies are exempt from compliance because the Ordinances' limited definition of financial institution does not include them. This disparate treatment of ATM operators under the Ordinances would put the Banks at a competitive disadvantage.

Upon passage of the Ordinances, the Banks, not surprisingly, suspended ATM service to non-depositors. On November 3, 1999, the Banks filed a complaint against the Cities seeking a declaratory judgment that the Ordinances are preempted by the National Bank Act. * * *

On January 20, 2000, the district court granted California Federal Bank's ("Cal Fed") motion to intervene as a plaintiff in this action. The following day, Cal Fed filed its complaint against the Cities seeking a declaratory judgment that the Ordinances are preempted by the Home Owners' Loan Act as applied to federal savings banks. * * *

The district court found that the HOLA and the Office of Thrift Supervision's ("OTS") regulations occupy the entire field of ATM fees with respect to federal savings banks. It also found that the HOLA and OTS regulations authorize federal savings banks to charge ATM fees. Thus, the district court held that HOLA preempt the Ordinances. The district court also held that the National Bank Act and the regulations of the Office of Comptroller of Currency ("OCC"), which permit nationally chartered banks to charge ATM fees, preempt the Ordinances.

Because of these findings, the district court permanently enjoined the Cities from enforcing the Ordinances. The Cities appeal. * * *

We find that the Ordinances are preempted by federal law and regulations and thus invalid by reason of the Supremacy Clause of the Constitution. In determining whether a municipal ordinance is preempted by federal law, our sole task is to ascertain the intent of Congress. Federal law may preempt state law in three different ways. First, Congress may preempt state law by so stating in express terms. Second, preemption may be inferred when federal regulation in a particular field is "so pervasive as to make reasonable the inference that Congress left no room for the States to supplement it." Rice v. Santa Fe Elevator Corp., 331 U.S. 218, 230 (1947). In such cases of field preemption, the "mere volume and complexity" of federal regulations demonstrate an implicit congressional intent to displace all state law. Third, preemption may be implied when state law actually conflicts with federal law. Such a conflict arises when "compliance with both federal and state regulations is a physical impossibility," Florida Lime & Avocado Growers, Inc. v. Paul, 373 U.S. 132, 142–43 (1963), or when state law "stands as an obstacle to the accomplishment and execution of the full purposes and objectives of Congress," Hines v. Davidowitz, 312 U.S. 52, 67 (1941).

The Cities contend that all preemption analysis begins with the presumption against preemption. This rests on the assumption that Congress did not intend to supplant state law. However, the presumption is "not triggered when the State regulates in an area where there has been a history of significant federal presence." United States v. Locke, 529 U.S. 89, 108 (2000).

Congress has legislated in the field of banking from the days of McCulloch v. Maryland, 17 U.S. 316, 325–26, 426–27 (1819), creating an extensive federal statutory and regulatory scheme. The history of national banking legislation has been "one of interpreting grants of both enumerated and incidental 'powers' to national banks as grants of authority not normally limited by, but rather ordinarily pre-empting, contrary state law." Barnett Bank v. Nelson, 517 U.S. 25, 32 (1996). Indeed, since the passage of the National Bank Act in 1864, the federal presence in banking has been significant. Similarly, since the passage of the HOLA in 1933, OTS regulations have governed the "powers and operations of every federal savings and loan association from its cradle to its corporate grave." de la Cuesta, 458 U.S. at 145. This court has recognized that regulation of federal savings associations by the OTS has been so "pervasive as to leave no room for state regulatory control." Conference of Fed. Sav. & Loan Ass'ns v. Stein, 604 F.2d 1256, 1260 (9th Cir. 1979), aff'd, 445 U.S. 921 (1980).

State regulation of banking is permissible when it "does not prevent or significantly interfere with the national bank's exercise of its powers." *Barnett Bank*, 517 U.S. at 33. Thus, states retain some power to regulate national banks in areas such as contracts, debt collection, acquisition and transfer of property, and taxation, zoning, criminal, and tort law. Nevertheless, because there has been a "history of significant federal presence" in national banking, the presumption against preemption of state law is inapplicable. *Locke*, 529 U.S. at 108.

* * * [W]e hold that the HOLA and OTS regulations together preempt conflicting state limitations on the authority of federal savings associations to collect fees for provision of deposit and lending-related electronic services and that prohibition of ATM fees by the Ordinances is therefore invalid under the Supremacy Clause of the Constitution. Because the ordinances are preempted for attempting to regulate the operations of federal savings banks, we do not discuss the alternate justifications for preemption including field preemption of deposit and lending-related activities as well as conflict pre-emption.

We also find that National Bank Act preempts the Ordinances.

National banks are "instrumentalit[ies] of the federal government, created for a public purpose, and . . . subject to the paramount authority of the United States." Marquette Nat'l Bank v. First of Omaha Serv. Corp., 439 U.S. 299, 308 (1978). State attempts to control the conduct of national banks are void if they conflict with federal law, frustrate the purposes of the National Bank Act, or impair the efficiency of national banks to discharge their duties. First Nat. Bank v. California, 262 U.S.

366, 369 (1923). The supremacy of the federal government in regulating national banks has long been recognized.

The National Bank Act of 1864 was enacted to protect national banks against intrusive regulation by the States. To fulfill this Congressional purpose, the Supreme Court has "interpret[ed] grants of both enumerated and incidental 'powers' to national banks as grants of authority not normally limited by, but rather ordinarily preempting, contrary state law." *Barnett Bank*, 517 U.S. at 32. Therefore, in determining the preemptive scope of federal statutes and regulations granting a power to national banks, the Supreme Court has adopted the view that "normally Congress would not want States to forbid, or to impair significantly, the exercise of a power that Congress explicitly granted." Id. at 33. * * *

The "business of banking" [in 12 U.S.C. § 24 (Seventh)] is not limited to the powers enumerated in § 24 (Seventh). NationsBank v. Variable Annuity Life Ins. Co., 513 U.S. 251, 258 n. 2 (1995). Therefore, the OCC "may authorize additional activities if encompassed by a reasonable interpretation of § 24 (Seventh)." Indep. Ins. Agents of Am., Inc. v. Hawke, 211 F.3d 638, 640 (D.C. Cir. 2000).

Incidental powers include activities that are "convenient or useful in connection with the performance of one of the bank's established activities pursuant to its express powers under the National Bank Act." M & M Leasing Corp. v. Seattle First Nat'l Bank, 563 F.2d 1377, 1382 (9th Cir. 1977), cert. denied, 436 U.S. 956 (1978). The incidental powers of national banks are thus not limited to activities deemed essential to the exercise of enumerated powers but include activities closely related to banking and useful in carrying out the business of banking.

OCC Regulation § 7.5002 authorizes national banks to "deliver through electronic means and facilities any ... service that [they are] otherwise authorized to ... provide." 12 C.F.R. § 7.5002. Also, Regulation § 7.4003 authorizes national banks to operate ATMs pursuant to their incidental powers under 12 U.S.C. § 24 (Seventh). 12 C.F.R. § 7.4003. Finally, Regulation § 7.4002(a) authorizes national banks to collect "non-interest charges and fees, including deposit account service charges." 12 C.F.R. § 7.4002(a). The establishment of such fees "are business decisions to be made by each bank ... according to sound business judgment and safe and sound banking principles." 12 C.F.R. § 7.4002(b)(2).[11] These regulations make no distinction between depositors and non-depositors with respect to a national bank's authority to collect fees for provision of

---

11. [n.6] Regulation § 7.4002(b)(2) further provides:

A national bank establishes non-interest charges and fees in accordance with safe and sound banking principles if the bank employs a decision-making process through which it considers the following factors, among others: (i) The cost incurred by the bank in providing the service; (ii) The deterrence of misuse by customers of banking services; (iii) The enhancement of the competitive position of the bank in accordance with the bank's business plan and marketing strategy; and (iv) The maintenance of the safety and soundness of the institution.

12 C.F.R. § 7.4002(b)(2). The OCC found that the Banks had properly considered these factors in deciding to charge ATM fees to non-depositors.

authorized services. It follows that national banks may charge ATM fees to non-depositors. * * *

We give "great weight" to any reasonable construction of a regulatory statute adopted by the agency charged with its enforcement. Clarke v. Secs. Indus. Ass'n, 479 U.S. 388, 403 (1987). "As the administrator charged with supervision of the National Bank Act, the [OCC] bears primary responsibility for surveillance of 'the business of banking' authorized by § 24 Seventh." *NationsBank*, 513 U.S. at 256.

In its *amicus* brief and in two interpretive letters issued following passage of the Ordinances, the OCC has construed the incidental powers of national banks under § 24 (Seventh) as encompassing the provision of ATM services to nondepositors at a charge. The OCC's position is reasonable and thus entitled to "great weight." *NationsBank*, 513 U.S. at 256–57.[12]

The depositing of funds and the withdrawal of cash are services provided by banks since the days of their creation. Indeed, such activities define the business of banking. Although the ATM is a relatively new technology, the deposit and lending-related services offered through ATMs are traditional banking functions. As we held in *M & M Leasing Corp.*, "the National Bank Act did not freeze the practices of national banks in their nineteenth century forms. . . . We believe the powers of national banks must be construed so as to permit the use of new ways of conducting the very old business of banking." 563 F.2d at 1382. In our view, the widespread use of ATMs by banks to deliver deposit and lending-related services exemplifies a "new way[]of conducting the very old business of banking." Id.

We find no support in the Cities' contention that the charging of ATM fees to non-depositors renders the provision of ATM services beyond the incidental powers granted to national banks under § 24 (Seventh). As held in First Union Nat'l Bank v. Burke, 48 F. Supp. 2d 132, 147 (D. Conn. 1999), the notion that "determination of state regulatory authority over national banks' ATM services is predicated on who accesses the . . . ATMs, is without legal authority or sound rationale. The ATM service offered to []non-depositors allows them to access their accounts at their own banks from a different geographic location and logically constitutes part of banking business."

The language of the National Bank Act provides no support for the Cities' position. To the contrary, Regulation § 7.4002(a) authorizes na-

---

12. [n.7] The Cities insist that the OCC's opinion letters and amicus briefs are not entitled to deference. As explained above, the Cities' argument lacks merit. We find the OCC's opinion letters to be both persuasive and consistent with the National Bank Act and OCC regulations and thus at least "entitled to respect." Christensen v. Harris County, 529 U.S. 576, 587 (2000). Moreover, that the OCC's construction of the National Bank Act comes to us in the form of an *amicus* brief does not make it "unworthy of deference." See Auer v. Robbins, 519 U.S. 452, 462 (1997) (noting that an agency's position in an *amicus* brief is not "unworthy of deference" when "[t]here is simply no reason to suspect that the interpretation does not reflect the agency's fair and considered judgment on the matter in question.").

tional banks to collect "non-interest charges and fees." 12 C.F.R. § 7.4002(a).

We hold that the National Bank Act and OCC regulations together preempt conflicting state limitations on the authority of national banks to collect fees for provision of deposit and lending-related electronic services and that prohibition of ATM fees by the Ordinances is therefore invalid under the Supremacy Clause of the Constitution.

The Cities contend that the EFTA authorizes states to regulate ATM fees as a consumer protection measure. This argument fails on two grounds. First, regulation of ATM fees is not the type of consumer protection measure contemplated by the EFTA. Second, the EFTA's anti-preemption provision does not preclude preemption of state laws by the HOLA and the National Bank Act.

The Ordinances purport to protect consumers against "excessive fees" and "anti-competitive" business practices that encourage consumers to hold their accounts at national banks who operate more ATMs in the Cities than state-chartered financial institutions. The Cities claim that prohibition of ATM fees is the type of consumer protection measure contemplated by the EFTA. However, the language and legislative history of the EFTA point to the contrary.

The stated purpose of the EFTA is to "provide a basic framework establishing the rights, liabilities, and responsibilities of participants in electronic fund transfer systems." 15 U.S.C. § 1693(b). The EFTA's "primary objective . . . is the provision of individual consumer rights." Id.

The language of the EFTA indicates that the consumer protection measures contemplated by it are aimed at promoting disclosure, preventing fraud, and allocating liability. See 15 U.S.C. § 1693c (requiring disclosure of terms and conditions of electronic transfers); § 1693d (requiring documentation of transfers); § 1693e (requiring a writing for preauthorized electronic fund transfers); § 1693f (establishing procedures for error resolution); § 1693g (outlining consumer liability); § 1693h (outlining the liability of financial institutions); § 1693i (establishing requirements for issuance of cards); § 1693j (suspending consumer obligations in instances of system malfunction); § 1693l (prohibiting waiver of consumer rights under the EFTA).

The EFTA's ambit thus extends to regulation of ATM transactions. 15 U.S.C. § 1693a(6). However, the EFTA does not regulate ATM fees. Prohibition of ATM fees is not the type of consumer protection measure contemplated by the EFTA. The EFTA was enacted to prevent fraud, embezzlement, and unauthorized disclosure in electronic fund transfers, not to regulate service fees charged by financial institutions.

This is evident from the passage of the ATM Fee Reform Act of 1999, which requires that ATM operators who impose a fee notify customers of imposition of the fee and of the amount and prohibits charging a fee unless the customer elects to continue with the transaction after receiving notice. 15 U.S.C. § 1693b(d)(3). By requiring that ATM operators notify customers of imposition of fees, Congress recognized that ATM operators can charge fees. Therefore, the prohibition of ATM fees is not the type of consumer protection measure contemplated by the EFTA.

The EFTA contains an anti-preemption provision which provides that state laws affording greater protection to consumers than the EFTA are not preempted by the EFTA. It provides:

> This subchapter does not annul, alter, or affect the laws of any State relating to electronic fund transfers, except to the extent that those laws are inconsistent with the provisions of this subchapter, and then only to the extent of the inconsistency. A State law is not inconsistent *with this subchapter* if the protection such law affords any consumer is greater than the protection afforded *by this subchapter*.

15 U.S.C. § 1693q (emphasis added).

The Cities insist that § 1693q empowers them to regulate ATM fees charged by national banks and federal savings associations as a consumer protection measure. They claim that the EFTA's anti-preemption provision saves the Ordinances against preemption by the HOLA and the National Bank Act. However, the plain language of § 1693q indicates that it is limited to the EFTA. Section 1693q's reference to "this subchapter" indicates that the EFTA's anti-preemption provision does not apply to other statutes.

In Bank One v. Guttau, 190 F.3d 844 (8th Cir. 1999), the Eighth Circuit rejected the same argument raised by the Cities here that the EFTA's anti-preemption provision authorizes states to regulate ATMs operated by national banks irrespective of whether the state regulations are preempted by the National Bank Act. The Eighth Circuit explained that the EFTA's "anti preemption provision is specifically limited to the provisions of the federal EFTA, and nothing therein grants the states any additional authority to regulate national banks." Id. at 850. It thus held that a state regulation restricting a national bank's placement of, and advertising on, ATMs was preempted by the National Bank Act notwithstanding the EFTA's anti-preemption provision. Id.

Because the EFTA's anti-preemption provision is limited to the EFTA, it does not save the Ordinances against preemption by the HOLA and the National Bank Act. * * *

We hold that the HOLA and OTS regulations preempt the Ordinances from prohibiting federal savings associations to charge ATM fees to non-depositors. We also hold that the National Bank Act and OCC regulations preempt the Ordinances from prohibiting national banks to do the same. We further hold that the EFTA does not rescue the Ordinances from preemption. * * *

The amendments to the Electronic Funds Transfer Act (EFTA) referred to in the *Bank of America* case were made in sections 702, 703 and 705 of GLBA. These amendments require disclosure of ATM surcharges. 12 C.F.R. pt. 205. An ATM surcharge must now be disclosed prominently and conspicuously on the ATM screen or on paper before the consumer has committed to the transaction.

After the Dodd–Frank Act, the BCFP has the authority to issue regulations identifying "unfair, deceptive, or abusive acts or practices." Consider how this broad mandate might be used to regulate overdraft fees or ATM fees.

QUESTIONS AND NOTES

1. Why might banks not be interested in developing products designed to attract the 8% of American families without bank accounts to the banking system? You may wish to compare the basic checking account products offered by local banks and local credit unions. Do some institutions offer substantially better accounts for low balance customers? What are the requirements to become a member of the local credit union? Why may credit unions often offer "better" account options than banks?

2. What is the penalty for withdrawing a certificate of deposit prior to its maturity date? Compare the interest rates offered by local depository institutions on different maturities of CDs for different amounts. Why do most banks pay higher interest on CDs with longer maturities?

3. There has been some litigation on whether banks may post checks for payment from customers' accounts based on amount, starting with the highest check. The effect of this high-to-low payment policy is that if the customer has insufficient funds in his account to honor all the checks presented for payment against the account, more checks are returned for insufficient funds (and more bank charges are incurred) than if the bank payed the checks starting with the lowest dollar amount checks. Banks have argued that often the highest dollar amount checks are more important to the customer (i.e., the mortgage check or car payment check) than the lower dollar items, and that therefore high-to-low represents the payment order preferred by most consumers. The Uniform Commercial Code provides in § 4–303(b) that items may be paid in "any order." Pursuant to this authority a bank's policy of paying checks in order from high-to-low has been upheld. Smith v. First Union National Bank, 958 S.W.2d 113 (Tenn. Ct. App. 1997).

A bank's practice of posting debit card transactions from high-to-low was found to be an unfair and fraudulent action in violation of California's Unfair Competition law, and not subject to preemption under the National Bank Act. Gutierrez v. Wells Fargo Bank, N.A., 2010 WL 3155934 (N.D. Cal. 2010). A multi-district class action is proceeding on similar issues related to high-to-low posting of debit transactions. See In re Checking Account Overdraft Litigation, MDL No. 2036, 694 F.Supp.2d 1302 (S.D. Fla. 2010).

4. Do ATM surcharges put small banks without extensive ATM networks at a competitive disadvantage with banks with a larger number of

ATMs? If ATM surcharge fees are used to pay for expanded ATM networks, does this justify their assessment and serve to advance the interests of consumers? Some smaller banks have decided to pay ATM surcharge fees for their customers using the ATMs of other banks. Although this presents some cost for the bank, it provides the customer with free access to any ATM. Surcharge–Free ATMs Help Smaller Banks Compete, US Banker, July 2006, at 34.

5. The United States Court of Appeals for Fifth Circuit determined that 12 C.F.R. § 7.4002(a), which permits national banks to "charge its customers non-interest charges and fees" for authorized services, preempted a Texas statute prohibiting banks in Texas (including national banks) from charging non-account holders for cashing checks drawn on the bank (so-called "on us" checks). Wells Fargo Bank of Texas N.A. v. James, 321 F.3d 488 (5th Cir. 2003). The court noted

> The primary ambiguity lies in whether non-account holding payees are "customers" for the purpose of the regulation. The OCC interprets "customers" to include any person who presents a check for payment. Certainly this is not he only reasonable interpretation of § 7.4002(a), and it is perhaps not even the most natural reading of "customer." For example, one might easily understand "customer" to ... include primarily those individuals with whom the Banks exchange services and remunerations, rather than payees seeking payment for executory negotiable instruments. Nevertheless, we find it neither unwarranted nor unreasonable to define customer as anyone who seeks payment for a check from the bank. In doing so, the payee avails himself of the servants and services of the bank. We conclude, therefore, that the OCC interpretation is not a clearly erroneous interpretation, and the district court properly deferred to it.

Id. at 495.

Wells Fargo and Bank of America settled lawsuits brought over fees they charged to noncustomers to cash paychecks in California. The cases were brought pursuant to a California labor statute which requires that paychecks "be negotiable and payable in cash, on demand, without discount." Jim Cole, In Brief: Wells Settles Calif. Paycheck Fee Suit, Am. Banker, Sept. 7, 2005. The banks may still charge the check-cashing fee to noncustomers, but agreed as part of the settlement to provide some deposit and account services to employers and employees for a specified period without fees.

6. Whether overdrafts may be assessed against public benefit payments, such as Social Security, directly deposited to a customer's account has also been hard-fought in California courts. In 2002, the Ninth Circuit held that federally chartered financial institutions could offset overdrafts against directly deposited Social Security payments. Lopez v. Washington Mutual Bank, FA, 302 F.3d 900 (9th Cir.), *opinion amended on denial of rehearing,* 311 F.3d 928 (9th Cir. 2002). The California Supreme Court held in Miller v. Bank of America, NT & SA, 207 P.3d 531 (Cal. 2009), that offsetting overdrafts and NSF fees from customers' benefit payments did not violate public policy or a state statute limiting the bank's ability to set off debt.

7. During 2009, it was estimated that banks earned $38.5 billion in overdraft fees. What is likely to happen to the amount of overdraft fees earned by banks following the Reg. E changes to overdraft protection programs and the litigation relating to high-to-low posting of debit card transactions?

(2) Check 21

The Check Clearing for the 21st Century Act (Check 21) (effective October 28, 2004) removes the requirement that banks process and route original checks and permits banks to transfer electronic images of checks. See Reg. CC, 12 C.F.R. pt. 229. Banks are not required to transmit or receive electronic images of checks, but if they cannot accept a digital images of a check they are required to accept an Image Replacement Document (IRD), which is also referred to as a "substitute check" and is a paper printout of the document's image. According to a report by the Fed submitted to Congress in 2007, the implementation of Check 21 was slowed by the investment necessary in technology to create and process images of checks and substitute checks.[13] Substantial increases in electronic and substitute checks began in 2006 and 2007. Check 21 also facilitates remote deposit capture in which a user scans checks it receives and transmits the scanned images to its bank for a digital deposit. The advantages of remote deposit capture are obvious for the user. A risk, however, is that the user or the bank presents multiple images of the same check for payment. See Frank Stokes, Don't Be Duped: Remote Checks Risky, Am. Banker, May 26, 2010, at 8.

(3) Deposit Interest Rate Regulation

After the 1929 stock market crash, Congress attempted to quell what it viewed as potentially ruinous competition among banks based on interest rates paid to depositors. Congress was also concerned with the New York "call" money market, in which New York City banks attracted deposits from country banks by paying interest. Those funds were then loaned to stockbrokers who reloaned the money to customers to finance the purchase of stock (i.e., margin loans). This practice was thought to have diverted funds from more important industrial uses and to have played a large role in the speculative excesses occurring before the stock market crash of 1929.[14] Interest rate competition and the call money market were addressed when, in the Banking Act of 1933, Congress forbade the payment of interest on demand deposits and placed a ceiling on the rate of interest that could be paid on savings accounts.

Because many banks subject to these ceilings experienced disintermediation during the inflation of the 1970s, Congress repealed the ceilings in 1980. With market interest rates well in excess of the interest rate ceilings, bank depositors withdrew their funds and reinvested in

---

13. Board of Governors of the Federal Reserve System, Report of the Congress on the Check Clearing for the 21st Century Act of 2003, at 11 (Apr. 2007).

14. Jerry W. Markham, A Financial History of the United States: J.P. Morgan to the Institutional Investor (1900–1970) 167 (2001).

money market mutual funds and other investments perceived as equally safe, but much more remunerative. Congress also approved the payment of interest on transaction accounts that were called NOW (negotiable order of withdrawal) accounts, although this type of account was available only to individual customers and not businesses.

Congress received numerous requests to repeal the prohibition on the payment of interest on demand deposits. The requests were often linked with a proposal that the Federal Reserve Banks pay interest to banks on the funds they held on deposit at the Federal Reserve Banks. Congress ultimately authorized the Federal Reserve Banks to begin paying interest on deposits, to begin in 2011. The effective date of this action was moved up to October 1, 2008 by the Emergency Economic Stabilization Act of 2008. The Dodd–Frank Act permits the payment of interest on commercial demand deposits, beginning on July 21, 2011. Dodd–Frank Act, § 627. The Act provides, however, at least a temporary incentive to maintain a non-interest bearing transaction account, and that is unlimited deposit insurance on non-interest bearing accounts through December 31, 2012. Dodd Frank Act, § 343. Thus, the cash management services described below, will continue at least through 2012, as banks assist their customers in reducing the amount of money kept on deposit in non-interest bearing accounts.

CF INDUSTRIES, INC. v. COMMISSIONER OF INTERNAL REVENUE

United States Tax Court, 1991.
T.C. Memo. 1991–568, *modified in part*, 995 F.2d 101 (7th Cir. 1993).

GOFFE, JUDGE.

* * * CF is the parent corporation of three operating subsidiaries * * * The parent and the subsidiaries operate on a nonexempt cooperative basis within the meaning of section 1381(a)(2) of subchapter T.

Ownership of CF is made up of 18 shareholder patrons. * * * Each shareholder patron owns one share of CF's common stock and the board of directors is composed of one representative from each of the shareholder patrons.

Petitioner's primary business is the manufacture and distribution of chemical fertilizers, specifically nitrogen, phosphate, and potash. During the years in issue, CF held approximately 20 percent of the domestic nitrogen and phosphate fertilizer markets and approximately 16 percent of the domestic potash market. CF also engages in mining and sales activities which pertain to its fertilizer business. * * *

A properly managed business with fluctuating capital must have procedures for administering operating cash. Because the fertilizer industry is so volatile, it is essential that operating cash be retained in a safe and readily available form. To meet its immediate needs, it is appropriate for a business to place its operating cash in safe, liquid, money-market instruments. Financial prudence requires that the business attempt, to the best of its ability, to stagger the maturities of its money-market instruments so that favorable terms can be obtained on cash which would otherwise be idle. The short-term placement, however, must not compromise safety and liquidity. * * *

CF employs a full-time cash manager, Eric Bergstrom, to manage cash flow. Mr. Bergstrom, in consultation with other management personnel at CF, continuously monitors and evaluates CF's cash needs, and when the company has more cash than is required to meet that day's business needs, he purchases short-term, liquid money-market instruments with that excess cash. When CF does not have sufficient cash to meet that day's business needs, Mr. Bergstrom arranges short-term borrowing. * * *

In order to accommodate the financial aspects of its operation, CF maintained a ''concentration banking account'' system with Continental Illinois National Bank (Continental Illinois) in Chicago, Illinois, for the various members of the consolidated group. The concentration account system was composed of a primary concentration account at Continental Illinois and numerous subaccounts at Continental Illinois and other banks. In addition, CF had numerous lockbox accounts at banks near the offices of CF's shareholder patrons.

Cash received from CF's operations was deposited into the concentration account, the lockbox accounts, or the subaccounts. Funds were generally disbursed from the subaccounts. Each of the subsidiaries of CF's cooperative group maintained one or more bank accounts in which there were some small balances. Other subaccounts were maintained as ''zero balance'' accounts. That is, balances in these accounts at the end of the day were transferred into the concentration account. When funds were required for payment, the amount was transferred from the primary concentration account to the appropriate sub-account.

The overall purpose of CF's concentration account system was to marshall as much of CF's cash resources as possible into one account. CF could then manage all of its cash efficiently and purchase money-market instruments when cash was not needed to cover checks that had already been written or to meet compensating balance requirements. Apart from the cash management just described, CF did not further divide its cash into categories. All of its cash was treated equally and it was not put into additional or different accounts or categories. Nor was CF's cash assigned labels for such items as operations, long-term investments, or other uses.

CF earned $6,552,362 in interest income in 1980 from placing temporarily surplus cash in 352 short-term money-market instruments. * * *

CF attempted to stagger the maturities of its money-market instruments so that the instruments would mature at, or near, the time the cash might be needed in CF's business. CF placed surplus cash in instruments with maturities longer than 1 month only when it had sufficient cash placed in instruments of shorter duration that could meet foreseeable business needs within that 1–month period. * * *

Patronage Sourced

The issue presented is whether the interest income from short-term money-market instruments earned by petitioner was derived from "business done with or for [its] patron[s]" within the meaning of section 1388(a)(1). If the interest income is patronage-sourced, then it is taxed only once, usually to the patron. If it is not patronage-sourced, then the income is fully taxable to the cooperative and, if paid out in dividends to the patrons, it is taxed as income to the patrons as well. Sec. 1382(b). * * *

[The court concluded, as modified by the Seventh Circuit, that the interest income which the petitioners received from short-term money market instruments was patronage-sourced and not taxable to the cooperative.]

QUESTIONS AND NOTES

1. Sweep accounts are those that sweep amounts on deposit in a non-interest bearing checking account into an interest-bearing account or investment at the end of each day. Will sweep accounts and cash management services still be used to keep the minimum amount of funds needed in transaction accounts even when they bear interest?

2. Lockbox arrangements assist bank customers in speeding up the collection of checks written to them. The bank assists its customer in setting up a lockbox in which payments made to the bank customers are sent. The bank controls the lockbox and deposits the checks as soon as they are received, providing faster collection than if the customer received payments at its business site and then took them to the bank for deposit. What effect is remote deposit capture likely to have on lockbox services?

C.　DEPOSIT INSURANCE

Federal deposit insurance was implemented by the Banking Act of 1933. It helps to prevent bank runs or panics because customers have no need to withdraw amounts on deposit at a bank—even if the bank is failing—if the government has guaranteed the depositor will receive back the amount of his deposit. Interestingly, President Roosevelt was not initially a proponent of federal deposit insurance.

Any system of insurance, including federal deposit insurance, is affected by "moral hazard." This is the term for taking excessive risks or hazards because the loss will not be borne directly by the risk-taker, but by the insuring entity. Furthermore, the depositors of federally insured depository institutions have little incentive to monitor the behavior of the debtor because they are covered by the federal deposit insurance guaran-
[th]is guarantee permits the bank to raise funds by offering a risk-free [r]eturn, even as the bank engages in increasingly risky behavior or [approa]ches insolvency.

[In] private insurance schemes, the moral hazard of insurance is [control]led by risk-adjusted premiums, deductibles, co-insurance, exclusions for intentional conduct, and limits on policy coverage. The deposit insurance system has always had coverage limits, but only began pricing premiums based on risk after the passage of FDICIA in 1991.

If a bank becomes insolvent, the FDIC guarantees that depositors will be compensated up to the coverage amount, which currently stands at $250,000. As a practical matter, most failed institutions are sold to another institution that purchases the assets and assumes the liabilities (including the uninsured deposits) of the failed institution. Thus, even those depositors with more than $250,000 on deposit in a single account often lose no money if their bank fails. Depositors, the largest category of bank creditors, therefore have little incentive to monitor the bank or its future prospects.

(1) Amount of Coverage

Federal deposit insurance is required for national banks and state member banks. Although there is no federal statutory mandate that state nonmember banks obtain federal deposit insurance, as a practical matter, all state banks have elected to obtain this coverage. Indeed, in many states federal deposit insurance coverage is a prerequisite to obtaining a state charter.

When begun in 1934, federal deposit insurance was in the amount of $2,500 per account. The amount steadily increased over the years until 1980, when the Depository Institutions Deregulation and Monetary Control Act of 1980 increased coverage from $40,000 per account to $100,000 per account. When the coverage limit was increased to $100,000, Congress felt the dramatic increase was necessary to attract back depositors who had withdrawn their funds from banks and put them in higher interest money market mutual funds.

Until 1989, thrift deposits were insured by the Federal Savings and Loan Insurance Corporation (FSLIC). That agency's functions were terminated and transferred to the FDIC when FSLIC became insolvent during the savings and loan crisis. Two separate funds, the Savings Association Insurance Fund (SAIF) and the Bank Insurance Fund (BIF), were then established. The Federal Deposit Insurance Reform Act of 2006 merged the two deposit funds into one fund called the Deposit Insurance Fund (DIF). Credit union deposits are insured by the National Credit Union Share Insurance Fund (NCUSIF).

In the Federal Deposit Insurance Reform Act of 2006, Congress set up a new Standard Maximum Deposit Insurance Amount (SMDIA) of $100,000 that would be subject to adjustment for inflation at the discretion of the FDIC and NCUA boards beginning in 2010, and subject to further adjustment every five years. 12 U.S.C.A. § 1821(a)(1)(E). In the same legislation the deposit insurance coverage for IRA retirement accounts maintained at insured depository institutions was increased to $250,000, also subject to inflationary adjustment at five-year intervals. 12 U.S.C.A. § 1821(a)(3)(A). The Emergency Economic Stabilization Act

(EESA) that was passed on October 3, 2008 at the height of the financial crisis temporarily increased the SMDIA to $250,000 to quell deposit runs on banks that were viewed in risk of failure by commercial customers with more than $100,000 on deposit. The EESA increase was to expire on December 31, 2009, but Congress subsequently extended the termination date to December 31, 2013. The Dodd–Frank Act made the temporary increase in the SMDIA permanent. Dodd–Frank Act, § 335. The increase was also made retroactive to cover failures that occurred after January 1, 2008, thus covering uninsured depositors of IndyMac Bank, FSB, which failed on July 11, 2008, prior to EESA's temporary deposit insurance increase on October 3, 2008. The credit union insurance coverage limits were also permanently increased to $250,000.

The FDIC expanded deposit insurance coverage further when it announced on October 14, 2008, not even two weeks after EESA's passage, the creation of its Temporary Liquidity Guaranty Program (TLGP). The TLGP provided unlimited deposit insurance coverage to non-interest bearing transaction accounts typically maintained by business customers (the Transaction Account Guarantee program or TAG) until December 31, 2009, later extended to June 30, 2010, and then to December 31, 2010. The FDIC cited the systemic risk exception as its authority for the TLGP. This exception, permitted FDIC assistance to a troubled insured institution, including open bank assistance, even when that is not the least costly resolution method, if the institution's failure would have "serious adverse effects on economic conditions or financial stability." 12 U.S.C.A. § 1823(c)(4)(G). The TAG program was voluntary and institutions were permitted to opt out of it and thus avoid the deposit insurance assessments on the additional insured deposits.[15] A large majority of institutions remained in this program, although some exercised their right to opt out. Effective December 31, 2010, the Dodd–Frank Act extended this program until December 31, 2012. Dodd–Frank Act, § 343. The Dodd–Frank Act does not provide an opt out right for this deposit insurance coverage.

(2) FDIC Reserves

Prior to 2006, the FDIC was required to maintain a reserve equal to 1.25% of all insured deposits (or $1.25 per $100 of insured deposits) to fund deposit insurance claims. When the reserve ratio was in excess of the

---

15. If the systemic risk authority was "meant to apply only to FDIC aid aimed at a *particular* institution rather than to potentially all financial institutions," this broad-based program might not fit well within the systemic risk provision. Lissa L. Broome, Extraordinary Government Intervention to Bolster Bank Balance Sheets, 13 N.C. Banking Inst. 150 (2009). The "voluntary nature of the participation in ... the Transaction Account Guarantee Program ... [might also] undercut the conclusion that not offering these programs would result in 'serious adverse effects on economic conditions or financial stability?' " Id. A GAO report evaluating this use of the FDIC's systemic risk authority concluded that there was some support for the position that the statute authorized assistance such as that provided under TLGP, but that there were questions about the broad program of direct assistance to "healthy" institutions and suggested that the statute might require some clarification. General Accountability Office, Federal Deposit Insurance Act: Regulators' Use of Systemic Risk Exception Raises Moral Hazard Concerns and Opportunities Exist to Clarify the Provision. GAO–10–100 (Apr. 15, 2010). Dodd–Frank explicitly extended the TAG program, providing legislative authorization for its temporary continuation.

required minimum, the FDIC was not permitted to assess premiums for the lowest risk banks. The Federal Deposit Insurance Reform Act of 2006 replaced the rigid 1.25% reserve ratio requirement with a range between 1.15% to 1.5% of insured deposits. Each year the FDIC board was to designate the reserve ratio applicable for the upcoming year. Rebates of deposit insurance assessments could be paid to banks by the FDIC if the reserve ratio exceeded 1.5% of insured deposits. If the reserve ratio was between 1.35% and 1.5%, institution would receive a rebate (called a dividend) of 50% of the excess. Insured banks in existence on December 31, 1996, that paid deposit insurance premiums prior to that date were eligible for an "assessment credit" based on their share of the assessment base as of that date. This provision of the 2006 Act ensured that the over 800 banks and thrifts established after the federal deposit insurance fund was recapitalized that had never paid for deposit insurance because the reserve ratio had, for their entire existence, been in excess of 1.25%, not enjoy a free ride off the established institutions which paid premiums that created the reserve.

The Dodd–Frank Act increased the minimum reserve ratio from 1.15% to 1.35% of estimated deposits or comparable asset-based assessment amount. Dodd–Frank Act, § 334. As explained further below, the Dodd–Frank Act permits the FDIC to calculate deposit insurance premiums based on an institution's assets or its insured deposits. The Act gives the FDIC until September 30, 2020, to increase the reserves to the 1.35% of estimated deposits amount. Further, Dodd–Frank permits the FDIC to suspend rebates or dividends of deposit insurance premiums to banks when the reserve ratio exceeds 1.5% (under prior law rebates were mandatory), and eliminated the possibility of rebates to insured banks when the reserve ratio is between 1.35% and 1.5% of estimated deposits. Dodd–Frank Act, § 332. The intent of this provision was to permit the FDIC to allow the reserve fund to accumulate funds during good times so that there would be sufficient funds on hand during times of stress and reduce the pro-cyclical effect of giving rebates in good times and increasing assessments in bad times, further straining the liquidity of struggling institutions.

The financial crisis took a tremendous toll on banks. While only three banks failed in 2007, the number of failures increased steadily to 26 in 2008, 140 in 2009, and 118 as of August 20, 2010. At the same time, the FDIC's list of problem institutions increased to 829 through the second quarter of 2010. The costs of resolving the failed institutions drained the FDIC's reserves. The reserve ratio fell below the 1.15% minimum in the second quarter of 2008, steadily declined, and became negative in the third quarter of 2009.

To ensure that the FDIC would continue to be able to meet its obligations to insured depositors, Congress increased the FDIC's line of credit with Treasury from $30 billion to $100 billion on May 20, 2009, and provided for a temporary increase in the line of credit to $500 billion until December 2010.[16]

(3) Deposit Insurance Assessments

The reserve fund is replenished by deposit insurance premiums, referred to as assessments. Prior to 1991, banks paid a flat rate of 12 cents per $100 of deposit for deposit insurance. The Federal Deposit Insurance Corporation Act (FDICIA) of 1991 instituted a system of risk-based deposit insurance premiums with the risk-adjusted premiums ranging between 0 and 27 cents per $100 of deposits. For a twenty-year period preceding the Federal Deposit Insurance Reform Act of 2006, approximately 95% of insured banks did not pay any deposit insurance assessments since the reserve amount equaled the required ratio of 1.25%. The Federal Deposit Insurance Reform Act of 2006 permitted the FDIC board use its discretion to charge assessments to well-capitalized and well-managed banks even when the insurance fund is at or exceeds its designated reserve ratio in an effort to avoid insurance assessment volatility when the required minimum ratio is not met.

To replenish the depleted reserve fund, the FDIC imposed a series of assessment increases. The first increase was in the amount of the regular quarterly deposit insurance assessment. The second increase was in the form of a special assessment due on September 30, 2009, but based on the amount of an institution's assets minus its Tier 1 capital (the bank's core capital that is discussed later in this Chapter), rather than on the typical assessment base of insured deposits.[17] Finally, the FDIC required prepayment by December 31, 2009, of three years of deposit insurance assessments. The FDIC permitted banks to record the prepayment as an asset and then record each quarter's assessment as an expense when the assessment came due.

The Dodd–Frank Act requires the FDIC to amend its regulations to redefine the assessment base upon which it calculates the required deposit insurance premiums from insured deposits to an institution's average consolidated total assets less its average tangible equity. Dodd–Frank Act, § 331. This change will most likely mean that larger institutions that rely more heavily on non-deposit funding sources than smaller institutions will bear a proportionally greater charge for FDIC insurance since the assessment is based on assets rather than deposits. Some large banks objected to this strategy arguing that the failure of small banks, not large banks, was draining the FDIC fund. FDIC Chairman Shelia Bair responded that larger banks were bailed out with a massive infusion of taxpayer funds through the TARP program, and thus it was not unfair to ask them to shoulder a greater portion of the deposit insurance funding burden. Congress provided further relief to smaller banks by requiring the FDIC to offset the effect of the increase in the minimum reserve ratio from

---

16. This increase was contained in the Helping Families Save Their Homes Act of 2009.

17. Peter S. Kim, Note, The FDIC's Special Assessment: Basing Deposit Insurance on Assets Instead of Deposits, 14 N.C. Banking Inst. 381 (2010).

1.15% to 1.35% for assessments on institutions with less than $10 billion in total consolidated assets.

(4) Who Is Covered

Deposit insurance is currently provided up to the SMDIA (now $250,000) per depositor at an institution. Federal deposit insurance coverage per *person* is unlimited, however. One individual could have an account at every insured institution, each of which would be fully guaranteed by the FDIC up to $250,000 in amount. Depositors of large sums of money may use the services of a deposit broker to divide their money among several different banks to gain expanded deposit insurance coverage and to seek the highest deposit interest rates available.

A depositor who has multiple accounts at one institution should be aware that the accounts will be aggregated for the purposes of determining federal deposit insurance coverage. Let's suppose Jerry has two accounts at First Bank as shown below.

First Bank

Account	Account Holder	Deposit Amount
Checking	Jerry	$40,000
Savings	Jerry	$220,000
TOTAL	Jerry	$260,000

Jerry's effective insurance coverage is $250,000, with $10,000 of his deposits being uninsured.

Let's suppose instead that Jerry and Marcia have joint accounts at First Bank as shown below.

First Bank

Account	Account Holder	Deposit Amount
Checking	Jerry & Marcia	$40,000
Savings	Jerry & Marcia	$220,000
TOTAL	Jerry & Marcia	$260,000

How much is Jerry and Marcia's effective insurance coverage? Each joint account holder receives up to $250,000 of insurance coverage. 12 C.F.R. § 330.9. Jerry's half of the accounts is $130,000, well within the coverage limit of $250,000. Jerry's interest in the joint accounts is fully insured. Marcia's half of the account is $130,000 and she is fully insured as well. If three people were on a joint account, there would be effective deposit insurance coverage up to $750,000.[18]

Only deposits are covered by deposit insurance. Customer balances in mutual funds sold by the bank or brokerage balances maintained in a securities affiliate are not insured by the FDIC.

(5) FDIC Guarantees

On October 14, 2008, the FDIC announced its Temporary Liquidity Guarantee Program (TLGP). In addition to the Transaction Account Guarantee (TAG), which provided on a temporary basis unlimited deposit insurance for non-interest bearing transaction accounts, the TLGP also provided a Debt Guarantee Program for unsecured bank debt issued on or before June 30, 2009 (later extended to October 31, 2009), with the guarantee extending to the earlier of the debt's maturity or June 30, 2012 (later extended to December 31, 2012). The FDIC then stated that it would consider applications for an emergency guarantee facility for senior unsecured bank debt issued before April 30, 2010. This program covered loans of up to three years maturity, but not commercial paper of less than thirty days maturity. Dodd–Frank eliminated any concerns over whether this program was justified under the FDIC's systemic risk exception (since it was for a group of banks and not limited to failing banks)[19] in section 1105 when it specifically authorized the FDIC, after consultation with the Fed, to "create a widely available program to guarantee the obligations of solvent insured depository institutions" or their solvent holding companies "during times of severe economic distress." Dodd–Frank Act, § 1105.

QUESTIONS AND NOTES

1. The FDIC's website contains a deposit insurance estimator program. It is called EDIE (Electronic Deposit Insurance Estimator), <www2.fdic.gov/edie/index.html>. You may wish to run the example given above for Jerry and Marcia through this program to see if it provides the same result, or devise your own example.

2. Should the amount of federal deposit insurance coverage be *per person* across all institutions? Is the FDIC insuring the depositor or the solvency of the institution which holds the deposit?

3. Small banks were especially grateful for the increase in the SMDIA to $250,000. Why do you think that small banks often care more about the deposit insurance amount than larger banks?

D. BROKERED DEPOSITS

Brokered deposits come to a bank from a deposit broker who is seeking to split a customer's deposits among institutions to obtain full

---

18. See also Timothy R. Zinnecker, When a Hundred Grand Just Isn't Enough: Fifty Hypotheticals that Explore the Contours of FDIC Deposit Insurance Coverage, 72 Tenn. L. Rev. 1005 (2005).

19. See supra note 15.

FDIC coverage and to earn the best interest rates available on those deposits. Brokered deposits are sometimes referred to as "hot money" because they are not a stable supply of funding for banks. If a higher interest rate is available elsewhere, the broker is likely to move the deposit to an institution offering a higher rate (if the deposit may be withdrawn without penalty).

GARY PLASTIC PACKAGING CORP. v. MERRILL LYNCH, PIERCE, FENNER & SMITH, INC.

shouldn't have dismissed

United States Court of Appeals, Second Circuit, 1985.
756 F.2d 230.

CARDAMONE, CIRCUIT JUDGE.

On this appeal we must determine whether a program devised by defendants Merrill, Lynch, Pierce, Fenner & Smith, Inc. (Merrill Lynch) and its wholly-owned subsidiary, Merrill Lynch Money Markets, Inc. (Money Markets), to sell bank certificates of deposit (CDs) is within the compass of the federal securities law. In Marine Bank v. Weaver, 455 U.S. 551 (1982), the Supreme Court held that a conventional CD purchased from an issuing bank is not a security under the antifraud provisions of the federal securities laws. Nonetheless, the Court stated that each transaction must be analyzed on the content of the particular instrument involved and the factual setting as a whole. The possibility that in certain circumstances a CD might be a security within the scope of the federal securities laws was specifically left open.

The complaint alleges that defendants publish the Money Market Information Bulletin, which tells prospective customers that Merrill Lynch has available negotiable, insured, and liquid $100,000 CDs, for which they will maintain a secondary market. Defendants advertise that they screen daily a large group of quality banks to provide their customers with CDs with "competitive" yields from a variety of issuers. They represent that they will monitor the creditworthiness of issuing banks on a regular basis, and they discourage potential customers from seeking to deal directly with those banks. If the allegations of plaintiff's amended complaint are true, this sales message might be characterized as artful, but certainly not candid.

Plaintiff, who purchased 12 of the $100,000 CDs, claims that these certificates are not those regularly available at the issuing banks. Instead, plaintiff asserts that these CDs are specially created, issued and sold only to Merrill Lynch customers. Most significantly, plaintiff alleges that the rates of interest on the Merrill Lynch CDs were lower than the rates paid by the banks on their ordinarily issued CDs and that defendants pocketed the difference between the rates as an <u>undisclosed commission</u>. From the gold that flows through a broker's hands, a small shaving may be taken as commission. Yet, credibility and confidence in the market may demand that the amount of this shaving be revealed to investors. At this early stage of the litigation, before any discovery, it is difficult to discern if there

ML IR's lower of Δ's pocketed the difference as undisclosed commission

is merit to plaintiff's claims against these defendants. It is sufficient to say that in our view plaintiff's complaint states a cause of action and should not have been dismissed on defendants' motion for summary judgment. * * *

When, in 1982, plaintiff ordered 12 CDs from Merrill Lynch, Money Markets contacted financial institutions in various parts of the country, and purchased the CDs. For each certificate of deposit purchased, Gary Plastic received an order ticket and a confirmation slip from Merrill Lynch. The actual CDs were held by the "delivery agent," Manufacturers Hanover Trust Company, and when they matured Gary Plastic received all principal and interest due it under the terms of the confirmation slips.

On May 20, 1983, plaintiff brought this action. The gravamen of the complaint was that the interest rates shown on the customer confirmation slips were lower than the interest rates actually paid by the banks according to the terms of the deposit certificates. The complaint further asserted that while defendants in the Money Market Information Bulletin purported to perform its services free of charge, they actually retained the difference between the rate shown on the confirmation slip and the actual certificate of deposit rate as an "excessive, undisclosed commission." Plaintiff further charged that the Bulletin omitted and misrepresented material facts in violation of the antifraud provisions of the 1933 and 1934 Acts and that in violation of § 5(a) of the 1933 Act, defendants sold the CDs when no registration statement was in effect.

On April 17, 1984 plaintiff's counsel met informally with Merrill Lynch employees and, for the first time, learned how Merrill Lynch operated its CD Program. Although the information plaintiff obtained during that meeting was far from complete, plaintiff realized that some of the factual assumptions upon which its complaint was based were incorrect. The complaint's premise that the confirmation slips and the certificates of deposit stated different rates of interest was inaccurate. In its proposed amended complaint plaintiff has set forth the facts that came to light during the meeting. Essentially, Merrill Lynch determines on a given day the lowest interest rate it can market (the "competitive" rate) and has its subsidiary Money Markets purchase CDs in bulk from various banks at that rate. The banks specially create these CDs for Money Markets and Merrill Lynch markets them to its customers. Money Markets pays a commission to Merrill Lynch for the sale. Merrill Lynch furnishes its customer with a confirmation slip indicating that it acted as agent on its customer's behalf.

Plaintiff claims that the wrong in all of this is that Merrill Lynch never informed customers that the issuing bank was actually paying on its regularly issued CDs a rate of interest higher than the rate set on the instruments created for and marketed by Merrill Lynch. For example, plaintiff introduced evidence that Pacific Federal offered 15% interest to customers who purchased CDs directly from it, as compared to the 13.8% interest paid plaintiff on the CD it bought through Merrill Lynch. Similarly, State Savings Stockton was offering 16.1%, while plaintiff received only 14.5%, and Northern California Savings was offering 14.75%, while plaintiff earned only 13.8%. Money Markets collects the difference between the rates a bank agrees to pay on its regular CDs and the lesser amount it pays on CDs marketed by Merrill Lynch. Thus, plaintiff claims Merrill Lynch pooled funds and used its market power not to obtain the best rates available that day for its customers, as its literature implied, but instead to advance its own economic advantage. * * *

In the present case, the certificates of deposit sold through the CD Program satisfy the *Howey* test [S.E.C. v. W.J. Howey Co., 328 U.S. 293 (1946)] for determining what constitutes an investment contract within the meaning of the Acts. Gary Plastic invested $1,200,000 in its CD purchases. By investigating issuers, marketing the CDs, and creating a secondary market, Merrill Lynch was engaged in a common enterprise within the meaning of *Howey*. Finally, investors such as Gary Plastic expect profits derived solely from the efforts of Merrill Lynch and the banks. Plaintiff's investment in the CD Program was motivated by the expectation of a return of cash investment, the potential for price appreciation due to interest rate fluctuations, and the liquidity of these highly negotiable instruments. * * *

Plaintiff's decision to invest is obviously made in reliance upon the efforts, knowledge and skill of Merrill Lynch. This is a significant factor that sets this case apart from *Marine Bank*. At the outset *Marine Bank* acknowledges that it is dealing with a "conventional certificate of deposit," 455 U.S. at 552. In the present case, defendant's executive vice-president is alleged to have characterized the CD created and sold through the CD Program as *wholly different* from an ordinary certificate of deposit. The Weavers dealt with the issuing bank. As a result, the FDIC protected them fully against any risk of loss due to the insolvency of the bank from which they expected to derive their profits. The CD Program investor relies not only on the future solvency of the issuing bank, but also on the future solvency of Merrill Lynch to enjoy the unique benefits of this investment opportunity. The federal banking laws, including the FDIC, do not eliminate the risk to the CD Program investor. These investors are not "abundantly protected" under the federal banking laws. Like the holder of an ordinary long-term obligation, the CD Program investor assumes the risk of insolvency of defendants as unregulated borrowers. Unlike *Marine Bank*, federal securities fraud protection in this case is not a double-coating. Rather, absent the securities laws, plaintiff has no federal protection against fraud and misrepresentation by the defendants in the marketplace. * * *

Accordingly, the judgment of the district court is reversed and the case is remanded with directions to reinstate the complaint, as amended, and for further proceedings consistent with this Opinion.

[On remand the case was dismissed for failure to prosecute. The dismissal was affirmed on appeal. 903 F.2d 176 (2d Cir. 1990)].

FAIC SECURITIES, INC. v. UNITED STATES

United States Court of Appeals, District of Columbia Circuit, 1985.
768 F.2d 352.

SCALIA, CIRCUIT JUDGE.

These appeals are from an order of the District Court declaring regulations promulgated by appellants, the Federal Deposit Insurance Corporation and the Federal Home Loan Bank Board, to be unlawful and enjoining their implementation. The regulations change the existing federal insurance coverage of $100,000 per depositor, per financial institution, by adding the qualification that coverage of funds deposited by or through a deposit broker is limited to $100,000 per broker, per financial institution. * * *

The stock market crash of 1929 and the Great Depression of the 1930's resulted in an almost total collapse of the nation's banking system, with the result that a large part of the public ceased placing their money in banks, and banks were unable to extend credit. To restore depositor confidence and stimulate economic growth, Congress in 1933 established the federal deposit insurance system for eligible banks, and created the FDIC to administer it. Banking Act of 1933, ch. 89, 48 Stat. 162 (1933). The statutory provisions currently governing the FDIC were enacted in the Federal Deposit Insurance Act of 1950, Pub. L. No. 81–797, 64 Stat. 873 ("FDIA"). In 1934, Congress established the Federal Savings and Loan Insurance Corporation ("FSLIC"), which operates under the management and direction of the appellant Bank Board, see 12 U.S.C. § 1725(a) (1982), to provide similar protection for eligible savings and loan associations. National Housing Act ("NHA"), ch. 847, 48 Stat. 1246 (1934).

Recent advances in technology, and Federal legislative and regulatory action, have given birth to the deposit brokerage industry. Deposit brokers assist two types of investors in placing deposits. Some assist the large institutional customer to deposit millions of dollars of funds, directly and in its own name, in certificates of deposit none of which, in any single financial institution, exceeds the value of $100,000—the limit on federal insurance. The principal advantage of this service for the large investor is that all its funds will be federally insured. This form of brokerage, known as "deposit splitting," is engaged in by appellee FAIC. Other deposit brokers, among them the members of appellee SIA, serve smaller, individual investors in one of two ways. First, the broker, acting on its own or at the request of a financial institution, may solicit deposits from its customers, to be deposited with the institution either directly by the customers or by the broker (in which latter case the broker is listed as a nominee or agent, and notifies the financial institution that the funds are actually payable to the broker's individual customers). Second, a broker may engage in what is called (apparently with no apologies for transitiving an intransitive verb) "participating" certificates of deposit to its customers.

"Participating" CDs.

Participating Certificates

Under this method a broker purchases a certificate of deposit, sells interests in the certificate to its customers, and then notifies the issuing financial institution that it has sold the participating units and requests that the deposits be registered in its name as nominee. Whichever of these methods is used, under existing law each customer receives federal deposit insurance up to the statutory limit of $100,000 per institution. The principal advantage of this service for the small investor is that the readily accessible broker can place his funds in distant banks with higher interest rates, or (at least according to the Bank Board) can negotiate higher rates by reason of its aggregation of funds.

In November 1983, the FDIC and the Bank Board issued a joint Advance Notice of Proposed Rule making soliciting comments on insured brokered deposits. 48 Fed. Reg. 50,339 (1983). The concern prompting the Notice was expressed as follows:

> [D]eposit-placement practices enable virtually all institutions to attract large volumes of funds from outside their natural market area irrespective of the institutions' managerial and financial characteristics. The ability to obtain *de facto* one-hundred-percent deposit insurance through the parceling of funds eliminates the need for the depositor to analyze institutions' likelihood of continued financial viability. The availability of these funds to all institutions, irrespective of financial and managerial soundness, reduces market discipline. This impediment to natural market forces results in increased costs to the FDIC and the FSLIC in the form of either greater insurance payments or higher assistance expenditures if the institutions are subsequently closed because of insolvency.

B/c they all get FDIC coverage, this reduces market discipline + ↑ costs to FDIC FSLIC

Id. at 50,340. Following an analysis of the comments received, on January 23, 1984 the FDIC and the Bank Board published a joint Notice of Proposed Rulemaking, 49 Fed. Reg. 2,787 (1984), and, after receipt and consideration of comments, jointly adopted the rule that is the subject of this appeal, Final Rule, Brokered Deposits; Limitations on Deposit Insurance, 49 Fed. Reg. 13,003 (1984) ("Final Rule"). It reads in relevant part as follows (unless otherwise indicated, italicized portions indicate language applicable only to the FDIC, and bracketed portions, language applicable only to the Bank Board):

> Notwithstanding any other provision of this Part [12 C.F.R. Part 330 (FDIC); 12 C.F.R. Part 564 (Bank Board)], funds *deposited into* [invested in] one or more *deposit* accounts by or through a deposit broker shall be added to any other deposits placed by or through that deposit broker and insured up to $100,000 in the aggregate.

Id. at 13,011, 13,012 (to be codified at 12 C.F.R. §§ 330.13 (b), 564.12(b)).
* * *

The FDIA provides that the FDIC "shall insure . . . the deposits of all banks which are entitled to the benefits of insurance under this chapter." 12 U.S.C. § 1811. An insured deposit is defined to be "the net amount due to any depositor" up to $100,000. 12 U.S.C. § 1813(m)(1). And the net amount due to any depositor is in turn clarified by provision that "in determining the amount due to any depositor there shall be added together all deposits in the bank maintained in the same capacity and the same right for his benefit either in his own name or in the names of others." Id.

✳ These provisions establish a clear and unequivocal mandate that the FDIC shall insure each depositor's deposits up to $100,000, determining the amount of those deposits by adding together all accounts maintained for the benefit of the depositor, whether or not in the depositor's name. There is no exception based upon the identity of the person opening, or responsible for opening, the account. Indeed, even the possibility of a (much more plausible) exception based upon the identity of the person in whose *name* the account of held is explicitly precluded. * * *

For the reasons stated, the District Court was correct in finding both regulations not in accordance with law, 5 U.S.C. § 706(2)(A). * * *

QUESTIONS AND NOTES

1. In 1991, Congress imposed restrictions on the ability of banks to accept brokered deposits. Banks that are not well capitalized are not allowed to accept deposits from deposit brokers. 12 U.S.C. § 1831f(a); 12 C.F.R. § 337.6.

2. To attract brokered deposits, an institution must offer competitive interest rates. If the interest rates that must be paid on brokered deposits are higher than those paid on core deposits, and if an institution accepts a substantial portion of its deposits from brokers, what is the effect on loans and investments by the bank?

3. The OCC, Fed, FDIC, and OTS issued a joint advisory on brokered and rate sensitive deposits. This advisory states that deposits "attracted over the Internet, through CD listing services, or through special advertising programs offering premium rates to customers without another banking relationship" may not fall within the technical definition of "brokered deposits" in 12 U.S.C.A. § 1831f and 12 C.F.R. § 337.6. Joint Agency Advisory on Brokered and Rate–Sensitive Deposits, available at <www.occ.treas.gov/ftp/advisory/2001–5a.pdf>. Why is that? Should the statute and regulation be broadened to include these deposits within their scope?

4. How will the increase in the SMDIA from $100,000 to $250,000 affect the use of brokered deposits? Should banks and regulators be concerned?

5. The FDIC is directed in the Dodd–Frank Act to complete a study on core deposits and brokered deposits. Dodd–Frank Act, § 1506. This study is to assess the differences between core deposits and brokered deposits and their role in the economy and in banking in the United States. After conducting this study, the FDIC is to report to Congress on what additional legislation, if any, is needed. In proposing such legislation, the FDIC must consider the potential stimulative effect on local economies of redefining core deposits. It must also consider the effect of any proposed legislation on the competitive

parity between large banks and community banks that could result from redefining core deposits.

E.   SET–OFF

There is a common law right of set-off of a bank deposit against a matured debt owed by the depositor. For instance, if depositor has $20,000 on deposit in a savings account and owes the depository bank $15,000 on an overdue car loan, the bank could accelerate the car loan and set off the $15,000 owed on the loan against the $20,000 in the depositor's account, leaving the account with a balance of $5,000. The set-off right is sometimes codified in a state statute.

FARMERS' NATIONAL BANK v. JONES

Supreme Court of Kentucky, 1930.
28 S.W.2d 787.

It's too extreme to Reg banks to Debt-off @ mat. of loan – can't set-off special deposits

DRURY, COMMISSIONER.

Majority

* * * The general rule regarding the right of a bank to apply deposits to payment of indebtedness to it is thus stated in 3 R. C. L. p. 588, sec. 217:

> "It may be stated as a general rule that when a depositor is indebted to a bank, and the debts are mutual—that is, between the same parties, and in the same right—the bank may apply the deposit, or such portion thereof as may be necessary, to the payment of the debt due it by the depositor, provided there is no express agreement to the contrary, and the deposit is not specifically applicable to some other particular purpose. While this right is frequently called a lien, strictly speaking it is not such, when applied to a general deposit; for a person cannot have a lien on his own property, but only on that of another; and, as is well understood, funds on general deposit in a bank are the property of the bank. This right of a bank with respect to general deposits is more accurately a right of set-off, for it rests upon and is coextensive with, the right to set off as to mutual demands."

In 7 C. J. p. 653, sec. 351, practically the same is said, and it is there stated this right of set-off is optional with the bank. This seems to be the majority rule, but there is a minority rule to this effect:

Minority

> "When the debt is in the shape of a note or other obligation owned by the bank, on which there are indorsers, sureties, or other parties not primarily liable, the bank is bound to apply the deposit for the protection of such parties. This duty, however, exists only where the depositor is primarily liable; where his deposit is sufficient to pay the debt at the time when it matures, the bank being under no obligation to apply subsequent deposits; and where the deposit has not been previously appropriated by the depositor to any other use." * * *

There are cases going even beyond the minority rule and holding that not only must a bank exercise its right of set-off when the paper matures, but which go further and hold that sureties are released if it fails to exercise this right if the principal debtor makes deposits subsequent to the maturity of the paper.

The states taking this extreme position are Delaware and Kentucky. See McDowell v. President, etc., of Bank of Wilmington, 1 Harr. 369; Bank of Taylorsville v. Hardesty, 91 S.W. 729; Burgess v. Deposit Bank, 97 S.W. 761.

This is a rather extreme position and this court so recognized it, in the case of Eades v. Muhlenberg Savings Bank, 163 S.W. 494, 496, where we said:

> "While it is true that where a bank is the holder of a note payable at the bank, and upon its maturity the maker has a cash deposit in the bank sufficient to pay it, not specially applicable to a particular purpose, the bank is bound to charge the amount of the note against the deposit, and its failure to do so will discharge an indorser or surety (German Nat. Bank v. Foreman, 21 A. 20), it is also well settled that the deposit must be sufficient at the time of the maturity of the note, and must not have been previously appropriated to any other purpose. Subsequent deposits will not raise the duty. Peoples' Bank v. Legrand, 103 Pa. 309; First Nat. Bank of Lock Haven v. Emil Peltz, 35 A. 218."

This question is squarely before us now, and, if these two opinions are sound, they are determinative of this case, but, after full consideration, we have reached the conclusion this position is too extreme—that these two opinions, Bank of Taylorsville v. Hardesty, 91 S.W. 729, and Burgess v. Deposit Bank, 97 S.W. 761, in so far as they hold a bank must exercise its right of set-off as to deposits made by a principal debtor subsequent to the maturity of his note, and while it is in the hands of the bank and past due, under pain of releasing the sureties on the note, are unsound and they are expressly overruled.

It is usually the desire of the surety to help, and not to cripple, his principal; usually it is some tie of kindred, friendship, or business relation that induces the surety to become such. The signature of the surety is a most solemn declaration of his desire to aid the principal debtor. It frequently happens that considerable time is consumed in renewing notes, and nothing could be more embarrassing to a struggling debtor than to have the bank compelled to grab every deposit he makes while his paper is past due. * * *

———

Setoff is also precluded for funds held on "special deposit" by one party for the benefit of another. A special deposit is one in which the bank is expected to maintain the exact items deposited as a trustee of them so that the bank is required to return the exact items deposited to the depositor when he demands them. Title to the items or funds deposited remains with the depositor. As one commentator noted:

A special-purpose account defeats a bank's right to setoff because a third party who is not a debtor of the bank has an interest in the account. Since a party other than the bank's debtor has an interest in the funds on deposit in a special account, the bank may not exercise its right to setoff the property not belonging to the debtor.

Comment, Bank's Right of Setoff in Virginia, 41 Wash & Lee L. Rev. 1603, 1619 (1984). See also Central National Bank v. Conn. Mut. L. Ins. Co., 104 U.S. 54, 63–64 (1881) (discussing special deposits).

F. ESCHEAT LAWS

State escheat statutes provide that bank deposits, dividends, interest, and securities that remained unclaimed for a certain period of time and after reasonable efforts to find the owner, escheat (or are transferred) to the state rather than remain in the hands of the intermediary.

DELAWARE v. NEW YORK* *the st. in which intermediary is gets the $*

Supreme Court of the United States, 1993.
507 U.S. 490.

MR. JUSTICE THOMAS delivered the opinion of the Court.

In this original action, we resolve another dispute among States that assert competing claims to abandoned intangible personal property. Most of the funds at issue are unclaimed securities distributions held by intermediary banks, brokers, and depositories for beneficial owners who cannot be identified or located. The Special Master proposed awarding the right to escheat such funds to the State in which the principal executive offices of the securities issuer are located. Adhering to the rules announced in Texas v. New Jersey, 379 U.S. 674 (1965), and Pennsylvania v. New York, 407 U.S. 206 (1972), we hold that the State in which the intermediary is incorporated has the right to escheat funds belonging to beneficial owners who cannot be identified or located.

This case involves unclaimed dividends, interest, and other distributions made by issuers of securities. Such payments are often channeled through financial intermediaries such as banks, brokers, and depositories before they reach their beneficial owners. By arrangement with the beneficial owners, these intermediaries frequently hold securities in their own names rather than in the names of the beneficial owners; as "record owners," the intermediaries are fully entitled to receive distributions based on those securities. This practice of holding securities in "nominee name" or "street name" facilitates the offering of customized financial services such as cash management accounts, brokerage margin accounts, discretionary trusts, and dividend reinvestment programs. Street name accounts also permit changes in beneficial ownership to be effected through book entries rather than the unwieldy physical transfer of securities certificates. See Brown, The Shareholder Communication Rules and the Securities and Exchange Commission: An Exercise in Regulatory

Utility or Futility?, 13 J. Corp. L. 683, 688–691 (1988). The economies of scale attained in the modern financial services industry are epitomized by the securities depository, a large institution that holds only the accounts of "participant" brokers and banks and serves as a clearinghouse for its participants' securities transactions. Because a depository retains record ownership of securities, it effectively "immobilizes" the certificates in its possession by allowing its participants to trade securities without the physical transfer of certificates. Most of the equity securities traded on the New York Stock Exchange are immobilized in this fashion. Cf. Securities and Exchange Commission, Division of Market Regulation, Progress and Prospects: Depository Immobilization of Securities and Use of Book–Entry Systems 4 (1985).

The intermediaries are unable to distribute a small portion of the securities to their beneficial owners. When an intermediary claims no property interest in funds so held, they become escheatable. Between 1985 and 1989, New York escheated $360 million in funds of abandoned securities held for more than three years by intermediaries doing business in New York, without regard to the last known address of the beneficial owner or the intermediary's State of incorporation. N. Y. Aband. Prop. Law § 511 (McKinney 1991). Alleging that certain of these securities were wrongfully escheated, Delaware sought leave in 1988 to initiate an original action in this Court against New York. We granted leave to file the complaint, 486 U.S. 1030 (1988), and appointed a Special Master, 488 U.S. 990 (1988). We granted Texas' motion to file a complaint as an intervening plaintiff, 489 U.S. 1005 (1989), and every State not already a party to this proceeding and the District of Columbia sought leave to intervene. * * *

In *Texas*, we considered and rejected a proposal to award the *primary* right to escheat to the State "where [the debtor's] principal offices are located." 379 U.S. at 680. Although we recognized that "this State is probably foremost in giving the benefits of its economy and laws to the company whose business activities made the intangible property come into existence," we rejected the rule because its application "would raise in every case the sometimes difficult question of where a company's 'main office' or 'principal place of business' or whatever it might be designated is located." Ibid. Even when we formulated the *secondary* rule, we looked instead to the debtor's State of incorporation. As in *Texas*, we find that determining the State of incorporation is the most efficient way to locate a corporate debtor. Exclusive reliance on incorporation permits the disposition of claims under the secondary rule upon the taking of judicial notice. Although "a general inquiry into where the principal executive office is located [may] see[m] neither burdensome nor complex," we cannot embrace a "rule leaving so much for decision on a case-by-case basis," *Texas*, supra, at 680. The mere introduction of any factual controversy over the location of a debtor's principal executive offices needlessly complicates an inquiry made irreducibly simple by *Texas'* adoption of a test based on the State of incorporation. * * *

We remand this case to the Master for further proceedings consistent with this opinion and for the preparation of an appropriate decree.

JUSTICE WHITE, with whom JUSTICE BLACKMUN and JUSTICE STEVENS join, dissenting. * * *

TIMOTHY L. O'BRIEN
FORMER OFFICIAL IN BANKERS TRUST
FRAUD CASE CLAIMS A SET–UP

N.Y. Times, March 15, 1999, § B, at 4.

B. J. Kingdon, a once high-powered executive at the Bankers Trust Corporation, is being unfairly singled out as the mastermind of a fraud at the bank by his former employer and the Federal Government, his lawyer contends.

The lawyer, Stanley Arkin, said that Bankers Trust withheld stock options and other benefits from Mr. Kingdon, who has yet to be charged with any crimes, to compel him to cooperate with the Federal investigation into corruption at the bank. Mr. Kingdon is now the chief target of that investigation.

Moreover, Mr. Arkin said, Bankers Trust only pleaded guilty to criminal fraud charges filed against it by the United States Attorney's Office in Manhattan to complete its merger with Deutsche Bank A.G. of Germany more rapidly. Had the merger not been in the works, Mr. Arkin speculated, Bankers Trust would have more forcefully contested the charges. * * *

Last week, Bankers Trust pleaded guilty to Federal criminal charges that senior officers and employees in Mr. Kingdon's division had illegally diverted $19.1 million in unclaimed checks and other credits owed to customers to the bank's own books to improve its financial performance from 1994 to 1996. * * *

Bankers Trust agreed to pay a $60 million fine to the Federal Government and a separate fine of $3.5 million to New York state authorities for the illegal scheme. Unclaimed bank funds fall under ''escheat laws'' that typically require such funds be turned over to the state. Instead, Bankers Trust used the funds to pad its performance at a time when the bank was mired in a scandal stemming from questionable sales tactics involving complex financial products known as derivatives.

Mr. Kingdon later pleaded guilty to charges in connection with this activity, but two other Bankers Trust executives were acquitted of all charges by a jury.[20]

---

20. Paul Beckett, Jury Acquits Ex–Officials of Bankers Trust in Diversion of Unclaimed Client Funds, Wall St. J. Nov. 14, 2000, at B16.

QUESTIONS AND NOTES

1. In collecting checks, banks are subject to the Uniform Commercial Code (UCC), as adopted in their state. Specifically, Article 3 on Negotiable Instruments and Article 4 on Bank Deposits and Collections are of importance. Federal law also affects check collection. The Fed's Regulation J applies to collection of checks and other items by Federal Reserve Banks. 12 C.F.R. pt. 210.

2. Congress was concerned that banks were holding checks (especially those drawn on out-of-state banks) for excessive periods before providing the customer credit for the amount of the check. The Congressional response was the Expedited Funds Availability Act of 1987, 12 U.S.C.A. §§ 4001–10, and its implementing regulation, Regulation CC, 12 C.F.R. pt. 229. Neither the UCC or the federal statutes and regulations relating to check collection are discussed extensively in this book. These matters are typically covered in courses on the UCC.

3. The OCC's pre-Dodd–Frank preemption regulation on deposit-taking, 12 C.F.R. § 7.4007(b)(2)(i), provides that a national bank's deposit taking powers are not limited by state laws concerning abandoned or dormant accounts. A footnote to that provision, however, excepts "the type of law upheld in Anderson National Bank v. Luckett, 321 U.S. 233 (1944)," that applies a Kentucky escheat statute to a national bank.

SECTION 2. NON–DEPOSIT LIABILITIES

A. FEDERAL FUNDS BOUGHT

[handwritten in left margin: Like an unsecured short term loan]

Federal funds may appear as "federal funds sold" on the asset side of a bank's balance sheet or as "federal funds bought" on the liability side. Federal funds sold are a bank's excess reserves maintained on deposit at the bank's regional Federal Reserve Bank, which it has loaned to another bank that needs additional reserves. The transaction is essentially an unsecured short-term loan. Federal funds bought are recorded as liabilities because this represents the bank's borrowing another bank's excess reserve funds. There is a sophisticated market for the buying and selling of federal funds. These sales are often done in connection with repurchase (or repo) transactions.

B. REPOS

SECURITIES AND EXCHANGE COMMISSION v. MILLER

United States District Court, Southern District of New York, 1980.
495 F.Supp. 465.

CANNELLA, DISTRICT JUDGE.

* * * This is a Rule 10b–5 case involving allegations of deceptive conduct in connection with a highly specialized type of securities transaction, one which is used exclusively by a relatively small class of sophisticated investors. It is therefore essential to develop an understanding of the nature and purposes of such transactions, the market in which they occur, and the expectations of the persons and institutions that engage in them.

The transaction is commonly known as a "repurchase agreement," or "repo" for short, although it is sometimes also called a "buy/buy back." It involves two parties, who, for reasons that may become clearer, may be deemed the "borrower" and "lender." Each agreement may also be viewed as comprising two distinguishable transactions, which, although agreed upon simultaneously, are performed at different times: (1) the borrower agrees to sell, and the lender agrees to buy, upon immediate payment and delivery, specified securities at a specified price; and (2) the borrower agrees to buy and the lender agrees to sell, with payment and delivery at a specified future date or, if the agreement is "open," on demand the same securities for the same price plus interest on the price. The parties customarily provide that any interest accruing on the securities between the dates of the initial purchase and subsequent "repurchase" remains the borrower's property.

From a purely economic perspective, therefore, a repo is essentially a short-term collateralized loan, and the parties to these transactions tend to perceive them as such. The element of the transaction over which the most bargaining usually occurs is the interest rate. The parties customarily refer to the underlying securities as "collateral," and the risk of a change in the value of the collateral remains with the borrower, even though the lender "owns" it for the term of the agreement.

Why, then, are these deals structured as sales and repurchases rather than straight loans? The answer appears to be threefold: (1) certain regulations of the Federal Reserve Bank (the "Fed"), which treat repos differently from ordinary loans; (2) a desire to circumvent the U.C.C. requirements and other legal obstacles to using ordinary collateralized loans; and (3) market convention.

In order to understand the repo market, a brief discussion of the "federal funds" market may be helpful, since the development of repos is by and large related to that of federal funds transactions, which they resemble considerably. Since the early days of the Fed, member banks have traded reserve balances[21] as a means of allowing those with reserves

---

21. [n.7] Regulation D of the Federal Reserve Bank [sic], 12 C.F.R. §§ 204.1–204.5 (1980), requires member banks to retain a certain specified percentage of their deposits as "reserves," which means, in essence, as uninvested funds. Reserves may be maintained in two forms, either as deposits by the member bank in its non-interest bearing reserve account at the Fed, or as currency and coin held by the member bank. 12 C.F.R. § 204.2 (1980).

Since failure to maintain adequate reserves to meet requirements will subject a bank to penalties, id. § 204.3(b), (d), whereas reserves in excess of requirements constitute unnecessarily idle assets, banks generally aim to meet their requirements as closely as possible. Bank deposits fluctuate, however, and member banks often find themselves with an unanticipated reserve surplus or deficit. In order to make short-term adjustments to their reserve positions, therefore, banks developed the practice of trading reserve balances. To effect such a trade, a bank simply instructs the Fed to transfer funds from its reserve account to that of another member. These transfers, which are usually overnight loans, are commonly known as "fed funds" transactions.

below their legal requirements to borrow reserves from those with reserves in excess of their legal requirements. This enables the borrowing bank to meet its reserve requirements without having to sell securities from its portfolio, and at relatively lost [sic] cost. Since reserve deficits and surpluses can often be brief, most member banks prefer to borrow or lend reserves for relatively short periods, usually overnight, which is possible since such loans are effected over the federal wire.[22] These transactions also benefit the lending banks, since any reserves in excess of their legal requirements are unnecessarily idle assets. And because of their short duration, they do not significantly impair the lending banks' liquidity. As with repos, such transactions are referred to as sales and purchases rather than loans. A borrowing of reserve balances which came to be known as "federal funds" or "fed funds" is usually characterized as a "purchase" with an agreement to resell, and a loan as a "sale" with an agreement to repurchase.

Apparently because of their purpose, the Fed treats fed funds transactions differently from either ordinary loans or deposits. Unlike ordinary loans, "sales" of federal funds are exempt from loan limits, and unlike ordinary deposits, "purchases" of federal funds are exempt from reserve requirements. The Fed has also acknowledged that certain borrowings by member banks from other institutions, such as savings banks, are essentially identical, and consequently, it has ruled that these, too, are exempt from reserve requirements. The phrase "federal funds transactions," therefore, now generally encompasses all unsecured "loans made in immediately usable funds, against which a commercial bank borrower isn't required to maintain reserves."

Repos are different from federal funds transactions in essentially only two ways. First, fed funds by definition can be traded only by institutions whose unsecured loans to member banks are exempt from reserve requirements, whereas repos can be done by anyone with enough money. Second, a fed funds transaction is essentially an unsecured loan, whereas a repo is essentially a secured loan. In all other respects, however, they are identical. Both are for very short duration, usually overnight. Both are settled in immediately available funds. And since one day's interest is a rather small fraction, both are done only for large amounts of money. Nevertheless, because of the speed with which they must be concluded, they are both done on the basis of an oral contract subject to a written confirmation. Moreover, so long as the collateral consists exclusively of government or agency securities, repos are exempt from loan limits and reserve requirements.

Repos also contain provisions for the treatment of collateral, which, of course, need not be included in fed funds agreements. Repos customarily

---

22. [n.9] Banks that are members of the Fed are linked by telephone wire to the Federal Reserve Bank for their region. In turn, these regional reserve banks are linked to the Fed's central computer in Culpepper, Virginia. Most transfers of funds therefore can be made by wire signal to the appropriate regional reserve bank which will then effect the transfers by bookkeeping entries. Consequently, paper drafts are unnecessary for transfers of funds between member banks. * * *

provide for a right of substitution, which means that the lender need not resell the identical securities purchased, but may substitute different securities of the same issue. Thus, the lender is not required to safekeep the collateral, but may sell, pledge, use or dispose of it in any manner for any purpose, so long as he resells acceptable securities on the repurchase date. Repos also customarily give added protection to the lender against fluctuation in the value of the collateral, by providing a "margin," that is, a spread between the value of the collateral and the amount of the loan. In other words, the lender will usually demand as collateral securities that are worth more than the amount of the loan.

For repos that last longer than a day, the lender may receive even further protection. "Term repos," which are those for a definite period longer than a day, and "open" repos, which are indefinite and may be terminated by either party on demand, customarily give the lender a right to demand additional collateral if the value of the original collateral declines significantly. In the event the borrower fails to honor such a demand, the lender may unilaterally terminate the agreement, sell the collateral on the open market, and hold the borrower liable for any difference between the amount of the loan plus interest and the recovery from the sale.

As noted above, the types of collateral most commonly used in repos are government and agency securities. One advantage of this is that the risk that the issuer will dishonor them is presumed to be nonexistent, and hence their value does not fluctuate significantly in periods of steady interest rates. Of course, like any other fixed-rate security, their value does fluctuate generally in relation to interest rates: when interest rates rise, their value declines; when interest rates decline, their value rises.

Another advantage of using government and agency securities is their ease of transfer. Most of them are not held in the form of certificates, but rather as bookkeeping entries at the Fed. Thus, they can be transferred without any physical deliveries. If a member bank wishes to transfer securities it owns to another bank, it simply wires instructions to the Fed, which debits one account and credits another. No certificates are necessary. Since the regional Federal Reserve Banks are all linked by wire, these transfers can be made almost instantaneously between member banks anywhere in the nation. And since immediately available funds may be transferred the same way, repos may be cleared very quickly. Regardless of the parties' locations, therefore, the funds and securities may be exchanged almost simultaneously shortly after they come to an agreement.

It is worth noting the different participants in the repo market. Most banks participate, both to adjust short-term cash and reserve positions, and as a continuing source of either funds or brief, highly liquid investments. Even the Federal Reserve Bank participates but only for the purpose of making short-term adjustments to the nation's money supply

Among the important lenders in the repo market are large corporations and state and local governments. These institutions regularly find themselves with vast amounts of idle cash for brief, often indefinite periods of time. At one time, they would simply have kept such assets in a checking account as demand deposits, which earn no interest. Within the last ten or fifteen years, however, they have grown much more sophisticated about managing their liquid cash positions, and have increasingly turned to short-term instruments such as Treasury bills, commercial paper, negotiable certificates of deposit, and repos as a means of earning profit on them.

Of all of these short-term instruments, repos are by far the most flexible. They can be structured as overnight deals and "rolled over" to whatever extent the money is not needed. Or they can be set up as open agreements. In either case they provide exactly what a money manager needs most: liquidity; security in the form of collateral; and a good return. Consequently, they have come to be viewed by many as "income-generating substitutes for demand deposits at commercial banks."

Among the significant net borrowers in the repo market are government securities dealers, who use repos to finance their holdings. Their activities warrant a somewhat detailed treatment, since the defendant in this case was operating as a dealer in government and agency securities. Most dealers run highly leveraged operations, which means that their investment positions in the securities they hold are significantly larger than their net capital. In other words, the dealers tend to borrow a very high percentage of the money they invest. According to one source, dealers as a whole "borrow 95 cents or more of every dollar used to buy securities, pledging the securities bought as collateral." According to another, "(t)he typical dealer is running a highly levered operation in which securities held in position may total 500 or 600 times capital."

Repos are a very convenient way to leverage capital in order to take large positions in a security. And it is easy to see how a repo can be used to borrow against either a long or short position. Simply stated, "long" means taking the risks of owning, while "short" means taking the risks of owing. When a dealer wants to leverage long, he can buy a large amount of a security and finance nearly all of its purchase price by immediately "hanging it out" on repo in other words, by borrowing the money and using the securities as collateral. Using repos to leverage short is slightly more complicated. The dealer sells securities he does not own, then lends the proceeds of the sale in a repo, receiving as collateral the same type of securities he has sold.[23] He then delivers the collateral to the initial

Log

---

23. [n.37] Market participants usually distinguish between "repos" and "reverse repos," or "reverses," but they are actually the same transactions viewed from different perspectives. Viewed from the position of the borrower, who first sells then "repurchases," the transaction is commonly called a "repurchase agreement" or "repo." Viewed from the perspective of the lender, who purchases then resells, the transaction is commonly called a "reverse repurchase agreement," or simply a "reverse." "Reversing securities in" means lending money and receiving the securities as collateral. Thus, using repos to leverage short is commonly called "reversing" or "running a reverse book."

purchaser to complete the transaction. Since all the parts of these transactions can be cleared over the federal wire, it is possible to arrange to have everything clear nearly simultaneously, thus enabling the dealer to avoid tying up much of his own money for long. * * *

Of course, these sources of profit entail risks, an understanding of which is essential to this case. The principal risks to anyone trading in securities are: (1) a "credit risk" that one's trading partner will prove uncreditworthy;[24] (2) a "price risk" that the securities involved will change in value against one's expectations; and (3) a "liquidity risk" that one will need cash at a time when it is difficult or disadvantageous to sell the securities or borrow money. These are not rules of law, but of the market.

As to credit risk, the best way to minimize it is to deal only with persons you know, either through prior experience or good reputation, and by contractual protections such as margin where possible. One protects oneself against liquidity risk by prudently tending one's own garden, and by paying attention to the various indicators of trends in the cost and availability of money.

Price risk is more difficult to minimize, because it depends entirely on prognostication. As noted above, for government and agency securities, the price risk is essentially the risk that interest rates will change. In general, once a fixed-rate debt security has been issued, its market value will vary inversely to changes in interest rates.

A highly leveraged position is very exposed to price risk. For example, if a dealer is leveraged long at 100 times capital in a particular security, a 1% drop in value will wipe out his equity in that position. To illustrate, if a dealer has used $10,000 of his own money and $990,000 of borrowed money to purchase $1 million of a bond at par 100, he can sustain no more than a one point loss without having to put up additional capital: if the price drops to 99, the bonds will be worth only $990,000, precisely what he has borrowed on them, so that his $10,000 would be gone. For short positions, the computations are similar, except that losses arise when the securities' value increases. * * *

Among dealers in government and agency securities are three special categories that are pertinent to this case. Certain dealers are known as "primary dealers," which the Fed describes as "institutions which buy new government securities directly from the Treasury and are ready to buy or sell outstanding U.S. government and agency securities." These, then, are the major marketmakers. Approximately thirty of these primary

---

Although the parties in this case used the term "reverse" as well as "repo," and usually distinguished them correctly, the Court finds "reverse" to be unnecessary, and sometimes confusing. Throughout this opinion, therefore, it has avoided using the terms "reverse repurchase agreement" and "reverse," and simply specified, where necessary, the borrower and lender.

24. "Credit risk" has two similar meanings. First, it is often used to refer to the creditworthiness of the issuer of securities, that is, the risk that the issuer will dishonor, or be unable to redeem, its securities. Second, it may be used to refer to the risk that a person with whom one trades will not perform his agreed obligations. The phrase is used in this Opinion only in the latter sense.

dealers regularly report their trading activities and positions to the Federal Reserve Bank of New York, and are therefore known as "reporting dealers." Finally, there is a group whom market participants call "recognized dealers," which are those reporting dealers with whom the Fed trades when it wishes to buy and sell government securities and do repos as part of its open market operations. * * *

[The court found that the defendant repo dealer's records were adequate. With respect to one individual, his failure to disclose his records was materially deceptive or manipulative, but an injunction was not justified, absent evidence that he committed securities fraud on any other occasion.]

MANUFACTURERS HANOVER TRUST CO. v. DRYSDALE SECURITIES CORP.

United States Court of Appeals, Second Circuit, 1986.
801 F.2d 13, *cert. denied*, 479 U.S. 1066 (1987).

PIERCE, CIRCUIT JUDGE.

The defendant accounting firm appeals from a judgment entered in the United States District Court for the Southern District of New York, Richard Owen, Judge, after a jury returned a verdict against it. The jury awarded plaintiff $17 million, to which the district judge added pre-judgment interest, post-judgment interest and costs, in a civil action seeking damages for losses that Manufacturers Hanover Trust Company ("Manufacturers" or "MHT") claimed to have suffered as a result of certain alleged misrepresentations that Arthur Andersen & Co. ("Andersen") made on behalf of Andersen's client, Drysdale Securities Corporation ("DSC") and its successor, Drysdale Government Securities, Inc. ("DGSI"). * * *

The mechanics of DGSI's repo business are not disputed. Ossorio and Heuwetter created a so-called "Ponzi" scheme that profited from the use of coupon interest on securities sold. The essence of the scheme was DGSI's exploitation of an important difference between government securities transactions in (1) the "securities" or "cash" market, in which securities are straight-forwardly purchased and sold at market prices, and (2) the "repo market," in which government securities are purchased and sold pursuant to repo or reverse repo transactions. In the securities market, the price of a government security, such as a United States Treasury note, includes the market price of a particular issue *and* the accrued "coupon interest" on the security (i.e., the value of government payments due on the security at the time of the sale). In the repo market, the accrued coupon interest is paid only on the repurchase (or resale) transaction; the initial "loan" of the security is made at a price that includes only the market value of the security. Before the security is repurchased, its price will be "marked to market" periodically to reflect changed value. By borrowing increasing volumes of government bonds through reverse repos, selling them in the cash market and utilizing the cash and temporarily obtained accrued coupon interest to meet obligations on previously borrowed bonds and to conduct other trades, DGSI managed to stay solvent between February 1, 1982 (when DGSI was created, with the liabilities it had inherited from DSC) and May 17, 1982, when DGSI's ultimate collapse occurred and investors lost some $300 million. * * *

[The court declined to decide whether repos are securities because section 10(b) and Rule 10b–5 applied in any event to the underlying security, and affirmed the district court's judgment in favor of the plaintiff. The court vacated the lower court's order permitting pre-judgment interest and remanded this issue to the district court for resolution.]

The collapse of another repo dealer, Lion Capital Group, cost investors $40 million.[25] Other unregistered government securities dealers that failed included Financial Corp. of Kansas City; Winters Government Securities; Bevell, Bresler & Schulman; Lombard–Wall; Comark; and Hibbard & O'Connor Government Securities. These failures were due in large measure to the fact that the government securities market was only loosely regulated. Although many broker-dealers in that market were registered with the SEC or subject to the oversight of the banking authorities, numerous participants—about 25 percent—were virtually unregulated.

Following these failures, the SEC proposed and adopted changes to its net capital rules to reduce the amount of leverage in repos, and imposed greater restrictions to avoid defaults. The SEC further required broker-dealers to make specific disclosures of risks in repo transactions to their customers. Congress responded to these failures by enacting the Government Securities Act of 1986. This legislation requires dealers in government securities to register with the SEC or, in the case of a financial institution otherwise regulated by the government, to file a notice with that agency. 15 U.S.C.A. § 78c. The Secretary of the Treasury was given authority to adopt rules governing the financial responsibility, custody and use of government securities owned by customers, transfer and control of government securities in repo transactions, and record keeping requirements. The SEC was given authority to enforce those regulations against government securities broker-dealers registered with the Commission; the agencies regulating other broker-dealers firms would enforce the rules against those firms.

---

25. Excerpted from Jerry W. Markham & Thomas Lee Hazen, Broker–Dealer Operations Under Securities and Commodities Law § 2.08[6] (1999).

BRYAN J. ORTICELLINOTE, CRISIS COMPOUNDED BY CONSTRAINT: HOW REGULATORY INADEQUACIES IMPAIRED THE FED'S BAILOUT OF BEAR STEARNS

42 Conn. L. Rev. 647 (2009).

* * * Prior to the summer of 2007, "the world experienced an unusual mix of financial conditions"[26] that resulted in a dramatic growth of a variety of consumer and financial markets, most notably the housing market and subprime mortgage loan industry. Large investment banks sought to capitalize on the boom in the housing market by not only buying considerable stakes in subprime mortgage loans, but also by "securitizing" and pooling these loans into structured assets that would be attractive to other investors based on anticipated return and risk exposure. These assets, known primarily as subprime mortgage-backed securities ("MBS") and collateralized debt obligations ("CDOs"), were particularly popular with two large hedge funds at Bear Stearns: the "High–Grade Structured Credit Strategies Fund" and the "High–Grade Structured Credit Strategies Enhanced Leverage Fund."

Despite their initial appeal, subprime MBS and CDOs turned toxic when the housing bubble burst starting in late 2006 and early 2007, and extending into 2008. Large losses from these investments quickly resulted in the evaporation of financing for private-label MBS, causing loss of investor confidence and the subsequent failure of many subprime lenders. As these problems continued to escalate in a vicious cycle throughout late 2007 and early 2008, consequences soon spread to Wall Street and Bear Stearns, which in the summer of 2007 attempted to save one of its hedge funds by injecting $1.6 billion into its reserves—ultimately to no avail as both funds eventually lost all value. * * *

To understand how Bear Stearns ultimately collapsed, it is first important to explain Bear's financing structure. As an investment bank, Bear relied on short-term (usually overnight) loans called repurchase agreements ("repos") to finance its daily activities and liquidity demands. Repos are secured by collateral (including MBS) that the borrowing institution promises to buy back at a specified date and at a specified price, "which typically includes interest at an agreed upon rate."[27] In essence, because repos were vital to Bear's daily operations, they left Bear at the mercy of lender sentiment. Thus, when the subprime mortgage crisis unfolded, lenders grew more fearful of entering into collateralized loans with Bear given the firm's large exposure to mortgage products. Instead, lenders hoarded their liquidity, uncertain about the health of their own balance sheets and those of their counterparties. "And it was the [eventual] refusal of Bear's repo lenders to extend overnight loans that confirmed that Bear had a liquidity crisis [in mid-March 2008]."[28]

---

26. [n. 25] Timothy F. Geithner, Former President, Fed. Reserve Bank of N.Y., Remarks at the Council on Foreign Relations Corporate Conference 2008: The Current Financial Challenges: Policy and Regulatory Implications (Mar. 6, 2008), available at http:// www.newyorkfed.org/news events/speeches/2008/gei080306.html.

27. [n. 42] See [Stephen A.] Lumpkin, [Repurchase and Reverse Repurchase Agreements, in Instruments of the Money Markets] 59, 62 [(Timothy Q. Cook & Robert K. Laroche eds., 1993)].

28. [n. 46] [Jose] Gabilondo, [Leveraged Liquidity: Bear Raids and Junk Loans in the New Credit Market, 34 J. Corp. L. 447 (2009).]

However, the growing failure of Bear to secure its vital repos in March 2008 was not the only factor that led to the firm's "liquidity crisis." While it may be said that Bear's repo problems kept it from pulling money in, Bear's exposure to a variety of deteriorating assets led to losses that eroded its already meager capital. * * *

Because Bear Stearns was an investment bank, it could not use its collateral to gain a direct loan from the Fed's "discount window," necessitating the utilization of emergency lending authority. Although technically the Fed did not lend directly to Bear, by providing the funds to JPMorgan to then re-issue to the firm, the Fed itself assumed the risk of the loan. "By any measure, this action was extraordinary," as the New York Fed provided Bear with approximately $12.9 billion, a move not seen since the Great Depression.[29] The twenty-eight day government guarantee was greeted with "high-fives" and cheers among Bear executives, who believed that the term of the loan would allow them enough time to find a private buyer for their firm. To the contrary, news of the loan was not nearly as welcomed by Bear's counterparties, or the market as a whole, as Friday saw Bear's common stock close down forty-seven percent, and the major ratings agencies (Standard & Poor's, Moody's, and Fitch) drastically downgraded Bear's long-and short-term credit ratings. Based on these developments, then-Secretary Paulson realized the loan was not a viable solution and contacted Mr. Schwartz [the CEO of Bear Stearns] that same evening, informing the CEO that the Fed-backed liquidity "would not be available on Monday morning."[30] Suddenly, twenty-eight days became two, as Paulson told Schwartz "[he] need[ed] to have a deal by Sunday night."[31] With most of Bear's customers and clients abandoning ship, there seemed to be only one likely suitor: JPMorgan. * * *

QUESTIONS AND NOTES

1. After much negotiation, JPMorgan did take over Bear Stearns at a price of $10 per share, up from an original $2 offer, down from Bear's market price of $170 per share a year earlier. Do you think the role of the Fed was appropriate in assuring that Bear Stearns avoided a bankruptcy filing that would have wiped out shareholder value entirely? See Chapter 3 for a discussion of the Fed's authority to make such emergency loans.

2. One commentator noted that:

In the [repo] market, a firm holding a security can make money on it (without parting with it for good) by pledging it as collateral for a loan. Due to market convention, the loans are styled as back-to-back purchase

---

29. [n. 90] [Stephen G.] Cecchetti, [Crisis and Responses: The Federal Reserve and the Financial Crisis of 2007–2008,] at 17 [(Nat'l Bureau of Econ. Res., Working Paper No. 14134, 2008), available at, http://www.nber.org/papers/w14134.pdf].

30. [n. 94] JPMorgan [Chase & Co., Definitive Proxy Statement (Form DEFM14A),] at 29 [(Apr. 28, 2008)].

31. [n. 95] [Kate] Kelly, [The Fall of Bear Stearns: Bear Stearns Neared Collapse Twice in Frenzied Last Days–Paulson Pushed Low–Ball Bid, Relented, Wall St. J., May 29, 2008, at A1].

and sale agreements, typically for a term of one day that gets rolled over into a longer effective term. The deal liquifies the security by letting the cash borrower convert the security to cash for the term of the loan, thereby enhancing the borrower's own funding liquidity. Especially for investment banks with large securities portfolios, the repo market is one of their most important ways of funding their activities day to day because repo (and reverse repo deals that are the mirror image of the transaction) let the firm reduce the carrying costs of their securities portfolios.

Jose Gabilondo, Leveraged Liquidity: Bear Raids and Junk Loans in the New Credit Market, 34 J. Corp. L. 447, 458 (2009). Bear Stearns and other participants in the repo market essentially used these overnight loans for long term permanent funding, which disappeared as liquidity concerns grew.

3. Another large investment bank, Lehman Brothers, also used the repo market for funding and faced problems similar to Bear Stearns. However, the federal government let Lehman Brothers fail, touching off a market panic in September 2008. Why did the Fed and the Treasury Department not arrange a rescue for Lehman Brothers? Fed chairman Bernanke testified before the Financial Crisis Inquiry Commission in September 2010 that the Fed did not have the power to save Lehman Brothers because Lehman did not have the collateral to support a loan, while AIG, an insurance company, did. How was that determination made?

4. As a result of concerns raised by the repo market freeze up during the financial crisis, The Dodd–Frank Act limits credit exposure for systemically significant financial companies to any unaffiliated company to 25% of capital stock and surplus (or any lower amount set by the Fed). Credit exposure includes repurchase agreements; securities borrowing or lending; guarantees, acceptances, or letters of credit. Dodd–Frank Act, § 165. Off-balance sheet activities, including sale and repurchase agreements, risk participations in bankers' acceptances, and standby letters of credit must be included in the computation of capital. Id. National bank lending limits include credit exposure from repurchase agreements, reverse repurchase agreements, and securities lending or borrowing transactions. Dodd–Frank Act § 610.

C. BANKERS' ACCEPTANCES

A bankers' acceptance is a negotiable instrument issued in the form of a "draft," which is simply an order to pay a stated amount of money to the holder of the draft on a specific date. The draft is drawn on, and accepted by, a bank. The accepting bank assumes responsibility to pay the draft at maturity. The Federal Reserve Act of 1913 sought to create a bankers' acceptance market in the United States in order to promote exports and trade.

A bankers' acceptance may be a "sight" draft that is payable on presentation. More frequently, the bankers' acceptance is a "time" draft payable a specific number of days after acceptance by the bank. A bankers' acceptance is redeemed at maturity for face value by the accepting bank.

Maturities on bankers' acceptances vary but typically are one, three and six months. Once accepted by a bank, a draft becomes a bankers' acceptance and is a negotiable instrument. It may be sold (discounted) by the party receiving the instrument upon endorsement and delivery, or the bankers' acceptance may be held until maturity. A bankers' acceptance may be eligible for discount or purchase by the Federal Reserve Board. The eligibility requirements have important implications for bank reserve requirements and banks' ability to issue bankers' acceptances. The restrictions imposed by the Federal Reserve Board on "eligible" discount acceptances are found at 12 C.F.R. § 250.165.

UNITED STATES v. DOUGHERTY

United States Court of Appeals, Eighth Circuit, 1985.
763 F.2d 970.

Woods, District Judge.

After a jury trial, the appellant, Richard A. Dougherty, was found guilty of twenty-five counts of misapplying $14,500,000 in funds of the First National Bank of St. Paul, Minnesota, and falsifying the bank's books and records. The nine counts of misapplication dealt with the improper issuance of bankers' acceptances in violation of 18 U.S.C. § 656. The remaining sixteen counts charged a violation of 18 U.S.C. § 1005 in that appellant willfully failed to record these transactions. Appellant was given concurrent sentences of a year and a day on three counts, five years of probation, and a $15,000 fine on the remaining counts by the trial judge. Appellant challenges the sufficiency of the evidence and the correctness of the jury instructions. We affirm the convictions.

Appellant was a vice president in charge of the International Banking Division of the third largest bank in the Ninth Federal Reserve District. The offenses charged were mainly related to the financial difficulties of a seafood processing venture by Transalaska Fisheries Corporation (Transalaska). Based in Seattle, the company proposed to convert a ship into a floating seafood processor and to harvest mainly king crab. In April, 1979, Dougherty secured approval of the bank's loan committee for a $3,500,000 advance for which Transalaska gave a term note. Conversion of the ship ran into delays and cost overruns, with the result that the ship was not ready for the 1979 king crab harvest. The 1980 season fell far below expectations. During conversion in September, 1979, Dougherty disbursed $350,000 beyond the approved limit, documenting the excess amount in a memo to the bank's president and in comments placed in the Transalaska credit file. Transalaska's financial difficulties worsened, and its officers began calling on Dougherty for more financing. He complied by using the device of unapproved bankers' acceptances.[32] The First National Bank of

---

32. [n.2] A bankers acceptance is a negotiable instrument, governed by 12 U.S.C. § 372 and applicable regulations and rulings of the Federal Reserve Board, which define and interpret the "eligibility" of the financing instrument. An "eligible" bankers acceptance is one which the Federal Reserve has authority to purchase. Eligible bankers' acceptances ordinarily, and for purposes of this case, are used to finance shipments of goods between foreign countries. The

St. Paul required approval of its senior loan committee for loans and credit extensions in excess of $100,000. Dougherty sat on the senior loan committee and participated in its weekly discussion and decisions on lending. He presented none of the bankers' acceptances for Transalaska to the loan committee for approval. Nor were they posted in the bank's general ledger. Proceeds of the acceptances were deposited into the company's checking account. On maturity date Dougherty paid off the maturing acceptance with a new one, in an amount equal to or greater than the maturing acceptance, since the customer was unable to meet the obligation on its due date. An overdraft would have resulted if he had allowed the account to be charged on the due dates. When a customer's account suffers an overdraft of $1,000 for five days, a computerized printout automatically goes to the loan review personnel. This pattern of roll-overs prevented what would have been a series of overdraft reports from coming to the attention of the loan review committee.

The same system of bankers' acceptances and concealment was used by Dougherty to finance the operation of David Noland, who was engaged in the restaurant business in the Minneapolis–St. Paul area. Dougherty extended Noland more than $400,000 in bankers acceptances during 1979 and 1980, none of which were paid. These advances were made in spite of the fact that Noland was a very poor credit risk. If anything, bankers' acceptances were more inappropriate in Noland's case than in the advances to Transalaska Fisheries.[33] Although the Transalaska and Noland transactions were not recorded in the bank ledger, Dougherty maintained a private desk drawer accounting of the transactions.

When it appeared that an audit in progress would uncover the concealed multi-million dollar losses of the bank, Dougherty went to the bank president and confessed that he had issued the unauthorized accept-

---

typical transaction involves an exporter who proves in some manner to the bank that he has a given amount of product which will be shipped to a foreign country. He must have goods or a firm contract at least equal to the amount of financing. The shipment must be consummated in 180 days or less. The bank may then agree to finance for whatever period of time the shipment will require by taking the exporter's promise to pay in the form of a written draft. The bank stamps the word "accepted" on the draft, and the authorized officer signs or initials the item. The document will provide for a given sum to be due on a given date, correlating with the completion of the shipment. An authorized officer then places on the face of the instrument an eligibility clause, describing the international transaction in goods which is represented by the acceptance. The proceeds of the shipment then are to be used to liquidate the transaction, without expectation of resorting to collateral or other security. The bank may choose to hold the acceptance until maturity, at which time the customer pays the bank. More commonly, however, the bank sells acceptances at a discount on the secondary market, with the bank paying the holder in the face amount upon maturity. The market maintains a high interest in the instrument because it is a secure, no-risk investment due to the bank's absolute obligation to pay upon maturity, regardless of the customer's ability to pay the proceeds from the transaction.

33. [n.4] In sum, the prerequisites to an eligible bankers' acceptance are:

(a) that there be a specific transaction involving the shipment of goods usually between foreign countries;

(b) that there be actual goods or a firm contract for sale of the goods, in either case, representing at least the face value of the acceptance;

(c) that the transaction take no longer than 180 days, to correlate to the time set forth on the acceptance; and

(d) that the acceptance be paid upon maturity with the proceeds of the transaction.

ances. Four days later he tendered his resignation. There is no evidence that appellant personally profited from any of these transactions or that he had any type of special relationship with the officers of Transalaska Fisheries Corporation or David Noland. * * *

D. LETTERS OF CREDIT

Another service rendered by banks to customers is the issuance of letters of credit. Letters of credit are instruments issued by banks that act very much like a guarantee of payment. As such, the letter of credit is a contingent liability and does not appear on the bank's balance sheet. If a bank is called to pay upon a letter of credit, a loan relationship may immediately arise with the account party who arranged for the bank to issue the letter of credit, pursuant to a prearranged agreement permitting the bank to be reimbursed by the account party on whose behalf the bank paid the letter of credit.

FEDERAL DEPOSIT INSURANCE CORP. v. PHILADELPHIA GEAR CORP.

Supreme Court of the United States, 1986.
476 U.S. 426.

MADAME JUSTICE O'CONNOR delivered the opinion of the Court.

We granted certiorari to consider whether a standby letter of credit backed by a contingent promissory note is insured as a "deposit" under the federal deposit insurance program. We hold that, in light of the longstanding interpretation of petitioner Federal Deposit Insurance Corporation (FDIC) that such a letter does not create a deposit and, in light of the fact that such a letter does not entrust any noncontingent assets to the bank, a standby letter of credit backed by a contingent promissory note does not give rise to an insured deposit.

Orion Manufacturing Corporation (Orion) was, at the time of the relevant transactions, a customer of respondent Philadelphia Gear Corporation (Philadelphia Gear). On Orion's application, the Penn Square Bank, N.A. (Penn Square) issued a letter of credit for the benefit of Philadelphia Gear in the amount of $145,200. The letter of credit provided that a draft drawn upon the letter of credit would be honored by Penn Square only if accompanied by Philadelphia Gear's "signed statement that [it had] invoiced Orion Manufacturing Corporation and that said invoices have remained unpaid for at least fifteen (15) days." Because the letter of credit was intended to provide payment to the seller only if the buyer of the invoiced goods failed to make payment, the letter of credit was what is commonly referred to as a "standby" or "guaranty" letter of credit. See, e.g., 12 CFR § 337.2(a), and n.1 (1985) (defining standby letters of credit and mentioning that they may " 'guaranty' payment of a money obligation"). A conventional "commercial" letter of credit, in contrast, is one in which the seller obtains payment from the issuing bank without looking to the buyer for payment even in the first instance. See ibid. (distinguishing standby letters of credit from commercial letters of credit).

On the same day that Penn Square issued the standby letter of credit, Orion executed an unsecured promissory note for $145,200 in favor of Penn Square. The purpose of the note was listed as "Back up Letter of Credit." Although the face of the note did not so indicate, both Orion and Penn Square understood that nothing would be considered due on the note, and no interest charged by Penn Square, unless Philadelphia Gear presented drafts on the standby letter of credit after nonpayment by Orion.

On July 5, 1982, Penn Square was declared insolvent. Petitioner FDIC was appointed its receiver. Shortly thereafter, Philadelphia Gear presented drafts on the standby letter of credit for payment of over $700,000 for goods delivered before Penn Square's insolvency. The FDIC returned the drafts unpaid.

Philadelphia Gear sued the FDIC in the Western District of Oklahoma. Philadelphia Gear alleged that the standby letter of credit was an insured deposit under the definition of "deposit" set forth at 12 U. S. C. § 1813(l)(1), and that Philadelphia Gear was therefore entitled to $100,000 in deposit insurance from the FDIC. See 12 U.S.C. § 1821(a)(1) (setting forth $100,000 as the maximum amount generally insured by the FDIC for any single depositor at a given bank). In apparent hopes of obtaining additional funds from the FDIC in the latter's capacity as receiver rather than as insurer, respondent also alleged that terms of the standby letter of credit allowing repeated reinstatements of the credit made the letter's total value more than $145,200. * * *

Title 12 U.S.C. § 1813(l)(1) provides:

"The term 'deposit' means—

> "(1) the unpaid balance of money or its equivalent received or held by a bank in the usual course of business and for which it has given or is obligated to give credit, either conditionally or unconditionally, to a commercial ... account, or which is evidenced by ... a letter of credit or a traveler's check on which the bank is primarily liable: Provided, That, without limiting the generality of the term 'money or its equivalent,' any such account or instrument must be regarded as evidencing the receipt of the equivalent of money when credited or issued in exchange for checks or drafts or for a promissory note upon which the person obtaining any such credit or instrument is primarily or secondarily liable...."

Philadelphia Gear successfully argued before the Court of Appeals that the standby letter of credit backed by a contingent promissory note constituted a "deposit" under 12 U.S.C. § 1813(l)(1) because that letter was one on which the bank was primarily liable, and evidenced the receipt by the bank of "money or its equivalent" in the form of a promissory note upon which the person obtaining the credit was primarily or secondarily liable. The FDIC does not here dispute that the bank was primarily liable on the letter of credit. Nor does the FDIC contest the fact that the backup note executed by Orion is, at least in some sense, a "promissory note." The FDIC argues rather that it has consistently interpreted § 1813(*l*)(1) not to include standby letters of credit backed only by a contingent promissory note because such a note represents no hard assets and thus does not constitute "money or its equivalent." Because the alleged "deposit" consists only of a *contingent* liability, asserts the FDIC, a standby letter of credit backed by a contingent promissory note does not give rise to a "deposit" that Congress intended the FDIC to insure. Under this theory, while the note here may have been labeled a promissory note on its face and may have been a promissory note under state law, it was not a promissory note for purposes of the federal law set forth in 12 U.S.C. § 1813(*l*)(1). * * *

When Congress created the FDIC, the Nation was in the throes of an extraordinary financial crisis. More than one-third of the banks in the United States open in 1929 had shut their doors just four years later. In response to this financial crisis, President Roosevelt declared a national banking holiday effective the first business day after he took office. Congress in turn responded with extensive legislation on banking, including the laws that gave the FDIC its existence.

Congress' purpose in creating the FDIC was clear. Faced with virtual panic, Congress attempted to safeguard the hard earnings of individuals against the possibility that bank failures would deprive them of their savings. Congress passed the 1933 provisions "[in] order to provide against a repetition of the present painful experience in which a vast sum of *assets and purchasing power* is 'tied up.'" S. Rep. No. 77, 73d Cong., 1st Sess., 12 (1933) (emphasis added). The focus of Congress was therefore upon ensuring that a deposit of "hard earnings" entrusted by individuals to a bank would not lead to a tangible loss in the event of a bank failure. * * *

Congress' focus in providing for a system of deposit insurance—a system that has been continued to the present without modification to the basic definition of deposits that are "money or its equivalent"—was clearly a focus upon safeguarding the assets and "hard earnings" that businesses and individuals have entrusted to banks. Congress wanted to ensure that someone who put tangible assets into a bank could always get those assets back. The purpose behind the insurance of deposits in general, and especially in the section defining deposits as "money or its equivalent," therefore, is the protection of assets and hard earnings entrusted to a bank.

This purpose is not furthered by extending deposit insurance to cover a standby letter of credit backed by a contingent promissory note, which involves no such surrender of assets or hard earnings to the custody of the bank. Philadelphia Gear, which now seeks to collect deposit insurance, surrendered absolutely nothing to the bank. The letter of credit is for Philadelphia Gear's benefit, but the bank relied upon Orion to meet the obligations of the letter of credit and made no demands upon Philadelphia Gear. Nor, more importantly, did Orion surrender any assets unconditionally to the bank. The bank did not credit any account of Orion's in exchange for the promissory note, and did not treat its own assets as increased by its acceptance of the note. The bank could not have collected on the note from Orion unless Philadelphia Gear presented the unpaid invoices and a draft on the letter of credit. In the absence of a presentation by Philadelphia Gear of the unpaid invoices, the promissory note was a wholly contingent promise, and when Penn Square went into receivership, neither Orion nor Philadelphia Gear had lost anything except the ability to use Penn Square to reduce Philadelphia Gear's risk that Philadelphia Gear would go unpaid for a delivery of goods to Orion.

Accordingly, the judgment of the court below is reversed, and the case is remanded for further proceedings consistent with this opinion.

JUSTICES MARSHALL, BLACKMUN, and REHNQUIST, dissent. * * *

CENTRIFUGAL CASTING MACHINE CO. v. AMERICAN BANK & TRUST CO.

United States Court of Appeals, Tenth Circuit, 1992.
966 F.2d 1348.

SEYMOUR, CIRCUIT JUDGE.

The United States appeals from the judgment entered in one of two consolidated diversity actions involving a letter of credit and a standby letter of credit. The letters were issued in connection with a contract between plaintiff-appellee Centrifugal Casting Machine (CCM) and State Machinery Trading Company (SMTC), an agency of the Iraqi government, under which CCM was to provide cast ductile iron pipe plant equipment to SMTC for a total contract price of $27,390,731. The contracting parties agreed that the payment mechanism from SMTC to CCM was to be an irrevocable letter of credit for the benefit of CCM in the contract amount, out of which CCM was entitled to draw ten percent as a down payment. This letter was isued by Central Bank of Iraq and confirmed by defendant-appellee Banca Nazionale del Lavorov (BNL).

The parties further agreed that a standby letter of credit in the amount of the $2.7 million down payment would be issued on behalf of CCM for the benefit of an agent of SMTC, and would be available to repay SMTC the amount of the down payment upon the requisite proof that CCM had not performed under the contract.[34] This standby letter was

---

34. [n.1] "The essential function of [a letter of credit] is to assure a party to an agreement that he will receive the benefits of his performance." Wood v. R.R. Donnelley & Sons Co., 888 F.2d 313, 317 (3d Cir. 1989).

"A variation on this arrangement is present where, as here, the bank issues a 'stand-by' letter of credit. The beneficiary of an ordinary letter may draw upon it simply by presenting documents that show that the beneficiary has performed and is entitled to the funds. In

issued by BNL to defendant-appellee American Bank of Tulsa (ABT), CCM's bank, as account party, and made payable to Rafidain Bank, which in turn issued a $2.7 million guarantee to SMTC. CCM drew its down payment under the letter of credit and deposited that amount with ABT as security to protect ABT against any obligation it might incur on the standby letter of credit. Although an attempt was subsequently made on behalf of SMTC to draw on the standby letter of credit, the attempt was not accompanied by proof of nonperformance by CCM, and was not honored before the expiration date set out in that letter.

The suits below involved claims to the $2.7 million down payment by CCM, ABT, and BNL, the bank that had confirmed the letter of credit in favor of CCM and had issued the standby letter of credit in favor of SMTC. The United States intervened, asserting that Iraq had a property interest in the down payment and therefore in the money deposited by CCM in ABT. The United States claimed that the bank account was a blocked account under the regulations implementing the Executive Orders freezing assets of the Iraqi government. * * *

We begin by observing that CCM received the funds at issue by drawing on an irrevocable letter of credit. We must therefore determine the particular characteristics of that financial instrument and ascertain the nature of the interest that it conveys. Because the term "letter of credit" is not defined in either the Executive Orders or the implementing regulations, we give it the meaning ordinarily attributed to it by courts and parties dealing with this document. See Propper v. Clark, 337 U.S. 472, 480 (1949).

> "[A] letter of credit involves three parties: (1) an issuer (generally a bank) who agrees to pay conforming drafts presented under the letter of credit; (2) a bank customer or 'account party' who orders the letter of credit and dictates its terms; and (3) a beneficiary to whom the letter of credit is issued, who can collect monies under the letter of credit by presenting drafts and making proper demand on the issuer."

Arbest Construction Co. v. First Nat'l Bank & Trust Co., 777 F.2d 581, 583 (10th Cir. 1985). A letter of credit thus involves three legally distinct relationships, that "between the issuer and the account party, the issuer and the beneficiary, and the account party and the beneficiary (this last relationship being the underlying business deal giving rise to the issuance of the letter of credit)." Id. In this case, CCM was the beneficiary of the letter which was issued by Central Bank of Iraq to fund the contract, BNL was the confirming bank which then became directly liable to CCM,[35] and SMTC was the bank customer or account party.

---

contrast, a 'stand-by' letter requires documents that show that the customer has defaulted on some obligation, thereby triggering the beneficiary's right to draw down on the letter." Id.

35. [n.4] "A 'confirming bank' is a bank which engages either that it will itself honor a credit already issued by another bank or that such a credit will be honored by the issuer or a third bank." Okla. Stat. tit. 12A, § 5–103(f). Here, BNL agreed to honor the credit itself. "A confirming bank by confirming a credit becomes directly obligated on the credit to the extent of its confirmation as though it were its issuer and acquires the rights of an issuer." Id. § 5–107(2).

Two interrelated features of the letter of credit provide it with its unique value in the marketplace and are of critical importance in our consideration of the United States's claim here. First, "[t]he simple result [of a letter of credit] is that the issuer substitutes its credit, preferred by the beneficiary, for that of the account party." Id.; see also Republic Nat'l Bank v. Fidelity & Deposit Co., 894 F.2d 1255, 1258 (11th Cir.) (letter gives beneficiary irrevocable right to payment, not from account party, who might become insolvent or refuse to pay, but from bank), cert. denied, 111 S. Ct. 308 (1990); Airline Reporting Corp. v. First Nat'l Bank, 832 F.2d 823, 826 (4th Cir. 1987) (issuer replaces customer's promise to pay with its own promise to pay); Pringle–Associated Mortgage Corp. v. Southern Nat'l Bank, 571 F.2d 871, 874 (5th Cir. 1978) (beneficiary's claim based on letter of credit, not on agreement between issuer and account party and not on the underlying contract). The issuing bank thus pays the beneficiary *out of its own funds*, and then must look to the account party for reimbursement. See generally Republic Nat'l Bank, 894 F.2d at 1257–58; Okla. Stat. tit. 12A, § 5–114(3) (issuer which has honored demand for payment entitled to immediate reimbursement).

Second, the issuer's obligation to pay on a letter of credit is completely independent from the underlying commercial transaction between the beneficiary and the account party. See Ward Petroleum Corp. v. FDIC, 903 F.2d 1297, 1299–1300 (10th Cir. 1990). Significantly, the issuer must honor a proper demand even though the beneficiary has breached the underlying contract, see id. at 1299; Okla. Stat. Ann. tit. 12A, § 5–114 Okla. comment (1); even though the insolvency of the account party renders reimbursement impossible, see Wood v. R.R. Donnelley & Sons Co., 888 F.2d 313, 318 (3d Cir. 1989); and notwithstanding supervening illegality, impossibility, war or insurrection, see KMW Int'l v. Chase Manhattan Bank, N.A., 606 F.2d 10, 16 (2d Cir. 1979). This principle of independence is universally viewed as essential to the proper functioning of a letter of credit and to its particular value, i.e., its certainty of payment. See, e.g., *Ward Petroleum*, 903 F.2d at 1299; Wood, 888 F.2d at 318. "Parties to a contract may use a letter of credit in order to make certain that contractual disputes wend their way towards resolution with money in the beneficiary's pocket rather than in the pocket of the contracting party." Itek Corp. v. First Nat'l Bank, 730 F.2d 19, 24 (1st Cir. 1984).

This assurance of payment gives letters of credit a central role in commercial dealings, see Bank of San Francisco, 817 F.2d at 1398–99, and gives them a particular value in international transactions, "in which sophisticated investors knowingly undertake such risks as political upheaval or contractual breach in return for the benefits to be reaped from international trade," Enterprise Int'l, Inc. v. Corporacion Estatal Petrolera Ecuatoriana, 762 F.2d 464, 474 (5th Cir. 1985). "Law affecting such an essential instrument of the economy must be shaped with sensitivity to its special characteristics." Bank of San Francisco, 817 F.2d at 1399. Accordingly, courts have concluded that the whole purpose of a letter of credit would be defeated by examining the merits of the underlying contract dispute to determine whether the letter should be paid. Andy Marine, Inc. v. Zidell, Inc., 812 F.2d 534, 537 (9th Cir. 1987); Itek, 730 F.2d at 24 (resort to underlying contract dispute risks depriving beneficiary "of the very advantage for which he bargained, namely that the dispute would be resolved while he is in possession of the money").

Because of the nature of a letter of credit, we conclude that Iraq does not have a property interest in the money CCM received under the letter. The United States contends in essence that Iraq has a property interest in this money because it was allegedly a contract payment made by Iraq, which Iraq should recover because CCM breached the contract. In so arguing, the United States makes a breach of contract claim on behalf of Iraq that Iraq has never made, creates a remedy for the contracting parties in derogation of the remedy they themselves provided, and, most importantly, disregards the controlling legal principles with respect to letters of credit. * * *

In rejecting the United States's position, we reiterate our recognition that blocked Iraqi property interests are to be broadly construed so as to effectuate the purposes underlying the blocking orders. We nonetheless are not at liberty to restructure the essential characteristics of a letter of credit in order to create a property interest that would not be recognized under the rules applicable to that internationally recognized financing instrument. Because those rules do not establish that Iraq has a legally cognizable property interest in the payment made to CCM under the letter of credit, the policies underlying the blocking of Iraqi assets are simply not implicated. The national interest is not furthered by creating a property interest out of conditions that would not otherwise generate such an interest, particularly when we must do so at the expense of a critical and unique device of international trade.

QUESTIONS AND NOTES

1. A standby letter of credit is sometimes referred to as a "suicide letter" because the issuer of the credit loses control of the ability to block payment even when payment is not actually due. This became a problem during the Iranian crisis when American diplomatic personnel were seized as hostages, American assets were then appropriated, and standby letters of credit called without justification. For a discussion of those events and the solutions imposed by the courts see American Bell International v. Islamic Republic of Iran, 474 F.Supp. 420 (S.D.N.Y. 1979), and Harris Corp. v. National Iranian Radio and Television, 691 F.2d 1344 (11th Cir. 1982).

2. How can a party protect itself from an unwarranted demand for payment under a standby letter of credit?

3. Letters of credit are "off-balance sheet" items. This means that the obligation is not reflected on the bank's balance sheet until the letter of credit is paid by the bank and a debt obligation is created for repayment by the customer. Should letters of credit be included on the balance sheet? Are banks

required to disclose this contingent liability on their financial statements? Are banks required to maintain capital against letter of credit obligations? What do banks charge for issuing a letter of credit?

4. There is no express authority in 12 U.S.C.A. § 24 for a national bank to issue a guarantee. Some cases hold that national bank, therefore, does not have the authority to issue guarantees of a third-party's debt. Ellis v. Citizens' Nat. Bank of Portales, 183 P. 34 (N.M. 1919) (and cases cited therein). Is a standby letter of credit any different from a guarantee?

5. Section 165 of the Dodd–Frank Act requires that systemically significant financial companies limit their credit exposure to any unaffiliated entity to 25% of capital stock and surplus. Credit exposure includes exposure to standby letters of credit. Moreover, off-balance-sheet exposures, including standby letters of credit, must be considered in the capital calculation for systemically significant institutions.

SECTION 3.   PAYMENT METHODS

Demand deposits and NOW accounts are important not only as sources of funds for bank loans and investments, but also as payment methods for account holders. Banks also provide other payment methods such as credit cards (which are short-term extensions of credit by the bank issuing the credit card), debit cards (which provide immediate electronic access to account funds), stored value or smart cards (on which value may be stored to facilitate later purchases), and electronic money. Some of these payment methods are described below.

A.   CREDIT AND DEBIT CARDS

NATIONAL BANCARD CORP. v. VISA, U.S.A.

United States District Court, Southern District of Florida, 1984.
596 F.Supp. 1231, *aff'd*, 779 F.2d 592 (11th Cir.),
cert. denied, 479 U.S. 923 (1986).

HOEVELER, DISTRICT JUDGE.

This case involves a claim by plaintiff, NaBanco that defendant, VISA has violated the Sherman Antitrust Act, causing plaintiff damages. Defendant issues the VISA card, used by many as a method of payment for goods and services, in connection with the transfer of transaction paper from a merchant through its bank to the card issuing bank. VISA regulations call for payment of an interchange fee ("IRF") if its exchange system is used. The interchange fee is set by the VISA Board of Directors. Plaintiff, among other things, asserts that the methods of setting and determining the interchange fee involves price fixing and are anti-competitive. Defendant asserts that the setting of the fee is reasonable, not only in method but in amount, and further that the VISA regulations encourage competition and are not in violation of the Act. The Court has determined that the plaintiff, NaBanco has failed to prove its case and that judgment shall be entered in favor of the defendant, VISA.

The last 150 years have witnessed the evolution of several distinct methods of payment for goods and services. Just as we once moved from an economy which relied heavily on barter as a primary means of exchange to an economy based on cash, so we now find ourselves increasingly becoming a "cashless" society. Today it is not unusual to find major sectors of the buying public foreseaking cash in favor of credit cards[36] and, even more recently, debit cards.[37] Unlike consumer currency purchases, however, these newer payment forms leave a residue of paper credits and debits which must somehow be cleared in order to complete a particular consumer transaction. * * *

The issues raised in this case can best be defined and understood in the context of the bank credit card industry and its history.

In the early 1800's, the two principal means of commercial transactions payment devices were bank notes issued by state banks and drafts. These payment forms satisfied the needs of commerce at a time in history when consumers and merchants would usually reside and do business in the same geographical area. Accordingly, payment media rarely had to be sent beyond the local area. Bank notes, issued by the local bank or banks, circulated through the immediate region and were used to a far greater degree than currency is used today. In the larger local transaction, and also in the relatively infrequent long-distance transaction, the draft was the typical medium used.

However, rapid technological changes in both transportation and communication in the mid–1800's, heightened the need for a medium of exchange which was acceptable to diverse and unknown persons across the country and which could travel easily and cheaply. The check was increasingly employed to meet these needs.

Despite the check's utility, other payment devices arose to meet more specific consumer needs. About a century after the check gained common acceptance, the bank credit card was introduced. The chief antecedents of this card were the retail merchant's "open book" account and the somewhat later-developed but more closely-analogous "travel and entertainment" cards. Unlike either of its two predecessors, however, the bank credit card has come to play a much more versatile role in the universe of payment systems. The bank credit card provides many of the same services as the personal check, but, in addition, provides retailers of goods and services an extra measure of protection from the risk of default. Incident to the system, and in most cases, the banks, not the retailers, are responsible for seeking payment from the retailers' customers.

---

36. [n.1] The term "credit card" is actually a misnomer. Not all so-called credit cards authorize the issuance of "credit," i.e., an opportunity to pay off amounts owed over an extended period of time at some rate of interest. To the extent that any credit card does not require a cardholder to pay for a purchase at the point of sale, however, a "free" or "convenience use" period is endemic to all credit card systems.

37. [n.2] A "debit" card typically accesses a cardholder's asset account at the card-issuing bank although a line of credit may be available as "overdraft" protection when the account balance reaches zero.

As in the case of the check, the bank credit card system is principally a four-party payment arrangement. It involves: (1) cardholders who use bank credit cards to purchase goods and services; (2) merchants who accept bank credit cards in exchange for goods and services; (3) financial institutions (issuer banks) which issue cards to, and contract with, cardholders; and (4) financial institutions (merchant banks) which contract with merchants to accept the bank credit card and thereafter manage the bank credit card accounts of these merchant clients.

A typical transaction can be most simply described as follows: Once a potential consumer has opened a bank credit card account with a particular issuing bank, he or she may use that bank credit card in lieu of cash to purchase goods and services from any merchant participating in that particular bank credit card system. The merchant, after a sale, then transmits the consumer/cardholder's draft evidencing this transaction (referred to in the parlance of the industry as "paper") to its merchant bank, this sum being immediately credited to the merchant's account minus a small charge agreed upon earlier by contract (called the "merchant discount"). If the merchant bank happens to be the same bank which issued the card, the consumer/cardholder's account in the bank will be processed "in-house" in what has been described as an "on-us" transaction. When the issuer bank differs from the merchant bank, the process becomes more complicated. First, the merchant bank sends the transactional paper to the issuer bank. The issuer bank then will either send the merchant bank the requisite sums due and owing from its cardholder, or will directly credit the merchant bank's account at the issuer bank, if the merchant bank has such an account. In either case, the issuer bank is ultimately responsible for the sums due and owing from its cardholders, and thus, absent a breach of agreed procedure by the merchant or merchant bank, the issuing bank bears the risk of default by the cardholder.

The process by which transactional paper is moved from the merchant bank to the issuer bank involves certain costs. In the system at issue here, the issuer bank withholds a small amount (called the "interchange fee") from the monies due and owing the merchant bank to cover the costs of this processing. Even more simply stated, the merchant bank (if not the issuer of the card used in a sale) must process the paper generated by the sale to realize both the small profit hopefully provided in the merchant's discount charge to the retailer and reimbursement for the sale amount credited to the account of the retail merchant. The paper then goes to the issuer bank which reimburses the merchant bank but only after the deduction of the interchange fee. This interchange fee is the subject of the dispute in this case.

One of the most successful three-party bank cards was the California-based Bank of America's ("BA's") local prototype credit card program, the BankAmericard. This program expanded in 1960 to a statewide system to take advantage of the ever-increasing pool of people amenable to credit card use within the state. This expansion increased the base over which the costs of the system could be spread. Still, the nationwide expansion of its principal competitors' operations (travel and entertainment cards) in conjunction with dramatic technological changes in data-processing and electronic communications soon led BA to develop its own national credit card program in 1966.

The BA network was achieved by means of a franchise program which permitted BA-licensed local banks across the country to issue credit cards bearing the BankAmericard name. The licensee banks actually owned the credit cards they issued, and created their own receivables by signing up local merchants who would accept the card. Licensees were also encouraged to engage other non-issuer banks as their agents to expand the merchant base still further.

With the advent of the BankAmericard licensing program came the concept of the interchange fee, referred to earlier as a means of paying for costs associated with transferring transactional paper. Included in the licensing agreement was a provision indicating the sum or "fee" licensees were entitled to receive when purchasing their cardholders' paper in interchange. The agreement provided that the merchant-servicing licensee had to send to the card-issuing licensee either the actual merchant discount earned in each interchange transaction, or the merchant bank's "average" merchant discount.

Between 1966 and early 1970, many of the BA licensees grew in size and expertise and accordingly moved for the creation of a system which could more accurately reflect their individual interests and concerns, as well as address some of the more pressing problems facing the licensee system. These concerns led to the formation of NBI, a for-profit, non-stock-membership corporation which was established in 1970. * * *

In 1977, NBI changed its name to VISA and exclusive rights to the name "BankAmericard" reverted to BA. To become a VISA member, of which there were approximately 13,400 in 1983, a financial institution must be eligible for federal deposit insurance. Upon proper application, any eligible institution can serve either as a proprietary member or as an agent of a proprietary member. There were 1866 proprietary members in 1983. Each can perform the function of issuing cards to cardholders and of signing merchants to participate in the VISA system. Proprietary members also elect VISA's governing Board of Directors which makes the rules under which the system operates. Agent members, 11,537 strong in 1983, elect only to contract with merchants on behalf of proprietary members; they are not eligible to vote for Board members and therefore do not play as significant a role as proprietary members in determining VISA policy. * * *

... [T]he Court makes and enters these additional and somewhat more specific findings of fact:

A. VISA lacks power in the relevant market. In the absence of such market power, VISA lacks the ability to impose any restraint detrimental to competition. * * *

IN RE VISA CHECK/MASTERMONEY ANTITRUST LITIGATION

United States Court of Appeals, Second Circuit, 2001.
280 F.3d 124, *cert. denied*, 536 U.S. 917 (2002).

SOTOMAYER, CIRCUIT JUDGE.

Defendants-appellants Visa U.S.A. Inc. ("Visa") and MasterCard International Incorporated ("MasterCard") appeal from an order of the United States District Court for the Eastern District of New York (Gleeson, J.) granting plaintiffs-appellees' ("plaintiffs") motion for class certification. We hold that the district court did not abuse its discretion by finding that plaintiffs had established that this action is maintainable as a class action under Federal Rule of Civil Procedure 23(b)(3). We therefore affirm.

Plaintiffs—a number of large and small merchants and three trade associations—bring this antitrust class action against defendants Visa and MasterCard, alleging that defendants have created a tying arrangement in violation of § 1 of the Sherman Antitrust Act, 15 U.S.C. § 1, by means of their "honor all cards" policy, which requires stores that accept defendants' credit cards to accept their debit cards as well. Plaintiffs also allege that defendants have attempted and conspired to monopolize the debit card market in violation of § 2 of the Sherman Act, 15 U.S.C. § 2.

* * * Although Visa and MasterCard are separate associations, their rules permit "duality," which allows banks to be members of both associations and to issue both brands of credit cards. There is a 95 percent overlap between Visa's and MasterCard's memberships, and virtually every retailer that accepts one of defendants' credit cards also accepts the other's credit cards. Additionally, as a result of the duality policy, Visa and MasterCard coordinate many of their policies.

Visa and MasterCard, through member banks, issue different types of payment cards, including credit cards and debit cards. Member banks, called card-issuing institutions, rather than defendants themselves, issue payment cards to consumers and set the cardholders' interest rates and fees. Other member banks, called acquiring institutions, contract on behalf of Visa and MasterCard with retailers to accept their payment cards. When a cardholder makes a purchase with his or her Visa or MasterCard payment card at a merchant's store, the acquiring institution reimburses the merchant the purchase price less a "discount fee" and the acquiring institution pays the card-issuing institution an "interchange fee." The interchange fee is set by Visa and MasterCard, and the discount fee is based largely on the interchange fee.[38] Plaintiffs allege that, because

---

38. [n.2] As the district court noted, the complaint includes the following illustration of the chain of transactions:

Bank A issues a Visa credit card to Consumer X, who purchases a garment for $100 at Store Y, which was "acquired" for Visa by Bank B. Visa rules mandate that Bank B must pay Bank A an interchange fee of 1.25% of the amount of the transaction, i.e., $1.25. Bank B will charge

of defendants' policy of duality, there is a high degree of uniformity in both the interest rates and fees charged by defendants' member banks to cardholders and in the discount rates charged by defendants' member banks to merchants accepting Visa and MasterCard payment cards.

This action centers around a class of debit cards issued by Visa and MasterCard. A debit card is an access device which enables a cardholder, among other things, to withdraw cash from his or her bank account at an automated teller machine and to make purchases at a point of sale ("POS") which are debited against the cardholder's bank account. POS debit card transactions can either be "on-line" or "off-line." In an on-line debit card transaction, the cardholder enters his or her "personal identification number" ("PIN") into a PIN pad and then, during the retail transaction, the card-issuing institution verifies that there are sufficient funds in the cardholder's account and electronically puts a hold on the funds needed for the transaction. Within a day, the funds are moved from the cardholder's account to the retailer's account. In contrast, in an off-line debit purchase, the cardholder signs a slip authorizing the purchase (rather than entering a PIN), the card-issuing institution does not necessarily verify that there are sufficient funds or put a hold on those funds, and the funds take approximately one to seven days to be moved to the retailer's account. Plaintiffs contend that there is a higher incidence of fraud in off-line POS debit transactions because they are authorized by signature, rather than by PIN. Visa offers an off-line POS debit card called "Visa Check" and MasterCard offers one called "MasterMoney," both of which are the subject of this litigation.

Defendants have an "honor all cards" policy, which requires any merchant accepting any of their credit cards to accept all of their payment cards, including Visa Check and MasterMoney. According to plaintiffs, retailers are even prohibited by the defendants' "honor all cards" policy from asking customers whether they would mind using a different payment system. Defendants have set the interchange fees for Visa Check and MasterMoney at or near the same level as the interchange fees for their respective credit cards despite the fact that, according to plaintiffs, credit card transactions—which rely on the extension of credit—involve far more risk. The interchange fees for competing on-line debit cards—where the risk of non-payment is substantially eliminated—is far lower.

Plaintiffs contend that if Visa Check and MasterMoney were not tied to defendants' credit cards by the "honor all cards" rule, retailers would refuse to pay the high Visa Check and MasterMoney fees, and as a result, defendants would have to lower those fees. Plaintiffs also allege that

---

Store Y a "discount fee" higher than $1.25 in order to recover the mandated interchange fee and other fees that Visa rules mandate Bank B to pay Visa on each and every Visa credit card (and debit card) transaction and to earn a profit for itself. Thus, Bank B may charge a discount fee of 1.60% of the transaction amount (or $1.60) to Store Y. When Store Y presents Consumer X's $100 Visa transaction to Bank B, the bank will credit Store Y's account for $98.40, send the Visa mandated $1.25 interchange fee to Bank A and retain the $.35 balance of the "discount fee."

In re Visa Check/MasterMoney Antitrust Litig., 192 F.R.D. 68, 72 n.3 (E.D.N.Y. 2000).

defendants have undertaken measures to deceive retailers into accepting their off-line debit cards. Specifically, plaintiffs contend that defendants designed their off-line debit cards to be indistinguishable from their credit cards by making them visually and electronically identical and by setting identical interchange fees for their credit and off-line debit cards.

Thus, plaintiffs allege that defendants have created an illegal tie between Visa Check and MasterMoney and defendants' credit cards and have attempted and conspired to monopolize the debit card market in violation of sections 1 and 2 of the Sherman Act. Plaintiffs request both injunctive relief and money damages.

Plaintiffs moved to certify a class pursuant to Rule 23 consisting of "all persons and business entities who have accepted Visa and/or Master-Card credit cards and therefore are required to accept Visa Check and/or MasterMoney debit cards under the challenged tying arrangements, during the fullest period permitted by the applicable statutes of limitations." * * *

[W]e affirm the district court's grant of plaintiffs' motion for class certification pursuant to Rule 23(b)(3).

JACOBS, CIRCUIT JUDGE, dissenting. * * *

avoiding c.l or regulation

Both MasterCard and Visa settled the litigation in the spring of 2003 on the eve of trial. The terms of the settlement eliminated the "honor all cards" requirement, reduced by one-third the fee charged on signature-based debit transactions (until January 1, 2004), and provide a $3 billion settlement fund, although one source estimates that after the attorneys fees are paid, each retailer who is a class member can likely expect only a few hundred dollars over the course of several years.[39] After the settlement, Visa agreed to lower the fees it charged to Wal–Mart (but not to other retailers), but MasterCard did not. On February 1, 2004, Wal–Mart stopped accepting MasterCard debit cards. On a $40 grocery purchase, a supermarket pays Visa 24 cents in fees if the customer pays with a debit card and PIN, 35 cents in fees for a signature debit card, and 50 cents or more for a credit card.[40]

Many banks have replaced their traditional ATM cards, which permitted the user access to other ATM networks through the use of a PIN, with Visa or MasterCard debit cards (that do not require a PIN for a debit transaction). Under the "honor all cards" regime in place before the settlement, banks earned significant interchange fees from merchants as a

---

39. William A. Cooper, Comment: Give Debit Issuers a Voice in Wal–Mart Settlements, Am. Banker, June 17, 2003; Stan Paur, Comment: Who Really Won Wal–Mart Suit? Follow the Money, Am. Banker, Sept. 4, 2003.

40. Robin Sidel, Cash Back: As Card Fees Climb Merchants Push PINs, Wall St. J., Jan. 16, 2007.

result of their customers' use of the debit cards in off-line debit transactions.

QUESTIONS AND NOTES

1. In separate litigation pursued by the U.S. Justice Department, the United States Court of Appeals for the Second Circuit affirmed the district court's finding that the current exclusivity rules, whereby banks using Visa and Mastercard are precluded from using competitors' cards, violates the Sherman Antitrust Act. United States v. Visa U.S.A., Inc., 344 F.3d 229 (2d Cir. 2003), *cert. denied,* 543 U.S. 811 (2004). The ruling was seen as a big win for American Express and Discover and a big loss for Visa and MasterCard. Banks have benefitted from the increased competition for their business. H. Michael Jalili & David Breitkopf, Two Years On, Gauging Effect of a Ruling, Am. Banker, Oct. 5, 2006.

2. Was an "honor all cards" requirement necessary to gain widespread use of debit cards?

3. See Chapter 11 for a discussion of the currency conversion fees charged by some credit card companies on foreign purchases. Competition authorities at the European Commission also charged that Visa was improperly excluding competitors from its network.

4. A number of suits were brought against MasterCard and Visa by merchants over interchange fees and rules barring surcharges to customers to cover credit card fees. The Dodd–Frank Act addressed some of these issues in the Durbin Amendment, although it was directed only to debit cards. Pursuant to section 1075, the Electronic Funds Transfer Act was amended to direct the Fed to adopt rules defining permissible interchange fees for debit cards. Since interchange fees are paid by a merchant bank selling a product to a bank that issued the customer the debit card, regulation of the fees charged does not directly impact consumers and is not, therefore, within the regulatory ambit of the BCFP. The interchange fees must be reasonable and proportional in relation to the actual costs incurred by the issuer. A significant exemption is that the fees do not apply to issuers with consolidated assets of less than $10 billion. The statute also affects certain network practices such as establishing a minimum or maximum amount for card use. It is permissible to establish a minimum purchase amount of $10 (with annual adjustments) and a maximum amount for institutions of higher education and federal agencies. Does this power to set fees turn banking regulation into a public utility like rate setting mechanism?

5. The Fed was further directed by section 1075 of the Dodd–Frank Act to prescribe regulations that prohibit operators of payment card networks from restricting the number of payment card networks on which a debit card transaction may be processed or imposing network routing restrictions. Payment card networks are also prohibited from restricting discounts by merchants favoring one payment method such as a debit card over another method such as a credit card so long as such discounts do not favor a particular credit card issuer or payment card network.

6.   As noted in Chapter 6, the Credit Card Accountability, Responsibility, and Disclosure Act of 2009 (CARD Act) restricted the ability of credit card companies to increase interest rates on pre-existing balances and required more disclosures on fees. It also prohibited automatic fees for cardholders who exceeded their credit limit. Instead, the customers would have to be given notice of the breach and fee, so that they could decide not to use the card in the future. Citigroup and other banks responded to that statute by sharply raising interest rates and fees in advance of the 2010 effective date of that legislation. Fed regulations under Regulation Z implementing the CARD Act have been issued in final form as various parts of the CARD Act became effective. See 75 Fed. Reg. 37526 (June 29, 2010) and 75 Fed. Reg. 7658 (Feb. 22, 2010) (codified at 12 C.F.R. pt. 226).

7.   MasterCard has become a public company, MasterCard, Inc., abandoning its association structure. See Isabelle Lindenmayer, A New Master-Card, Am. Banker, Sept. 1, 2005. Presumably the access to additional capital available to a public company is needed, in part, to deal with the litigation against the company. MasterCard could also enter new lines of businesses and compete more directly with banks as an entity independent from its bank members.

8.   Bank of America came under fire in 2007 for offering credit cards to immigrants in Los Angeles who were required to show only an identity card from the Mexican consulate to receive the card. Some critics charged that this program aided and abetted illegal immigration. Eunice Moscoso, More Illegal Immigrants File Returns; Taxes a Possible Boos to Future Legalization, Atlanta Journal–Constitution, Apr. 17, 2007, at 8D. The CEO of Bank of America responded that the bank had an obligation to serve all with authorized identification and that the Treasury Department's money laundering regulations permitted consulate cards to be used to open an account, or in this case, a secured credit card. Kenneth D. Lewis, Not in the Cards, Wall St. J., Feb. 22, 2007.

9.   The Dodd–Frank Act also requires disclosures on remittance transfers, including disclosures in foreign languages. Remittances are often used by recent immigrants to send money home to their families. Dodd–Frank Act, § 1073.

B.   SMART CARDS OR STORED VALUE CARDS

RICHARD R. HOLLEY, III
NOTE, ONE–CARD 101: WACHOVIA HITS
THE PIT AND BECOMES THE PARTNER BANK
OF THE UNC ONE CARD

4 N.C. Banking Inst. 371 (2000).

A "one-card" is a multifunction identification card issued by an institution designed to combine that institution's various card-related functions onto a single plastic card. In the United States, the one-card has found its greatest success in academia, with captive audiences highly dependent on identification cards. Industry experts estimate that out of the 3,500 four-year colleges and universities in North America, approximately 1,300 have some type of campus one-card program. Universities implement one-card programs to take advantage of the administrative efficiency inherent in combining identification, library, security, building, and food service access onto a single plastic card. * * *

There are two types of university one-card systems currently in use. The first is the magnetic stripe, or "mag-stripe," technology found on the back of all credit and debit cards. Approximately sixty-percent of United States checking account customers possess debit cards based on mag-stripe technology. The second type of university one-card system is based on "smart chip" technology, which implants a miniature microchip into the card. Many smart cards often feature a mag-stripe in addition to the smart chip. * * *

A "smart card" is a traditional plastic card containing an imbedded ultra-thin microchip. The chip on a smart card typically holds one thousand bytes of data, in comparison to a mag-stripe card, which usually has three sub-tracks holding 226 bytes total. The major difference between the two technologies is that smart chips can actually *process* data, such as separating and designating funds for certain purposes or calculating points earned in loyalty programs. The increased memory of a chip also allows for a greater encryption to prevent fraud. * * *

Merchants are interested in smart cards mostly for their potential for integrating loyalty programs. Merchants are not, however, as receptive to the idea of using smart cards to replace cash. Cash is convenient for merchants, since it does not burden the merchant with transaction fees or any delayed funding associated with card payment systems. Another important consideration, revealed during the 1996 Summer Olympics smart card program in Atlanta, is that cash, since it is untraceable, allows merchants to understate their receipts and subsequently lighten their tax load. This practice is not possible with smart cards, since a smart card system keeps a precise electronic record of all transactions. Franchisers, on the other hand, are more receptive to smart cards since the chip system will keep track of each franchisee's true revenues, allowing the franchiser to maximize its cut of the profits.

Smart cards remain in a prolonged stage of infancy in North America, which accounts for 0.5% of all smart cards in use, compared to 85% for Europe. Though the Global Smart Card Advisory Services Report predicts that the U.S. share of the smart card market will rise to 25% over the long term, adoption of the smart card market technology is occurring slowly and cautiously in America. Where adoption of smart card technology is occurring, colleges and universities could properly be characterized as the cradle of smart card technology in the United States. * * *

FDIC GENERAL COUNSEL'S OPINION NO. 8
INSURABILITY OF FUNDS UNDERLYING STORED
VALUE CARDSAND OTHER
NONTRADITIONAL ACCESS MECHANISMS
74 Fed. Reg. 67155 (Nov. 13, 2008).

* * * Stored value products, or "prepaid products," may be divided into two broad categories: (1) Merchant products; and (2) bank products.

A merchant card (also referred to as a "closed-loop" card) enables the cardholder to collect goods or services from a specific merchant or cluster of merchants. Generally, the cards are sold to the public by the merchant in the same manner as gift certificates. Examples are single-purpose cards such as cards sold by book stores or coffee shops. Another example is a prepaid telephone card.

Merchant cards do not provide access to money at a depository institution. When a cardholder uses the card, the merchant is not paid through a depository institution. On the contrary, the merchant has been prepaid through the sale of the card. In the absence of money at a depository institution, no insured "deposit" will exist under section 3(l) of the FDI Act.

Bank cards are different. Bank cards (also referred to as "open-loop" cards) provide access to money at a depository institution. In some cases, the cards are distributed to the public by the depository institution itself. In many cases, the cards are distributed to the public by a third party. For example, in the case of "payroll cards," the cards often are distributed by an employer to employees. In the case of multi-purpose "general spending cards" or "gift cards," the cards may be sold by retail stores to customers.

A bank card usually enables the cardholder to effect transfers of funds to merchants through point-of-sale terminals. A bank card also may enable the cardholder to make withdrawals through automated teller machines ("ATM's"). In other words, a bank card provides access to money at a depository institution. The money is placed at the depository institution by the card distributor (or other company in association with the card distributor), but is transferred or withdrawn by the cardholders. In some cases, the card is "reloadable" in that additional funds may be placed at the depository institution for the use of the cardholder.

This General Counsel's opinion does not address merchant cards because such cards do not involve the placement of funds at insured depository institutions. * * *

Under this opinion, all funds underlying stored value cards and other nontraditional access mechanisms will be treated as "deposits" to the extent that the funds have been placed at an insured depository institution. If the FDIC's standard recordkeeping requirements are satisfied, the holders of the access mechanisms will be treated as the insured depositors for the purpose of applying the insurance limit. Otherwise, the distributor of the access mechanisms (*i.e.*, the named accountholder) will be treated as the insured depositor.

This opinion is based upon the proposition that the form of the access mechanism is unimportant. Whether the mechanism is traditional, such as an ATM card, book of checks or official check, or nontraditional, such as a stored value product, the access mechanism is merely a device for withdrawing or transferring the underlying money. The "deposit" is the underlying money received by the depository institution and held for an accountholder.

The use of stored value cards as payroll cards has been popular with many employers, especially if a large number of employees do not have a bank account to which a paycheck can be automatically deposited. The Fed published a final rule providing that Regulation E applies to payroll cards established through an employer. The rule reduced the compliance requirements for employers, does not require the bank to send the employee written periodic statements, and does not extend Regulation E coverage to other types of stored value cards. 71 Fed. Reg. 54437 (Aug. 30, 2007) (codified at 12 C.F.R. pt. 205) (effective July 1, 2007). An OCC Advisory Letter outlines additional unsettled issues with respect to payroll cards. OCC Advisory Letter 2004–6 (May 14, 2004).

Stored value cards operate much like a prepaid cell phone and are a mechanism for banking persons with poor credit histories or those without bank accounts. See generally John T. Albers, Stored Value Cards: Should We Know the Holder?, 11 N.C. Banking Inst. 363 (2007). People who do not have a credit history or a means to open a checking account or apply for a credit card, find stored value cards useful. Wal–Mart is also issuing stored value cards as a means of entering the banking business and providing a service to its unbanked customers. Diana Middleton, Wal–Mart Banks on Its (Non) Bank, Florida Times Union (Jacksonville), July 1, 2007, at G–1. The Dodd–Frank Act subjected stored value cards to the regulatory jurisdiction of the new Consumer Financial Protection Bureau. Under section 1002 of the Act, selling, providing, or issuing a stored value card is a financial product or service so the provider is subject to BCFP oversight. Store gift cards are excluded from this definition of stored value cards.

C. ELECTRONIC TRANSFERS

The Electronic Funds Transfer Act of 1978 requires customers to be provided with documentation of electronic fund transfers, and limits their liability where a breach of security in an electronic funds transfer results in losses. 15 U.S.C. § 1693. The Depository Institution Deregulation and Monetary Control Act of 1980 allows the use of electronic payments among institutions that are in the Federal Reserve system.[41]

BISBEY v. D.C. NATIONAL BANK

United States Court of Appeals, District of Columbia Circuit, 1986.
793 F.2d 315.

EDWARDS, CIRCUIT JUDGE.

Sandra Bisbey challenges the refusal of the District Court to hold the District of Columbia National Bank ("the Bank") liable for a violation of the Electronic Fund Transfer Act of 1984 ("the Act"). The District Court found that the Bank, in its resolution of Ms. Bisbey's inquiry about her account, erroneously failed to deliver or mail to her an explanation of its investigative findings. However, the trial court concluded that the Act did not contemplate a finding of civil liability for this type of procedural mistake.

We reverse the District Court. Although there is no evidence of bad faith in this case, it is nonetheless clear that Bank officials failed to comply with provisions of the Act. Therefore, the case must be remanded for a determination of civil liability and attorney's fees.

Ms. Bisbey opened a checking account with the defendant Bank in January 1981. Subsequently, she authorized the Bank to debit her checking account for fund transfer directives submitted monthly by the New York Life Insurance Company ("NYLIC") for payment for her insurance premiums.

In September 1981, Ms. Bisbey's account lacked sufficient funds to cover the NYLIC directive, and no transfer was made. Thus, the September request was resubmitted by NYLIC in October, along with the latter month's directive. Appellant's funds were insufficient to satisfy either submission, both of which were covered by the Bank. As a result, two overdraft notices were sent to Ms. Bisbey, each in the amount of her monthly insurance premium. The appellant, having forgotten her nonpayment in September, believed that the Bank had erroneously made two payments in October.

At this point, Ms. Bisbey informed a customer representative of the Bank that she believed that an error had occurred with regard to these preauthorized transfers. Upon request by the Bank, she confirmed her inquiry by letter. Approximately ten days later, an official of the Bank telephoned appellant and orally explained that there had been no improper duplication of her premium payments. Ms. Bisbey, however, still considered the matter unresolved, and she filed suit under the EFTA.
* * *

In relevant part, the opinion of the District Court held that the Bank had failed to comply with its statutory obligation to provide written notice of its findings when it concluded that no electronic funds transfer error

---

41. Kimberly Kegler, Note, Electronic Banking: Security, Privacy, and CRA Compliance, 2 N.C. Banking Inst. 426 (1998).

had occurred. However, the trial court determined that section 915 of the Act, which provides for civil liability and attorney's fees for certain violations, was, by its own terms, not applicable to the mistake at issue. Finally, neither party was deemed to have acted in bad faith; thus, the District Court found that an award of attorney's fees was unwarranted. * * *

The Bank's foregoing failures to comply with the statute give rise to civil liability under section 915 of the Act. That section provides that "any person who fails to comply with any provision of [the Act] with respect to any consumer, except for an error resolved in accordance with section 908, is liable to such consumer" for actual damages or for a symbolic award. Thus, under the plain terms of the Act, civil liability attaches to all failures of compliance with respect to *any* provision of the Act, including section 908. * * *

It may seem odd that the Bank is held liable for a transaction that benefited the plaintiff. Ms. Bisbey's account contained insufficient funds to cover either of the premium requests submitted by NYLIC. Though she had no overdraft agreement, the Bank did not charge an overdraft fee. Thus, the effect of the Bank's payments was to provide her, at no cost, with insurance coverage she would not have had otherwise. Upon Bisbey's inquiry, the Bank gave her a correct report but neglected to send it in writing, as the statute requires. Ms. Bisbey conceded below that she had suffered no damage and the District Court's surmise that she may have been benefited seems correct. Despite this, the litigation has continued for nearly three years, and the statute compels a finding that the Bank is liable. Doubtless the discretion given the District Court to award only nominal damages and a "reasonable" attorney's fee was designed to mitigate the results of strict liability in cases such as this, involving a technical and non-damaging violation. * * *

EISENBERG v. WACHOVIA BANK, N.A.

United States Court of Appeals, Fourth Circuit, 2002.
301 F.3d 220.

BEEZER, SENIOR CIRCUIT JUDGE.

Eric Eisenberg ("Eisenberg")* * * was the victim of a fraudulent investment scheme perpetrated by Douglas Walter Reid ("Reid"). Reid falsely represented to Eisenberg that he was a senior vice president of Bear Stearns Companies, a large financial securities firm, and convinced Eisenberg to make a putative investment. At Reid's direction, Eisenberg transferred $1,000,000 via electronic wire to a Wachovia branch bank in North Carolina for deposit in an account bearing the name "Douglas Walter Reid dba Bear Stearns," "For Further Credit to BEAR STEARNS." The electronic transfer was made through the "Fedwire" wire service operated by the Federal Reserve Bank. Wachovia accepted the transfer and deposited the funds to the credit of the specified account, which had been opened by and was under the control of Reid. Reid withdrew almost all of Eisenberg's funds and converted them to his own use.

Wachovia's customer agreements do not restrict the name under which a new customer may open a bank account. The Wachovia employee who opened Reid's account did not verify that Reid was authorized to operate under the name Bear Stearns. Reid possessed no such authority and was not in any way affiliated with Bear Stearns.

Eisenberg filed a complaint against Wachovia in federal court on the basis of diversity jurisdiction, see 28 U.S.C. § 1332, asserting two claims of negligence. The first claim alleged that Wachovia negligently allowed Reid to establish and operate a fraudulent bank account and negligently failed to train its employees to detect fraud. The second claim alleged that Wachovia was vicariously liable for its employee's negligence in allowing Reid to open the bank account without proper verification. Both claims include the allegation that Wachovia breached a duty of care owed to people like Eisenberg, who transact with Wachovia customers, to detect and prevent the fraudulent use of its bank accounts.

Wachovia moved to dismiss the complaint pursuant to Federal Rule of Civil Procedure 12(b)(6). Wachovia argued that both negligence claims are preempted by Federal Reserve Board Regulation J ("Regulation J"), Subpart B, 12 C.F.R. §§ 210.25–210.32 (2002). Wachovia also argued, in the alternative, that the claims fail as a matter of law because Wachovia does not owe Eisenberg a duty of care. Agreeing that the claims are preempted, the district court granted Wachovia's motion and dismissed the complaint with prejudice. The court did not address Wachovia's alternative argument for dismissal based on the absence of a duty of care. * * *

We discussed the preemptive effect of Regulation J in Donmar Enterprises, Inc. v. Southern National Bank of North Carolina, 64 F.3d 944 (4th Cir.1995). Subpart B of Regulation J incorporates Article 4A of the Uniform Commercial Code to "provide [] rules to govern funds transfers through Fedwire." 12 C.F.R. § 210.25(a) (2002); see id. at § 210.25(a)-(b). The rules adopted from Article 4A serve as the exclusive means for determining the rights, duties and liabilities of all parties involved in a Fedwire funds transfer. Comm. on Sec. 210.25(b), 12 C.F.R. Part 210, Subpt. B., App. A (2002). Affected parties include senders, intermediary banks, receiving banks and beneficiaries. Id. The Federal Reserve Board intended Subpart B to create a "uniform and comprehensive national regulation of Fedwire transfers." Donmar, 64 F.3d at 949.

By its own terms, Regulation J "supersedes or pre-empts inconsistent provisions of state law." Comm. on Sec. 210.25, 12 C.F.R. Part 210, Subpt. B, App. A (2002). We held in Donmar that Regulation J preempts any state law cause of action premised on conduct falling within the scope of Subpart B, whether the state law conflicts with or is duplicative of Subpart B. 64 F.3d at 949–50. Determining if a state law claim is preempted by Regulation J turns on whether the challenged conduct in the state claim would be covered under Subpart B as well.

Eisenberg's negligence claims focus on several aspects of Wachovia's conduct in establishing Reid's account and crediting Eisenberg's funds transfer to that account. One instance of alleged negligence involves Wachovia "accepting and crediting the Wire Transfer to Mr. Reid's account when the wire instructions designated 'Bear Stearns' as the intended recipient." Eisenberg addressed the Fedwire transfer to "Wachovia Bank," "Beneficiary Account 1861296138," "For Further Credit to BEAR STEARNS." Subpart B applies here. When a transfer order identifies the beneficiary by an account number, the receiving bank may rely on the account number in crediting the account even though the transfer order identifies a person different from the holder of the account. See 12 C.F.R. § 210.27 (2002). Wachovia properly processed Eisenberg's funds transfer order under the standards of Subpart B.

Wachovia is not liable under Subpart B for the manner in which it received and credited Eisenberg's Fedwire funds transfer. Any state law claim that is premised on this same conduct would be either duplicative of or contradictory to Regulation J and is thus preempted. Eisenberg's negligence claims are preempted insofar as they challenge Wachovia's Fedwire transfer processing.

Eisenberg contends, however, that his negligence claims primarily challenge not the wire transfer processing but rather Wachovia's conduct in allowing Reid to open and operate the bank account under the name "dba Bear Stearns." The Fedwire transfer, according to Eisenberg, is only incidental to his negligence claims. Eisenberg thus urges that his negligence claims are not preempted by Regulation J. We agree.

Eisenberg's allegations of negligence are not limited to Wachovia's conduct in processing the Fedwire transfer order. Eisenberg also alleged that Wachovia is negligent by reason of allowing Reid to open the "dba Bear Stearns" bank account, failing to discover Reid's improper use of the account and failing to train its employees to recognize and prevent fraud. Subpart B has no application to Wachovia's conduct in these instances. Subpart B governs only Fedwire funds transfers, defined as "the series of transactions, beginning with the originator's payment order, made for the purpose of making payment to the beneficiary of the order." Comm. to Secs. 4A–102 & 4A–104, 12 C.F.R. Part 210, Subpt. B, App. B (2002). Subpart B does not address the duties, obligations and liabilities applicable to bank functions having nothing to do with a Fedwire transfer.

State law claims premised on conduct not covered by Subpart B cannot create a conflict with or duplicate the rules established in Subpart B. Permitting Eisenberg's claims to go forward would not create an obstacle to the fulfillment of Subpart B's purpose of establishing a uniform body of federal law to govern Fedwire transfers. See Fidelity Fed. Sav. & Loan Ass'n v. de la Cuesta, 458 U.S. 141, 153 (1982) (holding state law claim preempted if it "stands as an obstacle to the accomplishment and execution of the full purposes and objectives of Congress'') (internal quotations and citation omitted). A finding that Wachovia is negligent in opening Reid's account would not conflict with a finding that, under Subpart B of Regulation J, Wachovia properly credited the Fedwire transfer to the account. The two findings would touch on distinct and independent conduct by Wachovia.

We hold that Eisenberg's negligence claims, insofar as they challenge the opening and management of Reid's account, are not preempted by Regulation J.

Wachovia reasserts on appeal an alternative argument for dismissal, not decided by the district court, that Eisenberg fails to allege one essential element in a negligence claim. Wachovia contends that it does not owe Eisenberg a duty of care and therefore cannot be held liable in negligence for Eisenberg's injury.

Under North Carolina law, "[n]egligence is the failure to exercise proper care in the performance of a legal duty owed by a defendant to a plaintiff under the circumstances." Cassell v. Collins, 344 N.C. 160, 472 S.E.2d 770, 772 (1996). A necessary factor in proving negligence is the existence of a duty of care owed to the particular plaintiff by the defendant. Pinnix v. Toomey, 242 N.C. 358 (1955) ("Actionable negligence presupposes the existence of a legal relationship between parties by which the injured party is owed a duty by the other, and such duty must be imposed by law."). We consider whether a bank owes a duty of care to a noncustomer who is defrauded by the bank's customer through use of its services. We cannot find an applicable precedent from a North Carolina court and look to case law from other jurisdictions. We conclude that the North Carolina Supreme Court, if it were to decide this issue, would hold that Wachovia did not owe Eisenberg a duty of care under the facts presented.

Whether Wachovia owes a duty of care to Eisenberg depends on the relationship between them. See W. Page Keeton et al., Prosser and Keeton on Torts § 53 at 356 (5th ed. 1984) ("It is better to reserve 'duty' for the problem of the relation between individuals which imposes upon one a legal obligation for the benefit of the other....''). Eisenberg had no direct relationship with Wachovia. He was not a Wachovia bank customer and, so far as the allegations indicate, has never conducted business with Wachovia. Eisenberg instead transacted with Reid, a Wachovia bank customer.

Courts in numerous jurisdictions have held that a bank does not owe a duty of care to a noncustomer with whom the bank has no direct relationship* * * [and that] banks do not owe a duty of care to noncustomers even when the noncustomer is the person in whose name an account was fraudulently opened. * * *

Eisenberg was neither a Wachovia customer nor the person in whose name Reid's fraudulent bank account was opened. Bear Stearns would be the beneficiary of any duty of care which Wachovia might owe to a noncustomer. Eisenberg instead falls into the undefined and unlimited category of strangers who might interact with Wachovia's bank customer. * * *

The district court properly dismissed Eisenberg's complaint with prejudice. Eisenberg's negligence claims are not preempted by Subpart B of Regulation J. The negligence claims are instead dismissed because Wachovia does not owe Eisenberg a duty of care. Affirmed.

QUESTIONS AND NOTES

1. According to the Federal Reserve's 2007 payments study the percentage of noncash payments made by check declined from 46% in 2003 to 33% in 2006. The difference was made up by increases in the number of debit card and ACH (automated payment transactions through the Automated Clearing House) transactions.

2. Smart cards in varying forms are popular in Europe and on college campuses in America but have been slow to catch on elsewhere in America. A large scale experiment with smart cards conducted by Mondex and others in New York City at the end of the last century was not a success. Consumers were not eager to embrace this form of payment mechanism. Are smart cards really smart for the consumer? The funds on the card do not earn interest for the consumer. The Fed has issued regulations supplementing Regulation E regarding gift card transactions. 75 Fed. Reg. 16580 (Apr. 1, 2010) (to be codified at 12 C.F.R. pt. 205).

SECTION 4. BANK CAPITAL

65

Banks are highly leveraged institutions. This means they have a high proportion of liabilities to assets. Regulatory capital requirements, however, impose a limit on the amount of debt a bank may have on its balance sheet by mandating that certain minimum capital levels be maintained. To understand bank capital requirements, it is necessary to focus on the balance sheet of a bank. One side of the balance sheet lists the bank's assets (e.g., cash, investments, loans, buildings, and equipment). The other side of the balance sheet describes the source of those assets, which includes the bank's liabilities and capital. The liabilities are composed of deposits and other borrowings. Capital is shareholders' equity in the form of paid in capital (i.e., the amount paid for the bank's stock upon its original issuance) and earnings retained over time. At the end of each fiscal year the bank's income (net of expenses) earned during that year, less any dividends paid to shareholders, is added as retained earnings to the bank's capital account.

A bank's capital serves as a cushion out of which any losses are taken. If a bank has negative income for the year, the capital account is reduced by the amount of the loss. A bank is insolvent if its liabilities exceed its assets. Since the balance sheet must balance, the difference between the assets and liabilities is recorded as negative net worth. If a bank's capital is reduced to zero, in theory the bank's assets could be liquidated to satisfy the claims in full of all the depositors and other liability holders. In practice, however, it is often difficult to judge exactly the value of a bank's assets, especially if its loan portfolio is experiencing problems due to borrower defaults.

The FDIC, as the insurer of most of bank liabilities (through FDIC deposit insurance), is keenly interested in the amount of a bank's capital cushion. In the event of an insolvency and liquidation of a bank, the FDIC will pay the bank's depositors the amount of the depositors' effective deposit insurance coverage. The bank's assets are sold and the proceeds used first to reimburse the FDIC and then to pay the bank's uninsured creditors, leaving shareholders with a worthless investment. If the bank is severely insolvent, the value of the assets may not even be enough to fully reimburse the FDIC for its payments to insured depositors. With a greater equity cushion, more losses may be sustained by the bank before it enters into insolvency and the FDIC is less likely to suffer a loss as a result of the bank's liquidation.

A. EVOLUTION OF BANK CAPITAL REQUIREMENTS

(1) Inadequate Capital as an Unsafe and Unsound Practice

The evolution of capital regulation demonstrates that increasingly sophisticated regulatory scrutiny follows the development of more sophisticated risk management techniques. Cases from the early 1980s, however, demonstrate that imprecise capital requirements and unclear enforcement mechanisms made capital regulation relatively ineffective.

FIRST NATIONAL BANK OF BELLAIRE v. COMPTROLLER OF THE CURRENCY

United States Court of Appeals, Fifth Circuit, 1983.
697 F.2d 674.

GARZA, CIRCUIT JUDGE.

* * * The Notice of Charges alleges that "contrary to safe and sound banking practices, the Bank has been operating with inadequate capital." The Cease and Desist Order commands the Bank to adjust its equity and assets so as to raise the Bank's equity capital to total assets ratio (hereinafter EC to TA ratio) to not less than seven percent. The Bank asserts that the Comptroller's finding that the Bank's capital level was unsafe and unsound was not supported by substantial evidence. We agree. * * *

The Comptroller's finding was unreasonable because there was no rational relationship between the evidence, when looked at as a whole, and the finding. There is evidence in the record which, on its face, supports the Comptroller's finding. When this evidence is looked at in light of the entire record, however, it becomes clear that this evidence is not substantive. The Comptroller acted unreasonably in relying on these bits of evidence in light of the entire record.

Unsafe and unsound banking practices "encompass what may be generally viewed as conduct deemed contrary to accepted standards of banking operations which might result in abnormal risk or loss to a banking institution or shareholder." First National Bank of Eden, South Dakota v. Department of the Treasury, Office of the Comptroller of the Currency, [568 F.2d 610, 611 n.2 (8th Cir. 1978)]. In making its finding that the Bank's capital level was unsafe and unsound the Comptroller primarily relied on the testimony of Mr. Vaez, an expert called by the Comptroller. Mr. Vaez analyzed the Bank's capital adequacy in accordance with quantitative and qualitative factors underlying the Comptroller's policy. The Administrative Law Judge and the Comptroller gave great weight to this analysis. A closer look is, therefore, warranted.

Mr. Vaez's qualitative analysis did not indicate that problems existed. Mr. Vaez found the quality of the Bank's assets, the Bank's earnings and the Bank's liquidity and deposit structure to be basically strong. He found the Bank's management and ownership to be acceptable but did note problems in regard to planning and internal operating controls.

In June of 1980 the Comptroller's bank examiner rated the Bank on a one to five scale in regard to these same qualitative factors. The Bank received the highest possible one rating for quality of assets, liquidity and earnings and a two rating for management. These qualitative factors, therefore, indicated only slight problems in the Bank's operations.

Mr. Vaez also engaged in a quantitative analysis of the Bank's capital. Part of this analysis involved projections which showed future equity shortfalls. Based on Mr. Vaez's own testimony, we must discount the weight of these projections. These projections were based on estimates of the Bank's asset growth rate. The Comptroller's bank examiner projected the Bank's asset growth rate at ten to fifteen percent while Mr. Vaez used a twenty-one percent growth rate. While stating that the bank examiner was in a better position than himself to predict the rate of growth, Mr. Vaez termed the examiner's prediction as "purely conjectural." It is, therefore, clear that these projections were conjectural and cannot be given substantial weight.

The other aspect of Mr. Vaez's qualitative analysis involves a rather in-depth look at the Bank in relation to peer group banks with regard to a variety of equity related ratios. This analysis reveals two factors which Mr. Vaez finds to be significant. First, the Bank's EC to TA ratio was 5.28 percent which is well below the 7.0 percent level that Mr. Vaez deemed appropriate. Second, the Bank ranked near the bottom of its peer group in all of the equity related ratios. When these two factors are looked at in light of the entire record, they do not indicate that the Bank's capital level was unsafe or unsound.

Mr. Vaez's testimony does not demonstrate a correlation between the Bank ranking towards the bottom of its peer [group] in an analysis of equity related ratios and a finding that the Bank's capital level was unsafe and unsound. Obviously, this peer group analysis indicates that a majority of banks, approximately the same size as Bellaire Bank, maintain a higher level of equity than Bellaire Bank. This analysis may indicate that further investigation is needed. It does not, by itself, prove that the Bank's capital level was unsafe and unsound. It is very possible that all the banks in the peer group are maintaining a safe and sound capital level. Without a connection between the peer group analysis and a finding of unsafe and unsound capital levels, therefore, the peer group analysis does not support the Comptroller's finding that the Bank's capital level was unsafe and unsound. * * *

The record as a whole does not provide support for the Comptroller's finding that the Bank's capital level was unsafe and unsound. The record, in fact, is to the contrary. Two expert witnesses found the Bank's EC to TA ratio to be adequate. One of the experts stated that a bank's EC to TA ratio could be as low as four percent and be adequate. Furthermore, the EC to TA ratio for all banks in 1979 was 5.45 percent, and the Comptroller found this level to be acceptable. Finally, note that in the 1930's the EC to TA ratio for all banks was at its highest level and yet bank failures, also, hit a record high. * * *

Furthermore, statements by Comptroller Heimann do not support Mr. Vaez's statement. Comptroller Heimann has said that data on bank failures indicates that banks do not fail because of capital problems. This indicates that even if the Comptroller had proved capital inadequacy it would not necessarily indicate the Bank was in any danger. Comptroller Heimann, also, stated that consistent bank earnings are the key to healthy financial institutions and the principal factor in influencing capital adequacy. Since the Bank's earnings were strong, this would indicate that the Bank was not facing any serious risk due to equity shortfalls. * * *

[T]he Cease and Desist Order, as it relates to the Comptroller's finding that the Bank's capital level was unsafe and unsound, must be set aside. * * *

Judge Tate dissenting in part. * * *

Following the decision in *First National Bank of Bellaire,* Congress passed the International Lending Supervision Act of 1983, 12 U.S.C.A. § 3901, et seq.

FEDERAL DEPOSIT INSURANCE CORP. v. BANK OF COUSHATTA

United States Court of Appeals, Fifth Circuit, 1991.
930 F.2d 1122, *cert. denied*, 502 U.S. 857.

BARKSDALE, CIRCUIT JUDGE.

* * * Chartered by Louisiana, the Bank is federally insured, subject to the Federal Deposit Insurance Act, 12 U.S.C. § 1811, et seq., and FDIC rules and regulations. In July, 1989, it was operating under the FDIC capital forbearance program in an attempt to bring its capital to a minimum level. Under its second capital forbearance plan, the Bank had agreed to bring its primary capital ratio to 5.49% by year end. The FDIC determined that the Bank could not comply with the plan, because its loss classifications exceeded amounts projected for all of 1989. As a result, in July 1989, the FDIC issued a notice of intent, with preliminary findings of fact and conclusions of law, stating that the Bank's primary capital was lower than required by regulation and that the FDIC proposed to issue a capital directive requiring the Bank by December 31, 1989, to increase that capital by not less than $725,000 and to achieve ratios of primary and total capital to total assets of not less than 5.5% and 6.0% respectively. * * *

The FDIC issued the directive in September 1989, with supporting findings of fact and conclusions of law and a cover letter to the Board. The Bank was directed (1) by December 31, 1989, to restore its ratio of primary capital to total assets to at least 5.5% and enhance that capital by at least $725,000; and (2) within 30 days, to submit a plan for achieving the capital level. The directive stated that it was binding upon "the Bank [and] its directors," among others.

Because the Bank failed to comply, the FDIC filed a letter in May 1990, in the United States District Court in Louisiana, pursuant to 12 U.S.C. § 1818(i), requesting an order enforcing the directive against the Bank and Board. Attached to the letter was a Petition for Enforcement of Administrative Order, stamped filed on June 14, 1990. On July 13, 1990, the district court issued the requested ex parte order.

The FDIC's authority to issue capital directives is one of its regulatory tools for dealing with troubled banks. Most of these methods are set forth in 12 U.S.C. § 1818; however, authority for a directive is found in the International Lending Supervision Act of 1983 (ILSA), 12 U.S.C. § 3907, which provides in part:

> (a)(1) Each appropriate Federal banking agency shall cause banking institutions to achieve and maintain adequate capital by establishing minimum levels of capital for such banking institutions and by using such other methods as the appropriate Federal banking agency *deems* appropriate.

> (2) Each appropriate Federal banking agency shall have the authority to establish such minimum level of capital for a banking institution as

the appropriate Federal banking agency, *in its discretion, deems* to be necessary or appropriate in light of the particular circumstances of the banking institution.

(Emphasis added.) Moreover, failure to maintain the requisite capital "may be *deemed* by the appropriate Federal banking agency, *in its discretion*, to constitute an unsafe and unsound practice. . . ." 12 U.S.C. § 3907(b)(1) (emphasis added).

If a bank fails to maintain the required capital, the agency may issue a directive:

(B)(i) Such directive may require the banking institution to submit and adhere to a plan acceptable to the appropriate Federal banking agency describing the means and timing by which the banking institution shall achieve its required capital level.

(ii) Any such directive issued pursuant to this paragraph . . . shall be enforceable under the provisions of Section 1818(i) . . . to the same extent as an effective and outstanding order issued pursuant to Section 1818(b) . . . which has become final.

12 U.S.C. §§ 3907(b)(2)(B)(i) and (ii). * * *

Section 3907 was enacted to provide "a stronger, unambiguous statutory directive to the regulators to strengthen banks' capital positions." H.R.Rep. No. 98–175, 98th Cong., 1st Sess. 45, reprinted in 1983 U.S.Code Cong. & Admin.News 1768, 1928. * * *

Another congressional purpose behind § 3907 was in response to this court's decision in First Nat'l Bank of Bellaire v. Comptroller of Currency, 697 F.2d 674 (5th Cir. 1983), where the portion of a cease-and-desist order requiring a capital ratio was set aside as not being supported by substantial evidence. Congress was concerned that *Bellaire* "clouded the authority of the bank regulatory agencies to exercise their independent discretion in establishing and requiring the maintenance of appropriate levels of capital." * * *

The capital maintenance regulations define such terms as primary capital, secondary capital, total assets, assets classified loss and intangible assets. 12 C.F.R. § 325.2 (1990 ed.). They describe how the ratios are calculated, with the minimum capital requirement for "a bank" being ratios of total and primary capital to total assets of not less than the aforementioned 6% and 5.5% respectively. § 325.3. * * *

The Bank does not contend that the FDIC did not follow its procedures. Instead, it asserts that it is not allowed to dispute the underlying facts which make up the FDIC's determination that the Bank is not in compliance. However, the notice of intent states that the Bank could include "other relative evidence" which supported its position. The Bank could have responded to the notice with documentation that the FDIC's data was either in error or had changed. There is no limit on what a bank can say in its response. The Bank did not take full advantage of its opportunity to respond. Nor did it challenge any of the data provided it, including the report of examination. Needless to say, its failure to take such opportunity is not due to an inherent deficiency in the procedures. * * *

[The court affirmed the district court's order to enforce the capital directive.]

(2) Capital Ratios and the Basel Accord

The Bank for International Settlements (BIS) through its Basel Committee, a panel of central bankers and bank regulators from the major industrialized countries, recognized the need for uniform international capital standards. The Basel Accord of 1988 forms the backbone of the capital ratios required for United States banks today.[42] The Accord is used by regulators in over one hundred countries to measure capital adequacy.

A crude ratio for measuring capital was already in widespread use by 1988. That ratio–the leverage ratio—is calculated by dividing a bank's capital by its assets. The ratio is still used by bank regulators. For instance, if a national bank is rated in the highest category (1) on its CAMELS rating,[43] and is otherwise considered a strong organization, its leverage ratio must be 3% or greater. 12 C.F.R. § 3.6. National banks with a lower CAMELS rating must have a leverage ratio of 4% or greater. See also 12 C.F.R. pt. 225 (FRB) and 12 C.F.R. pt. 325 (FDIC).

The Basel Accord improved upon the leverage ratio in two important respects. First, the Accord recognized that not all assets are equally risky and that therefore the amount of capital that needs to be maintained for all assets should not be the same. Second, the Accord required that certain off-balance sheet activities be included in the capital adequacy calculation.

With regard to risk-weighting of assets, the Accord set forth four separate categories of assets and assigned to each a different risk weight. The risk weight is multiplied by the dollar amount of a bank's assets in that category to determine the bank's "risk-adjusted" assets. The sum of all risk-adjusted assets is then used as the denominator in calculating the risk-adjusted capital ratio. The federal bank regulatory agencies employ the Basel risk-adjusted capital ratios. 12 C.F.R. pt. 3, App. A (national banks) (included in the Statutory and Regulatory Supplement for this casebook); 12 C.F.R. pt. 225, App. A (bank holding companies and state member banks); 12 C.F.R. pt. 325, App. A (state nonmember banks).

The first weight is zero, meaning that assets in this category require no capital. As might be expected the assets in this category are those that

---

42. Basel Committee on Banking Regulations and Supervisory Practices, International Convergence of Capital Measurement and Capital Standards (1988), available at <www.bis.org/publ/bcbs04a.htm>.

43. CAMELS stands for Capital, Assets, Management, Earnings, Liquidity, and Sensitivity. Each bank is given a score in each category and a composite score as part of its periodic regulatory examination. See Chapter 8 for a more detailed discussion.

are virtually risk-free, such as cash, balances at Federal Reserve Banks, and United States government securities (including Treasury bills and notes) or debts fully guaranteed by the United States government. In the 20% weighting category are portions of loans guaranteed by the United States or one of its agencies, portions of loans collateralized by cash or deposits at the bank, and securities issued by government sponsored enterprises such as Fannie Mae and Freddie Mac. In the 50% risk-weighting category are loans secured by first mortgages on residential real estate. All other loans are included in the 100% risk-weighting category.

Off-balance sheet exposure is also factored into the Basel Accord's capital calculations. For instance, bank standby letters of credit (which function much like a bank guarantee of debt) carry a 100% credit conversion factor. Performance bonds or standby letters of credit related to a particular transaction have a 50% conversion factor, as do unused portions of loan commitments with an original maturity of longer than one year. Short-term trade-related and self-liquidating obligations, such as those represented by a documentary letter of credit, have a 20% conversion factor.

The Accord contemplates two different capital ratios—a ratio of Tier 1 capital to risk-adjusted assets and other off-balance sheet items of at least 4%, and a total capital ratio of at least 8%. Tier 1 capital includes stockholders' equity (valued at par plus the surplus paid when the stock was first offered to the public), some types of preferred stock, and retained earnings. Tier 2 capital includes the allowance for loan losses, cumulative perpetual preferred stock and subordinated debt. Before the ratios are calculated, however, certain deductions, including goodwill and other intangible assets, must be made from the Tier 1 capital amount. Since 1991, bank regulators classify banks into one of five categories based on their capital ratios.

Capital Category	Leverage Ratio	Tier 1 Risk-Based	Total Capital Risk-Based
Well-capitalized	5% or above	6% or above &	10% or above
Adequately capitalized	4% or above 3% (CAMELS 1)	4% or above &	8% or above
Undercapitalized	Under 4% or 3% (CAMELS 1)	Under 4% or	Under 8%
Significantly undercapitalized	Under 3% or	Under 4% or	Under 6%
Critically undercapitalized	Under 2%	Under 2%	Under 2%

BOARD OF GOVERNORS OF THE FEDERAL RESERVE SYSTEM, TRADING AND CAPITAL–MARKETS ACTIVITIES MANUAL CAPITAL ADEQUACY, SECTION 2110.1

<www.federalreserve.gov/boarddocs/supmanual/trading/200901/2000p2.pdf>.

The principal objectives of the risk-based capital measure are to (1) make regulatory capital requirements generally sensitive to differences in risk profiles among banking organizations; (2) factor off-balance-sheet exposures into the assessment of capital adequacy; (3) minimize disincentives to holding liquid, low-risk assets; and (4) achieve greater consistency in the evaluation of the capital adequacy of major banks throughout the world. The risk-based capital measure focuses primarily on the credit risk associated with the nature of banking organizations' on-and off-balance-sheet exposures and on the type and quality of their capital. It provides a definition of capital and a framework for calculating risk-weighted assets by assigning assets and off-balance-sheet items to broad categories of credit risk. A banking organization's risk-based capital ratio is calculated by dividing its qualifying capital by its risk-weighted assets. The risk-based capital measure sets forth minimum supervisory capital standards that apply to all banking organizations on a consolidated basis.

The risk-based capital ratio focuses principally on broad categories of credit risk. For most banking organizations, the ratio does not incorporate other risk factors that may affect the organization's financial condition. These factors may include overall interest-rate exposure; liquidity, funding, and market risks; the quality and level of earnings; investment or loan portfolio concentrations; the effectiveness of loan and investment policies; the quality of assets; and management's ability to monitor and control financial and operating risks. An overall assessment of capital adequacy must take into account these other factors and may differ significantly from conclusions that might be drawn solely from the level of an organization's risk-based capital ratio.

For risk-based capital purposes, a banking organization's capital consists of two major components: core capital elements (tier 1 capital) and supplementary capital elements (tier 2 capital). Core capital elements include common equity including capital stock, surplus, and undivided profits; qualifying noncumulative perpetual preferred stock (or, for bank holding companies, cumulative perpetual preferred stock, the aggregate of which may not exceed 25 percent of tier 1 capital); and minority interest in the equity accounts of consolidated subsidiaries. Tier 1 capital is generally defined as the sum of core capital elements less any amounts of goodwill, certain other intangible assets, disallowed deferred tax assets, interest-only strips, nonfinancial equity investments, investments in financial subsidiaries that do not qualify within capital, as well as any other investments in subsidiaries that the Federal Reserve determines should be deducted from tier 1 capital. Tier 1 capital represents the highest form of capital, namely permanent equity. Tier 2 capital consists of a limited amount of the allowance for loan and lease losses, perpetual preferred stock that does not qualify as tier 1 capital, mandatory convertible securities and other hybrid capital instruments, long-term preferred stock with an original term of 20 years or more, and limited amounts of term subordinated debt, intermediate-term preferred stock, and unrealized holding gains on qualifying equity securities, and unrealized gains (losses) on other assets. * * *

Each asset and off-balance-sheet item is assigned to one of four broad risk categories based on the obligor or, if relevant, the guarantor or type of collateral. The risk categories are 0, 20, 50, and 100 percent. The standard risk category, which includes the majority of items, is 100 percent. The appropriate dollar value of the amount in each category is multiplied by the risk weight associated with that category. The weighted values are added together and the resulting sum is the organization's risk-weighted assets, the denominator of the risk-based capital ratio.

Off-balance-sheet items are incorporated into the risk-based capital ratio by first being converted into a "credit-equivalent" amount. To accomplish this, the face amount of the item is multiplied by a credit conversion factor (0, 20, 50, or 100 percent). The credit-equivalent amount is then assigned to a risk category in the same manner as on-balance-sheet items. * * *

(3) Basel II

The Basel Committee considered a revision of the capital accord to recognize the development of enhanced risk measurement techniques and to respond to criticism leveled at the 1988 Accord. Critics noted that the 1988 Accord does not deal with operational risk and does not measure or account for portfolio risk. Further, the risk-weighting categories employed are crude at best. For instance, all commercial loans—including those to blue chip companies as well as those to risky start-up ventures—carry the same risk weighting even though the former are obviously less risky than the latter.

In response to such criticism, the Committee issued a preliminary proposal to amend the Accord in 1999. After receiving comments on that proposal, a massive revised version was issued in January 2001 (the Second Consultative Paper). An additional proposal was released in April 2003 (the Third Consultative Paper), and three quantitative studies related to the proposal were conducted. The final report, Basel II: International Convergence of Capital Measurement and Capital Standards: A Revised Framework (Basel Committee Publications No. 107),[44] was released in June 2004. Member countries are to undertake appropriate adoption procedures for their own countries. A number of countries implemented Basel II's standardized and foundation approaches at the beginning of 2007. In other jurisdictions legislation, regulation and supervisory guid-

---

44. Available at <www.bis.org/publ/bcbs107.htm>.

ance to implement the Framework was still in process at the time of the financial crisis.

Basel II was based on three pillars—a minimum regulatory capital charge, supervisory review, and market discipline. The Basel Committee attempted to respond to the criticism of the risk-adjusted capital calculation by making the minimum regulatory capital charge more risk sensitive. For instance, rather than weight all corporate loans equally at 100%, Basel II proposed that corporate loans receive a weighting of 20%, 50%, 100% or 150%, depending on the external credit rating (if any) of the corporate borrower. Borrowers without external credit ratings would be subject to the 100% risk weighting. Interestingly, the rating agencies, such as Standard & Poor's and Moody's, did not embrace this proposal, cautioning that their ratings were not designed for this purpose. Other critics note that rating agencies often downgrade ratings in economic downturns, which would result in banks being required to increase their capital during such downturns, perhaps exacerbating an overall credit contraction, as actually happened during the financial crisis. Others noted that unrated borrowers may well be more risky than those that have received a low credit rating, but that less capital was required for a loan to an unrated borrower than to a poorly rated borrower.

Basel II also offered as an alternative to the traditional risk-weighting of loans, an institution's internal rating of risk. Especially in the case of large, complex banking organizations, the Basel Committee believed that sophisticated internal risk models might be an acceptable (and perhaps even a superior) alternative risk measurement system to the one described above. The internal ratings-based (IRB) approach is described in two forms—a simpler, foundation format and a more advanced framework. The advanced approach provided an individual institution with much greater flexibility in measuring its risk. Some observers believed that allowing an institution to assess its own risk—even when subject to review by the appropriate regulator—was akin to asking the fox to guard the hen house. In addition, Basel II proposed to consider how credit risk mitigation techniques, such as guarantees, credit derivatives, and collateralized credit exposures, should factor into an IRB approach.

The risk-adjusted capital system upon which Basel II was built is basically a model that measures credit risk. A new risk element introduced by the Basel Committee was an operational risk charge intended to measure the risk of loss resulting from inadequate personnel, failed internal processes, or external events.

In the United States, only banks with more than $250 billion in assets or $10 billion in on-balance sheet foreign exposure—only about a dozen institutions—would have been required to implement the advanced IRB approach. The institutions required to run the advanced IRB approach were expected to run the new approach alongside the more traditional method in what was described as a "parallel running."

There were, of course, numerous concerns, including the concern that Basel II was too complex. An additional concern was that the advanced IRB approach would lower the capital required by the institutions employing that approach, increase systemic risk, and provide advanced IRB institutions with a competitive advantage over their competitors.

Some U.S. institutions worried that they would meet the capital requirements set forth in Basel II, but not be in compliance with the leverage ratio still required by U.S. regulators.

The federal banking agencies issued an Advance Notice of Proposed Rulemaking to solicit comments on capital calculations for institutions that were not required to adopt the IRB approach. This rulemaking is referred to by some as "Basel I–A," but was abandoned in July 2007 in favor of a standardized option to be "finalized before the core banks begin the first transition period year under the advanced approaches of Basel II." Joint Press Release, Banking Agencies Reach Agreement on Basel II Implementation, July 20, 2007, at <www.federalreserve.gov/newsevents/ press/bcreg/2007/20070720a.htm>.

(4) The Government's Response to the Financial Crisis–the Troubled Asset Relief Program (TARP)

Under the IRB approach of Basel II it was assumed that banks would be able to justify maintaining lower capital than under traditional approaches. The FDIC maintained that the leverage ratio, still in use in the United States, should become a part of the Basel II calculus. As these particulars were being debated, the financial crisis that began in 2007 gained momentum throughout 2008 and the largest banks suffered tremendous losses that strained their capital. The Basel II effort stopped dead in its tracks as bank regulators and Congress attempted to deal with a financial meltdown. The government intervened in the Emergency Economic Stabilization Act of 2009 and authorized extraordinary government investments[45] in financial institutions to shore up their capital positions.

LISSA L. BROOME
GOVERNMENT INVESTMENT IN BANKS: CREEPING NATIONALIZATION OR PRUDENT, TEMPORARY AID?

4 FIU L. Rev. 409 (2009).

In 2008, twenty-five banks failed, more than in any year since 1993. The pace of bank failure has accelerated in 2009, with the 2008 total of twenty-five matched by mid-April. Three of the four largest U.S. banking institutions were so at risk that one—Wachovia—was acquired by Wells Fargo, a smaller institution, and two—Citigroup and Bank of America— were forced to request governmental investments in excess of the initial government investments they received under the Troubled Asset Relief

---

45. The article excerpted below also discusses the government's investment in banks during the Great Depression by the Reconstruction Finance Corporation.

Program (TARP). The Federal Deposit Insurance Corporation's (FDIC) ratio of reserves-to-insured deposits slipped to just 0.4% as of year-end 2008, well below the statutory minimum of 1.15% and the lowest level since 1993. The aggressive responses to the crisis by Congress, the Treasury Department, the Federal Reserve Board of Governors (FRB), and the FDIC to help banks improve their capital positions and liquidity have dramatically altered the liability/equity sides of bank balance sheets. This unprecedented government assistance to prevent widespread bank failure and to provide support for those institutions "too big to fail" underscores the vital role that banks play in our economy. * * *

Congress' initial legislative response to the financial crisis was the Emergency Economic Stabilization Act of 2008 (EESA), enacted on October 3, 2008. The $700 billion in funds authorized by Congress in EESA to assist in the financial crisis clean-up, labeled "Troubled Asset Relief Program" (TARP), were quickly diverted by then-Treasury Secretary Henry Paulson from buying troubled mortgage-related assets held by banks to purchasing preferred, non-voting stock in banks under what is now called the Capital Purchase Program (CPP). The initial tranche of TARP funds was $350 billion, with $250 billion specifically set aside for bank stock purchases. A second bank investment program, the Targeted Investment Program (TIP), was announced on November 23, 2008, and has been used to fund additional preferred stock investments in Citigroup and Bank of America beyond the initial CPP investments. The Senate authorized the second tranche of TARP funds on January 15, 2009, prior to the change in administration pursuant to a request from President Bush made at the urging of President-elect Obama. The new Obama administration announced on February 10, 2009, the Financial Stability Plan—its new name for TARP—that would fund additional bank stock purchases under a new program called the Capital Assistance Program (CAP).

The first tranche of funds released by Congress for the TARP amounted to $250 billion, and all of it has been committed for CPP and TIP preferred stock purchases; as of March 31, 2009, $235.8 billion had actually been disbursed. Secretary Paulson deemed the CPP a more expeditious way to inject capital into the banking system than attempting to value and purchase troubled mortgage-related assets held by banks. Originally, Paulson strongly resisted government stock purchases, asserting that taking preferred stock in banks is "what you do when you have failure" and stating "this is about success." His opposition to government stock purchases was in stark contrast with the lead of other countries, including the United Kingdom, Germany, France, Spain, and Italy. But, he soon did an about face, announcing the CPP on October 14, 2008. * * *

As the CPP program was originally conceived, there were no specific requirements regarding how banks that received the government equity infusion should use it. The expectation by Treasury officials and perhaps Congress seems to have been that banks would use the additional capital to increase lending, when in fact much of it appears to have been used to shore up capital positions and, at least in one case, finance an acquisition of an institution that did not have its request for TARP funds honored. * * *

The statute did require that certain executive compensation arrangements for CPP recipients would be limited. In addition, banks receiving the investment money were required to sign a contract providing that the Treasury "may unilaterally amend any provision . . . to the extent required to comply with any changes after the Signing Date in applicable federal statutes." Some banks cited this open-ended commitment as the reason they elected not to apply for TARP money, have yet to decide whether to accept it, or have decided not to accept the funds.

Institutions accepting preferred stock investments by the United States also are required to pay quarterly dividends to the United States of five percent per year for the first five years of the investment and nine percent per year thereafter. The institution may repurchase the preferred stock three years after its issuance for the purchase price plus accrued and unpaid dividends. A repurchase is not permitted unless the investment is replaced by an equivalent amount of private capital. The government also receives warrants to buy common stock at a market price equal to fifteen percent of its preferred stock investment. The exercise price for the warrants is the common stock price on the date of the investment.

On November 23, 2008, the Treasury Department, FRB, and FDIC announced further actions to support Citigroup. This new effort included an additional $20 billion investment in Citigroup preferred stock carrying an eight percent dividend, as opposed to the five percent dividend due to the Treasury during the first five years on its initial $25 billion equity infusion. Pursuant to this second extraordinary infusion of equity, the Treasury imposed some additional conditions. First, dividends on common stock are limited to one cent per share per quarter for three years unless the Treasury consents to additional dividend payments. Second, there are additional restrictions on executive compensation, and, third, Citigroup must adopt the FDIC's mortgage modification procedures developed in the conservatorship of IndyMac. Bank of America received a similar package of benefits, in large part because of its acquisition of loss-plagued Merrill Lynch, including another $20 billion preferred stock investment, on January 16, 2009. These additional equity investments in Citigroup and Bank of America were pursuant to a new TARP program labeled the Targeted Investment Program (TIP). The purpose of TIP is to "foster market stability and thereby to strengthen the economy and protect American jobs, savings, and retirement security."[46]

The Obama Administration's Treasury Secretary Timothy Geithner announced on February 10, 2009, the outline of the administration's plans for the use of the second tranche of TARP funds authorized in the EESA, or Tarp 2. The TARP appellation, and any negative connotations it

---

46. Press Release, U.S. Treas. Dept., Treasury Releases Guidelines for Targeted Investment Program (Jan. 2, 2009), http://www.treas.gov/press/releases/hp1338.htm.

carried, were dropped by Secretary Geithner in favor of the "Financial Stability Plan." Among other proposals, the new plan calls for a "stress test" of the nineteen financial institutions whose assets exceed $100 billion, with commitments of additional capital to those of the large institutions identified as needing additional capital under the stress test scenarios. These institutions account for approximately two-thirds of all bank holding company assets.

The stress test is sometimes referred to as the "Forward–Looking Capital Assessment," and the "Supervisory Capital Assessment Program." The capital assessment requires bank holding companies to predict their losses over the next two years under two different economic scenarios: a "baseline" scenario that is supposed to mirror the consensus view about the length and severity of the recession and a "more adverse" scenario assuming a longer and more severe recession. Some observers worry, however, that the more adverse scenario "may not be dire enough" since it assumes: only a 3.3% contraction in the economy in 2009 with no additional contraction in 2010; that unemployment will hit 8.9% in 2009 and 10.3% in 2010; and that housing prices will lose 22% in 2009. Moreover, each covered financial institution carries out its own analysis under government supervision. Concerned observers worry that banks' incentives to minimize the capital they need may skew test results. The stress tests were completed by the end of April 2009 with banks afforded the opportunity to challenge the results before they are made public in early May 2009. Federal banking regulators, following discussions with the nineteen financial institutions, will determine whether each institution's capital is sufficient given the results of the stress tests. * * *

The results of the government's stress test results for U.S. banks were disclosed on May 7, 2009. Bank of America was found to need $33.9 billion in additional capital; Wells Fargo required $13.7 billion; GMAC $11.5 billion; Citigroup $5.5 billion; and Morgan Stanley $1.8 billion. Those not needing additional capital included JPMorgan Chase, Goldman Sachs, Bank of New York Mellon, and American Express.[47]

Critics noted that the government had weakened its stress tests in response to demands from the banks that were being tested. Among other things, the banks were allowed to value distressed CDOs by cash flow, rather than marking them to market. Nevertheless, the test results seemed to restore the market's confidence in financial institutions. Several financial institutions then officially notified the Treasury of their desire to repay TARP funds. They included Goldman Sachs, JPMorgan Chase, Morgan Stanley, Bank of New York Mellon, State Street Corp., and U.S. Bancorp. Morgan Stanley responded quickly to the government's demand that it increase its capital, raising $9.2 billion by May 20, 2009. Citigroup

---

47. See Jerry W. Markham, A Financial History of the United States, From the Subprime Crisis to the Great Recession (2006–2009) 453–54 (2010).

raised $5.5 billion by May 20, 2009, allowing it to meet its stress test shortfall. Wells Fargo raised $7.5 billion in equity on June 1. Bank of America was able to raise nearly $33 billion in capital during May and early June 2009.

The government added another hurdle for repayment of TARP funds on June 1, 2009, requiring all banks seeking to repay the funds to raise capital from private investors even if the stress tests indicated they had no need for additional capital. JPMorgan Chase and American Express objected to this market test. They had both passed the government's stress tests and saw no need for additional capital. Nevertheless, the bank regulators insisted that they prove their ability to raise additional capital, so both companies made equity offerings. JPMorgan Chase raised $5 billion and American Express raised $500 million. In total, the largest nineteen banks were able to increase their capital by $85 billion in May and early June 2009.

Ten banks were allowed to repay their TARP funds to the federal government on June 9, 2009. They included JPMorgan Chase, Morgan Stanley, Bank of New York Mellon, Goldman Sachs, State Street Corp., American Express, and BB & T Corp. In total, those ten banks repaid $68.3 billion of the total of $239.4 billion that had been injected into financial institutions by the TARP program. The government had been paid $1.8 billion in dividends for the TARP money injected into those ten banks.

The government also expected an additional profit of around $4 billion from warrants received from these banks as a condition for receiving the funds. Some banks tried to repurchase these warrants, but the Treasury Department demanded an unrealistic price. This angered the banking community, some of whom had taken the TARP funds only because the Treasury Department requested them to do so in order to avoid stigmatizing banks, like Citigroup, that really did need the funds. As Jamie Dimon, CEO of JPMorgan Chase stated, his bank "didn't ask for it, didn't want it, didn't need it." Indeed, JPMorgan had raised $11 billion in September 2008 from a stock offering in the private markets. Morgan Stanley repurchased its warrants from the government for $950 million in August 2009, giving the government a total return of $1.27 billion for its $10 billion bailout of Morgan Stanley, an annualized return of some twenty percent.

The federal government lost $2.3 billion in TARP funds as a result of the CIT bankruptcy In April 2010 total TARP losses were predicted to be less than $29 billion, which was some $100 billion less than the losses experienced during the savings and loan crisis in the 1980s. The TARP losses were concentrated mostly at Freddie Mac, Fannie Mae, and the automakers. By February 2010, banks had repaid $173 billion in TARP funds by February 2010 and the federal government had made some $10 billion from those investments.

(5) The Financial Crisis and Basel III

International bank regulators spent years developing the Basel I and Basel II capital requirements for banks, but those mandates failed to prevent many of the largest banks from leveraging themselves into a position that threatened their viability during the financial crisis. Indeed, subprime mortgage lending was actually encouraged by the Basel capital requirements, which were amended by regulators in the United States in 2001 to permit lower capital for mortgage-backed instruments (that were rated AA or AAA) than the capital required for individual mortgages or for commercial loans. Banks reacted to that inducement by purchasing large amounts of securitized mortgages. To their credit, even then most banks eschewed the AA mortgage-backs in favor of the Super Seniors that carried a AAA rating.

The Basel Committee on Banking Supervision responded to the financial crisis by turning away from the Basel II principles that were focused on reducing capital for sophisticated financial institutions whose internal modeling could show that they had sufficient capital to cover the risks contained in their portfolios. The focus returned to requiring more and higher quality capital. U.S. regulators followed suit. Fed Chairman Ben Bernanke announced in October 2009 that the Fed would also focus on increased capital.

The emphasis on increasing the quality and amount of capital highlighted another problem—regulators were sending mixed messages to banks as the financial crisis peaked. Banks were urged to lend the TARP funds supplied under EESA. At the same time, however, bank regulators were pressuring banks to increase their capital, requesting that Tier 1 capital be increased from six percent to eight percent and that core capital be increased from ten percent to twelve percent. Increased capital requirements removed funds that were needed for lending and added to the ongoing credit crunch.[48]

In December 2009 the Basel Committee introduced a package of proposals known as Basel III. Areas of emphasis included raising the quality of Tier 1 capital, introducing a leverage ratio (similar to that in effect in the United States), implementing a liquidity coverage ratio to ensure that the institution has sufficient liquidity to survive one month of acute stress, promoting build-up of capital in good times so that it could be drawn upon in times of stress, and requiring higher capital or risk weights to capture the risks of complex trading activities and securitization exposures. This initial Basel report was sharply criticized by the international banking community which argued that it would impose great costs on banks, dampen lending, and hurt the global economy. The Institute of International Finance estimated that these Basel reforms would require banks to raise $700 billion in common stock and issue $5.4 trillion in long-

---

48. A similar thing happened in 1937 when the Fed doubled bank reserve requirements, helping stop a nascent recovery in the economy. See Jerry W. Markham, A Financial History of the United States, From J.P. Morgan to the Institutional Investors (1900–1970) 234 (2002).

term debt over five years. The Basel Committee released its own study of the economic impact of the proposed reforms in August 2010. That study concluded that there would be a modest negative macroeconomic impact caused by the increase in capital, but concluded that the long-term benefits of the changes would outweigh these short-term costs.

Additional details regarding Basel III were agreed to by the Basel Committee in September 2010. U.S. federal banking agencies noted in a press release their endorsement of the new standards. Joint Press Release, Banking Agencies Express Support for Basel Agreement, Sept. 12, 2010 <www.federalreserve.gov/newsevents/press/bcreg/20100912a.htm>. The minimum Tier 1 capital ratio will increase during a phase-in period from 4% to 6%, and the proportion of Tier 1 capital represented by common equity will also increase. The minimum total capital ratio will remain at 8%, but the new standards will also impose a countercyclical capital buffer of 2.5% of common equity during periods of growth. So, in these times, total capital must be 10.5% with 8.5% in the Tier 1 category. Under existing capital standards, only 4% Tier 1 capital is required in the 8% total capital ratio. A 3% leverage ratio on total assets (versus risk-adjusted assets) will also be phased in. The Committee hoped to gain approval for these changes in approach in November 2010 when the leaders of the Group of 20 major economies were scheduled to meet in South Korea.

(6) The Dodd–Frank Act

The U.S. Congress continued the renewed emphasis on capital in the Dodd–Frank Act. That Act directs the Financial Stability Oversight Council (FSOC) to make recommendations to the Fed concerning the creation of heightened prudential standards for risk-based capital and leverage limits for systemically significant nonbank financial companies and systemically significant bank holding companies. Dodd–Frank Act, § 165(b)(1)(A)(i). The Fed is required to limit the leverage of systemically significant financial companies to a debt-to-equity ratio (to be distinguished from the capital-to-assets ratio that is referred to as the leverage ratio) of no more than 15 to 1, upon a determination by the FSOC that such company poses a "grave threat" to the U.S. financial system and that imposing this leverage limit is necessary to mitigate the risk presented by the company. Dodd–Frank Act, § 165(j).

The FSOC is to conduct a study of the feasibility and benefits of a contingent capital bond ("CoCo" bond) requirement, which is a bond that is convertible to equity in times of financial stress and would thus reduce debt and increase equity, both desirable results. Dodd–Frank Act, § 115(c). The Fed is directed to develop capital requirements to make capital requirements "countercyclical, so that the amount of capital required to be maintained by a company increases in times of economic expansion and decreases in times of economic contraction, consistent with the safety and soundness of the company." Dodd–Frank Act, § 616.

The Collins Amendment, section 171 of the Dodd–Frank Act, requires that all depository institution holding companies be subject to the same capital requirements and include the same regulatory capital components as their insured deposit institution subsidiaries. The effect of this provision is to dramatically cut back on the use by holding companies of certain hybrid securities, such as trust preferred securities, as a component of Tier 1 capital. Trust preferred securities are issued by a trust created by a bank holding company to sell long-term securities. Prior to Dodd–Frank, trust preferred securities could constitute up to 25% of Tier 1 capital. Although considered capital, the interest on the securities was tax deductible.[49] Thus, trust preferred securities provided Tier 1 capital without diluting existing shareholders. These securities were widely sold during the financial crisis by bank holding companies needing to quickly boost their Tier 1 capital when more traditional capital, like common stock, was more difficult to sell and would further dilute the battered shareholders. Trust preferred stock, however, was not a permanent source of capital.

Under the Collins Amendment, small holding companies with less than $15 billion in assets may continue to include in Tier 1 capital any existing trust-preferred securities. Those holding companies above the $15 billion asset threshold must phase out their inclusion of trust preferreds in Tier 1 capital. The Government Accountability Office is also ordered to prepare a study on the use of trust preferreds as a component of Tier 1 capital.

Stress tests, similar to those performed on certain large financial institution in the spring of 2009, are required by the Dodd–Frank Act. Specifically, the Fed must, in conjunction with the appropriate federal bank regulatory agency, test all systemically significant institutions under baseline, adverse, and severely adverse scenarios. Dodd–Frank Act, § 165. A summary of the results will be published. These institutions are required to conduct internal stress tests semi-annually, and all banks and holding companies with assets over $10 billion must conduct internal stress tests annually.

Finally, to close out the financial crisis the Dodd–Frank Act reduced the amount authorized under TARP from $700 billion to $475 billion and prohibits Treasury from beginning any new TARP programs after June 25, 2010. Dodd–Frank Act, § 1302. Furthermore, money that is repaid from TARP may not be used to fund ongoing TARP programs, but rather must be applied to reduce the deficit.

QUESTIONS AND NOTES

1. Adequate capital is important in other aspects of bank regulation. For instance, as part of the regular bank examination process a bank's capital position is assessed, along with other CAMELS factors—capital, assets, management, earnings, liquidity, and sensitivity to interest rate risk. Based on the CAMELS scores (which range from 1 to 5 on each factor, with 1 being the highest; and from 1 to 5 on the composite score), the bank may be subject to

---

49. See Todd H. Eveson & John H. Schramm, Bank Holding Company Trust Preferred Securities: Recent Developments, 11 N.C. Banking Inst. 105 (2007).

varying degrees of supervisory oversight. As capital declines, more intense and intrusive regulatory attention can be expected, triggering the imposition of what is called "prompt corrective action" by the bank regulatory agency.

The Gramm–Leach–Bliley Act (GLBA) required that all the depository institution subsidiaries of a bank holding company be well capitalized to be certified as a financial holding company. 12 U.S.C.A. § 1843(l)(1). It also required that a bank be well capitalized in order to establish a financial subsidiary that may exercise expanded powers under GLBA. 12 U.S.C.A. § 24a(2)(c). The Dodd–Frank Act added the requirement that the holding company be well capitalized. Dodd–Frank Act, § 606.

2. Bank A's balance sheet is set forth below. Calculate the bank's leverage ratio, Tier 1 capital ratio, and total capital ratio under the original Basel accord. Is Bank A in compliance? How would Bank Holding Company's capital calculations change under Dodd–Frank?

Bank Holding Company Balance Sheet
(in millions)

Assets		Liabilities and Capital	
Cash	4	Deposits	85
Fed. Res. deposits	6	Other liabilities	6
Loans		Subordinated debt	5
- Mortgage	40	Capital	
- Commercial	50	- Trust preferred stock	1
		- Common stock	2
		- Retained earnings	1
TOTAL	100	TOTAL	100

3. If one of Bank Holding Company's capital ratios gets too low, what steps can Bank Holding Company take to attempt to improve that ratio?

4. A final guidance on Concentrations in Commercial Real Estate Lending, 71 Fed. Reg. 74580 (Dec. 12, 2006) and 71 Fed. Reg. 75294 (Dec. 14, 2006) (OTS version), expressed the federal banking agencies concern that high concentrations of commercial real estate (CRE) loans at some banks would make them vulnerable to downturns in the CRE market. The agencies defined excessive concentration and cautioned that those institutions with CRE concentrations should engage in heightened risk management and retain capital in excess of the regulatory minimums. Many community bankers were concerned about the impact of this guidance on their banks because commercial real estate lending is one of few areas "where smaller banks compete

successfully with big banks." Lee Conrad, Lending: Banks Vent Rage Over Commercial RE Loan Rule, US Banker, June 2006, at 10. See also H. Gary Pannell & Robert L. Carothers, Jr., Regulatory Guidance on Concentrations in Commercial Real Estate Lending,11 N.C. Banking Inst. 33 (2007). The agencies turned out to be prophetic. Commercial real estate concentrations have contributed to the demise of many community banks during the financial crisis.

B. SPECIAL ISSUES

(1) Merchant Banking

GLBA authorizes financial holding companies to engage in merchant banking activities, which include the ability to hold equity in companies that are not publicly traded. These activities are described further in Chapter 11. The federal bank regulators issued proposed regulations requiring that such investments would be subject to a 50% capital charge.[50] Those in the banking industry who hoped to take advantage of this expanded investment authority objected to the proposed charge as inconsistent with Congress' intent to authorize financial holding companies to engage in these activities. Financial holding companies claimed that, at this level of capital, merchant capital investments would be too costly to hold.

The banking regulatory agencies dramatically revised the capital requirements, replacing the March 2000 proposed rule with another proposed rule in early 2001 that was finalized in 2002.[51] If the institution's merchant capital investment is equal to 15% or less of the institution's Tier 1 capital, then the investment is subject to the normal 8% capital charge. If the amount of the investment ranges between 15% and 25% of Tier 1 capital, then the capital charge for the investment would be 12% for the portion of the investment above 15% of Tier 1 capital. For any portion of a total merchant capital investment exceeding 25% of the institution's Tier 1 capital, a 25% capital charge would be applied.

(2) Securitizations

FASB's FIN 45–R, Consolidation of Variable Interest Entities, operated to consolidate some asset backed commercial paper (ABCP) programs onto the balance sheets of the sponsoring banks. An Interagency final rule, however, permitted sponsoring banks, bank holding companies and thrifts to exclude those ABCP program assets consolidated onto the sponsors' balance sheets from the sponsoring institutions' risk-weighted asset base for determining capital. 69 Fed. Reg. 44908 (July 28, 2004) (codified at 12 C.F.R. pt. 3; 12 C.F.R. pts. 208 & 225; 12 C.F.R. pt. 325; 12 C.F.R. pt. 567). FASB's revised accounting standards in FAS 166 and 167 required the banking agencies to amend their risk-based capital rules. 75

---

50. 65 Fed. Reg. 16,480 (Mar. 28, 2000).

51. 67 Fed. Reg. 3784 (Jan. 25, 2002) (codified at 12 C.F.R. pt. 3 (OCC); 12 C.F.R. pts. 208 & 225 (FRB); 12 C.F.R. pt. 325 (FDIC)).

Fed. Reg. 4636 (Jan. 28, 2010). ABCP program assets that are consolidated onto the bank's balance sheet under GAAP may no longer be excluded from the bank's risk-based assets. Other off-balance sheet structures, including securitizations in which the bank retains a residual interest and servicing rights will also be subject to risk-based capital requirements. The regulators have provided for an optional transition mechanism to delay and phase in the impact of these changes on risk-weighted assets.

The Basel Committee has also addressed the capital treatment appropriate to securitization transactions. See the working papers at <www.bis.org/publ/bcbs157.htm>.

(3) Subordinated Debt

The Fed was charged by Congress in GLBA to consider whether it would be "feasible and appropriate to require systemically important depository institutions and their holding companies to maintain some portion of their capital in subordinated debt."[52] Some commentators, who criticized Basel II as too complex, tout mandatory subordinated debt as a simpler way to regulate and monitor risky activities.

Subordinated debt is currently a portion of Tier 2 capital for those banks and holding companies—primarily the largest ones—that issue it. Since this debt is contractually subordinated to the claims of other creditors, subordinated debt holders have strong incentives to monitor the financial solvency of the bank or holding company. Indeed, one would expect the interest rate demanded by subordinated debt holders to serve as a good proxy for the market's judgment regarding the riskiness of a particular institution's practices and the likelihood that it will become insolvent. If the perceived risk is high, subordinated debt issuers will demand higher interest rates. The Fed's study urged further research and analysis into subordinated debt, but stopped short of recommending any mandatory subordinated debt policy. The objectives of a subordinated debt policy are set forth below.

BOARD OF GOVERNORS OF THE FEDERAL RESERVE SYSTEM, THE FEASIBILITY AND DESIRABILITY OF MANDATORY SUBORDINATED DEBT

December 2000.
<www.federalreserve.gov/boarddocs/RptCongress/debt/subord_debt_2000.pdf>.

* * * A subordinated debt policy could be designed to achieve varying degrees of five objectives. The policy could improve *direct market discipline* if an institution's expected cost of issuing subordinated debt became more directly related to purchasers' perceptions of the riskiness of that institution. The anticipation of higher funding costs from increased risk would provide an incentive for the issuing organization to refrain from taking excessive risk.

---

52. Board of Governors of the Federal Reserves System, The Feasibility and Desirability of Mandatory Subordinated Debt (Dec. 2000).

The objective of augmenting *indirect market discipline* would be exerted if a rise in secondary market subordinated debt yields were interpreted by investors and others as a signal of increased risk, leading them to demand higher returns on other liabilities or to otherwise limit their exposure to the bank or other type of depository institution. Depository institution supervisors could also exert indirect discipline if they took the increase in secondary market yields as a signal of potentially increased institution risk and took actions to address that possibility.

A third objective of subordinated debt policy would be to stimulate *improved transparency and disclosure* at depository institutions, thereby encouraging both direct and indirect market discipline. In order to price risk accurately, purchasers of subordinated debt need a clear picture of a depository institution's overall riskiness. If such a picture is not forthcoming from the issuing institution, purchasers may require higher yields than would otherwise be the case or perhaps not even be willing to buy an institution's subordinated debt at any price.

Issuance of subordinated debt might also achieve the objective of *increasing the size of the financial cushion provided to the federal deposit insurer.* When an institution fails, subordinated debt holders receive their funds only after the deposit insurer has been fully compensated. Thus, increased issuance of subordinated debt could increase the deposit insurer's financial cushion.

A fifth objective sometimes specified for issuance of subordinated debt is to *reduce the tendency for depository institution supervisors to forbear their resolution of a troubled institution.* Because subordinated debt holders receive their funds after the deposit insurer in a depository institution failure, they may have an incentive to encourage supervisors to take prompt corrective actions against a troubled depository institution. * * *

QUESTIONS AND NOTES

1. Should subordinated debt be required for large banking organizations? If subordinated debt is issued, should regulators rely on market forces to signal capital problems at a bank or should the regulator still monitor traditional capital adequacy ratios? Is there any danger to relying on subordinated debt as the exclusive barometer of the adequacy of a bank's capital?

CHAPTER EIGHT

SUPERVISION, ENFORCEMENT AND FAILED BANK RESOLUTION

■ ■ ■

SECTION 1. SUPERVISION

Bank regulation is based on safety and soundness:

Safety and soundness regulations for banks consist of basically five components: federal deposit insurance to reduce the likelihood of bank runs and panics; deposit interest ceilings to reduce the costs of bank deposits and weaken banks' incentives to invest in risky assets; regulatory monitoring to ensure that banks do not invest in excessively risky assets, have sufficient capital given their risk, have no fraudulent activities, and have competent management; capital requirements to provide incentives for banks not to take excessive risk; and portfolio restrictions to prohibit investment in risky assets

Walter W. Eubanks, Federal Financial Services Regulatory Consolidation: An Overview, Congressional Research Service, CRS–3 (Aug. 17, 2005).

A bank is required to submit quarterly financial data to its regulator. 12 U.S.C.A. §§ 161(a) & (c) (national banks); 1817(a) & (c) (state banks). This information, although self-reported, permits regulators to monitor bank performance on a continuous basis.

An on-site examination of a bank is usually performed once a year. 12 U.S.C.A. § 1820(d). Some small, well-managed institutions may be examined every 18 months. 12 C.F.R. § 337.12. The Financial Services Regulatory Relief Act of 2006 increased the asset threshold for a small institution from $250 million to $500 million. 12 U.S.C.A. § 1820(d)(4)(A). Some institutions may qualify for the FDIC's streamlined examination program called MERIT (Maximum Efficiency, Risk–Focused, Institution Target).[1] The Dodd–Frank Act requires annual, internal stress testing for financial companies with assets of greater than $10 billion. Dodd–Frank Act, § 165. The stress test definition and methodologies will be defined by regulations

---

1. Banks with $1 billion or less in assets and with satisfactory regulatory ratings may qualify. In 2004, the threshold asset size was increased from $250 million to $1 billion. Federal Deposit Insurance Corporation, FIL–13–2004 (Feb. 4, 2004), available at www.fdic.gov.

purposes of examination:
1) maintenance of public confidence
2) adherence to laws & regs
3) financial integrity of fed ins. fund

issued by the federal financial regulatory agencies. The test must include a baseline, adverse, and severely adverse scenario.

The OCC examines national banks. The FDIC alternates exams of state nonmember banks with the state regulatory authority. 12 U.S.C.A. § 1820(d)(3). The Fed alternates exams of state member banks with the state regulator as well. The FDIC has backup examination authority over national banks, state member banks, and all thrifts so that it may request information from other regulators and participate in exams, provided there is advance approval from the FDIC chairman. This authority is viewed as essential in assisting the FDIC in protecting the integrity of the federal deposit insurance system. Even before Dodd–Frank strengthened the FDIC's back-up authority, the FDIC revised its Memorandum of Understanding with the other federal financial agencies to improve its ability to access, understand, and evaluate its exposure to insured banks, particularly the largest institutions. FDIC, FDIC Board Votes to Revise MOU on Backup Supervision Authority, PR 153–2010 (July 12, 2010), www.fdic.gov/news/nes/press/2010/pr10153.html. At the very largest banks, on-site examination teams of around 100 may work at the bank full-time, with a dozen or so Fed examiners examining the holding company (often from off-site) full-time, and usually at least one FDIC representative if the FDIC is not the bank's primary federal regulator.

Under Dodd–Frank, back-up regulatory authority is provided for the Fed. The Fed may take supervisory or enforcement action against a depository institution subsidiary as if the subsidiary were a bank holding company if the Fed makes a written recommendation for action to the primary financial regulatory agency and that agency does not take action acceptable to the Fed within sixty days of receiving the recommendation. Dodd–Frank Act, § 605. Similarly, the FDIC has back-up enforcement authority over BHCs and their nonbank subsidiaries and may take action if the FDIC recommends to the appropriate federal financial agency to take action against a depository holding company and that agency does not take action within sixty days of receiving the FDIC's recommendation. The FDIC also has examination and enforcement authority over a depository institution holding company if the conduct or threat of conduct of that company poses a foreseeable and material risk of loss to the deposit insurance fund. Dodd–Frank Act, § 172. Moreover, if the FDIC board determines examination and enforcement authority is necessary to provide for the orderly liquidation of a systemically significant nonbank financial company, the FDIC may so act. Id.

The Fed has regulatory authority over BHCs and their nonbanking subsidiaries. After Dodd–Frank, as will be discussed in more detail below, the Fed also has authority over systemically significant nonbank financial companies. Under GLBA the Fed retained umbrella supervision over the nonbanking subsidiaries of financial holding companies, but embraced the concept of functional regulation for FHC subsidiaries that have their own regulator. 12 U.S.C.A. § 1844(c). Congress expressed its dissatisfaction with this supervisory framework in the Dodd–Frank Act. It expanded the authority of the Fed to examine functionally regulated subsidiaries and scaled back existing restrictions on the Fed's authority over such subsidiaries. Dodd–Frank Act, § 604. The authority of the Fed to examine and regulate the non-depository and non-functionally regulated subsidiaries of depository holding companies was expanded in Dodd–Frank to permit examination and regulation of the activities of these entities in the same fashion as if the activities were conducted in an insured depository institution. Dodd–Frank Act, § 605.

The Bureau of Consumer Financial Protection (BCFP), created by Dodd–Frank to regulate those who offer or provide a consumer financial product or service, was granted broad enforcement power over this aspect of a bank's activities if the bank's assets are in excess of $10 billion. Dodd–Frank Act, § 1025. In such cases, the primary federal financial regulatory of the bank will only have back-up regulatory authority regarding consumer financial products and services.[2] The primary federal regulator will remain in charge, however, for overseeing compliance with federal consumer financial protection laws for banks with less than $10 billion in assets. Dodd–Frank Act, § 1026. The BCFP may appoint its examiners to participate in examinations of these smaller institutions on a sampling basis. The Dodd–Frank Act also requires that the BCFP have access to any examination or other financial condition report of an entity that provides consumer financial products or services and that the banking agencies receive copies of BCFP reports. *FCPB - Financial Consumer Protection Bureau*

A. CAMELS RATING SYSTEM

FEDERAL DEPOSIT INSURANCE CORPORATION MANUAL OF EXAMINATION POLICIES

<www.fdic.gov/regulations/safety/manual/index.html>.

What are the purposes of bank examinations? Although many answers to this question could be given, several fundamental reasons can be identified.

(1) The first relates to the maintenance of public confidence in the integrity of the banking system and in individual banks. Such confidence is clearly essential because the system's customers serve as the source of funding, without which banks would be unable to meet their most fundamental objective of providing financial services. The existence of unhealthy or deteriorating conditions, which may threaten this integrity, should be disclosed through the examiner's evaluation of the bank's capital adequacy, asset quality, management, liquidity position, and earnings capacity.

(2) Second, the periodic on-premise examination provides the best means of determining the bank's adherence to laws and regulations. Compliance

---

2. At the time of Dodd–Frank's enactment, the FDIC supervised only twenty-one banks with assets exceeding $10 billion.

with statutory and regulatory requirements has traditionally been given high priority by bank supervisors, and Congress has frequently reaffirmed this posture.

(3) A third response to the question concerns the role examinations play in protecting the financial integrity of the deposit insurance fund. That is, the examination process can help prevent problem situations from remaining uncorrected and deteriorating to the point where costly financial assistance by the FDIC, or even a payoff of depositors, becomes unavoidable.

Finally, the examination supplies the supervisor with an understanding of the nature, relative seriousness and ultimate cause of a bank's problems, and thus provides a factual foundation to soundly base corrective measures, recommendations and instructions. The examination thus plays a very key role in the supervisory process itself. * * *

The Uniform Financial Institutions Rating System (UFIRS) was adopted by the Federal Financial Institutions Examination Council (FFIEC) on November 13, 1979 [with updates effective in 1997]. * * *

Under the UFIRS, each financial institution is assigned a composite rating based on an evaluation and rating of six essential components of an institution's financial condition and operations. These component factors address the adequacy of capital, the quality of assets, the capability of management, the quality and level of earnings, the adequacy of liquidity, and the sensitivity to market risk. Evaluations of the components take into consideration the institution's size and sophistication, the nature and complexity of its activities, and its risk profile.

Composite and component ratings are assigned based on a 1 to 5 numerical scale. A 1 indicates the highest rating, strongest performance and risk management practices, and least degree of supervisory concern, while a 5 indicates the lowest rating, weakest performance, inadequate risk management practices and, therefore, the highest degree of supervisory concern.

The composite rating generally bears a close relationship to the component ratings assigned. However, the composite rating is not derived by computing an arithmetic average of the component ratings. Each component rating is based on a qualitative analysis of the factors comprising that component and its interrelationship with the other components. When assigning a composite rating, some components may be given more weight than others depending on the situation at the institution. In general, assignment of a composite rating may incorporate any factor that bears significantly on the overall condition and soundness of the financial institution. Assigned composite and component ratings are disclosed to the institution's board of directors and senior management.

The ability of management to respond to changing circumstances and to address the risks that may arise from changing business conditions, or the initiation of new activities or products, is an important factor in evaluating a financial institution's overall risk profile and the level of supervisory attention warranted. For this reason, the management component is given special consideration when assigning a composite rating. * * *

Composite 1

Financial institutions in this group are sound in every respect and generally have components rated 1 or 2. Any weaknesses are minor and can be handled in a routine manner by the board of directors and management. * * *

Composite 2

Financial institutions in this group are fundamentally sound. For a financial institution to receive this rating, generally no component rating should be more severe than 3. Only moderate weaknesses are present and are well within the board of directors' and management's capabilities and willingness to correct. * * *

Composite 3

Financial institutions in this group exhibit some degree of supervisory concern in one or more of the component areas. These financial institutions exhibit a combination of weaknesses that may range from moderate to severe; however, the magnitude of the deficiencies generally will not cause a component to be rated more severely than 4. Management may lack the ability or willingness to effectively address weaknesses within appropriate time frames. * * *

Composite 4

Financial institutions in this group generally exhibit unsafe and unsound practices or conditions. There are serious financial or managerial deficiencies that result in unsatisfactory performance. The problems range from severe to critically deficient. The weaknesses and problems are not being satisfactorily addressed or resolved by the board of directors and management. * * *

Composite 5

Financial institutions in this group exhibit extremely unsafe and unsound practices or conditions; exhibit a critically deficient performance; often contain inadequate risk management practices relative to the institution's size, complexity, and risk profile; and are of the greatest supervisory concern. The volume and severity of problems are beyond management's ability or willingness to control or correct. * * *

Capital Adequacy

A financial institution is expected to maintain capital commensurate with the nature and extent of risks to the institution and the ability of management to identify, measure, monitor, and control these risks. The effect of credit, market, and other risks on the institution's financial condition should be considered when evaluating the adequacy of capital. The types and quantity of risk inherent in an institution's activities will determine the extent to which it may be necessary to maintain capital at levels above required regulatory minimums to properly reflect the potentially adverse consequences that these risks may have on the institution's capital.

The capital adequacy of an institution is rated based upon, but not limited to, an assessment of the following evaluation factors:

- The level and quality of capital and the overall financial condition of the institution.

- The ability of management to address emerging needs for additional capital.

- The nature, trend, and volume of problem assets, and the adequacy of allowances for loan and lease losses and other valuation reserves.

- Balance sheet composition, including the nature and amount of intangible assets, market risk, concentration risk, and risks associated with nontraditional activities.

- Risk exposure represented by off-balance sheet activities.

- The quality and strength of earnings, and the reasonableness of dividends.

- Prospects and plans for growth, as well as past experience in managing growth.

- Access to capital markets and other sources of capital, including support provided by a parent holding company. * * *

Asset Quality

The asset quality rating reflects the quantity of existing and potential credit risk associated with the loan and investment portfolios, other real estate owned, and other assets, as well as off-balance sheet transactions.[3] The ability of management to identify, measure, monitor, and control credit risk is also reflected here. The evaluation of asset quality should consider the adequacy of the allowance for loan and lease losses and weigh the exposure to counter-party, issuer, or borrower default under actual or implied contractual agreements. All other risks that may affect the value or marketability of an institution's assets, including, but not limited to, operating, market, reputation, strategic, or compliance risks, should also be considered. * * *

Management

The capability of the board of directors and management, in their respective roles, to identify, measure, monitor, and control the risks of an

---

3. [eds.] "The quality of the bank's assets is determined by assessing the bank's credit risk of loans in its portfolio, which are classified as good, substandard, doubtful, or loss." Walter W. Eubanks, Federal Financial Services Regulatory Consolidation: An Overview, Congressional Research Service, CRS–3 (Aug. 17, 2005).

institution's activities and to ensure a financial institution's safe, sound, and efficient operation in compliance with applicable laws and regulations is reflected in this rating. Generally, directors need not be actively involved in day-to-day operations; however, they must provide clear guidance regarding acceptable risk exposure levels and ensure that appropriate policies, procedures, and practices have been established. Senior management is responsible for developing and implementing policies, procedures, and practices that translate the board's goals, objectives, and risk limits into prudent operating standards. * * *

Earnings

This rating reflects not only the quantity and trend of earnings, but also factors that may affect the sustainability or quality of earnings. The quantity as well as the quality of earnings can be affected by excessive or inadequately managed credit risk that may result in loan losses and require additions to the allowance for loan and lease losses, or by high levels of market risk that may unduly expose an institution's earnings to volatility in interest rates. The quality of earnings may also be diminished by undue reliance on extraordinary gains, nonrecurring events, or favorable tax effects. Future earnings may be adversely affected by an inability to forecast or control funding and operating expenses, improperly executed or ill-advised business strategies, or poorly managed or uncontrolled exposure to other risks. * * *

Liquidity

In evaluating the adequacy of a financial institution's liquidity position, consideration should be given to the current level and prospective sources of liquidity compared to funding needs, as well as to the adequacy of funds management practices relative to the institution's size, complexity, and risk profile. In general, funds management practices should ensure that an institution is able to maintain a level of liquidity sufficient to meet its financial obligations in a timely manner and to fulfill the legitimate banking needs of its community. Practices should reflect the ability of the institution to manage unplanned changes in funding sources, as well as react to changes in market conditions that affect the ability to quickly liquidate assets with minimal loss. In addition, funds management practices should ensure that liquidity is not maintained at a high cost, or through undue reliance on funding sources that may not be available in times of financial stress or adverse changes in market conditions. * * *

Sensitivity To Market Risk

The sensitivity to market risk component reflects the degree to which changes in interest rates, foreign exchange rates, commodity prices, or equity prices can adversely affect a financial institution's earnings or economic capital. When evaluating this component, consideration should be given to: management's ability to identify, measure, monitor, and control market risk; the institution's size; the nature and complexity of its activities; and the adequacy of its capital and earnings in relation to its level of market risk exposure. * * *

The federal banking agencies permit CAMELS ratings to be shared with the institution's directors, officers, attorneys, and auditors, but not with insurance companies that might request the information in an institution's application for directors and officers liability insurance coverage. Interagency Advisory on the Confidentiality of Nonpublic Supervisory Information, SR 05–04 (Feb. 28, 2005).

B.   HOLDING COMPANY REGULATION

FEDERAL RESERVE BOARD OF GOVERNORS BANK HOLDING COMPANY RATING SYSTEM

SR 04–18 (Dec. 6, 2004).

To more closely align the supervisory rating system for bank holding companies (BHCs), including financial holding companies, with the Federal Reserve's current supervisory practices, on December 1, 2004, the Board of Governors approved for System-wide implementation the attached revised BHC rating system. The revised rating system becomes effective January 1, 2005 and is to be used for all inspections commencing after that date. * * *

While the Federal Reserve has a well-established emphasis on risk management in its supervisory processes for BHCs of all sizes, which it reenforced through the introduction of a risk management rating for all BHCs in the mid–1990s, the primary components of the BHC supervisory rating system known as BOPEC (Bank subsidiaries, Other subsidiaries, Parent, Earnings, Capital) do not directly reflect this emphasis. To align more closely the ratings with the supervisory processes, the Federal Reserve has developed a revised BHC rating system that emphasizes risk management; introduces a more comprehensive and adaptable framework for analyzing and rating financial factors; and provides a framework for assessing and rating the potential impact of the parent holding company and its nondepository subsidiaries on the subsidiary depository institution(s). * * *

Each BHC is assigned a composite rating (C) based on an evaluation and rating of its managerial and financial condition and an assessment of future potential risk to its subsidiary depository institution(s). The main components of the rating system represent: Risk Management (R); Financial Condition (F); and potential Impact (I) of the parent company and nondepository subsidiaries (collectively nondepository entities) on the subsidiary depository institution(s). While all BHCs are required to act as sources of strength to their subsidiary depository institutions, pursuant to the Board's rules and policies, the Impact rating focuses on downside risk—that is, on the likelihood of significant negative impact on the subsidiary depository institutions. A fourth component rating, Depository Institution (D), will generally mirror the primary regulator's assessment of the subsidiary depository institution(s), as has been the case for the Bank (B) rating under the BOPEC rating system. Thus, the primary component and composite ratings are displayed:

R F I / C (D)

In order to provide a consistent framework for assessing risk management, the R component is supported by four subcomponents that reflect the effectiveness of the banking organization's risk management and controls. The subcomponents are: Board and Senior Management Oversight; Policies, Procedures, and Limits; Risk Monitoring and Management Information Systems; and Internal Controls. The F component is similarly supported by four subcomponents reflecting an assessment of the quality of the banking organization's Capital; Asset Quality; Earnings; and Liquidity. A simplified version of the rating system that requires only the assignment of the risk management component rating and composite rating will be applied to noncomplex BHCs with assets below $1 billion.

Composite, component, and subcomponent ratings are assigned based on a 1 to 5 numeric scale. A 1 indicates the highest rating, strongest performance and practices, and least degree of supervisory concern; a 5 indicates the lowest rating, weakest performance, and highest degree of supervisory concern.

* * * [T]he risk management component and subcomponents should be viewed as the more forward-looking aspect of the rating system, and the financial condition component and subcomponents should be viewed as the current aspect of the rating system. * * *

The Dodd–Frank Act explicitly states that the Fed's exams of depository holding companies and their subsidiaries should inform the Fed about risks to the stability of the U.S. financial system as well as risks to the particular holding company and its depository institution subsidiaries. Dodd–Frank Act, § 604.

C. SYSTEMICALLY SIGNIFICANT FINANCIAL INSTITUTIONS

The FSOC, established in the Dodd–Frank Act, is charged with identifying systemically significant financial institutions. Included in this designation are systemically significant nonbank financial companies, Dodd–Frank Act, § 113, and large, interconnected depository institution holding companies with consolidated assets in excess of $50 billion, Dodd–Frank Act, § 115. The Fed is granted supervisory authority over these nonbank financial institutions, even though these institutions were not subject to Fed oversight prior to the enactment of Dodd–Frank. The Fed must also implement heightened prudential standards for these systemically significant bank holding companies and nonbank financial institutions. These standards include heightened capital, leverage, and liquidity requirements. Dodd–Frank Act, § 115. Periodic stress testing is also mandated. Dodd–Frank Act, § 165. The Fed must conduct annual stress tests under a baseline, adverse, and severely adverse scenario for the systemically significant financial institutions. These institutions must also perform internal stress tests semi-annually. Moreover, these systemic institutions must prepare resolution plans (sometimes called living wills) which provide a roadmap for a rapid and orderly resolution of the company in the case of its failure. Dodd–Frank Act, § 165. Among other things, this confidential plan must detail all the company's assets, liabilities, contractual obligations, counterparties, and other exposures.

The FDIC established an Office of Complex Financial Institutions (CFI) to provide continuous review of the systemically significant nonbank financial institutions and bank holding companies with more than $100 billion in assets.[4] Moreover, Dodd–Frank provides the FDIC expanded examination authority over systemically significant financial institutions whenever the board of the FDIC determines that a special examination is necessary to implement the FDIC's new authority regarding the orderly liquidation of a systemically significant institution. Dodd–Frank Act, § 172.

SECTION 2.　ENFORCEMENT POWERS

A.　HISTORY OF ENFORCEMENT ACTIVITIES

The primary regulator of a bank or thrift has a variety of enforcement powers that may be used against the institution and "institution-affiliated parties." Before 1966, regulators had two basic measures they could use to enforce the banking laws: moral suasion and the "death penalty." Moral suasion, sometimes referred to as "jawboning," describes a regulator's efforts to persuade a bank to undertake different or more rigorous practices. The death penalty refers to the ultimate, and drastic, sanction of ending the existence of the institution through forfeiting the charter, revoking federal deposit insurance coverage, entering receivership (followed by a sale or liquidation), or entering conservatorship (appointing a conservator to run the institution). Regulators felt that additional enforcement mechanisms, falling between the two extremes of moral suasion and the death penalty, would be helpful.

In 1966, Congress enacted the Financial Institutions Supervisory Act (FISA) which gave federal regulators the authority to issue cease and desist orders, and modified their removal and prohibition powers. 12

---

4. FDIC, FDIC Announces Organizational Changes to Help Implement Recently Enacted Regulatory Reform by Congress, PR–184–2010 (Aug. 10, 2010), | www.fdic.gov/news/news/press/ 2010/pr10184.htmlℭ.

U.S.C.A. § 1818. These powers were extended to all national and state banks, as well as federal and state thrifts. 12 U.S.C.A. § 1818(a)(5). In 1974, the Fed received similar authority with respect to its oversight of bank holding companies. The National Credit Union Administration received comparable enforcement powers over credit unions in 1970.

In 1989, in an attempt to deal with the savings and loan crisis and the massive numbers of thrift and bank failures, Congress enacted the Financial Institutions Reform, Recovery, and Enforcement Act of 1989 (FIRREA). This statute consolidated the enforcement authority previously found in the Federal Deposit Insurance Act, the Home Owners' Loan Act, and the National Housing Act in the Federal Deposit Insurance Act. 12 U.S.C.A. § 1818. Prior to FIRREA, enforcement actions could be brought against an institution's officers, directors, employees, agents, or others "participating in the affairs of the institution." The latter category was not defined and uncertainty existed as to whether this language permitted enforcement actions to be brought against a shareholder who owned a significant portion of the institution's stock, and was not a board member, but might nevertheless be using the institution for his own purposes. FIRREA permitted enforcement actions, including those seeking restitution or reimbursement, to be brought against "institution-affiliated parties," which could include shareholders. 12 U.S.C.A. § 1813(u). FIRREA added the power to order restitution, reimbursement, or other affirmative action. In addition, the FDIC was given "back-up" enforcement authority over all federally insured depository institutions in the event the primary regulator's enforcement authority was not vigorous enough. 12 U.S.C.A. § 1818 (f). The FDIC has yet to exercise this "back-up" enforcement authority.

The FDIC Improvement Act of 1991 (FDICIA) set forth a regulatory scheme based on the notion of "prompt corrective action." 12 U.S.C.A. §§ 1818(b)(6) & 1831o. The premise of this scheme was to lessen the overall loss suffered by the federal deposit insurance funds by empowering regulators to direct institutions to address their capital deficiencies prior to technical insolvency. Institutions with inadequate capital are required to complete a capital restoration plan. If the institution does not comply with the plan, it may be precluded from engaging in certain activities. In addition, regulators may, under such circumstances, exercise removal powers against the institution's officers and directors.

The Comprehensive Thrift and Bank Fraud Act of 1990, part of the Comprehensive Crime Control Act, provided authority for prejudgment attachment and injunctive relief. The Annunzio–Wylie Money Laundering Act of 1992 set forth separate grounds for removal and prohibition of officers and directors found to be involved in money laundering operations.

In the 2000s, banks have been increasingly willing to settle regulatory actions to provide certainty, put a ceiling on their potential liability, and to move forward without further damage to their reputation.[5] Financial institutions have also been subject in this period to increased enforcement activity by the SEC, criminal investigations and proceedings by the Department of Justice, and actions by state attorneys general.

B. TYPES OF ENFORCEMENT ACTIONS

Under FIRREA, the supervisory enforcement powers of the federal bank agencies may be used against the institution and, in appropriate cases, against "institution-affiliated" parties. 12 U.S.C.A. § 1813(u). This term is defined to include directors, officers, controlling shareholders, and agents (those parties who generally were "participating in management" under the prior statute), but adds to the list "any shareholder ... consultant, joint venture partner," as well as any

> independent contractor (including any attorney, appraiser, or account-ant) who knowingly or recklessly participates in (A) any violation of law or regulation; (B) any breach of fiduciary duty; or (C) any unsafe or unsound practice, which caused or is likely to cause more than a minimal financial loss to, or a significant adverse effect on, the insured depository institution.

12 U.S.C.A § 1813(u).

(1) Informal Supervisory and Enforcement Actions

The bank regulator's report of examination should identify any problems the institution is experiencing and put the bank's board of directors on notice as to potential corrective actions. This report can serve as an informal enforcement mechanism, outlining steps the bank should take to correct problems noted in the examination. Sometimes the regulator will determine it is necessary to go beyond the report of examination and will require written commitments from the bank's management and board to address identified problems, adopt specific board resolutions, or draft a memorandum of understanding (MOU).

(2) Formal Enforcement Mechanisms

Formal enforcement orders authorized under 12 U.S.C.A. § 1818 include:

Consent Orders

A consent order is an order by the regulatory agency to cease and desist and is entered into pursuant to 12 U.S.C.A. § 1818(b). The bank's board enters into this order on behalf of the bank. Consent orders are also signed by an agency official. Violations of a consent order may result in civil money penalties (CMPs) against directors, officers and other institu-

---

5. See Todd Davenport, *Years of Scandal Really Have Changed Banking: Here's How,* Am. Banker, July 8, 2005.

tion-affiliated parties. A consent order may also be enforced by petition to a U.S. district court.

Cease and Desist Orders

A cease and desist order has the same legal effect as a consent order, but it is imposed on an involuntary basis after issuance of a Notice of Charges, a hearing before an administrative law judge, and a final decision and order issued by the agency. A cease and desist order may be reviewed by a U.S. Court of Appeals. The cease and desist order may require the offender to cease and desist from the identified activity, take action to correct the adverse conditions resulting from the activity, make restitution or reimbursement, or indemnify or guarantee the institution against loss if the offender was unjustly enriched by the improper activity, or the activity involved reckless disregard for law regulation or prior order. 12 U.S.C.A. § 1818(b)(6)

Temporary Cease and Desist Orders

A temporary cease and desist order is an interim order issued by an agency under 12 U.S.C.A. § 1818(c) that is used to compel immediate action pending resolution of a cease and desist order.

Removal and Prohibition Orders

Removal and prohibition orders are not made unless a three part test is satisfied. 12 U.S.C.A. § 1818(e). The test requires a specific act, effect, and intent. The *act* must be a violation of law or regulation, including violation of a cease and desist order, a condition, or an agreement with the agency; an unsafe or unsound practice; or an act, omission or practice that constitutes a breach of fidelity. 12 U.S.C.A. § 1818(e)(1)(A). The *effect* realized from the act must be that the institution has suffered or probably will suffer loss or damage, the interests of the depositors have been prejudiced, or the offender received some financial gain or benefit from the improper act. 12 U.S.C.A. § 1818(e)(1)(B). Finally, the offender must have acted with the requisite *intent*, which includes either personal dishonesty, or willful or continuing disregard for the safety and soundness of the institution. 12 U.S.C.A. § 1818(e)(1)(C).

If granted, a removal and prohibition order might include an industry ban prohibiting the offender from participating in the affairs of any depository institution. 12 U.S.C.A. § 1818(e)(1)-(e)(7). The order might also prohibit the solicitation or vote of any proxies, prevent the offender from voting for directors, or prohibit the offender from serving as an institution-affiliated party. 12 U.S.C.A. § 1818 (e)(7).

Formal Written Agreements

A formal written agreement between the bank and the agency is similar to a consent order in form. 12 U.S.C.A. § 1818(b). Violations of a formal agreement may result in civil money penalties against directors, officers and other institution-affiliated parties. Unlike a consent order, a formal agreement is not enforceable through the federal courts.

PCA Directives

Insured banks are subject to mandatory and discretionary actions depending on the banks' capital category under the prompt corrective action scheme (PCA) set forth in 12 U.S.C.A. § 1831o. Mandatory restrictions are effective upon the bank's receipt of notice that it is in a particular PCA capital category. A PCA directive is the vehicle through which discretionary actions are imposed on the bank.

Safety and Soundness Orders

An agency may issue a notice of deficiency under 12 U.S.C.A. 1831p–1 to the bank finding it failed to meet the required standards for safety and soundness. The notice requires the bank to submit a safety and soundness compliance plan. If the bank fails to submit an adequate plan or fails to implement an approved plan, the agency may require the bank to correct its deficiencies.

Capital Directives

A capital directive is an order issued pursuant to the agency's capital requirements (e.g., 12 C.F.R. pt. 3 for the OCC). A capital directive may be issued without a hearing before an administrative law judge. The directive sets a capital level for the bank and may require certain actions relating to the bank's capital. In practice, capital directives are rarely used since most banks with capital problems have already been dealt with through the other enforcement mechanisms described above.

Civil Money Penalties

Civil money penalties (CMPs) were substantially strengthened in FIRREA to provide a maximum penalty of $1 million per day, 12 U.S.C.A. § 1818(i)(2), indexed for inflation. There are three tiers of penalties that may be assessed against any depository institution or institution-affiliated party:

Tier 1. Up to $5,000 per day, for violation of any law or regulation, any final agency order, any condition of an agency approval, or any written agreement.

Tier 2. Up to $25,000 per day, for commission of a First Tier violation, recklessly engaging in an unsafe or unsound practice, or breaching a fiduciary duty. However, the predicate act to constitute a Tier 2 penalty must be part of a pattern of misconduct that has caused or is likely to cause more than a minimal damage to the institution, or which results in pecuniary gain to the offender.

Tier 3. Up to $1 million per day, for the same predicate acts as for a Tier 2 violation, but the offender must have knowingly or recklessly caused substantial loss to a depository institution or substantial gain or benefit to the offender.

12 U.S.C.A. §§ 93(b) & 1818(i)(2).

Each agency has developed a CMP matrix to determine the amount of the penalty for different combinations of actions and consequences.[6]

Divestiture of Assets

If the Fed determines that a systemically significant financial institution poses a grave threat to the financial stability of the United States, the Fed may, upon a vote of not fewer than two-thirds of the voting members of FSOC, require the company to sell or transfer assets or off-balance sheet items to unaffiliated entities. Dodd–Frank Act, § 121.

(3) Conduct of the Administrative Process

The administrative process of seeking enforcement against a depository institution or institution-affiliated party is governed by the Administrative Procedure Act. 12 U.S.C.A. § 1818(h). The normal sequence of events is that the agency files a Notice of Charges or an Intent to Remove. The defendant must respond within 20 days. Limited discovery takes place, and the parties exchange prehearing statements, witness lists, and exhibit lists. A hearing is held before an Administrative Law Judge (ALJ), who, since FIRREA, is drawn from a pool of ALJs familiar with bank enforcement matters. The hearing may include oral testimony, cross examination, and the presentation of documentary evidence.

Thirty days after they have received the transcript of the hearing, the parties must submit to the ALJ proposed findings of fact and conclusions of law, along with proposed orders. A party may also submit a brief in response to the other party's submissions. Forty-five days after the reply briefs are due, the ALJ must file and certify a record of the proceeding and his recommended decision, and submit both to the head of the applicable agency. The parties are entitled to file exceptions to the recommended decision, and the agency head may permit oral argument on those exceptions. The agency head is required to make a final decision within ninety days of any oral argument or when the record is deemed to be complete. The agency head may accept, reject, or modify the ALJ's recommended decision.

The parties may file an application for review by a federal court of appeals within thirty days following the agency head's decision. The appeals court may upset the agency head's decision only if it is arbitrary, capricious, an abuse of discretion, or otherwise not in accordance with the law, if the decision is not based on substantial evidence, or if the decision is in excess of the agency head's statutory authority.

---

6. See Office of the Comptroller of the Currency, Policies and Procedures Manual PPM 5310–3 Appendix C (Nov. 19, 1993).

MATTER OF SEIDMAN

United States Court of Appeals, Third Circuit, 1994.
37 F.3d 911.

HUTCHINSON, CIRCUIT JUDGE.

In these consolidated cases, Lawrence Seidman ("Seidman") and John Bailey ("Bailey") petition for review of the order of the Director ("Director") of the Office of Thrift Supervision ("OTS") subjecting them to administrative sanctions for their part in a loan transaction Crestmont Federal Savings and Loan ("Crestmont") considered while Seidman was Chairman of Crestmont's Board of Directors ("Board") and Bailey was one of its officers. Specifically, Bailey petitions for review of that portion of the Director's order publicly directing him to cease and desist from participating in unsafe and unsound lending practices. Seidman's petition seeks review of that portion of the Director's order removing him from his office at Crestmont and banning him from further participation in the banking industry. * * *

Section 1818(b)(1) prohibits unsafe and unsound practices. OTS argues that Bailey's commitment to the Levine loan conflicts with Crestmont's policy of prohibiting purchase money loans on the security of real property in which a Crestmont officer or director had an interest. An officer's violation of a banking institution's policy, however, is not enough to justify a cease and desist order under section 1818(b)(1). While the statute gives the Director considerable discretion, it nevertheless requires substantial evidence showing that the violation of policy amounted to an unsafe and unsound practice.

Section 1818(b)(1) provides:

> If, in the opinion of the appropriate Federal Banking Agency ... any institution-affiliated party ... has engaged ... in an unsafe or unsound practice in conducting the business of [a] depository institution, ... the agency may issue and serve upon the ... party a notice of charges in respect thereof.... [I]f upon the record made at ... [a] hearing, the agency shall find that any ... unsafe or unsound practice specified in the notice of charges has been established, the agency may issue and serve upon ... the institution-affiliated party an order to cease and desist from any such ... practice.

12 U.S.C.A. § 1818(b)(1).

Because the statute itself does not define an unsafe or unsound practice, courts have sought help in the legislative history. In hearings before Congress prior to its adoption in the Financial Institutions Supervisory Act of 1966, Pub. L. No. 89–695 (1966) John Horne, Chairman of the Federal Home Loan Bank Board ("FLHBB"), OTS's predecessor, testified:

> Generally speaking, an "unsafe or unsound practice" embraces any action, or lack of action, which is contrary to generally accepted standards of prudent operation, the possible consequences of which, if continued, would be abnormal risk or loss or damage to an institution, its shareholders, or the agencies administering the insurance funds.

Financial Institutions Supervisory Act of 1966: Hearings on S. 3158 and S. 3695 Before the House Committee on Banking and Currency, 89th Cong., 2d Sess. 49–50 (memorandum submitted by John Horne) (citations omitted). Thus, courts have generally interpreted the phrase "unsafe or unsound practice" as a flexible concept which gives the administering agency the ability to adapt to changing business problems and practices in the regulation of the banking industry. See Groos Nat'l Bank v. Comptroller of the Currency, 573 F.2d 889, 897 (5th Cir. 1978) ("The phrase 'unsafe or unsound banking practice' is widely used in the regulatory statutes and in case law, and one of the purposes of the banking acts is clearly to commit the progressive definition and eradication of such practices to the expertise of the appropriate regulatory agencies.").

Ex: Among the specific acts that may constitute an unsafe and unsound practice are "paying excessive dividends, disregarding a borrower's ability to repay, careless control of expenses, excessive advertising, and inadequate liquidity." Gulf Federal Sav. & Loan Ass'n, 651 F.2d at 264. In *Gulf Federal*, the court had to decide whether a bank's breach of contract was an unsafe or unsound practice that justified an FHLBB order to cease and desist. The FHLBB concluded that the bank's potential liability for breach and possible "loss of public confidence in the institution" meant the breach was an unsafe and unsound practice that authorized the agency to order the bank to perform its contract. The court disagreed and held that a breach of contract is not an unsafe or unsound practice that threatens a bank's financial soundness. The court expressly rejected FHLBB's conclusion that liability for breach and consequent loss of public confidence in the bank's willingness to honor its commitments give rise to an unsafe or unsound practice that authorized a cease and desist order. It stated:

> Such potential "risks" bear only the most remote relationship to [the bank's] financial integrity and the government's insurance risk. . . . We fail to see how the [FHLBB] can safeguard [the bank's] finances by making definite and immediate an injury which is, at worst, contingent and remote.
>
> Approving intervention under the [FHLBB's] "loss of public confidence" rationale would result in open-ended supervision. . . . The [FHLBB's] rationale would permit it to decide, not that the public has lost confidence in [the bank's] financial soundness, but that the public may lose confidence in the fairness of the association's contracts with its customers. If the [FHLBB] can act to enforce the public's standard of fairness in interpreting contracts, the [FHLBB] becomes the monitor of every activity of the association in its role of proctor for public opinion. This departs entirely from the congressional concept of acting to preserve the financial integrity of its members.

Id. at 264–65 (footnote omitted).

In *Northwest National Bank* the court upheld the Comptroller of the Currency's ("Comptroller's") conclusion that evidence showing failure to maintain an adequate loan to loss reserve and inadequate capital, together with deficient loan administration, established unsafe or unsound banking practices. *Northwest Nat'l Bank*, 917 F.2d at 1113–14. The court agreed with FHLBB that the bank's failure to maintain adequate reserves and capital was an unsafe or unsound practice. The court defined the phrase "unsafe and unsound banking practices" in general terms similar to those that appear in the legislative history: "Unsafe and unsound banking practices are ... 'conduct deemed contrary to accepted standards of banking operations which might result in abnormal risk or loss to a banking institution or shareholder.' " Id. (quoting First Nat'l Bank of Eden v. Department of the Treasury, 568 F.2d 610, 611 n.2 (8th Cir. 1978) (per curiam)). The court in *Northwest National Bank* decided that the poor state of the bank's loan portfolio and the insufficient level of its capital and reserves permitted an inference that unsafe lending practices had occurred. Accordingly, it upheld the Comptroller's finding that the bank had engaged in unsafe and unsound banking practices. [S]ee also First Nat'l Bank of Eden, 568 F.2d at 611 (upholding Comptroller's issuance of cease and desist order for unsafe and unsound banking practices when record showed accumulation of unsafe assets, inadequate internal controls and auditing procedures, lack of credit information on certain bank investments in violation of federal regulations and payment of excessive bonuses to bank officers).

In MCorp Financial, Inc. v. Board of Governors, 900 F.2d 852 (5th Cir. 1990), aff'd in part, rev'd in part on other grounds, 112 S.Ct. 459 (1991), the Board of Governors of the Federal Reserve concluded that MCorp's failure to provide capital to its subsidiary banks was an unsafe or unsound practice and entered a cease and desist order directing MCorp to transfer assets to its banking subsidiaries. On review, the court of appeals concluded that Congress had failed to provide a clear definition of "unsafe or unsound practice." Id. at 862. Limited by Chevron U.S.A., Inc. v. Natural Resources Defense Council, Inc., 467 U.S. 837 (1984), but relying on *Gulf Federal Savings & Loan Association*, the court concluded that the Board of Governors' order directing MCorp to transfer assets to its troubled subsidiaries was itself contrary to " 'generally accepted standard[] of prudent operation.' " Id. at 863 (quoting *Gulf Federal Sav.*, 651 F.2d at 259). "Such a transfer of funds would require MCorp to disregard its own corporation's separate status; it would amount to a wasting of the holding company's assets in violation of its duty to its shareholders." Id.

We think at least one common element of an unsafe or unsound banking practice relating to the health of the institution can be deduced from these cases and the legislative history. The imprudent act must pose an abnormal risk to the financial stability of the banking institution. This is the standard that the case law and legislative history indicates we should apply in judging whether an unsafe or unsound practice has occurred. * * *

When Bailey issued the commitment letter, he made Crestmont responsible for the Levine loan. * * * When Levine accepted the commitment, Crestmont remained ineligible to make the loan. Thus, Crestmont became responsible for the loan despite the potential illegal conflict. We think this act was imprudent. Although all parties testified that their understanding was that the loan would not go through absent Seidman's complete withdrawal [from a business relationship with Levine], Bailey had nevertheless obligated Crestmont to a loan it might not be able to make. Obligating one's institution to transactions that might be illegal is not in accord with "generally accepted standards of prudent operation." See *MCorp Fin., Inc.*, 900 F.2d at 862. After Levine accepted the commitment letter, Crestmont either had to make the loan, breach the agreement to make it or place the loan with another institution regardless of Seidman's position. Although, as it turned out, Crestmont was able to place the loan without incident or loss, we recognize that a risk was present when Bailey issued the commitment. Obliging an institution to choose between covering fluctuations in the interest rate, engaging in an illegal transaction or breaching a binding agreement is not prudent.

Imprudence standing alone, however, is insufficient to constitute an unsafe or unsound practice. A cease and desist order is designed to prevent actions that if repeated would carry a potential for serious loss. Although issuance of even this single commitment exposed Crestmont to some potential risk of loss, that potential risk did not begin to approach the abnormal risk involved in *Northwest National Bank*, where the bank was exposed to a serious threat to financial stability by its general failure to monitor its loans adequately and to maintain adequate reserves and capital. The potential loss to which Bailey subjected Crestmont is rather like that present in *Gulf Federal*. Contingent, remote harms that could ultimately result in "minor financial losses" to the institution are insufficient to pose the danger that warrants cease and desist proceedings. *Gulf Fed. Sav. & Loan Ass'n*, 651 F.2d at 264. Though it is not particularly onerous to require a loan officer to satisfy himself that the institution may legally make a loan before the commitment is issued, we cannot conclude that the commitment Bailey authorized posed such an abnormal risk that Crestmont's financial stability was threatened. * * *

Courts have recognized that the power to remove a bank officer is an extraordinary power that should be carefully exercised in strict accordance with the law. Accordingly, we might expect that the statute under which OTS sought the far more serious sanction of Seidman's removal from office and his permanent prohibition from participation in the thrift industry, 12 U.S.C.A. § 1818(e), requires elements additional to those that justify the lesser sanction of a cease and desist order. We are not disappointed. By requiring a three part conjunctive test in section 1818(e)(1), Congress has imposed significant additional conditions before a banker can be deprived of his office and permanently barred from banking. Thus, before an agency regulating a banking institution can impose this ultimate administrative sanction on any banker, it must show by substantial evidence that: (1) the banker has committed an unlawful act; (2) the act has either an adverse effect on the regulated institution or its depositors or confers a benefit on the actor and (3) the act is accompanied by a culpable state of mind. The acts come in three varieties. The effects also divide into three subclasses, but there are only two kinds of culpable mental states. Under section 1818(e)(1), at least one of the prohibited acts, accompanied by at least one of the three prohibited effects and at least one of the two specified culpable states of mind, must be established by substantial evidence on the whole record before the regulatory agency can properly remove a person from office and ban him from the banking or thrift industries. * * *

We do not think every appearance of wrongdoing justifies the sanction of removal and prohibition. Rather, we believe such a drastic sanction should require some evidence of actual misconduct or evidence from which a reasonable person acquainted with the facts could conclude there was misconduct. Here, Crestmont never made any loan to an end-user on the FSA project [in which Seidman had a business interest], and Seidman told Bailey to stop considering any loans in which Seidman had an interest before OTS began its investigation. Seidman did so as soon as he realized he could not persuade OTS that his guarantee did not matter. Seidman's earlier attempts to persuade OTS to the contrary were not improper. Viewed as a whole, we think this record contains substantial evidence that Seidman acted to further the interests of Crestmont, not just his own, when he attempted to obtain a release from his guarantee, and therefore his actions did not constitute a breach of the fiduciary duty of loyalty contained in section 1818(e)(1)(A)(iii).

In summary, we hold Seidman's conduct in seeking a release from the [guarantee he made to another bank] did not violate any "law or regulation" under section 1818(e)(1)(A)(i)(I) or constitute an "unsafe or unsound" practice under section 1818(e)(1)(A)(ii) or a breach of fiduciary duty under section 1818(e)(1)(A)(iii). To the extent the Director relied on Seidman's conduct of seeking a release from his guarantee of FSA's indebtedness to UJB [United Jersey Bank] to support the order of removal and prohibition, the Director erred. * * *

We agree with the Director that hindering an OTS investigation is an unsafe or unsound practice as that term has come to be used in the banking industry. Section 1818(e)(1)(A) can be satisfied by evidence showing the conduct with which an affiliated person like Seidman is charged falls within section 1818(e)(1)(A)(ii)'s proscription of unsafe or unsound practices because it "is contrary to generally accepted standards of prudent operation" and "the possible consequences of [the act], if continued, would be abnormal risk or loss or damage to . . . the agency administering the insurance fund[]." *Gulf Federal Sav. & Loan Ass'n,* 651 F.2d at 264 (quotation omitted). We believe an attempt to obstruct an OTS investigation is such an act. OTS is statutorily charged with preserving the financial integrity of the thrift system. See 12 U.S.C.A. § 1462(a) (West Supp. 1994); id. § 1463(a). To meet that responsibility, OTS has the power to investigate. See 12 C.F.R. § 509.16 (1993). Where a party attempts to induce another to withhold material information from the agency, the agency becomes unable to fulfill its regulatory function. Such behavior, if continued, strikes at the heart of the regulatory function. Seidman's attempt to obstruct the investigation, if continued, would pose an abnormal risk of damage to OTS. Accordingly, we hold that an attempt to hinder an OTS investigation constitutes an "unsafe or unsound practice," thus satisfying the act requirement of section 1818(e)(1)(A).

Our conclusion that Seidman's attempts to obstruct the OTS investigation constitute a prohibited act does not end our section 1818(e) inquiry. The act must still have a prohibited effect with a culpable intent before the severe sanction of a removal and prohibition order may issue. Section 1818(e)(1)(C)'s culpability element of personal dishonesty is shown by the undisputed evidence that Seidman asked Risko [an employee of a loan broker handling negotiations between Seidman's business interest and the involvement of the other bank] to forget about the draft of the letter to UJB. The requirements of section 1818(e)(1)(B) remain.

The Director concluded that section 1818(e)(1)(B)'s requirement of an untoward or prohibited effect was satisfied because Seidman had benefitted from the release of his guarantee of FSA's loan to [the other bank]. We conclude, however, that none of Seidman's attempts to obstruct the OTS investigation resulted in any benefit to Seidman, the sole basis the Director relied on to satisfy section 1818(e)(1)(B)'s condition of an untoward or prohibited effect. The Director made no other finding concerning any effect of Seidman's conduct that could satisfy section 1818(e)(1)(B) other than his conclusion that "Seidman benefitted from his [attempt to obstruct the OTS investigation] by depriving OTS of reliable and material evidence, thwarting OTS enforcement action and hampering the prompt resolution of the self-dealing charges." Section 1818(e)(1)(B)(iii) proscribes an act from which the actor "*has received* financial gain or other benefit by reason of such violation, practice, or breach...." 12 U.S.C.A. § 1818(e)(1)(B)(iii) (emphasis added).

Seidman's attempt to solicit false testimony from Risko was rebuffed; therefore, Seidman received no benefit from his request that Risko forget about the draft letter. Similarly, Seidman's destruction of a draft letter that OTS already possessed and his unwillingness to volunteer information in his deposition failed to thwart the OTS investigation. * * *

We conclude only that OTS may not, on this record, impose the draconian sanction of removal and prohibition under section 1818(e) because all the conditions that statute imposes on that ultimate penalty have not been met. However, we believe, for the reasons discussed supra, that Seidman's attempts to obstruct the OTS investigation, * * * particularly his act of counseling Risko to withhold potentially material facts, do constitute an unsafe or unsound practice and so could support a cease and desist order and monetary penalties as authorized by section 1818(b)(1). While the notice of charges did not specifically request a cease and desist order with respect to Seidman's obstructionist conduct, it did ask for "[a]ny other relief deemed appropriate by the Director of OTS." Thus, we will remand so that the Director may consider whether a cease and desist order with accompanying civil penalties is appropriate in this instance. * * *

STAPLETON, CIRCUIT JUDGE, dissenting. * * *

QUESTIONS AND NOTES

1. What is an "unsafe and unsound" practice? Do the regulations required by FDICIA add any precision to this term? Is it good to preserve bank regulators' discretion with a flexible standard for dealing with wrongdoing?

2. How does such a flexible standard operate in the setting of a bank or financial holding company?

3. In an unusual decision the FDIC was sanctioned for $72 million in a blistering opinion by a United States district court judge who found that the FDIC conspired to take 4,400 acres of redwood trees in Northern California from a Texas businessman whom it alleged was involved in the failure of a savings and loan. FDIC v. Hurwitz, 384 F.Supp.2d 1039 (S.D. Tex. 2005). On appeal, the Fifth Circuit subjected the FDIC to Rule 11 sanctions finding that it prosecuted the suit in a manner calculated to delay the case and increase the costs of defense. 523 F.3d 566 (5th Cir. 2008).

4. The Financial Services Regulatory Relief Act of 2006 provides that a federal banking agency may enforce "any condition imposed in writing by the agency on the depository institution *or any institution-affiliated party*." Section 702 (emphasis added). Bank directors are concerned that if an agency conditioned its approval of a charter application upon a written agreement with the directors that a specific capital level be maintained, that the directors could later be forced by this new provision to contribute additional capital to the bank. Luke Mullins, Reg–Relief Bill to Put Boards on Capital Hook: Agencies like idea, but some see chilling effect on start-ups, Am. Banker, May 18, 2006. An FDIC representative admitted that although such a condition would be unusual with a start-up bank, it could possibly be required for a new bank with an aggressive business plan. Id.

SECTION 3. ORDERLY LIQUIDATION AUTHORITY FOR SYSTEMICALLY SIGNIFICANT FINANCIAL COMPANIES

Before Dodd–Frank, the bankruptcies of financial holding companies, bank holding companies, and nonbank financial companies were subject to the provisions of the federal Bankruptcy Act, as would be the case with the bankruptcy of any other corporation. The Dodd–Frank Act, however, provides that the systemically significant financial companies identified by FSOC, including BHCs with assets over $50 million and the systemically significant nonbank financial companies named by the FSOC, are subject to an "orderly liquidation" conducted by the FDIC as receiver, Dodd–

Frank Act, § 204, without the possibility for reorganization, Dodd–Frank Act, § 214. The FDIC must appoint SIPC to act as trustee for the liquidation of a broker-dealer. Dodd–Frank Act, § 205.

The Orderly Liquidation Authority will be funded by the institutions whom take advantage of it, Dodd–Frank Act, § 204, and, if necessary, risk-based assessments on other systemically significant financial companies with assets exceeding $50 billion, Dodd–Frank Act, § 210. See also Dodd–Frank Act, § 214.

In testimony before the Financial Crisis Inquiry Commission, FDIC Chairman Sheila Bair compared the failure of Washington Mutual (WaMu) on September 25, 2008, with the bankruptcy of Lehman Brothers on September 15, 2008, to illustrate the inadequacies of the Bankruptcy Code in dealing with the failure of large, complex financial companies. Even though WaMu closed one day earlier than the FDIC originally planned because of adverse market circumstances, the FDIC was able to complete the transfer of it and all of its branches—in excess of 2,300—to JPMorgan Chase by the next day. In contrast, eighteen months after Lehman Brothers' bankruptcy filing, it is still only able to offer a blueprint for its reorganization. Further, as of July 2010, the fees and expenses of the Lehman bankruptcy were up to $918 million.

STATEMENT OF SHEILA C. BAIR, CHAIRMAN FEDERAL DEPOSIT INSURANCE CORPORATION FINANCIAL CRISIS INQUIRY COMMISSION

(www.fdic.gov/news/news/speeches/chairman/spsep0210.html).Sept. 2, 2010.

* * * Large financial institutions pose a variety of special challenges when they fail because of their size, structure, counterparty relationships and activities. Perhaps most notably, large financial services organizations that are dominant players in certain specialized markets for financial assets can create a *systemic risk* simply by virtue of their extensive counterparty exposures. These exposures, and even linkages between business lines within a given organization, may not be readily apparent prior to failure. Without the necessary tools in place to understand and mitigate these exposures, the failure of such an institution could impose losses or liquidity stresses on counterparties that are so large and widespread that they would lead to still more failures and/or the disruption of the interbank lending market, thereby destabilizing the entire financial system. Large, complex institutions are also difficult to resolve because they have fewer potential acquirers (who themselves may be negatively impacted by the failure of the target institution), and may have franchises (such as broker dealer operations) whose value dissipates quickly following failure.

Another crucial barrier to accomplishing an orderly resolution of a failed financial institution involves the complexity of its structure. Large bank holding companies or other nonbank financial institutions frequently have many different business lines, any one of which may extend across different subsidiaries, other legal entities, or international jurisdictions. Under the resolution authority available in 2008, even if the FDIC were to be appointed receiver for an insured depository institution subsidiary of a bank holding company, many of the operations of that bank might lie wholly or partially outside of the insured institution and be subject to the Bankruptcy Code or the laws of a foreign country. Prompt and efficient resolution of a failed institution, which is essential to preserving financial market stability in a crisis, is very difficult to achieve under tight timeframes in the face of such complexities.

The U.S. bankruptcy process is highly effective in reorganizing or liquidating the operations of nonfinancial companies. However, as the FDIC has pointed out in previous testimony, it has some critical shortcomings when it is applied to large financial institutions. A bankruptcy court does not regularly resolve financial firms. Nor does it have the capacity to work with financial regulators to prepare in advance for such a firm's failure, as the FDIC does routinely. The standard bankruptcy process of debtor in possession and the appointment of new trustees or a creditors committee makes it impossible to undertake the type of extensive pre-planning that is essential to the FDIC's ability to provide continuity for critical operations, ensure a prompt acquisition of the failed institution and minimize economic disruption.

When large financial companies enter bankruptcy, they may be unable to complete settlements and access sources of liquidity. For example, about 100 hedge funds used Lehman as their prime broker and relied heavily on the firm for financing. As administrators took charge of the London business and the U.S. holding company filed for bankruptcy, positions held by those hedge funds at Lehman were frozen. Large financial firms are particularly dependent on short-term, market-based funding and their assets are highly vulnerable to a loss of market confidence. Like banks, financial firms (holding companies and their affiliates) can experience "runs" if their short-term liabilities come due and cannot be rolled over. The liquid assets of a large financial firm can dissipate quickly, and a protracted litigation process may seriously impair franchise value, increasing resolution costs and potentially destabilizing the financial system.

* * * In contrast to the high cost and long timeframe of the bankruptcy process, the relative speed and predictability of the receivership process provides a measure of certainty to financial markets, which can be essential in mitigating the effects of a market shock.

Large, complex banking institutions inevitably are part of complex holding company structures that include both banks and non-banks. While the Federal Deposit Insurance Act (FDI Act) provides a sound framework to resolve banks, the events of 2008 demonstrated that U.S. law did not provide a similar framework for the liquidation of a holding company or its non-bank subsidiaries. In addition, many complex activities were conducted through off-balance sheet vehicles and transactions that masked the extent of the exposures and their potential impact on other market participants. In a case where the failure of a bank could create systemic risks, the FDIC had adequate legal authorities in place in 2008 to address those risks under the FDI Act. Where the risks could be created by the failure of the broader holding company or non-bank subsidiaries, there was simply no alternative to the use of the Bankruptcy Code with the potential difficulties illustrated by the bankruptcy proceedings involving Lehman Brothers. * * *

The new liquidation authority in the Dodd–Frank Act is a fundamental part of why the new law provides the U.S. with the tools to end "Too Big to Fail." The reason is simple. It provides a framework for a liquidation process for the largest, non-bank financial firms that can prevent a disorderly collapse, while protecting taxpayers from any future bailouts. This framework consists of two vital components that must be mutually supporting. First, the Dodd–Frank Act includes supervisory and regulatory powers designed to give the FDIC, and other regulators, the information and cooperation from the largest financial firms that is necessary for more effective oversight and—most essential for any future liquidation—for effective advance planning for an orderly dissolution of the firm. Second, Title II incorporates the critical legal powers for an effective liquidation process–modeled on those used by the FDIC to resolve thousands of failing banks. These two components must be mutually supporting because an orderly liquidation is impossible without both. Even if the FDIC were given the legal powers of the Dodd–Frank Act, it cannot implement an effective liquidation process without access to information, cooperation from the largest financial firms and other regulators, and the opportunity to conduct extensive advance planning. In fact, without advance planning, the FDIC could not have effectively resolved the many insured banks that have failed during the current financial crisis.

Effective planning requires access to information through regulatory cooperation and through the back-up examination authority and resolution plans ("Living Wills") regulatory authority provided by the Dodd–Frank Act. Using this framework, it is essential that the FDIC, other federal regulatory agencies, and the largest financial firms work closely together to ensure effective planning for any future crisis. Such planning will ensure a credible resolution process to end "Too Big to Fail" and make sure that all market participants can operate with greater certainty. This will enhance market discipline and, through that discipline, promote a more resilient, efficient financial marketplace in the future.

The value of access to information through cooperation and back-up examinations is self-evident. The importance of the new resolution plan authority is even more essential for the orderly liquidation of large, complex financial conglomerates. A few examples will illustrate the point. First, large and complex financial firms are highly interconnected and operate through financial commitments and operational dependencies

both within the conglomerate structure and through connect'
other firms. Second, these firms operate through a web of trading, cɪ
and liquidity relationships in exchanges, clearing houses, custodians, lines
of credit, securities settlement structures, and other market infrastructure
elements that cannot be addressed for the first time upon insolvency.
Third, large financial firms operate across national borders and conduct
business around the clock. This creates a set of complex legal and
operational challenges during normal business times that will become
infinitely more complex during any insolvency. * * *

The provisions for resolution plans incorporated into Title I of the
Dodd–Frank Act provide the necessary framework. The statutory provisions require the FDIC and the FRB to jointly issue regulations within 18
months to implement the resolution planning and reporting requirements.
Importantly, the statute requires both periodic reporting of detailed information by the largest financial firms and development and submission of a
plan "for rapid and orderly resolution in the event of material financial
distress or failure." * * *

The process places the burden appropriately on the financial firms to
develop their own resolution plans, in consultation with the FDIC and the
FRB, which if necessary will assist in an orderly liquidation. Equally key
to this process is that it will require a great deal of information and
analytical cooperation by the financial firms so that the regulators can
make informed judgments about the proposed plan. This process will
require financial firms to look critically at the often highly complex and
interconnected structures that have developed. If a resolution plan is to be
credible, it almost inevitably will require clarity around such corporate
structures and business operations. This process ultimately will inure to
the financial benefit of investors, financial firms, and certainly the public
by cutting costs, improving resiliency, and reducing systemic risk.

Taken together, the new resolution powers, the enhanced regulatory
and supervisory cooperation mandated in the law, and the resolution
planning authority provide an infrastructure to end "Too Big to Fail."
This means that the critical path of implementation applying high standards for transparency and simplification of overly complex financial firms
must be pursued aggressively to make this a reality. * * *

SECTION 4.　FAILED BANK RESOLUTION

Banks, savings institutions, and credit unions may not file for protection under the federal bankruptcy code. 11 U.S.C.A. § 109(b)(2). Instead,
insolvent banks and savings institutions are resolved by the FDIC, pursuant to FDIC procedures. Insolvent credit unions are resolved under the
NCUA.

A. OPEN BANK ASSISTANCE

The FDIC may offer financial assistance to a bank before the bank becomes insolvent. Such open bank assistance may be provided in the FDIC's sole discretion and upon the terms and conditions it prescribes. 12 U.S.C.A. § 1823(c)(1). Pursuant to FDIC policy, however, no request for such assistance should be granted unless the FDIC determines that the "financial impact on executive management, directors, shareholders and subordinated debtholders is comparable to what would have occurred if the bank had actually closed."[7]

B. PROMPT CORRECTIVE ACTION

In 1983, Congress passed the International Lending Supervision Act (ILSA), which granted agencies the authority to issue capital directives to depository institutions with declining capital positions. 12 U.S.C.A. § 3907. FDICIA in 1991 provided a new regime for dealing with deteriorating capital positions by instituting enforcement based on prompt corrective action (PCA). 12 U.S.C.A. § 1831o. As the institution's capital position descends from well capitalized to critically undercapitalized, the bank agencies may bring more severe measures to bear. The minimum action required under the PCA regime is that the institution develop a recapitalization plan. 12 U.S.C.A. § 1831o(e)(2). The agency may also restrict the institution's activities, 12 U.S.C.A. § 1831o(e)(3), and can require an improvement in management, which permits the dismissal and replacement of senior management and board members. 12 U.S.C.A. § 1831o(f)(2)(F).

The capital categories are (1) well-capitalized, (2) adequately capitalized, (3) undercapitalized, (4) significantly undercapitalized, (5) critically undercapitalized.[8] 12 U.S.C.A. § 1831o(c)(3)(1). If the bank's leverage ratio (book value of capital to book value of assets) falls below 2%, 12 U.S.C.A. § 1831o(c)(3)(B)(i), a receiver may be appointed even though the bank still has positive capital and is not technically insolvent. 12 U.S.C.A. § 1831o(h)(3).

The prompt corrective action regime does not apply to the systemically significant financial institutions subject to the Fed's heightened prudential standards after Dodd–Frank, but a comparable system imposes "early remediation requirements." The Fed is required to establish regulations to implement this requirement after consultation with the FSOC and the FDIC. Dodd–Frank Act, § 166. These requirements, like prompt corrective action directives, must increase in stringency as the systemically significant financial institution's financial condition declines.

---

7. 48 Fed. Reg. 38,669, 38,670 (1983); see also 51 Fed. Reg. 44,122, 44,123 (1986) (the same is true with respect to open bank assistance to a bank that is part of a holding company).

8. See Chapter 7 for the criteria for each capital category.

C. CLOSURE OF BANK

The decision to close a bank is made by its primary regulator. 12 U.S.C.A. §§ 191, 203(a). The bank's shareholders are not entitled to any pre-closure notice. The usual ground for closure is that the bank is insolvent based on its balance sheet (its liabilities exceed its assets), or based on its liquidity (it is unable to meet its obligations as they become due). Under the PCA regime, however, a bank may be closed when its capital position is at 2% or below, even though the institution is not technically insolvent. This authority is intended to reduce the FDIC's cost in resolving the bank. The authority is granted based on the assumption that the bank's condition is likely to have deteriorated further from the date of closure to the date of resolution. The FDIC must consider the effects of any guarantees against losses required by the cross-guarantee provision (described later in this Chapter) before it determines that a bank is insolvent and should be closed. 12 U.S.C.A. § 1815(e). A bank may also be closed by voluntary dissolution pursuant to a provision in the bank's charter, or by creditors asserting unpaid judgments under 12 U.S.C.A. § 191. The FDIC is appointed as the conservator or receiver of a failed institution under 12 U.S.C.A. § 1821(c).

D. RESOLUTION METHODS

FDICIA imposed upon the FDIC the obligation to resolve a failed institution under the "least cost" method. 12 U.S.C.A. § 1823(c)(4). The method used to resolve the failed institution must be the "least costly to the deposit insurance fund of all possible methods for meeting the [FDIC's] obligations under this section." Id. The choices for resolution include a liquidation of the institution, a purchase and assumption transaction with another institution purchasing the failed bank's assets and assuming its liabilities, and in certain extraordinary cases, where the bank is deemed to be "too big to fail," assistance provided by the government to return the bank to solvency pursuant to the systemic risk exception.

LISSA LAMKIN BROOME
REDISTRIBUTING BANK INSOLVENCY
RISKS: CHALLENGES TO LIMITED
LIABILITY IN THE BANK HOLDING
COMPANY STRUCTURE

26 U.C. Davis L. Rev. 935 (1993).

* * * A bank's primary regulator is authorized to close it upon insolvency, and to appoint the FDIC as conservator or receiver to resolve the failed institution. During the twenty-year period from the mid–1960s to the mid–1980s, bank failures were resolved so that "all general credi-

tors were, in practice, afforded 100 percent insurance."[9] The two resolution methods most often employed by the FDIC are a liquidation of the insolvent institution and a purchase and assumption transaction in which another bank agrees to purchase the assets and assume the liabilities of the failed bank. Approximately seventy-five percent of insolvent banks have been resolved by a purchase and assumption transaction. In the past, all liabilities—including uninsured deposits, nondeposit claims, and contingent claims—were assumed by the institution purchasing the failed bank's assets so that the claims of all creditors were honored by the purchasing institution and bank creditors lost nothing as the result of extending credit to a bank that became insolvent. In more recent purchase and assumption transactions, the liabilities of nondeposit creditors have not been assumed, although all deposit liabilities (including uninsured deposits) have been assumed by the asset purchaser. A purchase and assumption transaction in which uninsured deposits are assumed shifts "losses from uninsured depositors to the FDIC."[10] Thus, bank depositors bear none of the consequences of the bank's insolvency.

To illustrate the distribution of the risks of a bank's insolvency among its shareholders and the FDIC, consider the following example. A bank holding company owns 100% of the outstanding stock of Bank A and Bank B. It has invested $100,000 in each bank. The bank holding company is owned by five shareholders, each of whom has invested $100,000 in the bank holding company for a total investment in the bank holding company of $500,000, $200,000 of which has been invested in Banks A and B. Assume for illustration a simplified balance sheet for Bank A in which it has $1,900,000 in insured deposits (recorded as liabilities on the balance sheet), which along with its $100,000 in capital are invested in $2,000,000 in loans (recorded as assets on the balance sheet). The balance sheet balances as the assets of $2,000,000 equal the liabilities of $1,900,000 plus the capital of $100,000. If Bank A writes off $250,000 in bad loans, this reduces its $2,000,000 in assets to $1,750,000. Its liabilities (deposits) presumably remain the same, and therefore, to keep the balance sheet in balance, the $250,000 loss must be charged against Bank A's capital account, reducing it from its $100,000 beginning balance to a negative position of $150,000, and rendering the bank insolvent.

If the FDIC elects to resolve the insolvent institution by arranging a purchase and assumption transaction, the FDIC will have to pay the institution that purchases the $1,750,000 in assets and assumes the $1,900,000 in liabilities, the difference between the two—$150,000. The greater Bank A's negative net worth, the greater the difference between the value of its assets and liabilities, and the greater the cost to the FDIC to resolve insolvent Bank A. Thus, the bank holding company, as Bank A's shareholder, will lose its $100,000 investment in Bank A, and the FDIC

---

9. [n.36] [Congressional Budget Office,] Reforming Deposit Insurance 63 [(1990)] (footnote omitted).

10. [n.43] [Department of the Treasury,] Modernizing the Financial System: [Recommendations for Safer, More Competitive Banks] 8 [(1991)].

will bear the remaining $150,000 loss. Bank B continues to operate with its $100,000 of capital intact.

An alternative resolution method is liquidation of the failed bank. The FDIC pays the insured depositors, sells the assets of the bank, and distributes the proceeds to satisfy the claims of uninsured depositors, nondeposit creditors, and itself for the amounts it paid to insured depositors. When the FDIC selects liquidation as the resolution method, the risk of the bank's insolvency is borne in part by uninsured depositors and nondeposit creditors who may sometimes receive only a portion of their claims.

The three factors described above combine to impose the loss resulting from a bank's insolvency primarily on bank shareholders and the FDIC. Although the shareholders' loss is limited to the amount of the bank's capital, the remaining loss—no matter how large—is borne by the FDIC. * * *

In failures following the financial crisis, the FDIC has often made the purchase of a failed bank attractive by retaining some of the failed bank's assets (often loans or other investments) and entering into a loss-share agreement on some other portion of the assets purchased by the acquiring institution. For instance, in the August 2009 purchase by BB&T of Winston–Salem, North Carolina of Colonial Bank in Montgomery, Alabama, BB&T agreed to purchase $22 billion of Colonial Bank's $25 billion in assets, with the FDIC retaining the remainder of the assets for later disposition.[11] The FDIC and BB&T also entered into a loss-share transaction on approximately $15 billion of the $22 billion of assets purchased. BB&T was to share with the FDIC in the losses on the asset pools covered by the loss-share arrangement. By keeping these assets in the private sector, however, rather that retaining them directly the FDIC hoped to maximize the returns on them, as well as eliminate any disruption for loan customers. The total cost to the FDIC of this proposed resolution was estimated to be $2.8 billion, and was considered to be the "least costly" resolution for Colonial Bank.

Prior to 1991, the FDIC provided assistance to prevent some banks from failing, as described below.

　　　The failure of the Continental Illinois bank system provides an example of systemic risk failure. In 1984, Continental had extensive (over 1,000) correspondent bank accounts, which means that other banks held their accounts with Continental. Sixty-six of those correspondent banks had uninsured deposits exceeding 100% of capital and 113 had deposits equaling 50–100% of capital. Had the FDIC chosen

---

11. See FDIC, BB&T, Winston–Salem, North Carolina, Assumes All of the Deposits of Colonial Bank, Montgomery, Alabama, Aug. 14, 2009, www.fdic.gov/news/news/press/2009/pr 09143.html.

not to protect Continental, that decision would have significantly weakened the correspondent banks. * * *

Between 1986 and 1991, the FDIC determined that only four banks were "too big to fail" and protected all depositors. Those institutions were First National Bank & Trust Co., Oklahoma City, Oklahoma (1986), FirstRepublic Bank, Dallas, Texas (1988); MCorp, Houston, Texas (1989); and Bank of New England, Boston, Massachusetts (1991). The cost of protecting the uninsured depositors of these institutions was less than one billion dollars or about 3.5% of the FDIC's total insurance losses over this time period.[12]

The notion that some banks were "too big to fail" obviously increased moral hazard at any institutions perceived to be within that category. Congress responded in FDICIA in 1991, stating that assistance may be provided by the FDIC to keep a bank open even if that is not consistent with the FDIC's mandate to resolve the bank at the "least cost" only in cases of systemic risk. 12 U.S.C.A. § 1823(c)(4)(G). Assistance under this section may only be provided if the Treasury Secretary in consultation with the President, following a written request from the FDIC and Fed, determine that the least cost resolution would result in "serious adverse effects on economic conditions or financial stability." Id. The first attempt to use this systemic risk exception took place during the financial crisis in a potential deal to sell Wachovia Bank to Citigroup. As explained in the excerpt below, Wachovia ultimately accepted a bid from Wells Fargo that did not require FDIC financial assistance.

SCOTT C. ALVAREZ
GENERAL COUNSEL, FEDERAL RESERVE
BOARD OF GOVERNORS
TESTIMONY BEFORE THE FINANCIAL CRISIS
INQUIRY COMMISSION

www.federalreserve.gov/newsevents/testimony/alvarez20100901a.htm.
Sept. 1, 2010.

* * * Wachovia was a financial holding company headquartered in Charlotte, North Carolina, that provided commercial and retail banking services and other financial services in the United States and internationally. At the end of the second quarter of 2008, Wachovia had assets of $812 billion, making it the fourth largest banking organization in the United States in asset terms. Wachovia's principal subsidiary was Wachovia Bank, which had assets of $671 billion. Wachovia also had two insured thrift subsidiaries with total assets of $105 billion. Thus, the assets of the lead national bank and two insured thrift subsidiaries comprised about 95 percent of the assets of the holding company. Wachovia's insured depository institution subsidiaries had a very large retail presence—serving more

---

12. Cassandra Jones Havard, Back to the Parent: Holding Company Liability for Subsidiary Banks—A Discussion of the Net Worth Maintenance Agreement, the Source of Strength Doctrine, and the Prompt Corrective Action Provisions, 16 Cardozo L. Rev. 2353, 2369 & n.64 (1995).

than 27 million deposit accounts totaling more than $400 billion—and operated a large mortgage business. * * *

Wachovia had been profitable continuously for more than a decade through year-end 2007. During the first half of 2008, Wachovia posted losses totaling $9.6 billion, reflecting write-downs on securities and high provisions for loan losses. In part, the provisions reflected significant expected losses on option adjustable-rate mortgages (ARMs), which Wachovia acquired in the 2006 purchase of Golden West Financial Corporation, a $125 billion federal thrift holding company based in California. The losses also reflected, to a lesser extent, declines in the value of commercial real estate mortgages originated and held by Wachovia. * * *

The troubles at Wachovia occurred during a period of extreme financial turbulence and distress. The nation's economy was in recession, with declining housing prices and stalled economic growth. The financial system was also deteriorating quickly. On September 7, 2008, the Federal Housing Finance Agency had placed Fannie Mae and Freddie Mac into conservatorship and the Treasury had used its authority, granted by Congress in July 2008, to make financial support available to these two government-sponsored entities. On September 15, Lehman Brothers had filed for bankruptcy after efforts had failed to organize private-sector assistance or arrange an acquisition by another company. The failure of Lehman Brothers ended efforts by private investors to provide liquidity to American International Group, Inc. (AIG), which faced its own mounting financial difficulties. On September 16, the Board acted to provide temporary liquidity to AIG under the emergency lending authority of section 13(3) of the Federal Reserve Act. Losses at a prominent money market mutual fund caused by the failure of Lehman Brothers sparked extensive withdrawals from a number of similar funds. These events caused extraordinary turbulence in financial markets: equity prices dropped sharply, the costs of short-term credit spiked upward, and liquidity dried up in many markets.

On September 25, 2008, the Federal Deposit Insurance Corporation (FDIC) seized and sold Washington Mutual Bank (WaMu), then the largest thrift in the United States. WaMu was the second largest holder of option ARMs at the time, and Wachovia was the largest holder of these assets. The failure of WaMu thus raised creditor concern about the health of Wachovia. Wachovia's stock price declined sharply and credit default swap spreads on its debt surged.

The day after the failure of WaMu, Wachovia Bank depositors accelerated the withdrawal of significant amounts from their accounts. In addition, wholesale funds providers withdrew liquidity support from Wachovia. It appeared likely that Wachovia would soon become unable to fund its operations. That week, Wachovia management, which had engaged in tentative discussions with potential merger partners earlier in the month, began discussions in earnest to sell the company. On September 27 and 28, both Citigroup and Wells Fargo, the second and fifth largest banking organizations in the United States, respectively, conducted due diligence investigations of Wachovia. Both Citigroup and Wells Fargo also contacted federal regulators indicating that government assistance would be needed in connection with each of their proposed bids to acquire Wachovia.

The FDIC judged that an assisted bid from either Citigroup or Wells Fargo could be more expensive than a liquidation of Wachovia Bank and the two insured thrifts. The Federal Deposit Insurance Act (FDI Act) requires the FDIC, as a general matter, to exercise its resolution authority over insured depository institutions in the method least costly to the deposit insurance fund. The act also provides that the FDIC may take other actions or provide assistance that would not meet the least-cost test if the Secretary of the Treasury, in consultation with the President, and based on the recommendation of both the board of directors of the FDIC and the Board of Governors of the Federal Reserve (each by a vote of two-thirds of its members), determine that compliance with the least-cost requirement would have adverse effects on economic conditions or financial stability and other action or assistance would avoid or mitigate those adverse effects.

The Board of Governors and the FDIC were concerned about the systemic complications of the failure of the fourth largest bank in the United States during this fragile economic period. The Board believed that a full or partial default by Wachovia and its subsidiaries on their debt would intensify liquidity pressures on other U.S. banking organizations. At the time, U.S. banking organizations were extremely vulnerable to a loss of confidence by wholesale suppliers of funds. Markets were already under considerable strain after the events involving Lehman Brothers, AIG, and WaMu. Investors were becoming increasingly concerned about the outlook for a number of U.S. banking organizations, putting downward pressure on their stock prices and upward pressure on their credit default swap spreads.

At the time, Wachovia was considered "well capitalized" by regulatory standards and until very recently had not generally been thought to be in danger of failure, so there were fears that the failure of Wachovia would lead investors to doubt the financial strength of other organizations in similar situations, making it harder for those institutions to raise capital and other funding. In addition, if a least-cost resolution did not support foreign depositors, the resolution would endanger what was a significant source of funding for several other major U.S. financial institutions.

Creditors would also be concerned about direct exposures of other financial firms to Wachovia or Wachovia Bank, since these firms would face losses in the event of a default. In particular, losses on debt issued by Wachovia and Wachovia Bank could lead more money market mutual funds to "break the buck," accelerating runs on these and other money funds. The resulting liquidations of fund assets—along with the further loss of confidence in financial institutions—could lead short-term funding markets to virtually shut down; these markets were already under extreme pressure in the fall of 2008.

The consequences of an insolvency and unwinding of Wachovia under the least-cost resolution test would also have disastrous effects for an already weakened economy. Business and household confidence would be undermined by the worsening financial market turmoil, and banking organizations would be less willing to lend due to their increased funding costs and decreased liquidity. These effects could contribute to materially weaker economic performance, higher unemployment, and reduced wealth.

For these reasons, on September 28, 2008, the Board by unanimous vote determined that compliance by the FDIC with the least-cost requirements of the FDI Act with respect to Wachovia Bank and its insured depository institution affiliates would have serious adverse effects on economic conditions and financial stability, and that action or assistance by the FDIC permitted under the systemic risk exception within the act would avoid or mitigate these adverse effects. Similar determinations were made by the board of directors of the FDIC and the Secretary of the Treasury, in consultation with the President, which allowed the FDIC to consider measures outside the least-cost resolution requirement to resolve Wachovia, including the provision of so-called "open bank" assistance.

On September 29, 2008, Citigroup proposed to acquire most of Wachovia's assets and liabilities, including Wachovia Bank, and assume senior and subordinated Wachovia debt, in exchange for approximately $2.1 billion in Citigroup stock. Citigroup proposed that the FDIC enter into a loss sharing arrangement with Citigroup with respect to a pre-identified pool of Wachovia loans totaling about $312 billion. Under the arrangement, Citigroup would absorb the first $42 billion of losses on the pool, and the FDIC would absorb any additional losses. Citigroup would grant the FDIC $12 billion in preferred stock and warrants to compensate the FDIC for bearing this risk.

Around the same time, Wells Fargo submitted a bid for Wachovia that the FDIC judged would require a greater amount of FDIC assistance. Consequently, the FDIC accepted the Citigroup bid as the prevailing bid.
* * *

On October 2, during the period Citigroup and Wachovia were negotiating a final merger agreement, the board of directors of Wachovia received a communication from Wells Fargo that included an offer from Wells Fargo to acquire all of Wachovia's stock by merger. Contrary to its original communication days before that FDIC assistance would be needed as part of a Wells Fargo bid, the new Wells Fargo proposal did not involve any direct financial assistance from the FDIC. Based on an IRS notice issued September 30, Wells Fargo had determined that certain U.S. federal income tax benefits resulting from the proposed Wachovia transaction would allow it to acquire Wachovia without FDIC assistance.

On October 3, 2008, Wachovia's board of directors voted to accept the Wells Fargo offer, and the parties signed a binding merger agreement. Upon becoming aware of this, Citigroup informed Wachovia and Wells Fargo that Citigroup considered the merger agreement to be a violation of the exclusive dealing agreement between Citigroup and Wachovia. * * *

Due to concerns that the competing legal claims of Citigroup and Wells Fargo could themselves become a destabilizing influence on those institutions, Wachovia, and the banking system generally, representatives of the Federal Reserve attempted to facilitate negotiations among Wachovia, Citigroup, and Wells Fargo to resolve their disagreements. * * *

The Wachovia–Wells deal was consummated on December 31, 2008.

The FDIC's systemic risk exception to the least cost resolution method was used by the FDIC to justify its Transaction Liquidity Guaranty Program, announced on October 14, 2008, and discussed further in Chapter 7, and then again to provide additional aid to Citigroup and Bank of America beyond their initial infusions of TARP stock.[13] Government Accountability Office, Federal Deposit Insurance Act: Regulators' Use of Systemic Risk Exception Raises Moral Hazard Concerns and Opportunities Exist to Clarify the Provision, April 2010, <www.gao.gov/news.items/d 10100.pdf>

E. CROSS-GUARANTEES, THE CONTROLLING COMPANY GUARANTEE PROVISION, AND SOURCE OF STRENGTH

LISSA LAMKIN BROOME
REDISTRIBUTING BANK INSOLVENCY RISKS: CHALLENGES TO LIMITED LIABILITY IN THE BANK HOLDING COMPANY STRUCTURE

26 U.C. Davis L. Rev. 935 (1993).

* * * In 1989, as part of the Financial Institutions Reform, Recovery, and Enforcement Act (FIRREA), Congress added to the Federal Deposit Insurance Act a "cross-guarantee" provision, which provides that commonly controlled depository institutions must pay to the FDIC the amount of loss that the FDIC suffers or expects to suffer as the result of the insolvency of a depository institution.[14] Depository institutions are commonly controlled if they are controlled by the same holding company, and are treated for this purpose as if they were branches of a single bank. The purpose of the cross-guarantee provision is "to ensure that the assets of

---

13. This was referred to as the Targeted Investment Program (TIP). See Lissa L. Broome, Government Investment in Banks: Creeping Nationalization or Prudent, Temporary Aid?, 4 FIU L. Rev. 409, 414 (2009).

14. [n.96] 12 U.S.C. § 1815(e). * * *

healthy depository institution subsidiaries within the same holding company structure ... will be available to the FDIC to help offset the cost of resolving the failed subsidiary."[15]

A bank's cross-guarantee liability for the FDIC costs of resolving an insolvent sister bank is subordinate to all other liabilities of the bank except for liabilities owed to affiliated institutions. Thus, in the event the guarantor bank is also insolvent, the FDIC's claim against the insolvent guarantor bank will not be satisfied until after satisfaction of the claims of all other non-affiliated creditors, including subordinated debtholders. Moreover, a waiver procedure permits the FDIC to waive the cross-guarantee liability if it determines that a liability exemption is in the best interests of the deposit insurance fund.

The impact of this risk-shifting provision may be best illustrated by returning to the example described earlier of the bank holding company operating under a system of limited liability and owning insolvent Bank A and solvent Bank B. Upon Bank A's insolvency, the FDIC suffers a $150,000 loss from a purchase and assumption transaction, and the bank holding company loses its $100,000 of Bank A capital. Bank B continues to operate with its $100,000 of capital intact, unaffected by the failure of Bank A. If the FDIC elects to assert its cross-guarantee authority, however, it reduces its loss from $150,000 to $50,000 by using the capital of Bank B ($100,000) to satisfy Bank B's guaranty to the FDIC for the FDIC's costs in resolving Bank A. The bank holding company loses not only its $100,000 investment in Bank A, but also its $100,000 investment in Bank B. Bank B is now also insolvent as a result of the exercise of the cross-guarantee provision.

The Federal Deposit Insurance Corporation Improvement Act (FDICIA) was enacted late in 1991. That Act was the modest result of what began as an effort to obtain very sweeping reforms of bank regulation. One proposal set forth was the extension of the cross-guarantee provision to bank holding companies. Many viewed this proposal as a statutory codification of a regulation promulgated by the Federal Reserve Board and termed the "source of strength" regulation which provides that a "bank holding company shall serve as a source of financial and managerial strength to its subsidiary banks."[16] An administrative enforcement proceeding brought to enforce the regulation, however, was enjoined by the United States Court of Appeals for the Fifth Circuit, which held that the source of strength regulation exceeded the Federal Reserve Board's statutory authority.[17] Although the Supreme Court reviewed this case, it did not reach the question of whether the source of strength regulation was

---

15. [n.98] Policy Statement, 55 Fed. Reg. 21,934, at 21,935 (1990). * * *

16. [n.108] 12 C.F.R. § 225.4(a)(1)(1992). A holding company's "failure to assist a troubled or failing subsidiary bank ... would generally be viewed as an unsafe and unsound banking practice." Policy Statement, 52 Fed. Reg. 15,707, at 15,707 (1987). * * *

17. [n.109] MCorp Fin v. Board of Governors, 900 F.2d 852 (5th Cir. 1990), aff'd in part and rev'd in part, 502 U.S. 32 (1991). * * *

within the statutory authority of the Federal Reserve Board, and the validity of this regulation remains unresolved.[18]

Congress did not extend the cross-guarantee provision to include bank holding companies along with commonly controlled depository institutions, but it did provide in certain instances for a limited guarantee by the bank holding company parent.[19] This provision of the Act became effective in December 1992. If a bank is found to be undercapitalized (i.e., unable to meet applicable minimum capital requirements), it must submit a capital restoration plan to its federal regulator. A condition to the FDIC's approval of an institution's capital restoration plan is that its controlling company (if any) guarantee that the institution will comply with the capital restoration plan until the institution has been adequately capitalized during each of four consecutive calendar quarters and provide "appropriate assurances of performance."[20] The controlling company's guarantee liability is statutorily limited, however, to the lesser of the amount needed to bring the depository institution into compliance with all capital standards as of the time it fails to comply with its capital restoration plan, or five percent of the institution's assets at the time it became undercapitalized. The purpose of the guarantee has been described as "seeking to induce a parent company to decide promptly whether to recapitalize the institution, sell it, or stand behind it until it recovers."[21] If the bank holding company enters a bankruptcy proceeding, the FDIC's claim on the guarantee will be granted a priority position with respect to other unsecured creditors of the bank holding company pursuant to recent amendments to the Bankruptcy Code.

There is no requirement that the controlling company submit a guarantee of the undercapitalized institution's capital restoration plan. If the guarantee is not executed, however, the FDIC will not approve the plan. An institution that fails to submit an acceptable capital restoration plan is subject to numerous restrictions on its activities, including restrictions on asset growth, acquisitions, additional branches, and new lines of business.

If the FDIC elects to utilize the new controlling company guarantee along with its cross-guarantee authority, the FDIC loss upon a bank's insolvency may be further minimized. Assume that Bank A had previously adopted a capital restoration plan upon being found undercapitalized, and that the bank holding company's guarantee of Bank A's capital restoration plan was limited to 5% of Bank A's assets at the time it became undercapitalized. Five percent of Bank A's assets (about $2,000,000 at the time it

---

    18.   [n.110] See Board of Governors, 112 S.Ct. at 461 ("Because we conclude that the District Court lacked jurisdiction to enjoin either regulatory proceeding, we do not reach the merits of MCorp's challenge to the regulation.").

    19.   [n.111] See 12 U.S.C. 1831o(e)(2)(C) (Supp. III 1991) (requiring controlling company to guarantee that failed institution will comply with capital restoration plan).

    20.   [n.114] [12 U.S.C.] § 1831o(e)(2)(C)(ii). * * *

    21.   [n.116] [Richard S.] Carnell, [Prompt Corrective Action Under the FDIC Improvement Act of 1991] 339 [(1992), reprinted in Litigating For and Against the FDIC and the RTC 1992 (Practising Law Inst. 1992)].

became undercapitalized) might approximate $100,000. Thus, the FDIC could look to the bank holding company as a potential source of $100,000 pursuant to the controlling company guarantee and to Bank B as a potential source of $100,000 pursuant to the cross-guarantee to satisfy its $150,000 loss. The FDIC would be able to reduce its expected loss as a result of Bank A's insolvency from $150,000 to zero. Depending on how the FDIC chose to make itself whole for its losses, Bank B might continue to exist with some portion of its former capital remaining, or it too might have to be closed upon reaching zero net worth if the FDIC elected to exercise its cross-guarantee authority to the fullest extent possible against Bank B. * * *

CASSANDRA JONES HAVARD
BACK TO THE PARENT: HOLDING COMPANY LIABILITY FOR SUBSIDIARY BANKS—A DISCUSSION OF THE NEW WORTH MAINTENANCE AGREEMENT, THE SOURCE OF STRENGTH DOCTRINE, AND THE PROMPT CORRECTIVE ACTION PROVISIONS

16 Cardozo L. Rev. 2353 (1995).

* * * The FRB chose as its parental guarantee the source of strength condition. Using § 3(c) of the BHCA, the agency exercised its authority to impose the condition as a part of the approval process of a holding company's acquisition of a banking subsidiary.[22] Before the FRB issued its policy statements elaborating its views on the source of strength doctrine, a potential acquiror challenged the FRB's statutory authority to impose the condition. In Board of Governors v. First Lincolnwood Corp.,[23] the U.S. Supreme Court upheld the doctrine as an integral part of the FRB's exercise of its regulatory authority.

After the *Lincolnwood* decision, the FRB promulgated regulations on the source of strength condition. Those regulations made failure to comply with the source of strength condition the basis for an enforcement action. In 1984, the FRB amended Regulation Y to include, specifically, the statutory language of § 1842(c).[24] Three years later, the FRB issued a policy statement indicating that a violation of Regulation Y would be grounds for an enforcement violation.[25] * * *

---

22. [n.86] The FRB based its authority on § 3(c) of the BHCA, 12 U.S.C. § 1843 (1988 & Supp. V 1993), and the Financial Institutions supervisory Act ("FISA"), which governs "unsafe and unsound" banking practices. 12 U.S.C. § 1818 (1988).

23. [n.87] 439 U.S. 234 (1978). * * *

24. [n.89] * * * The amendment to Regulation Y stated: "[A] bank holding company shall serve as a source of financial and managerial strength to its subsidiary banks and shall not conduct its operations in an unsafe or unsound manner." Revision of Regulation Y, 49 Fed. Reg. 794, 820 (1984) (to be codified at 12 C.F.R. § 225.4(a)(1)). * * *

25. [n.90] The 1987 Policy Statement provided, in part, that "[a] bank holding company's failure to meet its obligation to serve as a source of strength to its subsidiary bank(s), including an unwillingness to provide appropriate assistance to a troubled or failing bank will generally ... result in ... enforcement action." 52 Fed. Reg. 15,707, 15,708 (1987). * * *

In MCorp Financial, Inc. v. Board of Governors (MCorp), the Fifth Circuit Court of Appeals invalidated the FRB's authority to enforce the source of strength condition against a holding company as unsafe and unsound banking practices. MCorp, a multibank holding company, challenged the authority of the FRB to require it to make capital infusions into its failing subsidiary banks after an acquisition.

Federal court review of the FRB's authority to impose the source of strength condition after acquisition occurred for the first time in 1988. MCorp, a multibillion dollar bank holding company that owned twenty-five subsidiary banks in Texas, began experiencing financial difficulties that threatened the subsidiary banks. The parent company had substantial assets which led the FRB to issue a temporary cease and desist order directing MCorp to use all of its assets to provide capital support to its subsidiary banks in need of additional capital. When MCorp failed to comply with the FRB order, the Office of the Comptroller of the Currency ("OCC") declared twenty of MCorp's twenty-five subsidiaries insolvent and closed them. The FRB then initiated an administrative action (a source of strength proceeding) against MCorp claiming that it had failed to give financial support to the five remaining subsidiary banks. Within a short time, MCorp filed for voluntary bankruptcy.

The federal district court enjoined the FRB from continuing its administrative source of strength proceeding on the ground that the bankruptcy code's automatic stay provision barred the FRB's actions. This decision prohibited the FRB from pursuing its "source of strength" proceedings against MCorp and the FRB appealed this decision to the Fifth Circuit Court of Appeals.

On appeal, the Fifth Circuit Court of Appeals partially reversed, holding that judicial review provisions of 12 U.S.C. 1818 deprived the district court of jurisdiction until the FRB completed the administrative proceedings. The Fifth Circuit evaluated two grounds of the FRB's alleged authority: (1) unsafe and unsound banking practices; and (2) Regulation Y. After evaluating both grounds, the Fifth Circuit concluded that the FRB exceeded its authority when it adopted the source of strength policy statement. Specifically, the court found Regulation Y would require the parent company to waste its corporate assets and the FRB did not have the authority to require that.

An "unsafe and unsound practice," as defined by this court, would be any action or lack of action that is "contrary to generally accepted standards of prudent operation."[26] The court concluded that capital injections on the scale the FRB would require would in turn require MCorp to disregard its own separate corporate status. Thus, the court determined that MCorp's refusal to transfer funds to its troubled subsidiaries was not an "unsafe and unsound practice" because it would, among other things,

---

26. [n. 115] [MCorp, 900 F.2d at 863] (quoting Gulf Fed. Sav. & Loan Ass'n v. FHLBB, 651 F.2d 259, 264 (5th Cir. 1981), cert. denied 458 U.S. 1121 (1982)).

amount to a wasting of MCorp's assets violating its duty to its shareholders.

Under Regulation Y, the court denied the FRB's assertion that it had authority to take supervisory action to require a holding company to make financial assistance to a troubled subsidiary. The court ruled that the FRB has supervisory control over bank holding companies and bank subsidiaries as well as the power to approve the acquisition of banks by a holding company, but the FRB "does not [have] the authority to consider the financial and managerial soundness of subsidiary banks" after issuing an approval of an acquisition to a holding company.[27] Thus, the court found that the FRB had exceeded its statutory authority by promulgating and enforcing its source of strength doctrine, as set forth in Regulation Y and the 1987 Policy Statement.

The Fifth Circuit, in a footnote, indicated its approval of net worth maintenance agreements as an appropriate means of implementing the source of strength policy statement. Thus, the court was indicating that the FRB's source of strength requirement might be acceptable if, like the net worth maintenance agreement, the requirement is imposed as a condition to acquisition rather than simply an arbitrary imposition applied at some subsequent point of difficulty.[28] * * *

QUESTIONS AND NOTES

1. How difficult will it be for bank regulators to determine the least cost resolution method? Isn't this like trying to predict the future?

2. Is it proper for Congress to grant bank regulatory agencies authority to ignore long-standing principles of limited liability in the corporate setting and to impose FDIC losses on entities affiliated with the failed institution? Of the various mechanisms available to the FDIC to hold others in the holding company family liable, which is likely to be most effective?

3. Under Dodd–Frank, a bank holding company or savings and loan holding company must serve as a source of financial strength for any subsidiary that is a depository institution. Dodd–Frank Act, § 616. If an insured depository institution is not the subsidiary of a bank holding company or savings and loan holding company, then any company that directly or indirectly controls the insured depository institution must serve as a source of financial strength for such institution.

F. CREDITORS AND PRIORITIES

Bank insolvency law provides its own special rules for dealing with the claims of creditors of an insolvent institution. These rules often differ from those available to persons and nonbank corporate entities under the federal Bankruptcy Code.

---

27. [n.119] MCorp, 900 F.2d at 861.

28. [n.122] The FRB appealed to the Supreme Court. See 502 U.S. at 32. In its review, the Court did not reach the merits of the applicability of the source of strength condition. Instead, it found that the appellate court did not have jurisdiction to consider the merits of the parent company's claim. Citing the statutory scheme found in 12 U.S.C. § 1818(i) (1988), the Court held that the FRB administrative proceeding was not final, thereby precluding review of either the regulation or its application. MCorp, 502 U.S. at 42–45. * * *

PETER P. SWIRE
BANK INSOLVENCY LAW NOW THAT IT
MATTERS AGAIN

42 Duke L.J. 469 (1992).

* * * It is important, however, to grasp the general point that bank insolvency law overall is quite distinctive, and varies both from the law applying to banks pre-insolvency and from the insolvency law applying to non-bank corporations. * * *

A bankruptcy trustee or debtor, subject to the court's approval, has broad powers to repudiate executory contracts or unexpired leases. This power prevents "sweetheart" contracts that allow insiders to get higher priority than other claimants. The banking agencies have essentially the same powers as the trustee, but with two material additions. First, the agencies appear to retain almost unlimited discretion about whether to repudiate,[29] in contrast to the bankruptcy court's supervision of a trustee's decision. Second, the agencies need not pay the full measure of contract damages that repudiation in bankruptcy requires; instead, the receiver or conservator is excused from payment for lost profits on contracts and for future rent on leases.[30]

Three aspects of the fraudulent conveyance provision of the Crime Control Act of 1990 illustrate the extraordinary powers granted to the FDIC and RTC by that Act. First, the FDIC and RTC can avoid fraudulent transfers made five years before or after appointment of the receiver or conservator.[31] Second, the agencies may avoid transfers not only of the bank itself, but of all "institution-affiliated parties," a broad term including any director, officer, employee, controlling stockholder, or agent for a bank. Third, the rights of the agencies in the fraudulent transfer are superior to any rights of a bankruptcy trustee for the fraudulent transferee. The agencies will thus stand ahead of all other claimants, except federal agencies, on the estate of that transferee.[32]

The Crime Control Act of 1990 gave the FDIC and RTC the power to request a court to freeze the assets of any person, with the assets held by a trustee.[33] Recovery on the assets goes to the estate of the failed

---

29. [n.72] The chief statutory limit on agency discretion is that the repudiation be within a "reasonable" time. 12 U.S.C. § 1821(e)(2) (Supp. II 1990). * * *

30. [n.74] 12 U.S.C. § 1821(e)(3)-(4) (Supp. III 1991).

31. [n.76] 12 U.S.C. § 1821(d)(17)(A) (Supp. III 1991). This contrasts with bankruptcy law, which allows the trustee to avoid such transactions made only within one year before bankruptcy, 11 U.S.C. § 548(a) (1988), or to use state law, id. § 544(b), which may allow avoidance for a set number of years, often two or three, before insolvency.

32. [n.78] 12 U.S.C. § 1821(d)(17)(D). That is, the agency will apparently come even before administrative expenses of the estate. In a bankruptcy law dispute between a fraudulent transferor and a fraudulent transferee, which creditor first gets a judicial lien wins; in bank insolvencies, the agencies always win.

33. [n.79] 12 U.S.C. § 1821(d)(18) (Supp. III 1991). * * * A similar power to seek prejudgment attachment is also given to the FDIC as an enforcement power against open banks. 12 U.S.C. § 1818 (i)(4) (Supp. III 1991).

institution. The agencies may seek this prejudgment attachment under the injunction provisions of Rule 65 of the Federal Rules of Civil Procedure, but with one remarkable change: They are not required to make the usual showing that the injury is "irreparable and immediate."[34]

FIRREA granted the FDIC and RTC the power to discriminate among claims on the failed institution, in contrast to the traditional rule that all claims in the same class must receive the same percentage recovery. The agencies are obligated to pay only the amount a claimant would have received if the agencies had liquidated the assets and liabilities of the institution,[35] which is often a steep discount from full recovery. The agencies also retains [sic] discretion to select some claimants for additional payments,[36] thus enabling the agencies to treat insiders less well than other claimants.

Government agencies have wide-ranging enforcement powers both before and after insolvency, with no close analogues to creditor powers in bankruptcy. Notably, the FDIC and OTS can levy civil money penalties of up to $1 million per day for violations of banking rules.[37] And temporary cease-and-desist orders can freeze assets of institution-affiliated parties upon a mere prima facie showing that money penalties are appropriate.[38] Such enforcement actions have been allowed to go forward against a holding company despite the automatic stay provisions in bankruptcy.[39] Such enforcement proceedings can obviously enhance the ability of agencies to recover for losses arising from insolvent institutions.

The Crime Control Act of 1990 also gave the agencies new powers that trump rules otherwise applying in bankruptcy. In order to ensure that bank insiders do not benefit from their acts, the Act declared certain banking-related claims no longer dischargeable in bankruptcy.[40] In addition, the Act created new rules that apply to any entity, such as a bank holding company, that commits to maintain the capital of an insured bank. If the holding company later becomes bankrupt, the FDIC is given high priority to the amount of the commitment.[41] These rules became

---

34. [n.80] 12 U.S.C. § 1821(d)(19) (Supp. III 1991).

35. [n.82] 12 U.S.C. § 1821(i)(2) (Supp. III 1991).

36. [n.84] 12 U.S.C. § 1821(i)(3)(A).

37. [n.85] Id. § 1818(i)(2).

38. [n.86] Id. § 1818(c). This power was the basis of the freeze against the law firm Kaye, Scholer, Fierman, Hays & Handler.

39. [n.87] See Carlton v. Firstcorp, Inc., 967 F.2d 942, 945 (4th Cir. 1992) (bankruptcy court lacks jurisdiction to stop OTS enforcement action due to anti-injunction provision of 12 U.S.C. § 1818(i)(1)).

40. [n.89] Individuals' debts are not dischargeable if they arise from fraud or defalcation while acting in a fiduciary capacity to an insured depository institution, or from reckless failure to fulfill any commitment by the individual to maintain the capital of the institution. 11 U.S.C. § 523 (a)(11)-(12) (Supp. III 1991).

41. [n.90] 11 U.S.C. §§ 365(o), 507(a)(8) (Supp. III 1991). A Chapter 11 trustee or debtor is required to assume and immediately cure any deficit under any commitment by the debtor to banking agencies to maintain the capital of an insured depository institution. Id. § 365(o). Such obligations pursuant to assumed executory contracts are administrative expense claims given first priority under the Bankruptcy Code. Id. §§ 503(b)(1)(A), 507(a)(1). * * *

more important in 1991 with passage of FDICIA, which routinely requires such commitments by holding companies to maintain the capital of undercapitalized banks.[42]

In 1991, FDICIA established a regime for prompt corrective action for undercapitalized banks. A series of increasingly stringent rules now apply to banks as their capital levels fall below statutorily required levels towards insolvency. Most important for purposes of this Article, the Act introduces a new trigger for bank insolvency. Instead of waiting for banks to exhaust their capital, the Act requires that "severely undercapitalized" banks (those whose capital is less than two percent of assets) be closed within ninety days of becoming severely undercapitalized.[43] The bank is thus subject to the full range of agency receivership powers even before the usual definitions of insolvency are met. One solid rationale for this rule is that, due to accounting imperfections, banks reporting two-percent capital are actually likely to be insolvent.

The FDIC and RTC acting as receiver are exempt from all taxation imposed by any state or local taxing authority, except for certain real property taxes.[44] These agency advantages both reduce the costs to the insurance fund of a receivership, and, echoing *McCulloch v. Maryland*, prevent the FDIC and RTC from being subjected to state and local taxation.

The FDIC and RTC enjoy a number of special procedural rules that a bank would not have available pre-insolvency. The agencies have a broad right to remove to federal court,[45] and can remove a suit from state court without bond.[46] They can stay litigation against the bank for ninety days in the case of receivership and forty-five days for conservatorship. These last powers are similar, although far from identical, to the automatic stay in bankruptcy, and the use of a federal bankruptcy court to replace state proceedings by creditors. Additional advantages to the agencies acting as receiver or conservator are an extended statute of limitations,[47] and broad investigative powers, such as the ability to issue a subpoena or subpoena *duces tecum*.[48] * * *

---

42. [n.91] Federal Deposit Insurance Corporation Improvement Act of 1991, Pub. L. No. 102–242, § 131, 105 Stat. 2236, 2253–67 (codified at 12 U.S.C. § 1831o (Supp. III 1991)).

43. [n.92] 12 U.S.C. § 1831o(h)(3)(A) (Supp. III 1991).

44. [n.94] 12 U.S.C. § 1825(b)(1) (Supp. III 1991); see id. § 1441a(b)(1)(B). The agencies also are not subject to any penalty or fine arising from nonpayment of *ad valorem* taxes. Id. § 1825(b)(3). * * *

45. [n.97] See 12 U.S.C. § 1819(b)(2)(B) (Supp. III 1991). * * *

46. [n.98] 12 U.S.C. § 1819(b)(4) (Supp. III 1991).

47. [n.101] The applicable period is six years for contracts and three years for torts, or longer if permitted by state law. 12 U.S.C. § 1821(d)(14) (Supp. III 1991).

48. [n.102] 12 U.S.C. § 1821(d)(2)(I) (Supp. III 1991).

G. LIABILITY OF INSTITUTION–AFFILIATED PARTIES, INCLUDING OFFICERS, DIRECTORS, AND ATTORNEYS

(1) Cease and Desist Order Against Institution–Affiliated Party

The most notorious use of enforcement authority against an institution-affiliated party occurred in connection with the failure of Charles Keatings' Lincoln Savings and Loan Association and the subsequent order brought by the OTS against Lincoln's law firm, Kaye Scholer. This action was the subject of much legal commentary, including a Symposium in the Southern California Law Review entitled In the Matter of Kaye, Scholer, Fierman, Hays & Handler: A Symposium on Government Regulation, Lawyers' Ethics, and the Law. You may wish to review 12 U.S.C.A. § 1813(u) which sets forth the conditions under which an independent contractor, such as an attorney, may be the subject of a bank regulatory enforcement action.

JAMES O. JOHNSTON, JR. & DANIEL SCHOTT SCHECTER INTRODUCTION: KAYE, SCHOLER AND THE OTS— DID ANYONE GO TOO FAR?

66 S. Cal. L. Rev. 977 (1993).

* * * On March 1, 1992, the OTS filed a $275 million action against Kaye, Scholer for alleged violations of applicable thrift regulations during the firm's representation of Lincoln. On the same day, the OTS issued a temporary cease-and-desist order that, *inter alia*, forbade the partnership from dissolving, prevented partners from leaving the firm without posting security, and required the firm to place twenty-five percent of partners' earnings into escrow. Despite Kaye, Scholer's public claims of innocence, the firm capitulated within a week, agreeing to individual sanctions against three partners and to a $41 million settlement of the charges. * * *

Kaye, Scholer began representing Charles Keating's American Continental Corporation in 1977. In February 1984, ACC acquired Lincoln and hired Kaye, Scholer to represent the thrift on various matters. In early 1986, Lincoln retained the law firm of Jones, Day, Reavis & Pogue to represent it before the Federal Home Loan Bank Board in its semiannual examination of operations and financial condition ("1986 Examination"). Lincoln, however, became dissatisfied with Jones Day's cooperative, non-confrontational dealings with the FHLBB's examiners and soon replaced the firm with Kaye, Scholer.

Kaye, Scholer partner Peter M. Fishbein immediately composed a caustic five-page letter to the FHLBB, denouncing the "abusive and costly" practices of the examiners and demanding that all further requests for information be given to specified Kaye, Scholer attorneys. This demand baffled the FHLBB, the rules of which gave it the right to inspect thrift records at any time. The request "reflects a fundamental misunderstanding of the examination process," wrote B.J. Davis, the FHLBB's regulator in charge of the 1986 Examination, in response to Fishbein's letter. "Unfettered access, including the ability to appear at a regulated institution without advance notice, is essential to fulfillment of [the FHLBB's] function." Nevertheless, the FHLBB complied, and for the remainder of the 1986 Examination the ten Kaye, Scholer lawyers working with Lincoln took a consistently hard-line approach to FHLBB requests. "This was not a dialogue," noted one examiner. "This was a stiff-arm day in and day out."

In April 1987, the FHLBB issued a very negative report of examination ("1986 ROE") for Lincoln and received a confidential recommendation from the examiners to appoint a receiver for the thrift, which had invested heavily in high-risk takeover stocks, junk bonds, and speculative real estate. Kaye, Scholer responded to the 1986 ROE with a 768—page rebuttal, supplemented by more than 10,000 pages of exhibits, that portrayed Lincoln as a soundly managed, solvent institution. The FHLBB, faced with Kaye, Scholer's threats of litigation and pressure from several U.S. Senators, ultimately declined to pursue the matter.

In July 1988, the FHLBB once again began an examination of Lincoln, which continued to retain Kaye, Scholer. The regulators' subsequent report of examination ("1988 ROE"), issued in December of that year, was similarly negative, concluding that Lincoln was managed in "an aggressive risk prone manner that has resulted in a level of problem assets that severely strains capital and places the continued viability of the association in jeopardy." Also in December, the Securities and Exchange Commission issued a report stating that Lincoln had failed to meet its minimum capital requirements, prompting the resignation of Lincoln's accountant, Arthur Young & Company. Kaye, Scholer nevertheless responded to the 1988 ROE, in January 1989, by asserting that "Lincoln's managerial skill, its sound diversification of investments and its prudent underwriting are all demonstrated by the unqualified success of its investment program."

Just three months later, however, the FDIC (the predecessor to the OTS) seized Lincoln and found the thrift to be insolvent by more than $2.6 billion. Lincoln's subsequent challenge to the government takeover in federal court proved unsuccessful, as Judge Sporkin declared it to be "abundantly clear that Lincoln was in an unsafe and unsound condition to transact business and that [Lincoln] did in fact engage in numerous unsafe and unsound banking practices."[49] Judge Sporkin then proceeded to issue a blistering condemnation of Lincoln's professional advisers:

> The questions that must be asked are:
>
> > Where were these professionals . . . when these clearly improper transactions were being consummated?
>
> > Why didn't any of them speak up or disassociate themselves from these transactions?

---

49. [n.12] Lincoln Sav. & Loan Ass'n v. Wall, 743 F.Supp. 901, 905–06 (D.D.C. 1990).

Where also were the outside accountants and attorneys when these transactions were effectuated?

What is difficult to understand is that with all the professional talent involved (both accounting and legal), why at least one professional would not have blown the whistle to stop the overreaching that took place in this case.

... Here it is clear that the private sector was not willing to cooperate with the public oversight regulators. Indeed, the private sector at times impeded the regulatory authorities from discharging their duties. All too often [Charles] Keating and those individuals working with him adopted strategies to thwart and frustrate the regulatory process.[50]

Judge Sporkin's "Where were the professionals?" became a rallying cry at the OTS, which began to build a case against Kaye, Scholer. The seizure of Lincoln gave the OTS access to internal documents and the ability to waive the attorney-client privilege in order to use those documents against Kaye, Scholer, which it promptly did. More than a year and a half later, after a painstaking compilation of correspondence and depositions, the OTS filed a notice of ten claims against the firm. In brief, the OTS alleged the following:

(1) Kaye, Scholer knew that Lincoln's directors had misleadingly backdated documents in order to take advantage of a rule permitting grandfathering of direct investments when "definitive plans" had been made for those investments.

(2) Kaye, Scholer knowingly misrepresented the status of those direct investments to the FHLBB.

(3) Kaye, Scholer knowingly failed to disclose that Arthur Andersen & Company, Lincoln's accountant in 1986, had resigned from service because of concerns about Lincoln's operations and asset management.

(4) Kaye, Scholer knowingly omitted material facts in submissions to the FHLBB and engaged in obstructionist and improper conduct in its appearances before the agency.

(5) Kaye, Scholer knowingly failed to disclose the existence of numerous "linked" transactions that improperly inflated Lincoln's income and net worth.

(6) Kaye, Scholer knowingly failed to disclose that Lincoln had removed adverse documents and created favorable documents in preparation for the 1986 Examination.

(7) Kaye, Scholer knowingly failed to disclose facts indicating that Lincoln had participated in limited partnership investments in order to finance personal tax shelters for ACC's control persons.

---

50.   [n.13] Id. at 920.

(8) Kaye, Scholer urged the FHLBB to rely on the opinions of Lincoln's auditors regarding certain joint venture transactions when it knew that those opinions had been prepared without adequate investigation.

(9) Kaye, Scholer engaged in improper and unethical conduct by representing both ACC and Lincoln, thus creating a conflict of interest.

(10) Kaye, Scholer obtained an illegal loan from Lincoln for one of its partners on favorable terms and in violation of the thrift's internal procedures.

Declaring that these charges constituted a prima facie showing that Kaye, Scholer had a "proclivity to violate laws and regulations, breach their fiduciary duties of loyalty and care and engage in unsafe and unsound practices," the OTS concurrently issued the temporary cease-and-desist order.

On the same day, Kaye, Scholer released a memorandum deeming the charges to be a "completely groundless . . . attempt by the OTS to create and apply new standards for attorney conduct that are different from, and inconsistent with, generally accepted professional standards and ethical obligations for lawyers representing a client." In the release, the firm indicated an intent to "contest these charges vigorously and ultimately to prevail on the merits." Kaye, Scholer also released a nine-page summary of the opinion of Professor Geoffrey C. Hazard, Jr., a specialist in legal ethics. This document, which was prepared by Kaye, Scholer but signed by Professor Hazard, concluded, after nearly six pages of factual assumptions, with a ringing endorsement of the firm's conduct:

> Kaye, Scholer did not violate existing standards of ethical conduct and professional responsibility, and Kaye, Scholer acted in accord with its duties under the law. The disclosures and representations that the OTS alleges should have been made to the [FHLBB] by Kaye, Scholer in fact would have violated the standards of ethical conduct and professional responsibility generally recognized in its role as litigation counsel.

Despite Kaye, Scholer's protestations of innocence, however, the firm rapidly capitulated, settling with the OTS six days later. Kaye, Scholer's insurance covered only about half of the $41 million, leaving the firm's 110 partners to pay the rest. Because Kaye, Scholer did not give a reason for its rapid decision to accept this bitter pill, speculation has abounded. Some argue that the temporary cease-and-desist order gave the firm no other choice. "What the government wanted was to bludgeon [Kaye, Scholer] so they wouldn't have to prove the allegations," said Professor Dennis Aronowitz. "The most insidious part of the case was that aspect: the government throwing its weight around." Others, however, argue that the firm would have settled quickly even in the absence of the order. "It was a realization that the freeze was irrelevant," Susan Beck and Michael Orey have claimed. "Nothing else the firm could have done would have saved it from having to fight the OTS's $275 million claim.... The firm would likely have lost a long, public fight at the OTS."

Whatever the reason for the settlement, the Kaye, Scholer case continues to reverberate in the legal community and beyond. * * *

(2) Actions by Conservator or Receiver to Recover Losses from Officers or Directors

RESOLUTION TRUST CORP. v. WALDE

United States Court of Appeals, District of Columbia Circuit, 1994.
18 F.3d 943.

BUCKLEY, CIRCUIT JUDGE.

* * * In the 1980s, the savings and loan industry was threatened by a deluge of insolvencies. As a consequence, the federal government was confronted with tens of billions of dollars in claims from depositors whose savings had been insured by the Federal Deposit Insurance Corporation ("FDIC"). To instill some semblance of order and limit the calls on the federal treasury, Congress created the RTC [Resolution Trust Corporation] as part of the Financial Institutions Reform, Recovery, and Enforcement Act of 1989, Pub. L. No. 101–73, 103 Stat. 183 (codified as amended at 12 U.S.C. §§ 1441a, 1811 et seq. (West Supp. 1993)) ("FIRREA").

Under this statute, the Director of the Office of Thrift Supervision ("OTS") may appoint the RTC as conservator of failed savings and loan institutions ("S & Ls"). 12 U.S.C. § 1821(c)(6)(A) (Supp. III 1991). The RTC is granted the same powers that Congress granted the FDIC under 12 U.S.C.A. §§ 1821–23. 12 U.S.C. § 1441a(b)(4)(A) (West Supp. 1993). As conservator of a failed S & L, the RTC succeeds to all of its "rights, titles, powers, and privileges." 12 U.S.C. § 1821(d)(2)(A) (Supp. III 1991).

In discharging its stewardship, the RTC is to "preserve and conserve the assets and property of such institutions." Id.§ 1821(d)(2)(B)(iv). To these ends, it is empowered to avoid fraudulent asset transfers, 12 U.S.C.A. § 1821 (d)(17) (West Supp. 1993), assert claims against an S & L's directors and officers, 12 U.S.C. § 1821(k) (Supp. III 1991), seek a court order attaching assets, 12 U.S.C.A. § 1821(d)(18) (West Supp. 1993), and issue administrative subpoenas *duces tecum*, 12 U.S.C. § 1821(d)(2)(I) (Supp. III 1991) (authorizing RTC to employ powers listed in 12 U.S.C. § 1818(n)).

In 1974, William Walde founded Trustbank Savings, F.S.B., and subsequently served it as President, Chief Executive Officer, Chairman of the Board, and director. Mr. Walde's career with the company ended on January 25, 1991, when the OTS declared Trustbank insolvent and appointed the RTC as its conservator. The RTC launched an investigation, still ongoing, into whether Mr. Walde and other former Trustbank officials might be liable to the RTC as a result of their operation of the company.

The agency's "Amended Order of Investigation" states that its purpose is to determine whether

> (1) former officers, directors and others who provided services to, or otherwise dealt with, Trustbank ... may be liable as a result of any actions, or failures to act, in connection with or which may have affected Trustbank ... ; (2) the RTC should seek to avoid a transfer of any interests or an incurrence of any obligations; (3) the RTC should seek an attachment of assets; and (4) pursuit of such litigation would be cost-effective, considering the extent of the potential defendant's ability to pay a judgment in any such litigation.

On November 30, 1992, the RTC served a subpoena *duces tecum* on Mr. Walde calling for the production of "[a]ny and all documents in your possession, custody or control for the years 1975 through the present that reflect, refer or relate to the operations or management of Trustbank. . . ." The subpoena also sought extensive personal financial information. * * *

To determine whether the RTC has the statutory authority to subpoena the information at issue here, we must first determine whether the purposes set forth in the orders of investigation are sanctioned by FIRREA. If so, the next question is whether the various materials sought by the subpoenas are reasonably relevant to those purposes. In undertaking our analysis, we are mindful that "the standard for judging relevancy in an investigatory proceeding is more relaxed than in an adjudicatory one. . . . The requested material, therefore, need only be relevant to the investigation—the boundary of which may be defined quite generally. . . ." Id. 965 F.2d at 1090 (emphasis in original; citations omitted).

The orders issued in these cases describe four areas of investigation: possible liability of former officers and directors, evidence of illegal asset transfers, identification of attachable assets, and the cost-effectiveness of litigation against prospective defendants. We discuss these in turn.

None of the appellants argues that the RTC lacks the authority to subpoena material reasonably relevant to the issue of liability. We find that some of the personal financial information sought under the subpoenas is reasonably relevant to the potential liability of officers and directors. Bank statements of officers and directors, for example, might reveal secret payments from individuals whose loans they had approved.

These subpoenas clearly cast a wider net, however, and we agree with appellants that not all of the information sought by the RTC is relevant to the issue of liability. Much as we strain our imagination, we cannot find any way in which alimony payments or irrevocable trusts that predate appellants' association with a failed S & L and to which no assets may be transferred are relevant to whether appellants might be guilty of fraud, negligence, or breach of fiduciary duties. Nonetheless, this information may be relevant to the remaining purposes listed in the orders of investigation. * * *

Having concluded that the RTC is not required to make a preliminary determination of liability before subpoenaing information relevant to the attachment of assets or the avoidance of asset transfers, we must see whether the personal financial information sought is relevant to either of these purposes. Once again, we are mindful that "in light of the broad deference we afford the investigating agency, it is essentially the respondent's burden to show that the information is irrelevant." *Invention Submission*, 965 F.2d at 1090 (citation omitted). Appellants have satisfied us that at least some of the information sought under the subpoenas is not relevant to these two purposes. We again cite alimony payments as just one example. Thus we turn to the last of the objectives enumerated in the orders of investigation—a determination of the cost-effectiveness of litigation against potential defendants.

In essence, the RTC asserts that as the conservator for a failed S&L, it is authorized to serve a subpoena on each former officer and director for the *sole* purpose of determining whether that individual has a sufficient net worth to warrant suing, even in the absence of any reason to believe he may be liable to the S & L. The RTC draws this conclusion from the sections of FIRREA that direct it to "minimize[ ] the amount of any loss realized in the resolution of cases," 12 U.S.C.A .§ 1441a(b)(3)(C)(iv) (West Supp. 1993), and authorize it to "conserve the assets and property of [the failed] institution," 12 U.S.C. § 1821 (d)(2)(B)(iv) (Supp. III 1991), and to use its subpoena authority "for purposes of carrying out any power, authority or duty with respect to an insured depository institution," id. § 1821(d)(2)(I)(i).

To the RTC, the sum of these sections is a congressional mandate to carry out its mission in a manner that minimizes the costs to the U.S. taxpayer, and it finds an assessment of the cost-effectiveness of potential litigation to be integral to this endeavor. See Transcript of Oral Argument in Resolution Trust Corp. v. Walde at 22–23 (counsel for RTC contending it has "[a]n obligation to conduct investigations in a cost-effective manner" by making "preliminary determinations about the potential sources of recovery so that we don't insert resources in investigations that are not warranted.").

As we are well aware, when a statute "is silent or ambiguous with respect to [a] specific issue, the question for the court is whether the agency's answer is based on a permissible construction of the statute." Chevron U.S.A., Inc. v. Natural Resources Defense Council, 467 U.S. 837, 843 (1984) (footnote omitted). If it is, the court must defer to the agency's construction. Here, the language and history of FIRREA offer no clues as to whether Congress intended to authorize the RTC to use its subpoena powers for the purpose of determining which of the possible targets of an investigation were sufficiently wealthy to warrant pursuit. Therefore, we must defer to the RTC's construction of the scope of its subpoena powers so long as it is permissible.

The RTC asserts that its interpretation is reasonable, citing our decision in *Invention Submission*. In that case, we suggested that the Federal Trade Commission could compare a corporation's profits "with those of other [similar] companies, and of the revenues of the corporation's various regional sales offices with one another, . . . [so as to] help the Commission to allocate its limited investigative resources. . . ." *Invention Submission*, 965 F.2d at 1090. That case, however, involved the subpoenaing of corporate rather than personal records.

The Supreme Court reminds us that "corporations can claim no equality with individuals in the enjoyment of a right to privacy." *Morton Salt*, 338 U.S. at 652. That right extends to personal papers:

> It cannot be too often repeated . . . that the principles that embody the essence of constitutional liberty and security forbid all invasions on the part of the government and its employes [sic] of the sanctity of a man's home, and the privacies of his life. . . . [O]f all the rights of the citizen, few are of greater importance or more essential to his peace and happiness than the right of personal security, and that involves, not merely protection of his person from assault, *but exemption of his private affairs, books, and papers from the inspection and scrutiny of others.* Without the enjoyment of this right, all others would lose half their value.

Interstate Commerce Comm'n v. Brimson, 154 U.S. 447, 479 (1894) (citation and internal quotation marks omitted; emphasis added). In commenting on this right, Justice Holmes observed:

> Anyone who respects the spirit as well as the letter of the Fourth Amendment would be loath to believe that Congress intended to authorize one of its subordinate agencies to sweep all our traditions into the fire and to direct fishing expeditions into private papers on the possibility that they may disclose evidence of crime. We do not discuss the question whether it could do so if it tried, as nothing short of the most explicit language would induce us to attribute to Congress that intent.

Federal Trade Comm'n v. American Tobacco Co., 264 U.S. 298, 305–06 (1924) (citation omitted).

The RTC would no doubt remind us that the Court has traveled some distance since 1924, and that in defining the permissible scope of administrative subpoenas, the Supreme Court in *Morton Salt*, and we in *Invention Submission*, have permitted agencies the greatest latitude in seeking the information they deem relevant to their duties. We in turn, however, would remind the RTC that not only did those cases involve corporations rather than individuals, they dealt with the power to investigate suspicions of wrongdoing whereas in the cases now before us, the agency is attempting to subpoena information relevant to wealth rather than liability. This distinction leads squarely to the question of the reasonableness of the RTC's conclusion that in enacting FIRREA, majorities in each house of Congress intended to authorize the RTC to browse among the private papers of citizens whose only sin had been to serve as officers or directors of defunct S & Ls.

Because of the absence of any evidence that Congress intended so intrusive a grant of authority, and for the reasons stated by Justice Holmes, we conclude that it was not reasonable for the RTC to impute such an intent to Congress. Instead, we think that the RTC must have at least an articulable suspicion that a former officer or director is liable to the failed institution before a subpoena for his personal financial information may issue. Of course, in determining whether the RTC acted reasonably in issuing such a subpoena, the court must give "due weight ... to the specific reasonable inferences" that the RTC might draw from the information available to it in light of its experience investigating other failed institutions. See Terry v. Ohio, 392 U.S. 1, 27 (1968).

Reasonable suspicion should not turn upon whether particular conduct is unlawful, but upon "the degree of suspicion that attaches to particular types of noncriminal acts." Illinois v. Gates, 462 U.S. 213, 243–44 n.13 (1983). Thus, the RTC could found its suspicion of liability upon, for example, records of the failed institution showing a suspicious asset transfer or a questionable payment involving the target, or deposition testimony of other former officers and directors. If the RTC has no such specific basis, however, upon which to suspect that the target engaged in wrongdoing, then the subpoena cannot be enforced. We therefore hold that in cases such as these, where the RTC has no articulable suspicion to believe that the former officer or director is liable to S & Ls in its custody, the RTC may not subpoena his personal financial information for the purpose of assessing the cost-effectiveness of prospective litigation.

Having found that the RTC does not have the authority to subpoena private financial information for the purpose of assessing an individual's net worth, we will not reach appellants' Fourth Amendment challenge. * * *

(3) Special Standards for Professional Negligence Actions Brought by Conservators or Receivers

PATRICIA A. McCOY
A POLITICAL ECONOMY OF THE
BUSINESS JUDGMENT RULE IN BANKING:
IMPLICATIONS FOR CORPORATE LAW

47 Case W. Res. L. Rev. 1 (1996).

* * * In banking, as in other industries, directors who breach their duty of care to the corporation face liability for simple or gross negligence. Today's formulations of the duty of care in banking trace directly back to the U.S. Supreme Court's 1891 decision in *Briggs v. Spaulding*, where the Court charged bank directors with the care "which ordinarily prudent and diligent men would exercise under similar circumstances," taking into

account "the restrictions of the statute and the usages of business."[51] While there are individual variations on the *Briggs* rule today from state to state, the variations are largely minor, and a majority of states still subscribe at least nominally to it.

If the unvarnished duty of care were dispositive, directors could be liable for honest but mistaken judgment calls that factfinders found imprudent in the harsh glare of hindsight. Concerned that entrepreneurial spirit might be dampened as a result, courts grafted the business judgment rule onto the duty of care. Under the classic definition of the business judgment rule, directors are not liable for honest business decisions that turn out wrong, assuming those decisions are disinterested, informed and in compliance with all laws, corporate charter provisions, and by-laws. To qualify for protection under the business judgment rule, board decisions also must meet a minimum rationality standard by having at least some profit potential on their face. * * *

The bank and thrift crisis of the 1980's precipitated cutbacks to the business judgment rule in banking on a scale hitherto unimagined. In the 1980's and early 1990's, courts second-guessed financial institution decisions with respect to a new range of loan activities that had previously gone unquestioned. As a result, bank and thrift directors now face common-law negligence liability for loans that are inadequately secured, for over reliance on risky types of collateral, for pre-funded interest clauses, for failures to perfect security, and for rollovers of delinquent loans. In addition, for the first time ever, irrespective of statutes or by-laws, courts held financial institution directors liable for defective internal controls. The most important recent holdings in this regard penalize directors for eschewing or ignoring loan underwriting standards, for not analyzing borrower credit profiles, and for lax administration of loans and other investments. Thus, in banking, the common-law duty of care has significantly reduced board discretion to approve bank loans. * * *

The rush toward increased federalization of bank director standards also has been fueled by the fact that federal bank agencies have replaced shareholders, depositors, and state court receivers as the dominant plaintiff in bank director liability litigation. The vast majority of reported bank director negligence cases since 1945 has been brought by the FDIC, or its one-time sister agency, the Resolution Trust Corporation ("RTC"), either in their corporate capacities or as conservators or receivers. One important by-product of this phenomenon is that the principal forum for bank director liability cases has shifted from state courts to federal courts, due to the federal question jurisdiction and removal powers that agency lawsuits confer.

As a result, the de facto authority for defining the scope of the business judgment rule has decisively shifted from state courts and bankers to federal bank regulators. In their dual roles as law-givers and plaintiffs, federal bank regulators now promulgate the rules that later

---

51. [n.11] [141 U.S. 132,] 152 [(1891)]. * * *

provide the standard of care in professional negligence suits against directors. In doing so, federal bank regulators supply the banking expertise that courts formerly felt they needed (but lacked) in order to pare back the business judgment rule. The judiciary's deference to agency expertise is such that many courts regularly draw on the new, regulator-shaped law, even while maintaining the facade that state common law is the rule of decision.

The incorporation of codified federal standards into the standard of care has obvious ramifications for the debate over whether state law or federal common law should provide the rule of decision in failed bank litigation. * * *

ATHERTON v. FEDERAL DEPOSIT INSURANCE CORP.

Supreme Court of the United States, 1997.
519 U.S. 213.

MR. JUSTICE BREYER delivered the opinion of the Court.

The Resolution Trust Corporation (RTC) sued several officers and directors of City Federal Savings Bank, claiming that they had violated the legal standard of care they owed that federally chartered, federally insured institution. The case here focuses upon the legal standard for determining whether or not their behavior was improper. It asks where courts should look to find the standard of care to measure the legal propriety of the defendants' conduct—to state law, to federal common law, or to a special federal statute (103 Stat. 243, 12 U.S.C. § 1821(k)) that speaks of "gross negligence"?

We conclude that state law sets the standard of conduct as long as the state standard (such as simple negligence) is stricter than that of the federal statute. The federal statute nonetheless sets a "gross negligence" floor, which applies as a substitute for state standards that are more relaxed.

In 1989, City Federal Savings Bank (City Federal), a federal savings association, went into receivership. The RTC, as receiver, brought this action in the bank's name against officers and directors. (Throughout this opinion, we use the more colloquial term "bank" to refer to a variety of institutions such as "federal savings associations.") The complaint said that the defendants had acted (or failed to act) in ways that led City Federal to make various bad development, construction, and business acquisition loans. It claimed that these actions (or omissions) were unlawful because they amounted to gross negligence, simple negligence, and breaches of fiduciary duty. * * *

This Court has recently discussed what one might call "federal common law" in the strictest sense, i.e., a rule of decision that amounts, not simply to an interpretation of a federal statute or a properly promulgated administrative rule, but, rather, to the judicial "creation" of a special federal rule of decision. See Texas Industries, Inc. v. Radcliff

Materials, Inc., 451 U.S. 630, 640–643, (1981). The Court has said that "cases in which judicial creation of a special federal rule would be justified . . . are . . . 'few and restricted.' " O'Melveny & Myers v. FDIC, 512 U.S. 79, 87 (1994) (quoting Wheeldin v. Wheeler, 373 U.S. 647, 651 (1963)). "Whether latent federal power should be exercised to displace state law is primarily a decision for Congress," not the federal courts. Wallis v. Pan American Petroleum Corp., 384 U.S. 63, 68 (1966). Nor does the existence of related federal statutes automatically show that Congress intended courts to create federal common-law rules, for " 'Congress acts . . . against the background of the total corpus juris of the states. . . .' " Id., at 68 (quoting H. Hart & H. Wechsler, The Federal Courts and the Federal System 435 (1953)). Thus, normally, when courts decide to fashion rules of federal common law, "the guiding principle is that a significant conflict between some federal policy or interest and the use of state law . . . must first be specifically shown." 384 U.S. at 68. Indeed, such a "conflict" is normally a "precondition." *O'Melveny*, supra, at 87. See also United States v. Kimbell Foods, Inc., 440 U.S. 715, 728, (1979); Kamen v. Kemper Financial Services, Inc., 500 U.S. 90, 98 (1991). * * *

After President Madison helped to create the second Bank of the United States, for example, many States enacted laws that taxed the federal bank in an effort to weaken it. This Court held those taxes unconstitutional. McCulloch v. Maryland, 17 U.S. 316, 4 Wheat. 316, 431, (1819) ("[T]he power to tax involves the power to destroy"). See also Osborn v. Bank of United States, 22 U.S. 738, 9 Wheat. 738 (1824) (federal marshals acted lawfully in seizing funds from a state tax collector who had hurdled the counter at the Chilicothe Branch of the Bank of the United States and taken $100,000 from the vault). Still, 10 years later President Andrew Jackson effectively killed the bank. His Secretary of the Treasury Roger Taney (later Chief Justice), believing state banks fully able to serve the Nation, took steps to "ushe[r] in the era of expansive state banking." A. Pollard, J. Passaic, K. Ellis, & J. Daly, Banking Law in the United States 16 (1988). See also Briscoe v. Bank of Kentucky, 11 Pet. 257 (1837) (permitting state banks to issue paper money in certain circumstances).

During and after the Civil War a federal banking system reemerged. Moved in part by war-related financing needs, Treasury Secretary (later Chief Justice) Salmon P. Chase proposed, and Congress enacted, laws providing for federally chartered banks, Act of Feb. 20, 1863, ch. 43, 12 Stat. 655, and encouraging state banks to obtain federal charters. Act of June 3, 1864, ch. 106, 13 Stat. 99 (only federally chartered banks can issue national currency). See also Veazie v. Fenno, 75 U.S. 533, 8 Wall. 533 (1869) (opinion of Chase, C. J.) (upholding constitutionality of federal taxation of state banks). Just before World War I, Congress created the federal reserve system. Act of Dec. 23, 1913, ch. 6, 38 Stat. 251. After that war, it created several federal banking agencies with regulatory authority over both federal and state banks. Act of June 16, 1933, ch. 89, 48 Stat. 162. And in 1933, it provided for the federal chartering of savings banks. Act of June 13, 1933, ch. 62, 48 Stat. 128.

This latter history is relevant because in 1870 and thereafter this Court held that federally chartered banks are subject to state law. See *National Bank* v. Commonwealth, 76 U.S. 353, 9 Wall. 353, 361 (1870). In National Bank the Court distinguished *McCulloch* by recalling that Maryland's taxes were "used . . . to destroy," and it added that federal banks

> "are subject to the laws of the State, and are governed in their daily course of business far more by the laws of the State than of the nation. All their contracts are governed and construed by State laws. Their acquisition and transfer of property, their right to collect their debts, and their liability to be sued for debts, are all based on State law. It is only when the State law incapacitates the banks from discharging their duties to the government that it becomes unconstitutional." 9 Wall. at 362. * * *

We conclude that the federal common-law standards enunciated in cases such as *Briggs* did not survive this Court's later decision in *Erie v. Tompkins*. There is no federal common law that would create a general standard of care applicable to this case.

We now turn to a further question: Does federal *statutory* law (namely, the federal "gross negligence" statute) supplant any state-law standard of care? The relevant parts of that statute read as follows:

> "*A director or officer* of an insured depository institution *may be held personally liable for* monetary damages in any civil action by, on behalf of, or at the request or direction of the Corporation . . . acting as conservator or receiver . . . for *gross negligence, including* any similar conduct or conduct that demonstrates *a greater disregard of a duty of care* (than gross negligence) including intentional tortious conduct, as such terms are defined and determined under applicable State law. *Nothing in this paragraph shall impair or affect any right of the Corporation under other applicable law.*" 12 U.S.C. § 1821(k) (emphasis added). * * *

In our view, the statute's "gross negligence" standard provides only ⸢ floor—a guarantee that officers and directors must meet at least negligence standard. It does not stand in the way of a s⸢ that the laws of some States provide. * * *

For these reasons, the judgment of the Court and the case is remanded for proceedings consistent \ so ordered.

JUSTICE O'CONNOR, with whom SCALIA and THOMAS ˌ judgment. * * *

(4) Criminal Sanctions

JOHN J. BYRNE, DOUGLAS W. DENSMORE & JEFFREY M. SHARP
EXAMINING THE INCREASE IN FEDERAL REGULATORY REQUIREMENTS AND PENALTIES: IS BANKING FACING ANOTHER TROUBLED DECADE?

24 Cap. U.L. Rev. 1 (1995).

* * * Few offenses bring forth the public's wrath more than those of a dishonest banker. The high-profile prosecutions of those at the helm of large failed institutions fed the hunger of the news media, politicians, and social commentators. It follows that after the public had been provided a steady diet of bank and savings institution failures during the 1980's, coupled with several high-profile prosecutions, the next leap was a mere step for the political establishment. That leap was the assumption that the financial institution industry had been populated by criminals. While numerous theories have been advanced to explain the banking debacle of the 1980's, no empirical data has been presented that would suggest that widespread criminal behavior was the primary cause. However, the assumption of widespread criminality carried little political risk. No rational elected official, officer of the court, or legal scholar wants to be perceived as "soft on crime." Therefore, Congress, with the support of the President, enacted a series of laws that represented a radical departure in the way the criminal justice system viewed the banking and thrift industries. This becomes significant due to the unique nature of banking. Our banking process is complex, and Congress' regulatory system is enormous. The compliance burden challenges the acumen of the most thorough compliance system designers. Even under ideal circumstances, some loans will go unpaid and some accounts will be overdrawn. One must acknowledge that even the most talented individual with the best technological support can make an occasional mistake. Some reports will be completed incorrectly. Some regulations will be violated. In all but the rare case, these mistakes and violations will result from an oversight, innocent mistake, or possibly a mistake in business judgment. This business reality becomes more relevant due to the changes in the law outlined herein because the potential punishment is enormous. Coupling this with banking's evolving role as an instrument of law enforcement through anti-money laundering legislation, one finds a massive body of potential criminal penalties available for use against bank officers and directors. * * *

The first major change in this trend toward the increased threat of criminal penalties came from the passage of The Money Laundering Control Act of 1986. Under this provision,[52] which was amended in 1988 anti-drug legislation and by the Crime Control Act of 1990, financial

---

[n.62] 18 U.S.C. § 1956 (1988).

institutions face a broad array of potential violations. Fines and imprisonment for violations can yield a fine of not more than $500,000 or twice the value of the property involved in the transaction, which ever is greater, and/or imprisonment for not more than 20 years. A companion provision was enacted under the same 1986 legislation which targets those engaging in monetary transactions in property derived from a specified unlawful activity.[53] Violations of this provision can yield a fine under an appropriate section of Title 18 or an alternative fine of not more than twice the amount of the criminally derived property and/or a prison term of not more than 10 years.

Through the enactment of The Financial Institutions Reform, Recovery, and Enforcement Act of 1989 (FIRREA), the federal government increased the maximum prison term from 5 years to 20 years and the maximum fine from $5,000 to $1 million for violations of Title 18 provisions governing the following: (1) receipt of commissions for gifts for procuring loans;[54] (2) theft, embezzlement, or misapplication by bank officer or employee;[55] (3) lending, credit and insurance institutions;[56] (4) bank entries, reports and transactions;[57] (5) Federal Deposit Insurance Corporation transactions;[58] (6) loan and credit applications generally; renewal and discounts; crop insurance;[59] (7) frauds and swindles (if the violation affects a financial institution);[60] (8) fraud by wire, radio or television (if the violation affects a financial institution) and;[61] (9) bank fraud.[62]

Under FIRREA, the maximum fine for the violation of an agency order was increased from $5,000 to $1 million and the maximum prison sentence was increased to five years from one year.[63] FIRREA increased the fine for those who knowingly violate any provision of the laws governing bank holding companies; or violating a regulation or order. It established a possible prison sentence of not more than one year, there being no suggested imprisonment under the previous version. The fine was increased to a maximum of $100,000 per day, having been $1,000 per day under the previous provision.[64]

Those who, with intent to deceive, defraud, or profit significantly from a knowing violation of any provision of the statutes governing bank holding companies found that the maximum imprisonment was increased

---

53.   [n.65] 18 U.S.C. § 1957 (1988).

54.   [n.67] 18 U.S.C. § 215 (1988).

55.   [n.68] Id. § 656 (1988).

56.   [n.69] Id. § 657 (1988).

57.   [n.70] Id. § 1005 (1988).

58.   [n.71] Id. § 1007 (1988).

59.   [n.72] Id. § 1014 (1988).

60.   [n.73] Id. § 1341 (1988).

61.   [n.74] Id. § 1343 (1988).

62.   [n.75] Id. § 1344 (Supp. V 1993).

63.   [n.76] Id. § 1818(j) (Supp. IV 1992).

64.   [n.77] Id. § 1847 (Supp. IV 1992).

by FIRREA from one year to five years and the maximum fine was increased from $10,000 to not more than $1 million per day. In addition, FIRREA amended RICO[65] to include a violation of 18 U.S.C. § 1344 (financial institution fraud). Therefore, all fines and penalties associated with RICO are available to prosecutors investigating bank officers and directors for bank fraud.

FIRREA amended 18 U.S.C. § 1510 to include officers of financial institutions who, "with the intent to obstruct a judicial proceeding, directly or indirectly notif[y] any person about the existence or contents of a subpoena for records of that financial institution."[66] Violators are subjected to a fine and/or imprisonment for up to five years. If an officer of a financial institution directly or indirectly discloses the existence or contents of a grand jury subpoena to a customer of the financial institution whose records are sought by a grand jury subpoena or any other person named in that subpoena, that officer shall be fined and/or imprisoned for a term of not more than one year. Under this provision, an officer of a financial institution includes officers, directors, partners, employees, agents or attorneys of or for the financial institution.

In addition to directing the Federal Sentencing Commission to increase the guideline penalties for crimes affecting financial institutions,[67] Congress increased the statute of limitations to 10 years for the violation of the following sections of Title 18:[68] sections 215, 656, 657, 1005, 1006, 1007, 1008, 1014, and 1344; and sections 1341 and 1343 if the offense affects a financial institution.

Finding the increases in the maximum prison sentences set forth in FIRREA to be insufficient, Congress again raised the potential prison terms through the passage of The Crime Control Act of 1990. The maximum prison terms were extended to 30 years for violations of the following statutory provisions: (1) theft, embezzlement, or misapplication by bank officer or employee;[69] (2) lending, credit and insurance institutions;[70] (3) bank entries, reports and transactions;[71] (4) Federal Deposit Insurance Corporation transactions;[72] (5) loan and credit applications generally renewal and discounts crop insurance;[73] (6) frauds and swindles (if the violation affects a financial institution);[74] (7) fraud by wire, radio or television (if the violation affects a financial institution);[75] and (8) bank

---

65. [n.78] Id. §§ 1961–68 (Supp. V 1993).

66. [n.79] Id. § 1510 (Supp. V 1993).

67. [n.80] See 28 U.S.C. § 94 (note) (Supp. V 1993). * * *

68. [n.81] 18 U.S.C. § 3293 (Supp. V 1993).

69. [n.83] 18 U.S.C. § 656 (Supp. V 1993).

70. [n.84] Id. § 657 (Supp. V 1993).

71. [n.85] Id. § 1005 (Supp. V 1993).

72. [n.86] Id. § 1007 (Supp. V 1993).

73. [n.87] Id. § 1014 (Supp. V 1993).

74. [n.88] Id. § 1341 (Supp. V 1993).

75. [n.89] Id. § 1343 (Supp. V 1993).

fraud.[76]

With respect to criminal forfeitures, the Act required courts to order the criminal forfeiture of any property, real or personal, which represents or is traceable to the gross receipts obtained, directly or indirectly, from a violation of specified provisions, if the violation relates to the sale of assets acquired or held by the Resolution Trust Corporation or other conservator for a financial institution.[77] In addition, this legislation requires the Federal Sentencing Commission to set an offense level of 24 for violations of numerous crimes affecting financial institutions.

Moreover, The Crime Control Act of 1990 adds a number of new prosecutorial avenues for the federal government with respect to banking. First, section 225 prohibits engaging in a "continuing financial crimes enterprise."[78] This is defined as a series of violations under 18 U.S.C. §§ 215, 656, 657, 1005, 1006, 1007, 1014, 1032, or 1344 or §§ 1341 or 1343 affecting a financial institution, committed by at least four persons acting in concert. A violation of this provision calls for a fine of not more than $10 million for an individual and imprisonment for not less than 10 years to a maximum of life imprisonment. Second, section 1032 prohibits knowingly concealing or attempting to conceal assets from any of the insurance or regulatory bodies (acting as receiver or conservator), or corruptly impeding or attempting to impede the functions of these bodies or corruptly or endeavoring to place assets or property beyond the reach of these insurance and regulatory bodies.[79] Violations will yield a fine or imprisonment of not more than five years or both.

A third addition prohibits obstructing the examination of a financial institution.[80] This broadly worded prohibition provides: "Whoever corruptly obstructs or attempts to obstruct any examination of a financial institution by an agency of the United States with jurisdiction to conduct an examination of such financial institutions shall be fined under this title, imprisoned not more than five years, or both."[81] Fourth, The Crime Control Act of 1990 creates a system for "special rewards for information relating to certain financial institution offenses."[82] This handy tool in the hands of an aggressive prosecutor gives the Attorney General of the United States sole discretion to have payments made to persons who furnish information unknown to the government relating to a possible prosecution under 18 U.S.C. §§ 215, 287, 656, 657, 1001, 1005, 1006, 1007, 1014, 1032, 1341, 1343, or 1344 if it affects a depository institution insured by the FDIC or any other agency or entity of the United States, as

---

76. [n.90] Id. § 1344 (Supp. V 1993).

77. [n.91] Id. § 982 (Supp. V 1993). * * *

78. [n.93] 18 U.S.C. § 225 (Supp. V 1993).

79. [n.94] Id. § 1032 (Supp. V 1993).

80. [n.95] Id. § 1517 (Supp. V 1993).

81. [n.96] Id.

82. [n.97] Id. § 3059A (Supp. V 1993).

well as possible prosecutions for conspiracy to commit any such offense. The amount of payment shall not exceed $50,000.

Additional assistance was given to prosecutors under the Crime Control Act through the addition of 18 U.S.C. § 1963 (RICO) to those violations to which the 10 year statute of limitations[83] applies (to the extent that the racketeering activity involves a violation of 18 U.S.C. § 1344).

Beginning in the mid–1980's, those convicted of federal crimes have been sentenced under the terms of the United States Sentencing Guidelines. The United States Sentencing Guidelines Manual ("USSG" or "Guidelines") sets forth the term of imprisonment, probation, fine, or restitution to be imposed in light of the unique characteristics of the defendant, the crime, and its impact upon the victim and society. A notable difference under the Guidelines is its abolition of parole. With few exceptions, one convicted and sentenced under the Guidelines is expected to serve that term.[84] * * *

QUESTIONS AND NOTES

1. Given the array of civil and criminal sanctions institution-affiliated parties are subject to, why would anyone agree to serve as an officer, director, attorney, or accountant for a bank or savings institution?

2. The Sarbanes–Oxley Act of 2002, signed into law July 30, 2002, affects corporate governance of banks and their holding companies as well as imposing more rigorous reporting and disclosure requirements. See Chapter 4. for a discussion of the application of Sarbanes–Oxley to banking organizations.

3. Prosecutors have liberally used deferred prosecution agreements when seeking to enforce criminal statutes against banks and other business corporations. Under such an agreement, the company generally acknowledges its misconduct, pays a fine, agrees to cooperate with investigators, and implements appropriate procedures to ensure that the misconduct will not be repeated. If the agreement has been complied with for the requisite period, the prosecution will be dismissed.

H. CLAIMS BY DEBTORS

Often the FDIC, as receiver of a failed institution, brings an action against a borrower based on nonpayment of a loan. If the borrower raises an undocumented agreement as a defense to such an action, the FDIC will be able to defeat the defense by invoking the *D'Oench* "superpower" described below.

---

83. [n.98] Id. § 3293 (Supp. V 1993).

84. [n.99] In place of parole, the Guidelines authorize a sentence of probation when the minimum imprisonment term authorized is zero months. * * * U.S.S.G. § 5B1.1. * * *

PETER P. SWIRE
BANK INSOLVENCY LAW NOW THAT IT MATTERS AGAIN

42 Duke L.J. 469 (1992).

* * * Perhaps most surprising of all the agency superpowers are the *D'Oench* powers, which bar many claims and defenses against conservators and receivers that would have been valid against the bank itself. Three interrelated sources of law aid the agencies in increasing the value of the failed institution. First, the *D'Oench* case announced an equitable doctrine that prevents a person doing business with a bank from benefitting from any "secret agreement" undocumented in bank records and thus not discoverable by bank regulators.[85] Second, section 1823(e) of Title 12, a strict statutory version of the *D'Oench* doctrine, creates a specialized statute of frauds that defeats all claims or defenses against a bank except those based on contemporary approval by the bank's board of directors. The approval must also be continuously maintained in bank records. Finally, the "federal holder in due course" doctrine has developed judicially to allow agencies to win in related cases even where *D'Oench* and section 1823(e) may not apply.[86]

The upshot of these powers has been agency victories over borrowers, even in quite extreme cases, such as where the bank unilaterally altered the terms of a note, or forged the signature on a loan renewal and diverted the funds to a bank officer's use. *D'Oench* cases most often involve a borrower's defense against FDIC or RTC enforcement of a loan. The agencies routinely win, usually on summary judgment, even where the claim or defense would have been valid under state or federal law if proved. To date, the agencies have won against a notable list of claims and defenses that includes fraud in the inducement; various forms of misrepresentation; various lender liability claims; recklessness or negligence; material alteration of a promissory note; inaccurate recital of note terms; unrecorded agreement; improper notarization; mechanic's lien; failure of consideration; accord and satisfaction; novation; unjust enrichment, waiver, and estoppel; duress; lack of mental capacity; usury; violation of federal securities laws; and setoff rights of participating bank. * * *

MOTORCITY OF JACKSONVILLE, LTD. v. SOUTHEAST BANK N.A.

United States Court of Appeals, Eleventh Circuit, 1997 (en banc).
120 F.3d 1140, *cert. denied*, 523 U.S. 1093 (1998).

Anderson, Circuit Judge.

In this case, appellants Motorcity of Jacksonville, Ltd. and David S. Hess (collectively "Motorcity") contend that the district court erroneously

---

85. [n.47] D'Oench, Duhme & Co. v. FDIC, 315 U.S. 447 (1942).

86. [n.49] See, e.g., FSLIC v. Murray, 853 F.2d 1251, 1256–57 (5th Cir. 1988); Gunter v. Hutcheson, 674 F.2d 862, 873 (11th Cir.), cert. denied, 459 U.S. 826 (1982).

granted a motion to dismiss in favor of appellee Federal Deposit Insurance Corporation ("FDIC") based on the *D'Oench* doctrine. See D'Oench, Duhme & Co., Inc. v. FDIC, 315 U.S. 447 (1942). A panel of this court vacated the district court's dismissal. See Motorcity of Jacksonville, Ltd. v. Southeast Bank N.A., 39 F.3d 292 (11th Cir. 1994). On rehearing en banc, this court affirmed the district court's dismissal, holding that neither the Federal Deposit Insurance Act of 1950, Pub. L. No. 797, 64 Stat. 873, nor the Financial Institutions Reform, Recovery and Enforcement Act of 1989 ("FIRREA"), Pub. L. No. 101–73, 103 Stat. 183, displaced the federal common law *D'Oench* doctrine. See Motorcity of Jacksonville, Ltd. v. Southeast Bank N.A., 83 F.3d 1317, 1327–34 (11th Cir. 1996) (en banc). At the time of our en banc decision, the D.C. Circuit and the Eighth Circuit had held that FIRREA displaced the *D'Oench* doctrine. See Murphy v. FDIC, 314 U.S. App. D.C. 24, 61 F.3d 34, 40 (D.C. Cir. 1995) (holding that FIRREA supplanted the D'Oench doctrine); DiVall Insured Income Fund Ltd. Partnership v. Boatmen's First Nat'l Bank, 69 F.3d 1398, 1402 (8th Cir. 1995) (following the D.C. Circuit's holding in Murphy that FIRREA supplanted the *D'Oench* doctrine). Since the time of our decision, the Fourth Circuit has held that FIRREA does not displace the *D'Oench* doctrine. See Young v. FDIC, 103 F.3d 1180, 1187 (4th Cir. 1997) (following the holding in our en banc Motorcity decision that FIRREA does not abrogate the *D'Oench* doctrine). There is thus a split in the circuits on this issue. See FDIC v. Houde, 90 F.3d 600, 605 n.5 (1st Cir. 1996) (noting the split in the circuits).

The Supreme Court granted certiorari in this case, vacated our judgment, and remanded this case for further consideration in light of Atherton v. FDIC, 519 U.S. 213.

* * * *Atherton* does not address the question of whether a federal statute abrogates a previously established and long-standing federal common law doctrine. * * *

By contrast, the federal common law rule at issue in this case, the *D'Oench* doctrine, was first articulated by the Supreme Court in 1942, after *Erie*. The issue in this case therefore is not whether the *D'Oench* doctrine survived *Erie*, but rather whether Congress intended FIRREA to supplant the previously established and long-standing federal common law *D'Oench* doctrine. As explained in our previous en banc opinion, United States v. Texas, 507 U.S. 529 (1993), applies in this context and provides a presumption in favor of retaining existing federal common law unless a statutory purpose to the contrary is evident. See id. at 534, 113 S.Ct. at 1634; *Motorcity*, 83 F.3d at 1330–34.

In order to transform this case into one for which the analysis of *Atherton* and *O'Melveny* is appropriate, this court would be required to overrule the Supreme Court's decision in *D'Oench*, which we cannot do. "Federal district courts and circuit courts are bound to adhere to the controlling decisions of the Supreme Court." Jaffree v. Wallace, 705 F.2d 1526, 1532 (11th Cir. 1983), aff'd, 472 U.S. 38 (1985). The courts of appeals must follow Supreme Court precedent that has "direct application" in a case, even if it appears that the reasoning of the Supreme Court precedent has been rejected in other cases. Rodriguez De Quijas v. Shearson/American Express, Inc., 490 U.S. 477, 484, (1989). See also Florida League of Prof'l Lobbyists, Inc. v. Meggs, 87 F.3d 457, 462 (11th Cir.), cert. denied, 117 S.Ct. 516 (1996). Only the Supreme Court has "the prerogative of overruling its own decisions." *Rodriguez de Quijas*, 490 U.S. at 484.

Moreover, we detect no indications that *D'Oench* is ripe for overruling. It is true that in its post-*Erie* jurisprudence, the Supreme Court has explained that the creation of federal common law is appropriate only in the " 'few and restricted' " instances where the use of state law would pose a significant threat to or conflict with a federal policy or interest. *O'Melveny*, 114 S.Ct. at 2055 (quoting Wheeldin v. Wheeler, 373 U.S. 647, 651, 83 S.Ct. 1441, 1445, 10 L. Ed. 2d 605 (1963)). However, in *D'Oench*, the Court examined the Federal Reserve Act and identified a significant federal interest and policy which warranted the creation of a federal common law rule:

> Public policy requires that a person who, for the accommodation of the bank, executes an instrument which is in form a binding obligation, should be estopped from thereafter asserting that simultaneously the parties agreed that the instrument should not be enforced.... Those principles are applicable here because of the federal policy evidenced in this Act to protect [the FDIC] ... from misrepresentations made to induce or influence the action of [the FDIC], including misstatements as to the genuineness or integrity of securities in the portfolios of banks which it insures.... It would be sufficient in this type of case that the maker lent himself to a scheme or arrangement whereby the banking authority ... was or was likely to be misled.

D'Oench, 315 U.S. at 459–60, 62 S.Ct. at 680–81 (citations and internal quotations omitted).

For the foregoing reasons, we decline to accept Motorcity's invitation to overrule *D'Oench*. With the *D'Oench* doctrine safely in place as a long-standing federal common law rule, we conclude that the appropriate analysis for the statutory abrogation issue presented in this case is that articulated in *United States v. Texas*, and not that articulated in *Atherton* and *O'Melveny*. We continue to believe that the analysis set forth in our prior en banc opinion reflects the most reasonable reading of Congress's intent—i.e., that Congress did not intend FIRREA to displace the *D'Oench* doctrine, but rather intended to continue the harmonious, forty-year coexistence of the statute and the *D'Oench* doctrine.

Having carefully reconsidered our decision in light of *Atherton*, we reinstate our prior en banc opinion published at 83 F.3d 1317, and we reinstate our judgment affirming the district court's judgment granting the FDIC's motion to dismiss.

QUESTIONS AND NOTES

1. Is the *D'Oench* power properly characterized as a "superpower" for the FDIC?

2. What is the difference between the common law *D'Oench* doctrine and the statutory version? How can *Motorcity*'s holding recognizing the *D'Oench* doctrine as a "long-standing federal common law rule" be squared with the Supreme Court's decision in *Atherton*, excerpted earlier in this Chapter, rejecting the existence of a federal common law?

3. If a bank agrees to modify a loan contract after it is executed so that the contract is more favorable to the borrower, should the borrow rely on an oral modification or insist on a modification in writing?

CHAPTER NINE

GEOGRAPHIC EXPANSION, MERGERS, AND ANTITRUST

■ ■ ■

Unlike other business enterprises, banks and bank holding companies have historically been limited in the geographic areas in which they may operate. Most restrictions on bank location have been removed, but the historical limitations help explain much about our current banking markets, including why the United States has thousands of separately incorporated banks. In many countries, where geographic restrictions on growth were not present, banking is dominated by a handful of large institutions. As geographic restrictions have been lifted, mergers among existing banks have increased, consolidating to some degree the number of banks in the United States. Bank mergers are subject to some special considerations, as will be explored in this chapter.

SECTION 1. GEOGRAPHIC EXPANSION

The Riegle–Neal Interstate Banking and Branching Efficiency Act of 1994 dramatically expanded the geographic expansion possibilities for banks and bank holding companies. The statute was enacted, however, only after many of the existing restrictions limiting branching and interstate branching had become almost meaningless as a result of judicial interpretation. The history of the undermining of geographic restrictions is recounted in this Chapter as well as in Chapter 1.

RNIB+BEA

A. THE HISTORY OF IN–STATE BRANCHING PRIOR TO RIEGLE–NEAL

A state-chartered bank may establish a branch within the state as permitted by state law. Some states prohibited branching (sometimes referred to as unit banking), some limited branching to a specified geographic area (such as a city or a county or within a certain radius of a bank's principal office), and some permitted statewide branching.

A national bank's ability to establish a branch is determined by the McFadden Act, enacted in 1927 and amended in 1933. 12 U.S.C.A. § 36(c).

When enacted, the National Bank Act provided no authority for a national bank to establish a branch. The McFadden Act was passed to deter national banks from converting to state charters in states that permitted state chartered banks to establish branches. The McFadden Act provides that a national bank may establish a branch anywhere within the state in which it is located if state law specifically grants a state bank the authority to establish a branch at that location.

FIRST NATIONAL BANK IN PLANT CITY v. DICKINSON

Supreme Court of the United States, 1969.
396 U.S. 122.

MR. CHIEF JUSTICE BURGER delivered the opinion of the Court.

* * * The First National Bank in Plant City, Florida, is a national banking association organized and operated pursuant to the National Bank Act, 12 U. S. C. § 21 et seq.; it sought and received from the United States Comptroller of the Currency permission to operate two services for the convenience of customers; one was an armored car messenger service and the other an off-premises receptacle for the receipt of packages containing cash or checks for deposit. The Comptroller's letter authorizing the armored car messenger service relied upon paragraph 7490 of the Comptroller's Manual for National Banks, a relatively recent ruling which specifically authorizes such a service. A second letter authorizing construction of an off-premises receptacle authorized such a service "as an incident to" the bank's ordinary business. Both letters contained explicit instructions to First National designed to insure that deposits so received would not become bank liabilities until actually in the hands of the bank teller at the chartered office or regular "banking house"; and that checks cashed for customers would be deemed paid at the bank when the cash was handed to the messenger, not when the cash was delivered to the customer by the armored car teller.

Relying on these letters, First National offered an armored car service and a secured receptacle for receipt of monies intended as deposits. The bank advertised "Full Service Banking at your doorstep" ... and a "mobile drive-in ... where customers may be served...." A more detailed examination of the services shows that customers having an account with First National could, upon signing a "Comprehensive Dual Control Contract," arrange to have the armored car call at their place of business to pick up cash and checks for deposit, or to bring cash to them in exchange for checks delivered to the armored car teller. The contract provided that in each situation the bank's armored car messenger would be the agent of the customer. Additionally, proffered deposits were accompanied by a transmittal slip upon which the customer itemized the funds being deposited in the same manner as with deposits made at the chartered office of the bank. The transmittal slip contained a "Contract" which provided that in this off-premises transaction the bank was the agent of the customer, and that "the transmittal of said currency, coin and checks, shall not be deemed to be a deposit until delivered into the hands of the bank's tellers at the said banking house." * * *

The armored car was owned and controlled by the bank; the teller and driver-guard in the car were bank employees. The bank paid the cost of armored car operations and assumed complete responsibility for the monies, checks, and deposits during transit by means of an insurance policy bought and paid for by it to protect the customer and the bank. * * *

The stationary off-premises receptacle for receipt of monies intended for deposit was located in a shopping center one mile from First National's banking house in a space leased by the bank. * * *

On September 28, 1966, the Comptroller of the State of Florida, respondent herein, addressed a letter to First National advising it that the proposed depository then under construction and the provision of an armored car messenger service would each violate the prohibition under Florida law against branch banking. The letter requested that First National cease and desist all such operations. * * *

Against this background, we turn to the question whether the off- premises business activities conducted by First National amounted to "branch" banking within the meaning of the McFadden Act. Since national banks are "necessarily subject to the paramount authority of the United States," First National Bank in St. Louis v. Missouri, 263 U.S. 640, 656 (1924), we consult that part of the McFadden Act that defines the term "branch." 12 U. S. C. § 36 (f) provides:

> "(f) The term 'branch' as used in this section shall be held to include any branch bank, branch office, branch agency, additional office, or any branch place of business . . . (at which deposits are received) or checks paid, or money lent."

Although the definition may not be a model of precision, in part due to its circular aspect, it defines the minimum content of the term "branch"; by use of the word "include" the definition suggests a calculated indefiniteness with respect to the outer limits of the term. However, the term "branch bank" at the very least includes *any* place for receiving deposits or paying checks or lending money apart from the chartered premises; it may include more. It should be emphasized that, since § 36 (f) is phrased in the disjunctive, the offering of any one of the three services mentioned in that definition will provide the basis for finding that "branch" banking is taking place. Thus not only the taking of deposits but also the paying of checks or the lending of money could equally well provide the basis for such a finding. Although the District Court briefly discussed the possibility that checks were being paid, we confine ourselves to the question of whether deposits were received. Specifically, we must resolve the question whether the mobile armored car service and stationary deposit receptacle singly or together fall within the ambit of that section. As to the receiving of deposits, the functions of the two facilities are essentially the same, hence they may be considered together.

First National and the Comptroller of the Currency urge that the challenged activity does not amount to branch banking under § 36 (f). First National relies heavily, if indeed not entirely, upon carefully drawn contracts with its customers who use armored car or deposit receptacle services. The bank urges that, "deposit" being a word of art, the determination of when a deposit is made is not a casual one inasmuch as that determination fixes important legal relationships of the parties.

The bank also urges that creation of a deposit being purely a matter of intent, the issue is governed exclusively by the private contract. Since these contracts must be interpreted under state law, the argument runs, no "deposit" is actually received as such until monies delivered to the armored car or the receptacle are physically delivered into the hands of a bank teller at the chartered premises. Until such time the bank may not, under the contracts, be held to account for the customer's funds.

We have no difficulty accepting the bank's argument that the debtor-creditor relationship is a creature of contract and that the parties can agree that until monies are physically delivered to the bank no deposit will be credited to the customer's account. We are satisfied, however, that the contracts have no significant purpose other than to remove the possibility that the monies received will become "deposits" in the technical and legal sense until actually delivered to the chartered premises of the bank.

We do not challenge the right of the contracting parties to fix rights and risks as between themselves; nothing in the law precludes the parties from agreeing, for example, that the bank does not assume the status of bailee, with liability for loss of money in transit. But while the contracting parties are free to arrange their private rights and liabilities as they see fit, it does not follow that private contractual arrangements, binding on the parties under state law, determine the meaning of the language or the reach of § 36(f).

Because the purpose of the statute is to maintain competitive equality, it is relevant in construing "branch" to consider, not merely the contractual rights and liabilities created by the transaction, but all those aspects of the transaction that might give the bank an advantage in its competition for customers. Unquestionably, a competitive advantage accrues to a bank that provides the service of receiving money for deposit at a place away from its main office; the convenience to the customer is unrelated to whether the relationship of debtor and creditor is established at the moment of receipt or somewhat later.

We need not characterize the contracts as a sham or subterfuge in order to conclude that the conduct of the parties and the nature of their relations bring First National's challenged activities within the federal definition of branch banking. Here, penetrating the form of the contracts to the underlying substance of the transaction, we are satisfied that at the time a customer delivers a sum of money either to the armored truck or the stationary receptacle, the bank has, for all purposes contemplated by Congress in § 36(f), received a deposit. The money is given and received for deposit even though the parties have agreed that its technical status as a "deposit" which may be drawn on is to remain inchoate for the brief period of time it is in transit to the chartered bank premises. The intended deposits are delivered and received as part of a large-scale continuing mode of conducting the banking business designed to bring basic bank services to the customers.

Since the putative deposits are in fact "received" by a bank facility apart from its chartered place of business, we are compelled, in construing § 36 (f), to view the place of delivery of the customer's cash and checks accompanied by a deposit slip as an "additional office, or . . . branch place of business . . . at which deposits are received."

Here we are confronted by a systematic attempt to secure for national banks branching privileges which Florida denies to competing state banks. The utility of the armored car service and deposit receptacle are obvious; many States permit state chartered banks to use this eminently sensible mode of operations, but Florida's policy is not open to judicial review any more than is the congressional policy of "competitive equality." Nor is the congressional policy of competitive equality with its deference to state standards open to modification by the Comptroller of the Currency.

Justice Douglas, dissenting. * * *

CLARKE v. SECURITIES INDUSTRY ASS'N

Supreme Court of the United States, 1987.
479 U.S. 388.

Mr. Justice White delivered the opinion of the Court.

* * * In 1982, two national banks, Union Planters National Bank of Memphis (Union Planters) and petitioner Security Pacific National Bank of Los Angeles (Security Pacific), applied to the Comptroller of the Currency for permission to open offices that would offer discount brokerage services to the public.[1] Union Planters proposed to acquire an existing discount brokerage operation, and Security Pacific sought to establish an affiliate named Discount Brokerage. Both banks proposed to offer discount brokerage services not only at their branch offices but also at other locations inside and outside of their home States.

In passing on Security Pacific's application, the Comptroller was faced with the question whether the operation of Discount Brokerage would violate the National Bank Act's branching provisions. Those limitations, enacted as §§ 7 and 8 of the McFadden Act, 44 Stat. 1228, as amended, are codified at 12 U. S. C. § 36 and 12 U. S. C. § 81. Section 81 limits "the general business" of a national bank to its headquarters and any "branches" permitted by § 36. Section 36(c) provides that a national bank is

---

1. [n.1] Discount brokers execute trades on behalf of their customers but do not offer investment advice. As a result, the commissions they charge are substantially lower than those charged by full-service brokers. See Securities Industries Assn. v. Board of Governors, FRS, 468 U.S. 207, 209, n. 2 (1984).

permitted to branch only in its home State and only to the extent that a bank of the same State is permitted to branch under state law. The term "branch" is defined at 12 U. S. C. § 36(f) "to include any branch bank, branch office, branch agency, additional office, or any branch place of business ... at which deposits are received, or checks paid, or money lent."

The Comptroller concluded that "the non-chartered offices at which Discount Brokerage will offer its services will not constitute branches under the McFadden Act because none of the statutory branching functions will be performed there." He explained that although Discount Brokerage would serve as an intermediary for margin lending, loan approval would take place at chartered Security Pacific offices, so that Discount Brokerage offices would not be lending money within the meaning of § 36(f). Likewise, although Discount Brokerage would maintain, and pay interest on, customer balances created as an incident of its brokerage business, the Comptroller concluded that these accounts differ sufficiently in nature from ordinary bank accounts that Discount Brokerage would not be engaged in receiving deposits.[2] He further observed that treating offices conducting brokerage activities as branches under § 36(f) would be inconsistent with the "long-standing and widespread" practice of banks' operating nonbranch offices dealing in United States Government or municipal securities. Accordingly, the Comptroller approved Security Pacific's application.[3]

Respondent, a trade association representing securities brokers, underwriters, and investment bankers, brought this action in the United States District Court for the District of Columbia. Among other things, respondent contended that bank discount brokerage offices are branches within the meaning of § 36(f) and thus are subject to the geographical restrictions imposed by § 36(c). The Comptroller disputed this position on the merits and also argued that respondent lacks standing because it is not within the zone of interests protected by the McFadden Act. * * *

The District Court, relying on Association of Data Processing Service Organizations, Inc. v. Camp, 397 U.S. 150 (1970), held that respondent has standing and rejected the Comptroller's submission that national banks may offer discount brokerage services at nonbranch locations. A divided panel of the Court of Appeals affirmed in a brief per curiam opinion, 758 F.2d 739 (1985), and rehearing en banc was denied, with three judges dissenting. 765 F.2d 1196 (1985).

The Comptroller sought review by petition for certiorari, as did Security Pacific. We granted both petitions, and consolidated the cases.

---

2. [n.2] The Comptroller relied primarily on the fact that banks publicly solicit deposits and use deposited funds in lending, while credit balances maintained by brokers are not, as such, directly solicited from the public, and are subject to regulatory restrictions regarding use by brokers. See the Securities Investor Protection Act, 15 U. S. C. § 78aaa et seq. (restricting advertising, promotional, and selling practices of brokers regarding interest-bearing free credit balances); 17 CFR § 240.15c3–2 (1986) (regulating the use of credit balances by brokers). * * *

3. [n.3] A month later, the Comptroller approved without comment the application of Union Planters to acquire an existing brokerage firm.

475 U. S. 1044 (1986). We now affirm the judgment that respondent has *S.ct. not* standing, but reverse on the merits. * * *

branches

Respondent contends that the Comptroller's interpretation of the Bank Act is not entitled to deference because it contradicts the plain language of the statute. Respondent relies on 12 U. S. C. § 81, which provides:

> "The general business of each national banking association shall be transacted in the place specified in its organization certificate and in the branch or branches, if any, established or maintained by it in accordance with the provisions of section 36 of this title."

In respondent's view, the unambiguous meaning of § 81 is that "national banks may locate their business only at their headquarters or licensed branches within the same state." However, § 81 is considerably more ambiguous than respondent allows. The phrase "[t]he general business of each national banking association" in § 81 need not be read to encompass all the business in which the bank engages, but, as we shall explain, can plausibly be read to cover only those activities that are part of the bank's core banking functions.

Prior to 1927, the predecessor of § 81 (Rev. Stat. § 5190) provided that "the usual business of each national banking association shall be transacted at an office or banking-house located in the place specified in its organization certificate." In Lowry National Bank, 29 Op. Atty. Gen. 81 (1911), the Attorney General interpreted this statute to permit "a bank [to] maintain an [extra-office] agency, the power of which is restricted to dealing in bills of exchange, or possibly to some other particular class of business incident to the banking business," but to forbid "a bank to establish a branch for the transaction of a general banking business." Id., at 86. The Attorney General went on to cite cases which he viewed as "recogniz[ing] a vital distinction between a mere agency for the transaction of a particular business and a branch bank wherein is carried on a general banking business." Id., at 87. He summarized the distinction as follows:

> "An agency requires no division of the capital stock, and the details of the business are few and are easily supervised by the officers of the bank, while a branch bank requires, in effect, a division of the capital, the working force is organized, and the business conducted as if it were a separate organization, and it competes in all branches of the banking business with other banks in that locality the same as if it were an independent institution." Id., at 87–88.

The Court subsequently approved this interpretation of § 5190 in First National Bank in St. Louis v. Missouri, 263 U. S., at 658.

The *Lowry National Bank* opinion, which is part of the background against which Congress legislated when it passed the McFadden Act in 1927, does not interpret § 5190 as requiring national banks to conduct *all* of their business at the central office. The opinion equates "the usual business of banking" with "a general banking business," and envisions branching in terms of the performance of core banking functions.

Respondent attempts to sidestep the *Lowry* opinion by arguing that Congress changed the meaning of § 5190 when, in passing the McFadden Act, it changed the words "the usual business of each national banking association" to "the general business of each national banking association." Respondent has pointed to nothing in the legislative history of the McFadden Act, however, indicating that this change in the wording had substantive significance. We find reasonable the Comptroller's position that "the amendment simply codified the accepted notion that the 'usual business' of a bank was the 'general banking business.' "

Respondent's fallback position from its "plain language" argument is that the phrase "general business" in § 81 at least refers to all activities in which Congress has specifically authorized a national bank to engage, including the trading in securities that the McFadden Act authorized by the amendment of 12 U. S. C. § 24 Seventh. See McFadden Act, ch. 191, § 2, 44 Stat. 1226. However, petitioner Security Pacific has provided a counter-example to this general thesis: In § 2(b) of the McFadden Act, Congress specifically authorized national banks' involvement in the safe-deposit business, and in doing so deleted language from the bill that arguably would have limited the bank's authority "to conduct a safe deposit business" to activities "located on or adjacent to the premises of such association." 67 Cong. Rec. 3231 (1926). In floor debates, Representative McFadden, in response to the question from Representative Celler whether the bill as amended would permit "a safe-deposit business [to be] conducted a block away or a mile away from a national banking association," replied that the deletion of the language regarding location "removes the limitations which might be very embarrassing to an institution." Id., at 3232. In view of this exchange, we are not persuaded that Congress intended the locational restriction of § 81 and § 36 to reach all activities in which national banks are specifically authorized to engage. * * *

It is significant that in passing the McFadden Act, Congress recognized and for the first time specifically authorized the practice of national banks' engaging in the buying and selling of investment securities. See Act of Feb. 25, 1927, ch. 191, § 2, 44 Stat. 1226. Prior to 1927, banks had conducted such securities transactions on a widespread and often interstate basis, without regard to the locational restriction imposed by § 5190 on "the usual business of each national banking association." See, e. g., W. Peach, The Security Affiliates of National Banks 74 (1941); Perkins, The Divorce of Commercial and Investment Banking: A History, 88 Banking L. J. 483, 492, 494, n. 26 (1971). We find it unlikely that Congress, in recognizing and explicitly authorizing this practice, would have undertaken to limit its geographic scope through the branching law without specifically noting the restriction on the prior practice.

For the foregoing reasons, we conclude that Congress did not intend to subject a bank's conduct of a securities business to the branching restrictions imposed by 12 U. S. C. § 36(f). We do not view our decision today as inconsistent with our prior decisions interpreting 12 U. S. C. § 36(f) as embodying a policy of "competitive equality" between state and national banks. See, e. g., First National Bank in Plant City v. Dickinson, 396 U.S. 122 (1969). The Comptroller reasonably interprets the statute as requiring "competitive equality" only in core banking functions, and not in all incidental services in which national banks are authorized to engage. We are not faced today with the need to decide whether there are core banking functions beyond those explicitly enumerated in § 36(f); it suffices, to decide this case, to hold that the operation of a discount brokerage service is not a core banking function. * * *

JUSTICE STEVENS, with whom THE CHIEF JUSTICE and JUSTICE O'CONNOR join, concurring in part and concurring in the judgment. * * *

The McFadden Act allowed national banks to branch to the same extent as state banks. The Act also defined "state banks" to include institutions that carried on the business of banking. Thrift institutions did not offer checking accounts and commercial loans and thus were not considered "state banks" under the McFadden Act. When the Monetary Control Act of 1980 and the Garn–St Germain Act of 1982, however, authorized thrift institutions to exercise bank-like powers (such as offering checking accounts and making commercial loans), some national banks were able to use this expansion of thrift powers to expand national bank branching opportunities. The national banks argued that state thrifts were "state banks" under the McFadden Act definition since they now had the statutory authority to engage in a "banking" business. In many states, state chartered thrifts had the authority to branch statewide. Thus, because a national bank could establish a branch within the state to the same extent as a "state bank" and a state bank included a thrift (after the expansion of thrift powers), if thrifts could branch statewide, so could national banks. A state chartered bank, however, was still subject to the state's limitations on in-state branching.[4] It is no surprise that in states that authorized statewide branching for thrifts, but limited branching for banks, state chartered banks were soon at a distinct competitive disadvantage to national banks. Many of these states responded to pressure from

---

4. See Lissa Lamkin Broome, The Influence of Enhanced Thrift Institution Powers on Commercial Bank Market Expansion, 67 N.C. L. Rev. 795, 810–29 (1989) (discussing Department of Banking and Consumer Fin. v. Clarke (Deposit Guaranty), 809 F.2d 266 (5th Cir. 1987)). At the time of the *Deposit Guaranty* case Mississippi law permitted a state bank to establish a branch within the county in which the bank's principal office was located or within 100 miles of the principal office. Deposit Guaranty wished to establish a branch located in a different county than the county of its principal office and also located outside the 100 mile radius. The Fifth Circuit upheld the OCC's approval of the branch since Mississippi permitted state thrifts (which had recently been granted the same functional powers as banks) to branch statewide. A Mississippi state-chartered bank, however, was limited by the state branching limitations.

state banks and amended state laws to permit state chartered banks to branch statewide.

B. INTERSTATE BRANCHING PRIOR TO RIEGLE–NEAL

Prior to 1994, interstate branching for banks was available only in very limited circumstances. A handful of states had enacted legislation that permitted an out-of-state bank to establish an in-state branch. These statutes had little practical effect since so few states had them and those that did required reciprocity. National banks could not establish interstate branches pursuant to the McFadden Act since it only contemplated branching "within the state." National banks with main offices close to a state border were able to take advantage of a limited ability to relocate their main office across the state line and retain the former main office as an interstate branch. Section 30(b) of title 12 provided that a bank could change the location of its main office to any other location not more than thirty miles from the city where the main office was located. Before 1959, this statute authorized a home office relocation only "within the *same state* not more than 30 miles distant."[5] The OCC consistently interpreted the deletion of the requirement in 1959 that the location change be within the same state to manifest Congressional authorization of interstate branches for national banks in the case of a thirty mile main office relocation.[6]

While banks were effectively precluded from establishing interstate branches, in 1992 the OTS permitted federal thrifts that met the qualified thrift lender test to exercise interstate branching powers. 12 C.F.R. § 556.

CONFERENCE OF STATE BANK SUPERVISORS v. OFFICE OF THRIFT SUPERVISION

United States District Court, District of Columbia, 1992.
792 F.Supp. 837.

LAMBERTH, DISTRICT JUDGE.

* * * Although prior to the adoption of this rule [permitting interstate branching for federal thrifts], OTS's general policy prohibited interstate branching by federal savings associations, interstate branching in various forms has been authorized for some time.[7]

---

5. Synovus Financial Corp. v. Board of Governors of the Federal Reserve System, 952 F.2d 426, 428 n.1 (D.C. Cir. 1991) (citing Act of May 1, 1886, Ch. 73, § 2, 24 Stat. 18) (emphasis added).

6. Id. at 428 n.1.

7. [n.1] For example, since at least 1967, the Federal Home Loan Bank Board ("FHLBB"), OTS's predecessor agency, had permitted interstate branching by federal savings associations to the extent that state law permitted such branching by a similar, state chartered institution. 32 Fed. Reg. 20630 (Dec. 21, 1967). Since 1972, federal associations that had converted from a state charter were allowed to retain their pre-existing out-of-state facilities under certain conditions. 37 Fed. Reg. 3987 (Feb. 25, 1972).

On December 30, 1991, OTS published a proposed rule entitled "Policy Statement on Branching by Federal Savings Associations, for comment in the Federal Register." 56 Fed. Reg. 67236 (Dec. 30, 1991). This proposed rule introduced OTS's new policy that would permit nationwide branching of federal associations to the full extent allowed by federal law. The purpose of this proposal was to improve the safety and soundness of the industry. The proposed rule requested comments and required that any comments be submitted within 30 days. The summary of the proposed rule stated that:

> The ... [OTS] proposes to amend its policy statement on branching on federal savings associations. The proposed amendment deletes current regulatory restrictions on the branching authority of federal savings associations to permit nationwide branching to the extent allowed by federal statute. The amendment is intended to facilitate consolidation and geographic diversification among savings associations, and thereby foster safety and soundness, and to improve the quality of services available to customers. * * * 56 Fed. Reg. at 67236.

The notice of the proposed rule also reviewed the statutory authority for the rule. OTS noted that Congress had given the FHLBB and OTS "exceptionally broad authority to regulate from 'cradle to grave' the branching operations and other activities of federal thrifts." Id. at 67237 (footnote omitted) (referring to the Home Owners' Loan Act, 12 U.S.C. § 1464(r) ("HOLA"), which has been applicable to federal associations since the enactment of the Garn–St Germain Act of 1982). The notice then states that "[o]n numerous occasions the courts have confirmed that the OTS's authority in this respect is plenary and not bounded by any restrictions of state law." 56 Fed. Reg. 67237. Pursuant to this authority, therefore, federal savings associations may be allowed to branch on an interstate basis. Id. (footnote omitted). * * *

On April 9, 1992, OTS published the final rule which permitted interstate branching by federal associations. 57 Fed. Reg. 12203 (April 9, 1992). This rule became effective on May 11, 1992. The language of the final rule is virtually identical to that of the proposed rule. * * *

OTS then listed seven reasons for adopting the rule substantially as it was proposed. The first was that OTS has the authority to regulate branching. This authority is not challenged by plaintiffs in this matter and

---

In 1981, the FHLBB approved a policy statement which provided that under some circumstances it would approve mergers, consolidations or acquisitions resulting from interstate branch operations in order to prevent the failure of federally-insured institutions. Moreover, the Garn–St Germain Depository Institution Act of 1982, which was re-enacted in FIRREA, explicitly permits interstate branching by federal associations under certain circumstances. See 12 U.S.C. § 1464(r).

In addition, in 1981 the FHLBB permitted associations that had established a branch in a state other than its home state through a supervisory acquisition to establish additional branch offices in that state with the FHLBB's approval. See 47 Fed. Reg. 45120 (September 10, 1981). In 1986, the FHLBB further liberalized its interstate branching policy by permitting federal associations that are acquiring failing institutions to obtain branching rights in other states. See 51 Fed. Reg. 16286 (May 2, 1986). Also in 1986, the FHLBB permitted non-supervisory branching by federal thrifts if state law permitted such branching for state chartered thrifts. See 51 Fed. Reg. 16501 (May 5, 1986).

thus need not be discussed further. Second, according to OTS, interstate branching of federal associations will, "enhance safety and soundness by facilitating geographical diversity in both the operation and loan portfolios of insured institutions. This diversity will reduce the vulnerability of thrifts to declines in the economies of a particular state or region." Third, OTS asserts that this rule will allow many federal associations to reduce their operating costs by increasing their efficiency and developing economies of scale, such as consolidating personnel and operations functions.

The fourth reason that OTS provided for adopting this rule is that interstate branching is likely to "stimulate and increase" healthy competition among federal institutions by eliminating the barriers that heretofore have prevented out-of-state associations from competing in any given market. Fifth, OTS states that this increase in competition will also serve to improve the customer services that federal associations provide and encourage greater availability of customer services in many markets. Sixth, according to OTS, the increased financial stability that this rule affords will reduce the risk to the SAIF. Finally, OTS states that because this rule is designed to promote safety and soundness in the federal thrift industry and because the rule does not impose any new requirements that may increase the operating costs or otherwise hurt federal associations financially, this rule will not have any " 'significant economic impact' on small entities for purposes of the Regulatory Flexibility Act [RFA]." * * *

[The court rejected plaintiffs' procedural and substantive complaints about the rule, including the claim that the final rule is arbitrary because the OTS failed to provide adequate reasons for reversing its policy on interstate branching.]

An agency may always change its mind and alter its policies. When an agency reverses its policy, however, it must supply a reasoned analysis for the change. Motor Vehicle Mfrs. Ass'n v. State Farm Mutual, 463 U.S. 29, 41 (1983). The departure from past policy amplifies the need for an adequate explanation of the new policy. Simmons v. Interstate Commerce Commission, 829 F.2d 150, 156 (D.C. Cir. 1987). In the present case, OTS provided a reasoned basis for adopting the policy of allowing interstate branching by federal associations. OTS enumerated seven facially valid reasons for its decision to allow interstate branching by federal associations. Accordingly, summary judgment shall be granted for defendants on this ground and plaintiffs' motion shall be denied on this ground. * * *

Even though the explicit authority for brick-and-mortar interstate bank branches was quite limited, modern technology, including the proliferation of automated teller machines (ATMs), permitted many banking functions to take place on an interstate basis.

BANK ONE, UTAH, N.A. v. GUTTAU

United States Court of Appeals, Eighth Circuit, 1999.
190 F.3d 844, *cert. denied,* 529 U.S. 1087 (2000).

WOLLMAN, CHIEF JUDGE.

Bank One, Utah, N.A. (Bank One) appeals from the district court's denial of a preliminary injunction that would prevent the state of Iowa (the State) from enforcing Iowa statutes restricting Bank One's operation of automated teller machines (ATMs). Because we find that certain provisions of the Iowa Electronic Funds Transfer Act (EFTA), Iowa Code ch. 527, are preempted by section 36 of the National Bank Act (NBA), 12 U.S.C. §§ 21–216d, we reverse the district court's order and remand for the entry of a permanent injunction prohibiting enforcement of the relevant sections.

Bank One is a national bank organized under the NBA. Its main office is located in Salt Lake City, Utah, and it has no branch offices in Iowa. In 1997, Bank One installed ATMs at twenty-four retail store locations in Iowa, including eleven at Sears, Roebuck & Co. (Sears) stores throughout the state.

In October of 1997, the Iowa Superintendent of Banking ordered Sears to cease operation of the ATMs, citing multiple violations of the Iowa EFTA. On December 26, 1997, the State filed an action in state court against Sears to prevent the operation of the ATMs and to assess a fine. As a result, Sears instructed Bank One to remove all of its ATMs from Sears stores in Iowa. Bank One complied with Sears's request and placed the ATMs in storage pending the outcome of this litigation.

Bank One filed suit in district court, seeking a declaration that provisions of the Iowa EFTA restricting out-of-state banks from operating ATMs within Iowa are preempted by the NBA and praying for the issuance of a preliminary and permanent injunction. Bank One's complaint also alleged that the restrictions violate several provisions of the United States Constitution. The district court denied Bank One's motion for a preliminary injunction, finding that the challenged provisions of Iowa law were not preempted and concluding that Bank One was unlikely to succeed on any of its constitutional claims. * * *

The Iowa EFTA contains several provisions relevant to the placement and operation of ATMs within the state. Among other things, it contains an in-state office requirement for the establishment of ATMs: *Iowa ATM restrictions*

> A satellite terminal shall not be established within this state except by a financial institution whose principal place of business is located in this state, one which has a business location licensed in this state under chapter 536A, or one which has an office located in this state and which meets the requirements of subsection 4.

Iowa Code § 527.4(1) (citing id. § 527.4(4), which sets various restrictions on the operation of ATMs). * * *

In addition to the in-state office and approval requirements, the Iowa EFTA limits the advertising that may be placed on an ATM. It provides:

A satellite terminal in this state shall bear a sign or label identifying each type of financial institution utilizing the terminal. A satellite terminal location in this state shall not be used to advertise individual financial institutions or a group of financial institutions. However, a satellite terminal shall bear a sign or label no larger than three inches by two inches identifying the name, address, and telephone number of the owner of the satellite terminal. The administrator may authorize methods of identification the administrator deems necessary to enable the general public to determine the accessibility of a satellite terminal.

Id. § 527.5(5).

The NBA grants national banks the authority to exercise "all such incidental powers as shall be necessary to carry on the business of banking." First Nat'l Bank of E. Ark. v. Taylor, 907 F.2d 775, 777 (8th Cir. 1990) (quoting 12 U.S.C. § 24(Seventh)). Bank One argues that the NBA implicitly authorizes the placement of ATMs without restriction by the states. The provisions of the Iowa EFTA, it argues, impair the ability of a national bank to place its ATMs and to advertise thereon.

"Grants of both enumerated and incidental 'powers' to national banks [are] grants of authority not normally limited by, but rather ordinarily pre-empting, contrary state law." Barnett Bank v. Nelson, 517 U.S. 25 (1996). Where state law stands "as an obstacle to the accomplishment and execution of the full purposes and objectives of Congress," it may be found to be preempted. 116 S. Ct. at 1108 (quoting Hines v. Davidowitz, 312 U.S. 52, 67 (1941)). State regulations are not preempted, however, when Congress "accompan[ies] a grant of an explicit power with an explicit statement that the exercise of that power is subject to state law." 116 S. Ct. at 1109. Congress predicated the establishment of national bank branches upon compliance with state regulations. See 12 U.S.C. § 36(c). Therefore, in order to determine whether the NBA preempts the Iowa regulations, we must determine whether an ATM is a "branch" as defined in section 36.

In 1996, Congress amended section 36 to read, "[t]he term 'branch', as used in this section, does not include an automated teller machine or a remote service unit." See 12 U.S.C. § 36(j). Thus, whatever regulatory authority the states may retain with respect to national bank branches, the 1996 amendment clearly expresses Congress's intent that that authority no longer extends to national bank ATMs.

That intent is made even clearer in light of the assumption that Congress enacts legislation with knowledge of relevant judicial decisions. See Cannon v. University of Chicago, 441 U.S. 677, 696–99 (1979). Prior to the 1996 amendment, courts had held that because ATMs were branches they were subject to state restrictions. See Colorado ex rel. State Banking Bd. v. First Nat'l Bank of Ft. Collins, 540 F.2d 497, 499 (10th Cir. 1976) (finding state regulation applied because ATM was a branch); Independent Bankers Ass'n of America v. Smith, 534 F.2d 921, 948 (D.C. Cir. 1976) (same); cf. Independent Bankers Ass'n v. Marine Midland Bank, 757 F.2d 453, 463 (2d Cir. 1985) (finding that an ATM was not a branch within the meaning of the section 36 because it was owned by a grocery store and merely used by a national bank). By excluding ATMs from the definition of "branch," Congress eliminated the contingency that formed the basis of those decisions and thus signaled its intention to foreclose the states from imposing location and approval restrictions on a national bank's ATMs.

Likewise, the legislative history of the 1996 amendment makes clear Congress's intent in adopting the amendment, which was enacted as part of the Economic Growth and Regulatory Paperwork Reduction Act of 1996. The purpose of this act was to "strengthen our nation's financial institutions and to increase their competitiveness." S. Rep. No. 104–185, at 1 (1996). The legislation was intended to "allow financial institutions to devote additional resources to productive activities, such as making loans, rather than to compliance with unnecessary regulations." Id. "Section [36(j)] clarifies that an 'ATM' or 'remote service unit' is not considered a 'branch' for purposes of federal bank branching law and is therefore not subject to prior approval requirements or geographic restrictions." Id. at 24.

Finally, the interpretation given the 1996 amendment by the Office of the Comptroller of the Currency (OCC), which appears in this action as an amicus supporting Bank One, supports a finding that the relevant Iowa regulations are preempted. As we stated in *Taylor*, the Supreme Court has made it clear that the Comptroller's interpretation of the NBA is entitled to great weight. 907 F.2d at 777 (citing Clarke v. Securities Indus. Ass'n, 479 U.S. 388 (1987)). The OCC has ruled that "[a] national bank may perform, provide, or deliver through electronic means and facilities any activity, function, product, or service that it is otherwise authorized to perform, provide, or deliver." See 12 C.F.R. § 7.1019 (1998); see also OCC Interpretative Letter No. 821, 1998 LEXIS 15 at *10 (Feb. 17, 1998) (stating that section 36 preempts state geographic restrictions of ATMs). We conclude that the OCC's interpretation is a reasonable one.

Given the clear language of the 1996 amendment, its legislative history and the judicial decisions that formed the backdrop against which it was adopted, and the interpretation of the regulatory body charged with the responsibility of administering the national banking laws, we conclude that Bank One's ATMs are not subject to the restrictions contained in Iowa Code § 527.4(1).

Bank One also challenges that provision of Iowa law which states that ATMs "shall not be used to advertise individual financial institutions or a group of financial institutions." Iowa Code § 527.5(5). Assuming that this section has any validity as against a national bank ATM in light of our holding with respect to section 527.4(1), we conclude that it is preempted by the NBA. In Franklin National Bank v. New York, 347 U.S. 373 (1954), the Supreme Court held that a state law prohibiting national banks from using the word "saving" or "savings" was preempted by the NBA. In so holding, the Court noted that "[m]odern competition for business finds advertising one of the most usual and useful of weapons. We cannot believe that the incidental powers granted to national banks should be construed so narrowly as to preclude the use of advertising in any branch of their authorized business." Id. at 377 (referring to the incidental powers granted in 12 U.S.C. § 24 (Seventh)). In light of *Franklin*, we conclude that the State's attempt to regulate the advertisements on Bank One's ATMs is preempted. See *Barnett Bank*, 116 S. Ct. at 1108 (stating that grants of incidental powers to national banks normally preempt contrary state law).

Moreover, the OCC considered a similar Colorado EFTA provision requiring banks to remove their names from ATMs or to place the names of all other banks whose customers may use the machines. It declared in an interpretative letter that these regulations created a "significant burden on a national bank's right to engage in the business of banking by means of an ATM, as authorized by the [NBA]." OCC Interpretative Letter No. 789 [1997 Transfer Binder] Fed. Banking L. Rep. (CCH) ¶ 81-216 at 90,244 (June 27, 1997) (citing 12 U.S.C. § 24 (Seventh)). Once again giving deference to the OCC's interpretation of the national banking laws, we conclude that this provision of Iowa law must be held invalid as against national bank ATMs.

The State argues that the federal Electronic Funds Transfer Act, 15 U.S.C. §§ 1693-1693r permits the states to regulate the electronic transfer of funds. The federal EFTA was enacted in 1978 "to provide a basic framework establishing the rights, liabilities, and responsibilities of participants in electronic fund transfer systems." 15 U.S.C. § 1693(b). The primary objective of the federal EFTA "is the provision of individual consumer rights." Id. To achieve that goal, the act allows the states to retain control over electronic transfers:

> This subchapter does not annul, alter, or affect the laws of any State relating to electronic funds transfers, except to the extent that those laws are inconsistent with the provisions of this subchapter, and then only to the extent of the inconsistency. A State law is not inconsistent with this subchapter if the protection such law affords any consumer is greater than the protection afforded by this subchapter.

15 U.S.C. § 1693q. Despite the State's claims, this anti-preemption provision is specifically limited to the provisions of the federal EFTA, and nothing therein grants the states any additional authority to regulate national banks. State regulation of national banks is proper where "doing so does not prevent or significantly interfere with the national bank's exercise of its powers." *Barnett Bank*, 116 S. Ct. at 1109. Congress has made clear in the NBA its intent that ATMs are not to be subject to state regulation, and thus the provisions of the Iowa EFTA that would prevent

or significantly interfere with Bank One's placement and operation of its ATMs must be held to be preempted.

To be entitled to the grant of an injunction, Bank One must establish the existence of irreparable harm. We conclude that it has done so, for in the absence of an injunction the continued enforcement of the relevant provisions of the Iowa EFT would result in irreparable economic loss to Bank One. Accordingly, Bank One is entitled to the entry of a permanent injunction enjoining the enforcement of those provisions. * * *

BRIGHT, CIRCUIT JUDGE, dissenting.

The court today reverses the district court and orders it to enjoin the State from enforcing Iowa Code Chapter 527, in its entirety, against Bank One–or against any other national bank for that matter. The court does so because it concludes that, following Congress's 1996 changes to the statutory definition of "branch," as found in 12 U.S.C. § 36(j), Automated Teller Machines ("ATMs") are exempt from geographical branching requirements based in state law. While it is true that such requirements no longer pertain to ATMs, I cannot agree that this exemption controls the disposition of the case before us. Even if a national bank's ATMs need not comply with state law geographic restrictions, that does not mean other relevant and permissible state law restrictions are preempted thereby. Many of the sections of Iowa law at issue here are simply not geographical restrictions and ought not be analyzed as though they were.

In my view, those statutory restrictions imposed under Chapter 527 which are valid, evenhanded consumer protections are not preempted by federal law. Thus, I believe that the Superintendent is entitled to enforce them against banks, both state and national alike. I therefore respectfully dissent. * * *

Moreover, it is important to note that the statute before us applies with equal force against both state *and* national banks. *Every* bank is required to comply and no advantage is gained by state chartered institutions in the process. This latter point is critically important because the questions raised by consumerism might warrant a different analysis if Iowa's statute were constructed so as to favor state banks, giving them an advantage over their national bank counterparts in the ongoing competition for borrowers, deposits, and fees. After all, the National Bank Act ("NBA") has been repeatedly interpreted to prevent such competitive imbalances and to insure that national banks are allowed to compete on an even footing with state banks. See First Nat'l Bank of Logan, Utah v. Walker Bank & Trust Co., 385 U.S. 252, 261 (1966) ("Congress intended to place national and state banks on a basis of 'competitive equality'...."); First Nat'l Bank in Plant City, Florida v. Dickinson, 396 U.S. 122, 131 (1969) (The NBA "respond[s] to the competitive tensions inherent in a dual banking structure ... [and] reflects the congressional concern that neither system have advantages over the other....").

Ironically, the court's conclusion in this case is at odds with this important principle of competitive equality. State chartered banks remain bound by Iowa's consumer protection laws. To the extent that the court's decision today means that national banks are given a free pass, national banks thereby achieve a distinct and favored position under the law. Competitive equality this is not. * * *

QUESTIONS AND NOTES

1. The branching policy for national banks set forth in the McFadden Act showed deference to state law and state control over the conduct of banking business within the state's borders. If there is no specific deference to state law in the National Bank Act or the Homeowners' Loan Act, whether state law applies to a national bank or federally chartered savings association or savings bank depends on the preemption analysis discussed further in Chapter 4.

2. In the *North Arlington* case, excerpted in Chapter 2, the agency and the courts interpreted Congressional silence on federal thrift branching as permitting it to occur. The National Bank Act's silence on national bank branching prior to 1927, however, was interpreted as a ban on branching. Is there any justification for this difference in the analysis of Congressional silence?

C. THE HISTORY OF INTERSTATE BANKING PRIOR TO RIEGLE–NEAL

NORTHEAST BANCORP, INC. v. BOARD OF GOVERNORS OF THE FEDERAL RESERVE SYSTEM

Supreme Court of the United States, 1985.
472 U.S. 159.

MR. JUSTICE REHNQUIST delivered the opinion of the Court.

Respondents Bank of New England Corporation (BNE), Hartford National Corporation (HNC), and Bank of Boston Corporation (BBC) are bank holding companies which applied to the Federal Reserve Board to obtain approval for the acquisition of banks or bank holding companies in New England States other than the ones in which they are principally located. Petitioners Northeast Bancorp, Inc., Union Trust Company, and Citicorp opposed these proposed acquisitions in proceedings before the Board. The Board approved the acquisitions, and the Court of Appeals for the Second Circuit affirmed the orders of the Board. Petitioners sought certiorari, contending that the acquisitions were not authorized by the Bank Holding Company Act of 1956, 70 Stat. 133, as amended, 12 U. S. C. § 1841 et seq., and that, if they were authorized by that Act, the state statutes which permitted the acquisitions in each case violated the Commerce Clause and the Compact Clause of the United States Constitution. We granted certiorari because of the importance of these issues and we now affirm.

The Bank Holding Company Act (BHCA) regulates the acquisition of state and national banks by bank holding companies. The Act generally defines a bank as any institution organized under state or federal law which "(1) accepts deposits that the depositor has a legal right to withdraw on demand, and (2) engages in the business of making commercial loans." 12 U. S. C. § 1841(c). The Act defines a bank holding company as any corporation, partnership, business trust, association, or similar organization that owns or has control over a bank or another bank holding company. §§ 1841(a)(1), (b); see § 1841(a)(5). Before a company may become a bank holding company, or a bank holding company may acquire a bank or substantially all of the assets of a bank, the Act requires it to obtain the approval of the Federal Reserve Board. § 1842.

The Board will evaluate the proposed transaction for anticompetitive effects, financial and managerial resources, community needs, and the like. § 1842(c). In addition, § 3(d) of the Act, 12 U. S. C. § 1842(d), known as "the Douglas Amendment," prohibits the Board from approving an application of a bank holding company or bank located in one State to acquire a bank located in another State, or substantially all of its assets, unless the acquisition "is specifically authorized by the statute laws of the State in which such bank is located, by language to that effect and not merely by implication." Pursuant to the Douglas Amendment, a number of States recently have enacted statutes which selectively authorize interstate bank acquisitions on a regional basis. This case requires us to consider the validity of these statutes.

From 1956 to 1972, the Douglas Amendment had the effect of completely barring interstate bank acquisitions because no State had enacted the requisite authorizing statute. Beginning in 1972, several States passed statutes permitting such acquisitions in limited circumstances or for specialized purposes. For example, Iowa passed a grandfathering statute which had the effect of permitting the only out-of-state bank holding company owning an Iowa bank to maintain and expand its in-state banking activities, Iowa Code § 524.1805 (1983); see Iowa Independent Bankers v. Board of Governors, 511 F.2d 1288, cert. denied, 423 U.S. 875 (1975); Washington authorized out-of-state purchasers to acquire failing local banks, Wash. Rev. Code § 30.04.230(4)(a) (Supp. 1985); and Delaware allowed out-of-state bank holding companies to set up special purpose banks, such as credit card operations, in Delaware so long as they do not compete in other respects with locally controlled full-service banks, Del. Code Ann., Tit. 5, § 801 et seq. (Supp. 1984).

Beginning with Massachusetts in December 1982, several States have enacted statutes lifting the Douglas Amendment ban on interstate acquisitions on a reciprocal basis within their geographic regions. The Massachusetts Act specifically provides that an out-of-state bank holding company with its principal place of business in one of the other New England States (Connecticut, Maine, New Hampshire, Rhode Island, and Vermont), which is not directly or indirectly controlled by another corporation with its principal place of business located outside of New England, may establish or acquire a Massachusetts-based bank or bank holding company, provided that the other New England State accords equivalent reciprocal privileges to Massachusetts banking organizations. Mass. Gen. Laws Ann., ch. 167A, § 2 (West 1984). In June 1983, Connecticut followed suit by adopting a substantially similar statute. 1983 Conn. Pub. Acts 83–411.

The other New England States have taken different courses or have not acted. Rhode Island, in May 1983, authorized acquisition of local banks by out-of-state bank holding companies on a reciprocal basis similarly limited to the New England region, but this geographic limitation will expire on June 30, 1986, after which the authorization will extend nationwide subject only to the reciprocity requirement. R. I. Gen. Laws § 19–30–1 et seq. (Supp. 1984). Since February 1984, Maine has permitted banking organizations from all other States to acquire local banks without any reciprocity requirement. Me. Rev. Stat. Ann., Tit. 9–B, § 1013 (Supp. 1984–1985). At the other extreme, New Hampshire and Vermont have not enacted any statute releasing the Douglas Amendment's ban on interstate bank acquisitions.

One predictable effect of the regionally restrictive statutes will apparently be to allow the growth of regional multistate bank holding companies which can compete with the established banking giants in New York, California, Illinois, and Texas. See 740 F.2d 203, 209, and n. 16 (1984). The Massachusetts and Connecticut statutes have prompted at least 15 other States to consider legislation which, according to the Federal Reserve Board, would establish interstate banking regions in all parts of the country. 70 Fed. Res. Bull. 374, 375–376 (1984). At least seven of these States have already enacted the necessary statutes. * * *

The Douglas Amendment to the BHCA prohibits the Board from approving the application of a bank holding company or a bank located in one State to acquire a bank located in another State, or substantially all of its assets, unless the acquisition "is specifically authorized by the statute laws of the State in which such bank is located, by language to that effect and not merely by implication." § 1842(d). Clearly the proposed acquisitions with which we deal in this case must be consistent with the Douglas Amendment, or they are invalid as a matter of federal statutory law. If the Massachusetts and Connecticut statutes allowing regional acquisitions are not the type of state statutes contemplated by the Douglas Amendment, they would not lift the ban imposed by the general prohibition of the Douglas Amendment. While petitioners blend together arguments about the meaning of the Douglas Amendment with arguments about the effect of the Commerce Clause, U.S. Const., Art. I, § 8, cl. 3, we think the contentions are best treated separately.

The Board resolved the statutory issue in favor of the state statutes, concluding that they were the sort of laws contemplated by the Douglas Amendment. While the Board apparently does not consider itself expert on any constitutional issues raised, it is nonetheless an authoritative voice on the meaning of a federal banking statute. Securities Industry Assn. v.

Board of Governors of Federal Reserve System, 468 U.S. 207 (1984). The Board may have applied a higher standard than was necessary when it analyzed the Douglas Amendment to see whether there was a "clear authorization" for selective lifting of the ban, such as the Massachusetts and Connecticut statutes undertake to do. Whether or not so stringent a standard was applicable, we think the Board was correct in concluding that it was in fact met in this case.

The language of the Douglas Amendment plainly permits States to lift the federal ban entirely, as has been done by Maine. It does not specifically indicate that a State may partially lift the ban, for example in limited circumstances, for special types of acquisitions, or for purchasers from a certain geographic region. On the other hand, it also does not specifically indicate that a State is allowed only two alternatives: leave the federal ban in place or lift it completely. The Board concluded that the language "does not appear *on its face* to authorize discrimination" by region or "to meet the stringent test of explicitness laid down by" this Court in the dormant Commerce Clause cases. 70 Fed. Res. Bull., at 384. We need not resolve this issue because we agree with the Board that the legislative history of the Amendment supplies a sufficient indication of Congress' intent.

At the time of the BHCA, interstate branch banking was already prohibited by the McFadden Act. 12 U. S. C. § 36(c). The bank holding company device, however, had been created to get around this restriction. A holding company would purchase banks in different localities both within and without a State, and thereby provide the equivalent of branch banking. One of the major purposes of the BHCA was to eliminate this loophole. H. R. Rep. No. 609, 84th Cong., 1st Sess., 2–6 (1955); 101 Cong. Rec. 4407 (1955) (remarks of Rep. Wier); id., at 8028–8029 (remarks of Rep. Patman); 102 Cong. Rec. 6858–6859 (1956) (remarks of Sen. Douglas). As enacted by the House in 1955, the BHCA contained a flat ban on interstate bank acquisitions. The legislative history from the House makes it clear that the policies of community control and local responsiveness of banks inspired this flat ban. See 101 Cong. Rec. A2454 (1955) (remarks of Rep. Wier); id., at 8030–8031 (remarks of Rep. Rains); H. R. Rep. No. 609, supra, at 2–6.

The Douglas Amendment was added on the floor of the Senate. Its entire legislative history is confined to the Senate debate. In such circumstances, the comments of individual legislators carry substantial weight, especially when they reflect a consensus as to the meaning and objectives of the proposed legislation though not necessarily the wisdom of that legislation. The instant case is not a situation where the comments of an individual legislator, even a sponsor, is at odds with the language of the statute or other traditionally more authoritative indicators of legislative intent such as the conference or committee reports.

The bill reported out by the Senate Committee on Banking and Currency permitted interstate bank acquisitions conditioned only on approval by the Federal Reserve Board. This approach apparently was favored by many of the large bank holding companies which sought further expansion, see, e. g., Control of Bank Holding Companies, 1955: Hearings on S. 880 et al. before the Subcommittee of the Senate Committee on Banking and Currency, 84th Cong., 1st Sess., 132, 136 (1955) (testimony of Ellwood Jenkins, First Bank Stock Corp.), 298–299 (Baldwin Maull, Marine Midland Corp.), 320 (Cameron Thomson, Northwest Bancorporation), cf. 375, 385 (Frank N. Belgrano, Jr., Transamerica Corp.), and by some who thought the total ban in the House bill offensive to States' rights, see 102 Cong. Rec. 6752 (1956) (remarks of Sen. Robertson, floor manager of Committee bill, quoting Sen. Maybank).

The Douglas Amendment was a compromise between the two extremes that also accommodated the States' rights concern:

> "Our amendment would prohibit bank holding companies from purchasing banks in other States unless such purchases by out-of-State holding companies were specifically permitted by law in such States." Id., at 6860 (remarks of Sen. Douglas).

Accord, ibid. (remarks of Sen. Bennett in opposition to the Amendment).

Of central concern to this litigation, the Douglas compromise did not simply leave to each State a choice one way or the other–either to permit or bar interstate acquisitions of local banks–but to allow each State flexibility in its approach. Senator Douglas explained that under his amendment bank holding companies would be permitted to acquire banks in other States "only to the degree that State laws expressly permit them." Id., at 6858. Petitioners contend that by the phrase "to the degree" Senator Douglas intended merely a quantitative reference to the number of States which might lift the ban, and did not mean that a State could partially lift the ban. Petitioners' contention, however, is refuted by the close analogy drawn by Senator Douglas between his amendment and the McFadden Act, 12 U. S. C. § 36(c):

> "The organization of branch banks proceeded very rapidly in the 1920's, and to check their growth various States passed laws limiting, and in some cases preventing it, as in the case of Illinois. National banks had previously been implicitly prohibited from opening branches, and there was a strong movement to remove this prohibition and completely open up the field for the national banks. This, however, was not done. Instead, by the McFadden Act and other measures, national banks have been permitted to open branches only to the degree permitted by State laws and State authorities.
>
>   "I may say that what our amendment aims to do is to carry over into the field of holding companies the same provisions which already apply for branch banking under the McFadden Act—namely, our amendment will permit out-of-State holding companies to acquire banks in other States only to the degree that State laws expressly permit them; and that is the provision of the McFadden Act." Ibid.

See id., at 6860.

In enacting the McFadden Act in 1927, Congress relaxed federal restrictions on branch banking by national banks, but at the same time subjected them to the same branching restrictions imposed by the States on state banks. First National Bank v. Walker Bank & Trust Co., 385 U.S. 252, 258 (1966). Congress intended "to leave the question of the desirability of branch banking up to the States," ibid., and to permit branch banking by national banks " 'in only those States the laws of which permit branch banking, and only to the extent that the State laws permit branch banking.' " Id., at 259 (quoting Sen. Glass, 76 Cong. Rec. 2511 (1933)). The McFadden Act did not offer the States an all-or-nothing choice with respect to branch banking. As Senator Douglas observed, some States had *limited* intrastate branching by state banks, and others like Illinois had *prohibited* it altogether.

This variative approach to intrastate branching was nicely illustrated at the time by the structure in New York, which Senator Douglas described as follows: "In New York the State is divided into 10 zones. Branch banking is permitted within each of the zones, but a bank cannot have branches in another zone." 102 Cong. Rec. 6858 (1956). At the same time, Pennsylvania permitted branching in contiguous counties. Upper Darby National Bank v. Myers, 386 Pa. 12, 124 A. 2d 116 (1956). In view of this analogy to the McFadden Act and Senator Douglas' explanation of that Act, there can be no other conclusion but that Congress contemplated that some States might partially lift the ban on interstate banking without opening themselves up to interstate banking from everywhere in the Nation.

Not only are the Massachusetts and Connecticut statutes consistent with the Douglas Amendment's anticipation of differing approaches to interstate banking, but they are also consistent with the broader purposes underlying the BHCA as a whole and the Douglas Amendment in particular to retain local, community-based control over banking. Faced with growing competition from nonbank financial services that are not confined within state lines, these States sought an alternative that allowed expansion and growth of local banks without opening their borders to unimpeded interstate banking. The Connecticut General Assembly established a Commission in 1979 to study the problem. It concluded:

> "Both at the national and state levels the philosophy underlying our structure of bank regulation has been to promote a pluralistic banking system–a system comprised of many units, rather than a highly concentrated system made up of a few large banks. The promotion of local ownership and control of banks has as one of its objectives the preservation of a close relationship between those in our communities who need credit and those who provide credit. To allow the control of credit that is essential for the health of our state economy to pass to hands that are not immediately responsive to the interests of Connecticut citizens and businesses would not, we believe, serve our state well. Similarly, to expose our smaller banks to the rigors of unlimited competition from large out-of-state banking organizations–particular-

ly at a time when deregulation of banking products at the federal level is already putting strains on the resources of smaller banks–would not be wise." Report to the General Assembly of the State of Connecticut (Jan. 5, 1983), 4 App. in No. 84–4047 (CA2), pp. 1230, 1240–1241.

Rather, the Commission proposed "an experiment in regional banking" as a first step toward full interstate banking which "would afford the legislature an opportunity to make its own calculus of the benefits and detriments that might result from a broader program of interstate banking." Id., at 1241–1242. The Connecticut General Assembly adopted the Commission's recommendations, and we believe that Connecticut's approach is precisely what was contemplated by Congress when it adopted the Douglas Amendment.

We hold that the Connecticut and Massachusetts statutes are of the kind contemplated by the Douglas Amendment to lift its bar against interstate acquisitions.

Petitioners contend that the regional limitation in the Massachusetts and Connecticut statutes burdens commerce from without the region while permitting a free flow of commerce among the States within the region. They provide numerous citations to prove that one of the principal purposes of the Framers of the Constitution was to break up and forestall precisely this type of economic "Balkanization" into confederations of States to the detriment of the welfare of the Union as a whole. There can be little dispute that the dormant Commerce Clause would prohibit a group of States from establishing a system of regional banking by excluding bank holding companies from outside the region if Congress had remained completely silent on the subject. Lewis v. BT Investment Managers, Inc., 447 U.S. 27, 39–44 (1980). Nor can there be serious question that an individual State acting entirely on its own authority would run afoul of the dormant Commerce Clause if it sought to comprehensively regulate acquisitions of local banks by out-of-state holding companies. Sporhase v. Nebraska ex rel. Douglas, 458 U.S. 941 (1982).

But that is not our case. Here the commerce power of Congress is not dormant, but has been exercised by that body when it enacted the Bank Holding Company Act and the Douglas amendment to the Act. Congress has authorized by the latter amendment the Massachusetts and Connecticut statutes which petitioners challenge as violative of the Commerce Clause. When Congress so chooses, state actions which it plainly authorizes are invulnerable to constitutional attack under the Commerce Clause. Western & Southern Life Insurance Co. v. State Board of Equalization, 451 U.S. 648, 653–654 (1981). Petitioners' Commerce Clause attack on the challenged acquisitions therefore fails.

Petitioners maintain that the Massachusetts and Connecticut statutes constitute a compact to exclude non-New England banking organizations which violates the Compact Clause, U. S. Const., Art. I, § 10, cl. 3, because Congress has not specifically approved it. We have some doubt as to whether there is an agreement amounting to a compact. The two statutes are similar in that they both require reciprocity and impose a regional limitation, both legislatures favor the establishment of regional banking in New England, and there is evidence of cooperation among legislators, officials, bankers, and others in the two States in studying the idea and lobbying for the statutes. But several of the classic indicia of a compact are missing. No joint organization or body has been established to regulate regional banking or for any other purpose. Neither statute is conditioned on action by the other State, and each State is free to modify or repeal its law unilaterally. Most importantly, neither statute requires a reciprocation of the regional limitation. Bank holding companies based in Maine, which has no regional limitation, and Rhode Island, which will drop the regional limitation in 1986, are permitted by the two statutes to acquire Massachusetts and Connecticut banks. These two States are included in the ostensible compact under petitioners' theory, yet one does not impose the exclusion to which petitioners so strenuously object and the other plans to drop it after two years.

But even if we were to assume that these state actions constitute an agreement or compact, not every such agreement violates the Compact Clause. Virginia v. Tennessee, 148 U.S. 503 (1893).

> "The application of the Compact Clause is limited to agreements that are 'directed to the formation of any combination tending to the increase of political power in the States, which may encroach upon or interfere with the just supremacy of the United States.' " New Hampshire v. Maine, 426 U.S. 363, 369 (1976), quoting *Virginia v. Tennessee*, supra, at 519.

See United States Steel Corp. v. Multistate Tax Comm'n, 434 U.S. 452, 471 (1978).

In view of the Douglas Amendment to the BHCA, the challenged state statutes which comply with that Act cannot possibly infringe federal supremacy. To the extent that the state statutes might conflict in a particular situation with other federal statutes, such as the provision under which the Federal Deposit Insurance Corporation will arrange for the acquisition of failing banks by out-of-state bank holding companies, 12 U. S. C. § 1823(f), they would be pre-empted by those statutes, and therefore any Compact Clause argument would be academic. Petitioners also assert that the alleged regional compact impermissibly offends the sovereignty of sister States outside of New England. We do not see how the statutes in question either enhance the *political* power of the New England States at the expense of other States or have an "impact on our federal structure." *United States Steel Corp. v. Multistate Tax Comm'n*, supra, at 471, 473.

Petitioners argued before the Board and the Court of Appeals that the Massachusetts and Connecticut statutes violated the Equal Protection Clause, U.S. Const., Amdt. 14, § 2, by excluding bank holding companies from some States while admitting those from others. * * *

Here the States in question–Massachusetts and Connecticut–are not favoring local corporations at the expense of out-of-state corporations. They are favoring out-of-state corporations domiciled within the New England region over out-of-state corporations from other parts of the country, and to this extent their laws may be said to "discriminate" against the latter. But with respect to the business of banking, we do not write on a clean slate; recently in Lewis v. BT Investment Managers, Inc., 447 U.S., at 38, we said that "banking and related financial activities are of profound local concern." * * *

We _____ the _____ which spurred Massachusetts and Connecticut _____ rent as they are from those w_____ a statute in *Metropolitan*, me_____ qual protection claims under _____ chi, 443 U.S. 55, 67 (1979). _____

We _____ stion comply with the Dougla_____ the Commerce Clause, the Co_____ se of the United States Consti_____ s is therefore Affirmed.

MADAM ____

1. _____ cation that did not apply to othe_____

2. _____ e in interstate branching before banks were. Did ___ _____ uality between state and federal thrifts in states that did not authorize interstate branching for state thrifts?

3. The regional, reciprocal interstate banking state statutes or compacts at issue in the *Northeast Bancorp.* case caught on and fueled the interstate banking boom. Many bank holding companies took advantage of the authority to purchase banks outside their home states. The *Northeast Bancorp.* case suggested that one effect of the regional limitations contained in many states' laws was to permit regional bank holding companies to grow large enough to be able to compete with banks located in New York, California, Illinois, and Texas. Did regional bank holding companies achieve this competitive position?

SECTION 2. THE RIEGLE–NEAL ACT AND BEYOND

The Riegle–Neal Interstate Banking and Branching Efficiency Act of 1994, Pub. L. No. 103–328, 108 Stat. 2338, struck down the federal restrictions on interstate banking and interstate branching. As the House Report on the bill noted:

Many of the geographic constraints on banking have been in place for more than half a century. Since then, Americans have become more mobile, and revolutions in technology and communications have altered the way we do our banking, and invest our money. In response, the States have loosened geographic constraints on banks: 49 states and the District of Columbia presently permit some form of interstate banking, and 39 states now permit some variation of statewide intrastate branching. However, the basic federal restrictions remain in place.

> The Committee believes [the bill] is an appropriate and necessary federal response to ongoing changes in the structure and regulation of the United States banking system.[8]

The Committee Report noted that the elimination of these geographic restrictions would provide numerous benefits.

> "First, it will give banks an opportunity to structure themselves more efficiently, eliminate duplicative functions, and reduce expenses. Second it will promote a safer and sounder banking system. * * * Third, it will promote customer convenience. * * * Fourth, it will encourage competition by making it easier for institutions to enter markets that are not now fully competitive."[9]

A. REPEAL OF THE DOUGLAS AMENDMENT

The Riegle–Neal Act repealed the Douglas Amendment to the Bank Holding Company Act and replaced it with a provision that permitted a bank holding company to acquire a bank located in a state other than the holding company's home state "without regard to whether such transaction is prohibited under the law of any state." 12 U.S.C.A. § 1842(d)(1)(A). This language preempts state legislation creating regional, reciprocal interstate banking compacts, such as that at issue in *Northeast Bancorp*. States were not permitted to "opt out" of interstate banking, but were permitted to prohibit the acquisition of a new (or *de novo*) bank. The statute provides, however, that these "State age laws" will only be honored up to a maximum age for the target bank of five years. 12 U.S.C.A. § 1842(d)(1)(B). Many of the states that enacted "age laws" have since repealed them.[10]

B. INTERSTATE BRANCHING

Congress, recognizing that branching had historically been a matter of state law, subjected the two methods of interstate branching to some state control in the form of an "opt out" and "opt in" procedure.

The first method of establishing interstate branches is Riegle–Neal's authorization for bank holding companies with "adequately capitalized and adequately managed" bank subsidiaries to merge their banks in

---

8. H.R. Rep. No. 103–448, at 19, reprinted in 1994 U.S.C.C.A.N. 2039, 2042.

9. Id. 2042–43 (quoting Under Secretary of the Treasury Frank N. Newman).

10. Jennifer Gordon, States Easing Interstate Branch Curbs, Am. Banker, Mar. 19, 2001.

different states and operate the interstate offices as branches effective June 1, 1997. 12 U.S.C.A. § 1831u(f)(6). This authority, however, was subject to state "opt out" prior to June 1, 1997. Only two states–Montana and Texas–enacted opt out legislation. Texas prohibited interstate branching until September 1,1999, and Montana until October, 2001. Pursuant to this authority, many large bank holding companies with bank subsidiaries located in various states merged their banking operations into one or two bank subsidiaries.[11]

The second method of establishing interstate branches is by application for a *de novo* branch or acquisition of an existing bank branch. This authority, however, is subject to state "opt in." See 12 U.S.C.A. §§ 36(g), 1828(d)(4)(A), 1831u(a)(4)(A).[12] Many states did opt in to *de novo* interstate branching but only on certain conditions such as reciprocity. By 2004, only 18 states permitted an out-of-state bank to branch de novo, and 14 of those states conditioned de novo branching on reciprocal home state laws.[13] The remaining states allowed an out-of-state bank to establish an in-state branch but only upon the acquisition of an existing host-state institution. In many states the bank to be acquired must have been in existence for a minimum period of time which may be as high as five years. Because there was no comparable limitation on the ability of a federally chartered thrift institution to branch across state lines, some bank and financial holding companies added a federally chartered thrift institution to assist in interstate expansion into states where de novo bank branching was not permitted.

Riegle–Neal permitted an interstate bank merger so long as the resulting bank continued to be adequately capitalized and adequately managed upon the consummation of the merger. 12 U.S.C.A. § 1831u(b)(4). The Dodd–Frank Act increased the post-merger condition following an interstate bank merger to "well capitalized and well managed." Dodd–Frank Act, § 607.

The challenge of implementing interstate branching in a dual charter system was addressed in the Riegle–Neal Clarification Act of 1997. This statute permitted state banks to exercise the powers granted by their home states at interstate branches in host states, but only to the extent that national banks or the host state's state chartered banks could exercise the same powers. The purpose of this legislation was to ensure that national banks did not enjoy any significant advantage over state banks in establishing an interstate branch. The 1997 clarification further provided that host state laws only apply to the interstate branches of out-of-state state banks to the same extent that host state laws apply to

---

11. Some bank holding companies continued to maintain a separate bank in a state without interest rate limits–like Delaware or South Dakota–from which to issue the bank's credit cards.

12. Riegle-Neal repealed 12 U.S.C. § 30(b), which permitted headquarters relocation for a national bank within 30 miles of its former headquarters. This section had been used to relocate national bank offices across state lines and retain the former main office as an interstate branch.

13. Ben Jackson, Statehouse Report: Illinois Weighing Cost and Benefit of Old Defense, Am. Banker, Mar. 12, 2004.

interstate branches established by out-of-state national banks. 12 U.S.C.A. § 1831a(j)(1). The application of host state laws to interstate branches of national banks under Riegle–Neal is relevant to the preemption debate and is discussed further in Chapter 4.

The Dodd–Frank Act removed the remaining state control over interstate branching that was permitted in the Riegle–Neal Act. Dodd–Frank Act, § 613. A national bank or state insured bank is permitted to branch in a new state so long as the law of the state in which the new branch is located would permit establishment of the branch if the bank attempting to branch were a state bank chartered in that state.

C. THE BAN ON INTERSTATE BRANCHING FOR DEPOSIT PRODUCTION

The Riegle–Neal Act bans the use of interstate branches for deposit production. This is meant to preclude an out-of-state bank or bank holding company from draining deposits from the local community to fund loans in another state where the bank does business. The Act directed federal bank regulators to review a branch's loan portfolio if the ratio of the interstate branch's in-state loans to in-state deposits is less than half the state average. The purpose of such review is to determine whether the branch adequately meets the needs of the community. If the regulatory review finds that the branch is not reasonably helping to meet the credit needs of the communities it serves, it could be subject to regulatory sanction. This requirement was implemented by a joint final rule issued in September 1997.[14] 12 C.F.R. §§ 25 (OCC), 208 (FRB), 369 (FDIC).

QUESTIONS AND NOTES

1. What are the efficiencies of operating a single bank with multiple interstate branches rather than a multi-bank holding company with separately chartered banks in each state? See Allen N. Berger & Robert DeYoung, The Effects of Geographic Expansion on Bank Efficiency, 19 J. of Fin. Serv. Res. (2001) (concluding based on an empirical study that there may be no particular optimal geographic scope for banking organizations; some may operate efficiently within a single region, while others may operate efficiently nationwide or internationally).

2. According to a 2004 survey by the Conference of State Bank Supervisors, three states (Minnesota, Nebraska, and New York) still had some *intra*state branching limitations. Is there any reason states should continue to limit branching within their borders in a world of *inter*state branching?

3. Do you believe that there will be further consolidation of banks in the United States?

4. Where is a national bank with interstate branches "located" for purposes of diversity jurisdiction? See Wachovia Bank, N.A. v. Schmidt, 545

---

14. 62 Fed. Reg. 44,734 (Sept. 10, 1997). GLBA broadened this requirement to apply not only to interstate branches established pursuant to Riegle–Neal, but also to "any bank or branch of a bank controlled by an out-of-State bank holding company." 67 Fed. Reg. 46,842 (July 17, 2002).

U.S. 1113 (2005) in Chapter 4, which held that a national bank is "located" for diversity jurisdiction purposes in the state of its headquarters and not in every state in which it maintains a branch office.

See also OCC Interpretive Letter #952 (Feb. 2003) (concluding that Bank of America's corporate location is the bank's main office in Charlotte, N.C., not the place where it was located in the bank's historical organization certificate, San Francisco, CA).

5. Should bans on the use of interstate branches for deposit production be kept in place? Why should a bank be limited where it uses its deposits? Does this requirement duplicate the Community Reinvestment Act (discussed in Chapter 6)? Are both needed?

6. According to FDIC statistics, between 1934 and 1988 there were each year between 13,000 and 14,500, commercial banks operating in the United States. The high number was 14,496 banks in 1984. Since 1988, the number of commercial banks declined each year to 6,669 in 2010. The number of branches, however, grew steadily from 0 in 1934 to 41,799 in 1984 (the year with the largest number of banks) and continued to grow when the number of banks began to decline from the 1984 high. In 2010, there were 83,320 bank branches.

7. In response to Wal–Mart's application to charter an industrial loan company (ILC) (now abandoned) in Utah, some states have considered legislation to prohibit an ILC from branching into the state. Federal bank regulators have warned that such restrictions may not comply with the Riegle–Neal Act which requires that a state's branch policy apply equally to all banks. Thus, a ban on out-of state ILC branches could have the effect of excluding all in-state branching by out-of-state banks.

The regulators did suggest that a state law permitting all out-of-state banks to establish de novo branches in the state, but prohibiting all banks from having a branch on the premises of a commercial affiliate (i.e., Wal–Mart), would achieve the desired purpose and be consistent with the Riegle–Neal Act. Joe Adler, States Told ILC Bills Could Have Unintended Effect, Am. Banker, Aug. 7, 2006.

SECTION 3. BANK MERGERS AND ACQUISITIONS

The banking industry has experienced significant consolidation over the last several decades, as the number of banks is less than one-half of the number of banks in 1984. Some financial giants emerged from that consolidation process, including Bank of America, JPMorgan Chase, and Citibank.[15]

These mergers and acquisitions present a number of issues for lawyers. Corporate law issues are relevant in determining the form of the

---

15. Bank of America resulted from a combination between NationsBank and Bank of America. NationsBank had grown through an aggressive expansion strategy that included the acquisition of Republic Bank of Texas and Barnett Banks of Florida. J.P. Morgan Chase resulted from the combination of Chase and J.P. Morgan, which was preceded by the combination of Chase Manhattan and Chemical Bank. J.P. Morgan Chase merged with Bank One in 2004 in a $58 billion merger.

combination and required shareholder approvals. Securities law issues are implicated where shares of a publicly traded company are purchased or exchanged through a tender offer. Finally, the necessary regulatory approvals must be obtained from the appropriate bank regulatory agency, which, along with the Department of Justice and, in certain cases, the Federal Trade Commission, will review the antitrust implications of the proposed combination.

A. FORM OF COMBINATION

Business combinations may be effected in a number of ways. One method is a merger where one bank is merged into the other, which is then referred to as the surviving entity. The surviving entity assumes the liabilities and assets of the other bank. An existing holding company may acquire an existing bank. Such an acquisition could be structured through a reverse or forward triangular merger in which the acquiring bank holding company creates a new shell bank and the target bank is then merged with the shell bank. If the new subsidiary is the survivor, the transaction is a forward triangular merger; if the target bank is the survivor, the transaction is a reverse triangular merger. Two holding companies might merge and then elect to operate their banks as separate subsidiaries or merge the bank subsidiaries together. A variation is to form a new holding company which purchases two existing banks and either operates them as separate subsidiaries or merges them into one bank through one of the methods described above. A bank may expand its operations by purchasing a branch of another bank. This is usually accomplished through a purchase and assumption transaction in which the acquiring bank purchases the branch's assets and assumes its liabilities. Purchase and assumption transactions are frequently used when the FDIC has taken over an insolvent bank and sells it to a healthy institution. When the FDIC arranges the purchase and assumption of a failed institution, it sometimes agrees to indemnify the purchaser from some liabilities, buy back inferior quality assets, or to share in any losses incurred on certain pools of assets to induce the purchaser to rescue the insolvent institution.

Mergers and acquisitions raise a number of regulatory concerns. Shareholder approval may be required by state corporate laws. This requires that proxies be solicited from shareholders. Where the selling bank is a publicly held bank, the share purchase, either by cash or exchange of shares, may be accomplished through a public tender offer. This is simply an offer to purchase shares, usually conditioned on financing and the acquisition of a specified amount of shares that will assure control. This process is regulated under the federal securities laws and SEC rules.

Unlike the sometimes contentious fights that occur in other industries, most bank tender offers are not contested. Nevertheless, fights do occasionally arise. Twenty-three hostile takeovers occurred between 1984 and 1988.[16] In 2001, a highly publicized battle erupted over First Union's efforts to acquire control of Wachovia. A competing offer for Wachovia was made by SunTrust Banks, but First Union prevailed in this $14.7 billion merger after a stiff fight.[17]

B. BUSINESS ISSUES

The merger and acquisition process is a complicated one, both in the context of business requirements and legal restrictions. A key business consideration is the valuation of the transaction: how much is the buyer willing to pay? The valuation process is aided by investment bankers who analyze the target's financial position. The investment bankers issue opinions on the fairness of the price proposed for an acquisition. This "fairness opinion" has been the subject of litigation on such issues as whether an adequate investigation was made before the opinion was rendered. In determining whether the price is fair, investment bankers use a number of objective measures, including the price-to-earnings ratio, return on equity, and EBITA (earnings before interest, taxes, depreciation, and amortization). There may also be intangible factors, such as asset quality, management, and cost savings, to consider in the valuation process. A large bank may also be willing to pay more for a small bank than its earnings or other objective measures might warrant in order to gain access to a new market.

A decision must be made on how to fund the acquisition. Should there be an exchange of stock or a cash purchase? If the latter, what is the source of the funds and how will payments in cash or the incurrence of additional debt to fund the acquisition affect the acquiring bank's financial position? Tax issues must also be considered. Many acquisitions are structured as tax-free, stock-for-stock exchanges. Often, complex merger agreements set the exchange price values at particular ratios because the merging banks' respective stock prices may fluctuate during the period required for shareholder approval and regulatory review. The agreement may include a "walkaway" provision that will allow either party to cancel

---

16. One such takeover involved the acquisition of the Irving Bank by the Bank of New York (BONY) in 1988. BONY was unsuccessful in its 1998 hostile takeover attempt of Mellon Bank in Pittsburgh. Saul Steinberg's Leasco Data Processing Corp. was unsuccessful in its hostile bid to acquire control of Chemical Bank in 1969. In 1999, hostile takeover bids were mounted abroad by BNP for Paribas and Societe Generale, and by Bank of Scotland for Natwest. In 2004, Mitsubishi Tokyo and UFJ in Tokyo were considering a merger that would create the largest bank in the work with assets of $1.75 trillion. A competing bid for UFJ was made by Sumitomo Mitsui, which is partially owned by Goldman Sachs. This was Japan's first takeover fight involving a bank.

17. For a thoughtful opinion discussing this failed hostile attempt, see First Union Corp. v. SunTrust Banks, Inc., 2001 WL 1885686 (N.C. Super. Aug. 10, 2001), available at <www.ncbusi nesscourt.net>. See also Lijun K. Yang, First Union v. SunTrust Banks: The Fight for Wachovia and Its Impact on North Carolina Corporate Law, 6 N.C. Banking Inst. 335 (2002). Wachovia paid $37 million to settle charges brought by the SEC that it failed to properly disclose over $500 million of stock purchases of First Union stock. The First Union and SunTrust bids were stock bids, so the values of the competing offers fluctuated with the respective stock prices. The SEC alleged that the old Wachovia purchased First Union shares during the takeover battle and that these purchases may have increased First Union's stock price, making the First Union bid more attractive to the shareholders of the old Wachovia. SunTrust Banks later acquired Memphis-based National Commerce Financial Corporation.

the merger if the stock prices of the two banks become so disparate that the deal is no longer economically viable.

There are also a number of political issues to resolve in merger situations, and these can often make or break a deal. An important issue is which chief executive officer will lead the combined entity after a merger. The heads of large companies are often reluctant to step down in favor of their counterpart at the other institution. Sometimes the respective heads of the merger partners agree to be co-equals in the new enterprise, but that arrangement rarely works. The merger of Bank of America and NationsBank, and the merger of Citicorp and Travelers Group are two examples where such arrangements failed. Other political issues involve the name of the surviving entity. Many banks have long histories and are reluctant to see their name, and the corporate culture it denotes, disappear. The location of the new headquarters and the composition of the board of directors of the surviving entity are also often hotly negotiated.

When an agreement in principle is reached on a merger, the parties may memorialize that agreement in a letter of intent, which is followed by a more definitive merger agreement. The parties then prepare proxy materials for shareholder approval, and seek to obtain all necessary regulatory approvals. Due diligence investigations must be undertaken to assure the parties are receiving what they bargained for from each other. Due diligence involves an examination of the books and records of the company being acquired (or both parties in the event of a merger) and an inspection of important assets, particularly loans, to assure they are accurately represented.

Post merger operational issues must also be considered. An acquiring bank must determine how to combine its record keeping operations with those of the acquired bank. How will the two banks' computer systems interface? Are there duplicative branch offices that need to be closed? Is it possible to merge check clearing and other operations to save expenses? How many people will be laid off and how will those decisions be made?

Historically, an important issue in mergers was whether the "pooling of interests" method or "purchase" method of accounting would be used to reflect the acquisition. That decision had a serious effect on future earnings. Under the purchase method, any premium paid over the book value of the assets of the newly acquired bank was treated as goodwill that was required to be amortized as a charge against earnings over a maximum period of forty years. That charge operated as an expense and reduced earnings. For that reason, acquiring banks usually preferred to account for an acquisition under an alternative accounting method, the pooling of interests approach. In a pooling, the balance sheets of the two banks are combined at book value. Thus, no premium or goodwill is recognized and there is no reduction of earnings by amortization.

The pooling of interests method was criticized, however, for masking the actual accounting effect of an acquisition. In the early 1970s, the SEC attempted to require the use of the purchase method, but the agency's efforts to impose such a rule were unsuccessful, even though the United States was one of few countries worldwide that permitted pooling. The debate continued and the Financial Accounting Standards Board (FASB), the body responsible for setting accounting standards, proposed in 1999 that the pooling of accounts method should no longer be used to account for an acquisition, requiring instead the purchase method, and reducing the goodwill amortization period from forty to twenty years. The FASB proposal met opposition, and the FASB later adopted a different approach, eliminating pooling of interests accounting treatment for all mergers initiated after June 30, 2001, and eliminating the requirement that any goodwill resulting from the acquisition be amortized for all acquisitions consummated after June 30, 2001.[18] Goodwill must, however, be assessed annually (or more frequently if certain circumstances warrant) and charged against earnings if it is found to be impaired.

FASB's new rule had disastrous effects at some companies. World-Com, Inc. and Qwest Communications International were forced to take massive write-offs. Nortel Networks and JDS Uniphase Corp. collectively wrote off billions of dollars of merger goodwill. The AOL Time Warner merger proved to be unsuccessful, and FASB's new rule forced the company to announce in 2001 that in 2002 it would take a stunning $56 billion charge against earnings.

C. REGULATORY APPROVALS

Bank mergers and acquisitions must be approved by the boards of directors and shareholders of the institutions. A particular combination cannot be effected, however, until regulatory approval is received. The Bank Merger Act sets forth the procedure for review of mergers or other acquisitions of banks. 12 U.S.C.A. § 1828(c). This statute requires the prior written approval by the responsible bank regulatory agency for the acquiring or resulting entity. The agency must consider the effect of the combination on competition (discussed further below) and consider "financial and managerial resources and future prospects of the existing and proposed institutions, and the convenience and needs of the community to be served." 12 U.S.C.A. § 1828(c)(5). The Dodd–Frank Act adds a further requirement that the responsible agency consider the "risk to the stability of the United States banking or financial system." Dodd–Frank Act, § 604. Where a state chartered bank is involved in the combination, the state banking regulator must also approve the transaction.

The Bank Holding Company Act requires the Fed's prior written approval of any combination involving a bank holding company. 12 U.S.C.A. § 1842. The approval standards based on an analysis of competition and the convenience and needs of the community are comparable to

---

18. FASB Statement No. 141–Business Combinations (July 20, 2001) and FASB Statement No. 142—Goodwill and Other Intangible Assets (July 20, 2001).

those under the Bank Merger Act.[19] The Fed must consider when it approves the acquisition of any bank by a holding company the extent to which the acquisition, merger, or consolidation "would result in greater or more concentrated risks to the stability of the United States banking or financial system." Dodd–Frank Act, § 604. State corporate law is also relevant when two bank holding companies are merged.

QUESTIONS AND NOTES

1.   The merger of many large banks raises competitive concerns, but one result has been a strengthening of regional banks outside New York City and the development of strong national franchises.

2.   Do larger, well-capitalized banks pose a greater systemic threat than a large number of smaller, less well-capitalized banks?

SECTION 4.   ANTITRUST REVIEW

The standards for antitrust review to be conducted by the responsible bank regulatory agency are based on the Sherman Act and Clayton Act which govern combinations of nonbank businesses. The provisions of those statutes are virtually identical to the requirements of the Bank Merger Act and the Bank Holding Company Act. The responsible bank agency may not approve a combination "whose effect in any section of the country may be substantially to lessen competition." 12 U.S.C.A. §§ 1842(c)(1)(B) (BHCA) & 1828(c)(5)(B) (BMA). This standard mirrors section 7 of the Clayton Act. A unique aspect of bank combinations, however, is that the agency may approve a combination that would foreclose competition if "it finds that the anticompetitive effects of the proposed transaction are clearly outweighed in the public interest by the probable effect of the transaction in meeting the convenience and needs of the community to be served." 12 U.S.C.A. § 1842(c)(1)(B).

Once the merger has been reviewed and approved by the responsible agency, the merger is stayed for thirty days to permit an opportunity for the Department of Justice to challenge the approval. The Justice Department conducts its own review of the merger during the responsible agency's review. 12 U.S.C.A. § 1828(c)(4), (6) & (7). This period is shortened to fifteen days if the Department of Justice has not commented adversely with respect to the merger's effect on competition.[20] If the responsible agency denies approval of a merger or acquisition, the affected bank may seek judicial review. Irving Bank Corp. v. Board of Governors of the Federal Reserve System, 845 F.2d 1035 (D.C. Cir. 1988). If the agency approves the merger, but the Justice Department challenges it, court

---

19.   The Change in Bank Control Act of 1978, 12 U.S.C. § 1817(j), governs transactions that fall outside the Bank Merger Act or the Bank Holding Company Act, such as where an individual is acquiring control of a bank. This statute requires a report of changes in control to the appropriate federal banking regulator, which may disapprove the transaction.

20.   The 15–day period was added by the Riegle–Neal Act of 1994.

review of the Department of Justice action is de novo. United States v. First City National Bank of Houston, 386 U.S. 361 (1987).

In conducting the antitrust review, the responsible bank agency and the Department of Justice consider the section of the country (geographic market) and the line of commerce (product market) in which competition is likely to be foreclosed by the combination. Then they assess the lessening of competition that will result in that geographic and product market to determine if the concentration after the merger will be impermissibly high. Certain factors may be urged by the merging parties as mitigating the decrease in competition. Often in concentrated markets, divestitures of various branches must be made to satisfy antitrust concerns.

The Hart–Scott–Rodino Antitrust Improvements Act of 1976, 15 U.S.C. § 18a, establishes notification requirements and waiting periods for large acquisitions. When applicable, the statute requires notification to be made to the Justice Department and to the Federal Trade Commission (FTC). Most bank mergers and acquisitions are exempt from Hart–Scott–Rodino review if the transaction must be reviewed and approved by a federal banking regulator. The Gramm–Leach–Bliley Act (GLBA), however, extended application of Hart–Scott–Rodino to acquisitions of nonbank companies by financial holding companies and other transactions that do not require the prior approval of banking regulators.[21] After Dodd–Frank, exclusive Hart–Scott–Rodino review continues for acquisitions of nonbank entities by financial holding companies with assets of less than $10 billion, but acquisitions of companies that engage in financial in nature activities under section 4(k) of the BHCA (12 U.S.C.A. § 1843(k)) with more than $10 billion in assets are subject to premerger approval by the Fed and Hart–Scott–Rodino review. Dodd–Frank Act, § 604(a) (for acquisitions by FHCs of section 4(k) companies with assets exceeding $10 billion); Dodd–Frank Act, § 163 (for acquisitions by systemically significant financial companies of section 4(k) companies with assets exceeding $10 billion). Premerger notice for these large acquisitions of financial in nature companies under 12 U.S.C.A. § 1843(j) must include an evaluation of competitive concerns as well as an evaluation of systemic risk as required by Dodd–Frank. This marks the first time the Fed and the Department of Justice have been required to coordinate a review of nonbank acquisitions. It also marks the Fed's first experience in evaluating competitive concerns regarding nonbank product lines. In exercising its orderly liquidation authority over systemically significant financial companies, the Dodd–Frank Act provides that non-bank merger transactions initiated by the FDIC are subject to Hart–Scott–Rodino review, but that asset sales of nonbank entities may go forward without any approval or consent, mirror-

---

21. The Federal Trade Commission and the Department of Justice issued an interpretation concerning mixed mergers where only the baking aspects of the merger are subject to bank regulatory agency review under GLBA. In such instances, only the non-bank portion of the merger is subject to Hart–Scott–Rodino review. Federal Trade Commission, Formal Interpretation No. 17, 65 Fed. Reg. 17880 (Apr. 5, 2000).

ing the Hart–Scott–Rodino Act's exemption from review for transfers to or from a federal agency. Dodd–Frank Act, § 210.

A. DEFINITION OF THE RELEVANT MARKET

UNITED STATES v. PHILADELPHIA NATIONAL BANK

Supreme Court of the United States, 1963.
374 U.S. 321.

MR. JUSTICE BRENNAN delivered the opinion of the Court.

* * * Commercial banks are unique among financial institutions in that they alone are permitted by law to accept demand deposits. This distinctive power gives commercial banking a key role in the national economy. For banks do not merely deal in, but are actually a source of, money and credit; when a bank makes a loan by crediting the borrower's demand deposit account, it augments the Nation's credit supply. Furthermore, the power to accept demand deposits makes banks the intermediaries in most financial transactions (since transfers of substantial moneys are almost always by check rather than by cash) and, concomitantly, the repositories of very substantial individual and corporate funds. The banks' use of these funds is conditioned by the fact that their working capital consists very largely of demand deposits, which makes liquidity the guiding principle of bank lending and investing policies; thus it is that banks are the chief source of the country's short-term business credit.

Banking operations are varied and complex; "commercial banking" describes a congeries of services and credit devices.[22] But among them the creation of additional money and credit, the management of the checking-account system, and the furnishing of short-term business loans would appear to be the most important. For the proper discharge of these functions is indispensable to a healthy national economy, as the role of bank failures in depression periods attests.

The Philadelphia National Bank and Girard Trust Corn Exchange Bank are, respectively, the second and third largest of the 42 commercial banks with head offices in the Philadelphia metropolitan area, which consists of the City of Philadelphia and its three contiguous counties in Pennsylvania. The home county of both banks is the city itself; Pennsylvania law, however, permits branching into the counties contiguous to the

---

22. [n.5] The principal banking "products" are of course various types of credit, for example: unsecured personal and business loans, mortgage loans, loans secured by securities or accounts receivable, automobile installment and consumer goods installment loans, tuition financing, bank credit cards, revolving credit funds. Banking services include: acceptance of demand deposits from individuals, corporations, governmental agencies, and other banks; acceptance of time and savings deposits; estate and trust planning and trusteeship services; lock boxes and safety-deposit boxes; account reconciliation services; foreign department services (acceptances and letters of credit); correspondent services; investment advice. It should be noted that many other institutions are in the business of supplying credit, and so more or less in competition with commercial banks, for example: mutual savings banks, savings and loan associations, credit unions, personal-finance companies, sales-finance companies, private businessmen (through the furnishing of trade credit), factors, direct-lending government agencies, the Post Office, Small Business Investment Corporations, life insurance companies.

home county, and both banks have offices throughout the four-county area. PNB, a national bank, has assets of over $1,000,000,000, making it (as of 1959) the twenty-first largest bank in the Nation. Girard, a state bank, is a member of the FRS and is insured by the FDIC; it has assets of about $750,000,000. Were the proposed merger to be consummated, the resulting bank would be the largest in the four-county area, with (approximately) 36% of the area banks' total assets, 36% of deposits, and 34% of net loans. It and the second largest (First Pennsylvania Bank and Trust Company, now the largest) would have between them 59% of the total assets, 58% of deposits, and 58% of the net loans, while after the merger the four largest banks in the area would have 78% of total assets, 77% of deposits, and 78% of net loans. * * *

Appellees contended below that the Bank Merger Act, by directing the banking agencies to consider competitive factors before approving mergers, 12 U.S.C. (1958 ed., Supp. IV) § 1828 (c), immunizes approved mergers from challenge under the federal antitrust laws. We think the District Court was correct in rejecting this contention. No express immunity is conferred by the Act. Repeals of the antitrust laws by implication from a regulatory statute are strongly disfavored, and have only been found in cases of plain repugnancy between the antitrust and regulatory provisions. * * *

The statutory test is whether the effect of the merger "may be substantially to lessen competition" "in any line of commerce in any section of the country." We analyzed the test in detail in Brown Shoe Co. v. United States, 370 U.S. 294, and that analysis need not be repeated or extended here, for the instant case presents only a straightforward problem of application to particular facts.

We have no difficulty in determining the "line of commerce" (relevant product or services market) and "section of the country" (relevant geographical market) in which to appraise the probable competitive effects of appellees' proposed merger. We agree with the District Court that the cluster of products (various kinds of credit) and services (such as checking accounts and trust administration) denoted by the term "commercial banking," composes a distinct line of commerce. Some commercial banking products or services are so distinctive that they are entirely free of effective competition from products or services of other financial institutions; the checking account is in this category. Others enjoy such cost advantages as to be insulated within a broad range from substitutes furnished by other institutions. For example, commercial banks compete with small-loan companies in the personal-loan market; but the small-loan companies' rates are invariably much higher than the banks', in part, it seems, because the companies' working capital consists in substantial part of bank loans. Finally, there are banking facilities which, although in terms of cost and price they are freely competitive with the facilities provided by other financial institutions, nevertheless enjoy a settled consumer preference, insulating them, to a marked degree, from competition; this seems to be the case with savings deposits. In sum, it is clear that commercial banking is a market "sufficiently inclusive to be meaningful in terms of trade realities." Crown Zellerbach Corp. v. Federal Trade Comm'n, 296 F.2d 800, 811 (C. A. 9th Cir. 1961). * * *

[T]he four-county area in which appellees' offices are located would seem to be the relevant geographical market. Cf. *Brown Shoe Co.*, supra, at 338–339. In fact, the vast bulk of appellees' business originates in the four-county area. Theoretically, we should be concerned with the possibility that bank offices on the perimeter of the area may be in effective competition with bank offices within; actually, this seems to be a factor of little significance. * * *

Having determined the relevant market, we come to the ultimate question under § 7: whether the effect of the merger "may be substantially to lessen competition" in the relevant market. Clearly, this is not the kind of question which is susceptible of a ready and precise answer in most cases. It requires not merely an appraisal of the immediate impact of the merger upon competition, but a prediction of its impact upon competitive conditions in the future; this is what is meant when it is said that the amended § 7 was intended to arrest anticompetitive tendencies in their "incipiency." See *Brown Shoe* Co., supra, at 317, 322. Such a prediction is sound only if it is based upon a firm understanding of the structure of the relevant market; yet the relevant economic data are both complex and elusive. And unless businessmen can assess the legal consequences of a merger with some confidence, sound business planning is retarded. So also, we must be alert to the danger of subverting congressional intent by permitting a too-broad economic investigation. And so in any case in which it is possible, without doing violence to the congressional objective embodied in § 7, to simplify the test of illegality, the courts ought to do so in the interest of sound and practical judicial administration. This is such a case. We noted in *Brown Shoe Co.*, supra, at 315, that "the dominant theme pervading congressional consideration of the 1950 amendments [to § 7] was a fear of what was considered to be a rising tide of economic concentration in the American economy." This intense congressional concern with the trend toward concentration warrants dispensing, in certain cases, with elaborate proof of market structure, market behavior, or probable anticompetitive effects. Specifically, we think that a merger which produces a firm controlling an undue percentage share of the relevant market, and results in a significant increase in the concentration of firms in that market, is so inherently likely to lessen competition substantially that it must be enjoined in the absence of evidence clearly showing that the merger is not likely to have such anticompetitive effects. See United States v. Koppers Co., 202 F. Supp. 437 (D.C. W.D. Pa. 1962).

The merger of appellees will result in a single bank's controlling at least 30% of the commercial banking business in the four-county Philadelphia metropolitan area. Without attempting to specify the smallest market share which would still be considered to threaten undue concentration, we are clear that 30% presents that threat. Further, whereas presently the two largest banks in the area (First Pennsylvania and PNB) control between them approximately 44% of the area's commercial banking business, the two largest after the merger (PNB–Girard and First Pennsylvania) will control 59%. Plainly, we think, this increase of more than 33% in concentration must be regarded as significant. * * *

The judgment of the District Court is reversed and the case remanded with direction to enter judgment enjoining the proposed merger.

MR. JUSTICE WHITE took no part in the consideration or decision of this case. MR. JUSTICE HARLAN, whom MR. JUSTICE STEWART joins, dissents. * * *

UNITED STATES v. CONNECTICUT NATIONAL BANK

Supreme Court of the United States, 1974.
418 U.S. 656.

MR. JUSTICE POWELL delivered the opinion of the Court.

This case concerns the legality of a proposed consolidation of two nationally chartered commercial banks operating in adjoining regions of Connecticut. The United States brought a civil antitrust action challenging the consolidation under § 7 of the Clayton Act, 38 Stat. 731, as amended, 15 U.S.C. § 18. Following a lengthy trial and on the basis of extensive findings and conclusions, the United States District Court for the District of Connecticut dismissed the Government's complaint. The Government brought a direct appeal pursuant to the Expediting Act, 32 Stat. 823, as amended, 15 U.S.C. § 29, and the Court noted probable jurisdiction, 414 U.S. 1127 (1974).

The banks desiring to consolidate, Connecticut National Bank (CNB) and First New Haven National Bank (FNH), have offices in contiguous areas in the southwestern portion of Connecticut. CNB maintains its headquarters in the town of Bridgeport, which is situated on the Long Island Sound approximately 60 miles from New York City. CNB is the fourth largest commercial bank in the State. At year-end 1972, it held 6.2% of the deposits in commercial banks in Connecticut. CNB operates 51 offices located in Bridgeport and nearby towns in the extreme southwest section of Connecticut.

FNH has its headquarters in the town of New Haven, approximately 19 miles to the northeast of Bridgeport along the Long Island Sound. FNH is the eighth largest commercial bank in Connecticut. At the end of 1972, it held 4.1% of commercial bank deposits in the State. FNH operates 22 bank offices in New Haven and surrounding towns.

In Connecticut as a whole at the end of 1971, the five largest commercial banks held 61% and the 10 largest commercial banks held 83% of the deposits in such banks in the State. Two large commercial banks based in Hartford, Connecticut Bank & Trust Co. of Hartford and Hartford National Bank, operate essentially statewide. At year-end 1972, they had 41% of the total commercial bank deposits held by Connecticut banks.

CNB and FNH both have offices and are in direct competition in a so-called "four-town area" located between Bridgeport and New Haven.

The banks assured the District Court, however, that in implementing the consolidation they would divest themselves of a sufficient number of offices in the four-town area to render insignificant the degree of overlap of their areas of actual operation. The District Court held that this divestiture plan eliminated any antitrust difficulties presented by the merger of direct competitors. The United States has not pursued the point on appeal. Accordingly, the case has been presented to us strictly as a geographic market extension merger on the part of both banks. The proposed consolidation would join the banks under FNH's national charter (with headquarters in Bridgeport). It would have no effect on the number of banks operating in either the Bridgeport or New Haven area. * * *

The District Court concluded that the appropriate "line of commerce" within the meaning of § 7 included both commercial banks and savings banks. The court recognized that its conclusion departed from this Court's holdings in, e. g., United States v. Phillipsburg National Bank, 399 U.S. 350, 359–362 (1970), and United States v. Philadelphia National Bank, 374 U.S. 321, 356–357 (1963). But in the District Court's view the pronouncements in Phillipsburg National Bank and Philadelphia National Bank "were not intended to be ironclad, hard and fast rules which require a court to don blinders to block out the true competitive situation existing in every set of circumstances." 362 F.Supp., at 280. * * *

Two of the District Court's reasons may be dealt with briefly. The court erred as a matter of law in concluding that the absence of a "line of commerce" phrase in the Bank Merger Act of 1966 alters traditional standards under § 7 of the Clayton Act for defining the relevant product market in a bank merger case. United States v. Third National Bank, 390 U.S. 171, 182 n. 15 (1968). See *Phillipsburg National Bank*, 399 U.S., at 359–362. Moreover, the absence of significant competition from savings banks in *Philadelphia National Bank*, supra, and *Phillipsburg National Bank*, supra, is not determinative. The commercial banks in both of those cases faced significant competition from savings and loan associations and other credit institutions. The Court in both instances nevertheless viewed the business of commercial banking as sufficiently distinct from other credit institutions to merit treatment as a separate "line of commerce" under § 7. Analogous distinctions, although perhaps not as sharply defined, are controlling here.

We believe that the District Court overestimated the degree of competitive overlap that in fact exists between savings banks and commercial banks in Connecticut. To be sure, there is a large measure of similarity between the services marketed by the two categories of banks. In our view, however, the overlap is not sufficient at this stage in the development of savings banks in Connecticut to treat them together with commercial banks in the instant case. Despite the strides that savings banks in that State have made toward parity with commercial banks, the latter continue to be able to provide a cluster of services that the former cannot, particularly with regard to commercial customers, and this Court has repeatedly held that it is the unique cluster of services provided by commercial banks that sets them apart for purposes of § 7.

* * * From the vantage point of at least one significant consumer of bank services—the commercial enterprise—commercial banks in Connecticut offer a "cluster of products and services" that their savings bank counterparts do not. The facts of this case indicate that the differences in what commercial banks in the State can offer to that important category of bank customers are sufficient to establish commercial banking as a distinct line of commerce. * * *

We do not say, and *Phillipsburg National Bank*, supra, and *Philadelphia National Bank*, supra, do not say, that in a case involving a merger of commercial banks a court may never consider savings banks and commercial banks as operating in the same line of commerce, no matter how similar their services and economic behavior. At some stage in the development of savings banks it will be unrealistic to distinguish them from commercial banks for purposes of the Clayton Act. In Connecticut, that point may well be reached when and if savings banks become significant participants in the marketing of bank services to commercial enterprises. But, in adherence to the tests set forth in our earlier bank merger cases, which we are constrained to follow, we hold that such a point has not yet been reached. Accordingly, on remand the District Court should treat commercial banking as the relevant product market.

The District Court ruled that the relevant geographic market, or "section of the country," under § 7, is the State as a whole. We think the District Court erred on this point for several reasons. If the State were the relevant geographic market, it would then be appropriate to analyze this not as a potential-competition case but as a direct-competition case involving the consolidation of two firms holding an aggregate market share of approximately 10%. Even if this figure is "shaded" by a factor of 10% to account for the influence of banks in New York, the consolidation of CNB and FNH would create a firm holding a 9% share of statewide commercial-bank deposits. Mergers between direct competitors producing smaller shares of less concentrated markets have been held illegal under § 7.

The State cannot be the relevant geographic market, however, because CNB and FNH are not direct competitors on that basis (or for that matter on any other basis pertinent to this appeal). The two banks do not operate statewide, nor do their customers as a general rule utilize commercial banks on that basis. The offices of the two banks are restricted to adjoining sections of the southwest segment of Connecticut. Although the two banks presumably market a small percentage of their loans to large customers on a statewide or broader basis, it is undoubtedly true that almost all of their business originates locally. For example, "about 88% of

CNB's total deposit business derive[s] from the towns in which CNB has offices." 362 F.Supp., at 250. As the District Court noted in a finding that is inconsistent with its conclusion on the appropriate section of the country, "[c]ommon sense ... would indicate that the relevant market areas of CNB and FNH generally coincide with where each has established branch offices." Ibid.

* * * In recognition of the local character of the great majority of commercial bank activities, *Philadelphia National Bank* indicated that the relevant geographic market in bank-merger cases must be drawn narrowly to encompass the area where "the effect of the merger on competition will be direct and immediate." Id., at 357. Moreover, the geographic market must be delineated in a way that takes into account the local nature of the demand for most bank services. It "must be charted by careful selection of the market area in which the seller operates, and to which the purchaser can practicably turn for [alternatives]. ..." Id., at 359 (citations, internal quotations, and italics omitted). Because the economic scale of separate categories of consumers of bank services will vary, a workable compromise must be struck "to delineate the area in which bank customers that are neither very large nor very small find it practical to do their banking business. ..." Id., at 361.

On remand the District Court must determine pursuant to the localized approach denoted above the geographic market in which CNB operates and to which the bulk of its customers may turn for alternative commercial bank services. It must do the same with regard to FNH, for this case presents the unusual fact situation of a consolidation of two banks, each with a history of de novo geographic expansion, rather than the acquisition of a geographically stable bank as in *Marine Bancorporation*, ante, p. 602. The task is important, because the definition of the respective geographic markets determines the number of alternative avenues of entry theoretically open to CNB in piercing FNH's area of significant competitive influence and vice versa. * * *

The judgment is vacated and the case is remanded for further consideration consistent with this opinion.

JUSTICE WHITE, with whom JUSTICES DOUGLAS, BRENNAN, and MARSHALL join, concurs in part and dissents in part. * * *

LISSA LAMKIN BROOME
THE INFLUENCE OF ENHANCED THRIFT
INSTITUTION POWERS ON
COMMERCIAL BANK MARKET EXPANSION
67 N.C. L. Rev. 795 (1989).

* * * As demonstrated by *Connecticut National Bank* and *Phillipsburg National Bank*, in certain circumstances the OCC was willing to include thrifts as participants in the product market in evaluating the antitrust consequences of a commercial bank merger. Although the Supreme Court rebuffed these efforts, the federal banking agencies now routinely consider thrift institutions as competitors of commercial banks and include thrift institutions in the product market. The federal banking agencies have justified the addition of thrifts to the product market by the

statutory enhancement of the powers of thrift institutions in the early 1980s, a development subsequent to the Supreme Court's 1974 *Connecticut National Bank* decision refusing to include savings banks in the product market.

In recent merger decisions the OCC has conducted its analysis of the effect of the proposed merger on competition by including all "depository institutions" in the product market. The FDIC has also defined the product market broadly to include thrift institutions. The FRB has been willing to consider thrift institutions as competitors of commercial banks, but it normally includes only fifty percent of thrift institution deposits in the product market.

The Department of Justice, however, has abandoned the single product market composed of the cluster of commercial banking products and services in favor of a separate consumer (or retail) market and a business (or wholesale) market, each of which is composed of separate banking services that may themselves constitute relevant product markets. Thrift institutions providing comparable services are included in each separate product market. In the consumer banking market, the Department includes one hundred percent of the deposits of thrift institutions in its market share calculations. In the business banking market, however, the Department includes only twenty percent of the deposits of thrift institutions. * * *

The standards applied by the regulators for measuring the anticompetitive effects of bank mergers continued to evolve. In 1995, the Department of Justice began applying a 2 percent commercial loan-to-asset ratio test. If the ratio of a bank or thrift's commercial and industrial loans to total assets is less than 2 percent, the thrift or bank is not included in the Department's analysis. If the thrift or bank's ratio exceeds 2 percent, its deposits are included in the market analysis at 100 percent. In contrast, the Fed will discount thrift deposits from 50 percent to 100 percent as determined by its commercial loan-to-asset ratio, which slides on a scale from 3 to 6 percent.[23]

B. CONVENIENCE AND NEEDS OF THE COMMUNITY

COUNTY NATIONAL BANCORPORATION v. Board of Governors of the Federal Reserve System

United States Court of Appeals, Eighth Circuit, 1981 (en banc).
654 F.2d 1253.

HENLEY, CIRCUIT JUDGE.

County National Bancorporation (County National) and its nonoperating subsidiary, TGB Co., seek review of an order of the Board of

---

23. Edward D. Herlihy, et al., Financial Institutions Developments 2003: Building a Strong Base for Future Growth and Consolidation 395 (2004) (on file with the authors).

Governors of the Federal Reserve System (Board) denying their applications to acquire control of T. G. Bancshares Co. (TG) under the Bank Holding Company Act of 1956 (BHCA), as amended, 12 U.S.C. § 1841 et

seq. * * *

County National, generally recognized as a "suburban bank" and headquartered in St. Louis County, Missouri, is the tenth largest banking organization in the State of Missouri and the sixth largest banking organization in the St. Louis market. County National controls five banks with aggregate deposits of approximately 333.7 million dollars, representing around 1.6 per cent of the total deposits in commercial banks in the state and 3.2 per cent of the commercial bank deposits in the St. Louis market. County National's largest subsidiary or "lead" bank is the St. Louis County Bank which is one of the seven largest banks in the St. Louis market.

TG, generally recognized as a "city" bank and headquartered in the City of St. Louis, is the thirteenth largest banking organization in the state and the tenth largest banking organization in the St. Louis market. TG controls three subsidiary banks with aggregate deposits of approximately 225.6 million dollars which represent around 1.1 per cent of the total commercial deposits in the state and 2.3 per cent of the total commercial deposits in the St. Louis market. TG's largest subsidiary or "lead" bank is the Tower Grove Bank & Trust Co. (Tower Grove Bank) which has deposits of over 150 million dollars and is among the seven largest banks in the St. Louis market. * * *

The proposed merger would result in County National becoming the seventh largest banking organization in the state with 2.7 per cent of the total state-wide commercial bank deposits and the fourth largest banking organization in the St. Louis banking market with 5.6 per cent of the total market deposits.

* * * In determining whether to approve a proposed transaction, the Board is directed under section 3(c), 12 U.S.C. § 1842(c), as amended, to consider various matters including questions whether the proposal will violate certain antitrust standards.

Applying the statute to the present case, the Board by a divided vote denied the petitioners' applications. The Board found that the merger, if allowed, would result in the elimination of existing competition between two aggressive and effective competitors and a harmful concentration of banking resources in the state as well as in the St. Louis banking market.

The Board further determined that these adverse effects would not be offset by compensating benefits. The Board, however, did not affirmatively find that the proposed merger would violate the antitrust standards set forth in section 3(c)(1) and (2).

Petitioners contend that the Board may not consider anticompetitive factors more stringent than those mandated in sections 3(c)(1) and 3(c)(2). The Board, on the other hand, has taken the position that it may deny an acquisition on competitive grounds absent a finding of specific antitrust violations.

As originally enacted, the BHCA provided no definition of "convenience and needs" of the community, and section 3(c) did not emphasize specific antitrust standards. Instead, section 3(c) provided standards requiring the Board to consider various factors including the preservation of competition within the banking field.

In 1966, however, the language was amended to its present form. The legislative history of the provision indicates that the language was changed to conform the standards governing Board review of cases involving bank holding companies to the standards governing review by the Federal Deposit Insurance Corporation in cases involving mergers of individual banks under section 5 of the Bank Merger Act (BMA), 12 U.S.C. § 1828(c)(5), as amended. See S.Rep.No.1179, 89th Cong., 2d Sess. . . The language of section 3(c) of the BHCA is thus virtually identical to that of section 5 of the BMA.

The language of section 3(c) also closely parallels the language of certain antitrust standards. The antimonopoly language found in section 3(c)(1) is, of course, derived from section 2 of the Sherman Act. 15 U.S.C. § 2. Moreover, the language found in section 3(c)(2) incorporates, in part, other antitrust standards. The phrase "may be substantially to lessen competition, or to tend to create a monopoly" is identical to the standard imposed by section 7 of the Clayton Act, 15 U.S.C. § 18, while the "in restraint [of] trade" clause is lifted from section 1 of the Sherman Act, 15 U.S.C. § 1. Congress' substitution of specific competitive standards in the 1966 amendment for the general "preservation of competition" language used in the BHCA of 1956 arguably is strong indication that the antitrust standards were intended to be the sole measure of the competitive effects of a proposed transaction.

The thrust of the four-hour long debate of the 1966 amendment to the BMA on the House floor focused on whether the antitrust standards set out in section 1 of the Sherman Act and section 7 of the Clayton Act should be strictly applied to the banking industry or whether a "convenience and needs of the community" exception should be created. 112 Cong. Rec. 2440–67 (1966). Although the debate centered around the language of subsection B of section 5 of the BMA, there is no indication in the statute or its legislative history that the "convenience and needs of the community" language was intended to mean something different when used in subsection B than when it was used, only a few lines later, in the last sentence of section 5. Indeed, the Congressmen participating in the debate repeatedly spoke in terms of balancing the "competitive factor" against the "convenience and needs of the community." 112 Cong. Rec. 2440–67 (1966). Thus, while many Congressmen perceived competition, in this sense, to be a factor separate and distinct from the "convenience and needs of the community," only two, Congressmen Weltner and Todd, who opposed the statutory language of "convenience and needs of the community" and who voted in the minority, indicated in their statements that competition was part of the "convenience and needs of the community." See 112 Cong. Rec. 2457–59.

Two concerns developed after 1960 which Congress addressed with the 1966 amendment to the Bank Merger Act. The first was that bank regulatory agencies approved 90% of all merger applications filed between 1960 and 1966, 112 Cong. Rec. 2444 (remarks of Congressman Reuss), even though the 1960 BMA was passed to control the concentration of banking resources and the resulting decline in the number of commercial banks caused by unregulated mergers and consolidations. H.R. Rep. No.1416, 86th Cong., 2d Sess. Congress perceived the cause of this problem to be that competition was only one of six equally weighted factors which the agencies were required to consider and was not given special emphasis by the BMA. See H.R. Rep. No.1221, 89th Cong., 2d Sess., 112 Cong. Rec. 2441 (1966) (remarks of Congressman Patman). * * *

The second concern arose from the Supreme Court decision in United States v. Philadelphia National Bank, 374 U.S. 321 (1963). In that case the Court held that asset acquisition-type mergers are within the ambit of the Clayton Act and that bank mergers which violate the anticompetitive standards of that Act cannot be validated on the ground that they would benefit the overall public interest. This decision is inconsistent with Congress' recognition in 1960 that some mergers are beneficial to the overall public interest even though they violate the antitrust laws. H.R. Rep. No. 1416, 86th Cong., 2d Sess. (1960).

Congress sought to correct these two problems with the 1966 amendment to the BMA. The 1966 amendment created new standards by which the bank regulatory agencies are to evaluate applications and by which the courts subsequently evaluate the legality of mergers in antitrust actions brought by the Justice Department. Both the agencies and the courts must uniformly apply the same standards. 12 U.S.C. § 1828(c)(7)(B); H.R. Rep. No.1221, 89th Cong., 2d Sess. (1966). See 12 U.S.C. § 1849(b). These new standards give competition preeminent consideration by mandating that the agencies and courts first determine whether the proposed transaction violates the antitrust laws. They restrict an agency's discretion to approve transactions that have anticompetitive effects; thus, the standards foster Congress' desire to increase competition in the banking industry. It follows that a question is raised under the 1966 BMA amendment as to how far an agency may go to increase competition; may an agency, in its discretion, promulgate rules that promote a more competitive banking market than do the antitrust laws. The answer lies in Congress' method of correcting the problem created by *Philadelphia National Bank*.

By creating the "convenience and needs of the community" exception, Congress again recognized that some mergers that violate the antitrust laws are nevertheless in the public interest and that strict application of the antitrust laws by the courts is inappropriate for the banking industry. The exception requires the courts to mitigate the harsh consequences of strictly applying the antitrust laws. Given this purpose of the convenience and needs exception, it cannot be interpreted to allow the courts to apply a competitive standard that is more stringent than the antitrust standards. Since Congress specifically said that the courts and agencies are to apply identical standards, the conclusion must be that, like the courts, the bank regulatory agencies may not, in their discretion, apply a competitive standard that is more stringent than the antitrust standards.

In evaluating a proposed bank holding company transaction under its statutory mandate, the Board is first required to determine if a proposed transaction violates these antitrust provisions. If the proposed transaction "would result in a monopoly or . . . be in furtherance of any combination or conspiracy to monopolize or to attempt to monopolize the business of banking in any part of the United States," the Board must deny approval. Moreover, if the proposed transaction may have the effect "substantially to lessen competition," or "tend to create a monopoly," or "be in restraint [of] trade," the Board is again required to deny approval unless it finds that the anticompetitive effects of the proposed transaction "are clearly outweighed in the public interest" by the likelihood that the acquisition will further the convenience and needs of the community to be served. Finally, the closing sentence of section 3(c) directs that "in every case," the Board should consider various factors including the question whether the proposed transaction will serve the convenience and needs of the community. * * *

In sum, we hold that so far as anticompetitive factors are concerned the Board is limited to consideration of violations of the antitrust standards contained in section 3(c)(1) and (2) as it is under section 5 of the BMA.

It follows that the decision of the Board should be, and it is, vacated, and the cause remanded. Since the Board proceeded initially at least in part under an erroneous interpretation of legal criteria to be applied, we remand for de novo consideration of petitioners' application not inconsistent with this opinion.

HEANEY, CIRCUIT JUDGE, with whom BRIGHT and McMILLIAN, CIRCUIT JUDGES, join, dissents. * * *

As discussed in Chapter 6, the Community Reinvestment Act (CRA) requires that the appropriate Federal banking agency assess a bank's record of "meeting the credit needs of its entire community, including low-and moderate-income neighborhoods, consistent with the safe and sound operation of the institution." 12 U.S.C.A. § 2903(a)(1). Although each bank receives a public CRA rating, the CRA performance of a bank has its greatest effect at the time of a merger when the CRA record must be considered in evaluating the bank's application for expansion. 12 U.S.C.A. § 2903(a)(2).

JERRY W. MARKHAM
REGULATING CREDIT DEFAULT SWAPS
IN THE WAKE OF THE SUBPRIME CRISIS

A Working Paper Prepared for the International Monetary Fund Seminar on Current
Developments in Monetary and Financial Law, Washington, D.C.
Dec. 2, 2009.

* * * The Community Reinvestment Act (CRA) of 1977 required affirmative action by banks in meeting the credit needs of minorities in their service areas. Loans to subprime areas were made a statutory condition by the CRA for receiving regulatory approval for bank mergers. However, that legislation did not prove to be immediately effective in expanding subprime lending. This was because bank merger activity was slow in the 1970s, and banks continued to shy away from the credit risks associated with such loans. The Clinton administration sought to overcome that resistance through its National Homeownership Strategy, which had as its goal to increase the percentage of owner occupied residences from 64 to 67.5 percent by the year 2000. That strategy was to be carried out by increasing the availability of subprime mortgages. That lending was to be motivated by additional CRA requirements that, "in the words of the Federal Reserve Governor who wrote the [new] regulations, set up soft quotas on lending in underserved areas."[24]

The Clinton administration's CRA efforts led to an eighty percent increase in the number of subprime mortgages. Clinton was aided by an increase in bank merger activity that motivated banks to make some massive CRA commitments. For example, Washington Mutual made a CRA pledge of $120 billion in its 1998 acquisition of HF Ahmanson & Co. The merger of Citibank and the Travelers Group in 1999 resulted in a ten-year $115 billion CRA pledge. The explosive growth of subprime CRA pledges carried over into the Bush administration. Bank of America made a ten-year CRA pledge of $750 billion when it merged with FleetBoston Financial Corp. in 2003. JPMorgan Chase made a larger $800 billion CRA pledge when it merged with Bank One Corp. in 2004. One website, which is highly critical of CRA pledges, claims that total CRA commitments by

---

24. [n. 11] Congressional Senate Oversight Committee, Hearings on Regulation of the Financial Sector, Jan. 14, 2009.

banks reached the astonishing figure of $4.2 trillion by 2004.[25]

After being forced into the subprime market by the federal government, banks found the business to their liking. This was another unfortunate legacy of the CRA. As former Senator Phil Gramm has noted: "It was not just that CRA and federal housing policy pressured lenders to make risky loans—but that they gave lenders the excuse and regulatory cover" to enter what was appearing to be a lucrative business in which risks could be managed through securitizations. Subprime lenders were initially an industry unto themselves because large banks avoided such lending until the CRA pushed them into it. There were only ten lenders in the subprime market in 1994, but their numbers increased to fifty by 1998. By 2001, after motivation from the CRA, ten of the twenty-five largest subprime lenders were banks or bank affiliates.

As a result of efforts by the Clinton administration, "[s]ubprime mortgage originations grew from $35 billion in 1994 to $140 billion in 2000, indicating an average annual growth rate of 26%."[26] Clinton certainly laid the groundwork for the subprime crisis, but subprime lending exploded during the years of the George W. Bush administration. As one source points out:

> Some 80 percent of outstanding U.S. mortgages are prime, while 14 percent are subprime and 6 percent fall into the near-prime category. These numbers, however, mask the explosive growth of nonprime mortgages. Subprime and near-prime loans shot up from 9 percent of newly originated securitized mortgages in 2001 to 40 percent in 2006.[27]

The Federal Reserve Board has contended that the CRA did not cause the subprime crisis because many subprime loans did not have CRA credit. It has also been asserted that the CRA was not responsible for the subprime crisis because: (1) few CRA loan applications were denied, which it is claimed demonstrates they were good loans; (2) many of the players in the subprime market were not regulated banks; and (3) most subprime loans originated in California, Florida and Nevada, suggesting that, since CRA had little effect elsewhere, it was not to blame.[28] These claims overlook the fact that the CRA required, and thereby legitimatized, subprime lending by institutions that had previously shied away from such risky loans. As former Fed Chairman Alan Greenspan testified before Congress in October 2008: "It's instructive to go back to the early stages

---

25. [n. 17] See Steve Sailer, The Minority Mortgage Meltdown (cont.): Charting the CRA Crackup, VDARE.COM, Feb. 15, 2009, http://www.vdare.com/sailer/090215_cra.htm.

26. [n. 20] Subprime Mortgage Lending and the Capital Markets, RBSF Economic Letter, Dec. 28, 2001, http://www.frbsf.org/publications/.

27. [n. 21] Danielle DiMartino & John V. Duca, The Rise and Fall of Subprime Mortgages, 2 Econ. Letter—Insights from the Fed. Reserve Bank of Dallas 11, http://www.dallasfed.org/research/.

28. [n. 23] See Charles E. Daye, Stripping Off Market Accountability: Housing Policy Perspectives on the Crisis in the Financial System, 13 N.C. Bank. Inst. 105, 110–111 (2009).

of the subprime market, which has essentially emerged out of the CRA."[29]
* * *

The Federal Reserve Board admonished banks that CRA loans were to be made in a safe and sound manner. That admonition begged the question of how do you make a safe and sound subprime loan when, as Fed Chairman Ben Bernanke has candidly admitted, those borrowers pose a "high credit risk?"[30] The solution for this counterparty risk problem was solved by the Clinton administration when CRA regulations were amended in 1995 to allow CRA based subprime loans to be securitized. Securitization provided the banks with a way to move subprime loans off their balance sheets, and it allowed "lenders to shift mortgage credit risk and interest rate risk to investors who have greater risk tolerance."[31]

The amount of securitized subprime mortgages grew from about $11 billion in 1994 to over $100 billion in 2002. Bear Stearns made its first subprime securitization offering in 1997 for mortgages totaling $385 million, and it underwrote an additional $1.9 billion in CRA securitizations over the next ten months. "By 2005, almost 68 percent of home mortgage originations were securitized."[32] The FDIC noted, in 2006, that:

> A significant development in the mortgage securities market is the recent and dramatic expansion of "private-label," [mortgage-backed securities] MBS ... Total outstanding private-label MBS represented 29 percent of total outstanding MBS in 2005, more than double the share in 2003. Of total private-label MBS issuance, *two thirds comprised non-prime loans in 2005*, up from 46 percent in 2003.[33]

The securitization process was carried out through [MBS] that were distributed through "warehouse" operations, in which mortgages were purchased from non-bank originators by investment banks and then resold through securitizations. These warehousing operations became a part of an unregulated "shadow banking" system. * * *

---

29.   [n. 24] Phil Gramm, Deregulation and the Financial Panic, Wall St. J., Feb. 20, 2009, at A17. The newest twist on the CRA was Goldman Sach's announcement that it was giving $500 million to aid small businesses. That announcement was designed to deflect criticism of its massive bonus pool, but critics noted that this contribution would also allow Goldman, which had converted to a bank holding company during the crisis, to meet its CRA needs in future years. Francesco Guerrera & Tom Braithwaite, Goldman Boost From Business Aid Fund, Fin. Times (London), Nov. 20, 2009, at 15.

30.   [n. 27] Ben S. Bernanke, Chairman, Federal Reserve Board, The Subprime Mortgage Market, Address Before the Federal Reserve Bank of Chicago's 43rd Annual Conference on Bank Structure and Competition (May 17, 2007).

31.   [n. 28] Division of Insurance and Research of the Federal Deposit Insurance Corporation, Breaking New Ground in U.S. Mortgage Lending, FDIC Outlook (Fed. Deposit Ins. Corp.), Summer 2006, at 21.

32.   [n. 31] FDIC, Breaking New Ground in U.S. Mortgage Lending, FDIC Outlook 21 (Summer 2006) (emphasis supplied).

33.   [n. 32] Id.

C. MARKET CONCENTRATION

LISSA LAMKIN BROOME
THE INFLUENCE OF ENHANCED THRIFT INSTITUTION POWERS ON COMMERCIAL BANK MARKET EXPANSION
67 N.C. L. Rev. 795 (1989).

* * * Although there are "no definite quantitative or qualitative tests ... to determine whether [a merger] may 'substantially' lessen competition," market share figures and other relevant factors such as barriers to entry by new competitors help to gauge a merger's probable effect on competition. Thus, the applicable federal banking agency and the Department of Justice consider the market shares of the parties to the merger and the market shares of other participants in the same market. Market share figures reflect the extent to which the market is concentrated and the extent to which consummation of the proposed merger will increase market concentration. The more concentrated a market is, the more likely it is that one participant or a small group of participants could successfully exercise market power. * * *

In 1984 the Department of Justice issued revised merger guidelines applicable to mergers between all types of businesses. These guidelines endorse the use of the Herfindahl–Hirschman Index (HHI) as a measure of market concentration. The federal banking agencies also use the HHI in measuring market concentration. The HHI figures measure the presence of all firms in the market and give proportionately greater weight to those firms with large market shares. To calculate the HHI figures, the market share of each firm in the market is determined. Traditionally the market shares of banks have been approximated by the percentage of deposits held by each bank in the relevant geographic market. The individual market share percentages are squared and then summed. The resulting number is the HHI for the premerger market. The same calculation is then performed assuming that the proposed merger has taken place to determine the postmerger HHI. * * *

The Department of Justice's merger guidelines state that it is likely to challenge a merger as anticompetitive if the merger would increase the HHI by over 50 points and would result in a postmerger HHI of over 1800 points. The Department has indicated, however, that it will challenge a bank merger with a post-merger HHI of over 1800 points only if the merger would increase the HHI by over 200 points. The Department has explained that it uses higher-than-normal HHI thresholds for bank mergers to take account of "the competitive effect of limited-purpose lenders and other non-depository financial entities" that are not otherwise specifically considered in the HHI calculation. * * *

The Department of Justice and the Federal Trade Commission revised their horizontal merger guidelines on August 19, 2010. Department of

Justice & Federal Trade Commission, Horizontal Merger Guidelines (Aug. 19, 2010), <http://www.justice.gov/atr/public/guidelines/hmg–2010.pdf>. The guidelines revise the 1992 guidelines and deemphasize the market definition and market concentration tests. In addition, the HHI safe harbor thresholds are relaxed so that a highly concentrated market is defined as having an HHI above 2500 and an increase of the HHI in such a market by more than 200 points is likely to warrant additional scrutiny. This 2500/200 screen is substantially more favorable to merger participants than the prior Department standard of 2000/50. At the same time, however, an interagency agreement between the banking regulators and the Department issued in 1995, Bank Merger Competitive Review, was not modified. The 1995 document still finds a market to be highly concentrated if its HHI exceeds 1800, but would only scrutinize further a merger in such a market that increased the HHI by more than 200 points. Bank Merger Competitive Review, <http://www.justice.gov/atr/public/guidelines/6472.htm>. Thus, the bank merger concentration standard, previously more generous than the general horizontal merger standard, is now more onerous.

BOARD OF GOVERNORS OF THE FEDERAL RESERVE SYSTEM, DIVISION OF RESEARCH AND STATISTICS[34]

June 2, 1997.

The factors considered in evaluating the competitive effects of proposed horizontal bank mergers and acquisitions include:

1. An initial screening of structural effects.
2. Potential competition.
3. Thrift institutional competition.
4. Competitive viability of the firm to be acquired.
5. Economic conditions in the market and the need for exit.
6. Competition from other financial institutions in the market.
7. Competition from out-of-market financial institutions.
8. Financial weakness of the firm to be acquired.
9. Market shares of leading firms.
10. The post-merger level and trends in market competition.
11. Economies of scale in small mergers.
12. Other factors unique to the market.

Every proposed merger is subjected to an initial screening in which structural effects are examined. Any or all of the remaining eleven factors

---

34. An "informal listing" prepared by Board staff in the Division of Research and Statistics (on file with the authors).

are considered only in instances where the structural effects of a merger suggest that the effect on competition may be substantially adverse. Each of factors 2 through 12 may weigh in favor of approval or in favor of denial of a proposal, given the structural conditions found to exist in a market. Some elaboration on each of the factors is provided below.

Factor 1. This is an initial screening device. If the resulting Herfindahl index is greater than 1800 and, at the same time, the change in the Herfindahl index is more than 200, an application receives a more detailed analysis. If the Herfindahl index is under 1800 or the change is less than 200, and the resulting market share is less than 35 percent, the application is usually eligible for processing under delegated authority. This expedited procedure does not involve an intensive investigation of competition in a market or an analysis of the other factors relating to competition. These structural indexes are calculated with 50 percent of thrift deposits included.

Factor 2. If certain conditions exist, potential competition may be given significant weight. For example, if the relevant market is judged to be attractive for entry, there has been recent nonincidental entry, and there are limited legal impediments to entry, this weighs toward approval. If a market is unattractive for entry or there are significant impediments to entry, due to factors such as small market size, little if any weight is given to potential competition.

Factor 3. If there is substantial similarity between banks and thrifts in a market, more than 50 percent of thrift deposits may be included in the calculation of structural indexes. The exact percentage of thrift deposits included depends, in large part, on the degree to which thrifts are exercising their commercial lending, transactions account, and consumer lending powers.

Factor 4. If the firm to be acquired is, by all indications, a weak competitor, this might diminish the significance of the structural indexes. The profitability and market share of the firm over time are among the factors considered in evaluating its viability.

Factor 5. If the fundamental, long-term economic conditions in a given market appear to be deteriorating, and if the market appears to be unable to support existing financial institutions, structural considerations may be given less weight than usual. This factor is most likely to be relevant in rural markets. Among the criteria examined are changes in population, income, deposits, and employment in the market, as well as profitability of banks in the market.

Factor 6. If competition from other depository institutions such as credit unions, industrial banks, or co-operative banks is unusually intense, this lends some weight in favor of approval. Lack of membership restrictions for credit unions or the provision of commercial loans by any nonbank depository institutions are important considerations.

Factor 7. If it can be demonstrated that competition from out-of-market banks or nonbank competitors is unusually strong, for some reason, such as the presence of a unique type of institution or a demographically unique community, this weighs toward approval.

Factor 8. If it can be substantiated that the firm to be acquired is in imminent danger of failing, this weighs toward approval. This is especially true if it is demonstrated that other, less anticompetitive options for purchase of the failing institution do not exist.

Factor 9. If a market is dominated by one or two firms with unusually large market shares, this is considered a negative factor that weighs against approval of acquisitions involving one of the dominant firms.

Factor 10. If the resulting level of the HHI substantially exceeds 1800, this may raise questions about the competitive effects of a merger regardless of the magnitude of the change in the HHI.

Factor 11. If the resulting banking organization is less than roughly about $100 million is assets, economies of scale weigh toward approval unless the economies could be substantially achieved in a less anticompetitive manner.

Factor 12. If there are other relevant factors unique to a market, they are given consideration in the analysis of competition. These factors might include a large amount of government deposits with restricted use and indications of unusual competitive behavior. * * *

The Fed's concern with potential competition in Factor 2 should be contrasted with the proposed guidelines it published in 1982. Those guidelines set forth standards for evaluating whether a bank merger would discourage "potential" competition in the affected market in addition to the analysis of effects on *existing* competition.[35] The Fed later withdrew that proposal because changes in interstate banking restrictions and thrift powers had relaxed the barriers to potential competition that were the focus of the Fed's concern.[36]

FEDERAL RESERVE BOARD OF GOVERNORS ORDER APPROVING THE MERGER OF BANK HOLDING COMPANIES

Dec. 10, 1997.
84 Fed. Res. Bull. 129.

NationsBank Corporation and NB Holdings Corporation (collectively, "NationsBank"), bank holding companies within the meaning of the Bank Holding Company Act ("BHC Act"), have requested the Board's approval under section 3 of the BHC Act (12 U.S.C. § 1842) to merge with Barnett

------

35. 47 Fed. Reg. 9,017 (1982).

36. 53 Fed. Reg. 21,462 (1988).

Banks, Inc., Jacksonville, Florida ("Barnett"), and thereby acquire Barnett's subsidiary banks, Barnett Bank, National Association, Jacksonville, Florida ("Barnett Bank"), and Community Bank of the Islands, Sanibel, Florida ("Community Bank"). NationsBank also has requested the Board's approval under section 4(c)(8) of the BHC Act and section 225.24 of the Board's Regulation Y to acquire the nonbanking subsidiaries of Barnett and thereby engage in the nonbanking activities.

NationsBank, with total consolidated assets of approximately $240.4 billion, is the fifth largest commercial banking organization in the United States, controlling approximately 5 percent of total banking assets of insured commercial banks in the nation ("total banking assets"). The subsidiary banks of NationsBank operate in North Carolina, Arkansas, Delaware, the District of Columbia, Florida, Georgia, Illinois, Iowa, Kansas, Kentucky, Missouri, Maryland, New Mexico, Oklahoma, South Carolina, Tennessee, Texas, and Virginia. NationsBank also engages through other subsidiaries in a number of permissible nonbanking activities. Barnett, with total consolidated assets of approximately $44.7 billion, is the 23rd largest commercial banking organization in the United States, controlling less than 1 percent of total banking assets in the United States. Barnett owns one subsidiary bank that operates in Florida and Georgia and another that operates in Florida, and engages through subsidiaries in a variety of permissible nonbanking activities. * * *

On consummation of the proposal, and accounting for all proposed divestitures, NationsBank would become the third largest commercial banking organization in the United States, with total consolidated assets of approximately $285.1 billion, representing approximately 5.9 percent of total banking assets in the United States. NationsBank also would control 29.6 percent and 18.4 percent of the total deposits held by insured depository institutions ("total deposits") in Florida and Georgia, respectively

Section 3(d) of the BHC Act, as amended by Section 101 of the Riegle–Neal Interstate Banking and Branching Efficiency Act of 1994 ("Riegle–Neal Act"), allows the Board to approve an application by a bank holding company to acquire control of a bank located in a state other than the home state of such bank holding company, if certain conditions are met. For purposes of the BHC Act, the home state of NationsBank is North Carolina, and Barnett has operations in Florida and Georgia. * * *

The NationsBank/Barnett proposal would combine two banking organizations that compete in a large number of banking markets in Florida. These organizations are among the largest providers of banking services in these markets and have a significant competitive effect in many markets. Accordingly, the Board has taken special care in analyzing the effect of this transaction on competition in the relevant markets and the comments submitted regarding the competitive effects of this transaction. While in several markets this is a close case, the Board has taken particular account of the fact that Florida and the markets affected by this transaction are among the fastest growing and most attractive locations for entry by banking organizations in the United States. The attractiveness of many of the markets affected by this transaction has been demonstrated by recent *de novo* entry by banking organizations, including several large multi-state bank holding companies, as well as by entry through acquisition by banking organizations that include Florida and large multi-state bank holding companies.

The Board and the courts consistently have recognized that the appropriate product market for evaluating the competitive effects of bank mergers and acquisitions is the cluster of products and services offered by banking institutions. * * *

The Board previously has indicated that HHI levels are only guidelines that are used by the Board, the DOJ, and other banking agencies to help identify cases in which a more detailed competitive analysis is appropriate to assure that the proposal would not have a significantly adverse effect on competition in any relevant market.[37] A proposal that fails to pass the HHI market screen may, nonetheless, be approved because other information indicates that the proposal would not have a significantly adverse effect on competition. * * *

This is a difficult case in many respects and highlights some of the complexities of analyzing the competitive effects of mergers that affect a large number of local markets. As explained above, the proposal meets the criteria that the Board have traditionally applied to bank acquisition cases. The Board's experience in analyzing these cases, however, suggests that, in future cases, increased importance should be placed on a number of factors where the proposal involves a combination that exceeds the DOJ guidelines in a large number of local markets. In these cases, the Board believes that it is important to give increased attention to the size of the change in market concentration as measured by the HHI in highly concentrated markets, the resulting market share of the acquiror and the pro forma HHIs in these markets, the strength and nature of competitors that remain in the market, and the strength of additional positive and negative factors that may affect competition for financial services in each market. The Board believes that this refined focus would better address the challenges of analyzing the complex competitive effects of combinations that affect multiple markets. * * *

Despite the Fed's threat in the NationsBank application to tighten its review standards in large mergers, it continued to approve such mergers.

---

37. [nn. 11 & 12]* * * The DOJ has informed the Board that a bank merger or acquisition generally will not be challenged (in the absence of other factors indicating anticompetitive effects) unless the post-merger HHI is at least 1800 and the merger or acquisition increases the HHI by at least 200 points. The DOJ has stated that the higher than normal HHI thresholds for screening bank mergers or acquisitions for anticompetitive effects implicitly recognize the competitive effect of limited-purpose lenders and other nondepository financial institutions. Market concentration calculations include deposits of thrift institutions at 50 percent. * * *

The Fed often based its approval on findings of mitigating factors and divestitures of branches in areas with the greatest concentration of deposits following the merger.

D. MITIGATING FACTORS

CHAD F. BROWN
NOTE, BANK MERGERS IN CONCENTRATED MARKETS: THE ROLE OF MITIGATING FACTORS

2 N.C. Banking Inst. 345 (1998).

* * * Bank merger applications that could not initially meet the HHI Merger Guidelines gained the Board's approval in several ways. First, several applications used divestitures to meet Merger Guidelines and to fall within the HHI safe harbor. Second, numerous applications used mitigating factors or a combination of mitigating factors and divestitures to gain the Board's approval. * * *

During 1996–97, the Board approved twenty applications that initially exceeded Merger Guidelines and included divestitures as part of their proposal. Of those twenty applications, the Board approved eight that could not meet Merger Guidelines before divestitures but with divestitures were able to meet the market concentration guidelines as measured by the HHI. In those proposals, the merging banks generally only agreed to divest the number of branches necessary to allow the merger to meet HHI Merger Guidelines. As a result, the number of banks and the amount of deposits divested by each bank in the respective mergers varied greatly. Using divestitures to meet Merger Guidelines can be complicated and expensive, in terms of both lost bank business and costs associated with divestiture. Yet, when merger proposals do not present satisfactory mitigating factors, divestitures, if successfully used to meet Merger Guidelines, are a guaranteed way to gain the Board's approval.

Of the twenty applications approved by the Board during 1996–97 that included divestitures, twelve could not meet Merger Guidelines even with divestitures in local markets. Since these proposals could not meet Merger Guidelines with divestitures, the merging banks had to give the Board additional reasons not to deny their applications. Consequently, the Board was able to justify the approval of these twelve proposals only after concluding that other mitigating factors were present in addition to the divestitures. Most of the banks in the hybrid group used divestitures as a means solely to reduce their share of the market concentration. Thus, the banks were able to meet Merger Guidelines in most of the markets that exceeded the HHI safe harbor. The only difference between the hybrid proposals and the pure divestiture proposals is that the hybrids were not able to meet Merger Guidelines in *all* of the markets where the merging banks directly competed.

Banks involved in the hybrid proposals used divestitures to place their applications closer to meeting Merger Guidelines and to strengthen their arguments that the post-merger HHI ratios tended to overstate the merger's anti-competitive effects on the markets concerned. Furthermore, the divestitures showed that the merging banks realized the potential adverse effects on competition raised by their merger proposals, and that they were taking steps to reduce those effects. These steps, combined with the mitigating factors found in each merger, helped the merging banks convince the Board to approve their applications. * * *

During 1996–97, the Board approved nineteen merger applications that exceeded the HHI Merger Guidelines after concluding that there were sufficient mitigating factors present to minimize the proposed merger's potential adverse effects on competition. In those nineteen applications, numerous mitigating factors were cited. Factors such as the number of competitors remaining in the market, the attractiveness of the market for entry, and the amount the HHI exceeded Merger Guidelines were some of the most commonly cited. * * *

The Board approved thirty-one merger proposals during 1996–97 where the post-merger HHI substantially exceeded Merger Guidelines. Of those thirty-one, the Board approved nineteen after it concluded sufficient mitigating factors were present to minimize the potential adverse effects on competition threatened by the proposal. A combination of divestitures and various mitigating factors was used to gain approval in the other twelve applications. The Board cited fourteen different mitigating factors in those thirty-one proposals.

The most commonly cited mitigating factor was the number of competitors remaining in the market. In eighteen of the nineteen applications approved solely based on the presence of mitigating factors, and in all twelve hybrid proposals, the number of competitors remaining in the market was cited as a mitigating factor. Even more notable, within the twelve hybrid proposals, the Board considered the number of remaining competitors as a mitigating factor in all thirty markets where the Merger Guidelines threshold was exceeded. The number of competitors remaining in the market ranged form four to fifty-eight.

The Board considered not only the number of competitors remaining in the market but also the nature of those competitors. In seventeen of the thirty merger proposals where the number of remaining competitors was cited as a mitigating factor, the Board also considered the amount of market deposits controlled by the remaining competitors. Where the remaining competitors controlled a significant share of the market deposits, the Board considered the merger less likely to have adverse effects on market competition.

In addition to the market deposits controlled by the remaining competitors, the Board considered the size of the remaining competitors. Specifically, when the remaining competitors were bank holding companies, subsidiaries of bank holding companies, multi-billion dollar banking organizations, large multi-state banking organizations, or large in size relative to other banks in the state or in similar markets, the Board concluded that the merger was unlikely to adversely affect market competition.

The second most commonly cited mitigating factor was the market's attractiveness for entry. In numerous merger applications, this factor was instrumental in mitigating the potential adverse effects on competition threatened by the proposals. The Board cited numerous factors making a market attractive for entry. * * *

Another mitigating factor the Board considered was the amount the post-merger HHI exceeded Merger Guidelines. Changes in the HHI that only exceeded Merger Guidelines by a "small amount" were considered mitigating. The Board did not specifically state what would constitute a "small amount." It did, however, make note in two cases where it considered the HHI to exceed the Merger Guidelines by only a "small amount." In First Bank System, the HHI increased 222 points to 2207, and in Norwest Corporation, the HHI increased 201 points to 2066. Therefore, it seems safe to say that if the raw increase in HHI is 222 points or less and the post-merger HHI does not exceed 2207 points, the Board would consider the HHI only to have exceeded Merger Guidelines by a "small amount" and would give that factor some mitigating value. The fact that the Board found the small increase in HHI to be a mitigating factor is basically consistent with the representations made by the Board that mergers falling under a 2200/250 HHI ratio will face "clear sailing" through the review process.

In eight applications, the Board cited ease of entry into the market as a mitigating circumstance. Low state legal barriers to bank expansion was the most specific factor the Board noted as making a market easy to enter. Once the Board established that the state allowed for interstate and statewide banking it was quick to find low legal barriers to market entry in all eight applications. Since low legal barriers made it easy for banks to enter the markets in question, the Board gave less weight to the potential anti-competitive effects in those markets predicted by their high post-merger HHI ratios.

In several proposals, credit unions or savings and loan associations (thrifts) competing in a market also mitigated the anti-competitive effects of applications in numerous proposals. The Board considered credit union participation in a market as a mitigating factor if the credit union was large or made up a substantial portion of market deposits. When thrifts provided a full range of banking services and/or could compete with the market's commercial banks, the Board said this mitigated the merger's potential anti-competitive effects on competition. An interesting point to note is that part of the reason the guideline for raw HHI increase in bank mergers is 200, as opposed to 50 or 100 as it is in guidelines for other industries, is because the guidelines for bank mergers take into account limited purpose lenders, such as credit unions and thrifts, and other non-depository financial entities. By counting credit union and thrift participation in the markets as a mitigating factor, the Board may in essence be counting these institutions twice. This further supports the argument that in the past few years the Board has reviewed bank mergers leniently with regard to the HHI. * * *

E. DEPOSIT CAPS AND LIABILITY CONCENTRATION LIMITS

Bank mergers face another potential obstacle in the form of state and federal deposit caps. The Riegle–Neal Act of 1994 prohibited acquisitions that would cause the acquiring bank to control more than 30 percent of total in-state deposits or 10 percent of all deposits nationally. 12 U.S.C.A. § 1842(d)(2). Internal growth of an institution in excess of the statutory concentration level is permitted. There are various exceptions to the state deposit caps, including home state acquisitions and initial acquisitions in another state. The 30 percent in-state cap may also be increased or decreased by a particular state. State deposit caps range from 10% to 40% and vary considerably in their particular requirements. Dodd–Frank amended the Bank Merger Act, 12 U.S.C.A. § 1828(c), to provide that an interstate bank merger may not be approved if after consummation the resulting insured depository institution (including all insured depository affiliates) would control more than 10 percent of the total deposits of all insured depository institutions in the United States. Dodd–Frank Act, § 623.

NationsBank, now Bank of America, was accused of moving deposits from one state to another in order to avoid the effect of a state's deposit cap. After NationsBank combined with Bank of America, it came close to exceeding the national 10 percent deposit cap. Subsequent growth in insured deposits nationwide, however, reduced the overall percentage of deposits held by Bank of America. After its merger with FleetBoston Financial, Bank of America controlled nearly 10% of the nation's deposits. Its mergers thereafter with MBNA and LaSalle Bank Corp. Also raised the deposit cap issue. In each case, the merger application revealed that Bank of America and the target controlled over 10% of the nation's deposits. By the time the MBNA merger was approved by the regulators, however, deposits were below the 10% ceiling. The bank reduced the interest rates it paid on some of its higher-cost deposits, such as certificates of deposit, to push depositors to other institutions offering higher rates. See Jim Cole, How Deal for MBNA Altered One Market: Calif. competitors cite B of A retreat from aggressive CD rates, Am. Banker, Nov. 3, 2005.

Dodd–Frank also addressed excessive concentration for financial companies by imposing a 10 percent limit on the consolidated liabilities of the resulting entity. For this purpose, "financial companies" are defined to include insured depositories, depository institution holding companies, and the systemically significant nonbank financial companies that are supervised by the Fed. Dodd–Frank Act, § 622. The consolidated liabilities are defined as risk-weighted assets minus regulatory capital. The FSOC must prepare a study regarding how this concentration limit will affect financial stability, moral hazard, efficiency and competitiveness of U.S. financial firms, and the cost and availability of credit.

QUESTIONS AND NOTES

1. What are the dangers in the concentration of financial services? Are there any offsetting advantages?

2. Does the market serve as a better disciplinary force than the government does in acting through its antitrust powers?

3. Do you think that bank regulators have acted as a curb on consolidation of banking services in particular and financial services in general?

4. Will the Internet level the playing field for banking services or will it encourage concentration?

5. Is the disaggregated product market used by the Department of Justice superior to the "cluster of services" approach still employed by the bank regulatory agencies? How broad or narrow might the "cluster of services" be?

6. Why is prior antitrust approval required for a bank merger? In other mergers of nonbank entities, a merger is consummated subject to later antitrust challenge and potential divestiture. Would a divestiture of a merged bank be more problematic than a divestiture of any other recently acquired entity? Why?

7. Why do the bank statutes permit bank regulatory agencies to approve an anticompetitive merger if it is justified by the convenience and needs of the community?

8. As discussed in Chapter 6, merger approval may be denied by the Fed if a bank's Community Reinvestment Act (CRA) compliance is deficient. Such denials are rare, but do occur. See, e.g., Gore–Bronson Bancorp, 78 Fed. Res. Bull. 784 (1992); Farmers & Merchants Bank of Long Beach, 79 Fed. Res. Bull. 365 (1993).

9. If you look at the orders on the Fed's website approving mergers, <www.federalreserve.gov/newsevents/press/orders/2007orders.htm>, you will find that a large part of each order discusses concentration and a large part discusses Community Reinvestment Act performance.

10. What justifies statewide or nationwide deposit caps? Do other businesses have such limits on their ability to grow if they are not in violation of the antitrust laws? A position paper circulated in late 2006 advocating a repeal of the deposit cap. With no other bank controlling as much as 7% of the nation's deposits, however, Bank of America soon realized that other banks would not likely join it in this cause. The points argued in the paper included the following: the cap disadvantages U.S. banks in a global marketplace, competition is adequately protected by statewide deposit caps and antitrust laws, community banks are not threatened by global consolidation, large banks do not increase the risk to the financial system, the U.S. banking system is much less concentrated than other U.S. industries and banking in other countries, and the definition of deposit does not reflect the marketplace

for deposit products since it excludes credit union shares and money market mutual funds. How do you react to these arguments?

11. Will the concentration test set forth in section 622 of Dodd–Frank focused on a 10 percent liability cap for systemically significant financial companies be harder or easier to satisfy than the 10 percent deposit cap included in the Bank Holding Company Act?

12. Why do you think the 10 percent liability concentration cap was added in Dodd–Frank?

SECTION 5.   DIRECTOR INTERLOCKS

BANKAMERICA CORP. v. UNITED STATES

Supreme Court of the United States, 1983.
462 U.S. 122.

Mr. Chief Justice Burger delivered the opinion of the Court.

The question presented is whether Section 8 of the Clayton Act bars interlocking directorates between a bank and a competing insurance company.

In 1975, the United States brought these companion test cases (now consolidated) against 10 corporations and 5 individuals. The corporations were three banks and their three respective holding companies, and four mutual life insurance companies. The five individuals each served on the board of directors of one of the banks or bank holding companies and one of the insurance companies. It was stipulated that the interlocked banks and insurance companies compete in the interstate market for mortgage and real estate loans.

The Government asserts that interlocking directorates between banks and insurance companies violate Section 8 of the Clayton Act, 15 U.S.C. § 19. The fourth paragraph of Section 8, on which the Government relies, provides:

> "*No person* at the same time shall be a director in *any two or more corporations*, any one of which has capital, surplus, and undivided profits aggregating more than $1,000,000,[38] engaged in whole or in part in commerce, *other than banks, banking associations, trust companies, and common carriers* subject to the Act to regulate commerce, approved February fourth, eighteen hundred and eighty-seven, if such corporations are or shall have been theretofore, by virtue of their business and location of operation, competitors, so that the elimination of competition by agreement between them would constitute a violation of any of the provisions of any of the antitrust laws." (Emphasis added).

---

38. [eds.] This amount was increased to $10 million in 1990 and is adjusted by changes in GNP. Additional threshold levels were added, including a minimum of $1 million in sales as adjusted by changes in GNP. 15 U.S.C.A. § 19.

In short, this statute forbids a person from serving simultaneously on the boards of directors of two or more corporations that meet certain specifications, namely, that the corporations be engaged in commerce, at least one of them having capital, surplus, and undivided profits worth more than $1,000,000, that they be competitors, and that they be "other than banks, banking associations, trust companies, and common carriers...."

According to the Government, the language "[n]o person at the same time shall be a director in any two or more corporations ... other than banks" prohibits interlocking directorates between any two or more competing corporations, but excludes from this general prohibition interlocking directorates between banks. The Government argues that the purpose of the "other than banks" clause was simply to prevent overlapping regulation of interlocks between banks, which are separately regulated in the first three paragraphs of § 8. Thus, it interprets the fourth paragraph of § 8 to reach interlocks between banks and nonbanks, which interlocks are otherwise unregulated. Petitioners respond that the "other than banks" clause expressly excludes interlocking directorates involving banks from the scope of the fourth paragraph of § 8. * * *

The Clayton Act of 1914 was passed in a period when Congress was focusing on the perceived evils of corporate bigness and monopoly. President Wilson, for example, had made the "trusts" a core issue of his 1912 campaign; Congress followed up with the Pujo Committee investigation into the investment banking trust. See generally, Travers, Interlocks in Corporate Management and the Antitrust Laws, 46 Tex.L.Rev. 819, 824–829 (1968). Interlocks between large corporations were seen in the public debate as *per se* antagonistic to the public interest; many, including President Wilson, called for legislation that would, among other things, ban all kinds of interlocks. Interlocks were condemned regardless of whether the relationship between the corporations was horizontal or vertical; whether it was accomplished through the sharing of personnel, including directors and officers; or whether it was achieved through interlocking stock holdings or other indirect forms of domination. See, e.g., S. Rep. No. 698, 63d Cong., 2d Sess. 15 (1914); Hearings on Trust Legislation Before the House Comm. on the Judiciary, 63d Cong., 2d Sess. 816, 818–820, 823, 925 (1914). Plainly, these were policy matters appropriate for Congress to resolve.

However, when the Clayton Act was enacted, its scope was considerably less comprehensive than many of the proposals pressed upon Congress. Rather than enacting a broad scheme to ban all interlocks between potential competitors, Congress approached the problem of interlocks selectively, limiting both the classes of corporations and the kinds of interlocks subject to regulation.

Three classes of business organizations are regulated by the Clayton Act's provisions concerning corporate interlocks and each class is subject to different restraints. Clayton Act §§ 8 and 10; 15 U.S.C. §§ 19 and 20.

Section 10 regulates, but does not prohibit, certain types of interlocks between common carriers and various other corporations with which the carrier has a supplier or customer-relationship; it does not regulate horizontal interlocks between competing common carriers. The first three paragraphs of § 8 regulate interlocks between banks and trust companies that meet certain geographic and other requirements. These provisions bar a wide range of personnel interlocks, including common directors, officers, and employees. The fourth paragraph of § 8 concerns the class of competing corporations "other than banks, banking associations, trust companies, and common carriers"; it prohibits only shared directors between competing corporations and does not bar any other kind of personnel interlock or any kind of vertical interlock. It is against this pattern of specific and limited regulation of corporate interlocks that we approach the narrow statutory question presented.

The starting point, as always, is the language of the statute. The narrow question here is whether the fourth paragraph of § 8 of the Clayton Act bars interlocking directorates involving a bank and a non-banking corporation with which it competes. The language of the statute is unambiguous in prohibiting interlocking directorates between "two or more corporations . . . other than banks." The most natural reading of this language is that the interlocked corporations must all be corporations "other than banks." It is self-evident that a bank and a nonbanking corporation are not both corporations "other than banks." Thus, the fourth paragraph of Section 8 by its express terms does not prohibit interlocking directorates between a bank and a competing nonbanking corporation. This reading of the statute is reinforced both by the structure of the Clayton Act and by the structure of the fourth paragraph of § 8.

The Clayton Act selectively regulates interlocks with respect to three different classes of business organizations: those interlocks between banks are covered in the first three paragraphs of § 8 and those interlocks involving common carriers are covered by § 10. Viewed in this framework, the purpose of the "other than" clause in the fourth paragraph of § 8 was to exclude altogether interlocking directorates involving either banks or common carriers. Moreover, this interpretation is the only one consistent with the treatment of "common carriers" in the "other than" clause.

The Government does not dispute that the language "two or more corporations . . . other than banks, [or] common carriers" completely excludes from the fourth paragraph any interlocking directorates in which any of the corporations involved is a common carrier; it should follow, logically, that it also excludes interlocking directorates involving banks. Put another way, the language "two or more corporations . . . other than banks, [or] common carriers" means "two or more corporations *none of which is a common carrier*." To be consistent, that language must also be interpreted to mean "two or more corporations *none of which is a bank*."

In our view, it strains the meaning of ordinary words to read "two or more corporations other than *common carriers*" to mean something completely different from "two or more corporations other than *banks*," as the Court of Appeals did. 656 F.2d, at 442–443. * * *

It is not surprising that for more than a half century literally thousands of citizens in the business world have served as directors of both banks and insurance companies in reliance on what was universally perceived as plain statutory language. These citizens were reassured that the Government's reading of that language indicated that their conduct was lawful. The Government brushes this aside, saying in effect that it will not bring suits against those directors who resign within a reasonable time. However, those who elect to resign under this "amnesty" would nonetheless carry a stigma of sorts as violators of federal laws. Equally, and perhaps more important, such persons face possible civil liability in unknown amounts, liability against which the Government cannot, and does not purport to, render them immune. While it is arguable that wise antitrust policy counsels against permitting interlocking directorates between banks and competing insurance companies, that policy must be implemented by Congress, and not by a crabbed interpretation of the words of a statute which so many in authority have interpreted in accordance with its plain meaning for so long. If changes in economic factors or considerations of public policy counsel the extension of the Clayton Act to the categories of interlocking directorates implicated here, it is a simple matter for Congress to say so clearly. * * *

The judgment of the Court of Appeals is Reversed.

JUSTICE POWELL took no part in the decision of this case. JUSTICE WHITE, with whom JUSTICE BRENNAN and JUSTICE MARSHALL join, dissents. * * *

Congress later amended the Clayton Act and dropped the provisions in Section 8, 15 U.S.C. § 19, that are referred to in the *BankAmerica* case and which were specifically addressed to bank interlocks. That legislative action was taken after the enactment of the Depository Institution Management Interlocks Act. 12 U.S.C. § 3201 et seq., which prohibited management officials (which includes an employee or officer with management functions or a director) of a depository institution with total assets in excess of $2.5 billion from serving as a management official of any non-affiliated depository institution having assets in excess $1.5 billion. 12 U.S.C.A. § 3203. The systemically significant nonbank financial companies that are overseen by the Fed following Dodd–Frank will be treated as bank holding companies and subject to the restrictions of the Depository Institution Management Interlocks Act. Dodd–Frank, § 164. Further, the statute provides that the Fed may not exercise its authority under that Act to permit a management official of a systemically significant nonbank financial company overseen by the Fed from also serving as the management official of any bank holding company with consolidated assets exceeding $50 billion or with any other nonaffiliated systemically significant nonbank financial company overseen by the Fed. Id.

Section 32 of the Glass–Steagall Act prohibited interlocking directors between banks and brokerage firms. That provision was repealed by the Gramm–Leach–Bliley Act (GLBA). Restrictions in the Investment Company Act of 1940 continue to limit the number of bank directors on the boards of affiliated investment companies because they are viewed as "interested" directors. The SEC finalized rules to provide greater independence for boards of funds that rely on certain exemptions to permit transactions that would otherwise be conflicts of interest between the fund and its management company.[39]

QUESTIONS AND NOTES

1. The prohibition on interlocking directorates in the Clayton Act was added after a Congressional investigation was held to determine whether a "money trust" was controlling finance and industry in the United States. The Pujo Committee found that J.P. Morgan & Co., First National, the National City Bank, and a few other commercial and investment banks were controlling vast enterprises through their financing activities and their interlocking positions on the boards of the companies they dealt with as bankers. This small "inner group" of financiers held over 300 director positions in over 100 major corporations. Jerry W. Markham, A Financial History of the United States: From J.P. Morgan to the Institutional Investor (1900–1970) 49 (2001).

2. Do you think there is a danger, in our modern economy, that large banks might gain control of large companies through interlocking directorships?

3. Do you think state law restrictions on board members' conflicts of interest are adequate to deal with antitrust concerns?

---

39. Release No. IC–26520, 69 Fed. Reg. 46378 (Aug. 2, 2004) (codified at 17 C.F.R. pt. 270).

CHAPTER TEN

TRUST AND OTHER ACTIVITIES

■ ■ ■

SECTION 1. BANKS AS TRUSTEES

Many banks operate trust departments, which manage funds for individuals and pension funds. In 2005, trust institutions had more than $20 trillion in fiduciary assets and another $68 trillion in assets were held in safekeeping and custodial accounts.

National Banks are afforded trust powers pursuant to 12 U.S.C.A. § 92a, in those states "where State banks, trust companies, or other corporations which come into competition with national banks are permitted to act under the laws of the state in which the national bank is located." These trust powers are implemented through OCC regulations found at 12 C.F.R. § 5.26 and 12 C.F.R. pt. 9. National banks may also serve as limited purpose trust banks and not engage in all banking functions. State bank trust powers are granted by state law. Many states also permit nonbanks to exercise trust powers.

FIRST NATIONAL BANK OF BAY CITY v. FELLOWS

Supreme Court of the United States, 1917.
244 U.S. 416.

MR. CHIEF JUSTICE WHITE delivered the opinion of the Court.

* * * Section 11(k) of the Act of Congress approved December 23, 1913, establishing the Federal Reserve Board (38 Stat. 251, 262, c. 6), gives to that board authority "To grant by special permit to national banks applying therefor, when not in contravention of State or local law, the right to act as trustee, executor, administrator, or registrar of stocks and bonds under such rules and regulations as the said board may prescribe."

The First National Bank of Bay City having obtained the certificate required began the exercise of the powers stated. Thereupon certain trust companies which under the laws of Michigan had the authority to do the same character of business petitioned the Attorney General of the State to test the right of the national bank to use the functions on the ground that

700

its doing so was contrary to the laws of the State of Michigan and that the action of the Federal Reserve Board purporting to give authority was in contravention of the Constitution of the United States. The Attorney General then, on the relation of the trust companies, commenced in the Supreme Court of the State a proceeding in the nature of *quo warranto* to test the right of the corporation to exercise the functions. The bank in defense fully stated its federal charter, the rights given by the act of Congress and the action of the Federal Reserve Board taken thereunder. The Attorney General demurred to this defence, first, because Congress had no power to confer the authority which was called in question; second, because if it had the power, it was without right to delegate to the Reserve Board the determination of when it should be used; and third, because the exercise of the powers was in contravention of the laws and authority of the State and the Reserve Board therefore under the act had no power to grant the certificate.

The case was heard by the full court. In an opinion of one judge which, it would seem, was written before the opinion of the court was prepared, it was elaborately reasoned that the exercise by a national bank of the functions enumerated in the section of the act of Congress under consideration would be contrary to the laws of the State and therefore the Reserve Board under the terms of the act of Congress had no power to authorize their exertion. The opinion of the court, however, fully examining the grounds thus stated and disagreeing with them, expressly decided that corporations were authorized by the state law to perform the functions in question and that the mere fact that national banks were federal corporations did not render them unfit to assume and perform such duties under the state law because the mere difference existing between the general administrative rules governing national banks and state corporations afforded no ground for saying that it would be contrary to state law for national banks to exert the powers under consideration. The authority conferred by the act of Congress and the rights arising from the certificate from such point of view were therefore upheld. Looking at the subject, however, from a consideration of the legislative power of Congress in the light of the decisions in *McCulloch v. Maryland* and *Osborn v. Bank* and recognizing that it had been settled beyond dispute that Congress had power to organize banks and endow them with functions both of a public and private character, and in the assumed further light of the rule that every reasonable intendment must be indulged in favor of the constitutionality of a legislative power exercised, it was yet decided that Congress had no authority to confer the powers embraced in the section of the act under consideration and hence that the section was void. * * *

But we are of opinion that the doctrine thus announced not only was wholly inadequate to distinguish the case before us from the rulings in *McCulloch v. Maryland* and *Osborn v. Bank*, but on the contrary directly conflicted with what was decided in those cases, that is to say, disregarded their authority so as to cause it to be our duty to reverse. * * *

In other words, we are of opinion that as the particular functions in question by the express terms of the act of Congress were given only "when not in contravention of State or local law," the state court was, if not expressly, at least impliedly authorized by Congress to consider and pass upon the question whether the particular power was or was not in contravention of the state law, and we place our conclusion on that ground. We find no ambiguity in the text, but if it be that ambiguity is latent in the provision, a consideration of its purpose would dispel doubt especially in view of the interpretation which we have given the statute and the contrast between the clause governing the subject by the state law and the provision conferring administrative power on the Reserve Board. The nature of the subject dealt with adds cogency to this view since that subject involves the action of state courts of probate in a universal sense, implying from its very nature the duty of such courts to pass upon the question and the power of the court below within the limits of state jurisdiction to settle so far as the State was concerned the question for all such courts by one suit, thus avoiding the confusion which might arise in the entire system of state probate proceedings and the very serious injury to many classes of society which also might be occasioned. And our conclusion on this subject is fortified by the terms of § 57, c. 106, 13 Stat. 116, making controversies concerning national banks cognizable in state courts because of their intimate relation to many state laws and regulations, although without the grant of the act of Congress such controversies would have been federal in character.

As it follows from what we have said that the court below erred in declaring the section of the act of Congress to be unconstitutional, the judgment must be reversed and the case remanded for further proceedings not inconsistent with this opinion.

JUSTICE VAN DEVANTER, dissents. * * *

AMERICAN TRUST CO. v. SOUTH CAROLINA STATE BOARD OF BANK CONTROL

United States District Court, District of South Carolina, 1974.
381 F.Supp. 313.

BUTZNER, CIRCUIT JUDGE.

* * * NCNB Corporation is organized under the laws of North Carolina as a bank holding company within the meaning of the Bank Holding Company Act. 12 U.S.C. § 1841 et seq. (1970). It owns all of the stock, except the directors' qualifying shares of North Carolina National Bank, which is organized under the laws of the United States and maintains its principal offices in Charlotte, North Carolina. In addition to being one of the largest commercial banks in the southeastern part of the country, North Carolina National operates an extensive trust department. Its customers include a number of residents of South Carolina, who, in conformity with South Carolina law in effect at the time, named North Carolina National as their testamentary trustee. However, in 1970, South

Carolina excluded otherwise qualified corporations that are domiciled or licensed in North Carolina or Georgia from serving as testamentary trustees of estates of South Carolina decedents.

NCNB Corporation then formed a South Carolina corporation, American Trust Company, to transact trust business in South Carolina. Before NCNB could launch its proposal to provide trust services in South Carolina through American Trust, it was required by federal law to obtain the approval of the Board of Governors of the Federal Reserve System. Despite opposition from South Carolina banking interests, the Board of Governors concluded that it would be in the public interest for NCNB to engage in the trust business in South Carolina through its subsidiary, American Trust. The Board, however, was unable to give its unqualified approval because, while NCNB's application was pending American Trust was prohibited by newly enacted laws from serving as an executor, administrator, or testamentary trustee. Accordingly, the Board approved NCNB's request to the extent permitted by South Carolina law. This litigation was then instituted to test the constitutionality of South Carolina's restrictive statutes. * * *

American Trust principally relies on the equal protection clause in attacking §§ 19–592 and 67–53(a)(3) and (4) which prohibit it, as a domestic corporation, from serving as executor, administrator, or testamentary trustee because it is controlled by a North Carolina corporation. It charges that the classification of domestic corporations by the domicile of their corporate owners is irrelevant to any constitutionally permissible exercise of South Carolina's police powers. South Carolina asserts that the prohibition of foreign controlled domestic trust companies assures local control over fiduciaries and prevents destructive competition to native controlled corporations for the ultimate benefit of the public. The state emphasizes that South Carolina's estates and trusts should be administered by persons trained in South Carolina law, that trust companies should serve small as well as large accounts, and that it is to the advantage of South Carolina's economy to retain within the state both commercial and trust deposits. All of these objectives, the state contends, will be impaired by the operation of foreign controlled domestic trust companies. * * *

Undoubtedly, South Carolina has a legitimate interest in assuring that corporate fiduciaries serve the public faithfully. Laws prescribing the fiduciaries' financial resources, governing their conduct, and defining their responsibilities are appropriate means of controlling trust companies. The difficulty with the state's argument is that the challenged statutes do not bear a fair and substantial relation to the objectives that the state seeks. A domestic trust company, whether it be native or foreign owned, can be required to retain licensed South Carolina attorneys to conduct those aspects of its business which the state includes in the practice of law. But the challenged statutes do not contain this requirement. Similarly, nothing in the challenged statutes would prevent a native owned domestic corporation from seeking investment or legal advice from persons who

have offices in other states. A native owned domestic corporation is not barred from refusing small, uneconomic accounts, or from transferring funds out of the state if this is in the best interests of a trust's beneficiaries. The challenged statutes address none of these business practices. Contrary to the state's contention, the record fails to establish that a domestic trust company owned by a corporation domiciled or licensed in a state contiguous to South Carolina would be a less suitable testamentary trustee than a domestic company owned by a corporation domiciled in some other state. Nor does the proof demonstrate that a locally owned domestic trust company would better serve the public, or be more amenable to regulation, than a domestic company owned by a foreign corporation. Classification of domestic trust companies by the domicile or licensing of their corporate ownership bears no rational relation to the lawful discharge of their fiduciary duties or to the state's control over them.
* * *

North Carolina National places a value in excess of $32,000,000 on the estates of South Carolina residents who have requested it to act as testamentary trustee or as trustee of pour-over trusts into which the customers may eventually devise their estates. The Bank explained that it formerly transacted this business "through use of the mails, telephone, and personal visits between its trust officers and South Carolina residents establishing the trusts, the beneficiaries of such trusts, or their attorneys." We hold, for the purpose of this case, that the Bank's interstate activities as testamentary trustee for South Carolina decedents constituted interstate commerce. Cf. United States v. Philadelphia National Bank, 374 U.S. 321, 336 n.12 (1963). This aspect of the case, therefore, turns on the question whether the ban against the Bank is an impermissible burden on interstate commerce.

National banks can exercise only the authority that has been expressly or impliedly granted to them by Congress. Investment Company Institute v. Camp, 401 U.S. 617, 628 (1971). Federal law, 12 U.S.C. § 92a(a) and (b), authorizes a national bank to act as a fiduciary only "when not in contravention of State or local law." But a national bank does not act in contravention of state or local law if a competing state bank can serve as a fiduciary.[1] In this event, the national bank's authority is coextensive with the state bank's, but it is not enlarged. New Hampshire Bankers' Ass'n v. Nelson, 336 F. Supp. 1330 (D.N.H.), aff'd 460 F.2d 307 (1st Cir.1972). The

---

1. [n.14] Title 12 U.S.C. §§ 92a(a) and (b) (1970) provide:

(a) The Comptroller of the Currency shall be authorized and empowered to grant by special permit to national banks applying therefor, when not in contravention of State or local law, the right to act as trustee, executor, administrator, registrar of stocks and bonds, guardian of estates, assignee, receiver, committee of estates of lunatics, or in any other fiduciary capacity in which State banks, trust companies, or other corporations which come into competition with national banks are permitted to act under the laws of the State in which the national bank is located.

(b) Whenever the laws of such State authorize or permit the exercise of any or all of the foregoing powers by State banks, trust companies, or other corporations which compete with national banks, the granting to and the exercise of such powers by national banks shall not be deemed to be in contravention of State or local law within the meaning of this section.

term, "local law," as used in § 92a is defined as "the law of the state . . . governing the fiduciary relationship," 12 C.F.R. § 9.1(f) (1974), which in this instance is the law of South Carolina. See 1 Bogert, Trusts and Trustees 642 (1965). Section 67–53(a)(4) prohibits both North Carolina state banks and national banks located in North Carolina from serving as testamentary trustees of South Carolina decedents. In this respect it treats both types of banks equally.

Congress has paramount authority over national banks. McCulloch v. Maryland, 17 U.S. (4 Wheat.) 316 (1819). It can exercise its authority by incorporating restrictions found in state law. In 1927, when the McFadden Act, 12 U.S.C. § 36 (1970), authorized national banks to operate branches to the same extent that a state bank located in the same state could operate them, it intended to create "competitive equality" between state and national banks located in the same state. First Nat'l Bank v. Walker Bank and Trust Co., 385 U.S. 252, 261 (1966). It is apparent that in enacting § 92a, Congress intended to create the same kind of "competitive equality" with regard to trust services. Since South Carolina's ban on foreign testamentary trustees operates equally against state and national banks located in North Carolina, the exclusion of North Carolina National is not an impermissible burden on interstate commerce; Congress has allowed it by enacting § 92a. Furthermore, because the commerce clause is a grant, not a restriction, on the power of Congress "to regulate Commerce . . . among the several States . . ." the exclusion is constitutionally valid. Cf. Prudential Insurance Co. v. Benjamin, 328 U.S. 408, 423 (1946). * * *

The Office of the Comptroller of the Currency (OCC) adopted changes to its regulations, effective August 1, 2001, that permit national banks to conduct multi-state trust operations. 12 C.F.R. pts. 5 & 9. Those changes permit national banks to market trust services across state lines and to establish trust operations in any state that allows its own banks to act as trustees. A national bank must give notice to the OCC before trust activities are commenced in a new state. The OCC asserts that states may only restrict the trust operations of a national bank if the state places the same restrictions on its own state chartered trustees. State bank representatives had unsuccessfully argued that this rule would give national banks a competitive edge over state banks attempting to operate trust activities on an interstate basis. Fiduciary Activities of National Banks, 62 Fed. Reg. 34,792 (July 2, 2001) (codified at 12 C.F.R. pts. 5 & 9). The OCC ruled in an interpretive letter that Missouri could not require out-of-state national banks to acquire a "Reciprocity Certificate" from state officials before exercising fiduciary powers in Missouri. The OCC opined that such a requirement conflicted with the powers of national banks to act as fiduciaries under the federal law. OCC Interpretive Letter No. 1080 (May 2007).

The Conference of State Bank Supervisors (CSBS) has drafted a Model Multi–State Trust Institutions Act. Some fifteen states have incorporated elements of this Act into their trust statutes. CSBS has also developed an Interstate Trust Activities Application and Supervisory Addendum. See <www.csbs.org>. A Uniform Trust Code was adopted by the National Conference of Commissioners on Uniform State Laws in 2005. It has been enacted in over a dozen states.

MULLANE v. CENTRAL HANOVER BANK & TRUST CO.

Supreme Court of the United States, 1950.
339 U.S. 306.

MR. JUSTICE JACKSON delivered the opinion of the Court.

This controversy questions the constitutional sufficiency of notice to beneficiaries on judicial settlement of accounts by the trustee of a common trust fund established under the New York Banking Law. The New York Court of Appeals considered and overruled objections that the statutory notice [by newspaper publication] contravenes requirements of the Fourteenth Amendment and that by allowance of the account beneficiaries were deprived of property without due process of law. 87 N.E.2d 73. The case is here on appeal under 28 U.S.C. § 1257.

Common trust fund legislation is addressed to a problem appropriate for state action. Mounting overheads have made administration of small trusts undesirable to corporate trustees. In order that donors and testators of moderately sized trusts may not be denied the service of corporate fiduciaries, the District of Columbia and some thirty states other than New York have permitted pooling small trust estates into one fund for investment administration. The income, capital gains, losses and expenses of the collective trust are shared by the constituent trusts in proportion to their contribution. By this plan, diversification of risk and economy of management can be extended to those whose capital standing alone would not obtain such advantage.

Statutory authorization for the establishment of such common trust funds is provided in the New York Banking Law, § 100–c (c. 687, L. 1937, as amended by c. 602, L. 1943 and c. 158, L. 1944). Under this Act a trust company may, with approval of the State Banking Board, establish a common fund and, within prescribed limits, invest therein the assets of an unlimited number of estates, trusts or other funds of which it is trustee. Each participating trust shares ratably in the common fund, but exclusive management and control is in the trust company as trustee, and neither a fiduciary nor any beneficiary of a participating trust is deemed to have ownership in any particular asset or investment of this common fund. The trust company must keep fund assets separate from its own, and in its fiduciary capacity may not deal with itself or any affiliate. Provisions are made for accountings twelve to fifteen months after the establishment of a fund and triennially thereafter. The decree in each such judicial settlement of accounts is made binding and conclusive as to any matter set forth in the account upon everyone having any interest in the common fund or in any participating estate, trust or fund.

In January, 1946, Central Hanover Bank and Trust Company established a common trust fund in accordance with these provisions, and in March, 1947, it petitioned the Surrogate's Court for settlement of its first account as common trustee. During the accounting period a total of 113 trusts, approximately half *inter vivos* and half testamentary, participated in the common trust fund, the gross capital of which was nearly three million dollars. The record does not show the number or residence of the beneficiaries, but they were many and it is clear that some of them were not residents of the State of New York. * * *

The statutory notice to known beneficiaries is inadequate, not because in fact it fails to reach everyone, but because under the circumstances it is not reasonably calculated to reach those who could easily be informed by other means at hand. However it may have been in former times, the mails today are recognized as an efficient and inexpensive means of communication. Moreover, the fact that the trust company has been able to give mailed notice to known beneficiaries at the time the common trust fund was established is persuasive that postal notification at the time of accounting would not seriously burden the plan.

In some situations the law requires greater precautions in its proceedings than the business world accepts for its own purposes. In few, if any, will it be satisfied with less. Certainly it is instructive, in determining the reasonableness of the impersonal broadcast notification here used, to ask whether it would satisfy a prudent man of business, counting his pennies but finding it in his interest to convey information to many persons whose names and addresses are in his files. We are not satisfied that it would. Publication may theoretically be available for all the world to see, but it is too much in our day to suppose that each or any individual beneficiary does or could examine all that is published to see if something may be tucked away in it that affects his property interests. * * *

We hold that the notice of judicial settlement of accounts required by the New York Banking Law § 100–c (12) is incompatible with the requirements of the Fourteenth Amendment as a basis for adjudication depriving known persons whose whereabouts are also known of substantial property rights. Accordingly the judgment is reversed and the cause remanded for further proceedings not inconsistent with this opinion.

JUSTICE DOUGLAS took no part in the consideration or decision of this case. JUSTICE BURTON, dissents. * * *

QUESTIONS AND NOTES

1. A common or collective investment trust fund such as the one at issue in *Mullane* is sometimes likened to a mutual fund. In a mutual fund, investor funds are pooled and traded by an expert adviser, similar to the manner in which a common trust fund operates at a bank. There are, however, some

material differences between these two investment mediums. An investor in a mutual fund may select from some different trading strategies or investment objectives employed by various funds within a single mutual fund family. The investor may also liquidate the investment at any time by demanding that the mutual fund redeem the shares at their net asset value. In contrast, a beneficiary of a common trust fund is subject to the terms of the trust and may have little choice in choosing its investment strategy.

The differences between common trust funds and mutual funds also has some regulatory significance. The Securities and Exchange Commission regulates mutual funds under the rather complex provisions of the Investment Company Act of 1940, while the bank regulators oversee the operation of common and other trust funds held at banks. Before its repeal, the Glass–Steagall Act imposed restrictions on banks marketing trust products that operated in the same manner as mutual funds. Compare Investment Company Institute v. Camp, 401 U.S. 617 (1971) (national banks are prohibited by Glass–Steagall from operating what was effectively a mutual fund), with Investment Company Institute v. Conover, 790 F.2d 925 (D.C. Cir.), cert. denied, 479 U.S. 939 (1986) (banks could manage individual retirement accounts (IRAs) through a common trust fund). Those restrictions gradually eroded. At first, the banks sold mutual funds for independent sponsors; they then began buying mutual fund complexes and even selling their own private label mutual funds. See generally Jerry W. Markham, Mutual Fund Scandals—A Comparative Analysis of the Role of Corporate Governance in the Regulation of Collective Investments, 3 Hastings Bus. L.J. 67 (2006) (comparing regulation of mutual funds, bank trust funds, and other collective investments).

2.   Are investment losses in a common trust fund managed by a bank trust department covered by FDIC insurance? Are funds held in a common trust fund covered by FDIC insurance in the event the bank becomes insolvent? Are funds held in the trust department subject to the claims of other bank creditors?

3.   How are banks compensated for their trust activities?

4.   Who decides what investments are to be made in a common or other trust fund held at a bank?

5.   Do the OCC regulations confer an advantage to national banks over state banks in conducting interstate trust operations? How effective is the CSBS effort to encourage states to adopt model statutes and use common applications?

SECTION 2.   FIDUCIARY STANDARDS

Banks acting as trustees are subject to special obligations. Early English decisions allowed trustees to invest trust funds in real estate and joint-stock companies, including those of the East India Company. The South Sea Bubble changed the attitude of English courts, and trustees found themselves bound by regulations that restricted their investments mostly to government securities. In America, the decision of the Massachusetts court in 1830 in Harvard College v. Amory, 26 Mass. (9 Pick.) 446 (1830) imposed the "prudent man" rule on trust investments. This rule is quoted in the *First Alabama Bank of Montgomery* case excerpted later in this Chapter. Courts in America split on whether the prudent rule would permit investments in common stock. Some states adopted legislation that created "legal lists" specifying which securities were prudent investments for trustees. Initially, those lists did not include common stocks.

After World War II, changes in state law helped fiduciaries by permitting trustees to purchase stocks. Colorado amended its constitution in 1950 to allow trust funds to be invested in common stocks and corporate bonds. In 1963, twenty-two states enacted the Model Prudent Man Investment Act, which eased restrictions on fiduciary investments. Gradually, these statutes and court decisions allowed fiduciaries to invest greater amounts in corporate stocks. Other restrictions were also loosened. For example, restrictions on fiduciaries commingling the funds of trust estates for investment purposes were relaxed by court decisions and various statutes, allowing banks to operate common trust funds.

IN RE BANK OF NEW YORK

Court of Appeals of New York, 1974.
323 N.E.2d 700.

JONES, JUDGE.

We hold that on the record [...] guardian ad litem to certain inves[...] trustee of its own common trust fun[...] for summary judgment.

In 1952 Empire Trust Compan[...] trust fund pursuant to section 100–[...] with the provisions of that section [...] Empire was merged in 1966) as co[...] fund made a periodic accounting of [...] four-year period ending September [...] litem and attorney for principal que[...] trustee. * * *

We take occasion to commend [...] his investigation and, such investi[...] satisfaction, for his further readi[...] sensible procedural vehicle, at least in this case, for the disposition of the objections raised by him. The statutory requirement for accountings every four years with respect to common trust funds presents an occasion for the exercise of a particularly sagacious prudence. Primarily, we observe that most of the trust beneficiaries have so limited an economic interest in a common trust fund that it is unrealistic to place practical reliance on the disposition of any of them carefully to scrutinize a trustee's account. Thus the role of the guardian takes on a special significance, for the trust beneficiaries must be assured that the trustee's accounts will receive

[Handwritten marginal note:]
GAL questioned 4 inv. of the trust. Properly dismissed b/c: Acted in good faith & exercised due diligence. (No req. not to fail). No detailed discussion b/c "times change." (- kind of weird to not discuss)
Matter of Citibank
Nat'l bank - trustee. subj. to acc. Rule: Allows investment of com. trust fund assets if st. law allows.
NY law (p. 711 - bottom)
GAL argued violated b/c inv. in mutual funds when shld be limited to equity type investments. & fixed inc. inv.

careful and thorough review. At the same time if it is to serve the useful purpose for which it was designed, the common trust fund must be spared the adverse economic impact of the types of harassing litigation to which the mandatory four-year accounting requirement may expose it.

We turn then to the objections raised here. Initially we do not agree with what appears to have been in part the basis on which the majority at the Appellate Division reached its conclusion. The fact that this portfolio showed substantial overall increase in total value during the accounting period does not insulate the trustee from responsibility for imprudence with respect to individual investments for which it would otherwise be surcharged (cf. King v. Talbot, 40 N. Y. 76, 90–91; 3 Scott, Trusts [3d ed.], § 213.1, pp. 1712–1713). To hold to the contrary would in effect be to assure fiduciary immunity in an advancing market such as marked the history of the accounting period here involved. The record of any individual investment is not to be viewed exclusively, of course, as though it were in its own water-tight compartment, since to some extent individual investment decisions may properly be affected by considerations of the performance of the fund as an entity, as in the instance, for example, of individual security decisions based in part on considerations of diversification of the fund or of capital transactions to achieve sound tax planning for the fund as a whole. The focus of inquiry, however, is nonetheless on the individual security as such and factors relating to the entire portfolio are to be weighed only along with others in reviewing the prudence of the particular investment decisions. * * *

The guardian objected to the trustee's purchase, retention and sale of the shares of Parke, Davis & Company, its sale of the holding in Mercantile Stores Company, Inc., and its purchase of shares of The Boeing Company. We conclude that there is no sufficient basis for surcharge as to any of such objections. The record discloses that with respect to each investment the trustee acted in good faith and cannot be said to have failed to exercise " 'such diligence and such prudence in the care and management [of the fund], as in general, prudent men of discretion and intelligence in such matters, employ in their own like affairs' " (Matter of Clark, 257 N. Y. 132, 136; Costello v. Costello, 209 N. Y. 252, 261; cf. EPTL, Consol. Laws, c. 17–b, 11–2.2). It was not shown in any instance that the losses to the trust fund resulted from imprudence or negligence. There was evidence of attention and consideration with reference to each decision made. Obviously it is not sufficient that hindsight might suggest that another course would have been more beneficial; nor does a mere error of investment judgment mandate a surcharge. Our courts do not demand investment infallibility, nor hold a trustee to prescience in investment decisions. (Matter of Hubbell, 302 N. Y. 246, 257.)

Whether a trustee is to be surcharged in these instances, as in other cases, must necessarily depend on a balanced and perceptive analysis of its consideration and action in the light of the history of each individual investment, viewed at the time of its action or its omission to act. In our opinion no sufficiently useful purpose would be served by a detailed description of the analysis by which we reach the conclusion that there is no basis for surcharge with respect to any of the four investments here called into question. Procedures we now find acceptable with respect to these investments at the time of this accounting may not be satisfactory at another time in other circumstances. It suffices here to state that we do not find sufficient basis for surcharge in this case. * * *

Banks are facing increased competition in their trust activities from other financial services firms such as Vanguard, Fidelity, and MetLife. A survey showed that banks and savings and loans held only about forty percent of the trust services market in 2002.[2]

MATTER OF ONBANK & TRUST CO.

Appellate Division, New York, 1996.
649 N.Y.S.2d 592, *rev'd*, 688 N.E.2d 245 (1997).

BOEHM, JUDGE.

* * * The trustee of the common trust funds was, for the greater part of the accounting period, a national bank organized under the National Bank Act and, as such, was subject to the regulations of the Office of the Comptroller of the Currency (OCC). The parties agree, however, that this case is governed by New York law. The OCC regulations in any event require compliance with State law. Those regulations provide that investment by national banks of common trust fund assets in mutual funds is permitted, provided such investment is permitted for State banks organized under the laws of the State in which the national bank maintains its headquarters, in this case New York (OCC Trust Banking Circular No. 4 [Revised] [Sept. 29, 1976]).

The trust funds here were established as discretionary common trust funds in order to distinguish them from those funds that were required to limit their investments to the so-called "legal list". After New York enacted the "prudent man rule" to govern the investments of fiduciaries (EPTL 11–2.2) and abolished the legal list, Banking Law § 100–c was amended in 1972 to eliminate the distinction between discretionary and legal list common trust funds (L 1972, ch 805). Under the statutory framework, all common trust fund trustees were authorized to invest trust *St.·Law* assets in "such investments as [the trustee] may select in its discretion" (ibid.; see, Matter of Bank of N. Y. [Spitzer–Koenig], 43 A.D.2d 105, 107, aff'd 35 N.Y.2d 512).[3] * * *

OnBank's Plans of Operation, the instruments defining OnBank's powers, authorize OnBank to make such investments "as it may select in

---

2. Matt Ackermann, Sizing Up Shifts in Trust Biz Market Share, Am. Banker, Mar. 27, 2003.

3. [n.1] With respect to investments made on or after January 1, 1995, EPTL 11–2.2 has been superseded by the "Prudent Investor Act" (see, EPTL 11–2.3; L 1994, ch 609). All of the investments at issue were made prior to January 1, 1995.

its discretion." The guardians did not submit evidence of any prohibition against investing in mutual funds in the underlying trust instruments. Nevertheless, the guardians contend that OnBank violated the Plans of Operation by investing common trust funds in mutual funds because the Plans of Operation specifically limit investment to "equity type investments" in Fund "A" and to "fixed income investments" in Fund "B". We see no difference, however, between such investments held as individual securities and the same investments held in mutual funds.

The guardians also argue that, under the Banking Law, OnBank is prohibited from delegating its managerial responsibilities by shifting them to a mutual fund. Banking Law § 100–c(2), as originally enacted, provided that "[e]ach common trust fund shall, subject to law, be under the exclusive management and control of such trust company" (L 1937, ch 687, at 1562). One commentator wrote that such prohibition was "aimed directly at the evils of delegation of managerial functions" (Note, The Common Trust Fund Statutes–A Legalization of Commingling, 37 Colum L Rev 1384, 1386 [1937]). The Legislature did no more than codify the common-law prohibition against delegation (see, Restatement of Trusts § 171, comment h, at 444 [1935]). At common law, a trustee could not delegate duties that involved the exercise of judgment or discretion (see, Matter of Osborn, 252 App Div 438, 444).

In 1986, the Legislature amended Banking Law § 100–c and removed the provision in section 100–c (2) addressing the exclusive management of a common trust fund for the reason that it was "superfluous" (Mem of State Dept of Banking, 1986 McKinney's Session Laws of NY, at 2867). Simultaneous with the amendment, however, the Banking Department promulgated Regulation 22.20 (3 NYCRR 22.20), which adopted similar language. That regulation provides, "[a] trust company administering a common trust fund shall have the exclusive management thereof". Further, each of the Plans of Operation requires that OnBank "shall have the exclusive management and control of the Fund," and that the investments of each fund "shall be subject to the joint control of two or more duly authorized officers or employees of the Bank."

Nevertheless, the foregoing restrictions do not prohibit the investment of common trust funds in mutual funds. Such investments always remain subject to the "prudent man" rule of EPTL 11–2.2 and do not alter the trustee's fiduciary responsibilities. EPTL 11–2.2 (b) (1) expressly authorizes fiduciaries to invest in management type investment companies, and the legislative history of EPTL 11–2.2 (b) makes clear that the legislation was intended to clarify that such investment did not come within the common law's prohibition against delegation. As the Surrogate observed, the trustee still maintains the ultimate managerial control of the investment by retaining the paramount authority to buy, hold or sell the shares of a mutual fund investment. This interpretation is consistent with the position taken by the Comptroller of the Currency regarding the investment of common trust fund assets managed by national banks, which are governed by Federal regulations that also require exclusive management by the trustee (see, 12 CFR 9.18 [b] [12]). * * *

Although the mutual fund assumes the responsibility of choosing the individual investments, the trustee maintains control by choosing a mutual fund that is operated according to investment objectives consistent with those of the underlying trust. Additionally, shares of the mutual fund can be redeemed almost immediately after a request from the shareholder, which also enables the trustee to maintain close control over the investment. * * *

We, therefore, conclude that investment in mutual funds by the trustee of a common trust fund does not constitute an improper delegation of its management authority.

No one disputes that the mutual funds charge a fee for the management of the assets under their control. Indeed, the fee is disclosed in the prospectus of each of the funds annexed as exhibits to the parties' Agreed Statement of Facts. But OnBank's characterization of the mutual fund's management or advisory fee as being only a part of the investment, similar to the internal management costs of publicly traded companies, does not withstand scrutiny, nor does the attempt at comparison of a mutual fund share to a share in General Motors. Ownership of a share of General Motors carries with it attributes of ownership that do not exist with a share in a mutual fund, i.e., the right to vote for directors, to participate in certain corporate decisions, and the conferring of standing necessary to bring a derivative action against corporate management. Further, the ownership of a corporate share of stock is not burdened with an annual management fee.

Consistent with the broad purpose of the statute, the language of Regulation 22.20 prohibits not only the charging of a fee by the trustee but also that the trustee not "pay a fee, commission, or compensation out of the common trust fund for management." Thus, the underlying trusts are protected, not only from having to pay a double fee to the trustee, but also from having a fee imposed for a third party's services that fall within the scope of the trustee's management duties. * * *

There are obvious benefits that may be derived from investing in mutual funds. Those benefits are freely available to both the underlying trusts and the common trust fund. The difference is that the common trust funds are subject to the protection of the Banking Law and its regulations; that protection prevents the trustees of a common trust fund from paying or permitting the payment of a fee, whether to itself or to the investment advisor of a mutual fund. Any such fee must be absorbed by the trustee. If a change is sought, then such change must come from the Legislature. * * *

JUDGES PINE and LAWSON dissent in part. * * *

Subsequent to this decision, the New York Legislature amended the Banking Law to specifically authorize charging fees to a common trust for mutual fund investments. The New York Court of Appeals then applied that amendment retroactively to the fees charged by OnBank & Trust Co. See In the Matter of OnBank & Trust Co., 688 N.E.2d 245 (N.Y. Ct. App. 1997).

FIRST ALABAMA BANK OF MONTGOMERY, N.A. v. MARTIN

Supreme Court of Alabama, 1982.
425 So.2d 415, *cert. denied*, 461 U.S. 938 (1983).

TORBERT, CHIEF JUSTICE.

This is a class action. The plaintiffs are beneficiaries of approximately 1,250 individual trusts, of which the bank is trustee. As trustee of these individual trusts, the bank invested certain assets comprising the principal of those trusts in participating units of two common trust funds, a bond fund and an equity fund. * * *

In regard to the equity fund, the court found that the purchase of seventeen of the twenty-four designated equity fund securities had been imprudent. As to these seventeen securities, the court found it unnecessary to decide whether their sale was imprudent but did conclude that the sale of five of the remaining seven securities had been imprudent.

Evidence was introduced showing that in 1973 the board of directors of First Alabama reduced to writing what it considered to be minimum standards of safety. Al Byrne, the vice president and senior trust officer of the bank admitted, however, that these standards were followed prior to 1973 as unwritten guidelines and were generally so followed at the time in which the sales and purchases in question were made. These standards were: (1) A rating of B+ or better by the Standard and Poor ratings (S & P) (B+ being an average rating and B being a speculative rating); (2) a minimum of 1,500,000 shares of stock in the hands of the public; and (3) annual sales of at least $100 million. Byrne testified that the bank generally invested in companies with at least ten years' experience in business and a record of increased earnings. He stated that the companies would generally be rated by one of the rating services. First Alabama claimed that the bank's minimum standards were primarily designed for individual trusts, rather than common trust funds, yet Byrne stated that when purchases were made for the two common funds, bank policy required that those minimum standards adopted by the bank be followed. Evidence was also presented showing that deviations were permitted from these standards adopted by the board of directors with the approval of the trust investment committee so as to accomplish its goals.

The plaintiffs offered evidence that these standards had not been followed. For example, Associated Coca–Cola, Cox Broadcasting, Rust Craft Greeting Cards and Sealed Power were rated B+ but failed to meet the Bank's requirement of one hundred million dollars in annual sales. In addition, the following stocks failed to meet the minimum requirement of a B+ rating: American Garden Products; Ames Department Stores; Beverage Canners; CNA Financial; Elixir Industries; First Mortgage Investors; Hav-a-Tampa; Kinney Services; Loomis Corp.; Mortgage Associates; Transamerica Corp.; Universal Oil Products; and Wynn Oil Co.

Dr. Robert Johnston, chairman of the finance faculty of the School of Business of George Mason University and expert witness for the plaintiffs, testified that First Alabama, as trustee, should have invested defensively. According to Johnston, a trustee should first provide for the safety of the principal and then obtain an adequate return. He based his conclusions upon a treatise by Dr. Benjamin Graham, which stated seven criteria for testing the safety of investments. These criteria were (1) a minimum of $100 million in annual sales; (2) a current ratio of at least two to one (current assets should be twice current liabilities); (3) a net working capital to long-term debt ratio of at least one to one (net working capital being current assets less current liabilities and long-term debt meaning obligations that mature in more than one year); (4) earnings stability (positive earnings for the last ten years); (5) a good dividend record; (6) an earnings growth measure of at least one-third per share over a ten-year period, averaging the first three years and the last three years to remove extremes; (7) a moderate price earnings ratio of no more than fifteen to one; and (8) a moderate ratio of price to assets of no more than one and one half to one. Johnston believed that a trustee should not purchase stocks which failed to meet any one of these standards. * * *

The bank, however, contested Johnston's opinion by testimony from Walter McConnell, an investment banker from New York, who stated that Graham's book was intended for amateurs and not trustees. Also, Johnston on cross-examination was forced to admit that only five of the thirty stocks in the Dow Jones industrial average would meet these criteria. Johnston did not believe that a trustee could protect the principal against inflation by investing in common stocks. However, he did believe buying stocks in an old established company which paid high dividends is better than investing in a new venture.

Walter McConnell, as an expert witness for the bank, listed various criteria to be applied in testing the soundness of an investment. Among these were the stability of the company, its financial soundness, its debt/equity ratio, the quality of its management, the company's product, and its standing in the industry. He testified that those criteria would not be affected by market cycles or ups and downs in the market. He stated that in his opinion the investments were prudent, though he could not say that his company had recommended the purchase of these stocks while he was an adviser.

McConnell testified that he believed a trustee must take inflation into account in making trust investments. He stated that the most popular approach was to invest in the very best companies, i.e., the best "growth" companies. The idea was that with companies whose earnings and dividends were growing faster than inflation one would be protected against inflation. Another approach, according to McConnell, was not as popular but was still used by some large banks. This approach was to buy stocks in companies that were not well known, i.e., not well recognized and which were selling at much lower prices than the stocks of better known companies. McConnell analyzed the twenty-four stocks at issue and concluded they had a faster growing rate than the general market, and their earnings were also growing faster than the general market, but they were selling at a lower price-earnings ratio. He concluded that First Alabama used a rational investment approach and that the purchases of these twenty-four stocks were prudent. He further testified that S & P ratings were not intended to be used as investment recommendations and that experienced analysts do not use S & P ratings as a guide to sound investments. He further testified that it would be imprudent to buy or sell solely because of the S & P ratings, because one would not be using judgment in his decisions. Evidence was also introduced showing that the S & P ratings were issued with a warning that they should not be used solely as market recommendations.

Eldon Davis, a former trust investment officer of the bank, who was the trust investment officer at the time the investments were made, testified for First Alabama by deposition. He stated that in 1971 and 1972 the stock market was very high. The "Favorite 50" stocks were selling at extremely high prices so he decided to seek out securities that were undervalued in relation to the higher priced ones. He further stated that he did not rely on prospectuses, because the SEC requires a prospectus to be "plastered with a high degree of risk," and "will not let you say anything good about the securities," i.e., will not allow a prospectus to make favorable forecasts or projections. He likewise stated that he saw little difference in stocks rated B, or speculative, and B+, or median, since the rating services "just don't understand the business they are in." It was Davis's opinion that it is best to buy securities in the growth cycle of a company and not after it has matured. * * *

Substantial questions arose in regard to the bond fund concerning the purchase of securities of six real estate investment trusts (REIT's). REIT's are entities primarily engaged in mortgage lending on security of real estate, or in a combination of lending with the ownership and commercial development of real estate. One witness called REIT's "the mutual funds of real estate." In September 1971, First Alabama purchased the unsecured debentures of six REIT's for $2,608,443.00, which comprised 23.2 percent of the principal of the bond fund. First Alabama suffered a 47.03+% loss on these bonds when they were sold for $1,381,645.00, for a total loss of $1,226,798.00.

Questions were raised as to whether REIT's are safe trust investments. Kenneth Campbell, an expert witness for First Alabama, testified that the purchases of the REIT's were prudent investments. Yet he had called REIT's "shaky legal undertakings" in his book, New Opportunities in Real Estate Trusts 29 (1978).

Testifying for the plaintiffs, Dr. Johnston stated that REIT's were risky investments. He applied a test set out by Benjamin Graham in his book Security Analysis (4th ed. 1962), which included size of the company, ratio of income to fixed charges, ratio of income to fixed charges in the company's worst year, ratio of income to funded debt, value of property ratio, ratio of net assets to funded debt, and a debt to capital funds ratio. Johnston testified that Graham's standards required one to look at the record of an REIT for a period of seven to ten years before making the investment, in order to determine the ratio of income to fixed charges. This was impossible here, however, because all of the REIT's were "too new" to apply this test. Johnston concluded that all six of the REIT's failed to meet the test suggested by Graham. Johnston concluded it was a poor decision to purchase REIT's because there were other options available which were less risky.

The plaintiffs also offered the prospectuses of the REIT's, which contained several pages of risk factors. These risk factors pointed out: (1) That the issuers were mortgage trusts engaged in making high-risk development and construction loans; (2) the competition in that field; (3) the conflict of interest with the sponsor-adviser; and (4) the fact that they operated principally on a leverage basis (that is, borrowing capital to increase earnings). Plaintiffs' evidence showed that the REIT's were making high-risk loans dependent upon the borrower's ability to pay. The plaintiffs contended that if the borrower had good credit, it could borrow directly from the bank and not have to pay the REIT fee.

Campbell, testifying for the bank, stated that the REIT's concept has limited if not dangerous application for mortgage lending trusts. John Davis, hired by First Alabama to replace Eldon Davis as trust investment officer, testified that in his opinion the purchase of the six REIT's was imprudent because they were all leverage. Davis testified that the REIT's would not meet the standards of the Bank today.

Mr. Byrne testified that in 1972 First Alabama's standards for bond purchases were to buy bonds from companies that were well managed, that were generally AA or better, that had the ability to withstand industry trauma, and that were the larger companies available in the bond market. None of the six REIT's met those standards. * * *

The standard to be followed in determining whether a trustee has breached his duty to the trust was stated in Birmingham Trust National Bank v. Henley, 371 So. 2d 883 (Ala. 1979):

"The general definition of a trustee's investment duties was first stated by the Supreme Court of Massachusetts in Harvard College v. Amory, 9 Pick 446, 461, 26 Mass. 446, 461 (1830):

" 'All that can be required of a trustee to invest, is, that he shall conduct himself faithfully and exercise a sound discretion. He is to observe how men of prudence, discretion and intelligence manage their own affairs, not in regard to speculation, but in regard to the permanent disposition of their funds, considering the probable income, as well as the probable safety of the capital to be invested." * * *

The difference between speculation and investment is well described by Dr. Headley in Headley, Trust Investments, 97 Trusts & Estates 739 (1952), quoted above in the quotation from Birmingham Trust National Bank v. Henley, 371 So. 2d at 895. As Dr. Headley states, one who buys common stocks with the idea of selling them on the market for higher prices is speculating. One who is making a prudent investment examines the stocks' intrinsic values and purchases them for a long-term investment. Walter McConnell, testifying for the defendant, stated that one approach adopted by trust managers is to pick established stocks and not worry about subsequent turns in the market price. It is obvious that neither Headley's standards, nor those mentioned by McConnell, were consistently used by First Alabama. * * *

After careful consideration of the many issues presented on appeal, this Court has determined that the trial court did not err in finding for the plaintiffs. We reaffirm the "prudent man rule," which states that a trustee must only exercise *sound* discretion, conduct himself faithfully, and manage funds entrusted to him as men of prudence, discretion, and intelligence would manage their own affairs, having due regard for the safety of the corpus and probable income. Harvard College v. Armory, 26 Mass. (9 Pick) 446 (1830). See also, Birmingham Trust National Bank v. Henley, 371 So. 2d 883 (Ala. 1979). We conclude that the trial court applied the "prudent man rule." Based upon the foregoing principles and the ore tenus rule, the findings of the trial court are due to be affirmed.

Modern portfolio theory poses new challenges for trustees. This theory posits that stock price changes depend on new information in an "efficient market" and that this makes stock prices unpredictable. Market investment had previously been directed primarily at identifying particular stocks that would outperform other investments. Critics of that practice claimed that market prices were as predictable as a "random walk" down Wall Street, meaning that even the most astute investors could not outperform the market by picking individual securities. This encouraged "passive" investing, where institutional investors diversified their portfolios to reflect overall market performance, as represented by broad-based market indexes such as the S&P 500.[4] Modern portfolio theory also posits that a money manager should not be judged on the basis of performance of individual investments in the portfolio. Rather, the manager should be measured on the overall performance of the portfolio. This encourages diversification and allows the inclusion of at least a few more risky investments in a prudently managed fiduciary fund.

---

4. The S&P 500 is a stock index that includes the stock of 500 leading U.S. companies.

CENTRAL NATIONAL BANK OF MATTOON v. UNITED STATES DEPARTMENT OF TREASURY

United States Court of Appeals, Seventh Circuit, 1990.
912 F.2d 897.

POSNER, CIRCUIT JUDGE.

Central National Bank is one of two national banks in Mattoon, a town of 20,000 in downstate Illinois. After an investigation of the bank's trust department, the Comptroller of the Currency, who regulates national banks, issued in 1987 a notice of intent to revoke the bank's permission to provide trust services to its customers. The notice was issued pursuant to 12 U.S.C. § 92a(k), which authorizes the Comptroller, upon notice and hearing, to revoke trust powers that the bank has "unlawfully or unsoundly exercised." After a hearing before an administrative law judge, the judge found that the bank had committed many violations of the Comptroller's regulations and engaged in many imprudent practices, but decided that it would be enough to order the bank to cease and desist. On review of the administrative law judge's order the Comptroller upheld the judge's findings, but considering the remedy imposed too weak revoked the bank's trust powers. The bank asks us to set aside the Comptroller's order. 12 U.S.C. § 1818(h)(2). We can do that only if the Comptroller has violated a statute or regulation, made findings of fact unsupported by substantial evidence, or exercised his judgment in an arbitrary, which is to say unreasonable, fashion. Id.; 5 U.S.C. §§ 706(2)(A), (E); Larimore v. Conover, 775 F.2d 890, 895–96 (7th Cir. 1985), reversed en banc on other grounds, 789 F.2d 1244 (7th Cir. 1986). These precepts apply to choice of remedy, id.; del Junco v. Conover, 682 F.2d 1338, 1340 (9th Cir. 1982); First National Bank v. Comptroller of Currency, 697 F.2d 674, 680 (5th Cir. 1983)—in spades, as we shall see. * * *

We turn to the merits of the petition for review. The bank does not deny that it has engaged in improper practices in its trust department, but pleads a variety of mitigating circumstances. The improper practices not only are numerous but also reach back many years and were only partly corrected in previous remedial proceedings that resulted in the entry and subsequent dissolution of a cease and desist order in the early 1980s. The improprieties range in gravity from the technical (failure to comply with certain reporting requirements) through the mild (minor violations of the terms of trust instruments) to the grave (deliberately overvaluing securities in one of the bank's common trust funds, the consequence being to overcharge customers for units of the fund). The bank has very little to say in rebuttal to these charges, and nothing worth discussing. It trains all its guns on the alleged impropriety that precipitated the Comptroller's decision to order the bank to shut down its trust department—the purchase in 1985 of 20,000 shares of Eagle Bancorporation for a common trust fund administered by the bank's trust department.

The purchase price of $220,000 constituted more than 20 percent of the assets of the common trust fund. To finance the purchase, Malcolm O'Neill, the bank's trust officer, sold blue-chip stocks and bonds held in the common trust fund. Eagle was a modest (net worth of $14 million), unlisted company owning small, unlisted banks and seeking to acquire more of these; its stock was narrowly held and thinly traded. The president and (indirectly) principal stockholder of the Central National Bank of Mattoon, James Singer, owned stock in Eagle, as did another director of the bank and O'Neill himself. In addition, as O'Neill well knew, Eagle was trying to acquire another bank of which Singer was a major owner.

The Eagle shareholder from whom O'Neill had purchased the 20,000 shares for Central National Bank's common trust fund agreed in writing to repurchase the stock within one year, upon demand, at a price slightly above the bank's purchase price. Within that year an attempt by Eagle to raise money by a new offering of stock failed, and O'Neill belatedly began to worry about the prudence of the bank's investment. But he unaccountably failed to exercise his option to sell the stock back to the seller. He claims to have made an oral demand, which—assuming he did make it— was ignored. He made no effort to follow up with a written demand. So far as appears, the stock remains in the bank's portfolio to this day, having paid during this period a single dividend of $1,500.

The imprudence of the investment does not lie in the fact that Eagle is not a blue chip. It is a myth that prudent investing requires limiting one's portfolio to the stocks or other securities of the strongest companies, the companies least likely to go broke. The prices of the stocks of weak companies are bid down in the market until those stocks yield the same risk-adjusted expected return as the stocks of the strongest companies; otherwise no one would hold stock in a weak company—the prices of such stock would fall to zero. The risk to which we have just referred is the volatility of the stock in relation to the market, or in other words the stock's sensitivity to market swings. This "market risk," what finance theorists call "beta," is different from insolvency risk—that is, how weak the company is. But like insolvency risk, it is compensated risk, since most investors (including most beneficiaries of trusts) are risk averse and therefore demand a premium to hold a security that has an above-average market risk. The prices of stocks with high market risk are bid down accordingly, to compensate investors for holding the stock.

But the proposition that the price of a stock that involves above-average insolvency risk or above-average market risk will be bid down to compensate investors for bearing these risks assumes that there is an efficient market for the stock in question, that is, a market in which there are enough well-informed buyers and sellers, actual and potential, to ensure that prices reflect true values as affected by risk preference as well as by expected earnings and other factors. We do not know whether the market in stock of Eagle Bancorporation is efficient, but probably it is not. Its existing shares are thinly traded and its effort to sell additional shares flopped. The fact that in all of 1985 the only price at which Eagle stock changed hands was $11 (and there were several transactions during this period, not just the purchase by the bank's common trust fund), even though the value of a company is rarely constant over an entire year, is further evidence that the price of this stock is not a reliable market price. With O'Neill and his bosses owning stock in Eagle and the big boss owning stock in Eagle's target as well, there is no reason to suppose that O'Neill's decision to buy 20,000 shares in Eagle for the common trust fund reflected an informed and unbiased effort to determine the value of those shares relative to the market value of the stocks that O'Neill sold to pay for the shares. Nor is there evidence that O'Neill in fact made any such effort. The problem, then, is not that Eagle was not a blue chip company, but that, as a prudent investor in O'Neill's shoes would have realized, it may very well not have been worth as much as $11 a share.

The purchase also impaired the diversification of the bank's common trust fund. We pointed out earlier that to investors who are risk averse, unnecessary risk is a cost, which they will willingly bear, therefore, only if compensated by the prospect of an additional return on their investment. We identified two types of risk: insolvency risk, and market risk (beta). Both are compensated risk, in that price will adjust to make securities containing even large amounts of such risk just as good investments as securities with less such risk. There is, however, a third type of risk, which is uncompensated, and that is risk that can be diversified away simply by holding a larger, more balanced portfolio. It is uncompensated because it is not a real burden to the investor, since he can eliminate it at trivial cost by the design of his portfolio. By placing a large fraction of the trust fund's assets in the shares of a small company, itself undiversified (for some companies, of course, are highly diversified—they are like mutual funds), O'Neill significantly reduced the fund's diversification without conferring any offsetting benefit, in the form of a higher expected return, on the fund's beneficiaries. In time, if and when they discovered that the bank was failing to maintain a diversified portfolio, they might withdraw from the fund, but until then they were simply worse off as a consequence of the bank's purchase of Eagle stock.

We have wandered a bit afield, for the Comptroller, perhaps prudently, does not emphasize the effect of the Eagle purchase in reducing the diversification of the common trust fund. So far as the trust services of the Central National Bank of Mattoon, Illinois, are concerned, the propriety of the bank's practices is determined by the Illinois law of trusts, 12 C.F.R. § 9.11(a); and while the duty of a fiduciary to diversify his investment portfolio is generally recognized, Restatement (Second) of Trusts, § 228 (1959); Hamilton v. Nielsen, 678 F.2d 709, 712 (7th Cir. 1982), leading us to hazard a guess in Hamilton that the duty was a part of the Illinois prudent man rule, we acknowledged that there were no Illinois cases on point. Id. The Illinois Appellate Court has misread *Hamilton* as holding that "Illinois law does not impose a duty on a trustee to diversify the trust assets." McCormick v. McCormick, 536 N.E.2d 419, 428 (1988). This leaves the status of the duty to diversify in Illinois law in a fog that neither the statute itself ("in ... investing ... property for any trust ... the trustee shall exercise the judgment and care under the circumstances then prevailing which men of prudence ... exercise in the management of their own affairs," Ill. Rev. Stat. ch. 17, para. 1675(1)) nor the cryptic discussion of diversification in In re Estate of Pirie, 492 N.E.2d 884, 887 (1986), can penetrate. What is clear, though, is that the bank's failure to take reasonable steps to determine whether $11 was a fair estimate of the value of Eagle stock, and the fact that the bank was engaged in self-dealing in buying for the trust fund stock in a company in which the bank's insiders had a substantial stake, made the purchase imprudent, and therefore improper, under Illinois law and hence under federal law as well. Kinney v. Lindgren, 26 N.E.2d 471 (1940); Herget National Bank v. Lampitt, 478 N.E.2d 904 (1985). * * *

The petition to set aside the Comptroller's order revoking the bank's trust authority is denied.

QUESTIONS AND NOTES

1.   The OCC issued a notice of proposed rulemaking that sought comment on whether it should adopt uniform standards of care for the trust departments of national banks. 65 Fed. Reg. 75,872 (Dec. 5, 2000). The OCC was particularly concerned that the multi-state fiduciary operations of national banks might face conflicting state standards for the obligations of trustees. The OCC also sought comment on what uniform fiduciary standards should be adopted. Because of broad-ranging questions and concerns raised in comment letters responding to this proposal, the OCC decided to defer adoption of such a rule pending further study. 66 Fed. Reg. 34,792 (July 2, 2001).

2.   Does the OCC's proposal conflict with the requirements of 12 U.S.C. § 92a that limit national bank trust activities to those "not in contravention of State or local law"? By regulation, the OCC provides that a national bank shall invest funds in a fiduciary account "in a manner consistent with applicable law." 12 C.F.R. § 9.11.

3.   The Lincoln First Bank, which became a part of J.P. Morgan Chase, was found liable in 2004 for $21 million in losses from an estate it was managing. Liability was assessed because the bank's trust department had kept the trust assets invested solely in the stock of Eastman Kodak Co. The individual creating the trust had asked that the estate remain invested in Eastman Kodak stock, absent some compelling reason. A state judge ruled that the bank should have realized there was a compelling reason to invest elsewhere, starting in 1974 and continuing into this century, because it was apparent that Eastman Kodak was being mismanaged. On appeal, it was held that the plaintiff's substantive claims were barred by *res judicata* to the extent that the trust's activities had been approved in proceedings in a New York surrogate court. In re Estate of Hunter, 827 N.E.2d 269 (N.Y. Ct. App. 2005).

In another case, SunTrust Banks Inc. was charged with a conflict of interest in keeping a family trust highly concentrated in the stock of the

Coca–Cola Co., which had suffered a sharp drop in value. SunTrust itself owned Coca–Cola stock valued at more than $2 billion and had close business ties with Coca–Cola. Indeed, the only copy of the formula for the Coca–Cola drink is kept in a SunTrust safe deposit box. The plaintiffs claimed that SunTrust did not want to sell stock held in their trusts and other trusts managed by the bank because that would depress Coca–Cola stock, hurting the bank's own holdings. Paul Davis, Lawsuit Targets SunTrust's Ties to Coke, Am. Banker, June 14, 2005.

SECTION 3.　CUSTODIAL SERVICES

Another service offered by large banks is providing custodial services for keeping collateral and other assets in safekeeping:

> National banks' custody activities developed from providing safekeeping and settlement services to customers for a fee, and historically are viewed as permissible incidental activities under 12 U.S.C. § 24 (Seventh), and often are in conjunction with the delivery of fiduciary services. A custody relationship is a contractual arrangement, and the services performed for customers vary. Services traditionally provided include the settlement, safekeeping, and reporting of customers' marketable securities and cash. A custodian also may invest cash balances as directed, collect income, process corporate actions, price securities positions, and provide recordkeeping services. As custody services are contractual in nature, a bank must ensure compliance with the provisions of all applicable agreements. The custody industry has grown significantly in recent years, and now global custodians control trillions of dollars in assets in offices around the world.

Comptroller of the Currency, Administrator of National Banks, Interpretive Letter No. 1078 (May 2007).

COMPTROLLER OF THE CURRENCY
CUSTODY SERVICES: COMPTROLLER'S HANDBOOK

<www.occ.treas.gov/handbook/custodyservice.pdf>.
January 2002.

* * * The ability to gather assets, effectively employ technology, and efficiently process huge volumes of transactions is essential in the custody business today. With the growth of the investment industry during the past two decades, particularly in the mutual fund arena, the level of assets under custody has increased significantly. Competition for custody of those assets has been fierce, causing profit margins to shrink. At the same time, the industry has focused on using technology to improve efficiency. As a result, a handful of large banks now dominate the custody services industry.

Services provided by a bank custodian are typically the settlement, safekeeping, and reporting of customers' marketable securities and cash. A custody relationship is contractual, and services performed for a customer may vary. Banks provide custody services to a variety of customers, including mutual funds and investment managers, retirement plans, bank fiduciary and agency accounts, bank marketable securities accounts, insurance companies, corporations, endowments and foundations, and private banking clients. Banks that are not major custodians may provide custody services for their customers through an arrangement with a large custodian bank.

A custodian providing core domestic custody services typically settles trades, invests cash balances as directed, collects income, processes corporate actions, prices securities positions, and provides recordkeeping and reporting services.

A global custodian provides custody services for cross-border securities transactions. In addition to providing core custody services in a number of foreign markets, a global custodian typically provides services such as executing foreign exchange transactions and processing tax reclaims. A global custodian typically has a sub-custodian, or agent bank, in each local market to help provide custody services in the foreign country. The volume of global assets under custody has grown rapidly in recent years as investors have looked to foreign countries for additional investment opportunities.

A bank may offer securities lending to its custody customers. Securities lending can allow a customer to make additional income on its custody assets by loaning its securities to approved borrowers on a short-term basis. In addition, a custodian may contract to provide its customers with other value-added services such as performance measurement, risk measurement, and compliance monitoring. * * *

Bank custody services include segregation arrangements required by statute, or agency regulations, for the safekeeping of assets of customers of regulated financial institutions. For example, broker-dealers regulated by the Securities and Exchange Commission are required to deposit the free credit balances of their customers into specially designated bank accounts identifying the account as being held for the exclusive benefit of customers. 17 C.F.R. § 240.15c3–3. Investment advisers are also required to keep customer funds in safekeeping. 17 C.F.R. § 275.206(4)(2). The Commodity Exchange Act of 1936 requires customer funds held by futures commission merchants to be held in specially segregated accounts. 7 U.S.C. § 6b. These segregation requirements are intended to protect customer assets from the claims of general creditors in the event of the bankruptcy of the regulated entity and to prevent futures commission merchants from using customer funds for their own purposes, such as securing loans.

GREDE v. BANK OF NEW YORK MELLON

United States District Court, Northern District of Illinois, 2009.
2009 WL 188460.

Sentinel Management Group, Inc. was a registered futures commission merchant ("FCM") with the Commodities Futures Trading Commission ("CFTC") and a registered investment advisor with the Securities and Exchange Commission ("SEC"). Sentinel did nothing other than manage investments. Its income was derived from its management fees based on the assets it held under management. It marketed itself with an attractive and very commonplace objective: "to achieve the highest yield consistent with the preservation of principal and daily liquidity." Its clients were supposed to be sophisticated investors and included hedge funds, futures commission merchants, financial institutions, pension plans and so forth. Sentinel had customer funds and a house account for its own securities and the benefit of insider investors. * * *

BNY extended a line of credit to provide liquidity, facilitate redemptions, and purchase securities. Sentinel dealt with BNY for many years. It began its relationship as a client of BNY's custodial services division and, some months later, began to use BNY's client services division, which offered same-day settlements and credit arrangements. When Sentinel began to use these services, its custodial accounts were closed and new accounts were opened under a new set of contracts (the "1997 Agreements"). These accounts were in place for a decade and included accounts in which Sentinel client assets were segregated and accounts in which non-segregated assets were held.

BNY was Sentinel's clearing bank and its secured lender during that time. BNY provided daily loans and credit, and Sentinel pledged collateral to secure the debt. To pledge collateral, Sentinel had to transfer securities to Sentinel's non-segregated accounts—its street or clearing accounts. To transfer, Sentinel had to issue a desegregation instruction to the Bank. Only Sentinel had the power to issue the instruction and, as is common, had to make warranties to BNY each time it did so.

Sentinel warranted that (a) it was authorized to issue the instruction and any claims to the securities transferred by customers or counterparties were extinguished; (b) it owned all the transferred securities free and clear; (c) if any securities were beneficially owned by others, Sentinel had the right to pledge them free of any claim by those owners; (d) BNY's interest in the pledged assets was superior in all respects to all other claims on them by any other party; and (e) it agreed to take all steps that BNY requires to assure itself of its priority rights including notifying or obtaining consent of any owner of the assets.

In January 2003, Sentinel made further agreements in order to take its money management business into global markets. These agreements for clearing services were, for all practical purposes, no different than the 1997 Agreements and, as before, BNY's clearing service division executed

Sentinel's instructions concerning receipt, delivery and transfer of cash and securities. The Bank recorded these debits and credits in accounts and made loans to Sentinel after collateral was pledged.

In mid–2007, Sentinel went over the cliff. On August 13, it announced a halt of redemption of customer assets; four days later it filed here for Bankruptcy protection. The Bank filed a proof of claim for $312,247,000.

Less than two months after Sentinel filed for protection, Sentinel's trustee sued the principals of Sentinel. The trustee alleged, in an adversary action, that these individuals had perpetrated a fraud against Sentinel and its customers. Generally speaking, the alleged means of the fraud were diverting customer income and trading gains, and leveraging through bank loans; all of which was concealed and misrepresented. The trustee also alleges repeated and significant violation of clear custodial and segregation requirements with respect to customer accounts.

About five months after that complaint, Sentinel's trustee filed an adversary action against BNY claiming damages of over $550 million because the Bank "established a fundamentally flawed account structure for Sentinel's accounts in violation of its obligations under federal law and its duties to Sentinel." The trustee alleges that the Bank thereby enabled Sentinel's misuse of customer funds by allowing Sentinel to pledge customer assets to secure loans to Sentinel and to commingle customer assets with Sentinel assets.

The Bank moves for dismissal [of the complaint, which was granted in part and denied in part]. * * *

SECTION 4. PENSION FUND MANAGEMENT

In 1970, collective investment trust funds maintained by banks for pension asset management were excluded from the provisions of the Investment Company Act of 1940 that regulates mutual funds and other investment companies. 15 U.S.C. § 80a–3(c)(11). This allowed banks to expand their services as professional managers of pension funds. By 1982, banks and other professional advisers were managing about one-half of pension fund assets. III Jerry W. Markham, A Financial History of the United States, From the Age of Derivatives to the Internet (1970–2001) 98 (2002). In 1986, the District of Columbia Court of Appeals held in Investment Company Institute v. Conover, 790 F.2d 925 (D.C. Cir.), cert. denied, 479 U.S. 939 (1986), that national banks could be authorized by the OCC to manage individual IRA accounts through a common trust fund. That decision was followed by other circuits. See Curtis J. Polk, Banking and Securities Law: The Glass–Steagall Act—Has It Outlived Its Usefulness?, 55 Geo. Wash. L. Rev. 812 (1987). The OCC has also adopted a regulation to govern the operation of collective investment funds. 12 C.F.R. § 9.18. That regulation requires a written plan by the bank governing the operation of such funds, as well as audits and financial reports.[5] Certain conflicts of interests are prohibited and management fees are required to be reasonable.

LABORERS NATIONAL PENSION FUND v. NORTHERN TRUST QUANTITATIVE ADVISORS, INC.

United States Court of Appeals, Fifth Circuit, 1999.
173 F.3d 313, *cert. denied*, 528 U.S. 967.

DENNIS, CIRCUIT JUDGE.

The Laborers National Pension Fund (Fund) filed suit against American National Bank and Trust Company of Chicago (ANB) for damages because of breach of fiduciary duties as the Fund's investment manager under the Employment Retirement Income Security Act of 1974 (ERISA), 29 U.S.C. §§ 1001 et seq. After a bench trial, the district court determined that ANB's purchase of interest-only mortgage-backed securities (IOs) was not a prudent investment and rendered a money judgment for the Fund against ANB. We reverse and render judgment for ANB. * * *

Interest-only mortgage-backed securities (IOs) were created in the late 1980s. An IO is a right to receive a portion of the interest only from payments on mortgage loans. Each IO is paid from the stream of interest payments made on mortgage loans by a pool of homeowners. Thus, prepayment of mortgage loans by members of the pool tends to diminish or extinguish the yield on the related IO. The rate at which mortgages are paid off increases more than expected if interest rates on mortgage loans decline unexpectedly prompting an unanticipated higher number of homeowners to refinance. Given these characteristics, IOs can result in significantly greater price and yield volatility than traditional debt securities. See Olkey v. Hyperion 1999 Term Trust, Inc., 98 F.3d 2, 6 (2d Cir. 1996), cert. denied, 520 U.S. 1264 (1997). In addition, however, IOs can serve as a hedge to prevent significant losses in value due to interest rate changes because IOs generally increase as interest rates rise and mortgage-backed securities generally decline as interest rates rise. Id. at 3–4. * * *

ERISA was enacted to regulate employee benefit plans and protect the funds invested in such plans. 29 U.S.C. § 1302(a). ERISA assigns to plan

---

5. The written plan must contain the following:

   (i) Investment powers and policies with respect to the fund;

   (ii) Allocation of income, profits, and losses;

   (iii) Fees and expenses that will be charged to the fund and to participating accounts;

   (iv) Terms and conditions governing the admission and withdrawal of participating accounts;

   (v) Audits of participating accounts;

   (vi) Basis and method of valuing assets in the fund;

   (vii) Expected frequency for income distribution to participating accounts:

   (viii) Minimum frequency for valuation of fund assets;

   (ix) Amount of time following a valuation date during which the valuation must be made;

   (x) Bases upon which the bank may terminate the fund; and

   (xi) Any other matters necessary to define clearly the rights of participating accounts.

12 C.F.R. § 9.18(b).

fiduciaries "a number of detailed duties and responsibilities, which include 'the proper management, administration, and investment of [plan] assets, the maintenance of proper records, the disclosure of specified information, and the avoidance of conflicts of interest.' " Mertens v. Hewitt Associates, 508 U.S. 248, 251–52 (1993) (citation omitted).

In ERISA, "rather than explicitly enumerating all of the powers and duties of trustees and other fiduciaries, Congress invoked the common law of trusts to define the general scope of their authority and responsibility."[6] Central States, Southeast and Southwest Areas Pension Fund v. Central Transport, Inc., 472 U.S. 559, 570 (1985). The manner in which trustees and other fiduciaries may exercise their powers, however, is further defined in the statute through the provision of strict standards of conduct, also derived from the common law of trusts—most prominently a standard of loyalty and a standard of prudence. Id. at 570–71 (citing 29 U.S.C. § 1104(a)(1)(A) ("a fiduciary shall discharge his duties with respect to a plan solely in the interest of the participants and beneficiaries and for the exclusive purpose of: (i) providing benefits to participants and their beneficiaries; and (ii) defraying reasonable expenses of administering the plan") and 29 U.S.C. § 1104(a)(1)(B) (a fiduciary must act "with the care, skill, prudence, and diligence under the circumstances then prevailing that a prudent man acting in a like capacity and familiar with such matters would use in the conduct of an enterprise of a like character and with like aims")).

In determining compliance with ERISA's prudent man standard, courts objectively assess whether the fiduciary, at the time of the transaction, utilized proper methods to investigate, evaluate and structure the investment; acted in a manner as would others familiar with such matters; and exercised independent judgment when making investment decisions. Katsaros v. Cody, 744 F.2d 270, 279 (2d Cir.), cert. denied sub nom., 469 U.S. 1072 (1984). " '[ERISA's] test of prudence . . . is one of conduct, and not a test of the result of performance of the investment. The focus of the inquiry is how the fiduciary acted in his selection of the investment, and not whether his investments succeeded or failed.' " Donovan v. Cunningham, 716 F.2d 1455, 1467 (5th Cir. 1983), cert. denied, 467 U.S. 1251 (1984). Thus, the appropriate inquiry is "whether the individual trustees, at the time they engaged in the challenged transactions, employed the appropriate methods to investigate the merits of the investment and to structure the investment." Donovan v. Mazzola, 716 F.2d 1226, 1232 (9th Cir. 1983), cert. denied, 464 U.S. 1040 (1984).

The Secretary of Labor may prescribe such regulations as he finds necessary to carry out the provisions of ERISA. 29 U.S.C. § 1135. In 1979

---

6. [n.2] Traditionally, fiduciaries have abided by the common law of trusts which held that the riskiness of each investment in a portfolio must be measured in isolation. Leslie J. Bobo, Comment, Nontraditional Investments of Fiduciaries: Re–Examining the Prudent Investor Rule, 33 Emory L.J. 1067, 1078 (1984); see also Chase v. Pevear, 419 N.E.2d 1358, 1366 (Mass. 1981) and In re Bank of New York, 323 N.E.2d 700, 703 (N.Y. 1974) (stating that under common law, trustee must exercise prudence in making each investment and is chargeable with any loss for failing to do so).

the Secretary prescribed regulations under ERISA further defining a fiduciary's investment duties. 29 C.F.R. § 2550.404a–1. In general, the regulations provide that the fiduciary shall be required to act as a prudent investment manager under the modern portfolio theory rather than under the common law of trusts standard which examined each investment with an eye toward its individual riskiness. Specifically, they state that a fiduciary's investment duties under 29 U.S.C. § 1104(a)(1)(B) are satisfied if he has given appropriate consideration to facts he knows or should know to be relevant to the particular investment or investment course of action involved, "including the role the investment or investment course of action plays in that portion of the plan's investment portfolio with respect to which the fiduciary has investment duties" and has acted accordingly. 29 C.F.R. § 2550.404a–1(b)(1)(i)-(ii). For these purposes, "appropriate consideration" includes determining that the investment or investment course of action "is reasonably designed, as part of the portfolio (or, where applicable, that portion of the plan portfolio with respect to which the fiduciary has investment duties), to further the purposes of the plan, taking into consideration the risk of loss and the opportunity for gain (or other return) associated with the investment or investment course of action," and consideration of the following factors: "(A) The composition of the portfolio with regard to diversification; (B) The liquidity and current return of the portfolio relative to the anticipated cash flow requirements of the plan; and (C) The projected return of the portfolio relative to the funding objectives of the plan." 29 C.F.R. § 2550.404a–1(b)(2)(i)-(ii).

In investments, the term "derivative" refers to "financial instruments whose performance is derived in whole or in part from the performance of an underlying asset (such as a security index of securities)." See BNA Pension Benefits Report No. 23, at 1046 (Apr. 15, 1996) (citing Department of Labor–Comptroller Letter of Guidance and Statement on Derivatives signed by Assistant Labor Secretary Olena Berg on Mar. 28, 1996). Examples of these financial instruments include futures, options, options on futures, forward contracts, swaps, structured notes and collateral mortgage obligations, and interest-only and principal-only strips. In the Letter of Guidance and Statement on Derivatives, the Department of Labor and the Comptroller made the following statements:

> Investments in derivatives are subject to the fiduciary responsibility rules in the same manner as are any other plan investments.... In determining whether to invest in a particular derivative, plan fiduciaries are required to engage in the same general procedures and undertake the same type of analysis that they would in making any other investment decision. This would include, but not be limited to, a consideration of how the investment fits within the plan's investment policy, what role the particular derivative plays in the plan's portfolio, and the plan's potential exposure to losses. * * *

> Plan fiduciaries have a duty to determine the appropriate methodology used to evaluate market risk and the information which must

be collected to do so. Among other things, this would include, where appropriate, stress simulation models showing the projected performance of the derivatives and of the plan's portfolio under market conditions. Stress simulations are particularly important because assumptions which may be valid for normal markets may not be valid in abnormal markets, resulting in significant losses. . . . * * *

Investment managers are also charged with making investments in accordance with documents and instruments governing the plan insofar as the plan documents are consistent with the provisions of ERISA. 29 U.S.C. § 1104(a)(1)(D). The Fund investment guidelines in the present case, in pertinent part, provide:

> 1. Investments are limited to holdings which would be permitted under the prudent man rule as set forth in the Employee Retirement Income Security Act of 1974. * * *

> 4. Bond investments shall be limited to Federal or Federal Agency obligations or corporate bonds of the first three quality grades (at the time of purchase) as established by one or more of the nationally recognized bond rating services. . . .

> 5. The investment managers are not authorized to engage in investment transactions involving stock options, short sales, purchases on margin, letter stocks, private placement debt, commodities, venture capital. Future investments in foreign securities will not be made without prior consultation with, and approval by, the Board of Trustees. . . .

The parties treated the Pension Fund Investment Philosophy and General Policy on Investments as part of the plan documents. The Investment Philosophy, in pertinent part, provides:

> The Trustees of the Laborers National Pension Fund, in order to protect the interests of the participants and beneficiaries for the purpose of providing them with benefits and defraying the reasonable expenses of administering the Plan, are committed to protect the corpus of the Fund, meet the actuarial assumptions, and comply with applicable Federal and state laws. In order to accomplish these goals in a prudent manner, the Trustees believe that the investments of the Fund must be diversified among government securities, bonds, mortgages, common stock, real estate, insurance company contracts, money market instruments, and other appropriate investments. Therefore, it will be the policy of the Trustees to invest the assets of the Fund with care in those vehicles which should preserve the principal while recognizing the need for income and appreciation with a minimal risk. This policy will be carried out by the Trustees in a prudent manner with the assistance of reputable professional money managers, consultants, insurance companies and banks to make the investments. The performance of these investments will be reviewed at least quarterly using various evaluation techniques that prove reliable and face-to-face discussion and review among the parties. . . .

And the General Policy on Investments, in pertinent part, states that:

> (a) It is the intention of the Board of Trustees to allow the investment manager full discretion within the scope of the agreed upon investment guidelines and restrictions. The manager's performance in meeting the Fund's objectives will be reviewed on a regular periodic basis. Results based on a total rate of return (including both realized and unrealized gains and losses) will be evaluated quarterly by a professional service retained by the Trustees. * * *

> (c) All investment managers will be providing quarterly reports to the Trustees in the requested format. The reports include a review of previous actions, current status of the portfolio, recommendations, etc. If changing market or economic conditions or other events suggest that a special meeting or action of the Trustees is necessary it is expected that the manager will communicate with the Trustees promptly rather than waiting for submission of the scheduled report.

> (d) If in the judgment of the investment manager strict adherence to one or more of the following investment guidelines in connection with a specific transaction is not in the best interests of the Laborers National Pension Fund or would produce an undesirable investment result the manager shall consult with the Trustees before proceeding with the transaction.

The district court clearly erred in determining that ANB failed to consider Fund guidelines before purchasing IOs. During the period at issue, Tom Pierce was ANB's Director of Fixed Income. Before Mr. Pierce authorized the purchase of IOs in 1991 he and his ANB associates consulted the ANB documents that incorporated the Fund guidelines, reviewed general literature on IOs and discussed the merits of investing in IOs with brokers. Mr. Pierce also utilized electronic Bloomberg stress simulation models to project the performance of IOs and the Fund's portfolio under market conditions. The Bloomberg stress simulation models based their projections on the prepayment histories of various securities based upon interest rate changes. Mr. Pierce considered the whole universe of investment grade, fixed-income alternatives and evaluated the risks and rewards associated with these securities relative to a Lehman Brothers Aggregate Index.

Not only did Mr. Pierce consider the risks associated with IOs in the context of the goals of the Fund; ANB also convened an Account Review Committee which met quarterly to review client objectives and to ascertain whether ANB's investment decisions complied with these objectives. ANB invested in IOs on behalf of several pension plans covered by ERISA and the Account Review Committee approved the use of IOs in the Fund's fixed-income account prior to their purchase. In addition, Standard Valuations, the company retained by the Trustees to be responsible for monitoring ANB's compliance with the Fund guidelines, considered the IO investment permissible under the Fund guidelines. In fact, at least one other investment manager, Lazard Freres, made an IO investment for the Fund under the same investment guidelines during the same period of time.

As we read the plan documents and instruments, ANB's investment in IOs was not a violation of the investment guidelines or their spirit. The documents and instruments governing the plan must generally be construed in light of ERISA's policies, and those documents cannot excuse either the trustees or the investment managers from their duties under ERISA. Central States, 472 U.S. at 568. In interpreting the provisions of plan documents and instruments such as the investment guidelines with this view, we are also guided by the principles of trust law. Firestone v. Bruch, 489 U.S. 101, 111 (1989) (citing Central States Southeast and Southwest Areas Pension Fund v. Central Transport, Inc., 472 U.S. 559, 570 (1985)). As they do with contractual provisions, courts construe terms in trust agreements without deferring to either party's interpretation. " 'The extent of the duties and powers of a trustee is determined by the rules of law that are applicable to the situation, and not the rules that the trustee or his attorney believes to be applicable, and by the terms of the trust as the court may interpret them, and not as they may be interpreted by the trustee himself or by his attorney.' " Firestone, 489 U.S. at 112 (citing 3 William F. Fratcher, Scott on Trusts § 201, at 221 (1988)). "The terms of trusts created by written instruments are 'determined by the provisions of the instrument as interpreted in light of all the circumstances and such other evidence of the intention of the settlor with respect to the trust as is not inadmissible.' " Firestone, 489 U.S. at 112 (citing Restatement (Second) of Trusts § 4, Comment d (1959)). Giving the written words of the guidelines their plain meaning within the context of trust law principles and ERISA policies, we conclude that the guidelines neither expressly nor implicitly prohibit investments in IOs of the first three quality grades; and that there is no reasonable basis for reading such a prohibition into the plan documents.

On the other hand, we find the interpretation of the Fund guidelines by the district court and the Trustees to be unreasonable under the ordinary meaning of the words of the document and especially so in light of the ERISA policies and the principles of trust law. The Investment Philosophy requires the Trustees to "protect the interests of the participants and beneficiaries for the purpose of providing them with [pension and other] benefits ... protect the corpus of the Fund, meet the actuarial assumptions, and comply with applicable Federal and state laws ... diversif[y] [investments] among government securities, bonds, mortgages, common stock, real estate, insurance company contracts, money market instruments, and other appropriate investments ... [and] invest the assets of the Fund with care in those vehicles which should preserve the principal while recognizing the need for income and appreciation with a minimal risk." The Trustees contend that the last clause implies a ban against IOs because derivatives involve a risk of loss of principal. We do not think that ambiguous clause standing alone justifies such an inference. Reading it together with the balance of the Investment Philosophy and plan documents, we are certain that it does not. The clear words of the Investment Philosophy and other plan documents require the Trustees to invest in many types of assets involving the risk of loss of principal, such as common stocks, real estate, insurance contracts, and money market instruments. Indeed, the evidence indicates that the Fund's equity and fixed-income portfolios have long contained many investments having risk of principal losses. The goals of the plan are to provide sufficient growth in assets for the payment of future pensions and other benefits to large numbers of participants and beneficiaries and to protect the Fund against inflation and depreciation. These objectives dictate an investment policy of reasonable risk, healthy appreciation and appropriate diversification. ERISA and the federal regulations likewise impose prudent fiduciary duties of careful investments for the same purposes.

The Fund guidelines expressly prohibit investments "involving stock options, short sales, purchases on margin, letter stocks, private placement debt, commodities [or] venture capital...." IOs are not among the prohibited investments. The Fund guidelines stated that investments should be limited to federal agency obligations or corporate bonds of the first three quality grades. The IOs at issue met this requirement, as they were rated "AAA" at the time of their purchase. Furthermore, the Investment Philosophy indicated that investments should be diversified among "government securities, bonds, mortgages, common stock, real estate, insurance company contracts, money market instruments, and other appropriate investments." ANB's investment in IOs was reasonably designed as part of the Fund's portfolio to further the purposes of diversification as a hedge against possible interest rate hikes and consequent declines in values of fixed income securities. * * *

Under a proper application of the correct legal principles to the evidence in the present case, there is not a reasonable basis for concluding that ANB or Mr. Pierce acted imprudently or in violation of their fiduciary responsibilities with regard to the 1991 investments in IOs. ANB considered the characteristics of IOs and utilized stress simulation models to project the performance of IOs and the Fund's portfolio under various market conditions before investing in IOs. The Fund's expert witnesses, none of whom were active or experienced ERISA plan investment managers, failed to point out any specific violation by Mr. Pierce or ANB of a fiduciary duty required by the prudent investor and modern portfolio standards of ERISA and the related federal regulations and guidance. Instead, the Fund's experts based their opinions that ANB's IO investments were imprudent on analysis of those investments standing alone, in isolation from the relevant portfolio. Also, despite their ultimate conclusions, one or more of the Fund's expert witnesses conceded that IOs can serve as a hedge against countervailing risks of a portfolio, the Fund guidelines did not prohibit the investment in IOs, the investment community did not anticipate the sudden, unprecedented decrease in interest rates which accelerated the prepayment of mortgages in 1992, and Mr.

Pierce sufficiently investigated the available data on the nature of the particular IOs prior to purchasing them.

ANB's expert witness, Mr. Henderson, an experienced ERISA plan investment manager, testified that ANB's IO investments were not imprudent when analyzed under the prudent investor, modern portfolio principles of ERISA and the pertinent Department of Labor regulations and guidances. He was the only expert witness who properly assessed ANB's IO investments as of the time they were made using the correct prudent man, modern portfolio ERISA principles. Mr. Henderson testified that in forming his opinion, he reviewed the quarterly reports issued by ANB to the Fund in 1991 and 1992; the data on the pertinent IOs available to ANB prior to the 1991 IO investments; the portfolio and investment goals and guidelines; and Standard Valuations' assessment of ANB's IO investments and overall performance for 1992. Based upon the Fund guidelines, the economic conditions that prevailed in September 1991, the makeup of the Fund's portfolio and Mr. Pierce's objectives for the portfolio, Mr. Henderson concluded that the IO investments were appropriate.

From our review of the record, we conclude that the Trustees failed to produce evidence from which it reasonably could be found that Mr. Pierce or ANB acted imprudently or that the IO investments in the present case violated the guidelines or ERISA policies. Accordingly, we REVERSE the district court's judgment in favor of the Trustees and RENDER judgment in favor of the defendants-appellants and against the plaintiffs-appellees.

QUESTIONS AND NOTES

1. The stock market run-up during the 1990s saw a substantial increase in the value of retirement plans and trust funds as the Internet economy exploded. The subsequent implosion of many dot.com companies, and the crippling of the market by Fed interest rate increases saw market values plunge. A diversified portfolio would have increased during the run-up and decreased in the downturn, which may or may not have been offset by investments in non-equity instruments. Modern portfolio theory, nevertheless, posits that the market will in the long run increase and be more profitable than investments selected only on the basis of perceived future performance. Of course we should remember the admonition of the economist John Maynard Keynes: "in the long run, we are all dead." Indeed, it was not until late in 1954 that the stock market regained the high it had set not long before the 1929 stock market crash. When the Dow Jones Industrial Average (DJIA) crashed in 2000, it was not until October 3, 2006, that it exceeded the record high set on January 14, 2000. The DJIA was in excess of 14,000 in the fall of 2007 prior to the financial crisis. By March 2009, it had lost over half its value and was below 7,000. As of mid-September 2010, it had returned to above 10,000, not yet making up half of the value lost during the financial crisis.

2. Would you prefer that your retirement funds be invested under modern portfolio theory or in government insured investments such as certificates of deposit?

3. What value does a bank trust department add to investment selection under modern portfolio theory. Could this same result be achieved by investment in a diversified mutual fund?

SECTION 5. SAFE DEPOSIT BOXES

Another service rendered by banks is the leasing or rental of safe deposit boxes. They provide security that is unavailable in many homes. The use of such boxes raise several legal issues, including liability when they are robbed and how they are to be handled on the death of the owner.

NATIONAL SAFE DEPOSIT CO. v. STEAD

Supreme Court of the United States, 1914.
232 U.S. 58.

MR. JUSTICE LAMAR delivered the opinion of the Court.

The Illinois Inheritance Tax Law operates to seal safe deposit boxes for at least ten days after the death of the renter. In view of the uncertainty as to who might own the contents of boxes, standing in the joint name of the deceased and others, the statute sealed their boxes also for a like period. The act further provided that in neither case could the securities be removed except after notice to officers designated by the State, and even then the Company was required to retain possession of enough of the assets to pay the State's tax. The Deposit Company insists that this statute violated the Fourteenth Amendment, for that, without due process of law, it imposed upon the Company a duty as to property over which it had no control; required it to assume the risk of determining who was the true owner, and forced upon it the obligations and liabilities of a tax-collecting agent of the State. In the court below and on the argument here, the validity of the section under review was said to depend upon the relation between the Company and the renter—it being argued for the State that the contract was one of bailment where, on the death of the bailor, the Deposit Company, as bailee, was bound to surrender the securities to the owner or person having a right thereto, one of whom, in each case, was the State to the extent of its tax. On the other hand, the complainant insisted that if there was no possession in fact there could be no possession in law; and that if no possession existed it was beyond the power even of the legislature to charge the Company with liabilities that could only arise out of a possession actually existing.

This is one of that class of cases which illustrate the fact that, both in common speech and in legal terminology, there is no word more ambiguous in its meaning than Possession. It is interchangeably used to describe actual possession and constructive possession which often so shade into one another that it is difficult to say where one ends and the other begins. Union Trust Co. v. Wilson, 198 U.S. 530, 537. Custody may be in the servant and possession in the master; or title and right of control may be in one and the property within the protection of the house of another, as in Bottom v. Clarke, 7 Cush. 487, 489, where such possession of a locked trunk was held not to include possession of the contents. So that, as pointed out by Pollock and Wright in their work on the subject, controversies arising out of mixed possession have inevitably led to many subtle refinements in order to determine the rights of conflicting claimants, or to lay the proper charge of ownership in prosecutions for larceny of goods belonging to one in the custody of another or found by the defendant.

In the present case, however, the Federal question presented by the record does not call for a decision as to the exact relation between the parties during the life of the renter,—whether there was a strict bailment; whether the render was in possession of the box with the Deposit Company as guard over the contents; whether the property was in the custody of the Company with the renter having a license to enter the building and remove the securities; or whether, as held in People v. Mercantile Safe Deposit Co. (Sup. Ct. App. Div. 143 N.Y. Supp. 849), construing a similar statute of New York—the relation was that which exists between tenants and landlord of an office building who keeps under his control the general means of access to the building and offices therein, but as to which offices and their contents, the rights of the tenants are exclusive. The Illinois Supreme Court held that the relation created by the Deposit Company's contract was that of bailor and bailee. That construction by the state court is controlling, unless, as claimed by the complainant, it makes the statute violate the Fourteenth Amendment as being an arbitrary attempt to create liabilities arising out of possession, where there was no possession in fact.

Certainly the person who rented the box was not in actual possession of its contents. For the valuables were in a safe built into the company's vault and therefore in a sense "under the protection of the house." The owner could not obtain access to the box without being admitted to the vault, nor could he open the box without the use of the company's master key. Both in law, and by the express provisions of the contract, the company stood in such relation to the property as to make it liable if, during the lifetime of the owner, it negligently permitted unauthorized persons to remove the contents, even though it might be under color of legal process. Roberts v. Safe Deposit Company, 123 N.Y. 57; Mayer v. Brensinger, 180 Illinois, 110. After his death, it would be likewise liable if it permitted unauthorized persons, be they heirs, legal representatives, or joint-renters, to take the property of the decedent. In the exercise of its power to provide for the distribution of his property, the State could make it unlawful, except on conditions named, for his personal representative to receive or the holder to deliver, effects belonging, or apparently belonging, in whole or in part, to the deceased. As the State could provide for the appointment of administrators, for the distribution to heirs or legatees of all the property of the deceased and for the payment of a tax on the transfer, it could, of course, legislate as to the incidents attending the collection of the tax and the time when the administrator or executor could take possession. If, before representatives were appointed any one, having the goods in possession or control, delivered them to an unauthorized person he would be held liable as an executor de son tort. The fixing by this statute of the time and condition on which delivery might be made by a deposit company was also, in effect, a limitation on the right of the heir or representatives to take possession. If they had no right to receive except on compliance with the statutory conditions, neither could the Safe Deposit Company, as bailee or custodian, surrender the contents except upon like compliance with statutory conditions.

The contention that the Company could not be arbitrarily charged with the duty of supervising the delivery and determining to whom the securities belonged is answered by the fact that in law and by contract it had such control as to make it liable for allowing unauthorized persons to take possession. Both by the nature of its business and the terms of its contract it had assumed the obligation cast upon those having possession of property claimed by different persons. If the parties could not agree as to who owned the securities the Company had the same remedy by Bill of Interpleader that was afforded all others confronted with similar conditions. There was certainly nothing arbitrary or unreasonable in compelling one, who had received such control of property from another, to surrender it after his death only to those having the right thereto. Nor was there any deprivation of property, nor any arbitrary imposition of a liability, in requiring the Company to retain assets sufficient to pay the tax that might be due to the State. * * *

It is contended that the statute impaired the complainant's charter power to do a safe deposit business. But it no more interferes with the right of the Company to do that business than it does with the right of a private person to contract to take possession or control of securities belonging to another. But, having regard to the radical change wrought by the death of the owner and the subsequent duty to make delivery to one authorized by law to receive possession, the statute points out when and on what conditions such delivery may be made to the personal representative, surviving partners or persons jointly interested.

The objection that the act, in directing the state officers to inspect the contents of the box, operates as an unreasonable search and seizure raises no Federal question, since the prohibition on that subject in the Fourth Amendment, does not apply to the States. Ohio ex rel. Lloyd v. Dollison, 194 U.S. 445, 447.

The claim that the statute compels the company to break its contract with joint-renters and deprives the latter, for ten days, of access to the box and the right to use it or remove the contents is without merit. The Company, joint-renters or firms, each made the contract in the light of the State's power to legislate for the protection of the estate of any one of the joint-renters or partners, that might die during the term. * * * The boxes were leased with the knowledge that the State had so legislated as not only to protect the interests of one dying after the rental, but also to secure the payment of the state tax out of whatever might be found in the box belonging to the deceased. The inconvenience was one of the not unreasonable incidents of the joint-relationship.

MORGAN v. CITIZENS' BANK OF SPRING HOPE

Supreme Court of North Carolina, 1925.
129 S.E. 585.

CONNOR, JUSTICE.

Plaintiff insists that there was error in allowing defendant's motion for judgment as of nonsuit, and in rendering judgment in accordance with said motion, for the reason: First, that there was evidence of a special contract between plaintiff and defendant, by virtue of which defendant became responsible as an insurer for the safe-keeping and return of said bonds; Second, that the relationship of plaintiff and defendant, with respect to said bonds was that of bailor and bailee, and that, as the evidence tended to show that the bonds, the property of plaintiff, were delivered by him into the possession of defendant, under a contract of bailment, and that defendant had failed to return them to plaintiff, upon his demand, the burden was upon defendant to establish, by evidence, facts which, under the law, relieved him of liability for the return of the bonds or for damages for failure to return same.

The decided weight of authority is to the effect that the relationship between a bank and its customer, resulting from the rental by the former to the latter of a safety deposit box, with respect to the contents of said box, placed therein for safe-keeping, is that of bailor and bailee, the bailment being for hire or mutual benefit. Trustees v. Banking Company, 182 N.C. 298. The fact that the safety deposit box can be unlocked and opened, and access had to its contents, only by the joint action of the customer, who has possession of the individual key, and of the bank, which has possession of the master key, does not affect the character of the relationship. The ownership of the property deposited in the safety deposit box remains in the customer; under the contract it must be kept in the place designated and agreed upon by the parties, to which access can be had only by their joint action; the place in which the property shall be kept is not to be determined solely by the bank. This is the only element of the contract which seems to differentiate it from a pure bailment as defined by the text-writers and approved by judicial decisions. Hail on Bailments; Dobie on Bailments; 3 R. C. L. 72; 6 C. J. 1084. This element is not sufficient to affect the relationship between the parties, and it must be held, both upon authority and upon principle, that the relationship between the parties to this action, with respect to the bonds, was that of bailor and bailee, for mutual benefit.

The interesting suggestion is made by counsel for defendant, in their brief, that the relationship between a lessor bank and a lessee customer, with respect to a safety deposit box, on principle, is that of landlord and tenant, and that the bank's possession of the contents of the box is analogous to the possession which a landlord has of the contents of the house which he has rented to his tenant. It is conceded that the greater weight of authority sustains the proposition that the relationship is that of bailor and bailee. Under a contract by which the relationship of landlord and tenant is established, both title to and possession of the subject-matter of the contract is transferred to the tenant, during the term of the lease. During said term, the landlord has no rights or duties as between himself and his tenant with respect to the property leased. The contract between the bank and its customers does not affect the title to the property, which remains in the customer, but does result in the transfer of possession to the bank. The suggestion is interesting but not persuasive.

It was the duty of defendant as bailee of the bonds delivered to it by plaintiff, under a contract of bailment, for the mutual benefit of the parties, to use ordinary care and diligence in safeguarding the bonds, the property of plaintiff, bailor, and to return same to plaintiff, upon his demand. If it failed to return the bonds, and such failure was the result of a breach of duty imposed by law by reason of the relationship growing out of the contract of bailment, it is answerable to plaintiff in damages. If its failure to return the bonds, however, was not due to breach of such duty, i.e., negligence, it is not liable to plaintiff for the loss of said bonds, for the law does not hold defendant, as a bailee, liable as an insurer. 3 R. C. L. 96. It is liable only for loss resulting from its failure to exercise the care required by law of a bailee with respect to the property bailed. * * *

Upon all the evidence it appears that the bonds were stolen by burglars from the safety deposit box in which they had been deposited, during the night of 5 November, 1920; that the said box at the time the bonds were stolen was inside the vault, in defendant's bank building; that the steel door to the vault had been blown open by the use of high explosives; that the safety deposit boxes had been opened by the use of a sledge hammer and punch and a cold chisel; that the jacket or envelope in which the bonds had been placed was found, but the bonds were missing.

There was also evidence that the equipment used by defendant was of recognized, standard make, and reasonably safe, in the opinion of expert bankers; that said equipment was the same used by banks in towns of like population as Spring Hope; that the safety deposit boxes of defendant were of standard make and similar to those used in banks located in larger towns.

There was no evidence to the contrary. The facts established by all the evidence are undisputed. The inference of negligence arising from the failure to return the bonds upon plaintiff's demand is rebutted. The only inference to be drawn from all the undisputed evidence is that the failure to return the bonds was due to the burglary, and that said burglary was not the result of the negligence of defendant; Hinnant v. Power Co., 121 S.E. 540. Justice Clarkson, writing the opinion for the Court in that case, approves the principle that where the facts are undisputed and but a single inference can be drawn from them it is the exclusive duty of the Court to determine whether a loss or injury is the result of negligence.

No facts can be found from the evidence in the record, and no inference can be drawn from the facts established by the undisputed evidence, upon which the Court could hold as a matter of law that defendant's failure to return the bonds, deposited with it as bailee, was due to its failure to exercise ordinary care for the safe-keeping of the contents of the safety deposit box, in which, under the evidence, plaintiff's bonds were on deposit on the night of 5 November, 1920, when same were stolen by burglars, who entered said vault after blowing the steel door open by high explosives, and who then broke into the safety deposit box by the use of a sledge hammer and cold chisel. The judgment based upon motion for nonsuit, which was allowed at the close of all the evidence, is affirmed.

QUESTIONS AND NOTES

1.   Safe deposit boxes were traditionally used as a place to store securities. The use of "street name" securities (customer securities held in the broker's name for an individual's account), the creation of a central depository, and book-entry securities have undercut the need for safe deposit boxes to fulfill that traditional role. Today, safe deposit boxes are largely used to hold family mementos, important documents (such as deeds and birth records), jewelry, and other valuables that could be imperiled by theft, fire, or some other disaster. The reduced use of safe deposit boxes for storing securities was not all bad news for banks. As already discussed, banks are involved in custodial activities for securities and, as detailed in Chapter 11, transfer activities for securities.

2.   Do you or a member of your family own a safe deposit box? What is stored in that box? Who holds the key? What happens when the box holder dies?

3.   Would a personal safe be as effective as a safe deposit box in protecting your valuables?

4.   A large number of safe deposit boxes recovered from the rubble of the World Trade Center in the wake of the September 11 attacks at J. P. Morgan Chase & Co. were found to have suffered severe damage from heat from the fires generated by the terrorist attacks. Some of the jewelry and artifacts were melted or burned beyond recognition. The bank disclaimed all liability. Pamela Sebastian Ridge, Not–So–Safe Deposit Boxes, Wall St. J., Jan. 18, 2002.

SECTION 6.   FUND TRANSFER SERVICES

Banks provide a number of other services to their customers, including electronic (wire) transfers of funds. Time is money and such transfers facilitate business. There are a number of systems used for such transfers among banks. The Clearing House Interbank Payments System (CHIPS) is a wire system created by the clearing house for its member banks. In 1972, the Federal Reserve Bank of San Francisco began exchanging electronic payments with its Los Angeles branch. That service was expanded to all Federal Reserve Banks in 1978, and is now called the Fedwire. It is a real-time payment system that is operated by the Fed for banks that have reserve or clearing accounts with a regional Federal Reserve Bank. Internationally, the Society for Worldwide Interbank Financial Telecommunications (SWIFT), headquartered in Brussels, Belgium, provides a messaging system that facilitates inter-bank transfers and communications. It serves banks in over 100 countries.

BANCA COMMERCIALE ITALIANA, NEW YORK BRANCH v. NORTHERN TRUST INTERNATIONAL BANKING CORP.

United States Court of Appeals, Second Circuit, 1998.
160 F.3d 90.

WALKER, CIRCUIT JUDGE.

* * * On April 23, 1991, the London Branch of Banca Commerciale Italiana ("BCI–London") agreed by telephone to a currency swap with Wallace Smith Trust Co. Ltd. ("Wallace Smith") whereby BCI–London would sell £1,750,000 to Wallace Smith in exchange for $2,968,262.50. BCI–London agreed to send the pounds sterling that day to Wallace Smith's account at Midland Bank, and Wallace Smith agreed to send the dollars to BCI–NY for the account of BCI–London. BCI–London sent the £1,750,000 to Midland Bank by 9:06 a.m. Wallace Smith then issued instructions to Northern Trust to pay $2,968,262.50 to BCI–NY for the account of BCI–London.

Northern Trust issued a payment order to BCI–NY for the benefit of BCI–London in the requisite amount through the New York Clearing House Interbank Payments System ("CHIPS"). That order hit BCI–NY's CHIPS computer at 12:50:42 p.m., and was posted to the account of BCI–London by 3:16:44 p.m.

That same day, apparently after Northern Trust's payment order had been sent to BCI–NY, Wallace Smith telephoned Northern Trust to cancel the payment to BCI–NY for the account of BCI–London and at 4:17 p.m. confirmed that instruction by telex. This act set off a sequence of events that is at the heart of this dispute over who should bear the loss of the nearly $3 million at issue. Northern Trust called BCI–NY and followed up with a telex sent at 5:02 p.m., requesting that BCI–NY "refund the amount of USD 2,968,262.50 which was not intended for you." In the same telex, Northern Trust gave its guarantee that "in consideration of your complying with the terms of this indemnity we agree to indemnify you according to the Compensation Indemnity and Responses contained in the Council on International Banking[']s Guideline For Issuing and Responding to an Indemnity."

CHIPS transactions on the day in question settled at 5:21 p.m. At 5:48 p.m. the same day, BCI–NY returned $2,968,262.50 to Northern Trust via Fedwire wire transfer. Northern Trust credited the returned amount to the account of Wallace Smith.

Two days later, on April 25, 1991, in accordance with the rules of the Council on International Banking ("CIB"), Northern Trust asked that BCI–NY "release [it] from [its] guarantee as funds were returned sameday [sic] via your [Fedwire]." Although BCI–NY had not contacted BCI–London to obtain its debit authorization, on August 29, 1991 BCI–NY sent Northern Trust a transmission that read: "re YR TLX. GTY DD 4 23 91.... We hereby consider YR GTY as null and void as funds were refunded same day via our Fed [wire]." In an affidavit submitted to the district court, Rene Seghini, the head of the Investigations Department of BCI–NY, admitted that he

> sent the message [to Northern Trust] ... because my department made an error.... My department verified our return of the funds and simply assumed, without checking, that the request from Northern Trust had come early enough in the day for operations to have called BCI London and procured their consent to the return.

BCI–London apparently did not consent to the return of funds because BCI–NY alleges that it was later required to "re-credit[] to BCI London the amount of $2,968,262.50 upon demand of BCI London."

Within two weeks of Northern Trust's request for the return of funds, Wallace Smith's operations were suspended by the Bank of England, and insolvency proceedings ensued. In the wake of Wallace Smith's demise, its principal was imprisoned for six years for a £100 million fraud. * * *

Article 4–A of New York's Uniform Commercial Code governs the rights and liabilities of parties involved in commercial electronic funds transfers. BCI–NY's Article 4–A claim was brought pursuant to § 211(6), which provides:

> Unless otherwise provided in an agreement of the parties or in a funds-transfer system rule, if the receiving bank, after accepting a payment order, agrees to cancellation or amendment of the order by the sender or is bound by a funds-transfer system rule allowing cancellation or amendment without the bank's agreement, the sender, whether or not cancellation or amendment is effective, is liable to the bank for any loss and expenses, including reasonable attorney's fees, incurred by the bank as a result of the cancellation or amendment or attempted cancellation or amendment.

N.Y. U.C.C. § 4–A–211(6). Northern Trust argues that this section does not apply to the transaction at issue because it was governed by the CIB Rules, a "funds-transfer system rule." We need not address this argument, however, because we agree with the district court's conclusion that BCI–NY's Article 4–A claims were time-barred. * * *

Even assuming, as BCI–NY argues, that unresolved questions of fact remain as to BCI–NY's fraud and unjust enrichment claims, Northern Trust is nevertheless entitled to summary judgment on these common law claims because BCI–NY released them. BCI–NY informed Northern Trust that it "consider[ed Northern Trust's] guaranty as null and void" two days after returning the funds to Northern Trust. The district court interpreted this communication as a general release of BCI–NY's common law claims. We agree.

BCI–NY's first two arguments are that the communication, which does not use the word "release," was not intended as a release, or at any rate, is too ambiguous to be interpreted as a release. These arguments are without merit.

As we discussed above, Northern Trust invoked the CIB Rules in its 5:02 p.m. telex of April 23, 1991, which requested repayment and stated that "in consideration of your complying with the terms of this indemnity we agree to indemnify you according to [the CIB Rules]." As BCI–NY acknowledges, the CIB Rules did not obligate it to return the funds to Northern Trust. However, the CIB Rules provided that upon accepting Northern Trust's offer of indemnity, BCI–NY "agreed to contact [BCI–London] immediately to obtain its debit authorization. Upon receiving such debit authorization, [Northern Trust's] obligations under this Indemnity will cease and [BCI–NY] will notify [Northern Trust] of [its] release hereunder." Thus, as the district court noted, this agreement, as mandated by the CIB Rules, placed squarely on BCI–NY the obligation to contact BCI–London prior to releasing Northern Trust's guarantee.

As Mr. Seghini of BCI–NY admitted, when BCI–NY received the request for a release from Northern Trust, he mistakenly assumed that debit authorization had already been obtained from BCI–London. Although Mr. Seghini contends that he consciously did not intend to give a release, but merely wanted to inform Northern Trust that BCI–NY was no longer relying on the indemnity, we are hard-pressed to find an alternative interpretation of BCI–NY's telex other then that it constituted a release. BCI–NY has offered no reason for why it would not have given a release when it believed BCI–London had already consented (which, if true, would have obligated BCI–NY to give a release under the CIB Rules). Second, BCI–NY offers no alternative interpretation for the words it did use: your guaranty is null and void. Instead it says "the words mean just what they say." To us, these words mean that Northern Trust was released from its indemnity.

Next, BCI–NY renews its argument from below that the release should be invalidated on the ground of unilateral mistake—namely, BCI–NY's mistaken belief that BCI–London had consented to the return of funds. The *Middle East* court rejected this same argument based on the fact that there was no evidence that the sending bank in that case knew or had reason to know that the release had been sent in error, i.e., without the beneficiary's debit authorization. See [Middle East Banking Co. v.

State St. Bank Int'l,] 821 F.2d [897] at 906 [(2d Cir. 1987)]. The same reasoning applies here. We also agree with the district court that none of the cases cited by BCI–NY stands for the proposition that in the time since *Middle East* was decided, the New York courts have adopted a doctrine of unilateral mistake that does not require that the mistake is "one which is known or ought to have been known to the other party." Id. See, e.g., Gould v. Board of Educ., 616 N.E.2d 142 (1993) (applying doctrine of mutual mistake to rescission of contract).

Finally, BCI argues that even if its communication to Northern Trust was a release, the release was limited to Northern Trust's indemnification and did not constitute a general release of its common law claims. *Middle East* is instructive on this point. There the court held that because the indemnity was absolute, the release was also absolute, on the ground that the " 'release of the guarantee is considered equally as encompassing as the guarantee itself,' " 821 F.2d at 908 (quoting expert testimony), as well as the fact that the "burden is on the releasor to establish that the release should be limited," id. at 907. Although in other contexts we might hesitate to adopt such a broad rule, in the peculiar context of electronic funds transfers, where hundreds of billions of dollars are transferred daily via hundreds of thousands of electronic funds transfers, see *Banque Worms*, 77 N.Y.2d at 369–70 (discussing volume, costs, and efficiency of electronic funds transfers); *Middle East*, 821 F.2d at 900 n.1 (same), the need for certainty with respect to such unnegotiated interbank communications is paramount.

Accordingly, we agree with the *Middle East* court that the release should ordinarily be considered to be as broad as the indemnity and that the burden is on the releasor to establish that the release is more limited. In the present case, BCI–NY failed to meet its burden of establishing that the release was limited. The indemnity issued by Northern Trust provided that BCI–NY would be indemnified "against any and all claims, liabilities, losses, [and] expenses." Northern Trust then expressly requested to be released on its indemnity. The communication sent in response to this request did not indicate any limitations or qualifications, but simply stated that BCI–NY considered Northern Trust's indemnity to be "null and void." In the absence of any qualifications, BCI–NY should reasonably have expected Northern Trust to rely on BCI–NY's statement, by, for example, releasing the funds back to Wallace Smith. We therefore affirm the district court's holding that the communication sent by BCI–NY was as broad as the indemnity issued by Northern Trust. Because the indemnity applied to all claims, BCI–NY's communication constituted a general release barring BCI–NY's common law claims. * * *

QUESTIONS AND NOTES

1. If this claim had not been released, how would you decide the case?

2. The Bankhaus Herstatt created a crisis in the CHIPS system in 1974 when it became insolvent due to large losses in foreign currency operations.

The bank declared bankruptcy at the end of its business day in Europe, but trading continued in the United States. An issue arose as to whether the closed positions in Germany could be netted against offsetting contracts in the United States that were still open. See Delbrueck & Co. v. Manufacturers Hanover Trust Co., 609 F.2d 1047 (2d Cir. 1979). Herstatt accounts in the United States were frozen while this and other issues were sorted out, and wire transfers were stopped through CHIPS for the Herstatt account. Concern arose that there could be other failures, and CHIPS became grid-locked as banks waited for each other to pay. That impasse was finally resolved. Thereafter, CHIPS adopted a settlement rule that requires same day settlement in order to avoid such concerns.

3. As described in Chapter 14, the SWIFT payments system was used by the U.S. government to monitor terrorist financing activities, creating a storm of controversy.

4. The Dodd–Frank Act, §§ 801–814, identify payment and clearing systems as a matter of systemic risk concern. The Act imposed several regulatory responses to improve supervision in order to guard against systemic risk. See Chapter 11 for additional discussion.

CHAPTER ELEVEN

CAPITAL MARKET ACTIVITIES

■ ■ ■

The involvement of banks in securities activities has varied over time and been subject to a wide variety of legal limitations. The authority for bank ownership of investment securities is discussed in Chapter 5. The ability of banks to act as brokers in buying and selling securities for third parties and to act as underwriters in bringing securities offerings to market is discussed in this Chapter. This Chapter also discusses other activities associated with the securities business in which banks now engage, including commercial paper, mergers, and mutual funds.

SECTION 1. HISTORICAL LIMITATIONS

A. EARLY RESTRICTIONS

BLOCK v. PENNSYLVANIA EXCHANGE BANK

New York Court of Appeals, 1930.
170 N.E. 900.

CARDOZO, CHIEF JUDGE.

Plaintiffs, stockbrokers in the city of New York, bought shares of stock and subscription rights on the order of the defendant bank, which "was acting as agent for a third party or parties unknown at said times to the plaintiffs."

The bank declined to accept the certificates when tendered or to pay the purchase price. Upon this, the brokers sold what they had bought, and sued for the deficiency.

* * * "The central function of a commercial bank is to substitute its own credit, which has general acceptance in the business community, for the individual's credit, which has only limited acceptability" (Willis & Edwards, Banking and Business, p.74). A bank "manufactures credit by accepting the business paper of its customers as security in exchange for its own bank credit in the form of a deposit account" (Holdsworth, Money and Banking, p. 182). It stands ready to exchange its own credits for those of its customers. Whatever is an appropriate and usual incident to this

substitution or exchange of credits, instead of being foreign to the functions and activities of banking, is in truth of their very essence. It is the end for which a bank exists.

Indisputably the defendant would have kept within its charter if it had made a loan of money wherewith to enable a customer to buy securities for himself. It could not have done an act more characteristic of the banking business. Having power to loan, it had power as an incident to receive securities as collateral, and to use the proceeds of the loan, if so authorized by the borrower, in acquiring the securities and subjecting them thereafter to its possession and dominion. This would not be doubted if in ordering the securities, it had given up the name of its customer with the result that the brokers would look to the customer as principal. We think its power does not fail where it buys in its own name, the moneys being already in its coffers either through previous deposits or as the proceeds of a discount. We are told that in giving an order in its own name it augments the risk of the transaction. Negligence or mistake in the transmission of the order might lead the customer thereafter to repudiate the purchase, in which event the bank would hold the securities as owner. We may doubt whether the risk would be greatly different if the bank in transmitting the order were to give up the name of its customer as principal. There would go with the order even then an implied warranty of authority, and the customer might repudiate the purchase if there was a departure from his mandate. But risk without more does not serve as a decisive test of power and legality. The bank might have opened a credit in favor of the brokers, to be availed of by drafts when accompanied by shares of stock. The risk would be substantially the same, yet no one would doubt that the transaction would be within the range of banking power. Every day banks subject themselves to a like risk of liability when upon the instructions of a customer they take up drafts with bills of lading attached. * * *

There is no question that the practice of banking as it has developed in our day upholds the purchase of securities for the benefit of customers whose deposit accounts are sufficient, as the result of loans or otherwise, to justify the credit. The practice is so general that it may be the subject of judicial notice. In many banks special departments are organized for that very purpose. All this was elucidated in our opinion in Dyer v. Broadway Central Bank (supra). Hubbs, J., writing for the court, reminded us that many depositors are accustomed to deal directly with their banks in the purchase of securities; that the validity of the practice has had tacit recognition in our decisions (Central Nat. Bank v. White, 139 N.Y. 631; Le Marchant v. Moore, 150 N. Y. 209); that it has never been questioned by the Superintendent of Banks or other administrative agencies; and that "the transactions of banking in a great financial center are not to be clogged, and their pace slackened, by overburdensome restrictions" (Whiting v. Hudson Trust Co., 234 N. Y. 394, 406; cf. Empire Trust Co. v. Cahan, 274 U.S. 473, 480). At the same time the case of Jemison v. Citizens Sav. Bank of Jefferson (supra) was sufficiently distinguished (cf.

Hotchkin v. Third Nat. Bank, 219 Mass. 234). It is enough indeed to recall that a bank for savings, unlike a bank of discount, is merely a depository and not a medium for the exchange of credits. In principle at least, the line of demarcation is not doubtful, however much it may be blurred at times by the encroachments of obscuring facts. On the one side are speculative purchases for the benefit of the bank itself, or in aid of some transaction foreign to the banking function. On the other are transactions where the pledge of the credit of the bank is tributary to an exchange of credit for the accommodation of a customer. * * *

Although banks were allowed to broker securities on behalf of their customers, the Comptroller of the Currency ruled in 1902 that a national bank could not underwrite corporate security offerings, but could continue to underwrite corporate and government debt securities. In order to avoid the restriction on underwriting corporate securities, several large banks formed affiliates to conduct broad-based securities businesses.[1] One such affiliate, National City Co., was created by National City Bank, which eventually evolved into Citibank. In 1911, the United States Solicitor General and Attorney General advised National City Bank that the operation of the securities affiliate violated banking laws. The Secretary of the Treasury, however, took the opposite position and the matter was submitted to President William H. Taft, who decided to do nothing. National City Co. continued its operations and was in the forefront of underwriting and sales activities for retail customers during the market runup that preceded the stock market crash of 1929.

After the market crash, Congressional investigators found that National City Co. had engaged in numerous abusive sales practices and had participated as an underwriter in several offerings that became virtually worthless, resulting in large losses to customers. National City Bank also provided large amounts of credit to speculators trading on margin with National City Co., even while the Federal Reserve was trying to restrict such credit in the days before the stock market crash. The Bank of United States, which operated a large securities affiliate, also failed during this period, causing further concern with bank involvement in the securities business.[2]

B. THE GLASS–STEAGALL ACT

Congress enacted the Glass–Steagall Act as part of the Banking Act of 1933, in response to the perceived dangers posed to banks by their

---

1. The McFadden Act of 1927 explicitly authorized national banks to underwrite certain corporate and government debt securities.

2. For a discussion of the background and operation of these bank securities affiliates see Jerry W. Markham, A Financial History of the United States: From J.P. Morgan to the Institutional Investor (1900–1970) 23, 57–58, 150–153, 168–169 (2001).

securities affiliates. The legislative history of that act and a description of its relevant provisions are discussed in the next case.

SECURITIES INDUSTRY ASS'N v. BOARD OF GOVERNORS OF THE FEDERAL RESERVE SYSTEM

United States Court of Appeals, Second Circuit, 1988.
839 F.2d 47, *cert. denied*, 486 U.S. 1059.

CARDAMORE, CIRCUIT JUDGE.

* * * The whole of the Banking Act of 1933, ch. 89, Pub. L. No. 73–66, 48 Stat. 162 (1933) (codified as amended in scattered sections of 12 U.S.C.), is sometimes referred to as the Glass–Steagall Act. It is perhaps more accurate to consider §§ 16, 20, 21, and 32 of the Banking Act of 1933 in particular as the Glass–Steagall Act. These sections, the " 'Maginot Line' of the financial world," see Macey, Special Interest Groups Legislation and the Judicial Function: The Dilemma of Glass–Steagall, 33 Emory L.J. 1, 5 (1984) [hereinafter *Glass-Steagall Dilemma*] (quoting Bevis Longstreth, "Current Issues Facing the Securities Industry and the SEC," May 4, 1982 speech to the SIA), were meant to separate commercial and investment banking.

Section 16 of the Glass–Steagall Act applies to federally chartered banks and restricts their powers. In pertinent part, the statute as amended provides:

> The business of dealing in securities and stock by the [member bank] shall be limited to purchasing and selling such securities and stock without recourse, solely upon the order, and for the account of, customers, and in no case for its own account, and the [member bank] shall not underwrite any issue of securities or stock.... The limitations and restrictions herein contained as to dealing in, underwriting and purchasing for its own account, investment securities shall not apply to obligations of the United States, or general obligations of any State or of any political subdivision thereof....

12 U.S.C. § 24 (Seventh) (1982 & Supp. IV 1986).

As can be readily seen, § 16 forbids national banks from underwriting "any issue of securities or stock" and also limits their ability to deal in securities. As noted, it expressly excepts from its coverage underwriting and dealing in the obligations of the United States or general obligations of states or their political subdivisions, which we have termed "bank-eligible securities."

Section 21 seeks to draw the same line as § 16 does for commercial banks, but from the perspective of investment banks. Section 21 as amended reads in pertinent part:

> (a) After the expiration of one year after June 16, 1933, it shall be unlawful—(1) For any person, firm, corporation, association, business trust, or other similar organization, engaged in the business of

issuing, underwriting, selling, or distributing, at wholesale or retail, or through syndicate participation, stocks, bonds, debentures, notes, or other securities, to engage at the same time to any extent whatever in the business of receiving deposits subject to check or to repayment upon presentation of a passbook, certificate of deposit, or other evidence of debt, or upon request of the depositor: *Provided*, That the provisions of this paragraph shall not prohibit national banks or State banks or trust companies (whether or not members of the Federal Reserve System) or other financial institutions or private bankers from dealing in, underwriting, purchasing, and selling investment securities, or issuing securities, to the extent permitted to national banking associations by the provisions of section 24 of this title....

12 U.S.C. § 378(a)(1) (1982). Section 21 prohibits firms *"engaged"* in certain investment banking activities from undertaking commercial banking activities. As originally drafted and enacted it did not contain the § 16 proviso that allowed banks to underwrite and deal in bank-eligible securities. See Banking Act of 1933, § 21, 48 Stat. at 189. A 1935 amendment to § 21 made explicit that § 21 did not prohibit those activities permitted member banks under § 16. See Banking Act of 1935, Pub. L. No. 74–305, ch. 614, tit. III, § 303(a), 49 Stat. 684, 707 (1935).

Sections 32 and 20 are the Glass–Steagall Act's "remaining ramparts" in the line between commercial and investment banking. *Glass-Steagall Dilemma*, supra, at 6. Section 32 as amended reads in its entirety:

No officer, director, or employee of any corporation or unincorporated association, no partner or employee of any partnership, and no individual, *primarily engaged* in the issue, flotation, underwriting, public sale, or distribution, at wholesale or retail, or through syndicate participation, of stocks, bonds, or other similar securities, shall serve the same time as an officer, director, or employee of any member bank except in limited classes of cases in which the Board of Governors of the Federal Reserve System may allow such service by general regulations when in the judgment of the said Board it would not unduly influence the investment policies of such member bank or the advice it gives its customers regarding investments.

12 U.S.C. § 78 (1982) (emphasis added). Section 32 prohibits personnel "interlocks" between member banks and firms that are *"primarily engaged"* in the business of underwriting or dealing in securities. * * *

Finally, § 20 * * * provides in pertinent part:

After one year from June 16, 1933, *no member bank shall be affiliated* in any manner described in subsection (b) of section 221a of this title with any corporation, association, business trust, or other similar *organization engaged principally in the issue*, flotation, underwriting, public sale, or distribution at wholesale or retail or through syndicate participation of *stocks, bonds, debentures, notes, or other securities....*

12 U.S.C. § 377 (1982). * * *

The Act's legislative history reflects the notion that the underlying cause of the stock market crash in 1929 and subsequent bank insolvencies came about from the excessive use of bank credit to speculate in the stock market. See S. Rep. No. 77, 73d Cong., 1st Sess. 3–9 (1933) [hereinafter *1933 Senate Report*]; see also 75 Cong. Rec. 9883–84 (1932) (remarks of Sen. Glass) (criticizing transformation of the Federal Reserve System from a commercial banking system into one used for "stock-market speculative operations"). Bank affiliates were identified as a major factor in the overextension of credit for security loans. See *1933 Senate Report*, supra, at 9–10.

Congress' concern was not limited solely to how securities affiliates contributed to the excesses in bank credit; its apprehension was far more fundamental and structural. Senator Bulkley, for example, repeatedly stressed that the debate over affiliates should not obscure "[t]he important and underlying question [of] whether banking institutions receiving commercial and savings deposits ought to be permitted at all to engage in the investment-security business." 75 Cong. Rec. 9910 (1932). * * *

Two large problems attendant upon the involvement of a commercial bank in investment banking—either on its own or through use of an affiliate—were identified by Congress. The first was "the danger of banks using bank assets in imprudent securities investments." ICI, 450 U.S. at 66. The second "focused on the more subtle hazards that arise when a commercial bank goes beyond the business of acting as fiduciary or managing agent and enters the investment banking business either directly or by establishing an affiliate to hold and sell particular investments." Camp, 401 U.S. at 630. * * *

The next case marked the judicial high water mark for the Glass–Steagall Act. The Supreme Court held that a bank could not operate a mutual fund, distinguishing mutual funds from traditional collective trust funds, which were permitted. The Court also set forth the "subtle hazards" analysis alluded to in the prior case.

INVESTMENT COMPANY INSTITUTE v. CAMP

Supreme Court of the United States, 1971.
401 U.S. 617.

MR. JUSTICE STEWART delivered the opinion of the Court.

* * * The Glass–Steagall Act reflected a determination that policies of competition, convenience, or expertise which might otherwise support the entry of commercial banks into the investment banking business was outweighed by the "hazards" and "financial dangers" that arise when commercial banks engage in the activities proscribed by the Act.

The hazards that Congress had in mind were not limited to the obvious danger that a bank might invest its own assets in frozen or otherwise imprudent stocks or security investments. For often securities affiliates had operated without direct access to the assets of the bank. This was because securities affiliates had frequently been established with capital paid in by the bank's stockholders, or by the public, or through the allocation of a legal dividend on bank stock for this purpose. The legislative history of the Glass–Steagall Act shows that Congress also had in mind and repeatedly focused on the more subtle hazards that arise when a commercial bank goes beyond the business of acting as fiduciary or managing agent and enters the investment banking business either directly or by establishing an affiliate to hold and sell particular investments. This course places new promotional and other pressures on the bank which in turn create new temptations. For example, pressures are created because the bank and the affiliate are closely associated in the public mind, and should the affiliate fare badly, public confidence in the bank might be impaired. And since public confidence is essential to the solvency of a bank, there might exist a natural temptation to shore up the affiliate through unsound loans or other aid. Moreover, the pressure to sell a particular investment and to make the affiliate successful might create a risk that the bank would make its credit facilities more freely available to those companies in whose stock or securities the affiliate has invested or become otherwise involved. Congress feared that banks might even go so far as to make unsound loans to such companies. In any event, it was thought that the bank's salesman's interest might impair its ability to function as an impartial source of credit.

Congress was also concerned that bank depositors might suffer losses on investments that they purchase in reliance on the relationship between the bank and its affiliate. This loss of customer goodwill might "become an important handicap to a bank during a major period of security market deflation." More broadly, Congress feared that the promotional needs of investment banking might lead commercial banks to lend their reputation for prudence and restraint to the enterprise of selling particular stocks and securities, and that this could not be done without that reputation being undercut by the risks necessarily incident to the investment banking business. There was also perceived the danger that when commercial banks were subject to the promotional demands of investment banking, they might be tempted to make loans to customers with the expectation that the loan would facilitate the purchase of stocks and securities. There was evidence before Congress that loans for investment written by commercial banks had done much to feed the speculative fever of the late 1920's. * * *

In sum, Congress acted to keep commercial banks out of the investment banking business largely because it believed that the promotional incentive of investment banking and the investment banker's pecuniary stake in the success of particular investment opportunities was destructive of prudent and disinterested commercial banking and of public confidence in the commercial banking system. * * *

(1) Brokering Securities

Section 16 of the Glass–Steagall Act provided explicit authority for a national bank to broker securities. Section 16 of the Glass–Steagall Act also applied to state member banks. 12 U.S.C.A. § 335. The scope of securities activities available to state nonmember banks was determined by state law and the FDIC. The Securities Exchange Act of 1934 exempted banks from registration as broker-dealers. Over time, however, the ambit of bank brokerage operations expanded through regulatory interpretation and the exemption from broker-dealer registration was attacked.

AMERICAN BANKERS ASS'N v. SECURITIES AND EXCHANGE COMMISSION

United States Court of Appeals, District of Columbia Circuit, 1986.
804 F.2d 739.

WALD, CHIEF JUDGE.

* * * The current controversy arises over fifty years after Congress passed the Securities Exchange Act because of a change in the administrative interpretation of the Banking Act of 1933, commonly referred to as the Glass–Steagall Act. * * *

The Comptroller of the Currency, charged with the duty of regulating the corporate powers of national banks, took the lead in interpreting these provisions of the Glass–Steagall Act for enforcement purposes. In 1936, the Comptroller construed the Glass–Steagall Act to limit brokerage activities by national banks to purchase and sale transactions for "actual customers of the bank, which customer relationship exists independently and apart from the particular transaction in which the bank buys or sells upon the order and for the account of such 'customer.'" 1 Bulletin of the Comptroller of the Currency ¶ 36 (October 26, 1936). The Comptroller also ruled that a national bank "is not authorized to retain any commission, rebate, or discount obtained from others in purchasing for a customer [securities or stock] unless it does not exceed the cost of handling the transaction." Id. ¶ 10. The Comptroller justified limiting the charge for brokering a customer's securities or stock on the grounds that the purpose of § 16 of the Glass–Steagall Act was "to prevent national banks from engaging in the brokerage business for profit." Id. Thus, under the Comptroller's original interpretation of the Glass–Steagall Act, a national bank could engage in brokerage activities only as "an accommodation agent" for the convenience of existing customers of the bank's traditional banking services. For example, a bank could purchase or sell securities for a trust account that it managed, but it could not make any money on its trades for that account.

This original administrative construction of the Glass–Steagall Act has been dismantled piecemeal over the last fifty years. First, in 1957, the

Comptroller repudiated the requirement that national banks receive no profit from the brokerage transactions that they perform for the convenience of their customers. See Digest of Opinions of the Comptroller of the Currency ¶ 220A (August 1957 Edition) (quoted in [1973–1978 Transfer Binder] Fed. Banking L. Rep. (CCH) ¶ 96,272 at 81,357). Nevertheless, at that time, the Comptroller retained the notion that banks could not perform "functions [that] would amount to engaging in the brokerage ... business ... beyond the permissible scope of limited accommodation services." Id. Moreover, the Comptroller in 1957 explicitly reiterated its earlier requirement that bank brokerage services "must be limited to actual customers of the bank—that is, the customer relationship must exist independently of the particular securities transaction." Id.

Then, in 1974, the Comptroller interpreted Glass–Steagall to allow banks to offer and advertise computer-assisted stock purchasing services. See Comptroller of the Currency Opinion Letter (June 10, 1974), reprinted in [1973–1978 Transfer Binder] Fed. Banking L. Rep. (CCH) ¶ 96,272 at 81,353. Answering the argument that these services, and in particular, dissemination of advertising about them, controverted the concept of "limited accommodation services," the Comptroller noted that "the 'accommodation' concept is not contained in the statute." Id. at 81,360. Because, however, the automatic investment service was limited to customers of the bank's checking accounts, the Comptroller did not explicitly address whether bank could offer and advertise brokerage services for nonbanking customers.

Finally, in 1982, the Comptroller abandoned its interpretation that § 16 of the Glass–Steagall Act limited bank brokerage activities to customers of traditional banking services by allowing a national bank to establish a subsidiary to offer retail discount brokerage services, to banking and nonbanking customers alike, at branch offices of the bank.

See In re Security Pacific National Bank (August 26, 1982), reprinted in [1982–1983 Transfer Binder]Fed. Banking L. Rep. (CCH) ¶ 99,284 at 86,255. The Comptroller has subsequently made clear that its new interpretation of § 16 applies to the brokerage activities of a bank itself in addition to those of a bank subsidiary. See, e.g., Comptroller of the Currency Opinion Letter No. 363 (May 23, 1986); see also 50 Fed. Reg. 31,605 (August 5, 1985) (withdrawing proposed rule which would require national banks engaging in discount brokerage services to do so through a nonbanking subsidiary). Both the Board of Governors of the Federal Reserve Board and the Federal Deposit Insurance Corporation, acting pursuant to their respective authority to interpret the Glass–Steagall Act, have also recently interpreted §§ 16 and 21 to allow banks to engage in brokerage services for nonbanking customers. See Federal Reserve Board's Statement Concerning Applicability of the Glass–Steagall Act to the Commercial Paper Placement Activities of Bankers Trust Company (June 4, 1985); FDIC General Counsel's Opinion No. 6, 48 Fed. Reg. 22,989 (May 23, 1983).

The SEC never attempted to apply its broker-dealer regulations to banks that engaged in profitless accommodation transactions. Nor did the SEC attempt to regulate banks as broker-dealers after either the 1957 or the 1974 revisions in the Comptroller's interpretation. The dramatic surge of banks into the discount brokerage business, resulting from the post–1980 administrative reinterpretations of Glass–Steagall, however, prompted the SEC to subject banks engaging in brokerage business to the same broker-dealer regulation as nonbank brokers.

Thus, in 1985, the SEC issued Rule 3b–9. The Rule regulates as a broker-dealer a bank that either "[p]ublicly solicits brokerage business for which it receives transaction-related compensation" or "receives transaction-related compensation for providing brokerage services for trust, managing agency or other accounts to which the bank provides advice." 17 C.F.R. § 240.3b–9(a)(1)(2) (1986). The Rule goes on to define "transaction-related compensation" to "mean monetary profit to the bank in excess of cost recovery for providing brokerage execution services." Id. § 240.3b–9(d). In other words, the SEC Rule does not reach banks which engage only in the profitless accommodation brokerage service permitted by the Comptroller's original 1936 ruling. But it does cover banks that seek profit from their brokerage business, whether that business was generated from public solicitation or from their existing banking customers.

Rule 3b–9 proceeds on the premise that regulatory authority should be divided among government agencies according to the different financial functions performed by the regulated entity, and not according to the species of financial institution it is (as defined by its charter or even its *primary* function). While this regulatory philosophy enjoys favor in many circles and has received the endorsement of a special task force established to conduct a comprehensive evaluation of federal financial regulation, it is, unfortunately, not the approach taken by the 73rd Congress, which enacted the Securities Exchange Act of 1934. In that Act, as we shall see, Congress explicitly excluded banks from the rules governing brokers and dealers. * * *

Section 3 of the 1934 Act excludes banks from the statutory definitions of "broker" and "dealer." The Act states that "[t]he term 'broker' means any person engaging in the business of effecting transactions in securities for the account of others, *but does not include a bank*." 15 U.S.C. § 78c(a)(4) (emphasis supplied). Similarly, the statute states that "the term 'dealer' means any person engaged in the business of buying or selling securities for his own account ... *but does not include a bank* ...." 15 U.S.C. § 78c(a)(5) (emphasis supplied). * * *

In the end, all of the SEC's efforts to avoid the "plain meaning" of the definitions of "broker," "dealer" and "bank" fail. We give effect to the statutory language not simply because its meaning is as "plain" as can be, but because it reflects a basic decision by Congress on how to allocate responsibility among different federal agencies for regulating financial institutions and markets. Rule 3b–9, whatever its beneficial purpose or the regulatory need for some such authority, still represents an attempt by one federal agency to reallocate, on its own initiative, the regulatory responsibilities Congress has purposefully divided among several different agencies. It is tantamount to one of the regulatory players unilaterally changing the rules of the game. The SEC by itself cannot extend its jurisdiction over institutions expressly entrusted to the oversight of the Comptroller, the Board of Governors, the FDIC, and others. * * *

———————

Congress adopted a system of shared regulatory authority for the securities activities that banks had not been barred from by the provisions of the Glass–Steagall Act. In 1975, Congress allocated jurisdiction over stock transfer agents and security clearing agencies (entities that act as custodians or settle security payments) between the Securities and Exchange Commission (SEC) and the bank regulators. Banks engaged in those activities were required to register with their appropriate bank regulatory agency. Nonbank transfer agents and clearing agencies were required to register with the SEC and were subject to its jurisdiction. 15 U.S.C. § 78q–1.[3] In the case of municipal securities, the Municipal Securities Rule Making Board (MSRB) (a self-regulatory body) was given authority to regulate the dealer activities in state and municipal securities of banks and other institutions. That organization was placed under the oversight of the SEC, but the SEC was denied enforcement authority over banks acting as dealers. That enforcement authority was placed in the hands of the bank regulators. 15 U.S.C. §§ 78c(a)(30), (a)(34) & 78o–4. In another case of shared regulatory authority, banks acting as dealers in federal government securities were subject to regulation under the Government Securities Act of 1986, Pub. L. No. 99–571, 100 Stat. 3208. Under that legislation, the Secretary of the Treasury was given rulemaking authority, and bank regulators were given supervisory authority over banks dealing in this market. The SEC was given enforcement authority over non-bank dealers, including previously unregistered broker-dealers that had caused problems in the government securities market.

Bank holding companies were also able to broker securities. The Bank Holding Company Act of 1956 limited bank holding company affiliates in section 4 of that legislation to the ownership of nonbanking companies only if the activities of the company were "so closely related to banking ... as to be a proper incident thereto." 12 U.S.C.A. § 1843(c)(8). Since brokerage was permitted for banks, it was clearly "closely related to banking" and thus permitted for nonbanking subsidiaries of bank holding companies.

———————

3. See 23A Jerry W. Markham & Thomas Lee Hazen, Broker–Dealer Operations Under Securities and Commodities Law §§ 8.02 & 8.04 (2000) (describing jurisdictional fights over these provisions by the SEC and bank regulators).

SECURITIES INDUSTRY ASS'N v. BOARD OF GOVERNORS OF THE FEDERAL RESERVE SYSTEM

Supreme Court of the United States, 1984.
468 U.S. 207.

MR. JUSTICE POWELL delivered the opinion of the Court.

* * * BankAmerica Corp. (BAC) is a bank holding company within the meaning of the Bank Holding Company Act. In March 1982, BAC applied to the Federal Reserve Board (Board) for approval under § 4(c)(8) of the Act to acquire 100 percent of the voting shares of The Charles Schwab Corp., a company that engages through its wholly owned subsidiary, Charles Schwab & Co. (Schwab), in retail discount brokerage.[4] * * *

Section 4 of the Bank Holding Company Act (BHC Act) prohibits the acquisition by bank holding companies of the voting shares of nonbanking entities unless the acquisition is specifically exempted. The principal exemption to that prohibition is found in § 4(c)(8). That provision authorizes bank holding companies, with prior Board approval, to engage in nonbanking activities that the Board determines are "so closely related to banking ... as to be a proper incident thereto." 12 U.S.C. § 1843(c)(8). * * *

In this case, the Board concluded that Schwab's brokerage services were "closely related" to banking because it found that the services were "operationally and functionally very similar to the types of brokerage services that are generally provided by banks and that banking organizations are particularly well equipped to provide such services." 69 Fed. Res. Bull., at 107. The Board acted well within its discretion in ruling on such factors. Moreover, the Board's factual findings are substantially supported by the record.

Banks long have arranged the purchase and sale of securities as an accommodation to their customers. Congress expressly endorsed this traditional banking service in 1933. Section 16 of the Glass–Steagall Act authorizes banks to continue the practice of "purchasing and selling ... securities and stock without recourse, solely upon the order, and for the account of, customers, and in no case for [their] own [accounts]." 12 U.S.C. § 24 Seventh. The Board found that in substance the brokerage services that Schwab performs for its customers are not significantly different from those that banks, under the authority of § 16, have been performing for their own customers for years. See 69 Fed. Res. Bull., at 107–109. Moreover, the amendment to Regulation Y, added by the Board in 1983 to reflect its decision in this case, expressly limits the securities brokerage services in which a bank may engage "to buying and selling

---

4. [n.2] Schwab is known as a "discount" broker because of the low commissions it charges. Schwab can afford to charge lower commissions than full-service brokerage firms because it does not provide investment advice or analysis, but merely executes the purchase and sell orders placed by its customers.

securities solely as agent for the account of customers" and does not authorize "securities underwriting or dealing or investment advice or research services." 48 Fed. Reg. 37006 (1983). * * *

The Board expressly considered and rejected SIA's argument that BAC's acquisition of Schwab violates the Glass–Steagall Act. That Act comprises four sections of the Banking Act of 1933. Only one of those four sections is applicable here. That provision, § 20, as set forth in 12 U.S.C. § 377, provides in relevant part:

> [No] member bank shall be affiliated in any manner described in subsection (b) of section 221a of this title with any corporation, association, business trust, or other similar organization *engaged principally in the issue, flotation, underwriting, public sale, or distribution* at wholesale or retail or through syndicate participation of stocks, bonds, debentures, notes, or other securities ... (emphasis added).

A bank holding company's subsidiaries are bank affiliates within the meaning of § 20. 12 U.S.C. § 221a(b). Section 20, therefore, prohibits BAC's proposed acquisition if Schwab is "engaged principally" in any of the activities listed therein. * * *

The legislative history demonstrates that Congress enacted § 20 to prohibit the affiliation of commercial banks with entities that were engaged principally in "activities such as underwriting." *ICI*, 450 U.S., at 64; see *Camp*, supra, at 630–634. In 1933, Congress believed that the heavy involvement of commercial banks in underwriting and securities speculation had precipitated "the widespread bank closings that occurred during the Great Depression." One of the most serious threats to sound commercial banking perceived by Congress was the existence of "bank affiliates" that "devote themselves in many cases to perilous underwriting operations, stock speculation, and maintaining a market for the banks' own stock often largely with the resources of the parent bank." S. Rep. No. 77, 73d Cong., 1st Sess., 10 (1933).

Congressional concern over the underwriting activities of bank affiliates included both the fear that bank funds would be lost in speculative investments and the suspicion that the more "subtle hazards" associated with underwriting would encourage unsound banking practices. See *Camp*, 401 U.S., at 630. None of the more "subtle hazards" of underwriting identified in *Camp* is implicated by the brokerage activities at issue here. Because Schwab trades only as agent, its assets are not subject to the vagaries of the securities markets. Moreover, Schwab's profits depend solely on the volume of shares it trades and not on the purchase or sale of particular securities. Thus, BAC has no "salesman's stake" in the securities Schwab trades. It cannot increase Schwab's profitability by having its bank affiliate extend credit to issuers of particular securities, nor by encouraging the bank affiliate improperly to favor particular securities in the management of depositors' assets. Finally, the fact that § 16 of the Glass–Steagall Act allows banks to engage directly in the kind of brokerage services at issue here, to accommodate its customers, suggests that the activity was not the sort that concerned Congress in its effort to secure the Nation's banks from the risks of the securities market. * * *

(2) Underwriting Securities

Section 16 of the Glass–Steagall Act permitted national banks to underwrite certain types of government securities, referred to as "bank-eligible" securities. These securities include U.S. government and agency securities, and State and municipal securities (other than municipal revenue bonds). See 12 C.F.R. pt. 1. The statute, however, clearly prohibited underwriting of corporate debt or securities ("bank-ineligible" securities). Section 20 of the Act presented an opportunity for bank holding company subsidiaries to underwrite bank-ineligible securities. Section 21 precluded a securities firm from also receiving deposits.

SECURITIES INDUSTRY ASS'N v. BOARD OF GOVERNORS OF THE FEDERAL RESERVE SYSTEM

United States Court of Appeals, Second Circuit, 1988.
839 F.2d 47, *cert. denied*, 486 U.S. 1059.

CARDAMORE, CIRCUIT JUDGE.

We review on this appeal those provisions of the Banking Act of 1933 that separated the commercial and investment banking industries and are known as the Glass–Steagall Act. See Pub. L. No. 73–66, §§ 16, 20, 21, & 32, 48 Stat. 162 (1933). Demand for divorcing banking and securities activities followed in the wake of the stock market crash of 1929, which occurred, it was said, because a mountain of credit rested on only a molehill of cash. The actions of the Federal Reserve Board that we review today allow commercial and investment banking to compete in a narrow market, and to that extent dismantle the wall of separation installed between them by the Glass–Steagall Act. Whether Santayana's notion that those who will not learn from the past are condemned to repeat it fairly characterizes the consequences of the Board's action is not for us to say. Our task is to review the Glass–Steagall Act, the legislative history that surrounded its enactment, and its prior judicial construction to determine whether the Board reasonably interpreted the Act's often ambiguous terms.

The Securities Industry Association (SIA) and seven bank holding companies petition for review of six related orders of the Board of Governors of the Federal Reserve System (Board). The orders approved the bank holding companies' applications to utilize subsidiaries as the vehicle by which they can underwrite and deal in certain securities. The Board determined that the approved activities would not run afoul of § 20 of the Glass–Steagall Act, which proscribes affiliations of banks—here, the holding companies' member bank subsidiaries—with entities that are "engaged principally" in underwriting and dealing in securities. At the same time, the Board limited the scope of the approved activities. The decisions allowing bank subsidiaries to engage in securities transactions and the limitations that were imposed are the focus of the petitions seeking review. For the reasons set forth below, we deny the petitions for review save for the bank holding companies' cross-petition for review that seeks to eliminate the market share limitation.

On April 30, 1987 the Board approved the applications of Citicorp, J. P. Morgan & Co., Inc., and Bankers Trust New York Corp. to engage in limited securities activities through wholly-owned subsidiaries. 73 Fed. Reserve Bull. 473 (1987). At the time of the applications, the subsidiaries were engaged entirely in underwriting and dealing in U.S. government and agency securities and those of state and municipal governments. The holding companies sought to extend their subsidiaries' activities to underwriting and dealing in municipal revenue bonds, mortgage related securities, consumer receivables related securities, and commercial paper. With the exception of the consumer receivables, on which decision was deferred because of an insufficient record, the Board approved the applications by a vote of three to two. Limitations on the scope of the activities more restrictive than those initially proposed by the holding companies—to be discussed more fully below—were imposed.

* * * [T]he Board concluded that § 20 only proscribes member bank affiliation with firms "engaged principally in the issue, flotation, underwriting, public sale, or distribution" of *bank-ineligible* securities, those which banks are prevented under § 16 from dealing in themselves. Throughout this opinion we have adopted, for clarity's sake, the term "underwriting and dealing in" to refer to "the issue, flotation ..." language in § 20.

When called upon to interpret the Glass–Steagall Act, judges "face a virtually insurmountable burden due to the vast dichotomy between the ostensible legislative intent and the actual motivations of Congress." *Glass-Steagall Dilemma*, supra, at 1–2. Divining the aim of Congress in enacting § 20 is particularly formidable because the issue of the proper relationship between commercial banks and their affiliates caused considerable disagreement among legislators and experts who participated in the development of what became the Banking Act of 1933. See generally Perkins, The Divorce of Commercial and Investment Banking: A History, 88 Banking L.J. 483, 505–12 (1971) [hereinafter *Banking Divorce*]. Consequently, we approach the subject first by examining the legislative history of § 20, analyzing the Congressional compromise that resulted in the enactment of § 20, and then by looking at prior judicial construction of the Act. * * *

Sections 16 and 21 effectively barred commercial banks from *direct* engagement in investment banking, with the notable exception of government securities. Yet even before the 1929 crash, direct involvement by a bank had been considered "improper," see Camp, 401 U.S. at 629, but bank affiliates had developed as the medium for commercial banks' *indirect* entry into investment banking, see id. Even though the stock market debacle laid bare the dangers arising from the activities of securities affiliates, opinion was divided on how best to mitigate those dangers. * * *

Section 20 was Congress' solution to the problem of affiliates and establishes the boundary separating banks from their security affiliates. While § 21 prohibits firms "engaged" in investment banking activities from accepting deposits, § 20 prohibits commercial bank affiliation with firms "engaged principally" in underwriting and dealing in securities. The inference following from this different terminology is obvious: § 20 applies a "less stringent standard" than the absolute bar between commercial and investment banking laid down by §§ 16 and 21. *ICI*, 450 U.S. at 60 n.26. Nor can the difference in terminology be attributed to oversight. Section 21 originally contained the term "engaged principally." In offering the amendment that deleted "principally," Senator Bulkley argued that "it has become apparent that at least some of the great investment houses are engaged in so many forms of business that there is some doubt as to whether the investment business is the principal one." 77 Cong. Rec. 4180 (1933). Given that one of the leading advocates of Glass–Steagall recognized that "engaged" connoted a stricter standard than "engaged principally," it is inconceivable that the latter term could remain in § 20 by sheer happenstance. Thus, while the original impetus behind the Glass–Steagall bill on the floor of Congress may have been to sever completely the commercial and investment banking industries, it fell short of that goal—a victim of legislative compromise. * * *

Thus, it seems eminently reasonable to conclude from * * * the legislative history, that Congress' concern was primarily with bank affiliate activities in bank-ineligible securities. Bank affiliates often "devote[d] themselves ... to perilous underwriting operations, stock speculation, and maintaining a market for the banks' own stock often largely with the resources of the parent bank." *1933 Senate Report*, supra, at 10. According to Senator Glass, "[w]hat the committee had foremost in its thought was to exclude from commercial banking all investment securities except those of an undoubted character that would be surely liquidated; and for that reason we made an exception [in § 16] of United States securities and of the general liabilities of States and subdivisions of States." 76 Cong. Rec. 2092 (1933). Given that Glass–Steagall was a means to sever commercial banking only from more speculative, "perilous" investment activities, in which bank-eligible activities were not included, an interpretation of "securities" in § 20 that excludes bank-eligible securities from its reach is entirely consistent with Congress' aim.

The history of security affiliates in the United States also supports this view. Many banks formed security affiliates in order to handle the sale of government bonds used to finance World War I. Banks were "expected" to aid the government in distributing war loans and were "encouraged" to aid potential investors by lending them the purchase price of government bonds. It was not until the 1920's that affiliates began to expand into private debt and equity securities activities in response to the demands of the public and business. It was not the affiliate system as a concept that worried Congress, but the affiliate system as it had developed. The evil that Congress intended to attack was bank involvement in speculative securities, that is, bank-ineligible securities. We cannot attribute to Congress a purpose to limit *all* securities activities when it consistently made clear that it was only concerned with *one type.* * * *

savilla

Thus, the legislative history strongly supports the view that "securities" in § 20 only refers to bank-ineligible securities. * * *

We now turn to the Board's determination of when a security affiliate is "engaged principally" in activities covered by § 20. In their applications the bank holding companies sought to comply with the "engaged principally" standard of § 20 by proposing limitations on their underwriting and dealing in bank-ineligible securities. J.P. Morgan & Co., for example, proposed that its bank-ineligible securities activities would not exceed during any rolling two-year period 15 percent of its total business. It proposed a combination of accounting tests to measure its compliance with the 15 percent limitation. The other companies proposed total volume limits of ten to 15 percent of their total business.

The Board rejected these proposals. Following the analysis set forth in its *Bankers Trust* order, 73 Fed. Reserve Bull. 138 (1987), the Board concluded that "engaged principally" in § 20 denotes any "substantial" bank-ineligible activity. See 73 Fed. Reserve Bull. at 482. Measured quantitatively, the Board stated that an affiliate would not be principally or substantially engaged in bank-ineligible activities if: (1) the gross revenue from § 20 activities did not exceed five to ten percent of the affiliate's total gross revenues (gross revenue limitation or gross revenue test); and (2) the affiliate's activities in connection with *each* particular type of ineligible security did not account for more than five to ten percent of the total amount of that type of security underwritten domestically by all firms (or, with commercial paper, the average amount of dealer-placed commercial paper outstanding) during the previous calendar year (market share limitation or market share test). Applying this measure to the applications before it, the Board selected the lower five percent figure for both gross revenue and market share limitations. It recognized that this was a "conservative approach," but stated that it would review the limitations within one year of the implementation of its orders. 73 Fed. Reserve Bull. at 485. * * *

The term "engaged principally" is intrinsically ambiguous. As discussed above, we must uphold the Board's interpretation if it is reasonable. * * *

The Board's construction of "engaged principally" as denoting any substantial activity is reasonable. We do not conclude that because "engaged principally" in § 20 and "primarily engaged" in § 32 both denote "substantial activity" that the two terms are therefore synonymous. * * *

An example illuminates how equating "principally" in § 20 with "chief" or "first" begets the dangers foreseen by Congress. Such an interpretation would allow a member bank to become affiliated with any large integrated securities firm. One commentator has pointed out that reading "principally" as "chief" would allow a bank to be affiliated with Merrill Lynch & Co., Inc., one of the nation's largest investment bankers. See Plotkin, What Meaning Does Glass–Steagall Have for Today's Financial World?, 95 Banking L.J. 404, 414–16 (1977). It cannot be supposed that the Congress that enacted Glass–Steagall would have intended that § 20 not prohibit such affiliations. This is not to say that "principally" cannot in some contexts mean "chief" or "first," but rather that in § 20 the term must be given a definition that is both sensible *and* in harmony with legislative purpose. * * *

The Board determined that substantial activity, measured quantitatively, constituted five to ten percent of an affiliate's gross revenues over a two-year period. 73 Fed. Reserve Bull. at 485. It set the approved level of activity at the five percent end of this range, but stated its intent to review this level within a year after the order's effective date. Id.

Engaged principally

* * * [W]e defer to the Board's determination that § 20 allows an affiliate to engage in bank-ineligible securities activities so long as those activities do not exceed five to ten percent of the affiliate's gross revenue. This range is both reasonable and consistent with the statute. Because of the Board's expertise we also defer to its decision to set the gross revenue limitation at five percent.

The Board's second limitation on the subsidiaries' bank-ineligible securities activities provides that the subsidiaries' involvement in *each* activity may not exceed a five percent share of the total market for that activity. * * *

The bank holding companies argue that neither § 20 nor the legislative history of the Glass–Steagall Act provides a basis for the Board's market share test. They assert that § 20 mandates an inquiry only into activities *within* a subsidiary rather than one into the size of the subsidiary's activity in relation to the market as a whole. A market share test, they claim, is intended *sub silentio* to promote competition rather than to protect against the hazards of affiliation envisioned by Congress. * * *

We discern no support in § 20 for the Board's market share limitation. In the legislative history there is evidence that before the enactment of Glass–Steagall, banks and bank affiliates had acquired an increasingly large share of securities activity in relation to investment banks. * * *

In sum § 20 of the Glass–Steagall Act forbids member bank affiliation with firms that are "engaged principally" in underwriting or dealing in "securities." It was not Congress' plan to forbid affiliates from those activities that banks themselves could engage in without limitation. The Board's interpretation of § 20 under which government securities—those that banks may without limitation underwrite and deal in—are excluded from the prohibition contained in § 20 is therefore consistent with the

Congressional scheme. The Board's qualitative and quantitative constructions of the term "engaged principally" are reasonable, with the exception of the market share limitation. * * *

———————

The revenue limitation for bank-ineligible activities was accompanied by a requirement that a bank holding company obtain authorization from the Fed before starting a Section 20 subsidiary. The holding company was required to create managerial and operational infrastructure controls between the Section 20 subsidiary and the holding company's banks. These "firewalls" were designed to ensure that the holding company's banks and its Section 20 subsidiary maintained separate corporate identities, and to assure that the bank did not extend credit to the Section 20 subsidiary for its securities activities.

The Fed increased the revenue limitation for bank-ineligible securities first from five to ten percent. Ten percent soon proved too restricitive, and in December, 1996, the Fed announced an increase from ten to twenty-five percent. Firewalls were replaced by more liberal "operating standards." This regulatory expansion permitted large bank holding companies to acquire major securities firms and severely undermined the separation between commercial banking and investment banking at the heart of the Glass–Steagall Act.[5]

Section 20 subsidiaries were regulated by the Fed pursuant to the provisions of the Bank Holding Company Act. In a further effort to expand banks powers, the OCC permitted "operating subsidiaries" of national banks to engage in activities beyond those permitted for the national bank parent. 12 C.F.R. § 5.34. Thus, the OCC approved an application by Zions National Bank to underwrite and deal in municipal revenue bonds through an operating subsidiary even though the national bank itself was not then statutorily authorized to engage in that activity under § 16 of the Glass–Steagall Act.

Critics charged that the OCC did not have authority to approve securities activities in national bank operating subsidiaries because Congress had enacted the Bank Holding Company Act (administered by the Fed) to regulate the nonbanking activities of bank holding companies.

C. THRIFT SECURITIES ACTIVITIES

Thrift institutions were not subject to either the Glass–Steagall Act or the Bank Holding Company Act. Some thrifts also sought entry into the securities business, and met with regulatory success.

———————

5. For example, Bankers Trust purchased Alex. Brown, U.S. Bankcorp bought Piper Jaffrey Co., First Union acquired Wheat First Butcher, NationsBank Corporation purchased Montgomery Securities, and Wachovia purchased Interstate/Johnson Lane.

SECURITIES INDUSTRY ASS'N v. FEDERAL HOME LOAN BANK BOARD

United States District Court, District of Columbia, 1984.
588 F.Supp. 749.

Greene, District Judge.

* * * The material facts are not in dispute. On May 6, 1982, the [Federal Home Loan] Board adopted Resolution No. 82–327, which granted the applications of Coast Federal Savings and Loan Association, Perpetual American Federal Savings & Loan Association, and California Federal Savings & Loan Association to invest in new service corporation subsidiaries. Under the grant of approval, these wholly-owned service corporations will become shareholders in a separate new corporation–Savings Association Financial Corporation (SAFC)—which will create its own wholly-owned subsidiary, Savings Association Investment Securities (SAIS). Both SAFC and SAIS will be Delaware corporations with their principal place of business in Tampa, Florida.

SAIS, which will be a registered broker-dealer and a member of the National Association of Securities Dealers, Inc., will operate "investment centers" in the offices of participating S & Ls. Such centers will provide the following services: (1) the execution on behalf of and for the account of others of purchases, sales, and redemptions of debt and equity securities, municipal and public utility bonds, and shares in mutual funds; (2) provision to customers of investment advisory services, including portfolio analysis and valuation; and (3) the rendering of assistance to participating associations in the implementation of the brokerage program through marketing and training services, as well as advice and education about liquidity management. SAIS will charge a commission to customers for effecting securities transactions, and it will charge fees to customers for portfolio analysis and evaluations, investment counseling, and similar services. SAIS will also charge initiating fees and recurring subscription fees to participating associations.

SAIS representatives will function somewhat differently than do other registered brokers. Such representatives will receive salaries rather than commissions, and they will not independently research or analyze investment opportunities or offer advice or make recommendations based on their own views. Instead, a research firm will supply SAIS representatives with investment information and advice, and it will develop a standard investment plan for various strata of customers. Although SAIS representatives may effect transactions within the range of services offered by SAIS, they may not recommend any investment which has not been approved for an investor of the particular customer's statum [sic]. Finally, SAIS will not hold the funds or securities of customers but will act as an introducing broker, ordering a New York clearing broker to execute trades on behalf of its customers. * * *

The thrift industry has suffered serious financial difficulties in recent years due to inflation and high interest rates. The deterioration of that industry is due in large part to the difference between recent high and volatile interest rates and the low rates paid on long-term mortgage portfolios held by S & Ls. In its brief, the Board states that the average 30 year fixed rate mortgage portfolio of S & Ls yields 10.02 percent, whereas the cost of funds to these associations is approximately 11.53 percent. As a result of this difference S & Ls are losing substantial sums of money. In 1981 alone the net worth of the S & L industry was reduced by five billion dollars.

Moreover, the successful development and marketing of new accounts, such as the money market mutual funds marketed by brokerage houses, have contributed to the outflow of funds from commercial banks, savings banks, and S & Ls. If S & Ls are to exploit the new and competitive opportunities that emerge, and if they are to realize a profit, they must be permitted to engage in activities other than those expressly provided for in 1933 when HOLA was enacted. The financial services market is becoming increasingly competitive and the Board needs flexibility to adapt and respond to the changing economic circumstances.

The overriding fact is that the Congress charged the Board with the task of preserving the financial health and integrity of the S & L industry. Fidelity Federal S & L Ass'n de la Cuesta, supra, 458 U.S. at 168; Independent Bankers Assoc. of America v. FHLBB, 557 F. Supp. 23 (D.D.C. 1982). In approving the S & L applications in question, the Board reasonably exercised that responsibility and its authority under HOLA so as to ensure the future financial stability of these institutions. * * *

For these reasons, the Court concludes that the limited brokerage and investment advisory activities to be conducted by S & L service corporation subsidiaries do not violate either the HOLA or the Glass–Steagall Act. Judgment will be entered for the defendants.

QUESTIONS AND NOTES

1. Clearly, banks believed they could not operate successfully within the confines of Glass–Steagall. Why do you think Congress did not respond more immediately to repeal the Glass–Steagall restrictions on securities activities by bank affiliates?

2. Why should there be any restrictions on bank securities activities beyond those imposed on other types of institutions?

3. Economic studies have found that securities underwritten by commercial banks before the passage of Glass–Steagall Act were of higher quality and more seasoned than those underwritten by investment banks. Randall S. Kroszner & Raghuram G. Rajan, Is the Glass–Steagall Act Justified? A Study of the U.S. Experience With Universal Banking Before 1933, 84 Am. Econ. Rev. 810 (1994). See also Randall S. Kroszner & Raghuram G. Rajan, Organization Structure and Credibility: Evidence From Commercial Bank

Securities Activities Before the Glass–Steagall Act, 39 J. of Money 475 (1997) (study evidences that market forces recognize bank conflict interest and force banks to organize their securities activities in a way relieve those concerns). Examination of the claimed abuses in congressional hearings on the Glass–Steagall legislation were also said to be insufficient to support a need for the legislation. Jim Powell, FDR's Folly: How Roosevelt and His New Deal Prolonged the Great Depression 57–64 (2003). Does this suggest that the conflicts of interest claimed by those supporting that legislation were illusory?

SECTION 2.   THE GRAMM–LEACH–BLILEY ACT (GLBA)

A. BACKGROUND

Efforts to repeal the Glass–Steagall Act began not long after its passage. Senator Glass himself sought a repeal of the Act one year after its enactment. More determined efforts were made later in the century as banks' business bases changed and competition forced them into the securities arena. Success was not immediate. At least a dozen attempts were made in Congress to repeal Glass–Steagall before the Gramm–Leach–Bliley Act (GLBA) was adopted at the end of 1999. The impetus for the passage of GLBA was the merger between Citicorp and the Travelers Group to form Citigroup. That amalgamation created a financial services firm that crossed all regulatory boundaries.

Citigroup took advantage of a provision of the Bank Holding Company Act that grants a company that becomes a bank holding company by virtue of its acquisition of a bank a two-year period (subject to three additional one-year extensions at the Fed's discretion) in which to divest itself of operations that are not permissible for a bank holding company. 12 U.S.C.A. § 1842(a). Operation of an insurance underwriter (Travelers) was not then permissible for a bank holding company. Travelers owned Salomon Smith Barney and its bank-ineligible activities were potentially in excess of the existing twenty-five percent revenue limitation. The formation of Citigroup represented a big gamble that financial modernization legislation would be passed. The Citigroup combination was announced on April 6, 1998, and GLBA was enacted on November 12, 1999. GLBA permits financial holding companies to own banks, insurance companies, and securities firms. Some critics have characterized GLBA as the "Citigroup Relief Act."

The breadth of the Citigroup merger is described in the following excerpt from a case challenging the new entity's name.

CIT GROUP, INC. v. CITICORP
United States District Court, District of New Jersey, 1998.
20 F.Supp.2d 775.

DEBEVOISE, SENIOR DISTRICT JUDGE.

Plaintiff, The CIT Group, Inc., a Delaware corporation, ("CIT Group") instituted this trademark infringement action against defendant,

Citicorp, also a Delaware corporation, ("Citicorp"). On April 6, 1998 Citicorp and Travelers Group, Inc. ("Travelers") announced plans to merge, disclosing that the merged entity proposed to carry on the combined business of these two financial giants under the name CITIGROUP. CIT Group's complaint alleges that this use of the name would constitute a violation of its statutory and common law trademark rights, would dilute its trademark rights and would constitute unfair competition. * * *

Citicorp is a holding company which engages in a wide range of financial services businesses through many subsidiary operating corporations. The most prominent of these subsidiaries is Citibank. Citibank began business in 1812 when it was chartered in New York as City Bank of New York. Through the years it changed its name from time to time: National City Bank of New York, First National City Bank of New York, and then First National City Bank. In the 1960's it started using the name "Citibank" and registered it as a trademark.

The mark "CITI" was widely used and advertised. It became a prefix for many names of enterprises in the Citicorp empire, e.g., CITICARD, THE CITI NEVER SLEEPS, CITIGOLD, CITIPAY. Through Citibank and its other subsidiaries Citicorp engages in the full range of banking and financial services—lending, accepting deposits, issuing certificates of deposit, transferring money, engaging in retirement planning, performing corporate trust activities, providing investment advice and services, issuing letters of credit, serving as a fiduciary and providing a multitude of other financial services.

Citicorp's operations are worldwide. For example, it conducts branch banking in 100 countries. More than half the households in the United States have a business relationship with Citibank and 25 million households have Citibank credit cards. It is estimated that the entity resulting from the proposed merger of Citicorp and Travelers will have managed assets of $700 billion and net revenue of $50 billion. * * *

In the spring of 1998 Citicorp's chairman and chief executive officer John S. Reed and his counterpart at Travelers, Sanford I. Weill, agreed upon a merger of the banking and insurance giants. The merger would create the world's largest financial services company. It was to be a merger of equals. Citicorp's and Travelers' stockholders would share ownership of the new company; the chairmen were to serve as co-chairmen, and in all other respects the businesses and employees of the merged entities were to be on an equal footing. * * *

The famous name in the present case is CITI, whether used alone or as a prefix to other words. These marks have been registered in the Trademark Office. Registration of CITIBANK was obtained in January 1960, and registration of CITICORP use obtained in 1981. CITIGROUP is one more addition to the family of CITI names which, through extensive use and advertising have become internationally famous. CIT Group's first use of the name THE CIT GROUP was not until 1986. * * *

Further, there is no likelihood that use of the CITIGROUP mark will cause dilution of THE CIT GROUP mark. * * *

B.   BROKER–DEALER REGISTRATION

Endorsing the concept of functional regulation, GLBA removed the exemption from broker-dealer registration for banks contained in the Securities Exchange Act of 1934. 15 U.S.C.A. § 78c(a)(4) & (a)(5). These sections have been referred to as the "push-out" provisions, since their objective is to "push-out" of the bank the securities broker-dealer activities to an affiliate of the bank that is an SEC-registered broker-dealer. Such a scheme implements the GLBA concept of functional regulation of bank securities activities. GLBA carved out some fifteen securities activities that a bank could engage in without being required to register as a broker-dealer with the SEC. These include securities activities that relate to functions traditionally performed by banks and transactions that relate to traditional bank products, such as trust activities (unless the bank customer has discretionary trading authority), dealings in exempted securities (principally U.S. government and municipal securities), stock purchase plans, commercial paper, stock custody arrangements, certain asset-backed debt, dividend reinvestment plans, sweep accounts, private securities placements, and municipal securities. 15 U.S.C.A. § 78c(4) & (5).

A rather heated row broke out between the SEC and bank regulators after the SEC adopted interim rules and interpretative guidance that narrowly defined these exemptions. Exchange Act Release No. 442911 (May 11, 2001), 66 Fed. Reg. 27760 (May 18, 2001) (codified at 17 C.F.R. § 240.3a4–2 et seq.).

The bank regulators filed a joint comment letter criticizing the SEC's proposed Regulation B. In asking the SEC to take a fundamentally different approach, the bank regulators expressed particular concern with registration requirements for bank trust and fiduciary activities, custodial and safekeeping operations, and networking arrangements involving referral fees for referring business to a broker-dealer. The banking regulators stated that:

> the Proposed Rules reflect a profound misinterpretation of the language and purposes of the "broker" exceptions in the GLB Act. The Proposed Rules would require banks to make substantial changes in the way they conduct well established and already highly regulated lines of banking business and would impose a new, SEC-created regime of extraordinarily complex requirements and restrictions on longstanding banking functions and relationships.

Comment Letter Issued on the SEC's Proposed Broker Rules for Banks by the OCC, Fed and FDIC, Oct. 8, 2004.

Section 101 of the Financial Services Regulatory Relief Act of 2006 amended 15 U.S.C. § 78c(a)(4) to resolve this impasse by directing the SEC and the Fed to jointly issue rules to define the term "broker" within 180 days after the Act's enactment. The Act was signed by President Bush on October 13, 2006. The SEC and Fed published the final rule for "push out" registration requirements that seems to have met most concerns in the banking community. This regulation (renamed Regulation R) allows banks more flexibility in their trust and fiduciary activities and allows banks to pay their employees referral fees for business referred to a broker-dealer affiliate. 72 Fed. Reg. 56554 (Oct. 3, 2007) (codified at 12 C.F.R. pt. 218).

As the push-out rulemaking process exemplifies, functional regulation is likely to complicate regulatory compliance for banks. A bank that elects to offer insurance, securities, or futures along with its traditional bank products will be subject to multiple regulators and multiple regulatory requirements. Critics of functional regulation believe it will prove to be inefficient as well as burdensome.[6] Moreover, there will inevitably be regulatory turf battles over the classification of various products by function. Professor Jonathan Macey argues that critics who worry that it is not feasible to classify products into functional categories should be relieved if they consider that economically indistinguishable activities will be regulated by different agencies and that regulatory competition will likely ensue. Such regulatory competition, he argues, is a good result since, "[i]nnovating and competing regulatory agencies would be more likely to respond quickly to changing market conditions in order to maintain market share against rival regulatory agencies seeking to grab regulatory turf."[7]

A Presidential Working Group on Financial Markets was formed after the Stock Market Crash of 1987 to coordinate agency regulatory responses to market emergencies. That group is composed of the heads of the Treasury Department, the Fed, the SEC, and the CFTC. However, the representatives on that working group are often at odds with each other on appropriate regulatory responses to market events like the collapse of the Long Term Capital Management hedge fund. David Barboza & Jeff Gerth, Who's in Charge? Agency Infighting and Regulatory Uncertainty, N.Y. Times, Dec. 15, 1998, at C14.

QUESTIONS AND NOTES

1. The restrictions in the Glass–Steagall Act were gradually eroded and then largely repealed by the Gramm–Leach–Bliley Act. What happened to the concerns about the direct and subtle hazards of banks' involvement in the

---

6. See Lissa L. Broome & Jerry W. Markham, Banking and Insurance; Before and After the Gramm–Leach–Bliley Act, 25 J. Corp. L. 723, 779–84 (2000) (describing problems raised by functional regulation).

7. Jonathan R. Macey, The Business of Banking: Before and After Gramm–Leach–Bliley, 25 J. Corp. L. 691, 713 (2000).

securities business raised by the Court in Investment Company Institute v. Camp?

2. One of the issues addressed in Regulation R is to what extent unlicensed bank personnel may participate in the securities sales transactions to bank customers and be compensated for referrals to the securities affiliates. This has been referred to as the "networking" rule. One of the promises of GLBA is the opportunity for cross-selling financial products such as securities and insurance to bank customers. Does Regulation R permit banks to efficiently and economically engage in cross-selling of securities activities offered by bank affiliates to bank customers?

3. To what extent should banks be able to conduct trust operations without broker-dealer registration? The final rule permits the exemption if the bank is "chiefly compensated" through "relationship compensation" (such as annual fees based on the amount of assets managed by the trustee) rather than through "sales compensation" (commissions on securities sales made by the trustee).

C.   UNDERWRITING

Section 20 of the Glass–Steagall Act was repealed by GLBA. Now a financial holding company may own an underwriting firm without regard to the prior twenty-five percent limitation on revenue from bank-ineligible activities. 12 U.S.C.A. § 1843(k)(4)(A). A financial subsidiary of a bank may also act as an underwriter without being subject to the bank-ineligible revenue limit. 12 U.S.C.A. § 24a(a) (national banks) & § 1831a(a) (insured state banks). A remaining issue is whether a bank holding company that does not qualify as a financial holding company may still own a Section 20 subsidiary operating within the revenue limit. The answer is probably no since Section 20, the provision under which that limitation was adopted, was repealed by GLBA. The Fed reported that 40 of 45 bank holding companies with Section 20 subsidiaries before GLBA are now financial holding companies and operate their securities business without the Section 20 restrictions.[8]

GLBA added a provision to section 24 (Seventh) of the National Bank Act that permits national banks to deal in, hold, and underwrite municipal revenue bonds. 12 U.S.C. § 24 (Seventh). Prior to GLBA, operating subsidiaries of national banks had been authorized to underwrite municipal revenue bonds, but that authority did not extend to the bank itself. Historically, banks were excluded from such activity because municipal revenue bonds were viewed as simply another form of corporate finance for those entities using the proceeds to build or operate what often amounted to private enterprises. State banks are also authorized to engage in such activities if permitted by their state law. Community banks are particularly interested in this new power since it permits them to

---

8. Three foreign bank holding companies continue to operate Section 20 subsidiaries in the U.S. and the remaining two Section 20 subsidiaries are now operated as financial subsidiaries. Board of Governors of the Federal Reserve System, Report to the Congress on Financial Holding Companies under the Gramm–Leach–Bliley Act 8 & n.18 (Nov. 2003).

provide this service to their local governments, as well as to earn lucrative underwriting fees.

GLBA also repealed Section 32 of the Glass–Steagall Act, which prohibited interlocking or common directors or management between a bank and a firm "principally engaged" in investment banking activities.

QUESTIONS AND NOTES

1. Within two years of the passage of GLBA, Citigroup dethroned Merrill Lynch as the nation's largest underwriter of stocks and bonds. Citigroup underwrote $486 billion in securities versus Merrill Lynch's $432 billion in 2001. Merrill Lynch had been the number one underwriter since 1990. Randall Smith, Citigroup Unseats Merrill Lynch as Top Stock, Bond Underwriter, Wall St. J., Dec. 28, 2001. Wachovia Corp. acquired the A.G. Edwards Inc. brokerage firm in 2007. That acquisition pushed Wachovia into the number two position of broker-dealers, second only to Merrill Lynch & Co. Wachovia's client assets exceeded $1.1 trillion post-acquisition, with over 3,300 branch office nationwide. Matt Ackerman, Wachovia's National Path Runs Through Brokerage, Am. Banker, June 1, 2007. During the financial crisis, Bank of America purchased the struggling Merrill Lynch and Wachovia was saved from near failure when it was purchased by Wells Fargo.

2. Federal savings associations may underwrite and deal in general obligation bonds, municipal revenue bonds and municipal notes issued by states and local municipalities.

3. The collapse of Enron, the nation's seventh largest corporation, led to concerns about the investment banking activities of financial holding companies. Citigroup and JPMorgan Chase were closely involved in complex financing activities that were designed to improve Enron's financial statements. Both banks collectively wrote off over $7 billion to cover their Enron and other financial scandal exposures. One author has suggested that the adoption of GLBA set the stage for the involvement of those financial institutions with Enron. James A. Fanto, Subtle Hazards Revisited: The Corruption of a Financial Holding Company by a Corporate Client's Inner Circle, 70 Brook. L. Rev. 7 (2004). However, those institutions were actually involved in Enron's activities before the adoption of GLBA.

The Enron scandal proved costly to the banks that provided it with financing. In a class action lawsuit brought on behalf of Enron shareholders, the following settlements were reached: JPMorgan Chase, $2.2 billion; Citigroup, $2 billion; and Canadian Imperial Bank of Commerce, $2.4 billion. JPMorgan Chase settled Enron's bankruptcy claims under an agreement that would cost it about $1 billion and paid another $2 billion to settle claims over its role in the WorldCom scandal. Bank of America contributed another $460.5 million to settle WorldCom claims. But see Regents of the University of California v. Credit Suisse First Boston, 482 F.3d 372 (5th Cir. 2007) (dismissing shareholder class action claims against investment banking firms that were alleged to have aided Enron's accounting manipulations).

D. MERCHANT BANKING

Merchant banking is the practice of taking an equity position as an investment in a company that is not traded on the public marketplace. Banks were able to engage in this activity prior to GLBA only through small business investment corporations, Edge Act corporations (which engaged in foreign investments), or through authority that allowed bank holding companies to make investments in up to five percent of the voting shares of any company. GLBA permits financial holding companies to engage in merchant banking activities directly. 12 U.S.C.A. § 1843 (k)(4)(H) (defining merchant banking investments).

Although it allowed expanded merchant banking investments, GLBA sought to prevent commercial businesses from becoming controlled by a financial holding company. Thus, GLBA imposed conditions on the length of time that merchant banking investments could be held and restricted the financial holding company from becoming routinely involved in managing the company in which the investment is made, except to the extent necessary to obtain a reasonable return on the investment. Financial holding companies are allowed to conduct merchant banking investments directly or through any subsidiary other than a depository institution or the subsidiary of a depository institution. Financial subsidiaries of depository institutions were barred from making merchant banking investments at least until November, 2004, at which time the statutory moratorium could have been reconsidered. 12 U.S.C.A. § 24a(2)(B). No action has been taken, however, to permit financial subsidiaries to engage in merchant banking. Merchant banking under GLBA may be conducted only by a registered broker-dealer in the financial holding company structure or an investment advisory affiliate of an insurance company in that structure.

The Fed and the Secretary of the Treasury adopted regulations to govern merchant banking investments under GLBA. The rules allow a financial holding company to make merchant banking investments directly or through a private equity fund (sometimes referred to as a hedge fund) or other investment fund that makes investments in nonfinancial companies. The regulations limit the management role that banks may play in managing their investment and set forth maximum holding periods for merchant banking investments (those periods generally range from 10 to 15 years unless the Fed approves a longer period). These rules are set forth in 12 C.F.R. pt. 225.

The banking regulators were concerned with the safety and soundness of complex financial institutions. They feared that investment losses from merchant banking could endanger an insured institution in a financial holding company. The regulations adopted by the Fed and the Secretary of the Treasury require financial holding companies engaging in merchant banking investments to adopt appropriate risk management policies. 12 C.F.R. § 225.175. The Fed's initial capital proposal for merchant banking investments would have imposed a capital requirement of fifty cents for every dollar invested. That proposal was so heavily criticized that it was withdrawn. A revised rule imposes a sliding scale based on aggregate equity investments and tier 1 capital. It is described more fully in Chapter 7.

QUESTIONS AND NOTES

1. The merchant banking provisions of GLBA will undoubtedly play a large role in shaping the structure of financial institutions in the future. Banks are likely to be managed and run more like European banks that have traditionally been merchant banks as well as lenders and depositories. Another aspect of merchant banking is that equity investments entail significant market risks that increase the volatility of earnings. What, if any, dangers do you see in the growth of merchant banking by American banks? While the market turmoil during the financial crisis is still fresh, are banks likely to flock to merchant banking investments?

2. The United States has traditionally been concerned with the concentration of financial power in a few large institutions. Do you think there is any justification for that concern especially in the light of the expanded powers for merchant banking?

3. The merchant banking activities of banks are monitored through Y–12 reports filed with the twelve regional federal reserve banks. These reports disclose the amount of bank investment in non-financial companies. Barbara A. Rehm, New Data on Commitment to Invest in Nonfinancials, Am. Banker, Mar. 8, 2002. In November 2004, the Fed required the filing of Y–12 reports where merchant investments exceed the lesser of $100 million or five percent of the bank holding company's consolidated tier 1 capital. These levels are one-half of the prior reporting levels. Supporting Statement for the Consolidated Bank Holding Company Report of Equity Investments in Nonfinancial Companies, FR Y–12; OMB No. 7100–0300, available at <www.federalreserve.gov/boarddocs/reportforms/formsreview/FRY12.20040728.omb.pdf>.

4. Twenty-six bank financial holding companies reported merchant banking investments as of March 2003. Board of Governors of the Federal Reserve System, Report to the Congress on Financial Holding Companies under the Gramm–Leach–Bliley Act 15 (Nov. 2003).

5. Private equity investments proved lucrative for financial holding companies when the stock market peaked in 2000, but resulted in large losses in the ensuing market downturn. JPMorgan Chase announced in March 2005 that it was spinning off its JPMorgan Partners, which handled that activity for the holding company and at one point had attracted $20 billion from institutional investors. JPMorgan Partners had achieved large gains initially but then experienced large losses. It also posed conflicts with the bank's commercial banking activities for other large equity investors. Liz Moyer, Why Spinoff Makes Sense to JPM Chase, Am. Banker, Mar. 2, 2005.

The SEC charged Guillaume Pollet, a managing director at Societe Generale's SG Cowen, with short selling on information he obtained from his trading desk, which handled private investments in public equities (PIPEs). SEC v. Pollet, SEC Litigation Release No. 19,199 (E.D.N.Y Apr. 21, 2005).

In 2005, First National Bank of Pennsylvania created a new merchant banking subsidiary to provide private equity and subordinated debt financing to companies that posed too much credit risk to qualify for bank loans. The bank viewed this as a way to compete with investment banks. John Reosti, Why F.N.B. Corp. Opted for Merchant Banking, Am. Banker, Oct. 31, 2005. What risks do such investments pose to bank shareholders?

SECTION 3.   BANK SECURITIES SALES

Broker-dealers operated by financial holding companies fall within the functional regulation of the Securities and Exchange Commission (SEC). That agency has adopted a comprehensive scheme of regulation for broker-dealers. SEC broker-dealer regulation includes a "customer protection" rule requiring that customer funds be maintained in specially segregated bank accounts and that customer securities be accounted for and held in the possession and control of the broker-dealer. 17 C.F.R. § 240.15c3–3.

The SEC has also adopted a complex capital rule for broker-dealers that requires liquid excess net capital in order to assure that broker-dealers are able to meet their obligations to customers. 17 C.F.R. § 240.15c3–1. The SEC adopted amendments to its net capital rule to allow broker-dealers operated by large banks to use mathematical models to calculate net capital requirements for market and derivatives-related credit risk. Alternative Net Capital Requirements for Broker–Dealers That are Part of Consolidated Supervised Entities, 69 Fed. Reg. 34428 (June 21, 2004) (codified at 17 C.F.R. pts. 200 & 240). The mathematical models that may be used include value at risk models and scenario analysis used as a capital adequacy measurement consistent with the standards adopted by the Basel Committee on Banking Supervision. Application must be made to the SEC for this exemption. Firms qualifying for the exemption must have tentative capital of at least $1 billion and $500 million of net capital. An early warning notice to the SEC by an exempted bank is required where tentative capital falls below $5 billion.

The SEC rule was designed to reduce regulatory burdens on banks but was also in response to the European Union's requirement that consolidated supervision at the ultimate holding company level be equivalent to European Union consolidated supervision. The functional regulation created by GLBA did not provide for such consolidated regulation. Since many large banks had European operations, the SEC had to cede some regulation to the banking regulators in order for American banks to remain compliant in their European operations.

The next case highlights some of the special problems created for banks by the operation of a broker-dealer.

IN THE MATTER OF NATIONSSECURITIES AND NATIONSBANK, N.A.

Securities and Exchange Commission, May 4, 1998.
Securities Act of 1933, Release No. 7532.
<www.sec.gov/litigation/admin/337532.txt>.

This matter concerns flaws in the operation and sales activities of NationsSecurities and NationsBank, relating to two closed-end bond funds, called Term Trusts. Some of NationsSecurities' registered representatives used materially false and misleading sales practices, including mischaracterizing the Term Trusts as straightforward U.S. Government bond funds, when, in fact, they were highly leveraged and invested in interest-rate-sensitive derivatives. These NationsSecurities registered representatives received such information from some of their supervisors at the broker-dealer, the National Sales Manager ("Sales Manager") for the family of funds then advised by NationsBank, and wholesalers employed by Stephens, Inc., the underwriter for the Term Trusts.

NationsBank failed to implement adequate measures to avoid the potential for customer confusion inherent in the operation of a broker-dealer on the premises of a bank. Some employees of NationsBank and NationsSecurities engaged in marketing and sales practices that blurred the distinction between the bank and the broker-dealer and their respective products. The combination of improper sales practices and practices that blurred the distinction between the bank and the broker dealer and their respective products culminated in unsuitable purchases by investors.
* * *

Shares of both Term Trusts were sold to investors for $10 per share in the initial public offerings ("IPO"). In 1994, significant interest rate increases adversely affected the net asset value of the Term Trusts' portfolios. By November 18, 1994, Term Trust 2003 had fallen to a low of $6 per share on the NYSE, primarily due to rising interest rates. Similarly, by November 14, 1994, Term Trust 2004 had fallen to a low of $6.50 per share. This drop in share value generated a large number of complaints from investors who complained that they had not been informed by their registered representatives, at the time they purchased the Term Trusts, that their investments were sensitive to interest rate changes, and were uninsured. Both Term Trusts are currently trading in the range of $8.65625 per share, with a net asset value in the range of $9.74 per share.

Registered representatives were encouraged to, and did, solicit customers, who had formerly invested in certificates of deposit ("CDs"), to be investors in the Term Trusts. For example, during a taped conference call in which branch managers participated, a registered representative stated that, "I have developed a pretty successful referral program here in NationsBank with the CD folks." Another registered representative stated that, "[O]ne of the first questions I ask [customers] is do they invest in anything other than CDs. If they say no, they are a 2004 term trust candidate."

For many of the former CD investors, however, the Term Trusts were unsuitable investments. Many CD investors seek absolute safety of principal and thus sacrifice rate of return to obtain this security. In contrast, an investor in the Term Trusts was subject to a high degree of risk resulting from the Trusts' extreme sensitivity to interest rate changes, as well as the risk that shares of the Term Trusts would trade at a discount to their net asset values. Many closed-end funds frequently trade at a significant discount to their net asset values. An investor in the trusts also was subject to the additional risks resulting from the Term Trusts' investments in derivatives. Thus, there was a limited possibility that an investor in the Term Trusts not interested in holding until maturity could achieve full return of principal by selling into the secondary market given the likelihood that the funds, like most closed-end bond funds, would trade at a discount to their net asset value. The age, financial position and investment objectives of many of the investors made the Term Trusts an unsuitable investment. * * *

NationsBank and NationsSecurities engaged in practices that "blurred" the differences between the bank and the broker-dealer and between the FDIC-insured products sold by bank employees and riskier investment products sold by NationsSecurities registered representatives. Registered representatives were told by NationsSecurities' senior management, the Sales Manager and the wholesalers during orientation and subsequent meetings that bankers were trusted more than brokers and they should use their location in the bank to build on that trust.

The sales scripts also blurred the distinction between the bank and the broker-dealer and their respective products. The Branch Manager's misleading sales document advised registered representatives to tell potential customers that the Term Trust 2004 was an "account managed by [the] NationsBank Trust Department. Managed $since 1894."[sic] It stated that you used to have to be Texas A & M or have the wealth of Ross Perot to get access to this quality of management but, now, "NationsBank has made this expertise available to you, our retail customers." As one registered representative stated, "[t]he thrust of the [document] was to convince the customer that because the Term Trust was managed by NationsBank, he or she could trust the investment as being safe." The Branch Manager also encouraged registered representatives to "use fear to sell" securities. According to a registered representative's notes from an orientation meeting, the Branch Manager suggested that representatives could ask customers: "Is this your risky money or safe money-if this is risky I know a guy at Merrill or Dean Witter." This recommended approach falsely implied that securities purchased at a bank were somehow safer than securities purchased at a brokerage.

NationsSecurities encouraged its representatives during orientation sessions to make every effort to blend into the bank and to become "a face at the bank." Some NationsSecurities registered representatives sat at desks in NationsBank banking centers next to bank employees with no signage or other physical demarcation indicating they were NationsSecurities employees, or that the products they sold were not FDIC insured. NationsBank's practice of providing maturing CD lists to NationsSecurities representatives also created the risk of confusion that the representatives were employees of the bank when contacting potential investors. It was reasonable for customers to assume that these people calling "from the bank" with bank information were bank employees. * * *

This blurring conduct, taken together, created an atmosphere in which a bank customer could conclude that the NationsSecurities registered representative was a bank employee and that, therefore, the product purchased was a bank product. Indeed, numerous investor complaints reflect the belief that they were buying a bank product or that the NationsSecurities registered representative was a bank employee. * * *

NationsSecurities' supervisory and compliance system was inadequate to provide timely detection or prevention of improper sales practices. NationsSecurities required only annual visits by its branch managers to each spoke office. This decentralized and infrequent system of review failed to deter adequately improper sales practices by some individual representatives. The use of two hundred inexperienced representatives in spoke offices increased the potential for improper sales practices. There also was no effective mechanism in place to supervise the interactions of the registered representatives with the Sales Manager and the wholesalers.

NationsSecurities' supervisory and compliance systems were inadequate to prevent unsuitable sales. In many cases, NationsSecurities failed to collect sufficient data on customer risk tolerance and investment horizon or failed to properly utilize the information that had been received. Although management was aware of the suitability risks of price volatile proprietary closed-end funds, such as the Term Trusts, the broker-dealer failed to create controls to ensure suitability. In addition, NationsSecurities failed to maintain in a readily accessible fashion detailed and current customer information which made it difficult for branch managers to supervise adequately suitability determinations made by registered representatives at the spoke locations. * * *

[NationsSecurities agreed to pay a civil monetary penalty of $4 million to settle this case, and it and NationsBank, N.A agreed to a cease and desist order prohibiting similar violations in the future.]

Banks entering the securities business encountered other difficulties, including compliance with the rules of self-regulatory bodies in the securities industry, such as the stock exchanges and the National Association of Securities Dealers, Inc. (NASD). These self-regulatory organizations conduct much of the day-to-day regulation of broker-dealers, although they themselves are subject to the oversight of the SEC. In 2007, the NASD combined its self-regulatory functions with those of the New York Stock Exchange. The combined entity is now called the Financial Industry Regulatory Authority (FINRA).

NASD REGULATION FINES CITICORP SECURITIES $25,000; ORDERS $300,000 IN DISGORGEMENT

<www.finra.org/Newsroom/NewsRelease/1996/P010578>.
Aug. 21, 1996.

NASD Regulation, Inc. announced today that it has censured and fined Citicorp Securities, Inc. $25,000 and ordered it to comply with an undertaking to disgorge $300,000 for violating NASD Regulation's Continuing Education Requirements. This disciplinary action results from an investigation conducted by NASD Regulation's New York District office.

"The Continuing Education Requirements help to ensure that registered representatives stay current on products and markets, and, importantly, the rules that govern the industry," said NASD Regulation President Mary L. Schapiro. "NASD Regulation is committed to closely monitoring members' compliance with these essential rules and assisting members in achieving full compliance. We will continue to pursue disciplinary actions against those members, large or small, who fail to comply," Schapiro said.

NASD Regulation found that for certain periods between November 1995 and May 1996, Citicorp failed to insure that 19 of its employees completed the Regulatory Element of the NASD Regulation's Continuing Education Requirements within the prescribed time period. As a result of their failure to comply with these requirements, the individuals' registrations were deemed inactive. Nevertheless, these individuals were permitted by Citicorp to improperly continue to function in capacities which required registration. * * *

"In light of the increased complexity of the demands made upon securities professionals who deal with the public, it is essential that the brokers maintain maximum standards of competency and professionalism," Schapiro said. This case demonstrates how important it is for the membership to insure that its registered persons fully comply with the mandates of the Continuing Education Requirements."

Banks and holding companies are subject to a broad range of rules in their dealings with securities customers. These rules relate to required disclosures, limitations on securities recommendations that are not suitable for customers, and extensive record-keeping requirements.

PRESS v. CHEMICAL INVESTMENT SERVICES CORP.

United States Court of Appeals, Second Circuit, 1999.
166 F.3d 529.

OAKES, SENIOR CIRCUIT JUDGE.

* * * Plaintiff–Appellant Donald Press purchased a Treasury bill ("T-bill") in November 1995 through Defendant–Appellee Chemical Investment Services Corp., a registered securities broker-dealer, that is wholly owned by Defendant–Appellee Chase Manhattan Corporation. The trade was cleared through Defendant–Appellee Pershing, a division of Defendant–Appellee Donaldson, Lufkin & Jenrette Securities Corporation. Pershing and Donaldson, Lufkin are both registered securities broker-dealers. Press purchased the T-bill for $99,488.42, to mature in 6 months at $102,000.

After purchasing the T-bill, he had discussions with the appellees, requesting that the proceeds of the bill at maturity be express mailed to him or that he be able to pick up the proceeds on the day of maturity at one of the New York City Pershing or Chemical locations. (He purchased the bill through a New York City location.) He was told that he could not pick up a check for the proceeds in New York City, though they could be express mailed or wired for an additional fee. Otherwise he would have to wait for the check for the proceeds to arrive via regular mail. He opted to have the check express mailed to him at maturity for an additional fee. Four days (including a weekend) after the maturity date, he received a check for $101,985.

He maintains that the appellees fraudulently did not disclose that the funds at maturity would not be immediately available. Therefore, the period over which the yield should have been calculated was longer than the appellees represented, so the yield advertised was, he claims, fraudulently inaccurate. He contends that the appellees structured the transaction in this manner to allow themselves more time to use his funds.

Press was also not told that the appellees were taking a $158.86 markup[9] from the transaction. This, he argues, is an excessive fee relative to the bill's yield, such that the appellees had the obligation under the federal securities laws to disclose it. Moreover, he maintains that the appellees also had a fiduciary obligation to Press to disclose the fee. * * *

Although the district court was correct that the markup was not excessive, a more extensive examination was needed. We recently noted in

---

9. [n.2] A markup is the difference between the price charged to a customer for a security and the prevailing market price for the security, when the seller of the security is acting as a principal, holding ownership of the security and selling it to the customer. See Securities and Exchange Comm'n v. First Jersey Sec., Inc., 101 F.3d 1450, 1469 (2d Cir. 1996). The trade confirmation form, mailed to Press after he purchased the T-bill, indicated on the back side that Chemical Investment Services was acting as a principal in the transaction. Were Chemical acting as an agent, purchasing the T-bill for Press without actually taking ownership of the T-bill prior to transferring it to Press, the remuneration to Chemical for executing the transaction would be referred to as a commission, as opposed to a markup.

Grandon that the determination of excessiveness is to be done on a case-by-case basis, and a markup is excessive "when it bears no reasonable relation to the prevailing market price." *Grandon*, 147 F.3d at 190 (quoting Bank of Lexington & Trust Co. v. Vining–Sparks Secs., Inc., 959 F.2d 606, 613 (6th Cir. 1992)). We discussed various factors to assess when determining whether municipal bonds are excessive and mentioned that, in limited cases, "we anticipate ... that a trial court, as a matter of law, properly may conclude that a plaintiff has failed to state a claim that the markups were excessive." 147 F.3d at 193. * * *

While the district court arguably did not use a bright-line rule, it did not analyze relevant factors extensively in a manner contemplated in *Grandon*. To say that a specific range of mark-ups is acceptable for a given line of financial product is to paint with a dangerously broad brush. A ten percent markup on a T-bill might be virtually always excessive. A ten percent mark-up on an instrument that is difficult to obtain and priced accordingly might not be. Among the factors relevant to the determination of whether a markup is excessive are the expense associated with effectuating the transaction, the reasonable profit fairly earned by the broker or dealer, the expertise provided by the broker or dealer, the total dollar amount of the transaction, the availability of the financial product in the market, the price or yield of the instrument, the resulting yield after the subtraction of the markup compared to the yield on other securities of comparable quality, maturity, availability, and risk, and the role played by the broker or dealer. See generally *Grandon*, 147 F.3d at 190 (discussing relevant considerations in assessing excessiveness of markups on municipal securities). We can say as a matter of law that, had the district court considered these factors in more detail, it would have been clear that the markup was not excessive.

This was not a complex transaction, yet there were efforts expended on the part of appellees. They had to, among other things, identify the appropriate instrument to purchase, arrange for its purchase, transfer the instrument to Press, and complete the corresponding paperwork. While this was an essentially riskless transaction, Press presented no compelling evidence of a more appropriate fee to be paid when comparing this transaction to other riskless transactions. While Press argued that the markup was blatantly excessive as a percentage of the yield, that argument ignores the fact that the comparison between the yield and the markup is not determinative. We suppose there may be cases where a $158 markup would be excessive, but Press has pointed to no factor or medley of factors indicating that this is such a circumstance. We therefore affirm the district court's determination that the markup in this case is not excessive as a matter of law. * * *

Press contends that Chemical was acting as an agent in the T-bill transaction, such that Chemical had the obligation to disclose, under Rule 10b–10, 17 CFR § 240.10b–10(a)(2), the "remuneration received ... in connection with the transaction" and the "yield to maturity" of the bill.

17 CFR § 240.10b–10(a)(2)(i)(B). This argument is insupportable, on these facts.

The confirmation slip sent by Chemical to Press states that Chemical was acting as a "principal" in the T-bill transaction, as opposed to acting as an agent. Appellant maintains, however, that Chemical's own assertion on the confirmation slip that it was acting as a principal should not be determinative.

Without addressing whether Chemical's indication on the confirmation slip should be determinative, we conclude that Press has presented no compelling argument to support the position that Chemical was acting as an agent. While Chemical might have purchased the T-bill to fill Press's order, the telling point is that Chemical took ownership of the T-bill and then sold it from its own account to Press. Even according to Press's definitions, that would classify Chemical as a principal in this transaction. See Press v. Chemical Inv. Servs. (2d Cir. 1998) (98–7123) ("A 'principal' sells a security from its own account in order to fill a customer's order."). While the appellant would still maintain that under 17 CFR § 240.10b–10(a)(8)(i)(D) there is the obligation to disclose, we do not read this section so to mandate. The district court's dismissal of the Rule 10b–10 claims is affirmed. * * *

CHARTER HOUSE, INC. v. FIRST TENNESSEE BANK, N.A.

United States District Court, Middle District of Tennessee, 1988.
693 F.Supp. 593.

NIXON, DISTRICT JUDGE.

This action concerns alleged securities fraud and related claims in connection with the sale of municipal bonds. Before the Court is a motion for partial dismissal for failure to state a claim upon which relief can be granted, pursuant to Rule 12(b)(6) of the Federal Rules of Civil Procedure.

The facts, as alleged in the complaint and taken as true for purposes of this motion are as follows: Plaintiff, Charter House, Inc. ("Charter House"), allegedly relied on defendant William H. Kelly ("Kelly"), an employee of defendant First Tennessee Bank National Association ("the Bank"), to choose investments for Charter House. Charter House claims that it instructed Kelly to choose secure, short-term, tax exempt municipal bonds in which Charter House could invest funds held by it in trust. Kelly is alleged to have disregarded those instructions, investing Charter House's funds in long-term zero coupon municipal bonds without Charter House's consent. The bonds declined in value and Charter House sold them at a loss of $185,750. Charter House alleges that this conduct by Kelly gives rise to causes of action against him for securities fraud, common law fraud, Racketeer Influenced and Corrupt Organizations Act ("RICO") violations, breach of fiduciary duty, and violations of the Municipal Securities Rulemaking Board ("MSRB") Rule G–19. * * *

Section 15B(c)(1) of the Securities Exchange Act of 1934 (the "Exchange Act"), 15 U.S.C. § 78o–4(c)(1) . . . prohibits a municipal securities dealer from violating a rule of the MSRB. * * *

Charter House has alleged that Kelly and the Bank, as Kelly's employer, are liable for Kelly's alleged violations of MSRB Rule G–19, a combination "suitability" and "know your customer" rule. That rule provides, in pertinent part, as follows:

Rule G–19. (a) Account Information. Each broker, dealer and municipal securities dealer shall obtain at or before the completion of a transaction in municipal securities with or for the account of a customer a record of the information required by rule G–8(a)(xi).

(b) Knowledge of Customer. Each broker, dealer or municipal securities dealer at or before recommending the purchase, sale or exchange of a municipal security to a customer shall have knowledge or shall inquire about the customer's financial background, tax status, and investment objectives and any other similar information.

(c) Suitability of Recommendation. No broker, dealer or municipal securities dealer shall recommend the purchase, sale or exchange of a municipal security to a customer unless such broker, dealer, or municipal securities dealer, after reasonable inquiry,

(i) has reasonable grounds based upon information available from the issuer of the security or otherwise for recommending a purchase, sale or other transaction in the security; and

(ii)(A) has reasonable grounds to believe and does believe that the recommendation is suitable for such customer in light of the customer's financial background, tax status, and investment objectives and any other similar information concerning the customer known by such broker, dealer or municipal securities dealer, or

(B) has no reasonable grounds to believe and does not believe that the recommendation is unsuitable for such customer if all of such information is not furnished or known.

Notwithstanding the foregoing, if a broker, dealer or municipal securities dealer determines that a transaction in municipal securities or in specific municipal securities would not be suitable for a customer and so informs such customer, the broker, dealer or municipal securities dealer may thereafter respond to the customer's requests for investment advice concerning municipal securities generally or such specific securities and may execute transactions at the direction of the customer.

MSRB Rule G–19, reprinted in Fed. Sec. L. Rep. (CCH) ¶ 3591. Plaintiff has alleged that defendants wilfully violated this rule on at least nine occasions over the course of more than three months as part of a scheme to defraud plaintiff. * * *

Prior to 1975, most of the conduct of municipal securities professionals, including banks, was unregulated because municipal securities were included within the definition of an "exempted security" under the pre–1975 version of section 3(a)(12) of the Exchange Act. Moreover, banks are expressly excluded from the definitions of the terms "broker" and "dealer" and, therefore, are not subject to the broker-dealer regulatory provision of section 15 of the Exchange Act, 15 U.S.C. § 78o. Further, banks are not members of the National Association of Securities Dealers ("NASD"), the New York Stock Exchange ("NYSE"), or any other self-regulatory organization established pursuant to section 15A of the Exchange Act, 15 U.S.C. §§ 78f and 78o–3. Under prior law, for example, Securities and Exchange Commission ("SEC") rules promulgated pursuant to section 15(c)(1), 15 U.S.C. § 78o(c)(1), defining manipulative, deceptive, or otherwise fraudulent devices and contrivances, did not reach the municipal securities conduct of banks. See S. Rep. No. 75, 94th Cong., 1st Sess. 3, 42–43 (1975) [hereinafter "Senate Report"].

Congress enacted section 15B in 1975 as part of a comprehensive set of amendments to the Exchange Act known as the Securities Acts Amendments of 1975 ("the Amendments"). The Amendments were intended to "create a federal mechanism for the regulation of transactions in [municipal securities] and brokers and dealers and banks engaged in a municipal securities business." Senate Report, supra, at 3. The legislative history of section 15B indicates that Congress intended to curb the abuses of municipal securities professionals by subjecting them to the then-existing regulatory scheme governing brokers and dealers.

In recognition of what the Senate Banking, Housing and Urban Affairs Committee described as a "disturbing pattern" of professional misconduct that was "characterized by unconscionable mark-ups, churning of customers' accounts, misrepresentations concerning the nature and value of municipal securities, disregard of suitability standards, and scandalous high-pressure sales techniques," Congress decided to bring the activities of municipal securities professionals, including banks, under "the same regulatory scheme that applied to other securities activity." Senate Report, supra, at 43. To this end, Congress created the MSRB to establish high standards of practice and trade applicable to all municipal securities professionals. The MSRB performs this function by promulgating rules, including the "suitability" and "know your customer" rule allegedly violated in this case. * * *

[S]ection 15B(c)(1) does not in terms create civil liabilities, but merely proscribes certain conduct for which specific judicial and administrative means of enforcement have been provided by Congress. See 15 U.S.C. §§ 78o–4(c)(2)-(5),78u. Thus, detecting no express or implicit private right of action from the statute's language, structure, legislative history, or circumstances of enactment, the Court FINDS that no such right of action exists under section 15B(c)(1) of the Exchange Act. * * *

IN RE FIRST UNION SECURITIES, INC.

Securities and Exchange Commission, Oct. 24, 2000.
Securities Exchange Act of 1934 Release No. 43478.
<www.sec.gov/litigation/admin/34-43478.htm>.

The Securities and Exchange Commission (the Commission) deems it appropriate and in the public interest that public administrative proceedings be instituted pursuant to Sections 15(b)(4) and 21C of the Securities Exchange Act of 1934 (Exchange Act) against First Union Securities, Inc. (First Union Securities).

In anticipation of the institution of these proceedings, First Union Securities has submitted an Offer of Settlement which the Commission has determined to accept. Solely for the purposes of these proceedings and any other proceedings or actions brought by or on behalf of the Commission or to which the Commission is a party, First Union Securities, without admitting or denying the findings contained herein, except that it admits to the jurisdiction of the Commission over it and over the subject matter of these proceedings, consents to the issuance of this Order Instituting Proceedings Pursuant to Sections 15(b) and 21 C of the Exchange Act of 1934, Making Findings, Issuing a Cease-and-Desist Order and Imposing Remedial Sanctions (Order).

First Union Securities is a broker-dealer registered with the Commission pursuant to Section 15 of the Exchange Act. The firm is an indirect subsidiary of First Union Corporation. In 1995, when the conduct in this matter began, the firm was known as First Union Capital Markets Corp. (First Union Capital). First Union Corporation acquired Wheat First Butcher Singer, Inc. on January 31, 1998, at which time First Union Capital was merged with and into Wheat First Securities, Inc. On October 1, 1999, First Union Capital (formerly known as Wheat First Securities, Inc.) was merged with and into EVEREN Securities, Inc. Immediately thereafter, EVEREN Securities, Inc. changed its name to First Union Securities, Inc. * * *

Auctions of government securities are conducted on a periodic basis by the Treasury Department, in conjunction with the Federal Reserve Banks. Treasury securities can be purchased in an auction through either the competitive or noncompetitive bidding process. Competitive bidders submit sealed bids at a specified price for the amount of securities they want to purchase. Securities are awarded to the highest bidders until all the competitive securities are sold. In contrast, noncompetitive bidders specify only the amount of securities they want to purchase, up to a limit of $5 million of securities per auction. Noncompetitive bidders then pay the average price of the successful competitive bids for the amount of securities that the noncompetitive bidders requested. Uniform Offering Circular, 31 C.F.R. § 356.

In October 1983, the Treasury Department published a notice prohibiting agreements to sell securities purchased through the noncompetitive auction process prior to 1:00 p.m. on the day of the auction. This deadline was extended in January 1991. The revised Treasury notice provided:

> A noncompetitive bidder may not have entered into an agreement, nor made an agreement to purchase or sell or otherwise dispose of any noncompetitive awards of this issue being auctioned prior to the designated closing time for receipt of competitive tenders.

31 C.F.R. § 356.12(2). The deadline for receipt of competitive bids was usually just after 1:00 p.m.

The Treasury Department provides noncompetitive bidding to encourage the widespread, long-term distribution of Treasury securities, principally into the hands of smaller investors. The prohibition on prearranged sales is designed to minimize the use of noncompetitive bidding by bidders that more appropriately should bid competitively. See Department of the Treasury, Securities and Exchange Commission, and Board of Directors of the Federal Reserve System, Joint Report on the Government Securities Market, p. A–2 (Jan. 1992). As described below, First Union Securities violated Treasury's noncompetitive bidding rules by entering into pre-auction agreements with its customers to sell their noncompetitive awards as soon as possible after the auction deadlines.

A former trader in First Union Capital's Taxable Fixed Income Sales Department devised a Treasury securities trading strategy in the early 1990's. Pursuant to this trading strategy, First Union Securities customers purchased Treasury securities through the noncompetitive auction process and then sold those securities at or immediately after the applicable deadline. The former trader, who was familiar with the Treasury market, developed the strategy after observing that prices of noncompetitive Treasury securities increased following the close of the auction process. First Union Securities salesman using the strategy believed that, because the noncompetitive securities were sold at the average price of the competitive bids, and because the competitive bids were filled from highest bid to lowest bid, the noncompetitive bids would be priced slightly lower than the secondary trading market price of the securities, creating a potential for profit. The key component of the strategy was the sale of the noncompetitive bidders' securities as close to the deadline as possible, in order to capture the spread between the average price in the auction and the price offered in the secondary market thereafter. After the auction close, the opportunity for profit could be lost through changes in the market price of the auctioned securities.

In order to ensure that the noncompetitive securities would be sold as close to the deadline as possible, First Union Securities entered into pre-auction agreements with certain customers to liquidate the customers' securities at or immediately after the deadline. First Union Securities did not record the agreements on the order tickets for the transactions; nor did First Union Securities record the agreement in any of its other books or records.

Six First Union Securities salesmen used the trading strategy in 35 Treasury auctions during the period May 1995 through February 1998.

The salesmen solicited a number of individuals and small institutional customers to engage in the strategy. The salesmen explained the trading strategy to the customers generally, and told them that it presented little risk of loss, and an opportunity for a small but quick profit.

The salesmen usually contacted the customers on the morning of each auction to determine whether the customers would purchase securities in the auction that day. The customers relied on First Union Securities' expertise in engaging in the noncompetitive transactions; they had little knowledge of the details of the transactions. In order to maximize the profit opportunity that was available immediately after auction as described above, First Union Securities entered into pre-auction agreements with the customers to liquidate the customers' securities at or immediately after the deadline. In most instances, customers bid for the maximum $5 million allowable noncompetitive award. Once the customers were awarded the Treasury securities through the noncompetitive process, First Union Securities immediately purchased the securities from the customers pursuant to the pre-auction agreements it had entered into with them.

First Union Securities did not record on its books and records that fact that the pre-auction agreements with its customers were in place. First Union Securities' books and records therefore failed to reflect that the customers' order to purchase the Treasury securities was accompanied with an order to immediately sell the securities, and that the order to sell occurred at or before the time of the order to purchase.

The customers' purchase orders that were conditioned on the pre-auction agreements would not have occurred without the pre-auction agreements to sell the securities immediately. * * *

Section 17(a)(1) of the Exchange Act requires registered brokers and dealers to "make and keep ... such records ... as the Commission, by rule, prescribes as necessary or appropriate in the public interest, for the protection of investors...." Pursuant to this section, the Commission has promulgated Rule 17a–3. Rule 17a–3 specifies the types of records that broker-dealers are required to make and keep current, including a record of the terms and conditions attached to each other placed for the purchase or sale of securities. The Commission has emphasized the importance of records maintained by broker-dealers as the "keystone of the surveillance of brokers and dealers by our staff and by the industry's self-regulatory bodies." Edward J. Mawod & Co., 46 SEC 865, 873 n. 39 (1977), aff'd, Mawod v. SEC, 591 F.2d 588, 594 (10th Cir. 1979).

When First Union Securities offered the noncompetitive trading strategy to its customers, it entered into agreements with its customers for the sale of their noncompetitive securities immediately following each auction. These agreements between First Union Securities and its customers violated the Treasury Department's prohibition of pre-auction agreements to sell noncompetitive securities.

First Union Securities' failure to record on its books and records their pre-auction agreements with its customers constituted a violation of Section 17(a) of the Exchange Act and Rule 17a–3 promulgated thereunder. The order tickets relating to the customers' purchase of the Treasury securities should have recorded the pre-auction agreements between First Union Securities and its customers to sell the customers' noncompetitive Treasury securities as soon as possible after the auctions. Rule 17a–3 requires brokers and dealers to record the terms and conditions attached to each order placed for the purchase or sale of securities. The pre-auction agreements constituted a term or condition of the customers' orders to purchase the Treasury securities at auction, since those orders would not have been placed without the accompanying agreements to sell being in place. Accordingly, they should have been recorded on the order tickets pursuant to Exchange Act Rule 17a–3(a)(6). See, e.g., In the Matter of Cantor Fitzgerald & Co., 56 S.E.C. 812 (1994).

First Union Securities benefitted from the transactions by obtaining markdowns from its customers. Since First Union Securities violated the federal securities laws in connection with these transactions, it should disgorge any markdowns it made in these transactions. See *Cantor Fitzgerald*, supra, at 817.

QUESTIONS AND NOTES

1. The SEC and other regulators encountered a number of abuses in Treasury auctions. In one notable instance, Paul Mozer, a trader at Salomon Brothers, used the names of customers without their permission to acquire as much as 87 percent of the government securities being offered in an auction. He then forced up prices in the resale of these securities to other dealers that needed them in their operations. Mozer was sent to prison and Salomon Brothers was fined $290 million.

2. The Treasury changed its auction method after the Mozer debacle and began employing Dutch auctions. Do you know how those auctions work? This change in the auction procedure did not stop another squeeze in the Treasury market in 2005 using futures contracts. Deborah Lagomarsino, Treasury Department Scrutinizes Trading of a Futures Contract, Wall St. J., Aug. 9, 2005.

The Treasury market was again hit by concerns of manipulation in 2006 after some controversial trading involving repos by primary dealers. All of the twenty-two primary dealers were then called before the Interagency Working Group on Market Surveillance, which includes representatives from the Federal Reserve Board, the SEC, the Commodity Futures Trading Commission, and the Treasury Department, to discuss that issue. The New York Federal Reserve Bank subsequently announced that no primary dealer would be allowed to hold more than 35 percent of any single Treasury issue. Katie Benner, A Whiff of Scandal Threatens the Treasury Repurchase Market. Fortune, Dec. 11, 2006, at 40.

3. A conflict concern raised by bank involvement in the securities market is the breach of "Chinese Walls" separating information flows be-

tween lending operations and trading desks located elsewhere structure. There were complaints that bank loan departments advise desks of loan clients' problems. The trading desks could use this inform to profit from or protect positions. Henry Sender, Banking 'Firewalls' M. Have Some Cracks, Wall St. J., Dec. 26, 2002, at C1.

4. Bank involvement in the securities industry had other effects. Banks soon found themselves ensnared in conflicts in their securities operations between their investment banking operations and their stock analysts.

———

Stock analysts became prominent in the 1990s for touting stocks to investors, particularly Internet and telecommunications companies. They also began working closely with the investment banking operations of the broker-dealer employer, and the compensation of the analysts was often tied to the profits of the investment bankers, giving them a stake in assuring that the investment banking clients were kept happy by positive recommendations for their stock. Frank Quattrone, an analyst at Credit Suisse First Boston (CSFB) was convicted of obstructing justice and the State of Massachusetts charged CFSB with having its analysts promote stocks that they were privately disparaging and with issuing fraudulent research reports. Quattrone's conviction was, however, set aside on appeal.

Another scandal involved Jack Grubman at Citigroup. Grubman admitted in an internal email that he wanted to downgrade several of the companies that he was rating, and which were heading toward bankruptcy, but that he got a "huge pushback" from the investment bankers. Grubman's emails also contained several cynical comments that evidenced that he was rating stocks to keep the clients happy and not on the basis any fundamental or technical analyst. In one email he called a company a "pig" and warned that its stock was going to zero even though he had just published a positive research note on the company. Analysts in the unit where Grubman worked were told to adjust their earnings expectations downward for investment banking clients so that the companies would meet projections and thereby experience an increase in their stock price as investors responded.

More spectacular was Grubman's change in his views on AT & T. Grubman had maintained a neutral recommendation on AT & T. Sandy Weill, the head of Citigroup, was a member of AT & T's board of directors, and AT & T managers complained to him about Grubman's recommendations. Weill asked Grubman to take a "fresh look" at AT & T for a possible upgrade, which Grubman proceeded to do. Grubman then sought Weill's help in having Grubman's children admitted to the 92d Street Y preschool program, which in the world of the New York elite was equivalent to a Harvard admission. After advising Weill that there are "no bounds for what you do for your children," Grubman issued a thirty-six page report upgrading AT & T's stock. Grubman's favorable report helped

Salomon Smith Barney to become lead underwriter and joint book manager on the $10.62 billion tracking stock underwriting by AT & T. That task produced $45 million in investment banking fees for Citigroup. Grubman also noted in an email that the chief executive officer of AT & T served on Citigroup's board and that Weill needed that director's vote in a showdown over control with John Reed, who shared power with Weill at Citigroup. Reed was shouldered aside by Weill in a tense confrontation before the Citigroup board of directors. Grubman gleefully boasted that he and Weill had played AT & T "like a fiddle." For his part, Weill called a member of the 92d Street Y and said he would be "very appreciative" if the school would admit Grubman's children, an appreciation that the board member understood would be expressed in the form of a contribution to the school. Not surprisingly, Grubman's children were allowed to matriculate and as a "thank you," Citigroup donated $1 million to the 92d Street Y.

In December 2002, ten investment banking firms agreed to a $1.4 billion settlement with New York and other state, federal, and self-regulatory organizations in an action challenging analysts conflicts. Of that amount, $900 million was assessed as a penalty and $450 million was devoted to the creation of independent research. An additional $85 million was directed to investor education. Among the investment banks included in the settlement were Citigroup, CFSB, UBS AG, Deutsche Bank. Jack Grubman, the Citigroup analyst, agreed to pay $15 million for his indiscretions and was barred from the securities business for life. Two of Grubman's supervisors were also sanctioned by the SEC for failing properly to supervise his activities. They were each fined $120,000 and barred from acting in a supervisory capacity for fifteen months.

Under the settlement, the investment bankers agreed to separate their research and investment banking businesses, physically and through different reporting lines. The two groups must separate their legal and compliance staffs as well as their budgets, and the investment bankers are to have no say in what companies should be covered by the analysts. Analysts are barred from investment banking sales presentations in road shows showcasing initial public offerings before their issuance. Firewalls are to be created between the investment bankers and the analysts, and analysts' compensation may not be based on investment banking revenues or input from investment banking personnel. The settling firms agreed to make their ratings and price target forecasts by analysts publicly available and disclose any investment banking relationships with covered firms that might create a conflict of interest.

The firms also agreed to provide a termination report describing why they terminated coverage on particular securities, and to create websites showing the analysts' performance. The settlement required the firms to purchase independent research from at least three independent firms for a period of five years and to make those reports available to retail investors in order to allow them to better assess stock recommendations. Seven of the settling firms agreed to pay a total of $80 million to fund "Investor Education Funds" to be created by the states and the SEC.[10]

Banks encountered other problems in the securities business. JPMorgan Chase paid $25 million to the SEC to settle claims that its underwriting unit was using allocations in "hot" issue initial public offerings (IPOs) as an inducement for those customers receiving such allocations to buy more of the issue in the secondary market. This activity, called "laddering," helped support the market in the shares. The SEC charged that such activities violated its Rule 101 under Regulation M governing stabilizing activities during an underwriting. The bank also offered customers shares in "hot" IPOs if they would agree to buy shares in "cold" IPOs that did not have much interest from subscribers. See SEC v. J.P. Morgan Securities Inc., SEC Litigation Release No. 18,385 (D.D.C. Oct. 1, 2003) (by consent), available at <www.sec.gov/litigation/litreleases/lr18385.htm>. Investment bankers were also charged with "spinning," which involved allocating shares in hot issues to executives of other companies in order to induce them to place their investment banking business with the firm making the allocation. Another practice called "flipping" restricted sales of hot issues receiving allocations until the distribution was complete.

Banks' securities, derivatives and other non-traditional activities created problems in connection with the spectacular collapse of Enron and its ensuing bankruptcy. Three banks entered into settlements totaling $6.6 billion. Kristen Hays, Judge Gives Final Approval to $6.6 billion Enron Settlement, Law.com, May 25, 2006. Banks and other financial service firms paid a total of $13 billion to settle claims arising from the bankruptcy of WorldCom Inc. Charles Fleming & Carrick Mollenkamp, Insurers, Banks Clash Over Claims for Enron, WorldCom Settlements, Wall St. J., Dec. 23, 2005. This raised concerns that the GLBA had reopened the door to another disaster like the one that resulted in the passage of the Glass–Steagall Act, which GLBA repealed. Arthur E. Wilmarth, Jr., The Dark Side of Universal Banking: Financial Conglomerates and the Origins of the Subprime Financial Crisis, 41 Conn. L. Rev. 963 (2009). However, no major bank failures resulted from these calamities. Moreover, despite a sharp market downturn in 2000, the September 11, 2001, terrorist attacks, and these corporate scandals, the American economy remained strong.

IN THE MATTER OF DEUTSCHE ASSET MANAGEMENT, INC.

Securities and Exchange Commission, Aug. 19, 2003.
Investment Advisors Act of 1940, Release No. 2160.

The Securities and Exchange Commission ("Commission") deems it appropriate and in the public interest that public administrative and

---

10. These settlements are described in SEC Fact Sheet on Global Analyst Research Settlements, <www.sec.gov/news/speech/factsheet.htm> (Apr. 28, 2003). The NASD subsequently issued guidance on avoiding analysts' conflicts. NASD Notice to Members 04–18, 2004 WL 484586 (March 9, 2004).

cease-and-desist proceedings be, and hereby are, instituted pursuant to Sections 203(e) and (k) of the Investment Advisers Act of 1940 ("Advisers Act") against Deutsche Asset Management, Inc. ("DeAM" or the "Company") to determine whether DeAM violated Section 206(2) of the Advisers Act.

In anticipation of the institution of these proceedings, Respondent has submitted an Offer of Settlement ("Offer"), which the Commission has determined to accept. Solely for the purpose of these proceedings and any other proceedings brought by or on behalf of the Commission, or to which the Commission is a party, and without admitting or denying the findings herein, except as to the Commission's jurisdiction over it and the subject matter of these proceedings, which are admitted, Respondent consents to the entry of the Order Instituting Administrative and Cease-and-Desist Proceedings, Making Findings, and Imposing a Censure, a Cease-and-Desist Order and Penalties Pursuant to Sections 203(e) and 203(k) of the Investment Advisers Act of 1940, as set forth below.

This proceeding concerns the failure of DeAM, a registered investment adviser, to disclose a material conflict of interest prior to voting client proxies in a hotly contested merger. On March 19, 2002, DeAM, along with the other entities that comprise the investment advisory operations of Deutsche Bank AG ("Deutsche Bank"), voted proxies on behalf of advisory clients on approximately 17 million shares of Hewlett–Packard Company ("HP") stock in favor of a merger between HP and Compaq Computer Corporation ("Compaq").

At the time of this vote, DeAM had a material conflict of interest. Specifically, Deutsche Bank, through its investment banking division, had been retained to advise HP on the proposed merger and senior Deutsche Bank investment bankers had intervened in DeAM's voting process by requesting that HP have an opportunity to present its strategy to the DeAM Proxy Working Group. By failing to inform its advisory clients of the existence of this material conflict of interest, DeAM willfully violated Section 206(2) of the Advisers Act.

DeAM is an investment adviser registered with the Commission that provides investment advisory services to advisory clients, including its own mutual funds and to mutual funds marketed by other entities. DeAM is one of the entities that comprise the asset management division of Deutsche Bank.

Deutsche Bank is a multinational diversified financial institution organized under the laws of Germany whose stock is registered with the Commission pursuant to Section 12(b) of the Securities Exchange Act of 1934 and traded on the New York Stock Exchange.

Deutsche Bank Securities, Inc. ("DB Securities") is a broker-dealer registered with the Commission since 1973. Prior to April 2002, it was known as Deutsche Banc Alex. Brown.

In January 2002, HP Retained DB Securities to Advise HP on the Merger

In September 2001, HP management announced a proposed merger between HP and Compaq. A shareholder vote on the merger was set for March 19, 2002.

In January 2002, HP retained DB Securities to advise HP in connection with the proposed merger. HP agreed to pay DB Securities $1 million guaranteed, and another $1 million contingent upon the approval and completion of the merger. DB Securities' assignment was to assess shareholder sentiment concerning the vote, and provide market reconnaissance to HP.

In accordance with the confidentiality provision of the engagement letter, DB Securities did not disclose the merger consulting assignment publicly. Thus, DeAM's advisory clients (along with the rest of the public) were unaware that DB Securities was working for HP to secure approval of the proposed merger.

In mid-February 2002, a DB Securities investment banker contacted DeAM's then-Chief Operating Officer ("COO") and told her about the merger consulting assignment for HP. DeAM's COO then sent an email to the DeAM representative who was serving as the chairman of the Proxy Working Group, the DeAM committee that would cast the proxy votes on the merger. The email revealed the existence of the investment bankers' assignment for HP. The COO's email was subsequently forwarded to another member of the Proxy Working Group. Thus, in February two members of the Proxy Working Group knew that DB Securities was representing HP in connection with the proposed merger.

On March 11, 2002, the Proxy Working Group met to discuss how to vote proxies on approximately 17 million shares of HP stock held on behalf of DeAM clients in the proposed HP–Compaq merger. However, the Proxy Working Group decided to defer its vote until Friday, March 15, 2002, to allow further time to study the issues.

On March 15, the Proxy Working Group met again to vote its clients' HP proxies. After extensive discussion, the Proxy Working Group voted 3 to 1 to cast all DeAM-controlled HP proxies against the merger. Later that day, DeAM faxed its proxy cards to be processed.

On the afternoon of March 18, HP senior managers learned that DeAM (and the other entities in Deutsche Bank's asset management division) had voted their clients' approximately 17 million proxies against the merger. Three senior HP officials called their contacts at DB Securities about the situation. In particular, HP's Chief Financial Officer requested that HP be given the opportunity to make a presentation to the Proxy Working Group.

Later that day, two senior DB Securities investment bankers called DeAM's then-CIO ("Chief Investment Officer") and requested an opportunity for HP management to speak with the Proxy Working Group. The

CIO already knew that DB Securities was an adviser to HP on the merger. During the call, the CIO questioned whether the bankers were trying to pressure him, which they denied. The bankers stated that the HP relationship was important to the bank and that from a client relationship perspective it would be important to give HP the opportunity to talk to the Proxy Working Group about the deal. The CIO agreed to arrange the meeting, on the condition that a dissident HP shareholder who was leading opposition to the merger also be given a chance to make a presentation to the Proxy Working Group.

On the evening of March 18, the CIO notified the Proxy Working Group by email of what he referred to as an "urgent proxy meeting" the next day.

The Proxy Working Group met again on the morning of March 19, 2002, and heard first from the dissident HP shareholder. Following this presentation and after the shareholder had left the call, DeAM's CIO informed the members of the Proxy Working Group that "we have an enormous banking relationship with Hewlett Packard. And there has been some miscommunication that occurred that caused us not to meet with either the Hewlett–Packard management or ... with Walter Hewlett and Spencer Fleischer, who represent the opposing view." After acknowledging that the Proxy Working Group had already voted, the CIO told them:

> I have some very grave concerns that—and this is why this is taking place—that, we need to have very strong documentation in place as it relates to this vote. And I'm going to ask everyone to reconsider their vote based on the information they hear today. That does not mean they have to change their vote. It just means I want people to make sure that they have heard all the evidence and all the facts, and then with their—with that in mind, make a new vote.

The CIO stated that the committee still had time to change their vote and submit new proxies before the HP shareholders meeting.

Several minutes later, a DB Securities investment banker, who was identified by name only and not by title or affiliation, joined the call from San Francisco, followed by HP management. HP management presented its views on the proposed merger. The DB Securities investment banker did not participate in the discussion. Upon the completion of the HP management presentation, HP's CEO closed by saying that the success of the merger was "of great importance to our ongoing relationship." Then both HP management and the DB Securities investment banker left the call.

During the Proxy Working Group's subsequent discussion, the CIO informed the members that he believed that Deutsche Bank was one of HP's advisers on the proposed merger with Compaq. Following a discussion, the Proxy Working Group voted 4 to I to revoke their previous proxies and cast them instead in favor of the merger. On the afternoon of March 19, shortly before voting closed, DeAM personnel recast all 17 million of its clients' votes in favor of the merger.

At the time of the March 19 vote, the fact that HP had retained DB Securities to advise HP on its proposed merger with Compaq was not publicly known. Nor was it publicly known that senior DB Securities investment bankers had intervened in DeAM's voting process by requesting that HP be given an opportunity to make a presentation to the DeAM Proxy Working Group.

Section 206(2) of the Advisers Act makes it unlawful for an investment adviser "to engage in any transaction, practice or course of business, which operates as a fraud or deceit upon any client or prospective client." An adviser violates Section 206(2) by failing to disclose to its clients any material fact about a potential or actual conflict of interest that may affect its unbiased service to its clients. SEC v. Capital Gains Research Bureau, Inc., 375 U.S. 180, 195–97 (1963). Materiality is judged according to a reasonable investor standard. TSC Industries, Inc. v. Northway, Inc., 426 U.S. 438, 449 (1979). Negligence is sufficient to prove a violation of Section 206(2). SEC v. Steadman, 967 F.2d 636, 643 (D.C. Cir. 1992).

Whether a client was actually harmed by an adviser's failure to disclose a potential conflict of interest is irrelevant. See Capital Gains, 375 U.S. at 195; SEC v. Blavin, 760 F.2d 706, 711 (6th Cir. 1985) (no showing of actual harm required to establish violation of antifraud provisions of Advisers Act).

DeAM violated Section 206(2) by voting client proxies in connection with the HP–Compaq merger without first disclosing the circumstances of its investment banking affiliate's work for HP on the proposed merger and its intervention in DeAM's voting process. A reasonable advisory client would want to know that its fiduciary, which was called upon to vote client proxies on a merger, had been contacted by officials of its affiliated investment bank in connection with an engagement directly related to the subject of the proxy vote.

Based on the foregoing, DeAM willfully violated Section 206(2) of the Advisers Act.[11]

In view of the foregoing, the Commission deems it appropriate and in the public interest to impose the sanctions specified in the Respondent's Offer. * * *

By the Commission.

---

11. [n.2] In March 2002, a dissident HP shareholder brought suit in Delaware Chancery Court to block the merger based, in part, on the claim that HP improperly influenced the outcome of DeAM's March 19, 2002 proxy re-vote. The Chancery Court rejected this claim, stating that DeAM's Proxy Working Group acted in what the committee believed to be the best interests of its advisory clients. Hewlett v. Hewlett–Packard Co., C.A. No. 19513–NC, slip op. at 41 (Del. Ch. Apr. 30, 2002). Ultimately, DeAM's vote did not determine the outcome of the HP merger contest. For purposes of this Order, the Commission expresses no opinion as to whether DeAM's Proxy Working Group acted in what it believed were the best interests of its advisory clients. The Commission need not reach that issue in light of relevant law. As the Supreme Court explained in Capital Gains, 375 U.S. at 195, Section 206(2) does not "require proof of intent to injure and actual injury to the client" of an adviser. An adviser must disclose material potential or actual conflicts of interest so that the client can decide whether it wants the adviser to continue to act on the client's behalf, or whether the client wishes to take other steps to protect its interests. Id. at 196.

SECTION 4. MARGIN REQUIREMENTS

Prior to the enactment of the federal securities laws, banks operated a "call" money market in New York that loaned funds to broker-dealers, who in turn loaned the funds to customers in margin transactions. The New York banks obtained those funds from the country banks and interest was paid to the country banks on their deposits. The New York banks made a profit on the spread between their borrowing from the country banks and their loans to broker-dealers. This call money market was criticized for encouraging speculation through margin lending. In margin lending, only a small portion of the purchase price of a stock is paid by the customer, the rest is borrowed from the broker-dealer, using the stock being purchased as collateral. The margin loan leverages the position of the speculator because the speculator is able to buy much more stock with the same amount of capital than it could have acquired if the entire purchase price was paid in cash. It was thought that the excessive use of margin credit contributed to the speculative excesses before the stock market crash of 1929 and that such margin loans diverted credit from industries needing funds. Country banks also made withdrawals in times of financial crisis. The New York City banks would then call the money from the broker-dealers to whom it had been lent. The broker-dealers in turn would call in the loans of their customers. Those customers would have to sell their stocks to raise the money to repay the margin loan to the broker, placing further downward pressure on a market that was already under stress. In addition, the country banks would often withdraw their funds in the fall to meet their financing needs in the agricultural communities where most of them operated. The withdrawal of these funds caused liquidity problems in the stock market.

After the crash of 1929, Congress reacted to these problems by enacting Section 7 of the Securities Exchange Act of 1934, 15 U.S.C. § 78g. This section authorized the Fed to set minimum margin amounts for securities trading, and gave the SEC the authority to enforce the provisions. The Fed imposed its margin requirements through various regulations. Regulation T applies to broker-dealers. 12 C.F.R. § 220.1. Regulation U applies to banks that extend loans for the purpose of purchasing securities on margin. 12 C.F.R. § 221.2. Regulation G applies to persons, other than banks and broker-dealers, who extend margin credit. 12 C.F. R. § 207.1 et seq.

The Fed has set a 50 percent minimum initial margin requirement on publicly traded equity securities. It uses the concept of "good faith loan value" as the standard for margin requirements for debt and other fixed income instruments. This standard allows a bank or other creditor to set the margin amount based on the collateral value of the security.[12]

---

12. For a discussion of these margin requirements see Jerry W. Markham & Thomas L. Hazen, Broker–Dealer Operations Under Securities and Commodities Laws, Ch. 3 (2000).

SECURITIES AND EXCHANGE COMMISSION

Response to an inquiry from Senator John C. Danforth publicly available Jun. 25, 1982.
1982 WL 30043 (SEC No–Action Letter).

In a letter dated August 20, 1981, Senator John C. Danforth forwarded a letter from one of his constituents, Hugh V. Murray. In his letter Mr. Murray complains that the "SEC's 'initial minimum margin' requirement of $2,000 equity has discouraged small investors from becoming involved in the stock and options market." He cites three examples in his letter which purportedly demonstrate the unfairness of the margin rules to small investors. He suggests that the Commission "drop the minimum margin requirement and simply use the same percentage that they use for large investors for all investors." Mr. Murray's final idea, unrelated to his suggestion regarding the minimum margin requirement, is that the margin requirement on stock purchases should be determined by the "changes in the overall ratio of the selling prices of marginable securities with the book value of [such] marginable securities."[13]

It should initially be noted that the Commission has not set "initial minimum margin" requirements for public investors. A brief summary of the various applicable margin regulations is appropriate at this point.

The Board of Governors of the Federal Reserve System (the "Board") acting pursuant to sections 7 and 8(a) of the Securities Exchange Act of 1934 (the "Act") has promulgated Regulation T (12 C.F.R. 220.1 et seq.) which governs the amount of credit which brokers and dealers may advance to customers. The Board is charged with the responsibility of establishing appropriate margin standards in order to prevent the excessive use of credit in the purchase or carrying of securities. The Commission is responsible for enforcing those margin rules. * * *

The Board was vested with the power to control speculative loans through the institution of "initial" and "maintenance margin requirements."[14] The initial margin rule requires that the investor deposit with the broker or dealer cash and/or securities equal to 50% of the purchase price of the security purchased by the investor. However, such a simplified explanation of the initial margin requirements of Regulation T is mislead-

---

13. [n.1] The word "margin" refers to the collateral or security used in connection with the purchase of securities. Ordinarily, margin is the amount of money and/or securities deposited by a purchaser of stock with his broker. On initial purchases, it represents a certain percentage of the purchase price of the stock involved. The broker agrees to advance the balance of the purchase price ("credit") upon the condition that he be entitled to hold the stock purchased as security for his advance.

14. [n.4] Trading on margin is normally accomplished by one of two methods. Using the first method, the investor deposits a percentage of the purchase price with his broker in a margin account and the broker lends the investor the remainder of the purchase price. The broker will then return the purchased stock as collateral. The amount deposited by the investor at the time of purchase is the "initial margin" and the amount which must be maintained in accordance with a percentage of the market value is the "maintenance margin." Under the second method, an investor borrows directly from a bank, finance company or other lender with no formal margin account being established with the broker-dealer. Kelly & Webb, "Credit and Securities: The Margin Requirement," 24 Bus. Law. 1153–1154 (1969).

ing and somewhat inaccurate. An explanation of Sections 3(b) and 8, the key provisions of Regulation T, is helpful in attaining a more complete understanding of the margin rules.

Section 3(b) is the heart of Regulation T. It prohibits the broker or dealer from extending credit beyond the "maximum loan value"[15] of the securities in the customer general account. Section 3(b) makes it unlawful for a broker or dealer to

> effect for or with any customer in a general account ... any transaction which, in combination with the other transactions effected in such account on the same day, creates an excess of the adjusted debit balance of such account over the maximum loan value of the securities in such account, or increases any such excess, unless in connection therewith the creditor obtains, as promptly as possible and in any event before the expiration of 7 full business days following the date of such transaction, [a deposit in the account]. . . .

The deposit in the account must consist of "cash or securities in such amount that the cash deposited plus the loan value of the securities deposited equals or exceeds the excess so created or the increase so caused."

The maximum amount of credit a broker-dealer may extend to the investor is limited to the maximum loan value of those securities as set out in the Supplement to Regulation T, Section 8 (12 C.F.R. § 220.8). The maximum loan value for margin equity securities is 50% of their current market value. If an investor who has margin securities worth $1000 and $1000 in cash in his general account decides to purchase 100 shares of a $50 margin stock, the maximum loan value of the securities in the investor's account is $3,000, [50% of $5,000 (the amount of the purchase) + $1,000 (value of securities on deposit in the general account)]. The adjusted debit balance is $4,000, [$5,000 (the amount the investor owes the broker-dealer for the securities he is purchasing)—$1,000 (the amount of cash in his general account)]. Thus, under Section 3(b), the investor must deposit an additional $1,000 cash or $2,000 worth of margin securities within 7 business days from the date of the purchase of the $5,000 in margin securities.

While the Board was given the power by Congress to promulgate maintenance margin requirements, the Board has generally chosen not to exercise that power, relying instead on the maintenance requirements of the various stock exchanges to which most brokerage firms which carry margin accounts belong. The most important of the maintenance margin rules are those of the New York Stock Exchange (NYSE). All of the exchanges, as well as well as, the National Association of Securities Dealers, Inc. (NASD) have established margin rules very similar to Rule

---

15. [n.6] The maximum loan value of securities is the maximum amount of credit a broker or dealer can extend to a customer in a margin transaction as determined by the type (i.e., margin equity security, non-equity security, exempted security etc.), market value, and number of securities in the customer's general account.

431 of the NYSE. Paragraph (b), the key provision of the rule with respect to maintenance margin, requires that the margin to be maintained at all times in the margin accounts of customers be at least 25% of the market value of all securities "long" in the account. In the example above, the customer would have to maintain an equity of at least $1,500 (25% of $6,000) in his account.

In addition to the maintenance margin rules, the exchanges have established initial minimum equity requirements for all investors who trade on margin. Paragraph (a) of NYSE Rule 431 is illustrative of such rules. It requires that for the purpose of effecting new securities transactions, the margin required shall be at least the greater of the amount specified in the regulations of the Federal Reserve Board or such greater amount as the Exchange may from time to time require for specific securities, "with a minimum equity in the account of at least $2,000 except that cash need not be deposited in excess of the cost of any security purchased." Thus, when an investor desires to purchase a security on margin, he must deposit with the broker or dealer cash and/or securities worth $2,000, unless the investor makes full payment for the security.

The Rule does not require investors to deposit $2,000 equity for each and every margin transaction; rather, it requires that the customer's account must have an initial equity of at least $2,000 after each new commitment or margin transaction. Investors may make withdrawals from their account, but must have an equity balance of no less than $2,000 after the withdrawals.

If the equity in the account falls below $2,000 because of a decline in the market and no new transactions or commitments are effected or withdrawals made, no deposit or liquidation is necessary. Thus, for example, if an investor purchases margin securities for $4,000, Rule 431(a) would require the investor to deposit initially $2,000 cash or securities worth $2,000 into his account. If the market value of the purchased securities dropped to $3,000, no additional deposit would be required by Rule 431; the customer would have equity in his account of only $1,000, rather than, $2,000. The maintenance margin requirement, Rule 431(b), would be satisfied if the investor had deposited initially cash of $2,000 because the investor would still have equity in his account in excess of 25% of the market value of all the securities long in his account ($1,000 equity/$3,000 market value of securities = 33%). The $2,000 minimum equity requirement of Rule 431(a) is not applicable to the investor's position at this time because the decline in his account is due to market conditions and not the result of a new commitment. * * *

SCHY v. FEDERAL DEPOSIT INSURANCE CORP.

United States District Court, Eastern District of New York, 1977.
465 F.Supp. 766.

MISHLER, DISTRICT JUDGE.

Defendants, by a motion attacking the sufficiency of the claim pursuant to Rule 12(b)(6) F.R.Civ.P., challenge plaintiffs' right to prosecute this action. The Susquehanna Corporation complains that various loans made by the defendant banks to finance its tender offer for a control block of PASCO (Pan American Sulphur Co.) stock were indirectly secured in violation of section 7 of the Securities Exchange Act of 1934 and the margin requirements of regulation U promulgated thereunder. 12 C.F.R. § 221.1 et seq. Plaintiff seeks to recover the losses it suffered due to the decline in the stock's market value as well as the interest and fees paid in connection with the loans. In seeking dismissal, defendants argue that no private remedy for violations of the margin requirements may be implied in favor of plaintiffs.

Taken together, section 7 and regulation U recite a pervasive legislative scheme governing the terms under which banks may extend credit for the purchase of market securities. Section 221.1(a) of regulation U provides in part that:

> ... no bank shall extend any credit secured directly or indirectly by any stock for the purpose of purchasing or carrying any margin stock in an amount exceeding the maximum loan value of the collateral, as prescribed from time to time.... [16]

It is not disputed that the loans exceeded in amount the permissible limits as prescribed by the prevailing margin requirements. Defendants deny, however, that the loans were either directly or indirectly secured, a necessary element of any regulation U violation. Freeman v. Marine Midland Bank–New York, 494 F.2d 1334, 1338 (2d Cir. 1974). The several loan agreements make no express reference to direct security.

Plaintiffs' theory of action, rather, rests on a claim of indirect security which finds its basis in certain oral agreements and pre-existing written contracts that were incorporated by reference, which allegedly encumbered Susquehanna's ability to sell, pledge or otherwise dispose of the PASCO stock. * * *

In Pearlstein v. Scudder & German, 429 F.2d 1136 (2d Cir. 1970) (*Pearlstein I*), the court was confronted with the very question presented here. Pearlstein, a sophisticated individual speculator, made two separate bond purchases on his margin account kept with the defendant Scudder. He failed, however, to tender the necessary payment within seven business days of the transaction. Under regulation T, governing the extension of credit by brokers and dealers, Scudder was required to sell the bonds on Pearlstein's account. It did not, but rather sued for the amount due and secured a consent judgment. The price of the bonds plummeted causing

---

16. [n.2] Subsection (b) of 12 C.F.R. § 221.3 provides that:

The "purpose of a credit" is determined by substance rather than form.

(1) Credit which is for the purpose, whether immediate, incidental, or ultimate, of purchasing or carrying a margin stock is "purpose credit", despite any temporary application of funds otherwise.

(2) Credit to enable the customer to reduce or retire indebtedness which was originally incurred to purchase a margin stock is for the purpose of "carrying" such a security.

Pearlstein to sustain significant losses. Pearlstein sued to recoup his loss charging Scudder with a violation of regulation T.[17]

The court found that Pearlstein had an implied right of action against Scudder for its violation of the margin requirements, holding that while investor protection was only an incidental purpose of section 7, "... private actions by market investors are a highly effective means of protecting the economy as a whole from margin violations by [lenders]...." *Pearlstein I*, supra at 1140. * * *

Our consideration of the question must turn on an interpretation of *Pearlstein I* in light of subsequent legislation and decisional law. * * *

[S]ection 7 was amended in 1970 to add subsection (f), 15 U.S.C. § 78g(f), making it illegal for any person to obtain, receive or enjoy an unlawful extension of credit. The amendment was implemented by regulation X, 12 C.F.R. § 224 et seq., promulgated the following year by the Board of Governors of the Federal Reserve. Regulation X prohibits any person from obtaining credit when to do so would cause the creditor to violate regulations T (governing the extension of credit by brokers or dealers) or U (governing bank financing). Thus, responsibility for compliance now rests with the customer as well as the lender.

There is no firm evidence that the 1970 amendment was enacted in response to *Pearlstein*. Congress was concerned with the infusion of foreign credit into the American securities market; there was doubt as to whether section 7 reached lenders. In order to inject stability into, and maintain the fiscal integrity of the national securities and credit markets, Congress thought it sound to place the duty of compliance on the investor. Report of the House Committee on Banking and Currency, H.R.Rep. No.91–975, 91st Cong. 2d Sess. 4, reprinted in [1970] U.S. Code Cong. & Admin.News, pp. 4394, 4409.

The change has prompted widespread reanalysis of *Pearlstein I* principles. The court itself in Pearlstein v. Scudder & German, 527 F.2d 1141 (2d Cir. 1975) (*Pearlstein II*) observed:

> ... that in our prior opinion in this case, emphasis was placed on the fact that 'the federally imposed margin requirements forbid a broker to extend undue credit but do not forbid customers from accepting such credit.' 429 F.2d at 1141. However, the addition of section 7(f) to the Exchange Act in 1970, 15 U.S.C. § 78g(f), as well as the promulgation by the Federal Reserve Board of Regulation X, 12 C.F.R. § 224 (1975), have now made it unlawful to obtain credit in violation of the margin requirements. The effect of these developments is to cast doubt on the continued viability of the rationale of our prior holding.

---

17. [n.12] Regulation T, governing the extension of credit by brokers and dealers, is the companion to regulation U which regulates bank financing used to purchase securities. The second circuit has treated regulation T and regulation U cases interchangeably. See e.g. Freeman v. Marine Midland Bank–New York, supra; Stonehill v. Security National Bank, 68 F.R.D. 24 (S.D.N.Y.1975); National Bank of North America v. Quest, 425 F. Supp. 186 (E.D.N.Y.1977).

Id. at 1145 n. 3. (citations omitted). The tenth circuit has gone so far as to hold that the amendment operates to overturn the *Pearlstein I* doctrine thus stripping investors of their right to sue. See Utah State University of Agriculture and Applied Science v. Bear, Stearns & Co., 549 F.2d 164 (10th Cir. 1977). Although Congress did not primarily intend, with the enactment of section 7(f), to impose the burden of compliance on the investor using domestic money markets, the amendment, nevertheless, has had that effect. Congress' statement at the very least must be construed to suggest that private access should be sharply restricted. Bell v. J. D. Winer & Co., Inc., 392 F. Supp. 646, 654 (S.D.N.Y.1975). Certainly a private remedy should not be afforded the investor who was in a position to know of the violation. * * *

Accordingly, defendants' motion to dismiss is granted. * * *

———————

Ken Lay, the chief executive officer for the Enron Corp., was charged with bank fraud by obtaining loans on his Enron stock in violation of margin requirements set by the Federal Reserve Board in Regulations U and X . The government charged that Lay had used "non-purpose" lines of credit from his banks to margin Enron stock. Such non-purpose loans may not be used to for the purpose of margining stock. Rather, "purpose credit" is used for margin transactions and then only up to the margin value of the stock. In the case of Enron the margin value of the stock would be fifty percent. The non-purpose loans were secured by Enron stock and had a loan to value ratio of seventy to eighty percent, which the government claimed allowed Lay to reduce the margin on his stock from the fifty percent level required for purpose credit. Lay was convicted of those charges after a bench trial, but died before his appeal was completed and the conviction was then set aside.

SECTION 5. CLEARING AND SETTLEMENT

Banks play an important role in the clearing, settling and transfer of securities in the United States and abroad. Those activities also engender some legal problems.

ALEX. BROWN & SONS, INC. v. MARINE MIDLAND BANKS, INC.

United States District Court, Southern District of New York, 1997.
Fed. Sec. L. Rep. (CCH) ¶ 99,440.

SWEET, DISTRICT JUDGE.

* * * For the purpose of this motion to dismiss, the allegations of the complaint are taken as true. In September 1994, Alex. Brown was a clearing broker for Monness, Crespi, Hardt & Co., Inc. ("Monness Crespi"), a securities brokerage firm. In its capacity as a clearing broker, Alex.

Brown performed various functions in connection with securities transactions initiated through Monness Crespi, including the receipt and delivery of securities and of payment therefor on the Depository Trust Company ("DTC") automated trading settlement system.

Pursuant to contractual agreements, Marine acted as a custodian and paying agent for Stanley I. Berk and for Armor Pension Managers ("Armor") and Westside Partners ("Westside") (collectively, "Berk"), two entities controlled by Berk. Marine extended credit to Berk and paid for securities purchased by Berk, holding them on Berk's behalf in Berk's custody accounts at Marine. These transactions were collateralized by the securities kept in Berk's accounts.

In September 1994, Berk directed Monness Crespi to make several trades of over-the-counter biotechnological securities on Berk's behalf. The five trades which are the subject of this action were among those trades, and Alex. Brown acted as the clearing broker to facilitate the trades via the DTC system. All of these trades were "affirmed" by Marine, meaning that Marine reviewed the trades on the DTC system, determined that the quantity and price of securities being purchased, the net purchase money, and the account instructions comported with its instructions from Berk. Marine also represented to Alex. Brown, through its affirmations on the DTC system, that the trades would settle as scheduled.

Two of the trades, one on behalf of Armor for 150,000 shares of Intelligent Surgical Lasers, Inc. ("ISLS") and the other on behalf of Westside for 100,000 shares of Biosepra ("BSEP"), settled as scheduled on September 21, 1994. The securities were delivered electronically via DTC from Alex. Brown to Marine. Marine was debited in the amount of the purchase price and Alex. Brown was credited with the purchase price. On September 22, 1994, however, Blech & Company ("Blech"), a major underwriter and market-maker in over-the-counter biotechnological securities, closed its operations, causing the value of the stocks which it had underwritten, including ISLS, BSEP, Ariad Pharmaceuticals, Inc. ("Ariad") and La Jolla Pharmaceuticals Co. ("LJPC"), to decrease dramatically.

Alex. Brown alleges that Marine, having determined that the decline in the value of the Blech underwritten securities would cause a deficit in Berk's custody accounts, thereby decreasing the value of Marine's securities collateral, reversed the ISLS and BSEP settlements by sending a "new" delivery to Alex. Brown via DTC of the same securities which Marine had previously purchased. Marine allegedly thereby caused Alex. Brown's account to be debited and Marine's account to be credited for the monies Marine had previously paid to Alex. Brown. Marine did not convey its reason for the deliveries to Alex. Brown at this time, but Alex. Brown alleges Marine's motive was to "jam" Alex. Brown with the depreciating stock and to regain control over the purchase monies.

At approximately 10:30 a.m. on September 23, Marine's Vice President of Securities Client Services, Louis Pilato ("Pilato"), notified Berk that Berk's accounts were overdrawn by $4,554,647.89 and that if Marine did not receive funds to cover the overdraft by 10:45 a.m. that day, Marine would not honor any of Berk's trades. Berk did not cover the overdraft.

Not knowing why Marine had reversed the ISLS and BSEP trades, Alex. Brown contacted Marine on September 23, 1996 to discuss the matter. Pilato stated that he needed time to investigate the matter and would call Alex. Brown back later that day with an answer. Alex. Brown next heard from Marine on September 27, 1994, at which time Pilato informed Alex. Brown that as of September 23 Marine did not honor any of Berk's trades.

Between September 23 and September 27, Alex. Brown held the ISLS and BSEP securities, allegedly in reliance on Marine's failure to inform Alex. Brown that the value of the securities had plummeted as of September 23. When Alex. Brown attempted to deliver the ISLS and BSEP securities again to Marine on September 26 and to settle three other trades which Marine had previously affirmed, Marine DK'd those deliveries without comment.[18]

Alex. Brown alleges that, as a result of its reliance on Marine's failure to disclose the reason for the new deliveries, Alex. Brown suffered substantial losses. First, had Alex. Brown known on September 23 that Marine did not intend to take the ISLS and BSEP securities back, it could have protected itself by DK'ing the deliveries from Marine, or it could have immediately liquidated the securities by selling them on the market before the stock value continued to decrease. Instead, Alex. Brown held the securities until their value had substantially decreased, and was then forced to sell them at a substantial loss. * * *

Here, Marine contends that Alex. Brown has failed to state a claim for securities fraud for three reasons: Alex. Brown, as a clearing broker, is neither a purchaser nor a seller of securities, and therefore lacks standing; Alex. Brown has not properly alleged a fraud "in connection with" the sale of securities; and Alex. Brown has not properly alleged that the omissions and misrepresentations at issue fraudulently induced them to enter the transactions.

Section 10(b) and Rule 10b–5 proscribe the use of any deceptive or manipulative device, scheme or artifice "in connection with the purchase or sale of any security." 15 U.S.C. § 78(j)(b); 17 C.F.R. 240.10b–5. This standard is met "where accomplishment of the alleged scheme is 'directly related to the trading process.'" United States v. Newman, 664 F.2d 12, 18 (2d Cir. 1981); Perez–Rubio v. Wyckoff, 718 F. Supp. 217, 236 (S.D.N.Y. 1989). * * * Marine's alleged misrepresentations and omissions here were not made "in connection with" the purchase and purchase and sale of the securities in question, because they do not relate to the fundamental

---

18. [n.1] According to the Complaint, "DK" means that the purchasing Participant, in this case, Marine, does not know the trade—i.e, it will not accept (settle) the securities trade because of a problem with the trade as billed or formatted or because the stock was delivered altogether in error.

investment attributes of the securities. Instead, the alleged misrepresentations here relate to whether Berk had funds available to effectuate the purchases. * * *

IN THE MATTER OF THE CHASE MANHATTAN BANK, N.A.

Securities and Exchange Commission, Oct. 4, 1994.
Securities Exchange Act of 1934, SEC Release No. 34784.
1994 WL 559152.

The Office of the Comptroller of the Currency ("OCC") and the Securities and Exchange Commission ("SEC") today announced the settlement of a joint enforcement action against The Chase Manhattan Bank, N.A. ("Chase"), New York, New York. Chase, without admitting or denying the findings, consented to the entry of a joint Order requiring it to permanently cease and desist from committing or causing any violations or future violations of the provisions referred to below and to pay a civil money penalty of $100,000.

During the period 1982 to 1989, Chase, in its function as transfer agent, hired two disposal firms to destroy cancelled corporate bond certificates with a face value of over $6 billion. An unknown number of the cancelled certificates, however, were not destroyed. Since 1991, cancelled securities with a face value of approximately $7 million have surfaced in the U.S. and European markets. The cancelled certificates that have surfaced are perforated with the bank's initials, "CMB," on an edge of the certificates to signify Chase's cancellation.

When Chase learned such cancelled certificates had resurfaced, it failed to file timely Missing/Lost/Stolen/Counterfeit Securities Reports on form X–17f–1A ("Securities Reports") with the proper agency. * * *

Rule 17Ad–12 provides, in relevant part, as follows:

> Any registered transfer agent that has custody or possession of any funds or securities related to its transfer agent activities shall assure that: (1) All such securities are held in safekeeping and are handled, in light of all facts and circumstances, in a manner reasonably free from risk of destruction, theft or other loss ... In evaluating which particular safeguards and procedures must be employed, the cost of the various safeguards and procedures as well as the nature and degree of potential financial exposure are two relevant factors.

Chase failed to meet this standard of safeguarding securities in at least two respects. First, Chase failed to specifically mark the registered certificates with the word "cancelled" in a clear and distinct manner. Chase's perforations were especially difficult to detect when the certificates were photocopied or transmitted by facsimile.

Second, Chase failed to require reasonable security precautions regarding cancelled certificates sent to outside vendors for destruction, including verification that the documents had actually been destroyed.

Chase's failure to require that the vendors adopt security measures was unreasonable. * * *

Section 17(f)(1) and Rule 17f–1 provide, in pertinent part, that every registered transfer agent shall report to the Commission or its designee, the SIC [the Securities Information Center], among others, certain information about missing, lost, counterfeit or stolen securities certificates on a Securities Report. With regard to stolen or lost securities where there is a substantial basis for believing that criminal activity has been involved, a report must be filed within one business day of the discovery of the theft or loss and the certificate numbers, if not immediately ascertainable, are to be reported as soon as possible. Also, the discovery of the theft or loss of certificates where criminal activity is suspected must be promptly reported to the FBI. If criminal activity is not suspected, a report must be filed one day after the discovery of the loss when the certificates have been missing or lost for a period of two days.

Once Chase learned in November, 1991, that cancelled certificates from more than one issue of securities had resurfaced, and that the certificates were among those that were supposed to have been destroyed by the outside vendors, it had reason to believe that additional cancelled certificates sent to the outside vendors could be in circulation. Accordingly, Chase had an obligation under Section 17(f)(1) and Rule 17f–1 thereunder to promptly identify all issues of certificates sent to the outside vendors and to timely file Securities Reports with respect to those certificates. Chase failed, however, to file such timely Securities Reports. * * *

In 2001, the SEC instituted an action against Chase Manhattan Bank that alleged that Chase committed record keeping and reporting violations while acting as a registered transfer agent for municipal and corporate bond issues. The SEC charged that Chase failed to promptly reconcile discrepancies in its computerized bond record keeping system that totaled more than $48.6 billion. Chase consented to the SEC's request for a $1 million civil penalty, but did not admit or deny the allegations in the complaint. <www.sec.gov/litigation/admin/34–44835.htm> (N.D. Ill. Sept. 24, 2001).

FIDELITY PARTNERS, INC. v. FIRST TRUST CO. OF NEW YORK

United States Court of Appeals, Second Circuit, 1998.
142 F.3d 560.

NEWMAN, CIRCUIT JUDGE.

These consolidated appeals concern garnishment in the context of a form of ownership of financial interests that is becoming widely used in today's global economy. The subject of the litigation is an interest in bonds regulated through a "multi-tiered" or "indirect" holding system.

The system with which this litigation is concerned is Euroclear, a network of 2,400 participating financial institutions that engage in cross-border securities transactions. Key features of an indirect holding system are that interests in bonds are reflected on the books of various institutions, transfers are effected by electronic book-entry, and the need to transfer the instruments in which participating interests are held rarely arises.

The principal issue sought to be presented by this appeal is whether, under New York law, a judgment creditor can execute against an interest in bonds beneficially owned by a judgment debtor, where, pursuant to an indirect holding system like Euroclear, the bonds are payable in New York by the issuer's New York paying agent, but the judgment debtor's interest is recorded only on the books of a financial intermediary located abroad. * * *

After an unsuccessful effort to attach certain bank accounts of Philguarantee, Fidelity learned that Philguarantee owned an interest in certain Philippine Interest Reduction Bonds ("FLIRBs") that had been issued by the Republic of the Philippines in an offshore offering in 1992. The FLIRBs are dollar-denominated bonds purchased and traded through "Euroclear," which is a multi-tiered indirect holding and clearance system managed by Morgan Guaranty Trust Company ("Morgan"). At least at that time, Philguarantee held a $1.75 million participation interest in the FLIRBs through ING Bank of Manila ("ING Bank"). The only entity on whose books the interest of Philguarantee was then reflected was ING Bank. ING Bank, in turn, held its interest in the FLIRBs through Euroclear, where its interest is reflected in a book-entry credit to a securities account maintained by Morgan's Brussels branch office. Finally, Morgan's London office, as sub-custodian for Morgan Brussels, is the holder of Global Bearer Certificates representing the FLIRBs, and is the only recorded owner of the FLIRBs reflected on the books of First Trust, the New York-based fiscal and paying agent, registrar, transfer agent, and authenticating agent pursuant to the terms of three fiscal agency agreements entered into by the issuer.

In May 1997, Fidelity moved for an order of execution against what it described as "the debt owed to Philguarantee by the Republic of the Philippines, the issuer and obligor of the Philippine Interest Reduction Bonds owned by Philguarantee." * * *

Prior to Judge Stein's December 1 ruling dismissing the "turnover" action, ING Bank had agreed to abide by Judge Brieant's restraining order and to prevent Philguarantee from selling any interest in the FLIRBs that was held through ING Bank, even though Philguarantee and ING Bank had refused to participate in the proceeding based on their position that the Court could not exercise personal jurisdiction over them. However, on January 13, 1998, as the parties were preparing their briefs for these appeals, Morgan received a letter from an official at ING Bank indicating that ING Bank had sold Philguarantee's participation interest in the FLIRBs on December 6, 1997. * * *

Thus, all that remains for consideration is the factual issue of whether Philguarantee's interest in the FLIRBs was sold on December 6. We leave that issue for determination by the District Court. If the Court determines that the interest was sold on December 6, the entire controversy concerning Philguarantee's interest in the FLIRBs has become moot. In that event, the judgment in 97 Civ. 5184, which concerns Philguarantee's interest in the FLIRBs, should be vacated and the complaint dismissed. Whether 96 Civ. 407 should also be dismissed will depend on whether Fidelity can present the District Court with any valid basis for keeping alive its removed action to enforce the California judgment. If the Court determines that Philguarantee's interest was not sold on December 6 (or was sold during any time prior to December 1 or after December 24), then the pending appeals may be restored to this Court's docket by a letter request from any party filed within 10 days of the District Court's factual determination. * * *

Morgan Guaranty Bank began operations of Euroclear, an international clearing agency based in Brussels, Belgium, in 1968. Morgan later transferred ownership to the participating institutions and Euroclear was operated as a cooperative agency for clearing by large banks, broker-dealers, and other institutions. By the end of the twentieth century, Euroclear was handling almost two-thirds of all internationally traded debt securities. Cedel, formed by the Cedel bank in Luxembourg, is another international clearing agency. Cedel handles eurobonds, equities, warrants, money market instruments and other securities. Euroclear and Cedel have created an electronic bridge to cross-clear their transactions.

CIBC Mellon Trust Company, by consent, agreed to pay $6 million to settle SEC enforcement proceedings charging that it acted illegally as an unregistered broker-dealer for thirty-four companies in connection with its administration of "Stock Plans" (dividend reinvestments, stock purchase plans, employee stock purchase plans and odd lot programs) for U.S. citizens. SEC v. CIBC Mellon Trust Co., SEC Litigation Release No. 19081 (Feb. 16, 2005). The SEC staff thereafter granted limited exemptive relief to the company so that it could continue such activities. The SEC noted that banks registered as transfer agents are exempted from broker-dealer registration requirements for stock plan activities. However, CIBC Mellon Trust Company, a Canadian entity, was not registered as a transfer agent. Order Exempting CIBC Mellon Trust Company from Broker–Dealer Registration, Securities Exchange Act Release No. 51253 (Feb. 25, 2005).

The Dodd–Frank Act established regulatory supervision over payment, clearing and settlement activities conducted by financial institutions and financial market utilities (FMUs). Dodd–Frank Act, § 805. FMUs are defined as including a multilateral system for transferring, clearing or settling payments, securities or other financial transactions among financial institutions or between financial institutions and a person. Dodd–

Frank Act, § 803. This legislation recognizes that, while financial institutions that conduct or support payment, clearing, or settlement activities may reduce risks for the financial system, such utilities may also concentrate and create new risks. The FSOC may designate, by supermajority vote, those FMUs that are systemically significant. Dodd–Frank Act, § 804. The Fed has an enhanced role in the supervision of risk management standards for systemically important FMUs.

SECTION 6.   MERGER ACTIVITIES

Banks have discovered other niches in the securities business that allow them to use their financial expertise and resources to facilitate securities transactions. One such area is advising and financing mergers and acquisitions.

NORWEST BANK MINNESOTA v. SWEEN CORP.

United States Court of Appeals, Eighth Circuit, 1997.
118 F.3d 1255.

Gibson, Circuit Judge.

* * * Sween Corporation is a Minnesota corporation that develops and manufactures skin care products for the medical market. Norwest is a national bank established in Minneapolis, Minnesota pursuant to the National Bank Act as amended. Norwest provides investment advisory services related to mergers and acquisitions through a division of Norwest referred to as Norwest Corporate Finance. This division is not a separate legal entity. The common stock of Norwest is owned by Norwest Corporation, a bank holding company governed by the Bank Holding Company Act as amended. Jeffrey Maas, Peter Slocum, and D. Christian Osborne worked for Norwest in the Norwest Corporate Finance Division when Norwest Corporate Finance and Sween entered into the Engagement Agreement at issue. None of these three employees has ever been licensed as a Minnesota broker.

An Engagement Agreement between Sween Corporation, Sween, Brekke, and Norwest dated October 10, 1994, authorized Norwest to act as the exclusive advisor to initiate negotiations regarding the sale of all or part of Sween Corporation. Under the terms of the Engagement Agreement, upon the sale of Sween Corporation, Sween Corporation agreed to pay Norwest an advisory fee.

Immediately after October 10, 1994, Norwest prepared and circulated to prospective buyers an extensive brochure promoting Sween Corporation. Norwest contacted in excess of 135 potential buyers. By December 1994, Sween Corporation agreed to narrow the list to four prospective buyers. These buyers brought teams to Mankato for a week in December to meet with representatives of both Sween Corporation and Norwest for the purpose of investigating and evaluating Sween Corporation. Two top ranking executives of Coloplast A/S, one of the potential buyers, met with Sween personnel. * * *

The primary issue before us is whether Sween is obligated to pay Norwest the fee that he promised to pay under the Engagement Agreement. Sween argues that Minnesota law prohibits Norwest from collecting the fee. In formulating his argument, Sween first contends that Norwest is a broker under Minnesota law,[19] which Norwest does not dispute. Sween next points to a Minnesota statute that prohibits a person required to be licensed from bringing a suit for collection of compensation for the performance of acts for which a license is required, without proving that the person was licensed properly at the time the alleged action occurred. Minn. Stat. § 82.33, subd. 1 (1996). Sween argues that because neither Norwest Corporate Finance, nor its employees, were licensed as brokers under Minnesota law at the time the parties acted under the Engagement Agreement, Norwest cannot bring this suit to collect the advisory fee.

Norwest responds by first pointing to Minnesota Statute section 82.18(e), that exempts various entities, including banks, from the term "broker" when engaged in the transaction of business within the scope of their corporate powers as provided by law. Norwest then asserts that pursuant to the National Bank Act, as a national bank, it had federal authority to enter into the Engagement Agreement and to fulfill its duties under that agreement. See 12 U.S.C. § 24(Seventh) (1994). Sween responds that Norwest's acts went beyond the authority provided to Norwest under the Act. We review a grant of summary judgment de novo. See McKee v. Federal Kemper Life Assurance Co., 927 F.2d 326, 328 (8th Cir. 1991). We will affirm only if there is no genuine issue of material fact and the moving party is entitled to judgment as a matter of law. See Fed. R. Civ. P. 56(c); Celotex Corp. v. Catrett, 477 U.S. 317, 323 (1986).

The National Bank Act vests each national bank with the authority "[t]o exercise ... all such incidental powers as shall be necessary to carry on the business of banking." Id. Though the statute lists a few activities in which banks are authorized to engage, the incidental powers are not confined to activities that are considered essential to the exercise of express powers. See First Nat'l Bank v. Taylor, 907 F.2d 775, 778 (8th Cir.), cert. denied, 498 U.S. 972 (1990). Our analysis thus focuses on whether the acts conducted under the Engagement Agreement fall within the "incidental powers" necessary to carry on the business of a national bank. * * *

The Office of the Comptroller of the Currency, through 12 C.F.R. § 7.1002 (1997) and an amicus brief submitted in this appeal, has stated its view that Norwest's acts under the Engagement Agreement fall within a national bank's powers. In 1971 the Comptroller adopted 12 C.F.R.

---

19. [n.4] A broker is "any person who ... for another and for commission, fee, or other valuable consideration or with the intention or expectation of receiving the same directly or indirectly lists, sells, exchanges, buys, rents, manages, offers or attempts to negotiate a sale ... of any business opportunity or business, or its goodwill, inventory, or fixtures, or any interest therein." Minn. Stat. § 82.17, subd. 4(c) (1996).

§ 7.7200, a regulation that specifically authorized a national bank to act as a " 'finder' in bringing together a buyer and seller." The present version of this regulation provides that:

(a) General. A national bank may act as a finder in bringing together a buyer and seller.

(b) Qualification. Acting as a finder includes, without limitation, identifying potential parties, making inquiries as to interest, introducing or arranging meetings of interested parties, and otherwise bringing parties together for a transaction that the parties themselves negotiate and consummate. Acting as a finder does not include activities that would characterize the bank as a broker under applicable Federal law.

(c) Advertisement and fee. Unless otherwise prohibited, a national bank may advertise the availability of, and accept a fee for, the services provided pursuant to this section. 12 C.F.R. § 7.1002.

This regulation encompasses most of Norwest's activities under the Engagement Agreement which involved locating suitable buyers for Sween Corporation. In fact, Sween himself concedes in his brief that he "would be pressed if forced to point to significant doings of [Norwest] that would not arguably fit within subparagraph (b) of the amended regulation." In addition, the Office of the Comptroller of the Currency argues that Norwest's role in the negotiations between Sween Corporation and Coloplast is of no consequence because these additional activities also fall within a national bank's incidental powers under 12 U.S.C. § 24(Seventh). * * *

SECTION 7. MUTUAL FUNDS

Mutual funds are a popular form of investment for many individuals. The total amount of money held in mutual funds increased from $60 billion in 1972 to $11.2 trillion in 2007. By the end of the last century, there were over 6000 mutual funds. The popularity of mutual funds was due in part to the growth of money market funds for short term returns on idle cash. Mutual funds were also a way to invest in long term instruments such as stock and bonds. Mutual funds provide expertise in investment selection and portfolio diversification that most small investors are not able to achieve on their own. Mutual funds are also liquid investments that can be redeemed by investors at their net asset value.

A mutual fund is owned by its shareholders and overseen by a board of directors. The fund itself does not have any employees. Typically, a fund's board hires an advisory firm to manage the fund's money.

Mutual funds are regulated by the SEC under the Investment Company Act of 1940, which has been said to be "the most intrusive financial legislation known to man or beast." The Financial Services Revolution: Understanding the Changing Role of Banks, Mutual Funds, and Insurance Companies 382 (Clifford E. Kirsch ed. 1997). "It places substantive restrictions on virtually every aspect of the operations of investment companies; their valuation of assets, their governance and structure, their issuance of debt and other senior securities, their investments, sales and redemptions of their shares, and, perhaps most importantly, their dealings with service providers and other affiliates." Paul F. Roye, Remarks Before American Law Institute/American Bar Association Investment Company Regulation and Compliance Conference (Oct. 16, 2003). For a discussion of the regulation of hedge funds and mutual fund scandals see Jerry W. Markham, Mutual Fund Scandals—A Comparative Analysis of the Role of Corporate Governance in the Regulation of Collective Investments, 3 Hastings Bus. L.J. 67 (2006).

Not all collective investment mediums were required to register under the Investment Company Act. Among those exempted from registration, and hence regulation, under that statute were insurance companies, banks and "any common trust fund or similar fund maintained by a bank exclusively for the collective investment and reinvestment of monies contributed thereto by the bank in its capacity as a trustee, executor, administrator or guardian." 15 U.S.C. § 80a–3(c)(3). Also exempted were any qualified "employees' stock bonus, pension, or profit sharing trust." Id. at § 80a–3(c)(11). Bank management of common trust funds and pension funds is discussed in Chapter 10.

Investment companies registered under the Investment Company Act are required to provide the SEC with periodic financial reports. 15 U.S.C. § 80a–29 (sales literature must also be submitted to the SEC. 15 U.S.C. § 80a–24(b)). Those requirements are similar to those imposed on other issuers of securities, but the Investment Company Act goes far beyond that pattern with other provisions. Among other things, that statute governs the capital structure of investment companies, limiting the amount of their indebtedness acquired through "senior securities." I5 U.S.C. § 80a–18. The act regulates dividend polices of investment companies, a matter normally left to state regulation. I5 U.S.C. § 80a–19.

The Investment Company Act also requires that forty percent of an investment company's board of directors be independent outside directors. 15 U.S.C. § 80a–10. The SEC expanded this requirement to a majority of outside directors and, after some mutual fund scandals in 2003, adopted a rule requiring seventy-five percent as the minimum number of outside directors and requiring that the roles of chairman and chief executive officer be split. That action was set aside on two occasions by a federal appeals court because the SEC had not shown any justification for such requirements. Chamber of Commerce of the United States v. Securities and Exchange Commission, 412 F.3d 133 (D.C. Cir. 2005) and Chamber of Commerce of the United States v. Securities and Exchange Commission, 443 F.3d 890 (D.C. Cir. 2006).

IN THE MATTER OF THE BANK OF CALIFORNIA, N.A.

Securities Exchange Commission, 1993.
Administrative Proceedings File No. 3–8084.
1993 WL 243770 (S.E.C.).

* * * The Bank of California, N.A. is a national banking association whose headquarters are located in San Francisco, California. At all times relevant, the Bank served as the fund accountant for the investment portfolios of The HighMark Group, a registered investment company. In that capacity, the Bank was responsible for, among other things, calculating the net asset value per share of the Tax–Free Fund, a money market portfolio within The HighMark Group. In addition, the Bank served as investment adviser to The HighMark Group. * * *

This proceeding involves acts and omissions by the Bank which caused the Fund to violate the pricing and books and records provisions of the Investment Company Act. In August 1991, counsel for the Fund informed the staff of the Commission that, for approximately a five week period, the Bank had erroneously priced the Phoenix Bond in the Fund's portfolio at over 42% more than its market value. Consequently, the Bank incorrectly computed the Fund's net assets and the Fund sold and redeemed shares at a price other than its correct net asset value per share. The Bank's pricing error relating to the Phoenix Bond was primarily caused by the actions of an employee in the fund accounting department of the Bank. However, the Bank's internal control procedures and systems were inadequate in that they allowed the pricing problem to occur and remain undetected for a substantial period of time. As a result, the Bank caused the Fund to violate Sections 22(c) and 31(a) of the Investment Company Act and Rules 22c–1 and 31a–1 thereunder. * * *

Rule 22c–1, promulgated pursuant to Section 22(c) of the Investment Company Act, states, in pertinent part, that no registered investment company issuing redeemable securities "shall sell, redeem, or repurchase any such security except at a price based upon the current net asset value of such security...." Section 2(a)(41) of the Investment Company Act defines value, with respect to securities for which market quotations are readily available, as the fair market value of those securities. However, Rule 2a–7, promulgated pursuant to Section 2(a)(41) of the Investment Company Act, allows money market funds to value securities using the amortized cost method subject to certain conditions. One such condition imposes a limitation of 1/2 of 1 percent on the amount of allowable dilution as expressed by the difference between the market value of a fund's portfolio securities and the amortized cost value of those securities.

The Bank failed to accurately record the actual values obtained during the periodic mark-to-market valuation of the Fund's portfolio securities. The substantial decrease in the market value of the Phoenix Bond caused a decrease in the Fund's aggregate portfolio market value of over 3/5ths of 1%, well over the 1/2 of 1% maximum allowed in Rule 2a–7.

As a result, during the period between July 25, 1991 and August 28, 1991, over 20,000,000 shares were redeemed by the Fund at an inflated value, which diluted the value of the remaining shareholders' assets. During the same period, over 15,000,000 shares of the Fund were purchased at a price which exceeded the value of the assets purchased. The Fund violated Rule 22c–1 when it sold and redeemed shares at a value that did not reflect a correct net asset value. Because the Bank prepared the inaccurate valuation reports that were used to calculate the price of Fund shares, the Bank caused the Fund's violations of the pricing requirements of Rule 22c–1 of the Investment Company Act. * * *

As the twentieth century came to a close, banks found that they could no longer depend on customer deposits as an exclusive source of funds. By 1993, the amount of money in mutual funds exceeded the amount of commercial bank deposits, largely as the result of the growth of money market mutual funds. Banks responded to this threat by becoming vendors of mutual funds. As seen in Investment Company Institute v. Camp, 401 U.S. 617 (1971) (excerpted earlier in this chapter), banking restrictions slowed that effort, but those barriers gradually fell. Soon, a third of all mutual funds were sold through banks.

OLESH v. DREYFUS CORP.

United States District Court, Eastern District of New York, 1995.
Fed. Sec. L. Rep. (CCH) ¶ 98,907.

SIFTON, DISTRICT JUDGE.

This is an action brought by plaintiffs, Martin H. and Deborah W. Olesh, against defendant The Dreyfus Corporation ("Dreyfus"), Dreyfus Liquid Assets, Inc. ("DLA"), and Dreyfus Growth Opportunity Fund, Inc. ("DGO") arising out of a merger between Dreyfus and the Mellon Bank Corporation ("Mellon"). According to the caption of the complaint, plaintiffs have sued the last two named defendants both in defendants' individual capacity and on behalf of "the Dreyfus Family of Funds," an unincorporated association. Plaintiffs allege violations of sections 15(f) and 35(b) of the Investment Company Act ("ICA"), 15 U.S.C. § 80a–15(f), 35(b), and breach of a common law fiduciary duty. They seek monetary and declaratory relief. * * *

Defendant Dreyfus is the investment adviser to the more than 130 mutual funds that comprise the Dreyfus Family of Funds. The funds, which have approximately 1 million shareholders and a total of approximately $80 billion in investor assets, are registered investment companies under the ICA. Each fund has a separate board of directors, and Dreyfus advises each fund pursuant to separate advisory agreements pursuant to which Dreyfus receives fees for its advisory services to the fund. Plaintiffs are investors in two of the Dreyfus Funds, defendants Dreyfus Liquid Assets, Inc. and Dreyfus Growth Opportunity Fund, Inc.

Mellon, which is not a party to this litigation, is a publicly owned multi-bank holding company which provides a comprehensive range of financial products and services. It is the 23rd largest bank holding company in the United States, with total assets of $36.6 billion as of March 31, 1994. Mellon Bank, N.A. ("Mellon Bank"), a national bank, is a wholly-owned subsidiary of Mellon. Among other business and banking activities, Mellon provides investment and non-investment services to mutual funds.

On December 6, 1993, Dreyfus and Mellon publicly announced that they had entered into a merger agreement pursuant to which Dreyfus would merge with and become a wholly-owned subsidiary of Mellon Bank, in a stock-for-stock transaction approximately worth $1.85 billion, pursuant to which shares of Dreyfus would be exchanged for shares of Mellon.

As required by section 15(a) of the ICA, 15 U.S.C. § 80a–15(a)(4), the merger automatically terminated the investment advisory contracts Dreyfus then had with the funds. Accordingly, the "non-interested" directors of each fund, and each fund's shareholders or investors were required to approve new advisory agreements with Dreyfus. To this end, the merger agreement between Dreyfus and Mellon contained a clause known as the "90% Condition," under which the merger was conditioned on the approval of new investment advisory contracts by investors in funds owning 90% of all fund assets.

Because Mellon is regulated by the Office of the Comptroller of the Currency (the "OCC"), the OCC, among other agencies, had to approve Mellon's merger with Dreyfus. Among the issues considered by the OCC was the fact that Mellon, as a bank, is exempt from the Investment Advisers Act (the "IAA"), 15 U.S.C. § 80b, which places investment advisers under the jurisdiction of the Securities and Exchange Commission (the "SEC"). If Mellon were to choose not to operate Dreyfus as a separate company following the merger, the funds' investment adviser would, as a result, no longer be subject to the registration requirements of the IAA, to record-keeping and procedural requirements mandated by the SEC pursuant to the IAA, and in general, to oversight of its activities by the SEC under the IAA's mandate.

On May 4, 1994, the OCC announced that it had approved the Dreyfus–Mellon merger, subject to a number of conditions. A central condition was that Mellon commit to operating Dreyfus as an independent entity for at least two years subsequent to the acquisition. This commitment is also expressed in the merger agreement.

The directors of the funds identified by Dreyfus as non-interested approved new advisory agreements between Dreyfus and the funds. On June 6, 1994, Dreyfus disseminated to investors in all the funds a "Combined Proxy Statement," soliciting approval of new investment advisory contracts for the funds and of the election of Dreyfus nominees as directors of the funds. The proxy statement represented that all fund directors who were employees of Dreyfus would resign at the time of the merger and that other directors of the funds would continue to serve as directors. The proxy statement also represented that the "non-interested" directors of each fund approved the new advisory agreements. The fund shareholders approved the new advisory agreements at a special shareholders' meeting held during the week of August 1, 1994, satisfying the 90% Condition.

Dreyfus, of course, is paid fees for its investment advisory services. Dreyfus currently has in effect "waiver" agreements between Dreyfus and many of the funds pursuant to which Dreyfus has agreed to forego certain fees and expense reimbursements to which it would otherwise be entitled under its advisory contracts with the funds. It has been Dreyfus' policy to renew most of these waiver agreements as they expire. In 1993, Dreyfus received management, advisory, and administrative fees totalling $297,472,000 and waived fees aggregating $57,010,000. On December 6, 1993, Dreyfus and Mellon announced that they would phase out these waiver agreements. Dreyfus and Mellon subsequently confirmed this plan to government regulatory agencies. Plaintiffs allege that this decision is a "direct result" of Mellon's desire to recoup some of its investment in Dreyfus as well as the fact that in light of an analysis of Dreyfus undertaken by McKinsey & Company, a management consulting firm, Mellon needs to take drastic measures in order to close a revenue gap that has opened up between Dreyfus' actual financial results and those projected by McKinsey. The McKinsey report also recommended a number of other alternative revenue enhancement measures that would increase the fees to the Dreyfus funds.

Virtually all of the directors who were elected during the week of August 1, 1994, including those who were designated as non-interested, have close business relationships with Dreyfus and receive substantial compensation as directors of the funds. According to the plaintiffs, these purportedly "non-interested" directors sit on multiple boards of the funds and, in exchange for little work, are paid substantial sums of money. The complaint documents five individuals who each serve on the boards of no less than 15 funds, and who receive over $50,000 yearly in aggregate compensation. Moreover, the complaint alleges that Dreyfus officers, including Dreyfus Chairman Howard Stein, sit on the boards of the funds, thereby being in a position to develop personal and business relationships with the outside directors.

Plaintiffs allege that by virtue of this disproportionate compensation, the interlocking directorates, and the presence of Dreyfus officers, the non-interested directors are anything but disinterested, and in fact have an ongoing business relationship with Dreyfus that overcomes their ability to judge Dreyfus' conduct independently. Plaintiffs also allege that the boards of the funds voted in 1994 to approve new advisory agreements despite the plans of Mellon and Dreyfus to phase out fee waivers and the likelihood that Dreyfus would be compelled to institute increased advisory fees. These facts, they allege, state a claim that the merger has violated Section 15(f) of the ICA because the proportion of interested directors of the funds exceeds 25% and also because the prospective advisory fee increases constitute an unfair burden to the funds. Plaintiffs bring this claim both as a class action on behalf of themselves and other fund investors as well as derivatively on behalf of the nominal defendants. Plaintiffs seek declaratory relief that the merger does not comply with section 15(f) of the ICA. * * *

Section 15(f) of the ICA was enacted subsequent to the Second Circuit Court of Appeals' decision in Rosenfeld v. Black, 445 F.2d 1337 (2d Cir. 1971), cert. dismissed, 409 U.S. 802 (1972), which held that profits realized by an investment advisor from the sale of its office were recoverable by the investment company. See Meyer v. Oppenheimer Management Corp., 764 F.2d 76, 86 (2d Cir. 1985) (Meyer II). The new section, added in 1975, allowed the sale of the investment adviser's business upon certain statutory conditions. * * *

Section 15(f) of the ICA provides that an investment advisor may receive benefit for the sale of its business that involves assignment of investment advisory contracts if (a) seventy-five percent of the directors of the investment company are not "interested persons" of the investment adviser or the predecessor investment advisor and (b) the transaction does not impose an unfair burden on the investment company. 15 U.S.C. § 80a–15. Plaintiffs assert that the Mellon/Dreyfus merger fails both these conditions and, thus, that the merger is invalid. However, plaintiffs arguments and factual allegations are insufficient to mount a claim against the merger under § 15(f).

Plaintiffs claim that at least twenty-five percent of the directors of the boards of the nominal defendant funds are "interested" within the meaning of 15 U.S.C. § 80a–2(19). The basis of this claim is the allegation that many of the directors of individual Dreyfus funds sit on the boards of several funds and receive substantial aggregate compensation. Plaintiffs point to certain fund directors who sit on over fifteen boards and receive over $50,000 annually in compensation. * * *

The term "interested persons" was given a very specific definition in 1970 Amendments to the ICA. When used with respect to an investment adviser, a person is an "interested person" to that company if any one of six enumerated criteria is met. The first five such criteria are "per se" tests. For example, § 2(19)(B)(iv) classifies as interested "any person or partner or employee of any person who at any time since the beginning of the last two fiscal years of such investment company has acted as legal counsel for such investment advisor or principal underwriter." * * *

By its terms, this [sixth] section empowers the SEC to declare, by order, a person "interested." Plaintiffs are well aware of that power, having petitioned the SEC for such a declaration and having appealed its refusal to the D.C. Circuit Court of Appeals. However, plaintiffs also contend that this court has concurrent jurisdiction with the SEC and is thus also empowered to find the directors "interested" under the sixth criteria. Defendants respond that this section of the statute can only be read to convey jurisdiction over the § 2(19)(B)(vi) "material business or professional" determination to the SEC exclusively. Plaintiffs' arguments that the statute should be read otherwise are unpersuasive. * * *

As set forth above, § 36 of the ICA allows a suit for breach of "fiduciary duty with respect to the receipt of compensation for services, or of payments of a material nature, paid by such registered investment company, or by the security holders thereof, to such investment adviser." 15 U.S.C. § 80a–35.

Plaintiffs and defendants agree that this section is violated when the adviser charges "a fee that is so disproportionately large that it bears no reasonable relationship to the services rendered and could not have been the product of arm's length bargaining." Meyer II, 764 F.2d at 81 (quoting Gartenberg v. Merrill Lynch Asset Management, Inc., 694 F.2d 923, 928 (2d Cir. 1982), cert. denied, 461 U.S. 906 (1981)). The complaint nowhere alleges that the fee increases at issue here would violate that standard, and plaintiffs do not appear to be proceeding on that ground. Instead, plaintiffs allege that Dreyfus has violated these duties "by failing to obtain any benefits for the Funds (such as a reduction in fees) and by failing to obtain any protections concerning future fee increases (after the initial two year period following the merger) or concerning the phasing out or reduction in fee waiver agreements and waiver of expense arrangements." Plaintiffs contend that these breaches should be cognizable under § 36.

The failure of Dreyfus to negotiate reduced fees for its client funds is not a breach of fiduciary duty. Wexler at 98,925. Similarly, neither is the failure to obtain protections against future fee increases. All section 36(b) authorizes is for the court "to determine whether the investment adviser has committed a breach of fiduciary duty in determining or receiving the fee." S. Rep. No. 91–184, supra. The mere failure of an investment adviser to provide protections against fee increases or to negotiate reduced fees upon a merger does not state a claim, without some allegation to tie this failure to the imposition of excessive fees. * * *

See Chapter 9 for additional discussion of director interlocks. As discussed in Chapter 10, some banks have invested their common trust funds in mutual funds. Banks were also authorized by legislation enacted in 1996 to convert their common trust funds into mutual funds; thereby providing liquidity for the underlying trusts. Those conversions were facilitated by the Small Business Jobs Protection Act of 1996, Pub. L. No. 104–188, 110 Stat. 1755, which amended the tax treatment of conversions into mutual funds under Section 584 of the Internal Revenue Code of 1986. Many banks made such conversions, giving rise to litigation that the effects of such conversions had not been fully disclosed to trust beneficiaries. See Lori Pizzani, B of A, Wachovia Lawsuits May Shake Up Fund World, Am. Banker, July 13, 2006.

One commentator noted that:

> We're now starting to see the banks having second thoughts about whether it was a good idea to convert their collective funds to mutual funds. And some of them are going back and reconverting them back to collective funds. We're starting to see a movement where investment advisors are teaming up with bank trust departments and creating collective funds as investment options for 401(k) plans because the world has changed. Back then, collective funds did not have daily valuation. Today, you can get daily valuation in a collective fund. The values of a collective fund are not published in the newspaper, but any participant has easy access on the internet to go to a website and find the daily valuation of its interest in its collective fund. And while you cannot move the interest in your collective fund to another, to an IRA if a participant leaves its plan, leaves the employer, that seems to be of less concern today than the fact that the collective funds come in at lower costs than the mutual funds. And there's lots of debate as to why the collective funds are less expensive to maintain, whether they have less regulatory costs, whether . . . they don't have a distribution network in place and are less of a retail oriented product. Nevertheless, we see collective funds being offered . . . where the asset management fee and the other fees are less than comparable mutual funds. And that's providing significant competitive opportunity for these collective funds.

Remarks of Donald Myers, partner Reed Smith LLP, at the American Enterprise Institute Conference on The Regulation of Mutual Funds, Competition With other Investment Vehicles for Retirement Savings, Wash. D.C. (Jan. 3, 2006) available at <www.aei.org>.

Bank common trusts are often likened to mutual funds. However, there are some significant differences between those two investment formats. Mutual fund shareholders may select their own investment strategy, while the bank will usually make the investment decision for trust beneficiaries, perhaps with some guidelines from the trust deed. The investor in a mutual fund may freely redeem his holdings at their net asset value, while the trust beneficiary is subject to the terms of the trust, rendering the investment illiquid.

One disadvantage of a mutual fund is that a customer buying or selling receives the net asset value only as calculated at day's end rather than at the time sold. When mutual funds experienced a drop in their net asset values after the market bubble burst in 2000, they faced competition from the exchanges that offered products that were the equivalent of a diversified mutual fund, but permitted intra-day trading and pricing. The products were exchange-traded funds (ETFs), initially known as Standard and Poor's Depository Receipts (SPDRs or Spiders). In order to meet this competition and declining fees as net asset values dropped, mutual funds advisors began allowing hedge funds and other professional traders to engage in "market timing" and "late" transactions in exchange for "sticky" assets that would remain with the mutual fund.

As a general rule, mutual funds are not supposed to be used for "market timing" trading (i.e., buying and selling rapidly in order to take advantage of short-term market movements), but rather for long-term "buy and hold" strategies. This is because of the high fees associated with mutual fund transactions and because of their pricing at the close of trading only, which restricts the ability to take advantage of market movements. By permitting some large traders to trade at night at the preceding day's closing price, those traders were able to take advantage of overnight price movements at the preset price. Such market timing was not illegal per se, unless an unsophisticated investor was induced to market time to increase commissions for the salesman. Market timing transactions, nevertheless, increased transaction costs for the mutual fund, required it to maintain higher amounts of liquidity, and could dilute the holdings of other shareholders if the fund's shares were overpriced when the market timer liquidated.

The New York attorney general, Eliot Spitzer, exposed these problems in a suit against Edward J. Stern and a hedge fund Stern managed, Canary Capital Partners. Spitzer charged those defendants with improper late trading in the shares of mutual funds. Security Trust, a bank used to transfer mutual funds, was charged with helping Canary Capital and other hedge funds to late trade mutual funds. The bank was ordered to be dissolved by banking regulators. The SEC charged Strong Capital Management and Richard Strong with engaging in improper market timing transactions for Canary Capital. They agreed to settle that action for $140 million.[20]

BankOne Corp., which sponsored the OneGroup fund complex, Janus Capital Group, Inc. and Strong Capital, was also found to have allowed Canary Capital to late trade in their mutual funds. Another institution allowing late trading by Canary Capital was Bank of America's mutual fund complex that operated under the name of Nations Funds. The Nations Funds imposed a two percent redemption fee to discourage market timing transactions but waived the fee for Canary Partners. The SEC charged that an employee of Banc of America Securities LLC, had time stamped mutual fund order tickets for hedge funds in advance of the 4:00 p.m. cutoff so that it would appear that the orders had been entered before that time. That employee was acquitted of criminal charges for that conduct.

The SEC and New York attorney general Spitzer charged that traders for FleetBoston's mutual funds engaged in a total of $2.5 billion of market timing transactions in seven Columbia Funds sponsored by FleetBoston between 1998 to 2003.

---

20. In the Matter of Strong Capital Management, Inc., 2004 WL 1124933 (S.E.C. 2004).

Bank of America and FleetBoston later agreed to merge with each other and jointly settled their mutual fund problems. They agreed to pay $675 million to regulators in order to settle market timing and late trading claims. Of that amount, $160 million was to be used to reduce fees charged to mutual funds investors. Regulators collected over $3 billion in fines from the various offenders, including $125 million paid by the Canadian Imperial Bank of Commerce to settle SEC late trading and market timing charges. Several regulatory measures were also taken by the SEC to strengthen mutual fund regulation after these events, including proposed regulations for mutual fund governance,[21] requirements for disclosures about market timing and selective disclosure of portfolio holdings,[22] disclosures on transaction costs,[23] pricing of mutual funds,[24] compliance programs for investment companies and advisers,[25] and codes of ethics.[26] Some of these proposals proved to be more complicated than envisioned by the SEC and only limited reforms were adopted. See Jerry W. Markham, Mutual Fund Scandals—A Comparative Analysis of the Role of Corporate Governance in the Regulation of Collective Investments, 3 Hastings Bus. L.J. 67, 94 (2006) (describing problems with the proposals).

QUESTIONS AND NOTES

1. The Gramm–Leach–Bliley Act (GLBA) sought to strengthen the SEC's regulation of bank investment advisory activities for mutual funds. 15 U.S.C.A. § 80b–2(a). Banks engaging in advisory activities, once exempt from the Investment Advisors Act of 1940, are now subject to its provisions. Under GLBA, the bank or one of its designated departments must register with the SEC as an investment adviser if it is acting as an investment adviser to a mutual fund. The SEC was given authority to adopt regulations governing the operations of banks that are acting as advisers and custodians for mutual funds, and to regulate loans to mutual funds by bank affiliates. Persons selling mutual fund shares are prohibited from claiming that they are guaranteed by the FDIC or by a bank or other depository institution.

2. GLBA expanded the definition of "bank" in the Investment Company Act to include thrifts so that they might also be excepted from the Act's registration requirements. The Investment Advisors Act, however, was not amended by GLBA to include thrifts within the "bank" exemption. The SEC has issued a proposed rule to except a thrift from the Investment Advisors Act when it provides investment advice in its role as a fiduciary (trustee, executor, administrator or guardian). 69 Fed. Reg. 25777 (proposed May 7, 2004). The OTS and the thrift industry were concerned that the proposed exemption was

---

21. Investment Company Governance, 2004 WL 69152 (S.E.C. Jan. 15, 2004).

22. Securities Act Release No. 8408, April 6, 2004.

23. Request For Comments on Measures to Improve Disclosure of Mutual Fund Transaction Costs, 2003 WL 22988749 (S.E.C. Dec. 18, 2003).

24. Amendments to Rules Governing Pricing of Mutual Fund Shares, 2003 WL 22926831 (S.E.C. Dec. 11, 2003).

25. Compliance Programs of Investment Companies and Investment Advisers, 2003 WL 22971048 (S.E.C. Dec. 17, 2003).

26. SEC News Digest 2004–10, 2004 WL 65366 (S.E.C. Jan. 15, 2004).

too limited and not equivalent to the exemption afforded to banks. The proposed rule was not adopted.

3. Are you aware that your money market account (which is a mutual fund) is not insured by the FDIC unless it is maintained as a demand deposit account at an insured institution?

4. Are you aware that mutual funds are simply a method to trade a pool of funds and that profits will depend on the wisdom of the investment and the vagaries of the market?

5. The mutual fund activities of banks raise other regulatory issues, including safety and soundness concerns. For example, banks sponsoring mutual funds may sometimes cover losses in their funds in order to mitigate bad publicity from a poor investment or an already troubled banking situation, but the payment of such funds reduces the assets available to bank depositors. Federal bank regulators have warned banks that they need to adopt policies as to when bank funds may be used to support mutual funds by covering losses in those funds for reasons of reputation risk or to mitigate liability. Interagency Policy on Banks/Thrifts Providing Financial Support to Funds Advised by the Banking Organization or its Affiliates, OCC 2004–2 (Jan. 5, 2004).

SECTION 8.   HEDGE FUNDS AND PRIVATE EQUITY

There is no technical distinction between hedge funds and private equity. Typically, however, hedge funds are short-term traders of financial instruments, while private equity firms take control and manage the companies they buy, often for extended periods of time. However, hedge funds and private equity will sometimes cross these lines and some private equity groups operate their own hedge funds.

A.   HEDGE FUNDS

Hedge funds are usually formed by a limited number of investors who are required to invest a significant minimum amount. The fund may engage in aggressive trading strategies and is often highly leveraged since it is not subject to many of the restrictions that limit the activities of mutual funds. Hedge fund managers also usually collect a substantial percentage of the hedge fund's profits—often twenty percent—as part of their fee, as well as a two percent fee for the amount of funds under management. In 2007, hedge funds were estimated to have some $1.5 trillion under management in some 8,000 or more funds. The figure on funds under management may actually understate the buying power of hedge funds since they often trade with borrowed funds and highly leveraged instruments. The buying power of the hedge funds has been estimated to exceed that of mutual funds and private equity. The latter (private equity) is another growing phenomenon in finance.

The near failure of the Long Term Capital hedge funds (described in Chapter 3) raised concerns of systemic failure in the entire financial system. Such hedge funds are really investment companies that operate in many ways like a mutual fund except that redemption is usually limited. Those hedge funds were not previously required to register with the SEC under the Investment Company Act of 1940 because their participants were largely institutions or sophisticated investors who did not need the protection of that statute. Because of their role in the late trading and market timing scandals, however, the SEC, in a controversial decision, required those entities to register with it under the Investment Advisers Act of 1940. 17 C.F.R. pts. 275 and 279 (2004). The hedge fund investment adviser registration requirement was challenged in the District of Columbia Court of Appeals. That court concluded that the SEC had acted arbitrarily in defining clients to include hedge fund shareholders. Goldstein v. SEC, 451 F.3d 873 (D.C. Cir. 2006).

Then Fed Chairman Alan Greenspan noted that hedge funds provide some benefits:

> Hedge funds have become increasingly valuable in our financial markets. They actively pursue arbitrage opportunities across markets and in the process often reduce or eliminate mispricing of financial assets. Their willingness to take short positions can act as an antidote to the sometimes-excessive enthusiasm of long-only investors. Perhaps most important, they often provide valuable liquidity to financial markets, both in normal market conditions and especially during periods of stress. They can ordinarily perform these functions more effectively than other types of financial intermediaries because their investors often have a greater appetite for risk and because they are largely free from regulatory constraints on investment strategies.

Alan Greenspan, Chairman, Risk Transfer and Financial Stability, Remarks at the Federal Reserve Bank of Chicago's Forty-first Annual Conference on Bank Structure (May 5, 2005).

Hedge funds often have significant borrowing and other relationships with banks. In fact, large banks often use their affiliates to capture the trading, clearing, and other operations of hedge funds. One bank, UBS, was accused of running a "hedge fund hotel" by Massachusetts regulators in which the bank provided hedge funds with cheap office rent, secretaries, furniture, internet access, and entertainment. Keith Reed, Galvin Sues UBS Over Hedge Fund Perks, Boston Globe, June 28, 2007. Hedge funds also often seek to contract out their operations to bank affiliates. This may involve execution of trades through a broker-dealer affiliate of a bank as the hedge fund's "prime broker." A separate bank affiliate may be used to act as a hedge fund "administrator" for accounting and reporting changes in hedge fund net asset value ("NAV") to investors.

PENSION COMMITTEE OF THE UNIVERSITY OF MONTREAL PENSION PLAN v. BANC OF AMERICA SECURITIES LLC

United States Court of Appeals, Second Circuit, 2009.
568 F.3d 374.

LEVAL, CIRCUIT JUDGE.

Plaintiffs appeal from the judgment of the United States District Court for the Southern District of New York dismissing their claims against Banc of America Securities LLC ("BAS"), without leave to re-plead, for failure to state a claim upon which relief may be granted. Plaintiffs were investors in two hedge funds based in the British Virgin Islands, Lancer Offshore, Inc. and OmniFund Ltd. ("the Funds"). They brought this action to recover losses they suffered on the liquidation of the Funds. Plaintiffs alleged that their losses resulted from frauds committed by Michael Lauer, who managed the Funds through Lancer Management Group, LLC ("Lancer Management").

Plaintiffs' claims against BAS allege that, in its role as the prime broker for the Funds, BAS aided and abetted the frauds and breaches of fiduciary duty committed by Lauer and Lancer Management. The district court dismissed the claims, ruling that Plaintiffs failed to satisfy their burden of pleading proximate causation for their losses. We disagree. The complaint includes allegations that BAS knowingly and substantially assisted Lauer and Lancer Management in deceiving Plaintiffs as to the net asset values of the Funds by falsifying the values of the Funds' holdings on Position Reports, which BAS knew would be relied upon by the Funds' auditor and administrators in calculating and verifying the Funds' net asset values ("NAVs"). It alleges further that the Plaintiffs "reasonably relied upon the [false] representations regarding the Funds' NAVs [net asset values] ... in deciding to invest in and/or remain invested in the Funds," and that the falsely inflated net asset values were used to justify the payment of fees to Lauer, Lancer Management, and others, which drained the assets of the Funds. In our view, the complaint sufficiently pleaded that BAS's actions proximately caused the Plaintiffs' losses. * * *

Lauer was the founder, manager and sole shareholder of Lancer Management, which was the Funds' investment manager. Lauer and Lancer Management were responsible for all investment decisions for the Funds. Lancer Management managed the Funds in exchange for fees, which were based on the Funds' NAVs. Lauer and Lancer Management solicited investors in the Funds through personal contacts, third-party marketers or finders, and letters and other mailings, marketing materials, newsletters and private placement memoranda ("PPMs").

The PPMs represented that the majority of the Funds' assets would be invested in common stocks traded on the New York Stock Exchange, the American Stock Exchange or in the U.S. over-the-counter market.

However, Lauer and Lancer Management caused the Funds to pursue an increasingly risky strategy, investing the Funds' assets in restricted (and thus not freely marketable) shares, warrants, and non-equity investments of a small number of "micro-cap and small-cap companies … many of [which] were not publicly traded at all." The majority of the securities in which the Funds invested were not listed on any exchange and were quoted, if at all, on the Over-the-Counter Bulletin Board and/or pink sheets.

The PPMs provided that the NAVs of the Funds would be determined based on the market values of the securities held by the Funds. Specifically, the PPMs provided that listed or quoted securities were to "be valued at their last sales price on the date of determination." The PPMs also provided that listed or quoted securities not sold on the date of determination as well as unlisted securities were to "be valued at the mean between the 'bid' and 'asked' prices" of the most recent date on which such prices were quoted, and if no quotes had been [made] in the past 15 business days, then at a valuation assigned by the Board of Directors. The PPMs also contained a caveat that, in the event the directors determined that the listed valuation method did not represent its market value, the directors would value the securities.

As early as March 2000, the Funds began losing money on a massive scale. To hide the Funds' losses and show increasing NAVs, Lauer and Lancer Management embarked on a scheme to manipulate and inflate their valuation of the securities held by the Funds to the extent of hundreds of millions of dollars: Lauer and Lancer Management purchased for the Funds substantial and sometimes controlling stakes in companies whose shares were thinly-traded on the open market. The Funds' purchases were made in private transactions; they did not involve free-trading common stock, but rather securities not traded on the open market. Prior to the end of the Funds' reporting periods, Lauer and Lancer Management would purchase small amounts of the unrestricted, free-trading stock of these companies in such a manner as to drive up the "market price" of those shares. They would then improperly assign these artificially inflated values to the Funds' restricted holdings, thereby generating the appearance of large paper profits, and triggering payment of larger fees to Lauer and Lancer Management.

These false inflated valuations were used in calculating the Funds' NAVs, and the false NAVs were disseminated to investors each month and used to prepare the Funds' audited financial statements. Lancer Offshore's annual reports for 2000, 2002, and 2003 also included fraudulent NAV figures. The fraudulent NAV statements and audit reports were intended to and did induce Plaintiffs to invest, and remain invested, in the Funds and to artificially and improperly inflate the Fund management, incentive, and administrative fees, thereby draining the Funds' remaining assets. * * *

As the Funds' prime broker, BAS cleared and settled trades, provided portfolio management services, and served as the central custodian for some of the securities held by the Funds. BAS received a commission on each of the trades it cleared and settled. Because Lancer Management executed a high volume of trades through BAS and therefore generated substantial commissions for the bank, BAS provided Lauer with substantial goods and services, such as funding construction of, paying rent on, and providing the infrastructure for Lancer Management's Park Avenue office space.

Each month, BAS prepared monthly account statements ("Account Statements"), which purported to reflect the value of the securities held in its custody on behalf of the Funds. In order to collect the valuation information needed to generate account information, BAS received an electronic data feed from one or more third-party data providers who, in turn, obtained market prices from various securities exchanges and market makers.

BAS also permitted Lauer and Lancer Management to access reports from its computer system through a website called www.primebroker.com. Upon request from Lauer and Lancer Management, BAS periodically posted reports generated by BAS's computer system on its website. Using logins and passwords provided by BAS, Lauer and Lancer Management were able to access the BAS website on a "read-only" basis and view, download and print various reports posted by BAS, including Position Reports, which purported to show the Funds' holdings and the values of those holdings. The Position Reports were the only documents in existence that listed and depicted the values of both the Fund positions in BAS's custody and those held "away" from BAS.

The Position Reports contained BAS's name at the top of each page. When downloaded and printed, the Position Reports contained no disclaimer or other marking to suggest that they were anything other than official documents prepared by BAS and bearing its imprimatur. BAS also gave the Funds' service providers access to the BAS website so that they could view, download, and print Position Reports for the Funds.

Lauer and Lancer Management used Letters of Authorization ("LOAs") both to instruct BAS to transfer money for the purchase of securities and to instruct BAS how to input valuations and other information about the securities in the Funds' portfolios. * * *

BAS, according to the allegations of the complaint, participated and directly assisted in Lauer and Lancer Management's fraud by presenting false values of the Funds' holdings on the Position Reports at the request of Lauer and Lancer Management with actual knowledge that the information being supplied by Lauer and Lancer Management was false and was being used to mislead investors about the Funds' condition and performance. The Position Reports misrepresented the values of the Funds' holdings in at least five ways: (1) they overvalued unregistered warrants; (2) they valued securities at values higher than the last quoted public price for the shares; (3) they reported unrealistic and misleading increases in the values of unregistered shares and unregistered warrants; (4) they depicted unregistered shares and warrants which could not be publicly traded as registered, free-trading shares; and (5) they valued unregistered shares at the last quoted public price for the registered shares (although their unmarketable status necessarily gave them a lower value than otherwise identical marketable shares). * * *

According to the allegations of the complaint, BAS had actual knowledge that the Position Reports would be relied upon by the Funds' auditor and administrators in calculating and verifying the Funds' NAVs because: (a) BAS knew that the Position Reports were the only reports reflecting the entirety of the Funds' holdings by depicting the values of the positions held both in the custody of BAS and away from BAS; (b) BAS knew that Lauer and Lancer Management were downloading and printing the Position Reports and providing them to third parties, including the Funds' auditor and administrators; and (c) BAS itself provided these parties with direct access to the BAS computer system for the purpose of allowing them to review, download, and print the Position Reports generated and posted there by BAS. BAS also had actual knowledge that investors and potential investors would receive the NAV statements and audits based on the falsified valuations and rely on them in making investment decisions.

Moreover, Lauer and Lancer Management managed the funds in exchange for receiving certain fees, which were based on the Funds' NAVs. The fraudulent inflation of the Funds' NAVs, which BAS assisted, was intended to, and did, artificially and improperly inflate the management, incentive, and administrative fees claimed by Lauer, Lancer Management, and others. As an experienced prime broker for hedge funds, BAS knew the importance of portfolio valuations and NAV statements, and the ways that Lauer, Lancer Management, the Funds' auditors and administrators, investors, and potential investors would use them. * * *

Plaintiffs contend that the complaint sufficiently alleged proximate causation by setting forth that the investors' losses were the direct or reasonably foreseeable result of BAS's role in falsifying and disseminating the BAS reports that were used to prepare the NAV statements and audited financial statements on which the investors relied for financial decisions. We agree. The complaint did not contain merely "conclusory assertions." * * *

Specifically, the complaint pleads that, at the request of Lauer and Lancer Management, BAS placed false values of the Funds' holdings on the Position Reports, which contained BAS's name at the top of each page, without any disclaimer or other marking to suggest that they were anything other than official documents prepared by and bearing the imprimatur of BAS. The complaint provided specific examples of BAS's role in the fraud, involving BAS's participation in falsifying values for XtraCard warrants, Nu–D–Zine restricted shares, and a publicly traded stock (FFIRD). * * *

Whether the Plaintiffs will be able to prove the allegations set forth in the complaint is quite another matter. Since we are at the pleading stage, we need not resolve this question. Accepting all factual allegations in the complaint as true, and drawing all reasonable inferences from them in the Plaintiffs' favor, we must conclude that Plaintiffs have adequately pled that BAS aided and abetted frauds and breaches of fiduciary duty in a manner which proximately caused losses to the Plaintiffs.

For the reasons set forth above, the judgment of the district court is vacated and the case is remanded for further proceedings consistent with this opinion.

JERRY W. MARKHAM
SEC v. GOLDMAN SACHS & CO.—SERIOUS FRAUD
OR JUST MORE BANKER BASHING
30 Fut. & Deriv. L. Rep. 8 (2010).

The sensational "fraud" charges brought by the Securities and Exchange Commission (SEC) against Goldman Sachs & Co. in April 2010 made headlines around the world, caused a serious drop in the Dow Jones Industrial Average, and immediately cut the value of Goldman's stock by thirteen percent. * * * The SEC suit accuses Goldman and one of its employees, Fabrice Tourre, of fraudulently arranging a synthetic collateralized debt obligation (CDO). That CDO, which was called ABACUS 2007–AC1, was sold to IKB Deutsche Industriebank AG (IKB) in April 2007 after several months of negotiation.[27] The SEC alleges that Goldman misled IKB and its Portfolio Selection Agent, ACA Management LLC (ACA), about the true role played by a hedge fund, Paulson & Co., in the transaction.

Paulson & Co., which is managed by John Paulson, engaged in extended direct negotiations with ACA over which residential mortgage-backed securities (RMBS) would be referenced in the CDO. However, the SEC asserts that neither Paulson & Co. nor Goldman Sachs disclosed to ACA or IKB that Paulson & Co. was taking a short position against the CDO through credit default swaps (CDS) written by Goldman. The SEC further charges that Goldman committed fraud by misleading ACA into believing that Paulson & Co. was taking a long position in the transaction when in fact it was seeking to include mortgage-backed securities that it believed had the best chance of defaulting.

Although Paulson & Co. made nearly $1 billion from the transactions that were the subject of the SEC's charges, the SEC did not sue that hedge fund. According to the SEC, Paulson was not charged because it made no misrepresentations to the investors in the synthetic CDO. This was a requirement imposed in 2008 by the Supreme Court in Stoneridge Investment Partners LLC. v. Scientific–Atlanta Inc.[28] This means that the

---

27. [n. 3] SEC v. Goldman Sachs & Co., 10 CV 3229, Complaint at ¶ ¶ 52–59 (S.D.N.Y. April 15, 2010).

28. [n. 8] 552 U.S. 148 (2008).

alleged mastermind of the "fraudulent" scheme committed no crime and is entitled to keep its $1 billion in profits. * * *

Goldman Sachs asserts in its defense that the SEC charges were grounded neither in fact nor in law. Goldman Sachs also claims that it lost $90 million on the ABACUS 2007–AC1 deal, arguing that this evidenced that the firm had not believed that the long side of the deal was destined for failure. The press discounted this claim after it was learned that the loss was due to the fact that Goldman could not sell that piece of the deal and had to keep the exposure on its books. Still, that begged the question of why Goldman would expose itself to such a loss if it believed that the deal was designed to fail, especially since its fee was a comparatively small $15 million.

Some internal Goldman Sachs emails did provide grounds for some spirited banker bashing. Among other things, defendant Fabrice Tourre had referred to himself as the "Fabulous Fab" and stated jokingly to his girlfriend that he had been able to "sell a few abacus bonds to widows and orphans that I ran into at the airport." The case also appeared to be breaking down into a "he said, she said" slanging match between ACA personnel and Goldman. Tourre testified before Congress that he had never told ACA that Paulson & Co. would be an equity investor in the CDO or that it would take a long position, thus contesting the centerpiece of the SEC's case. Tourre further testified that he had informed ACA that Paulson would be taking a short position in the transaction. * * *

The Goldman Sachs' Wells submission to the SEC points out, that when negotiations began on the ABACUS 2007–AC1 transaction in January 2007, John Paulson was "relatively unknown" and that he was no Warren Buffet whose views might be material because they could move markets. It was only after the events in question that Paulson achieved true rock star status for earning $15 billion from shorting the subprime market, of which he personally kept $4 billion. That is all true, but there is much more to the story.

First, if due diligence had been conducted on Paulson & Co. when negotiations began over the ABACUS 2007–AC1 transaction in January 2007, it could have been discovered that Paulson & Co. was short the subprime market as early as the third quarter of 2006. The Alternative Investment News, a newsletter published by Euromoney, thus reported on September 15, 2006 that Paulson had created a fund that "will be short credit on the sub-prime U.S. residential market."[29] Second, while Paulson & Co. was still a relatively unknown hedge fund in January 2007, that status changed dramatically with the appearance in the financial press of a number of articles on Paulson's short position that were published well before the ABACUS 2007–AC1 transaction closed at the end of April in 2007. Those articles included reports in the Wall Street Journal, the New York Times, the Financial Times and Euromoney. * * *

---

29. [n. 30] US Hedge Fund Manager News; Paulson Launches Credit Fund, Alternative Investment News, Sept. 15, 2006.

To summarize what appears to be the facts in this case: ACA knew Paulson & Co. was the counterparty approving the RMBS to be included in ABACUS 2007–AC1. Paulson & Co. dealt directly with ACA in face-to-face negotiations and other communications in selecting the reference portfolio for that transaction. ACA even met in the offices of Paulson & Co., as well as those of ACA, to negotiate the reference portfolio. ACA was, therefore, fully advised that Paulson & Co. was the counterparty responsible for approving the RMBS for the reference portfolio.

It also seems clear that ACA was not a mere puppet of Goldman or Paulson. Paulson & Co. initially proposed a list of 123 RMBS, 62 of which ACA had previously purchased, for inclusion into the reference portfolio. ACA rejected all but 55 of the RMBS proposed by Paulson. ACA also proposed 31 alternative securities. Later, ACA and Paulson agreed on a list of 82 RMBS, and ACA proposed a list of 21 other RMBS to replace the others proposed by Paulson that ACA had rejected. Paulson & Co. accepted eight of those securities. In the end, after much negotiation, Paulson and ACA agreed on a portfolio of 90 RMBS for inclusion into ABACUS 2007–AC1.

In light of these negotiations and the widespread publicity of Paulson's short position before the closing of the ABACUS 2007–AC1 transaction, it will be hard to claim that Goldman Sachs was engaged in a furtive conspiracy to conceal Paulson's short position from ACA. The fact that the financial press had broadly reported that Paulson was shorting the subprime market long before ABACUS 2007–AC1 closed has other legal implications. There is a line of cases holding that there is no fraud if the information not disclosed was already publicly available.[30] Here, Paulson's short position and negative views on subprime paper were broadcast widely in the leading financial press before the ABACUS 2007–AC1 transaction closed * * *.

There are also some fundamental market structure issues raised by this case. The ABACUS 2007–AC1 transaction was reached through an arms-length negotiation between Paulson and ACA over the reference portfolio. ACA rejected several of the mortgage-backed securities Paulson proposed, and Paulson rejected several proposed by ACA through back and forth negotiations. Goldman, like any swap dealer, was acting as an intermediary between two sophisticated counterparties with differing investment outlooks. Goldman was seeking to match those counterparties through structured trades that would meet each trader's objectives. Such a dealer, at least before this case, had no duty to advise the counterparties of their respective investment objectives or even their identities. * * *

---

30. [n. 42] See e.g., Selbert v. Sperry Rand Corp., 586 F.2d 949, 952 (2d Cir. 1978) (no duty to disclose information to one who should reasonably be aware of it and citing numerous cases); Sailor v. Northern States Power Co., 4 F.3d 610, 612 (8th Cir. 1993) (Rule 10b–5 does not protect non-disclosed facts equally available to both parties); Heliotrope Gen. Inc. v. Ford Motor Co., 189 F.3d 971, 981, n. 18 (9th Cir. 1999) (taking judicial notice of newspaper articles in finding disclosure) * * *.

Goldman Sachs settled the SEC ABACUS case on July 15, 2010, agreeing to pay $550 million, most of which went to the alleged victims. This was the largest fine ever imposed by the SEC on a Wall Street firm, but was generally viewed as a victory for Goldman because pundits had been predicting a fine of $1 billion or more. The $550 million constituted only fourteen trading days of profit for Goldman in the first quarter of 2010. The SEC agreed as a part of the settlement to drop its intentional fraud charge and Goldman admitted only that it made a "mistake" in not disclosing Paulson's role. The SEC also agreed not to bring other cases it had under review against Goldman.

On the same day that the *Goldman* case was settled, the Senate approved the Conference Report leading the way to the enactment of the Dodd–Frank Act. That law addressed the SEC's claim in the *Goldman* by prohibiting conflicts of interest for one-year on the part of underwriters or placement agents of asset-backed securities, including synthetic CDOs. Dodd–Frank Act, § 621.

QUESTIONS AND NOTES

1. A prime broker:

clears and finances the trades of customers executed by other brokers at the customer's direction. The prime broker clears and executes the trades of the executing brokers for the customer. The customer maintains its funds and securities in an account with the prime broker. The executing brokers execute the trades in the name of the prime broker but for the benefit of the customer. The prime broker is responsible for margin requirements for the customer. The prime broker provides financing and clearing for the customer's securities transactions wherever they are executed. This means that the customer does not need to maintain funds at numerous broker-dealers. Prime broker arrangements are particularly popular with hedge funds.

23A Jerry W. Markham & Thomas Lee Hazen, Broker–Dealer Operations Under Securities and Commodities Law: Financial Responsibilities, Credit Regulation, and Customer Protection, § 13:15 (2d ed. 2007).

2. The SEC has expressed concerns with the "retailization" of hedge funds, i.e., an increasing number of relatively inexperienced and low net worth persons were investing in those vehicles through various pooling arrangements that allowed them collectively to meet the normally high minimum investment requirements of hedge funds. See Jerry W. Markham, Mutual Fund Scandals—A Comparative Analysis of the Role of Corporate Governance in the Regulation of Collective Investments, 3 Hastings Bus. L. J. 67, 99–121 (2006). The Dodd–Frank Act adjusted the accredited investor standard upward and excludes from the value of an individual's primary residence from the net worth calculation. Dodd–Frank Act, § 413. Further, the Act mandates that the Government Accountability Office complete a study and deliver a report on the appropriate criteria for accredited investor status. Dodd–Frank Act, § 415.

3. Following the *Goldstein* decision rejecting the SEC's efforts to compel hedge funds to register under the Investment Advisers Act, the President's Working Group on Financial Markets concluded that the regulation of hedge funds should be left to market discipline. Financial Regulation and the Invisible Hand, Remarks by Ben S. Bernanke, Chairman Federal Reserve Board, at the New York University Law School, New York, N.Y. (April 11, 2007). The SEC, nevertheless, adopted an anti-fraud rule for hedge funds under the Investment Advisers Act of 1940. 17 C.F.R. § 275.206(4)–8. The Dodd–Frank Act rejected the approach of the Presidential Working Group and required hedge fund managers to register with the SEC as investment advisers, if the assets they manage in the United States exceed $150 million. Dodd–Frank Act, §§ 403, 408. That action was undertaken after the discovery of the largest fraud on record from a hedge fund operated by Bernard Madoff, a once respected figure on Wall Street. Ironically, Madoff had registered as an investment adviser under the SEC hedge fund rule that was stricken by the D.C. Circuit. Unlike other hedge funds, however, Madoff had neglected to deregister. Yet, the SEC missed numerous opportunities to uncover Madoff's Ponzi scheme, and it came to light only after Madoff ran out of funds and confessed his scheme. Registered hedge fund managers must keep books and records that disclose the amount of assets under management, the degree of leverage in the funds they manage, any side pocket arrangements giving some investors greater rights than others, and trading practices. Dodd–Frank Act, § 404. In response to the Madoff Ponzi scheme, the SEC was authorized to make periodic and surprise examinations of registered hedge funds. Id.

4. Many hedge funds trade regulated commodity contracts. That trading activity initially led those funds to register with the Commodity Futures Trading Commission as commodity pool operators (CPOs) and commodity trading advisors (CTAs). However, "[i]n 1992, the CFTC adopted a key liberalizing measure, Rule 4.7, which preserved CPO registration requirements but provided an exemption from most regulatory requirements for pools offered only to highly accredited investors," which composed most of those persons investing in hedge funds. Susan C. Ervin, Letting Go: The CFTC Rethinks Managed Futures Regulation, 24 Futures & Derivatives L. Rep. 1, 8 & n.5 (May 2004). Similar relief was not given for CTA registration. However, the CFTC began rethinking its regulatory role after the enactment of the Commodity Futures Modernization Act of 2000. Pub. L. Rep. No. 106–554, 114 Stat. 2763 (2000). That statute was a statutory reflection of the CFTC's decision to deregulate the commodity markets for transactions in which only wealthy and sophisticated investors are involved. The CFTC was, therefore, receptive to a petition from the "Managed Funds Association . . . a trade association for hedge fund managers and CPOs" that sought "a 'sophisticated investor' exemption" from registration as a CTA for advisors advising only wealthy and sophisticated clients. Ervin, supra, at 3. That exemption was adopted by the CFTC on August 8, 2003. 68 Fed. Reg. 47221. This means that hedge funds remained largely unregulated until Dodd–Frank.

5. Many hedge funds are "offshore funds" that are based in tax havens around the world, thereby allowing foreign investors to invest without U.S. tax consequences. U.S. persons are subject to U.S. taxes but may still want to invest in those funds. This is accomplished by "feeder" funds in the U.S. that

in form are separate from the offshore fund (as if it were a separate account in the hedge fund) but are traded collectively. The Cayman Islands are a popular venue for these offshore funds; an estimated 75 percent of hedge funds are based in the Cayman Islands and are managed principally by one service company headquartered there. Lynnkley Browning, A Hampton's for Hedge Funds, N.Y. Times, July 1, 2007, § 3, at 1. The Dodd–Frank Act provides a limited exemption from registration for foreign private advisers. Dodd–Frank Act, § 403. The European Union proposed to require hedge funds to register and make disclosures on their operations. The finance ministers of the Group of 20 at their meeting in London in April 2009 considered the issue of how to regulate hedge funds. The U.S. and U.K. advocated for more disclosures, while Germany and France proposed regulating hedge funds in a manner similar to banks. The United States and Great Britain lobbied the European Union to drop some of its more onerous proposals for hedge funds and private equity, such as leverage limitations and stiff capital requirements. Especially controversial was a proposal that would exclude U.S. hedge funds from operating in Europe.

6. Hedge funds periodically encounter difficulties because of the high risks they take in order to obtain large profits. In 2007, Bear Stearns had to mount a multi-billion dollar rescue of some of its hedge funds that had invested heavily in subprime mortgages that were defaulting in unexpected large quantities. Those hedge funds eventually became worthless and Bear Stearns was sold to JPMorgan Chase with Fed assistance. Mark Trumbull, Will It be Harder to Get Credit? Christian Sci. Monitor, July 13, 2007, at 2. Hedge funds accounted for 58 percent of credit derivatives volume in 2007. This was another source of large losses during the financial crisis.

7. Banks may operate their own hedge funds, but they have not always been successful in such endeavors. See Eric Dash, A Citigroup Investment Chief is Shutting Hedge Fund, N.Y. Times, Sept. 6, 2007, at C3.

B. PRIVATE EQUITY

Private equity is another increasing source of banking business. See David Rubenstein, Beyond Wall Street: The Rise of Private Equity and the Future of Investing (2007). Banks supply private equity firms with "equity bridges" in which investment banking arms of banks buy equity stakes in leveraged buyouts that private equity firms could not sell elsewhere. Banks supplied private equity with over $100 billion in loans in 2007, to be funded through junk bond offerings. David Wighton, Dimon Slams "Equity Bridges," Fin. Tims (London), July 19, 2007, at 1.

Private equity is a reference to non-public, institutional investors that buy and manage existing companies, either private or public. These entities appeared in the 1980s and were often at the center of some famous takeover battles. See Bryan Burrough & John Helyar, Barbarians at the Gate (1990); George P. Baker & George David Smith, The New Financial Capitalists: Kohlberg Kravis Roberts and the Creation of Corporate Value (1998); George Anders, Merchants of Debt: KKR and the

Mortgaging of American Business (1993); and Dan Briody, The Iron Triangle, Inside the Carlyle Group (2004).

Private equity groups adopted a lower profile in the 1990s, but before the financial crisis began they went on a buying binge. Private equity became a source of escape for managers of public companies who sought ways to avoid the heavy costs imposed by the enactment of the Sarbanes–Oxley Act of 2002.[31] The costs imposed on public companies by that statute and the ever-increasing scrutiny of management by prosecutors, class action plaintiffs, and pension funds made life at a public company miserable for executive officers. Private equity-owned firms did not face those challenges, and private equity managers could pay themselves as much as they desired without worrying about criticism from the press or attacks from shareholders.

Between 2003 and 2006, about twenty-five percent of takeovers of public companies were by private equity investors. The value of companies going private trebled between 2004 and 2006. Over 2,100 private equity buyouts were consummated in the first ten months of 2006, at a total price of $583 billion, up $138 billion from the prior twelve months. The total buyouts of public companies in 2006 reached $709.8 billion by year-end. The total value of private equity investments reached $1.3 trillion in 2007. Private equity raised over $300 billion in equity commitments in 2007. More funds flowed into private equity in 2006 than equity mutual funds. Even public companies tapped the private equity market, receiving about $27.7 billion in financing from private equity and hedge funds in 2006 through "PIPEs" (private investments in public equity).

Between 2006 and 2007, nine of the ten largest acquisitions at the time were announced. Bain and Blackstone agreed to acquire Michaels Stores for $6 billion in July 2006. HCA Corp. went private in a $21.3 billion buyout in 2006 that included the assumption of $11.7 billion in debt. In 2006, private equity pools included the Blackstone Group, with $71 billion under management; the Carlyle Group, with $47 billion; Bain Capital—$40 billion; Kohlberg Kravis Roberts—$30 billion; Texas Pacific Group—$30 billion; and Cerberus Capital Management—$24 billion. These private equity pools attracted hedge fund investors and pension funds seeking alternative investments outside the public exchanges. This burgeoning alternative market gave rise to the development of private equity electronic exchanges by several broker-dealers in which pieces of private equity could be bought and sold. That effort was eventually abandoned in favor of using the NASDAQ Portal system for such trading, which operates under SEC Rule 144A that allows institutions to trade in unregistered securities.

Private equity groups traditionally were intensely private and sought to prevent any public or regulatory scrutiny of their activities. That benefit made them more nimble and exposed them to less regulatory costs,

---

31. For a further description of the role of private equity see Jerry W. Markham, VI A Financial History of the United States: The Subprime Crisis (2006–2009) 249–76 (2004).

including the shareholder class action lawsuits that every public company must now endure. However, in a surprising turnaround, some large private equity funds and hedge funds made public offerings of their own stock. See Dennis K. Berman & Henny Sender, KKR's IPO May Set Firm on Rugged Path, Wall St. J., July 5, 2007; Michael J. de la Merced & Jenny Anderson, Hedge Funds Continue Public Path, N.Y. Times, July 3, 2007, at C1. Congress considered legislation that would have more than doubled the tax on private equity profits known as "carried interest" that are presently taxed at capital gains rates. See Francesco Guerrera et al., Blackstone Faces IPO Challenge in the Senate, Fin. Times (London), June 15, 2007, at 1.

Cracks in the private equity market began appearing in June 2007, when Kohlberg Kravis & Roberts (KKR) encountered difficulties in obtaining needed financing through the leveraged loan market. Many private equity deals were announced on Mondays, coining the term "Merger Monday." On Monday June 25, 2007, however, only seven private equity acquisitions were announced, down from forty-three in the previous week, and further reduced from the eighty-four deals announced on June 4. Somewhat ominously, Bank of America CEO Kenneth Lewis stated publicly that his bank was turning down private equity deals that it might have previously financed. Those words presaged one of the worst credit crunches ever experienced in the United States.

The private equity buyout binge peaked in July 2007 as the credit crunch tightened and the financial crisis began. Leveraged loans to private equity groups were an early victim of that credit crunch. Banks that were willing to underwrite syndicated loans for billions of dollars shut down much of that lending because of concerns that losses could spread throughout the credit markets. Private equity deals virtually stopped in August 2007 as the credit crunch further tightened.

Another effect of the credit crunch was to disrupt closings of acquisitions agreed to before the credit crunch. Cerberus Capital Management walked away from a $6.6 billion takeover of United Rentals, an equipment leasing company; a suit against Cerberus over that walk away was dismissed. Cerberus also took a pounding from large investments in Chrysler and GMAC. Its $7.4 billion investment in Chrysler in 2007 was worth only $1.4 billion as 2008 ended. In another private equity retreat from an existing deal, KKR and Goldman Sachs backed out of an agreement to purchase Harman International for $8 billion. They claimed there was a material adverse change that could be used to invoke a walk away clause in the purchase agreement. The material change was that Harman's business was deteriorating. Walking away from a deal was practically unheard of previously on Wall Street, but the financial crisis and accompanying credit crunch changed the rules. The breakup fee for the transaction was $225 million plus expenses, for a total of $400 million.

Thomas H. Lee Partners and Bain Capital withdrew from a $19 billion purchase agreement for Clear Channel Communications. A consortium of six banks, which included Citigroup, Deutsche Bank and Wachovia, reneged on their deal to provide nearly $20 billion in financing to those two private equity firms. A misdirected e-mail disclosed that the banks formulated a plan to evade their commitment as the credit crunch worsened. The banks faced the fact that they could immediately lose $2.65 billion, which was the amount that such debt was being discounted for in the markets. An agreement was reached in May 2008 that allowed the buyout to be completed in July.

The leveraged loan market was disrupted further by the inability of Deutsche Bank and Bank of America to syndicate a $14 billion debt offering that was needed to finance the $20 billion buyout of Harrah's Entertainment by two private equity groups, Apollo Management LLC and Texas Pacific Group. Apollo Management sued Huntsman Corp. in an effort to withdraw from its pre-credit crunch agreement to purchase Huntsman for $6.5 billion and to assume $4.1 billion of its debt. Apollo claimed that Huntsman's financial condition had deteriorated and that a merger would render both companies insolvent. The parties finally agreed on a breakup fee of $1 billion, $675 million of which would be paid by Apollo, and the rest by some of the banks that had agreed to finance the deal. Apollo was given rights that would allow it to recover at least some of its payment.

C. DODD–FRANK ACT LIMITS ON HEDGE FUNDS AND PRIVATE EQUITY

The financial crisis that began in 2007 raised concerns that the securities and other non-traditional banking activities of large banks had exposed them to undue risk that threatened the entire financial system. Former Fed Chairman Paul Volcker, who was appointed to head President Obama's Economic Recovery Advisory Board, became an advocate for once again separating commercial banking from investment banking. He also sought a prohibition against commercial banks owning or trading risky securities. President Obama expressed his support for this "Volcker Rule." See Jerry W. Markham, The Subprime Crisis—A Test Match for the Bankers: Glass–Steagall vs. Gramm–Leach–Bliley, 12 U. Pa. J. Bus. L. 1081 (2010).

Senate Banking Committee Chairman Chris Dodd advocated also for the Volcker approach, but, as enacted, the Dodd–Frank Act cut back on the Volcker proposal. As discussed in Chapter 5, banking entities are generally banned from investing in or sponsoring private equity and hedge funds. Dodd–Frank Act § 619. The funds that are covered by this bank include those from an issuer that would be considered an investment company under the Investment Company Act (ICA) but for an exemption under the ICA in Section 3(c)(1) (exempting funds with fewer than 100 beneficial owners in the U.S.), Section 3(c)(7) (exempting funds with owners who are considered "qualified purchasers" such as institutions and individuals with large investment portfolios), or such other funds as designated by rule by the federal banking agencies, the CFTC, and the SEC. The Dodd–Frank Act bans on investments in these covered funds by banking entities, also prohibits banking entities from sponsoring such funds.

The Volcker Rule's ban on banking entities investing in or sponsoring private equity and hedge funds is subject to several exemptions. There is an exemption that permits banking entities to make *de minimis* investments so long as the entity's aggregate investment in all covered funds is less than three percent of the bank's Tier 1 capital. There is a fiduciary exemption that permits a banking entity to sponsor a private equity or hedge fund and serve as a general partner or managing member, subject to numerous conditions, including that the banking entity provides investment advisory or fiduciary services, does not have an equity interest in the fund greater than the three percent *de minimis* amount, and the fund is offered only to customers of the banking entity.

Banking entities are also restricted in Dodd–Frank from engaging proprietary trading. There are numerous exemptions for so-called "permitted activities" detailed further in Chapter 5.

SECTION 9. TRUST INDENTURES

The Trust Indenture Act of 1939 was enacted following a study by the SEC on abuses in public offerings of bonds. Trust indentures are master agreements that govern the terms and conditions of debentures (bonds) issued by corporations. Initially, trust indentures were used for mortgage bonds but were later extended to unsecured bonds. The bond or debenture itself is a simple document, but the trust indenture is a long, complex instrument. The trust indenture spells out the rights of bond holders. It also designates a trustee to make sure that the issuer's obligations are met and that the bondholders' rights are respected.

An SEC investigation and hearings by Congress during the 1930s determined that trustees often failed to assure that issuers met their obligations under the trust indenture agreement. Indenture agreements were often favorable to the issuing companies and sought to limit or disclaim all liability on the part of the trustees administering the terms of indenture agreements. The SEC and Congress found that indenture trustees seldom provided bondholders with basic information concerning default under the indenture agreement.

Congress was particularly concerned with "ostrich clauses," which allowed indenture trustees to assume that there was no default until they received notice from at least ten percent of the security holders. The trustee was allowed to make this assumption even if the trustee had actual knowledge of a default. In addition, Congress discovered that trustees often had financial interests that conflicted with the interests of bondholders.

The Trust Indenture Act of 1939 was enacted to clarify the role of trustees and to lessen conflicts between trustees and bondholders. The Act sought to provide full disclosure for issues of bonds, notes, and debentures. It requires the rights of debenture holders and the duties of the trustees to be specified in the indenture agreement and requires trustees to provide reports to debenture holders.

ZEFFIRO v. FIRST PENNSYLVANIA BANKING AND TRUST CO.

United States Court of Appeals, Third Circuit, 1980.
623 F.2d 290, *cert. denied*, 456 U.S. 1005 (1982).

ROSENN, CIRCUIT JUDGE.

The Trust Indenture Act of 1939, 15 U.S.C. § 77aaa et seq., regulates the terms of the agreement between debenture holders and the indenture trustee. This appeal presents to a United States Court of Appeals for the first time the question of whether the Act provides an injured investor with a cause of action in federal court against a trustee for breach of the agreement. We conclude, as did the district court, that a cause of action exists under the Act, allowing injured investors to bring suit in federal court.

Jay A. Zeffiro and Harry M. Bernard, Jr. each hold debentures issued in 1972 by Capital Equipment Leasing Corporation, a predecessor of defendant Capital First Corporation (Capital). The debentures were issued under a trust indenture which named First Pennsylvania Banking and Trust Company, a predecessor of defendant First Pennsylvania Bank, N.A. (First Pennsylvania), as indenture trustee. The indenture contained provisions mandated by the Act, detailing the duties of First Pennsylvania toward the debenture holders. In December 1976, Capital defaulted on its obligation to pay interest on the debentures and, subsequently, filed a petition under Chapter XI of the Bankruptcy Act. * * *

Before proceeding to a discussion of the merits, it may be useful to briefly outline the structure and background of the Trust Indenture Act. A study was conducted by the Securities Exchange Commission (SEC) in 1936 which revealed widespread abuses in the issuance of corporate bonds under indentures. The main problems identified by the study were that the indenture trustee was frequently aligned with the issuer of the debentures and that the debenture holders were widely dispersed, thereby hampering their ability to enforce their rights. Furthermore, courts frequently enforced broad exculpatory terms of the indenture inserted by the issuer, which offered the investors less protection than the traditional standards of fiduciary duty.

Rather than allow the SEC direct supervision of trustee behavior and thereby provide for a more overt intrusion into capital markets, the Act establishes a standard of behavior indirectly by refashioning the form of the indenture itself. The Act is structured so that before a debt security non-exempted from the Act may be offered to the public, the indenture under which it is issued must be "qualified" by the SEC. The indenture is deemed "qualified" when registration becomes effective. Before registration of the debenture is declared effective it must be qualified under the following conditions: (1) the security has been issued under an indenture; (2) the person designated as trustee is eligible to serve; and (3) the indenture conforms to the requirements of §§ 310–318, 15 U.S.C. §§ 77jjj–77rrr. Judge Bechtle aptly described the operative provisions of the Act, §§ 310–318, as follows.

> Sections 310 through 318 form the core of the Act in that they outline the substantive duties that the indenture must impose on the trustee. These sections are of three types. The first type is proscriptive in nature, prohibiting certain terms. For example, § 315, 15 U.S.C. § 77ooo (d), prohibits provisions in the indenture which would relieve or exculpate the trustee from liability for negligence. The second type of section is merely permissive in nature. An example of this type of section is § 315(a), 15 U.S.C. § 77ooo (a)(1), which states that the indenture may contain a provision relieving the trustee of liability except for the performance of such duties as are specifically set out in such indenture.

> The third type of section, and the most important for our purposes, is mandatory and prescriptive in nature. These sections begin with the phrase "indenture to be qualified shall provide" or "shall require." An example of this type of section is § 311, 15 U.S.C. § 77kkk, which states that the indenture shall require the trustee to establish certain accounts for the benefit of bond holders in the event the trustee also becomes a creditor of the issuer and the issuer defaults on the bonds.

473 F. Supp. at 206.

The SEC has no enforcement authority over the terms of the indenture once the registration statement becomes effective, and it cannot issue a stop order for violation of indenture provisions by the indenture trustee. After the effective date of the indenture the SEC's role is limited to general rulemaking and investigation. 15 U.S.C. §§ 77ddd(c), (d), (e); 77eee(a), (c); 77ggg; 77sss; 77ttt. The Act contains criminal liability for certain willful violations and misrepresentations and express civil liability for any omission or misstatement in the filing documents.

Enforcement of the terms of the indenture is left to the parties. The plaintiffs in this case contend that the Act necessarily allows for enforcement of the indenture in federal court to insure compliance with the Act. First Pennsylvania argues that, because the Act only mandates certain terms of the indenture in order for it to be qualified by the SEC, the remedy is contractual under state law and not one for federal jurisdiction. * * *

There are several reasons why a finding of a federal cause of action is necessary and helpful to the purposes of the Act. First, the Act sought to attack a national problem in a uniform way. Congress believed that the "inadequacy [of indentures] presents a national problem which cannot be dealt with effectively by the States...." A necessary means of facilitating the national uniformity goal of the Act would be through enforcement of the indenture in a federal forum. It is hard to believe that Congress would have established uniform standards to govern indentures and then paradoxically have allowed the application of those standards to depend on the law of the state of the suit. The interpretation of the indenture provisions mandated by the Act does not depend on ordinary contract principles—the intent of the parties—but depends on an interpretation of the legislation. It would be contrary to the purposes of the Act to have the trustee held to certain standards in one state court and potentially different standards in another. Thus, federal court jurisdiction is necessary to achieve the uniform standards intended by the Act. * * *

LAYTON, DISTRICT JUDGE, dissents. * * *

ELLIOTT ASSOCIATES v. J. HENRY SCHRODER BANK & TRUST CO.

Untied States Court of Appeals, Second Circuit, 1988.
838 F.2d 66.

ALTIMARI, CIRCUIT JUDGE.

* * * Appellant Elliott Associates ("Elliott") was the holder of $525,000 principal amount of 10% Convertible Subordinated Debentures due June 1, 1990 (the "debentures") which were issued by Centronics Data Computer Corporation ("Centronics") pursuant to an indenture between Centronics and J. Henry Schroder Bank and Trust Company ("Schroder"), as trustee. Elliott's debentures were part of an aggregate debenture offering by Centronics of $40,000,000 under the indenture which was qualified by the Securities Exchange Commission ("SEC") pursuant to the Act.

The indenture and debentures provided, inter alia, that Centronics had the right to redeem the debentures "at any time" at a specified price, plus accrued interest, but the indenture also provided that, during the first two years following the issuance of the debentures, Centronics' right to redeem was subject to certain conditions involving the market price of Centronics' common stock. To facilitate its right to redeem the debentures, Centronics was required to provide written notice of a proposed redemption to the trustee and to the debenture holders. Section 3.01 of the indenture required that Centronics give the trustee 50–day notice of its intention to call its debentures for redemption, "unless a shorter notice shall be satisfactory to the [t]rustee." Section 3.03 of the indenture required Centronics to provide the debenture holders with "at least 15 days but not more than 60 days" notice of a proposed redemption.

At the option of the debenture holders, the debentures were convertible into shares of Centronics' common stock. In the event Centronics called the debentures for redemption, debenture holders could convert their debentures "at any time before the close of business on the last

Business Day prior to the redemption date." Subject to certain adjustments, the conversion price was $3.25 per share. The number of shares issuable upon conversion could be determined by dividing the principal amount converted by the conversion price. Upon conversion, however, the debentures provided that "no adjustment for interest or dividends [would] be made."

Debenture holders were to receive interest payments from Centronics semi-annually on June 1 and December 1 of each year. Describing the method of interest payment, each debenture provided that

> [t]he Company will pay interest on the Debentures (except defaulted interest) to the persons who are registered Holders of Debentures at the close of business on the November 15 or May 15 next preceding the interest payment date. Holders must surrender Debentures to a Paying Agent to collect principal payments.

To insure the primacy of the debenture holders' right to receive interest, the indenture provided that "[n]otwithstanding any other provision of this Indenture, the right of the Holder of a Security to receive payment of ... interest on the Security ... shall not be impaired."

In early 1986, Centronics was considering whether to call its outstanding debentures for redemption. On March 12, 1986, Centronics' Treasury Services Manager, Neil R. Gordon, telephoned Schroder's Senior Vice President in charge of the Corporate Trust Department, George R. Sievers, and informed him of Centronics' interest in redeeming the debentures. Gordon told Sievers that Centronics "was contemplating redemption" of all of its outstanding debentures, subject to SEC approval and fluctuations in the market for Centronics' common stock. Specifically addressing the 50–day notice to the trustee requirement in section 3.01 of the indenture, Gordon asked Sievers how much time "Schroder would need once the SEC had Centronics' registration materials and an actual redemption date could therefore be set." Sievers responded that "Schroder would only need [one] week" notice of the redemption. Sievers explained that this shorter notice would satisfy section 3.01 because Centronics was proposing a complete rather than a partial redemption, and because there were relatively few debenture holders. Sievers explained that the shorter notice therefore would provide it with sufficient time to perform its various administrative tasks in connection with the proposed redemption.

Shortly thereafter, on March 20, 1986, Centronics' Board of Directors met and approved a complete redemption of all of its outstanding debentures and designated May 16, 1986 as the redemption date. On April 4, 1986—42 days prior to the redemption—Centronics' President, Robert Stein, wrote Schroder and informed the trustee that "pursuant to the terms of the Indenture, notice is hereby given that the Company will redeem all of its outstanding 10% Convertible Subordinated Debentures due June 1, 1990, on May 16, 1986." Centronics then proceeded to file registration materials with the SEC in order to receive clearance for the

CAPITAL MARKET ACTIVITIES

redemption. Schroder was furnished with copies of all the materials Centronics had filed with the SEC.

On May 1, 1986, the SEC cleared the proposed redemption. On that same day, pursuant to section 3.03 of the indenture, Centronics gave formal notice of the May 16, 1986 redemption to the debenture holders. In a letter accompanying the Notice of Redemption, Centronics' President explained that, as long as the price of Centronics' common stock exceeded $3.75 per share, debenture holders would receive more value in conversion than in redemption. In the Notice of Redemption, debenture holders were advised, inter alia, that the conversion price of $3.25 per share, when divided into each $1,000 principal amount being converted, would yield 307.69 shares of Centronics common stock. Based upon the April 30, 1986 New York Stock Exchange closing price of $5 3/8 per share of Centronics' common stock, each $1,000 principal amount of debenture was convertible into Centronics common stock having an approximate value of $1,653.83. Debenture holders were advised further that failure to elect conversion by May 15, 1986 would result in each $1,000 principal amount debenture being redeemed on May 16 for $1,146.11, which consisted of $1,000 in principal, $100 for the 10% redemption premium, and $46.11 in interest accrued from December 1, 1985 (the last interest payment date) to May 16, 1986 (the redemption date). Finally, the notice of redemption explained that accrued interest was not payable upon conversion:

> No adjustments for Interest or Dividends upon Conversion. No payment or adjustment will be made by or on behalf of the Company (i) on account of any interest accrued on any Debentures surrendered for conversion or (ii) on account of dividends, if any, on shares of Common Stock issued upon such conversion. Holders converting Debentures will not be entitled to receive the interest thereon from December 1, 1985 to May 16, 1986, the date of redemption. (emphasis in original).

On May 15, 1986, the last day available for conversion prior to the May 16, 1986 redemption, Centronics' common stock traded at $6 5/8 per share. At that price, each $1,000 principal amount of debentures was convertible into Centronics' common stock worth approximately $2,038. Thus, it was clear that conversion at $2,038 was economically more profitable than redemption at $1,146.11. Debenture holders apparently recognized this fact because all the debenture holders converted their debentures into Centronics' common stock prior to the May 16, 1986 redemption.

Elliott filed the instant action on May 12, 1986 and sought an order from the district court enjoining the May 16, 1986 redemption. Elliott alleged in its complaint that Schroder and Centronics conspired to time the redemption in such a manner so as to avoid Centronics' obligation to pay interest on the next interest payment date, i.e., June 1, 1986. This conspiracy allegedly was accomplished by forcing debenture holders to convert prior to the close of business on May 15, 1986. Elliott contended that, as part of this conspiracy, Schroder improperly waived the 50–day notice in section 3.01 of the indenture and thus allowed Centronics to proceed with the redemption as planned. Elliott claimed that Schroder waived the 50–day notice without considering the impact of that waiver on the financial interests of the debenture holders and that the trustee's action in this regard constituted, inter alia, a breach of the trustee's fiduciary duties. Finally, Elliott alleged that, had it not been for the trustee's improper waiver, debenture holders would have been entitled to an additional payment of $1.2 million in interest from Centronics. * * *

The central issue on this appeal is whether the district court properly held that the trustee was not obligated to weigh the financial interests of the debenture holders when it decided on March 12, 1986 to waive Centronics' compliance with section 3.01's 50–day notice requirement. We agree with the district court's conclusion that the trustee was under no such duty. See 655 F.Supp. at 1288–89. * * *

Our analysis here is therefore limited to determining whether the trustee fulfilled its duties under the indenture. As set forth above, section 3.01 requires that, when the company intends to call its debentures for redemption, it must provide the trustee with 50–day notice of the redemption, "unless a shorter notice shall be satisfactory to the [t]rustee." Section 3.02 of the indenture sets forth the manner in which the trustee selects which debentures are to be redeemed when the company calls for a partial redemption. The American Bar Foundation's Commentaries on Model Debenture Indenture Provisions (1971) (the "Commentaries") explains that "[n]otice of the Company's election to redeem *all* the debentures need not be given to the Trustee since such a redemption may be effected by the Company without any action on the part of the Trustee...." Id. at § 11–3, p. 493. Thus, it appears that section 3.01's notice requirement is intended for the trustee's benefit to allow it sufficient time to perform the various administrative tasks in preparation for redemption. While compliance with a full notice period may be necessary in the event of partial redemption, the full notice may not be required in the event of a complete redemption. We find that, although the trustee may reasonably insist on the full 50–day notice in the event of a complete redemption, it nevertheless has the discretion to accept shorter notice when it deems such shorter notice satisfactory. * * *

RACEPOINT PARTNERS, LLC V. JPMORGAN CHASE BANK, N.A.

Court of Appeals of New York, 2010.
928 N.E.2d 396.

PIGOTT, J.

On February 7, 2001, the energy company Enron executed an indenture agreement with Chase Manhattan Bank ("Chase"), naming Chase as the indenture trustee for the holders of certain Enron notes. The agreement contained, in section 4.02, a standard provision setting forth a covenant by Enron "[to] file with the Trustee [i.e. Chase], within 15 days after it files the same with the [Securities and Exchange Commission], copies of its annual reports and of the information, documents and other reports . . . which the Company [i.e. Enron] is required to file with the SEC pursuant to Section 13 or 15 (d) of the [Securities] Exchange Act. Delivery of such reports, information and documents to the Trustee is for informational purposes only and the Trustee's receipt of such information shall not constitute constructive notice of any information contained therein or determinable from information contained therein, including the Issuer's compliance with any of its covenants hereunder (as to which the Trustee is entitled to rely exclusively on Officers' Certificates). The Issuer also shall comply with any other provisions of Trust Indenture Act Section 314 (a)."

The agreement also set forth various circumstances or events that would constitute default by either party, including failure by Enron to comply with this provision, if not corrected within 60 days of notification by Chase.

In December 2001, in the wake of the major accounting fraud scandal with which it has become synonymous, Enron filed for bankruptcy. Thereafter, plaintiffs Racepoint Partners, LLC, and Willow Capital–II, L.L.C., bought approximately $1 billion of the notes from their holders. Plaintiffs, which, as secondary holders of the notes, are vested with the claims and demands of the sellers, then brought this common law action against Chase alleging, among other things, breach of contract. Plaintiffs claim, first, that Enron defaulted under the indenture agreement and, second, that Chase had actual knowledge of this default and that its failure to notify Enron and the noteholders of the default constituted breach of the agreement. The issue in this appeal is the allegation of contractual default by Enron in filing reports that were false.

Plaintiffs point to the fact that Enron agreed in section 4.02 to file with Chase copies of all reports that it was "required to file with the SEC pursuant to Section 13 or 15 (d) of the [Securities] Exchange Act." Section 13 of the Act requires publicly traded companies to keep records accurately reflecting their transactions and assets, and to file annual and quarterly reports with the Securities and Exchange Commission (see 15 USC § 78m). Plaintiffs argue that because the financial reports filed by Enron with Chase were inaccurate and did not comply with federal securities law, they were not the reports Enron was "required to file with the SEC." Plaintiffs posit that, by filing these same fraudulent reports with Chase, Enron failed to satisfy its section 4.02 covenant, and thus defaulted.

Chase moved to dismiss the complaint under CPLR 3211. Supreme Court denied Chase's motion. The Appellate Division reversed, granting the motion. We granted leave to appeal, and now affirm.

Section 4.02 of the indenture agreement is a mandated provision based on the requirements of § 314 (a) of the Trust Indenture Act of 1939:

"Each person who, as set forth in the registration statement or application, is or is to be an obligor upon the indenture securities covered thereby shall . . .

"file with the indenture trustee copies of the annual reports and of the information, documents, and other reports (or copies of such portions of any of the foregoing as the [Securities and Exchange] Commission may by rules and regulations prescribe) which such obligor is required to file with the Commission pursuant to section 13 or section 15(d) of the Securities Exchange Act of 1934 [15 USCS §§ 78m or 78o(d)]; or, if the obligor is not required to file information, documents, or reports pursuant to either of such sections, then to file with the indenture trustee and the [Securities and Exchange] Commission, in accordance with rules and regulations prescribed by the Commission, such of the supplementary and periodic information, documents, and reports which may be required pursuant to section 13 of the Securities Exchange Act of 1934 [15 USCS § 78m], in respect of a security listed and registered on a national securities exchange as may be prescribed in such rules and regulations (15 USCS § 77nnn [a] [1]).

Plaintiffs concede that the parties' intent in section 4.02 may be equated with Congressional intent with respect to § 314 (a) of the Trust Indenture Act of 1939. In drafting the Trust Indenture Act, Congress intended simply to ensure that an indenture trustee was provided with up-to-date reports on a company's financial status, by requiring the company to send the trustee a copy of filed financial reports. In the 1930s, when § 314 (a) was drafted, computer-based technologies, whereby copies of SEC reports can now be obtained, did not exist.

The legislative history of § 314 (a) suggests that Congress intended to create a delivery requirement and no more. The 1939 House Report highlighted the legislators' concern that trustees and bondholders at the time did not receive periodic reports from companies issuing bonds.

"In a substantial portion of indentures . . . the issuer was under no obligation to file an annual report with the indenture trustee. None of the indentures . . . required the transmission to the bondholders of periodic reports, such as stockholders customarily receive. None of them established machinery for the transmission of such reports . . . " (H. R. Rep. No. 1016, 35 [1939]).

It is apparent that § 314 (a) was designed to mandate such a mechanism of delivery of reports to indenture trustees. The same House Report, observing that in many cases a company "will already be required to file periodic reports with the [Securities and Exchange] Commission under Section 13 or Section 15 (d)," stated that the bill under consideration "merely requires that copies of such reports . . . be filed with the indenture trustee" (H. R. Rep. No. 1016, 35).

As federal courts have observed, when considering Indenture Agreement provisions very similar to the one at issue here, "the provision merely requires the company to transmit to the trustee copies of whatever reports it actually files with the SEC . . .

"[A]ny duty actually to file the reports is imposed 'pursuant to Section 13 or 15 (d) of the Exchange Act' and not pursuant to the indenture itself. The provision does not incorporate the Exchange Act; it merely refers to it in order to establish which reports must be forwarded. . . .

"[It] impose[s] nothing more than the ministerial duty to forward copies of certain reports, identified by reference to the Exchange Act, within fifteen days of actually filing the reports with the SEC."

It is clear therefore that indenture agreements containing the required delivery provisions pursuant to § 314 (a) refer to the Exchange Act only to identify the types of report that should be forwarded to indenture trustees. They do not create contractual duties on the part of the trustee to assure that the information contained in any report filed is true and accurate. That is simply not the mission or purpose of the trustee or the contract under which it undertakes its duties.

Of course, companies have a duty to file accurate reports with the SEC. That obligation, however, derives from the Securities Exchange Act, not from indenture agreements.

Our holding that section 4.02 of the indenture agreement simply embodies a delivery requirement, and does not imply a duty on the part of the trustee to assure the filing of accurate reports or risk default, is consistent with the limited, "ministerial" functions of indenture trustees and with the plain language of section 4.02, which states that "[d]elivery of such reports, information and documents [filed with the SEC] to the Trustee is for informational purposes only." Plaintiffs' proposed interpretation, on the other hand, would require indenture trustees to review the substance of SEC filings, so as to reduce the risk of liability, greatly expanding indenture trustees' recognized administrative duties far beyond anything found in the contract.

Accordingly, the order of the Appellate Division should be affirmed, with costs.

QUESTIONS AND NOTES

1. In 1990, the Trust Indenture Act was amended to prohibit the indenture trustee from becoming a creditor of the issuer. A trustee, however, is not required to resign its position in the event of a conflict of interest unless there is a default under the trust indenture agreement. See Efrat Lev, The Indenture Trustee: Does It Really Protect Bondholders?, 8 U. Miami Bus. L. Rev. 47 (1999).

2. Should trustees have more affirmative obligations to monitor these lending arrangements for the benefit of investors?

SECTION 10. COMMERCIAL PAPER

Commercial paper is simply a loan with a term of no longer than nine months evidenced by a promissory note. Most commercial paper has a maturity of between thirty and ninety days, is negotiable in form, and is issued as a discount note. It is an unsecured obligation; therefore, unless otherwise agreed, the lender is dependent entirely upon the ability of the issuing corporation to repay the debt from its general revenues on a timely basis. Issuers of commercial paper (borrowers) may be industrial corporations or other large institutions, including commercial banks.

"Direct paper" is commercial paper issued directly by the company that is borrowing the funds. "Dealer paper" is placed by dealers. The dealer usually acts as principal, purchases the paper for its own account from the issuer, and resells it at a discount. There is an active market in commercial paper because it is a popular short term investment for excess funds.

The use of commercial paper for short-term credit has, in some cases, replaced business borrowers' typical reliance on a bank line of credit. Thus, the commercial paper market presents a challenge to banks' traditional credit intermediation function. Banks, however, participate in this market as issuers, dealers, brokers, and purchasers.

[handwritten margin note: CP present challenge to bank intermed. function.]

RYDER INTERNATIONAL CORP. v. FIRST AMERICAN NATIONAL BANK

United States Court of Appeals, Eleventh Circuit, 1991.
943 F.2d 1521.

ENGEL, SENIOR CIRCUIT JUDGE.

On August 16, 1989, Ryder International Corporation filed suit in district court against First American National Bank, asserting violations of both federal and state securities laws, among other claims. The claims arose from the purchase by Ryder of approximately $400,000 of commercial paper issued by Integrated Resources, Inc., a publicly held company which defaulted on its commercial paper obligations in June of 1989. The Integrated commercial paper was one of a dozen or so securities offered by First American to those customers seeking higher returns than the yield produced by interest bearing instruments.

Ryder voluntarily dismissed all of its claims except one, which is based on section 12(2) of the Securities Act of 1933 and section 8–6–19(a) of the Alabama blue sky laws. After extensive discovery, the district court granted summary judgment for First American. The court concluded that the bank's conduct of providing financial information concerning the available commercial paper for sale by others and its mechanical act of executing Ryder's orders did not make the bank an "offeror" or a "seller" under section 12(2). For the reasons that follow, we affirm.

[handwritten margin note: lower ct. ruling / ct. affirms.]

Ryder is a manufacturing business which regularly makes short-term investments to earn interest on its excess cash. At the beginning of

Ryder's banking relationship with First American in 1987, Frank Ryder, the President of Ryder, briefly and orally gave First American "investment criteria" suggesting GMAC as an example of the desired type of commercial paper Ryder would later purchase through Wallace Case, a Vice President of Ryder, whom Frank Ryder trusted "to look after my interests." Frank Ryder also told the First American executives he met with that he "wasn't looking for any more risk than GMAC" of which he had little knowledge. Frank Ryder had no more documented involvement with Ryder's investments. The company has no written guidelines regarding Ryder's investments. Besides granting plenary authority to Wallace Case to make the investments, Frank Ryder retained Leo Krupp, a business consultant, to advise but not control Case with regard to the making and monitoring of investments. Over time, from 1984 to 1989, Case used millions of dollars of Ryder's excess money to make short term investments through several different institutions.

On two occasions, March 20, 1989 and April 19, 1989, Ryder (through Wallace Case) used First American to buy commercial paper issued by Integrated which would pay $400,000 at maturity in June, 1989. First American, in turn, bought the paper for Ryder from Drexel Lambert, the underwriter and exclusive dealer for Integrated. The issuer, Integrated, was at that time a New York Stock Exchange listed company, required by the Security Exchange Act to file and publicly disseminate annual, quarterly, and other periodic reports and information about its business. * * *

> Bank buys on behalf of the client

When a broker is an agent of the purchaser of the securities, he is in reality *buying* on behalf of the purchaser (rather than selling on behalf of the owner if he were an agent of the owner). See Merrill Lynch, Pierce, Fenner & Smith, Inc. v. Cheng, 697 F. Supp. 1224, 1228–29 (D.D.C.1988) ("Although it has been held that a 'seller' under § 12(2) is not necessarily just a person who conveys title and no one else, there is no reading of the statute that would broaden its application to the broker/defendant who *buys* on behalf of a customer/plaintiff.") (emphasis in original). "[A] broker executes orders for the purchase or sale of securities solely as agent," and if done on behalf of the buyer "it is the customer, rather than the [bank] who bears the risk of loss." Securities Indus. Ass'n, 468 U.S. at 218 & n. 18. We note that "risk of loss" is one of the criteria for determining ownership. As we find that First American did not pass title to the Integrated paper, something more than simple execution of Ryder's orders is required for defendant to fall within the ambit of section 12(2). * * * [As First American was neither a "seller" nor "offeror" of commercial paper within the civil liability provisions of the Securities Act of 1933, summary judgment in favor of First American was affirmed.]

QUESTIONS AND NOTES

(1) Before the adoption of the Gramm–Leach–Bliley (GLBA), the Supreme Court held that the Glass–Steagall Act prevented banks from distributing commercial paper for their corporate customers. Securities Industry Ass'n

v. Board of Governors of the Federal Reserve System, 468 U.S. 137 (1984). An appeals court later held that a bank could distribute commercial paper on an agency basis. Securities Industry Ass'n v. Board of Governors of the Federal Reserve System, 807 F.2d 1052 (D.C. Cir. 1986), cert. denied, 483 U.S. 1005 (1987). GLBA ensures that banks may participate in the commercial paper business and that they may do so under one of the carve outs for banks from broker-dealer registration.

GLBA allows banks to participate in CP mkts

2. Are you aware that your money market fund probably invests in commercial paper on your behalf? The Reserve Primary Fund, the nation's first and one of its largest money market funds, "broke-the-buck"[32] and caused losses to investors as the result of its investment in commercial paper issued by Lehman Brothers, a large investment bank that declared bankruptcy in September 2008. That loss set off a panic among money fund investors. Money market funds had a net outflow of $200 billion in the two-week period following the Reserve Primary Fund's problems. Of that amount, $125.2 billion was withdrawn during the week of September 17, 2008. In comparison, there was a net inflow of $28.4 billion in the prior month. The panic in the money market funds was quelled after the federal government announced on September 19 that it would provide $50 billion to temporarily guarantee money market funds against loss. The guarantee was set to expire on December 18, 2008, but was thereafter extended into 2009. Money market funds that wanted to participate in this program were charged a fee based on their net asset value as of September 19, 2008. The program covered more than $3 trillion of participating money market fund assets. The SEC amended its Rule 2a–7 governing money fund liquidity requirements to further assure liquidity and quality of money fund investments. Money Market Fund Reform, Investment Company Act Release N. 29,132 (Feb. 23, 2010) [75 Fed. Reg. 10060 (Mar. 4, 2010)], <www.sec.gov/rules/final/2010/_ic–29132fr.pdf>.

3. Because of its short term nature and the high credit ratings required of its issuers, commercial paper is usually viewed as a safe investment. Are you familiar with the bankruptcy of the Penn Central railroad a number of years ago? Its highly rated commercial paper, which had been issued in large amounts, went into default.

4. A reduction in the credit rating of a company issuing commercial paper may preclude its access to the commercial paper market. Banks, therefore, provide standby credit lines for such events. What danger does this present for the banks?

5. The commercial paper market grew from $1.5 trillion in 2005 to $2.25 trillion in August 2007. The asset-backed commercial paper market (ABCP) (which is described in Chapter 5) issued about $1.2 trillion of that amount, when the credit crunch and financial crisis began in 2007. That market shrank to a little over $800 million by December 2007, and many commercial paper programs were frozen resulting in massive losses. The failure of Lehman Brothers in September 2008 resulted in significant losses to its commercial paper holders, including the Reserve Primary Fund, referred to in Note 2 above. Among the steps the federal government took to restore

---

32. This means that the net asset value of one dollar invested by the mutual fund investor could only be redeemed for less than one dollar.

confidence in the commercial paper market were the creation of the Asset–Backed Commercial Paper Money Market Liquidity Facility (ABCP MMLF) that made non-recourse loans on ABCP commercial paper in order to curb the panic in money market funds after the failure of the Reserve Primary Fund; the Commercial Paper Funding Facility (CPFF) to purchase unsecured, asset-backed commercial paper from corporate issuers through a special purpose vehicle (SPV); and the Money Market Investor Funding Facility (MMIFF) to purchase up to $600 billion in assets from money market funds.

CHAPTER TWELVE

DERIVATIVES

■ ■ ■

SECTION 1. INTRODUCTION TO DERIVATIVES

Derivatives are instruments whose value "derives" from the price of an underlying asset or object of value. These instruments include forwards, futures, options, and swaps. Like other businesses, many banks use derivative transactions to hedge against investment risks. For example, a bank is subject to interest rate risk if it funds fixed-interest-rate loans with deposits whose interest costs float with market rates. A bank that has such an interest rate exposure from floating rates for funds it has borrowed may seek to offset that risk with a futures contract. In the event of interest rate changes, the bank may have a loss from increased interest rate payments, but that loss will be offset by profits from the futures position. Hedging and dealing in derivatives is an important part of the banking business as exemplified by the fact that the notional value of derivative contracts held by insured institutions has increased from $144.8 trillion in the first quarter of 2007 to $216.5 trillion in the first quarter of 2010.[1]

MERRILL LYNCH, PIERCE, FENNER & SMITH, INC. v. CURRAN

Supreme Court of the United States, 1982.
456 U.S. 353.

MR. JUSTICE STEVENS delivered the opinion of the Court.

* * * Prior to the advent of futures trading, agricultural products generally were sold at central markets. When an entire crop was harvested and marketed within a short timespan, dramatic price fluctuations sometimes created severe hardship for farmers or for processors. Some of these risks were alleviated by the adoption of quality standards, improvements in storage and transportation facilities, and the practice of "forward

---

1. Comptroller of the Currency, OCC's Quarterly Report on Bank Trading and Derivatives Activities.

contracting"–the use of executory contracts fixing the terms of sale in advance of the time of delivery.

When buyers and sellers entered into contracts for the future delivery of an agricultural product, they arrived at an agreed price on the basis of their judgment about expected market conditions at the time of delivery. Because the weather and other imponderables affected supply and demand, normally the market price would fluctuate before the contract was performed. A declining market meant that the executory agreement was more valuable to the seller than the commodity covered by the contract; conversely, in a rising market the executory contract had a special value for the buyer, who not only was assured of delivery of the commodity but also could derive a profit from the price increase.

The opportunity to make a profit as a result of fluctuations in the market price of commodities covered by contracts for future delivery motivated speculators to engage in the practice of buying and selling "futures contracts." A speculator who owned no present interest in a commodity but anticipated a price decline might agree to a future sale at the current market price, intending to purchase the commodity at a reduced price on or before the delivery date. A "short" sale of that kind would result in a loss if the price went up instead of down. On the other hand, a price increase would produce a gain for a "long" speculator who had acquired a contract to purchase the same commodity with no intent to take delivery but merely for the purpose of reselling the futures contract at an enhanced price.

In the 19th century the practice of trading in futures contracts led to the development of recognized exchanges or boards of trade. At such exchanges standardized agreements covering specific quantities of graded agricultural commodities to be delivered during specified months in the future were bought and sold pursuant to rules developed by the traders themselves. Necessarily the commodities subject to such contracts were fungible. For an active market in the contracts to develop, it also was essential that the contracts themselves be fungible.

The exchanges therefore developed standard terms describing the quantity and quality of the commodity, the time and place of delivery, and the method of payment; the only variable was price. The purchase or sale of a futures contract on an exchange is therefore motivated by a single factor–the opportunity to make a profit (or to minimize the risk of loss) from a change in the market price.

The advent of speculation in futures markets produced well-recognized benefits for producers and processors of agricultural commodities. A farmer who takes a "short" position in the futures market is protected against a price decline; a processor who takes a "long" position is protected against a price increase. Such "hedging" is facilitated by the availability of speculators willing to assume the market risk that the hedging farmer or processor wants to avoid. The speculators' participation in the market substantially enlarges the number of potential buyers and sellers of executory contracts and therefore makes it easier for farmers and processors to make firm commitments for future delivery at a fixed price. The liquidity of a futures contract, upon which hedging depends, is directly related to the amount of speculation that takes place.

Persons who actually produce or use the commodities that are covered by futures contracts are not the only beneficiaries of futures trading. The speculators, of course, have opportunities to profit from this trading. Moreover, futures trading must be regulated by an organized exchange. In addition to its regulatory responsibilities, the exchange must maintain detailed records and perform a clearing function to discharge the offsetting contracts that the short or long speculators have no desire to perform. The operation of the exchange creates employment opportunities for futures commission merchants, who solicit orders from individual traders, and for floor brokers, who make the actual trades on the floor of the exchange on behalf of futures commission merchants and their customers. The earnings of the persons who operate the futures market–the exchange itself, the clearinghouse, the floor brokers, and the futures commission merchants–are financed by commissions on the purchase and sale of futures contracts made over the exchange.

Thus, in a broad sense, futures trading has a direct financial impact on three classes of persons. Those who actually are interested in selling or buying the commodity are described as "hedgers"; their primary financial interest is in the profit to be earned from the production or processing of the commodity. Those who seek financial gain by taking positions in the futures market generally are called "speculators" or "investors"; without their participation, futures markets "simply would not exist."[2] Finally, there are the futures commission merchants, the floor brokers, and the persons who manage the market; they also are essential participants, and they have an interest in maximizing the activity on the exchange. The petitioners in these cases are members of this third class whereas their adversaries, the respondents, are speculators or investors.

Because Congress has recognized the potential hazards as well as the benefits of futures trading, it has authorized the regulation of commodity

---

2. [n.11] "Broadly speaking, futures traders fall into two general classifications, i.e. 'trade' hedging customers, and speculators. All orders which reach the trading floor originate with one or the other group of traders. The 'trade' customer is the hedger who seeks, at low cost, to protect himself or his company against possible loss due to adverse price fluctuations in the market place. Speculators, on the other hand, embrace all representatives of the general public, including some institutions, plus floor scalpers and position traders, who seek financial gain by taking positions in volatile markets. The principal role of the speculator in the markets is to take the risks that the hedger is unwilling to accept. The opportunity for profit makes the speculator willing to take those risks. The activity of speculators is essential to the operation of a futures market in that the composite bids and offers of large numbers of individuals tend to broaden a market, thus making possible the execution with minimum price disturbance of the larger trade hedging orders. By increasing the number of bids and offers available at any given price level, the speculator usually helps to minimize price fluctuations rather than to intensify them. Without the trading activity of the speculative fraternity, the liquidity, so badly needed in futures markets, simply would not exist. Trading volume would be restricted materially since, without a host of speculative orders in the trading ring, many larger trade orders at limit prices would simply go unfilled due to the floor broker's inability to find an equally large but opposing hedge order at the same price to complete the match."

futures exchanges for over 60 years. In 1921 it enacted the Future Trading Act, 42 Stat. 187, which imposed a prohibitive tax on grain futures transactions that were not consummated on an exchange designated as a "contract market" by the Secretary of Agriculture. The 1921 statute was held unconstitutional as an improper exercise of the taxing power in Hill v. Wallace, 259 U.S. 44 (1922), but its regulatory provisions were promptly reenacted in the Grain Futures Act, 42 Stat. 998, and upheld under the commerce power in Chicago Board of Trade v. Olsen, 262 U.S. 1 (1923). Under the original legislation, the principal function of the Secretary was to require the governors of a privately organized exchange to supervise the operation of the market. Two of the conditions for designation were that the governing board of the contract market prevent its members from disseminating misleading market information and prevent the "manipulation of prices or the cornering of any grain by the dealers or operators upon such board." The requirement that designated contract markets police themselves and the prohibitions against disseminating misleading information and manipulating prices have been part of our law ever since.

In 1936 Congress changed the name of the statute to the Commodity Exchange Act, enlarged its coverage to include other agricultural commodities, and added detailed provisions regulating trading in futures contracts. Commodity Exchange Act, ch. 545, 49 Stat. 1491. Among the significant new provisions was § 4b, prohibiting any member of a contract market from defrauding any person in connection with the making of a futures contract, and § 4a, authorizing a commission composed of the Secretary of Agriculture, the Secretary of Commerce, and the Attorney General to fix limits on the amount of permissible speculative trading in a futures contract. The legislation also required registration of futures commission merchants and floor brokers.

In 1968 the CEA again was amended to enlarge its coverage and to give the Secretary additional enforcement authority. Act of Feb. 19, 1968, 82 Stat. 26. The Secretary was authorized to disapprove exchange rules that were inconsistent with the statute, and the contract markets were required to enforce their rules; the Secretary was authorized to suspend a contract market or to issue a cease-and-desist order upon a showing that the contract market's rules were not being enforced. In addition, the criminal sanctions for price manipulation were increased significantly, and any person engaged in price manipulation was subjected to the Secretary's authority to issue cease-and-desist orders for violations of the CEA and implementing regulations.

In 1974, after extensive hearings and deliberation, Congress enacted the Commodity Futures Trading Commission Act of 1974. 88 Stat. 1389. Like the 1936 and the 1968 legislation, the 1974 enactment was an amendment to the existing statute that broadened its coverage and increased the penalties for violation of its provisions. The Commission was authorized to seek injunctive relief, to alter or supplement a contract market's rules, and to direct a contract market to take whatever action deemed necessary by the Commission in an emergency. The 1974 legislation retained the basic statutory prohibitions against fraudulent practices and price manipulation, as well as the authority to prescribe trading limits. The 1974 amendments, however, did make substantial changes in the statutory scheme; Congress authorized a newly created Commodities Futures Trading Commission to assume the powers previously exercised by the Secretary of Agriculture, as well as certain additional powers. The enactment also added two new remedial provisions for the protection of individual traders. The newly enacted § 5a(11) required every contract market to provide an arbitration procedure for the settlement of traders' claims of no more than $15,000. And the newly enacted § 14 authorized the Commission to grant reparations to any person complaining of any violation of the CEA, or its implementing regulations, committed by any futures commission merchant or any associate thereof, floor broker, commodity trading adviser, or commodity pool operator. This section authorized the Commission to investigate complaints and, "if in its opinion the facts warrant such action," to afford a hearing before an administrative law judge. Reparations orders entered by the Commission are subject to judicial review.

The latest amendments to the CEA, the Futures Trading Act of 1978, 92 Stat. 865, again increased the penalties for violations of the statute. The enactment also authorized the States to bring *parens patriae* actions, seeking injunctive or monetary relief for certain violations of the CEA, implementing regulations, or Commission orders.

Like the previous enactments, as well as the 1978 amendments, the Commodity Futures Trading Commission Act of 1974 is silent on the subject of private judicial remedies for persons injured by a violation of the CEA.

In the four cases before us, the allegations in the complaints filed by respondents are assumed to be true. The first involves a complaint by customers against their broker. The other three arise out of a malfunction of the contract market for futures contracts covering the delivery of Maine potatoes in May 1976, " 'when the sellers of almost 1,000 contracts failed to deliver approximately 50,000,000 pounds of potatoes, resulting in the largest default in the history of commodities futures trading in this country.' "3 * * *

One of the futures contracts traded on the New York Mercantile Exchange provided for the delivery of a railroad car lot of 50,000 pounds of Maine potatoes at a designated place on the Bangor and Aroostook Railroad during the period between May 7, 1976, and May 25, 1976. Trading in this contract commenced early in 1975 and terminated on May 7, 1976. On two occasions during this trading period the Department of

---

3. [n.39] 638 F.2d, at 285 (quoting National Super Spuds, Inc. v. New York Mercantile Exchange, 470 F.Supp. 1256, 1258 (SDNY 1979)). "The default was virtually unprecedented and, in the words of CFTC officials and members of the industry, shocked the commodity markets and the participants more than any other single event in recent years." H.R.Rep. No. 95–1181, p. 99 (1978).

Agriculture issued reports containing estimates that total potato stocks, and particularly Maine potato stocks, were substantially down from the previous year. This information had the understandable consequences of inducing investors to purchase May Maine potato futures contracts (on the expectation that they would profit from a shortage of potatoes in May) and farmers to demand a higher price for their potatoes on the cash market.

To counteract the anticipated price increases, a group of entrepreneurs described in the complaints as the "short sellers" formed a conspiracy to depress the price of the May Maine potato futures contract. The principal participants in this "short conspiracy" were large processors of potatoes who then were negotiating with a large potato growers association on the cash market. The conspirators agreed to accumulate an abnormally large short position in the May contract, to make no offsetting purchases of long contracts at a price in excess of a fixed maximum, and to default, if necessary, on their short commitments. They also agreed to flood the Maine cash markets with unsold potatoes. This multifaceted strategy was designed to give the growers association the impression that the supply of Maine potatoes would be plentiful. On the final trading day the short sellers had accumulated a net short position of almost 1,900 contracts, notwithstanding a Commission regulation limiting their lawful net position to 150 contracts. They did, in fact, default.

The trading limit also was violated by a separate group described as the "long conspirators." Aware of the short conspiracy, they determined that they not only could counteract its effects but also could enhance the price the short conspirators would have to pay to liquidate their short positions by accumulating an abnormally large long position—at the close of trading they controlled 911 long contracts—and by creating an artificial shortage of railroad cars during the contract delivery period. Because the long conspirators were successful in tying up railroad cars, they prevented the owners of warehoused potatoes from making deliveries to persons desiring to perform short contracts.[4]

Respondents are speculators who invested long in Maine futures contracts. Allegedly, if there had been no price manipulation, they would have earned a significant profit by reason of the price increase that free market forces would have produced. * * *

We granted certiorari. 450 U.S. 910, (1981). For the purpose of considering the question whether respondents may assert an implied cause of action for damages, it is assumed that each of the petitioners has violated the statute and thereby caused respondents' alleged injuries. * * *

In determining whether a private cause of action is implicit in a federal statutory scheme when the statute by its terms is silent on that

---

4. [n.45] "Because the long conspirators had successfully tied up all the freight cars of the Bangor & Aroostook, Incomco was unable to deliver its warehoused potatoes to persons seeking delivery to fulfill short contracts. As the warm weather set in, the 1,500,000 pounds of potatoes became rotten, and Incomco's total investment was lost." 638 F.2d, at 291.

issue, the initial focus must be on the state of the law at the time the legislation was enacted. More precisely, we must examine Congress' perception of the law that it was shaping or reshaping. When Congress enacts new legislation, the question is whether Congress intended to create a private remedy as a supplement to the express enforcement provisions of the statute. When Congress acts in a statutory context in which an implied private remedy has already been recognized by the courts, however, the inquiry logically is different. Congress need not have intended to create a new remedy, since one already existed; the question is whether Congress intended to preserve the pre-existing remedy. * * *

Prior to the comprehensive amendments to the CEA enacted in 1974, the federal courts routinely and consistently had recognized an implied private cause of action on behalf of plaintiffs seeking to enforce and to collect damages for violation of provisions of the CEA or rules and regulations promulgated pursuant to the statute. * * *

The inference that Congress intended to preserve the pre-existing remedy is compelling. As the Solicitor General argues on behalf of the Commission as *amicus curiae*, the private cause of action enhances the enforcement mechanism fostered by Congress over the course of 60 years. In an enactment purporting to strengthen the regulation of commodity futures trading, Congress evidenced an affirmative intent to preserve this enforcement tool. It removed an impediment to exchange rulemaking caused in part by the implied private remedy not by disapproving that remedy but rather by giving the Commission the extraordinary power to supplement exchange rules. And when several Members of Congress expressed a concern that the exclusive-jurisdiction provision, which was intended only to consolidate federal regulation of commodity futures trading in the Commission, might be construed to affect the implied cause of action as well as other court actions, Congress acted swiftly to dispel any such notion. Congress could have made its intent clearer only by expressly providing for a private cause of action in the statute. In the legal context in which Congress acted, this was unnecessary. * * *

The judgments of the Courts of Appeals are affirmed.

JUSTICE POWELL, with whom THE CHIEF JUSTICE, JUSTICE REHNQUIST, and JUSTICE O'CONNOR join, dissents. * * *

Following the decision of the Supreme Court in *Curran*, Congress acted to restrict the availability of a private right of action in federal courts under the Commodity Exchange to those most directly injured by a violation. 7 U.S.C. § 25.[5]

Until the end of the twentieth century, commodity futures transactions were regulated principally by the Commodity Futures Trading

---

5. See Jerry W. Markham, Commodities Regulation: Fraud, Manipulation and Other Claims, Ch. 21 (2000).

Commission (CFTC) under the Commodity Exchange Act. That legislation required all futures contracts to be traded on a regulated "contract market" such as the Chicago Mercantile Exchange. The Act was crafted for the regulation of agricultural products, but today most futures trading involves financial products such as interest rates, stock indexes, and now even individual stocks. Institutions found that the standardized terms in these contracts (e.g., delivery date, amount and point of delivery) and the rigid trading requirements imposed by the CFTC did not always comport with the needs of institutional traders. This led to the development of hybrid or "over-the-counter derivatives." For the most part, however, these contracts are simply derivations of the traditional option or futures contract.

GROUP OF THIRTY
GLOBAL DERIVATIVES STUDY GROUP
DERIVATIVES: PRACTICES AND PRINCIPLES

July 1993.

* * * In the most general terms, a derivatives transaction is a bilateral contract or payments exchange agreement whose value derives, as it name implies, from the value of an underlying asset or underlying reference rate or index. Today, derivatives transactions cover a broad range of "underlyings"—interest rates, exchange rates, commodities, equities, and other indices.

In addition to privately negotiated, global transactions, derivatives also include standardized futures and options on futures that are actively traded on organized exchanges, and securities such as call warrants. The term "derivative" also is used by some observers to refer to a wide variety of debt instruments that have payoff characteristics reflecting embedded derivatives, or have option characteristics, or are created by "stripping" particular components of other instruments such as principal or interest payments.

The array of derivatives contracts is not as complex as it first appears. Every derivative transaction can be built up from two simple and fundamental types of building blocks: forwards and options. Forward-based transactions include forwards and swap contracts, as well as exchange-traded futures. Option-based transactions include privately negotiated, OTC options (including caps, floors, collars, and options on forward and swap contracts) and exchange-traded options on futures. Diverse types of derivatives are created by combining the building blocks in different ways, and by applying these structures to a wide range of underlying assets, rates, or indices. * * *

The simplest derivative is the forward contract. A forward contract obligates one counterparty to buy, and the other to sell, a specific underlying at a specific price, amount, and date in the future. Forward markets exist for a multitude of underlyings, including the traditional agricultural or physical commodities, as well as currencies (referred to as foreign exchange forwards) and interest rates (referred to as forward rate agreements or "FRAs"). The change in the value of a forward contract is roughly proportional to the change in the value of its underlying. This distinguishes forward-based derivatives from option-based derivatives, which have a different payoff profile.

Forward contracts are customized with terms and conditions tailored to fit the particular business, financial, or risk management objectives of the counterparties. Negotiations often take place with respect to contract size, delivery grade, delivery locations, delivery dates, and credit terms. Forwards, in other words, are not standardized.

Forward contracts create credit exposures. Since the value of the contract is conveyed only at maturity, the parties are exposed to the risk of default during the life of the contract. The credit risk is two-sided. Only the party for whom the contract has a positive mark-to-market value can suffer a loss; but, since either party can ultimately end up in this situation, each party must evaluate the creditworthiness of its counterparty.

Since these contracts are typically large and the potential credit risk may be significant, the counterparties to forward contracts are usually corporations, financial institutions, institutional investors, or government entities.

As the name implies, a swap transaction obligates the two parties to the contract to exchange a series of cash flows at specified intervals known as payment or settlement dates. The cash flows of a swap are either fixed, or calculated for each settlement date by multiplying the quantity of the underlying (notional principle) by specified reference rates or prices. Depending upon the type of underlying, the great majority of these transactions are classified into interest rate, currency, commodity, or equity swaps. Except for currency swaps, the notional principal is used to calculate the payment stream but not exchanged. Interim payments are generally netted, with the difference being paid by one party to the other.

Swaps, like forwards, are bilateral agreements between sophisticated, institutional participants; they are entered into through private negotiations and give rise to credit exposures. Swaps are tailored, like forwards, to meet the specific risk management needs of the counterparties.

The cash flows from a swap can be decomposed into equivalent cash flows from a bundle of simpler forward contracts. Interest rate and currency swaps can also be analyzed in economic terms as back-to-back or parallel loans. Both of these decompositions have important implications for pricing and hedging. They imply pricing relationships and related arbitrage opportunities among swaps, forwards, and futures contracts and between derivatives in general and various cash market instruments. They also suggest the many ways in which the market risk of swaps can be hedged. For example, combinations of long and short positions in government or corporate securities, exchange-traded interest rate futures, or forward rate agreements can be used to hedge swap exposure—and vice versa.

The basic form of a futures contract is similar to that of a forward contract: a futures contract obligates its owner to buy a specified underlying at a specified price on the contract maturity date (or settle the value for cash). The payoff, or market risk, profile facing the owner of a futures contract is also similar to that of a forward contract. The volume of the newer financial futures contracts involving interest rates, currencies and equity indices now dwarfs the volume in traditional agricultural contracts.

Despite the similarity in payoff profiles, important economic differences distinguish futures from forwards and swaps. First, the contract terms of futures describing the quantity and quality of the underlying, the time and place of delivery, and the method of payment are fully standardized. Price is the only variable left to be determined. This standardization extends to the credit risk of futures. Credit risk is greatly reduced by marking the contract to market with daily (or more frequent) settling up of changes in value, and by requiring buyers and sellers alike to post margin as collateral for these settlement payments. This full standardization leads to fungibility–that is, contracts of the same maturity are perfect substitutes. These characteristics are designed to facilitate anonymous trading in an active and liquid exchange market.

Second, futures differ from forwards and swaps in that contractual obligations under futures contracts are entered into directly with the exchange clearinghouse and are generally satisfied through offset–the cancellation of an existing futures position through the acquisition of an equal but opposite position that leaves the clearinghouse with zero net exposures. The right to offset allows futures participants to readily cut their losses or take their profits, without negotiating with counterparties.[6]

Finally, the anonymous nature of futures trading and the relatively small contract size makes futures contracts accessible to members of the general public, including retail speculators, who are unable to transact in forwards and swaps.

The other derivatives building block is the option contract. In exchange for payment of a premium, an option contract gives the option holder the right *but not the obligation* to buy or sell the underlying (or settle the value for cash) at a price, called the strike price, during a period or on a specified date. Thus, the owner of the option can choose not to exercise the option and let it expire. The buyer benefits from favorable movements in the price of the underlying but is not exposed to corresponding losses.

---

6. [eds.] An important aspect of futures and options trading on organized markets is the role played by the clearing houses. These entities act as the buyer and seller of each contract and as guarantor of each contract's performance. The clearing house is supported by the credit of its members and by clearing funds that are generated from fees assessed on each trade. This support greatly reduces counter party risk in futures and options transactions.

Privately negotiated options exist on a multitude of underlyings, such as bonds, equities, currencies and commodities, and even swaps. Options also can be structured as securities such as warrants or can be embedded in securities such as certain commodity or equity-linked bonds with option-like characteristics.

Much as forwards can be bundled to create swaps, options can be bundled to create other option-based contracts called caps, floors, and collars. Like interest rate swaps, caps, floors, and collars are generally medium-to long-term transactions. A notional principal is used to calculate periodic cash flows. The buyer of the cap pays a premium, normally at inception. At each payment date, the seller must pay the buyer an amount based on the difference, if positive, between the reference and strike price (cap). A cap therefore protects a floating-rate borrower against a rise in interest rates. A floor contract is the opposite of a cap in that payment is made only if the difference is negative. A floor therefore protects a floating-rate investor against a decline in interest rates. Buying a collar is equivalent to buying a cap and selling a floor.

A swaption (or swap option) is an option on a swap. It gives the buyer the right, but not the obligation, to enter into a specified swap contract at a future date. In this case, the asset underlying the option contract is another derivatives transaction (i.e., a swap). A borrower can buy protection against the effect of a general rise in interest rates through the purchase of an option to enter into an interest rate swap. Swaptions now play an important role in the management of corporate debt, especially callable debt.

Options on futures contracts are to OTC options what futures contracts are to forward contracts and swaps. They have similar payoff profiles but differ from OTC options in that they are fully standardized (including credit terms), can be cancelled through offset, and can be traded by the general public.

The participants in derivatives activity can be divided into two groups—end-users and dealers. End-users consist of corporations, governmental entities, institutional investors, and financial institutions. Dealers consist mainly of banks and securities firms, with a few insurance companies and highly rated corporations (mainly energy firms) having recently joined the ranks. An institution may participate in derivatives activity both as an end-user and a dealer. For example, a money-center bank acts as an end-user when it uses derivatives to take positions as part of its proprietary trading or for hedging as part of its asset and liability management. It acts as a dealer when it quotes bids and offers and commits capital to satisfying customers' demands for derivatives.

Derivatives permit end-users and dealers to identify, isolate, and manage separately the fundamental risks and other characteristics that are bound together in traditional financial instruments. Desired combinations of cash flow, interest rate, currency, liquidity, and market source characteristics can be achieved largely by separable choices, each independent of the underlying cash market instrument. As a result, management is able to think and act in terms of fundamental risks. * * *

Global derivatives are now used widely by financial institutions to manage the interest rate and foreign exchange risk arising from a variety of activities. Eighty-four percent of the financial institutions responding to the Survey indicate that they use derivatives for hedging market risks arising from new financings, 77% use them to manage their existing assets and liabilities, 39% use them to offset option positions embedded in the institution's assets and liabilities, 39% use them to hedge transaction exposures, and 46% use them to hedge translation exposures.

Early in the evolution of OTC derivatives, financial institutions–including investment banks, commercial banks, merchant banks, and independent broker/dealers–acted for the most part as brokers finding counterparties with offsetting requirements with regard to notional amount, currencies, type of interest to be paid, frequency of payments, and maturity. They then negotiated on behalf of the two parties. Acting as agent or broker for a fee, the institutions took no principal position in the transactions and, hence, were not exposed to credit or market risk. * * *

Dealing in derivatives has tended to concentrate among principals possessing not only the requisite technology and know-how but also ample capital and credit appraisal experience. Banks have become the dominant derivatives players, but they hold no monopoly. Securities firms, insurance companies, and highly rated corporates (especially in the energy area) are deploying capital and credit experience to run swap books to profit from both dealing and position-taking activity.

The credit standing of the dealer is very important. Several dealers have created special purpose derivatives product companies which benefit from the support of a strong parent or shareholder. Some dealers have established separately capitalized triple-A rated, derivatives vehicles.

The risks to end-users and dealers involved in derivatives can be broadly categorized as market, credit, operation, and legal. These risks are of the same type that banks and securities firms have faced in their traditional lines of business–taking deposits and making loans, or purchasing and financing securities positions. The risks of derivatives, in other words, are not new. The management of derivatives activities, however, is more complex than it is for some of the traditional banking products. For derivatives activities, dealers have developed sophisticated risk management systems.

Some other banking products, such as residential mortgages with prepayment options, require a similarly sophisticated approach to risk management. An important by-product of derivatives activities has been that the knowledge dealers have gained about the assessment and management of risk has flowed out of derivatives groups into other areas, improving the general risk management techniques and policies of many firms. * * *

Questions and Notes

1. Can you explain the difference between a forward and a futures contract? Between a futures contract and an option contract?

2. What is the difference between a put option and a call option? Between a "short" and a "long" transaction?

3. What is the difference between a European option, an American option, and a Bermuda option?

4. What do you think caused the shift from agriculturally based futures trading to financial instruments? Note that futures trading fell under the jurisdiction of the agricultural committees in Congress because of its historical precedents. Do you think these committees have the requisite expertise or interest in regulating what are now largely financial based instruments?

SECTION 2.   BANKS ENTER THE DERIVATIVES BUSINESS

JERRY W. MARKHAM & DAVID J. GILBERG
FEDERAL REGULATION OF BANK ACTIVITIES IN THE COMMODITIES MARKETS

39 Bus. Law. 1719 (1984).

* * * Futures contracts on stock indexes, Treasury bills, Eurodollars and Government National Mortgage Association (GNMA) commitments have attracted a whole new range of participants in the commodity futures industry, including banks and other financial institutions. It has been stated that "banks and corporations throughout the world are actively using these contracts to minimize their exchange rate and interest rate risks" and "[e]very major bank in the United States will be trading these contracts." * * *

Commodity futures contracts are traded on margin, a concept that should not be confused with the use of margin in the securities industry. Margins for commodity futures contracts are good-faith deposits of money, designed to assure that the parties will perform upon their obligations under the contract. In contrast, margin in the securities industry is used as a limitation on the amount of credit that can be extended. Margin for a commodity futures contract represents only a small percentage of the purchase price of the contract, often less than ten percent. This permits a high degree of leverage and is therefore attractive to speculators seeking large profits with a recognition of the commensurate risk involved. * * *

In recent years, the emphasis in futures trading has shifted from agricultural commodities to the so-called "financial futures." * * * These include contracts on underlying securities such as stock index futures, GNMA pass-through certificates, and treasury obligations as well as on stock indexes. Simply stated, stock-index futures involve the purchase or sale of a theoretical portfolio of stocks contained in a securities index such as Standard & Poor's, allowing speculators, in effect, to purchase a diversified portfolio reflecting overall price movements in the market and permitting institutions to hedge their stock portfolios against market declines. Other financial futures such as GNMAs, commercial paper, Eurodollars, and Treasury bills may be used to speculate or to hedge against the risk of loss from interest-rate fluctuations. * * *

On November 2, 1976, the Comptroller of the Currency (Comptroller) published Banking Circular No. 79, which authorized national banks to engage in commodity futures trading in a limited manner. Specifically, national banks were allowed to participate in trading of GNMA mortgage futures on the Chicago Board of Trade and Treasury bill futures on the International Monetary Market in Chicago in "order to reduce the risk of interest rate fluctuation in the corresponding cash markets. . . . " * * *

The proliferation of futures contracts and their apparent popularity with banks and other financial institutions continued to concern the Board of Governors of the Federal Reserve System (FRB) and the Department of the Treasury after the issuance of Circular No. 79. Specifically, these agencies were concerned that these futures contracts could represent a threat to the financial stability of banks and the effective performance of the cash market for treasury securities. Therefore, in 1978, the Treasury and the FRB conducted a study (Treasury Study) on the use and effects of financial futures.

The Treasury Study found that many major financial institutions that had previously dealt in or traded treasury securities and other financial instruments had also begun to promote and trade financial futures. After first trading for their own account, the Treasury Study found that these firms had begun to service the needs of their customers as well, including banks, savings and loan associations and other financial and nonfinancial firms. The Treasury Study also found numerous advantages in trading commodity futures contracts. Among other things, futures markets allowed strangers to trade with each other without concern about their creditworthiness, that is, the credit risk was obviated by the clearinghouse guarantee. * * *

On July 1, 1982, the FRB approved the application of J.P. Morgan & Co., Inc. to establish a subsidiary registered with the CFTC as a futures commission merchant (FCM). The subsidiary, Morgan Futures Corp. (Morgan Futures), was granted permission to deal in futures contracts involving bullion, foreign exchange, United States government securities, domestic money-market instruments, and Eurodollar certificates of deposit. The FRB's approval of the operation of Morgan Futures as an FCM provided compelling confirmation of the increasingly active role of banks in the commodity futures markets but represented only the most recent step in a process begun as much as ten years earlier. * * *

Almost immediately after its approval of Morgan Futures' application, the FRB also granted permission to Bankers Trust New York Corporation to establish an FCM subsidiary, BT Markets Corp. (BTMC). The application similarly sought authorization for BTCM to trade for the accounts of customers in futures contracts on United States government securities, negotiable money-market interest, foreign exchange, and bullion. Based upon the Morgan Futures determination, the FRB noted, in a somewhat summary fashion, that the BTCM application presented a similar situation and was likewise permissible under the BHCA [Bank Holding Company Act]. * * *

FCMs are registered with and regulated by the CFTC under the CEA. The primary function of an FCM is the solicitation of customer orders and accounts and acceptance of customer funds for the purpose of trading in their behalf on designated contract markets. FCMs may conduct their operations through a sales force of employees, who must be registered with the CFTC as associated persons (APs), and are the equivalent of registered representatives of a securities broker-dealer. In the alternative, an FCM may operate through an independent sales force made up of introducing brokers (IBs), independent entities or individuals registered as IBs with the CFTC who are authorized to solicit customer orders or accounts on behalf of an FCM but may not accept any customer funds in connection therewith. * * *

FCMs are required to file a Statement of Financial Condition on form 1–FR with the registration application and must complete the same report periodically thereafter. The central portion of the financial statement is the computation of minimum financial requirements disclosing the amount of liquid net capital available to the FCM. The minimum financial regulations, which are roughly similar to the net capital regulations of the SEC, are designed to assure that FCMs maintain a specified amount of liquid assets in order to satisfy potential customer demands. * * *

The Act and CFTC regulations require FCMs to "treat and deal with all money, securities, and property received . . . to margin, guarantee, or secure the trades or contracts of any customer . . . as belonging to such customer." All customer funds held by an FCM for the purpose of commodity futures trading must, therefore, be maintained separately from the funds of noncommodities customers and from those of the FCM and its affiliates. Ordinarily segregated funds are maintained in a distinct bank account with a bank or other entity separate from the FCM itself, and the institution undertakes specific responsibilities.[7] * * *

The Dodd–Frank Act limits the derivatives activities of banks in several ways. First, there is a broad provision intended to "push out" swaps activities from banks to nonbank affiliates and to make any

---

7. [n.176] 17 C.F.R. § 1.21 (1983). With respect to a bank acting as a depository for segregated funds, the CFTC has stated that it must receive notice from the FCM as to the nature of the funds on deposit, may not use those funds to set off any liability of the FCM and must send an acknowledgment to the FCM that it is aware that the funds are segregated commodity funds. CFTC Interpretive Letter No. 79–1 [1977–1980 Transfer Binder] Comm. Fut. L. Rep. (CCH) ¶ 20,835 (May 29, 1979).

transactions between the bank and affiliate subject to the Federal Reserve Act's affiliate transaction rules discussed in Chapter 4. Dodd–Frank Act, § 716. The "push-out" is required because banks may not receive federal assistance and act as a "swaps entity." Federal assistance is defined broadly to include FDIC deposit insurance as well as accepting advances from the Fed's discount window. In a compromise inserted during the conference on Dodd–Frank, however, several important exemptions were added to this provision that permit banks to engage in swap activities that hedge the bank's risk, involve rates or reference assets permitted as national bank investments including interest rate swaps and currency swaps, or are CDS transactions cleared by a clearinghouse. Swaps based on commodities and equity securities as well as uncleared CDS must be pushed out to nonbank affiliates, unless the transactions have been entered into for hedging purposes. Second, an insured bank is also required to comply with the prohibition on trading in derivatives as required under section 619 of the Dodd–Frank Act. Dodd–Frank Act, § 716.

The third important aspect of Dodd–Frank for bank derivatives activities is that it requires that credit exposures from a derivative transaction be considered a "loan or extension of credit" subject to the National Bank Act's lending limits and insider trading limits. Dodd–Frank Act, § 610. In addition, an insured state bank may only engage in the permitted derivatives activities if its chartering state's lending limit law "takes into consideration" credit exposures from derivatives transactions. Dodd–Frank Act, § 610. The effective date of this provision is delayed so that states will have sufficient time to amend their lending limit statutes to accommodate this new provision.

QUESTIONS AND NOTES

1. The CFTC and the Securities and Exchange Commission (SEC) have frequently found themselves at odds over their respective jurisdictions for financial futures and options contracts in which the underlying commodity was a security. Compounding the confusion is that the SEC acquired regulatory control over the stock option exchanges, such as the Chicago Board Options Exchange, Inc. (CBOE), before the creation of the CFTC. Conflicts developed as to which exchange, the CBOE regulated by the SEC or the Chicago Board of Trade regulated by the CFTC, had the right to trade options or futures on GNMA pass-through securities.

After much acrimony and litigation, the chairmen of the SEC and CFTC reached an agreement in 1982 that allocated their respective jurisdictions. That agreement was subsequently enacted as law. The SEC was given jurisdiction over options on individual stocks, options on indexes of securities, and options on foreign currency when traded on a national securities exchange. The CFTC was given jurisdiction over all futures contracts, including those on exempted securities such as United States government securities. The CFTC was also given jurisdiction over options on futures on stock and other indexes and options and futures on foreign currency when not traded on a national securities exchange. For a discussion of the jurisdictional fights between the SEC and CFTC see Jerry W. Markham, The History of Commodity Regulation and its Regulation (1987); Jerry W. Markham & Rita McCloy Stephanz, The Stock Market Crash of 1987–The United States Looks at New Recommendations, 76 Geo. L.J. 1993 (1988).

The confusion created by this jurisdictional arrangement was compounded by the different regulatory approaches the SEC and CFTC take in their customer protection and trading requirements. For example, the SEC allows over-the-counter trading, while the CFTC did not. The SEC has adopted a suitability requirement that prohibits brokers from recommending trades not suitable for customers in light of their particular financial circumstances and needs. The CFTC has eschewed such a requirement in favor of risk disclosure statements that warn investors of the dangers of trading futures and options and advises investors to make their own determination as to whether the transaction is suitable for them. Banks involved in derivatives must contend with this regulatory morass, as well as deal with their own regulators.

2. Initially, futures on single stocks, such as IBM or General Motors, were prohibited. Congress, however, later authorized the trading of futures contracts on single stocks under a system in which both securities and futures markets may be involved. Commodity Futures Modernization Act of 2000, Pub. L. No. 106–554, 114 Stat. 2763.

SECTION 3. HEDGING

Banks are generally required to limit their activities in derivatives to hedging activities. This means that a bank trading in derivatives for its own account must use that trading to offset some other risk. Speculation is not allowed. The Dodd–Frank Act exempts from its general prohibition of derivatives activities by a bank receiving federal assistance through deposit insurance, discount window advances, or more explicit federal benefits "[h]edging and other similar risk mitigating activities directly related to the insured depository institution's activities." Dodd–Frank Act, § 716.

OCC BULLETIN 96–43
CREDIT DERIVATIVES: GUIDELINES
FOR NATIONAL BANKS

<www.occ.treas.gov/ftp/bulletin/96–43.txt>.

This bulletin informs bankers of a new set of derivative products and provides initial guidance on supervisory issues related to bank participation in the developing market for credit derivatives. The guidance is principally intended for end-user banks, rather than dealers, unless otherwise indicated.

Credit derivatives are new financial instruments marketed as an efficient way to manage credit exposure. Credit derivatives permit the transfer of credit exposure between parties—i.e., the buyer and seller of the credit protection–in isolation from other forms of risk. These derivatives represent a natural extension of the market for similar products that "unbundle" risks, such as certain interest rate and foreign exchange products.

When used properly, credit derivatives can help to diversify credit risk, improve earnings, and lower the risk profile of an institution. Conversely, the improper use of credit derivatives, similar to poor lending practices, can result in an imprudent credit risk profile. Although the current volume of credit derivative activity in U.S. banks is quite small and mainly limited to dealers, many banks have begun to evaluate these products as tools for credit risk management.

With a credit derivative, a bank can both acquire and hedge risk. When a bank acquires risk, it takes on a credit exposure. Unlike traditional loan assets, most credit derivatives, except for credit-linked notes (discussed below), are off-balance-sheet contracts. The risk acquiror (i.e., seller of credit protection) may have several reasons for assuming the risk of a specific reference credit. For example, the protection seller may be underloaned, and would like to take carefully targeted credit risk in order to improve earnings, while also diversifying credit risk by assuming a risk position that has a low correlation with existing portfolio risks.

When a bank hedges risk, it transfers a credit exposure, but not the asset itself, to a counterparty who agrees to make a payment under certain conditions. Thus, the buyer of credit protection can hedge an existing exposure, much as the bank can with a loan participation. With a credit derivative, however, the asset remains on the bank's books. Because the exposure, but not the asset itself, is sold, credit derivatives can assist banks in managing internal limits, while avoiding customer relationship problems that can arise if the bank sells the asset.

There are three principal types of credit derivatives: credit default swaps, total rate of return (TROR) swaps, and credit-linked notes. Credit default swaps and TROR swaps are off-balance-sheet transactions. Credit-linked notes are credit-sensitive, cash-market structured notes that appear on the balance sheet like any other security. While these three vehicles are currently the predominant types of credit derivative transactions, the OCC expects that many variations, as well as new product types, will develop.

Credit default swaps are similar to standby letters of credit. The risk hedger (i.e., buyer of credit protection) pays a fee, which effectively represents an option premium, in return for the right to receive a conditional payment if a specified "reference credit" defaults. A reference credit is simply the party whose credit performance will determine credit derivative cash flows. Typically, the reference credit has a borrowing relationship with the bank that is buying credit protection. The bank may diversify its portfolio by reducing its exposure to the borrower, and the swap enables it to do so without disturbing its relationship with the customer. The methods used to determine the amount of the payment that would be triggered by the default vary by instrument. In some contracts, the amount of the payment is agreed upon at the inception of the contract. In others, the amount paid is determined after the default event and is based upon the observed prices of similar debt obligations of the borrower in the corporate bond market. A default event typically must exceed a materiality threshold in order to trigger a payment under the swap contract.[8]

A TROR swap transfers the total economic performance of a reference asset (or index), which includes all associated cash flows, as well as capital appreciation or depreciation. The total return payer pays the total rate of return on a reference asset, which includes contractual payments plus any price appreciation, in return for a floating rate plus any depreciation on the reference asset. The total return payer has hedged its credit risk, while the total return receiver has accepted credit risk. If the reference asset depreciates, the total return payer will receive the depreciation amount from its counterparty. Although the hedger has transferred the risk of the asset, it does not transfer the asset itself. It retains the customer relationship and must continue to fund the earning asset. TROR swaps may, but need not, terminate upon a default event.

A credit-linked note is an on-balance-sheet, cash-market structured note often issued by a special purpose trust vehicle. The note represents a synthetic corporate bond or loan, because a credit derivative (credit default or TROR swap) is embedded in the structure. Depending upon the performance of a specified reference credit, and the type of derivative embedded in the note, the note may not be redeemable at par value. These notes are similar to variable principal redemption (VPR) bonds referenced in Advisory Letter 94–2, "Purchases of Structured Notes." The primary difference is that credit-linked notes have principal (par value) at risk depending upon the credit performance of a reference credit, whereas VPR bonds have principal at risk based upon changes in financial market rates. For example, the purchaser of a credit-linked note with an embedded default swap may receive only 60 percent of the original par value if a reference credit defaults. Investors in credit-linked notes assume credit risk of both the reference credit and the underlying collateral. The trust is generally collateralized with high-quality assets to assure payment of contractual amounts due. Like other structured notes, credit-linked notes allow an investor to take a customized investment view. Credit-linked notes may contain leverage that can magnify the risk and return of the asset.

When properly used, credit derivatives, like other financial derivatives, can provide national banks with substantial benefits. Most significantly, credit derivatives can allow banks to reduce concentration risks. For example, using a credit default swap, a bank may hedge a concentration risk by purchasing credit protection against a specific borrower's default. A bank can hedge against credit deterioration of a specific asset,

---

8. [eds.] See Eternity Global Master Fund Ltd. v. Morgan Guaranty Trust Co. of New York, 375 F.3d 168 (2d Cir. 2004) (discussed further in Section 5 of this chapter and describing some of the complexities that may arise as to when a credit default has occurred).

short of an actual default, by paying the total return on a TROR swap. Alternatively, banks can adjust their credit profile by purchasing credit protection (i.e., hedging risk) against borrowers in an industry where an undesired exposure exists and selling protection (i.e., acquiring risk) in another industry. Portfolio management techniques can allow banks to increase the return on a portfolio, for a given level of risk, by structuring the portfolio to diversify credit exposures. To effectively diversify credit exposures, however, banks should understand how their asset risks are correlated. For example, if a fall in commodity prices will affect land prices, credit portfolios exposed to both commodity and land prices will typically have greater risks than portfolios without such correlated credit exposures. Using credit derivatives to manage the risk/return trade-off in a portfolio is an appropriate use of these products. * * *

Banking Circular 277 provides guidance for financial derivatives activities, and is equally appropriate for users of credit derivatives. Proper control over derivatives activities begins with effective senior management and board oversight. The oversight process includes sound policies and procedures to govern the use of derivatives, systems to identify, measure, monitor, and control risks, and independent oversight systems, such as audit coverage, to identify deficiencies in internal controls or systems. * * *

GREENE COUNTY BANK v. FEDERAL DEPOSIT INSURANCE CORP.

United States Court of Appeals, Eighth Circuit, 1996.
92 F.3d 633, *cert. denied*, 519 U.S. 1109 (1997).

JACKSON, DISTRICT JUDGE.

The Greene County Bank appeals a cease and desist order issued by the Board of Directors of the Federal Deposit Insurance Corporation ("FDIC"). The order requires the Bank to comply with a February 12, 1992 Memorandum of Understanding ("MOU") regarding certain activities in the futures and securities markets, and was prompted by the alleged failure of the Bank to comply with the MOU. The Bank attacks the order as not supported by substantial evidence and as arbitrary and capricious. The Bank also argues that the FDIC applied an incorrect standard in determining that the Bank engaged in unsafe and unsound practices. We uphold the cease and desist order. * * *

At issue in this case is whether the process by which the Bank engaged in futures and securities market activities complied with the procedures set forth in the MOU. The MOU requires the Bank to (1) develop written policies for addressing interest rate risk exposure and governing the use of futures to reduce interest rate risk and (2) provide detailed justification each time the Bank uses futures to reduce interest rate risk. The MOU also incorporates the FDIC Policy Statement which, in part, requires the Bank's board of directors to approve any plan to engage in futures market activities. In his recommended decision, the ALJ concluded that the Bank had complied with the MOU in material respects but had not adopted an investment policy in compliance with Section 1(c). The ALJ, however, did not recommend the issuance of a cease and desist order. In its reversal of the ALJ decision, the FDIC found that the Bank had in fact failed to adhere to the MOU requirements by engaging in futures and securities market transactions without prior approval by the Bank's board of directors and without proper analysis and documentation. The FDIC concluded that in light of the risks involved in these types of transactions, complete compliance with the MOU was required, and the cease and desist order was necessary to ensure such compliance.

The record shows that the Bank failed to comply with the terms of the MOU and the FDIC Policy Statement when it did not properly document and obtain approval of the acquisition of a number of spread positions. The Bank began acquiring these positions in the Fall of 1992. However, these investments were not formally approved by the Board until March 29, 1993, months after they were made. The only document in the record which contained the Bank's explanation of its strategy for this type of investment was undated. The FDIC concluded that to the extent that any documents contained language that could be construed as authorizing the acquisition of these spread positions, such language was too vague to comply with the requirements of the FDIC Policy Statement. The testimony of the FDIC examiner in charge supports this conclusion.

The FDIC's decision was also based on substantial evidence of deficiencies regarding the Bank's calculation and analysis of interest rate risk exposure. The evidence revealed that the Bank did not calculate and analyze its interest rate risk exposure on a regular basis as the MOU required. Although the ALJ believed that this deficiency could be excused because the Bank was receiving gap analyses measuring the exposure from the FDIC and other examiners, clearly the terms of the MOU required regular monitoring by the Bank.

After reviewing the record as a whole, we find that the FDIC's determination that the Bank failed to fully comply with the conditions of the MOU is supported by substantial evidence. * * *

Finally, the Bank argues that the FDIC applied the wrong standard in determining that the Bank's failure to comply with the MOU constituted an unsafe and unsound practice. The Bank argues that application of the "unsafe and unsound practice" standard is limited to practices having a reasonably direct effect on the Bank's financial soundness, a situation not present in this case. See Matter of Seidman, 37 F.3d 911 (3rd Cir.1994). It is well-settled in this Circuit, however, that an "unsafe or unsound practice" exists where the conduct is "deemed contrary to accepted standards of banking operations which might result in abnormal risk or loss to a banking institution or shareholder." *Eden*, 568 F.2d at 611 n. 2. We conclude that the FDIC in this case applied the appropriate standard to determine whether the challenged action constituted an "unsafe or unsound practice."

The August 1, 1995 Decision and Order of the FDIC Board of Directors is affirmed.

QUESTIONS AND NOTES

1. Derivatives traded on stock indexes like the S & P 500 have proven to be particularly popular instruments for institutional trading. Futures and options contracts allow institutions to hedge against adverse changes in the stock markets. Controversy arose between the Comptroller of the Currency (OCC) and Representative Leach, then the House Banking and Financial Services Committee Chairman, over whether banks should be allowed to buy equity stocks to hedge derivative swaps. Chairman Leach thought that this would allow banks to evade restrictions on the ownership of equity securities as an investment. OCC Interpretive Letter No. 892 (Sept. 2000). Under Dodd–Frank, swaps based on equity securities would need to be pushed out to affiliated entities under section 716.

2. Should banks be allowed to invest in stocks like any other business? In the light of the easing of merchant banking restrictions in the Gramm–Leach–Bliley Act (see Chapter 11), do you agree with Chairman Leach that banks should be restricted from derivatives trading in equities?

3. What are the dangers of stock ownership by a bank? Could those risks be reduced by hedging?

4. Could banks use derivatives in a way that might convert their role from intermediary to trader?

5. A bank holding company may deal with its customers as principal in certain derivative transactions specified in Regulation Y under the Bank Holding Company Act. Such authority is intended to limit bank holding companies "to trading and investing in financial instruments rather than dealing directly in commodities." Bank Holding Companies and Change in Bank Control, 68 Fed. Reg. 39807, 39808 (July 3, 2003). The restrictions limit the ability of holding companies to take delivery of commodities, although the Federal Reserve Board permits delivery where title is taken in the contract on a pass-through basis without physical possession. Id.

Under the Dodd–Frank Act's push-out provision in section 716, would a national bank continue to be able to engage in these activities approved prior to Dodd–Frank: cash settled electricity derivatives transactions,[9] delivery of electricity derivative contracts where title is taken in the contracts on a pass-through basis without physical possession,[10] and derivatives that allow businesses to hedge inflation risks?[11]

6. Even small banks are using derivatives to protect themselves against the risks of adverse interest rate changes in long-term loans, allowing them to

---

9. OCC Interpretive Letter No. 937 (June 2002), available at <www.occ.treas.gov/interp/jun 02/int937.pdf>.

10. OCC Interpretive Letter No. 962 (May 2003), available at <www.occ.treas.gov/interp/may 03/int962.pdf>.

11. OCC Interpretive Letter No. 1079 (May 2007), available at <www.occ.treas.gov/interp/ may07/int1079.pdf>.

make larger loans with longer terms. Steve Garmhausen, Swaps Emerge as New Loan Tool for Small Banks, Am. Banker, Feb. 6, 2007.

7.   Some traders acting on behalf of banks have caused great losses. One famous trader was Nick Leeson, who destroyed the venerable Barings bank in 1995 after losing $1.3 billion from unauthorized trading in futures contracts. Jerome Kerviel, a mid-level employee at Société Générale SA ("SocGen") incurred $7.2 billion in trading losses on futures contracts in January 2008. Kerviel had taken huge bullish positions in the Dow Jones Euro Stoxx 50 index and the German DAX Index. When the bank dumped his positions it set off a market panic that destabilized markets around the world and caused the Fed in the U.S. to cut interest rates in a near record amount in order to bolster the market. Kerviel was a salaried employee, making less than $200,000. He covered up his trading losses by hacking into the bank's computers. Another French bank, Caisse d'Epargne, announced an unauthorized derivatives trading loss of over $800 million on October 17, 2008. See Jerry W. Markham, A Financial History of the United States, From the Suprime Crisis to the Great Recession (2006–2009) 475 (2010).

8.   Swaps and other derivatives receive special treatment under the Bankruptcy Code so that a counter-party does not have to both pay its obligations under the derivative contract to a bankrupt counter-party and forfeit payments due it from the bankrupt. Instead, the parties' obligations are netted out under "netting agreements." Will Cohen Bruckner, Legal and Regulatory Developments in Derivatives, 23 Rev. Bank. & Fin. Services 25, 25 (Mar. 2007).

SECTION 4.   THE TREASURY AMENDMENT

DUNN v. COMMODITY FUTURES TRADING COMMISSION

Supreme Court of the United States, 1997.
519 U.S. 465.

MR. JUSTICE STEVENS delivered the opinion of the Court.

The question presented is whether Congress has authorized the Commodity Futures Trading Commission (CFTC or Commission) to regulate "off-exchange" trading in options to buy or sell foreign currency.

The CFTC brought this action in 1994, alleging that, beginning in 1992, petitioners solicited investments in and operated a fraudulent scheme in violation of the Commodity Exchange Act (CEA), 7 U.S.C. § 1 et seq., and CFTC regulations. See 7 U.S.C. § 6c(b); 17 CFR § 32.9 (1996). The CFTC's complaint, affidavits, and declarations submitted to the District Court indicate that customers were told their funds would be invested using complex strategies involving options to purchase or sell various foreign currencies. Petitioners apparently did in fact engage in many such transactions. To do so, they contracted directly with international banks and others without making use of any regulated exchange or board of trade. In the parlance of the business, petitioners traded in the "off-exchange" or "over-the-counter" (OTC) market. No options were ever sold directly to petitioners' customers. However, their positions were tracked through internal accounts, and investors were provided weekly reports showing the putative status of their holdings. Petitioners and their customers suffered heavy losses. Subsequently, the CFTC commenced these proceedings.

The outcome of this case is dictated by the so-called "Treasury Amendment" to the CEA. 88 Stat. 1395, 7 U.S.C. § 2(ii). We have previously reviewed the history of the CEA and generally described how it authorizes the CFTC to regulate the "volatile and esoteric" market in futures contracts in fungible commodities. See Merrill Lynch, Pierce, Fenner & Smith, Inc. v. Curran, 456 U.S. 353, 356, 357–367 (1982). As a part of the 1974 amendments that created the CFTC and dramatically expanded the coverage of the statute to include nonagricultural commodities "in which contracts for future delivery are presently or in the future dealt in," see 88 Stat. 1395, 7 U.S.C. § 2 (1970 ed., Supp. IV), Congress enacted the following exemption, which has come to be known as the "Treasury Amendment":

> "Nothing in this chapter shall be deemed to govern or in any way be applicable to *transactions in foreign currency*, security warrants, security rights, resales of installment loan contracts, repurchase options, government securities, or mortgages and mortgage purchase commitments, unless such transactions involve the sale thereof for future delivery conducted on a board of trade." 7 U.S.C. § 2(ii) (emphasis added).

The narrow issue that we must decide is whether the italicized phrase ("transactions in foreign currency") includes transactions in options to buy or sell foreign currency. An option, as the term is understood in the trade, is a transaction in which the buyer purchases from the seller for consideration the right, but not the obligation, to buy or sell an agreed amount of a commodity at a set rate at any time prior to the option's expiration. We think it plain that foreign currency options are "transactions in foreign currency" within the meaning of the statute. We are not persuaded by any of the arguments advanced by the CFTC in support of a narrower reading that would exempt futures contracts (agreements to buy or sell a specified quantity of a commodity at a particular price for delivery at a set future date) without exempting options. * * *

Indeed, adopting the Commission's reading would deprive the exemption of the principal effect Congress intended.[12] The CFTC acknowledges

12. [n.8] The amendment was enacted on the suggestion of the Treasury Department at the time of a dramatic expansion in the scope of federal commodities regulation. The Department expressed concerns in a letter to the relevant congressional committee that this development might lead, *inter alia*, to the unintended regulation of the off-exchange market in foreign currency futures. See S. Rep. No. 93–1131, pp. 49–50 (1974) ("The Department feels strongly that foreign currency futures trading, other than on organized exchanges, should not be regulated by the new agency") (letter of Donald Ritger, Acting General Counsel). The Treasury Amendment, which tracks almost verbatim the language proposed by the Department, was included in the legislation to respond to these concerns. The CFTC is therefore plainly correct to reject the

that futures contracts fall squarely within the Treasury Amendment's exemption, and there is no question that the exemption of off-exchange foreign currency futures from CFTC regulation was one of Congress' primary goals. Yet on the CFTC's reasoning the exemption's application to futures contracts could not be sustained.

A futures contract is no more a transaction "in" foreign currency as the Commission understands the term than an option. The Commission argues that because a futures contract creates a legal obligation to purchase or sell currency on a particular date, it is somehow more clearly a transaction "in" the underlying currencies than an option, which generates only the right to engage in a transaction. This reasoning is wholly unpersuasive. No currency changes hands at the time a futures contract is made. And, the existence of a futures contract does not guarantee that currency will actually be exchanged. Indeed, the Commission concedes that, in most cases, futures contracts are "extinguished before delivery by entry into an offsetting futures contract." Adopting the CFTC's reading would therefore place both futures and options outside the exemption, in clear contravention of Congress' intent.

Furthermore, this interpretation would leave the Treasury Amendment's exemption for "transactions in foreign currency" without any significant effect at all, because it would limit the scope of the exemption to "forward contracts" (agreements that anticipate the actual delivery of a commodity on a specified future date) and "spot transactions" (agreements for purchase and sale of commodities that anticipate near-term delivery). Both are transactions "in" a commodity as the CFTC would have us understand the term. But neither type of transaction for *any* commodity was subject to intensive regulation under the CEA at the time of the Treasury Amendment's passage. See 7 U.S.C. § 2 (1970 ed., Supp. IV) ("term 'future delivery,' as used in this chapter, shall not include any sale of any cash commodity for deferred shipment or delivery"); J. Markham, The History of Commodity Futures Trading and Its Regulation 201–203 (1987). Our reading of the exemption is therefore also consonant with the doctrine that legislative enactments should not be construed to render their provisions mere surplusage. * * *

Justice Scalia concurs in part. * * *

The Commodity Futures Modernization Act of 2000 (CFMA) clarified the Treasury Amendment by making clear that transactions in Treasury Amendment instruments such as foreign currency, government securities, security warrants, security rights, resale and installment loan contracts, repurchase transactions and mortgages and mortgage commitments were not subject to the Commodity Exchange Act. The Commodity Exchange

---

suggestion of its *amici* that the Treasury Amendment's exemption be construed not to include futures contracts within its coverage.

Act still applies to futures or options on futures on the commodities otherwise exempted by the Treasury Amendment, if such transactions are traded on an "organized exchange." An organized exchange is one that permits trading by non-institutional participants or on other than a principal-to-principal basis. This change allows the Commodity Exchange Act to be applied to the retail firms that had sought to avoid CFTC jurisdiction under the Treasury Amendment. The CFTC has jurisdiction over foreign currency futures or options on foreign currencies traded by persons who are not institutions, unless the counter-party is a bank, broker-dealer, futures commission merchant, or other specified regulated entity. The United States Court of Appeals for the Seventh Circuit undercut that legislation by creating a loophole for "spot" transactions. Normally, spot transactions involve the purchase and sale of an actual commodity. However, the transactions at issue in that case rarely involved delivery and were usually offset in much the same fashion as futures or options traded on exchange. See CFTC v. Zelener, 373 F.3d 861 (7th Cir. 2004). This ruling allowed the forex firms to continue their fraud.

Congress acted to close the loophole opened by the Seventh Circuit decision through the CFTC Reauthorization Act of 2008. Those amendments gave the CFTC regulatory authority over all retail forex transactions offered on a leveraged or margin basis, or which the seller or its affiliates financed. The legislation created a new category of registrants, "retail foreign exchange dealers." Those dealers were required to have minimum adjusted net capital of $20 million. This net capital requirement was also applied to futures commission merchants acting as foreign-currency counterparties. The CFTC was given broad regulatory authority over other forex market participants, including commodity pool operators and commodity trading advisors.

A major part of the business mix of many large money center banks has been their foreign exchange (FX or forex) operations. The unfixing of exchange rates as a result of the collapse of the Bretton Woods agreement in 1971 led to large risks for companies engaged in foreign trade. For example, the drop in value of a foreign currency against the dollar could have serious consequences to a United States company when it exchanges funds earned in that foreign country for dollars. Since the U.S. company reports its earnings in dollars, a devaluation of its foreign currency payments could reduce earnings or even cause losses. Thus, U.S. companies engaged in foreign transactions may seek to hedge the exchange rate risk by buying dollars forward in the foreign currency. This will set a price for the currency and provide insurance against losses due to unfavorable fluctuations.

Large banks provide trading facilities for such operations, and make a two-sided market in most freely traded currencies. The participating banks are willing to buy or sell the currency at prices the banks believe reflect relative values. The banks quote a spread, buying the currency from customers at a price that is less than that which the banks are selling the same currency. This spread allows the banks to profit from the transactions. As seen from the preceding case, the interbank FX market is usually open only to large institutions or wealthy individuals.

Banks often buy and sell the same currency from the same customer as the customer's hedging needs change. This may result in offsetting transactions on the bank's books. Banks typically "net" such positions against each other. At issue, is whether such netting is allowed if the customer becomes bankrupt. If not, the bank could end up owing the customer on one side of offsetting contracts while receiving only a claim in bankruptcy for amounts due from the customer. The Bankruptcy Code and the Federal Deposit Insurance Act broadly allow netting for financial contracts entered into by banks and other financial institutions. Some questions, however, may still arise as to whether a particular institution or its contracts qualify for netting.

QUESTIONS AND NOTES

1.   Why has the CFTC sought so vigorously to keep individuals out of the interbank FX market?

2.   When you travel to Europe and exchange money at a foreign bank or currency exchange kiosk, you are not participating in the interbank FX market. Rather, this is a retail market that has much wider and less favorable spreads than those in the interbank market. The next time you travel abroad, compare the exchange rate you receive when you change money at a foreign bank with the exchange rate on your credit card transactions. Are the credit card transactions more favorable? If so, why is that the case?

3.   VISA and MasterCard came under attack for fees they charged to cardholders amounting to three percent or more on transactions requiring currency conversions. A California judge found that these fees had not been adequately disclosed and ordered refunds totaling $800 million to cardholders. Schwartz v. Visa Intern. Corp., No. 822404–4, 2003 WL 1870370 (Cal. Sup. Apr. 7, 2003), *review dismissed*, 154 P.3d 999 (Cal. Sup. 2007). The judgment was reversed based on the 2004 voter-approved Proposition 64 which bars lawsuits by individuals not harmed by the alleged actions. Schwartz v. Visa International Service Ass'n, 34 Cal.Rptr.3d 449 (2005). The court remanded to the trial court to determine whether to grant leave to amend the complaint. This practice was also the subject of several class action suits in federal court charging antitrust and Truth in Lending Act violations. In re Currency Conversion Fee Antitrust Litigation, 265 F.Supp.2d 385 (S.D.N.Y. 2003).

SECTION 5.   OVER–THE–COUNTER DERIVATIVES

Banks may play their traditional role as a financial intermediary in derivatives. Either directly or through a subsidiary, a bank may discern and match customer hedging needs from financial risks. Acting as a counter-party or intermediary, banks sold derivative interests that were tailored to the particular needs of customers. This proved to be a highly lucrative business and broker-dealers and investment banks rushed to form their own subsidiaries to compete in this business. Those subsidiaries had to be highly capitalized and have a AAA credit rating (they are sometimes called AAA subs) in order to remove counter-party risk concerns. After Dodd–Frank, banks must push-out derivatives activities to an affiliated nonbank entity unless they are OTC swaps based on rates or reference assets that are permissible for investment by a national bank under 12 U.S.C. § 24(7). Dodd–Frank Act, § 716.

PROCTER & GAMBLE CO. v. BANKERS TRUST CO.

United States District Court, Southern District of Ohio, 1996.
925 F.Supp. 1270.

Feikens, District Judge.

Plaintiff, The Procter & Gamble Company ("P&G"), is a publicly traded Ohio corporation. Defendant, Bankers Trust Company ("BT"), is a wholly-owned subsidiary of Bankers Trust New York Corporation ("BTNY"). BTNY is a state-chartered banking company. BT trades currencies, securities, commodities and derivatives. Defendant BT Securities, also a wholly-owned subsidiary of BTNY, is a registered broker-dealer. The defendants are referred to collectively as "BT" in this opinion. * * *

Financial engineering, in the last decade, began to take on new forms. A current dominant form is a structure known as a derivatives transaction. It is "a bilateral contract or payments exchange agreement whose value derives ... from the value of an underlying asset or underlying reference rate or index." Global Derivatives Study Group of the Group of Thirty, Derivatives: Practices and Principles 28 (1993). Derivatives transactions may be based on the value of foreign currency, U.S. Treasury bonds, stock indexes, or interest rates. The values of these underlying financial instruments are determined by market forces, such as movements in interest rates. Within the broad panoply of derivatives transactions are numerous innovative financial instruments whose objectives may include a hedge against market risks, management of assets and liabilities, or lowering of funding costs; derivatives may also be used as speculation for profit. Singher, Regulating Derivatives: Does Transnational Regulatory Cooperation Offer a Viable Alternative to Congressional Action? 18 Fordham Int'l. Law J. 1405–06 (1995).

This case involves two interest rate swap agreements. A swap is an agreement between two parties ("counterparties") to exchange cash flows over a period of time. Generally, the purpose of an interest rate swap is to protect a party from interest rate fluctuations. The simplest form of swap, a "plain vanilla" interest-rate swap, involves one counterparty paying a fixed rate of interest, while the other counterparty assumes a floating interest rate based on the amount of the principal of the underlying debt. This is called the "notional" amount of the swap, and this amount does not change hands; only the interest payments are exchanged.

In more complex interest rate swaps, such as those involved in this case, the floating rate may derive its value from any number of different securities, rates or indexes. In each instance, however, the counterparty with the floating rate obligation enters into a transaction whose precise value is unknown and is based upon activities in the market over which the counterparty has no control. How the swap plays out depends on how market factors change. * * *

During the fall of 1993, the parties began discussing the terms of an interest rate swap which was to be customized for P&G. After negotiations, the parties agreed to a swap transaction on November 2, 1993, which is referred to as the 5s/30s swap; the written Confirmation is dated November 4, 1993.

In the 5s/30s swap transaction, BT agreed to pay P&G a fixed rate of interest of 5.30% for five years on a notional amount of $200 million. P&G agreed to pay BT a floating interest rate. For the first six months, that floating rate was the prevailing commercial paper ("CP") interest rate minus 75 basis points (0.75%). For the remaining four-and-a-half years, P&G was to make floating interest rate payments of CP minus 75 basis points plus a spread.

In late January 1994, P&G and BT negotiated a second swap, known as the "DM swap", based on the value of the German Deutschemark. The Confirmation for this swap is dated February 14, 1994. For the first year, BT was to pay P&G a floating interest rate plus 233 basis points. P&G was to pay the same floating rate plus 133 basis points; P&G thus received a 1% premium for the first year, the effective dates being January 16, 1994 through January 16, 1995. On January 16, 1995, P&G was to add a spread to its payments to BT if the four-year DM swap rate ever traded below 4.05% or above 6.01% at any time between January 16, 1994, and January 16, 1995. If the DM swap rate stayed within that band of interest rates, the spread was zero. * * *

P&G unwound both of these swaps before their spread set dates, as interest rates in both the United States and Germany took a significant turn upward, thus putting P&G in a negative position vis-a-vis its counterparty BT. BT now claims that it is owed over $200 million on the two swaps, while P&G claims the swaps were fraudulently induced and fraudulently executed, and seeks a declaratory verdict that it owes nothing. * * *

Economic reality is the guide for determining whether these swaps transactions that do not squarely fit within the statutory definition are, nevertheless, securities. Reves [v. Ersnst & Young,] 494 U.S. at 62.[13]

---

13. [eds.] As the court explained:

In *Reves*, the Supreme Court set out a four-part "family resemblance" test for identifying notes that should be deemed securities. Those factors are: 1) the motivations of the buyer and seller in entering into the transaction (investment for profit or to raise capital versus commercial); 2) a sufficiently broad plan of distribution of the instrument (common trading for speculation or investment); 3) the reasonable expectations of the investing public; and 4) whether some factor, such as the existence of another regulatory scheme, significantly reduces the risk of the

Balancing all the *Reves* factors, I conclude that the 5s/30s and DM swaps are not notes for purposes of the Securities Acts. * * *

An option is the right to buy or sell, for a limited time, a particular good at a specified price.

Five-year notes and thirty-year Treasury bonds are securities; therefore, P & G contends that the 5s/30s swap is an option on securities. It argues that because the 5s/30s swap spread was based on the value of these securities, it falls within the statutory definition: "any put, call, straddle, option or privilege on any security, group or index of securities (including any interest therein or based on the value thereof)." It describes the 5s/30s swap as "a single security which can be decomposed into a plain vanilla swap with an embedded put option. The option is a put on the 30–year bond price with an uncertain strike price that depends on the level of the 5–year yield at the end of six months."

BT contends that the 5s/30s swap is not an option because no one had the right to take possession of the underlying securities. BT argues that although both swaps contained terms that functioned as options, they were not options because they did not give either party the right to sell or buy anything. According to BT, the only "option-like" feature was the spread calculation that each swap contained; that any resemblance the spread calculations had to options on securities does not extend to the underlying swaps themselves, which had no option-like characteristics. I agree that the 5s/30s swap was not an option on a security; there was no right to take possession of any security.

The definition of a "security" in the 1933 and 1934 Acts includes the parenthetical phrase "(including any interest therein or based on the value thereof)," which could lead to a reading of the statute to mean that an option based on the value of a security is a security. Legislative history, however, makes it clear that that reading was not intended. The U.S. House of Representatives Report ("House Report") on the 1982 amendments that added this parenthetical phrase provides that the definition of "security" includes an option on "(i) any security, (ii) any certificate of deposit, (iii) any group or index of securities (including any interest therein or based on the value thereof), and (iv) when traded on a national securities exchange, foreign currency." H.R. Rep. No. 626, 97th Cong., 2d Sess., pt. 2, at 4 (1982).

Thus, even though the statute jumbles these definitions together, it is clear from the House Report that the parenthetical phrase "(... based on the value thereof)" was intended only to modify the immediately preceding clause—"group or index of securities"—and not the words "any option" or "any security."

Two Orders by the Security and Exchange Commission must be considered. These rulings involve transactions between BT and Gibson Greetings, Inc. in swaps that have some similarities to the 5s/30s swap. In

---

instrument, thereby rendering application of the securities laws unnecessary. 925 F.Supp. at 1278.

re BT Securities Corp., Release Nos. 33–7124, 34–35136 (Dec. 22, 1994), and In the Matter of Mitchell A. Vazquez, Release Nos. 33–7269, 34–36909 (Feb. 29, 1996). In these cases, the SEC ruled that a "Treasury–Linked Swap" between BT and Gibson Greetings, Inc. was a security within the meaning of the federal securities laws. The SEC stated: "While called a swap, the Treasury–Linked Swap was in actuality a cash-settled put option that was written by Gibson and based initially on the 'spread' between the price of the 7.625% 30–year U.S. Treasury maturity maturing on November 15, 2022 and the arithmetic average of the bid and offered yields of the most recently auctioned obligation of a two-year Treasury note."

These SEC Orders were made pursuant to Offers of Settlement made by BT Securities and Vazquez. In both Orders, the SEC acknowledged that its findings were solely for the purpose of effectuating the respondents' Offers of Settlement and that its findings are not binding on any other person or entity named as a defendant or respondent in any other proceeding. They are not binding in this case, in part because of the differences between the transactions; nor do they have collateral estoppel effect. See also SEC v. Sloan, 436 U.S. 103, 118 (1978) (citations omitted) (The "courts are the final authorities on the issues of statutory construction and are not obliged to stand aside and rubber-stamp their affirmance of administrative decisions that they deem inconsistent with a statutory mandate or that frustrate the congressional policy underlying a statute.").

Even though both the Gibson Greetings, Inc. swap and the P&G 5s/30s swap derived their values from securities (Treasury notes), they were not options. While these swaps included option-like features, there is a missing essential element of an option. These swaps were exchanges of interest payments; they did not give either counterparty the right to exercise an option or to take possession of any security. Neither party could choose whether or not to exercise an option; the stream of interest payments under the swap was mandatory. Consequently, I conclude that the 5s/30s swap is not an option on a security or an option based on the value of a security. * * *

The Commodity Exchange Act ("CEA") includes in its definition of a commodity "all services, rights, and interests in which contracts for future delivery are presently or in the future dealt in." 7 U.S.C. § 1a(3). BT asserts that the swaps are not futures contracts; P&G claims that they are.

Under the CEA, The Commodity Futures Trading Commission has exclusive jurisdiction over "accounts, agreements ... and transactions involving contracts of sale of a commodity for future delivery traded or executed on a contract market ... or any other board of trade, exchange, or market, and transactions [in standardized contracts for certain commodities]." As of January 19, 1996, the CFTC had "not taken a position on whether swap agreements are futures contracts." Letter from Mary L. Schapiro, Chair of U.S. Commodity Futures Trading Commission to Congressmen Roberts and Bliley, p.4 (Jan. 19, 1996). This opinion does not decide that issue because the 5s/30s and DM swaps are within the Swaps Exemption to the CEA and because P & G has not stated a claim under § 4b, § 4o, or 17 C.F.R. § 32.9, as discussed below.

Even if the 5s/30s and DM swaps are defined as commodities, swap agreements are exempt from all but the antifraud provisions of the CEA under the CFTC Swap Exemption. Title V of the Futures Trading Practices Act of 1992 granted the CFTC the authority to exempt certain swaps transactions from CEA coverage. 7 U.S.C. § 6(c)(5).

In response to this directive, on January 22, 1993, the CFTC clarified its July 1989 safe-harbor policy regarding swap transactions[14] in order to "promote domestic and international market stability, reduce market and liquidity risks in financial markets, including those markets (such as futures exchanges) linked to the swap market, and eliminate a potential source of systemic risk. To the extent that swap agreements are regarded as subject to the provisions of the Act, the rules provide that swap agreements which meet the terms and conditions [of the rules] are exempt from all provisions of the Act, except section 2(a)(1)(B)." Exemption for Certain Swap Agreements, 58 Fed. Reg. 5587, 5588 (Jan. 22, 1993). * * *

The four criteria for exemption are: 1) The swap must be entered into solely between "eligible swap participants;" 2) the swap may not be part of a fungible class of agreements standardized as their material economic terms; 3) counterparty creditworthiness is a material consideration of the parties in entering into the swap agreement; and 4) the swap is not entered into and is not traded on or through an exchange market. 17 C.F.R. § 35.2 (1993).

The 5s/30s and DM swaps meet these criteria. * * *

[While the antifraud provisions may apply to exempt transactions, the court found no claims for P&G.]

P&G contends that a fiduciary relationship existed between it and BT. It argues that it agreed to the swap transactions because of a long relationship it had with BT and the trust that it had in BT, plus the assurance that BT would take on the responsibility of monitoring the transactions and that BT would look out for its interests.

P&G points to its trust in BT in that it divulged confidential corporate information to BT. By entering into complex swaps transactions with BT, which represented itself as experts in such transactions, P&G relied on that expertise and BT statements that it would tailor the swaps to fit P&G's needs. Even accepting these contentions as true, these contentions fail. New York case law is clear.

---

14. [n.5] The CFTC identified those swap transactions that would not be regulated as futures or commodity options transactions under the CEA to include those that had 1) individually-tailored terms; 2) an absence of exchange-style offset; 3) an absence of a clearing organization or margin system; 4) limited distribution with the transaction undertaken in conjunction with the parties' lines of business, thus precluding public participation; and 5) a prohibition against marketing to the public. Policy Statement Concerning Swap Transactions, 54 Fed. Reg. 30,694 (July 21, 1989).

In Beneficial Commercial Corp. v. Murray Glick Datsun, Inc., 601 F. Supp. 770, 772 (S.D. N.Y. 1985) that law is summarized with case citations as follows:

> New York law is clear that a fiduciary relationship exists from the assumption of control and responsibility and is founded upon trust reposed by one party in the integrity and fidelity of another. No fiduciary relationship exists . . . [where] the two parties were acting and contracting at arm's length. Moreover, courts have rejected the proposition that a fiduciary relationship can arise between parties to a business relationship.[15]

P&G and BT were in a business relationship. They were counterparties. Even though, as I point out hereafter, BT had superior knowledge in the swaps transactions, that does not convert their business relationship into one in which fiduciary duties are imposed. Thus, I grant summary judgment on Count IV in favor of BT.

This does not mean, however, that there are *no* duties and obligations in their swaps transactions.

Plaintiff alleges that in the negotiation of the two swaps and in their execution, defendants failed to disclose vital information and made material misrepresentations to it. For these reasons plaintiff has refused to make any payments required by the swaps transactions to defendants. Plaintiff requests that a jury verdict should declare that it owes nothing to defendants. Put another way, the damage which plaintiff claims is the amount of money it would have to pay to defendants if the jury verdict is against its position. * * *

I turn to the statute law of New York. The Uniform Commercial Code, as part of New York statute law, particularly Section 1–203, states: "Every contract or duty written in this Act imposes an obligation of good faith in its performance or enforcement." New York has also adopted the principles in the Restatement (Second) Contracts, § 205, that every contract imposes upon each party a duty of good faith and fair dealing in its performance and enforcement. Id.

New York case law establishes an implied contractual duty to disclose in business negotiations. Such a duty may arise where 1) a party has superior knowledge of certain information; 2) that information is not readily available to the other party; and 3) the first party knows that the second party is acting on the basis of mistaken knowledge. Banque Arabe et Internationale D'Investissement v. Maryland National Bank, 57 F.3d 146 (2d Cir. 1995). In that case, the U.S. Court of Appeals for the Second Circuit refers to New York cases which establish that implied duty. * * *

Thus, I conclude that defendants had a duty to disclose material information to plaintiff both before the parties entered into the swap

---

15. [eds.] Compare Societe Natonale D'Exploitation Industrielle Des Tabacs et Allumettes, 674 N.Y.S.2d 648 (1st Dept. App. 1998) (rejecting the *Banker's Trust* opinion that a confidential relationship cannot arise between parties to a business relationship).

transactions and in their performance, and also a duty to deal fairly and in good faith during the performance of the swap transactions. I confine these conclusions to the parameters outlined in this opinion.

One final point must be made. No matter how plaintiff proceeds to prove its case, under New York law the burden of proving fraud requires clear and convincing evidence, and not mere preponderance. See Almap Holdings v. Bank Leumi Trust Co. of N.Y., 601 N.Y.S.2d 319 (N.Y. App.Div. 1993), leave to appeal denied, 634 N.E.2d 979 (Ct. App. 1994). This evidentiary standard demands "a high order of proof" (George Backer Mgmt. Corp. v. Acme Quilting Co., 385 N.E.2d 1062 (1978)) and forbids the awarding of relief " 'whenever the evidence is loose, equivocal or contradictory.' " * * *

For another case dealing with the derivatives activities of Bankers Trust, see In the Matter of BT Securities Corp., [1994–95 Transfer Binder] Fed. Sec. L. Rep. (CCH) ¶ 85,477 (1994).

Numerous other institutions suffered losses from over-the-counter derivative transactions when interest rates experienced directional changes. Banking regulators responded with a requirement that banks assure that the derivative transactions recommended to customers be appropriate for those institutions.[16] The NASD adopted a similar requirement for broker-dealers dealing in derivatives.[17] This regulation has been criticized as unnecessary since institutions can protect themselves.[18]

The CFTC had for some time been concerned with the proliferation of over-the-counter derivative instruments. It adopted a regulation that prohibited some such "hybrid" instruments where options or futures components outweighed other elements. 17 C.F.R. § 34.1 et seq. This regulation did not apply to swaps and did little to slow the growth of other derivatives. The SEC also grew concerned because the broker-dealers it regulated were forming unregulated triple A subsidiaries to conduct derivatives business. The SEC was concerned that the operations of those affiliates could endanger the customers of the regulated broker-dealer in the event of a failure. The SEC, therefore, adopted a regulation that would allow those subsidiaries to register as "broker-dealer Lites," which meant that they would be subject to only minimal regulation. 17 C.F.R. § 240.3b–13. Only one firm chose to seek such regulation. Nevertheless, the CFTC viewed this regulation as an affront to its jurisdiction and began considering whether to promulgate its own regulation. The CFTC's action

---

16. See Office of the Comptroller of the Currency, Questions and Answers for Banking Circular 277, OCC Bull. 94–31 (May 10, 1994).

17. See Jerry W. Markham, Commodities Regulation: Fraud Manipulation and Other Claims § 27.06 (West Group 2000).

18. Jerry W. Markham, Protecting the Institutional Investor—Jungle Predator or Shorn Lamb? 12 Yale J. on Reg. 345 (1995).

was opposed by the SEC, the Treasury, the Fed, and ultimately by Congress.

The CFTC then did an about-face and sought to deregulate almost all aspects of derivatives transactions, including those on an exchange or electronic communications network, when only institutions are involved. Congress concurred in that effort, subsequently deregulating much of the trading in futures and derivatives by institutions on markets that do not invite public participation.[19] Congress sought the broadest possible exclusion from CFTC jurisdiction for derivative transactions entered into by banks and determined by the OCC to be bank products.

QUESTIONS AND NOTES

1. Would you like to have a derivative contract that would protect the value of your retirement portfolio in the event of a market downturn after you retire? How could such a contract be structured? What would be the cost for such protection?

2. In May 2005, then-Fed Chairman Alan Greenspan expressed concern over the concentration of risk by a few dealers in interest rate derivatives. Alan Greenspan, Risk Transfer and Financial Stability, Remarks at the Federal Reserve Bank of Chicago's Forty-first Annual Conference on Bank Structure (May 5, 2005). Nevertheless, he also noted that that "the growing array of derivatives and the related application of more-sophisticated methods for measuring and managing risks had been key factors underlying the remarkable resilience of the banking system, which had recently shrugged off severe shocks to the economy and the financial system." Id.

Greenspan would regret that remark after the subprime crisis was blamed largely on credit default swaps and the instruments they protected.

SECTION 6. CREDIT DEFAULT SWAPS

A centerpiece of the financial crisis that began in 2007 was the widespread use of credit default swaps (CDS) to protect against defaults on collateralized debt obligations (CDOs), which were the instruments used to securitize subprime mortgages. The following article addresses the concerns raised by these instruments.

JERRY W. MARKHAM
REGULATING CREDIT DEFAULT SWAPS IN
THE WAKE OF THE SUBPRIME CRISIS

A Working Paper Prepared for the International Monetary Fund Seminar on Current Developments in Monetary and Financial Law, Washington, D.C. Dec. 2, 2009.

* * * [A CDS is an agreement by one party to make a series of payments to a counter party, in exchange for a payoff, if a specified credit instrument goes into default] As one court defined these instruments:

---

19. Commodity Futures Modernization Act of 2000, Pub. L. No. 106–554, 114 Stat. 2763.

a common type of credit derivative in which the protection buyer makes a fixed payment to the protection seller in return for a payment that is contingent upon a "credit event"—such as a bankruptcy—occurring to the company that issued the security (the "reference entity") or the security itself (the "reference obligation"). The contingent payment is often made against delivery of a "deliverable obligation"—usually the reference obligation or other security issued by the reference entity—by the protection buyer to the protection seller. This delivery is known as the "physical settlement."[20]

Although CDS were widely used as a form of insurance against a default from that credit instrument, they were also used for speculation on whether a default will occur.[21] It was estimated that eighty percent or more of the giant CDS market was composed of theses "synthetic" speculative CDS. The CDS, in all events, proved to be a popular instrument. Outstanding notional value of the CDS was over $42 trillion in debt at year-end 2007.

CDS were used to enhance the creditworthiness of subprime securitizations. As an April 2008 UBS AG shareholder report noted, "[k]ey to the growth of the CDO structuring business was the development of the credit default swap ('CDS').... "[22] With the credit enhancement of a CDS, the credit rating agencies often gave the Super Seniors their highest triple-A rating. This was the same credit rating enjoyed by the federal government, which signaled to the world that a default on those Super Senior tranches was highly unlikely. Unfortunately, the rating agencies' risk models for awarding the triple-A rating on CDOs did not take into account the possibility of a major downturn in the real estate market. That flaw was not spotted until the subprime crisis arose.

A risk model developed by David Li did for CDOs what the Black–Scholes model did for options. Seemingly, it allowed a supposed precise mathematical computation of the risks posed by these instruments. That and other Gaussian Copula risk models failed, however, to predict the

---

20. [n. 41] Deutsche Bank AG v. AMBAC Credit Products LLC, 2006 WL 1867497 (S.D.N.Y. 2006). One scholar gave the following description of a credit default swap where: Bank A is trying to hedge its exposure from a $10 million loan to company B "by going to C, a dealer in these swaps, who agrees to pay the $10 million to A if B defaults, in exchange for paying an annual premium to C for the protection. A will want collateral from C to be sure it's good for the debt." L. Gordon Crovitz, When Even Good News Worsens a Panic, Wall St. J., Nov. 24, 2008, at A17.

21. [n. 42] An ABX Index was created to track the value of mortgaged-backed securities based on credit default swaps.

The ABX Index is a series of credit-default swaps based on 20 bonds that consist of subprime mortgages. ABX contracts are commonly used by investors to speculate on or to hedge against the risk that the underling mortgage securities are not repaid as expected. The ABX swaps offer protection if the securities are not repaid as expected, in return for regular insurance-like premiums. A decline in the ABX Index signifies investor sentiment that subprime mortgage holders will suffer increased financial losses from those investments. Likewise, an increase in the ABX Index signifies investor sentiment looking for subprime mortgage holdings to perform better as investments.

Housing Derivatives: ABX Index, available at http://www.housingderivatives.typepad.com/hous ing_ Derivatives/abx_index/. The CBOE also began trading credit default options in 2007 that were automatically exercised upon the occurrence of specified credit events.

22. [n. 46] See UBS AG, Shareholder Report on UBS's Write–Downs § 4.22 (2008).

massive losses sustained by commercial banks in the United States, and Europe, from their exposures to subprime CDOs.[23] Fail they did, but there was no cabal using a secret formula to deceive investors. Moody's actually published its CDO risk assessment model (CDOROM), which became the industry standard, on the Internet in 2004. The whole world was free to discover its flaws but, except for a few naysayers, the model went pretty much unchallenged.

The mathematical model used to rate CDOs proved to be badly flawed. Critics charged that these models were defective because they relied on historical prices generated by a rising market. That Pollyanna approach overlooked the possibility of a hundred-year, "perfect" storm, which arrived in the form of the subprime crisis. The possibility of such an unusual event was called a "fat tail" or "outlier." They were also called "black swans," as a metaphor for the widely held belief that there was no such thing as a black swan, until explorers reached Australia and found just such a bird.[24] The probability of an outlier was considered so small that they were ignored by the credit assessors. * * *

The high credit ratings given to the Super Senior tranches posed another problem. These securities were hard to market due to their lower interest rates, which was a function of their triple-A rating. That problem was solved after bank regulators in the United States allowed favorable capital treatment of Super Seniors on bank balance sheets, provided that the Super Senior had a triple-A credit rating. This regulatory blessing removed any residual concerns on the part of the banks of undue risk from Super–Seniors and created a demand for the Super Seniors by banks here and abroad. As a result, a large portion of the Super Senior tranches were held on the books of many major investment banks such as Citigroup, Merrill Lynch, UBS AG and Lehman Brothers. The twenty-five largest banks were also holding $13 trillion in CDS notionals on their books in March 2008.

A credit down grade at the American International Group, Inc. (AIG) in September 2008 raised concerns that large losses would be experienced in the financial community if AIG defaulted on its $500 billion CDS portfolio. This spurred the federal government to mount a $183 billion rescue of that firm. AIG entered the CDS market in a big way in 2005 through its division called AIG Financial Products (AIGFP), which had been founded by a group of traders from Drexel Burnham Lambert, the failed junk bond broker of Michael Milken fame. AIGFP's risk model predicted that, based on historic default rates, the economy would have to fall into depression before AIG would experience losses from its CDS exposures. AIGFP assured investors in August 2007 that "it is hard for us, without being flippant, to even see a scenario within any kind of realm of reason that would see us losing $1 in any of those transactions."

---

23.   [n. 47] These risk models were created by high IQ quants, but as Warren Buffett warned, "beware of Geeks . . . bearing models."

24.   [n. 50] See Nassim Nicholas Taleb, The Black Swan: The Impact of the Highly Improbable (2007).

AIG's share price dropped sharply after it reported a large 2007 fourth quarter loss that was accompanied by a $5.29 billion write-down of its mortgage related business, including a write-down of its credit CDS business by $4.88 billion. AIG reported a loss of $7.81 billion in the first quarter of 2008, largely due to a write down of $11 billion related to losses from Super Senior CDS written by the AIG Financial Products Corp. (AIGFP). Another $3.6 billion was written off by AIG for those instruments in the second quarter of 2008, adding to the $5.36 billion loss by AIG in that quarter. AIG reported a loss in the third quarter of $24.47 billion, including losses of $7.05 billion in AIGFP.

Fed chairman Ben Bernanke turned AIG and the CDS market into a pariah when he declared in congressional testimony that nothing had made him more angry than the AIG failure, which he attributed to AIG's exploitation of "a huge gap in the regulatory system." He asserted that AIGFP was nothing more than a hedge fund attached to large and stable insurance company that "made huge numbers of irresponsible bets, [and] took huge losses. There was no regulatory oversight because there was a gap in the system." Bernanke stated that the government was forced to expend billions of dollars to save AIG because its failure would have been "disastrous for the economy."

Actually, it appears that AIG's failure was the result of credit downgrades, prompted by AIG's write-downs of its CDS positions. Those write-downs were caused by a lack of a market that could accurately price the underlying Super Seniors. The subsequent credit downgrades caused large collateral calls that AIG did not have the liquidity to meet.

AIG's CEO, Martin Sullivan blamed mark-to-market accounting requirements for the losses sustained by AIGFP. Sullivan complained that AIG was required to markdown its inventories even though it had no intention of selling them. He may have had a point, as this was a common complaint in the industry. Fair value pricing was resulting in a procyclical progression of write-downs that bore no relation to actual value.
* * *

The CFTC issued a policy statement in 1989 exempting swaps among institutions from regulation. There was, however, some uncertainty over whether the CFTC had the power to adopt such an exemption. To provide more certainty, the Futures Trading Practices Act of 1992 authorized the CFTC to exempt swaps, which it did. The swaps market then grew rapidly. Thereafter, Congress directed the Presidential Working Group on Financial Markets to conduct a study of the OTC derivatives market and make recommendations on whether it should be regulated. That report was issued in 1999 and was followed by the enactment of the Commodity Futures Modernization Act of 2000 (CFMA). The CFMA exempted OTC instruments from regulation where the parties to the transactions were sophisticated counterparties. The exempted institutions included banks, investment bankers, pension funds, large businesses, and high net worth individuals.

The CFMA created an exemption and exclusions from most regulation for electronic trading facilities used by institutional traders. These facilities were called "exempt commercial markets" (ECMs). The ECM exclusion was often referred to as the "Enron loophole." This was because it was inserted into the CFMA at the last minute through the lobbying efforts of the Enron Corp., which was seeking to protect its popular electronic trading platform, EnronOnline, from regulation. Because of concerns over the explosion of energy prices in 2008, Congress closed the Enron loophole through amendments included in the CFTC Reauthorization Act of 2008.

The CDS market was unregulated before the subprime crisis, but the International Swaps and Derivatives Association, the industry trade group, provided a self-regulating structure for the business. Governmental intervention was occasionally required. The failure in 1998 of Long Term Capital Management LTCM, a large hedge fund that had a large swaps book, raised systemic concerns. This led the Fed Reserve Bank in New York to arrange a rescue by a group of investment bankers. The Fed also pumped large amounts of funds into the money market during this period of uncertainty, which followed economic turmoil abroad during the so-called Asian Flu crisis. It was thought the Fed was signaling with that action that it would flood the market with liquidity whenever a large institution was about to fail, a monetary policy referred to as the "Greenspan put."

Following the failure of LTCM, twelve large banks formed the Counterparty Risk Management Policy Group (CRMPG) to assess whether improvements were needed in the swaps market. CRMPG was chaired by E. Gerald Corrigan, a managing director at Goldman Sachs and former president of the New York Fed. CRMPG issued a report in June 1999 that considered counterparty credit assessment; risk management; measurement and reporting; market practices and conventions; and regulatory reporting for swaps. It recommended improvements in internal firm policies and procedures for documentation; more standardization in market practices and conventions; improved ability to measure aggregate counterparty credit exposure and use of collateral as a risk mitigant; and use of stress tests to evaluate potential exposures.

The CRMPG met again in 2005 with an expanded membership that included hedge funds and other money managers as well as the large banks. The CRMPG issued a report on July 27, 2005 that was amazingly prescient in predicting the precipitating factors and effects of a financial shock such as was experienced during the subprime crisis.[25] The CRMPG described its:

> goal of identifying additional measures to be taken by the financial community to "promote the efficiency, effectiveness and stability of the global financial system." While Policy Group members recognized

---

25. [n. 123] See The Report of the CRMPG II, Toward Greater Financial Stability: A Private Sector Perspective (2005), available at http://www.crmpolicygroup.org/crmpg2/.

that financial disturbances occur from time to time and do not generally lead to widespread systemic risk, they noted that "rare but potentially virulent financial shocks may occur with little, if any, warning." Such financial shocks can lead to sudden declines in asset prices and concerns about counterparty creditworthiness, position liquidations, and concerns about the adequacy of collateral, in turn causing liquidity to disappear as investors sell off positions.[26]

The swap market also encountered some concerns with its settlement practices. Because of the massive growth in trading volume in CDS there were significant backlogs in matching confirmations, which in many instances were done manually. The CRMPG recommended automating and integrating the transaction process through "straight through processing." Another issue concerning the CDS market were the occurrence of disputes over whether trigger events had occurred that would require the credit protection seller to either pay up or provide additional collateral. To resolve such issues, ISDA developed a protocol that required participants to submit their dispute to a determination committee of investors and swap dealers. AIG refused to sign the protocol, preferring to negotiate its wind-downs bilaterally with each counterparty. This immensely complicated its problems when it was taken over by the federal government.

The failure of Lehman Brothers during the height of the subprime crisis raised concerns that CDS written on its debt obligations could generate claims of up to $400 billion. However, that concern quickly dissipated after the obligations were netted, leaving an exposure of a more modest $5.2 billion. An auction was held to determine the value of Lehman's bonds in bankruptcy, and they were valued at about $.08 on the dollar, which meant that the paying party on these credit default obligations would have to pay $.92 on the dollar. Those payments had to be made within two weeks. Those claims were settled quickly and in an orderly fashion. Similarly, outstanding CDS on bankrupt General Motors' debt totaling $35 billion netted out to only $2.2 billion in exposure.

A report from the senior financial supervisors of the G–7 nations concluded that the credit default swap market functioned well in the second half of 2008, despite "an unprecedented 12 credit events"—or actions that obliged the sellers of credit protection to make payments to those who had bought protection. Nevertheless, the AIG failure, which resulted in a U.S. Government bailout of over $180 billion, placed political pressure worldwide for regulation of the CDS market. Initially, that effort was directed at requiring CDS to be listed on a central clearinghouse that would provide transparency and credit protection. * * *

A jurisdictional fight broke out among the SEC, CFTC and New York Federal Reserve Bank over who would approve and regulate such clearing-

---

26. [n. 124] See [Zdenka Seiner] Griswold, [Counterparty Risk Management Policy Group II: OTC Documentation Practices in a Changing Risk Environment, at http://files.ali-aba.org/thumbs/data/storage/skoobesruoc/pdf/CL047–ch08_thumb.pdf].

houses. These regulators tried to resolve this dispute through a memorandum of understanding that promised enhanced cooperation and information sharing among the Federal Reserve Board, the SEC and the CFTC, upon the development of such a facility. This truce did not last long, and the turf war continued. The SEC claimed that credit default swaps were securities subject to its jurisdiction. Using that regulatory handle, the SEC proposed to exempt from most of its regulation CDS clearinghouses that complied with its standards, including the exclusion of non-eligible swap participants.

In the meantime, the effort to create an OTC clearinghouse turned into a competition among the larger exchanges seeking to grab market share. ICE, the CME, which had a joint venture with the Citadel Investor Group, the Clearing Corporation, which was formerly the clearing house for the Chicago Board of Trade, Eurex Clearing; and NYSE Euronext/Liffe/LCH Clearnet, were all separately rushing to create CDS clearinghouses. * * *

———————

The Dodd–Frank Act imposed regulation over swaps. In general, the SEC and CFTC must consult with the federal banking regulators in developing regulations relating to swaps. Dodd–Frank Act, § 712. Banks may not act as a swaps entity for credit default swaps unless the "swaps or security-based swaps are cleared by a derivatives clearing organization ... or a clearing agency ... that is registered, or exempt from registration, as a derivatives clearing organization under the Commodities Exchange Act or as a clearing agency under the Securities Exchange Act." Dodd–Frank Act, § 716. The SEC was given jurisdiction over security based swaps and the CFTC was given jurisdiction over other swaps. If either agency believes that a final rule of the other conflicts with the agency's rulemaking authority as specified in Dodd–Frank, a petition for review may be filed in the D.C. Circuit Court of Appeals. Joint regulatory authority is given to both agencies for "mixed" swaps that have elements of both securities and commodities. Any disputes between the SEC and the CFTC regarding this joint rulemaking are to be resolved by the FSOC. Dodd–Frank Act, § 712. Most swaps will now be exchange traded and cleared through a regulated central counterparty. In order to prevent any future bailouts like the one at AIG, federal assistance to any swap related transaction or entity is prohibited. As previously discussed, insured depositories are allowed to engage in a number of swaps activities such as hedging and acting as a credit default swaps dealer if the swaps are centrally cleared. Dodd–Frank Act, § 716.

The Dodd–Frank Act allows regulators to impose capital and margin requirements on swap dealers and major swap participants, but not end users. Dodd–Frank Act, §§ 731 & 764. It establishes a code of conduct for all registered swap dealers and major swap participants when advising a swap entity. Id.

Swaps may not be regulated as insurance under state law, Dodd–Frank Act, § 722, and the Treasury Secretary is authorized to exempt foreign exchange swaps from the federal regulation imposed on other swaps, Dodd–Frank Act, § 721.

QUESTIONS AND NOTES

1. Concerns over CDS exposures were not limited to the United States. Banks in the European Union (EU) were severely damaged by the AAA rated "Super–Senior" subprime CDOs. By August 2008, write-offs at European banks included $44.2 billion at UBS; IKB Deutsche, $12.6 billion; Royal Bank of Scotland, $14.9 billion; Credit Suisse, $10.5 billion; Credit Agricole, $8 billion; Societe Generale, $6.8 billion; Bayerische Landesbank, $6.4 billion; ING Groep, $5.8 billion; Lloyds TSB, $5 billion; Dresdner, $4.1 billion; and BNP Paribas, $4 billion.

2. Charlie McCreevy, the European Commissioner in charge of the Internal Market and Services, declared in October 2008 that an immediate goal of the Commission was to require central clearing of CDS. The Commission sought the prompt creation of a central registry for such instruments that would record credit derivative instruments after trades have been confirmed. This would create a "golden" copy of those transactions. That goal was accomplished on July 31, 2009, when CDS on European reference entities began clearing through central counterparties regulated in the EU.

SECTION 7. ACCOUNTING FOR DERIVATIVES

Derivative transactions were not reported on a bank's balance sheet. They were among the items referred to as "off balance sheet" transactions. Derivative transactions can help to reduce the bank's underlying risk (or increase it if not being used properly). Therefore, it is important that derivative transactions be reported in some fashion to a bank's shareholders.

BASEL COMMITTEE ON BANKING SUPERVISION RECOMMENDATIONS FOR PUBLIC DISCLOSURE OF TRADING AND DERIVATIVES ACTIVITIES OF BANKS AND SECURITIES FIRMS

<www.bis.org/publ/bcbs60.htm>.
October 1999.

The US Financial Accounting Standard Board (FASB) Statement of Financial Accounting Standards No. 133 entitled Accounting for Derivative Instruments and Hedging Activities, effective 15 June 2000, establishes accounting and disclosure standards for derivative instruments and for hedging activities. In summary, it requires that an entity recognize all derivatives as either assets or liabilities and measure them at fair value. The entity must disclose its objectives for holding or issuing derivatives and indicate the entity's risk management policies, including a description of the items or transactions for which risks are hedged. For derivative instruments not designated as hedging instruments, the description should indicate the purpose of the derivatives. The Statement specifies the accounting treatment based on the designated use of the derivative and requires disclosure of the resulting effects.

MARK O. HENRY
NOTE, THE IMPACT OF STATEMENT OF
FINANCIAL ACCOUNTING STANDARDS 133
ON THE BANKING INDUSTRY

3 N.C. Banking Inst. 291 (1999).

On June 16, 1998, the Financial Accounting Standards Board (FASB) issued Statement of Financial Accounting Standards (SFAS) 133. This long awaited statement contains major changes to the accounting rules for trillions of dollars worth of derivative transactions. The accounting requirements contained in this standard will have a tremendous effect on the banking industry because financial institutions are generally the largest users and providers of derivatives and because of the unique accounting problems that result from managing the various risks inherent in the banking business. * * *

In order to understand fully the impact SFAS 133 will have on the use of and accounting for derivatives, it is helpful to examine how derivatives are frequently used. There are three main uses of derivatives today: speculation and arbitrage, reduction of funding costs, and risk management. For the most part, only dealers and traders use derivatives for speculation or arbitrage, however financial institutions may choose to use derivatives to speculate on the direction of various markets. When an institution uses derivatives for speculation, it is normally attempting to predict which way interest rates, commodity prices, equity prices or foreign exchange rates will move. On the other hand, arbitrage involves using derivatives to take two offsetting positions in order to take advantage of inefficient pricing in the market.

Derivatives are also often used to reduce funding costs. It has been estimated that over half of all new financings utilize derivatives. The most common use for derivative financial instruments in structured financings involves a borrower issuing either fixed or floating rate debt and then simultaneously entering into an interest rate swap. In this manner, a company can convert its fixed rate debt into a variable rate obligation, or convert a variable rate obligation into a fixed rate obligation. By utilizing derivatives in these transactions, it is possible to take advantage of differences in interest rates for different borrowers, usually due to differences in credit risk, and/or possible cross border tax differences that could not be achieved by just directly issuing debt.

Finally, the most common use for derivatives is to manage (hedge) risk. Financial institutions may use derivatives to manage several different types of risk. First, derivatives, usually options, may be used to protect against securities price risk. Derivatives may also be used to manage interest rate risk or to reduce a firm's exposure to fluctuations in foreign exchange rates or changes in the prices of commodities. Financial institutions also use derivatives to manage risks other than market risk, such as credit, operational, and/or liquidity risk.

Although SFAS 133 is a rather long and detailed statement—FASB Chairman Edmund Jenkins called it "250 pages of scintillating reading"—most of the basic concepts are fairly straightforward. The actual accounting for derivatives under SFAS 133 can be broken down into two general parts: initial recognition of derivatives and subsequent changes in fair value. For initial recognition, SFAS 133 requires all derivatives to be recognized as either assets or liabilities on the balance sheet. Recognition as an asset or liability will depend on the rights or obligations under the specific contracts. The value to be recognized on the balance sheet is the fair value of the financial instrument as determined by using the guidance provided in SFAS 107, "Disclosures About Fair Value of Financial Instruments." Recognition of all derivatives on the balance sheet at fair value represents a significant change from current accounting practices, which do not require certain derivatives such as interest rate swaps to be recognized on the balance sheet at all.

The accounting for subsequent changes in the fair values of derivatives recorded on the balance sheet will depend on the use of each financial instrument. First, an entity must determine if the derivative will be designated as a hedging instrument. If a derivative is not designated as a hedging instrument, then the change in fair value will be recognized in earnings as a gain or loss in the period when the change in value occurred. Financial institutions will use this method for derivatives that are used for speculation and/or arbitrage.

If the derivative is designated as a hedging instrument, there are three ways to account for a change in fair value depending on the specific classification of the hedge. First, a derivative used as a hedging instrument may be classified as a fair value hedge. In a fair value hedge, a derivative financial instrument is used to reduce exposure to changes in the fair value of either a recognized asset or liability. Subsequent changes in fair value of these hedges are recognized as gains or losses in earnings in the period the market value changed. The offsetting gains or losses on the recognized asset or liability being hedged are also recognized in earnings in this period. The effect of this treatment is to recognize in earnings the net gain or loss resulting from the ineffectiveness of the hedge in offsetting changes in fair value of the hedged item.

The second hedge classification is a cash flow hedge. For a derivative to be designated a cash flow hedge, it must be hedging a firm's exposure to variable cash flows from a forecasted transaction. Subsequent changes in fair value resulting from the effective portion of the hedge are initially recognized in other comprehensive income. Other comprehensive income is not a component of earnings, so the gains or losses resulting from changes in fair value of these instruments will initially only impact equity. However, these gains or losses are subsequently reclassed into earnings in the period when the forecasted transaction being hedged affects earnings. Gains or losses from any portion of the hedge deemed ineffective are reported in earnings immediately.

The final classification is a foreign currency hedge of a net investment in a foreign operation. If a derivative financial instrument is hedging this type of exposure, then any gain or loss resulting from a change in the fair value of the derivative is recognized as a component of other comprehensive income as part of the cumulative foreign currency translation adjustment.

* * * Upon adoption of the Standard, all hedging relationships should be designated and appropriately documented. SFAS 133 also requires companies to define the parameters of a "highly effective" hedging strategy in order for derivatives designated as hedges to qualify for hedge accounting. Thereafter, firms must assess the effectiveness of their hedging strategies on at least a quarterly basis. Any derivative financial instruments initially designated as hedges that subsequently fall outside these parameters will no longer qualify for hedge accounting, meaning that changes in fair value will have to be recognized in earnings in the period of change. Although the FASB has not provided official guidance on how to measure the effectiveness of a hedging strategy, it has indicated that the SEC would consider items to be "highly correlated" if the change in value of the hedge is within plus or minus 20% of the offsetting change in value of the hedged item. In adopting a highly effective hedge strategy, it is also permissible to hedge against a group of assets that are fairly consistent or homogeneous.

SFAS 133 will likely have the greatest impact on the banking industry as it generally includes the largest users and providers of derivatives and because of the unique accounting problems that result from managing the various risks inherent in the banking business. * * *

Although the banking industry has raised some valid concerns regarding the impact SFAS 133 will have on its members, a careful examination of the statement will demonstrate that, despite these concerns, the new standard will significantly improve the accounting for derivatives. Specifically, the new standard appropriately recognizes the fair value of derivatives on the balance sheet, represents a fair compromise with respect to the accounting for subsequent changes in the fair values of these financial instruments, and will not necessarily lead to investor uncertainty over volatility or the decline of prudent risk management strategies.

The most fundamental concept of SFAS 133 is that derivatives should be recorded on the balance sheet at fair value. All of the other complexities of the standard, which generally relate to the accounting for subsequent changes in fair value of these instruments, necessarily flow from this basic concept. The current accounting for derivatives does not require many derivatives to be recorded on the balance sheet.

This practice is neither an oversight of the accounting profession, nor the result of a previous decision that derivatives should not be recorded on the balance sheet. Rather, it is the result of the basic accounting model that requires assets and liabilities to be recorded at historical cost. Under this basic model, derivatives are not recorded on the balance sheet because they often involve no up front cash payment, and not because they have inconsequential economic effects. The current practice is simply an improper accounting method because derivatives represent either a contractual obligation to make a net payment or payments in the future, which is clearly a liability, or they represent the contractual right to receive a net payment or payments in the future, which is clearly an asset. Since derivatives often have little or no historical cost, the true economic effects of these instruments are not reflected in the financial statements under the historical cost method of accounting. Thus, the only way to record these assets or liabilities is to use the fair value of the instrument. * * *

FAS 133 was amended and clarified by FAS 137, Accounting for Derivative Instruments and Hedging Activities–Deferral of the Effective Date of FASB Statement No. 133–an amendment of FASB Statement No. 133 (issue Date 6/99); FAS 138, Accounting for Certain Derivative Instruments and Certain Hedging Activities-an amendment of FASB Statement No. 133 (issue Date 6/00); and FAS 149, Amendment of Statement 133 on Derivative Instruments and Hedging Activities (issue Date 4/03). All these statements are available at <www.fasb.org>. In addition, the Derivatives Implementation Group (DIG) was formed to anser questions regarding implementation of FAS 133. By mid–2004, this group had published 167 implementation issue statements.

QUESTIONS AND NOTES

1. A number of losses by large institutions during the early 1990s caused a great deal of concern that those firms were not properly managing their exposure to risks from complicated derivatives instruments. One institution that was destroyed was the 250–year-old Barings bank, which had helped the United States finance the Louisiana Purchase. See Jerry W. Markham, "Confederate Bonds," "General Custer," and the Regulation of Derivative Financial Instruments, 25 Seton Hall L. Rev. 1 (1994) (describing those losses). Industry and government regulators responded with better risk management systems such as value-at-risk programs that sought to measure risk from particular positions by historical analysis. Improved accounting methods and disclosures were also thought necessary in order to allow better shareholder and management monitoring of derivative positions. Even with increased protective measures, one rogue currency trader working for a U.S.

subsidiary of Allied Irish Banks managed to lose $691 million. See Abigail Rayner et al., AIB trader makes claims to investigators over huge loss, Fin. Times, Mar. 6, 2002, at 1. Jerome Kerviel, a low-level trader at the French bank Societe Generale, lost $6.9 billion through his rogue trading, causing a massive sell-off in the markets in January 2008.

2.   Does FAS 133 adequately disclose the risk to shareholders from derivative positions?

3.   Has the effort to make FAS 133 a principle-based statement been successful given that it has resulted in over 800 pages of accounting standards and implementation guidance? Is balancing basic principles with the need for rules to ensure consistent practices possible?

4.   Do you think non-financial institutions should be engaged in risky and complex derivative transactions?

5.   Derivatives were used during the Enron debacle to manipulate that company's balance sheets and those of Dynegy Inc. J.P. Morgan Chase and Citigroup agreed to pay a total of $255 million to settle SEC actions charging those banks with aiding Enron in that effort. The SEC described its action against J.P. Morgan Chase as follows:

> The Securities and Exchange Commission ("Commission") today charged J.P. Morgan Chase & Co. with aiding and abetting Enron Corp.'s securities fraud. The Commission's complaint, filed in U.S. District Court in Houston, alleges that J.P. Morgan Chase aided and abetted Enron's manipulation of its reported financial results through a series of complex structured finance transactions, called "prepays," over a period of several years preceding Enron's bankruptcy. These transactions were used by Enron to report loans from J.P. Morgan Chase as cash from operating activities. The structural complexity of these transactions had no business purpose aside from masking the fact that, in substance, they were loans from J.P. Morgan Chase to Enron. Between December 1997 and September 2001, J.P. Morgan Chase effectively loaned Enron a total of approximately $2.6 billion in the form of seven such transactions. * * *

> Specifically, the complaint alleges that between December 1997 and Enron's demise in 2001, J.P. Morgan Chase and Enron engaged in seven of these prepay transactions in order to disguise loans as commodity trades thus achieving Enron's desired accounting and reporting objectives. As the complaint alleges, the clearest indication that the J.P. Morgan Chase/Enron prepays were disguised loans was their structure. In general, in a prepay transaction (also known as a prepaid forward sale contract) the purchaser pays for a commodity upfront, in full, at the time the contract is made, and the seller agrees to deliver the subject commodity on future dates, often over the course of several years. In effect, the seller bets that the market price of the subject commodity would be lower at the time of delivery than at the time the contract is made. The purchaser bets the opposite way: that the market price of the commodity at the time of delivery will exceed the price it paid at the time of contracting. In a typical prepay transaction, therefore, each side assumes commodity price risk.

According to the complaint, the critical difference in the J.P. Morgan Chase/Enron prepays–and the reason that these transactions were in substance loans–was that they employed a structure that passed the counter-party commodity price risk back to Enron, thus eliminating all commodity risk from the transaction. This was accomplished through a series of simultaneous trades whereby Enron passed the counter-party commodity price risk to a J.P. Morgan Chase-sponsored special purpose vehicle called Mahonia, which passed the risk to J.P. Morgan Chase, which, in turn, passed the risk back to Enron.

As in typical prepays, the complaint alleges, Enron received cash upfront. In contrast to typical prepays, according to the complaint, with all elements of the structure taken together, Enron's future obligations were reduced to the repayment of cash it received from J.P. Morgan Chase with negotiated interest. The interest was calculated with reference to LIBOR. Since all price risk and, in certain transactions, even the obligation to transport a commodity were eliminated, the only risk in the transactions was Chase's risk that Enron would not make its payments when due, i.e., credit risk. In short, the complaint alleges, these seven prepays were in substance loans.

According to the complaint, Mahonia was included in the structure solely to effectuate Enron's accounting and financial reporting objectives. Enron told J.P. Morgan Chase that Enron needed Mahonia in the transactions for Enron's accounting. Mahonia was controlled by Chase and was directed by Chase to participate in the transactions ostensibly as a separate, independent, commodities-trading entity. As the complaint further alleges, in order to facilitate Enron's accounting objectives, J.P. Morgan Chase took various steps to make it appear that Mahonia was an independent third party.

The Commission alleges that J.P. Morgan Chase knew that Enron engaged in prepays to match its so-called mark-to-market earnings (paper earnings based on changes in the market value of certain assets held by Enron) with cash flow from operating activities. By matching mark-to-market earnings with cash flow from operating activities, Enron is alleged to have sought to convince analysts and credit rating agencies that its reported mark-to-market earnings were real, i.e., that the value of the underlying assets would ultimately be converted into cash.

The Commission further alleges that J.P. Morgan Chase also knew that prepays yielded another substantial benefit to Enron: they allowed Enron to hide the true extent of its borrowings from investors and rating agencies because sums borrowed in prepay transactions appeared as "price risk management liabilities" rather than "debt" on Enron's balance sheet. In addition, Enron's obligation to repay those sums was not otherwise disclosed. Significantly, according to the Commission's allegations, J.P. Morgan Chase considered prepays to be unsecured loans to Enron, rather than commodity trading contracts, and based its decisions to participate in these transactions primarily on its assessment of Enron's credit.

SEC v. J.P. Morgan Chase & Co., SEC Litigation Release No. 18252 (S.D. Tex. July 28, 2003) (consent order), available at <www.sec.gov/litigation/litreleases/lr18252.htm>.

The case against Citigroup made similar charges of structuring prepay arrangements for Enron and Dynegy. The Enron prepays at Citigroup were a bit more complex than those at J.P. Morgan Chase and used the capital markets to fund those transactions:

> The structure, called Project Yosemite, accomplished this goal by using proceeds of sales of privately placed notes to fund blind pool trusts that either funded prepay transactions or served as security for Citigroup's funding of prepay transactions. Specifically, Citigroup underwrote and privately placed certain notes with large sophisticated investors. The proceeds of those notes were deposited in trusts that were allowed to make certain permitted investments. These permitted investments could have taken a variety of forms generally consisting of highly rated securities or bank deposits, and certain obligations of Enron. The trusts were set up such that Citigroup made the periodic interest payments on the notes. In turn, Citigroup received the returns on permitted investments.

> Citigroup also entered into credit default swaps with the trusts whereby, in case of an Enron bankruptcy, Citigroup would deliver to the note holders senior unsecured obligations of Enron and Citigroup would receive the trust investments. In the first two structures, the trusts invested in prepay transactions by replacing Citigroup as the source of Delta's funding. In the later variation of this structure, Citigroup funded the prepays and the trusts invested in highly rated bank deposits. In this iteration of the structure, Citigroup's extension of credit to Enron under the prepay arrangement was fully secured with highly rated bank deposits by operation of the credit default swap with the relevant trust. Using the Yosemite structure, Enron and Citigroup raised approximately $2.3 billion in the capital markets, which provided the financing for additional Enron–Citigroup prepay transactions.

In the Matter of Citigroup, Inc., Securities Exchange Act Release of 1934 No. 48230 (S.E.C. July 28, 2003) (consent order), available at <www.sec.gov/litigation/admin/34–48230.htm>. The SEC also charged Citigroup with engaging in other projects for Enron that manipulated its financial statements:

> As Citigroup knew, because it helped structure the transaction, the purpose of Project Nahanni was to generate cash from operating activities by selling Treasury bills ("T-bills") bought with the proceeds of a loan. The transaction took place over approximately five weeks spanning Enron's 1999 fiscal year end. The project was structured as a business partnership between Enron and an "investor" entity arranged by Citigroup to engage in this transaction. The investor entity was capitalized with a $485 million loan from a

Citigroup affiliate and $15 million in equity contributed by a third party. The idea was that the "investor" entity would turn its capitalization into T-bills and contribute those T-bills into a partnership with Enron. The partnership would sell the T-bills (classified by Enron as "merchant investments"), thus generating cash flow from operating activities. Enron would consolidate the partnership's results on its financial statements and report the proceeds of T-bill sales as cash from operating activities on its consolidated statement of cash flows. The partnership was created in mid-December 1999. On December 29, 1999, Enron used this structure to increase its reported cash from operating activities by $500 million. Enron informed Citigroup that it would use this $500 million to decrease its reported debt by that amount. Three weeks later, in January 2000, Enron arranged to repay the $485 million loan in full with interest. Enron's purported disclosure of this transaction in its year-end 1999 filings failed to disclose fully that the partnership was created in December to fund a transaction that lasted just long enough to achieve a year-end financial reporting effect. Enron's disclosure was also misleading because it created the false impression that this transaction related to Enron's regular-course-of-business investments in energy and technology companies.

Project Bacchus was structured by Enron as a sale of an interest in certain of its pulp and paper businesses to a special purpose entity ("SPE") capitalized by Citigroup with a $194 million loan and $6 million in equity. Citigroup understood that the $6 million in equity represented the three percent minimum capital investment by an independent, third party (here, Citigroup) considered necessary under the then existing accounting literature to avoid consolidating this entity with Enron for accounting purposes. (To protect Citigroup's loan, Enron and the entity entered into a total return swap, the effect of which was to make Enron responsible for paying Citigroup an amount equal to the principal and interest on the $194 million loan.) Enron and Citigroup signed documents that supported Enron's accounting treatment. Simultaneously, however, Citigroup obtained oral representations from Enron that Citigroup would not lose money in connection with its three percent equity investment. Citigroup understood that reducing this representation to a written contractual term would have negated Enron's accounting treatment. Consequently, in substance, Citigroup was not at risk for its equity investment, thus rendering Project Bacchus a $200 million financing from Citigroup, which should have been accounted as such. At the end of December 2000, Project Bacchus generated $200 million of cash from operating activities and $112 million in pre-tax income for Enron. Four months before Project Bacchus' maturity date, the Project Bacchus structure was terminated and the pulp and paper assets were moved into a different structure involving Enron and Citigroup.

Id.

The SEC and bank regulatory authorities assembled a task force in 2004 to consider structured finance products sold by banks to corporations that were then used to manipulate the financial results of those companies. The task force proposed a requirement that banks develop procedures to identify structured products that could cause the banks embarrassment or liability. Interagency Statement on Sound Practices Concerning Complex Structured Finance Activities and Request for Public Comment, 69 Fed. Reg. 28980 (May 19, 2004).

The purpose was to make banks responsible for such abuses, eliminating the head in the sand, ostrich defense by the banks involved in the Enron scandal who claimed they were not responsible for the accounting treatment claimed by their customers.

SECTION 8.   FAIR VALUE ACCOUNTING[27]

"What many people do not realize is that mark-to-market accounting existed in the Great Depression and, according to Milton Friedman, was an important reason behind many bank failures. In 1938, Franklin Delano Roosevelt called on a commission to study the problem and the rule was finally suspended."[28] Even earlier, the Reconstruction Finance Corp. (RFC) dropped fair value accounting requirements in order to restart the banking system by allowing troubled banks to join the FDIC. Instead, the RFC "deemphasized the liquidity and marketability of bank assets, and evaluated high-grade securities at their potential, not market, value. The RFC gave book or cost value to the highest grade bonds, market value for bonds in default, face value for slow but sound assets, and a reasonable valuation for doubtful assets like real estate."[29]

Historical cost accounting was widely embraced following the Great Depression because of its perceived conservative approach to valuation. The SEC adopted historical cost accounting, but its shortcoming of ignoring market value in favor of purchase price was criticized by many. In December of 1975, FASB[30] issued FAS 12, which required companies to record their marketable equity securities at the lower-of-cost or fair-value, in an attempt to create some uniformity in accounting methods used to report these instruments.

In 1986, in response to the savings and loan crisis, FASB began working toward more market-based accounting. In 1993, FASB issued FAS 115, which sets forth mark-to-market accounting requirements for investments in equity securities with determinable fair market value and

---

27. This discussion is excerpted from Jerry W. Markham, VI A Financial History of the United States: The Subprime Crisis (2006–2009) 448–49, 715–21 (2011).

28. Brian S. Wesbury & Robert Stein, "Mr. President, Suspend Mark–To–Market," Forbes.com, Jan. 21, 2009, at http://www.forbes.com/2009/01/20/accounting-treasury-obama-oped-cx_bw_rs_0121wesburystein.html.

29. James Olson, Saving Capitalism, The Reconstruction Finance Corporation and the New Deal 79–80 (1988).

30. The Financial Accounting Standards Board (FASB) is a private body that sets accounting standards in the United States.

for all investments in debt securities. FAS 133, which was adopted in 1998, imposed fair value reporting requirements for derivatives.

An issue that arose during the financial crisis that began in 2007 was fair value accounting for financial instruments.

> The foundational ideas associated with fair value accounting were adopted by FASB in Statement of Financial Accounting Standards (FAS) 115 [in 1993]. The rule divided financial assets into three categories—those held "to maturity," those held "for trading purposes," and those "available for sale." Each of these categories is treated slightly differently. Assets held to maturity are valued at amortized cost; assets held for trading are marked to market, with unrealized gains or losses included in earnings; and assets deemed available for sale are marked to market, with unrealized gains or losses excluded from earnings but included in shareholders' equity.[31]

That concept was further advanced with FASB's SFAS 157, which was adopted in 2006, just as the subprime market peaked, and became effective for fiscal years beginning after November 15, 2007, just as the subprime crisis was in full bloom. SFAS 157 specified conditions on how fair value was to be determined, but placed the greatest emphasis on the use of market prices. This requirement meant that financial assets subject to fair valuation had to be written down whenever there was a decline in the market value of those instruments.

> Many subprime mortgage instruments were not actively traded and were difficult to value, particularly as foreclosures mounted and issues were downgraded by the credit rating agencies. Accounting firms, badly stung by the over-valuations at Enron and elsewhere, took a hard line and insisted on marking down the value of subprime securities. Since valuations were difficult, and any overstatement could lead to life in prison, many securities were marked down to levels well below their actual values. The result was a downward spiral further undermining subprime securitizations, creating more uncertainty, resulting in more markdowns, creating more uncertainty, and touching off a cascade effect that that would eventually undermine the entire economy.

Fair value pricing resulted in a pro-cyclical progression of write-downs that bore no relation to actual value. As one author noted in the midst of the subprime crisis:

> As losses mounted in subprime mortgage portfolios in mid–2007, lenders demanded more collateral. If the companies holding the assets did not have additional collateral to supply, they were compelled to sell the assets. These sales depressed the market for mortgage-backed securities (MBS) and also raised questions about the quality of the ratings these securities had previously received. Doubts about the quality of ratings for MBS raised questions about the quality of ratings for other asset-backed securities (ABS). Because of the com-

---

31. Peter Wallison, Fair Value Accounting: A Critique, American Enterprise Institute, July 2008.

plexity of many of the instruments out in the market, it also became difficult to determine where the real losses on MBS and ABS actually resided. As a result, trading in MBS and ABS came virtually to a halt and has remained at a standstill for almost a year. Meanwhile, continued withdrawal of financing sources has compelled the holders of ABS to sell them at distressed or liquidation prices, even though the underlying cash flows of these portfolios have not necessarily been seriously diminished. As more and more distress or liquidation sales occurred, asset prices declined further, and these declines created more lender demands for additional collateral, resulting in more distress or liquidation sales and more declines in asset values as measured on a mark-to-market basis. A downward spiral developed * * *.[32]

The effort to ease fair value accounting turned into trench warfare between corporate activists that wanted the requirement continued and much of the business community that wanted it suspended. "The difficulty in putting a value on loans, securities, and exotic financial instruments banks were carrying on their books became one of the most debilitating features of the Great Panic" in 2008.[33] The adoption of a mark-to-market accounting requirement for subprime securities seems strange since "fair value" accounting was pioneered by the Enron Corp. to inflate its earnings in order to run up its stock price. Equally interesting is the fact that regulators stoutly resisted easing fair value accounting requirements during the subprime crisis.

Critics of fair value accounting charged that, because liquidity in subprime investments had dried up as the subprime crisis blossomed, the only prices available for "fair value" accounting were fire sale prices from desperate sellers. Those prices did not reflect the actual value of the Super Seniors as measured by their cash flows or defaults. One accountant complained to the FASB that: "May the souls of those who developed FASB 157 burn in the seventh circle of Dante's Hell."[34] Warren Buffett likened mark-to-market requirements for measuring bank regulatory capital to throwing "gasoline on the fire in terms of financial institutions."[35]

The SEC gave some interpretative relief on September 23, 2008. The Emergency Economic Stabilization Act passed on October 3, 2008 required the SEC to conduct a study of mark-to-market accounting and authorized suspension of that requirement. A debate arose, however, over whether

---

32. Id.

33. David Wessel, In Fed We Trust, 128 (2009).

34. Accounting Principles, 40 Sec. Reg. & L. Rep. (BNA) 1767 (2008).

35. Holman W. Jenkins, Jr., Buffett's Unmentionable Bank Solution, Wall St. J., Mar. 11, 2009, at A13. As one author noted:

The argument against fair value is a compelling one: volatile markets make securities valuation difficult and undermine investors' confidence, forcing companies to mark down values, leading to greater illiquidity and further markdowns. The more the markdowns impair capital, the greater the loss of investor confidence, and the faster the churn of the self-reinforcing cycle.

Todd Davenport. Fair Value: Few Fans, But Fewer Alternatives; Despite Widespread Frustration, Changes Don't Seem Likely, Am. Banker 1 (Mar. 24, 2008).

suspension was appropriate, and the SEC subsequently decided not to suspend mark-to-market accounting. The SEC staff stated that the crisis was caused by a "run on the bank" at some institutions with counterparties reducing their credit and risk exposures at each bank, rather than the fair value method of accounting for assets.

The Bank for International Settlements' (BIS) Basel Committee on Banking Supervision published guidance on how banks should value financial instruments held in inventory. Its concern was that banks were using overly optimistic pricing models for instruments that did not have an ascertainable market price. BIS also wanted independent verification of prices. It later appeared that banks had become too pessimistic during the financial crisis in their valuations of subprime investments at prices lower than would be justified by a discounted cash flow analysis.

Chapter Thirteen

Insurance

■ ■ ■

SECTION 1.   INTRODUCTION TO INSURANCE

A.   THE BUSINESS OF INSURANCE

Traditionally, insurance has been used to guard against any number of risks. Insurance products insure, among other things, life, health, title, fidelity, and property and casualty. The business of insurance is based on the law of large numbers as described in the following case.

NEW YORK LIFE INSURANCE CO. v. STATHAM

Supreme Court of the United States, 1876.
93 U.S. 24.

* * * The first case is a bill in equity, filed to recover the amount of a policy of life assurance, granted by the defendant (now appellant) in 1851, on the life of Dr. A. D. Statham, of Mississippi, from the proceeds of certain funds belonging to the defendant attached in the hands of its agent at Jackson, in that State. It appears from the statements of the bill that the annual premiums accruing on the policy were all regularly paid, until the breaking out of the late civil war, but that, in consequence of that event, the premium due on the 8th of December, 1861, was not paid; the parties assured being residents of Mississippi, and the defendant a corporation of New York. Dr. Statham died in July, 1862. * * *

Each policy is in the usual form of such an instrument, declaring that the company, in consideration of a certain specified sum to it in hand paid by the assured, and of an annual premium of the same amount to be paid on the same day and month in every year during the continuance of the policy, did assure the life of the party named, in a specified amount, for the term of his natural life. Each contained various conditions, upon the breach of which it was to be null and void; and amongst others the following: "That in case the said [assured] shall not pay the said premium on or before the several days hereinbefore mentioned for the payment thereof, then and in every such case the said company shall not be liable to the payment of the sum insured, or in any part thereof, and this policy shall cease and determine." * * *

MR. JUSTICE BRADLEY delivered the opinion of the Court.

We agree with the court below, that the contract is not an assurance for a single year, with a privilege of renewal from year to year by paying the annual premium, but that it is an entire contract of assurance for life, subject to discontinuance and forfeiture for non-payment of any of the stipulated premiums. Such is the form of the contract, and such is its character. It has been contended that the payment of each premium is the consideration for insurance during the next following year,—as in fire policies. But the position is untenable. It often happens that the assured pays the entire premium in advance, or in five, ten, or twenty annual instalments. Such instalments are clearly not intended as the consideration for the respective years in which they are paid; for, after they are all paid, the policy stands good for the balance of the life insured, without any further payment. Each instalment is, in fact, part consideration of the entire insurance for life. It is the same thing, where the annual premiums are spread over the whole life. The value of assurance for one year of a man's life when he is young, strong, and healthy, is manifestly not the same as when he is old and decrepit. There is no proper relation between the annual premium and the risk of assurance for the year in which it is paid. This idea of assurance from year to year is the suggestion of ingenious counsel. The annual premiums are an annuity, the present value of which is calculated to correspond with the present value of the amount assured, a reasonable percentage being added to the premiums to cover expenses and contingencies. The whole premiums are balanced against the whole insurance.

But whilst this is true, it must be conceded that promptness of payment is essential in the business of life insurance. All the calculations of the insurance company are based on the hypothesis of prompt payments. They not only calculate on the receipt of the premiums when due, but on compounding interest upon them. It is on this basis that they are enabled to offer assurance at the favorable rates they do. Forfeiture for non-payment is a necessary means of protecting themselves from embarrassment. Unless it were enforceable, the business would be thrown into utter confusion. It is like the forfeiture of shares in mining enterprises, and all other hazardous undertakings. There must be power to cut off unprofitable members, or the success of the whole scheme is endangered. The insured parties are associates in a great scheme. This associated relation exists whether the company be a mutual one or not. Each is interested in the engagements of all; for out of the coexistence of many risks arises the law of average, which underlies the whole business. An essential feature of this scheme is the mathematical calculations referred to, on which the premiums and amounts assured are based. And these calculations, again, are based on the assumption of average mortality, and of prompt payments and compound interest thereon. Delinquency cannot be tolerated nor redeemed, except at the option of the company. This has always been the understanding and the practice in this department of business. Some companies, it is true, accord a grace of thirty days, or other fixed period, within which the premium in arrear may be paid, on certain conditions of continued good health, & c. But this is a matter of stipulation, or of discretion, on the part of the particular company. When no stipulation exists, it is the general understanding that time is material, and that the forfeiture is absolute if the premium be not paid. The extraordinary and even desperate efforts sometimes made, when an insured person is *in extremis*, to meet a premium coming due, demonstrates the common view of this matter.

The case, therefore, is one in which time is material and of the essence of the contract. Non-payment at the day involves absolute forfeiture, if such be the terms of the contract, as is the case here. Courts cannot with safety vary the stipulation of the parties by introducing equities for the relief of the insured against their own negligence. * * *

In the case of life insurance, besides the materiality of time in the performance of the contract, another strong reason exists why the policy should not be revived. The parties do not stand on equal ground in reference to such a revival. It would operate most unjustly against the company. The business of insurance is founded on the law of averages; that of life insurance eminently so. The average rate of mortality is the basis on which it rests. By spreading their risks over a large number of cases, the companies calculate on this average with reasonable certainty and safety. Any thing that interferes with it deranges the security of the business. If every policy lapsed by reason of the war should be revived, and all the back premiums should be paid, the companies would have the benefit of this average amount of risk. But the good risks are never heard from; only the bad are sought to be revived, where the person insured is either dead or dying. Those in health can get new policies cheaper than to pay arrearages on the old. To enforce a revival of the bad cases, whilst the company necessarily lose the cases which are desirable, would be manifestly unjust. An insured person, as before stated, does not stand isolated and alone. His case is connected with and correlated to the cases of all others insured by the same company. The nature of the business, as a whole, must be looked at to understand the general equities of the parties.

We are of opinion, therefore, that an action cannot be maintained for the amount assured on a policy of life insurance forfeited, like those in question, by non-payment of the premium, even though the payment was prevented by the existence of the war.

[The court did allow the plaintiffs to recover the equitable value of the premiums previously paid]

JUSTICES WAITE and STRONG concur. * * *

B. REGULATION OF INSURANCE— BACKGROUND AND HISTORY[1]

The insurance industry in America grew dramatically after the Civil War. By the end of the nineteenth century, insurance companies had amassed vast amounts of capital that had to be maintained as reserves for claims. The investment of those reserves brought them in close contact with the investment bankers (such as J.P. Morgan & Co.) who in turn were closely allied with the commercial banks (such as the National City Bank and the First National Bank in New York). Louis D. Brandeis, a future United States Supreme Court Justice, stated in 1905 that insurance companies were "the greatest economic menace of today" and that as "creditors of [the] great industries," they used their power "selfishly, dishonestly [and] inefficiently."[2] Increased criticism of the insurance industry led the New York legislature to appoint an investigating committee headed by Senator William Armstrong.[3]

The Armstrong Committee concluded that the insurance industry should be kept separate from the securities and banking industries. As a result of the committee's recommendations, the New York legislature enacted legislation that prohibited insurance companies from purchasing stock for investment and from underwriting securities as a part of a syndicate or otherwise. Insurance companies could not affiliate with banks since the legislation barred them from owning bank stocks. These restrictions effectively isolated insurance from banking and the securities industry.

The isolation of the insurance industry from banking and securities had a salutary effect following the 1929 stock market crash. Although insurance company reserves did not escape unscathed, they also were not devastated by the stock market crash. Moreover, insurance companies were not subjected to the pervasive federal regulation that was enacted during that period for banks and securities firms. The insurance industry rightfully claimed that it was uninvolved in the abuses that led to the banking and securities legislation. However, an investigation by Franklin Roosevelt's Temporary National Economic Committee (TNEC) in 1941, found that insurance company assets were highly concentrated in industrial bonds because of the restrictions on equity ownership. That concentration skewed and leveraged corporate balance sheets by encouraging debt over equity. Nevertheless, no federal legislation emerged.

---

1. The discussion of the history and background of banking and insurance in this chapter is based on Lissa L. Broome & Jerry W. Markham, Banking and Insurance: Before and After the Gramm–Leach–Bliley Act, 25 J. Corp. L. 723 (2000).

2. Morton Keller, The Life Insurance Enterprise, 1885–1920, at 32 (1963).

3. Charles Evan Hughes, a future United States Supreme Court Chief Justice, acted as the Armstrong Committee's counsel.

SCOTT A. SINDER
THE GRAMM–LEACH–BLILEY ACT AND
STATE REGULATION OF THE BUSINESS
OF INSURANCE

5 N.C. Banking Inst. 49 (2001).

* * * "Perhaps no modern commercial enterprise directly affects so many persons in all walks of life as does the insurance business. Insurance touches the home, the family, and the occupation or the business of almost every person in the United States."[4] "It is practically a necessity to business activity and enterprise."[5] Insurance serves a broad public interest far beyond its role in business affairs and its protection of a large part of the country's wealth. It is the essential means by which the "disaster to an individual is shared by many, the disaster to a community shared by other communities; great catastrophes are thereby lessened, and, it may be, repaired."[6] Thus, it is "the conception of the lawmaking bodies of the country without exception that the business of insurance so far affects the public welfare as to invoke and require governmental regulation."[7]

To meet the "imperative need" for regulation, state legislatures have enacted comprehensive bodies of law, dating back over one hundred years, to "control the insurance business."[8] State insurance law regulates every aspect of the business: insurance companies (including assets, liabilities, and investments), insurance policies and rates, the agents who solicit the sale of insurance on behalf of companies and the brokers who represent the insured on their purchase of insurance.

Until 1944, it was universally understood that the States maintained exclusive control over the regulation of insurance. This axiom of state regulation had existed since 1869 when the Supreme Court decided *Paul v. Virginia*,[9] a case involving an appeal by an insurance agent from a fine imposed for selling coverage for a New York insurer who was not properly licensed in Virginia. In rejecting the agent's argument that the Virginia licensing laws violated the Commerce Clause of the U.S. Constitution, the Court held that "issuing a policy of insurance is not a transaction of commerce" and is "governed by the local law." Subsequent cases have held the entire business of insurance was not interstate commerce subject to regulation by Congress. Like *Paul v. Virginia* itself, many of these cases involved state statutes governing licensure of insurance companies and their agents.

Consistent with this case law and understanding, Congress has routinely refused to extend federal authority over the conduct of the insurance business. Between 1902 and 1906, for example, numerous bills were

---

4. [n.10] United States v. South–Eastern Underwriters Association, 322 U.S. 533, 540 (1944).

5. [n.11] German Alliance Ins. Co. v. Lewis, 233 U.S. 389, 414 (1914) (upholding police power of State to regulate insurance).

6. [n.12] Id. at 413.

7. [n.13] Id. at 412.

8. [n.14] S.E. Underwriters, 322 U.S. at 544–45.

9. [eds.] 75 U.S. 168 (1869).

introduced providing for federal regulation of various aspects of the insurance industry, but the judiciary committees of both the House and Senate concluded such regulation was beyond Congress' constitutional power. In 1914, in recognition of Congress' lack of authority, resolutions were introduced in both the House and Senate proposing the Constitution be amended to give Congress the power to regulate the insurance industry.

Thus, prior to 1944, Congress did not even believe it had the constitutional authority to regulate the general conduct of the private-sector insurance business in this country; that power resided solely with the States. Consequently, "the States enjoyed a virtually exclusive domain over the insurance industry."[10]

All this changed in 1944 with the Supreme Court's decision in *South-Eastern Underwriters*, which held that insurance companies are engaged in interstate commerce and are therefore subject to the federal antitrust laws.[11] The decision, "naturally, was widely perceived as a threat to state power to tax and regulate the insurance industry."[12] Congress quickly enacted the McCarran–Ferguson Act.[13] Passed at the urging of the state insurance regulators directly affected by *South-Eastern*, McCarran "provides that regulation of the insurance industry is generally a matter for the States."[14]

* * * Section 2 of the Act provides:

(a) The business of insurance, and every person engaged therein, shall be subject to the laws of the several States which relate to the regulation or taxation of such business.

(2) No Act of Congress shall be construed to invalidate, impair, or supersede any law enacted by any State for the purpose of regulating the business of insurance, or which imposes a fee or tax upon such business, unless such Act specifically relates to the business of insurance: Provided, That after June 30, 1948, the Act ... known as the Sherman Act, and the Act ... known as the Clayton Act, and the Act ... known as the Federal Trade Commission Act ... shall be applicable to the business of insurance to the extent that such business is not regulated by State law.[15]

As the Supreme Court has noted, "[o]bviously Congress' purpose was broadly to give support to the existing and future state systems for regulating and taxing the business of insurance."[16] * * *

---

10. [n.22] St. Paul Fire & Marine Ins. Co., 438 U.S. 531, 539 (1978). * * *

11. [n.23] United States v. S.E. Underwriters Ass'n, 322 U.S. 533 (1944).

12. [n.24] United States Dep't of Treasury v. Fabe, 508 U.S. 491, 499–500 (1993).

13. [eds.] 59 Stat. 53, 15 U.S.C. § 11011–1015 (1944).

14. [n.26] Hartford Fire Ins. Co. v. California, 509 U.S. 764, 780 (1993).

15. [n.30] [15 U.S.C.A. § 1012].

16. [n.31] Prudential Ins. Co. v. Benjamin, 328 U.S. 408, 429 (1946).

C. INSURANCE EXPANDS ITS BORDERS

Insurance companies began to look for new products after World War II. They found that annuities and conventional life insurance policies were competing with securities, particularly mutual funds, as a mechanism for building an estate. To meet that competition, the insurance industry created the "variable" annuity contract. This was a variation of the traditional "fixed" annuity that payed a fixed amount each year to the annuitant for life. The fixed annuity prevented the annuitant from outliving his or her estate. The insurance company computed the amount of the annual payment on the basis of the annuitant's life expectancy and an assumed rate of return on the purchase price of the annuity. A problem with the fixed annuity, however, was that the value of the fixed payment could be sharply undercut by inflation. The variable annuity was created to deal with that concern.

In the simplest form of variable annuity, the purchaser makes a series of payments to the insurance company until retirement. Those funds are invested in stocks or other securities. Upon retirement, the annuitant receives a stream of payments for life. The amount of those payments depends on the annuitant's life expectancy and the amount of funds accumulated from contributions and increases, or decreases, from the investment of those funds. The variable annuity proved to be a popular product, but it was declared to be a security by the Supreme Court. This subjected it to regulation by the Securities and Exchange Commission (SEC).[17] These holdings presaged the cross-selling of insurance and securities products, throwing insurance companies back into the mainstream of finance from which the Armstrong Committee had removed them.

Insurance companies also sought to involve themselves in banking through loopholes in the federal statutes that generally prohibited the mixing of banking and insurance. The Savings and Loan Holding Company Act, 12 U.S.C. § 1730a, allowed a company, including an insurance company, to own a single thrift, provided that the thrift was a "qualified thrift lender" (QTL). A QTL is a thrift with at least 65 percent of its assets devoted to housing or consumer related lending. Several large insurance companies used that provision to operate their own thrifts. Another way to gain entry into banking before 1987 was through the operation of a nonbank bank (a "bank" that did not both accept deposits and make commercial loans). That loophole was closed in 1987, but the existing nonbank banks received limited grandfather rights. Still another means by which insurance companies entered banking was by operating a limited purpose trust company. A trust company is not considered a "bank" under the BHCA if the institution functions "solely in a trust or fiduciary capacity," accepts only trust funds (not demand deposits) as deposits, and does not offer FDIC insurance on these deposits.

---

17. SEC v. Variable Annuity Life Ins. Co. of America, 359 U.S. 65 (1959); SEC v. United Benefit Life Ins. Co., 387 U.S. 202 (1967).

1. What types of insurance products do you have? What other types of insurance products are available for purchase?

2. Insurance underwriting, sometimes also called producing, involves creating the insurance product and bearing the risk associated with the insurance product, such as the risk that a young man who has purchased a life insurance policy will die prematurely. This risk is often mitigated through another type of insurance, called reinsurance. Insurance agents sell insurance products to customers and retain a commission for facilitating the sale and for providing follow-up services to the customer. Insurance agents may be captive (sell the products of only one underwriter) or independent (sell the products of several insurance companies). Which insurance activity is riskier—acting as an agent or as an underwriter?

SECTION 2. BANK INSURANCE ACTIVITIES PRIOR TO GRAMM–LEACH–BLILEY

While insurance companies searched for ways to expand their banking activities, banks sought entry into the insurance industry. The fees and underwriting commissions from that business were attractive. Those products could round out the financial services banks offered to customers. Banks also had some competitive advantages that could be employed to sell insurance products.

MICHAEL D. WHITE
WHAT WILL IT TAKE FOR BANK INSURANCE TO SUCCEED IN THE UNITED STATES?

2 N.C. Banking Inst. 123 (1998).

* * * Supreme Court Justice Louis Brandeis certainly believed banks could meet the needs of an underinsured America. Retained in 1904 as counsel for The New England Equitable Policyholders Protective Committee during the Armstrong investigation of leading life insurance companies in New York, Brandeis was appalled, like many others, by the insurance companies' scandalously high premiums and commissions and low policy values and retention rates. In 1905, Brandeis introduced the idea of selling life insurance over-the-counter in mutual savings banks in Massachusetts. After much study, he concluded that mutual savings banks, with minor enlargements of their powers, would be the ideal vehicle to bring low-cost insurance to those of modest means. His plan for a Savings Bank Life Insurance (SBLI) system was enacted into law in 1907. In later years, Justice Brandeis referred to the creation of SBLI as his "greatest achievement."

From its birth as a social experiment, SBLI grew to become not only a successful business, but also to be known as one of the best life insurance buys in America. In addition to Massachusetts, New York (1938) and

Connecticut (1941) adopted SBLI systems. Today, the three SBLI systems insure close to one million people with total insurance-in-force close to $50 billion. Therefore, the U.S. banking industry can look to SBLI as a modest precedent of success for selling insurance. Moreover, the tremendous growth in bank insurance activities in Europe, where they refer to it as "bancassurance," bears witness generally to the ability of banks to become principal suppliers of insurance products and services. Surely, then, U.S. banks poised to enter the twenty-first century can succeed selling insurance. * * *

The traditional life insurance agency system is flawed with inherent structural weaknesses and deficiencies that include:

(1) Declining sales. LIMRA [Life Insurance Marketing Research Association] regards the number of policies sold as the most accurate measure of how the life insurance industry is doing. By its own criterion, the industry is in decline. Since their peak in 1983, new sales of ordinary life policies have declined twenty-five percent.

(2) Declining sales productivity. The average sales productivity of agents is also falling. For example, the average number of life policies sold annually by ordinary agents with more than five years of experience dropped from fifty-four in 1987 to forty-seven in 1992. LIMRA projects agent productivity will decline further to thirty-nine policies in 1997.

(3) Traditional distribution is insurers' greatest expense. Declines in productivity and service are indicative of an expensive distribution system. The traditional agent distribution system is the life insurance companies' greatest single expense because two-thirds of their expenses go to maintain this distribution system. Life insurance company CEOs are increasingly concerned about the excessive cost of distribution and low sales force productivity. Agent productivity has changed little in decades (except to decline inexorably), and average acquisition costs are estimated at a whopping 175 to 200 percent of each dollar of new life premium.

(4) Record declines in agent recruitment and retention. The life insurance industry uses several key measurements to assess the performance, health and potential of agents and the agency system. Among them are new agent recruitment rates and four-year agent retention rates. LIMRA describes these bellwethers as "either flat or heading south," indicating "a continued slow and painful decline." Overall, the number of new life agent recruits per year has declined by half since 1980. Worse yet, once new agents are recruited to the life business, few last long. The four-year agent retention rate now typically ranges from sixteen to eighteen percent. In other words, for every 100 new agents recruited, only sixteen remain in the business four years later. * * *

Access to life insurance is critical to our nation's economic and social well-being. However, nearly three times as many Americans (104 million) are without any form of life insurance than the thirty-seven million alleged to be without health insurance. As a result, households in which breadwinners have no life insurance protection are in financial jeopardy.

With uninsured Americans needing at least $5 trillion in life insurance coverage, there are many uninsured (and under insured) families and business owners to be protected and plenty of sales to be made. * * *

Banks can succeed selling insurance because they possess marketing and distribution advantages over traditional insurance agencies. These advantages include:

(1) Customer affinity for and proximity to banks is greater than for traditional agencies. Surveys repeatedly show that consumers have greater trust for their banks than for insurance companies and agents, and that banks are nearer to their customers, physically and psychically, than traditional agents.

(2) Banks have more frequent contact with customers and reach a broader range of client segments than do agents, allowing for improved consumer access to insurance products and services. Banks are a natural and, in many states, a long-standing, historical sales channel for insurance—witness SBLI in Connecticut, Massachusetts and New York and property-casualty insurance in Indiana. Bank insurance activities improve competition and customer service. They provide more product access, insurance alternatives, and choices for more consumers, especially middle and low-income earners.

(3) Banks are at the point of customer needs origination. Customer financial transactions, relationships and goals necessarily engender new insurable interests. In the rush of business, bankers must keep in mind that financial transactions often represent or signify important life events, relationships or decisions including: marriage, buying a new home, starting a family, paying for a child's college education, starting one's own business, and securing one's retirement.

Since banks are at the point of origination and fulfillment of many customers' financial needs, banks have a unique opportunity to serve the new insurance needs that many financial transactions engender and to meet the many personal goals that seemingly ordinary transactions signify. Consider two simple examples. A mortgage loan will require homeowners' insurance, possibly mortgage or flood insurance, and probably mortgage life or mortgage disability coverage. A small business loan may signify needs like key employee protection, a 303 stock redemption plan, an insured cross-purchase buy-sell agreement, or increased personal insurance for the company's executives.

(4) Banks are able to coordinate their marketing efforts. Insurance companies provide agents with little marketing support. Traditional insurance agents are generally responsible for their own marketing and prospecting efforts—this is what makes it so difficult for most agents to survive in the business. Banks can bring significant, coordinated and centralized marketing resources to bear on the insurance business, thereby freeing insurance agents to do what they should do best—meet customers' needs and sell insurance.

(5) Banks can employ database marketing, segment their customer base, and target markets. They have a greater capability to utilize customer information files (with appropriate respect for privacy and confidentiality). Banks clearly have greater financial and technological resources, a greater number of customers, and a higher frequency of extensive or multiple-account relationships with their customers than do the vast majority of insurance agents. Bank master customer information files are capable of being organized, analyzed and distributed to their sales forces.

Customers can be segmented into discrete kinds of potential buying units according to needs, buyer preferences, purchase transactions, incomes, and location-proximity to agents. They can be targeted as a market according to these and other criteria. Banks can know their customers better and, therefore, can help them in a highly professional fashion meet their insurance needs through the purchase of appropriate insurance products and services.

(6) Banks have available a wider variety of methods and techniques for marketing and selling insurance to customers than do traditional agents. Customer proximity and relationships, numerous bank-branch locations and advanced technologies produce—either face-to-face or remotely—more points of contact and greater frequency of contact between a bank and its customers than those between agents and their customers or the general public.

Banks can market and/or sell insurance through monthly customer statements, statement stuffers, branch signage, customer newsletters, bank brochures, financial education seminars, ATM receipts and screens, in-branch kiosks, WEB sites, home banking by phone or PC, direct mail, telemarketing, customer service call centers, personal banking relationships, mortgage loan officer relationships, commercial accounts, trust departments, investment centers and brokers or advisors, customer service representatives, and platform staff.

(7) Banks have an opportunity to earn larger margins than traditional insurance agencies by using more effective and lower cost distribution strategies. Banks can add insurance to their quiver of financial products, using them to raise branch productivity and output and to offset fixed unit costs and brick-and-mortar overhead. The closer bank-customer relationships and effective use of customer databases should more readily identify customer needs, producing many "warm" leads that improve sales closing ratios and sales productivity. A bank's capability to implement broader, more extensive and fully coordinated marketing efforts to assist its sales force should relieve the bank's sales force of much of the unproductive marketing and prospecting necessarily undertaken by traditional agents. Proper exercise of this capability should improve the effectiveness and lower the cost of insurance distribution, over time resulting in higher profit margins for bank-based agencies than for traditional agencies. * * *

A. NATIONAL BANKS

SAXON v. GEORGIA ASS'N OF INDEPENDENT INSURANCE AGENTS, INC.

United States Court of Appeals, Fifth Circuit, 1968.
399 F.2d 1010.

ELLIOTT, DISTRICT JUDGE.

These two actions were brought by Appellees (Plaintiffs below) to have declared unlawful Appellant Comptroller's 1963 Ruling No. 7110 and to enjoin Appellant Citizens and Southern National Bank's insurance agent and agency activities in Georgia cities of over 5,000 population. * * *

Two provisions of the National Bank Act (Title 12, U.S.C.A.) are involved:

Section 24(7), enacted in 1864, grants to national banks "all such incidental powers as shall be necessary to carry on the business of banking".

Section 92, enacted in 1916, provides that national banks "located and doing business in any place the population of which does not exceed five thousand inhabitants * * * may, under such rules as may be prescribed by the Comptroller of the Currency, act as the agent for any fire, life or other insurance company authorized by the authorities of the State in which such bank is located to do business in said State * * *."

In this statutory setting James J. Saxon (the original defendant below in Case No. 25050) was secretary of an Advisory Committee appointed by the United States Senate in 1956 to make a study of the national banking laws and to make suggestions concerning revisions. He and the Advisory Committee drafted and recommended passage of legislation which would have allowed national banks in cities of more than 5,000 population to act as insurance agents if state chartered banks could do so under State law. This legislation was proposed in Congress as the Financial Institutions Act of 1957. After consideration and debate by the Congress this legislative proposal as drafted and recommended by Mr. Saxon and the Committee of which he was a member was rejected by Congress.

In 1961 Mr. Saxon became Comptroller of the Currency and in 1962 Comptroller Saxon created a "National Advisory Committee on Banking Regulatory Policies and Practices," which committee was composed entirely of persons affiliated with the banking business. Comptroller Saxon asked this committee to make suggestions and recommendations to him for changes in the laws, policies and regulations affecting national banks. In due course Mr. Saxon's Advisory Committee recommended with regard to the insurance agency matter that "appropriate legislation should be enacted expressly to permit any National Bank to act as broker or agent in the writing of * * * insurance issued in connection with a loan by the bank, and to participate in premium experience refunds." * * * Instead of asking Congress for the "appropriate legislation" recommended by the committee, Comptroller Saxon in 1963 simply converted that recommendation into an administrative ruling, that being Ruling No. 7110, which is the subject of this inquiry, the full text of which provides:

> "Incidental to the powers vested in them under 12 U.S.C. Sections 24, 84 and 371, National Banks have the authority to act as agent in the issuance of insurance which is incident to banking transactions. Commissions received therefrom or service charges imposed therefor may be retained by the bank."

This ruling was not limited in scope to cities of 5,000 population or less and purported to authorize every national bank, regardless of where located, to enter the insurance agency field and to compete with Appellees and other insurance agents.

In 1964 by an exchange of letters Appellant C & S Bank requested and received Comptroller Saxon's specific approval of the Bank's entry "into the insurance agency business," and in 1965 the Bank in its Atlanta offices began selling to borrowers broad forms of automobile, home, casualty and liability insurance, and the program was subsequently extended to its national bank offices in the cities of Athens, Augusta, Macon, Savannah and Valdosta, each of which has a population in excess of 5,000.

To protect their business from what was alleged to be unlawful encroachment by the bank, Appellees brought suit against the Bank, federal jurisdiction being based upon 28 U.S.C. §§ 1331(a), 1348 and 1391, and against Comptroller Saxon, jurisdiction being based upon 28 U.S.C. §§ 1331(a) and 1391(e) and 5 U.S.C. § 1009.

After overruling Appellants' motion to dismiss (260 F. Supp. 802), the District Court granted Appellees' motions for summary judgment (268 F. Supp. 236), and subsequently entered judgments declaring Comptroller Saxon's Ruling No. 7110 unlawful and in excess of statutory authority and declaring unlawful the Bank's insurance agent and agency activities in cities of more than 5,000 population.

We affirm the judgments of the District Court. * * *

Does Section 92 of the National Bank Act impliedly prohibit national banks from carrying on the business of insurance agents in places of more than 5,000 population[?] * * *

Appellants contend that authority for national banks located in cities of over 5,000 population to act as insurance agents may be inferred from the general provisions contained in Section 24(7) of the Act, heretofore set out in pertinent part, this Section allowing national banks to exercise, subject to law, all such "incidental" powers as shall be "necessary" to carry on the business of banking. The District Court held that the specific grant of insurance agency power contained in Section 92 of the Act, heretofore set out, is the full extent of the insurance agency power possessed by national banks, and that an insurance agency power may not be inferred from the provisions of Section 24(7). Adjudication of the first question presented, therefore, hinges upon the proper construction to be given to these two sections of the Act.

Pertinent to consideration of these statutory provisions, we take note of the fact that prior to the 1916 enactment of Section 92 it seems to have been universally understood that no national banks possessed *any* power to act as insurance agents. Section 24(7) was contained in the original National Bank Act of 1864. Between that time and 1916 when Section 92 was enacted, the various administrative agencies charged by law with the administration of the Bank Act consistently ruled that national banks had no power to act as insurance agencies. * * *

The Comptroller then recommended to Congress that it grant insurance agency power to national banks located in small towns, submitting to Congress a draft of a proposed amendment to the National Bank Act which Congress enacted and is now Section 92 of the Act. 53 Cong.Rec. 11001 (1916).

In interpreting the meaning of one provision of an act it is proper that all other provisions in *pari materia* should also be considered. So, in construing the general authority contained in Section 24(7) we must give equal consideration to Section 92 as it specifically deals with the power of national banks to act as insurance agents, and when the general language in Section 24(7) dealing with "incidental" powers is construed in conjunction with the specific grant in Section 92 it is clear that application of the *expressio unius est exclusio alterius* rule requires the construction that national banks have no power to act as insurance agents in cities of *over* 5,000 population. * * *

Since Congress dealt specifically with the insurance agency power in Section 92, the *expressio unius* rule negates the existence of any other power to act as an insurance agent under the general provisions of Section 24(7). * * *

INDEPENDENT INSURANCE AGENTS OF AMERICA v. LUDWIG

United States Court of Appeals, District of Columbia Circuit, 1993.
997 F.2d 958.

BUCKLEY, CIRCUIT JUDGE.

This case is before us on remand from the Supreme Court. It concerns the interpretation of section 92 of the National Bank Act, which authorizes any bank located in a community with a population of 5,000 or less to sell insurance, subject to the regulations of the Comptroller of the Currency. The Comptroller determined that section 92 imposes no geographic limit on the insurance market so that, as long as it is located in a small town, a bank is free to solicit and serve insurance customers everywhere. We uphold the Comptroller's interpretation as permissible. * * *

In 1963, the Comptroller ruled that section 92 permits the branch of a national bank located in a community with a population of 5,000 or under ("small town") to sell insurance even though its principal office is located in a larger community. This policy is codified at 12 C.F.R. § 7.7100 (1993).

* * * In 1984, the United States National Bank of Oregon ("the Bank"), a subsidiary of U.S. Bancorp, proposed to sell insurance from its branch in Banks, Oregon, population 489, "to customers of U.S. Bank and others." * * *

In 1986, the agency * * * approved the Bank's proposal. A letter from Judith A. Walter, the Senior Deputy Comptroller for National Operations, explained:

> Based on our analysis of the relevant legal precedent, we have concluded that * * * a national bank or its branch which is located in a place of 5,000 or under population may sell insurance to existing and potential customers located anywhere. In other words, while the bank or bank branch must be located in a small town, it can sell insurance to persons and businesses located outside that town. * * *

We see no need, however, to canvass the landscape of banking regulation. The Fifty-third Congress expressly permitted small town banks to sell insurance, and the Comptroller has concluded that it did not impose a geographic limit on the insurance business they are allowed to conduct. To overturn the Comptroller's construction, we would have to conclude that it is "so inconsistent" with a "sufficiently clear" statutory policy as to demonstrate that "Congress' clear intent has been violated." Investment Co. Inst. v. Conover, 790 F.2d 925, 935 (D.C. Cir. 1986) (internal quotation marks and citation omitted). We find no basis for doing so. And, to the extent that subsequent developments have threatened to cause the section 92 exception to swallow any rules, the "solution," if there is to be one, lies with Congress, not the courts. * * *

After the Comptroller ruled that insurance customers need not be located in a place of five thousand, section 92 became a powerful tool for national banks seeking to sell insurance. While it is true that the statute only restricted the *bank's* location to the place of less than five thousand, many believed that the original intention of the section was to give small town banks an additional source of income, rather than to permit large banks or their branches to sell insurance nationwide.

In Barnett Bank of Marion County, N.A. v. Nelson, 517 U.S. 25 (1996) (excerpted in Chapter 4), the Supreme Court held that state legislation could not restrict national banks from selling insurance. The legislation in question was a Florida statute that prevented banks from being affiliated with entities selling insurance within the state. While the McCarran–Ferguson Act provided that regulation of insurance was relegated to the states and that federal law was not to preempt it, the Act excepts federal statutes *specifically* regulating insurance from this reverse-preemption rule. The Court found in *Barnett Bank* that section 92 of the NBA did specifically regulate insurance and therefore preempted the inconsistent Florida statute purporting to regulate insurance.

In 1996, the OCC issued an advisory letter stating that it would find state insurance regulation problematic where it treats or affects national banks offering insurance differently than other insurance agents. State statutes subsequently challenged by national banks included a Rhode Island statute that limited the ability of national banks to use customer information to solicit and sell insurance, a New York statute that barred national banks in small towns from selling insurance to their loan customers, and an Ohio statute that limited the ability of national banks to sell insurance to their customers.

OFFICE OF THE COMPTROLLER OF THE CURRENCY
OCC INTERPRETIVE LETTER

1996 WL 655026.

* * * The notification was filed on behalf of the First Union National Banks of North Carolina, South Carolina, Georgia, Florida, Tennessee, Virginia, Maryland, and First Union National Bank, Pennsylvania, a multi-state bank with branches in Pennsylvania, New Jersey and New York. The Banks intend to establish operating subsidiaries in each of the states where they are located. The Banks intend and expect that the Subsidiaries, and/or the Subsidiaries' employees engaged in selling insurance, will be appropriately licensed under applicable state law. The Subsidiaries will engage in general insurance agency activities pursuant to section 92 for all kinds of Insurance, including life, health, property and casualty insurance. The Banks have not at this time requested authority for the Subsidiaries to act as agent for the sale of title insurance. The Subsidiaries also may sell as agent fixed and variable annuities pursuant to 12 U.S.C. § 24(Seventh). * * *

Section 92 authorizes a bank that is "located and doing business in" a place with a population of less than 5,000 to solicit and sell insurance as agent for state-authorized insurance companies. Section 92 does not define what "located and doing business" means. By its terms, section 92 does not require the bank's insurance solicitation and sales activities to occur within the "place of 5,000." Specifically, there is no restriction as to either the identity of the customer or the methodology of sale. Any such restraints were expressly delegated by Congress to the OCC. * * *

[T]he first question we ask is a relatively simple one: Could a non-bank, non-bank-affiliated insurance agency based in a particular "place of 5,000" use the methods, tools and facilities the bank proposes to use to solicit and sell insurance? If state law would not so limit the marketing range, methods and facilities available for non-bank, non-bank-affiliated agencies, then that scope and those methods and facilities also should be permissible for a bank or bank-affiliated agency.

The second question draws on the history of section 92: Are the bank agency's operations inconsistent with the type of activities Congress accepted and authorized? On this issue, a brief recap of the historical perspective when Congress authorized national banks to act as insurance agents in 1916, * * * is helpful. At that time, nonbank insurance agents were soliciting and servicing insurance customers in territories that could encompass large geographic areas, such as whole states or several states. The insurance salesmen's general pattern was to personally solicit customers in any way possible, such as seeking out prospective customers at home, at the office, at the club, or elsewhere. The efficient and prosperous salesmen used any means available to seek out prospects. Similarly, the general business of banking was not limited to the confines of the bank's physical location. Bankers also engaged in personal solicitation of prospective customers.

In conducting their business, insurance salesmen and bankers alike used the latest devices and technology to sell their products, such as the mails, the telegraph, and the telephone. These activities extended beyond city and town boundaries. The clear emphasis for banks was to adopt progressive methods and strategies to sell the bank's services, similar to methods and strategies used in the commercial and industrial business spheres.

In particular, both the insurance and banking industry in 1916 used advertising to solicit business. Banks engaged in extensive advertising in a variety of forms, including local mediums such as newspapers, window displays, and streetcars, as well as nationally circulating trade journals and magazines.

The organizational structure of the "general insurance agency" usually resulted in agents being managed from a local agency, although agents were not necessarily based or present in the local office on a day-to-day basis. By 1916, the general agent acted as the local sales manager and was in charge of the activities of his agents. Salesmen typically were paid by the general agent from the local agency location. Similarly, bank employees typically were managed from the local bank location.

The local agency was the insurance salesmen's place of business for licensing purposes. Insurance agents and managers sent correspondence and applications from the local agency office to the home office while the home office sent the policies for delivery to the local agency offices. Soliciting agents were required to be licensed by the state for registration, tax, or regulatory purposes. Insurance companies also were subject to state licensing requirements.

Section 92 as enacted in 1916 generally described the ways national bank insurance agencies operated: by soliciting and selling, by collecting premiums, and by receiving commissions and fees for these services from the Insurance company. Congress knew how to, but conspicuously did not, delineate or curtail how these activities were to be conducted by bank insurance agencies. Thus, Congress permitted national banks to operate effectively in the insurance business that existed in 1916, and also did not restrain banks ability to modernize their solicitation and sales methods as needed to remain competitive as the insurance business evolved.

Thus, today, insurance agents enjoy expanded geographic flexibility, and employ technological innovations and contemporary marketing methods and facilities. The language of section 92, its legislative history, the practices of banks and insurance agents in 1916, the OCC's longstanding interpretive ruling, and recent cases all support the conclusion that a national bank insurance agency located in a "place of 5,000" should be permitted the same marketing range and be able to use the same marketing tools and facilities as generally available for licensed insurance agencies in the state(s) in which the bank agency operates.

Accordingly, the following general principles can be distilled from the foregoing analysis to define the scope of solicitation and sales activities permissible for national banks under section 92:

The agency located in the "place of 5,000" must, of course, be bona fide. In the present situation that will clearly be the case. Agents will be managed through the agency and the "place of 5,000" will be the agency's business location for licensing purposes. Each agency will be responsible for collecting commissions from insurance carriers and paying commissions to its licensed sales staff. The agency also generally will be responsible for processing insurance applications, delivery of insurance policies, and collection of premiums, where consistent with procedures of the relevant insurance carriers. In addition, business records of the agency, including copies of customer application and policy information, and licensing, customer complaint, and other compliance records, will be available at the "place of 5,000."

The bank agency and its agents may seek the same market range and use the same marketing tools and facilities as generally available for a licensed insurance agency, not affiliated with a bank, that is based in the "place of 5,000." This will generally allow the following:

- Meetings with customers and solicitations and sales of insurance by agents of the bank agency may take place at locations inside the "place of 5,000" as well as at locations outside that "place," provided the agents are managed and paid through the bank agency located in the "place of 5,000" and use that location as their place of business for licensing purposes. If an insurance company has adopted other procedures for its nonbank agents, however, the bank agency may follow the same procedures as other insurance agents selling the company's policies.

- Mailings to advertise and sell insurance may originate from inside or outside of the "place of 5,000," and brochures, leaflets, and other literature alerting potential customers to the bank's insurance activities may be distributed from locations both inside and outside of the "place of 5,000," including other branches of the same bank. Personnel of bank branches outside of the "place of 5,000" also may make referrals to the bank's insurance agency. Likewise, telephone and cybermarketing may be used and the calls and messages need not originate within the "place of 5,000."

• The bank may contract with third parties to assist the agency's sales activities. For example, third parties might provide advertising support, direct mail marketing services, telemarketing services, payments processing, or other types of "back office" support. * * *

QUESTIONS AND NOTES

1. Although the *Saxon* opinion, excerpted earlier in this section, indicated that Section 24(Seventh) does not permit national banks to act generally either as insurance agents or underwriters, the OCC recognized numerous exceptions. It approved underwriting of title insurance and credit life insurance, as well as agency for the sale of title insurance, credit life insurance, municipal bond insurance, and mortgage reinsurance.

2. National banks made further inroads into the insurance business in 1995 when the Supreme Court, in NationsBank of North Carolina v. Variable Annuity Life Insurance Co., 513 U.S. 251 (1995) (excerpted in Chapter 4), held that a national bank could sell fixed and variable rate annuities. The Court found that annuities were financial investment products (rather than insurance) for purposes of federal banking law and that banks may act as agents or brokers with respect to them.

3. Although annuities may not be insurance products under the NBA, the Seventh Circuit Court of Appeals held that fixed annuities remain insurance products for purposes of the McCarran–Ferguson Act so that their sale is subject to state insurance regulation. American Deposit Corp. v. Schacht, 84 F.3d 834, 842–43 (7th Cir. 1996), cert. denied, 519 U.S. 870 (1996) (holding that "Retirement CDs" were fixed annuities). The decision in *Schacht* was not the only blow to Retirement CDs. The Eleventh Circuit also held that underwriting Retirement CDs involves a type of risk shifting that is not part of the business of banking. Blackfeet National Bank v. Nelson, 171 F.3d 1237 (11th Cir.), cert. denied, 528 U.S. 1004 (1999). The Internal Revenue Service ended this fight when it issued regulations providing that interest could not accumulate tax free, effectively eliminating the justification for this product.

B. STATE BANKS

For years, a number of states allowed their own state-chartered banks to provide insurance services to their customers. South Dakota and Delaware led the way in authorizing expansive insurance activities for banks chartered in their states. On December 13, 1984, the FDIC proposed a rule amendment to prohibit insured banks, which would include most state banks, from directly engaging in real estate, underwriting insurance, reinsurance, and engaging in a surety business.[18] After receiv-

---

18. Powers Inconsistent With the Purposes of Federal Deposit Law, 49 Fed. Reg. 48,552 (Dec. 13, 1984).

ing over five hundred comments, the FDIC revised the proposal to, among other things, permit an insured bank to operate a life insurance underwriting department within the bank, subject to various conditions.[19] Over two years later, the FDIC withdrew the proposed rule, claiming that it had grown "stale" and needed updating.[20] More importantly, since there had been no systemic problems (i.e., bank failures), the FDIC decided to grant state banks a degree of leeway.

BB&T Corporation, headquartered in Winston–Salem, North Carolina, and parent company of state-chartered Branch Banking and Trust Company, has operated insurance agencies since 1922. It exemplifies a successful marriage of banking and insurance agency activities. Beginning in the mid–1980s, it expanded its insurance agency operations through a strategy of aggressive acquisition of independent agencies. The strategy was based on the assumption that there were opportunities for profit when agencies with duplicative back office operations were put under one roof, thereby reducing overall costs. BB&T owns the seventh largest retail insurance brokerage in the country. BB&T sells life, health, title, and property insurance products. Wells Fargo & Co., parent of Wells Fargo Bank, N.A., operates the nation's largest bank-owned insurance broker.

The Federal Reserve Board challenged an early Citicorp application requesting permission for its South Dakota bank to engage in insurance activities. The Fed was concerned that the South Dakota bank would primarily operate as an insurance agency, rather than a bank.[21]

CITICORP v. BOARD OF GOVERNORS OF THE FEDERAL RESERVE SYSTEM

United States Court of Appeals, Second Circuit, 1991.
936 F.2d 66.

NEWMAN, CIRCUIT JUDGE.

Once again we consider an aspect of the broad issue of the extent to which banks are authorized to engage in nonbanking activities. That issue was before us just two years ago in Independent Insurance Agents of America, Inc. v. Board of Governors, 890 F.2d 1275 (2d Cir. 1989) (*Merchants II*), cert. denied, 498 U.S. 810 (1990). We there ruled, in agreement with the Federal Reserve Board ("the Board" or "the Fed"), that the Bank Holding Company Act ("BHCA" or "the Act") did not preclude bank subsidiaries of a bank holding company from selling insurance. The question now before us is the one left open in *Merchants II*— whether the BHCA extends the regulatory authority of the Fed to the subsidiary of a holding company's bank subsidiary.

---

19. Powers Inconsistent With the Purposes of Federal Deposit Law, 50 Fed. Reg. 23,964 (June 7, 1985).

20. Powers Inconsistent With the Purposes of Federal Deposit Law, 52 Fed. Reg. 48,447 (Dec. 22, 1987).

21. Order Issued Under Bank Holding Company Act, Bank Merger Act, Bank Service Corp. Act, and Federal Reserve Act, 71 Fed. Res. Bull. 789 (1985).

The question arises on a petition for review filed by Citicorp challenging the Board's September 5, 1990, order. That order requires one of Citicorp's bank subsidiaries, Citibank Delaware, to terminate insurance activities that the bank subsidiary was conducting through its operating subsidiary, Family Guardian Life Insurance Co. ("Family Guardian"). Though mindful of the deference due an agency's construction of the statute it is administering, we conclude that, once the BHCA has been construed to leave the regulation of a holding company's subsidiary banks to their chartering authorities, the Act cannot sensibly be interpreted to reimpose the authority of the Fed on a generation-skipping basis to regulate the subsidiary's subsidiary. We therefore grant the petition for review and vacate the Board's order.

Before introducing the facts, it will be helpful to outline briefly the pertinent statutory provisions of the BHCA, the construction placed on those provisions at the Board's urging by this Court in *Merchants II*, the Board's regulation concerning operating subsidiaries, and the pertinent aspects of the Delaware regulatory framework.

The principal regulatory powers of the Fed concerning bank holding companies are set forth in sections 3 and 4 of the Act. 12 U.S.C. §§ 1842, 1843 (1988). Section 3 requires Board approval of the acquisition of ownership or control of any bank by a bank holding company, with narrow exceptions not here relevant. Section 3 sets forth factors governing acquisition approval, focusing on the competitive effect of the proposed acquisition, the financial and managerial resources of both the holding company and the acquired bank, and the convenience and needs of the community served. Id. § 1842(c).

Section 4 of the Act, the provision ultimately at issue in this litigation, contains two sets of prohibitions. First, it specifies, in what might be called the "ownership clause," that a bank holding company may not "retain direct or indirect ownership or control of any voting shares of any company which is not a bank or bank holding company." Id. § 1843(a) (2). Second, it provides, in what might be called the "activities clause," that a bank holding company may not "engage in any activities other than (A) those of banking or of managing or controlling banks ... and (B) those permitted under [section 4(c) (8) of the Act]...." Id. Section 4 (c) (8) sets forth the so-called "closely related to banking" exception to the nonbanking prohibition of the ownership and activities clauses. In relevant part, section 4(c) (8) states that the section 4(a) nonbanking prohibitions shall not apply to

> shares of any company the activities of which the Board after due notice and opportunity for hearing has determined (by order or regulation) to be so closely related to banking or managing or controlling banks as to be a proper incident thereto, but for purposes of this subsection it is not closely related to banking or managing or controlling banks for a bank holding company to provide insurance as a principal, agent or broker....

Id.

In 1989 the Board approved an application by Merchants National Corporation, a bank holding company, to permit two of its Indiana bank subsidiaries to engage in insurance activities. Merchants National Corp., 75 Fed. Res. Bull. 388 (1989). That ruling was vigorously challenged in this Court by insurance interests who contended that the BHCA was intended to accomplish a nearly complete separation of banking and nonbanking activities by precluding bank holding companies and all entities within their systems from engaging in nonbanking activities, other than the "closely related to banking" activities specifically identified in section 4(c)(8) of the Act. The Board took the position that Congress had not gone so far. In the Board's view, Congress had precluded non-banking activities by bank holding companies themselves but had not wished to displace the traditional authority of state and national bank chartering bodies to determine what nonbanking activities could appropriately be engaged in by banks that are subject to their regulatory authority, even though such banks were owned by a bank holding company under the jurisdiction of the Fed.

The dispute between the Board and the banking interests, on the one hand, and the insurance interests, on the other hand, was a substantial one. Ultimately, we ruled in favor of the Board. *Merchants II*, 890 F.2d at 1284. We acknowledged that the statute was not entirely clear and that arguments supporting each of the contending positions could plausibly be based on some of the language of the Act, some aspects of the structure of the Act, and some passages from the legislative history. Id. at 1281–84. After canvassing the available evidence, we concluded that the construction urged by the Board was a "reasonable interpretation" of the Act, "one that confides decisions concerning the scope of insurance and other nonbank activities of bank subsidiaries to their national and state chartering authorities." Id. at 1284.

In *Merchants II* we noted the Board's additional position that, although the Act denied the Board authority to preclude bank subsidiaries of a bank holding company from engaging in nonbank activities, it nonetheless empowered the Board to preclude the subsidiaries of bank subsidiaries from engaging in nonbank activities. Though the insurance interests pressed upon us the "apparent awkwardness and perhaps illogic," id. at 1282, of the Board's generation-skipping approach, we confined our ruling to approval of the Board's construction of the Act to permit nonbank activities by bank subsidiaries (the first generation after the holding company), and left for another day the issue of whether the Act could simultaneously be construed to bar nonbank activities by a subsidiary's subsidiaries (the second generation). That day has now arrived.

Long before the administrative and judicial rulings in *Merchants II*, the Board had issued Regulation Y, the so-called "operating subsidiary rule," which purports to govern the activities of subsidiaries of a bank holding company. See 12 C.F.R. Pt. 225 (1990) (current version). In general, such subsidiaries must limit their activities to those banking and "closely related to banking" activities permitted by section 4 of the Act. However, one provision of Regulation Y permits state-chartered banks, without the Board's prior approval, to acquire

> all ... of the securities of a company that engages solely in activities in which the parent bank may engage, at locations at which the bank may engage in the activity, and subject to the same limitations *as if the bank were engaging in the activity directly.*

Id. § 225.22(d) (2) (ii) (emphasis added). Thus, under Regulation Y and the Board's construction of section 4, as endorsed in *Merchants II*, a subsidiary of a state-chartered bank subsidiary of a holding company may engage in nonbank activities permitted to the bank under state law, provided that the activities are conducted under the same limitations that would apply if the bank were engaging in the activities "directly."

In May 1990, Delaware enacted the Bank and Trust Company Insurance Powers Act of 1989, 67 Del. Laws, c. 223 (1990) ("the Delaware statute"). The Delaware statute permits Delaware banks, under certain conditions, to engage in insurance activities (other than title insurance). The statute affords the banks the option of conducting insurance activities through a "department" or "division" of the bank or through a subsidiary of the bank. Whichever option is chosen, the statute requires substantial structural barriers between the bank's insurance activities and its banking activities.

For example, the statute requires that the assets of the bank may be applied only to satisfy the non-insurance liabilities of the bank and not those of the bank's insurance "division," id. § 8, and the assets of the insurance "division" may be applied only to satisfy the liabilities of that "division" and not the other liabilities of the bank, id. § 22. The statute places a 25 percent limit on the amount of the bank's total capital, surplus, and undivided profits that may be allocated to its insurance "division," id. § 10, and the minimum capital that the bank is required to maintain under Delaware banking law may not be used to meet the separate capital requirements of the "division" imposed by state insurance law, id. § 3. The statute provides that for purposes of the Delaware Insurance Code an insurance "division" of a bank is treated as an insurance company "in the same manner and to the same extent as if it were a separately incorporated subsidiary ... with separate capital accounts, assets and liabilities." Id. § 17.

In general, Delaware authorizes its bank commissioner to regulate the banking activities of state-chartered banks and authorizes its insurance commissioner to regulate the insurance activities of a bank's insurance "division." Id. §§ 5, 38. However, the statute permits the bank commissioner to supervise the insurance "division" whenever he determines that the "division's" activities are "likely to have a materially adverse effect on the safety and soundness of the bank." Id. § 5.

Citicorp is a bank holding company with assets of more than $200 billion. In 1982, Citicorp obtained a charter from Delaware for Citibank Delaware, a commercial bank wholly owned by Citicorp. Citibank Delaware has assets of more than $2 billion and serves customers in 35 states.

In 1986, with the approval of the Fed, Citicorp established Family Guardian as a wholly owned subsidiary to underwrite and sell certain credit-related insurance expressly authorized for bank holding companies by section 4(c)(8)(A) of the BHCA, 12 U.S.C. § 1843(c)(8)(A). The day after the Delaware statute was enacted, Citicorp transferred all of the voting shares of Family Guardian to Citibank Delaware in order to permit Family Guardian to transact the broader range of insurance activities authorized under the Delaware statute for insurance "divisions" and subsidiaries of Delaware banks. Family Guardian then began to expand its operations to include insurance underwriting and other insurance activities within the scope of Delaware law, though beyond the scope of the "closely related to banking" activities specified in section 4(c)(8) of the BHCA. * * *

Citicorp contends that the BHCA does not permit the Fed to regulate the activities of the subsidiary of a bank subsidiary of a holding company. Before the *Merchants II* litigation, that contention would have posed a substantial issue because a major controversy then existed as to whether the BHCA permitted non-banking activities (other than those specifically authorized by section 4(c)(8)) to be conducted anywhere in a system controlled by a bank holding company. The insurance interests in *Merchants II* contended that neither a holding company, nor a bank subsidiary, nor the subsidiary of a bank subsidiary could engage in nonbanking activities. However, the Fed disagreed with that interpretation of the Act and argued that the bank subsidiaries of a holding company were beyond the Board's regulatory authority. In the Fed's view, Congress intended to leave unimpaired the primary regulatory authority of state and national bank chartering agencies to determine the activities of institutions under their jurisdiction. We agreed with that construction of the statute.

Thus, in the aftermath of *Merchants II*, we take the Act as if it said in terms, "The Board is without authority to limit the activities of a bank subsidiary of a bank holding company." Now the question is whether the Board may nonetheless regulate the activities of a bank subsidiary's subsidiary. The rationale of the position that the Board successfully urged upon us in *Merchants II* requires an answer consistent with the interpretation the Board there urged us to adopt. The Board urged, and we agreed, that Congress wanted bank chartering agencies to regulate the activities of banks within their jurisdiction. By virtue of their authority over the banks that they charter, those agencies have ample authority to determine the permissible activities of the subsidiaries owned by the banks. We have been given no reason to believe that Congress wanted the jurisdiction of bank chartering authorities to end at the corporate structure of the bank itself, rather than extend throughout the chain of companies owned by the bank. Surely a bank chartering agency, charged with the responsibility to maintain the soundness of a bank, is vitally interested in the assets owned by a bank, including shares of wholly owned subsidiaries. In the pending case, Delaware has demonstrated that its regulatory authority over Delaware-chartered banks is not confined to activities occurring within the bank, but extends to insurance activities whether conducted within the bank (albeit in a separate "division") or in a subsidiary of the bank.

Moreover, the Board has provided no basis for believing that Congress wished to create two classes of state-chartered banks—those owned and those not owned by bank holding companies. Before *Merchants II*, such an argument was plausible; Congress might have wanted those state-chartered banks owned by holding companies to be confined to banking activities, leaving banks not so owned to have broader activity. But once the Board persuaded us to read the statute to leave all state-chartered banks free to sell insurance, subject to state, not Board, regulation, there is no basis for believing that Congress simultaneously adopted a generation-skipping approach and authorized the Board to bar the subsidiaries of state-chartered banks from selling insurance whenever those banks were in turn the subsidiaries of a holding company.

Neither of the two technical statutory arguments tendered by the Board supports the generation-skipping approach. Section 4(a) of the Act provides that no bank holding company shall acquire or retain "direct or indirect ownership or control of any voting shares of any company which is not a bank." 12 U.S.C. § 1843(a) (1), (2). That provision would plainly bar a holding company from using some entity other than a bank to acquire or retain control of a nonbanking company. A holding company may not directly acquire an insurance company, and it may not do so indirectly through some shell corporation, voting trust, or other nonbanking entity. But section 4 and the entire BHCA obviously contemplate that a holding company may own a bank, and if the Act permits the bank to sell insurance, subject to state regulation, it leaves the states equally free to permit bank subsidiaries to sell insurance. That is made explicit in section 7 of the Act, which provides:

> No provision of this chapter shall be construed as preventing any State from exercising such powers and jurisdiction which it now has or may hereafter have with respect to ... banks ... and subsidiaries thereof.

12 U.S.C. § 1846.

The Board also relies on section 2(g)(1) of the Act, which provides that "shares owned or controlled by any subsidiary of a bank holding company shall be deemed to be indirectly owned or controlled by such bank holding company." 12 U.S.C. § 1841(g)(1). There is no doubt that a literal application of this language would mean that Citicorp shall be deemed to own Family Guardian. But the question remains whether, in adding section 2(g)(1) in 1966, Congress intended to extend to the Board the authority to prevent a state-chartered bank like Citicorp Delaware from selling insurance through an operating subsidiary like Family Guardian. Citicorp contends, and we agree, that the purpose of section 2(g)(1) was to make clear that the BHCA applied when a holding company's *nonbank* subsidiaries controlled, but did not wholly own, another company. See Amend the Bank Holding Company Act of 1956: Hearings on S. 2353, S. 2418 and H.R. 7371 Before a Subcomm. of the Senate Comm. on Banking and Currency, Pt. 1, 89th Cong., 2d Sess. 342 (1966) ("Technical question[] ha[s] arisen" regarding applicability of phrase to situation in which a bank holding company "owns less than 50% of the voting shares of" a company that owns another company.). The 1966 amendment was noncontroversial and elicited no opposition from national or state bank regulators who surely would have objected, as they do now, to the contention that the amendment permits the Fed, and not these chartering regulators, to determine what activities may be engaged in by the operating subsidiary of a bank subject to their jurisdiction. * * *

The petition for review is granted, and the order of the Board is vacated.

In 1991, the Federal Deposit Insurance Corporation Improvement Act (FDICIA) limited the activities that state-chartered banks could engage in as *principal* to those activities permissible for national banks. 12 U.S.C.A. § 1831a(a). Nevertheless, state-chartered banks could still engage in *agency* activities authorized by their state chartering authorities. Other insurance activities, even as a principal, could be authorized under FDICIA if permitted under state law and if the FDIC found the bank to be well-capitalized and concluded that the proposed activity posed no risk to the safety and soundness of the federal deposit insurance fund. However, FDICIA specifically prohibited insurance underwriting by state banks, except to the extent permitted for national banks. 12 U.S.C.A. § 1831a(b). There was also a limited grandfather provision that allowed subsidiaries of state chartered banks to continue, but not expand, their previously permissible underwriting activities.

Between 1995 and 1998, the number of states that allowed state banks to operate insurance agencies increased from twenty-two to forty. All forty granted their state banks broad insurance powers, although in some instances state banks were entitled to expanded powers by virtue of so-called "wild card" statutes that permitted state banks to engage in all activities permissible for national banks. Several other states permitted banks to sell annuities or insurance. Seven states permitted insurance sales, but only in designated locations (such as places of less than 5,000 in population). Two states permitted insurance sales only in designated places, but permitted insurance products to be marketed throughout the state. One state, Massachusetts, did not permit state-chartered banks to engage in any insurance activities.

C. NONBANKING SUBSIDIARY OF A BANK HOLDING COMPANY

Bank holding companies could undertake expanded activities that were "closely related to banking" through their nonbanking subsidiaries. Prior to 1982, many bank holding companies had subsidiaries that performed insurance agency functions, and some even underwrote credit life, credit accident, and health insurance. The possibility for expansion of insurance activities through the holding company largely evaporated, however, with the passage of the Garn–St Germain Act of 1982.[22] That Act provided that "it is not closely related to banking ... for a bank holding company to provide insurance as a principal, agent, or broker," with certain exceptions. Among the exceptions were two grandfather provisions, including one for activities authorized before 1982. These grandfathered insurance sales provisions have been interpreted to be transferable upon acquisition. Moreover, an exception parallel to section 92 of the NBA exists for activities of the nonbanking subsidiary in a place of less than five thousand people. The Fed did not read this exception as expansively regarding nonbanking subsidiaries as the OCC read section 92 regarding national banks. Exceptions also existed for small bank holding companies with total assets of less than $50 million and for providing credit-related insurance as a principal or agent. Notwithstanding the many exceptions contained in the BHCA, the clear general rule forbidding bank holding companies from participating in insurance precluded the FRB from authorizing bank holding companies to engage in or affiliate with companies underwriting insurance. Some bank holding companies established offshore subsidiaries to engage in reinsuring insurance policies sold abroad—a practice similar to underwriting, although not as risky.

Even prior to the adoption of the Gramm–Leach–Bliley Act, seventy percent of all banks offered some insurance products ranging from annuities and credit-related insurance to property, life, and medical insurance. In the annuity market, banks were significant participants, accounting for twenty-five to thirty percent of all annuity sales. One-third of all fixed annuities and twelve percent of all variable annuity products were sold at banks.

QUESTIONS AND NOTES

1. Why do you think Massachusetts did not allow its banks to engage insurance activities?

2. How do you think the insurance companies responded to the intrusion of banks onto their turf?

---

22. The Garn–St Germain Depository Institutions Act of 1982, Pub. L. No. 97–320, 96 Stat. 1469.

SECTION 3. THE GRAMM–LEACH–BLILEY ACT

To many, the Gramm–Leach–Bliley Act (GLBA) is most notable for its repeal of the Glass–Steagall Act restrictions on commercial bank affiliates' investment banking activities. Of equal interest, however, are provisions that widen the entrance for banks into the insurance industry. Those provisions were not easily added. Initially, the trade association for independent insurance agents ferociously opposed bank intrusion into the insurance industry. Clearly, banks were a threat to the agents' existence. Independent agencies already faced competition from direct line purchasers that allowed consumers to buy insurance from the insurance underwriting company without having to pay an intervening agency. As one writer noted, "we are witnessing the virtual disappearance, nominally, of the 'life insurance agent' as this person is now being named 'financial planner.' "[23]

This transformation occurred because many insurance agents and securities brokers were cross-licensed, and many securities brokers selling insurance were working for a bank affiliate. The insurance lobby effectively capitulated to bank competition in 1997 when the Independent Insurance Agents of America announced that it would support legislation allowing the affiliation of banks and insurance firms if functional regulation of insurance activities by the traditional state regulator was retained, and if appropriate consumer protection measures were enacted. Perhaps the insurance underwriters decided that banks would function well as retail delivery vehicles for insurance products and that empowering more bank-affiliated insurance agents could improve insurance company sales.

The biggest bombshell in the world of banks and insurance arrived in April of 1998, when Citicorp announced that it was merging with Travelers Group, which also owned Salomon Smith Barney. The value of this merger was set at $83 billion. The combined firm's holding company became Citigroup, Inc. Citigroup had more than 100 million customers world wide and offered a wide range of products ranging from corporate finance to consumer banking, securities and insurance. The Fed's approval of the Citibank/Travelers merger was subject to a requirement that the new Citigroup divest itself of the Travelers insurance underwriting unit because of the restrictions on bank holding companies engaging in insurance underwriting activities. The divestiture period, however, was by statute a minimum of two years, with possible extension to a maximum of five years upon application to the Fed. 12 U.S.C.A. § 1843(a). This merger placed increased pressure on Congress to repeal restrictions on insurance activities, especially underwriting.

A. NONBANKING SUBSIDIARY OF A HOLDING COMPANY

GLBA significantly expanded the ability of banks to engage in insurance activities. A bank holding company that is designated as a financial

---

23. Howard J. Sachs, Merging of Life Insurance and Securities Industries Accelerates, 25 Est. Plan. 326 (1998).

holding company (FHC) may engage in activities that are (A) "financial in nature or incidental to such financial activity," or (B) "complementary to a financial activity" and do not present a substantial risk to the safety or soundness of the depository institution subsidiaries or the financial system. 12 U.S.C.A. § 1843(k)(1). Specifically listed as activities that are financial in nature are "[i]nsuring, guaranteeing, or indemnifying against loss, harm, damage, illness, disability, or death, or providing and issuing annuities, and acting as principal, agent, or broker for purposes of the foregoing, in any State." 12 U.S.C.A. § 1843(k)(4)(B). Moreover, it is permissible for a subsidiary of an FHC to own shares, assets, or ownership interests in a company or other entity if such ownership represents an investment made in the normal course of business by an insurance company in accordance with state law regulating such investments, and the FHC does not routinely manage or operate the company in which it holds the investment, except as necessary to ensure a reasonable return on the investment. 12 U.S.C.A § 1843(k)(4)(H) & (I).

Thus, GLBA legitimates Citigroup's ownership of both Citibank and Travelers Insurance Company. Bank holding companies that wish to expand into insurance underwriting need to qualify as an FHC and conduct underwriting activities in a subsidiary of the FHC. Numerous institutions have already filed as FHCs, enabling them to expand their financial activities when they desire.

B. NATIONAL BANKS AND NATIONAL BANK SUBSIDIARIES

Under GLBA, neither a national bank nor its subsidiary may underwrite insurance unless underwriting was permitted by enforceable OCC rulings as of January 1, 1999. 15 U.S.C.A. § 6712(a), (b). The OCC permits underwriting of credit-related insurance products. The Act, however, specifically prohibits the underwriting of title insurance or an annuity contract even if it has already been approved by the OCC. 15 U.S.C.A. § 6712(b)(3).

The financial subsidiaries of national banks, like the subsidiaries of an FHC, are authorized under GLBA to engage generally in activities that are "financial in nature or incidental to a financial activity." However, insurance underwriting, annuity issuance, real estate investment and development, and merchant banking are specifically excluded for a financial subsidiary even though all are permitted for an FHC subsidiary. 12 U.S.C.A. § 24a(a)(2). This curious distinction is apparently the result of a compromise in the turf war between the FRB (regulator of FHCs, bank holding companies, and their respective nonbank subsidiaries) and the OCC (primary regulator of national banks and national bank subsidiaries). The compromise was apparently premised on an assumption that certain financial activities were too risky to be placed in a financial subsidiary of a bank.

Section 92 of the NBA, permitting national banks to act as an insurance agent in a place of less than five thousand, was not repealed by GLBA, so presumably national banks may still conduct insurance agency activities in offices of the national bank located in a place of less than five thousand people. A financial subsidiary of a national bank is not subject to the place of five thousand limitation, however, and for this reason most national banks have transferred their insurance agency activities to a financial subsidiary.

In another curious restriction, GLBA forbids the sale of title insurance by a national bank unless authorized under state law for a state-chartered bank. 15 U.S.C.A. § 6713(a), (b)(1). In such a state, a national bank may sell title insurance, subject to the same restrictions applicable to the state-chartered bank. The title insurance sale restriction applies only to the national bank, so presumably, a financial subsidiary should be able to sell title insurance, which would provide an additional incentive to transfer insurance agency activities to a financial subsidiary of a national bank. A grandfather provision permits a national bank or its subsidiary to continue any title insurance activities (underwriting or sale) that were "actively and lawfully" conducted before the enactment of GLBA. 15 U.S.C.A. § 6713(c). However, a national bank with no affiliate other than a subsidiary that underwrites insurance may not directly engage in underwriting title insurance. In addition, if a national bank has an affiliate that underwrites insurance but is not a subsidiary of the bank, neither the bank nor its subsidiary may underwrite title insurance pursuant to the grandfather provision. Although a national bank's title insurance activities may continue pursuant to this grandfather provision, the grandfather provision in effect pushes the title insurance activities out of the bank into a separate existing subsidiary or affiliate engaged in insurance.

The possible preemption of state insurance laws that significantly interfere with the ability of a national bank or national bank subsidiary to engage in insurance activities is discussed further in Section D.

C.   STATE BANKS AND STATE BANK SUBSIDIARIES

State banks and their subsidiaries, as a general matter, are prohibited by the FDICIA from engaging in insurance underwriting even if permitted under state law, except to the extent that activity is permissible for national banks. 12 U.S.C.A. § 1831a. The new insurance underwriting restrictions for national banks in GLBA also restrict the underwriting ability of state banks. Thus, state banks cannot underwrite title insurance unless they fall within one of the limited exceptions provided in the FDICIA.

GLBA does not answer definitively whether state banks may issue annuities if so authorized under state law. GLBA clearly prevents national banks from issuing annuities. But if annuities are not insurance, then they are not subject to the underwriting prohibitions. Moreover, a state bank or its subsidiary could apply for the FDIC's permission to issue annuities as a principal.

Insurance agency activities, if permitted under state law, are not linked to national bank powers since the FDICIA only limits a state bank's activities as principal. In a state that authorizes title insurance sales for its state banks, those sales may continue under GLBA. Although national banks under GLBA generally may not engage in the underwriting or sale of title insurance, a national bank may sell title insurance in a particular state to the same extent as a state bank.

A state bank, to the extent permitted by state law, may own a subsidiary that engages in activities comparable to those permitted by GLBA for a national bank's financial subsidiary. 12 U.S.C.A. § 1831w. The conditions for establishing a financial subsidiary of a state bank mirror those for establishing a financial subsidiary of a national bank. In addition, a state bank may retain existing subsidiaries (that may not qualify as financial subsidiaries) and continue to engage in activities lawfully conducted by such subsidiaries as of the date of GLBA's enactment. Moreover, a state bank subsidiary may still apply to engage in new activities pursuant to section 24 of the Federal Deposit Insurance Act, bypassing the requirements necessary for establishing a financial subsidiary.

D.   STATE REGULATION OF INSURANCE

GLBA continues the McCarran–Ferguson Act's requirement that insurance be regulated at the state level. 15 U.S.C.A. § 6701(a), (b). The statute specifically addresses the interaction between state insurance regulators and federal banking regulators, anticipating the likely regulatory struggle. See 15 U.S.C.A. § 6714. The Act's adoption of a functional regulatory structure is likely to be put to the test in regulating the insurance activities of banking organizations.

SCOTT A. SINDER
THE GRAMM–LEACH–BLILEY ACT AND STATE REGULATION OF THE BUSINESS OF INSURANCE
5 N.C. Banking Inst. 49 (2001).

* * * GLBA explicitly "recogniz[es] the primacy and legal authority of the States to regulate the insurance activities of all persons."[24] The Act thus generally mandates that all insurance activities will be "functionally regulated" by the States regardless of the nature of the entity that is engaging in those activities. To implement this requirement, the Act specifically provides that:

---

24. [n.78] H.R. Rept. No. 106–434, at 156 (1999) (issuing a joint explanatory statement on the operation of state law).

- The McCarran–Ferguson Act remains good law;

- No person or entity may provide insurance as principal or agent in any State unless they are properly licensed to do so in accordance with the laws of that State;[25]

- "The insurance activities of any person or [entity] shall be functionally regulated by the States," subject to the preemption provisions discussed below;[26] and

- Small-town national banks selling insurance as agents under their Section 92 authority are fully subject to state regulation of those activities (thus eliminating the OCC's power to serve as the sole regulator of national bank insurance sales activities).

Section 104 of the Act limits the scope of permissible state "functional regulation" of insurance activities by establishing preemption standards. The Act thus generally prohibits any State from preventing or restricting any affiliation among bank holding company subsidiaries that is authorized under the Act.

The Act also generally dictates that a state non-sales insurance requirement cannot be preempted as long as it does not apply to the activities of insured depository institutions (except those selling savings bank life insurance). Although at first blush this limitation seems broad, the Act limits the insurance authority for national bank subsidiaries to sales activities. It also specifically prohibits bank subsidiaries from engaging in insurance activities "as principal," and it prohibits national banks from engaging in underwriting-related activities. The remaining question is whether there is some insurance activity in which the Comptroller could authorize national banks to engage "as principal" that is not underwriting-related. None have been identified to date.

Although the Act clarifies that State requirements of "general applicability" relating to corporate governance or antitrust concerns are generally preserved,[27] it also establishes a "nondiscrimination" preemption standard that prohibits a State from regulating the insurance activities authorized or permitted under the Act or any other provision of law in a manner that—

(1) overtly distinguishes between insured depository institutions and other persons engaged in insurance sales activities in any way adverse to an insured depository institution;

(2) as interpreted or applied, has or will have an impact on insured depository institutions that is substantially more adverse than its impact on other persons providing similar products and services;

25. [n.80] * * * 15 U.S.C. § 6701(b). * * *

26. [n.81] * * * 15 U.S.C. § 6711. * * *

27. [n.86] * * * 15 U.S.C. § 6701(f)(2).

(3) effectively prevents an insured depository institution from exercising its powers under this Act or federally law; or

(4) conflicts with the purpose of the GLBA.

For insurance sales, solicitation and cross-marketing activities, the primary rule is as follows:

> In accordance with the legal standards for preemption set forth in the decision of the Supreme Court in Barnett Bank of Marion County N.A. v. Nelson, [citation omitted] no State may, by statute, regulation, order, interpretation, or other action, prevent or significantly interfere with the ability of a depository institution, or an affiliate thereof, to engage, directly or indirectly, either by itself or in conjunction with any other person, in any insurance sales, solicitation, or cross-marketing activity.[28]

There are two noteworthy facets of this provision. First, it is not national bank specific in any way. It instead governs state regulation of all depository institutions and their affiliates. Second, the Act expressly incorporates the "prevent or significantly interfere" preemption standard articulated in *Barnett* and explicitly dictates that nothing in the Act is intended to amend or modify that standard in any way. Both the explicit reference to *Barnett* in the preemption provision itself and the subsequent construction provision declaring that "nothing in this paragraph [Section 104(d)] shall be construed . . . to limit the applicability of the decision" in *Barnett* make this absolutely clear.

The Act's preservation of the *Barnett* "prevent or significantly interfere" preemption standard is, however, subject to two important caveats. First, state insurance sales requirements enacted after September 3, 1998 also are subject to the "nondiscrimination" requirement discussed above. Second, any state consumer protection law that falls within one of the thirteen "safe harbor" provisions included in the Act and discussed below is specifically exempted from preemption under the Act.

The thirteen separate "safe harbor" provisions essentially permit a State to impose restrictions that are substantially the same as but no more burdensome or restrictive than the "safe harbor" provisions of the GLBA. Any state law that falls within a safe harbor cannot be preempted. The "safe harbors" apply to laws already in place as well as those that may be enacted in the future.[29] They protect state restrictions—

- Prohibiting the rejection of an insurance policy required in connection with a loan because it was sold by an unaffiliated agent.

- Prohibiting the imposition of extra charges on insurance policies required in connection with a loan that are purchased from unaffiliated agents.

---

28. [n.88] * * * 15 U.S.C. § 6701(d)(2)(A) (citing Barnett Bank of Marion County, N.A. v. Nelson, 517 U.S. 25 (1966)).

29. [eds.] 12 U.S.C. § 6701(d)(2)(B).

- Prohibiting misrepresentations regarding the insured or guaranteed status of any insurance product.

- Requiring that commissions can be paid only to licensed insurance agents.

- Prohibiting any referral fees paid to non-licensed individuals to be based on whether the referral results in a transaction.

- Prohibiting the release of insurance information to third parties without the express written consent of the customer.

- Prohibiting the use of health information obtained from insurance records without the express written consent of the customer.

- Prohibiting tying arrangements.

- Requiring the disclosure, prior to any insurance sale, that the product is—(1) not a deposit; (2) not insured by the FDIC; (3) not guaranteed by the financial institution or its subsidiaries or affiliates; and (4) where appropriate, involves investment risk, including loss of principal. This disclosure may be required to be in writing where a writing is practicable.

- Requiring the disclosure, when insurance is required in connection with a loan, that the purchase of insurance from an unaffiliated agent will not affect the loan decision or the credit terms in any way.

- Requiring the completion of credit and insurance transactions through separate documents.

- Prohibiting the inclusion of insurance premiums in a primary credit transaction without the express consent of the customer.

- Requiring the maintenance of separate insurance books and records that must be made available to state insurance regulators for inspection.

It is important to note that the Act precludes the drawing of any inference regarding whether a state insurance sales, solicitation or cross-marketing regulation is preempted under the *Barnett* "prevent or significantly interfere" standard by virtue of the fact that the regulation falls outside one of the thirteen "safe harbor" provisions. The Act thus makes absolutely clear that "nothing in this [Section 104(d)(2)] shall be construed ... to limit the applicability of *Barnett* ... or to create any inference with respect to any State statute, regulation, order, interpretation, or other action that is not described in this paragraph." In addition, as Senator Richard Bryan—the Senate sponsor of the amendment that included the Section 104(d) provisions—noted in comments on the Senate floor that the intent of the provision was to do nothing more than codify the *Barnett* standard, and Congress "intended to leave the development of the interpretation of that standard to the courts."

The new law thus has absolutely no impact on any of the bank sales of insurance consumer protection requirements already in place that are not protected by one of the safe harbor provisions; they are subject to the same "prevent or significant interference" *Barnett* test to which they were subject before enactment of the GLBA.

The Act also establishes a new "expedited dispute resolution" process that applies to any dispute between a State insurance commissioner and federal banking regulators on any insurance issues, including whether a state insurance sales requirement is preempted by this Act. Either regulator may bring a case in the appropriate U.S. Court of Appeals or U.S. Court of Appeals for the District of Columbia Circuit, and the court is required to act on the petition within 60 days. The Section also establishes an appeal right to the United States Supreme Court that must be taken "as soon as practicable." The appellate courts are required to decide all disputes "on their merits," without giving "unequal deference" to either regulator. This "standard of review" section is intended to clarify that the opinions of state insurance regulators are entitled to as much consideration as those of federal banking regulators in resolving these disputes.

In addition to the "safe harbor" protections for many state insurance sales consumer protections, the Act also includes several consumer protection requirements that apply to the insurance sales activities of all insured depository institutions that the federal banking agencies were required to implement within one year from the date of enactment of the Act.[30] These requirements establish federal minimum consumer protections that:

- Prohibit discrimination against non-affiliated agents by providing expedited or enhanced treatment if insurance is purchased from affiliated agents.

- Prohibit tying and other coercive practices.

- Prohibit misrepresentations regarding the federally insured or guaranteed status of any insurance product.

- Prohibit any action could mislead a consumer to believe that they were required to purchase an insurance product from a bank in order to receive a loan from that bank or that could mislead a consumer to believe that they were required to purchase insurance from any particular agent or broker.

- Require the separation of insurance and deposit-taking activities.

- Limit the payment of referral fees to a nominal amount that may not be based on whether the referral results in a transaction.

- Require the disclosure, prior to any insurance sale, that the insurance is—(1) not a deposit; (2) not insured by the FDIC; (3) not guaranteed by the financial institution or its subsidiaries or affiliates; and (4) where appropriate, involves investment risk, including loss of principal.

---

30. [n.113] * * * 12 U.S.C. §§ 1811–3222. * * * Consumer Protection for Depository Institutions Sale of Insurance, 65 Fed. Reg. 75,822 (Dec. 4, 2000). * * *

- Require that an acknowledgment be obtained whenever a disclosure is required from the customer verifying receipt of the disclosure.
- Prohibit any discrimination against an applicant for, or an insured under, any insurance product based on the fact that the person was a victim of domestic violence.

The Act clarifies that the federal insurance sales consumer protection provisions are not intended to be construed as limiting state insurance regulatory authority, and federal banking regulators are required to coordinate their efforts with those of state officials. Moreover, the Act also makes clear that if any State maintains a consumer protection requirement applicable to insured financial institutions that offers more consumer protection than the parallel federal requirement, the state requirement "preempts" the application of the federal requirement in that State. The federal banking regulators are required to determine jointly whether any parallel state consumer protection requirement is more protective; if it is not, the federal banking regulators must advise the State that the federal requirement will apply. The State may then "opt-out" of this preemption if it enacts a statute dictating that its less-restrictive state consumer protection requirement should apply in lieu of the federal requirement. * * *

Finally, the Act contains a set of provisions designed to alleviate the onerous and duplicative burdens associated with the multi-state licensing of insurance agents and brokers. To accomplish this, the Act contains provisions that would establish the National Association of Registered Agents and Brokers (NARAB) as a voluntary licensing clearinghouse for insurance agents and brokers seeking licensure in states in which they are not residents.[31] Under the terms of the legislation, however, if twenty-nine states enact fully uniform or reciprocal licensing statutes within five years (three years, and then an additional two-year grace period), NARAB's creation will be averted. NARAB thus creates a strong incentive for the states to streamline multi-state licensing requirements.

If NARAB does come into existence, it would operate in the following manner. First, an agent or broker must be licensed in his or her own state. Only then could the applicant apply for NARAB membership. Under the terms of the Act, the NAIC [National Association of Insurance Commissioners] would be empowered to establish the criteria and categories of membership in NARAB. According to the subtitle, the standard of professionalism for each of those categories must exceed the highest standard that currently exists in any state. Once a NARAB applicant meets those requirements, the applicant may use NARAB as a "clearinghouse" for multi-state licensing. NARAB would not actually be a federal "license" but, rather, would allow the NAIC to issue state licenses to NARAB members. NARAB members would have to indicate the states in which they wish to be licensed and remit state licensing fees to those states. All other areas of state insurance regulation—such as conformance

---

31.   [n.135] * * * 15 U.S.C. §§ 6751–6766.

with all unfair trade practices acts—would remain fully in force with no preemption granted to NARAB members. Membership in NARAB would be purely voluntary and self-funding, and would be open to all state-licensed insurance producers. * * *

Whether the states can avert the creation of NARAB is the pressing issue. In many ways, this is the most immediate threat to the perpetuation of a state-dominated insurance regulatory system. State insurance regulators are taking the threat seriously, as evidenced by the unprecedented speed with which they adopted a model-licensing act through the NAIC. State regulators believe that adoption of the NAIC model in at least twenty-nine states would satisfy the statutory threshold and avert the creation of NARAB. * * *

———————

The requisite number of jurisdictions enacted either uniform or reciprocal licensing requirements in time to avoid the creation of NARAB. Most of the state statutes contain a reciprocity provision, rather than uniform licensing standards.

Preemption by the OCC of state insurance statutes and regulations has already created much controversy. In Association of Banks in Insurance, Inc. v. Duryee, 270 F.3d 397 (6th Cir. 2001), the court considered a challenge brought by a national bank and several banking industry trade groups to provisions in the Ohio insurance law authorizing Ohio's Superintendent of Insurance to deny or revoke an insurance license upon determining that the principal purpose of the license is or has been to solicit or place insurance on the property or lives of persons in certain prohibited categories. For example, the statute provides that the state superintendent of insurance must be satisfied that "in applying for a license it is not the applicant's purpose or intention principally to solicit or place insurance on the applicant's own property or that of relatives, employers, or employees or that for which they or the applicant is agent, custodian, vendor, bailee, trustee, or payee." The court found that transactions between a bank and its customers commonly make the bank the "agent, custodian, vendor, bailee, trustee, or payee" of its customers, and that these relationships are not routinely created in the general insurance business. The court held that the impact of the statute on national banks would, therefore, be to "significantly interfere" with the national bank's authority to act as an insurance agent under 12 U.S.C. § 92, and also has an impact that is "substantially more adverse" on depository institutions than on others in the insurance business.

The OCC issued an opinion finding that some provisions of the West Virginia insurance laws were preempted. The state law provisions preempted included a prohibition on using information obtained in the loan process to solicit insurance, a requirement that insurance operations be kept physically separate from other financial operations, and a prohibition on banks soliciting credit insurance until after a loan is approved.

The OCC also ruled that the state's prohibition of the conditioning of a loan on the purchase of insurance was not preempted. OCC Preemption Opinion Doc. No. 01–22 (Sept. 24, 2001), available at 66 Fed. Reg. 51,502 (Oct. 9, 2001). The Independent Insurance Agents of America challenged the OCC's ruling in the federal district court for the District of Columbia, arguing that GLBA's functional regulatory scheme mandates oversight of insurance activities by state insurance regulators.[32] The Fourth Circuit Court of Appeals concluded in an unpublished opinion that deference should be given to the OCC's interpretation of the West Virginia statutes since they were enacted before September 3, 1998, GLBA § 104, 12 U.S.C.A. § 6701, and accordingly dismissed the petition for review brought by the West Virginia insurance commissioner. Cline v. Hawke, No. 01–2100, 2002 WL 31557392 (4th Cir. 2002), *cert. denied*, 540 U.S. 813 (2003).

The OCC issued another preemption determination on March 19, 2002, regarding national bank powers under a Massachusetts statute. OCC Preemption Opinion Doc. No. 02–03 (2002), available at 67 Fed. Reg. 13,405 (Mar. 22, 2002). The OCC concluded that federal law:

> (1) preempted certain provisions of the Massachusetts law that prohibited non-licensed bank personnel from referring potential customers to licensed insurance agents absent an inquiry by the customer;

> (2) prohibited non-licensed bank personnel from receiving additional compensation for a referral even if the compensation was not conditioned upon the sale of insurance products by the bank; and

> (3) prohibited banks from discussing insurance products available from the bank until the loan application was approved and, in the case of a home mortgage loan, until the customer had accepted the bank's written commitment to make the loan.

Further, the OCC found that the state law prohibitions were not within any of the GLBA safe harbors.

In June 2002, Massachusetts filed its petition objecting to the OCC's ruling with the United States Court of Appeals for the First Circuit, pursuant to the expedited review procedures of the GLBA. The First Circuit ruled in Bowler v. Hawke, 320 F.3d 59 (1st Cir. 2003), that the OCC's preemption letter was informal and did not carry the force of law. Therefore, there was no "regulatory conflict" for the court to consider. Further, the court suggested that the issue at hand would involve a factual determination of the extent to which the laws hinder banks in their sales and solicitation activities and that the inherent judgment calls in such a determination would better be made based on an evidentiary record created in a trial court. The Massachusetts Bankers Association then challenged the Massachusetts Consumer Protection Act's provisions relating to the sale of insurance by banks in federal district court. That

---

32. R. Christian Bruce, Independent Insurance Agents Sue OCC, Seek Reversal of Recent Preemption Ruling, 77 Banking Rep. (BNA) 825, 826 (2001).

court held that the state statute was preempted. Massachusetts Bankers Ass'n v. Bowler, 392 F.Supp.2d 24 (D. Mass. 2005).

IN RE LUTHERAN BROTHERHOOD VARIABLE INSURANCE PRODUCTS CO. SALES PRACTICES LITIGATION

United States District Court, District of Minnesota, 2000.
105 F.Supp.2d 1037.

MAGNUSON, DISTRICT JUDGE.

* * * The consolidated case currently before the Court arises out of a number of cases filed in both state and federal courts in Minnesota and Ohio. Plaintiffs in each of these actions seek to represent a class of persons who "have [had] an ownership interest in one or more permanent whole life, universal life or variable life policies issued by Defendants" anytime since 1982. Four of these cases, *Thompson*, *Eifler*, *Locke*, and *Watson*, were filed in state court and removed to federal court by Defendants Lutheran Brotherhood and Lutheran Brotherhood Variable Life Insurance Company (collectively "Lutheran Brotherhood") on the basis of federal question jurisdiction. Even though the Complaints did not explicitly state causes of action arising under federal law, Defendants justified removal by contending the variable insurance policies at issue were "registered securities" governed by the Securities Act of 1933, 15 U.S.C. §§ 77 et seq., and the Securities Litigation Uniform Standards Act of 1998, P.L. 105–353 ("SLUSA"). * * *

For the third time, Plaintiffs now move the Court to remand these cases to state court, asserting that federal law simply does not apply to the type of insurance contracts at issue in these cases. However, Plaintiffs have added a new wrinkle in their present motion, related to the recent enactment of the Gramm–Leach–Bliley Financial Modernization Act of 1999. In the alternative, Plaintiffs ask the Court to sever the claims of Plaintiffs who own only nonvariable insurance policies and remand those claims to state court. * * *

In recent years, Congress passed two statutes designed to alleviate the problems corporations suffered as a result of class action lawsuits. The first of these, the PSLRA, was designed to curb abuse in securities suits, particularly shareholder derivative suits in which the only goal was a windfall of attorney's fees, with no real desire to assist the corporation on whose behalf the suit was brought. See Greebel v. FTP Software, Inc., 194 F.3d 185, 191 (1st Cir. 1999). The PSLRA immediately drove many would-be plaintiffs to file their claims in state court, based on state law, in order to circumvent the strong requirements established by the statute. Motivated by a response to keep such lawsuits in federal court, Congress quickly passed SLUSA in order to "prevent plaintiffs from seeking to evade the protections that federal law provides against abuse litigation by filing suit in State, rather than federal, courts." H.R. Conf. Rep. No. 105–803 (Oct. 9, 1998). With some exceptions, SLUSA made the federal courts the exclusive fora for most class actions involving the purchase and sale of securities. Primarily, SLUSA mandates that any class action based on an allegation that a "covered security" was sold through misrepresentation, manipulation, or deception shall be removable to federal court. * * *

In this latest attempt to remand these cases to state court, Plaintiffs have added a new argument to their litany. Plaintiffs argue that through the Gramm–Leach–Bliley Financial Modernization Act of 1999, 15 U.S.C. § 6701 et seq. (2000), Congress made clear its "intent to preserve the states' functional regulation of variable insurance products." In Plaintiffs' view, this clear congressional mandate requires a reading of SLUSA and the PSLRA that preserves the regulation of insurance solely to state lawmakers.

The primary purpose of Gramm–Leach is well-known. Since the 1930's, the Glass–Steagall Act, 12 U.S.C. § 377 et seq., prevented organizations which engage in banking services from also engaging in the issuing, underwriting, sale, or distribution of securities. See 12 U.S.C. § 378(a)(1) (repealed 1999). After years of protest and lobbying by the financial services industry, Congress passed Gramm–Leach in late 1999 to repeal Glass–Steagall and once again allow intersectional combination in the financial industry. In the wake of this significant de-regulation, concerns arose about the effect of this federal action on the insurance industry. To assuage these concerns, Congress included in Gramm–Leach clear language that the McCarran–Ferguson Act, 15 U.S.C. §§ 1011–1015, "remains the law of the United States." 15 U.S.C. § 6701(a).

For fifty-five years, the McCarran–Ferguson Act, 15 U.S.C. §§ 1011–1015, has ensured that the states bear the primary responsibility of regulating insurance. McCarran–Ferguson creates a "clear statement" rule of federalism: no federal law will be read to "invalidate, impair, or supersede" state insurance law absent the clearest of Congressional intentions—according to the statute, only when the federal law "specifically relates to the business of insurance." 15 U.S.C. § 1012. The Supreme Court has identified three factors which must be examined in determining whether a federal statute preempts state insurance law: (1) whether the federal statute "specifically relates to the business of insurance"; (2) whether the state law at issue was "enacted for the purpose of regulating the business of insurance"; and (3) whether a proposed reading of a federal statute would "invalidate, impair, or supersede" state insurance law. Dep't of Treasury v. Fabe, 508 U.S. 491, 500 (1993).

These factors need not be examined in too much detail here, however, for it is resoundingly clear that McCarran–Ferguson does not bar application of SLUSA to Plaintiffs' claims in these circumstances. Two points are important here. First, the variable insurance policies to which SLUSA allegedly applies are simply not pure insurance products. The Supreme Court has long held that hybrid insurance-investment products, as variable policies could be characterized, cannot be deemed purely "insurance." See Securities and Exchange Comm'n v. United Ben. Life Ins. Co., 387

U.S. 202, 207, (1967). In part relying on this authority, the Securities and Exchange Commission has consistently subjected variable insurance products to federal securities laws. To the extent that an insurance policyholder does not enjoy a fixed benefit, and instead shares in the advantages and risks of equity investments, he owns a security, or at least a product with the qualities of both insurance and a security. See SEC Release No. 5360. Under the Court's understanding, these characteristics form the essence of the variable life insurance policies at issue in this case.

Second, even if variable polices were pure "insurance" products, an examination of the second *Fabe* factor compels the conclusion that the application of SLUSA to the variable policy claims does not offend McCarran–Ferguson. As discussed above, concerns about the application of McCarran–Ferguson are implicated when a federal act may invalidate, impair, or supersede a state law enacted for the purpose of regulating insurance. Nowhere in Plaintiffs' Complaints is any such state law relied on or discussed. Plaintiffs' causes of action include fraud, fraudulent inducement, breach of contract, breach of fiduciary duty, unjust enrichment, declaratory relief, reformation, and violations of Minnesota's false advertising, consumer fraud, and deceptive trade practices statutes. These causes of action certainly can apply to insurance policies, and their use may be a form of implicit, private regulation of the insurance industry. But it simply strains credulity to suggest that these general contract, tort, and consumer protection laws were *enacted* for the *purpose* of regulating insurance. McCarran–Ferguson protects states' well-crafted regimes of insurance regulation from unintentional federal intrusion; it does not somehow convert ageless causes of action of wide applicability into exclusively insurance-regulating weapons. See Meyer v. Employers Health Ins. Co., 722 F. Supp. 547, 553 (E.D. Wisc. 1989) (common law claims may "affect the insurance industry, [but] their origin is no doubt based on general principles of [law].") None of the cases Plaintiffs cite compel a different conclusion. * * *

Over the last decade, Congress has significantly amended the procedural hurdles putative class representatives must face in suits involving securities. Although Plaintiffs may not like the result, it is clear that these changes apply equally to suits involving variable life insurance policies. Furthermore, after considering the issues involved in this case and the burdens which would befall Plaintiffs and Lutheran Brotherhood if the state law claims were to be remanded, the Court concludes that exercise of supplemental jurisdiction over the Plaintiffs' state law claims is both legally acceptable and prudentially appropriate. * * * [The court denied plaintiffs' motion to remand and the motion to dismiss the plaintiffs who purchased only non-variable life insurance. The court granted plaintiffs additional time to file an amended complaint that complied with the Private Securities Litigation Reform Act of 1966.][33]

---

33. [eds.] For subsequent rulings in this litigation see In re Lutheran Brother. Variable Ins. Products Co. Sales Practices Litigation, No. 99–MD–1309 (PAM/JGL), 2004 WL 909741 (Apr. 28, 2004).

QUESTIONS AND NOTES

1. Although 17 domestic FHCs and 9 foreign FHCs reported that they engaged to some extent in insurance underwriting in the U.S., Citigroup and MetLife accounted for the bulk of FHC insurance underwriting activity in 2003. Board of Governors of the Federal Reserve System, Report to the Congress on Financial Holding Companies under the Gramm–Leach–Bliley Act 11–12 (Nov. 2003). Other insurance companies (not affiliated with FHCs) continued to engage in banking activities through grandfathered unitary thrift holding companies or through the establishment of limited purpose trust companies not classified as banks under the Bank Holding Company Act.

Traditional banking organizations that wished to continue to expand their insurance business have done so almost exclusively through agency acquisition. As of March 2003, 165 FHCs were engaged in insurance agency activities, often through a financial subsidiary. Id. at 13.

2. Rather than undertake joint ownership, many insurance companies and banks have entered strategic alliances to cross-sell their products. In one such venture, American International Group, Kemper Insurance Co., and Prudential Insurance Company announced a joint venture to sell their insurance products through banks and brokerage firms. What advantage is there to structuring bank and insurance combinations as joint marketing efforts rather than through common ownership under the privacy notice provisions of GLBA? See 65 Fed. Reg. 15,345 (March 19, 2001).

3. Some parties remain unhappy with the regulatory scheme set forth by GLBA. The American Bankers Insurance Association urges the creation of a federal charter option for insurance companies. Under the ABIA proposal, federal insurance companies would be regulated by a new agency to be housed in the Treasury Department, the Office of the National Insurance Commissioner. Additional information about the ABIA's proposal may be found at the ABIA wesbite, <www.aba.com/ABIA/ABIA_issues.htm>. See also Lissa Lamkin Broome, "A Federal Charter Option for Insurance Companies: Lessons from the Bank Experience," in Financial Modernization After Gramm–Leach–Bliley (Patricia A. McCoy ed. 2002), available at <ssrn.com>. Other industry participants urge more uniformity of state insurance laws. The Property Casualty Insurers Association, for instance, is touting proposed federal legislation to make the state-based insurance regulatory system more efficient and more uniform. See generally Robert H. Jerry, II & Steven E. Roberts, Regulating the Business of Insurance: Federalism in an Age of Difficult Risk, 41 Wake Forest L. Rev. 835 (2006) (describing role of government in managing risk and acting as an insurer in disasters).

4. A series of scandals involving accounting manipulations and undisclosed fees by some of the world's largest insurance companies renewed cries for a federal insurance charter. In one scandal, New York Attorney General Eliot Spitzer charged that Marsh & McLennan Corp., the world's largest insurance broker, defrauded its large corporate clients by accepting fees from insurance companies in exchange for directing business to those companies.

Spitzer further charged that Marsh & McLennan had engaged in bid rigging. American International Group Inc. (AIG), another large insurer, announced on March 30, 2005, that it was reducing its net worth by $1.7 billion as a result of various accounting manipulations using something called "finite" insurance. The scandal spread throughout the insurance industry. Among others, General Re, owned by Warren Buffett's Berkshire Hathaway, was under investigation by the SEC for selling insurance products that could be used to smooth earnings. The chief executive officer and others in that unit were later indicted for such practices.

Platinum Underwriters, a Bermuda reinsurer, unwound a "finite" insurance contract with a Berkshire Hathaway subsidiary, because of accounting concerns that side agreements negated the passing of risk. That product allowed purchasers to pay for losses with deductible insurance premiums in transactions that were structured to prevent the insurer from having any risk, thereby taking on aspects of a loan. In other words, the purchaser of the insurance paid extraordinarily high premiums over the life of the policy. Any funds paid in excess of actual claims were returned at the end of the contract period.

5. Do you think the "functional" regulatory system envisioned by GLBA is practical in light of the merging of financial services across product lines?

6. Have you seen advertisements by your bank for securities products or insurance? Were you made aware that these products were being sold by a separate subsidiary or affiliate?

7. Citigroup sold the property and casualty business of its Travelers insurance group because of the difficulty of cross-selling these insurance products through its banking and other operations. See David Boraks, In Focus: In this Storm, the Umbrella Worked, Am. Banker, Jan. 18, 2002. It later sold off much of its life insurance and annuity business to MetLife Inc. At the same time, MetLife expanded its deposit base by purchasing a branch of a small New Jersey bank in 2001 with deposits of $80 million. By 2004, deposits in the now renamed MetLife Bank, had increased to $2.3 billion. Lee Ann Gjertsen, For MetLife, Its Bank is a Distribution Engine, Am. Banker, Sept. 28, 2004.

8. The OCC adopted rules for the offer and sale of Debt Cancellation Contracts (DCC) and Debt Suspension Agreements (DSA). 67 Fed. Reg. 58,962 (Sept. 17, 2002) (effective June 13, 2003). These products are contracts in which the lender, for a fee, will cancel or suspend a borrower's loan payments in the event of the borrower's death or some other specified catastrophe. Although similar to credit insurance in many respects, DCCs and DSAs are, pursuant to the OCC rule, regulated as bank products rather than insurance products,[34] and any portion of the loan forgiven because of a DCA or DSA is taxable income to the borrower while proceeds from credit insurance policies are not taxable. Some consumer advocates allege that consumers have overpaid $2.5 billion in the aggregate for credit insurance and credit protection contracts, and that most borrowers do not need this coverage if they already have life insurance. The OCC rules contain provisions for consumer protection

---

34. Some state insurance commissioners, however, regulate DCAs and DSAs as insurance, suggesting a potential conflict in those states.

from abuses, including a prohibition on lump sum, single premium DCCs or DSAs in connection with residential mortgages. Nicole Duran, In Focus: Broader Critique of Credit Insurance Taking Shape, Am. Banker, Dec. 3, 2001; Richard Cowden, Questions Surround Rapid Transition from Credit Insurance to Debt Protection, 77 Banking Rep. (BNA) 875 (2001).

SECTION 4.   THE DODD–FRANK ACT

AIG, the world's largest insurance company, was also a casualty of the financial crisis.

FINANCIAL CRISIS INQUIRY COMMISSION PRELIMINARY STAFF REPORT: GOVERNMENTAL RESCUES OF "TOO–BIG–TO–FAIL" FINANCIAL INSTITUTIONS

Aug. 31, 2010.<www.fcic.gov/reports/pdfs/2010–0831–Governmental-Rescues.pdf>.

* * * Immediately after Lehman's failure [on September 15, 2008], the Treasury and the Fed confronted another severe crisis at AIG, the world's largest insurance organization, with more than $1 trillion in assets and operations in more than 130 countries. AIG was a diversified financial conglomerate, but it was not a financial holding company and therefore was not regulated by the Fed. Its Financial Products subsidiary (AIGFP) was a leading underwriter of credit default swaps (CDS), which provided protection against credit default events with respect to a variety of corporate debt obligations and structured securities, including AAA-rated tranches of nonprime-related CDOs. AIG (with its strong credit rating) guaranteed the CDS underwritten by AIGFP. However, AIG was required to post additional collateral with the CDS counterparties if its credit rating declined.

A number of the CDOs protected by AIGFP's CDS began to suffer ratings downgrades and losses by late 2007, and some of the counterparties demanded collateral from AIG. Standard & Poor's downgraded AIG from its previous "AA" rating in May 2008, and CDS counterparties increased their demands for collateral from AIG. By September 2008, AIG was forced to post more than $30 billion of collateral to meet its CDS obligations.

In addition, AIG was exposed to significant losses from its securities lending operation. That operation pooled investment securities held by AIG's life insurance subsidiaries and lent out those securities in exchange for cash collateral. The securities lending operation invested that cash collateral in a variety of securities, including $45 billion of MBS. As the MBS became illiquid in 2007, AIG was unable to sell the MBS to raise the cash needed to repay its securities lending counterparties. In early September 2008, counterparties demanded that AIG return $24 billion in cash, thereby aggravating AIG's liquidity problems.

On September 12, FRBNY President Geithner and Treasury Secretary Henry (or Hank) Paulson learned that AIG would be insolvent within a week if it could not raise additional capital. On September 16, Paulson and Geithner were advised that AIG could not secure the necessary funding to continue in operation. Faced with the imminent failure of AIG, the Fed decided to exercise its authority under Section 13(3) to make an emergency $85 billion loan to AIG, secured by the stock of AIG's major insurance subsidiaries and certain other financial instruments. In return, AIG gave the Treasury preferred stock and warrants convertible into a 79.9% ownership stake in AIG. * * *

The Congressional Oversight Panel reported in its Oversight Report on AIG that total government assistance reached $182 billion, which included the $85 billion loan, $49.1 billion in purchases of preferred stock and warrants under TARP, and additional funds from the Federal Reserve. Congressional Oversight Panel, June Oversight Report, The AIG Rescue, Its Impact on Markets, and the Government's Exit Strategy 7 (June 10, 2010), <cop.senate.gov/documents/cop–061010–report.pdf>. Although AIG's management is confident the federal government will be repaid in full, the Congressional Budget Office estimated in 2010, that the government would lose $36 billion from the AIG investment. Id. at 10.

After the Dodd–Frank Act, the Financial Stability Oversight Council (FSOC) (discussed further in Chapter 3) may designate a nonbank financial company, like AIG, as a systemically significant institution that will be subject to Fed oversight and prudential regulation that will include enhanced risk-based capital, and leverage and liquidity requirements. Further, such a company is subject to the Orderly Liquidation Authority (described in Chapter 8) in which the FDIC may be appointed as a receiver of the institution for its liquidation with no possibility of reorganization.

The Dodd–Frank Act also created a new Federal Insurance Office (FIO) in the Treasury Department that is to monitor all aspects of the insurance industry and to identify any issues that could pose a systemic risk to the industry or to the financial system as a whole. Dodd–Frank Act, § 502. Excluded from the jurisdiction of the FIO are health care insurance, certain long-term care insurance, and crop insurance. The director of the FIO and a state insurance commissioner will be nonvoting members of the FSOC. The FIO may recommend that the FSOC designate an insurance company for regulation as a systemically significant nonbank financial company. The FIO also has CRA-like monitoring authority over insurance products in its charge "to monitor the extent to which traditionally underserved communities and consumers, minorities . . . and low-and moderate-income persons have access to affordable insurance products regarding all lines of insurance, except health insurance." Dodd–Frank Act, § 313.

The FIO may preempt state laws that discriminate against foreign insurance companies, but substantive state insurance regulation is otherwise preserved. Notwithstanding this, the Act does require the FIO to prepare a report for the Senate Banking Committee and the House Financial Services Committee on how to modernize and improve the regulation of insurance in the United States that is to include a discussion of potential federal regulation of insurance (other than health insurance), and subjecting insurance companies to a federal resolution authority. Thus, the frequent calls for federal regulation of insurance or an optional federal insurance charter are likely to be analyzed further.[35]

Insurance companies are also subject to the reforms related to derivatives (described further in Chapter 12). Their use of derivative products could be subject to central clearing and exchange trading. Swaps, however, will not be considered insurance and subjected to state law regulation as insurance products. Dodd–Frank Act, § 722.

No state, other than the home state of an insured, may require any premium tax payment for commercial purchasers of non-admitted insurance (insurance sold by an insurance company domiciled outside the state of sale). Dodd–Frank Act, § 521. Such non-admitted insurers are subject to home state regulation only, and surplus lines brokers are subject to home state regulation. Limitations were also placed on the ability of the states to regulate reinsurance from other jurisdictions.

Questions and Notes

1. What are the advantages of federal regulation of insurance? Should there be a dual state and federal chartering system, an exclusive state chartering system (the current situation), or an exclusive federal charter?

2. Why should credit default swaps (CDS) be excluded from regulation as insurance? What costs would there be to subjecting CDS to regulation as an insurance product?

---

35. The Obama administration threatened to seek a repeal of the insurance industry's exemption from the antitrust laws under the McCarran–Ferguson Act in retaliation for the industry's opposition to his health care bill. The Treasury Department also recommended in 2008 the establishment of a federal insurance regulatory structure and the creation of an optional federal charter for insurance companies, similar to the dual-chartering system for banking. Treasury recommended that Congress establish a Federal Office of Insurance Oversight within Treasury to establish a federal presence in insurance for international and regulatory issues. Department of the Treasury, Blueprint for a Modernized Financial Regulatory Structure 126 (Mar. 2008).

CHAPTER FOURTEEN

INTERNATIONAL BANKING

■ ■ ■

SECTION 1. FOREIGN BANK OPERATIONS IN THE UNITED STATES

Foreign banks are formidable competitors with United States banks. Indeed, only three United States banks ranked in the largest twenty banks in the world as of the end of 2002. Three foreign bank holding companies based just on their United States assets rank in the top ten of all bank holding companies operating in the United States. The United States holding companies assets, however, are measured on their worldwide holdings. The three largest foreign bank holding companies based on their U.S. assets are Barclays, Deutsche Bank, and HSBC Holdings.

A. INTERNATIONAL BANKING ACT

Foreign banks may conduct business in the United States through a subsidiary, a branch office, an agency or a representative office. As described in the following case, the United States has struggled with the issue of how to regulate foreign bank operations in the United States.

UNITED STATES v. LEWIS
United States Court of Appeals, Ninth Circuit, 1995.
67 F.3d 225.

HALL, CIRCUIT JUDGE.

* * * In August, 1984 twenty-seven-year-old Larry Lewis became manager of the Portland, Oregon branch of the Hong Kong and Shanghai Bank ("HKSB"), a title he would hold until his resignation in June, 1988. Lewis, whose previous position at HKSB was limited to supervising tellers and assisting in import/export loans, had no prior experience in granting loans or in managing a bank. With his promotion came the weighty task of improving the revenues of the singularly unprofitable Portland branch. * * *

Lewis did not deny that he made unauthorized loans, that he granted credit exceeding approved limits or that he failed to obtain required collateral. In his defense, he claimed variously that he continued to extend unauthorized credit facilities to keep the borrowers from going out of business and to enable them to repay prior loans, that he relied in good faith on representations made by the companies, that certain of his misrepresentations were unintentional, and that he was acting in the best interests of HKSB. A jury convicted Lewis on all bank and wire fraud counts.

Prior to the commencement of the jury trial, Lewis filed an unsuccessful motion to dismiss the bank fraud counts for lack of jurisdiction, arguing that 18 U.S.C. § 1344 did not apply to HKSB. The version of § 1344 in effect during 1987 and 1988, the time period charged in the indictment, defines bank fraud as the knowing execution or attempted execution of "a scheme or artifice ... to defraud a federally chartered or insured financial institution." The essence of this case revolves around the meaning of the phrase "federally chartered ... financial institution," defined, in pertinent part, by § 1344(b)(5) as "a bank ... or other banking or financial institution organized or *operating under the laws of the United States.*" 18 U.S.C. § 1344(b)(5) (1988) (emphasis added). There is no dispute that HKSB is a foreign entity incorporated under the laws of the British Crown Colony of Hong Kong, and is thus not organized under the laws of the United States. It is also undisputed that the Portland branch has an Oregon state charter and is neither federally chartered nor federally insured. Thus, the only question is whether the bank is operated under the laws of the United States as that term is used in § 1344(b)(5). * * *

The International Banking Act of 1978 ("IBA"), 12 U.S.C. §§ 3101–3108 (1988), as it existed during the relevant time period of 1987 and 1988, and its legislative history provide further support for a narrow reading of § 1344(b)(5). The IBA, which is the principal federal law governing foreign bank operations, was enacted to eliminate various "competitive advantages" foreign banks operating in this country enjoyed over federally and state chartered domestic banks. S. Rep. 95–1073, 95th Cong., 1st Sess. 6 (1978). Specifically, unlike their domestic counterparts, branches of foreign banks, because not subject to the strictures of the McFadden Act and Bank Holding Company Act, were permitted the unfair advantage of establishing full service banking facilities capable of accepting deposits in more than one state.

To establish competitive equality between foreign and domestic banks, the IBA limits the domestic deposit-taking activities of a foreign bank to its designated "home" state, 12 U.S.C. § 3103(a) (1988), thus "provid[ing] foreign banks with 'national treatment' under which 'foreign enterprises ... are treated as competitive equals with their domestic counterparts.'" Conference of State Bank Supervisors v. Conover, 715 F.2d 604, 606 (D.C. Cir. 1983) (quoting 1978 U.S.C.C.A.N. 1421, 1422), cert. denied 466 U.S. 927 (1984). Until the enactment of the IBA, foreign banks operating branches in the United States did so only under state authority. 1978 U.S.C.C.A.N. 1421, 1426. Under the IBA, a branch of a foreign bank must choose between state or federal treatment and can expect, thereafter, to be subject to the same restrictions as a similarly situated domestic bank. See 12 U.S.C. § 3102(a) (1988) (subject to approval of the Comptroller of the Currency, a foreign bank may establish a federal branch in any state in which it is not operating a branch under state law, and in which the establishment of such branch is not prohibited by state law); see also 1978 U.S.C.C.A.N. 1421, 1426 (discussing "State–Federal option").

Because HKSB elected an Oregon state charter for its Portland branch, that branch was a "state branch," defined under the IBA as "a branch of a foreign bank *established and operating under the laws of any State*." 12 U.S.C. § 3101(12) (1988) (emphasis added). By contrast, the IBA defines a "federal branch" as one "established and operating under section 3102." 12 U.S.C. § 3101(6) (1988). Section 3102 provides, in turn, that a federal branch of a foreign bank is "subject to such rules, regulations, and orders as the Comptroller [of the Currency] considers appropriate," and that such a branch will, with certain exceptions, receive "the same rights and privileges as a national bank at the same location" under the National Bank Act. 18 U.S.C. § 3102(b) (1988).

The government recognizes that § 3101(12) appears linguistically to exclude HKSB's Portland branch from the effect of § 1344(b)(5)'s "operating under the laws of the United States" language. It contends, however, that the regulatory control exercised over state branches of foreign banks through the IBA is sufficient to bring the Portland branch within the bank fraud statute's purview. The government finds the regulatory authority of the Federal Reserve Board over such branches particularly persuasive, contending that the Federal Reserve exercises the same authority over state branches as it does over federally chartered branches. In actuality, the IBA's legislative history makes clear that the Federal Reserve's authority over a state branch of a foreign bank is secondary to the state's oversight. In sharp contrast, federal branches and federally insured state branches receive their principal oversight from federal sources–i.e., from the Comptroller of the Currency and the FDIC, respectively. As the legislative history of the IBA states:

> * * * Thus, Federal branches and agencies will be subject to examination by the Comptroller, federally insured State branches will be examined by the State agencies and by the FDIC, and *non-federally insured State branches ... will be examined by the appropriate State authorities or, if not so examined, by the Federal Reserve.* * * *

We cannot agree with the district court's view that the federal regulations applicable through the IBA are "significant," 838 F. Supp. at 477, enough to cause the Portland branch to fall within the bank fraud statute's definition of a "federally chartered" bank. The plain language of the IBA's text, which distinguishes between state and federal branches of foreign banks, and the IBA's legislative history, make clear that a state branch is "organized and operating under the laws of a state" even though it is subject to the Federal Reserve's secondary regulatory authority and other federal regulation under the IBA. We hold that HKSB's Portland branch was not "operating under the laws of the United States" within the meaning of § 1344(b)(5), and that the district court therefore erred in denying Lewis' motion to dismiss the bank fraud charges for lack of jurisdiction. By extension, we hold also that the district court misstated an element of the crime of bank fraud when it erroneously instructed the jury that a bank is "operating under the laws of the United States" if it is "subject to regulation, examination and supervision by the Federal Government" including regulation by the Federal Reserve. * * *

For the foregoing reasons, Lewis' conviction on the bank fraud counts is reversed. * * *

McHUGH v. WESTPAC BANKING CORP.

United States District Court, Northern District of Illinois, 1995.
1995 WL 243339.

NORDBERG, DISTRICT JUDGE.

Defendant Westpac Banking Corporation ("Defendant") brings the instant Motion to Dismiss asserting that this Court lacks subject matter jurisdiction over this action.

In his Complaint, Gary Spencer ("Plaintiff") alleges that the basis for this Court's jurisdiction over the instant action is diversity of citizenship, 28 U.S.C. § 1332(a)(2). Section 1332(a)(2) states, "the district court shall have original jurisdiction of all civil actions where the matter in controversy . . . is between citizens of a State and citizens or subjects of a foreign state." 28 U.S.C. § 1332(a)(2). Plaintiff is a resident of Illinois. Defendant is an Australian corporation with its principal place of business in Sydney, Australia. Thus, Plaintiff alleges that, as the present controversy is between an Illinois citizen and a subject of a foreign state, diversity jurisdiction is proper under 28 U.S.C. § 1332(a)(2).

In support of its Motion to Dismiss, Defendant asserts that, at the time Plaintiff filed his Complaint (May 20, 1993), Defendant operated a branch office in Chicago, Illinois, pursuant to a license from the Office of the Comptroller of the Currency Administrator of National Banks. In fact, Defendant operated its Chicago branch from October 1982 until September 30, 1993.

Defendant argues that, because of its license to operate a federal branch of a foreign bank, its citizenship must be determined by 28 U.S.C. § 1348, not 28 U.S.C. § 1332. Section 1348 reads, "all national banking associations shall, for the purposes of all other actions by or against them, be deemed citizens of the state in which they are respectively located." 28 U.S.C. § 1348. A national banking association is "located" wherever it maintains a branch office or a substantial presence. Bank of New York v. Bank of America, 861 F. Supp. 225, 230–31 (S.D.N.Y. 1994). See also Connecticut National Bank v. Iacono, 785 F. Supp. 30 (D.R.I. 1992) (relying on Citizens & Southern National Bank v. Bougas, 434 U.S. 35, 44 (1977) and holding that under § 1348, a national banking association is located in, and therefore a citizen of, every state in which it maintains branch banks.) Thus, Defendant argues that, as it maintained a branch in Chicago at the time Plaintiff filed his Complaint and was accordingly a citizen of Illinois pursuant to the terms of § 1348, complete diversity does not exist and this Court lacks subject matter jurisdiction.

Defendant cites § 3102(b) of the International Banking Act, 12 U.S.C. § 3102(b), in support of its argument that it should be treated as a "national banking association," for which the citizenship and jurisdiction is determined by § 1348, not § 1332. Section 3102 states in relevant part,

> Except as otherwise specifically provided in this chapter or in rules, regulations, or orders adopted by the Comptroller under this section, operations of a foreign bank at a Federal branch or agency shall be conducted with the same rights and privileges as a national bank at the same locations and shall be subject to all the same duties, restrictions, penalties, liabilities, conditions and limitations that would apply under the National Bank Act [12 U.S.C.A. § 21 et seq.] to a national bank doing business at the same location.

12 U.S.C. § 3102(b). Defendant claims that, as § 3102 directs that a federal branch of a foreign bank be conducted with and subject to the same rights, privileges, duties, liabilities and conditions as a national bank, a federal branch of a foreign bank should also be subject to the specific jurisdictional grant and designation of citizenship of § 1348 which by its terms applies to national banking associations.

This Court must look to the language, legislative history and purpose of both § 3102 and § 1348 in determining whether Congress intended § 3102(b) to extend § 1348 to federal branches of foreign banks. Prior to the enactment of the International Banking Act, a bank organized under the laws of a foreign country could only obtain a charter from a state authority because the federal government did not charter foreign banks. Conference of State Bank Supervisors v. Conover, 715 F.2d 604, 606 (D.C. Cir. 1983), cert. denied, 466 U.S. 927 (1984) (citing H.R.Rep. No. 910, 95th Cong., 2d Sess. 5 (1978)). The absence of federal charters for foreign banks caused the treatment of foreign banks to vary from state to state. Conover, 715 F.2d at 606. Thus, in support of the International Banking Act, the Senate Committee on Banking, Housing and Urban Affairs noted,

> There is, at this time, no uniform national policy concerning foreign banking operations in this country. As a result foreign banks may have competitive advantages over our domestic banks. This bill establishes the principal of parity of treatment between foreign and domestic banks in like circumstances.

Id. (quoting S. Rep. No. 1073, 95th Cong., 2d Sess. 2 (1978)). The Senate Committee on Banking, Housing and Urban Affairs noted further that, "the [International Banking Act] sought to provide foreign banks with 'national treatment' under which 'foreign enterprises ... are treated as competitive equals with their domestic counterparts.' " Id.

The legislative history of the International Banking Act clearly evidences Congress' concern with establishing competitive parity between domestic banks and foreign banks. However, neither the language of § 3102 nor the legislative history of the International Banking Act indicates that § 1348's specific grant of jurisdiction over and designation of the citizenship of national banking associations was meant to encompass both foreign banks and domestic national banks. See R.W. Sawant & Co. v. Ben Kozloff, Inc., 507 F. Supp. 614, 617 (N.D. Ill. 1981); Wright, Miller & Cooper, 13B Federal Practice and Procedure: Jurisdiction § 3571 (2d ed. 1984). * * *

Absent an indication from Congress that § 1348 applies to federal branches of international banks, the Court will not read § 3102(b)–subjecting federal branches of foreign banks to the same rights, privileges, duties, liabilities and conditions as national banks are subjected to under the National Bank Act–as implying that federal branches of international banks are citizens of every state in which they are located. * * *

Accordingly, this Court will not extend § 1348, which specifically applies to national banking associations, to foreign banks with federal branches. As Plaintiff is an Illinois resident and as Defendant is an Australian corporation with its principal place of business in Sydney Australia, this Court has [diversity] jurisdiction pursuant to § 1332(a)(2). * * *

QUESTIONS AND NOTES

1. As noted in Chapter 4, Wal–Mart was thwarted from chartering an industrial bank. It then obtained a bank charter in Mexico for one of its subsidiaries. Will Wal–Mart be able to carry out banking activities in the United States through that subsidiary? See generally Anna Gelpern, Wal–Mart Bank in Mexico: Money to the Masses and the Home–Host Hole, 39 Conn. L. Rev. 1513 (2007).

B. INTERNATIONAL COORDINATION OF REGULATION

The globalization of world trade has had a corresponding effect on banking regulation as regulators around the world became concerned that their regulations were uncoordinated and that gaps could allow large international banks to escape effective regulation. The failure of a large bank as a result of unregulated operations could threaten the international financial system. The Bank for International Settlements (BIS) assumed the role of encouraging cooperation among the central banks and facilitating effective regulation of expanded international banking operations. BIS is located in Basel, Switzerland, and is owned by the central banks of several countries. It was founded in 1930 to receive and monitor

World War I reparation payments from Germany. Later BIS expanded its operations to provide foreign exchange clearing facilities for its member banks. For a description of BIS and its ownership see First Eagle SoGen Funds, Inc. v. Bank for International Settlements, 252 F.3d 604 (2d Cir. 2001).

In addition, the International Lending Supervision Act of 1983, 12 U.S.C. §§ 3901–3911, requires the federal bank regulatory agencies to "consult with the banking supervisory authorities of other countries to reach understandings aimed at achieving the adoption of effective and consistent supervisory policies and practices with respect to international lending." 12 U.S.C. § 3901(b).

UNITED STATES GENERAL ACCOUNTING OFFICE INTERNATIONAL BANKING: STRENGTHENING THE FRAMEWORK FOR SUPERVISING INTERNATIONAL BANKS

Report to Congressional Committees.
Mar. 21, 1994.

* * * The expanding number, changing nature, and increasing complexity of international banks has brought to the forefront the need for effective coordination of international banking supervision. This need is particularly important, because although banking operates worldwide, no supranational regulator exists to monitor all international banks. Banks are locating operations in foreign markets or offering cross-border services whereby the lending bank and the borrower reside in different countries. They are conducting an array of activities that, for some of them, includes providing investment banking, insurance, leasing, mutual funds, and derivatives, as well as traditional commercial banking, through complex organizations known as "financial conglomerates." The resulting linkages among different markets and types of financial services mean that difficulties in one country's banking system can adversely affect the banking systems in other countries and, in the extreme, the worldwide banking system. In addition, because the stringency of national regulation varies and banking is global, problems experienced by a multinational bank in a less-regulated market can affect well-regulated markets. * * *

As banking activities become increasingly global in nature, problems in one bank or banking group can be detrimental to financial entities in multiple countries. "Systemic crisis" is a disruption that severely damages the operation of the financial system either within a country or across country borders and, at the extreme, causes the system to break down completely. A typical form of financial crisis occurs when the sudden failure of a financial institution leads to a lack of confidence not only in the failed firm, but also in any of its other financial institutions thought to have similar vulnerabilities. Investors, in turn, refuse to deal with these other financial institutions. Creditors demand immediate payment, causing a liquidity problem not only with the original firm, but also among its other financial institutions, threatening the entire group's solvency if the situation is not resolved quickly. Several factors have increased the potential for systemic failure in international banking. * * *

In 1974, the central bank governors of the G–10 countries established the Basle Committee on Banking Regulation and Supervisory Practices, which is now known as the Basle Committee on Banking Supervision. The committee's members are senior officials of the central banks and supervisory agencies of the G–10 and Luxembourg. The committee operates under the auspices of the Bank for International Settlements (BIS)[1] in Basle, Switzerland, where it meets 3–4 times a year. * * *

Four bank regulatory officials represent the United States at Basle Committee meetings–two from the Federal Reserve, and one each from the Office of the Comptroller of the Currency (OCC) and the Federal Deposit Insurance Corporation (FDIC). The Federal Reserve has appointed a senior official in its Banking Supervision and Regulation Division as its representative. Given the Federal Reserve Bank of New York's responsibility in money markets, the United States added the New York bank to its representation on the committee in late 1975. The Federal Reserve Bank of New York sends a senior official of its foreign banking department to Basle Committee meetings.

The United States added OCC to its representation in 1978. A senior deputy comptroller has usually been OCC's representative, although on occasion the Comptroller has attended. In 1984, FDIC became the third U.S. bank regulatory agency represented at committee meetings. FDIC is represented at committee meetings by the Executive Director of its Division of Supervision.

The Basle Committee is an advisory body whose recommendations require consensus agreement of all its representatives. It has no power to require implementation of its agreements in the laws or regulations of its member nations. Instead, it formulates broad supervisory standards and guidelines. It also recommends statements of "best practices," expecting that individual countries will implement them through arrangements that best suit their own national system. However, U.S. federal bank supervisory agencies, as well as bank supervisory agencies of other member countries, have committed themselves to work to implement committee principles. * * *

In almost 20 years since its formation, the Basle Committee on Banking Supervision has addressed sensitive bank supervisory issues, especially those that have arisen because of the expansion of foreign bank operations. In the original concordat (1975) and the revised concordat (1983), the committee apportioned responsibility for supervising foreign banking offices between countries in which the offices are located (host

---

1. [n.11] BIS is a bank and an international financial institution headquartered in Basle with three primary roles: it serves as a forum for promoting international monetary cooperation; it assists central banks in managing and investing some of their monetary reserves; and it acts as an agent or trustee for various international financial settlements.

countries) and those in which the banks are headquartered (parent countries). The revised concordat also introduced the concept of consolidated supervision. In the 1988 Capital Adequacy Accord, the committee established the minimum capital standard defining how much capital internationally active banks should maintain. * * *

The Basel Committee's efforts to coordinate international bank regulation failed with respect to operations of a bank called Bank of Credit and Commerce International (BCCI). That rogue bank operated in a netherworld of international banking that had no single regulator to regulate its criminal behavior or prevent its collapse.

UNITED STATES v. BCCI HOLDINGS (LUXEMBOURG), S.A.

United States District Court, District of Columbia, 1999.
69 F.Supp.2d 36.

GREEN, DISTRICT JUDGE.

At last! For nearly eight years I have been presiding over this fascinating, complex, and sobering case arising out of the collapse of Bank of Credit and Commerce International ("BCCI"), the largest bank failure in history. The Order that accompanies this Opinion is the final chapter in the longest-running forfeiture proceeding in the history of federal racketeering law. Against the odds, through the combined efforts of the United States Department of Justice, the Trustees appointed by this Court, the BCCI Court Appointed Fiduciaries, the Board of Governors of the Federal Reserve System, and the District Attorney for New York County, more than $1.2 billion has been realized from BCCI assets in the United States. Most of that sum has been forwarded for distribution to the victims of BCCI's collapse.

The worldwide liquidation proceeding conducted by the BCCI Court Appointed Fiduciaries remains ongoing. To date, the Court Appointed Fiduciaries have distributed approximately $4 billion worldwide to innocent depositors and creditors. In two dividends, they have repaid creditors a total of 46 percent on admitted claims. Additional dividends are expected, although the amounts will depend on future recoveries. In contrast to the pessimistic projections of 1991, creditors will certainly receive more than half of their money back.

But today's Final Order of Forfeiture brings to an end the criminal case against the BCCI corporations and its attendant forfeiture proceeding. This Opinion summarizes the landmark events in this case to explain why terminating the forfeiture proceeding at this juncture is appropriate. The United States Government has located all of the BCCI-related assets in this country that it could, all disputes regarding ownership of those assets have been resolved, and, thus, the Court's task is complete. * * *

BCCI was founded in 1972. The moving force behind its establishment was Agha Hasan Abedi ("Abedi"), a Pakistani banker who envisioned BCCI becoming an international Islamic bank. Abedi's chief lieutenant was Saiyid Mohammad Swaleh Naqvi ("Naqvi"). Abedi remained at the helm of BCCI until 1988, when he suffered a heart attack. Naqvi succeeded him for two years, until the sovereigns of Abu Dhabi took formal control of the bank in 1990.

Abu Dhabi took control in 1990

Abedi established the principal BCCI corporations in Luxembourg and the Cayman Islands. Although formally separate, the BCCI corporations were under the same management and were closely linked in their operations. At its peak, BCCI's coordinated international banking network had more than 400 branches in 69 countries. BCCI's depositors included large corporate interests as well as numerous small businesses and middle class households, particularly in England. * * *

As early as 1978, a group of shareholders of Financial General Bankshares, Inc.—the predecessor of First American Bank in Washington, D.C.—sued BCCI, among others, claiming that it was behind a hostile takeover attempt. Judge Oliver Gasch, of this Court, preliminarily enjoined any further stock purchases by BCCI. In the course of that lawsuit, BCCI retained the services of prominent Washington counsel, Clark M. Clifford ("Clifford") and Robert A. Altman ("Altman"). Shortly after an amended complaint was filed in 1980, BCCI and all but one defendant settled the claims; BCCI subsequently entered into a consent judgment with the Securities and Exchange Commission. See Financial General Bankshares, Inc. v. Metzger, 523 F.Supp. 744, 747 (D.D.C. 1981), vacated on juris. grds., 680 F.2d 768 (D.C. Cir. 1982).

Not long after BCCI had settled the *Financial General Bankshares* case, a new proposal was made to sell First American to Credit and Commerce American Investment, B.V. ("CCAI"), a Netherlands shell corporation wholly owned by Credit and Commerce American Holdings, N.V. ("CCAH"), a Netherlands Antilles corporation. The record shareholders of CCAH were wealthy individuals from the Persian Gulf. Although not apparent at the time, it now appears that nearly all of the money required for the purchase had been loaned to the investors by BCCI. Some of these loans were actual extensions of credit while others were false loans created to disguise BCCI's takeover of First American Bank.

In 1981, the Board of Governors of the Federal Reserve System held hearings to determine whether to approve the sale. Some of the proposed investors from the Middle East testified. See, e.g., BCCI Holdings (Luxembourg) S.A. v. Khalil, 56 F. Supp. 2d 14 (D.D.C. 1999). Clifford and Altman appeared as counsel in those proceedings. Ultimately, the Federal Reserve approved the sale. Shortly thereafter, Clifford and Altman were chosen by the shareholders to be Managing Directors of the shell corporations, CCAH and CCAI, as well as directors and senior officers of the rechristened First American Corporation, the holding company that controlled the largest bank in the Washington, D.C. area. See generally First American Corp. v. Al–Nahyan, 17 F. Supp. 2d 10, 13–14 (D.D.C. 1998).

BCCI again came to the fore in 1987 and 1988 in connection with investigations into narcotics trafficking by Panamanian General Manuel Noriega. It was known that Noriega had a banking relationship with BCCI and First American. Federal prosecutors, and then committees of the United States Senate and House of Representatives, investigated allegations that BCCI was laundering Noriega's drug proceeds. BCCI was indicted in the United States District Court in Tampa, Florida and pled guilty to launder- subsequently pled guilty to federal money laundering charges. Certain to ing BCCI employees also were indicted, tried, and convicted on money laundering charges. See United States v. Awan, 966 F.2d 1415 (11th Cir. 1992) (affirming convictions in large part).

Then in 1990 and early 1991, BCCI became the focus of attention in the United States and abroad. In this country, news reports in 1990, and intensifying in early 1991, indicated that the Federal Reserve was investigating rumors that BCCI had secretly been behind the takeover of First American. In December 1990, the Republic of Panama sued BCCI and First American in the United States District Court for the Southern District of Florida, alleging that BCCI illegally owned First American and that both sets of corporate entities had violated federal racketeering laws in laundering proceeds from narcotics trafficking for the benefit of General Noriega.

Abroad, the Bank of England received troubling information about BCCI's financial condition and integrity. In response, it commissioned a special audit, which "disclosed evidence of a complex and massive fraud at BCCI, including substantial loan and treasury account losses, misappropriation of funds, unrecorded deposits, the creation and manipulation of fictitious accounts to conceal bank losses, and concealment from regulatory authorities of BCCI's mismanagement and true financial position." Corrigan, Mattingly & Taylor, The Federal Reserve's Views on BCCI, 26 Int'l Law. 963, 970–71 (1992) (based on testimony before the Committee on Banking, Finance and Urban Affairs of the United States House of Representatives on September 3, 1991).

The results of the audit were shared with regulators in other countries, and, on July 5, 1991, banking regulators in the United Kingdom, Luxembourg and the United States, froze assets owned or controlled by BCCI. This included seizure of BCCI's deposit agencies by the Superintendent of Banks of the State of California (since retitled the Commissioner of Financial Institutions of the State of California) and the Superintendent of Banks of the State of New York. In addition, the New York Superintendent of Banks seized BCCI's assets at various New York banks, including those at the Bank of New York ("BNY") and Security Pacific Bank ("SPB"). By July 6th, eighteen countries had shut down BCCI's operations in their jurisdictions, and, as of July 29, 1991, forty-four countries had closed down BCCI branches. * * *

At the time of its failure, BCCI was the seventh largest privately owned bank in the world. It had over 400 offices and 1.3 million customers. Clark Clifford, advisor to several presidents, and former Secretary of Defense, and Robert Altman, the husband of Linda Carter (the television actress who played Wonder Woman), were indicted for their role in assisting BCCI in acquiring First American. Clifford could not be tried for health reasons and Altman was acquitted after a lengthy trial in a New York state court. Both Altman and Clifford reached settlements with United States banking authorities in which they agreed to pay $5 million and were barred from the banking business. Another major international scandal soon followed the BCCI debacle. It is described in the following case.

UNITED STATES v. DROGOUL

United States Court of Appeals, Eleventh Circuit, 1993.
1 F.3d 1546.

KRAVITCH, CIRCUIT JUDGE.

This interlocutory appeal stems from a pretrial dispute in the government's prosecution of appellee Christopher Drogoul. The sole question before us is whether the district court abused its discretion in denying the government's motion to take the depositions of several foreign nationals in Italy. We hold that it did and, accordingly, reverse.

Drogoul was manager of the Atlanta branch of Banca Nazionale del Lavoro (BNL), a bank headquartered in Rome, Italy and owned largely by the Italian government. He is charged in a multicount indictment with, *inter alia*, wire fraud, conspiracy, and making false statements to government agencies. The crux of the government's allegations is that Drogoul defrauded BNL by making and concealing unauthorized loans and credit extensions totalling several billion dollars to agencies and instrumentalities of the Republic of Iraq.

Drogoul pled guilty in June 1992 to sixty counts of a 347–count original indictment. The current trial-preparation phase of the litigation began on October 1, 1992, when the district court granted Drogoul's request to withdraw his guilty plea. Trial initially was set for April 5, 1993, but subsequently was rescheduled for September 8, 1993.

* * * At a sentencing hearing prior to the withdrawal of his guilty plea, Drogoul asserted that his former BNL superiors in Rome were fully aware of his loan activities regarding Iraq. Several pleadings which Drogoul has filed in the district court indicate strongly that this contention will be a central defense theory at trial. This defense goes to the very heart of the government's allegations that Drogoul went beyond the scope

of his lending authority in extending credit to agencies of Iraq. The government expects the testimony of the prospective Italian deponents directly to refute Drogoul on this issue. * * *

[The court ordered the district court to allow the depositions of the Italian witnesses.].

———————

The billions of dollars in loans made by Christopher Drogoul were purportedly employed to purchase arms used by Iraq in the First Gulf War against American soldiers. Drogoul eventually pled guilty to some federal charges against him and spent thirty-three months in prison. A court in Rome also found him guilty of violating Italian laws and sentenced him to prison.

In 1990, the Basel Committee responded to the BCCI debacle by adding to its Concordat a supplement that sought more structured coordination among banking supervisors around the world. In 1992, the Basel Committee issued a paper that set forth minimum standards for the supervision of international banking groups with cross-border operations, and sought consolidated supervision of all international banks. Legislation was also adopted in the United States.

(1) Foreign Bank Supervision Enhancement Act

UNITED STATES GENERAL ACCOUNTING OFFICE INTERNATIONAL BANKING: STRENGTHENING THE FRAMEWORK FOR SUPERVISING INTERNATIONAL BANKS

Report to Congressional Committees.
Mar. 21, 1994.

The Federal Reserve Board of Governors submitted to the Congress proposed legislation in May of 1991 designed to strengthen the supervision and regulation of foreign banks operating in the United States. The legislation was later introduced as [the Foreign Bank Supervision Enhancement Act of 1991] FBSEA and enacted on December 19, 1991, as title II, subtitle A, of the Federal Deposit Insurance Corporation Improvement Act of 1991 (P.L. 102–242, 105 stat. 2236, 2286–2305).

FBSEA gives the Federal Reserve Board enhanced supervisory and regulatory authority over foreign banks conducting banking in the United States through branches, agencies, commercial lending companies, and representative offices. The act was largely a response to problems discovered in the U.S. operations of BCCI and BNL and the perceived need for more federal oversight.

In the BCCI case, the Board was concerned about the bank's lack of consolidated supervision over its worldwide operations and BCCI's acquisition, without Board approval, of control of more than 25 percent of the voting shares of First American Bankshares and several other U.S. banking operations. The BNL case involved the discovery that BNL's state-licensed agency in Atlanta allegedly failed to report to bank examiners a large part of its banking business and may have kept this lending secret from the parent bank. As a result, the Board believed that it needed examination authority over BNL–Atlanta to fully investigate the case. The Board also wished to have clear authority to share bank examination information on a confidential basis with foreign bank supervisors.

FBSEA's major provisions give the Board authority to approve all branch, agency, or commercial lending company applications; terminate the activities of state banking offices of foreign banks and recommend to OCC that licenses of federal banking offices be terminated; conduct examinations of branches, agencies, and affiliates; and approve the establishment and examine the operations of representative offices. * * *

The FBSEA permits a foreign bank to operate in the United States only if the bank is subject to comprehensive supervision or regulation on a consolidated basis in its home country. Moreover, the Fed is empowered to close the foreign bank's U.S. operations if it reasonably believes that the bank or its affiliates violated the law or engaged in an unsafe and unsound banking practice. Professor Raj Bhala criticizes the FBSEA as protectionist by setting up barriers for the entry of foreign banks into the United States. He also criticizes the unilateral power of the Fed to shut down foreign bank operations without consultation with the foreign bank's regulator as an improper way to regulate in an increasingly global economy. Finally, he argues that the FBSEA does not respond to the BCCI problem, which he describes as lying to the government. Professor Bhala argues that a BCCI-type debacle should be dealt with by increasing the coordination among the world's banking regulators.[2]

American regulators created an interagency program for supervising the United States operations of foreign banking organizations (FBOs) in 1995.[3] The FBO supervision program is risk-focused and has four components: (1) understanding the FBO; (2) assessing its risks; (3) planning supervisory activities; and (4) determining the overall condition of the U.S. operations of the FBO. Among other things, U.S. regulators review the FBO's risk matrix and risk assessment as well as the home country's financial system and accounting practices. An examination program is established after a strength-of-support assessment is made. This assessment ranks the FBO based on several factors, such as its financial condition (including such things as capital ratios and U.S. dollar liquidity), its risk profile, and the strength of its home country regulator. A com-

---

2. Raj K. Bhala, Foreign Bank Regulation After BCCI (1994).

3. A description of this supervisory system is set forth in Enhancements to Supervision of U.S. Operations of Foreign Banking Operations, Board of Governors of the Federal Reserve System, SR 00–14 (SUP) (Oct. 23, 2000).

bined rating of "1" means that the FBO's operations are fundamentally sound in every respect, while a rating of "4" means that the FBO's combined U.S. operations have serious weaknesses. The FBO's rating will determine the amount of supervision and examination by U.S. regulators.

(2) The Gramm–Leach–Bliley Act (GLBA)

The International Banking Act of 1978, 12 U.S.C.A. § 3101 et seq., grandfathered the operations of foreign banks operating in the United States at the time its enactment. 12 U.S.C.A. § 3106(c). This allowed those banks to operate free from branching limitations and Bank Holding Company Act restrictions on permissible activities that applied to domestic banks and subsequent foreign bank entrants into the United States. Although the Gramm–Leach–Bliley Act (GLBA) eliminated those grandfather rights, GLBA allows most activities that were being undertaken pursuant to the grandfather provision to be conducted outright by financial holding companies. GLBA also requires subsidiaries of foreign banks to register as representative offices with the Fed. This may even require registration of broker-dealer subsidiaries. The Fed has adopted amendments to Regulation Y (12 C.F.R. pt. 225) with respect to foreign institutions that wish to be treated as financial holding companies. 12 C.F.R. §§ 225.90–.93.

(3) Regulatory Framework

The Federal Reserve Board's Regulation K, 12 C.F.R. pt. 211, implements the International Banking Act. Subpart B of Regulation K specifically applies to foreign banking organizations and their activities in the United States. The FRB is the primary U.S. federal regulator for the state branch, state agency, representative office or commercial lending company subsidiary of a foreign banking organization. Compliance with Regulation K, however, does not relieve the foreign bank of the responsibility of complying with the laws and regulations of the state licensing authority. 12 C.F.R. § 211.20(c). The FRB also oversees foreign banking organizations that have qualified as financial holding companies pursuant to Regulation Y, 12 C.F.R. pt. 225.

The OCC has regulatory authority over federal branches and agencies of foreign banking organizations. 12 C.F.R. §§ 28.10–.26. Recent revisions to the OCC regulations sought to clarify and simplify the regulatory procedures for foreign banks desiring to operate in the United States and to further conform the treatment of the Federal branches and agencies of foreign banks to the treatment of domestic national banks in a manner consistent with the principles of national treatment enunciated in the International Banking Act of 1978. 68 Fed. Reg. 70691 (Dec. 19, 2003) (codified at 12 C.F.R. pts. 5 & 28).

The FDIC has regulatory authority over insured and noninsured U.S. branches of foreign banks pursuant to its role as provider of deposit insurance. 12 C.F.R. §§ 347.201–.214. The FDIC amended its rules to address several issues concerning U.S. branches of foreign banks. Among other things, those rules adopt a risk-based asset pledge requirement and information and examination requirements for foreign banks that own branches or depository institution subsidiaries seeking FDIC deposit insurance. 70 Fed. Reg. 17550 (Apr. 6, 2005).

(4) The Dodd–Frank Act

Under the Dodd–Frank Act, the Financial Stability Council (FSOC) may identify and subject to Fed regulation and heightened prudential standards systemically significant foreign nonbank financial companies and bank holding companies with consolidated worldwide assets exceeding $50 billion. Dodd–Frank Act, § 113. With respect to foreign bank holding companies, however, the FSOC must consult with the appropriate non-U.S. regulatory authorities regarding imposing additional regulation and supervision on these institutions with due regard for preserving national treatment and consideration of whether the company is subject to home country oversight that is comparable to that applied to U.S. financial companies. Further, the Government Accountability Office is charged with coordinating a study of capital requirements for the U.S. intermediate holding companies of non-U.S. banks. Dodd–Frank Act, § 173.

QUESTIONS AND NOTES

1. Another international organization that is playing an increasingly important role in finance is the International Organization of Securities Commissions (IOSCO). That organization is concerned with international securities operations, including the creation of standards for and the effective surveillance of international securities transactions. IOSCO's activities affect banks as a result of their growing involvement in the securities markets.

2. A large number of protestors have turned out for international conferences on world trade and finance. Among other things, they oppose "globalization," its effects on the environment, and operations that exploit labor in lesser developed countries. Do you agree with the anti-globalization protesters? Do you think they will stop globalization?

3. Does globalization of finance and trade threaten America's position as a leading provider of financial services?

4. On April 23, 2002, the OCC, the Fed, the FDIC, and the OTS issued a joint statement concerning parallel-owned banking organizations that are not subject to the Bank Holding Company Act, i.e., a U.S. depository institution and a foreign depository institution controlled by the same person or group of persons, either directly or indirectly. The joint statement expressed concern with the policing of money laundering by such institutions, as well as the shifting of assets between institutions. Control may be found for the purpose of identifying a parallel-owned institution through such things as joint marketing strategies, as exemplified by linked web sites, sharing a similar name, overlapping officers and directors, as well as stock ownership. The regulators issuing the statement intend to create a system of coordinated supervision over the U.S. operations of these institutions, including unannounced inspections. U.S. institutions that contemplate becoming a part of a parallel-owned

organization are directed to notify their bank regulator. Joint Agency Statement on Parallel–Owned Banking Organizations, Apr. 23, 2002, at <www.federalreserve.gov/boarddocs/press/general/2002/20020423/attachment.pdf>.

5. The FDIC amended its international banking regulations in April 2005 to address the relocation of insured U.S. branches of foreign banks and to impose a risk-based asset pledge requirement for insured U.S. branches of foreign banks. The amendments further established information and examination requirements for foreign banks that own branches or depository institution subsidiaries seeking FDIC deposit insurance. The FDIC has also decided to maintain its existing position of denying FDIC deposit insurance for wholesale U.S. branches of foreign banks. 70 Fed. Reg. 17,550 (Apr. 6, 2005) (codified at 12 C.F.R. pts. 303, 325, 327 & 347).

6. The insolvency of foreign banks with U.S. operations also raises a number of complex issues on how those assets will be resolved. See Steven L. Schwarcz, The Confused U.S. Framework for Foreign–Bank Insolvency: An Open Research Agenda, 1 Rev. Law & Econ. 81 (2005); Michael Krimminger, Resolution of Cross–Border Banks (2006) (available at <ssrn.com>).

7. Foreign banks operating in the United States are required to file annual reports on their operations with the Fed, which uses the reports to monitor compliance with Bank Holding Company Act restrictions on non-banking activities of foreign banks. John E. Court, Foreign Bank Regulatory Reporting, 23 Bank. & Fin. Services 55 (May 2007).

SECTION 2. INTERNATIONAL OPERATIONS OF UNITED STATES BANKS

The Edge Act, the result of 1916 and 1919 amendments to the Federal Reserve Act, was enacted to assist American banks conducting international operations. It authorized the creation of federally chartered corporations that could engage in international banking and other international financial activities. 12 U.S.C. § 611 et seq. Edge Act corporations were authorized to deal in notes, drafts, checks, bankers acceptances, and also receive deposits, as long as they were not domestic in nature. 12 U.S.C. § 615(c). The only activities that could take place in the United States were those incidental to the international operations of the Edge Act company.

APFEL v. MELLON

United States Court of Appeals, District of Columbia Circuit, 1929.
33 F.2d 805, *cert. denied*, 280 U.S. 585.

MARTIN, CHIEF JUDGE.

This is an appeal from a final order of the lower court dismissing the appellants' petition for a writ of mandamus upon the allegations of the petition and answer.

The case arises under the Act of Congress of December 24, 1919 (41 Stat. 378), commonly known as the "Edge Act," first enacted as section 25(a) of the Federal Reserve Act. See title 12 USCA §§ 611 to 631.

The act provides that corporations may be organized for the purpose of engaging in international or foreign banking or other international or foreign financial operations, and may be formed by any number of natural persons not less than five; that such persons shall enter into articles of association which shall specify in general terms the objects for which the association is formed, and shall execute an organization certificate which shall set out the name assumed by the corporation, the place or places where its operations are to be carried on, the place in the United States where its home office is to be located, the amount of its capital stock and the number of shares into which it shall be divided, the names and places of business or residence of the persons executing the certificate and the number of shares to which each has subscribed, and the fact that the certificate is made to enable the subscribers and their successors to avail themselves of the advantages of the act. It provides also that no corporation shall be organized under the act with a capital stock of less than $2,000,000, one quarter of which shall be paid in before the corporation may be organized to begin business; that the persons signing the organization certificate shall duly acknowledge the execution thereof, and forward it to the Federal Reserve Board, and that after the articles of association and an organization certificate are duly made and filed, and "after the Federal Reserve Board has approved the same and issued the permit to begin business, the association shall become and be a body corporate," with certain specified powers including in general the right to engage in international or foreign banking or other financial operations. The act provides "that except such as is incidental and preliminary to its organization no such corporation shall exercise any of the powers conferred by this section until it has been duly authorized by the Federal Reserve Board to commence business as a corporation organized under the provisions of this section." It also provides that such a corporation may establish and maintain branches or agencies in foreign countries at such places as may be approved by the Federal Reserve Board and under such rules and regulations as the Board may prescribe.

In the instant case the appellants, as relators below, filed their petition against the appellees as members of the Federal Reserve Board, alleging that the relators had duly executed and filed with the respondents, a certificate for the organization of a corporation under the foregoing act for the purpose of engaging in international or foreign banking under the name "Foreign Financing Corporation," and that the certificate fully conformed with the requirements of the act; but that the respondents nevertheless had wrongfully refused to approve of the same or to issue a permit to relators to begin business as a body corporate under the act. The relators prayed for a writ of mandamus to compel the respondents acting as the Federal Reserve Board to approve the articles of incorporation and the organization certificate aforesaid, and to permit relators to begin business as a body corporate under the name "Foreign Financing Corporation," in accordance with the provisions of the act.

The respondents filed their answer admitting that the articles of association and organization certificate filed with the Board by relators were in proper legal form, but stating that the Board had refused to approve the same on the following grounds:

"That the Federal Reserve Board as a board, and the respondents as members thereof, deem it their duty carefully to inquire into the qualifications of the organizers of such proposed corporations and to refuse to approve the article of association and organization certificates of such proposed corporations and to issue a permit for such proposed corporations to do business, unless after investigation, said Board is of the opinion that the financial responsibility, experience, training, and other qualifications of the organizers of such proposed corporations are such as may reasonably be calculated to hold promise of the financial soundness, reliable and competent management, and proper and successful operation of such proposed corporation."

" * * * That relators do not possess the qualifications reasonably necessary to assure the financial soundness, reliable and competent management, or the proper or successful operations of a corporation organized under Section 25 (a) of the Federal Reserve Act to engage in the highly technical activities of international or foreign banking or other international or foreign financial operations and that it would detrimental to the public interest to approve such articles of association or organization certificate and to issue a preliminary permit for such proposed corporation to commence business; and that, therefore, the said Board refused to approve the articles of association and the organization certificate and refused to issue a permit to said proposed corporation to begin business." * * *

It is contended by appellees that the statute imposes the duty upon the Federal Reserve Board of exercising its judgment and discretion with respect to the approval or disapproval of the articles of association and organization certificates made and filed under the act, and that the Board's action in this instance is within the limits of that authority. On the other hand, appellants contend that "Congress has not undertaken to delegate to the Board the discretion it has assumed to exercise."

We agree with the contention of the appellees. The statute provides that an association formed under the act shall not become a body corporate until after the articles of association and organization certificate have been duly made and filed, and after the Federal Reserve Board has approved the same and issued a permit to it to begin business. The word "approved" naturally imports the exercise of judgment and discretion; and the power to approve ordinarily implies a power to disapprove. * * *

The International Banking Act of 1978 allowed foreign banks to own Edge Act corporations. Foreign banks could thus establish a base in the

United States without being subject to Bank Holding Company Act restrictions. Foreign banks could also operate a branch or agency with restricted banking powers under the IBA, if licensed by the Comptroller of the Currency.[4]

Domestic banks faced many challenges in their operations abroad. The following are a few examples.

ALLIED BANK INTERNATIONAL v. BANCO CREDITO AGRICOLA DE CARTAGO

United States Court of Appeals, Second Circuit, 1985.
757 F.2d 516.

MESKILL, CIRCUIT JUDGE.

* * * Allied is the agent for a syndicate of thirty-nine creditor banks. Defendants-appellees are three Costa Rican banks that are wholly owned by the Republic of Costa Rica and subject to the direct control of the Central Bank of Costa Rica (Central Bank). Allied brought this action in February 1982 to recover on promissory notes issued by the Costa Rican banks. The notes, which were in default, were payable in United States dollars in New York City. The parties' agreements acknowledged that the obligations were registered with Central Bank which was supposed to provide the necessary dollars for payment.

The defaults were due solely to actions of the Costa Rican government. In July 1981, in response to escalating national economic problems, Central Bank issued regulations which essentially suspended all external debt payments. In November 1981, the government issued an executive decree which conditioned all payments of external debt on express approval from Central Bank. Central Bank subsequently refused to authorize any foreign debt payments in United States dollars, thus precluding payment on the notes here at issue. In accordance with the provisions of the agreements, Allied accelerated the debt and sued for the full amount of principal and interest outstanding.

The Costa Rican banks moved the district court to dismiss the complaint, claiming lack of subject matter jurisdiction due to sovereign immunity, lack of *in personam* jurisdiction and insufficiency of process and service. Allied moved for summary judgment. The sole defense raised by appellees in response was the act of state doctrine.

The district court denied all of the motions. Reasoning that a judicial determination contrary to the Costa Rican directives could embarrass the United States government in its relations with the Costa Rican government, the court held that the act of state doctrine barred entry of summary judgment for Allied.

While the action was still pending before the district court, the parties began to negotiate a rescheduling of the debt. In July 1982, the suit was

---

4. See Douglas McPheters, Formation of Edge Act Corporations, 37 Bus. Law. 593 (1982).

dismissed by agreement after the parties stipulated that no issues of fact remained with respect to the act of state doctrine issue. In September 1983, appellees, Central Bank and the Republic of Costa Rica signed a refinancing agreement with the coordinating agent for Costa Rica's external creditors. Fidelity Union Trust Company of New Jersey, one of the members of the Allied syndicate, did not accept the agreement. On behalf of Fidelity, the only creditor that refused to participate in the restructuring, Allied has prosecuted this appeal. The refinancing went into effect nonetheless and appellees have been making payments to the remaining thirty-eight members of the syndicate.

In our previous decision, we affirmed the district court's dismissal. We did not address the question of whether the act of state doctrine applied because we determined that the actions of the Costa Rican government which precipitated the default of the Costa Rican banks were fully consistent with the law and policy of the United States. We therefore concluded that principles of comity compelled us to recognize as valid the Costa Rican directives.

Our interpretation of United States policy, however, arose primarily from our belief that the legislative and executive branches of our government fully supported Costa Rica's actions and all of the economic ramifications. On rehearing, the Executive Branch of the United States joined this litigation as *amicus curiae* and respectfully disputed our reasoning. The Justice Department brief gave the following explanation of our government's support for the debt resolution procedure that operates through the auspices of the International Monetary Fund (IMF). Guided by the IMF, this long established approach encourages the cooperative adjustment of international debt problems. The entire strategy is grounded in the understanding that, while parties may agree to renegotiate conditions of payment, the underlying obligations to pay nevertheless remain valid and enforceable. Costa Rica's attempted unilateral restructuring of private obligations, the United States contends, was inconsistent with this system of international cooperation and negotiation and thus inconsistent with United States policy.

The United States government further explains that its position on private international debt is not inconsistent with either its own willingness to restructure Costa Rica's intergovernmental obligations or with continued United States aid to the economically distressed Central American country. Our previous conclusion that the Costa Rican decrees were consistent with United States policy was premised on these two circumstances.

In light of the government's elucidation of its position, we believe that our earlier interpretation of United States policy was wrong. Nevertheless, if, as Judge Griesa held, the act of state doctrine applies, it precludes judicial examination of the Costa Rican decrees. Thus we must first consider that question.

The act of state doctrine operates to confer presumptive validity on certain acts of foreign sovereigns by rendering non-justiciable claims that challenge such acts. The judicially created doctrine is not jurisdictional; it is "a rule of decision under which an act meeting the definition ... is binding on the court." Restatement (Revised) of Foreign Relations Law § 428 comment c (Tent. Draft No. 4, 1983); Empresa Cubana Exportadora de Azucar y Sus Derivados v. Lamborn & Co., 652 F.2d 231, 239 (2d Cir.1981). The applicability of the doctrine is purely a matter of federal law. Banco Nacional de Cuba v. Sabbatino, 376 U.S. 398, 427 (1964).

* * * The Costa Rican banks conceded jurisdiction in New York and they agreed to pay the debt in New York City in United States dollars. Allied, the designated syndicate agent, is located in the United States, specifically in New York; some of the negotiations between the parties took place in the United States. The United States has an interest in maintaining New York's status as one of the foremost commercial centers in the world. Further, New York is the international clearing center for United States dollars. In addition to other international activities, United States banks lend billions of dollars to foreign debtors each year. The United States has an interest in ensuring that creditors entitled to payment in the United States in United States dollars under contracts subject to the jurisdiction of United States courts may assume that, except under the most extraordinary circumstances, their rights will be determined in accordance with recognized principles of contract law.

In contrast, while Costa Rica has a legitimate concern in overseeing the debt situation of state-owned banks and in maintaining a stable economy, its interest in the contracts at issue is essentially limited to the extent to which it can unilaterally alter the payment terms. Costa Rica's potential jurisdiction over the debt is not sufficient to locate the debt there for the purposes of act of state doctrine analysis. Cf. United Bank Ltd. v. Cosmic International, Inc., 542 F.2d 868, 874 (2d Cir. 1976).

Thus, under either analysis, our result is the same: the situs of the debt was in the United States, not in Costa Rica. Consequently, this was not "a taking of property within its own territory by [Costa Rica]." Sabbatino, 376 U.S. at 428, 84 S.Ct. at 940. The act of state doctrine is, therefore, inapplicable.

Acts of foreign governments purporting to have extraterritorial effect—and consequently, by definition, falling outside the scope of the act of state doctrine—should be recognized by the courts only if they are consistent with the law and policy of the United States. United States v. Belmont, 301 U.S. 324, 332–33. Thus, we have come full circle to reassess whether we should give effect to the Costa Rican directives. We now conclude that we should not.

The Costa Rican government's unilateral attempt to repudiate private, commercial obligations is inconsistent with the orderly resolution of international debt problems. It is similarly contrary to the interests of the United States, a major source of private international credit. The government has procedures for resolving intergovernmental financial difficulties. See, e.g., Foreign Assistance Act of 1961, Pub.L. No. 87–195, 75 Stat. 424 (1961) (codified as amended in scattered sections of 22 U.S.C.). With respect to private debt, support for the IMF resolution strategy is consistent with both the policy aims and best interests of the United States.

Recognition of the Costa Rican directives in this context would also be counter to principles of contract law. Appellees explicitly agreed that their obligation to pay would not be excused in the event that Central Bank failed to provide the necessary United States dollars for payment. This, of course, was the precise cause of the default. If we were to give effect to the directives, our decision would vitiate an express provision of the contracts between the parties.

The Costa Rican directives are inconsistent with the law and policy of the United States. We refuse, therefore, to hold that the directives excuse the obligations of the Costa Rican banks. The appellees' inability to pay United States dollars relates only to the potential enforceability of the judgment; it does not determine whether judgment should enter.

* * * The act of state doctrine was the only defense raised by the Costa Rican banks to Allied's motion and the only ground for the district court's denial of that motion. * * *

We vacate our previous decision * * * and direct the district court to enter judgment for Allied.

Compare Braka v. Bancomer, S.N.C., 762 F.2d 222 (2d Cir. 1985) (act of state doctrine barred recovery on losses caused by government decree on exchange rate for Mexican certificates of deposit).

CITIBANK, N.A. v. WELLS FARGO ASIA LTD.

Supreme Court of the United States, 1990.
495 U.S. 660.

MR. JUSTICE KENNEDY delivered the opinion of the Court.

At issue here is whether the home office of a United States bank is obligated to use its general assets to repay a Eurodollar deposit made at one of its foreign branches, after the foreign country's government has prohibited the branch from making repayment out of its own assets.

The case arises from a transaction in what is known in the banking and financial communities as the Eurodollar market. As the District Court defined the term, Eurodollars are United States dollars that have been deposited with a banking institution located outside the United States, with a corresponding obligation on the part of the banking institution to repay the deposit in United States dollars. P. Oppenheim, International Banking 243 (5th ed. 1987). The banking institution receiving the deposit can be either a foreign branch of a United States bank or a foreign bank.

A major component of the Eurodollar market is interbank trading. In a typical interbank transaction in the Eurodollar market, the depositing bank (Bank A) agrees by telephone or telex, or through a broker, to place a deposit denominated in United States dollars with a second bank (Bank X). For the deposit to be a Eurodollar deposit, Bank X must be either a foreign branch of a United States bank or a foreign bank; Bank A, however, can be any bank, including one located in the United States. To complete the transactions, most banks that participate in the interbank trading market utilize correspondent banks in New York City, with whom they maintain, directly or indirectly, accounts denominated in United States dollars. In this example, the depositor bank, Bank A, orders its correspondent bank in New York (Bank B) to transfer United States dollars from Bank A's account to Bank X's account with Bank X's New York correspondent bank (Bank Y). The transfer of funds from Bank B to Bank Y is accomplished by means of a wire transfer through a clearing mechanism located in New York City and known as the Clearing House Interbank Payments System, or "CHIPS." Repayment of the funds at the end of the deposit term is accomplished by having Bank Y transfer funds from Bank X's account to Bank B, through the CHIPS system, for credit to Bank A's account.

The transaction at issue here follows this pattern. Respondent Wells Fargo Asia Limited (WFAL) is a Singapore-chartered bank wholly owned by Wells Fargo Bank, N.A., a bank chartered by the United States. Petitioner Citibank, N.A. (Citibank), also a United States-chartered bank, operates a branch office in Manila, Philippines (Citibank/Manila). On June 10, 1983, WFAL agreed to make two $1 million time deposits with Citibank/Manila. The rate at which the deposits would earn interest was set at 10%, and the parties agreed that the deposits would be repaid on December 9 and 10, 1983. * * *

A few months after the deposit was made, the Philippine government issued a Memorandum to Authorized Agent Banks (MAAB 47) which provided in relevant part:

> " 'Any remittance of foreign exchange for repayment of principal on all foreign obligations due to foreign banks and/or financial institutions, irrespective of maturity, shall be submitted to the Central Bank [of the Philippines] thru the Management of External Debt and Investment Accounts Department (MEDIAD) for prior approval.' "

According to the Court of Appeals, "[a]s interpreted by the Central Bank of the Philippines, this decree prevented Citibank/Manila, an 'authorized agent bank' under Philippine law, from repaying the WFAL deposits with its Philippine assets, i.e., those assets not either deposited in banks elsewhere or invested in non-Philippine enterprises." As a result, Citibank/Manila refused to repay WFAL's deposits when they matured in December 1983. * * *

Little need be said respecting the operation or effect of the Philippine decree at this stage of the case, for no party questions the conclusion reached by both the District Court and the Court of Appeals that Philippine law does not bar the collection of WFAL's deposits from the general assets of Citibank in the State of New York. The question, rather, is whether Citibank is obligated to allow collection in New York, and on this point two principal theories must be examined. The first is that there was an agreement between the parties to permit collection in New York, or indeed at any place where Citibank has assets, an agreement implied from all the facts in the case as being within the contemplation of the parties. A second, and alternative, theory for permitting collection is that, assuming no such agreement, there is a duty to pay in New York in any event, a duty that the law creates when the parties have not contracted otherwise. See 3 A. Corbin, Contracts § 561, pp. 276–277 (1960). * * *

A fair reading of all of the testimony supports the conclusion that, at least in this trial, on the issue of the allocation of sovereign risk there was a wide variance of opinion in the international banking community. We cannot say that we are left with "the definite and firm conviction" that the District Court's findings are erroneous. United States v. United States Gypsum Co., 333 U.S. 364, 395 (1948). Because the Court of Appeals' holding relies upon contrary factual assumptions, the judgment for WFAL cannot be affirmed under the reasoning used by that court.

Given the finding of the District Court that there was no agreement between the parties respecting collection from Citibank's general assets in New York, the question becomes whether collection is permitted nonetheless by rights and duties implied by law. As is its right, see Dandridge v. Williams, 397 U.S. 471, 475–476, and n.6 (1970), WFAL seeks to defend the judgment below on the ground that, under principles of either New York or Philippine law, Citibank was obligated to make its general assets available for collection of WFAL's deposits. It is unclear from the opinion of the Court of Appeals which law it found to be controlling; and we decide to remand the case for the Court of Appeals to determine which law applies, and the content of that law.

One of WFAL's contentions is that the Court of Appeals' opinion can be supported on the theory that it is based upon New York law. We do not think this is a fair or necessary construction of the opinion. The Court of Appeals placed express reliance on its own opinion in Garcia v. Chase Manhattan Bank, N.A., 735 F. 2d 645 (CA2 1984), without citing or discussing Perez v. Chase Manhattan Bank, N.A., 463 N.E. 2d 5 (1984). In that case, the New York Court of Appeals was explicit in pointing out that its decision was in conflict with that reached two days earlier by the Second Circuit in *Garcia*, supra, a case that the Perez court deemed "similar on its facts." See 463 N.E. 2d, at 9, n.3. Given this alignment of authorities, we are reluctant to interpret the Court of Appeals' decision as resting on principles of state law. The opinion of the Court of Appeals, moreover, refers to "general banking law principles" and "United States law," 852 F.2d, at 660; whether this is the semantic or legal equivalent of the law of New York is for the Court of Appeals to say in the first instance.

Alternatively, if the Court of Appeals, based upon its particular expertise in the law of New York and commercial matters generally, is of the view that the controlling rule is supplied by Philippine law or, as Citibank would have it, by a federal common-law rule respecting bank deposits, it should make that determination, subject to any further review we deem appropriate. In view of our remand, we find it premature to consider the other contentions of the parties respecting the necessity for any rule of federal common law, or the pre-emptive effect of federal statutes and regulations on bank deposits and reserves. See 12 U.S.C. §§ 461(b)(6), 1813(1)(5)(a); 12 CFR § 204.128(c) (1990). All of these matters, of course, may be addressed by the Court of Appeals if necessary for a full and correct resolution of the case.

The judgment of the Court of Appeals is vacated, and the case remanded for further proceedings consistent with this opinion.

CHIEF JUSTICE REHNQUIST concurs. * * * JUSTICE STEVENS dissents. * * *

FEDERAL DEPOSIT INSURANCE CORPORATION THE GLOBALIZATION OF THE U.S. BANKING INDUSTRY

FDIC Outlook 25 (Summer 2005).

* * * Foreign-owned banking assets in the United States have exceeded international assets of U.S. banks since the mid–1980s. * * *

Citibank NA held the largest share of international assets (17 percent) of any U.S. bank, while the top five banks together held slightly more than half of all international assets reported by U.S. banks. Twenty years later, the share of international assets held by the top five banks had increased to 87 percent, and the single largest bank share, again held by Citibank NA, had increased to 42 percent. * * * The number of U.S. banks operating foreign offices has steadily declined from 266 banks in 1984 to 122 banks at year-end 2004. Three banks dominate the list of U.S. banks with foreign offices. At the end of 2004, Citigroup, JPMorgan Chase, and Bank of America collectively owned 651 (or 84 percent) of the 777 total foreign branches of U.S. banks.

* * * Citigroup and JPMorgan Chase, the two largest U.S. banks in terms of total assets, earned 53 percent and 48 percent, respectively, of their net income from operations outside of North America in 2004. * * *

International banking strategies may differ across banks in terms of geography or product choice. Several key objectives drive foreign expansion by U.S. banks, including

- increasing profits by expanding distribution channels into new, potentially high-growth geographic markets and across demographic groups;
- providing commercial lending and capital markets products and services to support global expansion plans of corporate and commercial clients;

- increasing revenue diversification; and

- cross-selling and leveraging existing product expertise in foreign markets.

Some banks limit their international operations to certain areas of expertise, while others establish a physical presence in foreign markets to offer a wider array of products to their foreign customers.

Geographically, U.S. banks have increasingly focused their international activities in Europe and Asia, while U.S. bank assets in Latin America and the Caribbean have declined. For example, at year-end 2004, Europe represented roughly half the foreign branch assets of U.S. banks, and Asia represented approximately one-quarter of these assets. * * *

Attracted by the opportunity to develop a strategic foothold in one of the world's largest economies, interest in China among U.S. and foreign-owned financial institutions is intensifying. As part of its 2001 accession into the World Trade Organization, China committed to remove restrictions on foreign participation in its financial industry over a five-year period. As the deadline for reform completion nears, reports suggest that interest from abroad in China's banking market has increased. Likewise, indications are that the Chinese government is becoming more receptive to foreign investment in that country's banking sector.

According to a 2004 special edition of The McKinsey Quarterly, China, the world's most populous nation, will represent "a golden opportunity" for foreign banks to provide credit card loans once foreign lending restrictions are lifted. * * * According to the report, partnerships with existing Chinese banks may be the best way to enter China's consumer lending market during this period. Foreign banks will not be able to accept deposits or issue cards until 2007, and card holders currently place little value on credit cards issued by foreign banks. * * *

Despite the growth of international activities among U.S. banks, most available financial indicators fail to show a performance advantage accruing to institutions with overseas operations. * * * For example, in 2004, the average return on assets (ROA) specifically attributed to international operations was 0.96 percent, compared with an overall 1.26 percent at all banks with international operations. Similarly, net interest income as a percentage of assets averaged 2.18 percent for international operations, compared with an overall average of 2.76 percent for domestic and foreign operations combined. * * *

The performance of international banks (that is, U.S. banks with more than $10 billion in assets and at least 25% of their assets in foreign offices) relative to the overall performance of the U.S. banking industry fails to show that sizable international operations have given a significant boos to overall performance. In fact, the international banks have earned less than the industry-average ROA in 14 of the past 15 years, and their return on equity has been below the industry average in eight of those years. * * *

Notwithstanding the motivations favoring expansion into foreign markets, the results for U.S. banks in recent years suggest that the international integration of the U.S. banking industry may be following, rather than leading, the wider expansion of global commerce. Indications are that better performance may be more easily attained in the domestic U.S. market, and most U.S. banks remain satisfied with a purely domestic focus. Overseas, a few large institutions continue to dominate the foreign banking activities of U.S.-based banks. * * * [A]s globalization bring foreign markets ever closer to us, more U.S. financial institutions will be motivated to consider the benefits and drawback of conducting international banking activities.

QUESTIONS AND NOTES

1. Under Regulation K, 12 C.F.R. pt. 211, the Fed regulates member banks (which includes national banks and state member banks) with respect to their foreign branches and investments in foreign branches. 12 C.F.R. §§ 211.1–13. The Fed also regulates pursuant to Regulation K Edge Act corporations (under 12 U.S.C. §§ 611–631), agreement corporations (under 12 U.S.C. §§ 601–604a), and the nonbanking activities of bank holding companies (under 12 U.S.C. § 1843(c)(13)). The Fed adopted revisions to Regulation K that make it easier for U.S. banks to branch internationally, expands the scope of permissible activities within foreign branches, and increases to 20% the amount of capital and surplus that banks can invest in Edge Act corporations. The final rule also removes some impediments and restrictions to foreign branching in the U.S. This rule had been proposed for several years before its adoption. 66 Fed. Reg. 54,399 (Oct. 26, 2001) (codified at 12 C.F.R. pts. 211 & 265). National banks operating abroad must also comply with the regulatory provisions in 12 C.F.R. §§ 28.1–5. Insured state nonmember banks are subject to the FDIC's regulations, 12 C.F.R. §§ 347.101–.110, with respect to their foreign branches and foreign investments.

2. Bank of America expanded its international operations by purchasing a minority interest in the China Construction Bank for $2.5 billion in June 2005. Bank of America sold much of its stake in this bank in May 2009 to boost its capital.

3. Foreign assets of U.S. banks held abroad are concentrated in a few large banks. The five largest U.S. banks held eighty-seven percent of those assets. Citibank N.A. alone held forty-two percent of such assets. The Globalization of the U.S. Banking Industry, FDIC Outlook 25 (Summer 2005).

SECTION 3. COMPARATIVE REGULATION

Banks in America have limited powers, whether they are nationally or state chartered. The activities conducted elsewhere in the holding company are also limited, although the Gramm–Leach–Bliley Act (GLBA) expanded the available activities from those "closely related to banking" to those that are "financial in nature." The latter formulation of permissible powers includes insurance and securities activities as agent or underwriter. GLBA endorsed the concept of "functional" regulation. As a result, banks and their holding companies are potentially subject to regulation by the various bank regulators (state, OCC, Fed and FDIC), the fifty state insurance commissions (plus the District of Columbia), the SEC, and the CFTC. An American bank involved in international operations will also have to face foreign regulators. The following is a discussion of comparative bank regulation in some of the important jurisdictions in which American banks may operate.

A. JAPAN

After World War II, American authorities occupying Japan imposed several U.S. statutes, including the federal securities laws and provisions of the Glass–Steagall Act, that separated investment banking from commercial banking. The Glass–Steagall provisions are found in Article 65 of the Japanese Securities and Exchange Law. An Anti–Monopoly Law prohibited banks from holding more than five percent of the stock of another company. In contrast to America, Japan did not permit bank holding companies. Despite those restrictions, banks joined the keiretsu movement that dominated the Japanese economy after the war. Keiretsu are groups of companies with close links that support each other. Banks joined such groups and provided banking services to other members. The keiretsu banks grew rapidly and several Japanese banks were soon among the largest in the world.

Japanese bank regulation was conducted through the Ministry of Finance (MOF). That regulation was intensive and penetrated nearly every aspect of banking operations. Japanese banks took few actions without the approval of the MOF, including opening new branches.

The Bank of Japan (BOJ) acted as a central bank and set monetary policy. The Japanese government did not allow banks to fail; rather, it arranged rescues of troubled banks. That policy has been criticized as supporting inefficient operations and concealing large numbers of bad loans.

BOJ controlled domestic interest rates closely after World War II, often holding them below international market rates, and preventing Japanese depositors from investing their funds abroad. Although those restrictions have been eased, at the end of the last century, as the result of a lasting recession, BOJ set a zero interest rate to help enhance growth.

A unique aspect of the Japanese financial system is the provision of postal savings accounts to consumers by the government. These accounts earn higher interest than bank deposits and receive favorable tax treatment. They are so popular that an estimated twenty percent of personal financial assets in Japan were held in postal savings accounts at the beginning of this century. The Japanese government used the deposits to help fund its operations, as an alternative to tax and other funding.

JERRY W. MARKHAM
SUPER REGULATOR: A COMPARATIVE ANALYSIS OF SECURITIES AND DERIVATIVES REGULATION IN THE UNITED STATES, THE UNITED KINGDOM, AND JAPAN

28 Brook. J. Int'l L. 319 (2003).

* * * In the 1980s, however, a "bubble economy" developed in Japan. The stock market boomed, and real estate prices more than doubled between 1986 and 1990. Scandals soon unfolded. In the "Recruit Cosmos" affair, Prime Minister Noboru Takeshita resigned after it was discovered that some 160 influential politicians had been given Recruit Cosmos stock at bargain prices in 1986, just before the company went public. In another scandal, the Hanshin Sogo Bank sold a large amount of stock it held in the Tateho Chemical Company the day before that company announced large losses. No wrongdoing was found, to the consternation of many. Nui Onoue, the "Bubble Lady" became famous for borrowing billions of dollars on her restaurants in order to invest in the stock market. The amounts she borrowed were greater than the value of those properties. She had also used forged certificates of deposit for her trading activities. Eventually, the Bubble Lady, who used séances to pick stocks, was sentenced to twelve years in prison.

The bursting of the Japanese bubble at the beginning of the 1990s had some horrific effects on the economy. The economy went into a recession that the country is still struggling with today—massive deflation was experienced; the Nikkei 225 index dropped from 39,000 to 11,000; land prices in large cities dropped eleven years in a row; government debt grew to 150% of GDP, as compared with 33% in the United States; and bad debt held by Japanese banks grew to be some 30% of GDP. The Hokkaido Takushokku Bank failed, the first to do so in Japan since World War II. Nineteen of Japan's largest banks had capital shortages that were threatening their ability to meet the Basel Committees guidelines for international banks. Yamaichi Securities, the fourth largest securities firm in Japan, also failed. Yamaichi had hid its losses in off-book accounts, apparently with the knowledge of at least one MoF official. In the early 1990s there were a series of "loss compensation" scandals, in which it was discovered that the country's four largest brokerage firms were covering the trading losses of important clients and politicians. In 1997, the nation's largest securities firm, Nomura, became mired in scandal, after it was discovered that the firm had covered the trading losses of a gangster and engaged in widespread abusive sales practices.

The Japanese government took several steps to deal with this deteriorating situation. The Japanese Diet passed the Financial Reform Act of 1992, which allowed the MoF to establish capital requirements for banks and allowed banks to own securities affiliates. The act also aimed to further competition among financial institutions. Furthermore, a Securities Exchange and Surveillance Commission ("SESC") was created in 1992 to police the securities markets. This legislation ostensibly reduced the MoF's role as the director agency for the placement of financial resources. In application, however, the MoF remained firmly in control of financial services firms and the SESC. Greater reform was attempted in 1996 by means of a "Japanese Big Bang" that sought to emulate the one in the U.K. and deregulate Japan's financial services. The Japanese Big Bang tried to ease market entry and remove non-competitive practices. Commissions were unfixed. The plan was formulated by a Financial System Research Council to allow banks, insurance companies, and brokerage firms to compete with each other without the prior restrictions that had kept these sectors separate. The government also announced a "Total Plan" to deal with the mass of non-performing debt in the economy and to dissolve bankrupt companies. Although public funds were used to shore up shaky banks, Japan's banks still maintain some $1.3 trillion in bad debts.

Another scandal arose after the Tokyo Prosecutor's Office staged a large-scale raid involving 100 investigators on the MoF offices in 1998. The Prosecutor was seeking information on bribes in the form of lavish entertainment and discount loans allegedly paid to MoF bank examiners by those being examined. Two examiners were arrested and a third committed suicide. More legislation followed in the form of a Financial Reconstruction Law for failed financial institutions and a Financial Early Strengthening Law that allowed public funds to be used to shore up weak or failing banks. These laws were to be administered by a five-member governmental body called the Financial Reconstruction Commission.

The SESC was transferred out of the MoF in 1998, along with an independent Financial Supervisory Agency, which was succeeded by the Financial Services Agency ("FSA–Japan") in 2000. The FSA–Japan was also given the power previously held by the MoF, to set securities policy and to regulate securities and banking. The SESC continued its operations under authority from FSA–Japan, which in turn was supervised by the Financial Reconstruction Commission. More reform legislation was adopted: the ban on holding companies was removed, and consumer protection was enhanced through the Law Concerning the Sale of Financial Products.

Some have expressed concern that all of these reforms may not have accomplished very much. The SESC lacked strong enforcement mechanisms–it is only an investigative agency. The SESC has no authority to impose sanctions, but may refer matters for sanctions. In practice, however, few referrals have been made to date. In 2001, the SESC had a relatively small staff, at least in comparison to the SEC in the U.S., and most of them had been transferred from the MoF. To be sure, the MoF does appear to retain some policy control. FSA–Japan also experienced a faltering start. When FSA–Japan did try to take aggressive action by urging vast bad debt write-offs, many small and medium-sized companies went bankrupt. FSA–Japan then eased off, pressuring the banks and using public funds to save the Daiei supermarket chain and Koizumi, a construction company, both of which had massive amounts of debt. However, there were no bailouts for small companies. The government nationalized the Long–Term Credit Bank of Japan and the Nippon Credit Bank, after those institutions could no longer be kept afloat. Public funds were also injected into all but one major bank.

FSA–Japan announced that it was undertaking inspections of large troubled banks in order to address their bad debt problems. This project was supposed to be a "Japanese sword" for dealing with the problem, but the result was mostly to shore up some troubled banks. Critics claimed that FSA–Japan was "whitewashing" the bad debt problem in Japan. After downgrading Japan's debt, a credit rating agency claimed that FSA–Japan was engaging in regulatory forbearance as a way to aid the economy "in the hope that something will turn up." The agency was waffling on reform in other areas. Japan dropped its insurance guaranty for customer funds held in time deposit accounts, limiting claims to about $83,000. This was intended to be assure more market discipline but it instead raised concerns that funds would be pulled out of all ready unstable institutions, weakening them further. When a similar proposal limiting deposit insurance on ordinary deposit accounts met political opposition FSA–Japan started backtracking. It then extended government insurance on some deposits, a breach of its promise to eliminate unlimited guarantees.

FSA–Japan seemed to be retreating from promised reform measures in the insurance industry and was stalling on allowing commercial banks, such as the one sought by Sony, to be licensed. The Japanese government continued the old MoF role of trying to manage the economy in other ways. Most recently, despite FSA–Japan's push for a market solution, the government suggested that more banks should merge and that it would offer a higher government guarantee to encourage such actions. In fact, several of Japan's largest banks did merge to form colossal enterprises, the largest being Mizuho Holdings, Inc., composed of Daiichi Bank, Fuji Bank, and the Industrial Bank of Japan.

FSA–Japan was accused of trying to manipulate the Nikkei 225 index through short sale restrictions, which were modeled after those of the SEC in the U.S. Like MoF, FSA–Japan has often been lenient, at least on Japanese banks. For example, FSA–Japan merely issued a warning to a Japanese bank that hid key information from inspectors. FSA–Japan has shown that it knows how to play tough, at least where foreigners are involved. FSA–Japan accused two American firms of improper short sales, in another attempt to support the market. In 1999, the Tokyo branch of Credit Suisse was excluded from engaging in the derivatives business in Japan after several abuses. FSA–Japan denied the consequent claims that it was discriminating against foreign firms.

The Nikkei 225 index remains 74% below its high in 1989. An advisory committee to FSA–Japan has recommended that stocks be sold at post offices as a means of shifting corporate financing away from bank loans and towards the equity markets in order to inflate the stock market. The committee also supported a continuing role for the government in bailing out troubled banks. The Bank of Japan followed up that proposal with an announcement that it would be buying the stock of companies held by banks. This action was said to be a "shocking" manipulation of the stock market designed for the benefit of the banks. The Bank of Japan, FSA–Japan, and the MoF were said to be at an impasse over policy disputes. On the positive side, the agency was seeking greater public disclosures from firms in precarious financial circumstances. It raised its bank capital adequacy threshold for intervention and correction, but capital levels at Japanese banks were still well below the Basel minimum international standard. FSA–Japan allowed banks to sell life and other insurance and announced that it was allowing bank affiliated brokers to do so as well. After some well publicized insurance firm failures, FSA–Japan increased regulatory controls over the industry, requiring, among other things, marked-to-market accounting and increasing solvency margins. At the same time barriers to entry were being lowered, allowing some foreign competition. * * *

––––––––––

For a discussion of Japan's efforts to deregulate its markets see Yoshiro Miwa & J. Mark Ramseyer, Deregulation and Market Response In Contemporary Japan: Administrative Guidance, *Keiretsu* and Main Banks, Harvard John M. Olin Discussion Paper Series No. 462 (Mar. 2004) (available at <www.law.harvard.edu/programs/olin_center>).

Japan enacted a new Financial Instruments and Exchange Law that went into effect October 2007. This new law expanded the government's regulation of securities and derivative transactions and increased disclosure requirements for unsophisticated investors. Following the American lead, exchange listed companies are now required to file quarterly financial reports and to establish internal controls. The government Post Office, Japan Post, is also being privatized, a move it is thought will push Japanese investors into stock and other private investment methods like mutual funds.

The Japanese Financial Services Agency announced rule proposals in January 2010 to regulate insurance and securities as corporate groups, rather than individually. This approach, favored by the European Union, proved unsuccessful in the United States as the result of the failure of several large investment banks (including Bear Stearns, Merrill Lynch, and Lehman Brothers) that were regulated on a consolidated basis by the SEC. The Japanese Financial Services Agency also sought greater regulation of hedge funds and centralized clearing of derivative contracts.

B. UNITED KINGDOM

The Bank of England, which was chartered in 1694, was responsible for bank regulation in England until 1997. Dubbed the "Little Old Lady on Threadneedle Street," the Bank of England used a "raised eyebrow" approach to regulation. More affirmative regulation was imposed after a number of banking scandals, including BCCI. Nevertheless, the Bank of England was stripped of its regulatory powers in 1998, in favor of the newly-created Financial Supervisory Authority (FSA). The Bank of England continues to set monetary policy in a role parallel to the role of the Federal Reserve in the United States.

This regulatory restructuring in the U.K. began in 1986 with the deregulation of securities services, the unfixing of commissions, and a greater opening of the London market to foreign competition. This process was dubbed the "Big Bang," and was prompted by a report by Professor Jim Gower on consumer protection and market practices. His report led to the adoption of the Financial Services Act of 1986. That legislation created the Securities and Investments Board (SIB). The SIB was loosely based on the American concept of the SEC, in which self-regulatory bodies are given primary regulatory responsibility. The SIB regulated insurance and commodities, however, as well as securities.

The FSA is the successor to the SIB. The creation of the FSA combines the regulation of financial services (banking, insurance, derivatives and securities) into one regulator. This is in stark contrast to the functional regulation approach in the United States that involves multiple regulators. As a super-regulator, the FSA should provide a case study on centralized versus functional regulation.[5]

FINANCIAL SERVICES AUTHORITY

<www.fsa.gov.uk/Pages/About/Who/index.shtml>.

The Financial Services Authority (FSA) is an independent non-governmental body, given statutory powers by the Financial Services and Markets Act of 2000.[6] We are a company limited by guarantee and financed by the financial services industry. The Treasury appoints the FSA Board, which currently consists of a Chairman, a Chief Executive Officer, three Managing Directors, and 9 non-executive directors (including a lead non-executive member, the Deputy Chairman). This Board sets our overall policy, but day-to-day decisions and management of the staff are the responsibility of the Executive.

---

5. For a discussion of changes in financial services in London see 4 David Kynaston, The City of London, A Club No More (1945–2000) (2001).

6. [eds.] Also the Financial Services Act of 1986 and the Banking Act of 1987 and certain other legislation.

FINANCIAL SERVICES AUTHORITY

<www.fsa.gov.uk/Pages/About/Who/History/index.shtml>.

The Chancellor of the Exchequer announced the reform of financial services regulation in the UK and the creation of a new regulator on 20 May 1997.

The Chancellor announced his decision to merge banking supervision and investment services regulation into the Securities and Investments Board (SIB). The SIB formally changed its name to the Financial Services Authority in October 1997.

The first stage of the reform of financial services regulation was completed in June 1998, when responsibility for banking supervision was transferred to the FSA from the Bank of England. In May 2000 the FSA took over the role of UK Listing Authority from the London Stock Exchange. The Financial Services and Markets Act, which received Royal Assent in June 2000 and was implemented on 1 December 2001, transferred to the FSA the responsibilities of several other organisations:

- Building Societies Commission
- Friendly Societies Commission
- Investment Management Regulatory Organisation
- Personal Investment Authority
- Register of Friendly Societies
- Securities and Futures Authority

In addition, the legislation gives us some new responsibilities–in particular taking action to prevent market abuse.

In October 2004, following a decision of the Treasury, we took on responsibility for mortgage regulation. In January 2005, to implement the Insurance Mediation Directive and in accordance with a Government announcement in 2004 we took on regulation of general insurance business.

FINANCIAL SERVICES AUTHORITY

<www.fsa.gov.uk/Pages/About/Aims/Stautory/index.shtml>.

The Financial Services and Markets Act gives us four statutory objectives:

- market confidence: maintaining confidence in the financial system;
- public awareness: promoting public understanding of the financial system;
- consumer protection: securing the appropriate degree of protection for consumers; and
- reduction of financial crime: reducing the extent to which it is possible for a business carried on by a regulated person to be used for a purpose connected with financial crime.

These are supported by a set of principles of good regulation which we must consider when achieving the objectives:

- using resources in the most economic and efficient way;
- the responsibilities of those who manage the affairs of authorised persons;
- being proportionate in imposing burdens or restrictions on the industry;
- facilitating innovation;
- taking into account the international character of financial services and the UK's competitive position; and
- not impeding or distorting competition unnecessarily.

The objectives:

- provide political and public accountability—our annual report contains an assessment of our achievement against them. Scrutiny of the FSA by Parliamentary Committees may focus on how we achieve our objectives. They are the goals against which our performance will be judged;
- govern the way we carry out our general functions e.g. rule-making, giving advice and guidance, and determining our general policy and principles. So, for example, we are under a duty to show how the draft rules we publish relate to our statutory objectives;
- provide legal accountability: where we interpret the objectives wrongly, or fail to consider them, we can be challenged in the courts through judicial review.

Before the financial crisis, the Financial Services Authority (FSA), Great Britain's single regulator, was a model for regulation around the world. Despite the reduced regulation imposed by the FSA, Great Britain was spared the Enron-era scandals that arose under functional regulation in the United States. London also grew as a financial services center as firms fled the United States to escape its onerous regulation. The FSA operated on a regulatory system based on six major principles, although its rule book was 8,500 pages in length. The FSA was further applauded after it adopted a unified approach to capital requirements and risk management. However, that program proved to be an empty shell during the financial crisis that began in 2007. The FSA was strongly criticized for failing to prevent a bank run on Northern Rock PLC during the subprime crisis, the first run on a bank in England in over 100 years. The English government nationalized that bank, putting up some $30 billion to rescue it and stop the panic. The House of Commons Treasury Committee subsequently issued a report criticizing the FSA for its laxness in regulating Northern Rock. The report asserted that the FSA had failed to allocate sufficient resources to monitor the bank. The committee recommended that the Bank of England be designated as the lead regulator when banks face financial difficulties.

The problems in the United Kingdom only mounted after the Northern Rock bank rescue. Barclays PLC took a $2.56 billion write-down in November of 2007 as a result of losses from its subprime activities. The Royal Bank of Scotland and Lloyds were effectively nationalized after they suffered staggering losses. After those failures, the U.K. government sought to increase the FSA's regulatory powers. Lord Turner of Ecchinswell, chairman of the FSA, filed a 122 page report recommending that the FSA abandon its "light touch" approach to regulation. Turner wanted to increase capital and liquidity requirements for banks in order to restrict their ability to take excessive risks. The Conservative party in the U.K. responded to the Turner report by promising to abolish the FSA once the party returned to power. The Conservative party was unable to obtain a majority in the May 2010 elections but was able to form a government coalition. They then announced plans to split the FSA into three new agencies and give the Bank of England overall leadership in dealing with systemic risk and in regulating large financial institutions.

The FSA promised more stringent regulation. Its head, Hector Sants, stated that the days of a financial services friendly regulation in London were over and that he intended to take strong action to assure that the business community would be frightened of the FSA. True to his word, the FSA began bringing high profile cases. The FSA set out to prove its new toughness with the announcement of the assessment of a record $4.06 million fine on Barclays Bank PLC for its failure to provide accurate transaction reports on 57.5 million transactions. In another action, the FSA fined an individual a record $1.5 million for insider trading. It also banned a Merrill Lynch trader from the securities business for mismarking his trading book by $100 million and fined Goldman Sachs $31 million. See Jerry W. Markham, A Financial History of the United States, From the Subprime Crisis to the Great Recession (2006–2009) 762–64 (2011).

QUESTIONS AND NOTES

1. For a discussion of England's efforts to deregulate its markets see Howell E. Jackson, An American Perspective on the U.K. Financial Services Authority: Politics, Goals & Regulatory Intensity, Harvard John M. Olin Discussion Paper Series No. 522 (Aug. 2005), available at <www.law.harvard.edu/programs/olin_center>.

2. The Financial Service Authority (FSA) in England attracted much interest in the United States because of concerns that the multiple layers of regulation in the U.S. makes U.S. markets less competitive. The Sarbanes–Oxley Act of 2002, enacted after the Enron and WorldCom scandals, caused public companies to incur an estimated $25 billion each year in additional compliance costs. Moreover, only one of the top twenty initial public offerings worldwide in 2006 was listed in the United States, down from sixty percent of such offerings five years earlier. The U.S. accounted for only twenty-eight percent of global equity raised in leading markets in 2006, down from forty-one percent in 1995. Is Wall Street Losing Its Competitive Edge?, Wall St. J., Dec. 2, 2006. As one critic has noted:

Between 1996 and 2001, the New York Stock Exchange averaged 50 new non-U.S. listings annually; in 2005, it was 19. In the same year, the London Stock Exchange, including its small company affiliate, the Alternative Investment Market, gained 139 new listings while Nasdaq attracted 19. Since the end of 2004, 30 foreign companies have left the NYSE and Nasdaq. Financial capital–the kind that finances mergers, acquisitions and new business formation–is also increasingly finding a more comfortable home abroad. Large offerings by Chinese, Korean and Russian companies–involving billions of dollars–have occurred in Hong Kong and London; meanwhile, large new foreign offerings this year by Russian aluminum producers and Kazakhstan oil and copper companies are planning to list in London.

Peter J. Wallison, Capital Punishment, Wall St. J., Nov. 4, 2006, at A7. However, the evidence on how much the U.S. markets are being undercut by regulatory costs is conflicting. One study showed that the premium for listing on a U.S. exchange had declined, but another study disagreed with that conclusion and found that a U.S. listing still carries a seventeen percent premium over foreign listings. Greg Ip, Maybe U.S. Markets are Still Supreme, Wall St. J. Apr. 27, 2007.

C. GERMANY

In Germany, banks rather than equity markets have traditionally dominated corporate finance. German banks supplied most corporate funding through commercial loans. Equity markets were traditionally weak, and banks filled the role of investment bankers in those markets. German financial markets were also highly regulated until 1994. Before then, this regulatory regime excluded Germans from many areas of finance. Futures trading, for example, was considered to be illegal gambling.[7] That bar was lifted and today Germany has one of the world's largest futures markets. German banks expanded into all areas of finance, including insurance. As Deutsche Bank's acquisition of Bankers Trust in New York and investment bank Morgan Grenfell in London illustrate, German banks have also aggressively expanded their international operations.

The Federal Banking Supervisory Office (FBSO) is now responsible for regulating banks in Germany. The Bundesbank, the German central bank, is responsible for monetary policy and regulating the money markets. Having seen the devastating effect of inflation in the aftermath of World War I, the Bundesbank has been stringent in its monetary policy in order to keep inflation under control.

THE NEW FEDERAL [GERMAN] FINANCIAL SUPERVISORY AUTHORITY (BAFIN)
.

Following the adoption on 22 April 2002 of the Law on Integrated Financial Services Supervision (Gesetz über die integrierte Finanzauf-

---

7. William P. Rogers & Jerry W. Markham, The Application of West German Statutes to United States Commodity Futures Contracts: An Unnecessary Clash of Policies, 19 Law & Pol'y Int'l Bus. 273, 285 (1987).

sicht—FinDAG), the German Financial Supervisory Authority (Bundesanstalt für Finanzdienstleistungsaufsicht–BAFin) was established on 1 May 2002. The functions of the former offices for banking supervision (Bundesaufsichtsamt für das Kreditwesen—BAKred), insurance supervision (Bundesaufsichtsamt für das Versicherungswesen—BAV) and securities supervision (Bundesaufsichtsamt für den Wertpapierhandel–BAWe) have been combined in a single state regulator that supervises banks, financial services institutions and insurance undertakings across the entire financial market and comprises all the key functions of consumer protection and solvency supervision. The new German Financial Supervisory Authority will make a valuable contribution to the stability of Germany as a financial centre and improve its competitiveness.

The BAFin is a federal institution governed by public law that belongs to the portfolio of the Federal Ministry of Finance and as such, has a legal personality. Its two offices are located in Bonn and Frankfurt/Main, where approximately 1,000 persons are employed. The BAFin supervises about 2,700 banks, 800 financial services institutions and over 700 insurance undertakings.

The decision to set up the BAFin was made basically in light of the fundamental changes on the financial markets which required a legislative response that would ensure the future stability of the German financial system.

An increasing number of clients of banks, financial services institutions and insurance companies are demanding integrated financial products. The providers of such products have adapted themselves to these demands and developed cross-sectoral products and strategies. The former distinctions between banking and financial services on the one hand and insurance business on the other are gradually disappearing: Insurance companies have entered the traditional banking business by offering integrated financial services, for instance within the scope of asset management, whereas at the same time banks have developed new lines of products and with these, are now dealing in core businesses once exclusively reserved for insurers. Consequently, suppliers are competing for the same clients with similar or even identical products. Furthermore, competition is intensified by the use of electronic distribution channels on the internet and by the savings potential involved. The client, in turn, is mainly interested in the product, i.e it is of minor importance to him whether it is offered by a bank or an insurance company.

As a result, there is a growing tendency among banks, financial services institutions and insurance undertakings to form cross-sectoral groups for whom it is easier to place broad product ranges effectively in the market. In the past, banks and insurance companies maintained only loose connections whereas today, powerful financial conglomerates have emerged in Germany which operate at a global level. Notable examples include the groups Allianz/Dresdner Bank and Münchner Rück/HypoVere-insbank, which in terms of market capitalisation rank among the world's largest financial conglomerates. The trend towards integrated bankassurance groups is expected to continue.

In view of these developments, the former separation of supervisory functions into the BAKred, BAV and BAWe has become obsolete: Over the last few years, a growing number of states have established modern integrated supervisory structures. Comprehensive powers and a full-scale overview of the market will enable the new German regulator to carry out supervision effectively and thus to contribute to the stability of Germany as a financial centre. This will help avoid imbalances in competition which can easily occur as a result of regulatory differences in a fragmented supervisory system.

The fact that the new German regulator is responsible for all market participants is also of major importance. Especially with regard to foreign companies this is an advantage that should not be underestimated, considering the fact that in the past they had to deal with several supervisory offices when trying to offer their products in Germany.

The foundation of a single regulator will also facilitate the exchange of information with supervisory authorities in other states. In addition, the voice of the new German regulator will carry more weight in international supervisory forums and as a result, German interests can be represented more effectively at an international level. This will help strengthen Germany as a financial centre.

As regards supervision in Germany, the new organisational structure will result in synergies. The integration of the former supervisory offices in a single body enables them to use their know-how and experience more efficiently, especially with regard to the trend towards product convergence and the emergence of financial conglomerates. Moreover, there is no further need for coordination between individual supervisory offices, which in the past was often time consuming and caused considerable expenses. However, although financial services supervision has been organised in a single body this does not mean that existing sectoral differences between the banking and insurance businesses will be disregarded. These differences have led to the development of specific supervisory methods and rules for banks and insurance companies which have proved to be successful. Thus, when creating the new structure the legislator decided not to change the substantive laws underlying supervision, for instance the German Banking Act (Gesetz über das Kreditwesen—KWG), the Insurance Supervision Law (Versicherungsaufsichtsgesetz—VAG) and the German Securities Trading Act (Gesetz über den Wertpapierhandel—WpHG).

The structure of the BAFin takes account of the sectoral differences: Separate organisational units were created for banking supervision, insurance supervision and securities supervision/asset management. Cross-sectoral tasks necessitated by the developments in the financial markets are carried out by several cross-sectoral departments which are organisationally separated from the traditional supervisory functions. The tasks of these departments include the supervision of financial conglomerates, coordination of the work in international supervisory forums and the fight against money laundering across all sectors. The latter has been of particular importance ever since the terrorist attacks in New York.

The new German Financial Supervisory Authority, as a single regulator, is better able than any other supervisory structure to develop equal rules for equal risks and thus to ensure equality of regulatory treatment and a level playing field. In addition, the new structure of German supervision helps strengthen Germany's role as a financial centre and its ability to compete on an international scale.

The BAFin has three main supervisory objectives: Its paramount aim is to ensure the functioning of the entire financial industry in Germany. From this objective, two others can be inferred: to safeguard the solvency of banks, financial services institutions and insurance undertakings—which in the past was mainly a task of the BAKred and the BAV—and to protect clients and investors.

Essentially, the BAFin comprises three supervisory directorates which now perform the supervisory tasks of the three formerly separate supervisory offices. They do not, however, deal with cross-sectoral issues; those have been assigned to three cross-sectoral departments. The directorates are each headed by a First Director.

The first directorate, Banking Supervision, has been assigned all regulatory powers in the framework of solvency-oriented supervision of banks. Banking supervision aims at securing the functioning of the banking industry in order to keep the economy stable, while at the same time it is intended to provide maximum protection for clients' capital deposited with banks. Banking supervision is essentially based on the German Banking Act (KWG) as well as on specific legislation such as the Mortgage Bank Act (Hypothekenbankgesetz) and the Building Societies Act (Bausparkassengesetz). The Deutsche Bundesbank will continue to be involved in the ongoing supervision of banks in accordance with section 7 of the Banking Act.

The tasks of the directorate for Banking Supervision are manifold, given that banks have to meet many legal requirements before they are allowed to provide banking services. For example, they must comply with the capital adequacy requirements and have an appropriate organisational structure as well as at least two professionally qualified and reliable managers. The BAFin monitors compliance with these requirements to make sure that banking services are provided only by undertakings that are solvent and can be expected to manage the business properly. The persons employed in the directorate for Banking Supervision monitor banks on an ongoing basis in order to verify their compliance with the capital adequacy requirements and if they maintain sufficient liquid funds. As regards the important lending business of banks, the BAFin checks if banks comply with statutory risk limits (e.g. large exposure limits) and if their bad debt provisions are in line with their risk exposure.

Growing complexity of banking business compels banks to take suitable measures for the purpose of controlling and monitoring the manifold risks involved in such transactions. As a result, the focus of supervision is on the banks' internal risk controlling and management systems. Furthermore, in line with this risk-oriented supervisory approach the banking supervisor has to be regularly informed about the economic situation of the respective institution, its business strategies and lines of business, as well as its project pipeline, and must evaluate these projects from a banking supervisory point of view.

The main sources of information available to the banking supervisory staff include a multitude of notifications and, in particular, the audit reports of annual accounts prepared by auditors or audit associations. Moreover, exceptional audits provide the BAFin with a better insight into a bank's economic situation. If clients' deposits entrusted to the bank are at risk the BAFin may take measures to avert these dangers, which may even go as far as withdrawing the authorisation to provide banking services. Moreover, the supervisory authority may dismiss unqualified managers.

The directorate for Banking Supervision consists of four departments plus one group and comprises 31 sections.

The second supervisory directorate is responsible for supervising insurance companies in accordance with the Insurance Supervision Law (VAG). The key objectives of insurance supervision consist in protecting the interests of the insured and in making sure that insurers are able to meet their future liabilities at all times.

Insurance companies are allowed to carry out insurance business only after obtaining an authorisation from the BAFin. Companies authorised to write insurance in Germany have to meet various requirements. Before granting the authorisation, the supervisor conducts a comprehensive legal and financial examination. For instance, the insurer is required to submit the operating plan as well as evidence of its own funds to the BAFin. Managers must furnish proof of their good repute and professional qualification. The BAFin monitors if insurance companies have set up sufficient provisions, have sufficient uncommitted funds and take out reinsurance to an appropriate degree to protect themselves against unexpected losses. Moreover, the insurance supervisory staff check if the annual accounts are drawn up correctly in accordance with applicable accounting standards and present a fair view of the insurer's financial situation. Finally, on-site inspections of insurance companies are carried out at regular intervals.

The Insurance Supervision Law provides the BAFin with various instruments to intervene in an insurer's operations for the purpose of preventing or eliminating irregularities or dangers. In the worst case, the authorisation may have to be withdrawn.

Insurance supervision is carried out by 6 departments which comprise a total of 33 sections.

The principal responsibility of the third directorate, Securities Supervision/Asset Management, consists in securing the functioning of German securities and derivatives markets in accordance with the Securities Trading Act (WpHG). In addition, the directorate has been assigned some of the duties of the former BAKred. Under the Securities Trading Act, taking advantage of inside knowledge and/or the unauthorised passing on of inside information is prohibited as this would undermine investors' confidence in fair and equal securities trading. The members of staff analyse trading patterns by means of securities trades reported to the BAFin in accordance with section 9 of the Securities Trading Act and evaluate them with regard to unusual price movements or turnover in order to be able to prosecute any cases of insider dealing they may discover. If indications of forbidden insider dealing are revealed the BAFin informs the public prosecutor. Insider offences are punishable by a fine or imprisonment of up to five years.

The reporting requirements stipulated in the Securities Trading Act play an important part in improving market transparency, given that both retail and professional investors require up-to-date and reliable information for their investment decisions. Thus, listed companies are obliged to publish immediately any new information that is likely to have a considerable effect on the stock market price (ad hoc disclosure). Moreover, owners of major holdings of voting rights in stock corporations whose shares are admitted to official trading or the regulated market must inform the public of the percentage of securities they hold as soon as certain thresholds are exceeded or dropped below. The BAFin may punish violations against these reporting requirements by imposing an administrative fine. Last but not least, the BAFin acts as a depository for prospectuses.

When providing securities services to customers, credit institutions and financial services institutions must comply with particular rules of conduct that serve the protection of investors. Compliance with these rules is checked once every year by external auditors on behalf of the BAFin. Information about the particular terms and risks of the products on offer as well as the costs involved enables investors to make their own, qualified investment decisions. The enterprises must have an appropriate organisational structure and establish internal control mechanisms to avoid conflicts of interest within the institutions.

Corporate takeovers have been supervised in accordance with the new Securities Acquisition and Takeover Act (Wertpapiererwerbs–und Übernahmegesetz–WpÜG) since 1 January 2002. The BAFin makes sure that takeover proceedings are in line with the regulations and monitors the offerors' compliance with the publication requirements.

Before the BAFin was founded, Asset Management and its sections belonged to the BAKred. Their responsibilities consist in monitoring both investment companies and financial services institutions as well as the marketing activities of foreign investment companies in accordance with the Foreign Investment Act (Auslandsinvestment–Gesetz). Their tasks being closely related to securities supervision, they were integrated into the third directorate when the supervisory authority was reorganised.

The directorate for Securities Supervision/Asset Management is comprised of four departments, one of which includes a separate group. The total number of units in the directorate is 25.

One source has summarized the German regulatory consolidation as follows:

> In 2002, Germany consolidated its banking, securities, and insurance regulators into BaFin, which was the federal banking regulator. The new structure kept the old divisions of financial services–banking, securities, and insurance. While the banking and insurance divisions are in Bonn, the securities division is in Frankfurt, home of Germany's stock market. As a federal agency, BaFin is under the oversight of the ministry of finance. It has a board of directors composed of the ministers of finance, economics, and justice, members of Parliament, officials of the Bundesbank, and representatives of the banking, insurance, and securities sectors. Like the other consolidated regulators, BaFin has an advisory council made up of industry, unions, and consumer representatives.

Walter W. Eubanks, Federal Financial Services Regulatory Consolidation: An Overview, Congressional Research Service, CRS–19 (Aug. 17, 2005).

German financial institutions took a battering during the financial crisis that began in 2007. Hypo Real Estate Holdings AG in Germany was about to fail when the German government came to the rescue and injected $142 billion to prop up the firm. Germany's second-largest bank, Commerzbank, was given a $10.4 billion injection of capital by the German government. Another German bank, HSH Nordbank AG, received a $45 billion guarantee from the German government in order to stabilize its condition. Germany also announced a guarantee of all consumer bank deposits. The German government pushed through a $750 billion rescue package for its financial institutions and approved a $39.6 billion economic stimulus package on December 5, 2008.

In August 2008, Germany's financial regulator, BaF in, required German banks to avoid compensation plans that encouraged undue risk taking or which rewarded short-term profits. BaFin also required increased stress testing of positions at all levels, tightened risk management controls, and directed that bank supervisory boards be given greater control over management. Earlier, in October 2008, Germany and Sweden acted to limit executive compensation for executives working at banks that were receiving government aid and guarantees. Germany limited compensation to about $670,000 for executives at its bailed out banks. The

German finance minister proposed a global tax on financial transactions in order to end "binge drinking" in risky financial services. He was supported in that claim by a BIS study that concluded that, since the big banks posed a systemic threat, they should pay higher taxes.

D. EUROPEAN UNION

The European Union (EU) is an international organization of 25 Member States, including the United Kingdom, Germany, France, Italy, Greece Spain, Denmark, Sweden, and Finland. The Member States have established some common institutions through the EU to which they delegate some of their sovereignty with respect to specific matters.

Under a Directive issued by the Council of Members, banks licensed in one member state in the EU must be given recognition by all member states. The bank is regulated and supervised by its home state.[8] The Banking Directive sought to create an EU-wide market for banking services. Similar action has also been ordered for securities activities.

Under the banking directive, banks in one member state may open branches or provide cross-border services in other member states and offer specified banking services there without the requirement of further authorization from the state where the branch is located. This directive thus creates a "passport" for European Union banks and other financial institutions to engage in cross-border operations in other EU countries. The home state notifies the state where one of its banks will be opening a branch or engaging in cross-border services. Banks and their affiliates in the EU are regulated as a consolidated group by the home country. Bank regulators in the EU, however, have adopted common supervisory standards, such as capital and exposure limits.

The Banking Directive defines banking services to include participation in share issues and portfolio management and advice. A bank licensed in one member state may conduct all banking services authorized in its home throughout the EU even if other member states do not allow its banks to engage in all of those activities. The Banking Directive places limits on banks affiliating with non-banks and financial institutions.

The EU adopted a Financial Services Action Plan in 1999 that sought a complete integration of financial services among member states. The Lisbon European Council set a deadline of 2005 for achieving the goals of that plan. A "Group of Wise Men" was appointed to assure progress. Among the items considered were standards for takeover bids, common accounting requirements, provisions for supervision of financial conglomerates, guidelines for cross-border use of collateral, prohibitions against

---

8. See Second Council Directive on the Co-ordination of Laws, Regulations and Administrative Provisions Relating to the Taking–Up and Pursuit of the Business of Credit Institutions and Amending Directive 77/780/EEC (effective Jan. 1993) (Banking Directive); M. Gruson & W. Feuring, A European Community Banking Law: The Second Banking and Related Directives, In the Single Market and the Law of Banking (R. Cranston ed. 1991).

market manipulation, rules for distance marketing, a prospectus directive, creation of a Securities Committee, and a European company statute.

Another European Union Directive ([2–2/87], Dec. 16, 2002) requires "supplementary" regulation for financial conglomerates" that offer multiple financial services such as credit, investment and insurance products. The directive seeks to assure uniform regulation so that such conglomerates do not carry out financial activities in separate subsidiaries that might escape regulation or avoid more stringent regulation intended for such services, a practice the Directive referred to as "regulatory arbitrage." The EU Directive required foreign financial services firms with operations in the EU to demonstrate holding company supervision that is equivalent to EU consolidated supervision. 70 Fed. Reg. 58985 (Oct. 11, 2005). Large American banks operated under such supervision but their broker-dealer and futures commission merchant affiliates were subject to separate capital rules that would not conform to the EU directive. The SEC and CFTC reacted to that directive by allowing such entities to used risk-based capital requirements on an entity basis as substitutes for the current net capital regimen. See generally Jorge E. Vinuales, The International Regulation of Financial Conglomerates: A Case–Study of Equivalence as an Approach to Financial Integration, 37 Cal. W. Int'l L.J. 1 (2006) (describing the European Union's Financial Conglomerates Directive and the SEC's response for consolidated supervised entities). The European Union also issued a Markets in Financial Instruments Directive that seeks to develop a single market in member states in all financial transactions. That directive includes a best execution requirement. Alan Jenkins, MiFid: Implications for Sell–Side Firms, Futures Industry Magazine 30 (May/June 2006). The directive (2004/39/EC) (MiFID) was one result of the activities of the "wise men" and sought to further the passporting concept to other financial services. It also required firms subject to MiFID to comply with another directive on capital requirements.

The EU has adopted a common currency for several of its member states—the euro. The euro has replaced the national currency for over 300 million individuals in Austria, Belgium, Finland, France, Germany, Greece, Ireland, Italy, Luxembourg, the Netherlands, Portugal, Slovenia, and Spain. The United Kingdom, as well as Sweden and Denmark, have not adopted the euro. The conversion of participating member states' coins and notes into euros occurred in 2002. The euro is now competing with the dollar as a leading national currency.

The European Central Bank (ECB) was created to administer the new currency. "The ECB's main task is to maintain the euro's purchasing power and thus price stability in the euro area." <www.ecb.int/ecb/html/index.en.html>. The ECB operates in conjunction with a European System of Central Banks (ESCB). Although banking regulation is left to each bank's home country, the ECB is given some supervisory authority to guard against systemic risk and has some limited powers to act as a lender of last resort in times of economic crisis.

Another pan-European instrument is the eurocheque, which is used like an American check but is widely accepted in the EU even when the drawer of the check lives in another member state. Another instrument, the EU card, may be used as an ATM and debit card across Europe.

Several large European banks made substantial investments in U.S. subprime mortgages and were severely crippled when those investments became illiquid during the subprime crisis. UBS AG, for example, was heavily involved in the U.S. subprime mortgage market through its Dillon Read Capital Management LLC (Dillon Read), which the Swiss Bancorp had acquired for $600 million before its merger with UBS. By the end of September 2007, the losses from the Dillon Read positions ballooned to over $3 billion. UBS losses associated with the U.S. residential mortgage market, mostly from CDOs, grew to $18.7 billion for all of 2007. See Jerry W. Markham, A Financial History of the United States, From the Subprime Crisis to the Great Recession (2006–2009) 257 (2011).

The European Central Bank (ECB) injected $210 billion into its financial markets on August 10 and 11, 2007, in order to provide liquidity as the subprime crisis spread to Europe. The Bank of England and the European Central Bank also worked in tandem with the Federal Reserve Board to make unlimited funds available to their banks in order to ease the credit crunch. On December 12, 2007, the Federal Reserve Board, the European Central Bank (ECB) in the European Union, the Bank of England, the Bank of Canada, and the Swiss National Bank announced that they would coordinate their efforts to provide liquidity to their banks. The ECB announced on December 18, 2007 that it would offer unlimited amounts of funds to its member banks at bargain interest rates. The ECB surprised observers when it disclosed that it had already pumped over $500 billion into 390 euro-zone private banks, twice the amount expected. Id. at 461.

The Obama administration clashed with the Europeans over the action needed to deal with the ongoing global financial crisis at Group of Twenty Conferences. President Obama believed increased spending was the best way to restart economies, while the Europeans wanted to concentrate on regulatory reform. In September 2009, the Group of Twenty had difficulty agreeing on increased capital requirements for banks. France resisted a proposal by the U.S. and the U.K to make significant increases in such requirements. As discussed in Chapter 7, the G20has reached agreement on the significantly tougher capital standards in Basel III. The Financial Stability Board, a group of regulators appointed by the G20 to design a more reliable financial system, recommended limits on bank employee bonuses until banks increased their capital.

The European Union announced to the Group of Twenty that it intended to create three pan-European regulatory bodies that would enforce common rules for banking, securities, and insurance. The three bodies would essentially involve beefing up three existing EU coordinating regulatory bodies for financial services. The proposed legislation would also create a European Systemic Risk Board, which would be composed of the twenty-seven central bank governors from the EU member states. In addition, a new European System of Financial Supervisors would be created to regulate particular banks. These proposals are analogous in many ways to the functions to be performed by the Financial Stability Oversight Council (FSOC) created in the United States by the Dodd–Frank Act of 2010. Id. at 765–66.

A renewed crisis broke out in Europe in early 2010. European markets fell in February over concerns about debt issued by the Greek government. Speculators using credit default swaps were blamed for worsening the situation, and it was claimed that Goldman Sachs and others arranged swaps that concealed Greece's true financial condition (and debt) when it sought approval from the European Union to use the euro as its currency. Greece was offered a $40 billion support package from the European Union, but it turned out that the Greek debt problem was even worse than expected. Greece then sought to increase the bailout to $60 billion, seeking funds from the European Union and the IMF. That amount proved to be inadequate and a $146.5 billion rescue package was agreed upon at the end of April. However, violent protests broke out in Greece after the government acted to impose the harsh austerity measures demanded as a condition for the loan. The financial crisis that began in Greece spread to Spain and Portugal. Id. at 685. That crisis nearly unhinged the euro as currency in the European Union.

The European Union announced a $1 trillion bailout for the affected countries on May 10, 2010. The EU was prodded into action by the Obama administration, which reopened a swap facility with the European Union Central Bank that had been employed during the subprime crisis to assure liquidity in Europe. The crisis drove down the euro and pushing gold to a new record of $1,219.90 per ounce. The euro hit a four-year low on May 19, 2010, falling to $1.21. Germany imposed restriction on naked short sales on that day as a renewed credit crunch struck European borrowers. This unilateral and unexpected action by Germany sent stock markets reeling and irritated other European Union members. Id. at 690.

QUESTIONS AND NOTES

1. Chapter 14 of the North America Free Trade Agreement (NAFTA) addresses the cross-border offering of financial services by firms in NAFTA member states (U.S., Mexico and Canada). It essentially requires NAFTA members to allow firms headquartered in other member states to establish offices and provide financial services within and across their borders. NAFTA generally adopts national treatment as the standard for regulating firms from other member states. This means that firms from other member states must be treated in the same manner as local firms. See generally Chapter 14 of NAFTA, available at <www-tech.mit.edu/Bulletins/nafta.html>. Canada, however, still limits foreign ownership of its larger banks to less than ten percent without prior permission of the Minister of Finance. Eric S. Gouvin,

The Political Economy of Canada's "Widely Held" Rule for Large Banks, 32 Law & Pol'y Int'l Bus. 391, 399 (2001).

2. Do you think the United States should centralize its financial services regulation into a single entity, as was done in Japan and the United Kingdom? The Senate bill that formed the basis for the Dodd–Frank Act originally proposed collapsing the four federal bank regulatory agencies (OCC, OTS, FDIC, and FRB) into one. As adopted, however, the Dodd–Frank Act eliminated only the OTS and transferred parts of its functions to the OCC, FDIC, and FRB.

3. Do you think United States banks will be at competitive disadvantage with those in the European Union? What, if any, competitive advantages are provided to banks in the single market of the European Union?

4. Some countries regulate banks more stringently than others. In September 2004, China executed four people for corruption involving amounts totaling $15 million. Those executed included employees from two of the larger state-owned banks. Nevertheless, China's booming economy attracted investments from U.S. banks. Kate Linebaugh, How Banks Scaled the Chinese Wall, Wall St. J., Feb. 23, 2006; David Barboza & Andrew Ross Sorkin, Citibank Expected to Land China Deal, nytimes.com, Dec. 31, 2005. China restructured its regulation to meet concerns of the World Trade Organization that it open its financial services market to foreign banks. James T. Areddy, Shift by Regulators Could Prove Unsettling, Blurring Differences in Structure With Local Lenders, Wall St. J., Feb. 23, 2006; Michael Goldhaber, Banking on China, law.com (Nov. 11, 2005). However, some regulatory changes were causing a dilution of the stakes purchased by U.S. Banks in Chinese banks. James T. Areddy, Citigroup Feels China's Bank Reform, Wall St. J., Feb. 28, 2006. China has been accused by members of the U.S. Congress of dragging its feet in opening its financial markets to foreign competition. China's Accession to WTO Fails to Bring Promised Benefits to U.S., Commission Says, 87 Banking Rep. (BNA) 797 (Nov. 20, 2006). An additional concern is the large amount of undisclosed non-performing loans on the books of Chinese banks. The Chinese government has spent $400 billion to cover some of these losses. David Barboza, Rare Look at China's Burdened Banks, NYTimes.com, Nov. 15, 2006. Yet, China remains a popular venue for U.S. banks. Citigroup Inc. led an effort to buy 85% of the Guangdong Development Bank for $3.1 billion, representative of a growing enthusiasm by U.S. banks for the Chinese market. Kate Linebaugh & James T. Areddy, Citigroup–Led Team is Poised to Win Guangdong Bank Battle, Wall St. J., Nov. 15, 2006.

6. Banks found that becoming global financial supermarkets exposed them to regulatory problems abroad as well as at home. The Tokyo branch of Credit Suisse was excluded from engaging in the derivatives business in Japan after several abuses in 1999. The Japanese government required Citigroup to close its private banking business in Japan, charging that it was being used for money laundering, misleading clients, and engaging in illegal tying arrangements. Citigroup also closed its Japanese trust unit after discovering more problems there.

Citigroup encountered trouble in Europe for massive trading in European government bonds on several electronic communications networks. This strategy was called "Dr. Evil," a reference culled from the Austin Powers spy movie spoof. German prosecutors later dismissed the case, concluding that the trades were not illegal manipulation. However, the Financial Services Authority in London fined Citigroup $25 million for failures in its internal controls that allowed the Dr. Evil transactions. Citigroup was also fined $10,000 by the Reserve Bank of India for allowing a forgery ring to operate an account at the bank. The Indian government arrested more than one hundred individuals who had forged financial documents valued at more than $600 million. Citigroup encountered problems with its manager for private equity investments in Brazil, and was forced to sever that relationship. With all these problems, an FDIC study concluded that United States banks were lagging foreign banks in expanding their international operations. Hanna Bergman, In Brief: FDIC Publishes Papers on Global Market, Am. Banker, June 27, 2005 (citing FDIC, The Globalization of the U.S. Banking Market, FDIC Outlook 25 (Summer 2005), excerpted earlier in this Chapter).

7. The NYSE merged in 2006 with Euronext, a combination of five European electronic exchanges that trade stocks and derivatives. In order to close that deal, the NYSE had to surrender half of its board seats to the Europeans, thus giving up control of one of the most venerated of U.S. financial institutions. George Ceron, NYSE to Split Board Evenly With Euronext, Wall St. J., Nov. 22, 2006. The SEC and European regulators have entered into a Memorandum of Understanding to coordinate their regulation of the merged entity. However, the merged entity was set up in a fashion that essentially allows the European exchanges to remove themselves from the merger if there is ever any effort to apply U.S. laws to those exchanges.

SECTION 4. INTERNATIONAL MONETARY SYSTEM

The present international monetary system evolved from debates over whether the United States and other countries should base their financial systems on a specie standard (i.e., whether the government's paper currency and private debts should be payable on demand in gold or silver). There was a subsidiary debate over whether silver should also be recognized as specie and valued at a certain ratio to gold. The United States played a central role in those debates and in the formulation of the international monetary system.

During our early history, most debts required payment in specie, even though bank bills were often accepted as a substitute payment. Specie payments were suspended at various times by banks in times of monetary stringency or crisis, including throughout the Civil War. After 1865, a debate raged over whether the United States should return to the requirement that government and private debts be payable in specie ("hard money") if demanded by the creditor. Populists, supported largely by the agricultural community, sought to inflate commodity prices and thus opposed a gold-only specie standard. The populists wanted to continue the use of greenbacks as legal tender and to have silver compete with gold as specie. The Resumption Act of 1875 declared the intention of the federal government to resume specie payments for government obligations, but specie payments were not actually resumed until 1879.

In the meantime, the struggle continued between hard money proponents and free silver and greenback advocates. In 1874, the Greenback, or National Party was created on a platform that sought a currency based solely on paper. Its adherents were joined by populists and free silver advocates. Thereafter, repeal of the Resumption Act was defeated by a single vote in the Senate. The Silver Coinage Act of 1878 required the Treasury Department to buy silver and coin it into silver dollars. The act authorized silver dollars to be deposited with the Treasury in exchange for silver certificates, which became a new form of paper currency. In another concession to the free silver movement, Congress enacted the Sherman Silver Purchase Act of 1890. This Act required the purchase by the federal government of up to 4.5 million ounces of silver per month, as well as the issuance of legal tender notes redeemable in gold or silver. The act declared that it was the policy of the United States to maintain gold and silver on a parity under existing legal ratios.

Agitation continued, and the Presidential election of 1896 turned into a struggle over the silver issue. The Democrats adopted a silver plank in their platform, and William Jennings Bryan was chosen as their candidate. In a famous political speech given at the 1896 Democratic convention in Chicago, he declared that the demand for a silver standard is "a cause as holy as the cause of humanity," and that "[h]aving behind us the producing masses of the nation and the world, supported by the commercial interests, the laboring interests, and the toilers everywhere, we will answer their demand for a gold standard by saying to them: You shall not press down upon the brow of labor this crown of thorns, you shall not crucify mankind upon a cross of gold."[9]

The "cross of gold" speech electrified the nation, but it was not enough to achieve victory for Bryan. The Gold Standard Act of 1900 declared gold to be the monetary standard of the United States and prescribed a minimum reserve of gold to be held by the Treasury for the redemption of currency. This officially put the United States on a gold standard.

The Great Depression following the Stock Market Crash of 1929 renewed concerns with the Gold standard, as commodity prices dropped to historical lows and farmers faced extreme hardship. The new President, Franklin Roosevelt, decided that action was necessary.

NORMAN v. BALTIMORE & OHIO RAILROAD CO.
Supreme Court of the United States, 1935.
294 U.S. 240.

MR. CHIEF JUSTICE HUGHES delivered the opinion of the Court.

These cases present the question of the validity of the Joint Resolu-

---

9. One reminder of the great debate is the Wonderful Wizard of Oz, which was originally written as an allegory of the bi-metal debate. The word "Oz" stood for ounce. Dorothy was the innocent American public. The yellow brick road was a path of gold. The cowardly lion was William Jennings Bryan. For a description of the history of the bi-metal debates in the United States see Jerry W. Markham, A Financial History of the United States: From Christopher Columbus to the Robber Barons (1492–1900) 339–350 (2001).

tion of the Congress, of June 5, 1933, with respect to the "gold clauses" of private contracts for the payment of money. 48 Stat. 112.

This Resolution * * * declares that "every provision contained in or made with respect to any obligation which purports to give the obligee a right to require payment in gold or a particular kind of coin or currency, or in an amount in money of the United States measured thereby" is "against public policy." Such provisions in obligations thereafter incurred are prohibited. The Resolution provides that "Every obligation, heretofore or hereafter incurred, whether or not any such provision is contained therein or made with respect thereto, shall be discharged upon payment, dollar for dollar, in any coin or currency which at the time of payment is legal tender for public and private debts." * * *

The Joint Resolution of June 5, 1933, was one of a series of measures relating to the currency. These measures disclose not only the purposes of the Congress but also the situations which existed at the time the Joint Resolution was adopted and when the payments under the "gold clauses" were sought. On March 6, 1933, the President, stating that there had been "heavy and unwarranted withdrawals of gold and currency from our banking institutions for the purpose of hoarding" and "extensive speculative activity abroad in foreign exchange" which had resulted "in severe drains on the Nation's stocks of gold," and reciting the authority conferred by § 5(b) of the Act of October 6, 1917 (40 Stat. 411), declared "a bank holiday" until March 9, 1933. On the same date, the Secretary of the Treasury, with the President's approval, issued instructions to the Treasurer of the United States to make payments in gold in any form only under license issued by the Secretary.

On March 9, 1933, the Congress passed the Emergency Banking Act. 48 Stat. 1. All orders issued by the President or the Secretary of the Treasury since March 4, 1933, under the authority conferred by § 5(b) of the Act of October 6, 1917, were confirmed. That section was amended so as to provide that during any period of national emergency declared by the President, he might "investigate, regulate or prohibit," by means of licenses or otherwise, "any transactions in foreign exchange, transfers of credit between or payments by banking institutions as defined by the President, and export, hoarding, melting, or earmarking of gold or silver coin or bullion or currency, by any person within the United States or any place subject to the jurisdiction thereof." The Act also amended § 11 of the Federal Reserve Act (39 Stat. 752) so as to authorize the Secretary of the Treasury to require all persons to deliver to the Treasurer of the United States "any or all gold coin, gold bullion, and gold certificates" owned by them, and that the Secretary should pay therefor "an equivalent amount of any other form of coin or currency coined or issued under the laws of the United States." By Executive Order of March 10, 1933, the President authorized banks to be reopened, as stated, but prohibited the removal from the United States, or any place subject to its jurisdiction, of "any gold coin, gold bullion, or gold certificates, except in accordance with regulations prescribed by or under license issued by the Secretary of the Treasury." By further Executive Order of April 5, 1933, forbidding hoarding, all persons were required to deliver, on or before May 1, 1933, to stated banks "all gold coin, gold bullion and gold certificates," with certain exceptions, the holder to receive "an equivalent amount of any other form of coin or currency coined or issued under the laws of the United States." Another Order of April 20, 1933, contained further requirements with respect to the acquisition and export of gold and to transactions in foreign exchange.

By § 43 of the Agricultural Adjustment Act of May 12, 1933 (48 Stat. 51), it was provided that the President should have authority, upon the making of prescribed findings and in the circumstances stated, "to fix the weight of the gold dollar in grains nine tenths fine and also to fix the weight of the silver dollar in grains nine tenths fine at a definite fixed ratio in relation to the gold dollar at such amounts as he finds necessary from his investigation to stabilize domestic prices or to protect the foreign commerce against the adverse effect of depreciated foreign currencies," and it was further provided that the "gold dollar, the weight of which is so fixed, shall be the standard unit of value," and that "all forms of money shall be maintained at a parity with this standard," but that "in no event shall the weight of the gold dollar be fixed so as to reduce its present weight by more than 50 per centum." * * *

The devaluation of the dollar placed the domestic economy upon a new basis. In the currency as thus provided, States and municipalities must receive their taxes; railroads, their rates and fares; public utilities, their charges for services. The income out of which they must meet their obligations is determined by the new standard. Yet, according to the contentions before us, while that income is thus controlled by law, their indebtedness on their "gold bonds" must be met by an amount of currency determined by the former gold standard. Their receipts, in this view, would be fixed on one basis; their interest charges, and the principal of their obligations, on another. It is common knowledge that the bonds issued by these obligors have generally contained gold clauses, and presumably they account for a large part of the outstanding obligations of that sort. It is also common knowledge that a similar situation exists with respect to numerous industrial corporations that have issued their "gold bonds" and must now receive payments for their products in the existing currency. It requires no acute analysis or profound economic inquiry to disclose the dislocation of the domestic economy which would be caused by such a disparity of conditions in which, it is insisted, those debtors under gold clauses should be required to pay one dollar and sixty-nine cents in currency while respectively receiving their taxes, rates, charges and prices on the basis of one dollar of that currency.

We are not concerned with consequences, in the sense that consequences, however serious, may excuse an invasion of constitutional right.

We are concerned with the constitutional power of the Congress over the monetary system of the country and its attempted frustration. Exercising that power, the Congress has undertaken to establish a uniform currency, and parity between kinds of currency, and to make that currency, dollar for dollar, legal tender for the payment of debts. In the light of abundant experience, the Congress was entitled to choose such a uniform monetary system, and to reject a dual system, with respect to all obligations within the range of the exercise of its constitutional authority. The contention that these gold clauses are valid contracts and cannot be struck down proceeds upon the assumption that private parties, and States and municipalities, may make and enforce contracts which may limit that authority. Dismissing that untenable assumption, the facts must be faced. We think that it is clearly shown that these clauses interfere with the exertion of the power granted to the Congress and certainly it is not established that the Congress arbitrarily or capriciously decided that such an interference existed.

The judgment and decree, severally under review, are affirmed.

JUSTICES MCREYNOLDS, VAN DEVANTER, SUTHERLAND, and BUTLER dissent.

* * *

Despite this ruling, the propriety of the invalidation of gold clauses was still being challenged in 1996, long after the prohibition on gold transactions had been lifted. Gold Clauses, 28 Sec. Reg. & L. Rep. (BNA) 1541 (Dec. 20, 1996).

The disruption of the international monetary system during the Great Depression led to calls for reform. An international monetary and financial conference was held at Bretton Woods, New Hampshire in 1944. That conference led to the "Bretton Woods Agreement," which sought to provide stabilization in international monetary affairs and exchange rates. The International Monetary Fund (IMF) was created to act as an international monetary authority that would stabilize currency exchange rates among members.[10] The plan involved the subscribing nations setting a par value for their currencies and maintaining that value. The United States dollar was designated as the bench mark for exchange rates, and participating currencies were exchangeable at set ratios to the American dollar. The entire plan was backed by a United States promise to pay for its dollars in gold at $35 per ounce. This promise was intended to keep the United States from inflating the dollar, and it meant that the dollar was backed by gold. The arrangement placed much of the world back on a gold standard.

---

10. For a description of the background and creation of the IMF, see Jerry W. Markham, A Financial History of the United States: From J.P. Morgan to the Institutional Investor (1900–1970) 275–77 (2001).

The IMF was given authority to protect its members from temporary deficiencies in their hard currency reserves that would affect their ability to maintain their currency at par. The IMF provided protection by making short term loans to member countries with deficits in their balance of payments. The amounts of these loans were set by quotas.

The Bretton Woods agreement came under attack in the 1960s, as worldwide inflation pushed up the price of gold and removed gold stocks from the United States. In 1971, President Richard Nixon announced that the United States would no longer remain on a gold standard and repealed the Bretton Woods agreement.

TRANS WORLD AIRLINES, INC. v. FRANKLIN MINT CORP.

Supreme Court of the United States, 1984.
466 U.S. 243.

MADAME JUSTICE O'CONNOR delivered the opinion of the Court.

The question presented in this litigation is whether an air carrier's declared liability limit of $9.07 per pound of cargo is inconsistent with the "Warsaw Convention" (Convention), an international air carriage treaty that the United States has ratified. As a threshold matter we must determine whether the 1978 repeal of legislation setting an "official" price of gold in the United States renders the Convention's gold-based liability limit unenforceable in this country. We conclude that the 1978 legislation was not intended to affect the enforceability of the Convention in the United States, and that a $9.07–per-pound liability limit is not inconsistent with the Convention.

* * * During the first 44 years of the United States' adherence to the Convention there existed an "official" price of gold in the United States, and the CAB's [Civil Aeronautics Board] task of supervising carrier compliance with the Convention's liability limit was correspondingly simple. The United States Gold Standard Act of 1900 set the value of the dollar at $20.67 per troy ounce of gold. On January 31, 1934, nine months before the United States ratified the Convention, President Roosevelt increased the official domestic price of gold to $35 per ounce. In 1945 the United States accepted membership in the International Monetary Fund (IMF) and so undertook to maintain a "par value" for the dollar and to buy and sell gold at the official price in exchange for balances of dollars officially held by other IMF nations. For almost 40 years the $35–per-ounce price of gold was used to derive from the Convention's Article 22(2) a cargo liability limit of $7.50 per pound. See, e. g., 14 CFR § 221.176 (1972).

When the central banks of most Western nations instituted a "two-tier" gold standard in 1968 the gold-based international monetary system began to collapse. Thereafter, official gold transactions were conducted at the official price, and private transactions at the floating, free market price. In August 1971 the United States suspended convertibility of foreign official holdings of dollars into gold. In December 1971 and then again in February 1973 the official exchange rate of the dollar against gold was increased. These changes were approved by Congress in the Par Value Modification Act, passed in early 1972 (increasing the official price to $38 per ounce) and in its 1973 reenactment (setting a $42.22–per-ounce price). Each time, the CAB followed suit by directing carriers to increase the dollar-based liability limits in their tariffs accordingly, first to $8.16 per pound, then to $9.07 per pound.

In 1975 the member nations of the IMF formulated a plan, known as the Jamaica Accords, to eliminate gold as the basis of the international monetary system. Effective April 1, 1978, the "Special Drawing Right" (SDR) was to become the sole reserve asset that IMF nations would use in their mutual dealings. The SDR was defined as the average value of a defined basket of IMF member currencies. In 1976 Congress passed legislation to implement the new IMF agreement, repealing the Par Value Modification Act effective April 1, 1978.

As these developments unfolded, the Convention signatories met in Montreal in September 1975. In No. 4 of the "Montreal Protocols," the delegates proposed to substitute 17 SDR's per kilogram for the 250 French gold francs per kilogram in Article 22 of the Convention. Although the United States supported this change, and signed Protocol No. 4, the Senate has not yet consented to its ratification.

The erosion and final demise of the gold standard, coupled with the United States' failure to ratify Montreal Protocol No. 4, left the CAB with the difficult task of supervising carrier compliance with the Convention's liability limits without up-to-date guidance from Congress. Although the market price of gold began to diverge from the official price in 1969, the CAB continued to track the official price in Orders converting the Convention's liability limit into dollars. Under CAB Order 74–1–16, promulgated in 1974, "the minimum acceptable figur[e] in United States dollars for liability limits applicable to 'international transportation' and 'international carriage' . . . [is $] 9.07 [per pound of cargo]." * * *

Despite the demise of the gold standard, the $9.07–per-pound liability limit retained since 1978 has represented a reasonably stable figure when converted into other Western currencies. This is easily established by reference to the SDR, which is the new, nonparochial, internationally recognized standard of conversion. On March 31, 1978, for example, one SDR was worth $1.23667; on March 23, 1979, $1.28626. At all times since 1978 a carrier that chose to set its liability limit at 17 SDR's per kilogram as suggested by Montreal Protocol No. 4 would have arrived at a liability limit in dollars close to $9 per pound. * * *

We recognize that this inquiry into the dollar's value relative to other currencies would have been unnecessary if the CAB had chosen to adopt the market price of gold for converting the Convention's liability limits into dollars. Since gold is freely traded on an international market its price always provides a unique and internationally uniform conversion rate. But reliance on the gold market would entirely fail to provide a stable unit of conversion on which carriers could rely. To pick one extreme example, between January and April 1980 gold ranged from about $490 to $850 per ounce. Far from providing predictability and stability, tying the Convention to the gold market would force every carrier and every air transport user to become a speculator in gold, exposed to the sudden and unpredictable swings in the price of that commodity. The CAB has correctly recognized that this is not at all what the Convention's framers had in mind. The 1978 decision by many of the Convention's signatories to exit from the gold market cannot sensibly be construed as a decision to compel every air carrier and air transport user to enter it. * * *

We reject the Court of Appeals' declaration that the Convention is prospectively unenforceable; the judgment of the Court of Appeals affirming the judgment of the District Court is Affirmed.

JUSTICE STEVENS, dissents. * * *

Subsequent changes were made in air carrier liability, including the use of IMF Special Drawing Rights as a measure of liability in the European Union.

As a result of the abandonment of the gold standard, currency prices were allowed to fluctuate, and most large banks began to trade in those currencies and provide them as a service for customers dealing in international commerce. The collapse of the Bretton Woods Agreement also resulted in a new role for the IMF.

ELLIOTT ASSOCIATES, L.P. v. BANCO DE LA NACION

United States Court of Appeals, Second Circuit, 1999.
194 F.3d 363.

MICHEL, CIRCUIT JUDGE.

Plaintiff–Appellant Elliott Associates, L.P. ("Elliott") appeals from the amended final judgments entered by the United States District Court for the Southern District of New York on September 3 and 15, 1998. The district court, after a bench trial, dismissed with prejudice Elliott's complaints seeking damages for the non-payment of certain debt by Defendants–Appellees The Republic of Peru ("Peru") and Banco de la Nacion ("Nacion") (together, the "Debtors") because it found that Elliott had purchased the debt in violation of Section 489 of the New York Judiciary Law ("Section 489"). * * *

Elliott is an investment fund with its principal offices located in New York City. Elliott was founded by Paul Singer in 1977 and he remains its sole general partner. One of the primary types of instruments that Elliott invests in is the securities of "distressed" debtors, that is, debtors that have defaulted on their payments to creditors. Singer testified that he invests in debt when he believes that the true or "fundamental" value of the debt is greater than the value accorded by the market. Elliott characterizes its approach to its investments as "activist." Thus, despite sometimes accepting the terms offered to other creditors, Elliott explains that it frequently engages in direct negotiations with the debtor and argues that, as a result, it has occasionally received a greater return than other creditors.

In August or September of 1995, Singer was approached by Jay Newman to discuss investing in distressed foreign sovereign debt. Newman, an independent consultant, had worked in the emerging market debt field at major brokerage houses Lehman Brothers, Dillon Read, and Morgan Stanley, as well as managing his own offshore fund, the Percheron Fund. The secondary market for such debt first developed in the early 1980s when the original lender banks began selling the non-performing debt of countries that had ceased servicing their external debt to other investors, including brokerage firms, in order to reduce the banks' exposure and to permit them to lend additional funds to developing countries.

At Newman's recommendation, in October 1995, Elliott purchased approximately $28.75 million (principal amount) of Panamanian sovereign debt for approximately $17.5 million. In July 1996, Elliott brought suit against Panama seeking full payment of the debt. Elliott obtained a judgment and attachment order and, with interest included, ultimately received over $57 million in payment.

At the time of Elliott's purchase of Panamanian debt, Panama was finalizing its Brady Plan debt restructuring program. The term "Brady Plan" derives from a March 1989 speech by Nicholas Brady, then Secretary of the United States Treasury, urging commercial lenders to forgive some of the debt that they were owed by less developed countries, restructure what remained, and continue to grant those countries additional loans. See generally, Ross P. Buckley, The Facilitation of the Brady Plan: Emerging Markets Debt Trading From 1989 to 1993, 21 Fordham Int'l L.J. 1802 (1998). Brady Plans contemplate that, in return for such voluntary partial debt forgiveness, the less developed country will submit to an economic austerity program supervised and monitored by the International Monetary Fund (the "IMF"). The purpose of implementing Brady Plans is to avoid the recurrence of debt defaults by less developed countries that have occurred from 1982 onwards. Typically, the terms of a Brady Plan are negotiated with the debtor country by an *ad hoc* committee of the nation's largest institutional creditors, generally known as the "Bank Advisory Committee." The members of the Bank Advisory Committee commit to restructuring the debt that they hold on the agreed terms and those terms are also offered to other creditors. However, while the members of the Bank Advisory Committee usually agree to be bound by the negotiated terms, the other creditors are under no such obligation to accept those terms.

In January 1996, Newman recommended that Elliott purchase Peruvian sovereign debt. Newman testified at trial that he believed that Peruvian sovereign debt was a good investment because of the sweeping economic reforms implemented by President Alberto Fujimori following his election in November 1990 in the wake of a severe six-year recession. Newman testified that he viewed Peru's Brady Plan, announced in October 1995, as undervaluing Peru's outstanding debt. In particular, Newman contended that the large commercial bank creditors that made up the Bank Advisory Committee had institutional incentives to accept reduced terms for the debt they held, such as the desire to make additional loans and to operate domestically within the country, and that he believed that the Bank Advisory Committee had not been privy to all material financial information, including Peru's rumored repurchase of a significant proportion of its debt.

Between January and March 1996, Elliott purchased from international banks ING Bank, N.V. ("ING") and Swiss Bank Corporation ("Swiss Bank") approximately $20.7 million (in principal amount) of the working capital debt of Nacion and Banco Popular del Peru ("Popular"), a bankrupt Peruvian bank. The debt was sold under a series of twenty-three letter agreements (the "Letter Agreements"). Elliott paid approximately $11.4 million for these debt obligations and all of the debt was guaranteed by Peru pursuant to a written guaranty dated May 31, 1983 (the "Guaranty"). Under their express terms, both the Letter Agreements and the Guaranty were governed by New York Law. * * *

The pivotal issue upon which this appeal necessarily turns is whether, within the meaning of Section 489 of the New York Judiciary Law, Elliott's purchase of Peruvian sovereign debt was "with the intent and for the purpose of bringing an action or proceeding thereon," thereby rendering the purchase a violation of law.

* * * After reviewing the pertinent New York state decisions interpreting Section 489, we are convinced that, if the New York Court of Appeals, not us, were hearing this appeal, it would rule that the acquisition of a debt with intent to bring suit against the debtor is not a violation of the statute where, as here, the primary purpose of the suit is the collection of the debt acquired. Consequently we must reverse the judgment of the district court. * * *

We hold that, in light of the pertinent New York precedent and compelling policy considerations, the district court erroneously interpreted Section 489 of the New York Judiciary Law. In particular, we hold that Section 489 is not violated when, as here, the accused party's "primary goal" is found to be satisfaction of a valid debt and its intent is only to sue absent full performance. Given that, notwithstanding the Section 489 issue, the district court found the Letter Agreements and Guaranty to have been breached by the Debtors, we remand only for the purpose of calculating damages more accurately than the approximate figures given in the district court's opinion and the possible resolution of other attendant damages-related issues.

Accordingly, the judgments of the district court are reversed and the case is remanded.

———————

United States banks loaned billions of dollars to various Latin American countries, apparently assuming that sovereign nations would always pay their debts. That assumption proved to be in error. American banks were forced to reschedule their debts with Mexico, Brazil and others in the early 1980s in order to avoid defaults which would have required massive charges against bank earnings. Some claimed the debt rescheduling concealed what were actual defaults that should have been accounted for as such. Congress responded with the International Lending Supervision Act of 1983 (ILSA), which required U.S. banks to increase their loan loss reserves for loans to defaulting countries. 12 U.S.C.A. § 3904.

QUESTIONS AND NOTES

1. Having lost its role in stabilizing exchange rates, the IMF became an international 911 rescue unit–a lender of last resort to countries in economic crisis. It provided $4.5 billion to Mexico after its 1982 debt default. That action was quickly followed by $5 billion in aid to Brazil. More aid was given to other Latin American countries as defaults began to spread. The size of these rescue efforts increased in the next decade. In 1995, a $50 billion rescue of Mexico was arranged. An economic crisis that spread across Asia in 1997 saw the IMF allocate $17.2 billion to Thailand, $30 billion to Indonesia, and $55 billion to South Korea. In 1998, the IMF provided $11.2 billion to Russia during its economic crisis.

2. IMF loans to countries involve the concept of "conditionality." This means the loans are granted on the condition that the receiving country will reform its economy, usually by reducing government spending. The IMF conditions often cause resentment on the part of those affected by them.

3. Should the IMF be directing government policies of foreign nations as a condition for credit?

4. The United States is the largest contributor to the IMF. Should it be involved in bailing out foreign governments whose failed economic policies have caused their collapse? Should countries borrowing money be permitted to declare bankruptcy like a corporation and erase their debts? The IMF rejected such a proposal in favor of "collective action" contract clauses in syndicated bank loans that allow the banks to renegotiate sovereign debt without requiring the agreement of all participating banks. In the past, negotiations over restructuring sovereign debt broke down because unanimous agreement could not be reached among the participating banks on the restructuring terms, causing the IMF to intercede and bail out the banks. Guidelines were also created setting forth the conditions under which the IMF

would bail out a defaulting country. John B. Taylor, Global Financial Warriors: The Untold Story of International Finance in the Post–9/11 World 111–32 (2007).

5.   The IMF appeared to be a dead letter as the new century began, but it reemerged as a powerhouse during the financial crisis that began in 2007. Among other things, the IMF created a $100 billion facility for making non-conditional loans to troubled economies. That loan facility was designed to attract Mexico, Brazil and South Korea, which had previously resented the conditional loans given to it by the IMF in prior crises. The IMF agreed in October 2008 to supply funds to the Ukraine in order to rescue its faltering economy. However, that program was stalled by Ukrainian unwillingness to submit to conditions imposed by the IMF for its loans, a problem common to IMF bailouts. The cost of refusing that aid was considerable. Ukraine's banking system nearly collapsed. Nine banks were taken over by the government. The IMF was able to grant Pakistan a $7.6 billion loan in November 2008. The IMF also prepared to establish monetary facilities to rescue the economies of countries in Latin America and elsewhere as the financial crisis spread around the world. At the request of U.S. Treasury Secretary Geithner, the Group of 20, at their meeting in London in April 2009, approved additional funding for the IMF, making a $1 trillion commitment to the IMF, quadruple its existing resources. Jerry W. Markham, A Financial History of the United States, From the Subprime Crisis to the Great Recession (2006–2009) 577 (2011).

6.   The IMF effectively acted as staff for the Group of 20 during the subprime crisis and functioned much like a global central bank. The IMF and the World Bank declared that the Group of 7 had become irrelevant and that the World Bank and IMF should play leading roles with the Group of 20 in global financial matters. In April 2010, the IMF announced its support for customized, higher capital requirements for banks posing systemic risk.

7.   During the financial crisis, China proposed the creation of a new global currency that would be administered by the IMF as the international reserve currency, replacing the U.S. dollar. Newly installed U.S. Treasury Secretary Tim Geithner caused a sharp drop in the dollar on March 25, 2009, after he casually remarked in an interview that he would be open to considering this proposal. Jerry W. Markham, A Financial History of the United States, From the Subprime Crisis to the Great Recession (2006–2009) 576 (2011).

SECTION 5.   MONEY LAUNDERING

The ever-increasing amounts of money generated through criminal activity affect legitimate financial institutions that are used to launder the proceeds received from illegal activities.[11] Federal regulation, however, attempts to prevent the use of financial institutions for money laundering.

Federal prosecutors frequently focus on money laundering as a means to curb trafficking in narcotics. Transfers of funds through financial

---

11.   Excerpted from Jerry W. Markham & Thomas L. Hazen, Broker–Dealer Operations Under Securities and Commodities Law, Ch. 11 (1999).

institutions to launder the proceeds of drug sales were said to be the "lifeblood" of the international drug trade,[12] that involves hundreds of billions of dollars. In 1997, it was estimated that as much as $500 billion was illegally laundered

Money laundering is not solely a byproduct of the drug trade. Funds used to finance terrorist activities are often transferred through financial institutions. "[M]oney laundering counts are now routinely added to insider trading and other securities fraud charges."[13] Money laundering has become the government's criminal charge of choice because it allows prosecutors to multiply penalties and apply broad forfeiture provisions. Federal sentencing guidelines impose penalties for money laundering that are consequently higher than those available for the underlying crimes. Often prosecutors try to couple money laundering charges with more routine prosecutions to increase potential penalties and prosecutorial bargaining power. Despite the dangers of such prosecutorial abuse, Congress continues to strengthen money laundering legislation.

Money laundering can take many forms. It is difficult to detect and regulate. Over time, money laundering techniques have become more sophisticated. As a result, Congress has taken various approaches to deal with the problem. For example, the Travel Act prohibits travel in or the use of the facilities of interstate or foreign commerce for the purpose of furthering specified unlawful activity such as gambling, liquor, prostitution, and narcotics. The Travel Act also prohibits interstate travel for the purpose of distributing the proceeds of such unlawful activity. 18 U.S.C. § 1952. Other statutes address money laundering more directly.

CALIFORNIA BANKERS ASS'N v. SHULTZ

Supreme Court of the United States, 1974.
416 U.S. 21.

MR. JUSTICE REHNQUIST delivered the opinion of the Court.

These appeals present questions concerning the constitutionality of the so-called Bank Secrecy Act of 1970 (Act), and the implementing regulations promulgated thereunder by the Secretary of the Treasury. The Act, 12 U.S.C. §§ 1730d, 1829b, 1951–1959, and 31 U.S.C. §§ 1051–1062, 1081–1083, 1101–1105, 1121–1122, was enacted by Congress in 1970 following extensive hearings concerning the unavailability of foreign and domestic bank records of customers thought to be engaged in activities entailing criminal or civil liability. Under the Act, the Secretary of the Treasury is authorized to prescribe by regulation certain record keeping and reporting requirements for banks and other financial institutions in this country. * * *

The express purpose of the Act is to require the maintenance of records, and the making of certain reports, which "have a high degree of

---

12.   132 Cong. Rec. S9938, S9986 (daily ed. July 31, 1996).

13.   United States v. Daccarett, 6 F.3d 37 (2d Cir. 1993), cert. denied, 510 U.S. 1191 (1994).

usefulness in criminal, tax, or regulatory investigations or proceedings." 12 U.S.C. §§ 1829b (a)(2), 1951; 31 U.S.C. § 1051. * * *

While most of the record keeping requirements imposed by the Secretary under the Act merely require the banks to keep records which most of them had in the past voluntarily kept and retained, and while much of the required reporting of domestic transactions had been required by earlier Treasury regulations in effect for nearly 30 years, there is no denying the impressive sweep of the authority conferred upon the Secretary by the Bank Secrecy Act of 1970. While an Act conferring such broad authority over transactions such as these might well surprise or even shock those who lived in an earlier era, the latter did not live to see the time when bank accounts would join chocolate, cheese, and watches as a symbol of the Swiss economy. Nor did they live to see the heavy utilization of our domestic banking system by the minions of organized crime as well as by millions of legitimate businessmen. The challenges made here to the Bank Secrecy Act are directed not to any want of legislative authority in Congress to treat the subject, but instead to the Act's asserted violation of specific constitutional prohibitions. * * *

[T]he regulations issued by the Secretary under the authority of Title II contain two essential reporting requirements with respect to foreign financial transactions. Chapter 3 of Title II of the Act, 31 U.S.C. §§ 1101–1105, and the corresponding regulation, 31 CFR § 103.23, require individuals to report transportation of monetary instruments into or out of the United States, or receipts of such instruments in the United States from places outside the United States, if the instrument transported or received has a value in excess of $5,000 [now $10,000]. Chapter 4 of Title II of the Act, 31 U. S. C. §§ 1121–1122, and the corresponding regulation, 31 CFR § 103.24, generally require United States citizens, residents, and businessmen to file reports of their relationships with foreign financial institutions.

The domestic reporting provisions of the Act as implemented by the regulations, in contrast to the foreign reporting requirements, apply only to banks and financial institutions. * * *

All of the bank and depositor plaintiffs have stressed in their presentations to the District Court and to this Court that the recordkeeping and reporting requirements of the Bank Secrecy Act are focused in large part on the acquisition of information to assist in the enforcement of the criminal laws. While, as we have noted, Congress seems to have been equally concerned with civil liability which might go undetected by reason of transactions of the type required to be recorded or reported, concern for the enforcement of the criminal law was undoubtedly prominent in the minds of the legislators who considered the Act. We do not think it is strange or irrational that Congress, having its attention called to what appeared to be serious and organized efforts to avoid detection of criminal activity, should have legislated to rectify the situation. * * *

JUSTICES POWELL and BLACKMUN concur. * * *

Justice Douglas, joined by Justices Brennan and Marshall, dissents.

* * * First, as to the record keeping requirements, their announced purpose is that they will have "a high degree of usefulness in criminal, tax, or regulatory investigations or proceedings," 12 U.S.C. §§ 1829b(a)(2), 1953(a). The duty of the bank or institution is to microfilm or otherwise copy every check, draft, or similar instrument drawn on it or presented to it for payment and to keep a record of each one "received by it for deposit or collection," 12 U.S.C. §§ 1829b(d)(1) and (2). The retention is for up to six years unless the Secretary determines that "a longer period is necessary," 12 U.S.C. § 1829b(g). The regulations issued by the Secretary show the depth and extent of the quicksand in which our financial institutions must now operate.

It is estimated that a minimum of 20 billion checks—and perhaps 30 billion—will have to be photocopied and that the weight of these little pieces of paper will approximate 166 million pounds a year.

It would be highly useful to governmental espionage to have like reports from all our bookstores, all our hardware and retail stores, all our drugstores. These records too might be "useful" in criminal investigations.

One's reading habits furnish telltale clues to those who are bent on bending us to one point of view. What one buys at the hardware and retail stores may furnish clues to potential uses of wires, soap powders, and the like used by criminals. A mandatory recording of all telephone conversations would be better than the recording of checks under the Bank Secrecy Act, if Big Brother is to have his way. The records of checks—now available to the investigators—are highly useful. In a sense a person is defined by the checks he writes. By examining them the agents get to know his doctors, lawyers, creditors, political allies, social connections, religious affiliation, educational interests, the papers and magazines he reads, and so on *ad infinitum*. These are all tied to one's social security number; and now that we have the data banks, these other items will enrich that storehouse and make it possible for a bureaucrat—by pushing one button—to get in an instant the names of the 190 million Americans who are subversives or potential and likely candidates.

It is, I submit, sheer nonsense to agree with the Secretary that *all bank records of every citizen* "have a high degree of usefulness in criminal, tax, or regulatory investigations or proceedings." That is unadulterated nonsense unless we are to assume that every citizen is a crook, an assumption I cannot make.

Since the banking transactions of an individual give a fairly accurate account of his religion, ideology, opinions, and interests, a regulation impounding them and making them automatically available to all federal investigative agencies is a sledge-hammer approach to a problem that only a delicate scalpel can manage. Where fundamental personal rights are involved—as is true when as here the Government gets large access to one's beliefs, ideas, politics, religion, cultural concerns, and the like—the Act should be "narrowly drawn" (Cantwell v. Connecticut, 310 U.S. 296, 307) to meet the precise evil. Bank accounts at times harbor criminal plans. But we only rush with the crowd when we vent on our banks and their customers the devastating and leveling requirements of the present Act. I am not yet ready to agree that America is so possessed with evil that we must level all constitutional barriers to give our civil authorities the tools to catch criminals. * * *

The Bank Secrecy Act (BSA), 12 U.S.C. § 5316 et seq., reporting requirements were a reflection of Congressional concern that "secret foreign bank accounts" were often serving as the "financial underpinning of organized criminal operations in the United States." H.R. Rep. No. 975, 91st Cong., 2d Sess. 12 (1970). The BSA provides for the forfeiture of funds that are not reported. Criminal and civil penalties are also available as sanctions for violations. The Act and its regulations require financial institutions to file a Currency Transaction Report (CTR), 31 C.F.R. § 103.22, whenever an aggregate of $10,000 or more is deposited or withdrawn from one account in a day. The Act also requires the filing of a Suspicious Activity Report (SAR) for any suspicious activity involving a transaction of $5,000 or more. 31 C.F.R. § 103.21. The financial institution is precluded from notifying the customer that a CTR or SAR has been filed.

The BSA did not prove to be effective in stopping money laundering. One problem was that the number of currency reports was overwhelming. Between 1987 and 1996, over 77 million reports were filed. The sheer number of those reports reduced their utility in detecting drug trafficking. "This deluge of paperwork resulted in a mere 580 convictions."[14] The reporting requirement also imposed a substantial burden on financial institutions, as each CTR required about twenty minutes to complete.

The BSA reporting requirements were designed to aid law enforcement officials in detecting other crimes, such as drug trafficking, and did not make money laundering itself a crime. The Money Laundering Control Act of 1986, remedied this omission. It provides that transactions involving more than $10,000 from illicit proceeds ("criminally derived property") are prohibited where the transaction involves a financial institution such as a bank. 18 U.S.C.A. § 1956. The 1986 Act also addressed "smurfing" or "structuring" transactions where individuals engaging in money laundering break financial transactions into small amounts in order to evade the CTR reporting threshold. 31 U.S.C.A. § 5324 and 31 C.F.R. § 103.53.[15]

---

14. Richard W. Rahn, "Financial Privacy in Peril," Wall St. J., June 1, 1999.

15. In Ratzlaf v. United States, 510 U.S. 135 (1994), the Supreme Court held that the statute's requirements of a "willful" violation to impose a criminal penalty meant that the government must show that the defendant acted with the knowledge that his conduct was

The Money Laundering Prosecution Improvements Act of 1988 prohibited financial institutions from issuing cashier's checks, traveler's checks, money orders, or bank checks to an individual in amounts of more than $3,000, without proper customer identification. Pub. L. No. 100–690, 102 Stat. 4354 (1988) (codified in scattered sections of 18 and 31 U.S.C.A.). Financial institutions including banks were required to collect and maintain information concerning domestic and international electronic fund transfers of $3,000 or more. Certain transfers among financial institutions were exempted from this requirement.

In 1990, the Treasury Department created the Financial Crimes Enforcement Network (FinCEN) to monitor money laundering activities. FinCEN acts as a central depository for the CTR and SAR reports filed by financial institutions. FinCen also coordinates enforcement activities with other agencies.

The BCCI debacle increased efforts to combat money laundering. The Secretary of the Treasury was given authority to require financial institutions to develop anti-money laundering procedures, compliance and audit programs, and employee training programs on money laundering. The Money Laundering Suppression Act of 1994 directed the Treasury to reduce the burden of currency transaction reports by exempting transactions among financial institutions. Pub. L. No. 103–325, 108 Stat. 2160 (1994) (codified at scattered sections of 31 U.S.C.A.).

The Financial Crimes Strategy Act of 1998 required the Department of Treasury and the Department of Justice to coordinate nationwide law enforcement efforts to stop money laundering. 31 U.S.C.A. § 5340.

The ever-increasing list of underlying illicit activities covered by the money laundering statutes include securities law violations, mail and wire fraud, drug trafficking, kidnaping, assassination, violence at airports, terrorism, the use of weapons of mass destruction, and violations of the Safe Drinking Water Act. 18 U.S.C.A § 1956(c)(7). Penalties for money laundering are severe. Money laundering legislation provides for fines of twice the value of the property involved in the transaction, or $500,000, whichever is greater, and imprisonment for not more than twenty years. 18 U.S.C. § 1956.

In one case, a Boston bank was fined $500,000 for failing to report more than 1,100 currency transactions that totaled over $1.6 billion. The Bank of New England was also prosecuted, but the bank tellers and customers, indicted for structuring transactions to avoid the Currency Transaction Report requirement, were acquitted. In the late 1980s, more than forty financial institutions were fined for Bank Secrecy Act reporting violations. In 1992, the Department of the Treasury imposed a fine of almost $1 million against the First National Bank of Maryland for failure to file currency transaction reports. Seven large Mexican and Venezuelan banks and over 150 individuals were indicted by American authorities as a

---

unlawful. The Money Laundering Suppression Act of 1994, however, removed the word "willful" from the structuring prohibition.

result of Operation Casablanca, a government sting operation that began in 1994 and targeted two Latin American drug cartels.

Money laundering statutes now apply to nearly all forms of financial transactions, including electronic fund transfers. 18 U.S.C. § 1956. Wire transfers, in particular, pose particular problems for anti-money laundering efforts. These transfers are most frequently sent through CHIPS, Fedwire, and SWIFT. The U.S. government used the facilities of the Society for Worldwide Interbank Financial Telecommunications (SWIFT), a wire service for international financial transactions, to monitor terrorist financial activities. Some critics claimed this was an unwarranted invasion of privacy. Do you agree? Other charged that disclosure of this program endangered American security. Treasury Official: Swift Disclosure "Very Damaging," Am. Banker, July 12, 2006. The European Commission was critical of this use of SWIFT by U.S. authorities, but an agreement was reached to let the program go forward. James Risen, U.S. Reaches Tentative Deal With Europe on Bank Data, N.Y. Times, June 29, 2007. See also Jeremy Shrader, Secrets Hurt: How SWIFT Shook Up Congress, the European Union, and the U.S. Banking Industry, 11 N.C. Banking Inst. 397 (2007).

Other financial transactions that are subject to money laundering legislation include sales; pledges; gifts; transfers; deposits; withdrawals; transfers between accounts; exchanges of currency; loans and other extensions of credit; and purchases or sales of stocks, bonds, certificates of deposits, or other monetary instruments.

The key self-enforcement mechanism advocated by regulators to guard against money laundering is a "know-your-customer" responsibility that is imposed on institutions that deal in cash and transfers of large amounts of funds. Banking regulators proposed regulations in 1998 that would have required banks and bank affiliates to adopt formal policies to identify their customers, verify the source of the deposits, and monitor accounts for unusual transactions. However, those proposals were met with over 250,000 letters and emails in opposition. In March 1999, federal bank regulators announced that the withdrawal of the proposed know-your-customer regulation.

The Treasury Department requires banks to file reports of suspicious financial transactions. 31 U.S.C. § 5318(g) and 31 C.F.R. § 103.21. Banks file the Suspicious Activity Report (SAR) with FinCEN when it appears there have been criminal violations of a federal law by the institution or its insiders or where there are potential money laundering violations involving specified amounts of funds. SARs must be filed within thirty days after detection, but filing in some circumstances may be delayed for an additional thirty days. 31 C.F.R § 103.21(b)(3). Banks are not allowed to disclose to their customers or any person involved in the transaction that a SAR has been filed. Banks are also prohibited from informing customers that their records have been subpoenaed or that customer information has been disclosed to a grand jury.

As money laundering statutes became a significant weapon in the war on drugs, banks found themselves acting as unofficial policemen in monitoring the activities of their customers. There is a clear conflict for a financial institution between its duty to protect the privacy of customers' financial transactions and the SAR reporting requirements of the anti-money laundering legislation. This conflict is highlighted in the case below, which should be compared with the *Lopez* case in Chapter 4. Considered together, the *Lee* and *Lopez* cases exemplify the courts' struggle to determine whether a bank is protected from claims of improper disclosure by the safe harbor provisions of the Annuzio–Wylie Act of 1992. *Lopez* imposed a requirement that the bank act in good faith before receiving the protection of the safe harbor.

LEE v. BANKERS TRUST CO.

United States Court of Appeals, Second Circuit, 1999.
166 F.3d 540.

McLaughlin, Circuit Judge.

In 1990, Bankers Trust Company ("Bankers Trust"), hired Let W. Lee as a Vice President for Global Retirement and Security Services. Later it promoted him to Managing Director. In April 1994, Bankers Trust asked Lee to work in its Global Security Services practice, and he agreed. Lee always worked in the New Jersey offices of Bankers Trust.

In Spring 1995, Lee asked two Bankers Trust employees, Harvey Plante and Gerard Callaghan, to look into Bankers Trust's older "custody credit" accounts. These accounts had been languishing unclaimed for long periods, and Lee asked Plante and Callaghan to determine whether Bankers Trust could properly keep some of this money rather than letting it escheat to the state. Plante told Callaghan and Lee that Bankers Trust had more than $3.9 million in the accounts that did not have to be escheated. Lee and Callaghan then told Plante that any non-escheatable funds that were properly documented should be transferred to a reserve account at Bankers Trust.

Plante was placed in charge of the reserve account. Lee maintains that he told Plante: (1) to clear all dealings with Bankers Trust's compliance department; (2) not to transfer any money that was not properly documented; (3) not to transfer any funds that might possibly be escheatable; and (4) to keep a detailed list of funds in the reserve account.

In March 1996, Bankers Trust became troubled by Plante's activities and questioned him about the reserve account. Shortly thereafter, Bankers Trust let Lee know that Plante claimed that Lee had told him to transfer escheatable funds into the reserve account. Lee denied this claim.

On March 21, 1996, Lee met with John Foos, John Peters and Elizabeth Hughes, all of whom worked in Bankers Trust's Securities Services practice. After meeting with this trio for over five hours, Lee signed a statement prepared by Bankers Trust. Bankers Trust then ordered Lee to stay out of his office while it conducted an investigation. Lee claims that by the end of March 21st, everyone at Bankers Trust was discussing his involvement in some kind of wrongdoing.

In early June 1996, Lee claims that Richard Coffina, Head of Human Resources at Bankers Trust, told him that the firm would like him to resign. Lee did resign on June 6, 1996. The press reported that Lee left Bankers Trust amid allegations of wrongdoing. Bankers Trust never made any public statement regarding Lee's activities or the reason for his departure. * * *

In his complaint, Lee alleged that Bankers Trust defamed him in an SAR [Suspicious Activity Report] filed with the United States Attorney's Office for the Southern District of New York. While refusing to confirm or deny the filing of an SAR, Bankers Trust counters that it has immunity for any allegedly defamatory statements made in such a filing. Lee recognizes that Bankers Trust enjoys some immunity for statements in an SAR, but argues that this immunity extends only to statements made in good faith. Lee is incorrect. * * *

The regulations promulgated under the Annunzio–Wylie Act (the "Act"), 31 U.S.C. § 5318(g), require financial institutions like Bankers Trust to file an SAR "no later than thirty (30) days after the initial detection of a known or suspected violation of federal law, a suspected transaction related to money laundering activity, or a violation of the Bank Secrecy Act." 12 C.F.R. § 208.20(d) (1997). Institutions are prohibited from acknowledging filing, or commenting on the contents of, an SAR unless ordered to do so by the appropriate authorities. See 12 C.F.R. § 208.20(j) & (g).

SAR filers are protected from civil liability by the "safe harbor" provision of the Act, which provides:

> Liability for disclosures. Any financial institution that makes a disclosure of any possible violation of law or regulation or a disclosure pursuant to this subsection or any other authority, and any director, officer, employee, or agent of such institution, shall not be liable to any person under any law or regulation of the United States or any constitution, law, or regulation of any State or political subdivision thereof, for such disclosure or for any failure to notify the person involved in the transaction or any other person of such disclosure.

31 U.S.C. § 5318(g)(3) (Supp. 1998). The safe harbor provision applies, regardless of whether the SAR is filed as required by the Act or in an excess of caution. See 12 C.F.R. § 208.20(k) (1998) (to be recodified at 12 C.F.R. § 208.62(k) (1999)).

Although the regulation does not say so, Lee argues that there is immunity only where the disclosures in the SAR were made in good faith. We disagree. * * *

The plain language of the safe harbor provision describes an unqualified privilege, never mentioning good faith or any suggestive analogue thereof. The Act broadly and unambiguously provides for immunity from *any* law (except the federal Constitution) for *any* statement made in an SAR by *anyone* connected to a financial institution. There is not even a hint that the statements must be made in good faith in order to benefit from immunity. Based on the unambiguous language of the Act, Bankers Trust enjoys immunity from liability for its filing of, or any statement made in, an SAR. * * *

The decision in Lee v. Bankers Trust Co. was followed in Stoutt v. Banco Popular de P.R., 320 F.3d 26, 30 (1st Cir. 2003). Compare, Coronado v. BankAtlantic Bancorp, 222 F.3d 1315, 1323 (11th Cir.), *cert. denied*, 531 U.S. 1052 (2000) (granting immunity where information was supplied pursuant to a grand jury subpoena).

UNITED STATES v. GIRALDI

United States Court of Appeals, Fifth Circuit, 1996.
86 F.3d 1368.

PARKER, CIRCUIT JUDGE.

Defendant–Appellant Antonio Giraldi ("Giraldi") was found guilty after a month long jury trial of 18 counts of money laundering, bank fraud, misapplication of funds and conspiracy. He was sentenced to 120 months in prison, $850 special assessment and released on a $700,000 bond pending appeal. Giraldi's co-defendant, Maria Lourdes Reategui, was convicted during the same trial, appealed, but dismissed her appeal after briefing. We affirm.

In 1989, Giraldi was an international private banker in the Mexico market with approximately two years of experience who worked for Bankers Trust Co. ("BT") in New York as a "relationship manager." His job was to recruit and service the bank accounts of wealthy Mexican individuals. He was also responsible for screening potential clients to determine if their wealth was legitimate.

Giraldi recruited a $2 million deposit from a new client named Aguirre in June 1989, that grew over the next several months to $21 million. There is no dispute that Aguirre was laundering drug money. The central question at trial and on appeal is whether Giraldi knew it was drug money.

Giraldi accepted Aguirre as a client without meeting him. A relationship manager could accept a client that he did not know and had not met if the potential client had a very strong recommendation from a known, reputable source. Giraldi circulated an interoffice memorandum ("the Benet memo") at BT that stated that Aguirre had been referred by Alberto Benet, whose family had been "Tier I clients" of Citibank for over 20 years. Giraldi was acquainted with Alberto Benet, a wealthy Mexican businessman and general director of ABSA, a Mexican financial services company, by virtue of having handled the Benet accounts at Citibank, Giraldi's former employer. In order to generate business, Giraldi had given Benet BT promotional literature and his (Giraldi's) business card. Benet testified that he had not, in fact, referred Aguirre to BT. There was evidence that the referral may have come from another ABSA employee, Laura Machuca, who had received Giraldi's literature from Benet. Further, the statement in the Benet Memo that Benet and his family had been Tier I clients (that is a client who had at least $10 million deposited with the bank) at Citibank for over 20 years was false. The Benet family had an account with Citibank from 1983 that was worth $3 million, and was never designated a Tier I client during 1983–1987. Because Giraldi handled Benet's Citibank account, he would have known that the information in his memo was false.

The signature card signed by the three account holders on Aguirre's account and Giraldi was dated 6–27–89 in New York. Giraldi's records showed that he was in Mexico City that day and could not have witnessed the signatures of the account holders.

Eight months after Aguirre opened his BT accounts, Giraldi was asked to resign from BT. He went to work for American Express Bank International (AEBI) and Aguirre moved his accounts to AEBI shortly thereafter.

The government also introduced evidence that Aguirre had no legitimate source of wealth, which Giraldi would have discovered had he investigated his background. Aguirre worked as a gas station manager in Mexico, was unsophisticated about financial matters, and had no banking references that showed wealth prior to 1989. Giraldi put on the bank forms that Aguirre's wealth was derived from the sale of Mexican ranch land, as well as interest in a car dealership, ranching, and a gas station. Later Aguirre purchased and ran a meat packing plant with part of the money from the accounts at issue in this case. The government introduced information from training seminars attended by Giraldi that described typical money laundering schemes that paralleled the techniques used to manage Aguirre's accounts, although these techniques were not per se illegal.

Other evidence showed that Giraldi and a myriad of other employees from both banks met with Aguirre over a two year period, and no one ever questioned his legitimacy. Aguirre was reported dead following a car wreck in March 1992. The Government implies that he did not die but went into hiding to avoid the legal consequences of his drug business.
* * *

Each count of conviction required the government to prove that Giraldi knew that Aguirre's funds were the proceeds of some form of unlawful activity. The money laundering conspiracy alleged in Count 1 and the substantive money laundering offenses in Counts 2 through 11, under 18 U.S.C. § 1956, require proof that,

Whoever, knowing that the property involved in a financial transaction represents the proceeds of some form of unlawful activity ...

Section 1956 also requires proof that the defendant knew the transaction was designed in whole or in part to conceal or disguise the nature, the location, the source, the ownership, or the control of the proceeds of specified unlawful activity. Absent sufficient proof of these elements, the convictions on Counts 1 through 11 are invalid.

The bank fraud allegations charged in Counts 13 and 14 require proof that Giraldi:

... knowingly executed or attempted to execute a scheme or artifice

(1) to defraud a financial institution; or

(2) to obtain any of the monies, funds, credits, assets, securities or other property owned by, or under the custody or control of, a financial institution, by means of false or fraudulent pretenses, representations or promises ...

* * * After a careful review of the record, we have concluded that the evidence is sufficient to sustain Giraldi's conviction. * * *

Money launderers have long used international transactions to frustrate the investigation of their activities. Several nations entered into a series of international agreements designed to curb money laundering. The United Nations Convention Against Illicit Traffic in Narcotic Drugs and Psychotropic Substances was adopted in 1988. It focused on curbing money laundering as a way to restrict the trafficking in illegal substances. This Convention was ratified by a large number of countries that agreed to make money laundering a crime. In 1988, the Basel Committee on Banking Supervision also adopted a Statement of Principles that set forth "best practices" for banks to prevent money laundering, including know-your-customer rules. The "Wolfsberg Principles" were developed by a group of eleven international banks as an aid in combating money laundering. Among other things, those principles establish know-your-customer standards, provide for heightened monitoring of accounts connected with high risk countries that do not have adequate money laundering standards, and establish guidelines for detecting and monitoring suspicious activity.

In 1989, the Group of Seven industrialized countries created a Financial Action Task Force on Money Laundering that made several recommendations to banks regarding money laundering, including reporting suspicious activity to law enforcement officials. The International Criminal Police Organization (Interpol, later Europol) also plays a role in the fight against money laundering. The Council of Europe adopted a Convention on Laundering, Search, Seizure, and Confiscation of Proceeds from Crime in 1990 that was signed by eighteen nations. This Convention sought to establish an enforcement system for detecting and prosecuting money laundering. The European Union issued a directive on money laundering in which its member states agreed to prohibit money laundering and to require financial institutions to adopt know-your-customer procedures.

The Organization of American States adopted model regulations for the prevention of money laundering that include a currency transaction reporting provision. Traditional foreign secrecy havens, including Switzerland, Luxembourg, the Bahamas, and Hong Kong, now prohibit money laundering. The International Financial Action Task Force, composed of over twenty-six nations, seeks to establish money laundering prevention programs, including know-your-customer policies, in its constituent countries.

Banks may even become involved in government efforts to stop terrorism.

UNITED STATES v. ONE 1997 E35 FORD VAN

United States District Court, Northern District of Illinois, 1999.
50 F.Supp.2d 789.

ANDERSEN, DISTRICT JUDGE.

The United States government filed this civil forfeiture action seeking to forfeit all funds contained in seven bank accounts and two safe deposit boxes on the theory that these funds were transferred to financial institutions within the United States from abroad with the intent to support the international terrorist activities of the HAMAS organization in violation of the Money Laundering Control Act of 1986, 18 U.S.C. § 1956. These activities allegedly include acts of extortion, kidnaping, and murder against the State of Israel and its citizens as part of HAMAS' alleged campaign to force Israel to cede physical and political control over the lands comprising Israel and the occupied territories of the West Bank and Gaza Strip. The government also seeks to forfeit a residence and one Ford Van because they were allegedly purchased with the illicit funds. The government alleges that the property is forfeitable pursuant to 18 U.S.C. § 981(a)(1)(A) which authorizes it to forfeit any property "involved in a transaction or attempted transaction in violation of section 1956 or 1957 ... or any property traceable to such property." * * *

On January 25, 1993, Mohamad Salah ("Salah"), a naturalized American citizen and Chicago area resident, was arrested by the Israeli government while in Israel allegedly to promote the activities of the HAMAS organization. In January 1995, Salah pled guilty in an Israeli military court to being a member of HAMAS and to channeling funds to HAMAS, including funds transferred through one of the subject bank accounts that he held jointly with his wife, Maryam Azita Salah. Salah was sentenced to a term of five years imprisonment. On February 10, 1995, the United States Treasury Department's Office of Foreign Asset Control, having reason to believe that Salah acted on behalf of HAMAS, which President

Clinton has designated in Executive Order 12947 as a terrorist organization threatening to disrupt the Middle East Peace Process, froze all known Salah bank accounts but on a monthly basis licensed Mrs. Salah to withdraw a living stipend. Also, on July 27, 1995, the Department added Salah to the list of Specially Designated Terrorists because of his alleged participation in terrorist activities in the Middle East. * * *

In November 1997, Salah was released from an Israeli prison and returned to the United States. On June 9, 1998, the government filed a verified complaint of forfeiture and resulting warrants of seizure and monition were executed for seven bank accounts, two bank safe deposit boxes, and one 1997 E35 Ford Van variously owned or controlled by the Salahs or QLI [Quranic Literacy Institute, a non-profit corporation which shared control of assets with Salah]. The bank accounts and safe deposit boxes include Standard Bank & Trust account nos. 5580349268 and 2393228806, and safe deposit box nos. 207 and 4019; First National Bank of Chicago account nos. 8060700 and 12310153; LaSalle Bank, F.S.B. account no. 022034532; Midland Federal Savings and Loan account no. 0010930021133; and First National Bank of Evergreen account no. 1412446. Also, a warrant for arrest in rem was executed for the Salahs' residence located at 9229 South Thomas, Bridgeview, Illinois. Salah, Mrs. Salah (on behalf of herself and her children), and QLI then each filed verified claims to the property. On October 19, 1998, each claimant moved to dismiss the complaint. * * *

The district court must necessarily assess the sufficiency of the forfeiture complaint with an eye toward the probable cause standard that the government must satisfy at trial. The government has the initial burden of establishing probable cause to believe that the property is subject to forfeiture. United States v. All Assets and Equip. of West Side Bldg. Corp., 58 F.3d 1181, 1188 (7th Cir. 1995). The government must show under the totality of the circumstances "a nexus," as compared to a "substantial connection," between the property and the illegal activity that is more than incidental or fortuitous. Id. at 1189 n.13. The government need not establish a criminal violation because probable cause requires only a probability or substantial chance of such activity. United States v. 6250 Ledge Rd., 943 F.2d 721, 725 (7th Cir. 1991). If the government establishes probable cause, the burden then shifts to the claimant to show by a preponderance of the evidence that the property is not subject to forfeiture. All Assets, 58 F.3d at 1189. If the claimant fails, the government's probable cause showing alone will support a judgment of forfeiture. Id. * * *

The complaint alleges that in January 1993, at the request of Abu Marzook, Salah traveled to Israel to help reorganize and restaff several HAMAS military cells after the Israeli government deported 415 HAMAS operatives. Abu Marzook allegedly instructed Salah to distribute to HAMAS operatives approximately $780,000 that Abu Marzook would wire to Salah's domestic bank accounts. The government alleges that, according to Salah, Abu Marzook directed Salah to distribute certain amounts to specific military cells throughout Israel and the Occupied Territories, with the remainder to be distributed according to Salah's assessment of the military and general requirements of HAMAS. Abu Marzook also ordered Salah to place certain individuals into leadership positions in various units to replace those who were deported and to meet with other operatives to coordinate responsive terrorists attacks against Israel.

The past activities of HAMAS leave little doubt as to what these terrorist attacks may have looked like. In October 1995, the United States filed an extradition action against Abu Marzook based on criminal charges pending in Israel for murder, attempted murder, and conspiracy. These charges stemmed from terrorist attacks allegedly sponsored by HAMAS on civilians in Israel and the Occupied Territories between July 1990 and October 1994. These ten terrorist attacks killed over 40 Israeli citizens, wounded scores of Israeli soldiers and citizens, and resulted in the kidnaping of several civilians. The United States District Court for the Southern District of New York found probable cause to believe that HAMAS was responsible for these attacks. In re Extradition of Marzook, 924 F. Supp. 565, 579–585 (S.D.N.Y. 1996). These incidents include the bombing of two passenger buses in April 1994 that together killed 14 people and injured 76 others. Id. at 583. The court also found probable cause to believe that Abu Marzook knew of these terrorist attacks and that he selected the leadership and supplied the money to enable the attacks to take place. Id. at 585–592. * * *

In conclusion, we find that the campaign of violence HAMAS allegedly undertook in the fall of 1992, which involved murders, kidnappings, and extortion under the direction of Abu Marzook, raises a reasonable inference that the defendant funds were transferred into the Salahs' accounts with the intent to promote and finance extortionate activities against Israel and its citizens. This inference is especially appropriate in light of the manner in which these funds were transferred into the United States and Salah's alleged admissions that he was coordinating and supporting terrorist attacks against Israel with HAMAS military operatives to whom he was also distributing funds. * * *

As a result of the terrorist attacks of September 11, 2001, and the boast of Osama bin Laden that terrorist funds could slip through the cracks of the U.S. financial system, money laundering has come under closer scrutiny by policymakers. On October 26, 2001, legislation known as the USA Patriot Act,[16] Pub. L. No. 107–56 (2001), was passed. Title III of that legislation–the International Money Laundering Abatement and Anti–Terrorist Financing Act of 2001 (IMLAFAT)–made sweeping reforms aimed at closing these cracks, both by statute and by strengthening the rulemaking power of the U.S. Treasury department. Broker-dealers are

---

16. USA Patriot is an acronym for United and Strengthening America by Providing Appropriate Tools Required to Intercept and Obstruct Terrorism.

now required to file Suspicious Activity Reports, as well as banks. Section 326 of IMLAFAT adopts a "Know Your Customer" standard in opening accounts. See Proposed Rule, 67 Fed. Reg. 48,290 (proposed July 23, 2002) (Department of Treasury issued jointly with the OCC, Fed, FDIC, OTS and NCUA). Section 321 expands the definition of "financial institution" to include, among others, credit unions and entities registered with the CFTC. Section 352 of the Act requires that entities falling under the statutory definition of financial institutions adopt policies to combat money laundering. These policies include designating a compliance officer to monitor adherence to the law, adopting internal audit programs, instituting employee training programs on money laundering, and developing an anti-money laundering program within the institution. Although the Secretary of Treasury already had the explicit authority to adopt such policies, he never did. The Act grants the Secretary the power to set additional minimum standards in each of these areas.

IMLAFAT addressed so-called correspondent banking accounts. These are accounts of U.S. financial institutions that are linked to an account with a foreign financial institution. Section 312 of the Act requires that financial institutions develop for these accounts (and for private banking accounts of non-U.S. persons) measures designed to detect money laundering. See Final Rule, 72 Fed. Reg. 44768 (Aug. 9, 2007) (regarding special due diligence for correspondent and private banking accounts). Further, Section 319(b) imposes on financial institutions an obligation to keep accurate and detailed records of correspondent accounts with foreign banks. Section 313 of the Act prohibits correspondent accounts with foreign shell banks, which are banks with no physical existence, making them an attractive vehicle for money laundering.

Final regulations were adopted on April 30, 2003 that specified the procedures and requirements for customer identification and verification by banks and other financial institutions. Among other things, those rules require banks to verify information on the identity of their customers, to maintain records on customer identities, and to check to see if the customer is listed as a suspected terrorist or terrorist group. Customers must be notified of verification efforts. Banks must obtain the customer's name, address, date of birth and an identification number. See Customer Identification Programs for Banks, Savings Associations, Credit Unions and Certain Non–Federally Regulated Banks, 68 Fed. Reg. 25,090 (May 9, 2003) (codified at 31 C.F.R. pt. 103).

The USA Patriot Act gives the government extraordinary powers that extend beyond terrorism. In United States v. Union Bank for Savings & Investment (Jordan), 487 F.3d 8 (1st Cir. 2007), the court upheld the seizure of $2.8 million attributed to a Canadian-based telemarketing fraud. The seized funds were cashiers checks that had passed through several hands and were awaiting collection in the correspondent account of a Jordanian bank at the Bank of New York. Forfeiture was allowed even though the Jordanian bank claimed that it could be liable to the depositors who were claiming to be holders in good faith. The court ruled that banks should contract with their customers to prevent such a result.

The Secretary of the Treasury is also authorized to take "special measures" against a country of financial institutions that the Department designates as a "primary" money laundering concern. Those measures may require U.S. banks to keep particular records and obtain additional information on the transactions of the country or institution so designated and correspondent accounts with such foreign institutions may be prohibited. The Treasury Department has used this measure against-Naura, a widely-reputed money laundering center; the Ukraine, because of widespread corruption; and Burma, which lacks any money laundering controls. Several foreign financial institutions have also been designated under this provision, including banks in North Cyprus, Latvia, and Belarus. Designation of a bank in Macao resulted in freezing $25 million in assets of North Korea, which in turn led to an apparent breakthrough in the negotiations seeking to stop that country's development of nuclear weapons. Douglas N. Greenburg, John Roth & Katherine A. Sawyer, Special Measures Under Section 311 of the USA Patriot Act, 23 Rev. Bank. & Fin. Services 65 (June 2007).

The effort to combat money laundering continues. Concern was was raised in 1999 when it was revealed that $7.5 billion was moved through nine accounts at the Bank of New York (BONY). Those funds originated in Russia. Three BONY employees were charged with other crimes, but were not indicted for money laundering. Riggs Bank was fined $25 million in May 2004 for failure to report suspicious transactions made by the Embassy of Saudi Arabia, a Riggs customer. An OCC official admitted in Congressional testimony that its supervisory actions with respect to Riggs "were not sufficient to achieve satisfactory and timely compliance with the BSA." Riggs had also allowed General Augusto Pinochet, the controversial former Chilean dictator, to conceal his identity on accounts holding more than $4 million. Riggs was acquired by PNC Financial Services Group in July 2004. Riggs agreed to pay $16 million to settle the Justice Department charges and paid another $8 million to Spain for failing to freeze Pinochet's assets as ordered by a Spanish court. Riggs also paid $3.8 million to settle shareholder lawsuits over these issues. A Senate report later found that Pinochet and his family had over 125 accounts in the United States at eight banks including Citigroup, Bank of America, and the Espirito Bank in Miami. Bank of America agreed in 2006 to pay $7.5 million to resolve charges by the Manhattan District Attorney that it allowed Brazilian money launderers to move $3 billion through one of its New York branches.

Following the problems at Riggs, AmSouth, an Alabama bank, was fined $50 million for failing to file a suspicious activity report with bank regulators that would have disclosed a Ponzi scheme that fleeced elderly investors of $10 million. The bank was given a deferred prosecution deal from the Justice Department and was forced to incur an additional $6 to

$9 million in compliance costs annually.[17] Banco Popular, a Puerto Rican bank, was fined $21.6 million for failing to file suspicious activity reports and money laundering failures under a deferred prosecution deal with the Justice Department. The New York branch of Arab Bank PLC was fined $24 million by bank regulators for money laundering violations. ABN Amro Holding NV severed relations with almost one hundred correspondent banks in Russia and Eastern Europe because of money laundering concerns by bank regulators in the United States and Europe.[18] Bank of America was under investigation for transferring funds tied to the drug trade in Uruguay. JPMorgan Chase was at the center of a probe into millions of dollars transferred by a small ice cream shop in Brooklyn to Al Qaeda supporters in Yemen. The Bank of New York negotiated a fine with regulators of over $20 million for failing to file suspicious activity reports.

Critics claimed that the Justice Department was trying to hijack bank regulation and criminalize even modest regulatory violations through money laundering controls. The OCC was also stepping up enforcement activity after being accused of going lightly on Wells Fargo & Co. and for failing to prevent the problems at Riggs. An internal review by the OCC of its own procedures found that banks often failed to correct money laundering deficiencies discovered by the agency. Rob Blackwell, OCC Reports Its Launder Enforcement Falls Short, Am. Banker, July 18, 2005. The OCC issued guidelines on its enforcement procedures for sanctioning banks without adequate anti-money laundering procedures. OCC Bulletin No. 2004–50 (Nov. 10, 2004). The Federal Financial Institutions Examination Council (FFIEC) issued an examination manual for bank regulators to be used by examiners beginning in October 2005. See also Interagency Statement on Enforcement of Bank Secrecy Act/Anti–Money Laundering Requirements (July 19, 2007), available at <www.federalreserve.gov/newsevents/press/bcreg/20070719a.htm>.

An investigation followed the discovery by American military forces in Baghdad, Iraq of $650 million in sequentially numbered $100 bills at a Saddam Hussein palace. Bank regulators discovered that the money had been shipped by three banks under a regulatory program called "Extended Custodial Inventory" (ECI) that was used to monitor and control international distribution of U.S. banknotes. "This is a particularly important function in light of the fact that almost two-thirds of the dollar value of all U.S. banknotes is in circulation overseas. As a result, only five specifically selected banks are permitted to participate in the program." Robert S. Pasley, Recent Developments in Bank Secrecy Enforcement, 9 N.C. Banking Inst. 61, 64 (2005).

---

17. A shareholder lawsuit against directors of AmSouth for this activity was dismissed by a Delaware court. Paul Davis, Ruling in AmSouth Case Offers Boards A Reprieve, Am. Banker, Mar. 9, 2006.

18. Glenn R. Simpson, How Top Dutch Bank Plunged Into World of Shadowy Money, Wall St. J., Dec. 30, 2005. Other foreign banks also experienced money laundering problems under the strict U.S. laws. Douglas N. Greenburg & Jonathan C. Su, Financial Institutions in the Cross-Hairs: Lessons From Recent Major Anti–Money Laundering Enforcement Cases, 22 Rev. Banking & Fin. Services 17 (2006).

QUESTIONS AND NOTES

1. A study by the Senate Permanent Subcommittee on Investigations in 2001 concluded that most banks do not have adequate procedures for monitoring money flows with high risk off-shore banks.

2. Do you think banks should be responsible for monitoring their clients' activities and reporting suspicious activity to the government? As a result of concerns over more stringent money laundering regulation, banks increased the number of suspicious activity reports they filed with regulators. The result was a forty percent increase in filings, which overwhelmed the ability of regulators to follow up on the activity being reported. The number of suspicious activity reports filed by financial service firms increased to over 500,000 in 2005, Damian Paletta, FinCEN '05 SAR Filings Surged Past Half Million, Am. Banker, Jan. 5, 2006, and to 567,000 in 2006.

3. UBS AG, the largest bank in Europe, was fined $100 million by the Federal Reserve Board for allowing funds to be sent to Cuba, Libya, Iran, and Yugoslavia, countries that were subject to sanctions by the United States and to whom money transfers were prohibited. Robert S. Pasley, Recent Developments in Bank Secrecy Act Enforcement, 9 N.C. Banking Inst. 61, 63 (2005).

SECTION 6.　FINANCIAL EMBARGOS

Banks sometimes find themselves in the middle of actions taken by the United States against hostile nations or foreign terrorists. This may involve embargos administered by the Office of Foreign Assets Control in the Department of the Treasury (OFAC).

DAMES & MOORE v. REGAN

Supreme Court of the United States, 1981.
453 U.S. 654.

MR. JUSTICE REHNQUIST delivered the opinion of the Court.

* * * On November 4, 1979, the American Embassy in Tehran was seized and our diplomatic personnel were captured and held hostage. In response to that crisis, President Carter, acting pursuant to the International Emergency Economic Powers Act, 91 Stat. 1626, 50 U. S. C. §§ 1701–1706 (1976 ed., Supp. III) (hereinafter IEEPA), declared a national emergency on November 14, 1979, and blocked the removal or transfer of "all property and interests in property of the Government of Iran, its instrumentalities and controlled entities and the Central Bank of Iran which are or become subject to the jurisdiction of the United States...." Exec. Order No. 12170, 3 CFR 457 (1980), note following 50 U. S. C. § 1701 (1976 ed., Supp. III). President Carter authorized the Secretary of the Treasury to promulgate regulations carrying out the blocking order. On November 15, 1979, the Treasury Department's Office of Foreign Assets Control issued a regulation providing that "[u]nless licensed or authorized ... any attachment, judgment, decree, lien, execution, garnish-

ment, or other judicial process is null and void with respect to any property in which on or since [November 14, 1979,] there existed an interest of Iran." 31 CFR § 535.203 (e) (1980). The regulations also made clear that any licenses or authorizations granted could be "amended, modified, or revoked at any time." § 535.805. * * *

On January 20, 1981, the Americans held hostage were released by Iran pursuant to an Agreement entered into the day before and embodied in two Declarations of the Democratic and Popular Republic of Algeria. The Agreement stated that "[i]t is the purpose of [the United States and Iran] ... to terminate all litigation as between the Government of each party and the nationals of the other, and to bring about the settlement and termination of all such claims through binding arbitration." In furtherance of this goal, the Agreement called for the establishment of an Iran–United States Claims Tribunal which would arbitrate any claims not settled within six months. Awards of the Claims Tribunal are to be "final and binding" and "enforceable ... in the courts of any nation in accordance with its laws." * * *

This Court has previously recognized that the congressional purpose in authorizing blocking orders is "to put control of foreign assets in the hands of the President...." Propper v. Clark, 337 U.S. 472, 493 (1949). Such orders permit the President to maintain the foreign assets at his disposal for use in negotiating the resolution of a declared national emergency. The frozen assets serve as a "bargaining chip" to be used by the President when dealing with a hostile country. * * *

Because the President's action in nullifying the attachments and ordering the transfer of the assets was taken pursuant to specific congressional authorization, it is "supported by the strongest of presumptions and the widest latitude of judicial interpretation, and the burden of persuasion would rest heavily upon any who might attack it." *Youngstown*, 343 U.S., at 637 (Jackson, J., concurring). Under the circumstances of this case, we cannot say that petitioner has sustained that heavy burden. A contrary ruling would mean that the Federal Government as a whole lacked the power exercised by the President, and that we are not prepared to say. * * *

BANQUE SAN PAOLO v. IRAQI STATE CO. FOR FOOD STUFF TRADING

United States District Court, Southern District of New York, 1996.
1996 WL 735505.

DUFFY, DISTRICT JUDGE.

This case arises out of the commercial transaction in which C.E.D. Viandes ("Viandes"), a French merchant, sold to the defendant Iraqi State Company for Food Stuff Trading ("Iraqi State Company") certain meat to be paid for in U.S. Dollars. The purchaser arranged for a letter of credit to be posted by the Rasheed Bank ("Rasheed") to cover the transaction. The letter of credit named Viandes as beneficiary and appointed, as negotiating bank, the Union De Banques Arabes et Francaises ("UBAF"), a French bank. The letter of credit also provided that UBAF would be reimbursed the U.S. Dollars from the Rasheed account at the Bank of New York ("BNY"), which was designated as the "reimbursing bank." * * *

The intervening events were the invasion of Kuwait by Iraq, the Gulf War, and a freeze on all Iraqi assets located in the United States by Presidential Order. The Presidential Order can be and has been lifted by licenses granted by the defendant United States Treasury Department, Office of Foreign Assets Control ("OFAC"). Such a license was applied for in this case and was denied. Rasheed's frozen account at the Bank of New York now contains $677,948.36, which is claimed by the plaintiff herein and also by Bergerco Canada, a Canadian corporation that commenced a totally unrelated lawsuit in the district court in Washington, D.C. (Bergerco Canada v. Iraqi State Company, et al., 92 Civ. 2781 (JHG). * * *

The International Emergency Economic Powers Act ("IEEPA") gives the President authority to "prohibit any ... transfer [of] ... any property in which any foreign country or a national thereof has any interest." 50 U.S.C. § 1702(a)(1)(B). On August 2, 1990 the President declared a national emergency and issued an order freezing

> [a]ll property and interests in property of the Government of Iraq, its agencies, instrumentalities and controlled entities and the Central Bank of Iraq that are in the United States, that hereafter come within the possession or control of United States persons, including their overseas branches....

Implementation of this part of the program of economic sanctions was left to OFAC. Count VI of the instant complaint is directed against OFAC and its refusal to grant a license unfreezing funds from Rasheed's account at Bank of New York. OFAC based its decision to deny the request for a license upon an agency regulation now codified in 31 C.F.R. § 575.510. That regulation restricts the issuance of a license for an export transaction of Iraqi funds to situations involving a letter of credit issued or confirmed by a United States bank, or a letter of credit reimbursement confirmed by a United States bank. The only United States bank involved here is the Bank of New York. * * *

Banque San Paolo makes three separate legal arguments: (1) OFAC's regulations illegally favor U.S. Banks and thus, are inconsistent with the underlying legislation; (2) OFAC's retroactive application of amendments to its general license is illegal and inconsistent with its own regulations; and, (3) the monies held by Bank of New York belong to the plaintiff and not Rasheed.

The supposed inconsistency between the underlying statute and the OFAC regulation on which the plaintiff bases its first argument is illusory at best. The underlying purpose of the IEEPA is not just to prohibit transfers to a particular foreign government and its entities; it also would permit the embargo of any payments of the debts of the foreign government. The statute and the blocking orders issued thereunder are intended to:

> put control of foreign assets in the hands of the President.... Such orders permit the President to maintain the foreign assets at his disposal for use in negotiating the resolution of a declared national emergency.

Dames & Moore v. Regan, 453 U.S. 654 (1981).

Banque San Paolo's argument that there has been an illegal retroactive application of OFAC's regulations is similarly without merit. At best, Banque San Paolo would have a complaint only if it was entitled to a license under prior regulations. Clearly it was not. The prior regulations permitted licenses only for "amounts owed to or for the benefit of a U.S. person." Neither Banque San Paolo nor its assignor can fit into that category. Banque San Paolo lost no vested right by the so-called illegal retroactive application.

The third and final formal argument made by San Paolo is based upon an expected judicial finding that the Bank of New York had confirmed its reimbursement of the letter of credit proceeds. Clearly, as set out above, such a confirmation was totally lacking from the transactions.

Plaintiff's attorneys have sprinkled their papers with suggestions that others have received licenses (without fully disclosing whether those situations fit under the guidelines, as apparently they do) and suggestions that the United States government would cheat these claimants because it is one of the principal claimants against Iraq. These allegations are of no benefit whatsoever to this plaintiff and indeed show, perhaps, how lacking in foundation its position is.

The motion for summary judgment made on behalf of the United States Treasury, Office of Foreign Assets Control is granted. Because there can be no license to permit any payment of these Iraqi debts at this time, it would appear that all of the other summary judgment motions made by the various parties in this action are premature. Accordingly, all other motions are denied and the case is to be sent to the Suspense Docket of this court. The matter can be restored to the active docket upon a showing that an appropriate license has been issued.

QUESTIONS AND NOTES

1. OFAC wants banks to have effective policies in place for monitoring accounts during an embargo. It will even forgive lapses, at least in some cases, if those policies and controls are adequate. Controls are needed because the United States frequently resorts to the imposition of financial embargos in times of international crisis. Usually, such actions are taken late at night to avoid disturbing the markets. This causes many difficulties for banks and other financial institutions that have ongoing financial transactions involving affected accounts. The banks must immediately identify the affected accounts and impose a freeze. This is sometimes difficult. For example, Kuwaiti assets

were frozen during the Gulf crisis to prevent them from being looted by Iraq. It was often difficult, however, to determine the account owner's nationality, as where a corporate account was owned by a non-Kuwait corporation, but was ultimately controlled by someone in Kuwait.

2. Another problem fueled by the United States when a financial embargo is imposed is that it may have to enforce the American embargo through foreign bank branches. This can raise conflicts with a foreign government that does not approve of the American policy at issue.

3. Should the seizure of foreign assets held in American bank accounts be used as a foreign policy tool? Do you think it makes American banks less attractive as a depository for foreign funds?

INDEX

References are to Pages

ACCOUNTING ISSUES
Balance Sheet, 173–174
Derivatives, 892–901
Income Statement, 172–173
Letters of Credit, 521–527
Pooling of interests, 665–666
Purchase method, 665–666

AFFILIATE TRANSACTIONS
Restrictions, 256–258

ANNUITIES
Fixed, 911
National Banks, 198–202
Variable, 198, 911

**ANNUNZIO-WYLIE ANTI–MONEY LAUN-
DERING CONTROL ACT OF 1992**
Description, 274–275, 1018

ANTITRUST
Change in Bank Control Act, 270, 667
Community needs, 676–683
Deposit caps, 693–695
Director interlocks, 695–699
Fed guidelines, 685–687
General, 633–693
Hart–Scott–Rodino, 668
Herfindahl–Hirschman Index, 684–687,
    689–693
Market concentration, 684–687
Mitigating factors, 690–693
Regulatory approvals, 666–695
Relevant market, 669–676
Reviews, 667–668

ANTI-TYING, 263–265

**ASSET-BACKED COMMERCIAL PAPER
MONEY MARKET MUTUAL FUND LI-
QUIDITY FACILITY**
Description, 165

ASSETS
Investments, 293–294
Loans, 302–314
Real Estate, 293
Securities trading, 294–296

ATMS
As branches, 645
Electronic Funds Transfer Act, 539–541, 648
Preemption of fees, 471
State Regulation, 475–477

BALANCE SHEETS
Explanation, 173

BANKERS ACCEPTANCES
Description, 518–521

**BANK FOR INTERNATIONAL SETTLE-
MENTS**
Description, 551, 956–958

BANK HOLDING COMPANIES
Antitrust review, 667–668
Background, 49
Business of banking, 198–199
Douglas amendment, 51
Interstate banking, 650–658
Investment banks applying to become, 244–246
Nonbank banks, 51–52
Permitted activities, 232–240
Regulatory structure, 225–226
Systemically significant, 246–247

BANK MERGER ACT OF 1966
Description, 666–667

BANK NOTES
Bank currency, 15
Shinplasters, 17–18
Stamp Payments Act, 17, 291

BANK OF THE UNITED STATES
First bank, 9–10
Second bank, 10–11

BANK SECRECY ACT OF 1970
Description, 1012–1015

BANK SERVICE CORP.
General, 224

BASEL COMMITTEE
See Capital

BASIC ACCOUNTS
Description, 466–467

BILLS OF CREDIT, 5–8

BOUNCED CHECKS
Bounce protection, 476–477
Fees, 477

BRADY BONDS
Description, 1008–1010

BRANCHING
ATMs, 645

BRANCHING—Cont'd
History, 44–49,633–658
Riegle–Neal, 54–55, 658–662
Thrifts, 642–644

BROKERED DEPOSITS
Description, 99, 175, 496–497

BUREAU OF CONSUMER FINANCIAL PROTECTION
Creation, 66
Powers, 222, 370–371, 487, 573
Privacy requirements, 282

BUSINESS METHOD PATENTS
Description, 285–286

CAPITAL
Basel II, 554–556
Basel III, 561–562
Concodant, 958–959, 963
Description, 956–960
Money Laundering, 1011–1012
Requirements, 551–552

CHARTERING
National bank, 188
State bank, 189–193

CHECK 21
Description, 487

CHECK CLEARING
Clearing houses, 28–30
Federal Reserve Board, 32–33

CHECKING ACCOUNTS
Interest, 433, 465–466
Overdraft fees, 472–477
Transaction accounts, 133–134

CIVIL MONETARY PENALTIES
Authority, 581–582

CLEARING HOUSES
History, 28–30

COLLATERALIZED DEBT OBLI-GATIONS
Description, 346–351

COMMERCIAL PAPER
Bank activities, 847

COMMERCIAL PAPER FUNDING FACIL-ITY
Description, 165

COMMODITY EXCHANGE ACT OF 1936
Description, 857–858

COMMODITY FUTURES MODERNIZA-TION ACT
Single stock futures, 867
Treasury amendment, 875–877

COMMODITY FUTURES TRADING COM-MISION
Creation, 854
Jurisdiction, 867

COMMUNITY REINVESTMENT ACT
Application, 431–432
Assessment area, 438
Financial Crisis, 681–683
Mergers, 437

COMPETITIVE EQUALITY BANKING ACT
Background, 104

CONSUMER FINANCIAL PROTECTION BUREAU
See Bureau of Consumer Financial Protection

CORPORATE GOVERNANCE
Generally, 230–231

COVERED BONDS
Description, 362

CREDIT CARDS
Credit Card Accountability, Responsibility, and Disclosure Act of 2009, 391–395
Debit cards, 533
Description, 528–531
Smart cards, 536–537

CREDIT DEFAULT SWAPS
Description, 885–886

CREDIT RATING AGENCIES
Description and proposed regulation, 356–359

CREDIT UNIONS
Common bond, 91–95
Comparison, 85–91
Federal Credit Union Act, 85
History, 85–91
National Credit Union Administration, 91

CRIME CONTROL ACT OF 1990
Fraudulent conveyances, 608–609

CRIMINAL ACTIONS
Penalties, 625–629

CUSTODIAL SERVICES
Description, 723

DATA SECURITY BREACH
Description, 290

DEBIT CARDS
Description, 533

DEPOSIT ACCOUNTS
Types of, 465–466

DEPOSIT BROKERS
FDIC coverage, 497

DEPOSIT CAPS
Applications, 693–695

DEPOSITORY INSTITUTIONS DEREGU-LATION AND MONETARY CONTROL ACT OF 1980
Background, 98

DERIVATIVES
Accounting treatment, 892–901

DERIVATIVES—Cont'd
Bank entry, 863–866
CFTC, 854, 863–866
Commodity Exchange Act, 854–855
Commodity Futures Modernization Act, 775, 867, 875, 888–889
Credit derivatives, 867–870
Dealers, 862–863
Description, 858–861
Dodd–Frank, see Dodd–Frank
End-users, 862–863
Forward contracts, 859
Futures, 859–860
Futures commission merchants, 864
Hedging, 867
Hybrids, 884
Jurisdictional disputes, 866–867
Margin, 863
Options, 860–861
Over-the-counter, 877–878
Single stock futures, 866–867
Swaps, 859–860, 878–884
Treasury amendment, 873–877

DIRECTOR INTERLOCKS
Antitrust concerns, 695–699
Mutual funds, 811–816

DISCOUNT BROKERS
Operation by bank, 757–762

DIVERSITY JURISDICTION
National banks, 219–221

DODD-FRANK ACT
Accredited investors, 831
Background, 61–65, 114, 948–949
Banks
    Holding companies, 247, 607
    Mergers, 662–664, 667, 693
    Reserves, 492–493
Board interlocks, 698
Bureau of Consumer Financial Protection, 66, 222, 282, 372
Business checking accounts, 133, 134, 467, 488
Capital requirements, 562
CDOs, 948
Clearing and settlement, 808–809
Corporate governance, 67, 232
Credit cards, 535
Deposit caps, 70, 693
Derivatives, 865–866, 891
Executive compensation, 67, 232
FDIC
    Emergency lending, 66
    Hedge funds, 67, 832–833
    Insurance, 490–491
    Powers, 167
Federal Insurance Office, 949
Fed powers, 66, 135, 166, 168, 257, 570
Financial holding companies, 240
Financial market utilities, 66
Financial Stability Oversight Council, 65, 70, 166, 167, 562, 949, 966
Hedge funds, 298
Hedging, 867

DODD-FRANK ACT—Cont'd
Industrial loan companies, 255
Lending authority during severe economic distress, 66
Lending limits, 307
Leverage ratios, 174
Liquidation authority, 65, 590, 592
Mortgage originators, 443
Non-bank financial companies, 66, 247, 253
OCC visitorial powers, 218
Office of Thrift Supervision, 114, 130, 999
Payment systems, 808
Predatory lending, 460
Preemption, 69, 82, 116, 117, 213–214, 221–222, 230
Private equity, 67
Proprietary trading, 298, 837
Rating agencies, 360
Reasons for, 67
Securities regulation, 67
Securitizations, 353
Stress testing, 568–569, 577
Swaps, 865, 878, 891, 950
Volcker rule, 68, 298, 836–837

D'OENCH DOCTRINE
Description, 629–632

EDGE ACT
Description, 967–970

ELECTRONIC BANKING
Description, 286–290

ELECTRONIC FUNDS TRANSFER ACT
ATM surcharges, 539–540

ELECTRONIC TRANSFERS
CHIPS, 741
FedWire, 1017
Herstatt risk, 745
Problems, 745
SWIFT, 741

EMERGENCY ECONOMIC STABILIZATION ACT OF 2008
Description, 64, 488, 557
    See Troubled Asset Relief Program

ENFORCEMENT
Administrative Process, 582
History, 577–579
Types of Enforcement Actions, 579–582

ENVIRONMENTAL CONCERNS
Lender liability, 315–319

EQUAL CREDIT OPPORTUNITY ACT
Burden of proof, 425–430
Description, 422–425
Unmarried couples, 422–425

ESCHEAT LAWS
Bankers Trust, 507–518
Description, 505–507

EURODOLLARS
Description, 973–974

FACT ACT, 281

FAILED BANKS
Cross-guarantee, 602–605
Director liability, 619–620, 621–623
D'Oench doctrine, 629–632
Living Wills, 168, 577
Priorities, 607–610
Resolution, 593–595
Risks, 595–602
Source of strength, 605–607

**FAIR CREDIT AND CHARGE CARD DIS-
CLOSURE ACT**
Description, 391–400

FAIR CREDIT BILLING ACT
Description, 397–400
Liabilities, 400–402

FAIR VALUE ACCOUNTING
Description, 319–320, 901–904

FANNIE MAE
Description, 331–336
Failure, 599

FED FUNDS
Description, 150, 508

**FEDERAL DEPOSIT INSURANCE COR-
PORATION**
Assessments, 494–495
Coverage, 490–496
Deposit brokers, 496–499
Enforcement powers, 577–582
History, 38
Moral hazard, 490
Numbers insured, 170–171
Orderly liquidation authority, 589–593
Reserves, 492–494
Structure, 38–39
Systemic risk exception, 492, 496

**FEDERAL DEPOSIT INSURANCE COR-
PORATION IMPROVEMENT ACT OF
1991**
Background, 105–106
Corrective actions, 578
Powers of state banks, 223–224

**FEDERAL DEPOSIT INSURANCE RE-
FORM ACT**
Coverage, 491–492

FEDERAL FUNDS
Description, 150

FEDERAL HOME LOAN BANK BOARD
Functions, 74
Replaced, 105

FEDERAL HOUSING FINANCE AGENCY
Functions, 331

FEDERAL INSURANCE OFFICE
Creation, 949

FEDERAL RESERVE SYSTEM
Birth, 30–31

FEDERAL RESERVE SYSTEM—Cont'd
Check clearing, 32–33
Currency, 33–34
Discount rate, 147–149
Federal Open Market Committee, 136, 142–147
Federal Reserve Banks, 137
Fed–Treasury Accord, 40–42
Greenspan, Alan, 154–155
Independence, 40–42
Martin, William McChesney, 41–42
Monetary policy, 35–37, 40–42, 134–135
Notes, 33–34
Open market operations, 134–135, 142–147
Purposes and functions, 137–138
Reserve requirements, 137–142
Systemic risks, 156–162

**FEDERAL SAVINGS AND LOAN INSUR-
ANCE CORPORATION**
Abolished, 105–106
Background, 74
Coverage, 98–99
Receivers, 96–98

**FINANCIAL CRIMES STRATEGY ACT
OF 1996**
Description, 1016

FINANCIAL EMBARGOS
Descriptions, 1029
Office of Foreign Assets Control, 1029–1033

FINANCIAL HOLDING COMPANIES
Affiliate transactions, 256–257
General, 240–248
Merchant banking, 565–566
Powers, 253–255

**FINANCIAL INSTITUTIONS REFORM,
RECOVERY AND ENFORCEMENT ACT**
Background, 105–106
Enforcement, 106
Failed institutions, 608–610

**FINANCIAL INSTITUTIONS REGULATO-
RY AND INTEREST RATE CONTROL
ACT OF 1976**
Background, 98–99

**FINANCIAL INSTITUTIONS SUPERVI-
SORY ACT**
Background, 577–578

FINANCIAL MARKET UTILITIES
Description, 808–809

**FINANCIAL SERVICES REGULATORY
RELIEF ACT**
Description, 200

**FINANCIAL STABILITY OVERSIGHT
COUNCIL**
Composition, 167
Creation, 65, 949
Powers, 70, 166, 576, 966

FINANCIAL SUBSIDIARIES
General, 230

FOREIGN BANK SUPERVISION EN-HANCEMENT ACT OF 1991
Description, 963–965
Requirements, 963–965

FOREIGN EXCHANGE
Netting, 876–877
Operations, 874–877
Treasury amendment, 873–877

FREDDIE MAC
Description, 331–335

FUNCTIONAL REGULATION
See Gramm–Leach–Bliley

GARN-ST GERMAIN DEPOSITORY IN-STITUTIONS ACT OF 1982
Background, 98–99

GEOGRAPHIC LIMITS
ATMs, 645
Douglas amendment, 51
General, 634–650
History, 44–45
Riegle–Neal, 54–55

GINNIE MAE
Description, 338–339

GLASS-STEAGALL ACT
History, 42–44
Director interlocks, 699

GOLD STANDARD
Descriptions, 1000–1011

GOLDSMITHS, 9

GRAMM-LEACH–BLILEY ACT
Antitrust issues, 667–669
Background, 767–769
Broker-dealer registration, 769–771
Commercial paper, 849–850
Financial holding companies, 240–243
Financial subsidiaries, 230
Foreign banks, 965
Functional regulation, 249–250
Insurance, 909–910
Investment advisors, 821–822
Merchant banking, 797–799
Overview, 57–59
Privacy, 278–280
Underwriting, 771–772
Unitary thrift holding companies, 127
Usury, 359

HART-SCOTT–RODINO ANTITRUST IM-PROVEMENTS ACT OF 1976
Application, 668–669

HEDGE FUNDS
Background, 822–823
CFTC regulation, 832
Dodd–Frank, See Dodd–Frank
Long Term Capital Management, 822–823
Offshore funds, 832–833
Prime brokers, 826, 831
SEC regulation, 832

HEDGE FUNDS—Cont'd
Systemic risks, 157–160

HOME EQUITY LOAN CONSUMER PRO-TECTION ACT
Home equity loans, 402–404

HOMEOWNERS EQUITY PROTECTION ACT
Description, 452, 454

INCOME STATEMENTS
Banks, 172–173

INSUFFICIENT FUNDS
Charges, 476–477

INSURANCE
Bank advantages, 912–915
Bank holding companies, 931–933
Federal Insurance Office, 949–950
Fixed annuities, 911–912
Gramm–Leach–Bliley, 931–950
History, 905–907
McCarran–Ferguson Act, 910
National banks, 916–923
National charters, 946–948
Nature of, 905–907
Place of 5000, 916–923
Preemption, 920–923
State banks, 923–924
State regulation, 935–943
Systemically significant, 949
Subsidiaries, 933–935
Underwriting, 932–935
Variable annuities, 911–912

INTEREST RATES
Deposit accounts, 44
Discount rate (Fed), 147–149
Usury, 8

INTERMEDIARIES
Bank as, 132–133

INTERNATIONAL BANKING ACT OF 1978
Description, 965
Edge Act Corporations, 967–970
Grandfather Provisions, 965

INTERNATIONAL LENDING SUPERVI-SION ACT OF 1983
Loan loss reserves, 957

INTERNATIONAL MONETARY FUND
Background, 1000–1011
Rescue operations, 957
Special Drawing Rights, 1004–1007

INTERNATIONAL REGULATION
Act of State, 971–972
Bank for International Settlements, 551, 956–957
Basel Committee, 551–556
BCCI, 959–962
BNL, 962–963
Comparative regulation, 978–1000
Coordination, 963–964

INTERNATIONAL REGULATION—Cont'd
Edge Act, 967–970
European Union, 995–998
FBO supervision, 964–965
Foreign Bank Supervision Enhancement Act of
    1991, 963–964
Germany, 988–995
Gramm–Leach–Bliley Act, 965
Grandfather provisions, 965
IOSCO, 966
Japan, 979–983
NAFTA, 998
Representative offices, 963
United Kingdom, 984–988

INTERNET BANKING
General, 283–292

INTERSTATE BANKING
Compacts, 650–658
Riegle–Neal, 658–662

IOSCO
Description, 966

KAYE, SCHOLER
Controversy, 611–615

**LAWYER LIABILITY FOR FAILED INSTI-
    TUTIONS**
Kaye, Scholer, 611–615

LEGAL TENDER, 3, 19–22

LETTERS OF CREDIT
Accounting treatment, 527–528
Description, 521–524
Stand-by letters, 521–525

LEVERAGED
Description, 324–328

LIFELINE ACCOUNTS
Description, 466–467

LIVING WILLS
See Resolution Plans

LOANS
Collateralized mortgage obligations, 344–348
Environmental liability, 315–319
Insider loans, 308–314
Lending limits, 302–308
Loan participations, 322–331
Loss reserves, 319–322, 1011–1012
Mortgage-backed, 338–344
Regulation, 302–319
Secondary loan market, 331–336
Securitization, 336–338, 348–354
Syndicated loans, 322–331

MARGIN REQUIREMENTS
Regulation T, 796–801
Regulation U, 796, 799–802
Regulation X, 799–802

McCARRAN-FERGUSON ACT
Background, 910

McFADDEN ACT
Application, 57–61
History, 46–49

MERCHANT BANKING
Capital, 565
GLBA provisions, 773–774

MERGERS AND ACQUISITIONS
Bank advisors, 809–811
Business concerns, 664–666
Conflicts, 258–264
Forms, 663
Hart–Scott–Rodino review, 668–669
Regulatory approvals, 666–667

MONETARY COMMISSION, 31

MONETARY POLICY
Discount rate, 147–149
Federal funds rate, 147–149
Federal Reserve Board, 33–36, 134–135
Open market operations, 142–147
Reserve requirements, 137–142

MONEY
Bills of credit, 5–8
Legal tender, 3, 19–22
Lenders, 8–9
Medium of payment, 2–3

MONEY LAUNDERING
Background, 272–278, 1011–1029
Bank Secrecy Act, 1013–1015
Currency transaction reports, 1023
FinCen, 1017
International efforts, 1022–1023
Know-your-customer, 1017, 1022–1023
Smurfing, 1015
Suspicious Activity Reports, 1015, 1019–1020
Travel Act, 1012

**MONEY LAUNDERING CONTROL ACT
    OF 1986**
Description, 1015

**MONEY LAUNDERING PROSECUTION
    IMPROVEMENTS ACT OF 1988**
Description, 1016

**MONEY LAUNDERING SUPPRESSION
    ACT OF 1994**
Description, 1016

MONEY MARKET ACCOUNTS
Cash Management Accounts, 52–54
History, 52

**MORTGAGE-BACKED PURCHASE PRO-
    GRAM**
Description, 166

MORTGAGE-BACKED SECURITIES, 294,
    331, 333

MORTGAGE LENDING
Foreclosures, 458
High-cost mortgage loans, 460
Nontraditional mortgage products, 454–455

MORTGAGE LENDING—Cont'd
Qualified mortgages, 460–461
Reverse mortgages, 462
Standards, 454
    See subprime

MUNICIPAL SECURITIES RULE MAKING BOARD
Bank regulation, 756
Suitability rule, 782–784

NATIONAL BANK ACT
History, 22–23

NATIONAL BANKS
Annuity sales, 198–202
Dealing in stocks, 23–25
Financial subsidiaries, 230–231
Insurance operations, 207–215, 916–918
Numbers, 169
Operating subsidiary, 224–231
Powers, 185–206
Preemption, 207–214, 211–249
Trust powers, 700–735
Usury, 373–383
Visitorial powers, 214–223

NATIONAL CURRENCY ACT, 22–23

NETTING
Herstatt risk, 745
Setoff, 503–505

NONBANK BANKS, 233–237

NONBANK FINANCIAL COMPANIES
See Systemically Significant Financial Institutions

OFFICE OF FEDERAL HOUSING ENTERPRISE OVERSIGHT
Description, 332–333
Creation, 330
Replaced, 331

OFFICE OF FOREIGN ASSETS CONTROL
Description, 1029–1033

OFFICE OF THE COMPTROLLER OF THE CURRENCY
History, 23

OFFICE OF THRIFT SUPERVISION
Abolishment, 114
Background, 114

OPERATING SUBSIDIARY
General, 224–225
Preemption, 225–231

ORDERLY LIQUIDATION AUTHORITY, 65–66, 671

OTHER DEPOSITORY INSTITUTIONS
Labor banks, 95
Morris Plans, 95
Postal Savings Banks, 95

PAYDAY LENDING
Description, 466
Preemption, 465–66
TILA, 466

PREEMPTION
Federal Savings Associations, 77–83
General, 207–214
Insurance, 919–920
Operating subsidiary, 225–240
State predatory lending laws, 449–450
Trust powers, 702–705

PRIVACY CONCERNS
Disclosures, 269–278
Gramm–Leach–Bliley, 278–283

PRIVATE EQUITY
Background, 833–836
Carried interest, 835
PIPEs, 834
Regulation, 834–835

REAL ESTATE SETTLEMENT PROCEDURES ACT
Description, 438–439
Mortgage brokers, 438–442

REDLINING
Description, 431–432

REGULATORY STRUCTURE
Description, 185–188
Dual regulation, 22–23, 185–188

REGULATORY THEMES
Branching, 69,120
Competition, 68–69, 120
Dual chartering, 68–69, 129
General, 67–71, 128–130
Grandfather provisions, 70–71, 130
Industrial banks, 68, 129
Limited entry, 68, 129
Regulatory arbitrage, 68, 129–130
Safety and soundness, 70, 130

REMOVAL ORDERS
Authority, 580

REPOS
Description, 508–510
Problems, 508–518

RESERVE REQUIREMENTS
Fed requirements, 137–142

RESOLUTION PLANS
Description, 168

RESOLUTION TRUST CORPORATION
Description, 615–619
Powers, 608–610, 615–619

RETIREMENT CDs
Description, 923

RIEGLE-NEAL INTERSTATE BANKING AND BRANCHING EFFICIENCY ACT OF 1994
Branch banking, 54–55

RIEGLE-NEAL INTERSTATE BANKING AND BRANCHING EFFICIENCY ACT OF 1994—Cont'd
Deposit production, 662
Interstate branching, 658–662

SAFE DEPOSIT BOXES
Liabilities, 735–740
Use, 740

SARBANES-OXLEY ACT, 231–232, 309, 628

SAVINGS AND LOAN HOLDING COMPANY ACT
Description, 701, 911

SAVINGS AND LOANS
See Thrifts

SAVINGS ASSOCIATIONS INSURANCE FUND
Creation, 105–106

SAVINGS BANKS
See Thrifts

SCHEME LIABILITY
Described, 369–370

SECURITIES ACTIVITIES
Broker-dealer registration, 753–756, 769–771
Clearing and settlement, 756, 802–809
Commercial paper, 847–850
Dodd–Frank, See Dodd–Frank
Glass–Steagall, 748–767
Government securities, 293–302, 756
Gramm–Leach–Bliley, 767–775
History, 746–769
Margin requirements, 796–802
Markups, 780–782
Merchant banking, 773–775
Merger advisers, 809–811
Municipal securities, 756
Mutual funds, 811–822
Record keeping, 785–789
Sales violations, 775–780
Shared regulatory authority, 756
SROs, 775–780
Stock analysts, 789–791
Suitability rules, 782–784
Thrifts, 764–767
Transfer agents, 805–806
Trust indentures, 837–846
Underwriting, 748–764, 771–772

SECURITIZATION
Commercial Paper, 348–349
Credit rating agencies, 360–361
Description, 336
Insolvency, 360–363
Rating agencies, 32–33
Risk retention, 353
Subprime mortgages, 458–459

SET-OFFS
Description, 503–505

SIVs
See Structured Investment Vehicles

SMART CARDS
Description, 536–539

SOURCE OF STRENGTH DOCTRINE
Description, 607

SPECIAL DEPOSITS
Description, 504–505

STAMP PAYMENTS ACT, 17–19, 25–28, 291

STATE BANKS
Bills, 15–17
Financial subsidiary, 230–231
History, 9–10
Numbers, 169
Powers, 223–224
Stamp Payments Act, 17–19, 25–28, 291
Usury, 383–389

STORED VALUE CARD
See Smart Cards

STRESS TESTS
Described, 559–560, 568–569

STRUCTURED INVESTMENT VEHICLES
Description, 62

SUBPRIME LENDING
Description, 443
Interagency Guidance, 455–457

SUPERVISION
CAMELS, 551, 563, 570–575
Regulators, 568

SURETY BONDS, 364–370

SWEEP ACCOUNTS
Description, 488–490

SYSTEMIC RISKS
General, 156–162, 590, 598

SYSTEMICALLY SIGNIFICANT FINANCIAL INSTITUTIONS
Bank holding companies, 50–51
Nonbank financial companies, 66, 247, 253, 589

TARP
See Troubled Asset Relief Program

TAXATION
Power of states, 11–14

TEMPORARY LIQUIDITY GUARANTEE PROGRAM
Description, 492

TERM ASSET–BACKED SECURITIES LOAN FACILITY
Description, 165, 352–354

TERM SECURITIES LENDING FACILITY
Description, 165

TERRORISM
Bank facilities, 1023–1029

THRIFTS
Accounting issues, 100, 108–115
Branching, 76–77, 642–644
Capital requirements, 571
CEBA, 105, 125
Conversion, 119–124
Crisis, 95–114
Demutualization, 119–124
Deposit insurance, 74–75, 105–106
DIDMCA, 98–100
FDICIA, 105–106
FIRIRCA, 98
FIRREA, 105–106, 126
Garn–St Germain, 98, 99–100
GLBA, 127
History, 72–74
Holding companies, 124–127
Interest rate ceilings, 98–99
OTS, 114
Powers, 115–116
Preemption, 77–82
Regulation, 74–75, 114–115
Regulatory themes, 128–131
Savings banks, 82–84
Unitary thrift holding companies, 124–127

TRADITIONAL BANKING
Changing businesses, 174–183
Changing regulatory views, 202–206

TROUBLED ASSET RELIEF PROGRAM
Description, 64, 164, 232, 242, 355, 556–558

TRUST INDENTURE ACT OF 1939
Description, 837–840, 844–845
Trustees, 837–840

TRUST POWERS
Common trust funds, 706–708
Description, 700–703
Fiduciary standards, 708–723
Modern portfolio theory, 718

TRUST POWERS—Cont'd
Pension fund management, 726–735
Prudent Man Rule, 709

TRUTH–IN–LENDING ACT
Arbitration, 413–422
Damages, 405–413
Description, 389
Open-end credit, 389–391
Payday lending, 462–464
Rescission, 405

TRUTH–IN–SAVINGS ACT
Description, 469

TYING
Restrictions, 264–269

UNFAIR AND DECEPTIVE ACTS AND PRACTICES
FTC Act, 444, 453–454
OCC, 451–453
State statuses, 445–449

UNSAFE AND UNSOUND PRACTICES
Description, 578–582

USA PATRIOT ACT
See Patriot Act

USURY
Credit cards, 337–353
GLBA, 388
Late fees, 380–383
Purgatory, 8
Regulation, 373–383
State preemption, 383–389

VISITORIAL POWERS, 214–223

VOLCKER RULE
Description, 836–837

YIELD SPREAD PREMIUMS
Description, 439–442

†